YOUNG ADULT FICTION
CORE COLLECTION

CORE COLLECTION SERIES

FORMERLY
STANDARD CATALOG SERIES

SHAUNA GRIFFIN, MLIS, GENERAL EDITOR

CHILDREN'S CORE COLLECTION
MIDDLE AND JUNIOR HIGH CORE COLLECTION
SENIOR HIGH CORE COLLECTION
PUBLIC LIBRARY CORE COLLECTION: NONFICTION
FICTION CORE COLLECTION
GRAPHIC NOVELS CORE COLLECTION

YOUNG ADULT FICTION
CORE COLLECTION
THIRD EDITION

EDITED BY

KENDAL SPIRES

AND

JULIE CORSARO

H. W. Wilson

A Division of EBSCO Information Services, Inc.

Ipswich, Massachusetts

2019

GREY HOUSE PUBLISHING

ISBN 978-1-64265-022-8

The Dewey Decimal Classification is © 2003-2017 OCLC Online Computer Library Center, Inc. Used with Permission. DDC, Dewey, Dewey Decimal Classification and WebDewey are registered trademarks/ service marks of OCLC Online Computer Library Center, Inc.

Young Adult Fiction Core Collection, Third Edition, published by Grey House Publishing, Inc., Amenia, NY, under exclusive license from EBSCO Information Services, Inc.

Publisher's Cataloging-In-Publication Data
(Prepared by The Donohue Group, Inc.)

Names: Spires, Kendal, editor. | Corsaro, Julie, editor.
Title: Young adult fiction core collection / edited by Kendal Spires and Julie Corsaro.
Other Titles: Core collection series.
Description: Third edition. | Ipswich, Massachusetts : H.W. Wilson, a division of EBSCO Information Services ; Amenia, NY : Grey House Publishing, 2019. | Includes indexes.
Identifiers: ISBN 9781642650228 (hardcover)
Subjects: LCSH: Young adult fiction--Bibliography. | Young adults--Books and reading--United States. | Best books.
Classification: LCC Z1037.A1 Y68 2019 | DDC 011.62/5--dc23

CONTENTS

PREFACE

YOUNG ADULT FICTION CORE COLLECTION is a curated list of collection development recommendations, created by librarians for librarians, for YA fiction collections in any kind of library. It is derived from the MIDDLE & JUNIOR HIGH and SENIOR HIGH CORE COLLECTION databases available on EBSCOhost, updated weekly.

What's in this Edition?

The third print edition of YOUNG ADULT FICTION contains nearly 3,200 fiction titles appropriate for the age range and reading level. Titles included in this edition represent the two top tiers of recommendation levels from the Core Collection databases.

A star (★) at the start of an entry indicates that a book is a "Most Highly Recommended" title. These titles constitute a short list of essential novels for young adults. Additional titles included represent the "Core Collection" recommendation level, a longer list of books for libraries with larger needs. Titles cover all fiction genres including science fiction, realistic fiction, mysteries, mythology, fantasy, and more.

History

Due to the growing popularity of young adult fiction—with readers at the middle, high school, and adult levels—and the ever increasing availability of new titles, librarians need more guidance than ever to select the highest quality works even with a limited budget. YOUNG ADULT FICTION CORE COLLECTION gives librarians an easy-to-use resource to strengthen their YA fiction collections with the most highly recommended titles available, saving the librarian time and money.

YOUNG ADULT FICTION CORE COLLECTION is derived from the MIDDLE & JUNIOR HIGH and SENIOR HIGH CORE COLLECTION databases. It has been curated by librarians at EBSCO Information Services in partnership with Grey House Publishing to present users with a curated list of the "Most Highly Recommended" and "Core Collection" level titles in YA fiction. Our team of librarians combed through thousands of titles published since the second edition, selecting the highest quality works to provide librarians with thoughtful collection development recommendations for young adult fiction.

Scope & Purpose

This Core Collection is intended to serve the needs of any library serving readers of YA fiction, at all age levels, regardless of library or patron type. Recommendations contained herein stand as a basic or "opening day" collection, with "Most Highly Recommended" and "Core Collection" titles. The newer titles help in identifying areas in a collection that can be updated or strengthened. Retention of useful material from the previous edition enables the librarian to make informed decisions about weeding a collection.

All books listed are published in the United States, or published in Canada or the United Kingdom and distributed in the United States. The Core Collection excludes non-English-language materials, with the exception of bilingual titles; graphic novels; and most works widely known as adult "classics." This was done as an effort to both save space and to concentrate on recommending titles that are perhaps less well-known. Additionally, extensive conversations with high school librarians indicated that inclusion of "classics" in senior high libraries were primarily based on local curricula, not on recommendations from the Core Collections product line.

With its alphabetical-by-author-then-title arrangement, complete bibliographical data, and descriptive and critical annotations, the YOUNG ADULT FICTION CORE COLLECTION provides useful information for teen librarians, public librarians, school media specialists, university librarians and collection development directors.

Organization

The Core Collection is organized into two parts: the List of Fictional Works; and an Author, Title, and Subject Index.

Part 1. List of Fictional Works

The List of Fictional Works is arranged alphabetically by author. The information supplied for each book includes bibliographic description, suggested subject headings, an annotation, and frequently, an evaluation from a notable source.

Each listing consists of a full bibliographical description. Prices, which are always subject to change, have been obtained from the publisher, when available, and are as current as possible. Entries include recommended subject headings derived from the *Sears List of Subject Headings*, a brief description of the contents, and, whenever possible, an evaluation from a quoted source.

The following is an example of a typical entry and a description of its components:

Chbosky, Stephen
★ The **perks** of being a wallflower; [by] Stephen Chbosky. Pocket Bks. 1999 213p pa $14
Grades: 9 10 11 12 **Fic**
1. School stories 2. Letters -- Fiction 3. Young men -- Social life and customs -- 20th century
ISBN 0-671-02734-4

LC 99-236288

This novel in letter form is narrated by Charlie, a high school freshman. "His favorite aunt passed away, and his best friend just committed suicide. The girl he loves wants him as a friend; a girl he does not love wants him as a lover. His 18-year-old sister is pregnant. The LSD he took is not sitting well. And he has a math quiz looming. . . . Young adult." (Time)

"Charlie, his friends, and family are palpably real. . . .This report on his life will engage teen readers for years to come." SLJ

The star at the start of the entry indicates this is a "Most Highly Recommended" title. The name of the author, Stephen Chbosky, is given in conformity with Anglo-American Cataloguing Rules, 2nd edition, 2002 revision. The title of the book is The perks of being a wallflower. The book was published by Pocket Books in 1999.

The book has 213 pages and does not contain illustrations. It is published in paperback, and sells for $14.00. (Prices given were current when the Collection went to press.) The book is recommended for any of the following grade levels: 9 10 11 12.

At the end of the last line of type in the body entry is Fic in boldface type. The notation "Fic" implies that the book is a work of fiction.

The numbered terms "1. School stories 2. Letters -- Fiction 3. Young men -- Social life and customs -- 20th century" are recommended subject headings for this book based on *Sears List of Subject Headings*.

The ISBN (International Standard Book Number) is included to facilitate ordering. The Library of Congress control number is provided when available.

Following are two notes supplying additional information about the book. The first is a description of the book's content, in this case, an excerpt from Time magazine. The second is a critical note from *School Library Journal*. Such annotations are useful in evaluating books for selection and in determining which of several books on the same subject is best suited for the individual reader. Additional notes may also appear to describe special features, such as a bibliography, sequels and companion volumes, editions available, awards, and publication history, if applicable.

Part 2. Author, Title, and Subject Index

The Index is a single alphabetical list of all the books entered in the Core Collection. Each book is entered under author; title (if distinctive); and subject. Appropriate added entries are made for joint authors and editors. "See" references are made from forms of names or subjects that are not used as headings. "See also" references are made to related or more specific headings.

The following are examples of Index entries for the book cited above:

Author	**Chbosky, Stephen**
	The perks of being a wallflower
Title	The **perks** of being a wallflower. Chbosky, S.
Subject	**LETTERS -- FICTION**
	Chbosky, S. The perks of being a wallflower

tandards Used

Anglo-American Cataloguing Rules, 2nd ed., 2002 revision, 2005 update. Chicago: American Library Association, 2005.

Bristow, Barbara A. and Kendal Spires, eds. *Sears List of Subject Headings*. 22nd ed. Ipswich, MA: The H. W. Wilson Company, 2018.

Dewey, Melvil. *Abridged Dewey Decimal Classification and Relative Index*. 15th ed. Edited by Joan S. Mitchell, et al. Dublin, Ohio: OCLC, 2012.

Additional Products

For additional recommendations of YA nonfiction, graphic novels, short stories, and more, librarians are encouraged to investigate these other databases and their print versions:

MIDDLE & JUNIOR HIGH CORE COLLECTION

SENIOR HIGH CORE COLLECTION

GRAPHIC NOVELS CORE COLLECTION

WAYS TO USE THE RECOMMENDATIONS IN THIS CORE COLLECTION:

As an aid in purchasing. The Core Collection is designed to assist in the selection and ordering of titles. Annotations are provided for each title along with information concerning the publisher, ISBN, price, and availability. In evaluating the suitability of a work each library will want to consider the special character of the school and/or community it serves.

As an aid to the reader's advisor. The work of the reader's advisor is furthered by the information about sequels and companion volumes and the descriptive and critical annotations in the List of Fictional Works, and by the subject access in the Index.

As an aid in verification of information. For this purpose, full bibliographical data are provided in the List of Fictional Works. Entries also include recommended subject headings based upon *Sears List of Subject Headings*. Notes describe editions available, awards, publication history, and other titles in the series.

As an aid in curriculum support. Subject indexing, grade levels, and annotations are helpful in identifying materials appropriate for lesson planning and classroom use.

As an aid in collection maintenance. Information about titles available on a subject facilitates decisions to rebind, replace, or discard items. If a book has been deleted from the Core Collection in this edition because it is no longer in print, that deletion is not intended as a sign that the book is no longer valuable or that it should necessarily be weeded from the collection. "Weeded" titles since the last edition are still visible in the Core Collection databases as "Archival Materials."

As an instructional aid. The Core Collection is useful in courses that deal with literature and book selection for young adults.

The Core Collections are an essential resource to enhance and enrich library collections with the highest quality titles available.

ACKNOWLEDGMENTS

EBSCO Information Services wish to express special gratitude to the following Advisory Board librarians who assisted in the selection and weeding of titles for this Core Collection:

Gail de Vos
Adjunct Associate Professor, SLIS
University of Alberta
Edmonton, Alberta, Canada

Francisca Goldsmith
Consulting Librarian
Worcester, Massachusetts

Joquetta Johnson
Library Media Specialist
Randallstown High School
Randallstown, MD

Angela Leeper
Director of Curriculum Materials Center
University of Richmond
Richmond, Virginia

Marcela Peres
Library Director
Lewiston Public Library
Lewiston, Maine

Linda Ward-Callaghan
Youth Services Manager
Joliet Public Library
Joliet, Illinois

The editors would also like to thank EBSCO/NoveList librarian Rebecca Honeycutt, who helped in the weeding of this edition.

YOUNG ADULT FICTION CORE COLLECTION
THIRD EDITION

50 Cent (Musician), 1975-

Playground; with Aura Moser. Razorbill 2011 314p $17.99

Grades: 7 8 9 10

1. Bullies -- Fiction

ISBN 978-1-59514-434-8; 1-59514-434-X

Thirteen-year-old Butterball doesn't have much going for him. He's teased about his weight. He hates the Long Island suburb his mom moved them to so she could go to nursing school and start her life over. He wishes he still lived with his dad in New York City where there's always something happening, even if his dad doesn't have much time for him. Still, that's not why he beat up Maurice on the playground.

"Readers who were ever confused about having a gay parent, or being overweight, or going through a parental breakup, or just wanting to fit in and be accepted by their peers, will relate to Butterball. 50 Cent's debut young adult novel is a quick read that will be great for discussions on a variety of important and timely topics." Voice Youth Advocates

Abawi, Atia

★ A **land** of permanent goodbyes. Atia Abawi. Philomel Books 2018 279 p.

Grades: 7 8 9 10 11 12

1. IS (Organization) -- Fiction; 2. Bombings -- Fiction; 3. Family life -- Syria -- Fiction; 4. Muslims -- Fiction; 5. Refugees -- Fiction; 6. Syria -- Fiction

9780399546839, $17.99; 9780399546846

LC 2017021847

In this novel, by Atia Abawi, "in a country ripped apart by war, Tareq lives with his...family...until the bombs strike. His city is in ruins. His life is destroyed.... In the wake of destruction, he's threatened by Daesh fighters and witnesses a public beheading.... As they travel as refugees from Syria to Turkey to Greece, facing danger at every turn, Tareq must find the resilience and courage to complete his harrowing journey." (Publisher's note)

"A heartbreaking, haunting, and necessary story that offers hope while laying bare the bleakness of the world Tareq leaves and the new one he seeks to join." Kirkus

Abdel-Fattah, Randa

★ **Does** my head look big in this? Orchard Books 2007 360p $16.99

Grades: 7 8 9 10 11 12

1. School stories 2. Muslims -- Fiction 3. Australia -- Fiction 4. Clothing and dress -- Fiction

ISBN 0-439-91947-9; 978-0-439-91947-0

LC 2006-29117

Year Eleven at an exclusive prep school in the suburbs of Melbourne, Australia, would be tough enough, but it is further complicated for Amal when she decides to wear the hijab, the Muslim head scarf, full-time as a badge of her faith—without losing her identity or sense of style. "Grades seven to ten." (Bull Cent Child Books)

"While the novel deals with a number of serious issues, it is extremely funny and entertaining." SLJ

The **lines** we cross. Randa Abdel-Fattah. Scholastic Press 2017 393 p.

Grades: 9 10 11 12

1. Emigration and immigration -- Fiction; 2. Ethnic relations -- Fiction; 3. Families -- Australia -- Fiction; 4. Family life -- Australia -- Fiction; 5. Interpersonal attraction -- Fiction; 6. Love -- Fiction; 7. Muslim families -- Australia -- Fiction; 8. Muslims -- Australia -- Fiction; 9. Refugees -- Australia -- Fiction; 10. Refugees -- Fiction; 11. Australia -- Ethnic relations -- Fiction; 12. Australia -- Fiction; 13. Australia -- Politics and government -- 21st century -- Juvenile literature; 14. Immigration and emigration -- Fiction

9781338118667, $18.99; 9781338118674

LC 2016040576

In this book, by Randa Abdel-Fattah, "Michael likes to hang out with his friends and play with the latest graphic design software. His parents drag him to rallies held by their anti-immigrant group, which rails against the tide of refugees flooding the country. And it all makes sense to Michael. Until Mina, a beautiful girl from the other side of the protest lines, shows up at his school, and turns out to be funny, smart -- and a Muslim refugee from Afghanistan." (Publisher's note)

"An engaging romance within a compelling exploration of the sharply opposing beliefs that tear people apart, and how those beliefs can be transformed through human relationships." Pub Wkly

First published 2016 in Pan by Pan Macmillan Australia Pty Ltd... Sydney, New South Wales, Australia.

Abrahams, Peter

Reality check. HarperTeen 2009 330p $16.99; lib bdg $17.89; pa $8.99

Grades: 7 8 9 10

1. School stories 2. Gambling -- Fiction 3. Social classes -- Fiction 4. Missing persons -- Fiction

ISBN 978-0-06-122766-0; 0-06-122766-8; 978-0-06-122767-7 lib bdg; 0-06-122767-6 lib bdg; 978-0-06-122768-4 pa; 0-06-122768-4 pa

LC 2008-22593

After a knee injury destroys sixteen-year-old Cody's college hopes, he drops out of high school and gets a job in his small Montana town, but when his ex-girlfriend disappears from her Vermont boarding school, Cody travels cross-country to join the search.

"Abrahams writes a fine thriller that is pitched to attract everyone from reluctant readers to sports fans to romantic idealists." Voice Youth Advocates

Acevedo, Elizabeth, ca. 1988-
★ The **poet** X: a novel. Elizabeth Acevedo. HarperTeen 2018 361 p.
Grades: 9 10 11 12
> 1. Adolescence -- Fiction; 2. Dominican Americans -- Fiction; 3. High school students -- Fiction; 4. Interpersonal relations -- Fiction; 5. Poetry slams -- Fiction; 6. Poets -- Fiction; 7. Schools -- Fiction; 8. Self-esteem -- Fiction; 9. Teenage girls -- Fiction; 10. Harlem (New York, N.Y.) -- Fiction; 11. Teenage girls -- Fiction; 12. Bildungsromans
> ISBN 9780062662828; 9780062662804, $17.99
> LC 2017943585

Boston Globe-Horn Book Award: Fiction and Poetry (2018); National Book Award: Young People's Literature (2018); Kirkus Prize Finalist: Young Readers' Literature (2018)

In this novel, by Elizabeth Acevedo, "Xiomara...feels unheard and unable to hide...Ever since her body grew into curves, she has learned to let her fists and her fierceness do the talking.... With Mami's determination to force her...to obey the laws of the church, Xiomara understands that her thoughts are best kept to herself. So when she is invited to join her school's slam poetry club, she doesn't know how she could ever attend without her mami finding out." (Publisher's note)

"Themes as diverse as growing up first-generation American, Latinx culture, sizeism, music, burgeoning sexuality, and the power of the written and spoken word are all explored with nuance. Poignant and real, beautiful and intense, this story of a girl struggling to define herself is as powerful as Xiomara's name: 'one who is ready for war.'" Kirkus

Aceves, Fred
The **closest** I've come. Fred Aceves. HarperTeen 2017 310 p.
Grades: 9 10 11 12
> 1. Friendship -- Fiction; 2. High schools -- Fiction; 3. Hispanic Americans -- Fiction; 4. Schools -- Fiction; 5. Single-parent families -- Fiction; 6. Tampa (Fla.) -- Fiction; 7. Hispanic Americans -- Fiction; 8. Prejudices -- Fiction
> 9780062488534, $17.99; 9780062489876

In this book, by Fred Aceves, "Marcos Rivas yearns for love, a working cell phone, and maybe a pair of sneakers that aren't falling apart. But more than anything, Marcos wants to get out of Maesta.... When Marcos is placed in a new after-school program, he meets Zach and Amy, whose friendship inspires Marcos to open up to his Maesta crew, too, and starts to think more about his future and what he has to fight for." (Publisher's note)

"It's a memorable, hard-hitting portrait of a teenager trying to shape his own destiny after being dealt a difficult hand." Pub Wkly

Adams, Richard
Watership Down; Scribner classics ed.; Scribner 1996 429p $30; pa $15
Grades: 6 7 8 9 10
> 1. Allegories 2. Rabbits -- Fiction
> ISBN 0-684-83605-X; 0-7432-7770-8 pa

First published 1972 in the United Kingdom; first United States edition 1974 by Macmillan

"Faced with the annihilation of its warren, a small group of male rabbits sets out across the English downs in search of a new home. Internal struggles for power surface in this intricately woven, realistically told adult adventure when the protagonists must coordinate tactics in order to defeat an enemy rabbit fortress. It is clear that the author has done research on rabbit behavior, for this tale is truly authentic." Shapiro Fic for Youth. 3d edition

Adeyemi, Tomi
★ **Children** of blood and bone. By Tomi Adeyemi. Henry Holt & Co. 2018 531 p. Map (Legacy of Orisha)
Grades: 9 10 11 12
> 1. Brothers and sisters -- Fiction; 2. Government, Resistance to -- Fiction; 3. Magic -- Fiction; 4. Prejudices -- Fiction
> 9781250170989; 9781250170972, $18.99
> LC 2017021080

Kirkus Prize Finalist: Young Readers' Literature (2018)

In this book in the Legacy of Orisha series, by Tomi Adeyemi, "Zélie Adebola remembers when the soil of Orïsha hummed with magic.... [But] under the orders of a ruthless king, maji were killed, leaving Zélie without a mother and her people without hope. Now Zélie has one chance to bring back magic and strike against the monarchy. With the help of a rogue princess, Zélie must outwit and outrun the crown prince, who is hell-bent on eradicating magic for good." (Publisher's note)

"Well-drawn characters, an intense plot, and deft writing make this a strong story. That it is also a timely study on race, colorism, power, and injustice makes it great." Kirkus

Includes bibliographical references (page 527).

Adlington, L. J.
★ The **diary** of Pelly D. Greenwillow Books 2005 282p hardcover o.p. pa $8.99
Grades: 7 8 9 10
> 1. Science fiction
> ISBN 0-06-076615-8; 0-06-076617-4 pa
> LC 2004-52258

"On the planet Home From Home, Toni V is a brute laborer, a barely educated member of the Demolition Crew that is busy pulverizing the bombed-out remains of City Five's central plaza. Pelly D is a hip member of the swank elite who used to live in an exclusive apartment fronting the plaza. Their stories come together when Toni V uncovers Pelly D's diary in the debris. . . . Middle school, high school." (Horn Book)

"Adlington has crafted an original and disturbing dystopian fantasy told in a smart and sympathetic teen voice." Booklist

Agard, John

The **young** inferno; written by John Agard; illustrated by Satoshi Kitamura. Frances Lincoln Children's 2009 un il $19.95

Grades: 8 9 10 11 12

    1. Novels in verse 2. Hell -- Fiction

    ISBN 978-1-84507-769-3; 1-84507-769-5

"The narrative poems in this short book are accessible and have important things to say about the state of the human race. . . . The hoodie-wearing protagonist . . . awakens in a strange and frightening forest. A dark man appears and introduces himself as the tale-teller Aesop: he is to be the teen's escort through Hell. . . . As the pair travels through the Circles of Hell, they see the sins of mankind. . . . The scribbled, heavy-lined black ink and watercolor illustrations convey exactly the right mood for a book about a modern-day expedition into Hell. This will be a great book to pair with a discussion about Dante's Inferno and/or poetic structure." SLJ

Ahdieh, Renée

Flame in the mist. Renee Ahdieh. G.P. Putnam's Sons 2017 392 p. (Flame in the Mist)

Grades: 7 8 9 10 11 12

    1. Arranged marriage -- Fiction; 2. Samurai -- Fiction; 3. Alchemy -- Fiction; 4. Adventure fiction

    9780399171635, $17.99

                          LC 2016057273

In this book, by Renee Ahdieh, "the daughter of a prominent samurai, Mariko has long known her place -- she may be an accomplished alchemist, . . .but because she is not a boy, her future has always been out of her hands. At just seventeen years old, Mariko is promised to Minamoto Raiden, the son of the emperor's favorite consort -- a political marriage that will elevate her family's standing. But en route to the imperial city of Inako, Mariko narrowly escapes a bloody ambush." (Publisher's note)

"Ahdieh delivers an elaborate fantasy set in feudal Japan, where a resilient young woman defies class conventions and gender roles in a quest for vengeance and autonomy." Pub Wkly

Another title in this series is: Smoke in the sun (2018)

The **rose** and the dagger. Renée Ahdieh. G.P. Putnam's Sons Books for Young Readers 2016 432 p. Map

Grades: 9 10 11 12

    1. Romance fiction 2. Fantasy fiction 3. Blessing and cursing -- Fiction

    9780399171628, $17.99; 9780698185906, $53.97

                          LC 2015049227

In this novel, by Renée Ahdieh, a sequel to "The Wrath and the Dawn," "Shahrzad has been torn from the love of her husband Khalid, the Caliph of Khorasan. She once believed him a monster, but his secrets revealed a man tormented by guilt and a powerful curse. . . . Reunited with her family, who have taken refuge with enemies of Khalid, and Tariq, her childhood sweetheart, she should be happy. But Tariq now commands forces set on destroying Khalid's empire." (Publisher's note)

"Shahrzad's brazen ingenuity and fiery devotion, and every other character's overflowing shame, rage, compassion, pain, loyalty, frustration, desire, loneliness, guilt, grief, and oily ambition. Above all there is the shattering, triumphant catharsis of love-between man and woman, parent and child, teacher and student, sisters and cousins, friends old and new." Kirkus

Sequel to: The wrath and the dawn

Smoke in the sun. Ahdieh, Renée. G.P. Putnam's Sons 2018 432 p.

Grades: 7 8 9 10 11 12

    1. Brothers and sisters -- Fiction; 2. Conduct of life -- Fiction; 3. Courts and courtiers -- Fiction; 4. Samurai -- Fiction; 5. Sex role -- Fiction; 6. Weddings -- Fiction; 7. Japan -- History -- Tokugawa period, 1600-1868 -- Fiction; 8. Siblings -- Fiction

    9781524738143, $18.99

                          LC 2018007928

In this novel in the Flame in the Mist series, by Renée Ahdieh, "after Okami is captured in the Jukai forest, Mariko has no choice -- to rescue him, she must return to Inako and face the dangers that have been waiting for her in the Heian Castle. She tricks her brother, Kenshin, and betrothed, Raiden, into thinking she was being held by the Black Clan against her will, playing the part of the dutiful bride-to-be to infiltrate the emperor's ranks." (Publisher's note)

Sequel to: Flame in the mist

The **wrath** and the dawn. Renée Ahdieh. Putnam-Juvenile 2015 416 p. Illustration; Map

Grades: 9 10 11 12

    Fairy tales 2. Love -- Fiction 3. Murder -- Fiction 4.Kings and rulers -- Fiction 5. Magic -- Fiction

    0399171614; 9780399171611, $17.99

                          LC 2014046249

In this book, by Renée Ahdieh, "the brave Shahrzad volunteers to marry the Caliph of Khorasan after her best friend is chosen as one of his virgin brides and is summarily murdered the next morning. She uses her storytelling skills, along with well-placed cliff-hangers, to keep herself alive while trying to discover a way to exact revenge on the Caliph. However, the longer she stays in the palace, the more she realizes there's more going on than just a murderous prince." (School Library Journal)

"It's not a completely faultless debut-the prose very occasionally turns purple, but that's a minor offense; the characters are redeemingly nuanced and well crafted. Even more impressive, Ahdieh is in complete control of her plot, tightly spooling out threads of the richly layered story just as surely as Shahrzad herself. The result is that the reader can't help but be absorbed by the time the crescendoing conclusion come-and in true Arabian Nights fashion, it's a cliff-hanger. Like the caliph, we will just have to wait for the rest."Booklist

Ahmed, Samira

★ Love, hate & other filters. Samira Ahmed. Soho Teen 2018 281 p. Illustration

Grades: 8 9 10 11

    1. Dating (Social customs) -- Fiction; 2. East Indian Americans -- Fiction; 3. Family life -- Illinois -- Chicago -- Fiction; 4. High schools -- Fiction; 5. Muslims -- Fiction; 6. Schools -- Fiction; 7. Terrorism -- Fiction; 8.

Chicago (Ill.) -- Fiction
9781616958473, $18.99; 9781616958480

LC 2017021616

In this book, by Samira Ahmed, "American-born seventeen-year-old Maya Aziz is torn between worlds. There's the proper one her parents expect for their good Indian daughter: attending a college close to their suburban Chicago home, and being paired off with an older Muslim boy her mom deems 'suitable.' And then there is the world of her dreams: going to film school and living in New York City -- and maybe (just maybe) pursuing a boy she's known from afar since grade." (Publisher's note)

"A well-crafted plot with interesting revelations about living as a secular Muslim teen in today's climate." Kirkus

Albert, Melissa

★ The **Hazel** Wood: a novel. Melissa Albert. Flatiron Books 2018 359 p. Illustration
Grades: 10 11 12

1. Fairy tales -- Fiction; 2. Imaginary places -- Fiction; 3. Inheritance and succession -- Fiction; 4. Magic -- Fiction; 5. Mothers and daughters -- Fiction; 6. Fairy tales
9781250147912; 9781250147905, $18.99

LC 2017041749

In this book, by Melissa Albert, "Alice and her mother have spent most of Alice's life on the road.... But when Alice's grandmother, the reclusive author of a cult-classic book of pitch-dark fairy tales, dies alone on her estate, the Hazel Wood, Alice learns how bad her luck can really get: Her mother is stolen away -- by a figure who claims to come from the Hinterland, the cruel supernatural world where her grandmother's stories are set." (Publisher's note)

"Highly literary, occasionally surreal, and grounded by Alice's clipped, matter-of-fact voice, it's a dark story that readers will have trouble leaving behind." Booklist

Albertalli, Becky

Leah on the offbeat. Becky Albertalli, edited by Donna Bray. Balzer + Bray, an imprint of HarperCollinsPublishers 2018 368 p.
Grades: 9 10 11 12

1. Friendship -- Fiction; 2. Identity (Psychology) -- Fiction; 3. High school students -- Fiction; 4. Bisexuals -- Fiction
9780062643803, $17.99

LC 2017934758

In this novel, by Becky Albertalli, edited by Donna Bray, "we follow Simon's BFF Leah as she grapples with changing friendships, first love, and senior year angst. When it comes to drumming, Leah Burke is always on beat -- but real life isn't always so rhythmic.... She loves to draw but is too self-conscious to show it. And even though her mom knows she's bisexual, she hasn't mustered the courage to tell her friends -- not even her openly gay BFF, Simon." (Publisher's note)

★ **Simon** vs. the Homo Sapiens agenda. Becky Albertalli. Balzer + Bray, an imprint of Harper Collins Publishers 2015 320 p.
Grades: 9 10 11 12

1. Friendship -- Fiction 2. Gays -- Fiction 3. High

schools -- Fiction 4. Pen pals -- Fiction 5. Schools -- Fiction 6. Secrets -- Fiction 7. Gay teenagers -- Fiction 8. School stories
0062348671; 9780062348678, $17.99

LC 2014022536

Morris Award (2016)

In this novel by Becky Albertalli, "sixteen-year-old and not-so-openly gay Simon Spier prefers to save his drama for the school musical. But when an email falls into the wrong hands, his secret is at risk of being thrust into the spotlight. Now change-averse Simon has to find a way to step out of his comfort zone before he's pushed out—without alienating his friends, compromising himself, or fumbling a shot at happiness." (Publisher's note)

"While Simon is focused on Blue, other characters go on journeys of their own, and the author is careful not only to wrap up Simon's story, but to draw attention to the stories the romance plot might overshadow in lesser hands. Funny, moving and emotionally wise." Kirkus

★ The **upside** of unrequited. Becky Albertalli. Balzer + Bray 2017 340 p.
Grades: 9 10 11 12

1. Twins -- Fiction; 2. Romance fiction; 3. Lesbian teenagers -- Fiction
9780062348708, $17.99; 9780062348722

LC 2016938957

This novel, by Becky Albertalli, is "about sisterhood, love, and identity. Seventeen-year-old Molly Peskin-Suso knows all about unrequited love. No matter how many times her twin sister, Cassie, tells her to woman up, Molly can't stomach the idea of rejection. So she's careful. Fat girls always have to be careful." (Publisher's note)

"Albertalli's keen ear for authentic teen voices will instantly make readers feel that they are a part of Cassie and Molly's world, filled with rich diversity..., love, support, and a little heartache." SLJ

★ **What** if it's us. Becky Albertalli and Adam Silvera. HarperTeen, an imprint of HarperCollinsPublishers 2018 448 p.
Grades: 9 10 11 12

1. Dating (Social customs) -- Fiction; 2. Fate and fatalism -- Fiction; 3. Gays -- Fiction; 4. New York (N.Y.) -- Fiction
9780062795250, $18.99

LC 2018013361

This book, by Becky Albertalli and Adam Silvera, is "about...two boys who can't decide if the universe is pushing them together -- or pulling them apart. ARTHUR is only in New York for the summer, but if Broadway has taught him anything, it's that the universe can deliver a showstopping romance when you least expect it. BEN thinks the universe needs to mind its business.... But when Arthur and Ben meet..., what exactly does the universe have in store for them...?" (Publisher's note)

"In the coauthors' capable hands, Arthur and Ben are distinct, empathetic heroes; Broadway-loving Arthur, who has Ivy League aspirations, adapts to the ways his recent coming out changed his friendships, while Ben struggles in school but dreams of writing, and sometimes isn't sure how to connect with his Puerto Rican heritage when he passes as white." Booklist

Alban, Andrea

Anya's war. Feiwel and Friends 2011 188p $16.99

Grades: 7 8 9 10

1. Jews -- China -- Fiction 2. Jewish refugees -- Fiction 3. Abandoned children -- Fiction 4. Sino-Japanese Conflict, 1937-1945 -- Fiction

ISBN 978-0-312-37093-0; 0-312-37093-8

LC 2010-37089

In 1937, the privileged and relatively carefee life of a fourteen-year-old Jewish girl, whose family emigrated from Odessa, Ukraine, to Shanghai, China, comes to an end when she finds an abandoned baby, her hero, Amelia Earhart, goes missing, and war breaks out with Japan. Based on the author's family history.

"Most moving are the scenes with the full cast of family characters, who are irritating, irritable, funny, surprising, mean, and prejudiced. Alban also explores the complexities of Anya's Jewish community. . . . An important addition to literature about WWII refugees." Booklist

Aldredge, Betsy

Sasquatch, love, and other imaginary things. Betsy Aldredge and Carrie DuBois-Shaw. Simon Pulse 2017 272 p.

Grades: 7 8 9 10

1. Competition (Psychology) -- Fiction; 2. Family life -- Fiction; 3. Jews -- United States -- Fiction; 4. Reality television programs -- Fiction; 5. Social classes -- Fiction; 6. Television -- Production and direction -- Fiction; 7. Yeti -- Fiction

9781507202814; 1507202806; 9781507202807, $19.99

LC 2017009581

This book, by Betsy Aldredge and Carrie DuBois-Shaw, is "about a loving, quirky family on the hunt for the mythical Sasquatch.... It's bad enough that Samantha's parents...have dragged their daughter... hunting for yetis. But now they're doing it on national TV, and worse, in front of an aristocratic prep-school crew including a boy who disdains Samantha's family. But when he scorns her humble Ohio roots, she becomes determined to take him down." (Publisher's note)

"Samantha's first-person narration is marked by her sarcastic, wry, and delightfully snarky humor. 'Squatching' doesn't get any funnier than this." Kirkus

Alegria, Malin

Estrella's quinceanera. Simon & Schuster Books for Young Readers 2006 272p $14.95

Grades: 7 8 9 10

1. Mexican Americans -- Fiction 2. Quinceañera (Social custom) -- Fiction

ISBN 0-689-87809-5

Estrella's mother and aunt are planning a gaudy, traditional quinceañera for her, even though it is the last thing she wants.

"Alegria writes about Mexican American culture, first love, family, and of moving between worlds with poignant, sharp-sighted humor and authentic dialogue." Booklist

Alender, Katie

Bad girls don't die. Hyperion Books 2009 352p $15.99

Grades: 7 8 9 10

1. School stories 2. Sisters -- Fiction 3. Demoniac possession -- Fiction

ISBN 978-1-4231-0876-4; 1-4231-0876-0

LC 2008-46179

When fifteen-year-old Lexi's younger sister Kasey begins behaving strangely and their old Victorian house seems to take on a life of its own, Lexi investigates and discovers some frightening facts about previous occupants of the house, leading her to believe that many lives are in danger.

This "novel is both a mystery and a trip into the paranormal. . . . With just enough violence, suspense, and romance to keep readers turning pages, this . . . will be a popular addition to any YA collection." Booklist

Followed by: From bad to cursed (2011)

The **dead** girls of Hysteria Hall. Point, an imprint of Scholastic Inc. 2015 336 p.

Grades: 7 8 9 10 11 12

1. Asylums -- fiction 2. Families -- Pennsylvania -- fiction 3. Family life -- Fiction 4. Ghost stories 5. Ghosts -- Fiction 6. Haunted houses -- Fiction 7. Horror stories 8. Horror tales 9. Psychiatric hospitals -- Fiction 10. Secrecy -- fiction 11. Secrets -- Fiction 12. Sisters -- Fiction 13. Horror fiction 14. Pennsylvania -- Fiction

9780545639996, $18.99

LC 2014046681

In this book, by Katie Alender, "Delia's new house isn't just a house. Long ago, it was the Piven Institute for the Care and Correction of Troubled Females—an insane asylum. . . . However, many of the inmates were not insane, just defiant and strong willed. Kind of like Delia herself. But the house still wants to keep "troubled" girls locked away. So, in the most horrifying way, Delia becomes trapped. And that's when she learns that the house is also haunted." (Publisher's note)

"Alender creates a fascinating, eerie world that turns on a nicely original use of time and features constantly interesting characters. Delia is likable and sympathetic even as she strikes out, and the house itself becomes a character, as readers wonder who or what is at the root of the evil that lurks there. The final confrontation will have readers curling their toes. A really scary and original ghost story, well told. Read it with the lights on." Kirkus

Alexander, Kwame

★ **Booked**. Houghton Mifflin Harcourt 2016 320 p.

Grades: 5 6 7 8 9

1. Soccer -- Fiction 2. Books and reading -- Fiction 3. Friendship -- Fiction

9780544570986, $16.99; 0544570987

LC 2015033312

In this novel by Kwame Alexander "soccer, family, love, and friendship, take center stage as twelve-year-old Nick learns the power of words as he wrestles with problems at home, stands up to a bully, and tries to impress the girl of his dreams. Helping him along are his best friend and sometimes teammate Coby, and The Mac, a rapping librarian who gives Nick inspiring books to read." (Publisher's note)

"Alexander scores again with this sports-themed verse novel, a companion to his Newbery Medal-winning The

Crossover. Eighth grader Nick, a devoted soccer player and fan, enjoys some friendly competition with his best friend, Coby. What Nick doesn't like is words-neither the ones in the dictionary that his linguistics professor father wrote (and is making him read) nor the ones he learns in his honors English class. But the school's quirky rapping librarian, Mr. Mac, helps Nick discover both a love of reading and a way to connect with the girl of his dreams. . . . Emotionally resonant and with a pace like a player on a breakaway, Nick's story will have readers agreeing: "The poems/ were cool./ The best ones were/ like bombs,/ and when all the right words/ came together/ it was like an explosion./ So good, I/ didn't want it to end." PW

★ The **crossover**; a basketball novel. by Kwame Alexander. Houghton Mifflin Harcourt 2014 240 p. $16.99

Grades: 7 8 9 10 11 12

1. Rap music 2. Novels in verse 3. Twins -- Fiction 4. Brothers -- Fiction 5. Basketball -- Fiction 6. Fathers and sons -- Fiction 7. African Americans -- Fiction
ISBN 0544107713; 9780544107717
LC 2013013810

Newbery Medal (2015)
Coretta Scott King Author Award Honor Book (2015)
In this novel, by Kwame Alexander, "12-year old Josh Bell . . . and his twin brother Jordan are awesome on the court. But Josh has more than basketball in his blood, he's got mad beats, too, that tell his family's story in verse. . . . Josh and Jordan must come to grips with growing up on and off the court to realize breaking the rules comes at a terrible price, as their story's . . . climax proves a game-changer for the entire family." (Publisher's note)

"Twins Josh and Jordan are junior high basketball stars, thanks in large part to the coaching of their dad, a former professional baller who was forced to quit playing for health reasons, and the firm, but loving support of their assistant-principal mom...Despite his immaturity, Josh is a likable, funny, and authentic character. Underscoring the sports and the fraternal tension is a portrait of a family that truly loves and supports one another. Alexander has crafted a story that vibrates with energy and heart and begs to be read aloud. A slam dunk." (School Library Journal)

He said, she said; by Kwame Alexander. Harper, an imprint of HarperCollinsPublishers 2013 336 p. (hardcover bdg.) $17.99

Grades: 9 10 11 12

1. High school students -- Fiction 2. Man-woman relationship -- Fiction 3. Love -- Fiction 4. Schools -- Fiction 5. High schools -- Fiction 6. African Americans -- Fiction 7. Protest movements -- Fiction
ISBN 006211896X; 9780062118967; 9780062118974
LC 2012043496

"Claudia Clarke--sharp, opinionated, and Harvard-bound--is the only girl who isn't impressed by quarterback Omar "T-Diddy" Smalls. Omar takes a bet that he can win Claudia over, and when his usual seduction tactics fail, he applies his social clout to Claudia's cause du jour. His burgeoning social awareness and transformation from carefree

jock to true campus leader are satisfying and convincing." (Horn Book)

Solo. Kwame Alexander with Mary Rand Hess. Blink 2017 458 p.

Grades: 7 8 9 10 11 12

1. Children of drug addicts -- Fiction; 2. Family secrets -- Fiction; 3. Fathers and sons -- Fiction; 4. Reconciliation -- Fiction; 5. Father-son relationship -- Fiction
9780310761839, $17.99; 9780310761907; 0310761832
LC 2016435234

In this book, by Kwame Alexander with Mary Rand Hess, "Blade never asked for a life of the rich and famous. In fact, he'd give anything not to be the son of Rutherford Morrison, a washed-up rock star and drug addict with delusions of a comeback. Or to no longer be part of a family known most for lost potential, failure, and tragedy, including the loss of his mother. The one true light is his girlfriend, Chapel, but her parents have forbidden their relationship." (Publisher's note)

"A contemporary hero's journey, brilliantly told." Kirkus

Swing. Kwame Alexander with Mary Rand Hess. Blink 2018 448 p.

Grades: 9 10 11 12

1. African Americans -- Fiction; 2. Baseball -- Fiction; 3. Best friends -- Fiction; 4. Friendship -- Fiction; 5. Letters -- Fiction; 6. Novels in verse
0310761913; 9780310761914, $18.99; 9780310761938; 9780310761945
LC 2018030417

This book in the Blink series, by Kwame Alexander and Mary Rand Hess, presents a "story about hope, courage, and love that speaks to anyone who's struggled to find their voice.... When America is not so beautiful, or right, or just, it can be hard to know what to do. Best friends Walt and Noah decide to use their voices to grow more good in the world, but first they've got to find cool." (Publisher's note)

Alexander, Shannon Lee

Love and other unknown variables. Shannon Lee Alexander. Entangled Teen 2014 329 p.

Grades: 9 10 11 12

1. Chemistry 2. Love stories 3. Physics 4. Terminally ill -- Fiction 5. Love -- Fiction
1622664671; 9781622664672, $16.99

This book by Shannon Lee Alexander "is told from the perspective of Charlie Hanson, a senior at Brighton School of Mathematics and Science. His life is planned out for him until he meets Charlotte Finch. She is ill, but this is a secret she does not immediately share. At Charlotte's urging and without knowing why, Charlie begins a prank campaign at Brighton in spite of the consequences to his future." (Library Media Connection)

"The characters' quirky affinities-Charlie's for math, Charlotte's for drawing, Ms. Finch's for literature-paint a world of passion and personality. A heartwarming YA story of love and entering the unknown territories of adulthood." Kirkus

Alexie, Sherman, 1966-

★ The **absolutely** true diary of a part-time Indian; art by Ellen Forney. Little, Brown 2007 229p il $18.99

Grades: 8 9 10

    1. School stories 2. Friendship -- Fiction 3. Family life -- Fiction 4. Native Americans -- Fiction

    ISBN 0316013684; 9780316013680

LC 2007-22799

National Book Award for Young People's Literature (2007)

    Boston Globe-Horn Book Award: Fiction and Poetry (2008)

Budding cartoonist Junior leaves his troubled school on the Spokane Indian Reservation to attend an all-white farm town school where the only other Indian is the school mascot. "Grades seven to ten." (Bull Cent Child Books)

"The many characters, on and off the rez, with whom he has dealings are portrayed with compassion and verve. . . . Forney's simple pencil cartoons fit perfectly within the story and reflect the burgeoning artist within Junior." Booklist

Ali, S. K.

★ **Saints** and misfits: a novel. S.K. Ali. Salaam Reads 2017 336 p.

Grades: 9 10 11 12

    1. Divorce -- Fiction; 2. Identity -- Fiction; 3. Muslims -- United States -- Fiction; 4. Sexual abuse -- Fiction; 5. Muslims -- Fiction

    9781481499248, $18.99; 9781481499255

LC 2016041455

William C. Morris Honor Book

This book, by S.K. Ali, is a "debut novel...starring a Muslim teen. There are three kinds of people in my world: 1. Saints, those special people moving the world forward.... 2. Misfits, people who don't belong. Like me -- the way I don't fit into Dad's brand-new family or in the leftover one composed of Mom and my older brother, Mama's-Boy-Muhammad. Also, there's Jeremy and me. Misfits. Because although..., Janna and Jeremy sound good together, we don't go together." (Publisher's note)

" Ali pens a touching exposition of a girl's evolution from terrified victim to someone who knows she's worthy of support and is brave enough to get it. Set in a multicultural Muslim family, this book is long overdue, a delight for readers who will recognize the culture and essential for those unfamiliar with Muslim experiences." (Booklist)

Almond, David, 1951-

★ **Clay**. Delacorte Press 2006 247p hardcover o.p. pa $8.99

Grades: 7 8 9 10

    1. Horror fiction 2. Supernatural -- Fiction

    ISBN 0-385-73171-X; 0-440-42013-X pa

LC 2005-22681

The developing relationship between teenager Davie and a mysterious new boy in town morphs into something darker and more sinister when Davie learns firsthand of the boy's supernatural powers.

"Rooted in the ordinariness of a community and in one boy's chance to play God, this story will grab readers with its gripping action and its important ideas." Booklist

Half a creature from the sea: A Life in Stories. David Almond; illustrated by Eleanor Taylor. Candlewick Press 2015 222 p. Illustration

Grades: 7 8 9 10

    1. England -- Fiction 3. Short stories -- Collections

    0763678775; 9780763678777, $16.99

LC 2015931431

In this book, author David Almond "presents a beautiful collection of short fiction, interwoven with pieces that illuminate the inspiration behind the stories. May Malone is said to have a monster in her house, but what Norman finds there may just be the angel he needs. Joe Quinn's house is noisy with poltergeists, or could it be Davie's raging causing the disturbance? Fragile Annie learns the truth about herself in a photograph taken by a traveling man near the sea." (Publisher's note)

"Taylor's illustrations help add depth, as do the interstitial author's notes offering glimpses into each story's autobiographical roots and other inspirations. Likely to appeal to aspiring writers and fans of The Tightrope Walkers." Horn Book

★ **Kit's** wilderness; 10th-anniversary edition; Delacorte Press 2009 229p $16.99

Grades: 6 7 8 9 10

    1. Ghost stories 2. Great Britain -- Fiction 3. Coal mines and mining -- Fiction

    ISBN 978-0-385-32665-0; 0-385-32665-3

    First published 1999

    Michael L. Printz Award, 2001

Thirteen-year-old Kit goes to live with his grandfather in the decaying coal mining town of Stoneygate, England, and finds both the old man and the town haunted by ghosts of the past

The author "explores the power of friendship and family, the importance of memory, and the role of magic in our lives. This is a highly satisfying literary experience." SLJ

★ **Skellig**; 10th anniversary ed.; Delacorte Press 2009 182p $16.99; pa $6.99

Grades: 5 6 7 8 9 10

    1. Fantasy fiction

    ISBN 978-0-385-32653-7; 0-385-32653-X; 978-0-440-41602-9 pa; 0-440-41602-7 pa

    First published 1998 in the United Kingdom; first United States edition 1999

    Michael L. Printz Award honor book

Unhappy about his baby sister's illness and the chaos of moving into a dilapidated old house, Michael retreats to the garage and finds a mysterious stranger who is something like a bird and something like an angel.

"The plot is beautifully paced and the characters are drawn with a graceful, careful hand. . . . A lovingly done, thought-provoking novel." SLJ

★ A **song** for Ella Grey. David Almond. Delacorte Press 2015 272 p.

    1. Friendship -- Fiction 2. Love -- Fiction 3. Mythology, Greek -- Fiction 4. Eurydice (Greek mythological character) -- Fiction 5. Orpheus (Greek mythological character) -- Fiction 6. England -- Fiction 7. Romance

fiction 8. England -- Fiction 9780553533590, $16.99; 9780553533606

LC 2014040181

This young adult novel, by David Almond, retells the story of Orpheus and Eurydice in contemporary England. It "is a tale of the joys, troubles, and desires of modern teens. It takes place in the ordinary streets of Tyneside and on the beautiful beaches of Northumberland. It's a story of first love, a love song that draws on ancient mythical forces. A love that leads Ella, Orpheus, and Claire to the gates of Death and beyond." (Publisher's note)

"Patient readers will likely be transfixed by this rhapsodic modern retelling of a classic tragedy." Booklist

Originally published in hardcover by Hodder Children's Books, London, in 2014.

★ The **tightrope** walkers. David Almond. Candlewick Press 2015 336 p.

Grades: 9 10 11 12

1. Bullying -- Fiction 2. Love stories 3. Shipbuilding -- Fiction 4. Teenagers -- Fiction 5. Bildungsromans 6. England -- Fiction

0763673102; 9780763673109, $17.99

LC 2014944915

In this book by David Almond, "Dominic Hall is the son of a shipbuilder, living in modest conditions in mid-20th century England. As he grows up, he finds himself torn between two influences—the dreamy intellectual artist girl next door and the brutal outcast boy who seems to cultivate a darker side of Dominic's nature. His coming-of-age is marked by the ramifications of his choices between the two." (School Library Journal)

"This brilliant novel follows Dom, a working-class boy in 1960s northern England, from ages five to seventeen. Dom forges his own values; succumbs to the lure of thug Vincent; falls in love with childhood pal Holly; discovers himself as a writer; and learns to walk a tightrope both literal and figurative. It's all unsettling emotion as Almond limns the nature of joy and rage." Horn Book

The **true** tale of the monster Billy Dean; David Almond. Viking 2011 255 p. $17.99

Grades: 9 10 11 12

1. Dystopian fiction 2. Children and war -- Fiction 3. Parent-child relationship -- Fiction

ISBN 0763663093; 9780763663094

LC 2012358384

This novel, by David Almond, is "about a hidden-away child who emerges into a broken world. Billy Dean is a secret child. . . . His father fills his mind and his dreams with mysterious tales and memories and dreadful warnings. But then his father disappears, and Billy's mother brings him out into the world at last. He learns the horrifying story of what was saved and what was destroyed on the day he was born, the day the bombers came to Blinkbonny." (Publisher's note)

"The opening scenes of this postapocalyptic, psychological novel describing the protagonist's confinement in a small, locked room is strongly reminiscent of Emma Donoghue's adult title Room (Little, Brown, 2010). Billy Dean's mother was seduced by an unethical priest, and young Billy is forced to suffer the consequences of their affair by being kept hidden. The compelling story is told from Billy's point of view and with the language and phonetic spelling of a child whose development has been stunted by his lifelong imprisonment... This challenging title demands to be read more than once, and even then it will leave questions unanswered." (School Library Journal)

Alsaid, Adi

Let's Get Lost. Adi Alsaid. Harlequin Books 2014 352 p.

Grades: 9 10 11 12

1. Adolescence 2. Bildungsromans 3. Friendship 4. Grief 5. Automobile travel -- Fiction 6. Teenagers -- Fiction 7. Interpersonal relations

0373211244; 9780373211241, $17.99

In this novel by Adi Alsaid "four teens across the country have only one thing in common: a girl named Leila. She crashes into their lives in her absurdly red car at the moment they need someone the most. Hudson, Bree, Elliot and Sonia find a friend in Leila. And when Leila leaves them, their lives are forever changed. But it is during Leila's own 4,268-mile journey that she discovers the most important truth—sometimes, what you need most is right where you started." (Publisher's note)

"With romantic interludes, witty banter, some exhilarating minor law breaking, occasional drinking, an empowering message, and satisfying conclusions for everyone involved, this will likely be a popular summer hit, especially for older teens about to embark on their own journeys of self-discovery." Booklist

Never Always Sometimes. Adi Alsaid. Harlequin Books 2015 352 p.

Grades: 9 10 11 12

1. High school students -- Fiction 2. Romance fiction 3. Friendship -- Fiction

0373211546; 9780373211548, $17.99

In this book by Adi Alsaid, "before beginning high school, best friends Dave and Julia create a list of cliches they plan to avoid: never run for prom king, never hook up with a teacher, etc. But after they get accepted to college, a slump sets in, and they decide to mix things up by tackling items on the list." (Booklist)

"There is a kernel of truth in every cliché, and Alsaid cracks the teen-lit trope of friends becoming lovers wide open, exposing a beautiful truth inside. He also perfectly captures the golden glow of senioritis, a period when teens are bored and excited and wistful and nostalgic all at once. Everything is possible in this handful of weeks, including making up for squandered time. A good romance is hard to come by. This is a great one." Kirkus

North of happy. By Adi Alsaid. Harlequin Teen 2017 296 p.

Grades: 9 10 11 12

1. Brothers -- Death -- Fiction; 2. Celebrity chefs -- Fiction; 3. Cooking -- Fiction; 4. Interpersonal relations -- Fiction; 5. Mexicans -- United States -- Fiction; 6. Father-son relationship -- Fiction; 7. Death -- Fiction; 8. Bildungsromans

9781488015359; 9780373212286, $18.99; 0373212283

In this book, by Adi Alsaid, "Carlos Portillo has always led a privileged and sheltered life. A dual citizen of Mexico and the United States, he lives in Mexico City with his wealthy family, where he attends an elite international school.... When his older brother, Felix -- who has dropped out of college to live a life of travel -- is tragically killed, Carlos begins hearing his brother's voice, giving him advice and pushing him to rebel against his father's plan for him." (Publisher's note)

"An exceptional tale of grief, ambition, love, and maturity." Kirkus

Alsenas, Linas

Beyond clueless. Linas Alsenas. Amulet Books 2015 256 p.

Grades: 7 8 9 10

1. Catholic schools -- Fiction 2. Coming out (Sexual orientation) -- Fiction 3. Gays -- Fiction 4. High schools -- Fiction 5. Interpersonal relations -- Fiction 6. Musicals -- Fiction 7. Schools -- Fiction 8. Theater -- Fiction 9. College and school drama 10. High school students -- Fiction 11. Friendship -- Fiction

9781419714962, $16.95; 1419714961

LC 2015005780

In this novel, by Linas Alsenas, "Marty Sullivan's life ends, basically, when her parents enroll her [in a] . . . private, Catholic, girls-only high school. Meanwhile, at their local public school, her best friend, Jimmy, comes out of the closet and finds himself a boyfriend and a new group of friends. Marty feels left out and alone, until she gets a part in the school musical . . . and Jimmy and his new crew are in it. Things start looking even better when Marty falls for foxy fellow cast member Felix Peroni. And Felix seems to like her back. But the drama is just beginning." (Publisher's note)

"Alsenas's title offers practical, kid-appropriate advice on the value of friendship and the importance of self-knowledge... A pleasing, humorous tale of relationship angst." SLJ

Altebrando, Tara

The **Leaving**. Tara Altebrando. Bloomsbury 2016 432 p.

Grades: 9 10 11 12

1. Identity -- Fiction 2. Kidnapping -- Fiction 3. Memory -- Fiction 4. Missing children -- Fiction 5. Mystery and detective stories 6. Mystery fiction

9781619638044, $42; 9781619638037, $17.99

LC 2015037730

In this novel, by Tara Altebrando, "eleven years ago, six kindergartners went missing without a trace. . . . Until . . . five of those kids return. They're sixteen, and they are . . . fine . . . , except they're entirely unable to recall where they've been or what happened to them. Neither of them remember the sixth victim, Max—the only one who hasn't come back." (Publisher's note)

"It's engrossing, both as a thriller and a meditation on memory-its limits, its loss, and the ways it deceives and constructs identity." Pub Wkly

Alvarez, Julia

★ **Before** we were free. Knopf 2002 167p $15.95; lib bdg $17.99; pa $5.99

Grades: 7 8 9 10

1. Family life -- Fiction 2. Dominican Republic --

History -- 1930-1961

ISBN 0-375-81544-9; 0-375-91544-3 lib bdg; 0-440-23784-X pa

LC 2001-50520

In the early 1960s in the Dominican Republic, twelve-year-old Anita learns that her family is involved in the underground movement to end the bloody rule of the dictator, General Trujillo

This "is a realistic and compelling account of a girl growing up too quickly while coming to terms with the cost of freedom." Horn Book

Amateau, Gigi

A **certain** strain of peculiar. Candlewick Press 2009 261p $16.99

Grades: 6 7 8 9

1. Ranch life -- Fiction 2. Grandmothers -- Fiction

ISBN 978-0-7636-3009-6; 0-7636-3009-8

Tired of the miserable life she lives, Mary Harold leaves her mother behind and moves back to Alabama and her grandmother, where she receives support and love and starts to gain confidence in herself and her abilities.

"Mary Harold is a wonderfully complex and honest character. . . . [Her] narrative is heartfelt and poignant, and the message that being 'different' is nothing to be ashamed of will resonate with readers." Voice Youth Advocates

Amato, Mary

Get happy. Egmont USA 2014 256 p.

Grades: 6 7 8 9

1. Families -- Fiction 2. Fathers and daughters -- Fiction 3. Friendship -- Fiction 4. Musicians -- Fiction 5. Father-daughter relationship -- Fiction 6. Family -- Fiction

1606845225; 9781606845226, $16.99

LC 2014008736

"Minerva has been raised by her single mother after her father left them both. On her 17th birthday, she is shocked to discover that he has been trying to keep in touch, but her mother has been sabotaging his attempts. Furious at her mom, she begins to investigate her dad, a famous marine biologist, only to discover that he has a new family, including a beloved, and perfect, stepdaughter—a girl Minerva already knows and despises." (Publisher's note)

"Though the book explores a heavy, fraught situation, the prose is light and the ending optimistic. Some readers may be frustrated with the lack of closure, as quite a bit is left unresolved. Overall, however, this is a moving, charged tale of family and identity." SLJ

Anderson, Jodi Lynn

★ **Midnight** at the Electric. Jodi Lynn Anderson. HarperTeen 2017 257 p.

Grades: 9 10 11 12

1. Friendship -- Fiction; 2. Interplanetary voyages -- Fiction; 3. Life change events -- Fiction; 4. Teenage girls -- Fiction

9780062393562; 9780062393548, $17.99

LC 2017932844

This novel, by Jodi Lynn Anderson, begins in "Kansas, 2065: Adri has been handpicked to live on Mars.... Oklahoma, 1934: Amid the...Dust Bowl, Catherine's family's situation is growing dire.... England, 1919:...Following World War I, Lenore tries to come to terms with her grief for her brother.... While their stories span thousands of miles and multiple generations, Lenore, Catherine, and Adri's fates are entwined." (Publisher's note)

"Anderson deftly tackles love, friendship, and grief in this touching exploration of resilience and hope." SLJ

★ **Tiger** Lily; Jodi Lynn Anderson. HarperTeen 2012 304 p. (trade bdg.) $17.99

Grades: 8 9 10 11

1. Love stories 2. Jealousy -- Fiction 3. Fairy tales 4. Peter Pan (Fictional character) 5. Love -- Fiction 6. Magic -- Fiction 7. Fairies -- Fiction

ISBN 0062003259; 9780062003256

LC 2011032659

This is the story of Tiger Lily, the girl Peter Pan spurned for Wendy. "Told from the perspective of Tinker Bell, the novel explores how Tiger Lily meets and falls in love with Peter, despite being betrothed to another villager, a man Tiger Lily despises. Tiger Lily and Peter's complicated inner conflicts emerge as they sort out their feelings about freedom, power, loyalty, and responsibility. When a girl from England arrives, Tiger Lily" feels jealous for the first time. (Publishers Weekly)

The **vanishing** season. Jodi Lynn Anderson; [edited by] Kari Sutherland. HarperTeen 2014 272 p.

Grades: 7 8 9 10 11 12

1. Detective and mystery stories 2. Murder -- Investigation -- Fiction 3. Door County (Wis.) -- Fiction 4. Teenage girls -- Fiction 5. Homicide -- Fiction

0062003275; 9780062003270, $17.99

LC 2014934799

In this teen novel, by Jodi Lynn Anderson, edited by Kari Sutherland, "for Maggie Larsen . . . what starts as an uneventful year suddenly changes. Someone is killing teen-aged girls, and the town reels from the tragedy. As Maggie's and Pauline's worlds collide and change around them, they will both experience love and loss. And by the end of the book, only one of them will survive." (Pubisher's note)

"For all the mythic overtones of Maggie and Pauline's friendship, Anderson still manages to give her characters authentic teen voices, striking an uneasy balance between naïveté and worldliness. The pace might be slow for some, but readers who like their romances tragic and dreamy should dive in." Booklist

Anderson, Katie D.

Kiss & Make Up. Amazon Childrens Pub 2012 307 p. (hardcover) $16.99

Grades: 7 8 9 10

1. Occult fiction 2. School stories

ISBN 076146316X; 9780761463160

This book focuses on Emerson Taylor, who "has a gift—or a curse. She can read a person's mind with the lightest of kisses. When her financially strapped aunt announces that Emerson will not be attending private school the following year if her grades don't improve, Emerson initializes Operation Liplock. She will begin study sessions with the geeky Ivys—those destined to attend Ivy League colleges—where

she will kiss them, allowing their knowledge to transfer to her mind." (School Library Journal)

Anderson, Laurie Halse, 1961-

★ **Chains**; seeds of America. Simon & Schuster Books for Young Readers 2008 316p $17.99

Grades: 6 7 8 9 10

1. Spies -- Fiction 2. Slavery -- Fiction 3. New York (N.Y.) -- Fiction 4. African Americans -- Fiction 5. United States -- History -- 1775-1783, Revolution -- Fiction

ISBN 1-4169-0585-5; 1-4169-0586-3 pa; 978-1-4169-0585-1; 978-1-4169-0586-8 pa

LC 2007-52139

After being sold to a cruel couple in New York City, a slave named Isabel spies for the rebels during the Revolutionary War. "Grades seven to ten." (Bull Cent Child Books)

"This gripping novel offers readers a startlingly provocative view of the Revolutionary War. . . . [Anderson's] solidly researched exploration of British and Patriot treatment of slaves during a war for freedom is nuanced and evenhanded, presented in service of a fast-moving, emotionally involving plot." Publ Wkly

Followed by: Forge (2010)

Fever, 1793. Simon & Schuster Bks. for Young Readers 2000 251p $17.99; pa $6.99

Grades: 5 6 7 8 9

1. Epidemics -- Fiction 2. Yellow fever -- Fiction 3. Philadelphia (Pa.) -- Fiction

ISBN 978-0-689-83858-3; 0-689-83858-1; 978-0-689-84891-9 pa; 0-689-84891-9 pa

LC 00-32238

In 1793 Philadelphia, sixteen-year-old Matilda Cook, separated from her sick mother, learns about perseverance and self-reliance when she is forced to cope with the horrors of a yellow fever epidemic. "Age ten and up." (N Y Times Book Rev)

"A vivid work, rich with well-drawn and believable characters. Unexpected events pepper the top-flight novel that combines accurate historical detail with a spellbinding story line." Voice Youth Advocates

Forge. Atheneum Books for Young Readers 2010 297p (Seeds of America) $16.99

Grades: 6 7 8 9 10

1. Slavery -- Fiction 2. Soldiers -- Fiction 3. Pennsylvania -- Fiction 4. African Americans -- Fiction 5. United States -- History -- 1775-1783, Revolution -- Fiction

ISBN 978-1-4169-6144-4; 1-4169-6144-5

LC 2010-15971

Sequel to: Chains (2008)

Separated from his friend Isabel after their daring escape from slavery, fifteen-year-old Curzon serves as a free man in the Continental Army at Valley Forge until he and Isabel are thrown together again, as slaves once more.

"Weaving a huge amount of historical detail seamlessly into the story, Anderson creates a vivid setting, believable characters both good and despicable and a clear portrayal of the moral ambiguity of the Revolutionary age. Not only can this sequel stand alone, for many readers it will be one of the best novels they have ever read." Kirkus

★ The **impossible** knife of memory; Laurie Halse Anderson. Viking, published by Penguin Group 2014 400 p. (hardback) $18.99
Grades: 9 10 11 12
  1. Father-daughter relationship -- Fiction 2. Iraq War, 2003-2011 -- Veterans -- Fiction 3. Post-traumatic stress disorder -- Fiction 4. Veterans -- Fiction 5. Family problems -- Fiction
  ISBN 0670012092; 9780670012091
                                    LC 2013031267
In this book, by Laurie Halse Anderson, "Hayley Kincaid and her father, Andy, have been on the road, never staying long in one place as he struggles to escape the demons that have tortured him since his return from Iraq. Now they are back in the town where he grew up so Hayley can attend school. Perhaps, for the first time, Hayley can have a normal life. . . . Will being back home help Andy's PTSD, or will his terrible memories drag him to the edge of hell, and drugs push him over?" (Publisher's note)
"With powerful themes of loyalty and forgiveness, this tightly woven story is a forthright examination of the realities of war and its aftermath on soldiers and their families." SLJ

★ **Speak**; 10th anniversary ed.; Speak 2009 197p pa $11.99
Grades: 7 8 9 10
  1. School stories 2. Rape -- Fiction
  ISBN 978-0-14-241473-6
                                    LC 2009-502164
First published 1999
A traumatic event near the end of the summer has a devastating effect on Melinda's freshman year in high school.
The novel is "keenly aware of the corrosive details of outsiderhood and the gap between home and daily life at high school; kids whose exclusion may have less concrete cause than Melinda's will nonetheless find the picture recognizable. This is a gripping account of personal wounding and recovery." Bull Cent Child Books

Twisted. Viking 2007 250p $16.99
Grades: 9 10 11 12
  1. School stories 2. Ohio -- Fiction 3. Family life -- Fiction
  ISBN 978-0-670-06101-3
                                    LC 2006-31297
After finally getting noticed by someone other than school bullies and his ever-angry father, seventeen-year-old Tyler enjoys his tough new reputation and the attentions of a popular girl, but when life starts to go bad again, he must choose between transforming himself or giving in to his destructive thoughts.
"This is a gripping exploration of what it takes to grow up, really grow up, against the wishes of people and circumstances conspiring to keep you the victim they need you to be." Bull Cent Child Books

★ **Wintergirls**. Viking 2009 288p $17.99
Grades: 8 9 10 11 12
  1. Death -- Fiction 2. Friendship -- Fiction 3. Self-mutilation -- Fiction 4. Anorexia nervosa -- Fiction
  ISBN 0-670-01110-X; 978-0-670-01110-0
                                    LC 2008-37452
Eighteen-year-old Lia comes to terms with her best friend's death from anorexia as she struggles with the same disorder.
"As events play out, Lia's guilt, her need to be thin, and her fight for acceptance unravel in an almost poetic stream of consciousness in this startlingly crisp and pitch-perfect first-person narrative." SLJ

Anderson, M. T., 1968-
  ★ The **astonishing** life of Octavian Nothing, traitor to the nation; the pox party. taken from accounts by his own hand and other sundry sources; collected by M.T. Anderson of Boston. Candlewick Press 2006 351p $17.99
Grades: 9 10 11 12
  1. Slavery -- Fiction 2. African Americans -- Fiction 3. United States -- History -- 1775-1783, Revolution -- Fiction
  ISBN 0763624020; 9780763624026
                                    LC 2006043170
Michael L. Printz Award honor book (2007), National Book Award for Young People's Literature (2006), Boston Globe-Horn Book Awards: Fiction and Poetry (2007)
This is the first of two volumes in The astonishing life of Octavian Nothing, traitor to the nation series. Various diaries, letters, and other manuscripts chronicle the experiences of Octavian, a young African American, from birth to age sixteen, as he is brought up as part of a science experiment in the years leading up to and during the Revolutionary War.
"Teens looking for a challenge will find plenty to sink into here. The questions raised about race and freedom are well developed and leave a different perspective on the Revolutionary War than most novels." Voice Youth Advocates
Followed by: The kingdom on the waves (2008)

The **astonishing** life of Octavian Nothing, traitor to the nation; v. #2 The kingdom on the waves. taken from accounts by his own hand and other sundry sources; collected by M.T. Anderson of Boston. Candlewick Press 2008 561p 2 maps (hardcover: alk. paper) $11.99
Grades: 9 10 11 12
  1. Freedom -- Fiction 2. African Americans -- Fiction 3. Slavery -- United States -- Fiction 4. United States -- History -- 1775-1783, Revolution -- Fiction 5. Slavery -- Fiction 6. Virginia -- History -- Revolution, 1775-1783 -- Fiction 7. United States -- History -- Revolution, 1775-1783 --Naval operations, British -- Fiction
  ISBN 0763646261; 9780763646264; 0763629502; 9780763629502
                                    LC 2008929919
Sequel to: The astonishing life of Octavian Nothing, traitor to the nation: the pox party (2006)
In this book, a Michael L. Printz Honor Book of 2009, "[f]earing a death sentence, Octavian and his tutor, Dr. Trefusis, escape through rising tides and pouring rain to find shelter in British-occupied Boston. Sundered from all he knows -- the College of Lucidity, the rebel cause -- Octavian hopes to find safe harbor. Instead, he is soon to learn

of Lord Dunmore's proclamation offering freedom to slaves who join the counterrevolutionary forces. . . . [Author] M. T. Anderson recounts Octavian's experiences as the Revolutionary War explodes around him, thrusting him into intense battles and tantalizing him with elusive visions of liberty." (Publisher's note)

"Elegantly crafted writing in an 18th-century voice, sensitive portrayals of primary and secondary characters and a fascinating author's note make this one of the few volumes to fully comprehend the paradoxes of the struggle for liberty in America." Kirkus

★ **Feed.** Candlewick Press 2002 237p hardcover o.p. pa $7.99
Grades: 8 9 10 11 12
    1. Satire 2. Science fiction
    ISBN 0-7636-1726-1; 0-7636-2259-1 pa
                   LC 2002-23738
In a future where most people have computer implants in their heads to control their environment, a boy meets an unusual girl who is in serious trouble

"An ingenious satire of corporate America and our present-day value system." Horn Book Guide

★ **Landscape** with invisible hand. M.T. Anderson. Candlewick Press 2017 149 p.
Grades: 9 10 11 12
    1. Survival -- Fiction; 2. Science fiction; 3. Extraterrestrial beings -- Fiction
    0763687898; 9780763697235; 9780763687892, $16.99
In this book, by M.T. Anderson, "when the vuvv first landed, it came as a surprise to aspiring artist Adam and the rest of planet Earth.... Can it really be called an invasion when the vuvv generously offered free advanced technology and cures for every illness imaginable? As it turns out, yes.... Soon enough, Adam must decide how far he's willing to go -- and what he's willing to sacrifice -- to give the vuvv what they want." (Publisher's note)

"Anderson takes issues of colonialism, ethnocentrism, inequality, and poverty and explodes them on a global, even galactic, scale. A remarkable exploration of economic and power structures in which virtually all of humanity winds up the losers." Pub Wkly

Anderson, Natalie C.

★ **City** of Saints & Thieves. Natalie C. Anderson. Penguin Group USA 2017 432 p.
Grades: 7 8 9 10
    1. Gangs -- Fiction 2. Sisters -- Fiction 3. Orphans -- Fiction 4. Refugees -- Fiction 5. Murder -- Fiction
    0399547584; 9780399547584, $18.99
                   LC 2016027799
In this novel, by Natalie C. Anderson, "after fleeing the Congo as refugees, Tina and her mother arrived in Kenya . . . to build a new life and home. Her mother quickly found work as a maid for a prominent family, headed by Roland Greyhill, . . . [whose] fortune was made from a life of corruption and crime. So when her mother is found shot to death in Mr. Greyhill's personal study, she knows exactly who's behind it." (Publisher's note)

"The novel is peppered with Swahili words and phrases, and Anderson makes an effort to paint a picture of the coun-try. A story full of twists and turns, proving nothing is ever as black and white as it may seem." Kirkus

Andreu, Maria E.

The **secret** side of empty; by Maria E. Andreu. Running Press Teens 2014 336p $16.95
Grades: 9 10 11 12
    1. Emigration and immigration-- Fiction 2. High school students-- Fiction 3. Teenage girls -- Fiction 4. United States —Immigration and emigration -- Fiction
    ISBN: 0762451920; 9780762451920
                   LC 2013950819
This book asks "what's it like to be undocumented? High school senior M.T. knows all too well. . . . M.T. was born in Argentina and brought to America as a baby without any official papers. And as questions of college, work, and the future arise, M.T. will have to decide what exactly she wants for herself, knowing someone she loves will unavoidably pay the price for it." (Publisher's note)

"An illegal immigrant, Monserrat Thalia has kept her status a secret for years. Despite her achievements in high school, now that she's a senior her future is uncertain and she's fighting for survival. Andreu draws from personal experience, and M.T.'s struggles with first love, depression, an abusive father, and the constant fear of deportation feel wholly real. A compelling and timely story." Horn Book

Andrews, Jesse

The **Haters**: a book about being in a band. Jesse Andrews. Amulet Books 2016 336 p.
Grades: 10 11 12
    1. Bands (Music) -- Fiction 2. Friendship -- Fiction 3. Musicians -- Fiction 4. Humorous fiction
    9781419720789, $18.95
                   LC 2015030408
In this book, by Jesse Andrews, "for Wes and his best friend, Corey, jazz camp turns out to be lame. It's pretty much all dudes talking in Jazz Voice. But then they jam with Ash, a charismatic girl with an unusual sound, and the three just click. It's three and a half hours of pure musical magic, and Ash makes a decision: They need to hit the road. Because the road, not summer camp, is where bands get good." (Publisher's note)

"At a jazz camp of "mostly dudes," bass player Wes and his drummer best friend Corey meet Ash, who has her own unique musical style and refuses to play with the condescending guys. Frustrated, she leaves—and Wes and Corey go with her. What follows is both a classic road-trip novel and an inventive teen adventure that subtly addresses race, family, and socioeconomics." Horn Book

Me & Earl & the dying girl; by Jesse Andrews. Amulet Books 2012 295 p. $16.95
Grades: 8 9 10
    1. Leukemia -- Fiction 2. Friendship -- Fiction 3. Family life -- Fiction 4. Pittsburgh (Pa.) -- Fiction 5. High school students -- Fiction 6. Humorous stories 7. Schools -- Fiction 8. High schools -- Fiction 9. Jews -- United States -- Fiction 10. Family life -- Pennsylvania -- Fiction
    ISBN 9781419701764
                   LC 2011031796

This book is a "confessional from a teen narrator who won't be able to convince readers he's as unlikable as he wants them to believe." It covers "[h]is filmmaking ambitions . . . his unlikely friendship with the . . . Earl of the title. And his unlikelier friendship with Rachel, the titular 'dying girl'. . . . He chronicles his senior year, in which his mother guilt-trips him into hanging out with Rachel, who has acute myelogenous leukemia." (Kirkus Reviews)

Munmun. Jesse Andrews. Amulet Books 2018 404 p. Illustration
Grades: 7 8 9 10 11 12
    1. Brothers and sisters -- Fiction; 2. Social classes -- Fiction; 3. Size -- Fiction; 4. Siblings -- Fiction
9781683352617; 9781419728716, $18.99
LC 2017043773
In this book, by Jesse Andrews, "Warner and his sister Prayer are destitute -- and tiny. Their size is not just demeaning, but dangerous: day and night they face mortal dangers that bigger richer people don't ever have to think about, from being mauled by cats to their house getting stepped on. There are no cars or phones built small enough for them, or schools or hospitals, for that matter.... [H]ow can two littlepoors survive in a world built against them?" (Publisher's note)

"Brilliant, savage, hilarious, a riveting journey through a harsh world that mirrors our own." Kirkus

Anstey, Cindy
    Carols and chaos. By Cindy Anstey. Swoon Reads 2018 336 p.
Grades: 7 8 9 10
    1. Christmas -- Fiction; 2. Counterfeits and counterfeiting -- Fiction; 3. Household employees -- Fiction; 4. Love -- Fiction; 5. Great Britain -- History -- George III, 1760-1820 -- Fiction; 6. Romance fiction
9781250174871, $10.99
LC 2018003012
In this book, by Cindy Anstey, "1817. The happy chaos of the Yuletide season has descended upon the country estate of Shackleford Park in full force, but lady's maid Kate Darby barely has the time to notice.... Matt Harlow is also rather busy.... Falling in love would be a disaster for either of them. But...when a devious counterfeiting scheme reaches the gates of Shackleford Park,...Kate and Matt are unwittingly swept up in the intrigue." (Publisher's note)
    Sequel to: Suitors and sabotage

Love, lies and spies. Cindy Anstey. Swoon Reads 2016 368 p.
Grades: 8 9 10 11
    1. Love -- Fiction 2. Spies -- Fiction 3. Great Britain -- History -- 1789-1820 -- Fiction 4. London (England) -- History -- 19th century -- Fiction 5. Romance fiction
9781250084033, $10.99; 9781250084064
LC 2015026917
In this novel, by Cindy Anstey, "in spite of the trappings of her time, Juliana is a lady of education and scientific interests thanks to her father. In London for her first season, she meets a young man who at first thinks she may be mixed up in some shady dealings that he's in town to investigate. No

new ground is covered in this tale: it follows the general formula of most Regency romances." (School Library Journal)

"A cute premise and cover make this a solid purchase for budding historical romance readers." SLJ

Anthony, Jessica
    Chopsticks; Jessica Anthony, Rodrigo Corral. Penguin/Razorbill 2012 304 p.
Grades: 9 10 11 12
    1. Mystery fiction 2. Musicians -- Fiction 3. Piano music -- Fiction 4. Mental illness -- Fiction 5. Missing children -- Fiction
ISBN 9781595144355
This "mystery [book] reveals the events leading up to the disappearance of Glory, a teenaged piano prodigy who goes missing after her struggle with mental illness that causes her to play the children's waltz 'Chopsticks' obsessively. Photographs, ephemera, and instant-message screenshots weave together the details of a forbidden romance with Francisco, the boy next door. . . . The story requires . . . visual literacy. . . . An example of the emerging trend of transmedia storytelling, this book will also be available in a 'fully interactive electronic version.' The inclusion of links to online media requires Internet access and a willingness to type . . . URLs, but the content of the links can be gleaned from context." (School Libr J)

Antieau, Kim
    Broken moon. Margaret K. McElderry Books 2007 183p $15.99
Grades: 7 8 9 10
    1. Pakistan -- Fiction 2. Siblings -- Fiction 3. Kidnapping -- Fiction
ISBN 978-1-4169-1767-0; 1-4169-1767-5
LC 2006-03780
When her little brother is kidnapped and taken from Pakistan to race camels in the desert, eighteen-year-old Nadira overcomes her own past abuse and, dressed as a boy and armed with knowledge of the powerful storytelling of the legendary Scheherazade, is determined to find and rescue him.

The author "presents important issues without letting them overtake the narrative, and the classic plot and sympathetic characters add up to an absorbing read." Horn Book

Arbuthnott, Gill
    The **Keepers'** tattoo. Chicken House 2010 425p $17.99
Grades: 6 7 8 9
    1. Fantasy fiction 2. Dreams -- Fiction 3. Uncles -- Fiction 4. Tattooing -- Fiction
ISBN 978-0-545-17166-3; 0-545-17166-0
LC 2009-26327
Months before her fifteenth birthday, Nyssa learns that she is a special member of a legendary clan, the Keepers of Knowledge, as she and her uncle try to escape from Alaric, the White Wolf, who wants to use lines tattooed on her to destroy the rest of her people.

Arbuthnott "writes with restraint and thoughtfulness, never condescending to her readers. Nyssa is a convincing mixture of ignorance, courage, and resourcefulness." Publ Wkly

Arcos, Carrie

★ **Out** of reach; Carrie Arcos. Simon Pulse 2012 250 p. (alk. paper) $16.99

Grades: 9 10 11 12

1. Siblings -- Fiction 2. Drug abuse -- Fiction 3. Families of drug addicts -- Fiction 4. Runaways -- Fiction 5. Methamphetamine -- Fiction 6. California, Southern -- Fiction

ISBN 1442440538; 9781442440531; 9781442440555

LC 2011044501

In this book by Carrie Arcos, "Rachel's older brother Micah is using crystal meth, and he is lying, stealing, and hurting those who love him in order to feed his addiction. . . . An anonymous e-mail warns Rachel that Micah is in serious trouble. So Rachel teams up with Micah's fellow band member . . . Tyler, to find her brother. . . . But, despite the heartache of the search, Rachel begins to see that her life isn't destroyed -- and that Tyler is surprisingly kind and caring." (Booklist)

There will come a time. Carrie Arcos. Simon Pulse 2014 315 p.

Grades: 9 10 11 12

1. Brothers and sisters -- Fiction 2. Death -- Fiction 3. Diaries -- Fiction 4. Family life -- California -- Los Angeles -- Fiction 5. Filipino Americans -- Fiction 6. Grief -- Fiction 7. Twins -- Fiction 8. Los Angeles (Calif.) -- Fiction 9. Suicide -- Fiction

1442495855; 9781442495852, $17.99

LC 2014002771

In this young adult novel by Carrie Arcos, "Mark knows grief. Ever since the accident that killed his twin sister, Grace, the only time he feels at peace is when he visits the bridge on which she died. Comfort is fleeting, but it's almost within reach when he's standing on the wrong side of the suicide bars. Almost. Grace's best friend, Hanna, says she understands what he's going through. . . . Hanna convinces Mark to complete Grace's bucket list from her journal." (Publisher's note)

" This nuanced story presents a close study on how different people react to loss while posing many thorny questions about relationships. Mark is Filipino American, and another character is Korean American, offering diversity for those wishing to widen their lists. Give this book to anyone who wants a rock-solid, character-driven story of finding one's footing after a life-changing event." Booklist

Armentrout, Jennifer L.

White Hot Kiss. By Jennifer L. Armentrout. Harlequin Books Teen 2014 400 p.

Grades: 9 10 11 12

1. Demonology -- Fiction 2. Supernatural -- Fiction 3. Gargoyles -- Fiction 4. Romance fiction

0373211104; 9780373211104, $9.99

In this book, "seventeen-year-old Layla just wants to be normal. But with a kiss that kills anything with a soul, she's anything but normal. Half demon, half gargoyle, Layla has abilities no one else possesses.Layla tries to fit in, but that means hiding her own dark side from those she loves the most. Especially Zayne, the . . . completely off-limits Warden she's crushed on since forever. Then she meets Roth—a tattooed, sinfully hot demon who claims to know all her secrets." (Publisher's note)

"With this first title in her new Dark Elements series, powerhouse author Armentrout delivers another action-packed, believably narrated ride through a paranormal world as seen by a teen... Intense, well plotted, and very readable, this title should fly into the hands of every paranormal reader out there." Booklist

Armistead, Cal

Being Henry David; by Cal Armistead. Albert Whitman 2013 312 p. (hardcover) $16.99

Grades: 8 9 10 11 12

1. Mystery fiction 2. Amnesia -- Fiction 3. Guilt -- Fiction 4. Runaways -- Fiction 5. Concord (Mass.) -- Fiction 6. Family problems -- Fiction 7. New York (N.Y.) -- Fiction 8. Street children -- Fiction

ISBN 080750615X; 9780807506158

LC 2012017377

In this book, a "boy wakes up in Penn Station, remembering nothing. He guesses that he's about 17, he has a head injury, and he is carrying only 10 dollars. Near at hand is a copy of Walden, so for want of anything better he calls himself Henry David (Hank). He heads to Concord, Massachusetts, to find, he hopes, some clues at Walden Pond. As his memories slowly return, he remembers who he was; as he copes with the memories, he discovers who he is and can be." (School Library Journal)

Armstrong, Kelley

Aftermath. Kelley Armstrong. Crown 2018 371 p.

Grades: 7 8 9 10

1. Best friends -- Fiction; 2. Brothers -- Death -- Fiction; 3. High school students -- Fiction; 4. Mass murder investigation -- Fiction; 5. School shootings -- Fiction; 6. Teenagers -- Fiction; 7. Brothers -- Fiction

0399550364; 9780399550362, $17.99; 9780399550386

In this book, by Kelley Armstrong, "three years after losing her brother Luka in a school shooting, Skye Gilchrist is moving home. But there's no sympathy for Skye and her family because Luka wasn't a victim; he was a shooter. Jesse Mandal knows all too well that the scars of the past don't heal easily. The shooting cost Jesse his brother and his best friend -- Skye. Ripped apart by tragedy, Jesse and Skye can't resist reopening the mysteries of their past." (Publisher's note)

The **summoning.** HarperCollinsPublishers 2008 390p (Darkest powers) $17.99; lib bdg $18.89

Grades: 7 8 9 10

1. Ghost stories 2. Supernatural -- Fiction

ISBN 978-0-06-166269-0; 0-06-166269-0; 978-0-06-166272-0 lib bdg; 0-06-166272-0 lib bdg

LC 2008-14221

After fifteen-year-old Chloe starts seeing ghosts and is sent to Lyle House, a mysterious group home for mentally disturbed teenagers, she soon discovers that neither Lyle House nor its inhabitants are exactly what they seem, and that she and her new friends are in danger.

"Suspenseful, well-written, and engaging, this page-turning . . . [novel] will be a hit." Voice Youth Advocates

Other titles in this series are:

The awakening (2009)

The reckoning (2010)

Armstrong, William Howard

★ **Sounder**; [by] William H. Armstrong; illustrations by James Barkley. Harper & Row 1969 116p il $15.99; pa $5.99

Grades: 5 6 7 8

1. Dogs -- Fiction 2. Family life -- Fiction 3. African Americans -- Fiction

ISBN 0-06-020143-6; 0-06-440020-4 pa

Awarded the Newbery Medal, 1970

"Set in the South in the era of sharecropping and segregation, this succinctly told tale poignantly describes the courage of a father who steals a ham in order to feed his undernourished family; the determination of the eldest son, who searches for his father despite the apathy of prison authorities; and the devotion of a coon dog named Sounder." Shapiro. Fic for Youth. 3d edition

Arnett, Mindee

Avalon. Balzer + Bray. 2014 432p $17.99

Grades: 8 9 10 11 12

1. Science fiction 2. Mercenary troops--Fiction

ISBN: 0062235591; 9780062235596

LC 2013005155

This novel is "about a group of teenage mercenaries who stumble upon a conspiracy that threatens the entire galaxy. Jeth Seagrave and his crew have made their name stealing metatech: the devices that allow people to travel great distances faster than the speed of light. . . . When he finds himself in possession of information that both government and the crime bosses are willing to kill for, he's going to find there's no escaping his past anymore." (Publisher's note)

"Jeth has one last job to complete before he can buy back his parents' spaceship from a crime boss. But the ship he was sent to find carries a deadly cargo that everyone in the galaxy wants. The strong bond between Jeth and his humorously motley crew of teenage mercenaries outshines the predictable plot and will appeal to Firefly-esque space-opera fans." Horn Book

Arnold, Alexandra

Love & other train wrecks. Leah Konen. Katherine Tegen Books 2018 359 p.

Grades: 7 8 9 10 11

1. Amtrak -- Fiction; 2. Children of divorced parents -- Fiction; 3. College students -- Fiction; 4. Interpersonal relations -- Fiction; 5. Railroad travel -- Fiction; 6. Strangers -- Fiction; 7. Winter storms -- Fiction; 8. New York (State) -- Fiction

9780062402509, $17.99; 9780062402523

LC 2017938600

In this book, author Leah Konen "spins a charming tale of two people who are meant to be, despite terrible first impressions. Alternating between Ammy and Noah's perspectives, Konen provides rich backstories for both characters while laying groundwork for a realistic love story that, like life, isn't always easy or perfect." (Publishers Weekly)

"An absurdly charming, funny, and romantic odyssey." Kirkus

Arnold, Elana K.

Infandous. By Elana K. Arnold. Carolrhoda Lab 2015 189 p.

Grades: 9 10 11 12

1. Mothers and daughters -- Fiction 2. Sculptors -- Fiction 3. Secrets -- Fiction 4. Sex -- Fiction 5. Single-parent families -- Fiction 6. Venice (Los Angeles, Calif.) -- Fiction 7. Mother-daughter relationship -- Fiction

1467738492; 9781467738491, $18.99; 9781467761802; 9781467776738; 9781467776745; 9781467776752

LC 2014008998

In this novel, by Elana K. Arnold, "Sephora Golding lives in the shadow of her unbelievably beautiful mother. Even though they scrape by in the seedier part of Venice Beach, she's always felt lucky. . . . But now, at sixteen, the fairy tale is less Disney and more Grimm. And she wants the story to be her own. Then she meets Felix, and the fairy tale takes a turn she never imagined. Sometimes, a story is just a way to hide the unspeakable in plain sight." (Publisher's note)

"Clocking in at just 200 pages, this is a story that packs no less of a punch for its brevity. Sephora's grim reimaginings of fairy tales are anti-Disney in the extreme (making this best suited for more mature readers). The strands are worked so surely into the narrative that they feel powerful instead of tired. Sephora herself is a narrator who defies convention, and her story, harsh and spare, is unforgettable." Booklist

What girls are made of. By Elana K. Arnold. Carolrhoda Lab 2017 200 p.

Grades: 9 10 11 12

1. Dating (Social customs) -- Fiction; 2. Family problems -- Fiction; 3. Girls -- Fiction; 4. Sex -- Fiction

9781512410242, $18.99; 9781512426946

LC 2016006372

National Book Award Finalist: Young People's Literature (2017)

In this book, by Elana K. Arnold, "when Nina Faye was fourteen, her mother told her there was no such thing as unconditional love. Nina believed her. Now she'll do anything for the boy she loves, to prove she's worthy of him. But when he breaks up with her, Nina is lost. What is she if not a girlfriend? What is she made of? Broken-hearted, Nina tries to figure out what the conditions of love are." (Publisher's note)

"Smart, true, and devastating, this is brutally, necessarily forthcoming about the crags of teen courtship." Booklist

Arnold, David

★ **Mosquitoland**. David Arnold. Viking, published by Penguin Group 2015 352 p.

Grades: 9 10 11 12

1. Mental illness -- Fiction 2. Mothers and daughters -- Fiction 3. Runaways -- Fiction 4. Stepfamilies -- Fiction 5. Voyages and travels -- Fiction 6. Mother-daughter relationship -- Fiction 7. Runaway teenagers

-- Fiction
045147077X; 9780451470775, $17.99

LC 2014009137

In this book, by David Arnold, "[a]fter the sudden collapse of her family, Mim Malone is dragged from her home in northern Ohio to . . . Mississippi, where she lives in a medicated milieu with her dad and new stepmom. Before the dust has a chance to settle, she learns her mother is sick back in Cleveland. So she ditches her new life and hops aboard a northbound Greyhound bus to her real home and her real mother, meeting a quirky cast of fellow travelers along the way." (Publisher's note)

Asher, Jay

The **future** of us; [by] Jay Asher and Carolyn Mackler. Razorbill 2011 356p $18.99
Grades: 8 9 10 11 12
    1. School stories 2. Computers -- Fiction 3. Supernatural -- Fiction
    ISBN 978-1-59514-491-1; 1-59514-491-9

In this book by Jay Asher and Carolyn Mackler, "it's 1996, before Facebook's been invented. Yet Emma's first computer leads her to her Facebook page from fifteen years in the future. She tells only her friend and would-be boyfriend Josh, and they contemplate their futures with concern. Can their current actions change who they become?" (Voice of Youth Advocates)

"It's 1996, and Emma Nelson has just received her first computer. . . . When Emma powers up the computer, she discovers her own Facebook page (even though Facebook doesn't exist yet) and herself in an unhappy marriage—15 years in the future. Alternating chapters from Josh and Emma over the course of five days propel this riveting read, as Emma discovers she can alter her future by adjusting her present actions and intentions." Booklist

Thirteen reasons why; a novel. Razorbill 2007 288p $16.99
Grades: 8 9 10 11 12
    1. School stories 2. Suicide -- Fiction
    ISBN 9781595141712

LC 2007-03097

When high school student Clay Jenkins receives a box in the mail containing thirteen cassette tapes recorded by his classmate Hannah, who committed suicide, he spends a bewildering and heartbreaking night crisscrossing their town, listening to Hannah's voice recounting the events leading up to her death.

"Clay's pain is palpable and exquisitely drawn in gripping casually poetic prose. The complex and soulful characters expose astoundingly rich and singularly teenage inner lives." SLJ

What light. Jay Asher. Penguin Group USA 2016 272 p.
Grades: 7 8 9 10
    1. Christmas -- Fiction 2. Love -- Fiction 3. Teenagers -- Fiction
    1595145516; 9781595145512, $18.99; 9780448493657, $56.97

LC 2016038795

In this book, by Jay Asher, "Sierra's family runs a Christmas tree farm in Oregon-it's a bucolic setting for a girl to grow up in, except that every year, they pack up and move to California to set up their Christmas tree lot for the season. So Sierra lives two lives: her life in Oregon and her life at Christmas. And leaving one always means missing the other. Until this particular Christmas, when Sierra meets Caleb, and one life eclipses the other." (Publisher's note)

"Sierra's story provides an interesting window into alternative schooling and living arrangements facing some teens whose families work in agriculture. Certain to please readers seeking an escapist, feel-good holiday read." Booklist

Ashton, Brodi

Everbound; an Everneath novel. Brodi Ashton. Balzer + Bray 2013 368 p. (Everneath) (hardcover bdg: alk. paper) $17.99
Grades: 7 8 9 10
    1. Love stories 2. Occult fiction 3. Future life -- Fiction 4. Hell -- Fiction 5. Love -- Fiction 6. Supernatural -- Fiction
    ISBN 0062071165; 9780062071163

LC 2012028327

This young adult paranormal story, by Brodi Ashton, is the sequel to "Everneath." "Nikki Beckett could only watch as . . . Jack . . . sacrificed himself to save her, taking her place in the Tunnels of the Everneath for eternity. . . . Desperate for answers, Nikki turns to Cole, the immortal bad boy who wants to make her his queen. . . . But his heart has been touched by everything about Nikki, and he agrees to help in the only way he can: by taking her to the Everneath himself." (Publisher's note)

Everneath; Brodi Ashton. 1st ed; Balzer + Bray 2012 370p. $17.99
Grades: 7 8 9 10
    1. Love stories 2. Occult fiction 3. Fantasy fiction
    ISBN 9780062071132 (trade bdg.)

LC 2011022892

This book tells the story of "Nikki Beckett [who] vanished, sucked into an underworld known as the Everneath. Now she's returned—to her old life, her family, her boyfriend—before she's banished back to the underworld . . . this time forever. She has six months before the Everneath comes to claim her, six months for good-byes she can't find the words for, six months to find redemption, if it exists. Nikki longs to spend these precious months forgetting the Everneath and trying to reconnect with her boyfriend, Jack, the person most devastated by her disappearance—and the one person she loves more than anything. But there's just one problem: Cole, the smoldering immortal who enticed her to the Everneath in the first place, has followed Nikki home. Cole wants to take over the throne in the underworld and is convinced Nikki is the key to making it happen." (Publisher's note)

Atkins, Catherine

The **file** on Angelyn Stark; by Catherine Atkins. 1st ed; Alfred A. Knopf 2011 250p.
Grades: 9 10 11 12
    1. Young women -- Fiction 2. Child sexual abuse --

Fiction 3. Teacher-student relationship -- Fiction
ISBN 9780375869068; 9780375969065 (lib. bdg.);
9780375899898 (ebook)

LC 2011016681

This book tells the story of "[f]ifteen-year-old Angelyn Stark [who] seems to relish her position as the head of a pack of bad girls, but her tough exterior covers a terrible secret. The summer she was 12, her stepfather, Danny, sexually molested her. The abuse stopped after a neighbor called police, but when her mom didn't believe her, Angelyn told investigators it never happened. . . . Angelyn's boyfriend, Steve, keeps pressuring her for sex, but she's only interested in her teacher, Mr. Rossi, the single adult in her life who encourages her. But Mr. Rossi is fighting demons of his own and rightly fears that a relationship with Angelyn will jeopardize his reputation." (Kirkus)

Atkins, Jeannine

★ **Stone** mirrors: the sculpture and silence of Edmonia Lewis. Jeannine Atkins. Atheneum Books for Young Readers 2017 172 p.
Grades: 9 10 11 12
1. Novels in verse; 2. Sculptors -- Fiction; 3. Women sculptors -- Fiction; 4. Lewis, Edmonia -- Fiction; 5. Biographical fiction
9781481459075;   9781481459051, $17.99;
9781481459068

LC 2016003598

This biographical verse novel, by Jeannine Atkins, is "about a half Native American, half African American sculptor working in the years following the Civil War.... Edmonia Lewis was...a sculptor, but she never spoke or wrote much about her past, and the stories that have come down through time are often vague or contradictory. Some facts are known...but the historical record is very thin." (Publisher's note)

"How this brave, driven young woman overcame prejudice and trauma to pursue her artistic calling to the highest level -- her work, once dismissed as démodé for its neoclassicism, now resides in top museums -- is a story that warrants such artful retelling." Booklist

Includes bibliographical references and index

Atwater-Rhodes, Amelia

Persistence of memory. Delacorte Press 2008 212p $15.99; lib bdg $18.99; pa $8.99
Grades: 8 9 10 11 12
1. Witches -- Fiction 2. Vampires -- Fiction 3. Supernatural -- Fiction 4. Schizophrenia -- Fiction
ISBN 978-0-385-73437-0; 0-385-73437-9; 978-0-385-90443-8 lib bdg; 0-385-90443-6 lib bdg; 978-0-440-24004-4 pa; 0-440-24004-2 pa

LC 2008-16062

Diagnosed with schizophrenia as a child, sixteen-year-old Erin has spent half of her life in therapy and on drugs, but now must face the possibility of weird things in the real world, including shapeshifting friends and her "alter," a centuries-old vampire.

"What sets this novel apart . . . are the two narrators— Erin, grown used to, and even comfortable with, the idea that she is mentally ill; and Shevaun, willing to do anything to protect the family she's cobbled together. Secondary char-

acters are equally compelling, and the world that Atwater-Rhodes has created is believable and intriguing." SLJ

Auch, Mary Jane

Guitar boy. Henry Holt 2010 260p $16.99
Grades: 6 7 8 9
1. Guitars -- Fiction 2. Musicians -- Fiction 3. Family life -- Fiction
ISBN 978-0-8050-9112-0; 0-8050-9112-2

LC 2009-50782

After his mother is severely injured in an accident and his father kicks him out of the house, thirteen-year-old Travis attempts to survive on his own until he meets a guitar maker and some musicians who take him in and help him regain his confidence so that he can try to patch his family back together.

"Budding musicians will be fascinated by the details, but all readers will find their heartstrings plucked by this story." Booklist

Avasthi, Swati

Chasing Shadows; by Swati Avasthi and illustrated by Craig Phillips. Random House Childrens Books 2013 320 p. $17.99
Grades: 9 10 11 12
1. Death -- Fiction 2. Teenage girls -- Fiction
ISBN 0375863427; 9780375863424

The book offers a "portrait of two girls teetering on the edge of grief and insanity. Two girls who will find out just how many ways there are to lose a friend . . . and how many ways to be lost. Holly and Savitri cope with the death of their friend Corey as they look for Corey's killer." (Publisher's note)

"Savitri's boyfriend Corey is killed and her best friend, Holly (Corey's sister), is injured by a seemingly senseless shooting. With the killer at large, Holly teeters on the brink of sanity. The narrative alternates among Savitri's voice; a second-person narrator; and Holly's perspective, told through first-person text and dramatic graphic novel style interludes. Avasthi delves deeply into the pysche of both girls." (Horn Book)

★ **Split.** Alfred A. Knopf 2010 282p $16.99; lib bdg $19.99
Grades: 10 11 12
1. Brothers -- Fiction 2. Child abuse -- Fiction
ISBN 978-0-375-86340-0; 0-375-86340-0; 978-0-375-96340-7 lib bdg; 0-375-96340-5 lib bdg

LC 2009-22615

A teenaged boy thrown out of his house by his abusive father goes to live with his older brother, who ran away from home years ago to escape the abuse.

"Readers seeking sensational violence should look elsewhere; this taut, complex family drama depicts abuse unflinchingly but focuses on healing, growth and learning to take responsibility for one's own anger." Kirkus

Avery, Lara

The **memory** book. Lara Avery. Little, Brown & Co. 2016 368 p.
Grades: 9 10 11 12
1. Friendship -- Fiction 2. Genetic disorders -- Fiction

3. Love -- Fiction 4. Memory -- Fiction 5. Terminally ill -- Fiction
9780316283748

LC 2015029157

"Resolving to graduate at the top of her class and leave her small town in spite of a rare genetic disorder that will eventually steal her memories and health, Sammie writes a journal to her future self so that she will recall her feelings of friendship, love and laughter. By the author of A Million Miles Away." (Publisher's note)

"When Sammie gets the diagnosis her senior year-that a genetic condition will rob her of her mind, the one thing she valued over everything else-it's just one more thing for her to overcome, with the help of her memory book, a diary that will remind her future self of the Sammie she once was. But as the realities of her condition become more glaring, Sammie has to reevaluate everything she thought made her who she is. . . . Though there are moments recorded in Sammie's book that seem like they were captured at a very unlikely time to journal, each entry adds to a story of self-discovery that's hard to put down." Booklist

Aveyard, Victoria

King's cage. Victoria Aveyard. HarperTeen, an imprint of HarperCollins Publishers 2017 512 p. (Red queen)

Grades: 7 8 9 10

1. Ability -- Fiction; 2. Blood -- Fiction; 3. Courts and courtiers -- Fiction; 4. Government, Resistance to -- Fiction; 5. Princesses -- Fiction; 6. Social classes -- Fiction; 7. Resistance to government -- Fiction
9780062310712; 9780062310699, $19.99

LC 2016478470

"In this breathless third installment to Victoria Aveyard's...Red Queen series, rebellion is rising and allegiances will be tested on every side. Mare Barrow is a prisoner.... She lives at the mercy of a boy she once loved.... Now a king, Maven Calore...attempt[s] to maintain control over his country -- and his prisoner. As Mare bears the weight of Silent Stone in the palace, her...band of newbloods and Reds continue organizing, training, and expanding." (Publisher's note)

Red queen. Victoria Aveyard. HarperTeen, an imprint of HarperCollins Publishers 2015 388 p. (Red queen trilogy)

Grades: 8 9 10 11

1. Blood -- Fiction 2. Resistance to government -- Fiction 3. Ability -- Fiction 4. Kings and rulers -- Fiction 5. Princesses -- Fiction 6. Teenage girls -- Fiction
0062310631; 9780062310637, $17.99

LC 2014952542

This book, by Victoria Aveyard, is the "sweeping tale of seventeen-year-old Mare, a common girl whose once-latent magical power draws her into the dangerous intrigue of the king's palace. Mare Barrow's world is divided by blood—those with common, Red blood serve the Silver- blooded elite, who are gifted with superhuman abilities. Mare is a Red, scraping by as a thief in a poor, rural village, until a twist of fate throws her in front of the Silver court." (Publisher's note)

"First-time author Aveyard has created a volatile world with a dynamic heroine, and while there are moments of romance, they refreshingly take a backseat to the action. Anticipation is already high for this debut, and with the movie rights already acquired and two sequels to come, it will likely only grow." Booklist

Avi, 1937-

★ **City** of orphans; with illustrations by Greg Ruth. Atheneum Books for Young Readers 2011 350p il $16.99

Grades: 5 6 7 8

1. Mystery fiction 2. Gangs -- Fiction 3. Immigrants -- Fiction 4. Family life -- Fiction 5. Homeless persons -- Fiction
ISBN 978-1-4169-7102-3; 1-4169-7102-5

LC 2010049229

In 1893 New York, thirteen-year-old Maks, a newsboy, teams up with Willa, a homeless girl, to clear his older sister, Emma, from charges that she stole from the brand new Waldorf Hotel, where she works. Includes historical notes.

"Avi's vivid recreation of the sights and sounds of that time and place is spot on, masterfully weaving accurate historical details with Maks' experiences." Kirkus

Includes bibliographical references

★ **Crispin**: the cross of lead. Hyperion Bks. for Children 2002 $15.99; pa $6.99

Grades: 5 6 7 8

1. Orphans -- Fiction 2. Middle Ages -- Fiction
ISBN 0-7868-0828-4; 0-7868-1658-9 pa

LC 2001-51829

Awarded the Newbery Medal, 2001

Falsely accused of theft and murder, an orphaned peasant boy in fourteenth-century England flees his village and meets a larger-than-life juggler who holds a dangerous secret

This "book is a page-turner from beginning to end. . . . A meticulously crafted story, full of adventure, mystery, and action." SLJ

Other titles in this series are:
Crispin at the edge of the world (2006)
Crispin: the end of time (2010)

★ **Nothing** but the truth; a documentary novel. Scholastic Inc. 2010 177p pa $6.99

Grades: 6 7 8 9

1. School stories
ISBN 978-0-545-17415-2

First published 1991 by Orchard Bks.

A Newbery Medal honor book, 1992

A ninth-grader's suspension for singing "The Star-Spangled Banner" during homeroom becomes a national news story.

"The book is effectively set entirely in monologue or dialogue; conversations, memos, letters, diary entries, talk-radio transcripts, and newspaper articles are all interwoven to present an uninterrupted plot. The construction is nearly flawless; the characters seem painfully human and typically ordinary. . . . A powerful, explosive novel that involves the reader from start to finish." Horn Book

★ **Traitor's** gate. Atheneum Books for Young Readers 2007 351p $17.99

Grades: 5 6 7 8

> 1. Spies -- Fiction 2. Poverty -- Fiction 3. Family life -- Fiction

ISBN 0-689-85335-1

When his father is arrested as a debtor in 1849 London, fourteen-year-old John Huffman must take on unexpected responsibilities, from asking a distant relative for help to determining why people are spying on him and his family.

"With plenty of period detail, this action-packed narrative of twists, turns, and treachery is another winner from a master craftsman." SLJ

Axelrod, Kate

The **law** of loving others: a novel. By Kate Axelrod. Razorbill 2015 240 p.

Grades: 9 10 11 12

> 1. Coming of age -- Fiction 2. Love -- Fiction 3. Mental illness -- Fiction 4. Mothers and daughters -- Fiction 5. Schizophrenia -- Fiction 6. Mother-daughter relationship -- Fiction 7. Romance fiction 8. Bildungsromans

1595147896; 9781595147899, $17.99

LC 2014032004

In this novel, by Kate Axelrod, "hours after Emma returns home from boarding school, she realizes that her mom is suffering from a schizophrenic break. Suddenly, Emma's entire childhood and identity is called into question. . . . In the span of just one winter break, Emma's relationships alter forever and she is forced to see the wisdom in a line from Anna Karenina: 'The law of loving others could not be discovered by reason, because it is unreasonable.'" (Publisher's note)

"In this candid, affecting portrait of a girl in crisis, debut author Axelrod nonjudgmentally and realistically captures the swirling ups and downs of anxiety, and the frantic, impotent grasp for control in the face of unpredictable, catastrophic change." Booklist

Ayarbe, Heidi

Compulsion. Balzer + Bray 2011 297p lib bdg $16.99

Grades: 10 11 12

> 1. School stories 2. Soccer -- Fiction 3. Obsessive-compulsive disorder -- Fiction

ISBN 978-0-06-199386-2

LC 2010027826

Poised to lead his high school soccer team to its third straight state championship, seventeen-year-old star player Jake Martin struggles to keep hidden his nearly debilitating obsessive-compulsive disorder.

"Ayarbe exercises both enormous skill and restraint getting to the root of just how debilitating OCD can become, juxtaposing descriptions of the ways the mind's compulsions can trip a trap of mental and physical anguish against a complex, credibly casted portrayal of teen social dynamics, which are treacherous enough on their own. A gripping, claustrophobic read." Booklist

Ayres, Katherine

North by night; a story of the Underground Railroad. Delacorte Press 1998 176p hardcover o.p. pa $4.99

Grades: 6 7 8 9

> 1. Diaries -- Fiction 2. Slavery -- Fiction 3. Fugitive slaves -- Fiction 4. Underground railroad -- Fiction

ISBN 0-385-32564-9; 0-440-22747-x pa

LC 98-10039

Presents the journal of Lucinda, a sixteen-year-old girl whose family operates a stop on the Underground Railroad

This "is an absorbing tale. Ayres slips in a lot of evocative detail about the hard work of running a farm and a household before the Civil War, as well as some rather charming musing about kissing and its myriad effects on the psyche." Booklist

Bacigalupi, Paolo

The **doubt** factory: a novel. Little, Brown & Co. 2014 484p

Grades: 9 10 11 12

> 1. Corporations -- Corrupt practices -- Fiction 2. Fathers and daughters -- Fiction 3. Whistle blowing--Fiction 4. Adventure fiction

ISBN: 0316220752; 9780316220750

LC 2014002543

This suspense novel "explores the . . . issue of how public information is distorted for monetary gain, and how those who exploit it must be stopped. Everything Alix knows about her life is a lie. At least that's what a mysterious young man who's stalking her keeps saying. But then she begins investigating the disturbing claims he makes against her father." (Publisher's note)

"This openly didactic novel asks challenging questions about the immorality of the profit motive and capitalism, but does so within the context of a highly believable plot . . . and well-developed, multifaceted characters." Pub Wkly

★ The **drowned** cities; by Paolo Bacigalupi. Little, Brown and Company 2012 448p. paperback $11.00

Grades: 9 10 11 12

> 1. Science fiction 2. Apocalyptic fiction 3. Refugees -- Fiction 4. War -- Fiction 5. Orphans -- Fiction 6. Soldiers -- Fiction 7. Survival -- Fiction 8. Conduct of life -- Fiction 9. Genetic engineering -- Fiction

ISBN 9780316056243; 9780316056229 paperback

LC 2011031762

This book takes place "[i]n a dark future America where violence, terror, and grief touch everyone, young refugees Mahlia and Mouse have managed to leave behind the war-torn lands of the Drowned Cities by escaping into the jungle outskirts. But when they discover a wounded half-man--a bioengineered war beast named Tool--who is being hunted by a vengeful band of soldiers, their fragile existence quickly collapses." (Publisher's note)

★ **Ship** Breaker; Bacigalupi, Paolo. Little, Brown and Co. 2010 326p $17.99

Grades: 8 9 10 11 12

1. Science fiction 2. Recycling -- Fiction
ISBN 0316056219; 9780316056212

LC 2009-34424

Michael L. Printz Award, 2011

In a futuristic world, teenaged Nailer scavenges copper wiring from grounded oil tankers for a living, but when he finds a beached clipper ship with a girl in the wreckage, he has to decide if he should strip the ship for its wealth or rescue the girl.

"Bacigalupi's cast is ethnically and morally diverse, and the book's message never overshadows the storytelling, action-packed pacing, or intricate world-building. At its core, the novel is an exploration of Nailer's discovery of the nature of the world around him and his ability to transcend that world's expectations." Publ Wkly

Tool of war. Paolo Bacigalupi. Little, Brown & Co. 2017 377 p. (Ship breaker)

Grades: 8 9 10 11 12

1. Genetic engineering -- Fiction; 2. Obedience -- Fiction; 3. Science fiction; 4. Soldiers -- Fiction; 5. Survival -- Fiction
9780316220835, $17.99; 9780316364775

LC 2016051846

In this book in the Ship Breaker series, by Paolo Bacigalupi, "Tool, a half-man/half-beast designed for combat, is capable of so much more than his creators had ever dreamed.... But he is hunted relentlessly by someone determined to destroy him, who knows an alarming secret: Tool has found the way to resist his genetically ingrained impulses of submission and loyalty toward his masters..." (Publisher's note)

"Tool is at center stage at last as readers move through Bacigalupi's exploration of the intricate relationships connecting hunter and prey, master and enslaved, human and monster. Masterful." Kirkus

Other titles in this series include:
Ship breaker (2010);
The Drowned Cities (2012)

Backes, M. Molly

The **princesses** of Iowa; M. Molly Backes. Candlewick Press 2012 442 p. $16.99

Grades: 9 10 11 12

1. Iowa -- Fiction 2. Schools -- Fiction 3. Popularity -- Fiction 4. High schools -- Fiction 5. Conduct of life -- Fiction
ISBN 0763653128; 9780763653125

LC 2011018622

This young adult novel follows "Paige Sheridan . . . she's pretty, rich, and popular, and her spot on the homecoming court is practically guaranteed. But when a night of partying ends in an it-could-have-been-so-much-worse crash, everything changes. Her best friends start ignoring her, her boyfriend grows cold and distant. . . . A charismatic new teacher . . . encourages students to be true to themselves. But who is Paige, if not the homecoming princess everyone expects her to be?" (Publisher's note)

"Backes addresses guilt, deceit, homophobia, loyalty, and the burden of keeping up appearances in a brutally believable high school setting." Pub Wkly

Badoe, Adwoa

Between sisters. Groundwood Books/House of Anansi Press 2010 205p $16.95

Grades: 9 10 11 12

1. School stories 2. Poor -- Fiction 3. Ghana -- Fiction 4. Family life -- Fiction
ISBN 978-0-88899-996-2

"When sixteen-year-old Gloria fails thirteen out of fifteen subjects on her final exams, her future looks bleak indeed. Her family's resources are meager so the entire family is thrilled when a distant relative, Christine, offers to move Gloria north to Kumasi to look after her toddler son, Sam. In exchange, after two years, Christine will pay for Gloria to go to dressmaking school. Life in Kumasi is more grand than anything Gloria has ever experienced. . . . [But] Kumasi is also full of temptations." Publisher's note

Bailey, Kristin

Legacy of the clockwork key; by Kristin Bailey. Simon Pulse 2013 416 p. (alk. paper) $17.99

Grades: 7 8 9 10

1. Inventions -- Fiction 2. Secret societies 3. Love -- Fiction 4. Science fiction 5. Orphans -- Fiction 6. Secret societies -- Fiction 7. London (England) -- History -- 19th century -- Fiction 8. Great Britain -- History -- Victoria, 1837-1901 -- Fiction
ISBN 1442440260; 9781442440265

LC 2011049871

In this book, "a teen girl unravels the mysteries of a secret society and their most dangerous invention. . . . When a fire consumes Meg's home, killing her parents . . . all she has left is the tarnished pocket watch she rescued from the ashes. But this is no ordinary timepiece. The clock turns out to be a mechanical key--a key that only Meg can use--which unlocks a series of deadly secrets and intricate clues that Meg has no choice but to follow." (Publisher's note)

Baldwin, Kathleen

A **School** for Unusual Girls: A Stranje House Novel. Kathleen Baldwin. St. Martin's Press 2015 352 p.

Grades: 9 10 11 12

1. Spy stories 2. School stories 3. Historical fiction
0765376008; 9780765376008, $17.99

LC 2015012225

In this young adult novel by Kathleen Baldwin, "It's 1814. Napoleon is exiled on Elba. Europe is in shambles. Britain is at war on four fronts. And Stranje House, a School for Unusual Girls, has become one of Regency England's dark little secrets. The daughters' of the beau monde who don't fit high society's constrictive mold are banished to Stranje House to be reformed into marriageable young ladies. Or so their parents think." (Publisher's note)

"The spunky, naive, and passsionate protagonist will resonate with readers, who will appreciate the lively, fast-paced narrative of personal discovery, maturing realizations, and understanding." SLJ

Bancks, Tristan

Mac Slater hunts the cool. Simon & Schuster Books for Young Readers 2010 203p $15.99

Grades: 6 7 8 9

1. School stories 2. Beaches -- Fiction 3. Weblogs

-- Fiction 4. Video recording -- Fiction
ISBN 978-1-4169-8574-7; 1-4169-8574-3

LC 2009-00152

Mac, an Australian youth, has one week to prove that he can be a "coolhunter," identifying emerging trends and posting images on a website, but he is competing against a classmate on whom he has a crush and dealing with resistance from his best friend and his own confusion over what "cool" means.

"Mac is a likable character who will appeal to a wide range of readers." Booklist

Mac Slater vs. the city. Simon & Schuster Books for Young Readers 2011 184p $15.99
Grades: 6 7 8 9

1. Inventors -- Fiction 2. Web sites -- Fiction 3. Inventions -- Fiction
ISBN 1-4169-8576-X; 978-1-4169-8576-1

LC 2010006858

Mac and his reluctant friend Paul head from Australia to Manhattan to continue their work for the Coolhunter website, and once there they discover a group of young inventors whose work is meant to be kept top-secret.

"The story takes twists and turns that are both surprising and rewarding. . . . An easy sell to many middle graders." SLJ

Bannen, Megan

The **bird** and the blade. Megan Bannen. Harpercollins Childrens Books 2018 432 p.
Grades: 7 8 9 10 11 12

1. Riddles -- Fiction; 2. Kings and rulers -- Fiction; 3. Secrecy -- Fiction; 4. Slavery -- Fiction
0062674153; 9780062674159, $17.99

In this novel, by Megan Bannen, "enslaved in Kipchak Khanate, Jinghua has lost everything: her home, her family, her freedom...until the kingdom is conquered by enemy forces and she finds herself an unlikely conspirator in the escape of Prince Khalaf and his...father across the vast Mongol Empire.... Jinghua hatches a scheme to use the Kipchaks' exile to return home, a plan that becomes increasingly fraught as her feelings for Khalaf evolve into an impossible love." (Publisher's note)

Bao, Karen

Dove arising. Karen Bao. Viking Books for Young Readers 2015 324 p. (Dove Chronicles)
Grades: 7 8 9 10

1. Government, Resistance to -- Fiction 2. Militia movements -- Fiction 3. Science fiction 4. Space colonies -- Fiction 5. Youths' writings 6. Moon -- Fiction 7. Space colonies 8. Children of prisoners -- Fiction
0451469011; 9780451469014, $17.99; 9780451476289

LC 2013041198

In this novel by Karen Bao, "Phaet Theta has lived her whole life in a colony on the Moon. She's barely spoken since her father died in an accident nine years ago. She cultivates the plants in Greenhouse 22, lets her best friend talk for her, and stays off the government's radar. Then her mother is arrested. The only way to save her younger siblings from the degrading Shelter is by enlisting in the Militia, the faceless army that polices the Lunar bases and protects them from at-

tacks by desperate Earth dwellers. Training is brutal, but it's where Phaet forms an uneasy but meaningful alliance with the preternaturally accomplished Wes, a fellow outsider. Rank high, save her siblings, free her mom: that's the plan. Until Phaet's logically ordered world begins to crumble..." (Publisher's note)

"Characters are well developed, especially strong-willed Phaet, and an even pace will keep teens turning pages. Fans of Orson Scott Card's Ender's Game (Tor, 1985), Veronica Roth's Divergent (HarperCollins, 2011) and Marie Lu's Legend (Putnam, 2011) should flock to this well-written debut effort by 19-year-old Bao." SLJ

Barakiva, Michael

One man guy. Michael Barakiva. Farrar, Straus & Giroux 2014 272 p.
Grades: 9 10 11 12

1. Armenian Americans -- Fiction 2. Coming out (Sexual orientation) -- Fiction 3. Gays -- Fiction 4. Love -- Fiction 5. Gay teenagers -- Fiction
0374356459; 9780374356453, $17.99

LC 2013033518

In this book, by Michael Barakiva, "being forced to attend summer school becomes a blessing in disguise for 14-year-old Alek Khederian when it sparks a romance with an older boy named Ethan, who runs with a crowd of skateboarders and perceived burnouts. Alek's Armenian heritage is the ever-present frame for the boys' budding relationship in suburban New Jersey." (Publishers Weekly)

"[D]eftly draws strong parallels between homosexuality and ethnicity that will resonate with audiences. East Coast teens will see themselves; Midwesterners will feel a little envy." Kirkus

Bardugo, Leigh

★ **Crooked** kingdom: A Sequel to Six of Crows. Leigh Bardugo. Henry Holt & Co. 2016 560 p.
Grades: 9 10 11 12

1. Thieves -- Fiction 2. Fantasy fiction
9781627797917, $60; 9781250076977; 9781627792134, $18.99; 9781627797917

LC 2016945089

In this book in the Six of Crows series, by Leigh Bardugo, "Kaz Brekker and his crew have just pulled off a heist, . . . [but are] back to fighting for their lives. Double-crossed and badly weakened, the crew is low on resources, allies, and hope. As powerful forces from around the world descend on Ketterdam to root out the secrets of the dangerous drug known as jurda parem, old rivals and new enemies emerge to challenge Kaz's cunning and test the team's fragile loyalties." (Publisher's note)

"This is dark and violent... but gut-wrenchingly genuine. Astonishingly, Bardugo keeps all these balls in the air over the 500-plus pages of narrative. How can such a hefty tome be un-put-down-able excitement from beginning to end?" Kirkus

The **language** of thorns: midnight tales and dangerous magic. By Leigh Bardugo ; illustrated by Sara Kipin. Imprint 2017 281 p. Color; Illustration
Grades: 9 10 11 12

1. Betrayal -- Fiction; 2. Magic -- Fiction; 3. Revenge

-- Fiction; 4. Sacrifice -- Fiction; 5. Short stories -- Collections; 6. Magic -- Fiction

9781250122520, $18.99; 9781250122537

LC 2017937768

In this book, by Leigh Bardugo, illustrated by Sara Kipin, "travel to a world of dark bargains struck by moonlight, of haunted towns and hungry woods, of talking beasts and gingerbread golems, where a young mermaid's voice can summon deadly storms and where a river might do a lovestruck boy's bidding but only for a terrible price." (Publisher's note)

"Bardugo may be best known for her exemplary world building, but here more than anything, it is her language, lovely and unsettling, that is on display, as well as the accompanying characters who, like the stories themselves, are never what they seem." Booklist

Ruin and rising; Leigh Bardugo. Henry Holt and Co. 2014 422p map (Grisha trilogy) $18.99

Grades: 8 9 10 11 12

1. Fantasy fiction 2. Love stories 3. Princes -- Fiction

ISBN: 080509461X; 9780805094619

LC 2013049306

Concluding volume of the author's Grisha Trilogy. "Deep in an ancient network of tunnels and caverns, a weakened Alina must submit to the dubious protection of the Apparat and the zealots who worship her as a Saint. Yet her plans lie elsewhere, with the hunt for the elusive firebird and the hope that an outlaw prince still survives." (Publisher's note)

"Alina and company have only one hope: if they can kill the Firebird, its magical bones can be used to break the Darkling's chokehold on Ravka. In this concluding volume, Alina must rely on her childhood friend Mal's preternatural tracking ability. Bardugo's longstanding theme of 'power corrupts' is developed organically; the magic she invents will surprise and delight readers." Horn Book

Shadow and bone; Leigh Bardugo. Henry Holt 2012 358 p. (Grisha trilogy) (hc) $17.99

Grades: 8 9 10 11 12

1. Fantasy fiction 2. Magic -- Fiction 3. Folklore -- Russia 4. Monsters -- Fiction 5. Slavic mythology 6. Ability -- Fiction 7. Orphans -- Fiction

ISBN 0805094598; 9780805094596

LC 2011034012

In this young adult novel, "[Leigh] Bardugo draws inspiration from Russian and Slavic myth and culture to kick off her 'Grisha' trilogy. In the nation of Ravka, Alina Starkov is a junior cartographer's assistant in the army, while her best friend Mai is an expert tracker. When a perilous mission into the magically created Shadow Fold goes wrong, Mai is gravely wounded and Alina manifests the rare ability to summon light. Immediately recruited into the order of the magic-using Grisha, Alina is taken under the wing of its intimidating and powerful leader, the Darkling, and heralded as the potential destroyer of the Shadow Fold. As she navigates Grisha politics and uncovers well-hidden secrets, she realizes that the fate of the nation rests on her shoulders and she may be in grave danger." (Publishers Weekly)

Siege and storm; Leigh Bardugo. 1st ed. Henry Holt and Co. 2013 448 p. (Grisha trilogy) (hardcover) $17.99

Grades: 8 9 10 11 12

1. Fantasy fiction 2. Russia -- Fiction 3. Monsters -- Fiction 4. Fantasy 5. Magic -- Fiction 6. Orphans -- Fiction

ISBN 0805094601; 9780805094602

LC 2012046361

This fantasy novel, by Leigh Bardugo, is book 2 of the "Grisha Trilogy." "Alina must try to make a life with Mal in an unfamiliar land, all while keeping her identity as the Sun Summoner a secret. But she can't outrun her past or her destiny for long. The Darkling has emerged from the Shadow Fold with a terrifying new power and a dangerous plan that will test the very boundaries of the natural world." (Publisher's note)

★ **Six** of crows. Leigh Bardugo. Henry Holt & Co. 2015 480 p. Illustration; Map

1. Fantasy 2. Criminals -- Fiction 3. Theft -- Fiction

9781250076960; 9781627792127, $18.99; 9781627795098

LC 2015005469

This book by Leigh Bardugo is set in the same universe as the author's Grisha Trilogy and is part of "a two-book story line called the Dregs. Six misfits and outcasts—a convict, a sharpshooter, a runaway, a spy, a magician, and a thief—join forces with criminal prodigy Kaz Brekker for a heist that could make them rich beyond imagination." (Booklist)

"Cracking page-turner with a multiethnic band of misfits with differing sexual orientations who satisfyingly, believably jell into a family." Kirkus

Sequel: Crooked Kingdom (2016)

Barnaby, Hannah

Wonder show; by Hannah Barnaby. Houghton Mifflin Books for Children 2012 viii, 274 p.p $16.99

Grades: 7 8 9 10 11 12

1. Carnivals 2. Orphanages 3. Runaway children -- Fiction 4. Fathers -- Fiction 5. Runaways -- Fiction 6. Sideshows -- Fiction 7. Orphanages -- Fiction 8. Depressions -- 1929 -- United States -- Fiction

ISBN 0547599803; 9780547599809

LC 2011052426

William C. Morris Award Finalist (2013)

In this book by Hannah Barnaby, "Portia Remini, 13 . . . escapes . . . from the McGreavey Home for Wayward Girls to search for her father. . . . She joins a carnival. . . . On the lam from sinister 'Mister,' who runs McGreavey's, Portia learns the stories of some of the carnival's strange troupe. . . . But . . . when Mister's dragnet closes in, Portia decides that to find the answers she seeks she must return to the horror of The Home." (School Library Journal)

Barnard, Sara

Fragile like us. Sara Barnard. Simon Pulse 2017 399 p.

Grades: 10 11 12

1. Best friends -- Fiction; 2. Depressed persons -- Fiction; 3. Friendship -- Fiction; 4. Teenagers -- Suicidal behavior -- Fiction; 5. Teenage girls -- Fiction; 6.

Friendship -- Fiction; 7. Teenagers -- Suicidal behavior -- Fiction

9781481486118; 9781481486125; 9781481486101, $17.99

LC 2016939293

In this novel, by Sara Barnard, "Caddy and Rosie have always been inseparable. But that was before Suzanne. Now the twosome has become a triangle with constantly shifting alliances. Caddy's ready to be more than just the quiet one. She wants something to happen. Suzanne is trying to escape her past and be someone different, someone free. But sometimes downward spirals have a momentum of their own. And no one can break your heart like a best friend." (Publisher's note)

"A beautiful, heartfelt appreciation of the importance of girls' friendships." Kirkus

Includes bibliographical references.

Barnes, Jennifer Lynn

The **Squad**: perfect cover. Delacorte Press 2008 275p pa $6.99

Grades: 7 8 9 10

1. School stories 2. Spies -- Fiction 3. Computers -- Fiction 4. Cheerleading -- Fiction

ISBN 978-0-385-73454-7 pa; 0-385-73454-9 pa

LC 2007-09352

High school sophomore Toby Klein enjoys computer hacking and wearing combat boots, so she thinks it is a joke when she is invited to join the cheerleading squad but soon learns cheering is just a cover for an elite group of government operatives known as the Squad.

"In addition to offering crafty plotting and time-honored, typical teen conflicts and rivalries, Barnes maintains a sharp sense of humor in this action-adventure series." Bull Cent Child Books

Another title in this series is:

The Squad: killer spirit (2008)

Barnes, John

★ **Tales** of the Madman Underground; an historical romance 1973. Viking 2009 532p $18.99; pa $9.99

Grades: 10 11 12

1. School stories 2. Ohio -- Fiction 3. Alcoholism -- Fiction 4. Friendship -- Fiction 5. Mother-son relationship -- Fiction

ISBN 978-0-670-06081-8; 0-670-06081-X; 978-0-14-241702-7 pa; 0-14-241702-5 pa

LC 2009-11072

ALA YALSA Printz Award Honor Book (2010)

In September 1973, as the school year begins in his depressed Ohio town, high school senior Kurt Shoemaker determines to be "normal," despite his chaotic home life with his volatile, alcoholic mother and the deep loyalty and affection he has for his friends in the therapy group dubbed the Madman Underground.

"Teens initially turned off by Barnes's liberal use of profanities and the book's length will be captured by the sharp, funny dialogue and crisp personalities of the Madmen. Even minor characters are distinctive. . . . [This] is an excellent selection for book clubs of older teens that like

sinking their teeth into longer stories with substance." Voice Youth Advocates

Barnholdt, Lauren

Through to you. Lauren Barnholdt. Simon Pulse 2014 278 p.

Grades: 9 10 11 12

1. Dating (Social customs) -- Fiction 2. Love -- Fiction

1442434635; 9781442434639, $17.99

LC 2013048226

In this book, by Lauren Barnholdt, it "starts with a scribbled note in class: I like your sparkle. . . . Harper's surprised by Penn's attention-and so is Penn. The last thing he needs is a girlfriend. Or even a friend-with-benefits. The note is not supposed to lead to anything. Oh, but it does. . . . But Penn and Harper have very different ideas about what relationships look like, in no small part because of their very different family backgrounds." (Publisher's note)

"Chapters alternate between the two characters' vantage points, providing an insightful and humorous look into the complex connections among feelings, actions and words and how easily they can be misconstrued. An absorbing, skillfully written depiction of two teens caught in a vortex of doubt, insecurity and miscommunication." Kirkus

Barratt, Mark

Joe Rat. Eerdmans Books for Young Readers 2009 307p pa $9

Grades: 7 8 9 10

1. Crime -- Fiction 2. Orphans -- Fiction 3. Mental illness -- Fiction

ISBN 978-0-8028-5356-1; 0-8028-5356-0

LC 2008055972

First published 2008 in the United Kingdom

In the dark, dank sewers of Victorian London, a boy known as Joe Rat scrounges for valuables which he gives to "Mother," a criminal mastermind who considers him a favorite, but a chance meeting with a runaway girl and "the Madman" transforms all their lives.

"The unraveling of the Madman's identity is but one of the pleasures of Barratt's leisurely and convincing historical fiction." Booklist

The **wild** man. Eerdmans Books for Young Readers 2010 341p pa $9

Grades: 7 8 9 10

1. Crime -- Fiction 2. Fathers -- Fiction 3. Orphans -- Fiction 4. Social classes -- Fiction 5. Impostors and imposture -- Fiction

ISBN 978-0-8028-5377-6 pa; 0-8028-5377-3 pa

LC 2010010937

In Victorian England, Joe Rat has escaped the clutches of the criminal mastermind, Mother, and is trying to make an honest living in a better part of London, but when a rich philanthropist tracks down a man claiming to be Joe's missing father—a British army deserter—he must determine where his loyalties lie.

"Barratt writes as if he is keeping an adjacent berth to Dickens; here's hoping scrappy Joe has a few more tricks up his ratty sleeves." Booklist

Barrett, Tracy

King of Ithaka. Henry Holt and Company 2010 261p map $16.99

Grades: 7 8 9 10

    1. Classical mythology -- Fiction 2. Odysseus (Greek mythology) -- Fiction

    ISBN 978-0-8050-8969-1; 0-8050-8969-1

                    LC 2009-50770

Sixteen-year-old Telemachos and his two best friends leave their life of privilege to undertake a quest to find Telemachos's father Odysseus. "Grades six to ten." (Bull Cent Child Books)

    "The exotic climes and vivid descriptions . . . give the story a sense of immediacy and color." Booklist

The **Stepsister's** Tale. By Tracy Barrett. Harlequin Books 2014 272 p.

Grades: 7 8 9 10

    1. Fantasy fiction 2. Poor -- Fiction 3. Stepfamilies -- Fiction 4. Stepsisters -- Fiction 5. Romance fiction

    037321121X; 9780373211210, $16.99

In this novel, by Tracy Barrett, "Jane Montjoy is tired of . . . pretending to live up to the standards of her mother's noble family—especially now that the family's wealth is gone. . . . When her stepfather suddenly dies, leaving nothing but debts and a bereaved daughter behind, it seems to Jane that her family is destined for eternal unhappiness. But a mysterious boy from the woods and an invitation to a royal ball are certain to change her fate." (Publisher's note)

    "Sometimes it feels like fairy-tale retellings are a dime a dozen, and this is certainly not the first or the last account of a misunderstood antagonist. But, Barrett's comparably quiet account of a household of women working to survive together as a family, sometimes in spite of one another, shines with soft, bucolic realism...Overall, this is an enjoyable read. The inclusion of discussion questions in the back makes it a solid choice for book clubs." VOYA

Barron, T. A.

★ The **lost** years of Merlin. Philomel Bks. 1996 326p $19.99; pa $7.99

Grades: 5 6 7 8

    1. Fantasy fiction 2. Merlin (Legendary character) -- Fiction

    ISBN 978-0-399-23018-1; 978-0-441-00668-7 pa

                    LC 96-33920

"A boy, hurled on the rocks by the sea, regains consciousness unable to remember anything—not his parents, not his own name. He is sure that the secretive Branwen is not his mother, despite her claims, and that Emrys is not his real name. The two soon find themselves feared because of Branwen's healing abilities and Emrys' growing powers. . . . Barron has created not only a magical land populated by remarkable beings but also a completely magical tale, filled with ancient Celtic and Druidic lore, that will enchant readers." Booklist

    Other titles in this series are:

    The seven songs of Merlin (1997)

    The fires of Merlin (1998)

    The mirror of Merlin (1999)

    The wings of Merlin (2000)

    The book of magic (2011)

Merlin's dragon. Philomel Books 2008 305p (Merlin's dragon) $19.99

Grades: 6 7 8 9

    1. Fantasy fiction 2. Magic -- Fiction 3. Dragons -- Fiction

    ISBN 978-0-399-24750-7; 0-399-24750-5

                    LC 2008-2469

Basil, a small, flying lizard who is searching for others like himself, discovers that there is more to him than he knows, as he becomes engaged in Avalon's great war between the evil Rhita Gawr and the forces of good.

    "Basil is an appealing, complex character. . . . This first book in a new series will captivate readers already familiar with the fantasist's Merlin chronicles." Booklist

    Other titles in this series are:

    Doomraga's revenge (2009)

    Utlimate magic (2010)

Bartoletti, Susan Campbell

★ The **boy** who dared. Scholastic Press 2008 202p $16.99

Grades: 5 6 7 8

    1. Courage -- Fiction 2. National socialism -- Fiction

    ISBN 978-0-439-68013-4; 0-439-68013-1

                    LC 2007014166

In October, 1942, seventeen-year-old Helmuth Hübener, imprisoned for distributing anti-Nazi leaflets, recalls his past life and how he came to dedicate himself to bringing the truth about Hitler and the war to the German people.

    Bartoletti "does and excellent job of conveying the political climate surrounding Hitler's ascent to power, seamlessly integrating a complex range of socioeconomic conditions into her absorbing drama." Publ Wkly

Barwin, Steven

Hardball. Steven Barwin. Orca Book Publishers 2014 192 p. (Orca sports)

Grades: 7 8 9 10

    1. Baseball players 2. Cousins 3. Hazing 4. School sports -- Fiction 5. Baseball -- Fiction 6. Cousins -- Fiction

    1459804414; 9781459804418, $9.95; 9781459804425; 9781459804432

                    LC 2014935389

"Griffin has college in his sights and plans to land himself a baseball scholarship. His determination causes him to turn a blind eye to the hazing of new players by the team captain, Wade. But when Griffin senses that his cousin Carson is getting the brunt of Wade's aggression, Griffin finally stands up to him." (Publisher's note)

    "Short, fast-paced chapters keep the narrative moving with a mix of baseball play-by-plays and sleuthing. A drug-dealing subplot adds a layer of suspense and raises the stakes well beyond troubles on the ball field. Ideal for reluctant readers, this book's gritty undertones will appeal to the intended high/low audience of sports fans." Booklist

Barzak, Christopher

The **gone** away place. Christopher Barzak. Alfred A. Knopf 2018 304 p.

Grades: 7 8 9 10

> 1. Dating (Social customs) -- Fiction; 2. Dead -- Fiction; 3. Family life -- Ohio -- Fiction; 4. Friendship -- Fiction; 5. Memory -- Fiction; 6. Tornadoes -- Fiction; 7. Ohio -- Fiction; 8. Ghost stories; 9. Family life -- Fiction
> 9780399556098, $17.99; 9780399556104
>
> LC 2017044047

In this book, by Christopher Barzak, "since the day when a rash of powerful tornadoes touched down in Newfoundland, Ohio -- killing more than half of the students in...[Ellie's] school,...she's been haunted: by the ghosts of her best friends.... [Then] a chance encounter with one ghost leads Ellie to discover a way to free the spirits that have been lingering since the storm, and she learns that she's not the only one seeing the ghosts -- it's a town-wide epidemic." (Publisher's note)

★ **Wonders** of the invisible world. Christopher Barzak. Alfred A. Knopf 2015 339 p.

Grades: 9 10 11 12

> 1. Blessing and cursing -- Fiction 2. Death -- Fiction 3. Farm life -- Ohio -- Fiction 4. Gays -- Fiction 5. Psychic ability -- Fiction 6. Supernatural -- Fiction 7. Ohio -- Fiction 8. Family secrets -- Fiction
> 0385392826; 9780385392792; 9780385392808; 9780385392822, $9.99
>
> LC 2014022809

Stonewall Book Award Honor Book, Youth (2016)

"Aidan Lockwood lives in a sleepy farming town. . . . But . . . Aidan begins to see . . . a world that is haunted by the stories of his past. Visions from this invisible world come to him unbidden: a great-grandfather on the field of battle; his own father, . . . and a mysterious young boy, whose whispered words may be at the heart of the curse that holds Aidan's family in its grip." (Publisher's note)

"With leisurely pacing and simple, expressive language, Barzak expertly balances magical realism, historical flashbacks, and contemporary teen romance in Aiden's journey of self-discovery. Give this to teen readers who want a quieter paranormal tale or a sincere love story between two boys." Booklist

Bashardoust, Melissa

Girls made of snow and glass. Melissa Bashardoust. Flatiron Books 2017 375 p.

Grades: 7 8 9 10

> 1. Magic -- Fiction; 2. Mothers and daughters -- Fiction; 3. Queens -- Fiction; 4. Stepmothers -- Fiction; 5. Fantasy fiction
> 9781250077745; 9781250077738, $18.99
>
> LC 2017022388

In this book, by Melissa Bashardoust, "at sixteen, Mina's mother is dead, her magician father is vicious, and her silent heart has never beat with love for anyone.... Fifteen-year-old Lynet looks just like her late mother, and one day she discovers why.... [The book] traces the relationship of two young women doomed to be rivals from the start. Only one can win all, while the other must lose everything -- unless both can find a way to reshape themselves and their story." (Publisher's note)

"Compellingly flawed characters, vivid world building, and pitch-perfect pacing make this utterly superb." Booklist

Baskin, Nora Raleigh

All we know of love. Candlewick Press 2008 201p $16.99

Grades: 6 7 8 9 10

> 1. Mothers -- Fiction 2. Loss (Psychology) -- Fiction 3. Voyages and travels -- Fiction
> ISBN 978-0-7636-3623-4; 0-7636-3623-1
>
> LC 2007-22396

Natalie, almost sixteen, sneaks away from her Connecticut home and takes the bus to Florida, looking for the mother who abandoned her father and her when she was ten years old.

"Baskin takes a familiar story line and examines it in a new and interesting way that will engage readers." Voice Youth Advocates

Bass, Karen

Graffiti knight. Orca Book Publishers 2014 272 p. $14.95

Grades: 7 8 9 10

> 1. Graffiti 2. Communist countries -- Fiction 3. Family life 4. Resistance to government
> ISBN 1927485533; 9781927485538

"Just as Ruta Sepetys revealed a different perspective of the Holocaust in Between Shades of Gray (2011), Bass introduces another view of history unknown to many American readers...This eye-opening story shows that war's end is never tidy." (Booklist)

Summer of fire; [edited by Laura Peetoom] Coteau Books for Teens 2009 267p pa $10.95

Grades: 9 10 11 12

> 1. Germany -- Fiction 2. Sisters -- Fiction 3. Runaway teenagers -- Fiction 4. World War, 1939-1945 -- Fiction
> ISBN 978-1-55050-415-6; 1-55050-415-0

"It is rare for a novel to offer a German civilian's viewpoint during Hitler's rise to power with such honesty. Alternating between Del's and Garda's voices, . . . the teen voices are immediate: Del's wry and self-aware; Garda's desperate and angry." Booklist

Bass, Ron

On thin ice. Red Deer Press 2006 348p pa $10.95

Grades: 8 9 10 11 12

> 1. Inuit -- Fiction 2. Polar bear -- Fiction 3. Greenhouse effect -- Fiction
> ISBN 978-0-88995-337-6; 0-88995-337-6

"Set in the remote Arctic village of Nanurtalik, this novel follows Ashley as she journeys on the shaman path chosen for her through the Inuit line of her father. Disturbed by haunting—sometimes frightening—dreams of a gigantic polar bear that seems bent on destroying her, Ashley furiously draws her dreams onto paper, capturing the very essence of the bear within. . . . This novel is told with richness of language, culture, and emotion, but its sense of place sparkles brightest." Voice Youth Advocates

Bassoff, Leah

Lost girl found; Leah Bassoff and Laura DeLuca. Groundwood Books/House of Anansi Press 2014 212p maps

Grades: 6 7 8 9 10

1. Refugees -- Fiction 2. Sudan -- History -- Civil War,1983-2005 -- Fiction 3. Mother-daughter relationship -- Fiction

ISBN: 1554984165; 9781554984169

LC bl2014008921

"For Poni life in her small village in southern Sudan is simple and complicated at the same time. But then the war comes and there is only one thing for Poni to do. Run. Run for her life. Driven by the sheer will to survive and the hope that she can somehow make it to the Kakuma refugee camp in Kenya, Poni sets out on a long, dusty trek across the east African countryside with thousands of refugees. . . In Kakuma she is almost overwhelmed by the misery that surrounds her. Poni realizes that she must leave the camp at any cost. Her destination is a compound in Nairobi." (Publisher's note)

"Poni wants to finish her education, and she has a chance to do so when she escapes the refugee camp. Poni is a fully realized and sympathetic character. This fast-paced novel covers a lot of ground and incorporates a good deal of historical background." Horn Book

Bastedo, Jamie

Cut Off. Jamie Bastedo. Red Deer Press 2015 320 p.

Grades: 7 8 9 10

1. Adventure fiction 2. Addiction -- Fiction 3. Internet and teenagers

0889955115; 9780889955110, $11.95

In this novel, by Jamie Bastedo, "fourteen-year-old Indio McCracken enjoys meteoric stardom as a guitar prodigy after his father posts a video of him playing. Things quickly go sour . Robbed of a normal childhood and already feeling alienated by his mixed Guatemalan-Canadian heritage, Indio desperately seeks escape online by creating a virtual identity. Facing school expulsion. . . unless he kicks his Internet habit, Indio is shipped off to a teen addictions rehab center." (Publisher's note)

"Indio's narration is completely believable throughout as he wrestles with identity and belonging. Bastedo gives readers who may be inclined to scoff at the addictive-cyberdevice premise the space to assess Indio's actions and reasoning and reach their own conclusions, all the while keeping the tension and pace high. A first-rate adventure with a powerful message." Kirkus

Bauer, Joan

★ **Hope** was here. Putnam 2000 186p $16.99; pa $7.99

Grades: 7 8 9 10

1. Aunts -- Fiction 2. Wisconsin -- Fiction 3. Restaurants -- Fiction

ISBN 0-399-23142-0; 0-14-240424-1 pa

LC 00-38232

A Newbery Medal honor book, 2001

When sixteen-year-old Hope and the aunt who has raised her move from Brooklyn to Mulhoney, Wisconsin, to work as waitress and cook in the Welcome Stairways diner, they become involved with G.T. Stoop, the diner owner, and his political campaign to oust the town's corrupt mayor. "Age twelve and up." (N Y Times Book Rev)

"Bauer manages to fill her heartfelt novel with gentle humor, quirky but appealing characters, and an engaging plot." Book Rep

Peeled. G.P. Putnam's Sons 2008 256p $16.99

Grades: 6 7 8 9 10

1. Ghost stories 2. School stories 3. Farm life -- Fiction 4. Journalism -- Fiction 5. New York (State) -- Fiction

ISBN 978-0-399-23475-0; 0-399-23475-6

LC 2007-42835

In an upstate New York farming community, high school reporter Hildy Biddle investigates a series of strange occurrences at a house rumored to be haunted.

This is "a warm and funny story full of likable, offbeat characters led by a strongly voiced, independently minded female protagonist on her way to genuine, well-earned maturity." SLJ

Bauman, Beth Ann

Rosie & Skate. Wendy Lamb Books 2009 217p $15.99; lib bdg $18.99

Grades: 9 10 11 12

1. Sisters -- Fiction 2. Alcoholism -- Fiction 3. New Jersey -- Fiction 4. Family life -- Fiction 5. Dating (Social customs) -- Fiction 6. Father-daughter relationship -- Fiction

ISBN 978-0-385-73735-7; 0-385-73735-1; 978-0-385-90660-9 lib bdg; 0-385-90660-9 lib bdg

LC 2009-10575

New Jersey sisters Rosie, aged fifteen, and Skate, aged sixteen, cope differently with their father's alcoholism and incarceration, but manage to stay close to one another as they strive to lead normal lives and find hope for the future.

"Bauman's prose is lovely and real. Vivid descriptions bring her characters to life, and the dialogue is both believable and funny. . . . The novel expertly captures the everhopeful ache of adolescents longing for love, stability and certainty." Kirkus

Bayard, Louis

★ **Lucky** strikes. Louis Bayard. Henry Holt & Co. 2016 320 p.

Grades: 6 7 8 9

1. Brothers and sisters -- Fiction 2. Depressions -- 1929 -- Fiction 3. Orphans -- Fiction 4. Poverty -- Fiction 5. Virginia -- History -- 20th century -- Fiction 6. Siblings -- Fiction

9781627793902, $16.99

LC 2015023829

In this novel, by Louis Bayard, "with her mama recently dead and her pa sight unseen since birth, Amelia is suddenly in charge of her younger brother and sister—and of the family gas station. Harley Blevins . . . is in hot pursuit to clinch his fuel monopoly. To keep him at bay and keep her family out of foster care, Melia must come up with a father—and fast. And so when a hobo rolls out of a passing truck, Melia grabs opportunity by its beard." (Publisher's note)

"Her foible-ridden supporting cast features more adults than kids, and in an interesting twist, they give young readers insight into grown-up issues that transcend those usually found in youth books. Most of all, though, this is a darn good yarn with plenty of room for rooting and more than a few laughs." Booklist

Beam, Cris

★ **I** am J. Little, Brown 2011 326p

Grades: 9 10 11 12

1. Friendship -- Fiction 2. Transgender people -- Fiction 3. Identity (Psychology) -- Fiction

ISBN 0-316-05361-9; 978-0-316-05361-7

LC 2010-08640

J, who feels like a boy mistakenly born as a girl, runs away from his best friend who has rejected him and the parents he thinks do not understand him when he finally decides that it is time to be who he really is.

"The book is a gift to transgender teens and an affecting story of self-discovery for all readers." Horn Book

Includes bibliographical references

Beard, Philip

Dear Zoe; a novel. Viking 2005 196p hardcover o.p. pa $13

Grades: 9 10 11 12

1. Death -- Fiction 2. Letters -- Fiction 3. Sisters -- Fiction 4. Bereavement -- Fiction

ISBN 0-670-03401-0; 0-452-28740-5 pa

LC 2004-57173

"On the morning planes hit the World Trade Center towers, Tess DeNunzio's three-year-old sister, Zoe, ran into the street and was killed by a car. Fifteen-year-old Tess, who was supposed to be watching Zoe, was consumed by guilt. This novel is written in the form of a letter from Tess to Zoe, chronicling the year after Zoe's death. . . . Beard captures the raw emotion of a 15-year-old girl with impressive dexterity, following Tess through the many stages of grief." Booklist

Beaudoin, Sean

Wise Young Fool; by Sean Beaudoin. Little, Brown and Co. 2013 448 p. $18

Grades: 10 11 12

1. Juvenile delinquency -- Fiction 2. Teenagers -- Fiction 3. Bands (Music) -- Fiction 4. Musicians -- Fiction 5. Juvenile detention homes -- Fiction

ISBN 0316203793; 9780316203791

LC 2012032472

In this book by Sean Beaudoin, protagonist "Ritchie grabs readers by the throat before (politely) inviting them along for the (max-speed) ride. A battle of the bands looms. Dad split about five minutes before Mom's girlfriend moved in. There's the matter of trying to score with the dangerously hot Ravenna Woods while avoiding the dangerously huge Spence Proffer--not to mention just trying to forget what his sister, Beth, said the week before she died." (Publisher's note)

"This coming-of-age story is told in alternating story lines, leading up to Ritchie Sudden's arrest and his time in a juvenile detention center... There are a lot of messages about the importance of safe driving and staying away from drugs and alcohol without being preachy. This is not a typical rock band story; it is actually interesting. The author does a brilliant job getting into the head of a troubled teen and does not shy away from racy topics." (School Library Journal)

Beaufrand, Mary Jane

The **rise** and fall of the Gallivanters. M.J. Beaufrand. Harry N. Abrams, Inc. 2015 288 p.

Grades: 9 10 11 12

1. Bands (Music) -- Fiction 2. Family problems -- Fiction 3. Friendship -- Fiction 4. Missing children -- Fiction 5. Punk rock music -- Fiction 6. Sick -- Fiction

1419714953; 9781419714955, $16.95

LC 2014013556

In this novel, by M. J. Beaufrand, "in Portland in 1983, girls are disappearing. Noah, a teen punk with a dark past, becomes obsessed with finding out where they've gone—and he's convinced their disappearance has something to do with the creepy German owners of a local brewery, the PfefferBrau Haus. . . . When the PfefferBrau Haus opens its doors for a battle of the bands, Noah pulls his band, the Gallivanters, back together in order to get to the bottom of the mystery." (Publisher's note)

"Beaufrand's masterful pace compels readers toward the satisfying though heartbreaking conclusion, prodding them to question throughout whether Noah's story takes place in reality or in a dissociative hellscape. A chilling yet poignant story about the suffering in front of us that we can't bear to see." Kirkus

★ **Useless** Bay. M. J. Beaufrand. Amulet Books 2016 240 p.

Grades: 8 9 10 11

1. Brothers and sisters -- Fiction 2. Family secrets -- Fiction 3. Islands -- Fiction 4. Missing children -- Fiction 5. Mystery and detective stories 6. Quintuplets -- Fiction 7. Mystery fiction

9781419721380, $17.95

LC 2016007659

In this novel, by M.J. Beaufrand, "on Whidbey Island, the Gray quintuplets are the stuff of legend. . . . Together, they serve as an unofficial search-and-rescue team for the island, saving tourists and locals alike from the forces of wind and sea. But, when a young boy goes missing, the mysteries start to pile up. While searching for him, they find his mother's dead body instead-and realize that something sinister is in their midst." (Publisher's note)

"Short in length but long on atmosphere, it's a gripping mystery with a supernatural overlay that makes its setting all the more haunting. But it's the irresistible Gray quints, subject to their own rumors and local mythos, who steal the show. " Pub Wkly

Bechard, Margaret

Hanging on to Max. Simon Pulse 2003 204p pa $6.99

Grades: 7 8 9 10

1. Infants -- Fiction 2. Teenage fathers -- Fiction

ISBN 0-689-86268-7

First published 2002 by Roaring Brook Press

When his girlfriend decides to give their baby away, seventeen-year-old Sam is determined to keep him and raise him alone.

"An easy read filled with practical wisdom, this book is highly recommended as an important edition for any adolescent classroom collection." ALAN

Bedford, Martyn

Flip. Wendy Lamb Books 2011 261p $16.99; lib bdg $19.99; ebook $10.99

Grades: 8 9 10 11 12

1. Supernatural -- Fiction 2. Great Britain -- Fiction
ISBN 978-0-385-73990-0; 0-385-73990-7; 978-0-385-90808-5 lib bdg; 0-385-90808-3 lib bdg; 978-0-375-89855-6 ebook; 0-375-89855-7 ebook

LC 2010-13158

A teenager wakes up inside another boy's body and faces a life-or-death quest to return to his true self or be trapped forever in the wrong existence.

"Bedford packs so much exhilarating action and cleanly cut characterizations into his teen debut that readers will be catapulted head-first into Alex's strange new world." Kirkus

Bell, Hilari

Fall of a kingdom; by Hilari Bell. Simon Pulse 2005 422 p. map (Farsala trilogy) (paperback) $6.99

Grades: 7 8 9 10

1. Fantasy fiction 2. Persian mythology -- Fiction
ISBN 0689854145; 9780689854149

LC 2005588003

This is the first book in Hilari Bell's Farsala trilogy. "Stories are told of a hero who will come to Farsala's aid when the need is greatest. But for thousands of years the prosperous land of Farsala has felt no such need. . . . Three young people are less sure of Farsala's invincibility. Jiaan, Soraya, and Kavi see Time's Wheel turning, with Farsala headed toward the Flames of Destruction. What they cannot see is how inextricably their lives are linked to Farsala's fate." (Publisher's note)

Forging the sword. Simon & Schuster Books for Young Readers 2006 494p (Farsala trilogy) $17.99

Grades: 7 8 9 10

1. Fantasy fiction
ISBN 978-0-689-85416-3; 0-689-85416-1

LC 2005017730

Farsalans, including Lady Soraya and her half-brother, Jiaan, Kavi, and others, work relentlessly and often secretly in their shared strategies regarding the ultimate defeat of the Hrum.

"Bell brings the Farsala Trilogy to a rousing conclusion. . . . The author maintains the complexity of her main characters and the intensity of the story line." Booklist

★ The **last** knight. Eos 2007 357p (Knight and rogue) $16.99; lib bdg $17.89

Grades: 7 8 9 10

1. Fantasy fiction 2. Knights and knighthood -- Fiction
ISBN 978-0-06-082503-4; 0-06-082503-0; 978-0-06-082504-1 lib bdg; 0-06-082504-9 lib bdg

LC 2006-36427

In alternate chapters, eighteen-year-old Sir Michael Sevenson, an anachronistic knight errant, and seventeen-year-old Fisk, his streetwise squire, tell of their noble quest to bring Lady Ceciel to justice while trying to solve her husband's murder.

"The novel is brimming with saved-by-a-hair escapades and fast-paced realistic action. . . . This well-created fantasy is a great read with worthwhile moral issues pertinent to its intended audience." SLJ

Other titles in this series are:
Rogue's home (2008)
Player's ruse (2010)

Bell, Joanne

Juggling fire. Orca Book Publishers 2009 171p pa $12.95

Grades: 7 8 9 10

1. Missing persons -- Fiction 2. Wilderness survival -- Fiction 3. Father-daughter relationship -- Fiction
ISBN 978-1-55469-094-7; 1-55469-094-3

"Sixteen-year-old Rachel's father disappeared years earlier from her family's home in the Yukon wilderness. . . . The teen sets off on a trek through the tundra and forest with only her dog as a companion, hoping to find clues about her father's disappearance. . . . Bell beautifully captures the natural world through descriptions of the mountainous terrain as well as nail-biting encounters with bears and wolves. Rachel is a smart, resourceful narrator." SLJ

Belleza, Rhoda

★ **Empress** of a thousand skies. Rhoda Belleza. Razorbill, an imprint of Penguin Random House 2017 313 p. (Empress of a Thousand Skies)

Grades: 7 8 9 10 11 12

1. Fugitives from justice -- Fiction; 2. Science fiction; 3. Princesses -- Fiction
1101999101; 9781101999103, $17.99; 9781101999127

LC 2016053016

In this novel, by Rhoda Belleza, "Rhee, also known as Crown Princess Rhiannon Ta'an, is the sole surviving heir to a powerful dynasty. She'll stop at nothing to avenge her family and claim her throne.... [When] Aly[,]...[the] star of a DroneVision show[,].... [was] falsely accused of killing Rhee, he's forced to prove his innocence to save his reputation -- and his life." (Publisher's note)

"This is a multiplanet, multiculture, multitech world and a timely tale. An exceptionally satisfying series opener." Kirkus

Followed by:
Blood of a Thousand Stars (2018)

Bennett, Holly

Shapeshifter. Orca Book Publishers 2010 244p il pa $9.95

Grades: 7 8 9 10

1. Fantasy fiction
ISBN 978-1-55469-158-6; 1-55469-158-3

In order to escape the sorceror who wants to control her gift of song, Sive must transform herself into a deer, leave the Otherworld and find refuge in Eire, the land of mortals.

This is a "rich, slightly revisionist retelling of an ancient Irish legend. Basic human emotions—fear, love, greed—move the tale along, and short first-person narratives that personalize the action are interspersed throughout." Booklist

Bennett, Jenn

★ **Alex**, approximately. By Jenn Bennett. Simon Pulse 2017 390 p.

Grades: 9 10 11 12

1. Dating (Social customs) -- Fiction; 2. Fathers and daughters -- Fiction; 3. Identity -- Fiction; 4. Moving, Household -- Fiction; 5. California -- Fiction; 6. Moving -- Fiction; 7. Father-daughter relationship -- Fiction

9781481478793; 9781481478779, $17.99

LC 2016028663

In this book, by Jenn Bennett, "classic movie buff Bailey 'Mink' Rydell has spent months crushing on a witty film geek she only knows online by 'Alex.' Two coasts separate the teens until Bailey moves in with her dad, who lives in the same California surfing town as her online crush. Faced with doubts (what if he's a creep in real life -- or worse?), Bailey doesn't tell Alex she's moved to his hometown." (Publisher's note)

"An irresistible tribute to classic screwball-comedy romances that captures the 'delicious whirling, twirling, buzzing' of falling in love." Kirkus

Starry eyes. Jenn Bennett. Simon Pulse 2018 417 p. Map

Grades: 9 10 11 12

1. Camping -- Fiction; 2. Dating (Social customs) -- Fiction; 3. Family problems -- Fiction; 4. Friendship -- Fiction; 5. Survival -- Fiction; 6. California -- Fiction

9781481478823; 9781481478809, $17.99

LC 2017025646

In this book, by Jenn Bennett, "best friends-turned-best enemies Zorie and Lennon have made an art of avoiding each other.... But when a group camping trip goes south, Zorie and Lennon find themselves stranded in the wilderness.... With no one but each other for company, Zorie and Lennon have no choice but to hash out their issues.... And as the two travel deeper into Northern California's rugged backcountry, secrets and hidden feelings surface." (Publisher's note)

"A layered adventure-love story that's as much about the families we have and the families we make ourselves as it is about romance." Booklist

Benway, Robin

★ **Far** from the tree. Robin Benway. HarperTeen 2017 384 p.

Grades: 7 8 9 10 11 12

1. Adopted children -- Fiction; 2. Family secrets -- Fiction

0062330624; 9780062330628, $17.99; 9780062330642

National Book Award: Young People's Literature (2017)

In this book, by Robin Benway, "being the middle child has its ups and downs. But for Grace, an only child who was adopted at birth, discovering that she is a middle child is a different ride altogether. After putting her own baby up for adoption, she goes looking for her biological family.... And when her adopted family's long-buried problems begin to explode to the surface, Maya can't help but wonder where exactly it is that she belongs." (Publisher's note)

Benway "delves into the souls of these characters as they wrestle to overcome feelings of inadequacy, abandonment,

and betrayal, gradually coming to understand themselves and each other." Pub Wkly

Benwell, Sarah

★ The **last** leaves falling. By Sarah Benwell. SSBFYR 2015 368 p.

Grades: 7 8 9 10 11 12

1. Amyotrophic lateral sclerosis -- Fiction 2. Assisted suicide -- Fiction 3. Friendship -- Fiction 4. Mothers and sons -- Fiction 5. Online chat groups -- Fiction 6. Single-parent families -- Fiction 7. Terminally ill -- Fiction 8. Japan -- Fiction 9. Mother-son relationship -- Fiction

9781481430654, $17.99; 9781481430661

LC 2014022950

This novel, by Sarah Benwell, is "infused with the haunting grace of samurai death poetry and the noble importance of friendship. Abe Sora is going to die, and he's only seventeen years old. Diagnosed with ALS (Lou Gehrig's disease), he's already lost the use of his legs, which means he can no longer attend school." (Publisher's note)

"References to samurai culture and snippets of poetry will leave readers at peace with the drifting ending. Benwell's gentle treatment of friendship and death with dignity will touch fans of John Green's The Fault in Our Stars (2012)." Kirkus

Berk, Ari

Death watch. Simon & Schuster Books for Young Readers 2011 527p (The Undertaken trilogy) $17.99

Grades: 7 8 9 10

1. Fantasy fiction 2. Father-son relationship -- Fiction

ISBN 978-1-4169-9115-1; 1-4169-9115-8

LC 2011006332

When seventeen-year-old Silas Umber's father disappears, Silas is sure it is connected to the powerful artifact he discovers, combined with his father's hidden hometown history, which compels Silas to pursue the path leading to his destiny and ultimately, to the discovery of his father, dead or alive.

"Berk's setting is atmospheric and creepy, fleshed out with a wealth of funereal traditions and folklore." Publ Wkly

Other titles in this series are:

Mistle Child (2013)

Lych Way (2014)

Bernard, Romily

Find me; Romily Bernard. HarperTeen, an imprint of HarperCollinsPublishers 2013 320 p. (hardback) $17.99

Grades: 7 8 9 10 11 12

1. Foster children -- Fiction 2. Teenagers -- Suicide -- Fiction 3. Computer hackers -- Fiction 4. Foster home care -- Fiction 5. Mystery and detective stories

ISBN 0062229036; 9780062229038

LC 2013021519

In this book, "Tessa Waye was Wicket Tate's best friend until five years ago when Wick's drug-dealing father drove them apart. When Tessa commits suicide and her diary is left on the teen's front steps, Wick suspects there might be a dark reason she jumped to her death. Wick and her sister,

Lily, are now free of their criminal father, living a shiny new life on the ritzy side of town with their foster parents. But Wick . . . fears her father will come back for them." (School Library Journal)

Berry, Julie

All the truth that's in me; by Julie Berry. Viking 2013 288 p. (hardcover: alk. paper) $17.99

Grades: 7 8 9 10 11 12

1. Truth -- Fiction 2. Kidnapping -- Fiction 3. Community life -- Fiction 4. War -- Fiction 5. Selective mutism -- Fiction

ISBN 0670786152; 9780670786152

LC 2012043218

In this book by Julie Berry, "sixteen-year-old Judith is still in love with Lucas, even after his father held her prisoner for two years and violently silenced her by cutting out part of her tongue. Another girl went missing at the same time and her body was found washed down a stream. Only Judith knows the truth of what happened to Lottie, but her muteness leaves her an outcast in the village, even from her own mother, and the truth stays bottled up inside her." (School Library Journal)

"Berry's novel is set in a claustrophobic village that seems to resemble an early American colonial settlement. Readers gradually learn "all the truth" from eighteen-year-old narrator Judith, who speaks directly (though only in her head) to her love, Lucas. Berry keeps readers on edge, tantalizing us with pieces of the puzzle right up until the gripping conclusion." (Horn Book)

★ The **passion** of Dolssa. By Julie Berry. Penguin Group 2016 496 p.

Grades: 7 8 9 10

1. Albigenses -- Fiction 2. Christian heresies -- Fiction 3. Faith -- Fiction 4. Inquisition -- Fiction 5. France -- History -- Louis IX, 1226-1270 -- Fiction 6. Provence (France) -- History -- 13th century -- Fiction 7. Christian heresies 8. Friendship -- Fiction 9. France -- Fiction

0451469925; 9780451469922, $18.99

LC 2015020814

Printz Honor Book (2017)

"Dolssa is an upper-crust city girl with a secret lover and an uncanny gift. Branded a heretic, she's on the run from the friar who condemned her mother to death by fire. . . . Botille is a matchmaker and a tavern-keeper, struggling to keep herself and her sisters on the right side of the law in their seaside town of Bajas. When their lives collide . . . Botille rescues a dying Dolssa and conceals her in the tavern." (Publisher's note)

"A (fictional) Catholic mystic, Dolssa de Stigata, escapes being burned as a heretic in 1241 France; mostly, this is the story of Botille, an enterprising young matchmaker from a tiny fishing village who rescues Dolssa. Botille's spirited character, the heart-rending suspense of events, and the terrifying context of the Inquisition in medieval Europe all render the novel irresistibly compelling." Horn Book

Includes bibliographical references

Berry, Nina

The **Notorious** Pagan Jones. Harlequin Books 2015 400 p.

Grades: 9 10 11 12

1. Berlin Wall (1961-1989) -- Fiction 2. Actresses -- Fiction 3. Cold war -- Fiction 4. Juvenile delinquency -- Fiction

0373211430; 9780373211432, $17.99

In this novel, by Nina Berry, "Pagan will be released from juvenile detention if she accepts a juicy role in a comedy directed by award-winning director Bennie Wexler. The shoot starts in West Berlin in just three days. If Pagan's going to do it, she has to decide fast—and she has to agree to a court-appointed 'guardian,' the handsome yet infuriating Devin, who's too young, too smooth and too sophisticated to be some studio flack." (Publisher's note)

"Scary in all the right places, with a strong setup for the sequel." Kirkus

Betts, A. J.

Zac and Mia. AJ. Betts. Houghton Mifflin Harcourt 2014 304 p.

Grades: 9 10 11 12

1. Cancer -- Fiction 2. Friendship -- Fiction 3. Cancer patients -- Fiction

0544331648; 9780544331648, $17.99

LC 2013050126

In this young adult novel by A. J. Betts, "seventeen-year-old Zac is recovering from a bone marrow transplant when a loud new patient moves into the room next door. While Zac thinks he knows all there is to know about cancer . . . Mia's arrival proves that he does not know everything. The two develop a friendship and learn to see beyond their own sickness and circumstances." (School Library Journal)

"Above average in this burgeoning subgenre; it's the healing powers of friendship, love and family that make this funny-yet-philosophical tale of brutal teen illness stand out." Kirkus

Originally published in Australia by Text Publishing in 2013.

Bick, Ilsa J.

The **Sin** eater's confession; by Ilsa J. Bick. Carolrhoda Lab 2013 320 p. (trade hard cover: alk. paper) $17.95

Grades: 9 10 11 12

1. Hate crimes -- Fiction 2. Homosexuality -- Fiction 3. Conduct of life -- Fiction 4. Murder -- Fiction 5. Wisconsin -- Fiction 6. Photography -- Fiction 7. Farm life -- Wisconsin -- Fiction

ISBN 0761356878; 9780761356875

LC 2012015291

In this novel, by Isla J. Bick, "Ben . . . likes helping the stern Mr. and Mrs. Lange and their 15-year-old son, Jimmy. When Jimmy wins a national photography contest with sensual photographs of his own father and Ben . . . , rumors . . . start circulating about Ben, who then distances himself from Jimmy. When Ben witnesses a horrific crime and does nothing, his life spins out of control; he begins to doubt himself, his senses, his motives . . . even his connection to reality." (Kirkus Reviews)

Bickle, Laura

The **hallowed** ones; Laura Bickle. Graphia 2012 311 p. (paperback) $8.99

Grades: 7 8 9 10 11 12

   1. Horror fiction 2. Amish -- Fiction 3. Terrorism -- Fiction 4. Family life -- Fiction 5. Bioterrorism -- Fiction 6. Coming of age -- Fiction 7. Christian life -- Fiction 8. Communicable diseases -- Fiction

ISBN 0547859260; 9780547859262

                  LC 2012014800

This book follows "Katie [who] is [about] to taste the freedom of rumspringa, [when] the elders close the gates of her small Amish community. . . . Katie daringly ventures Outside to find true horror: vampires have decimated a small nearby town and apparently much of the world's population. . . . Her situation is further complicated when she rescues Alex, a handsome Outsider who may or may not be a carrier of the contagion that seemingly caused the vampirism epidemic." (Bulletin of the Center for Children's Books)

The **outside**; Laura Bickle. Houghton Mifflin Harcourt 2013 320 p. (hardcover) $16.99

Grades: 7 8 9 10 11 12

   1. Horror fiction 2. Occult fiction 3. Vampires -- Fiction 4. Amish -- Fiction 5. Coming of age -- Fiction

ISBN 0544000137; 9780544000131

                  LC 2012040065

Sequel to: The hallowed ones

This book is a sequel to Laura Bickle's "The Hallowed Ones." Katie, an exile from an Amish community, travels with "Alex and Ginger, the two outsiders she's befriended, seeking other survivors of the vampire plague that's unmade their world. . . . Discovering a group that's genetically engineered with immunity to vampires raises tension between them, pitting science against religion: Are these vampires aliens or mutants spawned in labs, rather than manifestations of demonic evil?" (Kirkus Reviews)

Bigelow, Lisa Jenn

Starting from here; by Lisa Jenn Bigelow. Marshall Cavendish Children 2012 282 p. (hardcover) $16.99

Grades: 8 9 10 11 12

   1. School stories 2. Lesbians -- Fiction 3. Self-realization -- Fiction 4. Dogs -- Fiction 5. High schools -- Fiction 6. Fathers and daughters -- Fiction 7. Dating (Social customs) -- Fiction

ISBN 0761462333; 9780761462330; 9780761462347

                  LC 2011040129

In this book by Lisa Jenn Bigelow, "Colby is about ready to give up on people: her girlfriend Rachel dumps her and immediately moves onto Colby's opposite (a nice Jewish guy who does well in school), her mom is dead, and her dad is a frequently absent truck driver to whom she still hasn't come out. Only her best friend, Van, can bring her out of her shell. Then she adopts Mo, a friendly but wary stray dog, and life starts to move again." (Bulletin of the Center for Children's Books)

Bilen, Tracy

What she left behind; Tracy Bilen. Simon Pulse 2012 237 p. $9.99

Grades: 9 10 11 12

   1. Fathers -- Fiction 2. Missing persons -- Fiction 3. Domestic violence -- Fiction 4. Family violence --

Fiction

ISBN 1442439513; 9781442439511

                  LC 2011028989

This book follows Sara, whose mother goes missing just before their planned escape from her abusive father. "Sara works to protect herself while trying to find her mother. Her one lifeline in her increasingly isolated world is her friend Zach, her brother's former best friend. Negotiating her father's abuse, her missing mother, and a burgeoning romantic relationship with a new guy, Sara's juggling act takes all of her strength and wits to survive." (School Library Journal)

"Sharp prose and an increasingly tense plot make this debut a page-turner." Pub Wkly

Billingsley, Franny

Chime. Dial Books for Young Readers 2011 361p $17.99

Grades: 7 8 9 10 11 12

   1. Guilt -- Fiction 2. Twins -- Fiction 3. Sisters -- Fiction 4. Stepmothers -- Fiction 5. Supernatural -- Fiction

ISBN 0-8037-3552-9; 978-0-8037-3552-1

                  LC 2010-12140

Since her stepmother's recent death, 17 year old Briony Larkin know that if she can keep two secrets--that she is a witch and that she is responsible for the accident that left Rose, her identical twin, mentally compromised--and remember to hate her self alwaysalways, no other harm will befall her family in their Swampsea parsonage at the beginning of the twentieth century. The arrival of Mr. Claybourne, a city engineer, and his university-dropout son, Eric, make Briony's task difficult. (Booklist)

"Filled with eccentric characters—self-hating Briony foremost—and oddly beautiful language, this is a darkly beguiling fantasy." Publ Wkly

Bingham, Kelly

Formerly shark girl; Kelly Bingham. Candlewick Press 2013 352 p. (reinforced) $16.99

Grades: 7 8 9 10

   1. Artists -- Fiction 2. Shark attacks -- Fiction

ISBN 0763653624; 9780763653620

                  LC 2012952049

Sequel to Shark girl. While recovering from her injuries "Jane struggles with boyfriends and with her future: Will she become a nurse or continue as an artist even though she has lost her drawing hand? Her artwork continues to improve, but she feels obligated to give back to others what she received from the doctors and nurses who saved her life when she lost her right arm to a shark." (Kirkus)

Shark girl. Candlewick Press 2007 276p $16.99; pa $8.99

Grades: 7 8 9 10

   1. Novels in verse 2. Artists -- Fiction 3. Amputees -- Fiction

ISBN 978-0-7636-3207-6; 0-7636-3207-4; 978-0-7636-4627-1 pa; 0-7636-4627-X pa

                  LC 2006049120

After a shark attack causes the amputation of her right arm, fifteen-year-old Jane, an aspiring artist, struggles to come to terms with her loss and the changes it imposes on her day-to-day life and her plans for the future.

"In carefully constructed, sparsely crafted free verse, Bingham's debut novel offers a strong view of a teenager struggling to survive and learn to live again." Booklist

Bjorkman, Lauren

Miss Fortune Cookie; Lauren Bjorkman. Henry Holt and Co. 2012 279 p. (hardcover) $16.99
Grades: 9 10 11 12
    1. School stories 2. Female friendship -- Fiction 3. Friendship -- Fiction 4. Advice columns -- Fiction 5. Chinese Americans -- Fiction 6. San Francisco (Calif.) -- Fiction 7. Interpersonal relations -- Fiction 8. Chinatown (San Francisco, Calif.) -- Fiction
ISBN 0805089519; 9780805089516; 9780805096361
                LC 2012006327
In this book, "Erin and her best friends, Linny and Mei, live in San Francisco's Chinatown and are" deciding where to go to college. Mei was accepted to Harvard, but "would rather attend Stanford in order to be near her secret boyfriend, Darren . . . . When Erin, who anonymously writes the advice blog Miss Fortune Cookie, answers a letter that she believes is from Mei and Mei seems to follow the advice by announcing her plan to elope with Darren, Erin is shocked." (School Library Journal)

My invented life. Henry Holt 2009 232p $17.99
Grades: 9 10 11 12
    1. Poets 2. Authors 3. Dramatists 4. School stories 5. Sisters -- Fiction 6. Theater -- Fiction; 7. Shakespeare, William, 1564-1616 -- Fiction; 8. Shakespeare, William, 1564-1616. As you like it -- Fiction.
ISBN 978-0-8050-8950-9; 0-8050-8950-0
                LC 2008-50279
During rehearsals for Shakespeare's "As You Like It," sixteen-year-old Roz, jealous of her cheerleader sister's acting skills and heartthrob boyfriend, invents a new identity, with unexpected results.

"Narrator Roz is funny, well intentioned, and likable despite her cluelessness, and she is surrounded by a realistic cast of adult and teen characters representing a wide variety of viewpoints and sexual preferences. This is an enjoyable read that will be especially appealing to theater aficionados." SLJ

Black, Holly, 1971-

Black heart; Holly Black. Margaret K. McElderry Books 2012 296 p. (The curse workers) (hardcover) $17.99
Grades: 7 8 9 10
    1. Love stories 2. Science fiction 3. Brothers -- Fiction 4. Organized crime -- Fiction 5. Love -- Fiction 6. Criminals -- Fiction
ISBN 9781442403468; 9781442403482
                LC 2011028143
This book, the final volume of the Curse Workers trilogy, continues to follow "Cassel . . . [who has] figured out the truth about himself and signed on as a Fed-in-training, as has his charming and utterly unreliable older brother. But of course things don't go as planned; there are a lot of long cons Cassel has set in play or disrupted whose ripples are still being felt. And there's Lila, Cassel's best friend and the love of his life, who is also the rising head of a crime family" and who hates Cassel's guts." (Kirkus)

★ The **coldest** girl in Coldtown; by Holly Black. 1st ed. Little Brown & Co 2013 432 p. (hardcover) $19
Grades: 9 10 11 12
    1. Occult fiction 2. Vampires -- Fiction 3. Love -- Fiction
ISBN 0316213101; 9780316213103
                LC 2012043790
In this book by Holly Black, the vampires live in government-created ghettos called Coldtowns. "Seventeen-year-old Tana wakes up after a wild night of partying to discover that almost everyone in attendance has been killed by vampires. . . . Wandering through the carnage, she finds her infected ex-boyfriend, Aiden, and a mysterious, half-mad vampire named Gavriel chained in a bedroom. Escaping the massacre, Tana drives them to the nearest Coldtown," risking her life. (Publishers Weekly)

★ The **cruel** prince. Holly Black. Little, Brown & Co. 2018 370 p. Map (The folk of the air)
Grades: 9 10 11 12
    1. Courts and courtiers -- Fiction; 2. Fairies -- Fiction; 3. Fantasy; 4. Orphans -- Fiction; 5. Princes -- Fiction; 6. Sisters -- Fiction
9780316310277, $18.99; 9780316310307
                LC 2016049232
In this novel in The Folk of the Air series, by Holly Black, "Jude was seven years old when her parents were murdered and she and her two sisters were stolen away to live in the...High Court of Faerie. Ten years later, Jude wants nothing more than to belong there, despite her mortality. But many of the fey despise humans. Especially Prince Cardan, the youngest and wickedest son of the High King. To win a place at the Court, she must defy him -- and face the consequences." (Publisher's note)

"This is a heady blend of Faerie lore, high fantasy, and high school drama, dripping with description that brings the dangerous but tempting world of Faerie to life." Kirkus
Another title in this series is: The wicked king (2019)

Red glove. Margaret K. McElderry Books 2011 325p (The curse workers) $17.99
Grades: 7 8 9 10
    1. Science fiction 2. Magic -- Fiction 3. Brothers -- Fiction 4. Criminals -- Fiction 5. Swindlers and swindling -- Fiction
ISBN 1-4424-0339-X; 978-1-4424-0339-0
                LC 2010-31884
Sequel to: White cat (2010)
When federal agents learn that seventeen-year-old Cassel Sharpe, a powerful transformation worker, may be of use to them, they offer him a deal to join them rather than the mobsters for whom his brothers work.

This offers "a sleek a stylish blend of urban fantasy and crime noir." Booklist

★ The **white** cat. Margaret K. McElderry Books 2010 310p (The curse workers) $17.99

Grades: 7 8 9 10

1. Science fiction 2. Memory -- Fiction 3. Brothers -- Fiction 4. Criminals -- Fiction 5. Swindlers and swindling -- Fiction

ISBN 978-1-416-96396-7; 1-416-96396-0

LC 2009-33979

When Cassel Sharpe discovers that his older brothers have used him to carry out their criminal schemes and then stolen his memories, he figures out a way to turn their evil machinations against them.

This "starts out with spine-tingling terror, and information is initially dispensed so sparingly, readers will be hooked." Booklist

Blair, Jamie

Leap of Faith; Jamie Blair. Simon & Schuster 2013 240 p. (hardcover) $16.99

Grades: 9 10 11 12

1. Kidnapping -- Fiction 2. Children of drug addicts -- Fiction 3. Runaways -- Fiction 4. Parenting -- Fiction 5. Fugitives from justice -- Fiction

ISBN 1442447133; 1442447168; 9781442447134; 9781442447165

LC 2012043125

In this book, "17-year old Faith recounts her grim life with her abusive, drug-addicted mother and the circumstances that motivate her to flee. Although inured to her mother's frequent male visitors, Faith longs to save the baby her mother is carrying (for pay) for a guy that Faith considers 'drug-dealing scum.' Kidnapping the newborn from the hospital, Faith drives from Ohio to Florida, determined to start a new life with baby Addy." (Publishers Weekly)

Blair, Kate

Tangled planet. Kate Blair. Dancing Cat Books, an imprint of Cormorant Books Inc. 2018 259 p.

Grades: 8 9 10 11 12

1. Colonization -- Fiction; 2. Interplanetary voyages -- Fiction; 3. Life on other planets -- Fiction; 4. Murder -- Investigation -- Fiction; 5. Space travelers -- Fiction

9781770865051; 1770865047; 9781770865044, $14.95

LC 2017945945

In this book, by Kate Blair, "starship Venture has finally arrived at...Beta Earth, an uninhabited...planet. The first night seventeen-year-old engineer Ursa is on Beta Earth, she encounters a dead body. She's positive she saw a large creature with sharp teeth.... As injuries and bodies start piling up, Ursa must figure out who to trust when her fellow crewmates start taking sides between maintaining Venture's safety and the hope of creating a home on Beta Earth." (Publisher's note)

"A robust cast of secondary characters, each layered with their own motivations, histories, and perspectives, round out the novel and propel its fierce pace." SLJ

Blake, Ashley Herring

Girl made of stars. Ashley Herring Blake. Houghton Mifflin Harcourt 2018 295 p.

Grades: 9 10 11 12

1. Bisexuality -- Fiction; 2. Brothers and sisters -- Fiction; 3. Rape -- Fiction; 4. Sex crimes -- Fiction; 5. Teenagers -- Fiction; 6. Twins -- Fiction; 7. Rape -- Fiction; 8. Twins -- Fiction

9781328778239, $17.99; 9781328476692

LC 2017015661

In this book, by Ashley Herring Blake, "Mara and Owen are as close as twins can get, so when Mara's friend Hannah accuses Owen of rape, Mara doesn't know what to think.... Torn between her family and her sense of right and wrong, Mara feels lost.... As Mara, Hannah, and [Mara's ex-girlfriend] Charlie come together in the aftermath of this terrible crime, Mara must face a trauma from her own past and decide where Charlie fits into her future." (Publisher's note)

"The book explores so many topics -- consent, slut shaming, rape culture, what it means to move on from trauma -- but the tone never veers into pedantic territory, and the pace moves remarkably quickly for such heavy and emotional content." SLJ

Blake, Kendare

★ **Anna** Dressed in Blood. Tor 2011 320p $17.99

Grades: 8 9 10 11 12

1. Ghost stories 2. Horror fiction 3. Cats -- Fiction 4. Witches -- Fiction

ISBN 978-0-7653-2865-6; 0-7653-2865-8

LC 2011018985

"Blake populates the story with a nice mixture of personalities, including Anna, and spices it with plenty of gallows humor, all the while keeping the suspense pounding. . . . Abundantly original, marvelously inventive and enormous fun, this can stand alongside the best horror fiction out there. We demand sequels." Kirkus

Blankman, Anne

Conspiracy of blood and smoke. By Anne Blankman. Balzer + Bray, an imprint of HarperCollinsPublishers 2015 416 p.

Grades: 9 10 11 12

1. Love -- Fiction 2. Mystery and detective stories 3. Nazis -- Fiction 4. Hitler, Adolf, 1889-1945 -- Fiction 5. Germany -- History -- 1918-1933 -- Fiction 6. Mystery fiction 7. National socialism -- Fiction

0062278843; 9780062278845, $17.99

LC 2014038687

In this book, by Anne Blankman, "Gretchen Whitestone has a secret: She used to be part of Adolf Hitler's inner circle. More than a year after she made an enemy of her old family friend and fled Munich, she lives in England, posing as an ordinary German immigrant, and is preparing to graduate from high school. Her love, Daniel, is a reporter in town. . . . But then Daniel gets a telegram that sends him back to Germany, and Gretchen's world turns upside down." (Publisher's note)

"Suspenseful and clever, intertwining historical truth with action-packed shootouts." Kirkus

Includes bibliographical references; Sequel to: Prisoner of night and fog

Prisoner of night and fog; Anne Blankman. Balzer + Bray, an imprint of HarperCollinsPublishers 2014 416 p. (hardback) $17.99

Grades: 8 9 10 11 12

1. Love stories 2. National socialists -- Fiction 3.

Germany -- History -- 1918-1933 -- Fiction 4. Love -- Fiction 5. Nazis -- Fiction 6. Jews -- Germany -- Fiction 7. Munich (Germany) -- History -- 20th century -- Fiction

ISBN 0062278819; 9780062278814

LC 2013043071

This book, by Anne Blankman, is a "historical thriller set in 1930s Munich. . . . Gretchen Müller grew up in the National Socialist Party under the wing of her uncle Dolf, who has kept her family cherished and protected from the darker side of society ever since her father traded his life for Dolf's. But Uncle Dolf is none other than Adolf Hitler. And Gretchen follows his every command." (Publisher's note)

Blazanin, Jan

A **&** L do summer. Egmont USA 2011 273p pa $8.99

Grades: 7 8 9 10

1. Summer -- Fiction 2. Bullies -- Fiction 3. Friendship -- Fiction 4. Family life -- Fiction 5. Domestic animals -- Fiction

ISBN 978-1-60684-191-4 pa; 1-60684-191-2 pa; 978-1-60684-243-0 ebook

LC 2010-43616

In Iowa farm country, sixteen-year-old Aspen and her friend Laurel plan to get noticed the summer before their senior year and are unwittingly aided by pig triplets, a skunk, a chicken, bullies, a rookie policeman, and potential boyfriends.

"A series of mishaps add hilarity to the story. . . . All's well that ends well in this read perfectly suited for light refreshment on a hot summer day." Booklist

Bliss, Bryan

No parking at the end times. Bryan Bliss. Greenwillow Books, an imprint of HarperCollins Publishers 2015 272 p.

Grades: 9 10 11 12

1. Brothers and sisters -- Fiction 2. Faith -- Fiction 3. Family problems -- Fiction 4. Homeless persons -- Fiction 5. Swindlers and swindling -- Fiction 6. Twins -- Fiction 7. San Francisco (Calif.) -- Fiction

0062275410; 9780062275417, $17.99

LC 2014037503

In this book by Bryan Bliss, "Abigail and her twin brother, Aaron, live in a van in San Francisco, begging for meals from local churches and waiting for the end of the world with their fervently religious father and dutiful mother. After their zealot preacher's prediction falls short, the teens approach their breaking points, desperate for some semblance of normalcy." (Publishers Weekly)

"Bliss's depiction of a middle-class, suburban family's transition to life on the inhospitable San Francisco streets is nuanced and character-driven; the tightly focused first-person narration centers the story squarely on Abigail as she gathers the courage to choose between her family and her future. Bliss's debut explores family, sacrifice, and the power of everyday faith with a deft and sensitive hand." Horn Book

★ **We'll** fly away. Bryan Bliss. Greenwillow Books 2018 407 p.

Grades: 9 10 11 12

1. Abusive parents -- Fiction; 2. Best friends -- Fiction; 3. Death row -- Fiction; 4. Family problems -- Fiction; 5. High schools -- Fiction; 6. Schools -- Fiction; 7. Letters -- Fiction; 8. Prisoners -- Fiction; 9. Friendship -- Fiction

9780062494276, $17.99; 9780062494290; 0062494279

LC 2018008791

In this book, by Bryan Bliss, "best friends since childhood, Luke and Toby have dreamed of one thing: getting out of their dead-end town. Soon they finally will, riding the tails of Luke's wrestling scholarship, never looking back. If they don't drift apart first.... Tense and emotional, this hard-hitting novel explores family abuse, sex, love, and friendship, and how far people will go to protect those they love." (Publisher's note)

"A powerful story of loyalty, betrayal, and crippling family dysfunction." Pub Wkly

Block, Francesca Lia

Dangerous angels; the Weetzie Bat books. Revised paperback ed.; HarperTeen 2010 478p pa $9.99

Grades: 9 10 11 12

1. Friendship -- Fiction 2. Los Angeles (Calif.) -- Fiction

ISBN 978-0-06-200740-7

This compilation first published 1998

This is an omnibus edition of five Weetzie Bat books.

★ The **island** of excess love. Francesca Lia Block. Henry Holt and Company. 2014 214p $16.99

Grades: 8 9 10 11 12

1. Friendship -- Fiction 2. Love -- Fiction 3. Science fiction 4. Survival -- Fiction 5. Visions -- Fiction 6. Virgil. Aeneid -- Fiction 7. Los Angeles (Calif.) -- Fiction 8. Roman mythology 9. Adventure fiction

ISBN: 0805096310; 9780805096316

LC 2014005284

In this companion to Love in the time of global warming (2013) "Pen, Hex, Ash, Ez, and Venice are living in the pink house by the sea, getting by on hard work, companionship, and dreams. Until the day a foreboding ship appears in the harbor across from their home." (Publisher's note)

"Just as Block's earlier novel was loosely based on The Odyssey, this is even more loosely based on The Aeneid. The result is a mesmerizing, magical, and mysterious tale of love and loss, stories and visions, and betrayal and redemption, all told in the author''s signature lyrical voice." Booklist

★ **Love** in the time of global warming; Francesca Lia Block. Henry Holt and Co. 2013 240 p. (hardcover) $16.99

Grades: 8 9 10 11 12

1. Apocalyptic fiction 2. Voyages and travels -- Fiction 3. Love -- Fiction 4. Science fiction 5. Families -- Fiction 6. Survival -- Fiction 7. Earthquakes -- Fiction 8. Los Angeles (Calif.) -- Fiction

ISBN 0805096272; 9780805096279

LC 2012047808

Rainbow List (2014)

In this book, after "an earthquake and tidal wave destroy much of Los Angeles, Penelope—now going by Pen—sets out to find her family. In the course of a journey that explicitly parallels the one described in Homer's Odyssey, Pen navigates the blighted landscape with a crew of three other searchers. . . . Eventually they arrive in Las Vegas (the contemporary stand-in for the land of the dead) where Pen confronts the evil genius behind her world's destruction." (Publishers Weekly)

"In this Odyssey-inspired story, after the devastating Earth Shaker, Penelope sets out into the brutal Los Angeles landscape in search of her family. She meets an intriguing boy named Hex who joins her on her journey. Block's imagery is remarkable in this sophisticated melding of post-apocalyptic setting, re-imagined classic, and her signature magical realism." (Horn Book)

★ **Pretty** dead. HarperTeen 2009 195p $16.99; lib bdg $17.89

Grades: 9 10 11 12

1. Death -- Fiction 2. Vampires -- Fiction 3. Supernatural -- Fiction
ISBN 978-0-06-154785-0; 0-06-154785-9; 978-0-06-154786-7 lib bdg; 0-06-154786-7 lib bdg

LC 2008-45068

Beautiful vampire Charlotte finds herself slowly changing back into a human after the mysterious death of her best friend.

"Block takes what has up to now been the norm among vampire novels for teens and attempts to turn it on its head. This is a startlingly original work that drives a stake deep into the heart of typical vampire stories, revealing the deep loneliness and utter lack of romance in eternal life." SLJ

★ **Teen** spirit; Francesca Lia Block. Harper-Teen, an imprint of HarperCollinsPublishers 2014 240 p. (hardcover bdg.) $17.99

Grades: 9 10 11 12

1. Spirits -- Fiction 2. Grandparent-grandchild relationship -- Fiction 3. Dead -- Fiction 4. Grandmothers -- Fiction 5. Supernatural -- Fiction 6. Beverly Hills (Calif.) -- Fiction 7. Single-parent families -- Fiction 8. Dating (Social customs) -- Fiction
ISBN 0062008099; 9780062008091

LC 2013008057

In this novel, by Francesca Lia Block, when Julie's grandmother Miriam dies, "Julie's entire world is beginning to unravel. . . . [Then] she meets sweetly eccentric Clark, who is also mourning a loss. . . . One night, the two use a Ouija board . . . , believing it's a chance to reach out to her grandmother. But when they get a response, it isn't from Miriam. And Julie discovers that while she has been eager to regain her past, Clark is haunted by his." (Publisher's Note)

"Told in Block's signature, flowing prose, Teen Spirit is a layered story that's more about grief than it is about ghosts. Julie's narration is fast paced and accessible; readers won't be bogged down by intricate plots or complex ghost mythology. This is just a story about two kids learning to deal with loss. Julie realizes she cannot cling to the dead; she must hold her grandmother in her heart as she tries to live her own life. A beautiful story from a legendary young adult author." (School Library Journal)

The **waters** & the wild. HarperTeen 2009 113p $16.99; lib bdg $17.89

Grades: 7 8 9 10

1. School stories 2. Fairies -- Fiction
ISBN 978-0-06-145244-4; 0-06-145244-0; 978-0-06-145245-1 lib bdg; 0-06-145245-9 lib bdg

LC 2008031452

Thirteen-year-old Bee realizes that she is a fairy who has been switched at birth with another girl who now wants her life back.

"Fragments of poems by Yeats and Shelley are eerily apropos (and may provide an irresistible invitation for further reading). Haunting and thought provoking." Publ Wkly

Weetzie Bat. Harper & Row 1989 88p hardcover o.p. pa $7.99

Grades: 9 10 11 12

1. Friendship -- Fiction
ISBN 0-06-020534-2; 0-06-073625-9 pa

LC 88-6214

ALA YALSA Margaret A. Edwards Award (2005)

Follows the wild adventures of Weetzie Bat and her Los Angeles punk friends, Dirk, Duck-Man, and Secret-Agent-Lover-Man

"A brief, off-beat tale that has great charm, poignancy, and touches of fantasy. . . . This creates the ambiance of Hollywood with no cynicism, from the viewpoint of denizens who treasure its unique qualities." SLJ

Other titles about Weetzie Bat and her friends are:
Baby be-bop (1995)
Cherokee Bat and the Goat Guys (1992)
Missing Angel Juan (1993)
Necklace of kisses (2005)
Pink smog (2012)
Witch baby (1991)

Bloor, Edward

Taken. Alfred A. Knopf 2007 247p $17; pa $8.99

Grades: 6 7 8 9 10

1. Science fiction 2. Kidnapping -- Fiction 3. Social classes -- Fiction
ISBN 978-0-375-83636-7; 0-375-83636-5; 978-0-440-42128-3 pa; 0-440-42128-4 pa

LC 2006-35561

In 2036 kidnapping rich children has become an industry, but when thirteen-year-old Charity Meyers is taken and held for ransom, she soon discovers that this particular kidnapping is not what it seems.

"Deftly constructed, this is as riveting as it is thought-provoking." Publ Wkly

★ **Tangerine**. Harcourt Brace & Co. 1997 294p $17

Grades: 7 8 9 10

1. Soccer -- Fiction 2. Brothers -- Fiction
ISBN 0-15-201246-X

LC 96-34182

Twelve-year-old Paul, who lives in the shadow of his football hero brother Erik, fights for the right to play soccer despite his near blindness and slowly begins to remember the incident that damaged his eyesight

"Readers will cheer for this bright, funny, decent kid."
Horn Book Guide

Blume, Judy

Forever; a novel. Atheneum Books for Young Readers $17.99; pa $6.99

Grades: 9 10 11 12

1. Love stories 2. Sex -- Fiction 3. Families -- New Jersey -- Fiction

ISBN 0-689-84973-7; 0-671-69530-4 pa

A reissue of the title first published 1975 by Bradbury Press

ALA YALSA Margaret A. Edwards Award (1996)

The "story of a teenage senior-year love affair based primarily on physical attraction. Once Katherine Danziger and Michael Wagner meet at a party, they have eyes only for each other, and their romance progresses rapidly from kissing to heavy petting to lying together and finally to frequent sexual intercourse after Kath gets the Pill from a Planned Parenthood officer. . . . Characters—including adults and friends of the protagonists—are well developed, dialog is natural, and the story is convincing; however, the explicit sex scenes will limit this to the mature reader." Booklist

Tiger eyes; a novel. Bradbury Press 1981 206p $16.95; pa $6.99

Grades: 7 8 9 10

1. Death -- Fiction

ISBN 0-689-85872-8; 0-440-98469-6 pa

LC 81-6152

Resettled in the "Bomb City" with her mother and brother, Davey Wexler recovers from the shock of her father's death during a holdup of his 7-Eleven store in Atlantic City

"The plot is strong, interesting and believable. . . . The story though intense and complicated flows smoothly and easily." Voice Youth Advocates

Blumenthal, Deborah

Mafia girl. Deborah Blumenthal. Albert Whitman & Company. 2014 256p $16.99

Grades: 8 9 10 11

1. Identity--Fiction 2. Mafia--Fiction 3. Father-daughter relationship--Fiction

ISBN: 0807549118; 9780807549117

LC 2013028440

"Seventeen-year-old Gia, the daughter of New York City's most notorious Mafia boss, leads a privileged life, but what she wants most is to have a normal existence in which her family is safe. When she and her best friend are pulled over for underage drinking and driving, Gia is immediately attracted to the arresting police officer—despite his lack of interest. Not one to be denied, Gia does everything in her power to wear down his resistance, all the while running for school president, posing for Vogue, and surviving mob hits." SLJ

Gia's voice is an entertaining, effervescent stream-of-consciousness, but the book's frantic pace muddles too many competing plot lines." Horn Book

Blundell, Judy

What I saw and how I lied. Scholastic Press 2008 284p $16.99

Grades: 8 9 10 11 12

1. Mystery fiction 2. Florida -- Fiction

ISBN 978-0-439-90346-2; 0-439-90346-7

LC 2008-08503

In 1947, with her jovial stepfather Joe back from the war and family life returning to normal, teenage Evie, smitten by the handsome young ex-GI who seems to have a secret hold on Joe, finds herself caught in a complicated web of lies whose devastating outcome change her life and that of her family forever.

"Using pitch-perfect dialogue and short sentences filled with meaning, Blundell has crafted a suspenseful, historical mystery." Booklist

Blythe, Carolita

Revenge of a not-so-pretty girl; Carolita Blythe. Delacorte Press 2013 336 p. (library) $19.99; (hardcover) $16.99

Grades: 7 8 9 10 11 12

1. African American youth -- Fiction 2. Teenagers -- Conduct of life -- Fiction 3. Old age -- Fiction 4. Schools -- Fiction 5. Conduct of life -- Fiction 6. Family problems -- Fiction 7. Catholic schools -- Fiction 8. African Americans -- Fiction 9. Mothers and daughters -- Fiction 10. Brooklyn (New York, N.Y.) -- Fiction

ISBN 037599081X; 9780307978455; 9780375990816; 9780385742863

LC 2012012735

This novel, by Carolita Blythe, follows "an African American girl living in 1980s Brooklyn. . . . Evelyn Ryder used to be a beautiful movie star--never mind that it was practically a lifetime ago. . . . So if you think I feel guilty about mugging her, think again. But for something that should have been so simple, it sure went horribly wrong. . . . That's why I'm returning to the scene of the crime. . . . To see if I might be able to turn my luck around." (Publisher's note)

Bobet, Leah

Above; by Leah Bobet. Arthur A. Levine Books 2012 363 p.

Grades: 9 10 11 12

1. Fantasy fiction 2. Adventure fiction 3. Storytelling -- Fiction

ISBN 0545296706; 9780545296700

LC 2011012955

In this fantasy novel, "Safe is an underground refuge for the sick, the broken, and the freaks, far from the prying eyes of Above. Narrator Matthew is the Teller, responsible for remembering and guarding the stories of his friends and surrogate family. . . . When the only person ever to be exiled from Safe returns at the head of an army of shadows. . . . the group navigates the treacherous world of Above as they seek to reclaim Safe and come to terms with long-hidden truths" (Publishers Weekly)

An **inheritance** of ashes. By Leah Bobet. Clarion Books 2015 400 p. Map

Grades: 7 8 9 10 11 12

1. Fantasy 2. Farm life -- Fiction 3. Monsters -- Fiction 4. Secrets -- Fiction 5. Sisters -- Fiction 6. War --

Fiction 7. Fantasy fiction 8. War stories
9780544281110, $17.99

LC 2015006823

In this book, by Leah Bobet, the "strange war down south-with its rumors of gods and monsters-is over. And while sixteen-year-old Hallie and her sister wait to see who will return from the distant battlefield, they struggle to maintain their family farm. When Hallie hires a veteran to help them, the war comes home in ways no one could have imagined, and soon Hallie is taking dangerous risks-and keeping desperate secrets." (Publisher's note)

"Bobet repeatedly emphasizes the importance family-of blood or of choice-plays in surviving calamity. The satisfying yet realistic ending will leave readers hoping for more." Booklist

Bock, Caroline

LIE. St. Martin's Griffin 2011 211p pa $9.99
Grades: 8 9 10 11 12
    1. Homicide -- Fiction 2. Violence -- Fiction 3. Immigrants -- Fiction 4. Prejudices -- Fiction
    ISBN 978-0-312-66832-7; 0-312-66832-5

LC 2011019824

Seventeen-year-old Skylar Thompson is being questioned by the police. Her boyfriend, Jimmy, stands accused of brutally assaulting two young El Salvadoran immigrants from a neighboring town, and she's the prime witness.

"This effective, character-driven, episodic story examines the consequences of a hate crime on the teens involved in it. . . . Realistic and devastatingly insightful, this novel can serve as a springboard to classroom and family discussions. Unusual and important." Kirkus

Bodeen, S. A.

The **Compound**. Feiwel and Friends 2008 248p $16.95; pa $8.99
Grades: 7 8 9 10
    1. Twins -- Fiction 2. Fathers -- Fiction 3. Survival after airplane accidents, shipwrecks, etc. -- Fiction
    ISBN 0-312-37015-6; 0-312-57860-1 pa; 978-0-312-37015-2; 978-0-312-57860-2 pa

LC 2007-36148

After his parents, two sisters, and he have spent six years in a vast underground compound built by his wealthy father to protect them from a nuclear holocaust, fifteen-year-old Eli, whose twin brother and grandmother were left behind, discovers that his father has perpetrated a monstrous hoax on them all.

"The audience will feel the pressure closing in on them as they, like the characters, race through hairpin turns in the plot toward a breathless climax." Publ Wkly

Another title in this series is:
The Fallout (2013)

The **raft**; S.A. Bodeen. Feiwel and Friends 2012 231 p. $16.99
Grades: 7 8 9 10
    1. Survival skills -- Fiction 2. Wilderness survival -- Fiction 3. Survival after airplane accidents, shipwrecks, etc. -- Fiction
    ISBN 0312650108; 9780312650100

This novel, by S. A. Bodeen, is a plane crash survival story. "All systems are go until a storm hits during the flight. The only passenger, Robie doesn't panic until the engine suddenly cuts out and Max shouts at her to put on a life jacket. . . . And then . . . she's in the water. Fighting for her life. Max pulls her onto the raft. . . . They have no water. Their only food is a bag of Skittles. There are sharks. There is an island. But there's no sign of help on the way." (Publisher's note)

Bolden, Tonya

★ **Crossing** Ebenezer Creek. By Tonya Bolden. Bloomsbury 2017 230 p.
Grades: 7 8 9 10 11 12
    1. African Americans -- Fiction; 2. Brothers and sisters -- Fiction; 3. Freedmen -- Fiction; 4. Love -- Fiction; 5. Sherman's March to the Sea -- Fiction; 6. United States -- History -- Civil War, 1861-1865 -- Fiction; 7. Slavery -- Fiction; 8. Siblings -- Fiction
    9781619630550; 9781599903194, $17.99

LC 2016037742

In this book, by Tonya Bolden, "when Mariah and her young brother Zeke are suddenly freed from slavery, they join Sherman's march through Georgia.... [Then] she meets a free black named Caleb, [and] Mariah dreams in a way she never dared...of a future worth living and the possibility of true love. But even hope comes at a cost, and as the difficult march continues toward the churning waters of Ebenezer Creek, Mariah's dreams are as vulnerable as ever." (Publisher's note)

"A poetic, raw, and extraordinary imagining of a little-known, shameful chapter in American history." Kirkus

Includes bibliographical references, pages [225]-227.

Boll, Rosemarie

The **second** trial. Second Story Press 2010 319p pa $11.95
Grades: 6 7 8 9 10
    1. Wife abuse -- Fiction 2. Family life -- Fiction 3. Domestic violence -- Fiction 4. Parent-child relationship -- Fiction
    ISBN 978-1-897187-72-2 pa; 1-897187-72-6 pa

When his father's sentencing for domestic abuse isn't enough to protect them, Danny and his family are put into protective custody.

"This is a great story of upheaval and change, as well as the conflict a young person feels when his life is abruptly changed and he feels like he has lost control." Libr Media Connect

Bond, Gwenda

Fallout. By Gwenda Bond. Switch Press, a Capstone imprint 2015 304 p. (Lois Lane)
Grades: 9 10 11 12
    1. High schools -- Fiction 2. High schools -- Fiction 3. Reporters and reporting -- Fiction 4. Schools -- Fiction 5. Superheroes -- Fiction 6. Superman (Fictitious character) -- Fiction 7. Video gamers -- Fiction 8. Video games -- Fiction 10. Virtual reality -- Fiction 11. School stories
    1630790052; 9781630790059, $16.95

LC 2014026793

In this book, by Gwenda Bond, "Lois Lane is starting a new life in Metropolis. . . . A group known as the Warheads is making life miserable for another girl at school. They're messing with her mind, somehow, via the high-tech immersive videogame they all play. . . . Lois has her sights set on solving this mystery. But sometimes it's all a bit much. Thank goodness for her maybe-more-than-a friend, a guy she knows only by his screenname, SmallvilleGuy." (Publisher's note)

"Once these elements have been set up, it's pretty clear what steps will lead to the happy ending, but to Bond's credit, the dry wit of the narrative and the satisfyingly coy online romance between Lois Lane and Smallville Guy make each of those steps delightful." Booklist

Sequel: Double Down (2016)

Boone, Martina

Compulsion. Martina Boone. Simon Pulse 2014 433 p.

Grades: 9 10 11 12

1. Aunts -- Fiction 2. Blessing and cursing -- Fiction 3. Islands -- South Carolina -- Fiction 4. Orphans -- Fiction 5. Spirits -- Fiction 6. Supernatural -- Fiction 7. Vendetta -- Fiction 8. South Carolina -- Fiction

1481411225; 9781481411226, $17.99; 9781481411240

LC 2014027787

In this book, by Martina Boone, "Barrie Watson has been a virtual prisoner in the house where she lived with her shut-in mother. When her mother dies, Barrie promises to put some mileage on her stiletto heels. But she finds a new kind of prison at her aunt's South Carolina plantation instead—a prison guarded by an ancient spirit who long ago cursed one of the three founding families of Watson Island and gave the others magical gifts that became compulsions." (Publisher's note)

"Though the novel is grounded in the present day, there's an old-fashioned quality to Boone's dialogue and characters; she skillfully blends rich magic and folklore with adventure, sweeping romance, and hidden treasure, all while exploring the island and its accompanying legends. An impressive start to the Heirs of Watson Island series." Publishers Weekly

Sequel: Persuasion (2015)

Booth, Coe

Bronxwood. Push 2011 328p $17.99

Grades: 10 11 12

1. Drug traffic -- Fiction 2. Foster home care -- Fiction 3. African Americans -- Fiction 4. Bronx (New York, N.Y.) -- Fiction

ISBN 978-0-4399-2534-1

Sequel to Tyrell (2006)

"Action scenes combine with interpersonal exchanges to keep the pace moving forward at a lightning speed, but Booth never sacrifices the street-infused dialogue and emotional authenticity that characterize her works. She has created a compelling tale of a teen still trying to make the right choices despite the painful consequences." SLJ

★ **Tyrell**. PUSH 2006 310p hardcover o.p. pa $7.99

Grades: 9 10 11 12

1. Poor -- Fiction 2. Homeless persons -- Fiction 3.

African Americans -- Fiction 4. Bronx (New York, N.Y.) -- Fiction

ISBN 0-439-83879-7; 978-0-439-83879-5; 0-439-83880-0 pa; 978-0-439-83880-1 pa

LC 2005-37330

Fifteen-year-old Tyrell, who is living in a Bronx homeless shelter with his spaced-out mother and his younger brother, tries to avoid temptation so he does not end up in jail like his father.

"The immediate first-person narrative is pitch perfect: fast, funny, and anguished (there's also lots of use of the n-word, though the term is employed in the colloquial sense, not as an insult). Unlike many books reflecting the contemporary street scene, this one is more than just a pat situation with a glib resolution; it's filled with surprising twists and turns that continue to the end." Booklist

Followed by Bronxwood (2011)

Booth, Molly

★ **Saving** Hamlet. Molly Booth. Disner-Hyperion 2016 352 p.

Grades: 7 8 9 10

1. Theater -- Fiction 2. Time travel -- Fiction 3. Shakespeare, William, 1564-1616 Hamlet -- Fiction

1484752740; 9781484752746, $17.99

LC 2015045426

In this book, by Molly Booth, "Emma Allen couldn't be more excited to start her sophomore year. Not only is she the assistant stage manager for the drama club's production of Hamlet, but her crush Brandon is directing. . . . But soon after school starts, everything goes haywire. Emma's promoted to stage manager with zero experience, her best friend Lulu stops talking to her, and Josh—the adorable soccer boy who's cast as the lead—turns out to be a disaster. It's up to Emma to fix it all." (Publisher's note)

"Emma is an easy-to-root-for heroine whose struggles will resonate with teens, drama geeks or otherwise, and her forays into Shakespeare's London add insight into gender identity in the theater. A fun, imaginative debut." Booklist

Borris, Albert

Crash into me. Simon Pulse 2009 257p $16.99

Grades: 8 9 10 11 12

1. Suicide -- Fiction 2. Automobile travel -- Fiction

ISBN 978-1-4169-7435-2; 1-4169-7435-0

LC 2008-36225

Four suicidal teenagers go on a "celebrity suicide road trip," visiting the graves of famous people who have killed themselves, with the intention of ending their lives in Death Valley, California.

This "novel gives a spot-on portrayal of depressed and suicidal teens with realistic voices." Kirkus

Bow, Erin

★ **Plain** Kate. Arthur A. Levine Books 2010 314p $17.99

Grades: 7 8 9 10

1. Fantasy fiction 2. Cats -- Fiction 3. Magic -- Fiction 4. Orphans -- Fiction 5. Witchcraft -- Fiction 6. Wood carving -- Fiction

ISBN 978-0-545-16664-5; 0-545-16664-0

LC 2009-32652

Plain Kate's odd appearance and expertise as a wood-carver cause some to think her a witch, but friendship with a talking cat and, later, with humans help her to survive and even thrive in a world of magic, charms, and fear.

"Despite the talking animal . . . and graceful writing . . . this is a dark and complex tale, full of violence—knives cut a lot more than wood. . . . Kate is undeniably a sympathetic character deserving of happiness." Publ Wkly

★ The **Scorpion** Rules. By Erin Bow. Simon & Schuster 2015 384 p.

Grades: 9 10 11 12

1. Princesses -- Fiction 2. Artificial intelligence -- Fiction 3. Fantasy fiction 4. Hostages -- Fiction
1481442716; 9781481442718, $17.99

In this book, by Erin Bow, "Greta is a Duchess and a Crown Princess. She is also a Child of Peace, a hostage held by the de facto ruler of the world, the great Artificial Intelligence, Talis. This is how the game is played: if you want to rule, you must give one of your children as a hostage. Start a war and your hostage dies. . . . Greta will be free if she can make it to her eighteenth birthday. . . . But everything changes when Elian arrives at the Preceprture." (Publisher's note)

"Through Greta's conflicts, the author explores what it means to be human and gives readers a glimpse inside the mind of artificial intelligence." Booklist

Sequel: The Swan Riders (2016)

★ **Sorrow's** knot; Erin Bow. Arthur A. Levine Books 2013 368 p. (hardcover: alk. paper) $17.99

Grades: 8 9 10 11 12

1. Dead -- Fiction 2. Knots and splices -- Fiction 3. Magic -- Fiction 4. Identity -- Fiction 5. Fate and fatalism -- Fiction
ISBN 0545166667; 9780545166669; 9780545166676; 9780545578004

LC 2013007855

In this book, by Erin Bow, "the dead do not rest easy. Every patch of shadow might be home to something hungry, something deadly. Most of the people of this world live on the sunlit, treeless prairies. But a few carve out an uneasy living in the forest towns, keeping the dead at bay with wards made from magically knotted cords. The women who tie these knots are called binders. And Otter's mother, Willow, is one of the greatest binders her people have ever known." (Publisher's note)

"Sorrow's Knot is a dystopian novel that does not deal with the destruction of the broader world. Rather, it delves into the mythology of a group of people and how their prejudices and resistance to change came to be. Readers of suspense will love the dark tension of the story line, an ebb and flow that carries through to the very end." (School Library Journal)

Bowman, Akemi Dawn

Starfish. Akemi Dawn Bowman. Simon Pulse 2017 352 p.

Grades: 7 8 9 10

1. Artists -- Fiction; 2. Family problems -- Fiction; 3. Identity -- Fiction; 4. Mothers and daughters -- Fiction; 5. Racially mixed people -- Fiction; 6. Self-perception -- Fiction; 7. Sexual abuse -- Fiction; 8. Mother-daughter relationship -- Fiction
9781481487726, $17.99

LC 2016045829

William C. Morris Honor Book (2018)

In this novel, by Akemi Dawn Bowman, Kiko Himura's mother "makes her feel unremarkable and...[with] a half-Japanese heritage she doesn't quite understand, Kiko prefers to keep her head down.... When she receives an invitation from her childhood friend to leave her small town and tour art schools on the west coast, Kiko jumps at the opportunity in spite of the anxieties and fears that attempt to hold her back." (Publisher's note)

"The story will resonate deeply with readers who have experienced abuse of any kind, or who have been held back by social anxiety. This is a stunningly beautiful, highly nuanced debut." (Booklist)

Summer bird blue. Akemi Dawn Bowman. Simon Pulse 2018 384 p.

Grades: 7 8 9 10 11 12

1. Aunts -- Fiction; 2. Composers -- Fiction; 3. Death -- Fiction; 4. Grief -- Fiction; 5. Mothers and daughters -- Fiction; 6. Sisters -- Fiction; 7. Hawaii -- Fiction
9781481487757, $18.99

LC 2017048136

In this novel, by Akemi Dawn Bowman, "[Rumi Seto] wants to spend the rest of her life writing music with her younger sister, Lea. Then Lea dies in a car accident, and her mother sends her away to live with her aunt in Hawaii while she deals with her own grief.... With the help of...a teenage surfer named Kai...and an eighty-year-old named George Watanabe,...Rumi attempts to find her way back to her music." (Publisher's note)

Bradbury, Jennifer

Shift. Atheneum Books for Young Readers 2008 245p $16.99

Grades: 7 8 9 10 11 12

1. Travel -- Fiction 2. Cycling -- Fiction 3. Friendship -- Fiction 4. Missing persons -- Fiction
ISBN 978-1-4169-4732-5; 1-4169-4732-9

LC 2007-23558

When best friends Chris and Win go on a cross country bicycle trek the summer after graduating and only one returns, the FBI wants to know what happened.

"Bradbury's keen details . . . add wonderful texture to this exciting [novel.] . . . Best of all is the friendship story." Booklist

Wrapped. Atheneum Books for Young Readers 2011 309p $16.99

Grades: 7 8 9 10

1. Mystery fiction 2. Spies -- Fiction 3. Supernatural -- Fiction
ISBN 978-1-4169-9007-9; 1-4169-9007-0

"An 1815 parlor diversion leads to a fizzy, frothy caper. Agnes is a Regency debutante. . . . When she pockets the trinket she finds among the linens at her neighbor's mummy-wrapping party, she unwittingly sets off a series of catastrophes . . . that include burglaries, violent attacks and murder. . . . Bradbury weaves Egyptology, Napoleanic conquest and a flirtation with the supernatural into a spy thriller." Kirkus

Brande, Robin

Evolution, me, & other freaks of nature. Alfred A. Knopf 2007 268p hardcover o.p. pa $7.99

Grades: 7 8 9 10

1. School stories 2. Evolution -- Fiction 3. Christian life -- Fiction

ISBN 978-0-375-84349-5; 0-375-84349-3; 978-0-375-94349-2 lib bdg; 0-375-94349-8 lib bdg; 978-0-440-24030-3 pa; 0-440-24030-1 pa

LC 2006-34158

Following her conscience leads high school freshman Mena to clash with her parents and former friends from their conservative Christian church, but might result in better things when she stands up for a teacher who refuses to include "Intelligent Design" in lessons on evolution.

"Readers will appreciate this vulnerable but ultimately resilient protagonist who sees no conflict between science and her own deeply rooted faith." Booklist

Brant, Wendy

★ **Zenn** diagram. Wendy Brant. Kids Can Press 2017 315 p.

Grades: 8 9 10 11 12

1. Extrasensory perception -- Fiction; 2. Tutors and tutoring -- Fiction; 3. Psychic ability -- Fiction

9781771388566; 9781771387927, $17.95; 1771387920

In this novel, by Wendy Brant, "Eva Walker is a seventeen-year-old math genius. And if that doesn't do wonders for her popularity, there's another thing that makes it even worse: when she touches another person or anything that belongs to them from clothes to textbooks to cell phones she sees a vision of their emotions. She can read a person's fears and anxieties.... Then one day a new student walks into Eva's life." (Publisher's note)

"Though the plot coincidences stretch belief at times, they are forgiven in light of the strengths of the story, which include a unique premise, natural dialogue, and complex characters." Booklist

Brashares, Ann

Forever in blue; the fourth summer of the Sisterhood. Delacorte Press 2007 384p $18.99; lib bdg $21.99

Grades: 9 10 11

1. Friendship -- Fiction

ISBN 978-0-385-72936-9; 0-385-72936-7; 978-0-385-90413-1 lib bdg; 0-385-90413-4 lib bdg

LC 2006-18782

Fourth volume of the Traveling Pants books; Sequel to Girls in pants (2005)

As their lives take them in different directions, Lena, Tibby, Carmen, and Bridget discover many more things about themselves and the importance of their relationship with each other.

"This light read is a great ending to the series. Sisterhood followers who are eagerly awaiting this final book will not be disappointed." Voice Youth Advocates

Girls in pants; the third summer of the Sisterhood. Delacorte Press 2005 338p $16.95; lib bdg $18.99; pa $8.95

Grades: 9 10 11 12

1. Friendship -- Fiction

ISBN 0-385-72935-9; 0-385-90919-5 lib bdg; 0-553-37593-8 pa

LC 2004-15296

Third volume of the Traveling Pants books, previous titles The sisterhood of the travelling pants and The second summer of the sisterhood

"It's the summer before the Septembers go to college, a summer in which old and new boyfriends appear, families grow and change, crises occur and are resolved, and the pants continue their designated rounds. Despite their diverse schedules, the four friends . . . reunite one final weekend before they go off to four different colleges. Readers of the other books won't be disappointed with these new adventures." Booklist

Followed by Forever in blue (2007)

The **here** and now. Ann Brashares. Delacorte Press. 2014 256p $18.99

Grades: 8 9 10 11 12

1. High school students--Fiction 2. Time travel--Fiction 3. New York (N.Y.)--Fiction

ISBN: 0385736800; 9780385736800; 9780385906296

LC 2013018683

"Prenna and her doctor mom are not your average immigrants. No, they have immigrated to New York from the 2090s, a future of climate-change extremes and mosquito-borne plagues that wipe out entire families and civilizations. The few who have survived the plagues and the journey back to 2010 have been charged with two challenges: change the course of environmental history and assimilate into the culture without disclosing their origins or becoming intimate with the natives. Prenna knows her friendship with Ethan is 'red-flag behavior.' When an elderly homeless man warns her that she and Ethan must prevent a murder on May 17, 2014—just days away—she realizes she must defy the community and its counselors for civilization's greater good. . . . The book's environmental message won't be missed by readers, but this is a cautionary tale rather than a didactic screed." Booklist

The **second** summer of the sisterhood. Delacorte Press 2003 373p $15.95; lib bdg $17.99; pa $8.95

Grades: 9 10 11 12

1. Friendship -- Fiction

ISBN 0-385-72934-0; 0-385-90852-0 lib bdg; 0-385-73105-1 pa

LC 2003-535308

"Brashares has done an outstanding job of showing the four teens growing up and giving readers a happy, ultimately hopeful book, easy to read and gentle in its important lessons." Booklist

Followed by Girls in pants (2005)

The **sisterhood** of the traveling pants. Delacorte Press 2001 294p $14.95; pa $8.95; pa $9.99

Grades: 8 9 10

1. Friendship -- Fiction

ISBN 0-385-72933-2; 0-385-73058-6 pa; 9780385730587 pa

LC 2002-282046

"Four teenagers—best friends since babyhood—have different destinations for the summer and are distressed about disbanding. When they find a pair of 'magic pants'—secondhand jeans that fit each girl perfectly, despite their different body types—they take a solemn vow that the Pants 'will travel to all the places we're going, and they will keep us together when we are apart.' . . . Middle school, high school." (Horn Book)

"Four lifelong high-school friends and a magical pair of jeans take summer journeys to discover love, disappointment, and self-realization." Booklist

The **whole** thing together. Ann Brashares. Delacorte Press 2017 295 p.

Grades: 9 10 11 12

1. Families -- Fiction; 2. Interpersonal relations -- Fiction; 3. Vacation homes -- Fiction
9780399556005; 9780385736893, $18.99; 9780385906302

LC 2016026996

In this novel, by Ann Brashares, "summer for Sasha and Ray means the sprawling old house on Long Island. Since they were children, they've shared almost everything.... Sasha's dad was once married to Ray's mom, and...they had three daughters: Emma,...Mattie...and Quinn.... But the marriage crumbled and the bitterness lingered. Now there are two new families -- and neither one will give up the beach house that holds the memories, happy and sad, of summers past." (Publisher's note)

"Brashares's masterful orchestration of plot, multidimensional characters, and intriguing subplots will delight her fans and newcomers alike." Pub Wkly

Braxton-Smith, Ananda

★ **Merrow**. Ananda Braxton-Smith. Candlewick Press 2016 240 p.

Grades: 9 10 11 12

1. Self-realization -- Fiction 2. Mermaids and mermen -- Fiction 3. Mother-daughter relationship -- Fiction
9780763687106, $16.99; 9780763679248, $16.99

LC 2016947242

In this novel, by Ananda Braxton-Smith, "the people of Carrick Island have been whispering behind Neen's back ever since her father drowned and her mother disappeared. The townspeople say her mother was a merrow and has returned to the ocean. Neen, caught in her hazy new in-between self-not a child, but not quite grown up-can't help but wonder if the villagers are right. But if her mother was a merrow, then what does that make Neen?" (Publisher's note)

"A sparkling paean to the stories we tell-plain and embroidered, fantastical, amazing, true-that get us through the night." Kirkus

Bray, Libba

★ **Beauty** queens. Scholastic Press 2011 396p $18.99

Grades: 8 9 10 11 12

1. Beauty contests -- Fiction 2. Survival after airplane accidents, shipwrecks, etc. -- Fiction
ISBN 978-0-439-89597-2; 0-439-89597-9

LC 2011-02321

In this book by Libba Bray, "on their way to the Miss Teen Dream competition, a planeload of beauty pageant contestants crashes on what appears to be a deserted island. While the surviving Teen Dreamers valiantly cope with the basics (finding food, water, and shelter; practicing their pageant skills), they become pawns in a massive global conspiracy involving a rogue former Miss Teen Dream winner; a megalomaniacal dictator; and a Big Brother-ish pageant sponsor, The Corporation." (Horn Book Magazine)

"A full-scale send-up of consumer culture, beauty pageants, and reality television: . . . it makes readers really examine their own values while they are laughing, and shaking their heads at the hyperbolic absurdity of those values gone seriously awry." Bull Cent Child Books

★ The **diviners**; by Libba Bray. Little, Brown 2012 608 p. (hardback) $19.99

Grades: 9 10 11 12

1. Mystery fiction 2. Historical fiction 3. Occultism -- Fiction 4. Murder -- Fiction 5. Uncles -- Fiction 6. Psychic ability -- Fiction 7. Mystery and detective stories 8. New York (N.Y.) -- History -- 1898-1951 -- Fiction
ISBN 031612611X; 9780316126113

LC 2012022868

In this book by Libba Bray, "Evie O'Neill has been exiled from her boring old hometown and shipped off to the bustling streets of New York City. . . . The only catch is Evie has to live with her Uncle Will, curator of The Museum of American Folklore, Superstition, and the Occult. . . . When a rash of occult-based murders comes to light, Evie and her uncle are right in the thick of the investigation." (Publisher's note)

★ **Going** bovine. Delacorte Press 2009 480p $17.99; lib bdg $20.99

Grades: 9 10 11 12

1. Dwarfs -- Fiction 2. Automobile travel -- Fiction 3. Creutzfeldt-Jakob disease -- Fiction
ISBN 978-0-385-73397-7; 0-385-73397-6; 978-0-385-90411-7 lib bdg; 0-385-90411-8 lib bdg

LC 2008-43774

ALA YALSA Printz Award (2010)

In an attempt to find a cure after being diagnosed with Creutzfeldt-Jakob's (aka mad cow) disease, Cameron Smith, a disaffected sixteen-year-old boy, sets off on a road trip with a death-obsessed video gaming dwarf he meets in the hospital.

"Bray's wildly imagined novel, narrated in Cameron's sardonic, believable voice, is wholly unique, ambitious, tender, thought-provoking, and often fall-off-the-chair funny, even as she writes with powerful lyricism about the nature of existence, love, and death." Booklist

★ A **great** and terrible beauty. Delacorte Press 2004 403p $16.95

Grades: 9 10 11 12

1. Mystery fiction 2. Great Britain -- Fiction
ISBN 0-385-73028-4

LC 2003-9472

After the suspicious death of her mother in 1895, sixteen-year-old Gemma returns to England, after many years in India, to attend a finishing school where she becomes aware of her magical powers and ability to see into the spirit world.

"The reader will race to the end to discover the mysterious and realistic challenges of an exciting teenage gothic mystery." Libr Media Connect

Lair of dreams: a Diviners novel. Libba Bray. Little Brown & Co. 2015 704 p.

Grades: 9 10 11 12

1. Dreams -- Fiction 2. Mystery and detective stories 3. Psychic ability -- Fiction 4. Sleep -- Fiction 5. Supernatural -- Fiction 6. New York (N.Y.) -- History -- 1898-1951 -- Fiction 7. Mystery fiction 8. Psychics -- Fiction

9780316126045, $19

LC 2015010856

This book is the second in Libba Bray's Diviners series. "After a supernatural showdown with a serial killer, Evie O'Neill has outed herself as a Diviner. Now that the world knows of her ability to 'read' objects, and therefore, read the past, she has become a media darling, earning the title, 'America's Sweetheart Seer.' But not everyone is so accepting of the Diviners' abilities." (Publisher's note)

"A multilayered, character-driven, and richly rewarding installment to the paranormal historical fiction series." SLJ

Rebel angels. Delacorte Press 2005 548p $16.95; pa $9.99

Grades: 9 10 11 12

1. Mystery fiction 2. Magic -- Fiction 3. Great Britain -- Fiction

ISBN 0-385-73029-2; 0-385-73341-0 pa

LC 2005-3805

Sequel to A great and terrible beauty (2004)

Gemma and her friends from the Spence Academy return to the realms to defeat her foe, Circe, and to bind the magic that has been released.

"The writing never falters, and the revelations (such as Felicity's childhood of abuse, discreetly revealed) only strengthen the characters. Clever foreshadowing abounds, and clues to the mystery of Circe may have readers thinking they have figured everything out; they will still be surprised." SLJ

Followed by The sweet far thing (2007)

The sweet far thing. Delacorte Press 2007 819p $17.99; lib bdg $20.99

Grades: 9 10 11 12

1. Mystery fiction 2. Magic -- Fiction 3. Great Britain -- Fiction

ISBN 978-0-385-73030-3; 978-0-385-90295-3 lib bdg

LC 2007-31302

Sequel to Rebel angels (2005)

At Spence Academy, sixteen-year-old Gemma Doyle continues preparing for her London debut while struggling to determine how best to use magic to resolve a power struggle in the enchanted world of the realms, and to protect her own world and loved ones.

"The novel's fast-paced and exciting ending and Bray's lyrical descriptions of the decaying realms are sure to enchant readers who loved Gemma's previous exploits." SLJ

Brennan, Sarah Rees

The **demon's** lexicon. Margaret K. McElderry Books 2009 322p $17.99; pa $9.99

Grades: 9 10 11 12

1. Magic -- Fiction 2. Brothers -- Fiction 3. Demonology -- Fiction

ISBN 978-1-4169-6379-0; 1-4169-6379-0; 978-1-4169-6380-6 pa; 1-4169-6380-4 pa

LC 2008-39056

Sixteen-year-old Nick and his family have battled magicians and demons for most of his life, but when his brother, Alan, is marked for death while helping new friends Jamie and Mae, Nick's determination to save Alan leads him to uncover a devastating secret.

"A fresh voice dancing between wicked humor and crepuscular sumptuousness invigorates this urban fantasy. . . . The narrative peels back layers of revelation, deftly ratcheting up the tension and horror to a series of shattering climaxes." Kirkus

Other titles in this series are:

The demon's covenant (2010)

The demon's surrender (2011)

In other lands. Sarah Rees Brennan ; illustrated by Carolyn Nowak. Big Mouth House 2017 437 p.

Grades: 8 9 10 11 12

1. Bisexuality -- Fiction; 2. Diplomats -- Fiction; 3. Friendship -- Fiction; 5. Schools -- Fiction; 6. Soldiers -- Fiction; 7. Fantasy fiction

9781618731357; 9781618731203, $19.95

LC 2016059543

In this book, by Sarah Rees Brennan, illustrated by Carolyn Nowak, "the Borderlands aren't like anywhere else. Don't try to smuggle a phone or any other piece of technology over the wall that marks the Border -- unless you enjoy a fireworks display in your backpack.... There are elves, harpies, and...mermaids.... In Other Lands is.... a novel about...friendship, falling in love, diplomacy, and finding your own place in the world." (Publisher's note)

"Smart explorations of gender stereotypes, fluid sexuality, and awkward romance only add to the depth and delight of this glittering contemporary fantasy." PW Annex

Brewer, Zac

The **cemetery** boys. Zac Brewer. HarperTeen 2015 273 p.

Grades: 9 10 11 12

1. Brothers and sisters -- Fiction 2. Cults -- Fiction 3. Dating (Social customs) -- Fiction 4. Horror stories 5. Moving, Household -- Fiction 6. Peer pressure -- Fiction 7. Supernatural -- Fiction 8. Twins -- Fiction 9. Teenagers -- Fiction 10. Cemeteries -- Fiction

0062307886; 9780062307880, $17.99

LC 2014027404

In this novel by Heather Brewer "Stephen's summer starts looking up when he meets punk girl Cara and her charismatic twin brother, Devon. With Cara, he feels safe and understood. In Devon and his group, he sees a chance at making real friends. Only, as the summer presses on, and harmless nights hanging out in the cemetery take a darker turn, Stephen starts to suspect that Devon is less a friend than a leader. And he might be leading them to a very sinister end." (Publisher's note)

"The novel's final pages will surely shock readers: The author takes great glee in not just presenting a great reveal toward the end, but also twisting the knife. Keen-eyed readers may spot the twist, but few will predict just how far it goes. A slick, spooky, chilling mystery." Kirkus

The **chronicles** of Vladimir Tod: eighth grade bites. Dutton Children's Books 2007 182p (The chronicles of Vladimir Tod) $16.99
Grades: 6 7 8 9

1. School stories 2. Orphans -- Fiction 3. Vampires -- Fiction
ISBN 978-0-525-47811-9; 0-525-47811-6

LC 2006030455

For thirteen years, Vlad, aided by his aunt and best friend, has kept secret that he is half-vampire, but when his missing teacher is replaced by a sinister substitute, he learns that there is more to being a vampire, and to his parents' deaths, than he could have guessed.

This "is an exceptional current-day vampire story. The mix of typical teen angst and dealing with growing vampiric urges make for a fast-moving, engaging story." Voice Youth Advocates

Other titles in this series are:
Ninth grade slays (2008)
Tenth grade bleeds (2009)
Eleventh grade burns (2010)
Twelfth grade kills (2010)

Brezenoff, Steve

Brooklyn, burning. Carolrhoda Lab 2011 202p $17.95
Grades: 8 9 10 11

1. Musicians -- Fiction 2. Runaway teenagers -- Fiction 3. Brooklyn (New York, N.Y.) -- Fiction
ISBN 978-0-7613-7526-5

LC 2010051447

"Homelessness, queerness and the rougher sides of living on the street are handled without a whiff of sensationalism, and the moments between Kid, the first-person narrator, and Scout, addressed as 'you,' are described in language so natural and vibrant that readers may not even notice that neither character's gender is ever specified. . . . Overall, the tone is as raw, down-to-earth and transcendent as the music Scout and Kid ultimately make together." Kirkus

Guy in real life. Steve Brezenoff. Balzer + Bray. 2014 386p $17.99
Grades: 9 10 11 12

1. Fantasy games -- Fiction 2. Love -- Fiction 3. Role playing -- Fiction 4. Video games -- Fiction 5. Minnesota -- Fiction
ISBN: 0062266837; 9780062266835

LC 2013021584

"Sulky metal head boy meets artsy gamer girl. Awkward teenage love ensues. When Lesh's and Svetlana's worlds collide literally in Saint Paul, Minn., it precipitates a time-honored culture clash wherein magic happens, but that's where predictability ends. In a first-person narration that alternates between the boy in black and the girl dungeon

master, Brezenoff conjures a wry, wise and deeply sympathetic portrait of the exquisite, excruciating thrill of falling in love." Kirkus

Brignull, Irena

★ The **Hawkweed** Prophecy. Irena Brignull. Weinstein Books 2016 368 p.
Grades: 7 8 9 10

1. Witches -- Fiction 2. Magic -- Fiction 3. Individuality -- Fiction 4. Female friendship -- Fiction
9781602863019, $11.99; 1602863008; 9781602863002, $18.00

LC 2016037295

In this novel, by Irena Brignull, "Poppy Hooper and Ember Hawkweed couldn't lead more different lives. Poppy is a troubled teen, . . . causing chaos wherever she goes. . . . Ember is a young witch, struggling to find a place within her coven and prove her worth. Both are outsiders: feeling like they don't belong and seeking escape. Poppy and Ember soon become friends, and secretly share knowledge of their two worlds. Little do they know that destiny has brought them together." (Publisher's note)

"The third-person narration switches focus from character to character as they make frustrating, heart-rending, totally believable choices. Fantasy and nonfantasy readers alike will appreciate this gritty and intriguing coming-of-age story." Kirkus

Brockenbrough, Martha

Devine intervention; Martha Brockenbrough. Arthur A. Levine Books 2012 297 p.
Grades: 7 8 9 10 11

1. Soul -- Fiction 2. Angels -- Fiction 3. Heaven -- Fiction 4. Future life -- Fiction 5. High school students -- Fiction 6. Dead -- Fiction 7. Guardian angels -- Fiction
ISBN 0545382130; 9780545382137; 9780545382144

LC 2011039768

This book follows "Jerome . . . A hell raiser when alive and killed by his cousin in eighth grade in an unfortunate archery accident, he has spent his afterlife in Soul Rehab assigned to Heidi in an attempt to win his way into Heaven. Not that he's very committed to the notion; he lost his "Guardian Angel's Handbook" pretty much right away, but he sort of tries. Heidi has more or less enjoyed Jerome's company, though he could sometimes be annoying. When Heidi, having experienced unendurable humiliation in a high-school talent show, ventures onto thin ice and falls through, Jerome does his best to save her soul--as much for her own sake, he's surprised to find, as for his." (Kirkus Reviews)

The **game** of Love and Death. Martha Brockenbrough. Arthur A. Levine Books, an imprint of Scholastic Inc. 2015 352 p.
Grades: 9 10 11 12

1. African American teenage girls -- Washington (State) -- Seattle -- Fiction 2. African Americans -- Fiction 3. Death -- Fiction 4. Love -- Fiction 5. Man-woman relationships -- Fiction 6. Race relations -- Fiction 7. Teenage boys -- Washington (State) -- Seattle -- Fiction 8. Seattle (Wash.) -- History -- 20th century -- Fiction

9. Romance fiction
9780545668347, $17.99; 0545668344

LC 2014033339

In this novel, by Martha Brockenbrough, "Flora and Henry were born a few blocks from each other, innocent of the forces that might keep a white boy and an African American girl apart; years later they meet again and their mutual love of music sparks an even more powerful connection. But what Flora and Henry don't know is that they are pawns in a game played by the eternal adversaries Love and Death, here . . . reimagined as two extremely sympathetic and fascinating characters." (Publisher's note)

"There is a deliberately archetypal quality to the story, but the fully realized setting and characters make this more than just a modern fairy tale. It's a poignant reminder of how far we've come since the 1930s in terms of race, class, and sexual orientation—and how far we still have to go." Horn Book

Brooks, Bruce

The **moves** make the man; a novel. HarperCollins Pubs. 1984 280p hardcover o.p. pa $6.99
Grades: 7 8 9 10 11 12
1. Friendship -- Fiction 2. African Americans -- Fiction
ISBN 0-06-020679-9; 0-06-440564-8 pa
A Newbery Medal honor book, 1985

This is an "excellent novel about values and the way people relate to one another." N Y Times Book Rev

Brooks, Kevin

The **bunker** diary. By Kevin Brooks. Carolrhoda Lab 2015 260 p. Illustration
Grades: 9 10 11 12
1. Conduct of life -- Fiction 2. Diaries -- Fiction 3. Interpersonal relations -- Fiction 4. Kidnapping -- Fiction 5. Torture -- Fiction
146775420X; 9781467754200, $17.99

LC 2014026362

This book, by Kevin Brooks, is the winner of the 2014 Cilip Carnegie Medal. "Linus is a 16-year-old runaway living on the harsh English streets who wakes up one day in an unfamiliar underground bunker with no water or food while under constant surveillance by an unknown kidnapper. As each day passes, more people are kidnapped. . . . When Linus and the rest try to escape, . . . they realize that . . . they may have to resort to the ultimate horror to survive." (School Library Journal)

"Brooks' latest is not an easy novel, but it's one that begs for rereading to suss the intricacies of its construction of plot, character development and insight into the human condition. Not for everyone, this heady novel is worthy of study alongside existentialist works of the 20th century." Kirkus

First published in 2013 by Penguin Books Ltd, 80 Strand, London WC2R 0RL, England.

Brothers, Meagan

Weird Girl and What's His Name. Meagan Brothers. Three Rooms Press 2015 336 p.
Grades: 9 10 11 12
1. Friendship -- Fiction 2. Teenagers -- Sexual behavior -- Fiction 3. LGBT youth
1941110274; 9781941110270, $16.95

LC 2015935226

In this novel by Meagan Brothers "Rory and Lulu share an affinity for all things geek. When Lulu discovers that underage Rory had an explicit relationship with his divorced boss and hid it from Lulu because of her crush on him, she begins to question her own sexual orientation. After she is rebuffed by her favorite teacher, Lulu decides to hunt down the skeletons in her family's closet." (School Library Journal)

"Recommended for fans of realistic fiction with relationship drama and an LGBTQ focus." SLJ

Brouwer, Sigmund

Devil's pass; Sigmund Brouwer. Orca Book Publishers 2012 237 p. (pbk) $9.95
Grades: 6 7 8 9 10
1. Grandfathers -- Fiction 2. Voyages and travels -- Fiction 3. Grandparent-grandchild relationship -- Fiction 4. Canada -- Fiction 5. Street musicians -- Fiction 6. Canol Heritage Trail (N.W.T.) -- Fiction
ISBN 155469938X; 9781554699384

LC 2012938220

In author Sigmund Brouwer's book, "seventeen-year-old Webb's abusive stepfather has made it impossible for him to live at home, so Webb survives on the streets of Toronto. . . . When Webb's grandfather dies, his will stipulates that his grandsons fulfill specific requests. Webb's task takes him to the Canol Trail in Canada's Far North. . . . With a Native guide, two German tourists and his guitar for company, Webb is forced to confront terrible events in his grandfather's past and somehow deal with the pain and confusion of his own life." (Publisher's note)

Brown, Jaye Robin

Georgia peaches and other forbidden fruit. Jaye Robin Brown; [edited by] Tara Weikum. HarperTeen 2016 432 p.
Grades: 9 10 11 12
1. Father-daughter relationship -- Fiction 2. Lesbians -- Fiction 3. Romance fiction 4. Georgia -- Fiction
9780062270986, $17.99

LC 2016936318

In this novel by Jaye Robin Brown, "Joanna Gordon has been out and proud for years, but when her popular radio evangelist father remarries and decides to move all three of them from Atlanta to the more conservative Rome, Georgia, he asks Jo to do the impossible: to lie low for the rest of her senior year. And Jo reluctantly agrees. . . . Things get complicated when she meets Mary Carlson, the oh-so-tempting sister of her new friend at school." (Publisher's note)

"Joanna has always been out as a lesbian to her minister father, but now that he is remarrying and moving them from tolerant Atlanta to a small Georgia town, he asks her to 'lie low.' Initially, it doesn't seem so bad: it's only a year until she graduates from high school, and it turns out that finding friends who share her Christian faith is kind of great. Then one of Jo's new friends reveals that she has feelings for her, and that she isn't interested in hiding. . . . Faith matters in this book, but so do family, friends, and being funny. The dialogue is snappy—Joanna is sharp tongued and sometimes bratty—and the characters aren't types. Rather, they're individuals navigating a complicated world, which makes for a rich and satisfying read." Pub Wkly

No place to fall. By Jaye Robin Brown. Harper-Teen 2014 368 p.

Grades: 9 10 11 12

1. Dating (Social customs) -- Fiction 2. Family problems -- Fiction 3. High schools -- Fiction 4. Schools -- Fiction 5. Singers -- Fiction 6. North Carolina -- Fiction 7. Friendship -- Fiction 8. Family -- Fiction

0062270990; 9780062270993, $17.99

LC 2013051284

In this novel by Jaye Robin Brown "Amber decides that her dream—to sing on bigger stages—could also be her ticket to a new life. Devon's older brother, Will, helps Amber prepare. The more time Will and Amber spend together, the more complicated their relationship becomes. The bottom drops out of her family's world—and Amber is faced with an impossible choice between her promise as an artist and the people she loves." (Publisher's note)

"Amber could be the best friend you had in high school-she's funny and moody and truthful and absolutely the real deal, and readers will clamor for another well-paced story featuring her and her friends. Realistic treatment of social pot smoking, some drinking and (safe) sex make this title appropriate for mature teens." SLJ

Brown, Jennifer

Bitter end. Little, Brown 2011 359p $17.99

Grades: 10 11 12

1. Friendship -- Fiction 2. Bereavement -- Fiction 3. Abused women -- Fiction

ISBN 978-0-316-08695-0; 0-316-08695-9

LC 2010-34258

"Gritty and disturbing, this novel should be in all collections serving teens. It could be used in programs about abuse, as well as in psychology or sociology classes." SLJ

Hate list. Little, Brown and Co. 2009 408p $16.99

Grades: 9 10 11 12

1. School stories 2. Family life -- Fiction 3. School violence -- Fiction

ISBN 978-0-316-04144-7; 0-316-04144-0

LC 2008-50223

Sixteen-year-old Valerie, whose boyfriend Nick committed a school shooting at the end of their junior year, struggles to cope with integrating herself back into high school life, unsure herself whether she was a hero or a villain.

"Val's complicated relationship with her family, . . . the surviving victims, as well as how she comes to terms with Nick's betrayal, are piercingly real, and the shooting scenes wrenching. Her successes are hard-won and her setbacks . . . painfully true to life." Publ Wkly

Perfect escape; by Jennifer Brown. Little, Brown 2012 364 p. $17.99

Grades: 9 10 11 12

1. Siblings -- Fiction 2. Voyages and travels -- Fiction 3. Cheating (Education) -- Fiction 4. Obsessive-compulsive disorder -- Fiction 5. Automobile travel

-- Fiction 6. Brothers and sisters -- Fiction

ISBN 0316185574; 9780316185578

LC 2011027348

This book is a "road-trip drama" about brother and sister Grayson and Kendra. Kendra "defines herself by two things: her drive for academic and personal perfection, and her older brother Grayson's severe obsessive-compulsive disorder. . . . When a cheating scandal threatens to destroy Kendra's academic standing, she snaps, dragging Grayson on a cross-country trip from Missouri to California in an ill-defined attempt to 'fix' both their lives." (Publishers Weekly)

Brown, Skila

★ **Caminar**; Skila Brown. Candlewick Press 2014 208 p. $15.99

Grades: 6 7 8 9

1. War stories 2. Guatemala -- Fiction

ISBN 0763665169; 9780763665166

LC 2013946611

This book, by Skila Brown, is "set in 1981 Guatemala. . . . Carlos knows that when the soldiers arrive with warnings about the Communist rebels, it is time to be a man and defend the village, keep everyone safe. But Mama tells him not yet. . . . Numb and alone, he must join a band of guerillas as they trek to the top of the mountain where Carlos's abuela lives. Will he be in time, and brave enough, to warn them about the soldiers? What will he do then?" (Publisher's note)

"Unlike many novels in verse, which can read like conventional narratives with line breaks, Caminar contributes poetry that elevates the genre. In this story of a decimated Guatemalan village in 1981, readers will encounter a range of imagery, repetition, rhythms, and visual effects that bring to life the psychological experience of Carlos, a young boy caught in the violent clash between the government's army and the people's rebels...This is a much-needed addition to Latin American-themed middle grade fiction." (School Library Journal)

To stay alive. Skila Brown. Candlewick Press 2016 304 p.

Grades: 6 7 8 9 10

1. Donner party -- Fiction 2. Wilderness survival -- Fiction 3. Weather -- Fiction 4. Novels in verse -- Fiction

9780763678111, $17.99

LC 2016946911

"The journey west by wagon train promises to be long and arduous for nineteen-year-old Mary Ann Graves and her parents and eight siblings. Yet she is hopeful about their new life in California: freedom from the demands of family, maybe some romance, better opportunities for all. But when winter comes early to the Sierra Nevada and their group gets a late start, the Graves family, traveling alongside the Donner and Reed parties, must endure one of the most harrowing and storied journeys in American history. Amid the pain of loss and the constant threat of death from starvation or cold, Mary Ann's is a narrative, told beautifully in verse, of a girl learning what it means to be part of a family, to make sacrifices for those we love, and above all to persevere." (Publisher's note)

"The strong novel in verse uses beautiful, descriptive words to depict the vastness of the landscape and the emotional and mental toll of perpetual suffering. This is a well-crafted narrative in which readers get to know and empathize with Mary Ann as her adventure shifts to survival. However, it might be difficult to stomach the travelers' desperate choices: the book does not shy away from the Donner Party's well-known resort to cannibalism." SLJ

Bruchac, Joseph, 1942-

★ **Code** talker; a novel about the Navajo Marines of World War Two. Dial 2005 240p $16.99
Grades: 6 7 8 9 10

1. Navajo Indians -- Fiction 2. World War, 1939-1945 -- Fiction
ISBN 0-8037-2921-9

After being taught in a boarding school run by whites that Navajo is a useless language, Ned Begay and other Navajo men are recruited by the Marines to become Code Talkers, sending messages during World War II in their native tongue.

"Bruchac's gentle prose presents a clear historical picture of young men in wartime. . . . Nonsensational and accurate, Bruchac's tale is quietly inspiring." SLJ

Includes bibliographical references

Wolf mark. Lee & Low/Tu Books 2011 377p $17.95
Grades: 6 7 8 9

1. Spies -- Fiction 2. Supernatural -- Fiction 3. Native Americans -- Fiction 4. Father-son relationship -- Fiction
ISBN 1-60060-661-X; 978-1-60060-661-8; 978-1-60060-878-0 e-book

LC 2011014252

When Lucas King's covert-ops father is kidnapped and his best friend Meena is put in danger, Luke's only chance to save them—a skin that will let him walk as a wolf—is hidden away in an abandoned mansion guarded by monsters.

"Bruchac has created a tense, readable novel. He combines Native American lore, supernatural elements, genetic engineering, romance, geopolitics, and adventure in one story. . . . The mystery and edge-of-your-seat action are enough to keep readers hooked." SLJ

Bruton, Catherine

I Predict a Riot. Catherine Bruton. Trafalgar Square Books 2014 304 p.
Grades: 7 8 9 10

1. Gangs -- Fiction 2. Motion picture producers and directors -- Fiction
1405267194; 9781405267199, $12.99

This novel by Catherine Bruton is set on "Coronation Road—a kaleidoscope of clashing cultures and parallel lives. Amateur film-maker Maggie prefers to watch life through the lens of her camera. In Tokes, she finds a great subject for her new film. And when violence erupts, led by the Starfish gang, Maggie has the perfect backdrop. But as the world explodes around her, Maggie can't hide behind the lens anymore." (Publisher's note)

Maggie's video camera seems to represent all the stories that aren't told in the media, making this searing tale one that will get readers talking." Booklist

Bryant, Jennifer

Pieces of Georgia; a novel. [by] Jen Bryant. Knopf 2006 166p $15.95; lib bdg $17.99
Grades: 6 7 8 9

1. Artists -- Fiction 2. Bereavement -- Fiction
ISBN 0-375-83259-9; 0-375-93259-3 lib bdg

LC 2005-43593

In journal entries to her mother, a gifted artist who died suddenly, thirteen-year-old Georgia McCoy reveals how her life changes after she receives an anonymous gift membership to a nearby art museum.

"This is a remarkable book. . . . [The] story is a universal one of love, friendship, and loss and will be appreciated by a wide audience." SLJ

Bryant, Megan E.

Glow. Megan E. Bryant. Albert Whitman & Co. 2017 248 p.
Grades: 9 10 11 12

1. Factories -- Fiction; 2. Family life -- New Jersey -- Fiction; 3. Letters -- Fiction; 4. Painting, Modern -- Fiction; 5. Radiation -- Fiction; 6. Sisters -- Fiction; 7. New Jersey -- History -- 20th century -- Fiction; 8. Painting -- Fiction; 9. Radiation -- Physiological effect
080752963X; 9780807529638, $16.99; 9780807529645

LC 2017031988

In this book, by Megan E. Bryant, "when thrift-store aficionado Julie discovers a series of antique paintings with hidden glowing images that are only visible in the dark, she wants to learn more about the artist. In her search, she uncovers a century-old romance and the haunting true story of the Radium Girls, young women who used radioactive paint to make the world's first glow-in-the-dark products -- and ultimately became radioactive themselves." (Publisher's note)

"Bryant brilliantly lures readers into an engaging mystery, a page-turner that begins beneath layers revealed in both paintings and chapters. A riveting story of ambitious and self-sufficient women, both in the present and past." Kirkus

Includes bibliographical references (pages 255-256).

Bryce, Celia

Anthem for Jackson Dawes; by Celia Bryce. Bloomsbury USA Childrens 2013 240 p. (hardback) $16.99
Grades: 7 8 9 10

1. Hospitals -- Fiction 2. Cancer -- Patients -- Fiction 3. Cancer -- Fiction 4. Friendship -- Fiction 5. Family life -- Fiction 6. Medical care -- Fiction
ISBN 1599909758; 9781599909752

LC 2012024989

In this book, "after 13-year-old Megan Bright is diagnosed with a cancerous brain tumor, she's . . . determined to have everything remain as normal as possible during her time in the hospital. . . . Megan gets closer to the only other teenager there . . . and begins to acknowledge the emotions she's been keeping buried. Initially, Jackson rubs her the wrong way, but his positivity and determined interest in Megan teach her about optimism and taking control of what she can." (Publishers Weekly)

"Sensitive and honest, this novel addresses meaningful questions concerning mortality and soul searching, and its content is appropriate for younger teens." SLJ

Buckhanon, Kalisha

Upstate. St. Martin's Press 2005 247p hardcover o.p. pa $11.95

Grades: 9 10 11 12

1. Letters -- Fiction 2. Homicide -- Fiction 3. Prisoners -- Fiction 4. African Americans -- Fiction 5. Harlem (New York, N.Y.) -- Fiction

ISBN 0-312-33268-8; 0-312-33269-6 pa

LC 2004-56651

Set in the 1990's, this...[novel] features Harlem teenagers Antonio, who has been convicted of involuntary manslaughter for killing his father, and his bright and ambitious girlfriend, Natasha. With Antonio in jail, the two maintain their intense relationship through the written correspondence that makes up the text. Libr J

"This is a moving, uplifting story of love and hope in the face of adversity." Publ Wkly

Buckley-Archer, Linda

The **many** lives of John Stone. Linda Buckley-Archer. SSBFYR 2015 544 p. Illustration

Grades: 8 9 10 11

1. Identity -- Fiction 2. Longevity -- Fiction 3. Summer employment -- Fiction 4. Supernatural -- Fiction 5. England -- Fiction 6. England -- Fiction

9781481426374, $17.99; 9781481426381

LC 2014035641

In this book, by Linda Buckley-Archer, "Stella Park (Spark for short) has found summer work cataloging historical archives in John Stone's remote and beautiful house in Suffolk, England. . . . [W]hat kind of people live in the twenty-first century without using electricity, telephones, or even a washing machine? Additionally, the notebooks she's organizing span centuries-they begin in the court of Louis XIV in Versailles-but are written in the same hand." (Publisher's note)

"Spark's contemporary coming-of-age story is brilliantly heightened by the reader's understanding of her secret connection to John Stone. Exceptionally well orchestrated and a simply magnificent story." Booklist

Budhos, Marina Tamar

Ask me no questions; [by] Marina Budhos. Atheneum Books for Young Readers 2006 162p $16.95; pa $8.99

Grades: 7 8 9 10

1. School stories 2. Family life -- Fiction 3. Asian Americans -- Fiction 4. New York (N.Y.) -- Fiction

ISBN 1-4169-0351-8; 1-4169-4920-8 pa

LC 2005-1831

Fourteen-year-old Nadira, her sister, and their parents leave Bangladesh for New York City, but the expiration of their visas and the events of September 11, 2001, bring frustration, sorrow, and terror for the whole family.

"Nadira and Aisha's strategies for surviving and succeeding in high school offer sharp insight into the narrow margins between belonging and not belonging." Horn Book Guide

Tell us we're home; [by] Marina Budhos. Atheneum 2010 297p $16.95

Grades: 6 7 8 9 10

1. Immigrants -- Fiction 2. New Jersey -- Fiction 3. Social classes -- Fiction 4. Household employees -- Fiction 5. Mother-daughter relationship -- Fiction

ISBN 978-1-4169-0352-9; 1-4169-0352-6

LC 2009-27386

Three immigrant girls from different parts of the world meet and become close friends in a small New Jersey town where their mothers have found domestic work, but their relationships are tested when one girl's mother is accused of stealing a precious heirloom.

"These fully realized heroines are full of heart, and their passionate struggles against systemic injustice only make them more inspiring. Keenly necessary." Kirkus

Watched. Marina Budhos. Wendy Lamb Books 2016 272 p.

Grades: 9 10 11 12

1. Bangladeshi Americans -- Fiction 2. Muslims -- Fiction 3. New York (N.Y.) -- Fiction 4. New York (N.Y.) -- Fiction 6. Undercover operations -- Fiction

9780553534184, $17.99; 9780553534214; 9780553534191

LC 2015046828

"Naeem is far from the 'model teen.' Moving fast in his immigrant neighborhood in Queens is the only way he can outrun the eyes of his hardworking Bangladeshi parents and their gossipy neighbors. Even worse, they're not the only ones watching. Cameras on poles. Mosques infiltrated. Everyone knows: Be careful what you say and who you say it to. Anyone might be a watcher. Naeem thinks he can charm his way through anything, until his mistakes catch up with him and the cops offer a dark deal." (Publisher's note)

"Action takes second place to a deeper message, and room is left for readers to speculate on the fates of certain characters. While the absence of certainty may frustrate some readers, it also speaks to the underlying takeaway: you can never be sure what others' intentions are, even if you have made it your job to study them." Kirkus

Buffie, Margaret

Winter shadows; a novel. Tundra Books 2010 327p $19.95

Grades: 7 8 9 10

1. Manitoba -- Fiction 2. Prejudices -- Fiction 3. Family life -- Fiction 4. Stepmothers -- Fiction 5. Racially mixed people -- Fiction

ISBN 978-0-88776-968-9; 0-88776-968-3

"Hatred for their wicked stepmothers bonds two girls living in a stone house in Manitoba, Canada, more than 150 years apart. Grieving for her dead mother, high-school senior Cass is furious that she has to share a room with the daughter of her dad's new, harsh-tempered wife. Then she finds the 1836 diary of Beatrice, who is part Cree and faces vicious racism as a 'half-breed' in her mostly white community. . . . The alternating narratives are gripping, and the characters are drawn with rich complexity." Booklist

Bunce, Elizabeth C.

A **curse** dark as gold; [by] Elizabeth C. Bunce. Arthur A. Levine Books 2008 395p $17.99

Grades: 7 8 9 10

    1. Magic -- Fiction 2. Uncles -- Fiction 3. Orphans -- Fiction 4. Sisters -- Fiction 5. Factories -- Fiction

ISBN 978-0-439-89576-7; 0-439-89576-6

                    LC 2007019759

ALA YALSA Morris Award, 2009

Upon the death of her father, seventeen-year-old Charlotte struggles to keep the family's woolen mill running in the face of an overwhelming mortgage and what the local villagers believe is a curse, but when a man capable of spinning straw into gold appears on the scene she must decide if his help is worth the price.

"This is a rich, compelling story that fleshes out the fairy tale, setting it in the nonspecific past of the Industrial Revolution. Readers unfamiliar with 'Rumplestilskin' will not be at a disadvantage here." KLIATT

Liar's moon. Arthur A. Levine Books 2011 356p $17.99

Grades: 8 9 10 11 12

    1. Fantasy fiction 2. Mystery fiction 3. Magic -- Fiction 4. Thieves -- Fiction 5. Homicide -- Fiction 6. Social classes -- Fiction

ISBN 978-0-545-13608-2; 0-545-13608-3

                    LC 2011005071

In a quest to prove her friend, Lord Durrel Decath, innocent of the murder of his wife, pickpocket Digger stumbles into a conspiracy with far-reaching consequences for the civil war raging in Lllyvraneth, while also finding herself falling in love.

"A solid fantasy sequel embroils its irresistible heroine in mystery, intrigue and romance. . . . A darn good read." Kirkus

Star crossed. Arthur A. Levine Books 2010 359p $17.99

Grades: 8 9 10 11 12

    1. Fantasy fiction 2. Magic -- Fiction 3. Thieves -- Fiction 4. Religion -- Fiction 5. Social classes -- Fiction 6. Kings and rulers -- Fiction

ISBN 978-0-545-13605-1; 0-545-13605-9

                    LC 2010-730

In a kingdom dominated by religious intolerance, sixteen-year-old Digger, a street thief, has always avoided attention, but when she learns that her friends are plotting against the throne she must decide whether to join them or turn them in.

"Couching her characters and setting in top-notch writing, Bunce . . . hooks readers into an intelligent page-turner with strong themes of growth, determination, and friendship." Publ Wkly

Followed by: Liar's moon (2011)

Bunker, Lisa

Felix Yz. Lisa Bunker. Viking 2017 288 p.

Grades: 5 6 7 8 9

    1. Blogs -- Fiction; 2. Extraterrestrial beings -- Fiction; 3. Family life -- Fiction; 4. People with disabilities -- Fiction; 5. Schools -- Fiction; 6. Science fiction

9780425288504, $16.99

                    LC 2016029068

In this book, by Lisa Bunker, "when Felix Yz was three years old, a hyperintelligent fourth-dimensional being became fused inside him after one of his father's science experiments went terribly wrong. The creature is friendly, but Felix -- now thirteen -- won't be able to grow to adulthood while they're still melded together. So a risky Procedure is planned to separate them...but it may end up killing them both instead." (Publisher's note)

"Joyful, heartbreaking, completely bonkers, and exuberantly alive." Kirkus.

Bunting, Eve

The **pirate** captain's daughter; written by Eve Bunting. Sleeping Bear Press 2011 208p $15.95; pa $8.95

Grades: 7 8 9 10

    1. Pirates -- Fiction 2. Sex role -- Fiction 3. Seafaring life -- Fiction 4. Father-daughter relationship -- Fiction

ISBN 978-1-58536-526-5; 1-58536-526-2; 978-1-58536-525-8 pa; 1-58536-525-4 pa

                    LC 2010032409

Upon her mother's death, fifteen-year-old Catherine puts her courage and strength to the test by disguising herself as a boy to join her father, a pirate captain, on a ship whose crew includes men who are trying to steal a treasure from him.

"This is a gripping and entertaining novel that will have readers sucked in until the last page. Even teens who are not fond of historical fiction will enjoy." Voice Youth Advocates

Burd, Nick

★ The **vast** fields of ordinary. Dial Books 2009 309p $16.99

Grades: 10 11 12

    1. Iowa -- Fiction 2. Gay teenagers -- Fiction 3. Dating (Social customs) -- Fiction

ISBN 978-0-8037-3340-4; 0-8037-3340-2

                    LC 2008-46256

ALA GLBTRT Stonewall Book Award (2010)

The summer after graduating from an Iowa high school, eighteen-year-old Dade Hamilton watches his parents' marriage disintegrate, ends his long-term, secret relationship, comes out of the closet, and savors first love.

"A refreshingly honest, sometimes funny, and often tender novel." SLJ

Burg, Ann E.

★ **All** the broken pieces; a novel in verse. Scholastic Press 2009 218p $16.99

Grades: 7 8 9 10

    1. Novels in verse 2. Adoption -- Fiction 3. Vietnamese Americans -- Fiction 4. Vietnam War, 1961-1975 -- Fiction

ISBN 978-0-545-08092-7; 0-545-08092-4

                    LC 2008-12381

Two years after being airlifted out of Vietnam in 1975, Matt Pin is haunted by the terrible secret he left behind and, now, in a loving adoptive home in the United States, a series of profound events forces him to confront his past.

This is written "in rapid, simple free verse. . . . The intensity of the simple words . . . will make readers want to rush to the end and then return to the beginning again to make connections between past and present, friends and enemies." Booklist

Burgess, Melvin

The **hit**; Melvin Burgess. Chicken House/Scholastic Inc. 2014 304 p. $17.99
Grades: 9 10 11 12
    1. Death -- Fiction 2. Teenagers -- Drug use -- Fiction 3. Drugs -- Fiction 4. Death 5. Manchester (England) -- Fiction 6. Family life -- England -- Fiction
ISBN 0545556996; 9780545556996; 9780545557009
                  LC 2013013792

In this novel, by Melvin Burgess, "a new drug is on the street. Everyone's buzzing about it. Take the hit. Live the most intense week of your life. Then die. . . . Adam thinks it over. He's poor, and doesn't see that changing. . . . His brother Jess is missing. And Manchester is in chaos, controlled by drug dealers and besieged by a group of homegrown terrorists who call themselves the Zealots. . . . Adam downs one of the Death pills." (Publisher's note)

"Burgess' dystopian novel posits a near-future world in which the gap between rich and poor has grown to an unbridgeable chasm. In their despair, many have-nots are taking a new drug called Death that offers seven days of euphoric bliss followed by the oblivion of death...the novel is viscerally exciting and emotionally engaging. Best of all, it is sure to excite both thoughtful analysis and heated discussion among its readers. A clear winner from Burgess." (Booklist)

Smack. Holt & Co. 1997 327p hardcover o.p. pa $8.99
Grades: 9 10 11 12
    1. Drug abuse -- Fiction 2. Great Britain -- Fiction 3. Runaway teenagers -- Fiction
ISBN 0-8050-5801-X; 0-312-60862-4 pa
                  LC 97-40629

First published 1996 in the United Kingdom with title: Junk

After running away from their troubled homes, two English teenagers move in with a group of squatters in the port city of Bristol and try to find ways to support their growing addiction to heroin

"Although the omnipresent British slang (most but not all of which is explained in a glossary) may put off some readers, lots of YAs will be drawn to this book because of the subject. Those who are will quickly find themselves absorbed in an honest, unpatronizing, unvarnished account of teen life on the skids." Booklist

Burns, Laura J.

Crave; [by] Laura J. Burns & Melinda Metz. Simon & Schuster BFYR 2010 278p pa $9.99
Grades: 8 9 10
    1. Sick -- Fiction 2. Vampires -- Fiction
ISBN 978-1-4424-0816-6; 1-4424-0817-3

Seventeen-year-old Shay, having suffered from a rare blood disorder her entire life, starts receiving blood transfusions from her stepfather who is a physician, and, when she begins to see visions through the eyes of a vampire, she decides to investigate. She discovers a teenage vampire locked up in the doctor's office to whom she becomes attached and sets free, only to be kidnapped by the creature, who wants revenge.

This "is a fast-paced, action-packed vampire thriller with an original and refreshing story line. Gabriel's life is beautifully revealed through Shay's visions, and the well-written plot conveys depth and feeling while exploring important issues like friendship, loyalty, trust, love, and betrayal. A satisfying read with a shocking cliffhanger ending." SLJ

Butcher, Kristin

Cheat; written by Kristin Butcher. Orca Book Publishers 2010 107p (Orca currents) pa $9.95
Grades: 7 8 9 10
    1. School stories 2. Cheating (Education) -- Fiction
ISBN 978-1-55469-274-3; 1-55469-274-1

Laurel investigates a cheating scam at her high school.

"This novel is a realistic portrayal of high school students' attitudes towards cheating. . . . This is a well-written narrative that will challenge readers to make a decision about what's right and what's wrong." Libr Media Connect

Buzo, Laura

Love and other perishable items; Laura Buzo. Alfred A. Knopf 2012 243 p. (trade) $17.99
Grades: 9 10 11 12
    1. Love -- Fiction 2. Work -- Fiction 3. Friendship -- Fiction 4. Australia -- Fiction 5. Maturation (Psychology) -- Fiction
ISBN 0375870008; 9780307929747; 9780375870002; 9780375970009; 9780375986741
                  LC 2011037579

Originally published as: Good oil. Crows Nest, N.S.W.: Allen & Unwin, 2010.

William C. Morris Award Finalist (2013)

In this book, Laura Buzo presents a love story centered on Amelia. "From the moment she sets eyes on Chris, she is a goner. Lost. Sunk. Head over heels infatuated with him. It's problematic, since Chris, 21, is a sophisticated university student, while Amelia, 15, is 15. . . . Working checkout together at the local supermarket, they strike up a friendship. . . . As time goes on, Amelia's crush doesn't seem so one-sided anymore." (Publisher's note)

Cabot, Meg

Airhead. Scholastic/Point 2008 340p $16.99
Grades: 7 8 9 10
    1. Fashion models -- Fiction 2. New York (N.Y.) -- Fiction 3. Transplantation of organs, tissues, etc. -- Fiction
ISBN 978-0-545-04052-5; 0-545-04052-3
                  LC 2007-38269

Sixteen-year-old Emerson Watts, an advanced placement student with a disdain for fashion, is the recipient of a "whole body transplant"; and finds herself transformed into one of the world's most famous teen supermodels.

"Cabot's portrayal of Emerson is brilliant. . . . Pure fun, this first series installment will leave readers clamoring for the next." Publ Wkly

Other titles in this series are:
Being Nikki (2009)
Runaway (2010)

★ **All**-American girl. HarperCollins Pubs. 2002 247p hardcover o.p. pa $7.99
Grades: 7 8 9 10

1. Presidents -- Fiction
ISBN 0-06-029469-8; 0-06-029470-1 lib bdg; 0-06-147989-6 pa

LC 2002-19049

A sophomore girl stops a presidential assassination attempt, is appointed Teen Ambassador to the United Nations, and catches the eye of the very cute First Son. "Grades six to ten." (Bull Cent Child Books)

There's "surprising depth in the characters and plenty of authenticity in the cultural details and the teenage voices—particularly in Sam's poignant, laugh-out-loud narration." Booklist

★ The **princess** diaries. Avon Bks. 2000 238p $15.95; lib bdg $15.89; pa $6.99
Grades: 6 7 8 9

1. Fathers and daughters 5. Princesses -- Fiction
ISBN 0-380-97848-2; 0-06-029210-5 lib bdg; 0-380-81402-1 pa

LC 99-46479

Fourteen-year-old Mia, who is trying to lead a normal life as a teenage girl in New York City, is shocked to learn that her father is the Prince of Genovia, a small European principality, and that she is a princess and the heir to the throne

"Readers will relate to Mia's bubbly, chatty voice and enjoy the humor of this unlikely fairy tale." SLJ

Other titles about Princess Mia are:
Forever princess (2008)
Party princess (2006)
Princess in pink (2004)
Princess in the spotlight (2001)
Princess in training (2005)
Princess in waiting (2003)
The princess present (2004)
Sweet sixteen princess (2006)
Valentine princess (2006)

Caine, Rachel

Ash and quill. Rachel Caine. Berkley 2017 341 p. (The Great Library)
Grades: 10 11 12

1. Alexandrian Library -- Fiction; 2. Libraries -- Fiction; 3. Fantasy fiction
9780698180833; 9780451472410, $17.99

LC 2016058978

In this book in The Great Library series, by Rachel Caine, "Jess Brightwell and his band of exiles have fled London, only to find themselves imprisoned in Philadelphia.... But Jess and his friends have a bargaining chip: the knowledge to build a machine that will break the Library's rule. Their time is running out. To survive, they'll have to choose to live or die as one, to take the fight to their enemies -- and to save the very soul of the Great Library." (Publisher's note)

"A strong ensemble adventure, grim, gritty, and genuinely enjoyable." Kirkus

Ink and bone: the Great Library. Rachel Caine. New American Library 2015 355 p.

Grades: 8 9 10 11 12813/.6

1. Alexandrian Library -- Fiction 2. Libraries -- Fiction 3. Alternative histories 4. Dystopian fiction
9780451472397, $17.99; 045147239X

LC 2015001509

In this young adult alternative history novel, by Rachel Caine, "the Great Library [of Alexandria] is now a presence in every major city, governing the flow of knowledge to the masses. . . . When he inadvertently commits heresy by creating a device that could change the world, Jess discovers that those who control the Great Library believe that knowledge is more valuable than any human life—and soon both heretics and books will burn." (Publisher's note)

"Caine has created a Dickensian future with an odd mix of technologies and elements of sorcery. A strong cast of characters and nail-biting intensity make for a promising start to this new series." SLJ

Prince of Shadows: a novel of Romeo and Juliet. Rachel Caine. NAL, New American Library. 2014 354p $17.99
Grades: 7 8 9 10 11 12

1. Families -- Fiction 2. Love -- Fiction 3. Vendetta -- Fiction 4. Italy -- History -- 1559-1789 -- Fiction 5. Verona (Italy) -- History -- 16th century -- Fiction; 6. Shakespeare, William, 1595-1616 -- Romeo and Juliet; 7. Shakespeare, William, 1595-1616 -- Fiction
ISBN: 0451414411; 9780451414410

LC 2013033482

The star-crossed tale of Romeo and Juliet, told through the eyes of Romeo's cousin, Benvolio, a thief known as the Prince of Shadows.

"Choosing Romeo and Juliet as her base, Caine expands the story from the viewpoint of Benvolio, Romeo's Montague cousin. While Shakespeare's plot clearly anchors Caine's, the novel focuses on providing context for the well-known story rather than embellishing it. . . . Most impressive is the author's simulation of Shakespeare's language in her prose. Never too obscure for modern readers, it retains the flavor of Shakespearean dialogue throughout, lending an atmosphere of verisimilitude that's reinforced by the detailed city setting. Simply superb." Kirkus

Calame, Don

Beat the band; by Don Calame. 1st ed. Candlewick Press 2010 390 p. (reinforced) $16.99
Grades: 9 10 11 12

1. School stories 2. Humorous fiction 3. Popularity/Fiction
ISBN 0763646334; 9780763646332

LC 2010006607

Sequel to: Swim the fly.

This book, a sequel to "Swim the Fly," follows friends Coop, Matt, and Sean in tenth grade. "Right off the bat they are assigned partners for a semester-long health-class project. To his horror, Coop is paired with 'Hot Dog' Helen, the school outcast, and assigned to research contraceptives. Immediately dubbed 'Corn Dog Coop,' he is desperate for a way to salvage his social status. An upcoming Battle of the Bands presents the perfect opportunity for him to" do so. (School Library Journal)

"Creative sexual slang and bathroom humor begin on page one, but Coop is mostly just talk. Messages about bullying and consequences of teen sex (included via the health project) add just the right note of gravitas to this rockin' romp." SLJ

Swim the fly; by Don Calame. 1st ed. Candlewick Press 2009 345 p. (reinforced) $16.99; (paperback) $7.99

Grades: 9 10 11 12

    1. Swimming -- Fiction 2. Adolescence -- Fiction

ISBN 076364157X; 0763647764; 9780763641573; 9780763647766

LC 2009920818

Sequel: Beat the Band

In this book, fifteen-year-old Matt Gratton and his two best friends, Coop and Sean, have set themselves a summer goal of seeing "a real-live naked girl for the first time—quite a challenge, given that none of the guys has the nerve to even ask a girl out on a date. But catching a girl in the buff starts to look easy compared to Matt's other summertime aspiration: to swim the 100-yard butterfly . . . as a way to impress Kelly West, the sizzling new star of the swim team." (Publisher's note)

"Fifteen-year-old Matt has two summer goals: attract his crush Kelly's attention by learning to swim the fly and see a real girl naked. Matt and pals Cooper and Sean cook up several plots to catch a betty in the buff, but all attempts fail. . . . Fully realized secondary characters, realistically raunchy dialogue and the scatological subject matter assure that this boisterous and unexpectedly sweet read will be a word-of-mouth hit." Kirkus

Caletti, Deb

★   **Essential** maps for the lost. Simon Pulse 2016 336 p.

Grades: 9 10 11 12

    1. Grief -- Fiction 2. Love -- Fiction 3. Secrets -- Fiction 4. Depression (Psychology) -- Fiction 5. Books -- Fiction

1481415166; 9781481415163, $17.99

LC 2015024672

In this novel, by Deb Calettti, Mads "is trying her best to escape herself during one last summer away from a mother who needs more from her than she can give. The body Mads collides with in the middle of the water on a traumatic morning . . . changes everything. The son of the woman in the water, Billy . . . is struggling to find his way . . . in the shadow of grief. When three lives (and one special, shared book) collide, strange things happen." (Publisher's note)

"A moving story about rescuing yourself as well as finally being found." Booklist

The **fortunes** of Indigo Skye. Simon & Schuster Books for Young Readers 2008 304p pa $9.99

Grades: 9 10 11 12

    1. Wealth -- Fiction 2. Family life -- Fiction 3. Restaurants -- Fiction 4. Washington (State) -- Fiction 5. Single parent family -- Fiction 6. Waiters and waitresses -- Fiction

ISBN pa; 978-1-4169-1008-4 pa

LC 2007-08744

Eighteen-year-old Indigo is looking forward to becoming a full-time waitress after high school graduation, but her life is turned upside down by a $2.5 million tip given to her by a customer. "Grades nine to twelve." (Bull Cent Child Books)

The author "builds characters with so much depth that readers will be invested in her story. . . . Caletti spins a network of relationships that feels real and enriching." Publ Wkly

A **heart** in a body in the world. Deb Caletti. Simon Pulse 2018 368 p.

Grades: 9 10 11 12

    1. Grief -- Fiction; 2. Massacre survivors -- Fiction; 3. Post-traumatic stress disorder -- Fiction; 4. Running -- Fiction; 5. School shootings -- Fiction; 6. Social action -- Fiction

9781481415200, $18.99

LC 2017038192

Printz Honor Book (2019)

In this novel, by Deb Caletti, "when everything has been taken from you, what else is there to do but run? So that's what Annabelle does -- she runs from Seattle to Washington, DC, through mountain passes and suburban landscapes, from long lonely roads to college towns. She's not ready to think about the why yet, just the how.... Annabelle becomes a reluctant activist as people connect her journey to the trauma from her past." (Publisher's note)

★ The **last** forever; Deb Caletti. Simon Pulse 2014 336 p. (hardback) $17.99

Grades: 8 9 10 11 12

    1. Love 2. Death 3. Grief 4. Father-daughter relationship -- Fiction 5. Love -- Fiction 6. Death -- Fiction 7. Grief -- Fiction 8. Friendship -- Fiction

ISBN 1442450002; 9781442450004

LC 2013031010

This book, by Deb Caletti, is a "novel of love and loss. . . . Nothing lasts forever, and no one gets that more than Tessa. After her mother died, it's all she can do to keep her friends, her boyfriend, her happiness from slipping away. And then there's her dad. He's stuck in his own daze, and it's hard to feel like a family when their house no longer seems like a home. Her father's solution? An impromptu road trip that lands them in a small coastal town." (Publisher's note)

"After a trying bout with cancer, Tess's mother has died, but she's left behind a one-of-a-kind pixiebell plant. "My mother vowed that the last pixiebell would never die on her watch, and now that I have it, it isn't going to die on mine, either," Tess vows... Featuring sharp-witted first-person narration, some fascinating facts about plants and seeds, relatable characters, and evocative settings, Caletti's (The Story of Us) inspiring novel eloquently depicts the nature of mutability. As with her previous books, this love story reverberates with honesty and emotion." (Publishers Weekly)

The **secret** life of Prince Charming. Simon & Schuster Books for Young Readers 2009 322p $16.99; pa $9.99

51

Grades: 8 9 10 11 12

   1. Divorce -- Fiction 2. Fathers -- Fiction

ISBN 978-1-4169-5940-3; 1-4169-5940-8; 978-1-
4169-5941-0 pa; 1-4169-5941-6 pa

               LC 2008-13014

Seventeen-year-old Quinn has heard all her life about how untrustworthy men are, so when she discovers that her charismatic but selfish father, with whom she has recently begun to have a tentative relationship, has stolen from the many women in his life, she decides she must avenge this wrong.

"This is a thoughtful, funny, and empowering spin on the classic road novel. . . . Because of its strong language and the mature themes, this is best suited to older teens, who will appreciate what it has to say about love, relationships, and getting what you need." SLJ

  ★ The **six** rules of maybe. Simon Pulse 2010 321p $16.99

Grades: 8 9 10 11 12

   1. Oregon -- Fiction 2. Sisters -- Fiction 3. Pregnancy -- Fiction 4. Family life -- Fiction

ISBN 978-1-4169-7969-2; 1-4169-7969-7

               LC 2009-22232

Scarlet, an introverted high school junior surrounded by outcasts who find her a good listener, learns to break old patterns and reach for hope when her pregnant sister moves home with her new husband, with whom Scarlet feels an instant connection.

"Reminiscent of the best of Sarah Dessen's work, this novel is beautifully written, deftly plotted, and movingly characterized." SLJ

  Stay. Simon Pulse 2011 313p $16.99; ebook $9.99

Grades: 8 9 10 11 12

   1. Islands -- Fiction 2. Washington (State) -- Fiction 3. Dating (Social customs) -- Fiction 4. Father-daughter relationship -- Fiction

ISBN 978-1-4424-0373-4; 1-4424-0373-X; 978-1-4424-0375-8 ebook; 1-4424-0375-6 ebook

               LC 2010021804

"Fear tinges this summer romance and underscores the issue of abusive and claustrophobic relationships among teens." SLJ

Callahan, Erin

  The **art** of escaping. Erin Callahan. Amberjack Publishing 2018 324 p.

Grades: 9 10 11

   1. Escapes (Amusements) -- Fiction; 2. Family life -- Rhode Island -- Fiction; 3. High schools -- Fiction; 4. Magic tricks -- Fiction; 5. Recluses -- Fiction; 6. Schools -- Fiction; 7. Secrets -- Fiction; 8. Rhode Island -- Fiction; 9. Friendship -- Fiction; 10. Secrecy -- Fiction; 11. Magic -- Fiction

9781944995652, $12.99

               LC 2017057654

In this book, by Erin Callahan, "seventeen-year-old Mattie has a hidden obsession: escapology. Emphasis on hidden. If anyone from school finds out, she'll be abandoned to her haters. Facing a long and lonely summer, Mattie finally seeks out Miyu, the reclusive daughter of a world-renowned escape artist. Following in Houdini's footsteps, Miyu helps Mattie secretly transform herself into an escapologist and performance artist." (Publisher's note)

Cameron, Peter

  ★ **Someday** this pain will be useful to you. Farrar, Straus and Giroux 2007 229p $16

Grades: 9 10 11 12

   1. Conduct of life -- Fiction 2. New York (N.Y.) -- Fiction

ISBN 0-374-30989-2; 978-0-374-30989-3

               LC 2006-43747

Eighteen-year-old James, a gay teen living in New York City with his older sister and divorced mother, struggles to find a direction for his life.

"James makes a memorable protagonist, touching in his inability to connect with the world but always entertaining in his first-person account of his New York environment, his fractured family, his disastrous trip to the nation's capital, and his ongoing bouts with psychoanalysis. In the process he dramatizes the ambivalences and uncertainties of adolescence in ways that both teen and adult readers will savor and remember." Booklist

Cameron, Sharon

  The **dark** unwinding; by Sharon Cameron. Scholastic Press 2012 318 p. (jacketed hardcover) $17.99

Grades: 6 7 8 9

   1. Alternative histories 2. Fantasy fiction 3. Eccentrics and eccentricities -- Fiction 4. Toys -- Fiction 5. Uncles -- Fiction 6. Inventions -- Fiction 7. Inheritance and succession -- Fiction 8. Great Britain -- History -- Victoria, 1837-1901 -- Fiction

ISBN 0545327865; 9780545327862

               LC 2011044431

This steampunk novel, by Sharon Cameron, begins "when Katharine Tulman's inheritance is called into question by the rumor that her eccentric uncle is squandering away the family fortune. . . . But . . . Katharine discovers . . . [he is a] genius inventor with his own set of rules, who employs a village of . . . people rescued from the workhouses of London. Katharine is now torn between protecting her own inheritance and preserving the . . . community she grows to care for deeply." (Publisher's note)

  The **Forgetting**. By Sharon Cameron. Scholastic 2016 416 p.

Grades: 8 9 10 11

   1. Friendship -- Fiction 2. Memory -- Fiction 3. Science fiction 4. Amnesia -- Fiction

0545945216; 9780545945219, $18.99

               LC 2016007978

In this book, by Sharon Cameron, "what isn't written, isn't remembered. Even your crimes. Nadia lives in the city of Canaan, where life is safe and structured, hemmed in by white stone walls and no memory of what came before. But every twelve years the city descends into the bloody chaos of the Forgetting, a day of no remorse, when each person's memories—of parents, children, love, life, and self—are lost. Unless they have been written." (Publisher's note)

"Every 12 years, the orderly city of Canaan undergoes the chaotic, bloody time known as the Forgetting. During these brief hours, people's memories are erased. If it were not for the books in which inhabitants are required by law to record the events of their lives, they would have no way of knowing what happened before the Forgetting, or even of knowing their names or who their families are. Nadia is different. She remembers. The next Forgetting is a few weeks away. The teen is determined to keep her family together and away from the ensuing anarchy, but how? . . . This excellent work belongs in every collection." SLJ

The **knowing**. Sharon Cameron. Scholastic Press 2017 438 p. (Forgetting)
Grades: 8 9 10 11 12
> 1. Amnesia -- Fiction; 2. Conspiracy -- Fiction; 3. Friendship -- Fiction; 4. Memory -- Fiction; 5. Secrecy -- Fiction; 6. Science fiction
> 9780545945257; 9780545945240, $18.99
>   LC 2017022644

In this book, by Sharon Cameron, "Samara is one of the Knowing, and the Knowing do not forget. Hidden deep in the comfort and splendor of her underground city, a refuge from the menace of a coming Earth, Samara learns what she should have never known and creates a memory so terrible she cannot live with it. So she flees, to Canaan, the lost city of her ancestors, to Forget." (Publisher's note)

"In this companion novel to The Forgetting, Cameron once again fashions an elaborate dystopian narrative that fairly prickles with suspense" SLJ

Sequel to: The Forgetting (2016)

Rook. Sharon Cameron. Scholastic Press 2015 456 p.
Grades: 7 8 9 10 11 12
> 1. Adventure and adventurers -- Fiction 2. Adventure stories 3. Rescues -- Fiction 4. Secrets -- Fiction 5. France -- Fiction 6. Paris (France) -- Fiction 7. Suspense fiction 8. Revolutions -- Fiction 9. Romance fiction
> 0545675995; 9780545675994, $17.99
>   LC 2014038853

In this novel, by Sharon Cameron, "centuries after a shifting of the Earth's poles, the Sunken City that was once Paris is in the grips of a revolution. All who oppose the new regime are put to the blade, except for those who disappear from their prison cells, a red-tipped rook feather left in their place. Is the mysterious Red Rook a savior of the innocent or a criminal? When the search for the Red Rook comes straight to her doorstep, Sophia discovers that her fiancé is not all he seems. Which is only fair, because neither is she." (Publisher's note)

"Still, the novel's 456 pages mostly fly by thanks to the nonstop intrigue and the occasional swoon-worthy kiss. Full of derring-do and double crosses, this romantic adventure is thoroughly engrossing." Kirkus

Cameron, Sophie
Out of the blue. Sophie Cameron. Roaring Brook Press 2018 280 p.
Grades: 7 8 9 10 11
> 1. Angels -- Fiction; 2. Mothers -- Death -- Fiction; 3.

Edinburgh (Scotland) -- Fiction; 4. Grief -- Fiction; 5. Mothers -- Fiction; 6. Paranormal fiction
> 1250149916; 9781250149909; 9781250149916, $17.99
>   LC 2017957297

In this novel, by Sophie Cameron, "Jaya's life has completely fallen apart. Her mother is dead, her dad is on an obsessive wild goose chase, and mysterious winged beings are falling from the sky. For the past nine months, none of the them have survived the plummet to Earth, but when a female being lands near Jaya -- and is still alive -- she doesn't call the authorities. She hides the being and tries to nurse her back to health." (Publisher's note)

"A strong infusion of magic and wonder distinguish this debut novel." Kirkus

Canales, Viola
The **tequila** worm. Wendy Lamb Books 2005 199p hardcover o.p. pa $7.99
Grades: 6 7 8 9 10
> 1. Texas -- Fiction 2. Mexican Americans -- Fiction
> ISBN 0-375-84089-3 pa; 0-385-74674-1
>   LC 2004-24533

Sofia grows up in the close-knit community of the barrio in McAllen, Texas, then finds that her experiences as a scholarship student at an Episcopal boarding school in Austin only strengthen her ties to family and her "comadres."

"The explanations of cultural traditions . . . are always rooted in immediate, authentic family emotions, and in Canales' exuberant storytelling, which . . . finds both humor and absurdity in sharply observed, painful situations." Booklist

Cann, Kate
Consumed. Point 2011 325p $16.99
Grades: 10 11 12
> 1. Supernatural -- Fiction 2. Good and evil -- Fiction 3. Great Britain -- Fiction 4. Historic buildings -- Fiction 5. Household employees -- Fiction 6. Racially mixed people -- Fiction 7. Dating (Social customs) -- Fiction
> ISBN 978-0-545-26388-7
>   LC 2010-20171

Sequel to Possessed (2010)

A new manager brings many changes to Morton's Keep, capitalizing on its gothic atmosphere and history, but Rayne sees ominous signs indicating that the one thing that has not changed is the evil presence she had thought was destroyed.

"Eccentric characters are well-matched by absorbing writing and a satisfactory ending. Cann effectively builds both romantic and dramatic tension in a captivating gothic atmosphere, as Rayne struggles to reconcile her modern sensibilities with myths and legends that refuse to be laid to rest." Publ Wkly

Possessed. Point 2010 327p $16.99
Grades: 10 11 12
> 1. Supernatural -- Fiction 2. Good and evil -- Fiction 3. Great Britain -- Fiction 4. Historic buildings -- Fiction
> ISBN 978-0-545-12812-4; 0-545-12812-9
>   LC 2009-20977

Sixteen-year-old Rayne escapes London, her mother, and boyfriend for a job in the country at Morton's Keep, where she is drawn to a mysterious clique and its leader, St.

John, but puzzles over whether the growing evil she senses is from the manor house or her new friends.

"This atmospheric and deliciously chilling British import gets off to a quick start, and readers will empathize with the very likable 16-year-old protagonist, who is clearly out of her element. . . . With a minimum of actual bloodshed, this supernatural delight can even be enjoyed by the faint of heart." Booklist

Followed by Consumed (2011)

Cantor, Jillian

The **September** sisters. HarperTeen 2009 361p $16.99

Grades: 7 8 9 10 11 12

1. Sisters -- Fiction 2. Family life -- Fiction 3. Missing persons -- Fiction

ISBN 978-0-06-168648-1; 0-06-168648-4

LC 2008-7120

A teenaged girl tries to keep her family and herself together after the disappearance of her younger sister.

"Cantor treats the shape of Abby's agony with poignant credibility. . . . This is a sensitive and perceptive account of the way tragedy unfolds both quickly and slowly and life reassembles itself around it." Bull Cent Child Books

Card, Orson Scott, 1951-

★ **Ender's** game. TOR Bks. 1991 xxi, 226p $24.95; pa $6.99

Grades: 7 8 9 10 11 12 Adult

1. Science fiction 2. Interplanetary voyages -- Fiction

ISBN 0-312-93208-1; 0-8125-5070-6 pa

A reissue of the title first published 1985

ALA YALSA Margaret A. Edwards Award (2008)

"The key, of course, is Ender Wiggin himself. Mr. Card never makes the mistake of patronizing or sentimentalizing his hero. Alternately likable and insufferable, he is a convincing little Napoleon in short pants." N Y Times Book Rev

Other titles in the author's distant future series about Ender Wiggin include:

Children of the mind (1996)

Ender in exile (2008)

Ender's shadow (1999)

Shadow of the giant (2005)

Shadow of the Hegemon (2001)

Shadow of the giant (2005)

Shadow puppets (2002)

Speaker for the dead (1986)

A war of gifts (2007)

Xenocide (1991)

Pathfinder. Simon Pulse 2010 662p $18.99

Grades: 6 7 8 9 10

1. Science fiction 2. Time travel -- Fiction 3. Parapsychology -- Fiction 4. Space colonies -- Fiction 5. Interplanetary voyages -- Fiction

ISBN 978-1-4169-9176-2; 1-4169-9176-X

LC 2010-23243

Thirteen-year-old Rigg has a secret ability to see the paths of others' pasts, but revelations after his father's death set him on a dangerous quest that brings new threats from those who would either control his destiny or kill him.

"While Card delves deeply into his story's knotted twists and turns, readers should have no trouble following the philosophical and scientific mysteries, which the characters are parsing right along with them. An epic in the best sense, and not simply because the twin stories stretch across centuries." Publ Wkly

Ruins; Simon Pulse 2012 544p (hardback) $18.99

Grades: 7 8 9 10 11 12

1. Evolution -- Fiction 2. Time travel -- Fiction 3. Space colonies -- Fiction 4. Science fiction

ISBN 1416991778; 9781416991779

LC 2011052745

Sequel to: Pathfinder

In this book by Orson Scott Card, part of the Pathfinders series, "three time-shifters discover that the secrets of the past threaten their world with imminent obliteration. Rigg, his sister, Param, and best friend, Umbo, have joined their abilities to slip through time . . . circumventing the invisible Wall that divides their planet into 19 independent evolutionary experiments." (Kirkus Reviews)

Cardi, Annie

The **chance** you won't return. Annie Cardi. Candlewick Press. 2014 344p $16.99

Grades: 9 10 11 12

1. Mentally ill -- Fiction 2. Mother-daughter relationship -- Fiction

ISBN: 0763662925; 9780763662929

LC 2013946619

In this book, protagonist Alex's "mother believes herself to be Amelia Earhart. As Alex's mother's delusion becomes more persistent, she is hospitalized, but Alex's father's insurance isn't enough, and the family has to take care of her at home. . . .When she realizes that her mother is working on a timeline that will eventually lead to her disappearance . . . her confession closes the distance she has been maintaining between herself and her friends." (Bulletin of the Center for Children's Books)

"The author creates nuanced characters and presents them with their flaws and strengths intact, including a character with a mental disorder who never loses her humanity or becomes a caricature.... This novel delivers something far more rare: a well-written, first-person narrative about negotiating life's curve balls that has a realistic ending. An honest, uncompromising story." - Kirkus

Carey, Edward

Heap House; written and illustrated by Edward Carey. Overlook Press 2014 c2013 404p illus (Iremonger, book 1) $16.99

Grades: 5 6 7 8 9 10

1. Family secrets -- Fiction 2. Orphans -- Fiction 3. Boys —Fiction 4. London (England) -- Fiction 5. Houses -- Fiction 6. Great Britain -- History -- Victoria, 1837-1901 -- Fiction

ISBN: 1468309536; 9781468309539

First published 2013 in the United Kingdom

In this first book of a trilogy, "Clod is an Iremonger. He lives in the Heaps, a vast sea of lost and discarded items collected from all over London. At the centre is Heap House, a puzzle of houses, castles, homes and mysteries reclaimed from the city and built into a living maze of staircases and scurrying rats. The Iremongers are a mean and cruel family, robust and hardworking, but Clod has an illness. He can hear the objects whispering." (Publisher's note)

"Living among sentient trash heaps, Clod Iremonger has always been able to hear the voices of the objects that his family members carry, but the arrival of serving girl Lucy imbues the objects with a new and dangerous energy. Descriptive prose and black-and-white portraits create a unique cast of characters in a bleak, dilapidated home. Fans of Joan Aiken will flock to this dark mystery." Horn Book

Other titles in this series are:
Foulsham (2015)
Lungdon (2015)

Carey, Janet Lee

Dragon's Keep. Harcourt 2007 302p $17
Grades: 7 8 9 10
　　1. Fantasy fiction 2. Dragons -- Fiction 3. Princesses -- Fiction 4. Mother-daughter relationship -- Fiction 5. Great Britain -- History -- 1066-1154, Norman period -- Fiction
　　ISBN 978-0-15-205926-2; 0-15-205926-1
　　　　　　　　　　　　　　　　LC 2006-24669
In 1145 A.D., as foretold by Merlin, fourteen-year-old Rosalind, who will be the twenty-first Pendragon Queen of Wilde Island, has much to accomplish to fulfill her destiny, while hiding from her people the dragon's claw she was born with that reflects only one of her mother's dark secrets.

This is told "in stunning, lyrical prose. . . . Carey smoothly blends many traditional fantasy tropes here, but her telling is fresh as well as thoroughly compelling." Booklist

Dragonswood; by Janet Lee Carey. Dial Books 2012 403p.
Grades: 7 8 9
　　1. Love stories 2. Occult fiction 3. Fantasy fiction 4. Fantasy 5. Dragons -- Fiction 6. Fairies -- Fiction
　　ISBN 9780803735040
　　　　　　　　　　　　　　　　LC 2011021638
This juvenile fantasy novel tells the story of "Wilde Island [which] is not at peace. The kingdom mourns the dead Pendragon king and awaits the return of his heir; the uneasy pact between dragons, fairies, and humans is strained; and the regent is funding a bloodthirsty witch hunt, hoping to rid the island of half-fey maidens. Tess, daughter of a blacksmith, has visions of the future, but she still doesn't expect to be accused of witchcraft, forced to flee with her two best friends, or offered shelter by the handsome and enigmatic Garth Huntsman, a warden for Dragonswood. But Garth is the younger prince in disguise and Tess soon learns that her true father was fey." (Publisher's note)

In the time of dragon moon. By Janet Lee Carey. Kathy Dawson Books, an imprint of Penguin Group (USA) LLC 2015 472 p.
Grades: 9 10 11 12
　　1. Dragons -- Fiction 2. Fairies -- Fiction 3. Fantasy 4. Healers -- Fiction 5. Kidnapping -- Fiction 6. Kings, queens, rulers, etc. -- Fiction 7. Racially mixed people -- Fiction 8. British Isles -- History -- 13th century --

Fiction 9. Fantasy fiction
0803738102; 9780803738102, $17.99
　　　　　　　　　　　　　　　　LC 2014032216
In this medieval fantasy novel, by Janet Lee Carey, "Uma serves as her father's apprentice and dreams of succeeding him as Adan one day, but Euit tribal law forbids a woman as a healer. . . . When she becomes the queen's designated healer, Uma is soon embroiled in deadly court intrigues involving dragons and the fey folk. She also finds herself involved with Jackrun, a Pendragon prince who is part dragon and struggles to control the fire within him." (School Library Journal)

"The author's world-building is detailed and fascinating, and Uma is a strong, admirable heroine. This is a must-purchase for libraries owning the earlier installments and a great choice for where teen fantasy is popular." SLJ

The **beast** of Noor. Atheneum Books for Young Readers 2006 497p $16.95
Grades: 6 7 8 9
　　1. Fantasy fiction
　　ISBN 978-0-689-87644-8; 0-689-87644-0
　　　　　　　　　　　　　　　　LC 2005-17731
Fifteen-year-old Miles Ferrell uses the rare and special gift he is given to break the curse of the Shriker, a murderous creature reportedly brought to Shalem Wood by his family's clan centuries

"Carey delivers an eerie, atmospheric tale, full of terror and courage, set in a convincingly realized magical realm." Booklist

Carleson, J. C.

The **tyrant's** daughter; J.C. Carleson. Alfred A. Knopf 2014 304 p. (trade) $17.99
Grades: 8 9 10 11 12
　　1. Teenagers -- Fiction 2. Middle East -- Fiction 3. Kings and rulers -- Fiction 4. Exiles -- Fiction 5. Schools -- Fiction 6. Dictators -- Fiction 7. Immigrants -- Fiction 8. High schools -- Fiction 9. Middle East -- Politics and government -- Fiction
　　ISBN 0449809978; 9780449809976; 9780449809983; 9780449809990
　　　　　　　　　　　　　　　　LC 2013014783
"Removed from her unnamed Middle Eastern country after her father is murdered during a coup, 15-year-old Laila is now living near Washington D. C. with her mother and brother...This is more than just Laila's story; rather, it is a story of context, beautifully written (by a former undercover CIA agent), and stirring in its questions and eloquent observations about our society and that of the Middle East." (Booklist)

Carriger, Gail

★ **Curtsies** & conspiracies; Gail Carriger. Little, Brown and Co. 2013 320 p. (Finishing school) $18
Grades: 7 8 9 10 11 12
　　1. Steampunk fiction 2. Espionage -- Fiction 3. Conspiracies -- Fiction 4. Science fiction 5. Robots -- Fiction 6. Schools -- Fiction 7. Etiquette -- Fiction 8. Boarding schools -- Fiction 9. Great Britain -- History

-- George VI, 1936-1952 -- Fiction
ISBN 031619011X; 9780316190114

LC 2012048520

In this book, by Gail Carriger, "Sophronia's first year at Mademoiselle Geraldine's Finishing Academy for Young Ladies of Quality . . . is training her to be a spy. A conspiracy is afoot--one with dire implications for both supernaturals and humans. Sophronia must rely on her training to discover who is behind the dangerous plot—and survive the London Season with a full dance card." (Publisher's note)

"With the school's dirigible heading toward London for a liaison with an inventor studying aetherospheric travel, Sophronia (Etiquette & Espionage) is convinced that her professors are Up To Something. Is the academy affiliated with vampire hives, werewolf packs, the anti-supernatural Picklemen, or the Crown--all of whom would benefit from controlling aether technology? A witty and suspenseful steampunk romp." (Horn Book)

★ **Etiquette** & espionage; by Gail Carriger. Little, Brown 2013 320 p. (alk. paper) $17.99
Grades: 7 8 9 10 11 12

1. Spy stories 2. School stories 3. Assassins -- Fiction 4. Science fiction 5. Robots -- Fiction 6. Schools -- Fiction 7. Espionage -- Fiction 8. Etiquette -- Fiction 9. Boarding schools -- Fiction 10. Great Britain -- History -- George VI, 1936-1952 -- Fiction
ISBN 031619008X; 9780316190084

LC 2012005498

In this book, Sophronia's mother is "desperate for her daughter to become a proper lady. So she enrolls Sophronia in Mademoiselle Geraldine's Finishing Academy for Young Ladies of Quality. But Sophronia soon realizes the school is not quite what her mother might have hoped. At Mademoiselle Geraldine's, young ladies learn to finish . . . everything. Certainly, they learn the fine arts of dance, dress, and etiquette, but they also learn to deal out death, diversion, and espionage." (Publisher's note)

Carson, Rae

★ The **bitter** kingdom; by Rae Carson. Greenwillow Books 2013 448 p. (hardcover) $17.99
Grades: 8 9 10 11 12

1. Fantasy fiction 2. Magic -- Fiction 3. Queens -- Fiction 4. Love -- Fiction 5. Prophecies -- Fiction 6. Kings, queens, rulers, etc. -- Fiction
ISBN 0062026542; 9780062026545

LC 2013011912

Sequel to: The crown of embers

This is the final book in Rae Carson's Girl of Fire and Thorns trilogy. Here, "young Queen Elisa and her companions trek into enemy territory to rescue the man she loves, while a traitor back home attempts to overthrow her. Elisa's journeys take her to . . . Invierne, where she hopes to destroy the source of the Inviernos' magic and bargain for peace; to the Basajuan desert, where only her most audacious plans have any chance to stop the war; and home to try to regain her throne." (Publishers Weekly)

★ The **crown** of embers; by Rae Carson. Greenwillow Books 2012 410 p. (hardcover) $17.99

Grades: 8 9 10 11 12

1. Fantasy fiction 2. Adventure fiction 3. Love -- Fiction 4. Magic -- Fiction 5. Prophecies -- Fiction 6. Kings, queens, rulers, etc. -- Fiction
ISBN 0062026518; 9780062026514

LC 2012014125

Sequel to the Morris, Cybils, and Andre Norton Award finalist book The Girl of Fire and Thorns. "Elisa is a hero. . . . [But] to conquer the power she bears once and for all, Elisa must follow the trail of long-forgotten--and forbidden--clues from the deep, undiscovered catacombs of her own city to the treacherous seas. With her goes a one-eyed spy, a traitor, and the man who--despite everything--she is falling in love with." (Publisher's note)

★ The **girl** of fire and thorns. Greenwillow Books 2011 423p $17.99
Grades: 8 9 10 11 12

1. Fantasy fiction 2. Magic -- Fiction 3. Prophecies -- Fiction 4. Kings and rulers -- Fiction
ISBN 978-0-06-202648-4; 0-06-202648-8

LC 2010042021

Morris Award Finalist (2012)

Once a century, one person is chosen for greatness. Elisa is the chosen one. But she is also the younger of two princesses. The one who has never done anything remarkable, and can't see how she ever will. Now, on her sixteenth birthday, she has become the secret wife of a handsome and worldly king...And he's not the only one who seeks her. Savage enemies, seething with dark magic, are hunting her. A daring, determined revolutionary thinks she could be his people's savior. Soon it is not just her life, but her very heart that is at stake." (Publisher's note)

"This fast-moving and exciting novel is rife with political conspiracies and machinations." SLJ

Walk on Earth a Stranger. Rae Carson. Greenwillow books 2015 448 p. Map
Grades: 7 8 9 10

1. California -- Gold discoveries 2. Magic -- Fiction
0062242911; 9780062242914, $17.99

LC 2015015751

In Rae Carson's novel "Lee Westfall has a secret. She can sense the presence of gold in the world around her. Veins deep beneath the earth, pebbles in the river, nuggets dug up from the forest floor. The buzz of gold means warmth and life and home—until everything is ripped away by a man who wants to control her. Lee disguises herself as a boy and takes to the trail across the country. Gold was discovered in California, and where else could such a magical girl find herself, find safety?" (Publisher's note)

"Carson's story is simply terrific-tense and exciting, while gently and honestly addressing the brutal hardships of the westward migration. Even minor characters are fully three-dimensional, but it's Leah who rightfully takes center stage as a smart, resourceful, determined, and realistic heroine who embodies the age-old philosophy that it isn't what happens to you, but how you react to it that matters." Pub Wkly

Other titles in this series are:
Like a River Glorious (2016)
Into the Bright Unknown (2017)

Carter, Ally

Embassy row #1: all fall down. Ally Carter; [edited by] David Levithan. Scholastic Press 2015 320 p.
Grades: 7 8 9 10

    1. Mother-daughter relationship -- Fiction 2. Revenge -- Fiction 3. Murder -- Fiction 4. Ambassadors -- Fiction
0545654742; 9780545654746, $17.99

                  LC 2014947739

In this book, by Ally Carter, "Grace Blakely is absolutely certain of three things: 1. She is not crazy. 2. Her mother was murdered. 3. Someday she is going to find the killer and make him pay. As certain as Grace is about these facts, nobody else believes her—so there's no one she can completely trust. Not her grandfather, a powerful ambassador. Not her new friends, who all live on Embassy Row. . . . But they can't control Grace." (Publisher's note)

"This exciting first book in the Embassy Row series features sixteen-year-old Grace, who has moved into the United States Embassy on the coast of Adria with her ambassador grandfather. It is the first time in three years that she has been back to Adria, since her mother's tragic death in a fire... Her quest to find the truth is one that readers will love to follow, through the twists and turns of Embassy Row and with a diverse array of characters. Some help her, and some stand in her way . . . but Grace is a fighter, and she will stop at nothing to find out what happened to her mother. Readers will love this first book in what promises to be an exciting, thrilling mystery series from best-selling author Carter." VOYA

    Other titles in this series are:

    See how they run (2015)

    Take the key and lock her up (2016)

Heist Society. Hyperion 2010 287p il map
Grades: 7 8 9 10

    1. Thieves -- Fiction

    ISBN 1-4231-1639-9; 978-1-4231-1639-4

                  LC 2009-40377

A group of teenagers conspire to re-steal several priceless paintings and save Kat Bishop's father from a vengeful collector who is accusing him of art theft. "Grades six to ten." (Bull Cent Child Books)

    Carter "skillfully maintains suspense. . . . This is a thoroughly enjoyable, cinema-ready adventure." Booklist

    Another title about Kat is:

    Uncommon criminals (2011)

    Perfect scoundrels (2013)

Not if I save you first. Ally Carter. Scholastic Press 2018 293 p.
Grades: 8 9 10 11

    1. Best friends -- Fiction; 2. Fathers and daughters -- Fiction; 3. Forgiveness -- Fiction; 4. Friendship -- Fiction; 5. Kidnapping -- Fiction; 6. Rescues -- Fiction; 7. Survival -- Fiction; 8. Wilderness survival -- Fiction; 9. Alaska -- Fiction; 10. Father-daughter relationship -- Fiction
9781338134148, $18.99; 9781338134162

                  LC 2017049072

In this book, by Ally Carter, "Maddie thought she and Logan would be friends forever. But when your dad is a Secret Service agent and your best friend is the president's son, sometimes life has other plans. Before she knows it, Maddie's dad is dragging her to a cabin in the middle of the Alaskan wilderness." (Publisher's note)

    "A tightly plotted thriller helmed by a firecracker that never loses her spark." Kirkus

Perfect scoundrels; a Heist society novel. by Ally Carter. 1st ed. Disney/Hyperion Books 2013 328 p. (hardcover) $17.99
Grades: 7 8 9 10

    1. Crime -- Fiction 2. Theft -- Fiction 3. Wealth -- Fiction 4. Detective and mystery stories 5. Dating (Social customs) -- Fiction 6. Swindlers and swindling -- Fiction 7. Inheritance and succession -- Fiction
ISBN 1423166000; 9781423166009

                  LC 2012032405

This book is an installment of Ally Carter's Heist society series. "When Hale suddenly inherits his grandmother's billion-dollar company, it's pretty obvious that he and Kat can't be up to their old tricks anymore. But can Hale trust Kat not to dip her hand in the cookie jar and steal the company's fortune—even though he knows she's prepared to do the impossible?" (Dolly Magazine)

Carter, Caela

Me, him, them, and it; by Caela Carter. Bloomsbury Distributed to the trade by Macmillan 2013 320 p. (hardcover) $16.99
Grades: 9 10 11 12

    1. Teenage pregnancy -- Fiction 2. Dysfunctional families -- Fiction 3. Pregnancy -- Fiction 4. Family problems -- Fiction 5. Emotional problems -- Fiction
ISBN 1599909588; 9781599909585

                  LC 2012014331

In this novel, by Caela Carter, "when Evelyn . . . [upset] her parents with a bad reputation, she wasn't planning to ruin her valedictorian status. She also wasn't planning to fall for Todd—the guy she was just using for sex. And she definitely wasn't planning on getting pregnant. When Todd turns his back on her, Evelyn's not sure where to go." (Publisher's note)

Carvell, Marlene

Sweetgrass basket. Dutton Childrens Books 2005 243p $16.99
Grades: 7 8 9 10

    1. School stories 2. Sisters -- Fiction 3. Mohawk Indians -- Fiction
ISBN 0-525-47547-8

                  LC 2004-24374

In alternating passages, two Mohawk sisters describe their lives at the Carlisle Indian Industrial School, established in 1879 to educate Native Americans, as they try to assimilate into white culture and one of them is falsely accused of stealing.

    "Carvell has put together a compelling, authentic, and sensitive portrayal of a part of our history that is still not made accurately available to young readers." SLJ

Who will tell my brother? Hyperion Bks. for Children 2002 150p hardcover o.p. pa $5.99

Grades: 7 8 9 10
  1. School stories 2. Mohawk Indians -- Fiction
  ISBN 0-7868-0827-6; 0-7868-1657-0 pa
                                    LC 2001-51759
During his lonely crusade to remove offensive mascots
from his high school, Evan, part-Mohawk Indian, learns
more about his heritage, his ancestors, and his place in
the world
  "The blank verse format will be appealing, especially to
reluctant readers. . . . [A] lovely, heart-wrenching and profound little book." Voice Youth Advocates

Casanova, Mary
  Frozen; Mary Casanova. University of Minne-
sota Press 2012 264 p. (hc/j: alk. paper) $16.95
Grades: 7 8 9 10
  1. Voice -- Fiction 2. Conduct of life -- Fiction 3.
Mother-daughter relationship -- Fiction 4. Memory --
Fiction 5. Families -- Fiction 6. Identity -- Fiction
7. Selective mutism -- Fiction 8. Minnesota -- History
-- 20th century -- Fiction
  ISBN 0816680566; 9780816680566; 9780816680573
                                    LC 2012019376
Author Mary Casanova tells the story of a young girl's
life after her mother dies. "Sixteen-year-old Sadie Rose
hasn't spoken in eleven years—ever since she was found in
a snowbank the night her mother died under strange circumstances . . . Like her voice, her memories of her mother and
what happened that night were frozen . . . [The book] is a
suspenseful, moving testimonial to the power of family and
memory and the extraordinary strength of a young woman
who has lost her voice in nearly every way, but is determined
to find it again." (Publisher's note)

Casella, Jody
  Thin space; Jody Casella. Simon Pulse 2014
256 p. (hardcover: alk. paper) $16.99
Grades: 9 10 11 12
  1. Occult fiction 2. Fantasy fiction 3. Dead -- Fiction
4. Twins -- Fiction 5. Schools -- Fiction 6. Brothers
-- Fiction 7. High schools -- Fiction 8. Supernatural
-- Fiction 9. Conduct of life -- Fiction 10. Interpersonal
relations -- Fiction
  ISBN 158270435X; 9781582703923; 9781582704357
                                    LC 2012045691
In this book, for "three months, high school junior Marsh
Windsor has been refusing to wear shoes, ignoring school-
work and friends, and getting into fights. His parents and
teachers—even his former girlfriend—tolerate his bizarre
behavior as an inability to cope with the car wreck that
seriously injured Marsh and killed his twin, Austin. Only
the new girl, Maddie, knows that Marsh is seeking a 'thin
space,' a portal between the realms of the living and the
dead." (Kirkus Reviews)

Cashore, Kristin
  ★ **Bitterblue**; Kristin Cashore. Dial Books
2012 563 p.
Grades: 9 10 11 12
  1. Fantasy fiction 2. Queens -- Fiction 3. Brainwashing

-- Fiction 4. Conspiracies -- Fiction 5. Fantasy
  ISBN 0803734735; 9780803734739
                                    LC 2011035026
"Sequel to Graceling, companion to Fire"-Jkt
  This young adult fantasy novel "grapples with the messy
aftermath of destroying an evil overlord. Nine years after
Bitterblue took the crown, the young queen and her realm
are still struggling to come to terms with the monstrous
legacy of her father. . . . Bitterblue discovers that her people
have not healed as much as she has been told. . . . [She] must
draw upon all her courage, cleverness and ferocious compassion to reveal the truth -- and to care for those it shatters."
(Kirkus Reviews)

  ★ **Fire**; a novel. Dial Books 2009 461p map
$17.99
Grades: 9 10 11 12
  1. Fantasy fiction
  ISBN 978-0-8037-3461-6; 0-8037-3461-1
                                    LC 2009-5187
  In a kingdom called the Dells, Fire is the last human-
shaped monster, with unimaginable beauty and the ability to
control the minds of those around her, but even with these
gifts she cannot escape the strife that overcomes her world.
  "Many twists propel the action . . . [and] Cashore's
conclusion satisfies, but readers will clamor for a sequel to
the prequel—a book bridging the gap between this one and
Graceling." Publ Wkly

  ★ **Graceling**. Harcourt 2008 471p map $17;
pa $9.99
Grades: 8 9 10 11 12
  1. Fantasy fiction
  ISBN 978-0-15-206396-2; 0-15-206396-X; 978-0-
547-25830-0 pa; 0-547-25830-5 pa
                                    LC 2007045436
ALA YALSA Morris Award Finalist, 2009
  In a world where some people are born with extreme
skills called Graces, Katsa struggles for redemption from
her own horrifying Grace, the Grace of killing. She teams up
with another young fighter to save their land from a corrupt
king. "Age fourteen and up." (N Y Times Book Rev)
  "This is gorgeous storytelling: exciting, stirring, and accessible. Fantasy and romance readers will be thrilled." SLJ

  Jane, unlimited. Kristin Cashore. Kathy Dawson
Books 2017 453 p. Illustration; Map
Grades: 8 9 10 11 12
  1. Decision making -- Fiction; 2. Grief -- Fiction; 3.
Islands -- Fiction; 4. Orphans -- Fiction
  0803741499; 9780698158894; 9780803741492, $18.99
                                    LC 2017030463
  In this novel, by Kristin Cashore, "Jane has lived an ordinary life, raised by her aunt Magnolia -- an adjunct professor
and deep sea photographer.... But Aunt Magnolia was lost
a few months ago in Antarctica on one of her expeditions.
Now, with no direction, a year out of high school, and obsessed with making umbrellas that look like her own dreams
(but mostly just mourning her aunt), she is easily swept
away by Kiran Thrash -- a glamorous, capricious acquaintance." (Publisher's note)

"Creation, compassion, and choice repeatedly emerge as themes in this ambitious, mind-expanding novel." Booklist

Castan, Mike

Fighting for Dontae; Mike Castan. Holiday House 2012 150 p. (hardcover) $16.95
Grades: 6 7 8 9 10 11 12
1. Gangs -- Fiction 2. Reading -- Fiction 3. Children with disabilities -- Fiction 4. Schools -- Fiction 5. California -- Fiction 6. Middle schools -- Fiction 7. Conduct of life -- Fiction 8. Family problems -- Fiction 9. Mexican Americans -- Fiction 10. People with disabilities -- Fiction 11. People with mental disabilities -- Fiction
ISBN 0823423484; 9780823423484
LC 2011042115

This book is the story of seventh-grader Javier, who "does not really want to be in a gang," but thinks he must join the Playaz gang to be cool, which he desperately wants to be. "When he is assigned to work with the special-ed class at school, Javier knows that his days as a cool kid are officially over. He does not expect to enjoy it, but reading to Dontae, a severely disabled boy, becomes the one thing Javier looks forward to." (Children's Literature)

Castellucci, Cecil

Beige. Candlewick Press 2007 307p $16.99; pa $8.99
Grades: 7 8 9 10
1. Musicians -- Fiction 2. Punk rock music -- Fiction 3. Los Angeles (Calif.) -- Fiction 4. Father-daughter relationship -- Fiction
ISBN 978-0-7636-3066-9; 0-7636-3066-7; 978-0-7636-4232-7 pa; 0-7636-4232-0 pa
LC 2006-52458

Katy, a quiet French Canadian teenager, reluctantly leaves Montréal to spend time with her estranged father, an aging Los Angeles punk rock legend.

This a "a good read and an interesting look at the world of punk and alternative rock." Kliatt

Boy proof. Candlewick Press 2005 203p $15.99; pa $7.99
Grades: 7 8 9 10
1. Motion pictures -- Fiction 2. Los Angeles (Calif.) -- Fiction
ISBN 0-7636-2333-4; 0-7636-2796-6 pa
LC 2004-50256

Feeling alienated from everyone around her, Los Angeles high school senior and cinephile Victoria Denton hides behind the identity of a favorite movie character until an interesting new boy arrives at school and helps her realize that there is more to life than just the movies.

This "novel's clipped, funny, first-person, present-tense narrative will grab teens . . . with its romance and the screwball special effects, and with the story of an outsider's struggle both to belong and to be true to herself." Booklist

First day on Earth. Scholastic Press 2011 150p $17.99
Grades: 7 8 9 10
1. Children of alcoholics -- Fiction 2. Extraterrestrial

beings -- Fiction
ISBN 978-0-545-06082-0; 0-545-06082-6

"Mal's spare first-person narration is wistful and raw, reflecting the feelings of anyone who's ever felt misunderstood or abandoned. . . . Castellucci also creates vibrant secondary characters. . . . A simple, tender work that speaks to the alien in all of us." Kirkus

The **queen** of cool. Candlewick Press 2006 166p $15.99
Grades: 9 10 11 12
1. School stories 2. Zoos -- Fiction
ISBN 0-7636-2720-8
LC 2005-50174

Bored with her life, popular high school junior Libby signs up for an internship at the zoo and discovers that the "science nerds" she meets there may have a few things to teach her about friendship and life.

The author "offers a refreshingly nuanced and credible look at what lies behind the facade of cool." Bull Cent Child Books

Castle, Jennifer

You look different in real life; Jennifer Castle. HarperTeen, an imprint of HarperCollinsPublishers 2013 368 p. (hardback) $17.99
Grades: 7 8 9 10
1. School stories 2. Documentary films -- Fiction 3. Identity -- Fiction 4. Celebrities -- Fiction 5. New York (State) -- Fiction
ISBN 0061985813; 9780061985812
LC 2012051743

This book follows five ordinary 16-year-olds who have been the subjects of two documentaries at ages 6 and 11. Now, many "changes have occurred since the last time they were filmed" so the "producers struggle to find usable footage and resort to staging some scenes, which in previous years was unnecessary." (School Library Journal)

Castor, H. M.

VIII; H.M. Castor. Simon & Schuster Books for Young Readers 2013 399 p. (hardcover) $17.99
Grades: 8 9 10 11 12
1. Great Britain -- History -- 1485-1603, Tudors 2. Kings, queens, rulers, etc. -- Fiction 3. Great Britain -- History -- Henry VII, 1485-1509 -- Fiction 4. Great Britain -- History -- Henry VIII, 1509-1547 -- Fiction
ISBN 1442474181; 9781442474185; 9781442474208
LC 2012021550

This book is a biography of Henry VIII of England. As a second son, Henry's youth is full of "fighting, jousting and gambling. When his elder brother, Arthur, unexpectedly dies, Hal realizes that . . . he now has a straight line to the throne. However . . . the difficulties of producing a royal heir, together with the thwarting of his overweening military ambition against the French by Spanish Catherine's family and his own . . . advisers cause Henry to become increasingly cynical and desperate." (Kirkus Reviews)

Catmull, Katherine

The **radiant** road: a novel. By Katherine Catmull. Dutton Books, an imprint of Penguin Random House LLC 2016 368 p.

Grades: 7 8 9 10

1. Fairies -- Fiction 2. Good and evil -- Fiction 3. Identity -- Fiction 4. Magic -- Fiction
9780525953470, $17.99

LC 2015020678

In this book, by Katherine Catmull, "Clare Macleod and her father are returning to Ireland, where they'll inhabit the house Clare was born in-a house built into a green hillside with a tree for a wall. For Clare, the house is not only full of memories of her mother, but also of a mysterious boy with raven-dark hair and dreamlike nights filled with stars and magic. Clare soon discovers that the boy is as real as the fairy-making magic." (Publisher's note)

"Catmull has created an eerily lovely story, writing with an old-fashioned style that at times sings like a lullaby. An excellent addition to either teen or juvenile collections of all sizes." Booklist

Cavallaro, Brittany

★ The **Last** of August. Brittany Cavallaro. Harpercollins Childrens Books 2017 336 p.

0062398946; 9780062398949

In this second Charlotte Holmes novel, by Brittany Cavallaro, "Jamie and Charlotte are looking for a winter break reprieve in Sussex. . . . But nothing about their time off is proving simple, including Holmes and Watson's growing feelings for each other. When Charlotte's beloved Uncle Leander goes missing from the Holmes estate-after being oddly private about his latest assignment in a German art forgery ring-. . . Charlotte throws herself into a search for answers." (Publisher's note)

Other titles in this series are:

A study in Charlotte (2016)
The case for Jamie (2018)
A question of Holmes (2019)

Chaltas, Thalia

Because I am furniture. Viking Children's Books 2009 352p $16.99

Grades: 8 9 10 11

1. School stories 2. Novels in verse 3. Guilt -- Fiction 4. Child abuse -- Fiction 5. Child sexual abuse -- Fiction
ISBN 978-0-670-06298-0; 0-670-06298-7

LC 2008-23235

The youngest of three siblings, fourteen-year-old Anke feels both relieved and neglected that her father abuses her brother and sister but ignores her, but when she catches him with one of her friends, she finally becomes angry enough to take action.

"Incendiary, devastating, yet—in total—offering empowerment and hope, Chaltas's poems leave an indelible mark." Publ Wkly

Chambers, Aidan

★ **Dying** to know you; Aidan Chambers. Amulet Books 2012 275 p.

Grades: 9 10 11 12

1. Authors -- Fiction 2. Dyslexia -- Fiction 3.

Friendship -- Fiction 4. Elderly men -- Fiction 5. Self-perception -- Fiction 6. Interpersonal relations -- Fiction
ISBN 1419701657; 9781419701658

LC 2012000843

This young adult novel is "a story told in . . . first-person voice by a 75-year-old man. . . . Karl approaches the older man, an author, with a request. His new girlfriend, Fiorella, has tasked him with providing a series of written answers to questions . . . so that she can find out more about him. But Karl, an 18-year-old plumber who's no longer in school, is dyslexic. . . . The friendship . . . form[s] as Karl gradually gains knowledge of himself that isn't based on the previous failures in his life." (Kirkus)

★ **Postcards** from no man's land. Dutton Children's Bks. 2002 312p.

Grades: 11 12

1. World War, 1939-1945 -- Fiction 2. Netherlands -- Fiction
0-525-46863-3; 0-14-240145-5 (pa), $8.99

LC 2002-16562

Printz Award (2003)

"In Holland in 1944, Dutch teenager Geertrui fell passionately in love with a wounded young British soldier, and she hid him from the enemy. That soldier's grandson, Jacob, a British teenager, is now in Amsterdam to visit the grave of the grandfather he never knew, and he falls in love with a beautiful young woman, even as he's attracted to an openly gay young man." Booklist

"This novel is beautifully written, emotionally touching, and intellectually challenging." Voice Youth Advocates

First published 1999 in the United Kingdom

Chan, Crystal

All that I can fix. By Crystal Chan. Simon Pulse 2018 314 p.

Grades: 7 8 9 10 11

1. Family problems -- Fiction; 2. Racially mixed people -- Fiction; 3. Family life -- Fiction
9781534408906; 9781534408883, $18.99

LC 2017039196

In this novel, by Crystal Chan, "in Makersville, Indiana, people know all about Ronney -- he's from that mixed-race family with the dad who tried to kill himself, the pill-popping mom, and the genius kid sister.... [Then t]he local eccentric at the edge of town decided one night to open up all the cages of his exotic zoo...and then shoot himself dead.... Can Ronney figure out a way to hold it together as all his worlds fall apart?" (Publisher's note)

"A superbly entertaining read that weaves issues of mental health and gun control with adolescent angst." Kirkus

Chan, Gillian

The **disappearance**. Gillian Chan. Annick Press 2017 Ix, 197 p.

Grades: 8 9 10 11 12

1. Brothers -- Death -- Fiction; 2. Friendship -- Fiction; 3. Group homes -- Fiction; 4. Mutism -- Fiction; 5. Scars -- Fiction; 6. Selective mutism -- Fiction
9781554519835, $15.99; 9781554519859; 9781554519842; 9781554519828; 1554519837

This novel, by Gillian Chan, "centers on the unlikely friendship between two boys, Jacob Mueller and Mike Mc-Callum.... After mystifying experts and doctors, who finally decide that he is an elective mute, Jacob ends up in a juvenile group home, isolated and withdrawn.... Mike exists in his own private hell. Scarred physically and emotionally after the murder of his younger brother, his one aim is to survive the system until he is legally old enough to get out." (Publisher's note)

"Reluctant highly capable readers will be enticed, as will fans of R. L. Stine, Ripley's Believe It or Not, and ghost stories." VOYA

Chapman, Fern Schumer

★ **Is** it night or day? Farrar, Straus, Giroux 2010 205p $17.99

Grades: 6 7 8 9 10

1. Jewish refugees -- Fiction 2. Jews -- Germany -- Fiction 3. Holocaust, 1933-1945 -- Fiction 4. World War, 1939-1945 -- Fiction 5. Jews -- United States -- Fiction
ISBN 0-374-17744-9; 978-0-374-17744-7

LC 2008055602

In 1938, Edith Westerfeld, a young German Jew, is sent by her parents to Chicago, Illinois, where she lives with an aunt and uncle and tries to assimilate into American culture, while worrying about her parents and mourning the loss of everything she has ever known. Based on the author's mother's experience, includes an afterword about a little-known program that brought twelve hundred Jewish children to safety during World War II.

"In Edith's bewildered, sad, angry voice, the words are eloquent and powerful." Booklist

Chapman, Lara

Flawless. Bloomsbury 2011 258 p. $16.99; pa $9.99

Grades: 7 8 9 10

1. Love stories 2. School stories 3. Friendship -- Fiction 4. Personal appearance -- Fiction
ISBN 1599906317; 1599905965; 9781599906317; 9781599905969

LC 2010049102

In this modern take on the Cyrano story, brilliant and witty high school student Sarah Burke, who is cursed with an enormous nose, helps her beautiful best friend try to win the heart of a handsome and smart new student, even though Sarah wants him for herself.

"This retelling of Cyrano de Bergerac is great fun.... The ending is predictable but satisfying. Each chapter begins with thoughtful quotes about love. This novel will attract both reluctant readers and literature lovers." SLJ

Charbonneau, Joelle

Graduation day; Joelle Charbonneau. Houghton Mifflin Harcourt 2014 304 p. (hardback) $17.99

Grades: 7 8 9 10 11 12

1. Dystopian fiction 2. Love -- Fiction 3. Loyalty -- Fiction 4. Survival -- Fiction 5. Adventure and adventurers -- Fiction 6. Government, Resistance to

-- Fiction
ISBN 0547959214; 9780547959214

LC 2013034743

"Charbonneau concludes her dystopian Testing trilogy with this action-packed finale, which sees Cia Vale secretly tasked by the President of the United Commonwealth to remove the officials behind the lethal Testing process that has claimed so many young lives...As in the previous books, Charbonneau remains focused on philosophical worries and moral tests over spectacle and bloodshed, with multiple layers and twists to keep readers forever guessing. Enough potential threads are left dangling to leave room for future stories." (Publishers Weekly)

Independent study; by Joelle Charbonneau. Houghton Mifflin, Houghton Mifflin Harcourt 2014 320 p. (The testing) (hardback) $17.99

Grades: 7 8 9 10 11 12

1. Adventure and adventurers 2. Love -- Fiction 3. Survival -- Fiction 4. Examinations -- Fiction 5. Government, Resistance to -- Fiction 6. Universities and colleges -- Fiction
ISBN 0547959206; 9780547959207

LC 2013004815

In this book, by Joelle Charbonneau, "sixteen-year-old Cia Vale was chosen by the United Commonwealth government as one of the best and brightest graduates of all the colonies.... [Now], Cia is a freshman at the University in Tosu City with her hometown sweetheart, Tomas—and though the government has tried to erase her memory of the brutal horrors of The Testing, Cia remembers. Her attempts to expose the ugly truth behind the government's murderous programs put her ... in a world of danger." (Publisher's note)

"Fans of The Testing will be thrilled with this new installment and will be anxiously waiting for the story's conclusion." (School Library Journal)

★ The **Testing**; by Joelle Charbonneau. Houghton Mifflin Harcourt 2013 344 p. (hardcover) $17.99

Grades: 7 8 9 10 11 12

1. Examinations -- Fiction 2. Survival skills -- Fiction 3. Schools -- Fiction 4. Missing persons -- Fiction 5. Graduation (School) -- Fiction 6. Universities and colleges -- Fiction
ISBN 0547959109; 9780547959108

LC 2012018090

In this book by Joelle Charbonneau, "Cia Vale is one of four teens chosen to represent her small colony at the annual Testing, an intensive mental and physical examination aimed at identifying the best and brightest, who will go on to the University and help rebuild their shattered world. Forewarned not to trust anyone, Cia nonetheless forms a tentative partnership with resourceful Tomas, with whom she shares an unexpected emotional connection." (Publishers Weekly)

Charlton-Trujillo, E.

★ **Fat** Angie; E. E. Charlton-Trujillo. Candlewick Press 2013 272 p. $16.99

Grades: 9 10 11 12

1. School stories 2. Obesity -- Fiction 3. Lesbians

-- Fiction

ISBN 0763661198; 9780763661199

LC 2012942623

Lambda Literary Awards Finalist (2014)

Stonewall Book Award-Mike Morgan and Larry Romans Children's & Young Adult Literature Award (2014)

This teenage novel, by E. E. Charlton-Trujillo, follows Angie, an overweight high school student who is bullied and dealing with grief over her sister, a presumed dead prisoner of the Iraq War. After entering into a friendship and lesbian relationship with a gothic new girl named KC Romance, Angie comes to rediscover her self confidence.

Chayil, Eishes

Hush. Walker 2010 359p $16.99

Grades: 8 9 10 11 12

1. Judaism -- Fiction 2. Suicide -- Fiction 3. Conduct of life -- Fiction 4. Child sexual abuse -- Fiction 5. Jews -- New York (N.Y.) -- Fiction 6. Brooklyn (New York, N.Y.) -- Fiction

ISBN 978-0-8027-2088-7; 0-8027-2088-9

LC 2010-10329

"The author balances outrage at the routine cover-up of criminal acts with genuine understanding of the community's fear of assault on their traditions by censorious gentiles. Moreover, she delivers her central message in an engaging coming-of-age story in which tragedy is only one element in a gossipy milieu of school and career decisions and arranged marriages, designer shoes and tasteful cosmetics, and sneak peaks out from a world of restraint and devotion into the world of Oprah." Bull Cent Child Books

Chbosky, Stephen

★ The **perks** of being a wallflower; [by] Stephen Chbosky. Pocket Bks. 1999 213p pa $12

Grades: 9 10 11 12

1. School stories 2. Letters -- Fiction 3. Young men -- Social life and customs -- 20th century

ISBN 0-671-02734-4

LC 99-236288

This novel in letter form is narrated by Charlie, a high school freshman. "His favorite aunt passed away, and his best friend just committed suicide. The girl he loves wants him as a friend; a girl he does not love wants him as a lover. His 18-year-old sister is pregnant. The LSD he took is not sitting well. And he has a math quiz looming. . . . Young adult." (Time)

"Charlie, his friends, and family are palpably real. . . . This report on his life will engage teen readers for years to come." SLJ

Chee, Traci

★ The **Reader**. By Traci Chee. Penguin 2016 464 p. (Sea of ink and gold)

Grades: 8 9 10 11 12

1. Kidnapping -- Fiction 2. Fantasy fiction 3. Adventure fiction 4. Murder -- Fiction

0399176772; 9780399176777, $19.99

LC 2015039924

"Fleeing into the wilderness after her father's brutal murder, Sefia learns how to hunt, track and steal in order to survive before embarking on a quest to rescue the beloved aunt who is her mentor, an effort that is shaped by a magnificent book that is unheard of in her otherwise illiterate society." (Publisher's note)

"This cleverly layered fantasy leaves more questions than it answers, but fortunately, it's only the first of what promises to be an enchanting series." Kirkus

Other titles in this series are:

The speaker (2017)

The storyteller (2018)

The **speaker**. Traci Chee. G.P. Putnam's Sons 2017 487 p. Map (Sea of ink and gold)

Grades: 8 9 10 11 12

1. Books and reading -- Fiction; 2. Kidnapping -- Fiction; 3. Nightmares -- Fiction; 4. Orphans -- Fiction; 5. Fantasy fiction

9780698410633; 0399176780; 9780399176784, $19.99

LC 2017016556

In this book, by Traci Chee, "having barely escaped the clutches of the Guard, Sefia and Archer are back on the run, slipping into the safety of the forest to tend to their wounds and plan their next move. Haunted by painful memories, Archer struggles to overcome the trauma of his past with the impressors, whose cruelty plagues him whenever he closes his eyes. But when Sefia and Archer happen upon a crew of impressors in the wilderness, Archer finally finds a way to combat his nightmares." (Publisher's note)

"Filled with even more magic and intrigue than its predecessor, this is a gripping follow-up that will leave readers speculating and wanting more." Kirkus

Chen, Justina

Return to me; by Justina Chen. Little, Brown and Co. 2013 352 p. (hardcover) $17.99

Grades: 7 8 9 10

1. Moving -- Fiction 2. Family life -- Fiction 3. Clairvoyance -- Fiction 4. Love -- Fiction 5. Architecture -- Fiction 6. Family problems -- Fiction 7. Moving, Household -- Fiction 8. Self-actualization (Psychology) -- Fiction

ISBN 0316102555; 9780316102551

LC 2012001549

In this book, "moving away from her Washington home seems to be a logical part of Reb's life plan; after the summer, she'll start at Columbia University, studying to be a corporate architect in the family firm, while her family moves to New Jersey for her father's new job. All that unravels upon their arrival on the East Coast, when her father announces that he's leaving the family to be with another woman, forcing Reb to question everything." (Bulletin of the Center for Children's Books)

Cheva, Cherry

DupliKate; a novel. HarperTeen 2009 242p $16.99

Grades: 7 8 9 10

1. School stories 2. Computer games -- Fiction 3. Virtual reality -- Fiction

ISBN 978-0-06-128854-8; 0-06-128854-3

LC 2009-18292

When she wakes up one morning to find her double in her room, seventeen-year-old Kate, already at wit's end with college applications, finals, and extracurricular activities, decides to put her to work.

This is a "light and funny novel. . . . Though this is lightweight territory, there is a strong message here about being true to yourself and balancing fun and work in your life. . . . This is sure to fly off the shelves." SLJ

Chibbaro, Julie

Deadly. Atheneum Books for Young Readers 2011 293 p. $16.99

Grades: 6 7 8 9 10

1. Sick -- Fiction 2. Domestics -- Fiction 3. Diaries -- Fiction 4. Sex role -- Fiction 5. Epidemiology -- Fiction 6. Typhoid fever -- Fiction 7. Interpersonal relations -- Fiction 8. New York (N.Y.) -- History -- 1898-1951 -- Fiction

ISBN 0689857381; 9780689857386; 978-0-689-85738-6; 0-689-85738-1

LC 2010002291

"A deeply personal coming-of-age story set in an era of tumultuous social change, this is topnotch historical fiction that highlights the struggle between rational science and popular opinion as shaped by a sensational, reactionary press." SLJ

Childs, Tera Lynn

Oh. My. Gods. Dutton Books 2008 224p $16.99

Grades: 7 8 9 10

1. School stories 2. Running -- Fiction 3. Stepfamilies -- Fiction 4. Classical mythology -- Fiction

ISBN 978-0-525-47942-0; 0-525-47942-2

LC 2007-28294

When her mother suddenly decides to marry a near-stranger, Phoebe, whose passion is running, soon finds herself living on a remote Greek island, completing her senior year at an ancient high school where the students and teachers are all descended from gods or goddesses.

"Childs does a great job of character development and creating a fast-paced plot to keep readers engaged." Voice Youth Advocates

Sweet venom. Katherine Tegen Books 2011 345p $17.99

Grades: 7 8 9 10

1. Sisters -- Fiction 2. Monsters -- Fiction 3. Fate and fatalism -- Fiction 4. Classical mythology -- Fiction 5. San Francisco (Calif.) -- Fiction 6. Medusa (Greek mythology) -- Fiction

ISBN 978-0-06-200181-8; 0-06-200181-7

LC 2010050525

As monsters walk the streets of San Francisco, unseen by humans, three teenaged descendants of Medusa, the once-beautiful gorgon maligned in Greek mythology, must reunite and embrace their fates.

"Childs clearly has a sequel (or more) in mind and uses this book to ably set up an appealing conflict, introduce quite likable characters, and get readers ready for intrigue in the romance and fate-of-the-world departments." Booklist

Chima, Cinda Williams

The **Crimson** Crown; a Seven Realms novel. Cinda Williams Chima. Hyperion 2012 598 p. (hardback) $18.99

Grades: 7 8 9 10 11 12

1. Fantasy fiction 2. Queens -- Fiction 3. Magicians -- Fiction 4. Fantasy 5. Wizards -- Fiction 6. Kings, queens, rulers, etc. -- Fiction

ISBN 1423144333; 9781423144335

LC 2011053079

In this fantasy novel by Cinda Williams Chima, book 4 of the Seven Realms series, "the Queendom of the Fells seems likely to shatter apart. For young queen Raisa . . . , maintaining peace even within her own castle walls is nearly impossible; tension between wizards and Clan has reached a fevered pitch. . . . Raisa's best hope is to unite her people against a common enemy. But that enemy might be the person with whom she's falling in love." (Publisher's note)

★ The **Demon** King; a Seven Realms novel. Disney Hyperion 2009 506p map (Seven Realms) $17.99

Grades: 7 8 9 10 11 12

1. Fantasy fiction 2. Princesses -- Fiction 3. Witchcraft -- Fiction

ISBN 978-1-4231-1823-7; 1-4231-1823-5

LC 2008-46178

Relates the intertwining fates of former street gang leader Han Alister and headstrong Princess Raisa, as Han takes possession of an amulet that once belonged to an evil wizard and Raisa uncovers a conspiracy in the Grey Wolf Court.

"With full-blooded, endearing heroes, a well-developed supporting cast and a detail-rich setting, Chima explores the lives of two young adults, one at the top of the world and the other at the bottom, struggling to find their place and protect those they love." Publ Wkly

Other titles in this series are:
The exiled queen (2010)
The Gray Wolf Throne (2011)

The **warrior** heir. Hyperion Books for Children 2006 426p hardcover o.p.

Grades: 7 8 9 10 11 12

1. Fantasy fiction 2. Magic -- Fiction

ISBN 0-7868-3916-3; 0-7868-3917-1 pa; 978-0-7868-3916-2; 978-0-7868-3917-9 pa

LC 2005-52720

After learning about his magical ancestry and his own warrior powers, sixteen-year-old Jack embarks on a training program to fight enemy wizards. "Grades seven to ten." (Bull Cent Child Books)

"Twists and turns abound in this remarkable, nearly flawless debut novel that mixes a young man's coming-of-age with fantasy and adventure. Fast paced and brilliantly plotted." Voice Youth Advocates

Other titles in this series are:
The wizard heir (2007)
The dragon heir (2008)
The enchanter heir (2013)
The sorcerer heir (2014)

Choi, Sook Nyul

★ **Year** of impossible goodbyes. Houghton Mifflin 1991 171p hardcover o.p. pa $5.99

Grades: 5 6 7 8

    1. Korea -- Fiction

    ISBN 0-395-57419-6; 978-0-440-40759-1 pa

                    LC 91-10502

Sookan, a young Korean girl survives the oppressive Japanese and Russian occupation of North Korea during the 1940s, to later escape to freedom in South Korea

    "Tragedies are not masked here, but neither are they overdramatized. . . . The observations are honest, the details authentic, the characterizations vividly developed." Bull Cent Child Books

    Other titles about Sookan are:

    Echoes of the white giraffe (1993)

    Gathering of pearls (1994)

Chokshi, Roshani

The **star-touched** queen. Roshani Chokshi. St. Martin's Griffin 2016 352 p.

Grades: 9 10 11 12

    1. Queens -- Fiction 2. Arranged marriage -- Fiction 3. Fantasy fiction

    9781250085474, $18.99

                   LC 2016001958

In this book, by Roshani Chokshi, "Maya is cursed. With a horoscope that promises a marriage of Death and Destruction, she has earned only the scorn and fear of her father's kingdom. Content to follow more scholarly pursuits, her whole world is torn apart when her father, the Raja, arranges a wedding of political convenience to quell outside rebellions. Soon Maya becomes the queen of Akaran and wife of Amar. Neither roles are what she expected." (Publisher's note)

    "A unique fantasy that is epic myth and beautiful fairy tale combined." Booklist

Chupeco, Rin

The **Girl** from the Well. Rin Chupeco. Sourcebooks Fire 2014 272 p.

Grades: 9 10 11 12

    1. Ghost stories 2. Good and evil 3. Horror stories 4. Revenge 5. Horror fiction 6. Dead -- Fiction

    140229218X; 9781402292187, $16.99

In this horror novel by Rin Chupeco, "Okiku is a lonely soul. She has wandered the world for centuries, freeing the spirits of the murdered-dead. Once a victim herself, she now takes the lives of killers with the vengeance they're due. But releasing innocent ghosts from their ethereal tethers does not bring Okiku peace. Still she drifts on. Such is her existence, until she meets Tark. Evil writhes beneath the moody teen's skin, trapped by a series of intricate tattoos." (Publisher's note)

    "Told in a marvelously disjointed fashion from Okiku's numbers-obsessed point of view, this story unfolds with creepy imagery and an intimate appreciation for Japanese horror, myth, and legend. The tropes Chupeco invokes will be familiar to any fan of J-horror, but the execution is spine-tingling, relying more on cinematic cuts than outright gore." Publishers Weekly

    Companion: The Suffering (2015)

Cisneros, Sandra

★ The **house** on Mango Street. Knopf 1994 134p $24

Grades: 7 8 9 10

    1. Chicago (Ill.) -- Fiction 2. Mexican Americans -- Fiction

    ISBN 0-679-43335-X

                   LC 93-43564

Originally published by Arte Público Press in 1984. Verso of title page

    This is "a composite of evocative snapshots that manages to passionately recreate the milieu of the poor quarters of Chicago." Commonweal

Clare, Cassandra

City of ashes. Margaret K. McElderry Books 2008 453p (The mortal instruments) $17.99; pa $9.99

Grades: 9 10 11 12

    1. Horror fiction 2. Devil -- Fiction 3. Supernatural -- Fiction 4. New York (N.Y.) -- Fiction

    ISBN 978-1-4169-1429-7; 1-4169-1429-3; 978-1-4169-7224-2 pa; 1-4169-7224-2 pa

                 LC 2007-14714

Sequel to City of bones (2007)

    "In this sequel to City of Bones, sixteen-year-old Clary is still coming to terms with her abilities as a demon killer, with her mother's comatose state, and with her horror over the discovery that her father, Valentine, is a power-hungry and evil exile in Downworld, a realm that exists outside of New York City. . . . Grades nine to twelve." (Bull Cent Child Books)

    "The whole book is like watching a particularly good vampire/werewolf movie, and it leaves readers waiting for the next in the series. Watch this one fly off the shelves." SLJ

    Followed by City of Glass (2009)

City of bones. Margaret K. McElderry Books 2007 485p (The mortal instruments) $17.99; pa $9.99

Grades: 9 10 11 12

    1. Horror fiction 2. Devil -- Fiction 3. Supernatural -- Fiction 4. New York (N.Y.) -- Fiction

    ISBN 1-4169-1428-5; 1-4169-5507-0 pa; 978-1-4169-1428-0; 978-1-4169-5507-8 pa

                 LC 2006-08108

Suddenly able to see demons and the Darkhunters who are dedicated to returning them to their own dimension, fifteen-year-old Clary Fray is drawn into this bizzare world when her mother disappears and Clary herself is almost killed by a monster.

    "This version of New York, full of Buffyesque teens who are trying to save the world, is entertaining and will have fantasy readers anxiously awaiting the next book in the series." SLJ

City of fallen angels; by Cassandra Clare. 1st ed. Margaret K. McElderry Books 2011 424 p. (hardcover) $21.99

Grades: 9 10 11 12

    1. Vampires -- Fiction 2. Supernatural -- Fiction 3.

Magic -- Fiction 4. Demonology -- Fiction 5. New York (N.Y.) -- Fiction
ISBN 9781442403543; 1442403543

LC 2010041132

In this book, part of author Cassandra Clare's Mortal Instruments series, "Jace is plagued with horrifying nightmares of killing Clary as the pair investigates the source of demon babies. Simon, a rare Daylighter vampire, struggles to figure out who is trying to kill him. Camille, an ancient vampire, tempts Simon, while an ancient source of evil manipulates them all to an unthinkable end." (Booklist)

City of Glass. Margaret K. McElderry Books 2009 541p (The mortal instruments) $17.99
Grades: 9 10 11 12

1. Horror fiction 2. Devil -- Fiction 3. Supernatural -- Fiction 4. New York (N.Y.) -- Fiction
ISBN 978-1-4169-1430-3; 1-4169-1430-7

LC 2008-39065

Sequel to City of ashes (2008)

Still pursuing a cure for her mother's enchantment, Clary uses all her powers and ingenuity to get into Idris, the forbidden country of the secretive Shadowhunters, and to its capital, the City of Glass, where with the help of a newfound friend, Sebastian, she uncovers important truths about her family's past that will not only help save her mother but all those that she holds most dear.

"An experienced storyteller, Clare moves the plot quickly to a satisfying end." Booklist

City of lost souls; Cassandra Clare. Margaret K. McElderry Books 2012 535 p. (Mortal instruments) (hardback) $19.99
Grades: 9 10 11 12

1. Fantasy fiction 2. Siblings -- Fiction 3. Interpersonal relations -- Fiction 4. Horror stories 5. Magic -- Fiction 6. Vampires -- Fiction 7. Demonology -- Fiction 8. Supernatural -- Fiction 9. New York (N.Y.) -- Fiction
ISBN 9781442416864; 9781442416888

LC 2011042547

This book is the fifth in the Mortal Instruments series by Cassandra Clare. In it, "Clary's long-lost brother Sebastian, raised to be an evil overlord by their father (and Jace's foster father), has kidnapped Jace. . . . The narrative zips from one young protagonist to another, as they argue with the werewolf council, summon angels and demons, fight the 'million little paper cuts' of homophobia, and . . . negotiate sexual tension." (Kirkus)

Clockwork prince; Cassandra Clare. 1st ed. Margaret K. McElderry Books 2011 528 p. (The infernal devices) (hardcover) $19.99
Grades: 6 7 8 9 10 11 12

1. Orphans -- Fiction 2. Demonology -- Fiction 3. Supernatural -- Fiction 4. London (England) -- Fiction 5. Secret societies -- Fiction 6. Identity -- Fiction 7. London (England) -- History -- 19th century -- Fiction
ISBN 9781416975885; 9781442431348

LC 2011017869

In this book, a #1 New York Times Bestseller, set "[i]n the magical underworld of Victorian London, Tessa Gray has at last found safety with the Shadowhunters. But that safety proves fleeting when rogue forces in the Clave plot to see her protector, Charlotte, replaced as head of the Institute. If Charlotte loses her position, Tessa will be out on the street—and easy prey for the mysterious Magister, who wants to use Tessa's powers for his own dark ends. With the help of the handsome, self-destructive Will and the fiercely devoted Jem, Tessa discovers that the Magister's war on the Shadowhunters is deeply personal. . . . To unravel the secrets of the past, the trio journeys from mist-shrouded Yorkshire to a manor house that holds untold horrors, from the slums of London to an enchanted ballroom where Tessa discovers that the truth of her parentage is more sinister than she had imagined." (Publisher's note)

Clockwork princess; Cassandra Clare. 1st ed. Margaret K. McElderry Books 2013 592 p. (The infernal devices) (hardcover) $19.99
Grades: 6 7 8 9 10 11 12

1. Love stories 2. Fantasy fiction 3. Orphans -- Fiction 4. Demonology -- Fiction 5. Supernatural -- Fiction 6. Secret societies -- Fiction 7. London (England) -- History -- 19th century -- Fiction 8. Great Britain -- History -- Victoria, 1837-1901 -- Fiction
ISBN 141697590X; 9781416975908

LC 2012048910

This is the third installment of Cassandra Clare's The Infernal Devices trilogy. Here, "Tessa leads the fight against Mortmain (a.k.a. the Magister) and his army of clockwork automatons that threaten to wipe out the Shadowhunter race," automatons that are "reanimated with demon souls." Also of note are "Tessa's tangled relationships with her fiancé, Jem Carstairs, who has a terminal demon-related illness, and Jem's blood brother, Will Herondale, who's also in love with her." (Entertainment Weekly)

Clark, Kathy

Guardian angel house. Second Story Press 2009 225p il map (Holocaust remembrance book for young readers) pa $14.95
Grades: 6 7 8 9 10

1. Nuns -- Fiction 2. Jews -- Hungary -- Fiction 3. Holocaust, 1933-1945 -- Fiction
ISBN 978-1-89718-758-6; 1-89718-758-0

When Mama decides to send Susan and Vera to a Catholic convent to hide from the Nazi soldiers, Susan is shocked. Will the two Jewish girls be safe in a building full of strangers?

"Based on the experiences of her mother and aunt, Clark provides a compelling, fictionalized account documenting the courage and compassion of these nuns. . . . Black-and-white photographs and an afterword help to bring the story and history to life." SLJ

Clark, Kristin Elizabeth

★ **Freakboy**; by Kristin Elizabeth Clark. Farrar, Straus and Giroux 2013 448 p. (hardcover) $18.99
Grades: 8 9 10 11 12

1. Gender role 2. Identity (Psychology) 3. Teenagers -- Sexual behavior 4. Novels in verse 5. Schools -- Fiction 6. Wrestling -- Fiction 7. Family life -- Fiction 8. High schools -- Fiction 9. Sexual orientation --

Fiction 10. Transgender people -- Fiction
ISBN 0374324727; 9780374324728

LC 2012050407

Rainbow List (2014)

"High school wrestler Brendan likes girls "too much, / and not in / the same / way / everyone / else / does." Brendan's story weaves together with his girlfriend Vanessa's and that of transgender woman Angel in three-part verse-harmony. Each individual has a unique personality all his or her own in this sincere, profound rendering of sexuality, queerness, and identity." (Horn Book)

Clayton, Dhonielle

★ The **Belles**. Dhonielle Clayton. Freeform Books 2018 434 p. (Belles)

Grades: 9 10 11 12

1. Beauty, Personal -- Fiction; 2. Magic -- Fiction; 3. Nobility -- Fiction; 4. Teenage girls -- Fiction; 5. Personal appearance -- Fiction
1484728491; 9781484728499, $17.99

LC 2016054241

Sequel: The Everlasting Rose (2019)

In this novel, by Dhonielle Clayton, "Camellia Beauregard is a Belle. In the opulent world of Orleans, Belles are revered, for they control Beauty, and Beauty is a commodity coveted above all else. In Orleans, the people are born gray, they are born damned, and only with the help of a Belle and her talents can they transform and be made beautiful." (Publisher's note)

"With a refreshingly original concept, this substantial fantasy, the first in a duology, is an undeniable page-turner." Kirkus

Clement-Davies, David

The **sight**. Dutton Bks. 2002 465p hardcover o.p. pa $8.99

Grades: 7 8 9 10 11 12 Adult

1. Fantasy fiction 2. Wolves -- Fiction
ISBN 0-525-46723-8; 0-14-240874-3 pa

LC 2002-16572

In Transylvania during the Middle Ages, a pack of wolves sets out on a perilous journey to prevent their enemy from calling upon a legendary evil one that will give her the power to control all animals.

"The narrative is rich, complex, and most importantly, credible, but it requires a thoughtful and perceptive reader." Voice Youth Advocates

Followed by Fell (2007)

Clements, Andrew, 1949-

Things not seen. Philomel Bks. 2002 251p $15.99; pa $5.99

Grades: 7 8 9 10

1. Science fiction 2. Blind -- Fiction 3. People with disabilities
ISBN 0-399-23626-0; 0-14-240076-9 pa

LC 00-69900

When fifteen-year-old Bobby wakes up and finds himself invisible, he and his parents and his new blind friend Alicia try to find out what caused his condition and how to reverse it.

"The author spins a convincing and affecting story." Publ Wkly

Other titles in this series are:
Things hoped for (2006)
Things that are (2008)

Things that are; [by] Andrew Clements. Philomel Books 2008 224p $16.99

Grades: 7 8 9 10

1. Science fiction 2. Blind -- Fiction
ISBN 978-0-399-24691-3; 0-399-24691-6

Still adjusting to being blind, Alicia must outwit an invisible man who is putting her family and her boyfriend, who was once invisible himself, in danger.

"Clements tells a riveting tale, made all the more intriguing by the choice of narrator, who experiences and describes the world differently because she cannot see.

Clinton, Cathryn

A **stone** in my hand. Candlewick Press 2002 191p hardcover o.p. pa $6.99

Grades: 8 9 10 11

1. Family life -- Fiction 2. Palestinian Arabs -- Fiction
ISBN 0-7636-1388-6; 0-7636-4772-1 pa

LC 2001-58423

Eleven-year-old Malaak and her family are touched by the violence in Gaza between Jews and Palestinians when first her father disappears and then her older brother is drawn to the Islamic Jihad

"With a sharp eye for nuances of culture and the political situation in the Middle East, Clinton has created a rich, colorful cast of characters and created an emotionally charged novel." SLJ

Cluess, Jessica

A **poison** dark and drowning. Jessica Cluess. Random House 2017 417 p. (Kingdom on fire)

Grades: 7 8 9 10

1. Demonology -- Fiction; 2. Magic -- Fiction; 3. Great Britain -- History -- Victoria, 1837-1901 -- Fiction; 4. Demonology -- Fiction
9780553535945, $17.99; 9780553535952; 9780553535969

LC 2016043364

In this book in the Kingdom on Fire series, author "Jessica Cluess delivers her signature mix of magic, passion, and teen warriors fighting for survival. Henrietta doesn't need a prophecy to know that she's in danger. She came to London to be named the...first female sorcerer in centuries,...who would defeat the Ancients. Instead, she discovered...[that she] is not the chosen one. Still, she must play the role in order to keep herself and Rook...safe." (Publisher's note)

"As in the previous volume, Cluess keeps the action moving in the right direction. Fans will anxiously wait for the conclusion to this romantic and magical fantasy series." SLJ

Sequel to: A Shadow Bright and Burning (2016)

★ A **shadow** bright and burning. Jessica Cluess. Random House 2016 416 p. (Kingdom on fire)

Grades: 7 8 9 10

    1. Fantasy 2. Magic -- Fiction 3. Fantasy fiction
9780553535907, $17.99; 9780553535914;
9780553535921, $53.97

                              LC 2015014593

In this novel, by Jessica Cluess, "Henrietta Howel can burst into flames. Forced to reveal her power to save a friend, she's shocked when instead of being executed, she's invited to train as one of Her Majesty's royal sorcerers. Thrust into the glamour of Victorian London, Henrietta is declared the chosen one, the girl who will defeat the Ancients, bloodthirsty demons terrorizing humanity. " (Publisher's note)

"Cluess' clever prose employs Dickensian names and rolls along at a speedy and compelling clip. Expect a demand for future series titles." Booklist

Coakley, Lena

★ **Witchlanders**. Atheneum Books for Young Readers 2011 400p $16.99

Grades: 7 8 9 10 11 12

    1. War stories 2. Fantasy fiction 3. Witches -- Fiction
ISBN 978-1-4424-2004-5; 1-4424-2004-9

                              LC 2010051922

After the prediction of Ryder's mother, once a great prophet and powerful witch, comes true and their village is destroyed by a deadly assassin, Ryder embarks on a quest that takes him into the mountains in search of the destroyer.

"Plot twists unfold at a riveting pace, the boys' characters are compellingly sketched, and Coakley explores her subject matter masterfully without falling prey to safe plot choices." Publ Wkly

Coates, Jan L.

A **hare** in the elephant's trunk; [by] Jan L. Coates. Red Deer Press 2010 291p il map pa $12.95

Grades: 8 9 10 11 12

    1. Refugees -- Fiction 2. Sudan -- History -- Civil War, 1983-2005 -- Fiction
ISBN 978-0-88995-451-9

Inspired by the real life experiences of a Sudanese boy, follows Jacob Akech Deng's journey as he flees his home under the threat of war, and, guided by the memory of his mother, tries to survive in a refugee camp.

"This novel, based on the life of the real Jacob Deng, provides insight into the struggles of the Sudan as well as a strong, clear voice. Coates gives an unflinching and poetic glimpse into the life of a boy who chose hope in the face of adversity." SLJ

Coben, Harlan, 1962

Seconds away; a Mickey Bolitar novel. Harlan Coben. G. P. Putnam's Sons 2012 352 p. (hardback) $18.99

Grades: 8 9 10 11 12

    1. High schools 2. Mystery fiction 3. Adventure fiction 4. Murder -- Fiction 5. Uncles -- Fiction 6. Schools -- Fiction 7. Fiction
ISBN 9780399256516; 0399256512

                              LC 2012026728

This young adult adventure novel, by Harlan Coben, is the second book in his Mickey Bolitar series. "Mickey . . . continues to hunt for clues about the Abeona Shelter and the mysterious death of his father--all while trying to navigate the challenges of a new high school. . . . Now, not only does Mickey need to keep himself and his friends safe from the Butcher of Lodz, but he needs to figure out who shot [his classmate] Rachel." (Publisher's note)

Shelter; a Mickey Bolitar novel. G. P. Putnam's Sons 2011 304p $18.99

Grades: 8 9 10 11 12

    1. School stories 2. Mystery fiction 3. Moving -- Fiction 4. Uncles -- Fiction 5. Missing persons -- Fiction
ISBN 9780399256509

                              LC 2011009004

After tragic events tear Mickey Bolitar away from his parents, he is forced to live with his estranged Uncle Myron and switch high schools, where he finds both friends and enemies, but when his new girlfriend, Ashley, vanishes, he follows her trail into a seedy underworld that reveals she is not what she seems to be.

This is a "suspenseful, well-executed spin-off of [the author's] bestselling Myron Bolitar mystery series for adults. . . . Coben's semi-noir style translates well to YA, and the supporting cast is thoroughly entertaining." Publ Wkly

Cohen, Joshua C.

Leverage. Dutton Children's Books 2011 425p $17.99

Grades: 10 11 12

    1. School stories 2. Bullies -- Fiction 3. Football -- Fiction 4. Violence -- Fiction 5. Gymnastics -- Fiction
ISBN 978-0-525-42306-5

                              LC 2010-13472

High school sophomore Danny excels at gymnastics but is bullied, like the rest of the gymnasts, by members of the football team, until an emotionally and physically scarred new student joins the football team and forms an unlikely friendship with Danny.

"Sports fans will love Cohen's style: direct, goal oriented, and filled with sensory detail. Characters and subplots are overly abundant yet add a deepness rarely found in comparable books. Drugs, rape, language, and violence make this book serious business, but those with experience will tell you that sports is serious business, too." Booklist

Cohn, Rachel

Dash & Lily's book of dares; by Rachel Cohn & David Levithan. Alfred A. Knopf 2010 260p

Grades: 9 10 11 12

    1. Love stories 2. New York (N.Y.) -- Fiction
ISBN 9780375866593; 9780375966590 lib bdg

                              LC 2009054084

Told in the alternating voices of Dash and Lily, two sixteen-year-olds carry on a wintry scavenger hunt at Christmas-time in New York, neither knowing quite what—or who—they will find.

"Full of crisp vocabulary and diverse media and literary references, this light-hearted romance should have broad appeal." Voice Youth Advocates

Gingerbread. Simon & Schuster Bks. for Young Readers 2002 172p $15.95

Grades: 9 10 11 12
1. Parent-child relationship -- Fiction
ISBN 0-689-84337-2

LC 00-52225

After being expelled from a fancy boarding school, Cyd Charisse's problems with her mother escalate after Cyd falls in love with a sensitive surfer and is subsequently sent from San Francisco to New York City to spend time with her biological father.

"Cohn works wonders with snappy dialogue, up-to-the-minute language, and funny repartee. Her contemporary voice is tempered with humor and deals with problems across two generations. Funny and irreverent reading with teen appeal that's right on target." SLJ

Naomi and Ely's no kiss list; a novel. [by] Rachel Cohn and David Levithan. Alfred A. Knopf 2007 230p $16.99
Grades: 7 8 9 10 11 12
1. Gay teenagers -- Fiction 2. New York (N.Y.) -- Fiction 3. Dating (Social customs) -- Fiction
ISBN 978-0-375-84440-9

LC 2006-39727

Although they have been friends and neighbors all their lives, straight Naomi and gay Ely find their relationship severely strained during their freshman year at New York University.

"Even readers who long for the pair's glamorous downtown lifestyle will sympathize with the vulnerable young people living it." Bull Cent Child Books

★ **Nick** & Norah's infinite playlist; [by] Rachel Cohn & David Levithan. Knopf 2006 183p $16.95
Grades: 9 10 11 12
1. Rock musicians -- Fiction 2. New York (N.Y.) -- Fiction
ISBN 978-0-375-83531-5; 0-375-83531-8

LC 2005-12413

High school student Nick O'Leary, member of a rock band, meets college-bound Norah Silverberg and asks her to be his girlfriend for five minutes in order to avoid his ex-sweetheart.

"The would-be lovers are funny, do stupid things, doubt themselves, and teens will adore them. F-bombs are dropped throughout the book, but it works. These characters are not 'gosh' or 'shucks' people." Voice Youth Advocates

Shrimp. Simon & Schuster Books for Young Readers 2005 288p $15.95
Grades: 9 10 11 12
1. School stories
ISBN 0-689-86612-7

LC 2003-23992

Sequel to Gingerbread (2002)

Back in San Francisco for her senior year in high school, seventeen-year-old Cyd attempts to reconcile with her boyfriend, Shrimp, making some girlfriends and beginning to feel more a part of her family in the process.

"Cohn's humor is right on. . . . The joy of the book can be found in the familiar characters and meeting new ones, and this title leaves open the possibility for a third installment." SLJ

Followed by Cupcake (2007)

Cokal, Susann
★ The **Kingdom** of little wounds; Susann Cokal. Candlewick Press 2013 576 p. $22.99
Grades: 10 11 12
1. Queens -- Fiction 2. Princesses -- Fiction
ISBN 0763666947; 9780763666941

LC 2013933162

Printz Honor Book (2014)

In this book, by Susann Cokal, it's "the eve of Princess Sophia's wedding [and] the Scandinavian city of Skyggehavn prepares to fete the occasion with a sumptuous display of riches. . . . Yet beneath the . . . celebration, a shiver of darkness creeps through the palace halls. . . . When [the] . . . prick of a needle sets off a series of events that will alter the course of history, the fates of seamstress Ava Bingen and mute nursemaid Midi Sorte become . . . intertwined with that of mad Queen Isabel." (Publisher's note)

"Despite the challenging content, the book's lyrical writing, enthralling characters, and compelling plot will give older readers lots to ponder." Booklist

Coker, Rachel, 1997-
Chasing Jupiter; Rachel Coker. Zondervan 2012 224 p. $15.99
Grades: 9 10
1. Faith -- Fiction 2. Autism -- Fiction 3. Brothers and sisters -- Fiction 4. Farm life -- Georgia -- Fiction 5. Moneymaking projects -- Fiction 6. Family life -- Georgia -- Fiction 7. Georgia -- History -- 20th century -- Fiction
ISBN 031073293X; 9780310732938

LC 2012051600

In this book, "16-year-old Scarlett Blaine . . . struggles to be the perfect family member and caregiver for her autistic younger brother, Cliff. . . . When Cliff sees Neil Armstrong's Moon walk, he wants to fly to Jupiter and enlists Scarlett and Frank, the local peach farmer's son, to help build a rocket. Scarlett loves Frank, but his crush on her free-spirited, older sister and her parents' fighting leave the teen wondering how to cope with a world turned upside down." (School Library Journal)

Colbert, Brandy
★ **Little** & Lion. By Brandy Colbert. Little, Brown & Co. 2017 336 p.
Grades: 9 10 11 12
1. Bisexuality -- Fiction; 2. Brothers and sisters -- Fiction; 3. Dating (Social customs) -- Fiction; 4. Family life -- California -- Fiction; 5. Manic-depressive illness -- Fiction; 6. Mental illness -- Fiction; 7. California -- Fiction
9780316349000, $17.99

LC 2016019838

Stonewall Book Award: Children's & Young Adult Literature (2018)

In this novel, by Brandy Colbert, "when Suzette comes home to Los Angeles from her boarding school in New England, she isn't sure if she'll ever want to go back.... Her stepbrother, Lionel, who has been diagnosed with bipolar disorder, needs her emotional support.... When Lionel's disorder spirals out of control, Suzette is forced to confront her past mistakes and find a way to help her brother before he hurts himself -- or worse." (Publisher's note)

"One of many notable strengths here is Colbert's subtle, neatly interwoven exploration of intersectionality: Lion is desperate to be defined by something other than his bipolar disorder, and Suzette learns to navigate key elements of her identity -- black, Jewish, bisexual -- in a world that seems to want her to be only one thing. This superbly written novel teems with meaningful depth, which is perfectly balanced by romance and the languid freedom of summer." (Booklist)

Cole, Brock

The **goats**; written and illustrated by Brock Cole. Farrar, Straus & Giroux 1987 184p il hardcover o.p. pa $5.99

Grades: 7 8 9 10

1. Camps -- Fiction 2. Friendship -- Fiction
ISBN 0-374-32678-9; 0-374-42575-2 pa

LC 87-45362

Stripped and marooned on a small island by their fellow campers, a boy and a girl form an uneasy bond that grows into a deep friendship when they decide to run away and disappear without a trace.

"This is an unflinching book, and there is a quality of raw emotion that may score some discomfort among adults. Such a first novel restores faith in the cultivation of children's literature." Bull Cent Child Books

Cole, Kresley

Poison princess; Kresley Cole. 1st ed. Simon & Schuster Books For Young Readers 2012 369 p. (hardcover) $18.99

Grades: 9 10 11 12

1. Love stories 2. Occult fiction 3. Tarot -- Fiction 4. Ability -- Fiction 5. Prophecies -- Fiction 6. Supernatural -- Fiction
ISBN 9781442436640; 1442436646; 9781442436664

LC 2012000919

This paranormal romance novel, by Kresley Cole, is book one in the "Arcana Chronicles" series. "When an apocalyptic event decimates her Louisiana hometown, Evie realizes her hallucinations were actually visions of the future--and they're still happening. . . . An ancient prophesy is being played out, and Evie is not the only one with special powers. A group of twenty-two teens has been chosen to reenact the ultimate battle between good and evil." (Publisher's note)

Coles, Jay

Tyler Johnson was here. Jay Coles. Little, Brown & Co. 2018 304 p.

Grades: 9 10 11 12

1. African Americans -- Fiction; 2. Brothers -- Fiction; 3. Death -- Fiction; 4. Grief -- Fiction; 5. Police shootings -- Fiction; 6. Racism -- Fiction; 7. Single-parent families -- Fiction; 8. Twins -- Fiction
9780316440776, $17.99

LC 2017027423

In this novel, by Jay Coles, "when Marvin Johnson's twin, Tyler, goes to a party, Marvin decides to tag along to keep an eye on his brother. But what starts as harmless fun turns into a shooting, followed by a police raid. The next day, Tyler has gone missing, and it's up to Marvin to find him. But when Tyler is found dead, a video leaked online tells an even more chilling story: Tyler has been shot and killed by a police officer." (Publisher's note)

Colfer, Eoin, 1965-

★ **Airman**; [by] Eoin Colfer. Hyperion Books for Children 2008 412p $17.99; pa $7.99

Grades: 5 6 7 8 9

1. Adventure fiction 2. Airplanes -- Fiction 3. Inventors -- Fiction 4. Prisoners -- Fiction
ISBN 978-1-4231-0750-7; 1-4231-0750-0; 978-1-4231-0751-4 pa; 1-4231-0751-9 pa

LC 2007-38415

In the late nineteenth century, when Conor Broekhart discovers a conspiracy to overthrow the king, he is branded a traitor, imprisoned, and forced to mine for diamonds under brutal conditions while he plans a daring escape from Little Saltee prison by way of a flying machine that he must design, build, and, hardest of all, trust to carry him to safety.

This is "polished, sophisticated storytelling. . . . A tour de force." Publ Wkly

Collins, Pat Lowery

Hidden voices; the orphan musicians of Venice. Candlewick Press 2009 345p $17.99

Grades: 8 9 10 11 12

1. Composers 2. Violinists 3. Orphans -- Fiction 4. Musicians -- Fiction 5. Venice (Italy) -- Fiction
ISBN 978-0-7636-3917-4; 0-7636-3917-6

LC 2008-18762

Anetta, Rosalba, and Luisa, find their lives taking unexpected paths while growing up in eighteenth century Venice at the orphanage Ospedale della Pieta, where concerts are given to support the orphanage as well as expose the girls to potential suitors.

"Collins's descriptive prose makes Venice and a unique slice of history come alive as the three connecting narrative strains create a rich story of friendship and self-realization." SLJ

Collins, Suzanne, 1962-

Catching fire. Scholastic Press 2009 391p $17.99

Grades: 7 8 9 10

1. Science fiction 2. Survival -- Fiction 3. Dystopian fiction
ISBN 978-0-439-02349-8; 0-439-02349-1

LC 2008-50493

Sequel to: Hunger Games (2008)

This dystopian young adult novel, volume 2 of the Hunger Games trilogy, takes place after a televised, state-sponsored duel known as the Hunger Games. "Katniss Everdeen has won . . . with fellow district tribute Peeta Mellark. But it was a victory won by defiance of the Capitol and their harsh rules. Katniss and Peeta should be happy. After all, they have just won for themselves and their families a life of safety and plenty. But there are rumors of rebellion among the subjects, and Katniss and Peeta, to their horror, are the faces of that rebellion." (Publisher's note)

"Beyond the expert world building, the acute social commentary and the large cast of fully realized characters, there's action, intrigue, romance and some amount of hope in a story readers will find completely engrossing." Kirkus

Followed by: Mockingjay (2010)

★ The **Hunger** Games. Scholastic Press 2008 374p $17.99; pa $8.99

Grades: 7 8 9 10

    1. Science fiction   2. Survival -- Fiction   3. Dystopian fiction

ISBN 978-0-439-02348-1; 0-439-02348-3; 978-0-439-02352-8 pa; 0-439-02352-1 pa

                                   LC 2007-39987

In this dystopian young adult novel, "in the ruins of a place once known as North America lies the nation of Panem, a shining Capitol surrounded by twelve outlaying districts. The Capitol . . . keeps the districts in line by forcing them all to send one girl and one boy between the ages of twelve and eighteen to participate in the annual Hunger Games, a fight to the death on live TV. Sixteen-year-old Katniss Everdeen . . . regards it as a death sentence when she is forced to represent her district in the Games." (Publisher's note)

"Collins's characters are completely realistic and sympathetic. . . . The plot is tense, dramatic, and engrossing." SLJ

Mockingjay. Scholastic Press 2010 390p (Hunger Games) $17.99

Grades: 7 8 9 10

    1. Science fiction   2. Survival -- Fiction   3. Dystopian fiction

ISBN 978-0-439-02351-1; 0-439-02351-3

                                   LC 2008-50493

Sequel to: Catching fire (2009)

This dystopian novel, volume 3 of the Hunger Games trilogy, takes place after heroine Katniss Everdeen has "survived the Hunger Games twice. But now that she's made it out of the bloody arena alive, she's still not safe. . . . The Capitol wants revenge. Who do they think should pay for the unrest? Katniss. And what's worse, President Snow has made it clear that no one else is safe either. Not Katniss's family, not her friends, not the people of District 12." (Publisher's note)

"This concluding volume in Collins's Hunger Games trilogy accomplishes a rare feat, the last installment being the best yet, a beautifully orchestrated and intelligent novel that succeeds on every level." Publ Wkly

Combres, Elisabeth

Broken memory; a novel of Rwanda. translated by Shelley Tanaka. Groundwood Books/House of Anansi Press 2009 139p $17.95

Grades: 6 7 8 9 10

    1. Rwanda -- Fiction 2. Orphans -- Fiction 3. Genocide -- Fiction 4. Hutu (African people) -- Fiction 5. Tutsi (African people) -- Fiction

ISBN 978-0-88899-892-7; 0-88899-892-9

Original French edition, 2007

"This is a quiet, reflective story; neither laden with detail nor full of historical descriptions, it is simply one girl's horrific tale of personal tragedy. . . . Combres' story offers readers intimate access to this chapter of history as well as considerable potential for discussion." Bull Cent Child Books

Combs, Sarah

Breakfast served anytime. Sarah Combs. Candlewick Press. 2014 272p $16.99

Grades: 7 8 9 10 11 12

    1. Bildungsromans   2. Gifted children -- Fiction   3. Kentucky —Fiction   4. Camps -- Fiction

ISBN: 0763667919; 9780763667917

                                   LC 2013944002

In this book, by Sarah Combs, "when Gloria sets out to spend the summer before her senior year at a camp for gifted and talented students, she doesn't know quite what to expect. Fresh from the heartache of losing her grandmother and missing her best friend, Gloria resolves to make the best of her new circumstances. But some things are proving to be more challenging than she expected." (Publisher's note)

"At a summer college program in Kentucky, a classroom of gifted students studying "The Secrets of the Written Word" grapples with life's big questions. Mercurial, dreamy, and verbose, protagonist Gloria narrates with intellectual enthusiasm and attention to emotional detail. Although the plot meanders, Gloria's open, genuine voice carries this debut novel to the end of a life-changing summer." Horn Book

Conaghan, Brian

When Mr. Dog bites. Brian Conaghan. Bloomsbury 2014 368 p.

Grades: 10 11 12

    1. Family life -- England -- Fiction 2. Interpersonal relations -- Fiction 3. Schools -- Fiction 4. Terminally ill -- Fiction 5. Tourette syndrome -- Fiction 6. England -- Fiction 7. School stories 8. Family life -- Fiction

1619633469; 9781619633469, $17.99

                                   LC 2013044567

In this book, by Brian Conaghan, "[a]ll Dylan Mint has ever wanted is to keep his Tourette's in check and live life as a 'normal' teenager. The swearing, the tics, the howling 'dog' that escapes when things are at their worst. . . . But a routine hospital visit changes everything-Dylan overhears that he's going to die. In an attempt to claim the life he's always wanted, he decides to grant himself parting wishes." (Publisher's note)

"Dylan's habitual use of Cockney slang may make for a tough reading experiencing for American teenagers, but Dylan is smart and caring, and beneath his realistically portrayed condition, he is a normal teenager with relatable concerns. As Dylan would say, this one is 'A-mayonnaise-ing.'" Booklist

First published in Great Britain in January 2014 by Bloomsbury Publishing Plc.

Condie, Ally

Crossed; Ally Condie. Dutton Books 2011 367p map $17.99

Grades: 7 8 9 10

    1. Fantasy fiction   2. Resistance to government -- Fiction

ISBN 978-0-525-42365-2; 0-525-42365-6

                                   LC 2011016442

Sequel to: Matched (2010)

Seventeen-year-old Cassia sacrifices everything and heads to the Outer Provinces in search of Ky, where she is confronted with shocking revelations about Society and the promise of rebellion.

"Newcomers will need to read the first book for background, but vivid, poetic writing will pull fans through as Condie immerses readers in her characters' yearnings and hopes." Publ Wkly

Matched; Ally Condie. Dutton Books 2010 369p $17.99
Grades: 7 8 9 10
    1. Fantasy fiction
    ISBN 978-0-525-42364-5; 0-525-42364-8

All her life, Cassia has never had a choice. The Society dictates everything: when and how to play, where to work, where to live, what to eat and wear, when to die, and most importantly to Cassia as she turns 17, who to marry. When she is Matched with her best friend Xander, things couldn't be more perfect. But why did her neighbor Ky's face show up on her match disk as well?

"Condie's enthralling and twisty dystopian plot is well served by her intriguing characters and fine writing. While the ending is unresolved . . . , Cassia's metamorphosis is gripping and satisfying." Publ Wkly

Followed by: Crossed (2011)

Reached; Ally Condie. Dutton 2012 512 p. (Matched trilogy) (hardcover) $17.99
Grades: 7 8 9 10
    1. Epidemics -- Fiction 2. Resistance to government -- Fiction 3. Government, Resistance to -- Fiction
    ISBN 9780525423669; 0525423664
                              LC 2012031916

"This final story in the 'Matched' trilogy finds Cassia, Ky, and Xander all working for the Rising, but in different locations and for different reasons. The Rising has introduced a plague into the cities for which they have the cure. They are easily able to take control as they cure people. An unexpected mutation of the illness catches the Rising off guard, and the Pilot (the Rising's leader) realizes he could quickly lose all that has been gained." (Voice of Youth Advocates)

Connelly, Neil O.

Into the hurricane. Neil Connelly. Arthur A. Levine Books, an imprint of Scholastic inc. 2017 228 p.
Grades: 7 8 9 10
    1. Friendship -- Fiction; 2. Hurricanes -- Fiction; 3. Interpersonal relations -- Fiction; 4. Suicide -- Fiction; 5. Survival -- Fiction; 6. Louisiana -- Fiction
    9780545853873; 9780545853811, $17.99
                              LC 2017009604

In this book, by Neil Connelly, "Eli and Max both have good reasons to go to the lighthouse on Shackles Island. For Max, it's...the right place to scatter her dad's ashes. For Eli, it...[has] the clearest view of the rocks where his sister died -- so it's the right place to end his own life as well. But neither of them expected the other, nor the storm." (Publisher's note)

Connor, Leslie

The **things** you kiss goodbye. Leslie Connor. Katherine Tegen Books, an imprint of HarperCollinsPublishers 2014 368 p.
Grades: 9 10 11 12
    1. Dating violence -- Fiction 2. Greek Americans -- Fiction 3. Love -- Fiction 4. Abused women -- Fiction 5. Romance fiction 6. Teenage girls -- Fiction
    0060890916; 9780060890919, $17.99
                              LC 2013043191

In this teen novel, by Leslie Connor, "Bettina falls in love . . . , but when school starts up again, Brady unexpectedly changes for the worse. Unable to give up on her first love just yet, she finds herself trapped in an abusive relationship. Then she meets . . . a smoldering older guy. . . . Yet he is everything Brady is not. . . . When tragedy strikes, Bettina must tell her family the truth—and kiss goodbye the things she thought she knew about herself and the men in her life." (Publisher's note)

" Connor lets the story, and Bettina's realization of the situation, play out slowly, a choice that adds multiple subplots but also deepens characterization and elevates the book above simple problem-novel territory. Bettina begins finding herself through her art; her ensuing pride in her work is convincingly portrayed. A melodramatic ending and tendency to tie up all plot threads are somewhat distracting, but Bettina's situation creates much food for thought." Horn Book

Cook, Eileen

★ **With** malice. By Eileen Cook. Houghton Mifflin Harcourt 2016 320 p.
Grades: 9 10 11 12
    1. Accidents -- Fiction 2. Amnesia -- Fiction 3. Best friends -- Fiction 4. Friendship -- Fiction 5. Mystery and detective stories 6. Italy -- Fiction
    9780544805095, $17.99; 9780544829305, $17.99
                              LC 2015039039

In this novel by Eileen Cook, "eighteen-year-old Jill Charron's senior trip to Italy was supposed to be the adventure of a lifetime. And then the accident happened. Waking up in a hospital room, . . . Jill comes to discover she was involved in a fatal accident in her travels abroad. . . . Wondering not just what happened but what she did, Jill tries to piece together the events of the past six weeks before she loses her thin hold on her once-perfect life." (Publisher's note)

"Cook (Remember) believably portrays the struggles of girl who had it all and is left to pick up the pieces of a life she isn't sure is hers." Pub Wkly

Cook, Trish

A **really** awesome mess; Trish Cook and Brendan Halpin. Egmont USA 2013 288 p. (hardcover) $17.99
Grades: 9 10 11 12
    1. Private schools -- Fiction 2. Chinese Americans -- Fiction 3. Emotionally disturbed children -- Fiction 4. Schools -- Fiction 5. Psychotherapy -- Fiction 6. Boarding schools -- Fiction 7. Emotional problems -- Fiction
    ISBN 160684363X; 9781606843635
                              LC 2012045978

In this book, "a group of teens at a live-in institution for troubled young people bond, pull off a caper and overcome their issues. . . . Emmy, adopted from China by white parents, feels out of place and unwanted in her family. She is sent to Heartland Academy after retaliating against a tormentor at school. . . . Justin, who resents his father's absence, comes to Heartland following a suicide attempt and after being caught receiving oral sex from a girl he met earlier that day." (Kirkus Reviews)

"Having found themselves at Heartland Academy, a reform school for troubled youth, Justin, Emmy, and a band of misfit teens attempt to sneak out for one really awesome night of fun and adventure. With Eleanor & Park-esque protagonists and a cast reminiscent of Girl, Interrupted, this is a satisfying story about trauma and laughter, and the power of friendship." (Horn Book)

Cooney, Caroline B., 1947-

Code orange. Delacorte 2005 200p hardcover o.p. pa $6.99

Grades: 7 8 9 10

1. School stories 2. Smallpox -- Fiction 3. New York (N.Y.) -- Fiction
ISBN 0-385-90277-8; 0-385-73260-0 pa
LC 2004-26422

While conducting research for a school paper on smallpox, Mitty finds an envelope containing 100-year-old smallpox scabs and fears that he has infected himself and all of New York City.

"Readers won't soon forget either the profoundly disturbing premise of this page-turner or its likable, ultimately heroic slacker protagonist." Booklist

Diamonds in the shadow. Delacorte Press 2007 228p $15.99; pa $8.99

Grades: 7 8 9 10 11 12

1. Refugees -- Fiction 2. Connecticut -- Fiction 3. Family life -- Fiction 4. Africans -- United States -- Fiction
ISBN 978-0-385-73261-1; 978-0-385-73262-8 pa
LC 2006-27811

The Finches, a Connecticut family, sponsor an African refugee family of four, all of whom have been scarred by the horrors of civil war, and who inadvertently put their benefactors in harm's way.

"Tension mounts in a novel that combines thrilling suspense and a story about innocence lost." Booklist

The **face** on the milk carton. Delacorte Press 2006 184p $15.95; pa $6.99

Grades: 7 8 9 10

1. Kidnapping -- Fiction
ISBN 978-0-385-32328-4; 0-385-32328-X; 978-0-440-22065-7 pa; 0-440-22065-3 pa

A photograph of a missing girl on a milk carton leads Janie on a search for her real identity.

Cooney "demonstrates an excellent ear for dialogue and a gift for portraying responsible middle-class teenagers trying to come to terms with very real concerns." SLJ

A reissue of the title first published 1990 by Bantam Books

If the witness lied. Delacorte Press 2009 213p $16.99; lib bdg $19.99

Grades: 6 7 8 9 10

1. Orphans -- Fiction 2. Siblings -- Fiction 3. Bereavement -- Fiction 4. Connecticut -- Fiction
ISBN 978-0-385-73448-6; 0-385-73448-4; 978-0-385-90451-3 lib bdg; 0-385-90451-7 lib bdg
LC 2008-23959

Torn apart by tragedies and the publicity they brought, siblings Smithy, Jack, and Madison, aged fourteen to sixteen, tap into their parent's courage to pull together and protect their brother Tris, nearly three, from further media exploitation and a much more sinister threat.

"The pacing here is pure gold. Rotating through various perspectives to follow several plot strands . . . Cooney draws out the action, investing it with the slow-motion feel of an impending collision. . . . This family-drama-turned-thriller will have readers racing, heart in throat, to reach the conclusion." Horn Book

Janie face to face; Caroline B. Cooney. Delacorte Press 2013 352 p. (Janie Johnson) (ebk) $20.99; (trade hardcover) $17.99

Grades: 7 8 9 10

1. Love stories 2. Kidnapping -- Fiction 3. Family life -- Fiction 4. Love -- Fiction 5. Identity -- Fiction 6. Authorship -- Fiction 7. New York (N.Y.) -- Fiction 8. Universities and colleges -- Fiction
ISBN 0385742061; 9780375979972; 9780375990397; 9780385742061
LC 2012006145

This book, by Caroline B. Cooney, is the conclusion to the "Janie Johnson" series which begun in 1990. "All will be revealed as readers find out if Janie and Reeve's love has endured, and whether or not the person who brought Janie and her family so much emotional pain and suffering is brought to justice." (Publisher's note)

The **voice** on the radio. Delacorte Press 1996 183p hardcover o.p. pa $6.99

Grades: 7 8 9 10

1. Radio programs -- Fiction
ISBN 0-385-32213-5; 0-440-21977-9 pa
LC 96-3688

"Janie is a high-school junior and in love with Reeve. She finally feels that her life is somewhat normal and begins to reconcile with her biological family, but the voice on the radio destroys her trust. Cooney plots an engaging and realistic picture of betrayal, commitment, unconditional love, and forgiveness." ALAN

What Janie found. Delacorte Press 2000 181p pa $6.99

Grades: 7 8 9 10

1. Kidnapping -- Fiction 2. Parent-child relationship -- Fiction
ISBN 0-385-32611-4; 0-440-22772-0 pa
LC 99-37409

While still adjusting to the reality of having two families, her birth family and the family into which she was kidnapped as a small child, seventeen-year-old Janie makes a shocking discovery about her long-gone kidnapper

"Readers of the previous books will find this a satisfying closure to the unsettling circumstances of Janie's life." Booklist

Whatever happened to Janie? Delacorte Press 1993 199p hardcover o.p. pa $6.99
Grades: 7 8 9 10
    1. Kidnapping -- Fiction
    ISBN 0-385-31035-8; 0-440-21924-8 pa
                       LC 92-32334
The members of two families have their lives disrupted when Jane who had been kidnapped twelve years earlier discovers that the people who raised her are not her biological parents
"However strange the events of this book, the emotions of its characters remain excruciatingly real." Publ Wkly

Cooper, Susan
   ★ **Over** sea, under stone; illustrated by Margery Gill. Harcourt Brace Jovanovich 1966 252p il $19; pa $5.99
Grades: 5 6 7 8
    1. Fantasy fiction 2. Good and evil -- Fiction
    ISBN 0-15-259034-X; 0-689-84035-7 pa
    First published 1965 in the United Kingdom
Three children on a holiday in Cornwall find an ancient manuscript which sends them on a dangerous quest for a grail that would reveal the true story of King Arthur and that entraps them in the eternal battle between the forces of the Light and the forces of the Dark.
"The air of mysticism and the allegorical quality of the continual contest between good and evil add much value to a fine plot, setting, and characterization." Horn Book
    Other titles in this series are:
    The dark is rising (1973)
    Greenwitch (1974)
    The grey king (1975)
    Silver on the tree (1977)

Cooper, T.
   Changers book one: Drew; by T. Cooper and Allison Glock-Cooper. Black Sheep/Akashic Books. 2014 285p il $11.95
Grades: 7 8 9 10 11 12
    1. Science fiction 2. High school students --Fiction 3. Identity (Psychology) --Fiction 4. Fantasy fiction
    ISBN: 1617751952; 9781617751950; 9781617752070
    9781617752117
                   LC 2013938807
"Ethan wakes up on his first day of high school to discover that he is no longer the same person he was when he went to sleep overnight he was transformed into a beautiful girl. His parents inform him that his father was a Changer and that this is the first of four transformations. He will experience each year of high school in a new body, and at the end of his senior year, he will get to choose which body he will live in for the rest of his life...By the end of this book, readers will be invested in this character and will want to know what Ethan's future holds and how he will physically and emotionally transform over the next installments." SLJ

Córdova, Zoraida
   Labyrinth lost. Zoraida Cordova. Sourcebooks Fire 2016 336 p. Map
Grades: 9 10 11 12
    1. Families -- Fiction 2. Hispanic Americans -- Fiction 3. Magic -- Fiction 4. Supernatural -- Fiction 5. Witches -- Fiction 6. Latinos (U.S.) -- Fiction
    9781492620945, $17.99; 9781492620952, $9.99
                   LC 2016000723
In this book, part of the Brooklyn Brujas series by Zoraida Cordova, "Alex is a bruja, the most powerful witch in a generation . . . and she hates magic. At her Deathday celebration, Alex performs a spell to rid herself of her power. But it backfires. Her whole family vanishes into thin air, leaving her alone with Nova, a brujo boy she can't trust. . . . The only way to get her family back is to travel with Nova to Los Lagos." (Publisher's note)
"A compelling must-have for teens." SLJ

Cormier, Robert
   ★ **After** the first death. Dell Publishing 1991 233p pa $6.50
Grades: 7 8 9 10
    1. Terrorism -- Fiction
    ISBN 0-440-20835-1
    First published 1979 by Pantheon Bks.
    ALA YALSA Margaret A. Edwards Award (1991)
"A busload of children is hijacked by a band of terrorists whose demands include the exposure of a military brainwashing project. The narrative line moves from the teenage terrorist Milo to Kate the bus driver and the involvement of Ben, whose father is the head of the military operation, in this confrontation. The conclusion has a shocking twist." Shapiro. Fic for Youth. 2d editionp

   Beyond the chocolate war; a novel. Dell 1986 278p pa $6.99
Grades: 9 10 11 12
    1. School stories
    ISBN 0-440-90580-X
    First published 1985
Dark deeds continue at Trinity High School, climaxing in a public demonstration of one student's homemade guillotine. Sequel to "The Chocolate War."

   ★ The **chocolate** war; a novel. Pantheon Bks. 1974 253p rpt $8.99; $19.95
Grades: 7 8 9 10
    1. School stories
    ISBN 9780375829871 rpt; 0-394-82805-4
    ALA YALSA Margaret A. Edwards Award (1991)
"In the Trinity School for Boys the environment is completely dominated by an underground gang, the Vigils. During a chocolate candy sale Brother Leon, the acting headmaster of the school, defers to the Vigils, who reign with terror in the school. Jerry Renault is first a pawn for the Vigils' evil deeds and finally their victim." Shapiro. Fic for Youth. 3d edition
    Followed by Beyond the chocolate war (1985)

   ★ **I** am the cheese; a novel. Pantheon Bks. 1977 233p hardcover o.p. pa $6.50

Grades: 7 8 9 10 11 12
  1. Intelligence service -- Fiction
  ISBN 0-394-83462-3; 0-440-94060-5 pa
LC 76-55948
ALA YALSA Margaret A. Edwards Award (1991)
Adam Farmer's mind has blanked out; his past is revealed in bits and pieces—partly by Adam himself, partly through a transcription of Adam's interviews with a government psychiatrist. Adam's father, a newspaper reporter, gave evidence at the trial of a criminal organization which had infiltrated the government itself. He and his family, marked for death, came under the protection of the super-secret Department of Re-Identification, which changed the family's name and kept them under constant surveillance. Now an adolescent, Adam is finally let in on his parents' terrible secret." SLJ

"The suspense builds relentlessly to an ending that, although shocking, is entirely plausible." Booklist

Cornwell, Betsy

Mechanica. Betsy Cornwell. Houghton Mifflin Harcourt 2016 320 p.
Grades: 5 6 7 8 9 10
  1. Fairy tales 2. Inventions -- Fiction 3. Magic -- Fiction 4. Inventors -- Fiction 5. Fractured fairy tales
  0544668685; 9780544668683, $8.99
LC 2015001336
This young adult novel, by Betsy Cornwell, is a retelling of the story of Cinderella. "Nicolette's awful stepsisters call her 'Mechanica.' . . . When she discovers a secret workshop in the cellar on her sixteenth birthday—and befriends Jules, a tiny magical metal horse—Nicolette starts to imagine a new life for herself. . . . Determined to invent her own happily-ever-after, Mechanica seeks to wow the prince and eager entrepreneurs alike." (Publisher's note)

"Though the premise will beg comparisons to Marissa Meyer's Cinder (2011), Nick and her friends travel a very different journey, sidestepping typical romantic structures to find their own way. A smart, refreshing alternative to stale genre tropes." Kirkus

Tides; by Betsy Cornwell. Clarion Books 2013 304 p. (hardcover) $16.99
Grades: 7 8 9 10 11 12
  1. Love stories 2. Selkies -- Fiction 3. Internship programs -- Fiction 4. Love -- Fiction 5. Isles of Shoals (Me. and N.H.) -- Fiction
  ISBN 054792772X; 9780547927725
LC 2012022415
In this teen novel, by Betsy Cornwell, "high school senior Noah Gallagher and his adopted teenage sister, Lo, go to live with their grandmother in her island cottage for the summer. . . . Noah has landed a marine biology internship, and Lo wants to draw and paint, perhaps even to vanquish her struggles with bulimia. But then things take a dramatic turn for them both when Noah mistakenly tries to save a mysterious girl from drowning." (Publisher's note)

Venturess. Betsy Cornwell. Clarion Books/ Houghton Mifflin Harcourt 2017 311 p.

Grades: 5 6 7 8 9 10
  1. Fairy tales; 2. Inventors -- Fiction; 3. Magic -- Fiction
  9780544319271, $17.99; 9780544319295
LC 2016032623
In this book, by Betsy Cornwell, "inventor Nicolette Lampton is living her own fairy-tale happy ending. She's free of her horrible stepfamily, running a successful business, and is uninterested in marrying the handsome prince, Fin. Instead, she, Fin, and their friend Caro venture to the lush land of Faerie, where they seek to put an end to the bloody war their kingdom is waging." (Publisher's note)

"This unexpected sequel hits a sweet spot for fairy tale and steampunk lovers alike." Booklist
  Sequel to: Mechanica (2015)

Corthron, Kara Lee

★ The **truth** of right now. Kara Lee Corthron. Simon Pulse 2017 279 p.
Grades: 9 10 11 12
  1. Families -- Fiction; 2. Romance fiction; 3. Interracial dating -- Fiction; 4. Friendship -- Fiction
  9781481459471, $17.99; 9781481459488; 9781481459495
LC 2016018605
In this novel, by Kara Lee Corthron, "Lily is returning to her privileged Manhattan high school after a harrowing end to her sophomore year and it's not pretty.... Enter Dari (short for Dariomauritius), the artistic and mysterious transfer student, adept at cutting class.... Dari is everything that Lily needs: bright, creative, honest, and unpredictable.... When tragedy becomes reality, can friendship survive even if romance cannot?" (Publisher's note)

"A powerhouse of storytelling that feels timely and timeless." Kirkus

Cosimano, Elle

Holding Smoke. Elle Cosimano. Disney-Hyperion 2016 336 p.
Grades: 9 10 11 12
  1. Juvenile detention homes -- Fiction 2. Supernatural -- Fiction 3. Paranormal fiction -- Fiction
  9781484725979, $17.99; 9781484728147; 9781484729007, $17.99
LC 2015030628
In this novel by Elle Cosimano, "John 'Smoke' Conlan is serving time for two murders—but he wasn't the one who murdered his English teacher, and he never intended to kill the only other witness to the crime. . . . After a near death experience leaves him with the ability to shed his physical body at will, Smoke is able to travel freely outside the concrete walls of the Y, gathering information for himself and his fellow inmates while they're asleep in their beds." (Publisher's note)

"As in many prison dramas, the difference between good guys and bad guys isn't set in stone; Smoke is a complicated, sympathetic character, and his redemption feels earned." Booklist

Coulthurst, Audrey

★ **Of** Fire and Stars. By Audrey Coulthurst, illustrated by Jordan Saia. Harpercollins Childrens Books 2016 400 p. Illustration; Map

Grades: 8 9 10 11

1. Princesses -- Fiction 2. Man-woman relationships -- Fiction 3. Fire -- Fiction 4. Magic -- Fiction
0062433253; 9780062433251, $17.99; 9780062433275, $16.99

In this book, by Audrey Coulthurst, illustrated by Jordan Saia, Princess Dennaleia, "betrothed since childhood to the prince of Mynaria, . . . has always known what her future holds. Her marriage will seal the alliance between Mynaria and her homeland, protecting her people from other hostile kingdoms. But Denna has a secret. She possesses an Affinity for fire—a dangerous gift for the future queen of a land where magic is forbidden." (Publisher's note)

"A worthy debut that succeeds as both an adventure and a romance." Booklist

Cousins, Dave

Waiting for Gonzo. Dave Cousins. Flux 2015 288 p.

Grades: 7 8 9 10

1. Brothers and sisters -- Fiction 2. Family life -- England -- Fiction 3. High schools -- Fiction 4. Moving, Household -- Fiction 5. Practical jokes -- Fiction 6. Pregnancy -- Fiction 7. Schools -- Fiction 8. England -- Fiction 9. Family life -- Fiction 10. Moving -- Fiction
073874199X; 9780738741994, $9.99

LC 2014031277

In this book, by Dave Cousins, "[t]hings could be going better for Oz. He's just moved miles from all his friends. A prank at his new school puts him in the crosshairs of 'Psycho' Isobel Skinner, a bully who also happens to be his mum's new best friend. And he's driven off the only other kid who will have anything to do with him: a Tolkien-obsessed boy in desperate need of a decent playlist." (Publisher's note)

"In a darkly comic story written as Marcus's monologue to his unborn nephew (whom he nicknames Gonzo), Cousins (15 Days Without a Head) offers a vibrant, highly visual account of teen angst and backfiring schemes. Marcus makes more than a few mistakes at school and at home, but readers will never doubt that his heart is in the right place." Publishers Weekly

Originally published by Oxford University Press, Oxford, UK, 2013.

Coventry, Susan

The **queen's** daughter. Henry Holt and Company 2010 373p map $16.99

Grades: 8 9 10 11 12

1. Queens 2. Princesses -- Fiction 3. Middle Ages -- Fiction 4. Sicily (Italy) -- Fiction 5. Great Britain -- History -- 1154-1399, Plantagenets -- Fiction
ISBN 978-0-8050-8992-9; 0-8050-8992-6

LC 2009-24154

A fictionalized biography of Joan of England, the youngest child of King Henry II of England and his queen consort, Eleanor of Aquitaine, chronicling her complicated relationships with her warring parents and many siblings, particularly with her favorite brother Richard the Lionheart, her years as Queen consort of Sicily, and her second marriage to Raymond VI, Count of Toulouse.

"Fans of historical fiction, and especially historical romance, will devour this volume." SLJ

Cowan, Jennifer

★ **Earthgirl**. Groundwood Books 2009 232p $17.95

Grades: 8 9 10 11 12

1. Weblogs -- Fiction 2. Environmental movement -- Fiction
ISBN 978-0-88899-889-7; 0-88899-889-9

Sabine Solomon undergoes a transformation when she joins the environmental movement and becomes involved with activist Vray Foret, but when his activities involve something that is potentially illegal, she begins to question her identity and values.

This "novel with enormous teen appeal will inspire readers to question Sabine's tactics and their own impact on the earth." Kirkus

Cox, Suzy

The **Dead** Girls Detective Agency; Suzy Cox. Harper 2012 355 p. (trade bdg.) $9.99

Grades: 7 8 9 10

1. Future life 2. Ghost stories 3. Mystery fiction 4. Dead -- Fiction 5. Murder -- Fiction 6. New York (N.Y.) -- Fiction 7. Mystery and detective stories
ISBN 0-06-202064-1; 9780062020642

LC 2012006567

This novel, by Suzy Cox, follows the ghost of a teenager seeking to solve her own murder. "Meet the Dead Girls Detective Agency: Nancy, Lorna, and Tess--not to mention Edison, the really cute if slightly hostile dead boy. Apparently, the only way out of this limbo is to figure out who killed me, or I'll have to spend eternity playing Nancy Drew. Considering I was fairly invisible in life, who could hate me enough to want me dead? And what if my murderer is someone I never would have suspected?" (Publisher's note)

Coyle, Katie

Vivian Apple at the end of the world. By Katie Coyle. Houghton Mifflin Harcourt 2015 272 p.

Grades: 9 10 11 12

1. Coming of age -- Fiction 2. End of the world -- Fiction 3. Fundamentalism -- Fiction 4. Religion -- Fiction 5. Bildungsromans 6. Christian fundamentalism -- Fiction
0544340116; 9780544340114, $17.99

LC 2013050206

In this book, "seventeen-year-old Vivian Apple never believed in the evangelical Church of America, unlike her recently devout parents. But when Vivian returns home the night after the supposed 'Rapture,' all that's left of her parents are two holes in the roof. Suddenly, she doesn't know who or what to believe. With her best friend Harp and a mysterious ally, Peter, Vivian embarks on a desperate cross-country roadtrip through a paranoid and panic-stricken America to find answers." (Publisher's note)

"Coyle's debut (first published in Great Britain in 2013) is a unique and unpredictable apocalypse story steeped in tension and creepy atmosphere, with intelligent commentary on Fundamentalism and corporate influence in America; it's also an empowering coming-of-age adventure starring a relatable protagonist who successfully becomes 'the hero of [her] own story.'" Horn Book

Originally published in Great Britain by Hot Key Books in 2013 under title: Vivian Apple versus the apocalypse.

Vivian Apple needs a miracle. By Katie Coyle. Houghton Mifflin Harcourt 2015 304 p.

Grades: 9 10 11 12

1. Coming of age -- Fiction 2. End of the world -- Fiction 3. Fundamentalism -- Fiction 4. Missing persons -- Fiction 5. Religion -- Fiction 6. Revolutionaries -- Fiction 7. Christian fundamentalism -- Fiction 8. Bildungsromans

9780544390423, $17.99

LC 2014046783

In this book, by Katie Coyle, the "predicted Rapture by Pastor Frick's Church of America has come and gone, and three thousand Believers are now missing or dead. Seventeen-year-old Vivian Apple and her best friend, Harpreet, are revolutionaries, determined to expose the Church's diabolical power grab . . . and to locate Viv's missing heartthrob, Peter Ivey." (Publisher's note)

"Coyle adeptly handles an exceptionally multifaceted plot, easily seguing from snarky social criticism to heart-pounding action to stomach-fluttering romance, creating a breathless whirlwind that keeps the pages flying until the very end. A distinctive, complex, and thoughtful page-turner certain to leave readers clamoring for more." Kirkus

Sequel to: Vivian Apple at the end of the world

Crane, E. M.

Skin deep; [by] E. M. Crane. Delacorte Press 2008 273p $16.99; lib bdg $19.99

Grades: 7 8 9 10 11 12

1. Dogs -- Fiction 2. Death -- Fiction 3. Friendship -- Fiction

ISBN 978-0-385-73479-0; 0-385-73479-4; 978-0-385-90477-3 lib bdg; 0-385-90477-0 lib bdg

When sixteen-year-old Andrea Anderson begins caring for a sick neighbor's dog, she learns a lot about life, death, pottery, friendship, hope, and love.

"Teenage girls who can empathize with Andrea's journey of self-discovery and its triumphs and losses will find a well-written story, with lyrical explorations of nature, and memorable characters." Voice Youth Advocates

Cranse, Pratima

All the major constellations. By Pratima Cranse. Viking 2015 336 p.

Grades: 9 10 11 12

1. Christian life -- Fiction 2. Coma -- Fiction 3. Friendship -- Fiction

0670016454; 9780670016457, $17.99

LC 2014044806

In this book, by Pratima Cranse, "Andrew is leaving high school behind and looking ahead to a fresh start at college and distance from his not-so-secret infatuation: Laura Lettel. But when a terrible accident leaves him without the companionship of his two best friends, Andrew is cast adrift and alone--until Laura unexpectedly offers him comfort, friendship, and the support of a youth group of true believ-

ers, fundamentalist Christians with problems and secrets of their own." (Publisher's note)

"Andrew is prepared to graduate from high school, work his summer job, and finally escape his alcoholic father. His plans are thrown for a loop when one of his best friends, Sara, is in a coma after a car accident and his other best friend, Marcia, becomes distant as she helps to care for Sara. The fact that Andrew's older, baseball-star, bully brother is coming home from college only makes his home life more unbearable. A note slipped to him from his longtime crush, Laura, leads Andrew to a fundamentalist Christian youth group. . . . Older fans of realistic fiction will enjoy riding along with Andrew." SLJ

Crocker, Nancy

★ **Billie** Standish was here. Simon & Schuster Books for Young Readers 2007 281p $16.99

Grades: 7 8 9 10

1. Rape -- Fiction 2. Friendship -- Fiction 3. Child abuse -- Fiction

ISBN 978-1-4169-2423-4; 1-4169-2423-X

LC 2006-32688

When the river jeopardizes the levee and most of the town leaves, Miss Lydia, an elderly neighbor, and Billie form a friendship that withstands tragedy and time.

"This story is beautiful, painful, and complex, and the descriptions of people, events, and emotions are graphic and tangible. The rape scene is described but not sensationalized." SLJ

Croggon, Alison

Black spring; Alison Croggon. Candlewick Press 2013 288 p. $16.99

Grades: 9 10 11 12

1. Revenge -- Fiction 2. Witches -- Fiction 3. Social classes -- Fiction

ISBN 0763660094; 9780763660093

LC 2012950560

This book by Alison Croggon is "an homage to 'Wuthering Heights,' trading the English moors of the original for the remote northern wilds of Elbasa, a land of powerful wizards and strict rules concerning vendetta. . . . . It's a fantasy setting, but Croggon maintains the north/south, high/low, and male/female class divisions Brontë explores; Lina, born a witch, takes the place of Catherine, while 'swarthy' Damek il Haran has his analogue in Heathcliff." (Publishers Weekly)

"Violet-eyed witch Lina, daughter of a powerful lord, is subject to the wrath of the wizards of the North, who seek to suppress any competing powers--especially those found in women. Seemingly cursed, Lina only finds strength once she sheds the control of domineering men, including her love, Damek. The magical slant of this poetic Wuthering Heights reimagining is compelling." (Horn Book)

The **Naming**. Candlewick Press 2005 492p map (Pellinor) $17.99

Grades: 7 8 9 10

1. Fantasy fiction

ISBN 0-7636-2639-2

LC 2004-45165

First published 2002 in the United Kingdom with title: The gift

In this first book in the Pellinor series, a manuscript from the lost civilization of Edil-Amarandah chronicles the experiences of sixteen-year-old Maerad, an orphan gifted in the magic and power of the Bards, as she escapes from slavery and begins to learn how to use her Gift to stave off the evil Darkness that threatens to consume her world.

"Unbelievably fine, this book represents fantasy storytelling at its best. This exemplary novel is sure to appeal to all fantasy fans." Voice Youth Advocates

Other titles in this series are:

The Crow (2007)

The Riddle (2006)

The Singing (2009)

Cronn-Mills, Kirstin

Beautiful Music for Ugly Children; Kirstin Cronn-Mills. Flux 2012 271 p. $9.99

Grades: 9 10 11 12

 1. Disc jockeys -- Fiction 2. High schools -- Fiction 3. Schools -- Fiction 4. Transgender people -- Fiction

ISBN 1590207203; 9780738732510

          LC 2012019028

Stonewall Book Award-Mike Morgan and Larry Romans Children's & Young Adult Literature Award

In author Kirstin Cronn-Mills's book, "it is only after hearing Gabe's friend and neighbor John . . . use Gabe's birth name that readers learn that Gabe is transgender. Being trans, Gabe opines, is like being a 45 record with an A side and a B side. When the story opens, only a few people know about Gabe's B side; the rest see him as a girl. When Gabe's radio show becomes an underground hit, generating a . . . cadre of fans calling themselves the Ugly Children Brigade, Gabe's B side is pushed further into public view." (Kirkus Reviews)

Crossan, Sarah

Breathe; Sarah Crossan. Greenwillow Books 2012 373 p. (hardback) $17.99

Grades: 7 8 9 10 11 12

 1. Friendship -- Fiction 2. Dystopian fiction 3. Science fiction 4. Survival -- Fiction 5. Insurgency -- Fiction 6. Adventure and adventurers -- Fiction 7. Environmental degradation -- Fiction

ISBN 0062118692; 9780062118691

          LC 2012017496

In author Sarah Crossan's book, "Alina has been stealing for a long time . . . Quinn should be worried about Alina and a bit afraid for himself, too, but . . . it isn't every day that the girl of your dreams asks you to rescue her. Bea wants to tell him that none of this is fair; they'd planned a trip together, the two of them, and she'd hoped he'd discover her out here, not another girl. And as they walk into the Outlands with two days' worth of oxygen in their tanks, everything they believe will be shattered. Will they be able to make it back? Will they want to?" (Publisher's note)

Moonrise. Sarah Crossan. Bloomsbury 2018 383 p.

Grades: 9 10 11 12

 1. Brothers -- Fiction; 2. Capital punishment -- Fiction; 3. Death row -- Fiction; 4. Family problems -- Fiction; 5.

Novels in verse; 6. Prisoners' families -- Fiction

9781681193670; 1681193663; 9781681193663, $17.99

          LC 2017025085

In this novel author Sarah Crossan "explores life, death, love and forgiveness. Seventeen-year-old Joe hasn't seen his brother in ten years. Ed didn't walk out on the family, not exactly. It's something more brutal. Ed's locked up -- on death row. Now his execution date has been set, and the clock is ticking. Joe is determined to spend those last weeks with his brother, no matter what other people think...and no matter whether Ed committed the crime." (Publisher's note)

"Crossan's (We Come Apart, 2017, etc.) eloquent usage of language in this deeply affecting novel puts readers right at the heart of a very sensitive and timely story." Kirkus

One. By Sarah Crossan. Greenwillow Books, an imprint of HarperCollinsPublishers 2015 400 p.

Grades: 8 9 10 11 12

 1. Conjoined twins -- Fiction 2. Family problems -- Fiction 3. High schools -- Fiction 4. Novels in verse 5. Schools -- Fiction 6. Sisters -- Fiction 7. Twins -- Fiction

9780062118752, $17.99; 0062118757

          LC 2015004714

"Life for 16-year-old Grace and her sister Tippi hasn't been easy: they're conjoined twins—literally joined at the hip. They've spent their lives dealing with staring strangers and invasive questions, but the girls are happy together and wouldn't have it any other way. Grace and Tippi have been home-schooled until now, but when the state decides to pay for the girls to attend a private high school instead, they begin their junior year among peers. . . . When Grace is diagnosed with a bad heart, the twins have a difficult decision to make: risk the dangerous separation surgery so Grace can qualify for a transplant, or stay together and get sicker until they both die." (Kirkus)

"Crossan trusts her characters and her readers to find their better selves through her gently paced story." Booklist

Crossley-Holland, Kevin

★ **Crossing** to Paradise. Arthur A. Levine Books 2008 339p $17.99

Grades: 7 8 9 10

 1. Kings 2. Singing -- Fiction 3. Literacy -- Fiction 4. Middle Ages -- Fiction 5. Christian life -- Fiction 6. Pilgrims and pilgrimages -- Fiction 7. Great Britain -- History -- 1154-1399, Plantagenets -- Fiction

ISBN 978-0-545-05866-7; 0-545-05866-X; 978-0-545-05868-1 pa; 0-545-05868-6 pa

          LC 2007-51853

First published 2006 in the United Kingdom with title: Gatty's tale

Gatty, the field-girl who appeared in the author's trilogy about King Arthur, is now an orphan. When she is selected for a pilgrimage, she travels from her home on an English estate to London, Venice, and eventually Jerusalem. "Grades six to ten." (Bull Cent Child Books)

"Gatty, the irrepressible peasant girl first introduced in Crossley-Holland's 'Arthur' trilogy . . . comes into her own in this sweeping, vibrant story." SLJ

Crowder, Melanie

Audacity. Melanie Crowder. Philomel Books 2015
400 p. Illustration

Grades: 9 10 11 12

1. Immigrants -- United States -- Fiction 2. Jews --
United States -- Fiction 3. Labor movement -- Fiction
4. Novels in verse 5. Russian Americans -- Fiction
6. Women in the labor movement -- New York (State)
-- New York -- Fiction 7. Lemlich, Clara, 1886-1982
-- Fiction 8. New York (N.Y.) -- History -- 1898-1951
-- Fiction

0399168990; 9780399168994, $17.99

LC 2014018466

This novel, by Melanie Crowder, "is inspired by the real-
life story of Clara Lemlich, a spirited young woman who
emigrated from Russia to New York at the turn of the twentieth century and fought tenaciously for equal rights. Bucking
the norms of both her traditional Jewish family and societal
conventions, Clara refuses to accept substandard working
conditions in the factories on Manhattan's Lower East Side."
(Publisher's note)

"Crowder breathes life into a world long past and provides insight into the achievements of one determined woman who knows she will 'give / without the thought / of ever
getting back, / to ease the suffering of others. / That, / I think,
/ I will be doing / the rest of my life.' Compelling, powerful
and unforgettable."

Includes bibliographical references

Crowe, Chris

Mississippi trial, 1955. Penguin Putnam 2002
231p pa $5.99; $17.99

Grades: 7 8 9 10

1. Racism 2. Till, Emmett, 1941-1955 -- Fiction 3.
Grandfathers 4. Fathers and sons 5. Racism -- Fiction
6. Grandfathers -- Fiction 7. Mississippi -- Race
relations -- Fiction

ISBN 0-14-250192-1 pa; 0-8037-2745-3

LC 2001-40221

In Mississippi in 1955, a sixteen-year-old finds himself at odds with his grandfather over issues surrounding
the kidnapping and murder of a fourteen-year-old African
American from Chicago. "Grades seven to ten." (Bull Cent
Child Books)

"By combining real events with their impact upon a single fictional character, Crowe makes the issues in this novel
hard-hitting and personal. The characters are complex."
Voice Youth Advocates

Crowley, Cath

Words in deep blue. Cath Crowley. Alfred A.
Knopf 2017 269 p.

Grades: 8 9 10 11

1. Bookstores -- Fiction; 2. Love -- Fiction; 3. Australia
-- Fiction; 4. Romance fiction

9781101937662;   9781101937648, $17.99;
9781101937655

LC 2016001071

In this book, by Cath Crowley, "years ago, Rachel had
a crush on Henry Jones. The day before she moved away,
she tucked a love letter into his favorite book in his family's
bookshop. She waited. But Henry never came. Now Rachel

has returned to the city -- and to the bookshop -- to work
alongside the boy she'd rather not see, if at all possible, for
the rest of her life. But Rachel needs the distraction. Her
brother drowned months ago, and she can't feel anything
anymore." (Publisher's note)

"This journey is original, wise, and essential...This love
story is an ode to words and life." Kirkus

Originally published in Sydney by Pan Macmillan Australia in 2016.

Crowley, Suzanne

The stolen one. Greenwillow Books 2009 406p
$17.99; lib bdg $18.89

Grades: 8 9 10 11 12

1. Orphans -- Fiction

ISBN 978-0-06-123200-8; 0-06-123200-9; 978-0-06-
123201-5 lib bdg; 0-06-123201-7 lib bdg

LC 2008-15039

After the death of her foster mother, sixteen-year-old Kat
goes to London to seek the answers to her parentage, and surprisingly finds herself invited into Queen Elizabeth's court.

"Intrigue, romance, and period details abound in this riveting story of Tudor England. . . . The sophisticated writing
flows well, and the author does a terrific job of integrating
historical details." SLJ

Crutcher, Chris

★ Deadline. Greenwillow Books 2007 316p
$16.99; lib bdg $17.89; pa $8.99

Grades: 8 9 10 11 12

1. School stories 2. Death -- Fiction 3. Terminally ill
-- Fiction

ISBN 978-0-06-085089-0; 0-06-085089-2; 978-0-06-
085090-6 lib bdg; 0-06-085090-6 lib bdg; 978-0-06-
085091-3 pa; 0-06-085091-4 pa

LC 2006-31526

Given the medical diagnosis of one year to live, high
school senior Ben Wolf decides to fulfill his greatest fantasies, ponders his life's purpose and legacy, and converses
through dreams with a spiritual guide known as "Hey-Soos."

"Ben's sensitive voice uses self-deprecating humor, philosophical pondering, and effective dramatic irony." Voice
Youth Advocates

Ironman; a novel. Greenwillow Bks. 1995 181p
$16.99; pa $6.99

Grades: 8 9 10 11 12

1. School stories 2. Triathlon -- Fiction 3. Father-son
relationship -- Fiction

ISBN 0-688-13503-X; 0-06-059840-9 pa

LC 94-1657

While training for a triathlon, seventeen-year-old Bo attends Mr. Nak's anger management group at school which
leads him to examine his relationship with his father.

"Through Crutcher's masterful character development,
readers will believe in Bo, empathize with the other members of the anger-management group, absorb the wisdom of
Mr. Nak and despise, yet at times pity, the boy's father. This
is not a light read, as many serious issues surface, though the
author's trademark dark humor (and colorful use of street
language) is abundant." SLJ

Period 8; by Chris Crutcher. Greenwillow Books 2013 288 p. (hardback) $17.99

Grades: 7 8 9

    1. School stories 2. Missing persons -- Fiction 3. Clubs -- Fiction 4. Bullies -- Fiction 5. Schools -- Fiction 6. Kidnapping -- Fiction 7. High schools -- Fiction 8. Sexual abuse -- Fiction 9. Missing children -- Fiction 10. Mystery and detective stories

    ISBN 0061914800; 9780061914805; 9780061914812

                      LC 2012046726

In this book, high school teacher "Bruce Logsdon's Period 8 session, held during the regular lunch period, is a place for Heller High School students to talk about their concerns and feelings. . . . When quiet, unassuming Mary Wells (called the 'Virgin Mary' by other students due to her outwardly prudish behavior) goes missing, Period 8 must grapple with the fact that their safe space has been compromised." (School Library Journal)

Running loose. Greenwillow Bks. 1983 190p hardcover o.p. pa $8.99; pa $6.99

Grades: 7 8 9 10

    1. School stories

    ISBN 9780060094911 pa; 0-688-02002-X; 0-06-009491-5 pa

                      LC 82-20935

ALA YALSA Margaret A. Edwards Award (2000)

"Louie Banks tells what happened to him in his senior year in a small town Idaho high school. Besides falling in love with Becky and losing her in a senseless accident, Louie takes a stand against the coach when he sets the team up to injure a black player on an opposing team, and learns that you can't be honorable with dishonorable men. . . . Grade seven and up." (Voice Youth Advocates)

★ **Staying** fat for Sarah Byrnes. Greenwillow Bks. 1993 216p hardcover o.p. pa $6.99

Grades: 7 8 9 10

    1. Obesity -- Fiction 2. Swimming -- Fiction 3. Friendship -- Fiction 4. Child abuse -- Fiction

    ISBN 0-688-11552-7; 0-06-009489-3 pa

                      LC 91-40097

ALA YALSA Margaret A. Edwards Award (2000)

"An obese boy and a disfigured girl suffer the emotional scars of years of mockery at the hands of their peers. They share a hard-boiled view of the world until events in their senior year hurl them in very different directions. A story about a friendship with staying power, written with pathos and pointed humor." SLJ

Stotan! HarperTempest 2003 261p pa $6.99

Grades: 7 8 9 10

    1. Swimming -- Fiction

    ISBN 0-06-009492-3

                      LC 85-12712

First published 1986

ALA YALSA Margaret A. Edwards Award (2000)

A high school coach invites members of his swimming team to a memorable week of rigorous training that tests their moral fiber as well as their physical stamina.

"A subplot involving the boys' fight against local Neo-Nazi activists provides some immediate action, while the various characters' conflicts tighten the middle and ending. The pace lags through the story's introduction; nevertheless, this is a searching sports novel, with a tone varying from macho-tough to sensitive." Bull Cent Child Books

Whale talk. Greenwillow Bks. 2001 220p $15.99; pa $8.99

Grades: 7 8 9 10

    1. School stories 2. Swimming -- Fiction 3. Racially mixed people -- Fiction

    ISBN 0-688-18019-1; 0-06-177131-7 pa

                      LC 00-59292

Intellectually and athletically gifted, TJ, a multiracial, adopted teenager, shuns organized sports and the gung-ho athletes at his high school until he agrees to form a swimming team and recruits some of the school's less popular students

"This remarkable novel is vintage Crutcher: heart-pounding athletic competitions, raw emotion, an insufferable high school atmosphere that allows bullying and reveres athletes, and a larger-than-life teen hero who champions the underdog while skewering both racists and abusers with his rapier-sharp wit." Book Rep

Cummings, Priscilla

Blindsided. Dutton Children's Books 2010 226p $16.99

Grades: 7 8 9 10

    1. School stories 2. Blind -- Fiction 3. Maryland -- Fiction

    ISBN 978-0-525-42161-0; 0-525-42161-0

                      LC 2009-25092

"Natalie, 14, knows that her future is becoming dimmer as the loss of her eyesight is a nightmare she can't avoid. . . . Part of going from denial to acceptance is attending a boarding school for the blind. . . . Natalie is a credible character and her fear is palpable and painful. . . . Readers will enjoy the high drama and heroics." SLJ

The **journey** back; Priscilla Cummings. Dutton Children's Books 2012 243 p. (hardcover) $16.99

Grades: 7 8 9 10

    1. Camping 2. Voyages and travels 3. Fugitives from justice 4. Camping -- Fiction 5. Maryland -- Fiction 6. Coming of age -- Fiction 7. Conduct of life -- Fiction 8. Voyages and travels -- Fiction 9. Fugitives from justice -- Fiction 10. Juvenile detention homes -- Fiction

    ISBN 0525423621; 9780525423621

                      LC 2012003818

In this novel by Priscilla Cummings Digger is "escaped and on the run. . . His bold escape from a juvenile detention facility nearly kills him, but soon an angry fourteen-year-old Digger is . . . hijacking a tractor trailer, 'borrowing' a bicycle, and stealing a canoe. When injuries stop him, Digger hides at a riverside campground . . . New friends, a job caring for rescued horses, and risking his life to save another make Digger realize that the journey back is not just about getting home." (Publisher's note)

Red kayak; Priscilla Cummings. 1st ed; Dutton Children's Books 2004 209p $15.99; pa $6.99

Grades: 7 8 9 10
  1. Death -- Fiction 2. Friendship -- Fiction
  ISBN 0-525-47317-3; 0-14-240573-4 pa
  LC 2003-63532
Living near the water on Maryland's Eastern Shore, thirteen-year-old Brady and his best friends J.T. and Digger become entangled in a tragedy which tests their friendship and their ideas about right and wrong.
  "This well-crafted story will have broad appeal." SLJ

Cypess, Leah
Death sworn. Greenwillow Books. 2014 346p. 2014 $17.99
Grades: 7 8 9 10 11 12
  1. Assassins -- Fiction 2. Magic— Fiction 3. Secrets -- Fiction 4. Fantasy fiction 5. Love stories
  ISBN: 0062221213; 9780062221216
  LC 2013037379
"As seventeen-year-old Ileni's magic begins to fade, she's sent to the Black Mountain to tutor assassins in sorcery. With the help of Sorin, her student and assigned protector, she must discover who killed her predecessors before someone kills her. Ileni proves a compelling protagonist, and the blend of romance, assassins, magic, and murder-mystery consistently raises the stakes." Horn Book

Mistwood. Greenwillow Books 2010 304p $16.99
Grades: 7 8 9 10
  1. Fantasy fiction 2. Magic -- Fiction 3. Kings and rulers -- Fiction
  ISBN 978-0-06-195699-7; 0-06-195699-6
  LC 2009-23051
Brought back from the Mistwood to protect the royal family, a girl who has no memory of being a shape-shifter encounters political and magical intrigue as she struggles with her growing feelings for the prince.
  "A traditional premise is transformed into a graceful meditation on the ramifications of loyalty, duty and purpose. . . . Astonishing and inspiring." Kirkus

Nightspell. Greenwillow Books 2011 326p $16.99
Grades: 7 8 9 10
  1. Ghost stories 2. Dead -- Fiction 3. Sisters -- Fiction 4. Kings and rulers -- Fiction
  ISBN 978-0-06-195702-4; 0-06-195702-X
  LC 2010012637
Sent by her father, the king of Raellia, who is trying to forge an empire out of warring tribes, Darri arrives in Ghostland and discovers that her sister, whom she planned to rescue, may not want to leave this land where the dead mingle freely with the living.
  "Swordfights, blood, and double-dealing pack the pages as this action-filled story races to a surprising conclusion." Booklist

Daley, James Ryan
Jesus Jackson. James Ryan Daley. Poisoned Pencil Press 2014 Viii, 267
Grades: 8 9 10 11 12
  1. Brothers -- Death -- Fiction 2. Brothers and sisters

-- Fiction 3. Death -- Fiction 4. Faith -- Fiction 5. Teenage boys -- Fiction 6. Religion -- Fiction 7. Mystery fiction 8. High school students -- Fiction
  1929345062; 9781929345069, $10.95
  LC 2014938496
"Jonathan Stiles is a 14-year-old atheist who is coping with his first day of ninth grade at the fervently religious St. Soren's Academy when his idolized older brother Ryan is found dead at the bottom of a ravine behind the school. As his world crumbles, Jonathan meets an eccentric stranger who bears an uncanny resemblance to Jesus Christ (except for his white linen leisure suit and sparkling gold chains)." (Publisher's note)
  "The book excels, sidestepping holier-than-thou rhetoric and addressing the pain of loss head-on as well as painting a wonderful depiction of a young man coming to terms with how he was raised and how he wants to lead his own life. The mystery element and minor romance are icing on the cake: well-executed and finely tuned, complementing the book's major themes in all the right ways.Smart and sweet, comforting and moving. " Kirkus

Damico, Gina
Croak; by Gina Damico. Houghton Mifflin Harcourt 2012 311 p. $8.99
Grades: 7 8 9 10
  1. Mystery fiction 2. Soul -- Fiction 3. Death -- Fiction 4. Justice -- Fiction 5. Future life -- Fiction
  ISBN 9780547608327
  LC 2011017125
This book tells the story of "sixteen-year-old bad girl Lex Bartleby [who] is shipped off to her uncle Mort's farm, supposedly to figure out her anger issues with the help of manual labor. Instead, she learns that "farmer" Mort is a reaper of another kind entirely and that, as mayor of Croak, a small collection of Grim Reapers, he will be teaching Lex the family business. Although she initially takes to ferrying souls into the Afterlife with aplomb, Lex begins to question the roles of Reapers as silent witnesses to the world's injustices, especially when their knowledge of people's deaths would allow them to wreak karmic justice upon the murderers and rapists that otherwise get away with their crimes." (Bulletin of the Center for Children's Books)

Hellhole. By Gina Damico. Houghton Mifflin Harcourt 2014 368 p. Illustration
  1. Conduct of life -- Fiction 2. Devil -- Fiction 3. Humorous stories 4. Interpersonal relations -- Fiction 5. Mothers and sons -- Fiction 6. Sick -- Fiction 7. Single-parent families -- Fiction 8. Hell -- Fiction
  0544307100; 9780544307100, $17.99
  LC 2013042827
"Squeaky-clean Max Kilgore . . . accidentally unearths a devil. The big red guy has a penchant for couch surfing and junk food—and you should never underestimate evil on a sugar high. With the help of Lore, a former goth girl who knows a thing or two about the dark side, Max is racing against the clock to get rid of the houseguest." (Publisher's note)
  "Damico's blend of bleak humor and harsh reality lends itself well to Max's social awkwardness and Lore's biting cynicism." Pub Wkly

Rogue; by Gina Damico. Graphia 2013 336 p. (paperback) $8.99

Grades: 8 9 10

    1. Future life -- Fiction 2. Grim Reaper (Symbolic character) -- Fiction 3. Death -- Fiction 4. Humorous stories 5. Ghosts -- Fiction

    ISBN 0544108841; 9780544108844

LC 2013004154

This book by Gina Damico follows a "band of surly teenage grim reapers risking everything on their mission to save the Afterlife. Uncle Mort's plan to save the Afterlife by enlisting Junior Grims to help destroy the portals that access it is full of risks, loopholes and secrets—and fiery-tempered, impulsive Lex is the plan's unstable lynchpin." (Kirkus Reviews)

Scorch; Gina Damico. Houghton Mifflin Harcourt 2012 332 p. (paperback) $8.99

Grades: 7 8 9 10

    1. Fantasy fiction 2. Death -- Fiction 3. Humorous stories 4. Future life -- Fiction

    ISBN 0547624573; 9780547624570

LC 2012014799

In this novel by Gina Damico "Lex is a full-time teenage grim reaper -- but now has the bizarre ability to Damn souls. . . . [S]he and her friends embark on a wild road trip to DeMyse. Though this sparkling desert oasis is full of luxuries and amusements, it feels like a prison to Lex. Her best chance at escape would be to stop all the senseless violence that she caused—but how can she do that from DeMyse, where the Grims seem mysteriously oblivious to the bloodshed?" (Publisher's note)

Wax. Gina Damico. Houghton Mifflin Harcourt 2016 368 p.

Grades: 8 9 10 11

    1. Humorous stories 2. Mystery and detective stories 3. Supernatural -- Fiction 4. Wax figures -- Fiction 5. Mystery fiction 6. Humorous fiction

    9780544633186, $17.99; 9780544633155, $17.99

LC 2015035202

In this book, by Gina Damico, "Paraffin, Vermont, is home to the Grosholtz Candle Factory. There, seventeen-year-old Poppy finds something dark and unsettling: a room filled with dozens of startlingly lifelike wax sculptures. Later, she's shocked when one of the figures-a teenage boy who doesn't seem to know what he is-jumps naked and screaming out of the trunk of her car. Poppy wants to return him to the factory, but before she can, a fire destroys the mysterious workshop." (Publisher's note)

"With witty characters, a campy premise, and a creepy setting, this exciting, entertaining horror-mystery will appeal to readers who like their comedy on the dark side." Booklist

Danforth, Emily M.

    ★ The **miseducation** of Cameron Post; emily m. danforth. 1st ed. Balzer + Bray 2012 480p

Grades: 9 10 11 12

    1. Bildungsromans 2. Lesbians -- Fiction 3. Christian fundamentalism -- Fiction 4. Gays -- Fiction 5.

Montana -- Fiction 6. Orphans -- Fiction

    ISBN 9780062020567 (trade bdg.)

LC 2011001947

William C. Morris Award Finalist (2013)

This book offers a story about "coming of age as a lesbian in Miles City, Montana, in the early '90s, and . . . [focuses on] teen life in a pray-away-the-gay camp. Adopted by her born-again aunt Ruth after her parents' deaths, Cameron finds her first sexual explorations result in a betrayal that lands her in a re-education program called God's Promise." Bulletin of the Center for Children's Books)

Daniels, April

    ★ **Dreadnought**. April Daniels. Diversion Books 2017 279 p. (Nemesis)

Grades: 8 9 10 11 12

    1. Coming out (Sexual orientation) -- Fiction; 2. Transgender people -- Identity -- Fiction; 3. Transgender youth -- Fiction; 4. Women superheroes -- Fiction; 5. Superheroes -- Fiction; 6. Fantasy fiction; 9. Transgender people -- Fiction

    9781682300688, $14.99; 9781682300671; 1682300684

In this book in the Nemesis series, by April Daniels, "Danny Tozer has a problem: she just inherited the powers of Dreadnought, the world's greatest superhero. Until Dreadnought fell out of the sky and died right in front of her, Danny was trying to keep people from finding out she's transgender. But before he expired, Dreadnought passed his mantle to her, and those secondhand superpowers transformed Danny's body into what she's always thought it should be." (Publisher's note)

"A thoroughly enjoyable, emotionally rich, action-packed story with the most exciting new superheroes in decades." Kirkus

Danticat, Edwidge

    Untwine: a novel. Edwidge Danticat. Scholastic Press 2015 320 p.

Grades: 9 10 11 12

    1. Bereavement -- Fiction 2. Family life -- Florida -- Miami -- Fiction 3. Grief -- Fiction 4. Grief -- Fiction 5. Haitian American families -- Florida -- Miami -- Fiction 6. Haitian Americans -- Fiction 7. Sisters -- Fiction 8. Traffic accidents -- Fiction 9. Twins -- Fiction 10. Miami (Fla.) -- Fiction

    9780545423038, $16.99

LC 2014046787

NAACP Image Award Nominee: Outstanding Literary Work- Youth/Teens (2016)

In this book, by Edwidge Danticat, "Giselle Boyer and her identical twin, Isabelle, are as close as sisters can be, even as their family seems to be unraveling. Then the Boyers have a tragic encounter that will shatter everyone's world forever. Giselle wakes up in the hospital, injured and unable to speak or move. Trapped in the prison of her own body, Giselle must revisit her past in order to understand how the people closest to her . . . have shaped and defined her." (Publisher's note)

"There's a lot quietly packed into this novel-Giselle's Haitian heritage, her parents' imminent separation, the complications and thrills of first love, music, and art-yet most interesting is Danticat's rendering of identical twins as unique individuals. This is a poignant story for thoughtful teens that explores what it means to be a twin and how to say good-bye without losing oneself." Booklist

Dao, Julie C.

Forest of a thousand lanterns. Julie C. Dao. Philomel Books 2017 363 p. (Rise of the empress)
Grades: 9 10 11 12
    1. Witches -- Fiction; 2. Empresses -- Fiction
9781524738303; 9781524738297, $18.99
              LC 2017008021
In this Rise of the Empress novel, by Julie C. Dao, "eighteen-year-old Xifeng is beautiful. The stars say she is destined for greatness, that she is meant to be Empress of Feng Lu. But only if she embraces the darkness within her.... Xifeng longs to fulfill the destiny,...but...in order to achieve greatness, she must spurn the young man who loves her and exploit the callous magic that runs through her veins." (Publisher's note)
    "A dark and savage fairy-tale epic with all the trappings of imperial Asia." Kirkus
    Another title in this series is: Kingdom of the blazing phoenix (2018)

Darrows, Eva

The Awesome. By Eva Darrows. Simon & Schuster 2015 352 p.
Grades: 9 10 11 12
    1. Teenage girls -- Fiction 2. Interpersonal relations -- Fiction 3. Supernatural -- Fiction 4. Demonology -- Fiction 5. Monsters -- Fiction
178108324X; 9781781083246, $9.99
In this book, by Eva Darrows, "Seventeen-year-old Maggie Cunningham is tough, smart, and sassy. She's also not like other girls her age, but then, who would be when the family business is monster hunting? . . . Maggie's concerns in life slant more toward survival than fashion or boys. Which presents a problem when Maggie's mother informs Maggie that she can't get her journeyman's license for hunting until she loses her virginity." (Publisher's note)
    "Maggie's profanity-laced, snarky, deeply loving, yet antagonistic relationship with her mother is delightful. Maggie's adventurous baptism-by-undead provides enough complications to set up a sequel-readers will not want to wait long for it." Kirkus

Dead little mean girl. Eva Darrows. Harlequin Books 2017 250 p.
Grades: 7 8 9 10
    1. Bullying -- Fiction; 2. Death -- Fiction; 3. Grief -- Fiction; 4. Stepsisters -- Fiction; 5. Teenage girls -- Fiction
0373212410; 9780373212415, $18.99
              LC 2017296991
In this book, by Eva Darrows, "a proud geek girl, Emma loves her quiet life on the outskirts.... When her nightmare of a new stepsister moves into the bedroom next door, her world is turned upside down. Quinn is a queen bee with a nasty streak who destroys anyone who gets in her way.... Emma wants nothing more than to get this girl out of her life, but when Quinn dies suddenly, Emma realizes there

was more to her stepsister than anyone ever realized." (Publisher's note)
    "Darrows' (The Awesome, 2015) new YA novel is a seriously smart, funny, and empathetic look at how someone's manufactured exterior might be hiding inner turmoil, and ultimately advocates for looking past labels and categories." Booklist

Dashner, James

The kill order; James Dashner. Delacorte Press 2012 329 p. $17.99
Grades: 7 8 9 10 11 12
    1. Viruses -- Fiction 2. Survival skills -- Fiction 3. Natural disasters -- Fiction 4. Science fiction 5. Survival -- Fiction 6. Virus diseases -- Fiction
ISBN 9780307979117; 9780375990823; 9780385742887; 0385742886
              LC 2012016790
In this book by James Dashner "sun flares hit the earth and mankind fell to disease. Mark and Trina were there when it happened, and they survived. But surviving the sun flares was easy compared to what came next. Now a disease of rage and lunacy races across the eastern United States, and there's something suspicious about its origin. Worse yet, it's mutating, and all evidence suggests that it will bring humanity to its knees." (Publisher's note)

The maze runner. Delacorte Press 2009 375p $16.99; lib bdg $19.99
Grades: 7 8 9 10 11 12
    1. Science fiction 2. Amnesia -- Fiction
ISBN 0-385-73794-7; 0-385-90702-8 lib bdg; 978-0-385-73794-4; 978-0-385-90702-6 lib bdg
              LC 2009-1345
Sixteen-year-old Thomas wakes up with no memory in the middle of a maze and realizes he must work with the community in which he finds himself if he is to escape.
    "With a fast-paced narrative steadily answering the myriad questions that arise and an ever-increasing air of tension, Dashner's suspenseful adventure will keep readers guessing until the very end." Publ Wkly
    Other titles in this series are:
    The scorch trials (2010)
    The death cure (2011)

Daswani, Kavita

Indie girl. Simon Pulse 2007 232p pa $8.99
Grades: 7 8 9 10
    1. Fashion -- Fiction 2. Journalists -- Fiction 3. East Indian Americans -- Fiction
ISBN 1-4169-4892-9
    "What sets this novel apart is Daswani's nuanced take on her character's Indian-American subculture, the pressure she feels to be like her more conventional cousins, her desire for independence, American-style, and her pride in her heritage. Indie is a heroine worth meeting." Publ Wkly

Daugherty, C. J.

Night School; C.J. Daugherty. Katherine Tegen Books 2013 432 p. (hardcover) $17.99
Grades: 9 10 11 12
    1. School stories 2. Mystery fiction 3. Supernatural

-- Fiction 4. Conduct of life 5. Boarding schools -- Fiction 6. Interpersonal relations -- Fiction
ISBN 0062193856; 9780062193858

LC 2012022151

In this book, "upset over the loss of her brother, Christopher, Allie's vandalism gets her expelled from school" and she is sent to the mysterious boarding school Cimmeria Academy. Students are "not to enter the woods after dark; computers and cellphones are forbidden. A few [students] . . . attend the mysterious Night School but refuse to discuss it. Even Allie's best friend, Jo, keeps secrets from her." (Kirkus)

Davenport, Jennifer

Anna begins. Black Heron Press 2008 148p $21.95

Grades: 9 10 11 12

1. Alcoholism -- Fiction 2. Authorship -- Fiction 3. Child abuse -- Fiction 4. Eating disorders -- Fiction
ISBN 978-0-930773-83-0

This book's "two thematically paired novellas portray unrelated teenagers who are dealing with a variety of realistic teen problems. In the first work, Anna Begins, Melissa has a body image problem, a mother who is self-absorbed and not really in her children's lives, and a crush—maybe—on her best friend's ex-boyfriend or her older stepbrother. Melissa relates these events by writing a story about them, and seeks criticism about her story from others. In A Million Miles Up, Scott is a high school junior who, in an attempt to overcome his depression and be popular, takes up binge drinking. He shares some thoughts with Elly who has problems of her own. Although it is not overtly discussed, the implications are that she is being abused by her father and is acting out by being promiscuous. . . . This book will be one of those that will be recommended and talked about between teen readers." Voice Youth Advocates

David, Keren

Lia's guide to winning the lottery; Keren David. Frances Lincoln Children's Books 2012 339 p. ill. $16.99

Grades: 9 10 11 12

1. School stories 2. Family -- Fiction 3. Friendship -- Fiction 4. Lottery winners -- Fiction
ISBN 1847803318; 9781847803313

This book follows "Lia Latimer, [who] is more than ready to take her future in her own hands when she wins eight million pounds in the lottery. She'll drop out of school, buy a flat, leave her annoying family behind. What could go wrong? Plenty, of course . . . Her father's struggling bakery needs a cash infusion; her mother would like a boob job; sister Natasha longs for singing lessons. Jack (the winning ticket was his 16th-birthday present to Lia) wants an Italian motor bike; his mother demands half Lia's winnings. . . . Her romance with mysterious, gorgeous Raf is a bright spot--unless he's just after her winnings." (Kirkus Reviews)

Davies, Anna

Identity Theft. Point Horror 2013 250 p. $9.99

Grades: 9 10 11 12

1. Mystery fiction 2. Identity theft -- Fiction
ISBN 0545477123; 1480613169; 9780545477123; 9781480613164

In this book, "Hayley Westin knows exactly what she wants from life. As an overachiever who is determined to land a prestigious college scholarship, the high school senior doesn't have time for friends, sports, dating, or social media. So when she discovers that a fake Facebook account has been created in her name, she's convinced that someone is out to ruin her chances for the scholarship." But things might be even more malicious than they first appear. (School Library Journal)

Davies, Jacqueline

Lost. Marshall Cavendish 2009 242p $16.99

Grades: 7 8 9 10

1. Sisters -- Fiction 2. Factories -- Fiction 3. Bereavement -- Fiction 4. New York (N.Y.) -- Fiction 5. Triangle Shirtwaist Company, Inc. -- Fiction
ISBN 978-0-7614-5535-6; 0-7614-5535-3

LC 2008-40560

In 1911 New York, sixteen-year-old Essie Rosenfeld must stop taking care of her irrepressible six-year-old sister when she goes to work at the Triangle Waist Company, where she befriends a missing heiress who is in hiding from her family and who seems to understand the feelings of heartache and grief that Essie is trying desperately to escape.

The "unusual pacing adds depth and intrigue as the plot unfolds. There are many layers to this story, which will appeal to a variety of interests and age levels." SLJ

Davies, Jocelyn

The **odds** of lightning. Jocelyn Davies. Simon Pulse 2016 384 p.

Grades: 9 10 11 12

1. Friendship -- Fiction 2. Lightning -- Fiction 3. Magic realism (Literature)
9781481440554, $15.99; 9781481440530, $17.99

LC 2016013155

In this novel, by Jocelyn Davies, "Tiny, Lu, Will and Nathaniel used to be best friends . . . before high school tore them apart. . . . But fate weaves their lives together again . . . during a wild thunderstorm that threatens to shut down New York City. . . . The four teens embark on an epic all-night adventure to follow their dreams, fall in and out of love, reconcile the past, and overcome the fears that have been driving them since that one lost summer." (Publisher's note)

"As these four teens crisscross the city, contemplating who they really are and what makes them worthy of friendship and love, readers will be hard-pressed not to reflect on similar questions themselves." Pub Wkly

Davies, Stephen

★ **Outlaw.** Clarion Books 2011 192p $16.99

Grades: 7 8 9 10

1. Siblings -- Fiction 2. Terrorism -- Fiction 3. Kidnapping -- Fiction 4. Social problems -- Fiction
ISBN 978-0-547-39017-8; 0-547-39017-3

LC 2011009643

The children of Britain's ambassador to Burkina Faso, fifteen-year-old Jake, who loves technology and adventure, and thirteen-year-old Kas, a budding social activist, are abducted and spend time in the Sahara desert with Yakuuba Sor, who some call a terrorist but others consider a modern-day Robin Hood.

"Stephen Davies has crafted a novel full of intrigue, fast-paced action, and sly humor. The fast moving story will draw in many readers, including those who usually shy away from books." Voice Youth Advocates

Davis, Lane

I swear; Lane Davis. Simon & Schuster Books For Young Readers 2012 279 p. (hardcover) $16.99

Grades: 9 10 11 12

1. Suicide -- Fiction 2. Litigation -- Fiction 3. Cyberbullying -- Fiction 4. Bullying -- Fiction
ISBN 1442435062; 9781442435063

LC 2011046310

In this book by Lane Davis, "after years of abuse from her classmates, Leslie Gatlin decided she had no other options and took her own life. Now her abusers are dealing with the fallout. When Leslie's parents file a wrongful death lawsuit against their daughter's tormenters, the proceedings uncover the systematic cyber bullying and harassment that occurred. . . . Leslie may have taken her own life, but her bullies took everything else." (Publisher's note)

Davis, Rebecca Fjelland

Chasing AllieCat. Flux 2011 277p pa $9.95

Grades: 7 8 9 10

1. Violence -- Fiction 2. Bereavement -- Fiction 3. Mountain biking -- Fiction
ISBN 978-0-7387-2130-9; 0-7387-2130-1

LC 2010038217

When she is left with relatives in rural Minnesota for the summer, Sadie meets Allie, a spiky-haired off-road biker, and Joe, who team up to train for a race, but when they find a priest badly beaten and near death in the woods, Allie mysteriously disappears leaving Sadie and Joe to discover the dangerous secrets she is hiding.

Davis "constructs a succinct, compelling story that combines romance, suspense, and the theme of overcoming challenges. The strong sense of place, character development, and love triangle dynamics should engage cycling enthusiasts as well as a broader audience." Publ Wkly

Davis, Tanita S.

Happy families; by Tanita S. Davis. Alfred A. Knopf 2012 234 p. (hardcover) $16.99

Grades: 9 10 11 12

1. Twins -- Fiction 2. Family -- Fiction 3. Transgender parents -- Fiction 4. Fathers -- Fiction 5. Transgender people -- Fiction 6. Brothers and sisters -- Fiction
ISBN 9780375869662; 9780375969669; 9780375984570

LC 2011026546

In this book, "twins Ysabel and Justin struggle with the revelation that their father has begun living as a woman. . . . For spring break, Ysabel and Justin's parents arrange for the twins to stay with their father for the first time after the big news. Both the tension and the deep caring among Ysabel, Justin and Christine are palpable as the family . . . attends daily therapy sessions . . . and embarks on a guided raft-ing trip with other transgender parents and their children." (Kirkus Reviews)

A la carte. Alfred A. Knopf Books for Young Readers 2008 288p $15.99; lib bdg $18.99

Grades: 7 8 9 10

1. Cooking -- Fiction 2. African Americans -- Fiction
ISBN 978-0-375-84815-5; 0-375-84815-0; 978-0-375-94815-2 lib bdg; 0-375-94815-5 lib bdg

LC 2007-49656

Lainey, a high school senior and aspiring celebrity chef, is forced to question her priorities after her best friend (and secret crush) runs away from home.

"The relationships and characters in this book are authentic. The actions and dialogue seem true to those represented. Even though it is a quick read, the story is a meaningful one." Voice Youth Advocate

Mare's war. Alfred A. Knopf 2009 341p $16.99; lib bdg $19.99

Grades: 7 8 9 10

1. Alabama -- Fiction 2. Sisters -- Fiction 3. Grandmothers -- Fiction 4. African Americans -- Fiction 5. Automobile travel -- Fiction 6. World War, 1939-1945 -- Fiction 7. United States -- Army -- Women's Army Corps -- Fiction
ISBN 978-0-375-85714-0; 0-375-85714-1; 978-0-375-95714-7 lib bdg; 0-375-95714-6 lib bdg

LC 2008-33744

ALA EMIERT Coretta Scott King Author Award Honor Book (2010)

Teens Octavia and Tali learn about strength, independence, and courage when they are forced to take a car trip with their grandmother, who tells about growing up Black in 1940s Alabama and serving in Europe during World War II as a member of the Women's Army Corps.

"The parallel travel narratives are masterfully managed, with postcards from Octavia and Tali to the folks back home in San Francisco signaling the shift between 'then' and 'now.' Absolutely essential reading." Kirkus

Dawn, Sasha

Oblivion. Sasha Dawn. Egmont USA 2014 400 p.

Grades: 9 10 11 12

1. Compulsive behavior -- Fiction 2. Dating (Social customs) -- Fiction 3. Foster home care -- Fiction 4. Mental illness -- Fiction 5. Missing persons -- Fiction 6. Recovered memory -- Fiction 7. Illinois -- Fiction 8. Mentally ill -- Fiction
1606844768; 9781606844762, $17.99

LC 2013018267

In this young adult novel by Sasha Dawn, "all [Callie] knows is that her father, the reverend at the Church of the Holy Promise, is missing, as is Hannah, a young girl from the parish. Their disappearances have to be connected and Callie knows that her father was not a righteous man. Since that fateful night, she's been plagued by graphomania—an unending and debilitating compulsion to write." (Publisher's note)

"The story works on two levels: as a psychological mystery and as a story of Callie's rocky relationships with her sister and boyfriends, always grounding her difficulties in reality. Thoroughly compelling." Kirkus

Splinter. By Sasha Dawn. Carolrhoda Lab 2017 304 p.

Grades: 8 9 10 11

    1. Identity -- Fiction 2. Missing persons -- Fiction 3. Mothers and daughters -- Fiction 4. Mystery and detective stories

    9781512411515

                                          LC 2016008994

In this book, by Sasha Dawn, "Sami hasn't seen her mother in ten years--and neither has anyone else. The police suspect Sami's father had something to do with her mom's disappearance, but Sami's never believed that. . . . Now, evidence has emerged about another missing woman who used to be involved with Sami's dad. Coincidence--or evidence that the cops have been right all along? As Sami investigates, she's forced to question everything she thought she knew about the dad." (Publisher's note)

Dawson, Delilah S.

    Servants of the storm. Delilah S. Dawson. Simon Pulse 2014 384 p.

Grades: 9 10 11 12

    1. Demonology -- Fiction 2. Supernatural -- Fiction 3. Savannah (Ga.) -- Fiction 4. Fantasy fiction 5. Ghost stories

    1442483784; 9781442483781, $17.99

                                          LC 2013031587

In this Southern gothic fantasy novel by Delilah S. Dawson, "a year ago, Hurricane Josephine swept through Savannah, Georgia, . . . taking the life of Dovey's best friend, Carly. Since that night, Dovey has been in a medicated haze, numb to everything around her. But recently she's started . . . seeing things that can't be real. . . . Determined to learn the truth, Dovey stops taking her pills. And the world that opens up to her is unlike anything she could have imagined." (Publisher's note)

"The plot here is deep and twisting, and the mystery that lurks beneath it all is eerie. Though the ending is a tad abrupt, Dawson's atmospheric southern gothic spook-fest still pleases." Booklist

Dayton, Arwen Elys

    Stronger, faster, and more beautiful. Arwen Elys Dayton. Delacorte Press 2018 384 p.

Grades: 9 10 11 12

    1. Human beings -- Fiction; 2. Perfection -- Fiction; 3.Science fiction;

    ISBN 9780525580959, $18.99; 9780525580966

                                          LC 2018022928

In this book, by Arwen Elys Dayton, "tomorrow has different rules. The future is no longer about who we are—it's about who we want to be. If you can dream it, you can be it. Science will make us smarter, healthier, flawless in every way. Our future is boundless. . . . This is a story that begins tomorrow. It's a story about us. It's a story about who comes after us. And it's a story about perfection. Because perfection has a way of getting ugly." (Publisher's note)

De Goldi, Kate

    The **10** p.m. question. Candlewick Press 2010 245p $15.99

Grades: 7 8 9 10 11 12

    1. School stories 2. Worry -- Fiction 3. Agoraphobia -- Fiction 4. Family life -- Fiction 5. New Zealand -- Fiction 6. Eccentrics and eccentricities -- Fiction

    ISBN 978-0-7636-4939-5; 0-7636-4939-2

                                          LC 2009-49726

First published 2008 in New Zealand

Twelve-year-old Frankie Parsons has a quirky family, a wonderful best friend, and a head full of worrying questions that he shares with his mother each night, but when free-spirited Sydney arrives at school with questions of her own, Frankie is forced to face the ultimate ten p.m. question.

"De Goldi's novel is an achingly poignant, wryly comic story of early adolescence. . . . Nearly every character . . . is a loving, talented, unforgettable eccentric whose dialogue, much like De Goldi's richly phrased narration, combines heart-stopping tenderness with perfectly timed, deliciously zany humor." Booklist

De la Cruz, Melissa

    ★ **Blue** bloods. Hyperion 2006 302p hardcover o.p. pa $8.99

Grades: 9 10 11 12

    1. Vampires -- Fiction 2. New York (N.Y.) -- Fiction

    ISBN 978-0-7868-3892-9; 0-7868-3892-2; 978-1-4231-0126-0 pa; 1-4231-0126-X pa

                                          LC 2005-44786

Select teenagers from some of New York City's wealthiest and most socially prominent families learn a startling secret about their bloodlines.

"History, mythology, and the contemporary New York prep-school and club scene blend seamlessly in this sexy and sophisticated riff on vampire lore that never collapses into camp." Bull Cent Child Books

    Other titles in this series are:

Lost in time (2011)

Masquerade (2007)

Misguided angel (2010)

Revelations (2008)

The Van Alen legacy (2009)

Gates of Paradise (2013)

Keys to the Repository (2010)

    Someone to love. Melissa de la Cruz. Harlequin Teen 2018 389 p.

Grades: 9 10 11 12

    1. Bulimia -- Fiction; 2. Children of politicians -- Fiction; 3. Teenage girls -- Fiction; 4. Self-perception -- Fiction; 5. Teenagers -- Fiction

    0373212364; 9780373212361, $18.99

In this book, by Melissa de la Cruz, "Olivia 'Liv' Blakely knows how important it is to look good. Her father is running for governor and Liv is thrust into the bright media spotlight.... Liv's sunny, charming facade hides an inner voice that will settle for nothing less than perfection.... But as the high price of perfection takes a toll, Liv realizes that the love she feels for herself is more important than all the 'likes' in the world." (Publisher's note)

"Filled with a great deal of teenage angst, this tale will be relevant to many young adults trying to survive daily pressures. De la Cruz might be best known for her fantasy work, but her realist work is strong as well." Booklist

De la Peña, Matt

Ball don't lie. Delacorte Press 2005 280p hardcover o.p. pa $7.99

Grades: 9 10 11 12

1. Basketball -- Fiction 2. Race relations -- Fiction 3. Foster home care -- Fiction 4. Los Angeles (Calif.) -- Fiction 5. Obsessive-compulsive disorder -- Fiction

ISBN 0-385-73232-5; 0-385-73425-5 pa

LC 2004-18057

Seventeen-year-old Sticky lives for basketball and plays at school and at the Lincoln Rec Center in Los Angeles but he is unaware of the many dangers—including his own past—that threaten his dream of playing professionally.

"The prose moves with the rhythm of a bouncing basketball and those who don't mind mixing their sports stories with some true grit may find themselves hypnotized by Sticky's grim saga." Publ Wkly

The living; Matt de la Peña. Delacorte Press 2013 320 p.

Grades: 8 9 10 11 12

1. Cruise ships -- Fiction 2. Natural disasters -- Fiction 3. Survival after airplane accidents, shipwrecks, etc. -- Fiction 4. Diseases -- Fiction 5. Survival -- Fiction 6. Mexican Americans -- Fiction

ISBN 9780375989919; 9780385741200

LC 2012050778

Pura Belpre Author Award (2014)

In this book, by Matt de la Peña, "Shy took [a] summer job to make some money. In a few months on a luxury cruise liner, he'll rake in the tips and be able to help his mom and sister out with the bills. . . . But everything changes when the Big One hits. Shy's only weeks out at sea when an earthquake more massive than ever before recorded hits California, and his life is forever changed. The earthquake is only the first disaster. Suddenly it's a fight to survive for those left living." (Publisher's note)

"Shy Espinoza's summer job on Paradise Cruise Lines is, literally, a disaster. A series of catastrophes befall the cruise and eventually threaten civilization as he knows it; Shy finds himself on a life raft in the Pacific Ocean with a racist "spoiled-ass blond chick." Readers wanting a fast-paced survival story with plenty of action won't mind the over-the-top plot." (Horn Book)

Mexican whiteboy. Delacorte Press 2008 249p $15.99; lib bdg $18.99

Grades: 8 9 10 11 12

1. Cousins -- Fiction 2. California -- Fiction 3. Mexican Americans -- Fiction 4. Racially mixed people -- Fiction

ISBN 978-0-385-73310-6; 0-385-73310-0; 978-0-385-90329-5 lib bdg; 0-385-90329-4 lib bdg

LC 2007-32302

Sixteen-year-old Danny searches for his identity amidst the confusion of being half-Mexican and half-white while spending a summer with his cousin and new friends on the baseball fields and back alleys of San Diego County, California.

"The author juggles his many plotlines well, and the portrayal of Danny's friends and neighborhood is rich and lively." Booklist

We were here. Delacorte Press 2009 357p $17.99; lib bdg $20.99

Grades: 7 8 9 10 11 12

1. Brothers -- Fiction 2. California -- Fiction 3. Friendship -- Fiction 4. Runaway teenagers -- Fiction 5. Juvenile delinquency -- Fiction

ISBN 978-0-385-73667-1; 0-385-73667-3; 978-0-385-90622-7 lib bdg; 0-385-90622-6 lib bdg

LC 2008-44568

Haunted by the event that sentences him to time in a group home, Miguel breaks out with two unlikely companions and together they begin their journey down the California coast hoping to get to Mexico and a new life.

"The contemporary survival adventure will keep readers hooked, as will the tension that builds from the story's secrets." Booklist

De Lint, Charles

The blue girl; Charles de Lint. Viking 2004 368p hardcover o.p. pa $7.99

Grades: 7 8 9 10

1. Ghost stories 2. School stories 3. Fairies -- Fiction

ISBN 0-670-05924-2; 0-14-240545-0 pa

LC 2004-19051

New at her high school, Imogene enlists the help of her introverted friend Maxine and the ghost of a boy who haunts the school after receiving warnings through her dreams that soul-eaters are threatening her life

"The book combines the turmoil of high school intertwined with rich, detailed imagery drawn from traditional folklore and complex characters with realistic relationships. . . . This book is not just another ghost story, but a novel infused with the true sense of wonder and magic that is De Lint at his best. It is strongly recommended." Voice Youth Advocates

Dingo. Firebird 2008 213p $11.99

Grades: 9 10 11 12

1. Twins -- Fiction 2. Sisters -- Fiction 3. Wild dogs -- Fiction 4. Supernatural -- Fiction 5. Space and time -- Fiction

ISBN 978-0-14-240816-2; 0-14-240816-6

LC 2007-31716

Seventeen-year-old Miguel Schreiber and a long-term enemy are drawn into a strange dream world when they fall in love with shapeshifting sisters from Australia—twins hiding from a cursed ancestor who can only be freed with the girls' cooperation.

"The fated love angle will certainly draw in romance readers, and while they may be perfectly content with just following Miguel and Lainey's connection through to its expected happy ending, the intriguing details about shapeshifting, dingoes, and Aboriginal traditions may also lead them to dig a bit further into Australian myths and culture." Bull Cent Child Books

Little (grrl) lost. Viking 2007 271p hardcover o.p. pa $8.99

Grades: 7 8 9 10

    1. Fantasy fiction 2. Size -- Fiction 3. Moving -- Fiction 4. Friendship -- Fiction 5. Runaway teenagers -- Fiction

ISBN 978-0-670-06144-0; 0-670-06144-1; 978-0-14-241301-2 pa; 0-14-241301-1 pa

LC 2007-14832

Fourteen-year-old T. J. and her new friend, sixteen-year-old Elizabeth, a six-inch-high "Little" with a big chip on her shoulder, help one another as T. J. tries to adjust to her family's move from a farm to the big city and Elizabeth tries to make her own way in the world.

"De Lint mixes marvelous fantastical creatures and realities as he taps into young women's need to feel unique, understood, and valued." Booklist

De Quidt, Jeremy

★ The **toymaker**; with illustrations by Gary Blythe. David Fickling Books 2010 356p il $16.99; lib bdg $19.99

Grades: 5 6 7 8

    1. Adventure fiction 2. Toys -- Fiction

ISBN 978-0-385-75180-3; 0-385-75180-X; 978-0-385-75181-0 lib bdg; 0-385-75181-8 lib bdg

"Mathias . . . upon the death of his conjurer grandfather, is spirited away from the decrepit carnival they called home. His unknown new guardian appears to be after the secret contained on an inherited piece of paper, which is now in Mathias' possession. . . . Moving briskly across an atmospheric Germanic setting, the characters are chased by howling wolves, a dangerous dwarf, and unforgiving cold in a bloody, mysterious, and darkly thrilling quest." Booklist\

Deebs, Tracy

Tempest rising. Walker & Co. 2011 344p $16.99

Grades: 8 9 10 11 12

    1. War stories 2. Mermaids and mermen -- Fiction

ISBN 978-0-8027-2231-7; 0-8027-2231-8

LC 2010-34339

On her seventeenth birthday, Tempest must decide whether to remain a human and live on land or submit to her mermaid half, like her mother before her, and enter into a long-running war under the sea.

"Tempest is a gutsy, independent heroine with more than enough agency to save herself from danger. . . . For readers wanting a solid, familiar, but slightly different paranormal romance." Booklist

Deedy, Carmen Agra

★ The **Cheshire** Cheese cat; a Dickens of a tale. Peachtree Publishers 2011 228p il $16.95

Grades: 5 6 7 8

    1. Cats -- Fiction 2. Mice -- Fiction

ISBN 978-1-56145-595-9; 1-56145-595-4

LC 2010052275

"The vagaries of tavern life in 19th-century London come alive in this delightful tale. . . . The fast-moving plot is a masterwork of intricate detail that will keep readers enthralled, and the characters are well-rounded and believable.

Language is a highlight of the novel; words both elegant and colorful fill the pages. . . . Combined with Moser's precise pencil sketches of personality-filled characters, the book is a success in every way." SLJ

Delaney, Joseph

A **new** darkness; 1. Joseph Delaney. Greenwillow Books, an imprint of HarperCollinsPublishers 2014 352 p. (Starblade Chronicles)

Grades: 7 8 9 10

    1. Apprentices -- Fiction 2. Horror stories 3. Monsters -- Fiction 4. Supernatural -- Fiction 5. Witches -- Fiction 6. Horror fiction

0062334530; 9780062334534, $17.99

LC 2014011963

"Tom Ward is the Spook, the one person who can defend the county from bloodthirsty creatures of the dark. But he's only seventeen, and his apprenticeship was cut short when his master died in battle. . . . [F]ifteen-year-old . . . Jenny . . . is a seventh daughter of a seventh daughter, and she wants to be Tom's first apprentice. . . . Together, Tom and Jenny will uncover the grave danger heading straight toward the county." (Publisher's note)

"A plethora of action involving ghastly creatures, sword fights, and magic coupled with just enough backstory and description make this novel engaging enough to keep even the most reluctant reader turning pages until the end. Tom's story has a doozy of a cliff-hanger that is sure to bring teens back for more." - SLJ Reviews

Delsol, Wendy

Stork. Candlewick Press 2010 357p $15.99; pa $8.99

Grades: 7 8 9 10

    1. School stories 2. Minnesota -- Fiction 3. Supernatural -- Fiction

ISBN 978-0-7636-4844-2; 0-7636-4844-2; 978-0-7636-5687-4 pa; 0-7636-5687-9 pa

LC 2009-51357

After her parents' divorce, Katla and her mother move from Los Angeles to Norse Falls, Minnesota, where Kat immediately alienates two boys at her high school and, improbably, discovers a kinship with a mysterious group of elderly women—the Icelandic Stork Society—who "deliver souls."

"This snappy, lighthearted supernatural romance blends Norse mythology and contemporary issues with an easy touch." Booklist

Other titles in this series are:

Frost (2011)

Flock (2012)

Demetrios, Heather

Bad romance. Heather Demetrios. Henry Holt & Co. 2017 360 p.

Grades: 10 11 12

    1. Dating (Social customs) -- Fiction; 2. High schools -- Fiction; 3. Love -- Fiction; 4. Psychological abuse -- Fiction; 5. Schools -- Fiction; 6. Romance fiction

9781627797733; 9781627797726, $17.99

LC 2016035854

In this book, by Heather Demetrios, "Grace wants out. Out of her house,...out of her California town,...[and] out of her life, and into the role of Parisian artist, New York director -- anything but scared and alone. Enter Gavin: charming, talented, adored. Controlling. Dangerous. When Grace and Gavin fall in love, Grace is sure it's too good to be true. She has no idea their relationship will become a prison she's unable to escape." (Publisher's note)

"A realistic, worthwhile look at dating violence and unhealthy relationships." Kirkus

Something real; Heather Demetrios. Henry Holt and Co. 2014 416 p. (hardback) $17.99
Grades: 9 10 11 12
    1. Family -- Fiction 2. Reality television programs -- Fiction 3. Family life -- Fiction
    ISBN 0805097945; 9780805097948
LC 2013030798

In this book, by Heather Demetrios, Bonnie "and her twelve siblings are the stars of one-time hit reality show Baker's Dozen. Since the show's cancellation, Bonnie has tried to live a normal life. But it's about to fall apart . . . because Baker's Dozen is going back on the air. Bonnie's mom and the show's producers won't let her quit and soon the life that she has so carefully built for herself, with real friends (and maybe even a real boyfriend), is in danger." (Publisher's note)

"It's been four years since the reality television show Baker's Dozen went off the air. Bonnie Baker, 17, feels lucky to have survived the tension and challenges from constantly being in the limelight with her 12 siblings... With likable protagonists and snappy dialogue, Something Real credibly zooms in on reality TV's impact on unwilling subjects-a shoo-in for teens drawn to contemporary romance and drama. It will especially attract those who liked the similarly compelling reality show fictional exposés Reality Boy by A. S. King (Little, Brown, 2013) and The Real Real by Emma McLaughlin and Nicola Kraus (HarperCollins, 2009)." (School Library Journal)

Dennard, Susan

Something strange and deadly; Susan Dennard. 1st ed. Harpercollins Childrens Books 2012 388 p. (hardback) $17.99; (paperback) $9.99
Grades: 7 8 9 10 11 12
    1. Fairs 2. Ghost stories 3. Zombies -- Fiction 4. Horror stories 5. Dead -- Fiction 6. Magic -- fiction 7. Brothers and sisters -- Fiction 8. Philadelphia (Pa.) -- History -- 19th century -- Fiction
    ISBN 0062083260; 9780062083265; 9780062083272
LC 2011042114

Author Susan Dennard's protagonist Eleanor Fitt "and her dear Mama have just about run out of funds, and she misses [her brother] Elijah terribly [while he is on a] . . . three-year odyssey abroad. So when . . . he's been detained, she is mightily distressed. The next day, the determined teen is off for some help from the Spirit-Hunters. . . . Her can-do attitude finds her at one point systematically disabling a throng of zombies by smashing their kneecaps with her parasol." (Kirkus Reviews)

Followed by A Darkness Strange and Lovely (2013)

Truthwitch. By Susan Dennard. St. Martin's Press 2016 416 p.

Grades: 8 9 10 11 12
    1. Fantasy fiction 2. Witches -- Fiction 3. Friendship -- Fiction
    0765379287; 9780765379283, $18.99
LC 2015031484

In this book, by Susan Dennard, "Safiya is a Truthwitch, able to discern truth from lie. . . . Iseult, a Threadwitch, can see the invisible ties that bind and entangle the lives around her—but she cannot see the bonds that touch her own heart. Her unlikely friendship with Safi has taken her from life as an outcast into one of of reckless adventure, where she is a cool, wary balance to Safi's hotheaded impulsiveness." (Publisher's note)

"A great choice for fans of fantasy adventure and strong female characters." SLJ

Deracine, Anat

Driving by starlight. Anat Deracine. Godwin Books 2018 280 p.
Grades: 8 9 10 11 12
    1. Best friends -- Fiction; 2. Teenage girls -- Fiction; 3. Teenagers -- Saudi Arabia -- Fiction; 4. Women -- Saudi Arabia -- Fiction; 5. Saudi Arabia -- Fiction; 6. Friendship -- Fiction; 7. Women -- Fiction
    9781250133427, $17.99; 9781250133434
LC 2017957736

In this novel, by Anat Deracine, "sixteen-year-olds Leena and Mishie are best friends. They delight in small rebellions against the Saudi cultural police -- secret Western clothing, forbidden music, flirtations. But Leena wants college, independence -- she wants a different life. Though her story is specific to her world..., ultimately it's a story about friendship, family, and freedom that transcends cultural differences." (Publisher's note)

"The fast-paced narrative and unexpected twists make for an engaging yet educational novel with a powerful message about the complexities of being a woman in a man's world." Kirkus

Derting, Kimberly

The **body** finder. Harper 2009 329p $16.99
Grades: 7 8 9 10 11 12
    1. Mystery fiction 2. Dead -- Fiction 3. Supernatural -- Fiction 4. Extrasensory perception -- Fiction
    ISBN 978-0-06-177981-7; 0-06-177981-4
LC 2009-39675

"Violet Ambrose can find dead bodies. Their aura of sound, color, or even taste imprints itself on their murderers, and Violet's extrasensory perception picks up on those elements. . . . Derting has written a suspenseful mystery and sensual love story that will captivate readers who enjoy authentic high-school settings, snappy dialogue, sweet romance, and heart-stopping drama." Booklist

Followed by: Desires of the dead (2011)

Desires of the dead. HarperCollins 2011 358p $16.99
Grades: 7 8 9 10
    1. School stories 2. Homicide -- Fiction 3. Friendship -- Fiction 4. Supernatural -- Fiction 5. Washington

(State) -- Fiction 6. Extrasensory perception -- Fiction 7. United States -- Federal Bureau of Investigation -- Fiction

ISBN 978-0-06-177984-8; 0-06-177984-9

LC 2010017838

Sequel to: The body finder (2010)

Sixteen-year-old Violet Ambrose's ability to find murder victims and their killers draws the attention of the FBI just as her relationship with Jay, her best-friend-turned-boyfriend, heats up.

"The author paces the story beautifully, weaving together several story lines as she inches up to the final, desperate scene. . . . Imaginative, convincing and successful suspense." Kirkus

The **last** echo; Kimberly Derting. Harper 2012 360 p. (hbk.) $17.99

Grades: 7 8 9 10 11 12

1. Love stories 2. Parapsychology -- Fiction 3. Serial killers -- Fiction 4. Dead -- Fiction 5. Schools -- Fiction 6. Friendship -- Fiction 7. Best friends -- Fiction 8. High schools -- Fiction 9. Serial murders -- Fiction 10. Psychic ability -- Fiction 11. Washington (State) -- Fiction

ISBN 0062082191; 9780062082190

LC 2011044633

Sequel to: Desires of the dead (2011)

This book, "the third installment of the Body Finder series," begins with protagonist Violet "working for a secret agency that specializes in using paranormal powers to fight crime. . . . She still loves her normal boyfriend Jay, so she worries about the strong physical response she feels whenever she touches Rafe, a member of the team. Meanwhile, Violet doesn't know she's become the target of a terrifying serial killer." (Kirkus Reviews)

"As always, this author writes a gripping tale... Personalities come across quite strongly, as several of the characters tend toward the eccentric." Kirkus

The **pledge**. Margaret K. McElderry Books 2011 323p $16.99

Grades: 7 8 9 10

1. Fantasy fiction 2. Ability -- Fiction 3. Social classes -- Fiction 4. Language and languages -- Fiction

ISBN 978-1-4424-2201-8; 1-4424-2201-7; 978-1-4424-2202-5 e-book

LC 2010053773

In a dystopian kingdom where the classes are separated by the languages they speak, Charlaina 'Charlie' Hart has a secret gift that is revealed when she meets a mysterious young man named Max.

Derting "keeps her story consistently engaging through vivid description and brisk pacing. . . . Great suspense from a prolific new writer with a vibrant imagination." Kirkus

Desai Hidier, Tanuja

★ **Born** confused. Scholastic Press 2002 413p hardcover o.p. pa $7.99

Grades: 8 9 10 11 12

1. Friendship -- Fiction 2. East Indian Americans -- Fiction

ISBN 0-439-35762-4; 0-439-51011-2 pa

LC 2002-4515

Seventeen-year-old Dimple, whose family is from India, discovers that she is not Indian enough for the Indians and not American enough for the Americans, as she sees her hypnotically beautiful, manipulative best friend taking possession of both her heritage and the boy she likes

"This involving story . . . will reward its readers. The family background and richness in cultural information add a new level to the familiar girl-meets-boy story." SLJ

Despain, Bree

The **dark** Divine. Egmont USA 2010 372p $17.99; lib bdg $20.99

Grades: 7 8 9 10 11

1. School stories 2. Family life -- Fiction 3. Supernatural -- Fiction 4. Christian life -- Fiction

ISBN 978-1-60684-057-3; 1-60684-057-6; 978-1-60684-065-8 lib bdg; 1-60684-065-7 lib bdg

LC 2009-18680

Grace Divine, almost seventeen, learns a dark secret when her childhood friend—practically a brother—returns, upsetting her pastor-father and the rest of her family, around the time strange things are happening in and near their small Minnesota town.

"Despain raises complex issues of responsibility and forgiveness and offers no easy answers. Atmospheric and compelling." Booklist

Dessen, Sarah

Along for the ride; a novel. Viking 2009 383p $19.99

Grades: 7 8 9 10

1. Divorce -- Fiction 2. Infants -- Fiction 3. Stepfamilies -- Fiction 4. Dating (Social customs) -- Fiction

ISBN 978-0-670-01194-0; 0-670-01194-0

LC 2009-5661

When Auden impulsively goes to stay with her father, stepmother, and new baby sister the summer before she starts college, all the trauma of her parents' divorce is revived, even as she is making new friends and having new experiences such as learning to ride a bike and dating.

"Dessen explores the dynamics of an extended family headed by two opposing, flawed personalities, revealing their parental failures with wicked precision yet still managing to create real, even sympathetic characters. . . . [This book] provides the interpersonal intricacies fans expect from a Dessen plot." Horn Book

★ **Just** listen; a novel. Viking 2006 371p $17.99

Grades: 9 10 11 12

1. School stories 2. Friendship -- Fiction 3. Family life -- Fiction

ISBN 0-670-06105-0; 978-0-670-06105-1

LC 2006-472

Isolated from friends who believe the worst because she has not been truthful with them, sixteen-year-old Annabel finds an ally in classmate Owen, whose honesty and passion for music help her to face and share what really happened at the end-of-the-year party that changed her life.

The author "weaves a sometimes funny, mostly emotional, and very satisfying story." Voice Youth Advocates

Lock and key; a novel. Viking Children's Books 2008 422p $18.99

Grades: 7 8 9 10

1. Child abuse -- Fiction 2. Family life -- Fiction 3. Abandoned children -- Fiction

ISBN 978-0-670-01088-2; 0-670-01088-X

LC 2007-25370

When she is abandoned by her alcoholic mother, high school senior Ruby winds up living with Cora, the sister she has not seen for ten years, and learns about Cora's new life, what makes a family, how to allow people to help her when she needs it, and that she too has something to offer others.

"The dialogue, especially between Ruby and Cora, is crisp, layered, and natural. The slow unfolding adds to an anticipatory mood. . . . Recommend this one to patient, sophisticated readers." SLJ

The **moon** and more; by Sarah Dessen. Viking 2013 384 p. (hardcover) $19.99

Grades: 7 8 9 10

1. Bildungsromans 2. Dating (Social customs) -- Fiction 3. Father-daughter relationship -- Fiction 4. Beaches -- Fiction 5. Resorts -- Fiction 6. Coming of age -- Fiction 7. Fathers and daughters -- Fiction 8. Family-owned business enterprises -- Fiction 9. Documentary films -- Production and direction -- Fiction

ISBN 0670785601; 9780670785605

LC 2012035720

In this novel, by Sarah Dessen, "Luke is the perfect boyfriend. . . . But now, in the summer before college, Emaline wonders if perfect is good enough. Enter Theo, a super-ambitious outsider. . . . Emaline's . . . father, too, thinks Emaline should have a bigger life. . . . Emaline is attracted to the bright future that Theo and her father promise. But she also clings to the deep roots of her loving mother, stepfather, and sisters." (Publisher's note)

"Dessen's characters behave as deliciously unpredictably as people do in real life, and just as in real life, they sometimes have to make difficult choices with not-so-predictable outcomes... Completely engaging." Kirkus

Once and for all. Sarah Dessen. Viking 2017 357 p.

Grades: 9 10 11 12

1. Dating (Social customs) -- Fiction; 2. Summer employment -- Fiction; 3. Romance fiction; 4. Weddings -- Fiction

9780425290330, $19.99; 9780425290347

LC 2016043458

In this novel, by Sarah Dessen, "Louna's summer job is to help brides plan their perfect day, even though she stopped believing in happily-ever-after when her first love ended tragically. But charming girl-magnet Ambrose isn't about to be discouraged now that he's met the one he really wants. Maybe Louna's second chance is standing right in front of her." (Publisher's note)

"Romance, humor, kindhearted characters, and a touch of painful reality make this another sure bet for Dessen fans." Kirkus

Saint Anything: a novel. Sarah Dessen. Viking Juvenile 2015 432 p.

Grades: 9 10 11 12

1. Brothers and sisters -- Fiction 2. Dating (Social customs) -- Fiction 3. Family life -- Fiction 4. Family problems -- Fiction 5. Friendship -- Fiction 6. Self-perception -- Fiction 7. Family -- Fiction 8. Self-acceptance -- Fiction

0451474708; 9780451474704, $19.99

LC 2014039813

In Sara Dessen's novel "Sydney has always felt invisible. She's grown accustomed to her brother, Peyton, being the focus of the family's attention. Now, after a drunk-driving accident that crippled a boy, Peyton's serving some serious jail time, and Sydney is on her own, questioning her place in the family and the world. Then she meets the Chatham family. Drawn into their warm, chaotic circle, Sydney experiences unquestioning acceptance for the first time." (Publisher's note)

"Once again, Dessen demonstrates her tremendous skill in evoking powerful emotions through careful, quiet prose, while delivering a satisfying romance. The author's many devotees are sure to enjoy this weighty addition to her canon." Pub Wkly

That summer. Orchard Books 1996 198p hardcover o.p. pa $8.99

Grades: 7 8 9 10

1. Sisters -- Fiction 2. Weddings -- Fiction

ISBN 0-531-09538-X; 0-531-08888-X lib bdg; 978-0-14-240172-9 pa; 0-14-240172-2 pa

LC 96-7643

During the summer of her divorced father's remarriage and her sister's wedding, fifteen-year-old Haven comes into her own by letting go of the myths of the past

"Dessen adds a fresh twist to a traditional sister-of-the-bride story with her keenly observant narrative full of witty ironies. Her combination of unforgettable characters and unexpected events generates hilarity as well as warmth." Publ Wkly

The **truth** about forever. Viking 2004 382p $16.99; pa $6.50

Grades: 7 8 9 10

1. Death -- Fiction 2. Catering -- Fiction

ISBN 0-670-03639-0; 0-440-21928-0 pa

LC 2003-28298

The summer following her father's death, Macy plans to work at the library and wait for her brainy boyfriend to return from camp, but instead she goes to work at a catering business where she makes new friends and finally faces her grief.

"All of Dessen's characters . . . are fully and beautifully drawn. Their dialogue is natural and believable, and their care for one another is palpable. . . . Dessen charts Macy's navigation of grief in such an honest way it will touch every reader who meets her. " SLJ

What happened to goodbye. Viking 2011 402p $19.99

Grades: 8 9 10 11 12

    1. School stories 2. Divorce -- Fiction

    ISBN 978-0-670-01294-7; 0-670-01294-7

                     LC 2010-41041

"The novel nimbly weaves together familiar story lines of divorce, high-school happiness and angst, and teen-identity struggles with likable, authentic adult and teen characters and intriguing yet credible situations." Booklist

DeStefano, Lauren

    Fever; Lauren DeStefano. Simon & Schuster 2012 341 p. (The Chemical Garden trilogy)

Grades: 9 10 11 12

    1. Science fiction 2. Dystopian fiction 3. Escapes -- Fiction 4. Viruses -- Fiction 5. Genetic engineering -- Fiction 6. Orphans -- Fiction

    ISBN 9781442409071

                     LC 2011016961

This young adult novel is the second installment in Lauren DeStefano's "Chemical Garden Trilogy." "Having recently escaped the compound where she was forced to marry, take on sister wives and ultimately become her evil father-in-law Vaughn's scientific experiment in the name of finding a cure for the virus that kills off men and women at a young age, Rhine, along with former servant and love interest Gabriel, finds herself in trouble again. Plotting another escape from a heartless 'First Generation' who runs a brothel out of an abandoned carnival site, continuing to evade Vaughn, picking up a malformed and mute girl and trying to find Rhine's twin brother should be adventurous. And finally being able to communicate freely should bring out the intimacy between Rhine and Gabriel." (Kirkus)

    Perfect ruin; by Lauren DeStefano and illustrated by Teagan White. Simon and Schuster Books for Young Readers 2013 368 p. (The Internment chronicles) (hardcover: alk. paper) $17.99

Grades: 7 8 9 10

    1. Utopias 2. Imaginary places 3. Criminal investigation -- Fiction 4. Science fiction 5. Utopias -- Fiction

    ISBN 1442480610; 9781442480612

                     LC 2013014392

In this book by Lauren DeStefano "Morgan Stockhour knows getting too close to the edge of Internment, the floating city in the clouds where she lives, can lead to madness. Then a murder, the first in a generation, rocks the city. With whispers swirling and fear on the wind, Morgan can no longer stop herself from investigating, especially once she meets Judas. Betrothed to the victim, he is the boy being blamed for the murder, but Morgan is convinced of his innocence." (Publisher's note)

    Sever; Lauren DeStefano. Simon & Schuster 2013 384 p. (The Chemical Garden trilogy) (hardcover: alk. paper) $17.99

Grades: 9 10 11 12

    1. Love stories 2. Science fiction 3. Genetic engineering

-- Fiction 4. Orphans -- Fiction 5. Survival -- Fiction

ISBN 1442409096; 9781442409095; 9781442409101; 9781442409132

                     LC 2012015702

This young adult dystopian romance novel, by Lauren DeStefano, is the "conclusion to the New York Times bestselling Chemical Garden Trilogy. . . . While Gabriel haunts Rhine's memories, Cecily is determined to be at Rhine's side, even if Linden's feelings are still caught between them. Meanwhile, Rowan's growing involvement in an underground resistance compels Rhine to reach him before he does something that cannot be undone." (Publisher's note)

    Wither. Simon & Schuster Books for Young Readers 2011 358p (The Chemical Garden trilogy) $17.99

Grades: 9 10 11 12

    1. Science fiction 2. Orphans -- Fiction 3. Marriage -- Fiction 4. Kidnapping -- Fiction 5. Genetic engineering -- Fiction

    ISBN 978-1-4424-0905-7

                     LC 2010-21347

After modern science turns every human into a genetic time bomb with men dying at age twenty-five and women dying at age twenty, girls are kidnapped and married off in order to repopulate the world.

"This beautifully-written . . . fantasy, with its intriguing world-building, well-developed characters and intricate plot involving flashbacks as well as edge-of-the-seat suspense, will keep teens riveted to the plight of Rhine and her sister wives. . . . This thought-provoking novel will also stimulate discussion in science and ethics classes." Voice Youth Advocates

Deuker, Carl

    Gym candy. Houghton Mifflin Company 2007 313p $16

Grades: 7 8 9 10 11 12

    1. School stories 2. Football -- Fiction 3. Steroids -- Fiction 4. Washington (State) -- Fiction 5. Father-son relationship -- Fiction

    ISBN 978-0-618-77713-6; 0-618-77713-X

                     LC 2007-12749

Groomed by his father to be a star player, football is the only thing that has ever really mattered to Mick Johnson, who works hard for a spot on the varsity team his freshman year, then tries to hold onto his edge by using steroids, despite the consequences to his health and social life.

"Deuker skillfully complements a sobering message with plenty of exciting on-field action and locker-room drama, while depicting Mick's emotional struggles with loneliness and insecurity as sensitively and realistically as his physical ones." Booklist

    High heat. Houghton Mifflin 2003 277p $16; pa $6.99

Grades: 7 8 9 10

    1. School stories 2. Fathers -- Fiction

    ISBN 0-618-31117-3; 0-06-057248-5 pa

                     LC 2002-15324

When high school sophomore Shane Hunter's father is arrested for money laundering at his Lexus dealership, the star pitcher's life of affluence and private school begins to fall apart

This is "a story that delivers baseball action along with a rich psychological portrait, told through a compelling first-person narration." SLJ

Painting the black. Avon Books 1999 248p pa $5.99

Grades: 8 9 10 11 12

1. School stories 2. Baseball -- Fiction

ISBN 0-380-73104-5

First published 1997 by Houghton Mifflin

"After a disastrous fall from a tree, senior Ryan Ward wrote off baseball. But he is swept back into the game when cocky, charismatic Josh Daniels—a star quarterback with the perfect spiral pass as well as a pitcher with a mean slider—moves into the neighborhood. . . . The well-written sports scenes—baseball and football—will draw reluctant readers, but it is Ryan's moral courage that will linger when the reading is done." Booklist

★ **Payback** time. Houghton Mifflin Harcourt 2010 298p $16

Grades: 7 8 9 10

1. School stories 2. Courage -- Fiction 3. Obesity -- Fiction 4. Football -- Fiction 5. Journalists -- Fiction

ISBN 978-0-547-27981-7; 0-547-27981-7

LC 2010-6779

Deuker "really cranks up the suspense in his newest page-turner. . . . The game action alone is riveting . . . but Deuker enriches the tale with several well-tuned subplots and memorable narrator/protagonist." Booklist

Runner. Houghton Mifflin 2005 216p $16; pa $7.99

Grades: 7 8 9 10

1. Smuggling -- Fiction 2. Terrorism -- Fiction 3. Alcoholism -- Fiction

ISBN 0-618-54298-1; 0-618-73505-4 pa

LC 2004-15781

Living with his alcoholic father on a broken-down sailboat on Puget Sound has been hard on seventeen-year-old Chance Taylor, but when his love of running leads to a high-paying job, he quickly learns that the money is not worth the risk

"Writing in a fast-paced, action-packed, but at the same time reflective style, Deuker . . . uses running as a hook to entice readers into a perceptive coming-of-age novel." SLJ

Swagger; Carl Deuker. Houghton Mifflin Harcourt 2013 304 p. $17.99

Grades: 7 8 9 10 11 12

1. Basketball -- Fiction 2. Child sexual abuse -- Fiction 3. Sexual abuse -- Fiction

ISBN 0547974590; 9780547974590

LC 2012045062

In this book, by Carl Deuker, "high school senior Jonas moves to Seattle [and] is glad to meet Levi, a nice, soft-spoken guy and fellow basketball player." Then, readers are introduced to "Ryan Hartwell, a charismatic basketball coach and sexual predator. When Levi reluctantly tells Jonas that

Hartwell abused him, Jonas has to decide whether he should risk his future career to report the coach." (Publisher's note)

"When his family moves to Seattle, high school basketball star Jonas befriends new neighbor Levi, who plays power forward. Assistant coach Ryan Hartwell appreciates Jonas's fast-breaking style, but something about Hartwell feels wrong. Eventually his misdeeds lead to tragedy, and Jonas must find the courage to do what's right. Basketball fans will love the realistic hardwood action and the story's quick pacing." (Horn Book)

DeVillers, Julia

Lynn Visible. Dutton Children's Books 2010 278p il $16.99

Grades: 6 7 8 9

1. School stories 2. Fashion -- Fiction

ISBN 978-0-525-47691-7; 0-525-47691-1

LC 2009-23058

"Lynn Vincent knows all the latest trends and isn't afraid to flaunt her funky style. The problem is, in small-town Pennsylvania, being fashion forward makes Lynn socially backward. . . . But when one of Lynn's unique creations makes it into the hands of a famous designer and onto the runway, it seems that Lynn might finally get her moment in the spotlight." Publisher's note

Devine, Eric

Press play. Eric Devine. Running Press Book Publishers 2014 368 p.

Grades: 9 10 11 12

1. Documentary films -- Fiction 2. School sports -- Corrupt practices -- Fiction 3. Hazing -- Fiction 4. School stories

0762455128; 9780762455126, $9.95

LC 2014937889

In this book by Eric Devine, "at nearly 400 pounds, Greg is determined to shed his excess weight while making a documentary of the process. One day, Greg and his friend, Quinn, witness the lacrosse team involved in brutal hazing rituals, which Greg captures on film. Quinn wants to go to the principal, who is also the coach, but Greg convinces his friend that they need to record more evidence." (School Library Journal)

"It's thrilling to watch Greg enter the lion's den himself-the lacrosse team's Hell Week-for the bruising finale. A tough, smart look at weight issues, self-respect, and our intrinsic desire to belong at all costs." Booklist

Devlin, Calla

Tell me something real. Calla Devlin. Atheneum Books for Young Readers 2016 304 p.

Grades: 9 10 11 12

1. Betrayal -- Fiction 2. Family secrets -- Fiction 3. Leukemia -- Fiction 4. Mothers and daughters -- Fiction 5. Sisters -- Fiction

9781481461160; 9781481461153, $17.99

LC 2015039224

Morris Award Finalist (2017)

In this book, by Calla Devlin, "there are three beautiful blond Babcock sisters: gorgeous and foul-mouthed Adrienne, observant and shy Vanessa, and the youngest and best-loved, Marie. Their mother is ill with leukemia and the girls spend a lot of time with her at a Mexican clinic across the border from their San Diego home so she can receive alternative treatments." (Publisher's note)

"This is an intense read that explores the way illness can seep into the lives of everyone it touches, leaving behind confusion, fear, and anger, and a thoroughly engrossing story that will keep readers reevaluating everything they thought they knew about the Babcock family." SLJ

DeWoskin, Rachel

Blind. Rachel DeWoskin. Viking, published by Penguin Group 2014 394 p.

Grades: 9 10 11 12

1. Blind -- Fiction 2. Family life -- Fiction 3. High schools -- Fiction 4. Interpersonal relations -- Fiction 5. People with disabilities -- Fiction 6. Schools -- Fiction 7. Teenagers -- Fiction

0670785229; 9780670785223, $17.99

LC 2013041189

In this young adult novel by Rachel DeWoskin, "when Emma Sasha Silver loses her eyesight in a nightmare accident, she must relearn everything from walking across the street to recognizing her own sisters to imagining colors. . . . Emma used to be the invisible kid, but now it seems everyone is watching her. And just as she's about to start high school and try to recover her friendships and former life, one of her classmates is found dead in an apparent suicide." (Publisher's note)

"The life of a formerly sighted teen blossoms in Emma's strong voice as she explores the world, conquers fears, and attempts living everyday life again with her large, bustling, Jewish suburban family. A gracefully written, memorable, and enlightening novel." Booklist

Dhar, Payal

★ **Eat** the sky, drink the ocean. Edited by Kirsty Murray, Payal Dhar, and Anita Roy. Margaret K. McElderry Books 2017 Ix, 225 p. Illustration

Grades: 8 9 10 11 12

1. Boys -- Fiction; 2. Girls -- Fiction; 3. Short stories

9781481470575, $17.99; 9781481470599; 1481470574

This collection, edited by Kirsty Murray, Payal Dhar and Anita Roy, "is about connections: between men and women, boys and girls, between the past, the present, and the future. Through short stories, graphic novellas, and a play, the reader will discover new worlds where the strengths of women and men are celebrated and honored, and where magical realism is blended with self-confidence." (Publisher's note)

"Writers and artists from Australia and India worked together to create this thoughtful and nuanced collection of speculative short fiction in a variety of formats." SLJ

Diederich, Phillippe

Playing for the Devil's Fire. By Phillippe Diederich. Cinco Puntos Press 2016 232 p.

Grades: 7 8 9 10 11 12

1. Abandoned children -- Fiction 2. Coming of age -- Fiction 3. Criminals -- Fiction 4. Missing persons -- Fiction 5. Mexico City (Mexico) -- Fiction 6. Organized crime -- Fiction 7. Bildungsromans 8.

Mexico -- Fiction

9781941026298, $16.95; 9781941026304

LC 2015024951

In this young adult novel, by Phillippe Diederich, "nothing ever happens in the small Mexican town of Izayoc, where 13-year-old Boli spends his time playing marbles with his friends . . . and reading about the luchadores, who not only wrestle but fight crime, too.... When Boli's parents fail to return from their trip to request federal assistance, he sets out to discover the truth behind their disappearance with the help of washed-up wrestler El Chicano Estrada." (School Library Journal)

"Striking imagery and symbolism, along with the timeliness of the subject, make this title a natural for classroom discussion, and a Spanish glossary will aid English-only speakers. Diederich, who grew up in Mexico City, brings firsthand experience as well as tremendous compassion to this poignant coming-of-age novel." Booklist

Dickerson, Melanie

The **merchant's** daughter. Zondervan 2011 284p pa $9.99

Grades: 7 8 9 10 11 12

1. Love -- Fiction 2. Middle Ages -- Fiction 3. Christian life -- Fiction 4. Contract labor -- Fiction

ISBN 978-0-31072761-3

LC 2011034338

In 1352 England, seventeen-year-old Annabel, granddaughter of a knight and a would-be nun, eludes a lecherous bailiff but falls in love with Lord Le Wyse, the ferocious and disfigured man to whom her family owes three years of indentured servitude, in this tale loosely based on Beauty and the Beast.

Dickerson "manages a heartfelt romance that will stick with readers, not only for its morality but also for the exploration of a woman's place within fourteenth-century English Christianity." Booklist

Dickinson, Peter

★ **Eva**. Delacorte Press 1989 219p hardcover o.p. pa $6.50; pa $7.99

Grades: 7 8 9 10

1. Science fiction 2. Chimpanzees -- Fiction

ISBN 0-385-29702-5; 0-440-20766-5 pa; 9780440207665 pa

LC 88-29435

"Eva wakes up from a deep coma that was the result of a terrible car accident and finds herself drastically altered. The accident leaves her so badly injured that her parents consent to a radical experiment to transplant her brain and memory into the body of a research chimpanzee. With the aid of a computer for communication, Eva slowly adjusts to her new existence while scientists monitor her progress, feelings, and insight into the animal world." Voice Youth Advocates

★ The **ropemaker**. Delacorte Press 2001 375p $15.95; pa $7.95

Grades: 7 8 9 10

1. Fantasy fiction 2. Magic -- Fiction

ISBN 0-385-72921-9; 0-385-73063-2 pa

LC 2001-17422

Michael L. Printz Award honor book, 2002

When the magic that protects their Valley starts to fail, Tilja and her companions journey into the evil Empire to find the ancient magician Faheel, who originally cast those spells

"The suspense does not let up until the very last pages. While on one level this tale is a fantasy, it is also a wonderful coming-of-age story." SLJ

Dimaline, Cherie

★ The **marrow** thieves. Cherie Dimaline. Dancing Cat Books, an imprint of Cormorant Books Inc. 2017 260 p.

Grades: 9 10 11 12

1. Fantasy fiction; 2. Dreams -- Fiction; 3. Procurement of organs, tissues, etc.; 4. First Nations -- Fiction
9781770864863, $14.95

LC 2016945346

Kirkus Prize: Young Readers' Literature (2017)

In this book, by Cherie Dimaline, "the only people still able to dream are North America's Indigenous people, and it is their marrow that holds the cure for the rest of the world. But getting the marrow, and dreams, means death for the unwilling donors. Driven to flight, a fifteen-year-old and his companions struggle for survival, attempt to reunite with loved ones and take refuge from the 'recruiters' who seek them out to bring them to the marrow-stealing 'factories.'" (Publisher's note)

"A dystopian world that is all too real and that has much to say about our own." Kirkus

Dinnison, Kris

You and me and him. By Kris Dinnison. Houghton Mifflin Harcourt 2015 288 p.

Grades: 9 10 11 12

1. Friendship -- Fiction 2. Gays -- Fiction 3. High schools -- Fiction 4. Love -- Fiction 5. Schools -- Fiction 6. Gay teenagers -- Fiction 7. School stories
9780544301122, $17.99

LC 2014011663

In this young adult novel, by Kris Dinnison, "Maggie and Nash are outsiders. She's overweight. He's out of the closet. The best of friends, they have seen each other through thick and thin, but when Tom moves to town at the start of the school year, they have something unexpected in common: feelings for the same guy." (Publisher's note)

"Stilted and sometimes clunkily expository dialogue also reveals little, making several of the book's many interpersonal conflicts more confusing than compelling. The (mostly) fat-positive message is important, but its delivery falters." Kirkus

Dirkes, Craig

Sucktown, Alaska: a novel. Craig Dirkes. Switch Press, a Capstone imprint 2017 341 p.

Grades: 9 10 11 12

1. Interpersonal relations -- Fiction; 2. Marijuana -- Fiction; 3. Newspapers -- Fiction; 4. Reporters and reporting -- Alaska -- Fiction; 5. Alaska -- Fiction; 6. Marijuana -- Fiction; 7. Reporters and reporting -- Fiction
9781630790554, $17.95

LC 2016046406

In this novel, by Craig Dirkes, "Freshman year, Eddie Ashford had it all. Friends, parties, Taco Bell.... And he flunked out. Now he wants to redeem himself.... He takes a job in tiny Kusko, Alaska, and promises to stay a year. His intentions are pure, but soon he's lonely, low on cash, and desperate to escape the tundra.... Eddie's life becomes a dog-sled ride along a line between youth and experience, bravery and recklessness, right and wrong." (Publisher's note)

"The author paints vivid, detailed pictures of life, both in rural Alaska and in the mind of a young man." VOYA

Dixon, Heather

★ **Entwined**. Greenwillow Books 2011 472p

Grades: 7 8 9 10

1. Fantasy fiction 2. Dance -- Fiction 3. Death -- Fiction 4. Magic -- Fiction 5. Princesses -- Fiction 6. Kings and rulers -- Fiction 7. Father-daughter relationship -- Fiction
ISBN 0-06-200103-5; 978-0-06-200103-0

LC 2010-11686

Confined to their dreary castle while mourning their mother's death, Princess Azalea and her eleven sisters join The Keeper, who is trapped in a magic passageway, in a nightly dance that soon becomes nightmarish.

"The story gracefully explores significant themes of grief and loss, mercy and love. Full of mystery, lush settings, and fully orbed characters, Dixon's debut is both suspenseful and rewarding." Booklist

Doctorow, Cory

For the win. Tor 2010 475p $17.99

Grades: 8 9 10 11 12

1. Science fiction 2. Internet games -- Fiction
ISBN 978-0-7653-2216-6; 0-7653-2216-1

LC 2010-18644

A group of teens from around the world find themselves drawn into an online revolution arranged by a mysterious young woman known as Big Sister Nor, who hopes to challenge the status quo and change the world using her virtual connections.

The author "has taken denigrated youth behavior (this time, gaming) and recast it into something heroic. He can't resist the occasional lecture—sometimes breaking away from the plot to do so—but thankfully his lessons are riveting. With its eye-opening humanity and revolutionary zeal, this ambitious epic is well worth the considerable challenge." Booklist

★ **Homeland**; Cory Doctorow. 1st ed. Tor Teen 2013 396 p. (hardcover) $17.99

Grades: 9 10 11 12

1. Adventure fiction 2. Hacktivism -- Fiction 3. Civil rights -- Fiction 4. Counterculture -- Fiction 5. Computer hackers -- Fiction 6. Politics, Practical -- Fiction 7. San Francisco (Calif.) -- Fiction 8. United States. Dept. of Homeland Security -- Fiction
ISBN 0765333694; 9780765333698

LC 2012037366

This is a follow-up to Cory Doctorow's "Little Brother." Here, California's economy collapses, but Marcus's hacktivist past lands him a job as webmaster for a crusading politician who promises reform. Soon his former nemesis

Masha emerges from the political underground to gift him with a thumbdrive containing a Wikileaks-style cable-dump of hard evidence of corporate and governmental perfidy" and Marcus must choose whether to release it to the public. (Publisher's note)

★ **Little** brother. Tor Teen 2008 380p
Grades: 8 9 10 11 12
    1. Computers -- Fiction 2. Terrorism -- Fiction 3. Civil rights -- Fiction 4. San Francisco (Calif.) -- Fiction 5. United States -- Dept. of Homeland Security -- Fiction
    ISBN 0765319853; 9780765319852
                        LC 2008-1827
After being interrogated for days by the Department of Homeland Security in the aftermath of a terrorist attack on San Francisco, California, 17-year-old Marcus, released into what is now a police state, decides to use his expertise in computer hacking to set things right. "High school." (Horn Book)
"The author manages to explain naturally the necessary technical tools and scientific concepts in this fast-paced and well-written story. . . . The reader is privy to Marcus's gut-wrenching angst, frustration, and terror, thankfully offset by his self-awareness and humorous observations." Voice Youth Advocates

Pirate cinema; Cory Doctorow. 1st ed. Tor Teen 2012 384 p. (hardback) $19.99; (paperback) $9.99; (audiobook) $24.00
Grades: 7 8 9 10
    1. Copyright 2. Runaway teenagers -- Fiction 3. Science fiction 4. England -- Fiction 5. Internet -- Fiction 6. Protest movements -- Fiction 7. Motion pictures -- Production and direction -- Fiction
    ISBN 0765329085; 9780765329080; 9781429943185; 9780765329097; 9780307879585
                        LC 2012019871
In this book, author Cory Doctorow tells the story of Trent McCauley, a boy who "has an irrepressible drive to create . . . [films] through illegal downloading, and when he's caught, . . . [he] runs away to London, where he's taken under the wing of streetwise Jem Dodger. . . . He meets 26 and creates the persona Cecil B. DeVil. Pulled by 26 into the politics of copyright and the lobbyist money that purchases laws, Cecil becomes a creative figurehead for reform against escalating laws that aggressively jail kids." (Kirkus Reviews)

Dogar, Sharon
   ★ **Annexed**. Houghton Mifflin Harcourt 2010 333p $17
Grades: 8 9 10 11 12
    1. Children 2. Diarists 3. Holocaust victims 4. Netherlands -- Fiction 5. Holocaust, 1933-1945 -- Fiction; 6. Frank, Anne, 1929-1945 -- Fiction; 7. Pels, Peter van, 1926-1945 -- Fiction
    ISBN 978-0-547-50195-6; 0-547-50195-1
                        LC 2010-282410
"On July 13, 1942, 15-year-old Peter van Pels and his parents entered the attic that became their home for two years. Peter is angry that he is hiding and not fighting Nazis. He is also not happy to be sharing cramped living quarters with the Franks, especially know-it-all Anne. In this novel, Dogar 'reimagines' what happened between the families who lived in the secret annex immortalized in Anne Frank's diary. In doing so, she creates a captivating historical novel and fully fleshes out the character of Peter, a boy whom teens will easily relate to." SLJ

Doktorski, Jennifer Salvato
   Famous last words; Jennifer Salvato Doktorski. Henry Holt and Company 2013 288 p. (hardcover) $17.99
Grades: 7 8 9 10
    1. Women journalists -- Fiction 2. Internship programs -- Fiction 3. Journalism -- Fiction 4. Newspapers -- Fiction 5. Self-perception -- Fiction 6. Dating (Social customs) -- Fiction
    ISBN 0805093672; 9780805093674
                        LC 2012046312
In this book, "aspiring reporter Sam D'Angelo, 16, is interning at her local New Jersey paper for the summer, stuck writing obituaries with her occasionally annoying, college-age fellow intern AJ. When she's not taking phone calls about dead people, Sam writes humorous imaginary obits (including one for herself); spends time with her grandmother; lusts after the 'incredibly hot' features intern, Tony Roma; and covertly investigates the shady mayor with AJ." (Publishers Weekly)
"Something of a love note to print journalism, the story is nevertheless snappy and contemporary, furthered by Sam's wry, self-deprecating narration and convincingly colloquial dialogue. Cleverly titled, realistically written, and on the whole engaging and sympathetic, this story rings true." Kirkus

   The **summer** after you and me. Jennifer Salvato Doktorski. Sourcebooks Fire 2015 304 p.
Grades: 9 10 11 12
    1. Dating (Social customs) -- Fiction 2. Family life -- New Jersey -- Fiction 3. Summer resorts -- Fiction 4. Twins -- Fiction 5. New Jersey -- Fiction 6. Family life -- Fiction 7. Resorts -- Fiction 8. New Jersey -- Fiction 9. Summer -- Fiction
    1492619035; 9781492619031, $9.99
                        LC 2014044296
In this book, by Jennifer Salvato Doktorski, "[f]or Lucy, the Jersey Shore isn't just the perfect summer escape, it's home. As a local girl, she knows not to get attached to the tourists. . . . Still, she can't help but crush on charming Connor Malloy. . . . Then Superstorm Sandy sweeps up the coast, bringing Lucy and Connor together for a few intense hours. Except nothing is the same in the wake of the storm, and Lucy is left to pick up the pieces of her broken heart and her broken home." (Publisher's note)
"Doktorski has crafted a rich, multilayered novel with a strong sense of place and a good mix of characters and problems." Booklist

Dole, Mayra L.
   ★ **Down** to the bone; [by] Mayra Lazara Dole. HarperTeen 2008 384p $16.99; lib bdg $17.89

Grades: 8 9 10 11 12

    1. Lesbians -- Fiction 2. Cuban Americans -- Fiction

ISBN 978-0-06-084310-6; 0-06-084310-1; 978-0-06-084311-3 lib bdg; 0-06-084311-X lib bdg

LC 2007-33270

Laura, a seventeen-year-old Cuban American girl, is thrown out of her house when her mother discovers she is a lesbian, but after trying to change her heart and hide from the truth, Laura finally comes to terms with who she is and learns to love and respect herself.

"Using Spanish colloquialisms and slang, this debut author pulls off the tricky task of dialect in a manner that feels authentic. As Dole tackles a tough and important topic, her protagonist will win over a range of teen audiences, gay and straight." Publ Wkly

Doller, Trish

The devil you know. By Trish Doller. Bloomsbury 2015 256 p.

Grades: 10 11 12

    1. Camping -- Fiction 2. Fathers and daughters -- Fiction 3. Murder -- Fiction 4. Psychopaths -- Fiction 5. Single-parent families -- Fiction 6. Florida -- Fiction 7. Florida -- Fiction 8. Father-daughter relationship -- Fiction

1619634163; 9781619634169, $17.99

LC 2014023032

In this book, by Trish Doller, "[e]ighteen-year-old Arcadia wants adventure. Living in a tiny Florida town with her dad and four-year-old brother, Cadie spends most of her time working, going to school, and taking care of her family. So when she meets two handsome cousins at a campfire party, . . . [they] invite her . . . to join them on a road trip, and it's just the risk she's been craving. . . . But . . . she discovers that one of them is not at all who he claims to be." (Publisher's note)

"Cadie, 18, lives in a tiny Floridian town with her widowed dad and kid brother. She's spent the last couple years pining for an adventure to take her away from her boring home. When two cute cousins, Matt and Noah, show up at a campfire party, Cadie is so strongly attracted to Noah that it thrills and scares her. The next day, the guys invite her and her old friend to join them on their road trip. Even though they're not much more than strangers, Cadie just can't say no. What the teen thought was going to be a sexy and temporary getaway slowly turns out to be a dangerous, terrifying, and deadly experience. . . . This dark thriller features a strong female lead and a heap of sexy; a must-buy for readers looking for a healthy dose of drama." SLJ

Something like normal; Trish Doller. Bloomsbury Pub. Children's Books 2012 216 p. (hardback) $16.99

Grades: 9 10 11 12

    1. Love stories 2. Military personnel -- United States -- Fiction 3. Triangles (Interpersonal relations) -- Fiction 4. Love -- Fiction 5. Brothers -- Fiction 6. Veterans -- Fiction 7. Afghanistan -- Fiction 8. Family problems -- Fiction 9. Afghan War, 2001- -- Fiction 10. United States. Marine Corps -- Fiction 11. Post-traumatic stress disorder -- Fiction

ISBN 1599908441; 9781599908441

LC 2011035511

In this book, "Travis is home in southwest Florida, on leave from Afghanistan and dealing with the death of his best friend and fellow soldier Charlie, the breakup of his parents' marriage, and his girlfriend having left him for his brother. While processing all of this, he meets Harper, a girl whose reputation he destroyed years ago, and the two slowly start to connect." (Publishers Weekly)

Dominy, Amy Fellner

OyMG. Walker & Co. 2011 247p $16.99

Grades: 6 7 8 9

    1. Camps -- Fiction 2. Prejudices -- Fiction 3. Jews -- United States -- Fiction

ISBN 978-0-8027-2177-8; 0-8027-2177-X

LC 2010-34581

Fourteen-year-old Ellie will do almost anything to win a scholarship to the best speech school in the country, but must decide if she is willing to hide her Jewish heritage while at a Phoenix, Arizona, summer camp that could help her reach her goal.

"Readers will be pulled into the thoughtful exploration of one girl's emotional connection to her religion and family heritage, her struggle to balance ambition with honesty and self respect, and her delicate negotiation of being different when that difference isn't outwardly apparent." Bull Cent Child Books

Donaldson, Julia

Running on the cracks. Henry Holt 2009 218p $16.99

Grades: 6 7 8 9

    1. Orphans -- Fiction 2. Runaway teenagers -- Fiction 3. Child sexual abuse -- Fiction 4. Racially mixed people -- Fiction

ISBN 978-0-8050-9054-3; 0-8050-9054-1

LC 2008-50278

After her parents are killed in an accident, English teenager Leonora Watts-Chan runs away to Glasgow, Scotland, to find her Chinese grandparents

"The characters in Donaldson's . . . YA debut are well drawn and their imperfections are authentic, particularly Mary's battle with mental illness. Despite heavy themes, the story is neither bleak nor gritty. The fast pace and short chapters should appeal to readers, who will celebrate the hopeful ending." Publ Wkly

Donnelly, Jennifer

A **northern** light. Harcourt 2003 389p $17; pa $8.95

Grades: 9 10 11 12

    1. Farm life -- Fiction

ISBN 0-15-216705-6; 0-15-205310-7 pa

LC 2002-5098

Michael L. Printz Award honor book, 2004

In 1906, sixteen-year-old Mattie, determined to attend college and be a writer against the wishes of her father and fiance, takes a job at a summer inn where she discovers the truth about the death of a guest. Based on a true story.

"Donnelly's characters ring true to life, and the meticulously described setting forms a vivid backdrop to this finely crafted story. An outstanding choice for historical-fiction fans." SLJ

★ **Revolution**. Delacorte Press 2010 471p $18.99; lib bdg $21.99

Grades: 9 10 11 12

1. Princes 2. Diaries -- Fiction 3. Musicians -- Fiction 4. Bereavement -- Fiction 5. Family life -- Fiction 6. Paris (France) -- Fiction 7. France -- History -- 1789-1799, Revolution -- Fiction
ISBN 978-0-385-73763-0; 0-385-73763-7; 978-0-385-90678-4 lib bdg; 0-385-90678-1 lib bdg

LC 2010-08993

An angry, grieving seventeen-year-old musician facing expulsion from her prestigious Brooklyn private school travels to Paris to complete a school assignment and uncovers a diary written during the French revolution by a young actress attempting to help a tortured, imprisoned little boy—Louis Charles, the lost king of France.

"The ambitious story, narrated in Andi's grief-soaked, sardonic voice, will wholly capture patient readers with its sharply articulated, raw emotions and insights into science and art; ambition and love; history's ever-present influence; and music's immediate, astonishing power." Booklist

Includes bibliographical references

These shallow graves. Jennifer Donnelly. Delacorte Press 2015 496 p.

Grades: 7 8 9 10

1. Death -- Fiction 2. Fathers and daughters -- Fiction 3. Sex role -- Fiction 4. Social classes -- Fiction 5. New York (N.Y.) -- History -- 19th century -- Fiction 6. New York (N.Y.) -- History -- Fiction 7. Gender role -- Fiction 8. Father-daughter relationship -- Fiction
9780385737654, $19.99

LC 2014047825

In this book, by Jennifer Donnelly, "Jo Montfort . . . [will] graduate from finishing school and be married off to a wealthy bachelor. Which is the last thing she wants. Jo dreams of becoming a writer. . . . Wild aspirations aside, Jo's life seems perfect until tragedy strikes: her father is found dead. Charles Montfort shot himself while cleaning his pistol. One of New York City's wealthiest men . . . Jo knows he was far too smart to clean a loaded gun." (Publisher's note)

"Melodrama and intrigue drive this fast-paced thriller with a Wharton-esque setting and a naïve young protagonist willing to be exposed to the shadier side of life-prostitutes, uncouth men, and abject poverty-on her way to solving a mystery and asserting her right to claim her future for herself. The author keeps the clues coming at a rate that allows readers to be one small step ahead of Jo as the story races to its surprising conclusion. Readers who love costume dramas will relish this one." Kirkus

Donovan, John

I'll get there, it better be worth the trip; 40th anniversary edition; Flux 2010 228p pa $9.95

Grades: 7 8 9 10 11

1. Alcoholism -- Fiction 2. Friendship -- Fiction 3. LGBT youth -- Fiction
ISBN 978-0-7387-2134-7 pa; 0-7387-2134-4 pa

LC 2010014266

First published 1969 by Harper & Row

While trying to cope with his alcoholic mother and absent father, a lonely New York City teenager develops a confusing crush on another boy.

"Donovan's novel is startlingly outspoken and honest in its presentation of a young teen questioning his sexuality. . . . Such is the author's skill that the reader knows this young man's journey of self-discovery will get him to his 'there,' wherever it may be. This welcome fortieth-anniversary edition of a YA classic is an essential purchase for all libraries." Voice Youth Advocates

Dooley, Sarah

Body of water. Feiwel and Friends 2011 324p $16.99

Grades: 7 8 9

1. Arson -- Fiction 2. Camping -- Fiction 3. Family life -- Fiction 4. Homeless persons -- Fiction
ISBN 978-0-312-61254-2; 0-312-61254-0

LC 2011023523

After their trailer home and all their belongings are burned, twelve-year-old Ember and her Wiccan family move to a lakeside campground where Ember's anguish over losing her dog, as well as her friendship with the boy she fears started the fire, stops her from making new friends and moving on.

"Dooley puts readers directly into the center of Ember's plight with a heartfelt first-person narration. An enthralling tale that demystifies Wicca, humanizes homeless families and inspires reflection on friendship, forgiveness and moving forward." Kirkus

Livvie Owen lived here. Feiwel and Friends 2010 229p $16.99

Grades: 6 7 8 9 10

1. School stories 2. Autism -- Fiction 3. Family life -- Fiction
ISBN 978-0-312-61253-5; 0-312-61253-2

LC 2010-13009

Fourteen-year-old Livvie Owen, who has autism, and her family have been forced to move frequently because of her outbursts, but when they face eviction again, Livvie is convinced she has a way to get back to a house where they were all happy, once.

"This novel is an interesting perspective of what a teenage girl with autism might experience, but also a heartwarming story of how a family binds together during emotional and financial turmoil." Libr Media Connect

Dos Santos, Steven

The **culling**; Steven Dos Santos. Flux 2013 432 p. (The torch keeper) $9.99

Grades: 9 10 11 12

1. Dystopian fiction 2. LGBT youth -- Fiction 3. Resistance to government -- Fiction 4. Science fiction 5. Orphans -- Fiction 6. Contests -- Fiction 7. Survival -- Fiction 8. Brothers and sisters -- Fiction
ISBN 073873537X; 9780738735375

LC 2012041699

Rainbow List (2014)

In this young adult dystopian novel, by Steven dos Santos, book one of "The Torch Keeper" series, "for Lucian . . .

Recruitment Day means the . . . totalitarian government will force him to . . . compet[e] to join the ruthless Imposer task force. Each Recruit participates in increasingly difficult and violent military training . . . those who fail must choose . . . a family member to be brutally killed." (Publisher's note)

Dowd, Siobhan

★ **Bog** child. David Fickling Books 2008 321p
Grades: 8 9 10 11 12

1. Mummies -- Fiction 2. Prisoners -- Fiction
3. Terrorism -- Fiction 4. Family life -- Fiction 5. Northern Ireland -- Fiction
ISBN 0-385-75170-2 lib bdg; 978-0-385-75169-8; 0-385-75169-9; 978-0-385-75170-4 lib bdg

LC 2008-2998

This novel is set in Northern Ireland in 1981. 18-year-old Fergus is distracted from his upcoming A-level exams by the discovery of a girl's body in a peat bog, his imprisoned brother's hunger strike, and the stress of being a courier for Sinn Fein. "Grades eight to twelve." (Bull Cent Child Books)

"Dowd raises questions about moral choices within a compelling plot that is full of surprises, powerfully bringing home the impact of political conflict on innocent bystanders." Publ Wkly

★ **Solace** of the road. David Fickling Books 2009 260p $17.99; lib bdg $20.99
Grades: 9 10 11 12

1. Great Britain -- Fiction 2. Foster home care -- Fiction 3. Runaway teenagers -- Fiction 4. Voyages and travels -- Fiction
ISBN 978-0-375-84971-8; 0-375-84971-8; 978-0-375-94971-5 lib bdg; 0-375-94971-2 lib bdg

LC 2008-44603

While running away from a London foster home just before her fifteenth birthday, Holly has ample time to consider her years of residential care and her early life with her Irish mother, whom she is now trying to reach.

"A compelling psychological portrait of a girl's journey from denial to facing the facts that will let her move beyond her troubled past. . . . Readers will root for her to find her balance and arrive safely at the right destination." Publ Wkly

A **swift** pure cry. David Fickling Books 2007 309p hardcover o.p. pa $8.99
Grades: 9 10 11 12

1. Fathers -- Fiction 2. Ireland -- Fiction 3. Pregnancy -- Fiction 4. Family life -- Fiction
ISBN 978-0-385-75108-7; 0-385-75108-7; 978-0-440-42218-1 pa; 0-440-42218-1 pa

LC 2006-14562

Coolbar, Ireland, is a village of secrets and Shell, caretaker to her younger brother and sister after the death of their mother and with the absence of their father, is not about to reveal hers until suspicion falls on the wrong person.

"This book, with its serious tone and inclusion of social issues, will have appeal for American readers desiring weightier material, and teachers might find it useful in the classroom." Voice Youth Advocates

Dowell, Frances O' Roark

Ten miles past normal. Atheneum Books for Young Readers 2011 211p $16.99
Grades: 6 7 8 9 10

1. School stories 2. Farm life -- Fiction 3. Bands (Music) -- Fiction
ISBN 1-4169-9585-4; 978-1-4169-9585-2

LC 2010-22041

Because living with "modern-hippy" parents on a goat farm means fourteen-year-old Janie Gorman cannot have a normal high school life, she tries joining Jam Band, making friends with Monster, and spending time with elderly former civil rights workers.

"Janie narrates her first year in high school with her sure, smart, sarcastic voice. . . . Dowell gets all the details of ninth grade right." Horn Book

Downes, Patrick

★ **Fell** of dark: a novel. Patrick Downes. Philomel Books, an imprint of Penguin Group (USA) 2015 208 p.
Grades: 9 10 11 12

1. Good and evil -- Fiction 2. Hallucinations and illusions -- Fiction 3. Mental illness -- Fiction
0399172904; 9780399172908, $17.99

LC 2014037606

In this young adult novel, by Patrick Downes, "Erik is often silenced by headaches and suffers from more mysterious afflictions including stigmatalike bleeding. . . . Thorn is plagued by demons and the voices that come from within. Eventually, the stories of these two deeply disturbed young men collide. . . . At the . . . end . . . Erik must stop Thorn from doing something terrible." (School Library Journal)

"This debut novel jumps between first-person narrators Erik (sexually abused after his father's death) and Thorn (blamed by his parents for his sister's death). The story reaches a crescendo when the teens finally meet—on opposite ends of a gun outside an elementary school. This unflinching exploration of loss, abuse, and mental illness occasionally stumbles under the weight of its stylistic techniques." Horn Book

★ **Ten** miles one way. Patrick Downes. Philomel Books 2017 199 p.
Grades: 8 9 10 11 12

1. Traffic accidents -- Fiction; 2. Mental illness -- Fiction; 3. Love -- Fiction; 4. Manic-depressive illness -- Fiction
9780399544996, $17.99; 9780399545016

LC 2015041653

In this book, by Patrick Downes, "Nest and Q walk through the city. Nest speaks and Q listens. Mile by mile, Nest tells Q about her life, her family, her past...and her Chimaera, the beast that preys on her mind and causes her to lose herself. Q knows only that his love for Nest runs deeper than the demon that plagues her thoughts, that he loves her in spite of -- or perhaps because of -- the personal battle she fights every day. A beautifully-written, haunting story." (Publisher's note)

"Part romance, part poetry, and part monologue, perceptive teens will devour this one." Booklist

Downham, Jenny

★ **Before** I die. David Fickling Books 2007 326p hardcover o.p. pa $9.99

Grades: 8 9 10 11 12

    1. Death -- Fiction 2. Terminally ill -- Fiction

    ISBN 978-0-385-75155-1; 978-0-385-75183-4 pa

                LC 2007-20284

A terminally ill teenaged girl makes and carries out a list of things to do before she dies.

"Downham holds nothing back in her wrenchingly and exceptionally vibrant story." Publ Wkly

★ **You** against me. David Fickling Books 2011 412p $16.99; lib bdg $19.99; ebook $10.99

Grades: 9 10 11 12

    1. Rape -- Fiction 2. Guilt -- Fiction 3. Siblings -- Fiction 4. Great Britain -- Fiction 5. Social classes -- Fiction

    ISBN 978-0-385-75160-5; 978-0-385-75161-2 lib bdg; 978-0-375-98938-4 ebook

                LC 2010038226

When eighteen-year-old Mikey's younger sister claims to have been raped and he seeks to avenge the crime, he meets Ellie, the sister of the accused, and befriends her, complicating the situation considerably for all of them.

"Crisp, revealing dialogue, measured pacing and candid, unaffected prose round out this illuminating novel in which any reader can find someone to root for or relate to." Kirkus

★ **Unbecoming**. By Jenny Downham. David Fickling Books/Scholastic Inc. 2016 384 p. Illustration

Grades: 9 10 11 12

    1. Alzheimer's disease -- Fiction 2. Brothers and sisters -- Fiction 3. Family life -- Fiction 4. Grandmothers -- Fiction 5. Mothers and daughters -- Fiction 6. Secrets -- Fiction 7. England -- Fiction 8. Mother-daughter relationship -- Fiction 9. Family secrets -- Fiction

    0545907179; 9780545907170, $17.99

                LC 2015036012

Stonewall Book Award Honor Book, Youth (2017)

"Katie's life is falling apart: her best friend thinks she's a freak, her mother, Caroline, controls every aspect of her life, and her estranged grandmother, Mary, appears as if out of nowhere. Mary has dementia and needs lots of care, and when Katie starts putting together Mary's life story, secrets and lies are uncovered. . . As the relationship between Mary and Caroline is explored, Katie begins to understand her own mother's behavior, and from that insight, the terrors about her sexuality, her future, and her younger brother are all put into perspective." (Publisher's note)

"Downham keenly weaves together musings, revelations, confrontations, and poignancy. Her prose gets right down inside human fragility, tenderness, fury, gusto, and strength-leaving sweet, sharp images that are impossible to forget. Exceptional. (Fiction. 14 & up)." Kirkus

"First published in the United Kingdom in 2015 by David Fickling Books"—Copyright page.

Dowswell, Paul

The **Auslander**. Bloomsbury Children's Books 2011 295p $16.99

Grades: 7 8 9 10

    1. Orphans -- Fiction 2. Adoption -- Fiction 3. Insurgency -- Fiction 4. Berlin (Germany) -- Fiction 5. National socialism -- Fiction 6. World War, 1939-1945 -- Fiction 7. Germany -- History -- 1933-1945 -- Fiction

    ISBN 1599906333; 9781599906331

                LC 2010035626

First published 2009 in the United Kingdom

German soldiers take Peter from a Warsaw orphanage, and soon he is adopted by Professor Kaltenbach, a prominent Nazi, but Peter forms his own ideas about what he sees and hears and decides to take a risk that is most dangerous in 1942 Berlin.

"The characters are rich and nuanced; . . . the action is swift and suspenseful; and the juxtaposition of wartime nobility and wartime cruelty is timeless." Horn Book

Doyle, Brian

Boy O'Boy. Douglas & McIntyre 2003 161p hardcover o.p. pa $12.95

Grades: 6 7 8 9

    1. Child sexual abuse -- Fiction

    ISBN 0-88899-588-1; 0-88899-590-3 pa

Living in Ottawa in 1945, Martin O'Boy must deal with a drunken father, an overburdened mother, a disabled twin brother, and a sexual predator at his church.

"Martin O'Boy is an expert observer and narrator. . . . Martin's world is believably real. Even the description of the sexual encounter seems like what a confused 11 or 12-year-old might say. " SLJ

Pure Spring. Groundwood Books 2007 158p $16.95; pa $8.95

Grades: 6 7 8 9

    1. Canada -- Fiction

    ISBN 978-0-88899-774-6; 978-0-88899-775-3 pa

It's spring in post-World War II Ottawa and Martin has found a true home. He's also working even though he had to lie about his age to get the job. Martin is also in love, but his boss is robbing the family of the one he loves.

"Doyle lovingly shapes his characters. . . . Doyle rounds out the grimness with comedic scenes." Horn Book

Doyle, Marissa

Bewitching season. Henry Holt 2008 346p $16.95; pa $8.99

Grades: 7 8 9 10

    1. Magic -- Fiction 2. Twins -- Fiction 3. Sisters -- Fiction 4. Missing persons -- Fiction

    ISBN 978-0-8050-8251-7; 0-8050-8251-4; 978-0-312-59695-8 pa; 0-312-59695-2 pa

In 1837, as seventeen-year-old twins, Persephone and Penelope are starting their first London Season they find that their beloved governess, who has taught them everything they know about magic, has disappeared.

"Doyle takes as much care with characters . . . as with story details. This [is a] delightful mélange of genres." Booklist

Other titles in this series are:

Betraying Season (2009)

Courtship and Curses (2012)

Doyle, Roddy

A **greyhound** of a girl; Roddy Doyle. Amulet Books 2012 208 p. (hbk.) $16.95

Grades: 7 8 9 10 11 12

1. Dog racing -- Fiction 2. Family life -- Fiction 3. Dublin (Ireland) -- Fiction 4. Women -- Ireland -- Fiction 5. Death -- Fiction 6. Ghosts -- Fiction 7. Ireland -- Fiction 8. Grandmothers -- Fiction 9. Voyages and travels -- Fiction 10. Mother-daughter relationship -- Fiction

ISBN 9781407129334 Marion Lloyd; 1407129333 Marion Lloyd; 9781419701689 Amulet; 1419701681 Amulet

LC 2011042200

This book tells the story of "Twelve-year-old Mary O'Hara," an Irish girl who "is surrounded by good-humored women . . . her mum at home, her mum's mum, who is dying in Dublin's Sacred Heart Hospital, and her mum's mum's mum, who has just materialized as a ghost on her street. . . . [Roddy] Doyle divides up the novel by character, giving readers first-hand glimpses into the nature of each woman through time." (Kirkus)

Wilderness. Arthur A. Levine Books 2007 211p $16.99

Grades: 6 7 8 9

1. Mothers -- Fiction 2. Sledding -- Fiction 3. Wilderness survival -- Fiction

ISBN 978-0-439-02356-6; 0-439-02356-4

LC 2007-11688

As Irish teenager Gráinne anxiously prepares for a reunion with her mother, who abandoned the family years before, Gráinne's half-brothers and their mother take a dog-sledding vacation in Finland.

"The drama and adventure are leavened by generous helpings of Doyle's characteristic charm, laugh-out-loud humor, and wonderful way with words." SLJ

Draper, Sharon M. (Sharon Mills), 1948-

The **Battle** of Jericho. Atheneum Books for Young Readers 2003 297p $16.95; pa $6.99

Grades: 7 8 9 10

1. School stories 2. Clubs -- Fiction 3. Death -- Fiction 4. Cousins -- Fiction

ISBN 0-689-84232-5; 0-689-84233-3 pa

LC 2002-8612

When Jericho is invited to pledge for the Warriors of Distinction, he thinks his life can't get any better. As the most exclusive club in school, the Warriors give the best parties, go out with the hottest girls, and sail through their classes. And when Arielle, one of the finest girls in his class, starts coming on to him once the pledge announcements are made, Jericho is determined to do anything to become a member.

"This title is a compelling read that drives home important lessons about making choices." SLJ

Other titles in this series are:

Just another hero (2009)

November blues (2007)

Copper sun; [by] Sharon Draper. Atheneum Books for Young Readers 2006 302p $16.95

Grades: 8 9 10 11 12

1. Slavery -- Fiction 2. African Americans -- Fiction

ISBN 0-689-82181-6

LC 2005-05540

Two fifteen-year-old girls—one a slave and the other an indentured servant—escape their Carolina plantation and try to make their way to Fort Moses, Florida, a Spanish colony that gives sanctuary to slaves.

"This action-packed, multifaceted, character-rich story describes the shocking realities of the slave trade and plantation life while portraying the perseverance, resourcefulness, and triumph of the human spirit." Booklist

Double Dutch. Atheneum Bks. for Young Readers 2002 183p $16; pa $4.99

Grades: 6 7 8 9

1. Friendship -- Fiction 2. Rope skipping -- Fiction 3. African Americans -- Fiction

ISBN 0-689-84230-9; 0-689-84231-7 pa

LC 00-50247

Three eighth-grade friends, preparing for the International Double Dutch Championship jump rope competition in their home town of Cincinnati, Ohio, cope with Randy's missing father, Delia's inability to read, and Yo Yo's encounter with the class bullies

"Teens will like the high-spirited, authentic dialogue . . . the honest look at tough issues, and the team workout scenes that show how sports can transform young lives." Booklist

★ **Fire** from the rock. Dutton Children's Books 2007 229p $16.99

Grades: 6 7 8 9

1. School stories 2. Race relations -- Fiction 3. African Americans -- Fiction

ISBN 978-0-525-47720-4; 0-525-47720-9

LC 2006-102952

In 1957, Sylvia Patterson's life is disrupted by the impending integration of Little Rock's Central High when she is selected to be one of the first black students to attend the previously all white school.

"This historical fiction novel is a must have. It keeps the reader engaged with vivid depictions of a time that most young people can only imagine." Voice Youth Advocates

Panic; Sharon Draper. 1st ed. Atheneum Books for Young Readers 2013 272 p. (hardcover) $17.99

Grades: 9 10 11 12

1. Kidnapping -- Fiction 2. Ballet dancers -- Fiction 3. Dance -- Fiction 4. Sexual abuse -- Fiction 5. African Americans -- Fiction

ISBN 1442408960; 9781442408968; 9781442408982

LC 2012016339

In this book, "after teenage Diamond makes a disastrously foolish mistake, she is abducted and finds herself in terrible danger. Will she survive? Will her life ever be the same? Told from multiple points of view, 'Panic' is not only Diamond's story but also that of three of her friends, all of them students at the Crystal Pointe Dance Academy." (Booklist)

Tears of a tiger. Atheneum Pubs. 1994 162p $16.95; pa $5.99

Grades: 7 8 9 10

1. Death -- Fiction 2. Suicide -- Fiction 3. African Americans -- Fiction
ISBN 0-689-31878-2; 0-689-80698-1 pa

LC 94-10278

The death of African American high school basketball star Rob Washington in a drunk driving accident leads to the suicide of his friend Andy, who was driving the car

"The story emerges through newspaper articles, journal entries, homework assignments, letters, and conversations that give the book immediacy; the teenage conversational idiom is contemporary and well written. Andy's perceptions of the racism directed toward young black males . . . will be recognized by African American YAs." Booklist

Duane, Diane

So you want to be a wizard. Diane Duane. HMH Books for Young Readers 2001 400 p. (Young Wizards)

Grades: 6 7 8 9 10

1. Bullies -- Fiction 2. Wizards -- Fiction
015216250X; 0385293054; 9780152162504, $7.99; 9780385293051, $14.95

LC 83005216

"Kit, 12, and Nita, 13, turn to magic in desperation as a way to protect themselves from bullies who beat them up regularly. They and Fred, a white mole they called up, jump through a worldgate into an alternate Manhattan where malevolent machines attack them at every turn. Their task is to rescue The Book of Night with Moon, which the evil Starsnuffer has hidden." (Voice of Youth Advocates)

Originally published 1983; Other titles in this series are:
Deep wizardry (1985);
High wizardry (1990);
A wizard abroad (1997);
The wizard's dilemma (2001);
A wizard alone (2002);
Wizard's holiday (2003);
Wizards at war (2005);
A wizard of Mars (2010);
Games wizards play (2016)

Duble, Kathleen Benner

Phantoms in the snow. Scholastic Press 2011 226p $17.99

Grades: 6 7 8 9

1. Uncles -- Fiction 2. Orphans -- Fiction 3. Pacifism -- Fiction 4. Soldiers -- Fiction 5. Military bases -- Fiction 6. World War, 1939-1945 -- Italy -- Fiction
ISBN 978-0-545-19770-0; 0-545-19770-8

LC 2010016898

In 1944, fifteen-year-old Noah Garrett, recently orphaned, is sent to live at Camp Hale, Colorado, with an uncle he has never met, and there he finds his pacifist views put to the test.

"Duble has created a likable character in Noah, whose struggles to find out who he is and where he belongs in a world at war are convincingly portrayed and realistically resolved." Kirkus

Dubosarsky, Ursula

★ The **golden** day; by Ursula Dubosarsky. Candlewick 2013 160 p. $15.99

Grades: 7 8 9 10

1. Mystery fiction 2. Friendship -- Fiction 3. Missing persons -- Fiction
ISBN 0763663999; 9780763663995; 9781742374710

LC 2012452201

In this novel by Ursula Dubosarsky "eleven schoolgirls embrace their own chilling history when their teacher abruptly goes missing on a field trip. Who was the mysterious poet they had met in the Garden? What actually happened in the seaside cave that day? And most important—who can they tell about it?" (Publisher's note)

"Spare and well written, this slim novel covers the days following a teacher's disappearance during a class outing. Eleven girls must make their way back to school where they are determined to keep their teacher's rendezvous with the local park's gardener a secret. The book's chilling atmosphere and mature tone are best suited for older readers." (Horn Book)

Dudley, David L.

Caleb's wars. Clarion Books 2011 263p $16.99

Grades: 7 8 9 10

1. Georgia -- Fiction 2. Germans -- Fiction 3. Family life -- Fiction 4. Segregation -- Fiction 5. Race relations -- Fiction 6. Prisoners of war -- Fiction 7. African Americans -- Fiction 8. World War, 1939-1945 -- Fiction
ISBN 978-0-547-23997-2; 0-547-23997-1

LC 2011009644

Fifteen-year-old Caleb's courageous commitment to justice grows as he faces a power struggle with his father, fights to keep both his temper and self-respect in dealing with whites, and puzzles over the German prisoners of war brought to his rural Georgia community during World War II.

"Caleb is compelling and believable, and Dudley's rich writing is impressive, clearly showing the various wars black Americans were fighting in the 1940s, both abroad and closer to home." SLJ

Duey, Kathleen

Sacred scars. Atheneum Books for Young Readers 2009 554p il (A resurrection of magic) $17.99

Grades: 7 8 9 10

1. School stories 2. Fantasy fiction 3. Magic -- Fiction
ISBN 978-0-689-84095-1; 0-689-84095-0

LC 2008-56044

In alternate chapters, Sadima works to free captive boys forced to copy documents in the caverns of Limori, and Hahp makes a pact with the remaining students of a wizards' academy in hopes that all will survive their training, as both learn valuable lessons about loyalty.

"The text so successfully portrays Hahp's experience in this grueling, cold-blooded wizard 'academy'—isolation, starvation, abuse and constant, unsolvable puzzles—that readers may absorb his strain, confusion and desolation themselves. . . . Absorbing and unwaveringly suspenseful." Kirkus

Duiker, K. Sello

The **hidden** star. K. Sello Duiker. Cassava Republic Press 2018 210 p.

Grades: 5 6 7 8

    1. Friendship -- Fiction; 2. Magic -- Fiction; 3. Bullies -- Fiction

191111543X; 9781911115434, $10.99

In this novel, by K. Sello Duiker, "Nolitye lives in a shack with her mother Thembi in Phola, a dusty township on the edge of Johannesburg. She is good at maths and likes collecting stones.... One day, Nolitye finds a special stone that has the power to make people feel happy and laugh. Her mission from now on is to gather together the other pieces of the stone and reunite them, to stop darkness from taking control of her world." (Publisher's note)

Dunagan, Ted M.

The **salvation** of Miss Lucretia. Ted M. Dunagan. NewSouth Books 2014 208 p.

Grades: 6 7 8 9

    1. Race relations -- Fiction 2. Vodou -- Fiction 3. Alabama -- History -- 1819-1950 -- Fiction 4. Historical fiction 5. Friendship -- Fiction 6. Southern States -- Fiction

1588382931; 9781588382931, $21.95; 9781603062558

                        LC 2014933021

In this book, by Ted M. Dunagan, "young friends Ted and Poudlum continue their friendship despite the racial divide in the rural segregated South of the 1940s. On a trip to the forest . . . they stumble upon Miss Lucretia, the last of the voodoo queens. . . . Through a series of adventures, Ted and Poudlum resolve to follow their own unique moral compasses and do what's right despite the pressures of the time in which they live." (Publisher's note)

Duncan, Lois

I know what you did last summer. Little, Brown 1973 199p hardcover o.p. pa $6.50

Grades: 7 8 9 10 11 12

    1. Mystery fiction

ISBN 0-440-22844-1 pa

ALA YALSA Margaret A. Edwards Award (1992)

Four teen-agers who have desperately tried to conceal their responsibility for a hit-and-run accident are pursued by a mystery figure seeking revenge.

This book "has vivid characterization, good balance, and the boding sense of impending danger that adds excitement to the best mystery stories." Bull Cent Child Books

★ **Killing** Mr. Griffin. Dell 1990 223p hardcover o.p. pa $6.50

Grades: 7 8 9 10

    1. School stories 2. Kidnapping -- Fiction

ISBN 0-440-94515-1 pa

First published 1978 by Little, Brown

ALA YALSA Margaret A. Edwards Award (1992)

A teenager casually suggests playing a cruel trick on the English teacher, but did he intend to end it with murder?

The author's "skillful plotting builds layers of tension that draws readers into the eye of the conflict. The ending is nicely handled in a manner which provides relief without removing any of the chilling implications." SLJ

Locked in time. Little, Brown 1985 210p hardcover o.p. pa $6.50

Grades: 7 8 9 10

    1. Mystery fiction

ISBN 0-316-19555-3; 0-440-94942-4 pa

                        LC 85-23

This "is the story of a domineering mother, Lisette, and her two teenage children, Gabe and Josie, who have all drunk from the cup of eternal youth. Seventeen-year-old Nore Robbins goes to visit her father, Charles, and her new stepfamily, Lisette, Gabe and Josie, at Lisette's beautiful old estate deep in the Louisiana bayou country. Nore discovers her stepfamily's secret and, in an attempt to expose this knowledge, becomes Lisette's target for death. . . . Grades seven to ten." (SLJ)

"The writing style is smooth, the characters strongly developed, and the plot, which has excellent pace and momentum, is an adroit blending of fantasy and realism." Bull Cent Child Books

Stranger with my face. Little, Brown 1981 250p hardcover o.p. pa $8.95

Grades: 7 8 9 10

    1. Twins -- Fiction 2. Supernatural -- Fiction

ISBN 0-440-98356-8

                        LC 81-8299

"There are small things, at first—a face in the mirror, a presence in an empty room, a beckoning figure on treacherous rocks—that portend 17-year-old Laurie's confrontation with the astral projection of her previously unknown, malevolent identical twin. . . . The jealous twin, Lia, pursues her, prodding her to explore astral projection so that Lia may enter Laurie's body." SLJ

"The ghostly Lia is deliciously evil; the idea of astral projection—Lia's method of travel—is novel; the island setting is vivid; and the relationships among the young people are realistic in the smoothly written supernatural tale." Horn Book

Dunkle, Clare B.

The **house** of dead maids; illustrations by Patrick Arrasmith. Henry Holt and Co. 2010 146p il $15.99

Grades: 8 9 10 11 12

    1. Ghost stories 2. Orphans -- Fiction 3. Great Britain -- Fiction 4. Household employees -- Fiction

ISBN 978-0-8050-9116-8; 0-8050-9116-5

                      LC 2009-50769

Eleven-year-old Tabby Aykroyd, who would later serve as housekeeper for thirty years to the Brontë sisters, is taken from an orphanage to a ghost-filled house, where she and a wild young boy are needed for a pagan ritual.

"The author manages to stay true to the essence of Wuthering Heights while creating a deliciously chilling ghost story that stands on its own. Readers do not have to be at all familiar with Brontë's gothic story of destructive love to be scared out of their wits by this one: cognoscenti, though, will recognize a few sly nods to the original." Bull Cent Child Books

Dunlap, Susanne Emily

In the shadow of the lamp; [by] Susanne Dunlap. Bloomsbury Children's Books 2011 293p $16.99

Grades: 7 8 9 10

1. Nurses -- Fiction 2. Crimean War, 1853-1856 -- Fiction

ISBN 978-1-59990-565-5; 1-59990-565-5

LC 2010-21158

Sixteen-year-old Molly Fraser works as a nurse with Florence Nightingale during the Crimean War to earn a salary to help her family survive in nineteenth-century England.

"Dunlap has written a story with roots deep in research about Florence Nightingale and the women who served as nurses during the Crimean War. . . . [She] . . . delivers another extraordinary novel that feels relevant even today." Libr Media Connect

The **musician's** daughter; [by] Susanne Dunlap. Bloomsbury 2009 322p $16.99

Grades: 8 9 10 11 12

1. Composers 2. Mystery fiction 3. Gypsies -- Fiction 4. Homicide -- Fiction 5. Musicians -- Fiction 6. Vienna (Austria) -- Fiction

ISBN 978-1-59990-332-3; 1-59990-332-6

LC 2008-30307

In eighteenth-century Vienna, Austria, fifteen-year-old Theresa seeks a way to help her mother and brother financially while investigating the murder of her father, a renowned violinist in Haydn's orchestra at the court of Prince Esterhazy, after his body is found near a gypsy camp.

"Dunlap skillfully builds suspense until the final page. . . . Readers will root for courageous Theresa through the exciting intrigue even as they absorb deeper messages about music and art's power to lift souls and inspire change." Booklist

Dunmore, Helen

Ingo. HarperCollins Pubs. 2005 328p $16.99; lib bdg $17.89

Grades: 6 7 8 9

1. Mermaids and mermen -- Fiction

ISBN 978-0-06-081852-4; 0-06-081852-2; 978-0-06-081853-1 lib bdg; 0-06-081853-0 lib bdg

LC 2005-19079

As they search for their missing father near their Cornwall home, Sapphy and her brother Conor learn about their family's connection to the domains of air and of water.

"Strong character development combines with an engaging plot and magical elements to make this a fine choice for fantasy readers, who will look forward to the next installments in this planned trilogy." SLJ

Other titles about Sapphire are:

The tide knot (2008)

The deep (2009)

Durst, Sarah Beth

Ice. Margaret K. McElderry Books 2009 308p $16.99

Grades: 7 8 9 10

1. Fairy tales 2. Polar bear -- Fiction 3. Scientists -- Fiction 4. Supernatural -- Fiction 5. Arctic regions -- Fiction

ISBN 978-1-4169-8643-0; 1-4169-8643-X

LC 2009-8618

A modern-day retelling of "East o' the Sun, West o' the Moon" in which eighteen-year-old Cassie learns that her grandmother's fairy tale is true when a Polar Bear King comes to claim her for his bride and she must decide whether to go with him and save her long-lost mother, or continue helping her father with his research

"Told in a descriptive style that perfectly captures the changing settings, Durst's novel is a page-turner that readers who enjoy adventure mixed with fairy-tale romance will find hard to put down." Booklist

Vessel; Sarah Beth Durst. Margaret K. McElderry Books 2012 424 p. (hardcover) $16.99

Grades: 7 8 9 10

1. Deserts -- Fiction 2. Fantasy fiction 3. Adventure fiction 4. Fantasy 5. Survival -- Fiction 6. Goddesses -- Fiction 8. Fate and fatalism -- Fiction

ISBN 1442423765; 9781442423763; 9781442423787

LC 2011044691

In this book by Sarah Beth Durst, "Liyana has trained all her life to be the vessel for her desert tribe's goddess Bayla. . . . "Bayla never shows up, but the trickster god Korbyn appears in human form and gives Liyana some startling news: the gods have all been imprisoned in false vessels, and he and Liyana must retrieve the various tribes' unsuccessful vessels, figure out where the deities are being held, and rescue them." (Bulletin of the Center for Children's Books)

Duyvis, Corinne

★ **Otherbound.** By Corinne Duyvis. Amulet Books 2014 400 p.

Grades: 9 10 11 12

1. Fantasy 2. Household employees -- Fiction 3. Mute persons -- Fiction 4. Shapeshifting -- Fiction 5. Fantasy fiction

1419709283; 9781419709289, $17.95

LC 2013029536

In this young adult novel by Corinne Duyvis, "Nolan doesn't see darkness when he closes his eyes. Instead, he's transported into the mind of Amara, a girl living in a different world. Nolan's life in his small Arizona town is full of history tests, family tension, and laundry; his parents think he has epilepsy, judging from his frequent blackouts. Amara's world is full of magic and danger—she's a mute servant girl who's tasked with protecting a renegade princess." (Publisher's note)

"Whenever seventeen-year-old Nolan closes his eyes, he's transported into the body of Amara, a mute slave girl on an alien world who acts as decoy against would-be assassins of a princess. After years of being a helpless witness, Nolan suddenly becomes a player in the action. Duyvis keeps tensions high in both Nolan's Arizona and Amara's Dunelands. A humdinger of an adventure." Horn Book

Easton, T. S.

Boys Don't Knit. T.S. Easton. Feiwel & Friends 2015 272 p.

Grades: 9 10 11 12

1. Knitting -- Competitions 2. Conduct of life 3.

Families -- England 4. Humorous stories 5. Teenagers -- Fiction

1250053315; 9781250053312, $16.99

In this novel by T.S. Easton, "after an incident regarding a crossing guard and a bottle of Martini & Rossi (and his friends), 17-year-old worrier Ben Fletcher must develop his sense of social alignment, take up a hobby, and do some community service to avoid any further probation. He takes a knitting class . . . [that] helps ease his anxiety and worrying. The only challenge now is to keep it hidden from his friends, his crush, and his soccer-obsessed father." (Publisher's note)

"Despite some unnecessary Americanization of the text, this wonderfully funny novel is infused with British slang, including dozens of terms easily understood in context. Wacky characters, a farcical plot and a fledgling romance are all part of the fun in this novel that will appeal to fans of Angus, Thongs, and Full-Frontal Snogging." Kirkus

★ **Eat the sky, drink the ocean.**

Edited by Kirsty Murray, Payal Dhar, and Anita Roy. Margaret K. McElderry Books 2017 Ix, 225 p. Illustration

Grades: 8 9 10 11 12

1. Boys -- Fiction; 2. Girls -- Fiction; 3. Short stories

9781481470575, $17.99; 9781481470599; 1481470574

This collection, edited by Kirsty Murray, Payal Dhar and Anita Roy, "is about connections: between men and women, boys and girls, between the past, the present, and the future. Through short stories, graphic novellas, and a play, the reader will discover new worlds where the strengths of women and men are celebrated and honored, and where magical realism is blended with self-confidence." (Publisher's note)

"Writers and artists from Australia and India worked together to create this thoughtful and nuanced collection of speculative short fiction in a variety of formats." SLJ

Edwards, Janet

★ **Earth** girl; by Janet Edwards. Pyr 2013 350 p. (Earth girl trilogy) $17.95

Grades: 9 10 11 12

1. Science fiction 2. People with disabilities -- Fiction 3. Children with disabilities -- Abuse of -- Fiction

ISBN 1616147652; 9781616147655

LC 2012044570

In this young adult novel set in the future, Jarra and other Handicapped are discriminated against by the Norms. "Jarra decides to show them that she is just as good as they are and applies to an off-world college conducting an archaeology dig on the abandoned buildings of New York. Reinventing herself as Jarra Military Kid, JMK watches vids and takes combat lessons. . . . Since she grew up on Earth and has been to the New York digs many times, her skills quickly allow her to shine." (School Library Journal)

"The future that Edwards constructs is creative and the dig descriptions are well thought out... The "person against nature" conflict with unstable dig conditions and solar flares makes a refreshing change." SLJ

★ **Earth** star; Janet Edwards. Pyr, an imprint of Prometheus Books 2014 360 p. (hardback) $17.99

Grades: 7 8 9 10 11 12

1. Children with disabilities -- Abuse of -- Fiction

ISBN 1616148977; 9781616148973

LC 2013040057

"This far-future science-fiction sequel skips tired genre tropes to offer a fresh and thrilling adventure about hazardous archaeological excavation, a mystery in the sky and a potential threat to all of humanity...Nitty-gritty archaeology details are vivid, and easy slang creates color ("Twoing" is dating; "amaz" means amazing). Edwards shows that speculative fiction needn't be dystopic, conspiracy-filled or love-triangled to be riveting and satisfying. Amaz—simply amaz." (Kirkus)

Edwardson, Debby Dahl

★ **Blessing's** bead. Farrar, Straus & Giroux 2009 178p $16.99

Grades: 6 7 8 9 10

1. Inupiat -- Fiction 2. Villages -- Fiction 3. Influenza -- Fiction 4. Alcoholism -- Fiction

ISBN 978-0-374-30805-6; 0-374-30805-5

LC 2008-26726

In 1917, Aaluk leaves for Siberia while her sister Nutaaq remains in their Alaskan village and becomes one of the few survivors of an influenza epidemic, then in 1986, Nunaaq's great-granddaughter leaves her mother due to a different kind of sickness and returns to the village where they were born

"It's the Nutaag's rhythmic, indelible voices—both as steady and elemental as the beat of a drum or a heart—that will move readers most. A unique, powerful debut." Booklist

★ **My** name is not easy. Marshall Cavendish 2011 248p $17.99; e-book $17.99

Grades: 7 8 9 10

1. School stories 2. Native Americans -- Fiction

ISBN 978-0-7614-5980-4; 0-7614-5980-4; 978-0-7614-6091-6 e-book

LC 2011002108

"Edwardson's skillful use of dialogue and her descriptions of rural Alaska as well as boarding-school life invoke a strong sense of empathy and compassion in readers. . . . Edwardson is to be applauded for her depth of research and her ability to portray all sides of the equation in a fair and balanced manner while still creating a very enjoyable read." SLJ

Efaw, Amy

Battle dress. HarperCollins Pubs. 2000 291p hardcover o.p. lib bdg $16.89

Grades: 7 8 9 10

1. Military education -- Fiction 2. Women in the armed forces -- Fiction 3. Military education -- New York (State) -- West Point

ISBN 0-06-028411-0 lib bdg; 0-06-053520-2

LC 99-34516

As a newly arrived freshman at West Point, seventeen-year-old Andi finds herself gaining both confidence and self esteem as she struggles to get through the grueling six weeks of new cadet training known as the Beast

"This book by a West Point graduate is a gripping, hard-to-put-down look at a young woman's struggle to succeed in a traditionally all-male environment." Voice Youth Advocates

Egan, Catherine

★ **Julia** vanishes. Catherine Egan. Alfred A. Knopf 2016 375 p. Map (Witch's child)

Grades: 9 10 11 12

    1. Fantasy 2. Magic -- Fiction 3. Murder -- Fiction 4. Robbers and outlaws -- Fiction 5. Witches -- Fiction

9780553524864, $53.97; 0553524844; 0553524852; 9780553524840, $17.99; 9780553524857; 9781524700843

                    LC 2016299696

In this book in the Witch's Child series, by Catherine Egan, "Julia has the unusual ability to be . . . unseen. Not invisible, exactly. Just beyond most people's senses. It's a dangerous trait in a city that has banned all forms of magic and drowns witches in public Cleansings. But it's a useful trait for a thief and a spy. . . . She's being paid very well indeed to infiltrate the grand house of Mrs. Och and report back on the odd characters who live there." (Publisher's note)

"A beautifully rendered world and an exquisite sense of timing ensure a page-turning experience." Pub Wkly

Other titles in this series are:

Julia Defiant (2017)

Julia Unbound (2018)

Ehrenhaft, Daniel

Friend is not a verb; a novel. HarperTeen 2010 241p $16.99

Grades: 7 8 9 10

    1. Siblings -- Fiction 2. Rock music -- Fiction 3. Family life -- Fiction 4. Bands (Music) -- Fiction 5. New York (N.Y.) -- Fiction

ISBN 978-0-06-113106-6; 0-06-113106-7

                    LC 2009-44006

While sixteen-year-old Hen's family and friends try to make his supposed dreams of becoming a rock star come true, he deals with the reality of being in a band with an ex-girlfriend, a friendship that may become love, and his older sister's mysterious disappearance and reappearance.

"Offbeat characters, an intriguing mystery, and a sweet romance make Ehrenhaft's . . . coming-of-age story stand out. . . . The mystery—and romance—wrap up rather neatly, but readers should be impressed by the clever surprise ending." Publ Wkly

Elkeles, Simone

How to ruin my teenage life. Flux 2007 281p pa $8.95

Grades: 7 8 9 10 11 12

    1. Jews -- Fiction 2. Israelis -- Fiction 3. Chicago (Ill.) -- Fiction 4. Father-daughter relationship -- Fiction

ISBN 978-0-7387-0961-1; 0-7387-1019-9

                    LC 2007005535

Living with her Israeli father in Chicago, seventeen-year-old Amy Nelson-Barak feels like a walking disaster, worried about her "non-boyfriend" in the Israeli army, her mother, new stepfather, and the baby they are expecting, a new boy named Nathan who has moved into her apartment building and goes to her school, and whether or not she really is the selfish snob that Nathan says she is.

"This book has laugh-out-loud moments. . . . Amy's thoughtfulness and depth raise this book above most of the chick-lit genre." Voice Youth Advocates

Other titles in this series are:

How to ruin a summer vacation (2006)

How to ruin your boyfriend's reputation (2009)

Perfect chemistry. Walker 2009 360p $16.99; pa $9.99

Grades: 9 10 11 12

    1. School stories 2. Gangs -- Fiction 3. Social classes -- Fiction 4. Dating (Social customs) -- Fiction

ISBN 978-0-8027-9823-7; 0-8027-9823-3; 978-0-8027-9822-0 pa; 0-8027-9822-5 pa

                    LC 2008-13769

When wealthy, seemingly perfect Brittany and Alex Fuentes, a gang member from the other side of town, develop a relationship after Alex discovers that Brittany is not exactly who she seems to be, they must face the disapproval of their schoolmates—and others.

"Brittany's controlling parents and sister with cerebral palsy are well drawn, but it is Elkeles rendition of Alex and his life that is particularly vivid. Sprinkling his speech with Spanish, his gruff but tender interactions with his family and friends feel completely genuine. . . . This is a novel that could be embraced by male and female readers in equal measure." Booklist

Followed by Rules of attraction (2010)

Ellen, Laura

Blind spot; Laura Ellen. Houghton Mifflin Harcourt 2012 332 p. $16.99

Grades: 9 10 11 12

    1. Mystery fiction 2. Homicide -- Fiction 3. Teenagers -- Fiction 4. Blind -- Fiction 5. High schools -- Fiction 6. Mystery and detective stories 7. People with disabilities -- Fiction

ISBN 0547763441; 9780547763446

                    LC 2012028976

Author Laura Ellen presents a murder mystery. "When AP student Roz discovers she's in a special ed class because of her visual 'disability,' she is furious. . . . Everything about Life Skills is awful, especially junkie Tricia, who, on the first day of school, somehow manages to get Roz to buy pot for her with the help of hottie Jonathan Webb. This isn't all bad, as soon Jonathan is . . . taking her to parties. Meanwhile, Roz . . . slowly comes to appreciate her fellow Life Skills classmates. And then Tricia goes missing after a calamitous party and is discovered dead months later." (Kirkus)

Elliott, David

★ **Bull.** By David Elliott. Houghton Mifflin Harcourt 2017 200 p.

Grades: 9 10 11 12

    1. Minotaur (Greek mythology) -- Fiction; 2. Minotaur (Greek mythology) -- Fiction; 3. Mythology, Greek -- Fiction; 4. Novels in verse; 5. Theseus, King of Athens -- Fiction; 6. Theseus, King of Athens -- Fiction; 7. Minotaur (Greek mythology); 8. Theseus (Greek mythology)

9781328698933, $17.99; 0544610601; 9780544610606,

$17.99

LC 2016014200

This book, by David Elliott, "turns a classic on its head in form and approach, updating the timeless story of Theseus and the Minotaur for a new generation. A rough, rowdy, and darkly comedic young adult retelling in verse, Bull will have readers reevaluating one of mythology's most infamous monsters." (Publisher's note)

"Effective both for classrooms and pleasure reading, this modernization brings new relevancy to an old story." Booklist

Elliot, Laura, 1957-

Across a war-tossed sea; L.M. Elliot. Disney-Hyperion Books. 2014 247p $16.99

Grades: 7 8 9 10

    1. British -- United States -- Fiction 2. Brothers -- Fiction 3. World War, 1939-1945 -- United States -- Fiction 4. Virginia -- Fiction

ISBN: 1423157559; 9781423157557

LC 2013035303

"This follow-up to Under a War-Torn Sky (2001) picks up the story of British brothers Charles, 14, and Wesley, 10, as they learn to live as Yanks in Virginia following their escape from the firebombings and U-boat disasters of the UK. As the battle in Europe continues to rage, Charles struggles to understand American culture while looking out for Wesley, whose usually cheery nature is punctuated with traumatic memories. The book feels like it could have been written 50 years ago—and that's not a bad thing—as Elliott leads us through a series of misadventures and straight-up adventures as the boys go hunting, hold a haunted house, contribute to the war effort, and even conduct a few acts of outright heroism. Serious issues of intolerance (religious freedom in Europe, racism in America, cruelty to German POWs) permeate the story without overwhelming it, making this a breezy and enlightening read." Booklist

Hamilton and Peggy!: a revolutionary friendship. L.M. Elliott. Katherine Tegen Books 2018 436 p.

Grades: 7 8 9 10 11 12

    1. Friendship -- Fiction; 2. Sisters -- Fiction; 3. Van Rensselaer, Margarita, 1758-1801; 4. United States -- History -- Revolution, 1775-1783 -- Fiction; 5. Hamilton, Alexander, 1757-1804 -- Fiction

9780062671325; 9780062671301, $17.99

LC 2017944492

In this novel, edited by Katherine Tegen, author Laura Elliott "successfully navigates the challenge of maintaining historical accuracy while upholding the personalities popularized by the musical ['Hamilton!']. [Peggy] is showcased as a strong protagonist who is confident in the best possible ways. Her memorable story will keep readers interested from start to finish." (Booklist)

Includes bibliographical references (pages 427-436).

Elliott, Patricia

The **Pale** Assassin. Holiday House 2009 336p $17.95

Grades: 7 8 9 10

    1. Adventure fiction 2. Siblings -- Fiction 3. France

-- History -- 1789-1799, Revolution -- Fiction

ISBN 978-0-8234-2250-0; 0-8234-2250-X

LC 2009-7554

In early 1790s Paris, as the Revolution gains momentum, young and sheltered Eugenie de Boncoeur finds it difficult to tell friend from foe as she and the royalist brother she relies on become the focus of "le Fantome," the sinister spymaster with a long-held grudge against their family.

"The best aspect of this excellent work of historical fiction is Eugenie herself. Her gradual coming of age and growing political awareness provides resonant depth to what becomes a highly suspenseful survival tale." Booklist

Followed by: The traitor's smile (2011)

The **traitor's** smile. Holiday House 2011 304p $17.95

Grades: 7 8 9 10

    1. Adventure fiction 2. Cousins -- Fiction 3. France -- History -- 1789-1799, Revolution -- Fiction

ISBN 978-0-8234-2361-3; 0-8234-2361-1

Sequel to: The Pale Assassin (2009)

First published 2010 in the United Kingdom

As the French Revolutin rages around her, wealthy and beautiful Eugenie de Boncoeur is no longer safe in her own country. She flees the bloody streeets of Paris for her cousin Hetta's house in England, narrowly excaping the clutches of the evil Pale Assassin, who is determined to force her to marry him.

Ellis, Ann Dee

Everything is fine. Little, Brown and Co. Books for Young Readers 2009 154p il $16.99

Grades: 6 7 8 9 10

    1. Mothers -- Fiction 2. Bereavement -- Fiction 3. Family life -- Fiction 4. Depression (Psychology) -- Fiction

ISBN 978-0-316-01364-2; 0-316-01364-1

LC 2008-5847

When her father leaves for a job out of town, Mazzy is left at home to try to cope with her mother, who has been severely depressed since the death of Mazzy's baby sister.

"What makes [this book] so extraordinary is the narrative device that Ellis employs to searing effect. . . . [This] is a story so painful you want to read it with your eyes closed. It is a stunning novel." Voice Youth Advocates

★ **This** is what I did. Little, Brown 2007 157p $16.99

Grades: 6 7 8 9

    1. School stories 2. Bullies -- Fiction

ISBN 978-0-316-01363-5; 0-316-01363-3

LC 2006-01388

Bullied because of an incident in his past, eighth-grader Logan is unhappy at his new school and has difficulty relating to others until he meets a quirky girl and a counselor who believe in him.

"Part staccato prose, part transcript, this haunting first novel will grip readers right from the start. . . . A particularly attractive book design incorporates small drawings between each segment of text." Publ Wkly

Ellis, Deborah

Bifocal; [by] Deborah Ellis and Eric Walters. Fitzhenry & Whiteside 2007 280p $18.95; pa $12.95

Grades: 7 8 9 10

1. School stories 2. Muslims -- Fiction 3. Prejudices -- Fiction

ISBN 978-1-55455-036-4; 1-55455-036-X; 978-1-55455-062-3 pa; 1-55455-062-9 pa

When a Muslim boy is arrested at a high school on suspicion of terrorist affiliations, growing racial tensions divide the student population.

"The story is told in the alternating voices of two students. . . . Their individual struggles to understand the flaring prejudice and their journeys toward self-discovery are subtle and authentic. . . . This is a story that will leave readers looking at their schools and themselves with new eyes." Booklist

My name is Parvana. Groundwood Books/House of Anansi Press 2012 201 p. $16.95

Grades: 5 6 7 8

1. Afghanistan -- Fiction 2. Interrogation -- Fiction 3. Women -- Afghanistan -- Fiction

ISBN 1554982979; 9781554982974

In this novel by Deborah Ellis "15-year-old Parvana is imprisoned and interrogated as a suspected terrorist in Afghanistan. . . . Parvana's captors" read "aloud the words in her notebook to decide if the angry written sentiments of a teenage girl can be evidence of guilt. . . . The interrogation, the words of the notebook and the effective third-person narration combine for a . . . portrait of a girl and her country." (Kirkus Reviews)

★ **No** safe place. Groundwood Books/House of Anansi Press 2010 205p $16.95

Grades: 9 10 11 12

1. Iraq -- Fiction 2. France -- Fiction 3. Refugees -- Fiction 4. Great Britain -- Fiction

ISBN 978-0-88899-973-3

Fifteen-year-old Abdul, having lost everyone he loves, journeys from Baghdad to a migrant community in Calais where he sneaks aboard a boat bound for England, not knowing it carries a cargo of heroin, and when the vessel is involved in a skirmish and the pilot killed, it is up to Abdul and three other young stowaways to complete the journey.

"Ellis deftly uses flashbacks to fill in the backstories of each character, reminding readers of how they can never really know where people are coming from emotionally. Her writing is highly accessible, and yet understated. Orphans of the world and victims of human trafficking need all the press they can get, and this book does a great job of introducing the topic and allowing young people to see beyond the headlines of 'Another illegal accidentally dies in Chunnel.'" SLJ

Ellis, Kat

Breaker. Kat Ellis. Running Press 2016 336 p.

Grades: 9 10 11 12

1. Children of murder victims -- Fiction 2. Serial killers -- Fiction 3. Interpersonal relations -- Fiction 4.

Suspense fiction 5. Mystery fiction

0762459085; 9780762459087, $9.95; 9780762459094, $9.99

LC 2015951853

In this novel by Kat Ellis, "Kyle Henry has a new name, a new school, and a new life-one without the shadow of the Bonebreaker hanging over him. It's been a year since his serial killer father's execution. . . . Naomi Steadman . . . does not know he is the son of the man who murdered her mother. What she does know is she and Kyle have a connection with each other. . . . Soon after Kyle's arrival, the death count on campus starts to rise." (Publisher's note)

"Packed full of suspense, red herrings, and creepy taxidermy, this is an intriguing murder mystery and a compelling look at the ties that bind." Booklist

Ellsworth, Loretta

★ **Unforgettable**. Walker Books for Young Readers 2011 256p $16.99

Grades: 6 7 8 9

1. School stories 2. Memory -- Fiction 3. Synesthesia -- Fiction 4. Dating (Social customs) -- Fiction

ISBN 978-0-8027-2305-5; 0-8027-2305-5

LC 2010049590

When Baxter Green was three years old he developed a condition that causes him to remember absolutely everything, and now that he is fifteen, he and his mother have moved to Minnesota to escape her criminal boyfriend and, Baxter hopes, to reconnect with a girl he has been thinking about since kindergarten.

"A lot is going here—an exploration of of synesthesia and memory, a crime story, an environmental drama, family relationships and a sweet, earnest love story. . . . But everything works." Kirkus

Elwood, Tessa

Split the sun: An Inherit the Stars Novel. Tessa Elwood. Running Press Kids 2016 288 p.

Grades: 8 9 10 11

1. Terrorism -- Fiction 2. Mothers and daughters -- Fiction

9780762458479, $9.95

LC 2016940454

In this novel, by Tessa Elwood, "the Ruling Lord of the House of Galton is dead and the nation is divided. Kit Franks, a nobody escalated to infamy since her mother bombed the House capitol city, wishes she were dead, too. Then Mom-the-terrorist starts showing up on feeds and causing planet-wide blackouts and Kit becomes a target. . . . Everyone from family to government enforcers seems to have a vision for Kit's future. The question is, does Kit have a vision for herself?" (Publisher's note)

"This sequel to Inherit the Stars (2015) offers plenty of action, and readers will be swept away and kept guessing along with Kit as she hurtles towards that uncertain future." Booklist

Elston, Ashley

The **rules** for disappearing; Ashley Elston. 1st ed. Hyperion 2013 320 p. (reinforced) $16.99

Grades: 7 8 9 10 11 12

1. Witnesses -- Fiction 2. Friendship -- Fiction 3.

Dysfunctional families -- Fiction 4. High schools -- Fiction 5. Moving, Household -- Fiction 6. Natchitoches (La.) -- Fiction 7. Witness protection programs -- Fiction
ISBN 1423168976; 9781423168973

LC 2012035122

In this book by Ashley Elston, "seventeen-year-old Meg Jones . . . and her family are in the witness protection program, and they've changed towns six times in less than a year. . . . Meg's mother is an alcoholic, her father is depressed and secretive, and her 11-year-old sister is having trouble coping with all of the change. Fed up, Meg wants out of the program and will do anything to save her family, including digging up what her father did to get them into this mess." (Publishers Weekly)

"The fresh first-person narration serves the story well, providing grounding in reality as events spin out of control. Though the plot may seem a bit far-fetched at times, the realistic setting, believable romance and spunky protagonist will make this one worth the trip for mystery and romance fans." Kirkus

Emond, Stephen

Bright lights, dark nights. Stephen Emond. Roaring Brook Press 2015 384 p. Illustration
Grades: 7 8 9 10

1. Best friends -- Fiction 2. Dating (Social customs) -- Fiction 3. Fathers and sons -- Fiction 4. Friendship -- Fiction 5. High schools -- Fiction 6. Race relations -- Fiction 7. Schools -- Fiction 8. Single-parent families -- Fiction
1626722064; 9781626722064, $17.99

LC 2014047413

In this novel, by Stephen Emond, "Walter Wilcox has never been in love. That is, until he meets Naomi, and sparks, and clever jokes, fly. But when his cop dad is caught in a racial profiling scandal, Walter and Naomi, who is African American, are called out at school, home, and online. Can their bond (and mutual love of the Foo Fighters) keep them together?" (Publisher's note)

"Readers coming to this story for romance may feel shortchanged, as the relationship here is more true-to-life and awkward than swooningly romantic, but that's what sets Emond's book apart. A real slice of contemporary teenage life that's painfully honest about the below-the-surface racism in today's America." Booklist

Happyface. Little, Brown and Co. 2010 307p il $16.99
Grades: 7 8 9 10

1. School stories 2. Diaries -- Fiction 3. Divorce -- Fiction 4. Dating (Social customs) -- Fiction
ISBN 978-0-316-04100-3; 0-316-04100-9

LC 2008-47386

After going through traumatic times, a troubled, socially awkward teenager moves to a new school where he tries to reinvent himself.

"The illustrations range from comics to more fleshed-out drawings. Just like Happyface's writing, they can be whimsical, thoughtful, boyishly sarcastic, off-the-cuff, or achingly beautiful." Publ Wkly

★ **Winter** town; Story and art by Stephen Emond. Little, Brown 2011 336p il $17.99
Grades: 7 8 9

1. Love stories 2. Teenagers -- Fiction 3. High school students -- Fiction 4. Cartoons and caricatures -- Fiction
ISBN 9780316133326; 978-0-316-13332-6

LC 2011012966

Evan and Lucy, childhood best friends who grew apart after years of seeing one another only during Christmas break, begin a romance at age seventeen but his choice to mindlessly follow his father's plans for an Ivy League education rather than becoming the cartoonist he longs to be, and her more destructive choices in the wake of family problems, pull them apart.

This is a "remarkable illustrated work of contemporary fiction. . . . Interspersed throughout are both realistic illustrations and drawings of a comic strip being created by Evan and Lucy; these black-and-white, almost chibi-style panels form an effective parallel with the plot and appeal mightily on their own. Compelling, honest and true—this musing about art and self-discovery, replete with pitch-perfect dialogue, will have wide appeal." Kirkus

Engdahl, Sylvia Louise

★ **Enchantress** from the stars; foreword by Lois Lowry. Firebird 2003 288p pa $6.99
Grades: 7 8 9 10 11 12

1. Science fiction
ISBN 0-14-250037-2

A reissue of the title first published 1970 by Atheneum Pubs.

A Newbery Medal honor book, 1971

When young Elana unexpectedly joins the team leaving the spaceship to study the planet Andrecia, she becomes an integral part of an adventure involving three very different civilizations, each one centered on the third planet from the star in its own solar system

"Emphasis is on the intricate pattern of events rather than on characterization, and readers will find fascinating symbolism—and philosophical parallels to what they may have observed or thought. The book is completely absorbing and should have a wider appeal than much science fiction." Horn Book

Engle, Margarita

★ **Firefly** letters; a suffragette's journey to Cuba. Henry Holt & Co. 2010 151p $16.99
Grades: 7 8 9 10 11 12

1. Authors 2. Novelists 3. Novels in verse 4. Cuba -- Fiction 5. Slavery -- Fiction 6. Sex role -- Fiction
ISBN 978-0-8050-9082-6; 0-8050-9082-7

LC 2009-23445

"This engaging title documents 50-year-old Swedish suffragette and novelist Fredrika Bremer's three-month travels around Cuba in 1851. Based in the home of a wealthy sugar planter, Bremer journeys around the country with her host's teenaged slave Cecilia, who longs for her mother and home in the Congo. Elena, the planter's privileged 12-year-old daughter, begins to accompany them on their trips into the countryside. . . . Using elegant free verse and alternating among each character's point of view, Engle offers powerful glimpses into Cuban life at that time. Along the way, she comments on slavery, the rights of women, and the stark contrast between Cuba's rich and poor." SLJ

Hurricane dancers; the first Caribbean pirate shipwreck. Henry Holt and Co. 2011 145p $16.99
Grades: 6 7 8 9 10

> 1. Novels in verse 2. Pirates -- Fiction 3. Shipwrecks -- Fiction 4. Caribbean region -- Fiction 5. Native Americans -- West Indies -- Fiction
> ISBN 978-0-8050-9240-0; 0-8050-9240-4
>
> LC 2010-11690

This is an "accomplished historical novel in verse set in the Caribbean. . . . The son of a Taíno Indian mother and a Spanish father, [Quebrado] is taken in 1510 from his village on the island that is present-day Cuba and enslaved on a pirate's ship, where a brutal conquistador . . . is held captive for ransom. When a hurricane destroys the boat, Quebrado is pulled from the water by a fisherman, Naridó, whose village welcomes him, but escape from the past proves nearly impossible. . . . Engle fictionalizes historical fact in a powerful, original story. . . . Engle distills the emotion in each episode with potent rhythms, sounds, and original, unforgettable imagery." Booklist

★ The **Lightning** Dreamer; Cuba's Greatest Abolitionist. Margarita Engle. Houghton Mifflin Harcourt 2013 192 p. $16.99
Grades: 6 7 8 9 10

> 1. Historical fiction 2. Novels in verse 3. Authors -- Fiction 4. Feminists -- Fiction 5. Abolitionists -- Fiction 6. Cuba -- History -- 1810-1899 -- Fiction
> ISBN 0547807430; 9780547807430
>
> LC 2013003913

Pura Belpre Author Honor Book (2014)

This book is a "work of historical fiction about Cuban poet, author, antislavery activist and feminist Gertrudis Gómez de Avellaneda. Written in free verse, the story tells of how Tula, which was her childhood nickname, grows up in libraries, which she calls 'a safe place to heal/ and dream . . .,' influenced by the poetry of Jose Maria Heredia." (School Library Journal)

Includes bibliographical references.

Silver people: voices from the Panama Canal; Margarita Engle. Houghton Mifflin Harcourt. 2014 272p $17.99
Grades: 5 6 7 8

> 1. Novels in verse 2. Racism -- Fiction 3. Rain forests —Fiction 4. Segregation -- Fiction 5. Panama Canal (Panama) -- History -- Fiction 6. Migrant labor -- Fiction
> ISBN: 0544109414; 9780544109414
>
> LC 2013037485

An "exploration of the construction of the Panama Canal. . . . Mateo, a 14-year-old Cuban lured by promises of wealth, journeys to Panama only to discover the recruiters' lies and a life of harsh labor. However, through his relationships with Anita, an 'herb girl,' Henry, a black Jamaican worker, and Augusto, a Puerto Rican geologist, Mateo is able to find a place in his new land." (Kirkus Reviews)

"In melodic verses, Engle offers the voices of the dark-skinned workers (known as the 'silver people'), whose back-breaking labor helped build the Panama Canal, along with

the perspective of a local girl. Interspersed are occasional echoes from flora and fauna as well as cameo appearances by historical figures. Together, they provide an illuminating picture of the project's ecological sacrifices and human costs." Horn Book

★ **Tropical** secrets; Holocaust refugees in Cuba. Henry Holt 2009 199p $16.95
Grades: 7 8 9 10 11

> 1. Novels in verse 2. Jews -- Fiction 3. Refugees -- Fiction 4. Holocaust, 1933-1945 -- Fiction
> ISBN 978-0-8050-8936-3; 0-8050-8936-5
>
> LC 2008-36782

Escaping from Nazi Germany to Cuba in 1939, a young Jewish refugee dreams of finding his parents again, befriends a local girl with painful secrets of her own, and discovers that the Nazi darkness is never far away.

"Readers who think they might not like a novel in verse will be pleasantly surprised at how quickly and smoothly the story flows. . . . The book will provide great fodder for discussion of the Holocaust, self-reliance, ethnic and religious bias, and more." Voice Youth Advocates

Ephron, Delia
Frannie in pieces; drawings by Chad W. Beckerman. HarperTeen 2007 374p il $16.99; pa $8.99
Grades: 7 8 9 10

> 1. Puzzles -- Fiction 2. Bereavement -- Fiction 3. Father-daughter relationship -- Fiction
> ISBN 978-0-06-074716-9; 0-06-074716-1; 978-0-06-074718-3 pa; 0-06-074718-8 pa
>
> LC 2007-10909

When fifteen-year-old Frannie's father dies, only a mysterious jigsaw puzzle that he leaves behind can help her come to terms with his death.

"This is a tender, moving story dealing with grief and growing up and the power of art to heal." SLJ

The **girl** with the mermaid hair. HarperTeen 2010 312p $16.99
Grades: 7 8 9 10

> 1. Family life -- Fiction 2. Personal appearance -- Fiction 3. Perfectionism (Personality trait) -- Fiction
> ISBN 978-0-06-154260-2; 0-06-154260-1
>
> LC 2009-03061

A vain teenaged girl is obsessed with beauty and perfection until she uncovers a devastating family secret.

"A solid and perceptive realistic drama, this will particularly satisfy readers beginning to reconsider their own familial assumptions." Bull Cent Child Books

Epstein, Robin
God is in the pancakes. Dial Books 2010 265p $16.99
Grades: 7 8 9 10

> 1. Old age -- Fiction 2. Sisters -- Fiction 3. Religion -- Fiction 4. Euthanasia -- Fiction 5. Dating (Social customs) -- Fiction
> ISBN 978-0-8037-3382-4; 0-8037-3382-8

Fifteen-year-old Grace, having turned her back on religion when her father left, now finds herself praying for help with her home and love life, and especially with whether she should help a beloved elderly friend die with dignity.

"Everything comes together in an authentic, breezy read that asks difficult questions and doesn't shy away from direct answers, or the reality that answers may not exist. With well-developed adults and a teen seeking help from God and anyone she perceives as wise, this memorable novel offers food for thought and sustenance for the soul." Booklist

Erskine, Kathryn

Quaking. Philomel Books 2007 236p $16.99

Grades: 7 8 9 10

1. School stories 2. Patriotism -- Fiction 3. Toleration -- Fiction 4. Family life -- Fiction 5. Society of Friends -- Fiction

ISBN 978-0-399-24774-3; 0-399-24774-2

LC 2006-34563

In a Pennsylvania town where antiwar sentiments are treated with contempt and violence, Matt, a fourteen-year-old girl living with a Quaker family, deals with the demons of her past as she battles bullies of the present, eventually learning to trust in others as well as herself.

"This is a compelling story, which enfolds the political issues into a deeper focus on the characters' personal stories." Booklist

Esckilsen, Erik E.

The last mall rat. Houghton Mifflin 2003 182p $15; pa $5.95

Grades: 7 8 9 10

1. Shopping centers and malls -- Fiction

ISBN 0-618-23417-9; 0-618-60896-6 pa

LC 2002-14436

Too young to get a job at the Onion River Mall, fifteen-year-old Mitch earns money from salesclerks to harrass rude shoppers

"Realistic dialogue and a keen sense of what matters to teens will draw them to this quick read." Booklist

Eulberg, Elizabeth

Revenge of the Girl With the Great Personality; Elizabeth Eulberg. Scholastic 2013 272 p. (hardcover) $17.99

Grades: 7 8 9 10

1. Sisters -- Fiction 2. Beauty contests -- Fiction

ISBN 9780545476997; 0545476992

In this novel, by Elizabeth Eulberg, "Everybody loves Lexi. She's popular, smart, funny . . . but she's never been one of . . . the pretty ones who get all the attention from guys. And on top of that, her seven-year-old sister, Mackenzie, is a terror in a tiara. . . . Lexi's sick of it. . . . The time has come for Lexi to step out from the sidelines. Girls without great personalities aren't going to know what hit them. Because Lexi's going to play the beauty game." (Publisher's note)

Eshbaugh, Julie

Obsidian and stars. Julie Eshbaugh. HarperTeen 2017 359 p. (Ivory and bone)

Grades: 7 8 9 10

1. Prehistoric peoples -- Fiction; 2. Teenagers -- Fiction; 3. Clans -- Fiction

9780062399304; 9780062399298; 9780062399281,

$17.99

LC 2016961162

In this book, by Julie Eshbaugh, "after surviving the battle that erupted after Lo and the Bosha clan attacked, now Mya is looking ahead to her future with Kol.... But the same night as Kol and Mya's betrothal announcement, Mya's brother Chev reveals his plan to marry their youngest sister, Lees, to his friend Morsk.... In an effort to protect her sister, Mya whisks Lees away to a secret island." (Publisher's note)

Eves, Rosalyn

Blood Rose Rebellion. Random House Childrens Books 2017 416 p.

Grades: 7 8 9 10

1101935995; 9781101935996

"Sixteen-year-old Anna Arden is barred from society by a defect of blood. . . . She is Barren, unable to perform the simplest spells. . . . But her fate takes another course when, after inadvertently breaking her sister's debutante spell—an important chance for a highborn young woman to show her prowess with magic—Anna finds herself exiled to her family's once powerful but now crumbling native Hungary." (Publisher's note)

Fahy, Thomas Richard

The unspoken; [by] Tom Fahy. Simon & Schuster Books for Young Readers 2008 166p $15.99

Grades: 8 9 10 11 12

1. Horror fiction 2. Cults -- Fiction

ISBN 978-1-4169-4007-4; 1-4169-4007-3

LC 2007-00850

Six teens are drawn back to the small, North Carolina town where they once lived and, one by one, begin to die of their worst fears, as prophesied by the cult leader they killed five years earlier, and who they believe poisoned their parents.

"Teeth-clenching suspenseful at times and deliciously creepy at others, Fahy . . . delivers a classic horror story." Publ Wkly

Falkner, Brian

Brain Jack. Random House 2010 349p $17.99; lib bdg $20.99

Grades: 7 8 9 10

1. Science fiction 2. Computers -- Fiction 3. New York (N.Y.) -- Fiction

ISBN 978-0-375-84366-2; 0-375-84366-3; 978-0-375-93924-2 lib bdg; 0-375-93924-5 lib bdg

LC 2008-43386

In a near-future New York City, fourteen-year-old computer genius Sam Wilson manages to hack into the AT&T network and sets off a chain of events that have a profound effect on human activity throughout the world.

"This fast-paced, cyber thriller is intelligent, well-written, and very intuitive to the possibilities and challenges we may face in our ever changing digital society." Libr Media Connect

The project. Random House 2011 275p $17.99

Grades: 6 7 8 9 10

1. Adventure fiction 2. Time travel -- Fiction 3. National socialism -- Fiction 4. World War, 1939-1945

-- Fiction

ISBN 978-0-375-96945-4; 0-375-96945-4

LC 2010033449

After discovering a terrible secret hidden in the most boring book in the world, Iowa fifteen-year-olds Luke and Tommy find out that members of a secret Nazi organization intend to use this information to rewrite history.

"The wacky unbelievability of this story in no way detracts from its enjoyment. It reads like an action movie, with plenty of chases, explosions, and by-a-hair escapes." SLJ

Falls, Kat

Inhuman; Kat Falls. Scholastic Press 2013 384 p. $17.99

Grades: 7 8 9 10

1. Dystopian fiction 2. Apocalyptic fiction 3. Science fiction 4. Survival -- Fiction 5. Quarantine -- Fiction 6. Virus diseases -- Fiction 7. Father-daughter relationship--Fiction

ISBN 054537099X; 9780545370998

LC 2013026360

In this dystopian novel by Kat Falls, "the United States east of the Mississippi has been abandoned. Now called the Feral Zone, a reference to the virus that turned millions of people into bloodthirsty savages, the entire area is off-limits. . . . [Protagonist] Lane gets the shock of her life when she learns that someone close to her has crossed into the Feral Zone." (Publisher's note)

"Years ago, the U.S. was bisected by a pandemic (spread by biting) that causes humans to mutate into feral human-animal hybrids. When pampered teenager Lane is blackmailed into the Feral Zone, she joins the search for a cure and discovers the gray area between human and feral. While Lane and her love triangle are bland, the zombie-apocalypse-meets-wereanimals-gone-wild setup captures the imagination." (Horn Book)

Fantaskey, Beth

Buzz kill; Beth Fantaskey. Houghton Mifflin Harcourt. 2014 362p $17.99

Grades: 8 9 10 11 12

1. Coaches (Athletics) -- Fiction 2. Dating (Social customs) --Fiction 3. High schools -- Fiction 4. Murder -- Fiction 5. Mystery and detective stories

ISBN: 0547393105; 9780547393100

LC 2013011423

"When the head football coach is killed, seventeen-year-old Millie, a school reporter obsessed with Nancy Drew, sets out to learn the truth and clear her assistant-coach father of any suspicion. She gets some unexpected help from dreamy quarterback Chase, who's hiding some secrets. This entertaining sleuth story is a good choice for teens now graduated from books featuring Millie's literary hero." Horn Book

Jessica's guide to dating on the dark side. Harcourt 2009 354p $17

Grades: 8 9 10 11 12

1. Vampires -- Fiction

ISBN 978-0-15-206384-9; 0-15-206384-6

LC 2007-49002

Seventeen-year-old Jessica, adopted and raised in Pennsylvania, learns that she is descended from a royal line of Romanian vampires and that she is betrothed to a vampire prince, who poses as a foreign exchange student while courting her.

"Fantaskey makes this premise work by playing up its absurdities without laughing at them. . . . The romance sizzles, the plot develops ingeniously and suspensefully, and the satire sings." Publ Wkly

Farinango, Maria Virginia

★ The **Queen** of Water. Delacorte Press 2011 352p $16.99; lib bdg $19.99

Grades: 8 9 10 11 12

1. Ecuador -- Fiction 2. Social classes -- Fiction

ISBN 978-0-385-73897-2; 0-385-73897-8; 978-0-385-90761-3 lib bdg; 0-385-90761-3 lib bdg

LC 2010-10512

"The complexities of class and ethnicity within Ecuadorian society are explained seamlessly within the context of the first-person narrative, and a glossary and pronunciation guide further help to plunge readers into the novel's world. By turns heartbreaking, infuriating and ultimately inspiring." Kirkus

Farish, Terry

★ The **good** braider; by Terry Farish. Marshall Cavendish 2012 221 p. (hardcover) $17.99

Grades: 9 10 11 12

1. Refugees -- Fiction 2. Sudanese Americans -- Fiction 3. Mother-daughter relationship -- Fiction 4. Immigrants -- Fiction 5. Portland (Me.) -- Fiction 6. Mothers and daughters -- Fiction 7. Sudan -- History -- Civil War, 1983-2005 -- Fiction

ISBN 0761462678; 9780761462675; 9780761462682

LC 2011033659

In this novel by Terry Farish, written "in . . . free verse," protagonist Viola tells "the story of her family's journey from war-torn Sudan, to Cairo, and finally to Portland, Maine. Here, in the sometimes too close embrace of the local Southern Sudanese Community, she dreams of South Sudan while she tries to navigate the strange world of America . . . a world that puts her into sharp conflict with her traditional mother." (Publisher's note)

Farizan, Sara

★ **If** you could be mine; a novel. Sara Farizan. Algonquin 2013 256 p. (hardcover) $16.95

Grades: 8 9 10 11 12

1. Sex reassignment surgery -- Fiction 2. Iran -- Social conditions -- Fiction 3. Iran -- Fiction 4. Love -- Fiction 5. Lesbians -- Fiction 6. Friendship -- Fiction 7. Best friends -- Fiction

ISBN 1616202513

LC 2013008931

17-year-old Sahar, who has wanted to marry her best friend Nasrin since they were six years old, dreams of living openly with her lover. Nasrin prefers to accept an arranged marriage, while intending to continue their illicit affair. Exposed to a world of sexual diversity by her gay cousin and made desperate by Nasrin's impending marriage, Sahar explores the one legal option for the two of them to be together: her own sex reassignment surgery." (Publishers Weekly)

"Rich with details of life in contemporary Iran, this is a GLBTQ story that we haven't seen before in YA fiction." SLJ

Tell me again how a crush should feel; Sara Farizan. Algonquin Young Readers. 2014 304p $16.95
Grades: 9 10 11 12

1. Friendship -- Fiction 2. High schools -- Fiction 3. Iranian Americans -- Fiction 4. Lesbians -- Fiction
ISBN: 161620284X; 9781616202842
LC 2014021580

The protagonist is "sixteen-year-old Iranian American Leila Azadi. . . . Afraid to tell her best friends and her conservative family that she is gay, Leila finds herself in a secret relationship with Saskia, a gorgeous, sophisticated new girl with a decidedly wicked side. As Saskia reveals herself to be a master manipulator, Leila turns to an unexpected ally, Lisa, an old friend who recently lost her brother in a car accident." (Horn Book Magazine)

"Farizan fashions an empowering romance featuring a lovable, awkward protagonist who just needs a little nudge of confidence to totally claim her multifaceted identity." Booklist

Farmer, Nancy
★ The **Ear,** the Eye, and the Arm; a novel. Puffin Books 1995 311p pa $6.99
Grades: 6 7 8 9 10

1. Science fiction 2. Zimbabwe -- Fiction
ISBN 978-0-14-131109-8; 0-14-131109-6
LC 95019982

First published 1994 by Orchard Books
A Newbery Medal honor book, 1995

In 2194 in Zimbabwe, General Matsika's three children are kidnapped and put to work in a plastic mine while three mutant detectives use their special powers to search for them

"Throughout the story, it's the thrilling adventure that will grab readers, who will also like the comic, tender characterizations." Booklist

A **girl** named Disaster. Orchard Bks. 1996 309p $19.95; pa $7.99
Grades: 6 7 8 9

1. Adventure fiction 2. Supernatural -- Fiction
ISBN 0-531-09539-8; 0-14-038635-1 pa
LC 96-15141

A Newbery Medal honor book, 1997

While journeying from Mozambique to Zimbabwe to escape an arranged marriage, eleven-year-old Nhamo struggles to escape drowning and starvation and in so doing comes close to the luminous world of the African spirits

"This story is humorous and heartwrenching, complex and multilayered." SLJ

★ The **house** of the scorpion. Atheneum Bks. for Young Readers 2002 380p $17.95; pa $7.99
Grades: 7 8 9 10

1. Science fiction 2. Cloning -- Fiction
ISBN 0-689-85222-3; 0-689-85223-1 pa
LC 2001-56594

A Newbery Medal honor book, 2003

In a future where humans despise clones, Matt enjoys special status as the young clone of El Patrón, the 140-year-old leader of a corrupt drug empire nestled between Mexico and the United States.

"This is a powerful, ultimately hopeful, story that builds on today's sociopolitical, ethical, and scientific issues and prognosticates a compelling picture of what the future could bring." Booklist

★ The **lord** of Opium; Nancy Farmer. Atheneum Books for Young Readers 2013 432 p. (hardcover) $17.99
Grades: 7 8 9 10

1. Fantasy fiction 2. Drug traffic -- Fiction 3. Science fiction 4. Cloning -- Fiction 5. Environmental degradation -- Fiction
ISBN 1442482540; 9781442482548
LC 2012030418

Sequel to: House of the scorpion (2002)

Here, "Matt was a clone of El Patrón, drug lord of Opium, but with El Patrón dead, Matt is now considered by international law to be fully human and El Patrón's rightful heir. But it's a corrupt land . . . ruled over by drug lords and worked by armies of Illegals turned into 'eejits,' or zombies. Matt wants to bring reform." (Kirkus Reviews)

Farrey, Brian
With or without you. Simon Pulse 2011 348p pa $8.99; ebook $7.99
Grades: 9 10 11 12

1. Wisconsin -- Fiction 2. Friendship -- Fiction 3. Hate crimes -- Fiction 4. Homosexuality -- Fiction 5. Gay teenagers -- Fiction
ISBN 978-1-4424-0699-5 pa; 978-1-4424-0700-8 ebook
LC 2010-38722

When eighteen-year-old best friends Evan and Davis of Madison, Wisconsin, join a community center group called "chasers" to gain acceptance and knowledge of gay history, there may be fatal consequences.

"Farrey paces his story beautifully, covering many contemporary issues for teens about coming out, friendship, relationships, and following a dangerous crowd simply for a sense of belonging." SLJ

Fawcett, Heather
Even the darkest stars. Heather Fawcett. Balzer + Bray 2017 427 p.
Grades: 8 9 10 11 12

1. Imaginary places -- Fiction; 2. Magic -- Fiction; 3. Mountaineering -- Fiction; 4. Fantasy fiction
9780062463388, $17.99; 9780062463401
LC 2017932797

In this novel by Heather Fawcett, "Kamzin has always dreamed of becoming one of the Emperor's...elite climbers.... [Explorer] River Shara,...hire[s] Kamzin...for his next expedition. The challenges of climbing Raksha are unlike anything Kamzin expected.... And as dark secrets are revealed, Kamzin must unravel the truth of their mission and of her companions -- while surviving the deadliest climb she has ever faced." (Publisher's note)

"Add in a detailed, well-realized setting, an unsettling villain that lingers just off the page, and buckets of danger to result in an utterly inventive and wholly original debut." Booklist

Followed by: All the wandering light (2018)

Federle, Tim

★ The **great** American whatever. Tim Federle. Simon & Schuster Books for Young Readers 2016 288 p.

Grades: 9 10 11 12

    1. Gays -- Fiction 2. Grief -- Fiction 3. Screenwriters -- Fiction 4. Gay men -- Fiction

9781481404099, $17.99; 9781481404105; 9781481404112

                                       LC 2015015712

In this book, by Tim Federle, "Quinn Roberts is a six-teen-year-old smart aleck and Hollywood hopeful whose only worry used to be writing convincing dialogue for the movies he made with his sister Annabeth. Of course, that was all before—before Quinn stopped going to school, be-fore his mom started sleeping on the sofa...and before the car accident that changed everything. Enter: Geoff, Quinn's best friend who insists it's time that Quinn came out-at least from hibernation." (Publisher's note)

"It is cleverly plotted and smoothly written with many scenes presented in screenplay style. More important, while it has its serious aspects, it is whimsical, wry, and unfail-ingly funny-a refreshing change from the often dour nature of much LGBTQ literature. Bright as a button, this is a treat from start to finish." Booklist

Fehlbaum, Beth

Big fat disaster; Beth Fehlbaum. Merit Press, an imprint of F+W Media, Inc. 2014 288 p. (pb) $17.99

Grades: 7 8 9 10

    1. Moving -- Fiction 2. Family life -- Fiction 3. Eating disorders -- Fiction 4. Overweight teenagers -- Fiction 5. Texas -- Fiction 6. Schools -- Fiction 7. High schools -- Fiction 8. Family problems -- Fiction 9. Compulsive eating -- Fiction 10. Moving, Household -- Fiction 11. Overweight persons -- Fiction 12. Family life -- Texas -- Fiction

ISBN 1440570485; 9781440570483

                                       LC 2013044512

"Colby's life as the heavy daughter of a disapproving former Miss Texas beauty queen is difficult enough, but it gets worse very quickly once she discovers a photo of her politician father kissing another woman...Colby's experi-ences, while extreme, ring true, and the fast pace, lively and profane dialogue, and timely topic make it a quick and en-joyable read." (Kirkus)

Fehler, Gene

Beanball; by Gene Fehler. Clarion Books 2008 119p $16

Grades: 7 8 9 10

    1. School stories 2. Novels in verse 3. Baseball -- Fiction

ISBN 0-618-84348-5; 978-0-618-84348-0

                                       LC 2007013058

Relates, from diverse points of view, events surround-ing the critical injury of popular and talented high school athlete, Luke "Wizard" Wallace, when he is hit in the face by a fastball.

This is a "moving baseball novel in free verse. . . . This swift read will appeal to both reluctant readers and baseball players." KLIATT

Feinstein, John

Last shot; a Final Four mystery. Knopf 2005 251p $16.95; lib bdg $18.99

Grades: 6 7 8 9

    1. Mystery fiction 2. Basketball -- Fiction 3. Journalists -- Fiction

ISBN 0-375-83168-1; 0-375-93168-6 lib bdg

                                       LC 2004-26535

After winning a basketball reporting contest, eighth graders Stevie and Susan Carol are sent to cover the Final Four tournament, where they discover that a talented player is being blackmailed into throwing the final game.

"The action on the court is vividly described. . . . Mys-tery fans will find enough suspense in this fast-paced narra-tive to keep them hooked." SLJ

Other titles in this series are:

Vanishing act (2006)

Cover-up (2007)

Change-up (2009)

Rivalry (2010)

Foul trouble; by John Feinstein. Alfred A. Knopf 2013 400 p. (trade) $16.99

Grades: 8 9 10 11 12

    1. College basketball -- Fiction 2. High school students -- Fiction 3. Basketball -- Fiction 4. African Americans -- Fiction

ISBN 0375869646; 9780375869648; 9780375871696; 9780375982460

                                       LC 2012042982

In this basketball novel by John Feinstein, "Danny Wil-cox is Terrell's best friend and teammate, and a top prospect himself, but these days it seems like everyone wants to get close to Terrell: the sneaker guys, the money managers, the college boosters. They show up offering fast cars, hot girls, and cold, hard cash. They say they just want to help, but their kind of help could get Terrell disqualified." (Publish-er's note)

"Danny works to guide his friend and teammate, Terrell Jamerson, through the trials and temptations of the college recruiting process, as agents, boosters, and other 'dudes' look to hitch a ride with the top recruit. Engaging charac-ters (including real-life cameos), intense basketball action, and sports-writer Feinstein's behind-the-scenes background provide an authentic view of a system that can both promote and exploit young athletes." (Horn Book)

Feldman, Ruth Tenzer

Blue thread; Ruth Tenzer Feldman. Ooligan Press 2012 302 p. $12.95

Grades: 7 8 9 10

    1. Historical fiction 2. Jewish women -- Fiction 3. Women's rights -- Fiction

ISBN 1932010416; 9781932010411

                                       LC 2011024382

This young adult novel focuses on Miriam, a young Jewish girl in 1912 Portland, Oregon. "While her mother plans their trip to New York City to find her a husband, Miriam gets caught up in the fight for women's suffrage. At first she's nervous about going against her parents' wishes, but curiosity gets the better of her . . . . However, after a mysterious girl named Serakh whisks Miriam back to biblical times, her desire to be a larger part of the movement becomes stronger." (School Library Journal)

Felin, M. Sindy

Touching snow. Atheneum Books for Young Readers 2007 234p $16.99

Grades: 9 10 11 12

> 1. Child abuse -- Fiction 2. Stepfathers -- Fiction 3. New York (N.Y.) -- Fiction 4. Haitian Americans -- Fiction
> ISBN 978-1-4169-1795-3; 1-4169-1795-0
>> LC 2006-14794

After her stepfather is arrested for child abuse, thirteen-year-old Karina's home life improves but while the severity of her older sister's injuries and the urging of her younger sister, their uncle, and a friend tempt her to testify against him, her mother and other well-meaning adults persuade her to claim responsibility.

"Although the resolution is brutal, this story is a compelling read from an important and much-needed new voice. Readers will cheer for the young narrator." SLJ

Fergus, Maureen

Recipe for disaster. Kids Can Press 2009 252p $18.95; pa $8.95

Grades: 7 8 9

> 1. Baking -- Fiction 2. Friendship -- Fiction
> ISBN 978-1-55453-319-0; 1-55453-319-8; 978-1-55453-320-6 pa; 1-55453-320-1 pa

Francie was born to bake and dreams of one day starring in her own baking show. Her life is almost perfect until the new girl at school shows up.

"Francie is a delight. Her own special brand of humor touches every aspect of the tale. . . . This breezy, appealing read covers personal growth, the sacrifices of friendship, and the mistakes made along the way." SLJ

Ferraiolo, Jack D.

★ **Sidekicks**. Amulet 2011 309p $16.95

Grades: 6 7 8 9

> 1. Superheroes -- Fiction
> ISBN 978-0-8109-9803-2; 0-8109-9803-3

"By all outward appearances, Bright Boy is an average middle-school student, but at night, he becomes the sidekick to superhero Rogue Warrior. . . . Ferraiolo is delightfully unafraid to inject irreverence into the superhero formula, adding plenty of humor to the high-adventure high jinks." Booklist

Ferris, Jean

Of sound mind. Farrar, Straus & Giroux 2001 215p hardcover o.p. pa $6.95

Grades: 7 8 9 10

> 1. Deaf -- Fiction 2. Family problems 3. Friendship -- Fiction 4. American Sign Language 5. People with

disabilities
ISBN 0-374-35580-0; 0-374-45584-8 pa
>> LC 00-68123

Tired of interpreting for his deaf family and resentful of their reliance on him, high school senior Theo finds support and understanding from Ivy, a new student who also has a deaf parent. "Grades seven to ten." (Bull Cent Child Books)

"Both a thought-provoking study of just when being deaf matters and when it does not, and an unusually rich coming-of-age story that explores universal issues of family responsibility, emotional maturation, love, and loss." Booklist

Fforde, Jasper

★ The **last** Dragonslayer; Jasper Fforde. Hodder & Stoughton 2010 281 p. (The Chronicles of Kazam) $16.99; (hbk.) $16.99

Grades: 7 8 9 10

> 1. Magic -- Fiction 2. Dragons -- Fiction 3. Employment agencies -- Fiction
> ISBN 9780547738475; 1444707175; 1444707191; 9781444707175; 9781444707199
>> LC 2010551874

In this book by Jasper Fforde, part of the Chronicles of Kazam series, "magic is fading. . . . Fifteen-year-old foundling Jennifer Strange runs Kazam, an employment agency for magicians -- but it's hard to stay in business when magic is drying up. And then the visions start, predicting the death of the world's last dragon at the hands of an unnamed Dragonslayer. If the visions are true, everything will change for Kazam—and for Jennifer." (Publisher's note)

Other titles in this series are:
The Song of the Quarkbeast (2013)
The Eye of Zoltar (2014)

Fichera, Liz

Hooked; Liz Fichera. Harlequin Books 2013 368 p. $9.99

Grades: 9 10 11 12

> 1. Love stories 2. Golf -- Fiction 3. School sports -- Fiction
> ISBN 0373210728; 9780373210725

Fred Oday finds herself as the first girl on her school's golf team. She is worried about being assigned to the boys' team and what it will do to her popularity, but she also can't help noticing the attractive Ryan Berenger who she's been assigned to work with by the coach.

Played. Liz Fichera. Harlequin Books 2014 352 p.

Grades: 9 10 11 12

> 1. Romance fiction
> 0373210949; 9780373210947, $9.99
>> LC 2014001537

"Sam Tracy likes to stay under the radar and hang out with his friends from the Rez. But when he saves rich suburban princess Riley Berenger from falling off a mountain, she decides to try to save him. Riley promises to help Sam win the heart of the girl he can't get over, and suddenly Sam is mad popular and on everyone's hot list. Except now Riley's trying out some brand-new bad-girl moves." (Publisher's note)

Fine, Sarah

Of Metal and Wishes. Sarah Fine. Margaret K. McElderry 2014 336 p.

Grades: 9 10 11 12

1. Ghost stories 2. Love stories 3. Prejudices -- Fiction 4. Steel-works -- Fiction 5. Teenage girls -- Fiction 6. Wishes -- Fiction 7. Romance fiction 8. China -- Fiction

144248358X; 9781442483583, $17.99

In this novel by Sarah Fine, "sixteen-year-old Wen assists her father in his medical clinic, housed in a slaughterhouse staffed by the Noor, men hired as cheap factory labor. Wen often hears . . . a ghost in the slaughterhouse, a ghost who grants wishes to those who need them most. And after one of the Noor humiliates Wen, the ghost grants an impulsive wish of hers—brutally. Guilt-ridden, Wen befriends the Noor, including the outspoken leader, a young man named Melik." (Publisher's note)

"Fine creates a memorable atmosphere of desperation, deftly weaving together numerous subplots that intersect in a grisly and satisfying climax." Publishers Weekly

Sequel: Of Dreams and Rust (2015)

Fink, Mark

The **summer** I got a life. WestSide 2009 196p $15.95

Grades: 7 8 9

1. Love stories 2. Wisconsin -- Fiction 3. People with disabilities

ISBN 978-1-934813-12-6; 1-934813-12-5

"Andy is pumped that his freshman year is over and his vacation is about to begin. Then his dad's promotion changes everything. Instead of Hawaii, Andy is spending two weeks on a farm in Wisconsin with his somewhat odd, but well-meaning, aunt and uncle. Once there, though, he finds that things aren't so bad particularly when he spots 'the most incredible-looking girl he has ever seen.' . . . Andy discovers that an accident at age four has left Laura confined to a wheelchair. . . . This is an engaging novel filled with life lessons, a little romance, humor, sports, and fraternal love." SLJ

Finn, Mary

★ **Belladonna**. Candlewick Press 2011 371p $16.99

Grades: 7 8 9 10

1. Artists 2. Painters 3. Horses -- Fiction

ISBN 978-0-7636-5106-0; 0-7636-5106-0

LC 2010038707

This novel is set in "rural England in 1757, [where] Thomas Rose is on the verge-of becoming a man. Clever, but unable to learn reading and writing . . . Tom meets the enigmatic Hélène, a circus performer who goes by the name of Ling . . .Enchanted with Ling's stories of her life in the circus as much as with the girl herself, Tom commits to helping her find her beloved horse, Belladonna . . . Their search leads them to George Stubbs, known in the village as a horse butcher . . . the teens discover that Stubbs is a painter who is completing an anatomical study of horses that involves dissection of the animals. Stubbs takes Tom on as an apprentice and secures Ling a position in the household of the wealthy family that purchased Belladonna, not knowing that

the girl's ultimate goal is to escape with her horse." (School Libr J)

"A touch of intrigue and interesting details about horses, early necropsy, and everyday life add a rich frame to this historical coming-of-age story, unique in both its setting and subject." Booklist

Finneyfrock, Karen

Starbird Murphy and the world outside. By Karen Finneyfrock. Viking 2014 384 p.

Grades: 9 10 11 12

1. Communal living -- Fiction 2. Cults -- Fiction 3. High schools -- Fiction 4. Schools -- Fiction 5. Waiters and waitresses -- Fiction 6. Washington (State) -- Fiction

0670012769; 9780670012763, $17.99

LC 2013027007

This young adult novel by Karen Finneyfrock describes how "In her sixteen years of life, Starbird has . . . never been in a car. She's never used a cell phone. That's because Starbird has always lived on the Free Family Farm, a commune in the woods of Washington State. But all that is about to change. When Starbird gets her 'Calling' to be a waitress at the Free Family's restaurant in Seattle, she decides to leave behind the only home she's ever known." (Publisher's note)

"My breath caught in my throat. Io didn't believe in the Translations?" When Starbird leaves the Free Family Farm commune to work at the cult's cafe, she begins to uncover details about the life she shares with her Family that some members would rather remained hidden. An unwitting catalyst, Starbird's voice remains strong as her worldview begins to change." Horn Book

The **sweet** revenge of Celia Door; by Karen Finneyfrock. Viking 2013 272 p. (hardcover) $16.99

Grades: 7 8 9 10

1. School stories 2. Revenge -- Fiction 3. Teenagers -- Fiction 4. Gays -- Fiction 5. Poetry -- Fiction 6. Schools -- Fiction 7. High schools -- Fiction 8. Hershey (Pa.) -- Fiction 9. Family life -- Pennsylvania -- Hershey -- Fiction

ISBN 0670012750; 9780670012756

LC 2011047221

In this teen novel, by Karen Finneyfrock, "Celia Door enters her freshman year . . . with giant boots, dark eyeliner, and a thirst for revenge against Sandy Firestone. . . . But then Celia meets Drake, the cool new kid from New York City who entrusts her with his deepest, darkest secret. When Celia's quest for justice threatens her relationship with Drake, she's forced to decide which is sweeter: revenge or friendship." (Publisher's note)

Fisher, Catherine

The **dark** city. Dial Books for Young Readers 2011 376p (Relic master) $16.99

Grades: 6 7 8 9

1. Fantasy fiction 2. Apprentices -- Fiction

ISBN 978-0-8037-3673-3; 0-8037-3673-8

LC 2010028801

"Relic Master Galen injured both his body and his mind when he dismantled an ancient technological artifact. While his physical injuries have healed, the loss of his psychic gifts has left him reluctantly dependent on his talented young apprentice, Raffi. Together they travel the dangerous road to the ruined Antaran city of Tasceron, where Galen hopes to reclaim his abilities from a shadowy figure known only as the Crow." Booklist

Darkwater; by Catherine Fisher. Penguin Group USA 2012 229p (hardcover) $16.99
Grades: 6 7 8 9 10 11 12
    1. Sin -- Fiction 2. Teenagers -- Fiction 3. Private schools -- Fiction 4. Soul -- Fiction 5. Twins -- Fiction 6. England -- Fiction 7. Schools -- Fiction 8. Brothers -- Fiction 9. Supernatural -- Fiction 10. Great Britain -- History -- Edward VII, 1901-1910 -- Fiction
    ISBN 9780803738188
                                                    LC 2011048063
In author Catherine Fisher's book, "Sarah Trevelyan would give anything to regain the power and wealth her family has lost, so she makes a bargain with Azrael, Lord of Darkwater Hall. He gives her one hundred years and the means to accomplish her objective--in exchange for her soul. Fast-forward a hundred years to Tom, a fifteen-year-old boy who dreams of attending Darkwater Hall School but doesn't believe he has the talent. Until he meets a professor named Azrael, who offers him a bargain. Will Sarah be able to stop Tom from making the same mistake she did a century ago?" (Publisher's note)

The **door** in the moon. Catherine Fisher. Dial Books for Young Readers 2015 352 p. (Obsidian mirror)
Grades: 9 10 11 12
    1. Fairies -- Fiction 2. Fantasy 3. Magic mirrors 4. Mirrors 5. Time travel -- Fiction 6. Fantasy fiction
    0803739710; 9780803739710, $17.99
                                                    LC 2014028161
In this novel, by Catherine Fisher, the third volume in the Obsidian Mirror series "it's Midsummer Eve, and as Wintercombe Abbey is under siege by the Shee and their heartless faery queen, Jake and Sarah are snatched by a gang of time-traveling thieves and thrust into the chaos of the Reign of Terror. Meanwhile Janus, the tyrant of a dystopian future, is reaching back through the magical, inscrutable obsidian mirror to secure his power." (Kirkus Reviews)
    "Fisher's genre mixing is as successful as ever, and while the labyrinthine story is challenging and a little crowded, it has lost none of its addictive appeal. Though readers might be flummoxed by the twisty plot, at this point they are likely in it for the long haul." Booklist

The **hidden** Coronet. Dial Books for Young Readers 2011 421p (Relic master) $16.99
Grades: 6 7 8 9
    1. Fantasy fiction 2. Apprentices -- Fiction
    ISBN 978-0-8037-3675-7; 0-8037-3675-4
                                                    LC 2010039315
Sixteen-year-old Raffi and Master Galen continue to evade the Watch as they seek the Coronet, a potent ancient relic that could be their only hope for defeating the power that is destroying Anara.

"The climactic integration of visionary mysticism and gee-whiz gadgetry, rendered bittersweet by all-too human failures, leads directly to a cliffhanger ending." Kirkus

Incarceron. Dial Books 2010 442p $17.99
Grades: 7 8 9 10
    1. Fantasy fiction 2. Prisoners -- Fiction
    ISBN 978-0-8037-3396-1; 0-8037-3396-8
                                                    LC 2008-46254
First published 2007 in the United Kingdom
To free herself from an upcoming arranged marriage, Claudia, the daughter of the Warden of Incarceron, a futuristic prison with a mind of its own, decides to help a young prisoner escape.
    "Complex and inventive, with numerous and rewarding mysteries, this tale is certain to please." Publ Wkly
    Followed by Sapphique (2011)

The **lost** heiress. Dial Books for Young Readers 2011 375p (Relic master) $16.99
Grades: 6 7 8 9
    1. Fantasy fiction 2. Apprentices -- Fiction
    ISBN 978-0-8037-3674-0; 0-8037-3674-6
                                                    LC 2010038156
Even though the city of Tasceron and its emperor have fallen, when Master Galen and his sixteen-year-old apprentice Raffi hear a rumor that the heiress to the throne still lives, they must try to find her and keep her safe.
    "Separate plot threads intertwine in a satisfying climax, posing puzzles to keep readers ensnared while providing pleasing narrative momentum to the overall series." Kirkus

The **Margrave**. Dial Books for Young Readers 2011 464p (Relic master) $16.99
Grades: 6 7 8 9
    1. Fantasy fiction 2. Apprentices -- Fiction
    ISBN 978-0-8037-3676-4; 0-8037-3676-2
                                                    LC 2010043237
Their quest to find a secret relic with great power leads Master Galen and his sixteen-year-old apprentice Raffi into the Pit of Maar and the deep evil world at the heart of the Watch.
    "The conclusion to Fisher's science-fantasy quartet satisfies." Kirkus

The **obsidian** mirror; by Catherine Fisher. Dial Books 2013 384 p. (hardcover) $17.99
Grades: 7 8 9 10 11 12
    1. Fantasy fiction 2. Science fiction 3. Fathers -- Fiction 4. Time travel -- Fiction 5. Missing persons -- Fiction
    ISBN 0803739699; 9780803739697
                                                    LC 2012019459
This book is the first in a trilogy from Catherine Fisher. The "mirror of the title, a dangerous gateway to other time periods, is being pursued by not one but three equally unpleasant and obsessive mad scientists. One of them, Oberon Venn, is the master of spooky Wintercombe Abbey. . . . Jake Wilde, Venn's teenage godson and his equal in arrogance, has been expelled from boarding school and shipped off to Wintercombe, where the boy plans to accuse Venn of having murdered Jake's father." (Publishers Weekly)

The **oracle** betrayed; book one of The Oracle Prophecies. by Catherine Fisher. 1st American ed; Greenwillow Books 2004 341p (Oracle prophecies) $16.99; lib bdg $17.89; pa $6.99

Grades: 7 8 9 10

    1. Fantasy fiction

    ISBN 0-06-057157-8; 0-06-057158-6 lib bdg; 0-06-057159-4 pa

LC 2003-48498

After she is chosen to be "Bearer-of-the-god," Mirany questions the established order and sets out, along with a musician and a scribe, to find the legitimate heir of the religious leader known as the Archon.

"This [is] a well-developed world with its own culture, some sharply realized settings, and several strong, distinctive characters." Booklist

Other titles in this series :

Day of the scarab: book three of The Oracle Prophecies (2006)

The Sphere of Secrets: book two of The Oracle Prophecies (2005)

Sapphique. Dial Books 2011 460p $17.99

Grades: 7 8 9 10

    1. Fantasy fiction 2. Computers -- Fiction 3. Prisoners -- Fiction 4. Identity (Psychology) -- Fiction

    ISBN 978-0-8037-3397-8; 0-8037-3397-6

LC 2009-31479

Sequel to: Incarceron (2010)

After his escape from the sentient prison, Incarceron, Finn finds that the Realm is not at all what he expected, and he does not know whether he is to be its king, how to free his imprisoned friends, or how to stop Incarceron's quest to be free of its own nature.

"Fisher's superb world-building marks this title, effectively drawing the reader in to a place so rife with secrets even its inhabitants don't entirely understand the depth of its illusions." Bull Cent Child Books

Fishman, Seth

The **well's** end; Seth Fishman. G.P. Putnam's Sons. 2014 347pp $17.99

Grades: 9 10 11 12

    1. Boarding schools -- Fiction 2. Father-daughter relationship -- Fiction 3. Colorado -- Fiction 4. Viruses -- Fiction 5. Science fiction

    ISBN: 0399159908; 9780399159909

LC 2013022716

"When a bizarre disease that accelerates aging locks down her boarding school's campus, sixteen-year-old Mia and her friends stage a daring escape. If they can reach her father's secretive, subterranean office at mysterious Fenton Electronics, they will find a cure--and, hopefully, an explanation. This suspenseful sci-fi adventure ends with a cliffhanger that will leave readers eager for another installment." Horn Book

Fitzpatrick, Becca

Black ice. Becca Fitzpatrick. Simon & Schuster Books for Young Readers 2014 400 p.

Grades: 9 10 11 12

    1. Hostages -- Fiction 2. Love -- Fiction 3. Survival -- Fiction 4. Blizzards -- Fiction 5. Wilderness survival -- Fiction

    1442474262; 9781442474260, $19.99; 9781442474277

LC 2014004913

In this book, by Becca Fitzpatrick, "Britt Pheiffer has trained to backpack the Teton Range, but she isn't prepared when her ex-boyfriend, who still haunts her every thought, wants to join her. Before Britt can explore her feelings for Calvin, an unexpected blizzard forces her to seek shelter in a remote cabin, accepting the hospitality of its two very handsome occupants—but these men are fugitives, and they take her hostage." (Publisher's note)

"While the romance between Britt and one of her captors is soapy, it dovetails nicely with the murder mystery. With an action-packed conclusion, capped off with a fairy-tale ending, this finds a good intersection between romance and suspense." Booklist

Fitzpatrick, Huntley

My life next door; by Huntley Fitzpatrick. Dial Books 2012 394 p.

Grades: 9 10 11 12

    1. Love stories 2. Teenagers -- Fiction 3. Family life -- Fiction 4. Love -- Fiction 5. Conduct of life -- Fiction 6. Politics, Practical -- Fiction

    ISBN 0803736991; 9780803736993

LC 2011027166

This novel by Huntley Fitzpatrick is "about family, friendship, first romance, and how to be true to one person you love without betraying another . . . The Garretts are everything the Reeds are not. Loud, numerous, messy, affectionate. And every day from her balcony perch, seventeen-year-old Samantha Reed wishes she was one of them . . . until one summer evening, Jase Garrett climbs her terrace and changes everything. As the two fall fiercely in love, Jase's family makes Samantha one of their own. Then in an instant, the bottom drops out of her world and she is suddenly faced with an impossible decision." (Publisher's note)

What I thought was true; by Huntley Fitzpatrick. Dial. 2014 409p $17.99

Grades: 9 10 11 12

    1. Dating (Social customs)--Fiction 2. Islands--Fiction 3. Social classes--Fiction 4. Connecticut--Fiction 5. Love stories

    ISBN: 0803739095; 9780803739093

LC 2013027029

A "love story [that] shows the clash between classes in a New England beach community. . . Gwen, whose mother is a house cleaner, has . . . [a poor] reputation among the members of the boys' swim team, including rich Cass. . . . After a humiliating run-in with him at a party, it's hard for Gwen to believe that he wants more from her than a quick fling, but over the course of the summer, he gradually wins her trust and her heart." (Publishers Weekly)

"A teenage girl struggles with class divisions, sex and the tricky art of communication. Gwen . . . is an islander, while Cass Somers is a rich boy . . . The two have had some romantic moments, but miscommunication, misinterpretation and fear keep them from moving forward. . . . Whatstarts out as snappy chick-lit writing quickly becomes deeper and more complex . . . A late revelation will surprise readers as much as it does Gwen; natural dialogue and authentic characters abound. Much deeper than the pretty cover lets on." Kirkus

Fixmer, Elizabeth

Down from the mountain. By Elizabeth Fixmer. Albert Whitman & Co. 2015 272 p.

Grades: 9 10 11 12

1. Christian life -- Fiction 2. Cults -- Fiction 3. Fanaticism -- Fiction 4. Mothers and daughters -- Fiction 5. Polygamy -- Fiction 6. Mother-daughter relationship -- Fiction

0807583707; 9780807583708, $16.99

LC 2014027714

In this book, by Elizabeth Fixmer, "Eva is mostly content with her life in Righteous Path, an isolated religious compound led by Ezekiel, a man who claims to speak directly with God. . . . Once she witnesses the kindness and generosity of the 'heathens' in the city, however, as well as Ezekiel's growing egomania and paranoid, misogynistic behavior, she starts to question whether he is as holy as he claims." (Booklist)

"Teen readers fascinated by religious cults will be drawn in by Eva's story." Booklist

Flack, Sophie

★ **Bunheads**. Poppy 2011 294p $17.99

Grades: 8 9 10 11 12

1. Ballet -- Fiction 2. New York (N.Y.) -- Fiction 3. Dating (Social customs) -- Fiction

ISBN 978-0-316-12653-3; 0-316-12653-5

LC 2011009715

Hannah Ward, nineteen, revels in the competition, intense rehearsals, and dazzling performances that come with being a member of Manhattan Ballet Company's corps de ballet, but after meeting handsome musician Jacob she begins to realize there could be more to her life.

"Readers, both dancers and 'pedestrians' (the corps' term for nondancers), will find Hannah's struggle a gripping read." Publ Wkly

Flake, Sharon G.

Bang! Jump at the Sun/Hyperion Books for Children 2005 298p hardcover o.p. pa $7.99

Grades: 8 9 10 11 12

1. Violence -- Fiction 2. Family life -- Fiction 3. African Americans -- Fiction

ISBN 0-7868-1844-1; 0-7868-4955-X pa

LC 2005-47434

A teenage boy must face the harsh realities of inner city life, a disintegrating family, and destructive temptations as he struggles to find his identity as a young man.

"This disturbing, thought-provoking novel will leave readers with plenty of food for thought and should fuel lively discussions." SLJ

Pinned; Sharon G. Flake. Scholastic Press 2012 228 p. $17.99

Grades: 9 10 11 12

1. Friendship -- Fiction 2. Best friends -- Fiction 3. High schools -- Fiction 4. African Americans -- Fiction 5. Learning disabilities -- Fiction 6. People with

disabilities -- Fiction

ISBN 0545057183; 9780545057189; 9780545057332

LC 2012009239

This novel by Sharon G. Flake is "about a teen boy and girl, each tackling disabilities. Autumn is outgoing and has lots of friends. Adonis is shy and not so eager to connect with people. But even with their differences, the two have one thing in common--they're each dealing with a handicap. For Autumn, who has a learning disability, reading is a painful struggle that makes it hard to focus in class. . . . Adonis is confined to a wheelchair. But he's a strong reader who loves books." (Publisher's note)

Fleischman, Paul

Seek. Simon Pulse 2003 167p pa $7.99

Grades: 7 8 9 10

1. Radio -- Fiction 2. Fathers -- Fiction

ISBN 0-689-85402-1

First published 2001 by Front St./Cricket Bks.

Rob becomes obsessed with searching the airwaves for his long-gone father, a radio announcer.

"Fleischman has orchestrated a symphony that is both joyful and poignant with this book designed for reader's theatre." Voice Youth Advocates

Fletcher, Christine

★ **Ten** cents a dance. Bloomsbury U.S.A. Children's Books 2008 356p $16.95

Grades: 9 10 11 12

1. Dancers -- Fiction 2. Poverty -- Fiction 3. Chicago (Ill.) -- Fiction 4. Conduct of life -- Fiction 5. World War, 1939-1945 -- Fiction

ISBN 978-1-59990-164-0; 1-59990-164-1

LC 2007-50737

In 1940s Chicago, fifteen-year-old Ruby hopes to escape poverty by becoming a taxi dancer in a nightclub, but the work has unforeseen dangers and hiding the truth from her family and friends becomes increasingly difficult.

"The descriptions of nightlife are lively and engaging, and they bring to light race, class, and gender issues in 1940s Chicago, which are fodder for discussion. Leisure readers will enjoy this novel, but it will also be useful in the classroom as a historical snapshot." Voice Youth Advocates

Fletcher, Susan

Alphabet of dreams. Atheneum Books for Young Readers 2006 294p map $16.95

Grades: 6 7 8 9 10

1. Iran -- Fiction 2. Dreams -- Fiction 3. Zoroastrianism -- Fiction

ISBN 0-689-85042-5

Fourteen-year-old Mitra, of royal Persian lineage, and her five-year-old brother Babak, whose dreams foretell the future, flee for their lives in the company of the magus Melchoir and two other Zoroastrian priests, traveling through Persia as they follow star signs leading to a newly-born king in Bethlehem. Includes historical notes

"The characters are vivid and whole, the plot compelling, and the setting vast." Voice Youth Advocates

Ancient, strange, and lovely. Atheneum Books for Young Readers 2010 315p il (The dragon chronicles) $16.99

Grades: 6 7 8 9

1. Fantasy fiction 2. Dragons -- Fiction 3. Poaching -- Fiction

ISBN 978-1-4169-5786-7; 1-4169-5786-3

LC 2009053797

Fourteen-year-old Bryn must try to find a way to save a baby dragon from a dangerous modern world that seems to have no place for something so ancient.

"This book offers a wondrous mix of dystopic science fiction and magical fantasy. . . . Fletcher has done an outstanding job of creating a believable place and space for this story to unfold. The plot flows smoothly and quickly with a lot of action." SLJ

Dragon's milk. Atheneum Pubs. 1989 242p hardcover o.p. pa $5.99

Grades: 7 8 9 10

1. Fantasy fiction 2. Dragons -- Fiction

ISBN 0-689-31579-1; 0-689-71623-0 pa

LC 88-35059

Kaeldra, an outsider adopted by an Elythian family as a baby, possesses the power to understand dragons and uses this power to try to save her younger sister who needs dragon's milk to recover from an illness

"High-fantasy fans will delight in the clash of swords, the flash of magic, the many escape-and-rescue scenes." Booklist

Other titles in this series are:

Flight of the Dragon Kyn (1993)

Sign of the dove (1996)

Flinn, Alex

Beastly. HarperTeen 2007 304p $16.99; lib bdg $17.89; pa $8.99

Grades: 6 7 8 9 10

1. Fantasy fiction

ISBN 978-0-06-087416-2; 0-06-087416-3; 978-0-06-087417-9 lib bdg; 0-06-087417-1 lib bdg; 978-0-06-196328-5 pa; 0-06-196328-3 pa

LC 2006-36241

A modern retelling of "Beauty and the Beast" from the point of view of the Beast, a vain Manhattan private school student who is turned into a monster and must find true love before he can return to his human form.

This "is creative enough to make it an engaging read. . . . [This is an] engrossing tale that will have appeal for fans of fantasy and realistic fiction." Voice Youth Advocates

★ **Breathing** underwater. HarperCollins Pubs. 2001 263p hardcover o.p. pa $8.99

Grades: 9 10 11 12

1. Domestic violence -- Fiction

ISBN 0-06-029198-2; 0-06-447257-4 pa

LC 00-44933

Sent to counseling for hitting his girlfriend, Caitlin, and ordered to keep a journal, sixteen-year-old Nick recounts his relationship with Caitlin, examines his controlling behavior and anger, and describes living with his abusive father.

"This book attempts to understand the root of domestic violence. Flinn has created sympathetic characters who are struggling with their insecurities. While it is difficult at first to be sympathetic towards Nick, it becomes easier as he examines his life and relationships. This is a good book to use in discussion with teens who have anger issues." Book Rep

Followed by Diva (2006)

Cloaked. HarperTeen 2011 341p $16.99

Grades: 6 7 8 9

1. Fairy tales 2. Magic -- Fiction 3. Shoes -- Fiction 4. Animals -- Fiction 5. Princesses -- Fiction 6. Missing persons -- Fiction

ISBN 978-0-06-087422-3; 0-06-087422-8

LC 2009-53387

Seventeen-year-old Johnny is approached at his family's struggling shoe repair shop in a Miami, Florida, hotel by Alorian Princess Victoriana, who asks him to find her brother who was turned into a frog.

"A diverting, whimsical romp through fairy-tale tropes." Bull Cent Child Books

A **kiss** in time. HarperTeen 2009 384p $16.99; pa $8.99

Grades: 7 8 9 10 11 12

1. Witches -- Fiction 2. Princesses -- Fiction

ISBN 978-0-06-087419-3; 0-06-087419-8; 978-0-06-087421-6 pa; 0-06-087421-X pa

LC 2008-22582

Sixteen-year-old Princess Talia persuades seventeen-year-old Jack, the modern-day American who kissed her awake after a 300-year sleep, to take her to his Miami home, where she hopes to win his love before the witch who cursed her can spirit her away.

This is a "clever and humorous retelling of 'Sleeping Beauty.' . . . Alternating between the teenagers' distinctive points of view, Flinn skillfully delineates how their upbringings set them apart while drawing parallels between their family conflicts. Fans of happily-ever-after endings will delight in the upbeat resolution." Publ Wkly

Flood, Nancy Bo

Soldier sister, fly home. Nancy Bo Flood. Charlesbridge 2016 176 p. Illustration

Grades: 5 6 7 8

1. Families -- Arizona -- Fiction 2. Family life -- Arizona -- Fiction 3. Horses -- Fiction 4. Indians of North America -- Arizona -- Fiction 5. Navajo Indians -- Fiction 6. Sisters -- Fiction 7. Arizona -- Fiction

9781607348214, $49.99; 9781580897020, $16.95

LC 2015018819

In this book, by Nancy Bo Flood, "thirteen-year-old Tess is having a hard enough time understanding what it means to be part white and part Navajo, but now she's coping with her sister Gaby's announcement that she's going to enlist and fight in the Iraq war. Gaby's decision comes just weeks after the news that Lori Piestewa, a member of their community, is the first Native American woman in US history to die in combat, adding to Tess's stress and emotions." (Publisher's note)

"Flood lived and taught on the Navajo Nation for 15 years, and this quietly moving story of Tess's growing maturity as she searches for her cultural identity resounds with authenticity." Pub Wkly

Flores-Scott, Patrick

★ **American** road trip. Patrick Flores-Scott. Christy Ottaviano Books, Henry Holt & Co. 2018 336 p.

Grades: 7 8 9 10 11 12

1. Automobile travel -- Fiction; 2. Brothers -- Fiction; 3. Coming of age -- Fiction; 4. Conduct of life -- Fiction; 5. Mexican Americans -- Fiction; 6. Post-traumatic stress disorder -- Fiction; 7. Siblings -- Fiction
9781627797412, $17.99

LC 2018004255

In this book, by Patrick Flores-Scott, "with a strong family...and a budding romance with the girl of his dreams, life shows promise for Teodoro 'T' Avila. But he takes some hard hits the summer before senior year when his...brother, Manny, returns from a tour in Iraq with a devastating case of PTSD. In a desperate effort to save Manny from himself and pull their family back together, T's fiery sister, Xochitl, hoodwinks her brothers into a cathartic road trip." (Publisher's note)

"After Teodoro's older brother, Manny, left for Iraq, the Avila family began to fall apart...Featuring a diverse cast of delightful characters, this novel bursts with much-needed optimism." (Kirkus)

Jumped in; Patrick Flores-Scott. Christy Ottaviano Books, Henry Holt and Company 2013 304 p. (hardback) $16.99

Grades: 8 9 10

1. Gangs 2. Friendship 3. Slam poetry 4. Poetry -- Fiction 5. Schools -- Fiction 6. High schools -- Fiction 7. Mexican Americans -- Fiction 8. Des Moines (Wash.) -- Fiction 9. Interpersonal relations -- Fiction 10. Family life -- Washington (State) -- Fiction
ISBN 0805095144; 9780805095142

LC 2013018844

In this book, "grunge-rock devotee Sam has been trying to avoid the attention of teachers and other students ever since his mom left town two years earlier. Then the equally quiet Luis Cárdenas arrives in Sam's English class.... Sam doesn't see Luis' true colors until Ms. Cassidy announces that the class will have a poetry slam. Luis not only throws himself into creating a poem, he inspires Sam to do the same." (Kirkus Reviews)

Floreen, Tim

Willful machines. Tim Floreen. Simon Pulse 2015 368 p.

Grades: 9 10 11 12

1. Computer programs -- Fiction 2. Gays -- Fiction 3. Presidents -- Family -- Fiction 4. Science fiction 5. Terrorism -- Fiction 6. Gay men -- Fiction 7. Presidents -- United States -- Fiction
9781481432771, $17.99; 9781481432788

LC 2014030181

In this book, by Tim Floreen, "scientists create what may be a new form of life: an artificial human named Charlotte. All goes well until Charlotte escapes, transfers her consciousness to the Internet, and begins terrorizing the American public. Charlotte's attacks have everyone on high alert-everyone except Lee Fisher, the closeted son of the US president. . . . But when attacks start happening at his school, Lee realizes he's Charlotte's next target." (Publisher's note)

"An excellent debut thriller that will reach a wide range of readers." SLJ

Fogelin, Adrian

The **big** nothing; 1st ed; Peachtree 2004 235p $14.95

Grades: 7 8 9 10

1. Pianists -- Fiction 2. Family life -- Fiction
ISBN 1-56145-326-9

LC 2004-6327

Thirteen-year-old Justin Riggs struggles to cope with major family problems, including a brother who might be heading for the Persian Gulf, but finds an escape in piano lessons and the dream of a romance with a popular girl.

"Serious and humorous by turns, this seemingly simple story is actually quite complex but not weighty and will be enthusiastically embraced." SLJ

The **real** question. Peachtree 2006 234p $15.95

Grades: 7 8 9 10

1. Father-son relationship -- Fiction
ISBN 1-56145-383-8

LC 2006013996

Fisher Brown, a sixteen-year-old over-achiever, is on the verge of academic burnout when he impulsively decides to stop cramming for the SATs for one weekend and accompany his ne'er-do-well neighbor to an out-of-town job repairing a roof.

"Fisher's first-person narration is dead-on. . . . This amazing title . . . should be required reading for every teen . . . who feels the weight of a parent's expectations but cannot quite figure out what to do about it." Voice Youth Advocates

Foley, Jessie Ann

★ The **Carnival** at Bray: a novel; Jessie Ann Foley. Elephant Rock Books. 2014 235p $12.95

Grades: 9 10 11 12

1. Bildungsromans 2. Ireland--Fiction 3. Rock music--Fiction 4. Teenage girls--Fiction 5. Americans--Ireland--Fiction
ISBN: 0989515591; 9780989515597

LC 2014937608

Printz Honor Book (2015)

"This promising debut, set in the heyday of grunge, tells the story of Maggie Lynch, a displaced Chicagoan and grunge music fan, living in a quiet town (Bray) on the Irish Sea. Maggie was uprooted from her friends, her music scene, and her beloved Uncle Kevin when her romantically fickle mother married her latest boyfriend, resulting in a move to his hometown. During her time of difficult adjustment to Ireland, Maggie falls in love with Eion the very moment a devastating loss hits her family, leading to rebellion and a journey to Rome to see Nirvana and fulfill Uncle Kevin's wish for her...Foley has also populated Bray with a host of quirky, loving, and memorable background characters, which enriches the story. Recommended for teens who enjoy travelogue romance stories or novels about rock music." SLJ

Neighborhood girls. By Jessie Ann Foley. HarperTeen 2017 363 p.

Grades: 9 10 11 12

1. Children of police -- Fiction; 2. Children of prisoners -- Fiction; 3. Friendship -- Fiction; 4. High school students -- Fiction; 5. Loss (Psychology) -- Fiction; 6. Police corruption -- Illinois -- Chicago -- Fiction; 7. Teenage girls -- Fiction; 8. Chicago (Ill.) -- Fiction; 9. Bildungsromans; 10. Teenage girls -- Fiction

9780062571854, $17.99; 9780062571908

LC 2017939014

In this book, by Jessie Ann Foley, "Foley delivers a compelling story about a confused girl who remains likable even as she follows through on bad choices and keeps mistaking carelessness for connection. A riveting tale about a troubled teen finding her way through the wilds of high school life." (Kirkus Reviews)

"This is a thoughtful, moving portrait of a complex girl on the verge of finding her moral compass, set against a strong backdrop of a dynamic working-class Chicago neighborhood." Horn Book

Fombelle, Timothée de, 1973-

The **book** of Pearl. Timothée de Fombelle ; translated by Sarah Ardizzone and Sam Gordon. Candlewick Press 2018 355 p.

Grades: 7 8 9 10 11 12

1. Memory -- Fiction; 2. Teenagers -- Fiction; 3. Europe -- History -- 1918-1945 -- Fiction; 4. Paris (France) -- History -- 1870-1940 -- Fiction; 5. Teenagers -- Fiction; 6. Fairy tales

9780763691264, $17.99; 9780763694081; 0763691267

In this book, by Timothée de Fombelle. "Joshua Pearl comes from a world that we no longer believe in -- a world of fairy tale. He knows that his great love waits for him there, but he is stuck in an...old-world marshmallow shop in Paris on the eve of World War II. As his memories begin to fade, Joshua seeks out strange objects: tiny fragments of tales that have already been told, trinkets that might possibly help him prove his own story before his love is lost forever." (Publisher's note)

"A luminous, haunting, intriguingly intricate modern fairy tale." Kirkus

A **prince** without a kingdom. Timothee de Fombelle. Candlewick Press 2015 464 p. (Sequel to Vango)

Grades: 7 8 9 10 11 12843; 843/.92

1. Orphans -- Fiction 2. Adventure fiction 3. Europe -- Fiction

9780763679507, $17.99; 076367950X

LC 2014957056

In this novel, by Timothée de Fombelle and translated by Sarah Ardizzone, "fleeing dark forces and unfounded accusations across Europe in the years between World Wars, . . . Vango has been in danger for as long as he can remember. He has spent his life . . . evading capture across Russia, Paris, New York, and Italy. Narrow escapes, near misses, and a dash of romantic intrigue will rivet [readers] to their seats as Vango continues to unravel the mysteries of his past." (Publisher's note)

"The story runs from 1936 through 1942, which means that it is touched by WWII and the German occupation of France, where meaningful portions of the story are set. But whatever the setting, the story is rich in mysteries, enlivened by surprises, and suffused with suspense. It is so beautifully wrought, it reminds us why we love to read, and there can be no higher praise." Booklist

Vango: between sky and earth. By Timothee de Fombelle. Candlewick Press. 2014 432p $17.99

Grades: 9 10 11 12

1. False accusation -- Fiction 2. Clergy -- Fiction 3. Friendship— Fiction 4. Historical fiction 5. Adventure fiction

ISBN: 9780763671969; 0763671967

LC 2013955696

"Minutes from joining the priest hood in 1934, Vango, who was found washed ashore on a tiny Italian island as a toddler, must suddenly avoid both arrest and a simultaneous assassination attempt. Establishing his innocence while on the run across Europe requires untangling his mysterious past." (Kirkus Reviews)

"de Fombelle has written a brilliant, wonderfully exciting story of flight and pursuit, filled with colorful characters and head-scratching mystery. As the novel proceeds, the suspense is ratcheted up to breathtaking levels as the boy remains only one step ahead of his relentless pursuers." Booklist

Fontes, Justine

Benito runs. Darby Creek 2011 104p (Surviving Southside) lib bdg $27.93; pa $7.99

Grades: 7 8 9 10

1. Fathers -- Fiction 2. Hispanic Americans -- Fiction 3. Post-traumatic stress disorder -- Fiction

ISBN 978-0-7613-6151-0 lib bdg; 0-7613-6151-0; 978-0-7613-6165-7 pa; 0-7613-6165-0 pa

LC 2010023820

"Running away is the only option.Benito's father, Xavier, had been in Iraq for more than a year. When he returns, Benito's family life is not the same. Xavier suffers from PTSD--post-traumatic stress disorder--and yells constantly. He causes such a scene at a school function that Benny is embarrassed to go to back to Southside High. Benny can't handle seeing his dad so crazy, so he decides to run away." Publisher's note

This "well-written [story reinforces] the importance of family, friends, values, and thoughtful decision-making. . . . [An] excellent [purchase, this book] will attract and engage reluctant readers." SLJ

Ford, John C.

★ The **morgue** and me. Viking 2009 313p $17.99

Grades: 8 9 10 11 12

1. Mystery fiction 2. Homicide -- Fiction 3. Michigan -- Fiction 4. Journalists -- Fiction 5. Criminal investigation -- Fiction

ISBN 978-0-670-01096-7; 0-670-01096-0

LC 2009-1956

Eighteen-year-old Christopher, who plans to be a spy, learns of a murder cover-up through his summer job as a morgue assistant and teams up with Tina, a gorgeous newspaper reporter, to investigate, despite great danger.

"Ford spins a tale that's complex but not confusing, never whitewashing some of the harsher crimes people commit. The result is a story that holds its own as a mainstream mystery as well as a teen novel." Publ Wkly

Ford, Michael, 1980-

The **poisoned** house. Albert Whitman 2011 319p $16.99

Grades: 6 7 8 9 10

1. Ghost stories 2. Supernatural -- Fiction 3. London (England) -- Fiction 4. Household employees -- Fiction 5. Great Britain -- History -- 19th century -- Fiction

ISBN 978-0-8075-6589-6; 0-8075-6589-X

LC 2010048250

As the widowed master of an elegant house in Victorian-era London slips slowly into madness and his tyrannical housekeeper takes on more power, a ghostly presence distracts a teenaged maidservant with clues to a deadly secret.

"This ghost story is light fare, chilling, and suspenseful." SLJ

Ford, Michael Thomas

Suicide notes; a novel. HarperTeen 2008 295p $16.99; pa $8.99

Grades: 9 10 11 12

1. Suicide -- Fiction 2. Homosexuality -- Fiction 3. Psychiatric hospitals -- Fiction 4. Gay teenagers -- Fiction

ISBN 978-0-06-073755-9; 0-06-073755-7; 978-0-06-073757-3 pa; 0-06-073757-3 pa

LC 2008-19199

Brimming with sarcasm, fifteen-year-old Jeff describes his stay in a psychiatric ward after attempting to commit suicide.

Ford's "characterizations run deep, and without too much contrivance the teens' interactions slowly dislodge clues about what triggered Jeff's suicide attempt." Publ Wkly

Z. HarperTeen 2010 276p $16.99; lib bdg $17.89

Grades: 7 8 9 10

1. Science fiction 2. Games -- Fiction 3. Zombies -- Fiction

ISBN 978-0-06-073758-0; 0-06-073758-1; 978-0-06-073759-7 lib bdg; 0-06-073759-X lib bdg

LC 2009-44005

In the year 2032, after a virus that turned people into zombies has been eradicated, Josh is invited to join an underground gaming society, where the gamers hunt zombies and the action is more dangerous than it seems.

"This book is a thriller, and the clever plot and characters will have readers hoping for more." SLJ

Forman, Gayle

I have lost my way. By Gayle Forman. Viking 2018 258 p.

Grades: 9 10 11 12

1. Interpersonal relations -- Fiction; 2. Loss (Psychology) -- Fiction; 3. Runaway teenagers -- Fiction; 4. Self-actualization (Psychology) -- Fiction; 5. Singers --

Fiction; 6. Central Park (New York, N.Y.) -- Fiction; 7. New York (N.Y.) -- Fiction

9780425290798; 9780425290774, $18.99; 9780425290781

LC 2017058302

In this book, by Gayle Forman, "a fateful accident draws three strangers together over the course of a single day: Freya who has lost her voice.... Harun who is making plans to run away from everyone he has ever loved. Nathaniel who has just arrived in New York City.... As the day progresses, their secrets start to unravel and they begin to understand that the way out of their own loss might just lie in helping the others out of theirs." (Publisher's note)

"Tightly woven and, in places, heartbreaking, this is a masterful exploration of human emotion that will appeal to adults as well as older teens." Booklist

I was here; Gayle Forman. Viking. 2015 288p $18.99

Grades: 9 10 11 12

1. Friendship -- Fiction 2. Grief -- Fiction 3. Mystery and detective stories 4. Suicide -- Fiction 5. Washington (State) —Fiction 6. Secrets -- Fiction 7. Female friendship -- Fiction

ISBN: 0451471474; 9780451471475

LC 2014011445

"Cody struggles to figure out why Meg took her own life and puzzles over a suspicious line in her friend's suicide email. The distraught but determined teen begins to encrypt files on Meg's laptop, which lead her to a suicide support group and posts from . . . a Pied Piper-type character who encourages suicide. As she goes further down the rabbit hole, Cody comes to the realization that she needs to forgive Meg, and, more importantly, herself." (School Library Journal)

"An engrossing and provocative look at the devastating finality of suicide, survivor's guilt, the complicated nature of responsibility and even the role of the Internet in life-and-death decisions." Kirkus

★ **If** I stay; a novel. Dutton Children's Books 2009 201p $16.99

Grades: 7 8 9 10

1. Coma -- Fiction 2. Death -- Fiction 3. Oregon -- Fiction 4. Medical care -- Fiction

ISBN 978-0-525-42103-0; 0-525-42103-3

LC 2008-23938

While in a coma following an automobile accident that killed her parents and younger brother, seventeen-year-old Mia, a gifted cellist, weights whether to live with her grief or join her family in death.

"Intensely moving, the novel will force readers to take stock of their lives and the people and things that make them worth living." Publ Wkly

Followed by: Where she went (2011)

Just one day; Gayle Forman. Dutton Books 2013 320 p. (hardcover: alk. paper) $17.99

Grades: 9 10 11 12

1. Love stories 2. Voyages and travels -- Fiction 3. Europe -- Fiction 4. Actors and actresses -- Fiction 5.

Self-actualization (Psychology) -- Fiction
ISBN 0525425918; 9780525425915

LC 2012030798

In this story, recent high school graduate Allyson meets Dutch actor Willem and "the two take an impulsive trip to Paris, but Willem disappears and Allyson is left stranded. Back in the U.S., Allyson is unable to wipe Willem from her mind, and her carefully planned future takes unexpected turns. . . . In college, Allyson breaks away from her mother's expectations, realizes her passion for theater and language, and tries to gather clues about Willem's whereabouts." (Publishers Weekly)

Where she went. Dutton Books 2011 264p $16.99

Grades: 7 8 9 10

    1. Musicians -- Fiction 2. Rock music -- Fiction 3. Violoncellos -- Fiction 4. New York (N.Y.) -- Fiction
ISBN 978-0-525-42294-5; 0-525-42294-3

LC 2010-13474

In this sequel to If I stay, Adam, now a rising rock star, and Mia, a successful cellist, reunite in New York and reconnect after the horrific events that tore them apart when Mia almost died in a car accident three years earlier.

"Both characters spring to life, and their pain-filled back story and current realities provide depth and will hold readers fast." Kirkus

Forster, Miriam

  ★ **City** of a Thousand Dolls; Miriam Forster. HarperTeen 2013 368 p. (hardcover) $17.99

Grades: 9 10 11 12

    1. Fantasy fiction 2. Mystery fiction 3. Orphans -- Fiction
ISBN 0062121308; 9780062121301

LC 2012004289

In this book, "Nisha has lived in the City of a Thousand Dolls for 10 years, ever since her parents abandoned her there. Unlike the other girls there, she was never placed in one of the city's Houses to be trained. Nisha's only status comes from her position as the assistant to the Matron, a placement that allows her access to any house on the grounds. When someone begins killing girls on the eve of the Royal Prince's arrival to claim his bride, terror and chaos ensue." (School Library Journal)

Fowley-Doyle, Moïra

  ★ The **accident** season. Moïra Fowley-Doyle. Kathy Dawson Books 2015 304 p.

    1. Accidents -- Fiction 2. Families -- Fiction 3. Supernatural -- Fiction 4. Family secrets -- Fiction 5. Love -- Fiction
0525429484; 9780525429487, $17.99

LC 2014047858

In this novel by Moïra Fowley-Doyle, "every October for Cara and her family is the accident season. Broken bones, cuts, scrapes, and even death can occur during those long thirty-one days. This year's accident season is coming to a close, and it seems like a typical year . . . until they realize that it is not as normal as they thought. This year is bad, and not all the injuries they accrue are surface level—some are more than skin deep." (Voice of Youth Advocates)

"Beautifully crafted and atmospheric, the magic realism of this book gradually peels away to expose secrets and reveal unexpected truths. Readers will be swept away by Fowley-Doyle's lyrical writing and entrancing premise in this tale of forbidden love and magic." Booklist

Foxlee, Karen

  The **anatomy** of wings. Alfred A. Knopf 2009 361p $16.99; lib bdg $19.99

Grades: 8 9 10 11 12

    1. Sisters -- Fiction 2. Suicide -- Fiction 3. Australia -- Fiction 4. Bereavement -- Fiction 5. Family life -- Fiction
ISBN 978-0-375-85643-3; 0-375-85643-9; 978-0-375-95643-0 lib bdg; 0-375-95643-3 lib bdg

LC 2008-19373

First published 2007 in Australia

After the suicide of her troubled teenage sister, eleven-year-old Jenny struggles to understand what actually happened.

Jenny's "observations are . . . poetic and washed with magic realism. . . . With heart-stopping accuracy and sly symbolism, Foxlee captures the small ways that humans reveal themselves, the mysterious intensity of female adolescence, and the surreal quiet of a grieving house, which slowly and with astonishing resilience fills again with sound and music." Booklist

  The **midnight** dress; Karen Foxlee. Alfred A. Knopf 2013 288 p. $16.99

Grades: 9 10 11 12

    1. Magic -- Fiction 2. Female friendship -- Fiction 3. Clothing and dress -- Fiction 4. Sewing -- Fiction 5. Schools -- Fiction 6. Australia -- Fiction 7. Alcoholism -- Fiction 8. Friendship -- Fiction 9. Mystery and detective stories 10. Single-parent families -- Fiction 11. Eccentrics and eccentricities -- Fiction
ISBN 0375856455; 9780375856457; 9780375956454; 9780449818213

LC 2012029108

In this book by Karen Foxlee, "Rose doesn't expect to fall in love with the . . . town of Leonora. Nor does she expect to become fast friends with . . . Pearl Kelly, organizer of the high school float at the annual Harvest Festival parade. Pearl convinces Rose to visit Edie Baker, once a renowned dressmaker, now a rumored witch. Together Rose and Edie hand-stitch [a dress] for Rose to wear at the Harvest Festival--a dress that will have long-lasting consequences." (Publisher's note)

"After arriving in Australian beach town Leonora, self-contained, morose Rose is befriended by outgoing Pearl. Pearl tells Rose about the annual harvest festival and urges her to start thinking about a gown. Enter the enigmatic Edie Baker, an old dressmaker. There are many story lines within Foxlee's complex novel; they coalesce into a dreamlike, eerie whole told in mesmerizing, sensuous prose." (Horn Book)

Frank, E. R.

  Dime. E.R. Frank. Atheneum Books for Young Readers 2015 336 p.

Grades: 9 10 11 12

1. African Americans -- Fiction 2. Families -- Fiction 3. Prostitution -- Fiction 4. African American teenage girls -- Fiction 5. Juvenile prostitution -- Fiction
1481431609; 9781481431606, $17.99; 9781481431613
LC 2014023579

In this novel, by E. R. Frank, "as a teen girl in Newark, New Jersey, lost in the foster care system, Dime just wants someone to care about her, to love her. A family. And that is exactly what she gets—a daddy and two 'wifeys.' So what if she has to go out and earn some coins to keep her place? It seems a fair enough exchange for love. Dime never meant to become a prostitute. It happened so gradually, she pretty much didn't realize it was happening until it was too late." (Publisher's note)

"Dime's desire to save her friend transcends artifice and approaches heroism, making for a tremendously affecting novel." Kirkus

Life is funny; a novel. Puffin Books 2002 263p pa $7.99

Grades: 7 8 9 10

1. Family life -- Fiction 2. Brooklyn (New York, N.Y.) -- Fiction
ISBN 0-14-230083-7
LC 2001-48436

First published 2000 by DK Ink

The lives of a number of young people of different races, economic backgrounds, and family situations living in Brooklyn, New York, become intertwined over a seven year period.

"The voices ring true, and the talk is painful, vulgar, rough, sexy, funny, fearful, furious, gentle." Booklist

Wrecked. Atheneum Books for Young Readers 2005 247p $15.95

Grades: 8 9 10 11 12

1. Bereavement -- Fiction 2. Traffic accidents -- Fiction
ISBN 0-689-87383-2
LC 2004-18448

After a car accident seriously injures her best friend and kills her brother's girlfriend, sixteen-year-old Anna tries to cope with her guilt and grief, while learning some truths about her family and herself.

"This story is compulsively readable both because Anna is likable and imperfect and because Frank's writing is so fluid." SLJ

Frank, Lucy

Two girls staring at the ceiling. Lucy Frank. Schwartz & Wade 2014 272 p.

Grades: 9 10 11 12

1. Crohn's disease -- Fiction 2. Friendship -- Fiction 3. Hospitals -- Fiction 4. Novels in verse 5. Teenage girls -- Fiction
0307979741; 9780307979742, $16.99; 9780307979759
LC 2013023236

"This novel-in-verse—at once literary and emotionally gripping—follows the unfolding friendship between two very different teenage girls who share a hospital room and an illness. Chess, the narrator, is sick, but with what exactly, she isn't sure. And to make matters worse, she must share a hospital room with Shannon, her polar opposite. Where Chess is polite, Shannon is rude." (Publisher's note)

"Carefully rendered details (instead of magazines, Chess requests "running shoes, / a black bikini, a bottle of sriracha, / a kite, a Bernese mountain dog") characterize Chess and Shannon well beyond their shared diagnosis of Crohn's disease. A sympathetic and illuminating story of illness, friendship, and resilience." Horn Book

Franklin, Emily

The **half** life of planets; a novel. [by] Emily Franklin and Brendan Halpin. Disney Hyperion Books 2010 247p $16.99

Grades: 7 8 9 10

1. Astronomy -- Fiction 2. Rock music -- Fiction 3. Bereavement -- Fiction 4. Family life -- Fiction 5. Asperger's syndrome -- Fiction
ISBN 978-1-4231-2111-4; 1-4231-2111-2
LC 2010-4606

An unlikely romance develops between a science-minded girl who is determined to reclaim her reputation and a boy with Asperger's Syndrome.

"The discursive story favors dialogue and introspection over action and can border on melodrama, but the characters' candid perspectives ring true and the romance should have readers longing for connections as deeply felt." Publ Wkly

The **other** half of me. Delacorte Press 2007 247p $15.99; pa $6.50

Grades: 8 9 10 11 12

1. Artists -- Fiction 2. Sisters -- Fiction 3. Identity (Psychology) -- Fiction
ISBN 978-0-385-73445-5; 0-385-73445-X; 978-0-385-73446-2 pa; 0385-73446-8 pa
LC 2006-36825

Feeling out of place in her athletic family, artistic sixteen-year-old Jenny Fitzgerald, whose biological father was a sperm donor, finds her half sister through the Sibling Donor Registry and contacts her, hoping that this will finally make her feel complete.

"Franklin offers readers an engaging protagonist whose humor and unusual situation highlight the lonely and displaced feelings common to many teens." SLJ

Frazier, Angie

The **Eternal** Sea. Scholastic Press 2011 362p $17.99

Grades: 8 9 10 11 12

1. Adventure fiction 2. Egypt -- Fiction 3. Supernatural -- Fiction
ISBN 978-0-545-11475-2; 0-545-11475-6

Sequel to: Everlasting (2010)

Realizing that the magic of Umandu, the stone that grants immortality, is not done, seventeen-year-old Camille accompanies Oscar, Ira, and Randall to Egypt, where all their lives are in grave danger.

"Readers who enjoy sea romances won't go wrong." SLJ

Everlasting. Scholastic Press 2010 329p $17.99

Grades: 8 9 10 11 12

1. Adventure fiction 2. Australia -- Fiction 3. Shipwrecks -- Fiction 4. Supernatural -- Fiction 5.

Seafaring life -- Fiction 6. Father-daughter relationship -- Fiction
ISBN 978-0-545-11473-8; 0-545-11473-X

LC 2009-20519

In 1855, seventeen-year-old Camille sets out from San Francisco, California, on her last sea voyage before entering a loveless marriage, but when her father's ship is destroyed, she and a friend embark on a cross-Australian quest to find her long-lost mother who holds a map to a magical stone.

"Although this novel takes place in the nineteenth century, many of the themes are relevant for today's teens. The author does a nice job of developing strong and funny characters while keeping the plot moving at a readable pace." Voice Youth Advocates

Followed by: The eternal sea (2011)

Fredericks, Mariah

Crunch time. Atheneum Bks. for Young Readers 2006 317p $15.95

Grades: 9 10 11 12

1. School stories 2. Friendship -- Fiction
ISBN 0-689-86938-X

LC 2004-20008

Four students, who have formed a study group to prepare for the SAT exam, sustain each other through the emotional highs and lows of their junior year in high school. "Grades seven to ten." (Bull Cent Child Books)

"Fredericks writes about high school academics and social rules with sharp insight and spot-on humor." Booklist

The **girl** in the park; Mariah Fredericks. Schwartz & Wade Books 2012 217 p. $16.99

Grades: 10 11 12

1. Mystery fiction 2. Crime -- Fiction 3. Girls -- Fiction 4. New York (N.Y.) -- Fiction 5. Murder -- Fiction 6. Schools -- Fiction 7. High schools -- Fiction 8. Mystery and detective stories
ISBN 0375868437; 9780375868436; 9780375899072; 9780375968433

LC 2011012309

This young adult mystery novel by Mariah Frederick follows teenage social life in New York City. "When Wendy Geller's body is found in Central Park after the night of a rager, . . . Shy Rain, once Wendy's best friend, knows there was more to Wendy than just 'party girl.' As she struggles to separate the friend she knew from the tangle of gossip and headlines, Rain becomes determined to discover the truth about the murder." (Publisher's note)

Head games. Atheneum Books for Young Readers 2004 260p $15.95

Grades: 7 8 9 10

1. School stories 2. Dating (Social customs) -- Fiction
ISBN 0-689-85532-X

LC 2003-17012

Two teenagers connect online in a roleplaying game which leads them into their own face-to-face, half-acknowledged courtship.

"This novel realistically portrays young adults trying to find themselves, fit in, and resist the labels put on them." SLJ

Freitas, Donna

★ The **possibilities** of sainthood. Farrar, Straus & Giroux 2008 272p $16.95

Grades: 7 8 9 10 11 12

1. School stories 2. Saints -- Fiction 3. Catholics -- Fiction 4. Family life -- Fiction 5. Rhode Island -- Fiction 6. Italian Americans -- Fiction
ISBN 978-0-374-36087-0; 0-374-36087-1

LC 2007-33298

While regularly petitioning the Vatican to make her the first living saint, fifteen-year-old Antonia Labella prays to assorted patron saints for everything from help with preparing the family's fig trees for a Rhode Island winter to getting her first kiss from the right boy.

"With a satisfying ending, this novel about the realistic struggles of a chaste teen is a great addition to all collections." SLJ

The **Survival** Kit. Farrar Straus Giroux 2011 351p $16.99

Grades: 7 8 9 10

1. Death -- Fiction 2. Bereavement -- Fiction
ISBN 978-0-374-39917-7; 0-374-39917-4

LC 2010041294

After her mother dies, sixteen-year-old Rose works through her grief by finding meaning in a survival kit that her mother left behind.

"The premise of the survival kit, a real-life tradition from Freitas's own mother, begs to be discussed and glued-and-scissored with friends, students, teachers, and librarians. A copy of The Survival Kit would be a worthy addition for a teen coping with her own loss or struggling to help friends or family cope with theirs." Voice Youth Advocates

This gorgeous game. Farrar, Straus and Giroux 2010 208p $16.99

Grades: 9 10 11 12

1. Priests -- Fiction 2. Authorship -- Fiction 3. Sexual harassment -- Fiction 4. Colleges and universities -- Fiction 5. Teacher-student relationship -- Fiction
ISBN 978-0-374-31472-9; 0-374-31472-1

LC 2009-18309

Seventeen-year-old Olivia Peters, who dreams of becoming a writer, is thrilled to be selected to take a college fiction seminar taught by her idol, Father Mark, but when the priest's enthusiasm for her writing develops into something more, Olivia shifts from wonder to confusion to despair.

"Young women who have found themselves the object of obsession will relate to the protagonist's ordeal and be inspired by her decision to speak out no matter the consequences." Publ Wkly

French, Gillian

Grit. Gillian French. HarperTeen, an imprint of HarperCollinsPublishers 2017 294 p.

Grades: 9 10 11 12

1. City and town life -- Fiction; 2. Cousins -- Fiction; 3. High school students -- Fiction; 4. Rape -- Fiction; 5. Reputation -- Fiction; 6. Secrecy -- Fiction; 7. Secrets -- Fiction; 8. Summer -- Fiction; 9. Teacher-student relationships -- Fiction; 10. Maine -- Fiction; 11. Missing

persons -- Fiction
0062642553; 9780062642578; 9780062642554, $17.99

LC 2017288834

In this book, by Gillian French, "seventeen-year-old Darcy Prentiss has long held the title of 'town slut.' She knows how to have a good time, sure, but she isn't doing anything all the guys haven't done. But when you're a girl with a reputation, every little thing that happens seems to keep people whispering -- especially when your ex-best friend goes missing. But if anyone were to look closer at Darcy, they'd realize there's a lot more going on beneath the surface." (Publisher's note)

"Gorgeously written and helmed by a protagonist with an indelibly fierce heart." Kirkus

Freymann-Weyr, Garret

★ **After** the moment. Houghton Mifflin Harcourt 2009 328p $16

Grades: 8 9 10 11 12

1. Stepfamilies -- Fiction 2. Dating (Social customs) -- Fiction

ISBN 978-0-618-60572-9; 0-618-60572-X

LC 2008-36109

When seventeen-year-old Leigh changes high schools his senior year to help his stepsister, he finds himself falling in love with her emotional disturbed friend, although he is still attached to a girl back home.

"This is an expertly crafted story about a complicated first love." Publ Wkly

My heartbeat. Houghton Mifflin 2002 154p $15

Grades: 7 8 9 10

1. Siblings -- Fiction 2. Bisexual people -- Fiction 3. Gay teenagers -- Fiction

ISBN 0-618-14181-2

LC 2001-47059

Michael L. Printz Award honor book, 2003

As she tries to understand the closeness between her older brother and his best friend, fourteen-year-old Ellen finds her relationship with each of them changing

"This beautiful novel tells a frank, upbeat story of teen bisexual love in all its uncertainty, pain, and joy. . . . The fast, clipped dialogue will sweep teens into the story, as will Ellen's immediate first-person, present-tense narrative." Booklist

Stay with me. Houghton Mifflin 2006 308p $16

Grades: 9 10 11 12

1. Sisters -- Fiction 2. Suicide -- Fiction 3. New York (N.Y.) -- Fiction

ISBN 0-618-60571-1; 978-0-618-60571-2

LC 2005-10754

When her sister kills herself, sixteen-year-old Leila goes looking for a reason and, instead, discovers great love, her family's true history, and what her own place in it is.

"This novel pushes the markers of YA fiction onward and upward." Booklist

Friedman, Aimee

Two Summers. Aimee Friedman. Point 2016 368 p.

Grades: 7 8 9 10

1. Choice -- Fiction 2. Fathers and daughters -- Fiction 3. Mothers and daughters -- Fiction 4. Secrets -- Fiction 5. Self-confidence -- Fiction 6. Sisters -- Fiction 7. on 8. France -- Fiction 9. New York (State) -- Fiction 10. Provence (France) -- Fiction 11. Choice (Psychology) -- Fiction

9780545518079, $17.99

LC 2015036385

In this book, by Aimee Friedman, "when Summer Everett makes a split-second decision, her summer divides into two parallel worlds. In one, she travels to France, where she dreamed of going: a land of chocolate croissants, handsome boys, and art museums. In the other, she remains home, in her ordinary suburb, where she expects her ordinary life to continue but nothing is as it seems. In both summers, she will fall in love and discover new sides of herself." (Publisher's note)

"Summer Everett is boarding a plane headed to Marseilles for a summer of culture, food, and reconnection with her distant father-until her cell phone rings with a drastic change of plans. In this Sliding Doors-style story, readers see two possibilities for Summer's vacation and the ripple effects that follow. . . . This sunny and quick read will appeal to fans of Jennifer E. Smith, and its gentle portrayal of first crushes and high school parties make this suitable for all YA readers." SLJ

The **year** my sister got lucky. Scholastic 2008 370p $16.99

Grades: 7 8 9 10

1. Moving -- Fiction 2. Sisters -- Fiction 3. Country life -- Fiction 4. New York (State) -- Fiction 5. City and town life -- Fiction

ISBN 978-0-439-92227-2; 0-439-92227-5

LC 2007-16416

When fourteen-year-old Katie and her older sister, Michaela, move from New York City to upstate New York, Katie is horrified by the country lifestyle but is even more shocked when her sister adapts effortlessly, enjoying their new life, unlike Katie.

"Friedman gets the push and pull of the sister bond just right in this delightful, funny, insightful journey." Booklist

Friend, Natasha

★ **Bounce**; [by] Natasha Friend. Scholastic Press 2007 188p $16.99

Grades: 6 7 8 9

1. Moving -- Fiction 2. Remarriage -- Fiction 3. Stepfamilies -- Fiction

ISBN 978-0-439-85350-7; 0-439-85350-8

LC 2006038126

Thirteen-year-old Evyn's world is turned upside-down when her father, widowed since she was a toddler, suddenly decides to remarry a woman with six children, move with Ev and her brother from Maine to Boston, and enroll her in private school.

The author "presents, through hip conversations and humor, believable characters and a feel-good story with a satisfying amount of pathos." SLJ

For keeps. Viking 2010 267p $16.99

Grades: 8 9 10 11 12

1. School stories 2. Massachusetts -- Fiction 3. Father-daughter relationship -- Fiction 4. Mother-daughter relationship -- Fiction

ISBN 978-0-670-01190-2; 0-670-01190-8

LC 2009-22472

Just as sixteen-year-old Josie and her mother finally begin trusting men enough to start dating seriously, the father Josie never knew comes back to town and shakes up what was already becoming a difficult mother-daughter relationship.

"The book discusses sex and abortion, and includes adult language and underage drinking. Many readers will be able to relate to this protagonist, whose strength and maturity set a positive example. Friend skillfully portrays the challenges of adolescence while telling an engaging story with unique and genuine characters." SLJ

How we roll. By Natasha Friend. Farrar, Straus & Giroux 2018 272 p.

Grades: 7 8 9 10 11

1. Alopecia areata -- Fiction; 2. Amputees -- Fiction; 3. Dating (Social customs) -- Fiction; 4. Family life -- Massachusetts -- Fiction; 5. People with disabilities -- Fiction; 6. Self-acceptance -- Fiction; 7. Massachusetts -- Fiction

9780374305666, $17.99

LC 2017042313

In this book, by Natasha Friend, "Quinn is a teen who loves her family, skateboarding, basketball, and her friends, but after she's diagnosed with a condition called alopecia which causes her to lose all of her hair, her friends abandon her. Jake was once a star football player, but because of a freak accident -- caused by his brother -- he loses both of his legs. Quinn and Jake meet and find the confidence to believe in themselves again, and maybe even love." (Publisher's note)

My life in black and white; by Natasha Friend. Penguin Group USA 2012 294 p. (hardcover) $17.99; (paperback) $8.99

Grades: 8 9 10 11

1. Sisters 2. Self-perception 3. Self-consciousness 4. Boxing -- Fiction 5. Friendship -- Fiction 6. Peer pressure -- Fiction 7. Self-acceptance -- Fiction 8. Beauty, Personal -- Fiction 9. Dating (Social customs) -- Fiction

ISBN 067001303X; 9780670013036; 9780670784943

LC 2011021436

Author Natasha Friend tells the story of Lexi and her best friend Taylor. "After finding her boyfriend . . . and Taylor making out at a party, . . . an argument quickly escalates, leading to an accident that changes Lexi's life forever. . . . It isn't until her sister, Ruthie, and [friend] Theo . . . are honest with her that Lexi starts peeling away the plastic life she once had and discovers the real one underneath." (Kirkus Reviews)

The other F-word. Natasha Friend. Farrar Straus & Giroux 2017 328 p.

Grades: 7 8 9 10 11 12

1. Identity (Psychology) -- Fiction; 2. Fertilization in vitro -- Fiction; 3. Children of gay parents -- Fiction

9780374302351; 9780374302344, $17.99

LC 2016009256

In this book, by Natasha Friend, "Milo has two great moms, but he's never known what it's like to have a dad. When Milo's doctor suggests asking his biological father to undergo genetic testing to shed some light on Milo's extreme allergies, he realizes this is a golden opportunity to find the man he's always wondered about." (Publisher's note)

"This is a joyful, emotional story full of love, humor, and the messiness of family, no matter the shape it takes." Pub Wkly

Perfect. Milkweed Editions 2004 172p $16.95; pa $6.95

Grades: 6 7 8 9

1. Bulimia -- Fiction 2. Bereavement -- Fiction

ISBN 1-57131-652-3; 1-57131-651-5 pa

LC 2004-6371

Following the death of her father, thirteen-year-old Isabelle uses bulimia as a way to avoid her mother's and ten-year-old sister's grief, as well as her own.

"Isabelle's grief and anger are movingly and honestly portrayed, and her eventual empathy for her mother is believable and touching." Booklist

Friesen, Gayle

The **Isabel** factor. KCP Fiction 2005 252p $16.95; pa $6.95

Grades: 7 8 9 10

1. Camps -- Fiction 2. Friendship -- Fiction

ISBN 1-55337-737-0; 1-55337-738-9 pa

"Anna and Zoe are inseparable—at least until Zoe breaks her arm and Anna finds herself on her way to summer camp without her best friend. . . . By the time Zoe arrives at camp (with her arm still in a sling), Anna is already embroiled in keeping peace between the individualistic Isabel and everyone else in Cabin 7. . . . Girls addicted to friendship stories will welcome this particularly well-crafted novel." Booklist

Friesner, Esther M.

Nobody's princess; [by] Esther Friesner. Random House 2007 305p hardcover o.p. pa $7.99

Grades: 6 7 8 9 10

1. Adventure fiction 2. Sex role -- Fiction 3. Classical mythology -- Fiction 4. Helen of Troy (Legendary character) -- Fiction

ISBN 978-0-375-87528-1; 0-375-87528-X; 978-0-375-87529-8 pa; 0-375-87529-8 pa

LC 2006-06515

Determined to fend for herself in a world where only men have real freedom, headstrong Helen, who will be called queen of Sparta and Helen of Troy one day, learns to fight, hunt, and ride horses while disguised as a boy, and goes on an adventure throughout the Mediterranean world.

This "is a fascinating portrait. . . . Along the way, Friesner skillfully exposes larger issues of women's rights, human bondage, and individual destiny. It's a rollicking good story." Booklist

Other titles in this series are:

Nobody's prize (2008)

Sphinx's princess (2009)

Sphinx's queen (2010)
Spirit's princess (2012)
Spirit's chosen (2013)
Deception's princess (2014)
Deception's pawn (2015)

Threads and flames. Viking 2010 390p $17.99
Grades: 6 7 8 9 10

1. Jews -- Fiction 2. Fires -- Fiction 3. Immigrants
-- Fiction 4. New York (N.Y.) -- Fiction 5. Polish
Americans -- Fiction 6. Triangle Shirtwaist Company,
Inc. -- Fiction
ISBN 978-0-670-01245-9; 0-670-01245-9

After recovering from typhus, thirteen-year-old Raisa
leaves her Polish shtetl for America to join her older sister,
and goes to work at the Triangle Shirtwaist factory.

"Friesner's sparkling prose makes the immigrant experience in New York's Lower East Side come alive. . . .
Readers will turn the pages with rapt attention to follow
the characters' intrepid, risk-all adventures in building new
lives." Booklist

Frost, Gregory

Shadowbridge; [by] Gregory Frost. Ballantine
Books 2008 255p pa $14
Grades: 9 10 11 12

1. Fantasy fiction 2. Orphans -- Fiction
ISBN 978-0-345-49758-1 pa; 0-345-49758-9 pa
LC 2007033139

"Orphaned 16-year-old Leodora, a talented puppeteer
and storyteller, is forced to hide her identity and gender
as she travels the spans and tunnels of the ocean-crossing
Shadowbridge in Frost's exciting first of a diptych. . . . Frost
(Fitcher's Brides) draws richly detailed human characters
and embellishes his multilayered stories with intriguing
creatures—benevolent sea dragons, trickster foxes, death-
eating snakes and capricious gods—that make this fantasy a
sparkling gem of mythic invention and wonder." SLJ

Frost, Helen

★ The **braid**. Farrar, Straus and Giroux 2006
95p $16
Grades: 7 8 9 10

1. Novels in verse 2. Canada -- Fiction 3. Sisters --
Fiction 4. Scotland -- Fiction 5. Immigrants -- Fiction
ISBN 0-374-30962-0
LC 2005-40148

Two Scottish sisters, living on the western island of
Barra in the 1850s, relate, in alternate voices and linked narrative poems, their experiences after their family is forcible
evicted and separated with one sister accompanying their
parents and younger siblings to Cape Breton, Canada, and
the other staying behind with other family on the small island of Mingulay.

"The book will inspire both students and teachers to go
back and study how the taut poetic lines manage to contain
the powerful feelings." Booklist

★ **Crossing** stones. Farrar, Straus and Giroux
2009 184p $16.99
Grades: 6 7 8 9 10

1. War stories 2. Novels in verse 3. Soldiers -- Fiction

4. Family life -- Fiction 5. Women -- Suffrage -- Fiction
6. World War, 1914-1918 -- Fiction
ISBN 0-374-31653-8; 978-0-374-31653-2
LC 2008-20755

In their own voices, four young people, Muriel, Frank,
Emma, and Ollie, tell of their experiences during the first
World War, as the boys enlist and are sent overseas, Emma
finishes school, and Muriel fights for peace and wom-
en's suffrage.

"Beautifully written in formally structured verse. . .
. This [is a] beautifully written, gently told story." Voice
Youth Advocates

Hidden. Farrar Straus Giroux 2011 147p $16.99
Grades: 6 7 8 9 10

1. Novels in verse 2. Camps -- Fiction 3. Friendship
-- Fiction
ISBN 0-374-38221-2; 978-0-374-38221-6
LC 2010-24854

When Wren Abbott and Darra Monson are eight years
old, Darra's father steals a minivan. He doesn't know that
Wren is hiding in the back. Years later, in a chance encounter
at camp, the girls face each other for the first time.

"This novel in verse stands out through its deliberate use
of form to illuminate emotions and cleverly hide secrets in
the text." Booklist

Keesha's house. Frances Foster Bks./Farrar,
Straus & Giroux 2003 116p hardcover o.p. pa $8
Grades: 7 8 9 10

1. Home -- Fiction
ISBN 0-374-34064-1; 0-374-40012-1 pa
LC 2002-22698

Michael L. Printz Award honor book, 2004

Seven teens facing such problems as pregnancy, closeted homosexuality, and abuse each describe in poetic forms
what caused them to leave home and where they found
home again

"Spare, eloquent, and elegantly concise. . . . Public, private, or correctional educators and librarians should put this
must-read on their shelves." Voice Youth Advocates

Frost, Mark

Alliance; Mark Frost. Random House Inc 2014
352 p. (The Paladin Prophecy) (hardback) $17.99
Grades: 7 8 9 10

1. Supernatural -- Fiction 2. Secret societies -- Fiction
3. Superheroes -- Fiction 4. Good and evil -- Fiction
ISBN 0375870466; 9780375870460
LC 2013041891

"This second entry in the Paladin Prophecy trilogy
brings readers up to date and includes a list in the first chapter to show the strengths possessed by the main characters.
Basically, this is another book involving the adventures of a
group of young people against the forces of evil, set against
a school backdrop...There are discoveries, including caves
and a hidden lab, very real threats, and of course, more villains in book two, which ends on a cliff-hanger—with the
final confrontation for the fate of the world still to come in
the third book." (VOYA)

Fukuda, Andrew

The **Prey**; Andrew Fukuda. St Martins Press 2013 336 p. $18.99
Grades: 7 8 9 10 11 12

    1. Horror fiction 2. Occult fiction 3. Survival skills -- Fiction
ISBN 1250005116; 9781250005113

LC 2013002667

This teen horror thriller, by Andrew Fukuda, is book 2 of the "Hunt" series. "With death only a heartbeat away, Gene and the remaining humans must find a way . . . to escape the hungry predators chasing them through the night. . . . Their escape takes them to a refuge of humans living high in the mountains. Gene and his friends think they're finally safe, but not everything here is as it seems." (Publisher's note)

Funke, Cornelia, 1958-

Fearless; Cornelia Funke. Little, Brown Books for Young Readers 2013 432 p. (hardcover) $19.99
Grades: 6 7 8 9

    1. Fantasy fiction 2. Brothers -- Fiction 3. Blessing and cursing -- Fiction 4. Fantasy 5. Magic -- Fiction 6. Adventure and adventurers -- Fiction
ISBN 0316056103; 9780316056106

LC 2012028742

This fantasy novel, by Cornelia Funke, translated by Oliver Latsch, is part of the "Mirrorworld" series. "Jacob Reckless has . . . tried everything to shake the Fairy curse that traded his life for his brother's. . . . But . . . they hear of one last possibility . . .: a crossbow that can kill thousands, or heal one, when shot through the heart. But a Goyl treasure hunter is also searching for the prized crossbow." (Publisher's note)

"Adroitly building on layers of European fairy tale, Funke's original, rapid-fire narrative fearlessly transports Jacob and a bevy of ominous, multifaceted fantastical characters through a dark, decaying landscape in which death waits and honor is rare. Provocative, harrowing, engrossing." Kirkus

★ **Reckless**; written and illustrated by Cornelia Funke; translated by Oliver Latsch. Little, Brown 2010 394p il $19.99
Grades: 6 7 8 9

    1. Fantasy fiction 2. Adventure fiction 3. Magic -- Fiction 4. Brothers -- Fiction
ISBN 978-0-316-05609-0; 0-316-05609-X; 031605609X; 9780316056090

LC 2010006877

Jacob and Will Reckless have looked out for each other ever since their father disappeared, but when Jacob discovers a magical mirror that transports him to a warring world populated by witches, giants, and ogres, he keeps it to himself until Will follows him one day, with dire consequences.

"The fluid, fast-paced narrative exposes Jacob's complex character, his complicated sibling relationship and a densely textured world brimming with vile villains and fairy-tale detritus." Kirkus

Gagnon, Michelle

Don't let go; Michelle Gagnon. Harper. 2014 335p $17.99

Grades: 7 8 9 10 11 12

    1. Dystopian fiction 2. Computer hackers--Fiction 3. Conspiracies--Fiction 4. Experiments--Fiction 5. Foster home care--Fiction 6. Abandoned children--Fiction
ISBN: 0062102966; 9780062102966

LC 2014001880

"This novel by Michelle Gagnon is the "finale to the Don't Turn Around trilogy," in which "Noa Torson is out of options. On the run with Peter and the two remaining teens of Persephone's Army, and with quickly failing health, she is up against immeasurable odds. The group is outnumbered, outsmarted, and outrun. But they will not give up. They know they must return to where this all began." (Publisher's note)

"A look into a future marred by what powerful people will do to fulfill their needs and wants is a little scary. It is heartening to see that young people who discover the truth can band together and battle what seems like overwhelming odds to triumph in the end." VOYA

Don't Look Now; Michelle Gagnon. Harpercollins Childrens Books 2013 336 p. $17.99
Grades: 7 8 9 10 11 12

    1. Computer hackers -- Fiction 2. Abandoned children -- Fiction 3. Experiments -- Fiction 4. Foster home care -- Fiction 5. Dystopian fiction
ISBN 0062102931; 9780062102935

LC 2013021823

In this book, by Michelle Gagnon, "Noa Torsen is on the run. Having outsmarted the sinister Project Persephone, Noa and her friend Zeke now move stealthily across the country . . . Back in Boston, Peter anxiously follows Noa's movements from his computer, using his hacker skills to feed her the information she needs to stay alive. . . . It will take everything Noa and Peter have to bring down the Project before it gets them first." (Publisher's note)

"Still suffering strange side effects from her stint as a human lab rat at Pike & Dolan, Noa (Don't Turn Around) leads a group of homeless teens bent on sabotaging the corporation. In Boston, her "hacktivist" friend Peter and his ex-girlfriend, Amanda, uncover new evidence that places them all in danger. This tense, suspenseful tech-thriller will engage readers from beginning to end." (Horn Book)

Don't turn around; by Michelle Gagnon. Harper 2012 320 p. (trade bdg.) $17.99
Grades: 7 8 9 10 11 12

    1. Dystopian fiction 2. Teenagers -- Fiction 3. Conspiracies -- Fiction 4. Computer hackers -- Fiction 5. Experiments -- Fiction 6. Foster home care -- Fiction 7. Abandoned children -- Fiction
ISBN 0062102907; 9780062102904

LC 2012009691

This book tells the story of "[t]eenage hackers Noa and Peter." Orphan Noa escapes a hospital after waking up from an operation she has no memory of. After having his computer seized when he investigated his father's files, "Peter enlists his hacktivist group /ALLIANCE/ (of which Noa is a member) to" investigate and counterattack. "The attack only serves to dig the teens in deeper when they uncover a frightening conspiracy of human experimentation and corporate malfeasance." (Kirkus Reviews)

Strangelets; by Michelle Gagnon. Soho Teen 2013 1 p. (alk. paper) $17.99
Grades: 8 9 10 11 12
1. Horror fiction 2. Mystery fiction 3. Science fiction 4. Escapes -- Fiction 5. Survival -- Fiction 6. Near-death experiences -- Fiction
ISBN 1616951370; 9781616951375
LC 2012038333
This book by Michelle Gagnon shows the "horror endured by six teens trapped in a hospital-like bunker. They come from every point on the globe: cancer-stricken Sophie from California, petty thief Declan from Ireland, military trainee Anat from Israel, hiker Nico from Switzerland, shy Yosh from Japan, and studious Zain from India." They must figure out why they are there. (Publishers Weekly)

Gaiman, Neil

Interworld; [by] Neil Gaiman [and] Michael Reaves. Eos 2007 239p $16.99; lib bdg $17.89
Grades: 6 7 8 9 10
1. Science fiction 2. Space and time -- Fiction
ISBN 978-0-06-123896-3; 978-0-06-123897-0 lib bdg
LC 2007-08617
At nearly fifteen years of age, Joey Harker learns that he is able to travel between dimensions. Soon, he joins a team of different versions of himself, each from another dimension, to fight the evil forces striving to conquer all the worlds.
This offers "vivid, well-imagined settings and characters. . . . [A] rousing sf/fantasy hybrid." Booklist

★ The **Sleeper** and the Spindle. Neil Gaiman; illustrated by Chris Riddell. Harpercollins Childrens Books 2015 72 p. Illustration
Grades: 5 6 7 8 9 10
1. Fantasy fiction 2. Fractured fairy tales 3. Sleep -- Fiction
0062398245; 9780062398246, $19.99
LC 2015033123
"Three dwarves discover a realm in which everyone has fallen asleep, and they cross into the next country to warn its queen [Snow White] of the great plague that threatens her people. . . . Traveling to the cursed kingdom, the queen and dwarves encounter threatening zombie sleepers and more." (Publishers Weekly)
"Each page is packed with marvelous details—vines claustrophobically twist everywhere and expressions convey far more emotion than the words let on. Gaiman's narrative about strength, sacrifice, choice, and identity is no simple retelling; he sends readers down one path then deliciously sends the story veering off in an unexpected direction." SLJ

Galante, Cecilia

The **summer** of May. Aladdin 2011 252p $16.99
Grades: 5 6 7 8
1. Anger -- Fiction 2. Summer -- Fiction 3. Teachers -- Fiction 4. Loss (Psychology) -- Fiction 5. Mother-

daughter relationship -- Fiction
ISBN 1-4169-8023-7; 978-1-4169-8023 0
LC 2010-15879
An angry thirteen-year-old girl and her hated English teacher spend a summer school class together, learning surprising things about each other.
"May's voice is sometimes humorous, at times heartbreaking, and always authentic. . . . A taut and believable novel." SLJ

The **sweetness** of salt. Bloomsbury 2010 311p $16.99
Grades: 9 10 11 12
1. Sisters -- Fiction 2. Vermont -- Fiction 3. Family life -- Fiction 4. Self-perception -- Fiction
ISBN 978-1-59990-512-9; 1-59990-512-4
LC 2010-03477
After graduating from high school, class valedictorian Julia travels to Poultney, Vermont, to visit her older sister, and while she is there she learns about long-held family secrets that have shaped her into the person she has grown up to be.
"What makes this novel great is its simplicity. It is poignant without becoming overbearing; it is quiet yet speaks volumes. It contains a realness that is almost uncomfortable to face at times. . . . This is an excellent novel, one that deserves to be read." Voice Youth Advocates

Gansworth, Eric

Give me some truth: a novel with paintings. By Eric Gansworth. Arthur A. Levine Books, an imprint of Scholastic Inc. 2018 403 p. Illustration
Grades: 8 9 10 11 12
1. Adolescence -- Fiction; 2. Indian artists -- Fiction; 3. Indian families -- New York (State) -- Fiction; 4. Indian musicians -- Fiction; 5. Indian teenagers -- Fiction; 6. Indians of North America -- New York (State) -- Fiction; 7. Tuscarora Indians -- Fiction; 8. New York (State) -- History -- 20th century -- Fiction; 9. Tuscarora Nation Reservation (N.Y.) -- Fiction; 10. Bildungsromans; 11. Teenagers -- Fiction; 12. Native Americans -- Fiction
9781338143553; 1338143549; 9781338143546, $18.99
LC 2017042555
In this novel, by Eric Gansworth, "Carson Mastick is entering his senior year of high school and desperate to make his mark, on the reservation and off.... Maggi Bokoni has just moved back to the reservation with her family. She's dying to stop making the same traditional artwork her family sells to tourists.... Carson and Maggi...will navigate loud protests...and first love in this stirring novel about coming together in a world defined by difference." (Publisher's note)
"A rich, honest story of family and friends, of a Nation within a nation." Horn Book

Gant, Gene

The **Thunder** in His Head. Lightning Source Inc 2012 200 p. (paperback) $14.99
Grades: 9 10 11 12
1. Divorce -- Fiction 2. Gay teenagers -- Fiction
ISBN 1613725728; 9781613725726
In this book, "Kyle Manning is a tall, strong, openly gay sixteen-year-old who makes decent grades and plays on his

school's basketball team. He's a good kid who cares deeply about his family and friends. But his life has become a mess" due to his parents' divorce. "As Kyle struggles with his fear and frustration, he grows angrier and more erratic. Then he meets Dwight Varley, a buff, attractive athlete from another school." Will having Dwight make things better or worse? (Publisher's note)

Gantos, Jack

The **trouble** in me. Jack Gantos. Farrar, Straus & Giroux 2015 224 p.

Grades: 6 7 8 9 10

1. Behavior -- Fiction 2. Friendship -- Fiction 3. Humorous stories 4. Juvenile delinquency -- Fiction 5. Moving, Household -- Fiction 6. Florida -- Fiction 7. Florida -- Fiction 8. Humorous fiction 9. Moving -- Fiction

9780374379957, $17.99

LC 2015013115

This autobiographical novel, by Jack Gantos, "opens with an explosive encounter in which Jack first meets his awesomely rebellious older neighbor, Gary Pagoda, just back from juvie for car theft. Instantly mesmerized, Jack decides he will do whatever it takes to be like Gary. As a follower, Jack is eager to leave his old self behind, and desperate for whatever crazy, hilarious, frightening thing might happen next. But he may not be as ready as he thinks." (Publisher's note)

"Gantos has won a Newbery Medal, Printz Honor, Sibert Honor, and countless hearts. Readers will want to know how he became one of a kind." Booklist

Garber, Stephanie

★ **Caraval**. Stephanie Garber. St. Martin's Press 2016 416 p. Illustration

Grades: 8 9 10 11

1. Sisters -- Fiction 2. Magic -- Fiction 3. Fantasy fiction

1250095255; 9781250095251, $18.99; 9781250095275, $60

LC 2016055697

In this novel, by Stephanie Garber, "Scarlett's father has arranged a marriage for her, and Scarlett thinks her dreams of seeing Caraval, the far-away, once-a-year performance where the audience participates in the show, are over. But . . . with the help of a mysterious sailor, [her sister] Tella whisks Scarlett away to the show. Only, as soon as they arrive, Tella is kidnapped by Caraval's mastermind organizer, Legend." (Publisher's note)

"Garber's rich, vivid scene setting and descriptions make for entertaining reading, and the conclusion hints at a sequel focused on Tella. A colorful, imaginative fantasy with some steamy romance for good measure." Booklist

García, Cristina, 1958-

Dreams of significant girls. Simon & Schuster Books for Young Readers 2011 238p $16.99

Grades: 9 10 11 12

1. School stories 2. Summer -- Fiction 3. Friendship -- Fiction 4. Switzerland -- Fiction

ISBN 978-1-4169-7920-3; 1-4169-7920-4

LC 2010002585

In the 1970s, a teenaged Iranian princess, a German-Canadian girl, and a Cuban-Jewish girl from New York City become friends when they spend three summers at a Swiss boarding school.

"The girls' personal awakenings feel organic, and the narrative handles mature themes well, including abortion, family connections to Nazis, and sexual awakenings. García's boarding school setting feels vibrantly alive, an international home away from home that readers should find as magical as do the protagonists." Publ Wkly

Garcia, Kami

Beautiful creatures; by Kami Garcia & Margie Stohl. Little, Brown and Co. 2010 563p $17.99

Grades: 7 8 9 10

1. Love stories 2. School stories 3. Supernatural -- Fiction 4. South Carolina -- Fiction 5. Extrasensory perception -- Fiction 6. United States -- History -- 1861-1865, Civil War -- Fiction

ISBN 0-316-04267-6; 978-0-316-04267-3

LC 2008-51306

ALA YALSA Morris Award Finalist, 2010

This novel is set in a small South Carolina town. Ethan is powerfully drawn to Lena, a new classmate with whom he shares a psychic connection and whose family hides a secret that my be revealed on her sixteenth birthday. "Grades eight to ten." (Bull Cent Child Books)

"The intensity of Ethan and Lena's need to be together is palpable, the detailed descriptions create a vivid, authentic world, and the allure of this story is the power of love. The satisfying conclusion is sure to lead directly into a sequel." SLJ

Followed by Beautiful darkness (2010)

Beautiful darkness; by Kami Garcia & Margaret Stohl. Little, Brown 2010 503p $17.99; pa $9.99

Grades: 8 9 10 11 12

1. Love stories 2. Supernatural -- Fiction 3. South Carolina -- Fiction 4. Extrasensory perception -- Fiction

ISBN 978-0-316-07705-7; 0-316-07705-7; 978-0-316-07704-0 pa; 0-316-07704-6 pa

LC 2010-7015

Sequel to: Beautiful creatures (2010)

In a small southern town with a secret world hidden in plain sight, sixteen-year-old Lena, who possesses supernatural powers and faces a life-altering decision, draws away from her true love, Ethan, a mortal with frightening visions.

"The southern gothic atmosphere, several new characters, and the surprising fate of one old favorite will keep readers going until the next book, which promises new surprises as '18 moons' approaches." Booklist

Garden, Nancy

Endgame. Harcourt 2006 287p $17

Grades: 8 9 10 11 12

1. School stories 2. Bullies -- Fiction 3. Violence -- Fiction 4. Family life -- Fiction

ISBN 0-15-205416-2; 978-0-15-205416-8

LC 2005-19486

Fifteen-year-old Gray Wilton, bullied at school and ridiculed by an unfeeling father for preferring drums to hunting, goes on a shooting rampage at his high school.

"This is a hard-hitting and eloquent look at the impact of bullying, and the resulting destruction of lives touched by the violence." SLJ

Gardner, Faith

★ The **second** life of Ava Rivers. Faith Gardner. Razorbill 2018 368 p.

Grades: 9 10 11 12

1. Family problems -- Fiction; 2. Identity -- Fiction; 3. Missing children -- Fiction; 4. Sisters -- Fiction; 5. Twins -- Fiction; 6. California -- Fiction

9780451478306, $17.99

LC 2018003873

In this book, by Faith Gardner, "Vera Rivers' life is split in two: before her twin sister Ava disappeared twelve years ago and after.... Now, at eighteen, Vera is counting down the days until she starts her new life at college in Portland, Oregon, far away from the dark cloud she and her family have lived under for twelve years. But all that changes when a girl shows up at the local hospital. Her name is Ava Rivers and she wants to go home." (Publisher's note)

"A teen girl's life is turned upside down when her missing twin reappears after 12 years... A deftly written examination of familial relationships, trauma, and post-adolescence." (Kirkus Reviews)

Gardner, Sally

The **door** that led to where. Sally Gardner. Delacorte Press 2016 288 p.

Grades: 7 8 9 10

1. London (England) -- Fiction 2. Mystery and detective stories 3. Time travel -- Fiction 4. Mystery fiction

9780399549991, $53.97; 9780399549977, $17.99; 9780399549984

LC 2015034396

In this novel, by Sally Gardner, "AJ Flynn has just failed all but one of his major exams. . . . So when he's offered a junior clerk position at a London law firm, he hopes his life is about to change. . . . While on the job, AJ finds an old key labeled with his birth date, and he's determined to find the door it will open. When he does just that, AJ and his group of scrappy friends begin a series of amazing journeys to the past-1830, to be exact." (Publisher's note)

"Gardner's prose, peppered with colorful metaphors and period language, moves the plot along quickly, sketching out a pungent, vivid world in both present and past." Horn Book

★ **Maggot** moon; Sally Gardner. Candlewick Press 2013 288 p. (reinforced) $16.99

Grades: 7 8 9 10 11 12

1. Dystopian fiction 2. Alternative histories

ISBN 0763665533; 9780763665531

LC 2012947247

Costa Children's Book Award Winner 2012

In this dystopian novel, "Standish Treadwell, 15, has lost parents, neighbors, best friend: All disappeared from Zone Seven, a post-war occupied territory, into the hellish clutches of the Motherland. Now a new horror approaches. . . . Standish and [his friend] Hector spin fantasies about the far-off tantalizing consumer culture they glimpsed on television

(now banned), but they lack a vision of the future beyond vague dreams of rescue." (Kirkus Reviews)

★ The **red** necklace; a story of the French Revolution. Dial Books 2008 378p $16.99

Grades: 8 9 10 11 12

1. Adventure fiction 2. Gypsies -- Fiction 3. Orphans -- Fiction 4. Social classes -- Fiction 5. France -- History -- 1789-1799, Revolution -- Fiction

ISBN 978-0-8037-3100-4; 0-8037-3100-0

LC 2007-39813

In the late eighteenth-century, Sido, the twelve-year-old daughter of a self-indulgent marquis, and Yann, a fourteen-year-old Gypsy orphan raised to perform in a magic show, face a common enemy at the start of the French Revolution.

"Scores are waiting to be settled on every page; this is a heart-stopper." Booklist

Followed by: The silver blade (2009)

The **Silver** Blade. Dial Books 2009 362p $16.99

Grades: 8 9 10 11 12

1. Adventure fiction 2. Magic -- Fiction 3. France -- History -- 1789-1799, Revolution -- Fiction

ISBN 978-0-8037-3377-0; 0-8037-3377-1

LC 2009-9282

Sequel to: The red necklace (2008)

As the Revolution descends into the ferocious Reign of Terror, Yann, now an extraordinary practioner of magic, uses his skills to confound his enemies and help spirit refugees out of France, but the question of his true identity and the kidnapping of his true love, Sido, expose him to dangers that threaten to destroy him.

"A luscious melodrama, rich in sensuous detail from horrific to sublime, with an iridescent overlay of magic." Kirkus

Gardner, Scot

★ The **dead** I know. By Scot Gardner. Houghton Mifflin Harcourt 2015 201 p.

Grades: 9 10 11 12

1. Dreams -- Fiction 2. Emotional problems -- Fiction 3. Funeral homes -- Fiction 4. Memories -- Fiction 5. Sleepwalking -- Fiction 6. Senile dementia -- Fiction 7. Undertakers and undertaking -- Fiction

0544232747; 9780544232747, $17.99

LC 2013050162

In this book by Scot Gardner, "faced with recurring nightmares, uncontrollable sleepwalking, threats from gangs, and a mother suffering from dementia, Aaron Rowe becomes assistant to a funeral director. He retrieves and prepares bodies. John Barton, the funeral director, considers Aaron a valued member of his household and provides the teen with a strong, healthy environment. Extremely violent encounters require Aaron to make some difficult decisions." (Library Media Connection)

"Aaron has trouble connecting with people. He suffers from recurring nightmares—horrific memories of a dead woman—that have been locked away, and most nights he sleepwalks away from his home and into a caravan park where the majority of residents are drug addicts. When the teen gets a funeral director apprenticeship with Mr. Barton, it is not the dead bodies that make him nervous, but Mr. Barton's family and the grieving mourners instead...With humorous interactions and their unwavering belief that Aaron is worthwhile, Mr. Barton and his daughter, Skye, help him appreciate life in the midst of death and tragedy. A darkly funny book..." SLJ

Originally published in Australia by Allen & Unwin in 2011.

Gardner, Whitney

★ **You're** Welcome, Universe. Whitney Gardner. Alfred A. Knopf 2017 304 p. Illustration

Grades: 8 9 10 11 12

1. Deaf culture -- Fiction; 2. Young adult literature; 3. Children of gay parents -- Fiction; 4. Graffiti -- Fiction
9780399551420, $20.99; 9780399551444, $9.99; 9780399551413, $17.99; 9780399551437; 0399551417
LC 2017286263

Schneider Family Book Award (2018)

"When Julia finds a slur about her best friend scrawled across the back of the Kingston School for the Deaf, she covers it up with a beautiful (albeit illegal) graffiti mural. Her supposed best friend snitches, the principal expels her, and her two mothers set Julia up with a one-way ticket to a 'mainstream' school in the suburbs, where she's treated like an outcast as the only deaf student.... Out in the 'burbs, Julia paints anywhere she can, eager to claim some turf of her own. But Julia soon learns that she might not be the only vandal in town." (Publisher's note)

"Gardner brings together Deaf culture, discrimination, sexuality, friendship, body image, trust, betrayal, and even a potential Banksy spotting for this fresh novel, brightened by black-and-white illustrations from Julia's notebooks." Booklist

Garner, Em

Contaminated; by Em Garner. Egmont USA 2013 336 p. (hardcover) $17.99; (ebook) $17.99

Grades: 7 8 9 10

1. Horror fiction 2. Dystopian fiction 3. Horror stories 4. Science fiction 5. Mothers -- Fiction
ISBN 1606843540; 9781606843543; 9781606843550
LC 2012024472

This book is set two years after "a diet drink with genetically modified ingredients transformed countless Americans into mindlessly violent animals" Now, "the Contaminated are controlled by electronic collars, and the unclaimed are housed in kennels like that in which Velvet Ellis, 17, finds her mother." Velvet and her sister's "shaky hold on normal life is finally upended when Velvet brings their mother home, facing anger and fear from neighbors and eviction from their landlord." (Kirkus Reviews)

Mercy mode. Em Garner. Egmont USA 2014 352 p. (Contaminated)

Grades: 9 10 11 12

1. Government -- Resistance to -- Fiction 2. Horror stories 3. Science fiction 4. Survival -- Fiction 5. Dystopian fiction
1606843567; 9781606843567, $17.99
LC 2014007247

In this dystopian young adult novel by Em Garner, part of the Contaminated series, "seventeen-year-old Velvet, her little sister, Opal, their mom, who is recovering from the Contamination, and Velvet's sweet boyfriend, Dillon, are attempting to build a new life amid the rationing and regulations of the post-outbreak nation. But the outbreak isn't over: more people turning into 'Connies,' more madness erupting, more killings occurring." (Publisher's note)

"Velvet's complexity and thoughtfulness make her an especially interesting dystopian heroine, and the intense and horrifying plot comes to an exciting conclusion that satisfies but provides some enticing threads to continue in the next installment." Horn Book

Garsee, Jeannine

Say the word. Bloomsbury Children's Books 2009 360p $16.99

Grades: 9 10 11 12

1. Ohio -- Fiction 2. Lesbians -- Fiction 3. Bereavement -- Fiction 4. Family life -- Fiction
ISBN 978-1-59990-333-0; 1-59990-333-4
LC 2008-16476

After the death of her estranged mother, who left Ohio years ago to live with her lesbian partner in New York City, seventeen-year-old Shawna Gallagher's life is transformed by revelations about her family, her best friend, and herself.

"This sensitive and heart-wrenching story slowly unfolds into a gripping read featuring realistically flawed characters who undergo genuine growth." Booklist

Gaughen, A. C.

Reign the earth. By A.C. Gaughen. Bloomsbury 2018 438 p. Map (Elementae)

Grades: 9 10 11 12

1. Ability -- Fiction; 2. Four elements (Philosophy) -- Fiction; 3. Fantasy fiction; 4. Magic -- Fiction
9781681191119, $17.99; 9781681191126
LC 2017024397

"Shalia is a proud daughter of the desert, but after years of devastating war with the adjoining kingdom, her people are desperate for an end to the violence that has claimed so many of their loved ones. Willing to trade her freedom to ensure the safety of her family, Shalia becomes Queen of the Bone Lands, a country where magic is outlawed and the Elementae -- those that can control earth, air, fire and water -- are traitors, subject to torture...or worse. Before she is even crowned, Shalia discovers that she can bend the earth to her will. Trapped between her husband's irrational hatred of the Elementae and a dangerous rebellion led by her own brother, Shalia must harness her power and make an impossible choice: save her family, save the Elementae, or save herself." (Publisher's note)

"Gaughen...delivers a tale of staggering magic, cutthroat royalty, and lethal intrigue." Booklist

Another title in this series is: Imprison the sky (2019)

Gavin, Rohan

3 of a kind. Rohan Gavin. Bloomsbury Children's Books 2016 272 p. (Knightley and Son)

Grades: 5 6 7 8 9

1. Fathers and sons -- Fiction 2. Missing persons -- Fiction 3. Mystery and detective stories 4. Las Vegas (Nev.) -- Fiction 5. Father-son relationship -- Fiction 6. Adventure fiction -- Fiction 7. Las Vegas (Nev.) --

Fiction 8. Mystery fiction -- Fiction
9781619638303, $16.99

LC 2015037726

In this book by Rohan Gavin, "Darkus Knightley is . . . an extraordinary solver of crimes. . . . Despite trying to leave his detective ways behind to lead a normal teenage life, when his father's loyal housekeeper, Bogna, goes missing, Darkus must return to the family fold and follow the clues to America and the bright lights of Las Vegas. Alongside his father, Alan, and stepsister, Tilly, Darkus must once again face the deadly criminal organisation, the Combination." (Publisher's note)

"There's plenty of mystery, suspense, and humor here, but series fans will mainly enjoy watching the many idiosyncratic characters in action once again." Booklist

Gee, Maurice

★ **Salt**. Orca Book Publishers 2009 252p map (The Salt trilogy) $18; pa $12.95

Grades: 6 7 8 9 10

1. Fantasy fiction 2. Extrasensory perception -- Fiction
ISBN 978-1-55469-209-5; 1-55469-209-1; 978-1-55469-369-6 pa; 1-55469-369-1 pa

"Hari lives in Blood Burrow, a hellacious, rat-infested slum. . . . Pearl is a pampered daughter of Company, her only purpose in life to be married off to cement one of her father's political alliances. When both young people, who share rare psychic gifts, revolt against their fates, they find themselves on a desperate journey across a hostile landscape, with the forces of Company at their heels. . . . A compelling tale of anger and moral development that also powerfully explores the evils of colonialism and racism." Publ Wkly

Other titles in this series are:
Gool (2010)
The Limping Man (2011)

Geiger, J. C.

Wildman. J. C. Geiger. Disney-Hyperion 2017 327 p.

Grades: 9 10 11 12

1. Conduct of life -- Fiction; 2. Interpersonal relations -- Fiction; 3. Self-actualization (Psychology) -- Fiction; 4. Self-realization -- Fiction
148474957X; 9781484749579, $17.99; 9781484758526

LC 2016029359

In this book, by J. C. Geiger, "when Lance's '93 Buick breaks down in the middle of nowhere, he tells himself Don't panic. After all, he's valedictorian of his class. First-chair trumpet player. Scholarship winner. Nothing can stop Lance Hendricks. But the locals don't know that. They don't even know his name. Stuck in a small town, Lance could be anyone: a delinquent, a traveler, a maniac. One of the townies calls him Wildman, and a new world opens up." (Publisher's note)

"A thought-provoking, hilarious, eloquent story of a young man realizing that the world is much larger than the one set up for him." Kirkus

Gensler, Sonia

The **revenant**. Alfred A. Knopf 2011 336p $16.99; lib bdg $19.99

Grades: 7 8 9 10

1. Ghost stories 2. School stories 3. Oklahoma -- Fiction 4. Teachers -- Fiction 5. Cherokee Indians -- Fiction 6. Cherokee National Female Seminary -- Fiction
ISBN 978-0-375-86701-9; 0-375-86701-5; 978-0-375-96701-6 lib bdg; 0-375-96701-X lib bdg

LC 2010-28701

When seventeen-year-old Willemina Hammond fakes credentials to get a teaching position at a school for Cherokee girls in nineteenth-century Oklahoma, she is haunted by the ghost of a drowned student.

"Gensler makes a solid debut with an eerie and suspenseful work of historical fiction in which everyone is a murder suspect. . . . The layers of detail address the complex social structure of the period, and Gensler's characters and dialogue are believably crafted." Publ Wkly

George, Jessica Day

★ **Princess** of glass. Bloomsbury Children's Books 2010 266p $16.99

Grades: 6 7 8 9 10

1. Fairy tales 2. Princesses -- Fiction
ISBN 978-1-59990-478-8; 1-59990-478-0

In the midst of maneuverings to create political alliances through marriage, sixteen-year-old Poppy, one of the infamous twelve dancing princesses, becomes the target of a vengeful witch while Prince Christian tries to save her.

"In a clever reworking of the Cinderella story, George once again proves adept at spinning her own magical tale." Booklist

★ **Princess** of the midnight ball. Bloomsbury Children's Books 2009 280p $16.99

Grades: 6 7 8 9 10

1. Fairy tales
ISBN 978-1-59990-322-4; 1-59990-322-9

LC 2008-30310

A retelling of the tale of twelve princesses who wear out their shoes dancing every night, and of Galen, a former soldier now working in the king's gardens, who follows them in hopes of breaking the curse.

"Fans of fairy-tale retellings . . . will enjoy this story for its magic, humor, and touch of romance." SLJ

Sun and moon, ice and snow. Bloomsbury 2008 336p $16.95

Grades: 7 8 9 10 11 12

1. Fairy tales 2. Fantasy fiction
ISBN 1-59990-109-9; 978-1-59990-109-1

LC 2007030848

A girl travels east of the sun and west of the moon to free her beloved prince from a magic spell.

"George has adapted Norse myths and fairy tales to create this eerily beautiful, often terrifying world. . . . Mystery, adventure, and the supernatural, and a touch of love are woven together to create a vivid, well-crafted, poetic fantasy." Booklist

George, Madeleine

The **difference** between you and me; Madeleine George. Viking 2012 256 p.

Grades: 9 10 11 12

    1. Schools -- Fiction 2. Lesbians -- Fiction 3. High schools -- Fiction 4. Protest movements -- Fiction
ISBN 9780670011285

LC 2011012192

This young adult novel uses a trio of alternating narrators to tell the story of "self-proclaimed misfit and outspoken manifesto-author Jesse [who] deals daily with the hazards of being out and proud in high school. She's also carrying on a secret affair with image-conscious Emily, the girlfriend of a popular boy at school. Meeting weekly in the bathroom of the local public library, the two experience an inexplicable chemistry, even though Emily will barely acknowledge Jesse at any other time. Switching perspective among Emily, Jesse and a third girl, Esther, this . . . tale . . . explor[es] . . . attraction and shame. Jesse hides her relationship from her warmly quirky and accepting parents not because it is with a girl, but because she knows they will disapprove of its secrecy." (Kirkus)

    ★ **Looks**. Viking 2008 240p $16.99; pa $7.99
Grades: 8 9 10 11 12

    1. School stories 2. Obesity -- Fiction 3. Friendship -- Fiction 4. Anorexia nervosa -- Fiction
ISBN 978-0-670-06167-9; 0-670-06167-0; 978-0-14-241419-4 pa; 0-14-241419-0 pa

LC 2007-38218

"Meghan and Aimee are on opposite ends of the outcast spectrum. Meghan is extremely overweight. . . . Aimee, on the other hand, is classic anorexic. Both girls have been hurt by one of the popular girls at school. They join forces to bring Cara down in a stunning bit of public humiliation. . . . The story will make readers think about the various issues touched upon, and it is difficult to put down." SLJ

Geras, Adele

    ★ **Troy**. Harcourt 2001 340p hardcover o.p. pa $6.95
Grades: 7 8 9 10

    1. Trojan War -- Fiction
ISBN 0-15-216492-8; 0-15-204570-8 pa

LC 00-57262

"Mythology buffs will savor the author's ability to embellish stories of old without diminishing their original flavor, while the uninitiated will find this a captivating introduction to a pivotal event in classic Greek literature." Publ Wkly

Gibney, Shannon

    Dream country. By Shannon Gibney. Dutton 2018 368 p.
Grades: 10 11 12

    1. African Americans -- Fiction; 2. Americans -- Liberia -- Fiction; 3. Family life -- Liberia -- Fiction; 4. Family life -- Minnesota -- Fiction; 5. Liberian Americans -- Fiction; 6. Refugees -- Fiction; 7. Slavery -- Fiction; 8. Liberia -- History -- 1847-1944 -- Fiction; 9. Liberia -- History -- To 1847 -- Fiction; 10. Minneapolis (Minn.) -- Fiction; 11. Racism -- Fiction; 12. Family life -- Fiction
9780735231672, $17.99

LC 2017055923

This book, by Shannon Gibney, "begins in suburban Minneapolis at the moment when seventeen-year-old Kollie Flomo begins to crack under the strain of his life as a Liberian refugee.... When his frustration finally spills into violence and his parents send him back to Monrovia to reform school, the story shifts. Like Kollie, readers travel back to Liberia, but also back in time, to the early twentieth century and the point of view of Togar Somah." (Publisher's note)

    See no color. Shannon Gibney. Carolrhoda Lab 2015 186 p.
Grades: 7 8 9 10

    1. Adoption -- Fiction 2. African Americans -- Fiction 3. Baseball -- Fiction 4. Family life -- Fiction 5. Identity -- Fiction 6. Self-acceptance -- Fiction 7. Adopted children -- Fiction 8. Baseball players -- Fiction
1467776823; 9781467776820, $18.99

LC 2015001619

In Shannon Gibey's novel "for as long as she can remember, sixteen-year-old Alex Kirtridge has known two things: 1. She has always been Little Kirtridge, a stellar baseball player, just like her father. 2. She's adopted. But now, things are changing: she meets Reggie, the first black guy who's wanted to get to know her; she discovers the letters from her biological father that her adoptive parents have kept from her; and her body starts to grow into a woman's, affecting her game." (Publisher's note)

    "Recommended for purchase, particularly by libraries serving less diverse communities, where it will provide welcome education and support." SLJ

Gier, Kerstin

    ★ **Ruby** red. Henry Holt 2011 330p $16.99
Grades: 7 8 9 10

    1. Family life -- Fiction 2. Time travel -- Fiction 3. London (England) -- Fiction 4. Secret societies -- Fiction
ISBN 978-0-8050-9252-3; 0-8050-9252-8

LC 2010-49223

"Sixteen-year-old Londoner Gwyneth Shepherd comes from a family of time travelers. The gene was supposed to have skipped Gwen, but sneaks up on her unexpectedly in the middle of class one day and hurls her way back to the 18th century, where she meets an insufferable-turns-lovable time-traveling boy named Gideon." TeenVogue.com

    "Adventure, humor, and mystery all have satisfying roles here." Booklist

    Other titles in this series are:
Sapphire blue (2012)
Emerald green (2013)

Gilbert, Kelly Loy

    Conviction. Kelly Loy Gilbert. Disney-Hyperion 2015 352 p.
Grades: 9 10 11 12

    1. Faith -- Fiction 2. Fathers and sons -- Fiction 3. Trials (Murder) -- Fiction 4. Trials (Homicide) -- Fiction 5. Father-son relationship -- Fiction
1423197380; 9781423197386, $17.99

LC 2014042087

William C. Morris Award Finalist (2016)

In this young adult novel by Kelly Loy Gilbert, "Braden has always measured himself through baseball. . . . Now the rules of the sport that has always been Braden's saving grace are blurred in ways he never realized, and the prospect of playing against Alex Reyes, the nephew of the police officer his father is accused of killing, is haunting his every pitch." (Publisher's note)

Picture us in the light. Kelly Loy Gilbert. Hyperion 2018 353 p.

Grades: 9 10 11 12

    1. Artists -- Fiction; 2. Chinese Americans -- Fiction; 3. Family life -- California -- Fiction; 4. Immigrants -- Fiction; 5. California -- Fiction; 6. Unauthorized immigrants -- Fiction

9781484735282; 9781484726020, $17.99

LC 2017034519

In this book, by Kelly Loy Gilbert, "Danny Cheng has always known his parents have secrets. But when he discovers a taped-up box in his father's closet filled with old letters and a file on a powerful Silicon Valley family, he realizes there's much more to his family's past than he ever imagined.... [Danny] uncovers a secret that disturbs the foundations of his family history and the carefully constructed facade his parents have maintained begins to crumble." (Publisher's note)

"Family, art, love, duty, and longing collide in this painfully beautiful paean to the universal human need for connection." Kirkus

Giles, Amy

Now is everything. Amy Giles. HarperTeen 2017 362 p.

Grades: 7 8 9 10

    1. Child abuse -- Fiction; 2. Dysfunctional families -- Fiction; 3. Teenage girls -- Fiction; 4. Domestic fiction; 5. Family secrets -- Fiction; 6. Suicide -- Fiction

9780062495754; 9780062495730, $17.99

LC 2017932865

In this book, by Amy Giles, "the McCauleys look perfect on the outside. But nothing is ever as it seems, and this family is hiding a dark secret. Hadley McCauley will do anything to keep her sister safe from their father. But when Hadley's forbidden relationship with Charlie Simmons deepens, the violence at home escalates.... When Hadley attempts to take her own life,...the investigator on the case want to know why." (Publisher's note)

"Once readers pick up Hadley's story, they will have difficulty putting it down, desperately rooting for her to win. An admirably crafted debut that will haunt readers." Booklist

Giles, Gail

Dark song. Little, Brown 2010 292p $16.99

Grades: 8 9 10 11 12

    1. Criminals -- Fiction 2. Family life -- Fiction

ISBN 978-0-316-06886-4; 0-316-06886-1

LC 2010-06888

After her father loses his job and she finds out that her parents have lied to her, fifteen-year-old Ames feels betrayed enough to become involved with a criminal who will stop at nothing to get what he wants.

"Suspense lovers will savor this fast-paced psychological thriller." Voice Youth Advocates

Girls like us; Gail Giles. Candlewick Press 2014 224 p. $16.99

Grades: 9 10 11 12

    1. Roommates -- Fiction 2. Friendship -- Fiction 3. People with disabilities -- Fiction

ISBN 0763662674; 9780763662677

LC 2013944011

" In compelling, engaging, and raw voices, 18-year-olds Biddy and Quincy, newly independent, intellectually disabled high-school graduates, narrate their growing friendship and uneasy transition into a life of jobs, real world apartments, and facing cruel prejudice... Giles (Dark Song, 2010) offers a sensitive and affecting story of two young women learning to thrive in spite of their hard circumstances." (Booklist)

Right behind you. Little, Brown 2007 292p hardcover o.p. pa $7.99

Grades: 8 9 10 11 12

    1. Homicide -- Fiction 2. Family life -- Fiction 3. Psychotherapy -- Fiction

ISBN 978-0-316-16636-2; 0-316-16636-7; 978-0-316-16637-9 pa; 0-316-16637-5 pa

LC 2007-12336

After spending over four years in a mental institution for murdering a friend in Alaska, fourteen-year-old Kip begins a completely new life in Indiana with his father and stepmother under a different name, but not only has trouble fitting in, he finds there are still problems to deal with from his childhood.

"The story-behind-the-headlines flavor gives this a voyeuristic appeal, while the capable writing and sympathetic yet troubled protagonist will suck readers right into the action." Bull Cent Child Books

Shattering Glass. Simon Pulse 2003 215p pa $7.99

Grades: 7 8 9 10

    1. School stories 2. Violence -- Fiction

ISBN 978-0-689-85800-0; 0-689-85800-0

First published 2002 by Roaring Brook Press

When Rob, the charismatic leader of the senior class, turns the school nerd into Prince Charming, his actions lead to unexpected violence.

"Tricky, surprising, and disquieting, this tension-filled story is a psychological thriller as well as a book about finding oneself and taking responsibility." Booklist

★ **What** happened to Cass McBride? a novel. Little, Brown and Company 2006 211p $16.99; pa $7.99

Grades: 11 12

    1. Suicide -- Fiction 2. Kidnapping -- Fiction 3. Family life -- Fiction

ISBN 978-0-316-16638-6; 0-316-16638-3; 978-0-316-16639-3 pa; 0-316-16639-1 pa

LC 2005-37298

After his younger brother commits suicide, Kyle Kirby decides to exact revenge on the person he holds responsible.

"Often brutal, this outstanding psychological thriller is recommended for older teens." Voice Youth Advocates

Giles, Lamar

Fake ID; L.R. Giles. Amistad 2014 320 p. (hardback) $17.99

Grades: 8 9 10 11 12

    1. Homicide -- Fiction 2. Witnesses -- Fiction 3. Conspiracies -- Fiction 4. African Americans -- Fiction 5. Mystery and detective stories 6. Witness protection programs -- Fiction

    ISBN 0062121847; 9780062121844

LC 2013032149

"Nick Pearson's real name is Tony Bordeaux. A high schooler in Witness Protection, this is the fourth new identity and home for Nick in the last few years. It's all because his father keeps falling into his old criminal habits...Teen readers will especially relate to the likable everyman and African American main character. His burgeoning relationship with Reya, despite being grounded in tragedy, is one of the more charming aspects of the plot. A twist reveal at the novel's climax will shock many and will leave fans of mystery and suspense books extremely satisfied." (School Library Journal)

★ **Fresh** ink: an anthology. Edited by Lamar Giles. Crown 2018 208 p. Illustration

Grades: 9 10 11 12

    1. Short stories; 2. Identity (Psychology); 3. Literature -- Collections; 4. American short stories

    9781524766283; 9781524766290, $20.99; 9781524766313

LC 2018006762

In this book, edited by Lamar Giles, "thirteen of the most accomplished YA authors deliver a label-defying anthology that includes ten short stories, a graphic novel, and a one-act play about topics like gentrification, acceptance, untimely death, coming out, and poverty and ranging in genre from contemporary realistic fiction to adventure and romance. This collection will inspire you to break conventions, bend the rules, and color outside the lines." (Publisher's note)

"United by vivid descriptions of food, language, and cultural norms, the collection will serve as both mirror and window to teens from all walks of life." Kirkus

Gill, David Macinnis

Black hole sun. Greenwillow Books 2010 340p $16.99

Grades: 8 9 10 11 12

    1. Science fiction 2. Miners -- Fiction 3. Mars (Planet) -- Fiction

    ISBN 978-0-06-167304-7; 0-06-167304-8

LC 2009-23050

"Durango is the 16-year-old chief of a team of mercenaries who eke out a living on Mars by earning meager commissions for their dangerous work. Their current job, and the main thrust of this high-energy, action-filled, science-fiction romp, is to protect South Pole miners from the Dræu, a cannibalistic group who are after the miners' treasure. . . . Throughout the novel, the dialogue crackles with expertly delivered sarcastic wit and venom. . . . Readers will have a hard time turning the pages fast enough as the body count rises to the climactic, satisfying ending." Booklist

Other titles in this series are:

Invisible sun (2012)

Shadow on the sun (2013)

Soul enchilada. Greenwillow Books 2009 368p $16.99; lib bdg $17.89

Grades: 7 8 9 10

    1. Devil -- Fiction 2. Grandfathers -- Fiction 3. Racially mixed people -- Fiction

    ISBN 978-0-06-167301-6; 0-06-167301-3; 978-0-06-167302-3 lib bdg; 0-06-167302-1 lib bdg

LC 2008-19486

When, after a demon appears to repossess her car, she discovers that both the car and her soul were given as collateral in a deal made with the Devil by her irascible grandfather, eighteen-year-old Bug Smoot, given two-days' grace, tries to find ways to outsmart the Devil as she frantically searches for her conveniently absent relative.

"Bug is a refreshingly gutsy female protagonist with an attitude that will win over readers searching for something different." Booklist

Gilman, Charles

Professor Gargoyle; Charlie Ward. Quirk Books 2012 175 p. (hardcover) $13.99

Grades: 7 8 9 10

    1. Horror fiction 2. School stories 3. Monsters -- Fiction 4. Teachers -- Fiction 5. Middle schools

    ISBN 1594745919; 9781594745911

LC 2011946052

In this novel by Charles Gilman "Strange things are happening at Lovecraft Middle School. Rats are leaping from lockers. Students are disappearing. The school library is a labyrinth of secret corridors. And the science teacher is acting very peculiar -- in fact, he just might be a monster-in-disguise. Twelve-year-old Robert Arthur knew that seventh grade was going to be weird, but this is ridiculous!"(Publisher's note)

Gilman, David

The devil's breath. Delacorte Press 2008 391p (Danger zone) $15.99; lib bdg $18.99

Grades: 7 8 9 10 11 12

    1. Adventure fiction 2. Namibia -- Fiction 3. Environmental protection -- Fiction

    ISBN 978-0-385-73560-5; 978-0-385-90546-6 lib bdg

LC 2007-46744

When fifteen-year-old Max Gordon's environmentalist-adventurer father goes missing while working in Namibia and Max becomes the target of a would-be assassin at his school in England, he decides he must follow his father to Africa and find him before they both are killed.

"The action is relentless. . . . Gilman has a flair for making the preposterous seem possible." Booklist

Other titles in this series are:

Ice claw (2010)

Blood sun (2011)

Gilmore, Kate

The **exchange** student. Houghton Mifflin 1999 216p $15; pa $6.95

Grades: 7 8 9 10

   1. Science fiction 2. Endangered species -- Fiction 3. Wildlife conservation -- Fiction 4. Extraterrestrial beings -- Fiction

   ISBN 0-395-57511-7; 0-618-68948-6 pa

                    LC 97-47162

When her mother arranges to host one of the young people coming to Earth from Chela, Daria is both pleased and intrigued by the keen interest shown by the Chelan in her work breeding endangered species

"Gilmore makes a farfetched premise seem more reasonable with everyday details of life in the twenty-first century, sympathetic characters, and logical consequences. . . . A story that will appeal to readers on many levels." Booklist

Girard, M.-E.

  ★ **Girl** Mans Up. M-E Girard. Harpercollins Childrens Books 2016 384 p.

Grades: 9 10 11 12

   1. Children of immigrants -- Fiction 2. Gender identity -- Fiction 3. Friendship -- Fiction 4. Lesbian teenagers -- Fiction

   0062404172; 9780062404190, $16.99; 9780062404176, $17.99

                 LC 2016013197

Morris Finalist (2017)

In this novel by M-E Girard, "all Pen wants is to be the kind of girl she's always been. So why does everyone have a problem with it? They think the way she looks and acts means she's trying to be a boy—that she should quit trying to be something she's not. . . . Old-world parents, disintegrating friendships, and strong feelings for other girls drive Pen to see the truth—that in order to be who she truly wants to be, she'll have to man up." (Publisher's note)

"A strong genderqueer lesbian character, imperfect, independent, and deserving of every cheer." Kirkus

Gläser, Mechthild

The **book** jumper. Mechthild Gläser; [translated by Romy Fursland]. Henry Holt & Co. 2017 384 p.

Grades: 8 9 10

   1. Books and reading -- Fiction 2. Characters in literature -- Fiction 3. Books and reading -- Fiction 4. Characters and characteristics in literature -- Fiction

   9781250086662, $17.99; 9781250086679, $60

                 LC 2016007363

In this book, by Mechthild Gläser, translated by Romy Fursland, "Amy Lennox . . . and her mother . . . [leave] for Scotland, heading to her mother's childhood home of Lennox House. . . . Amy must read while she resides at Lennox House—but not in the usual way. It turns out that Amy is a book jumper, able to leap into a story and interact with the world inside. As thrilling as Amy's new power is, it also brings danger: someone is stealing from the books she visits." (Publisher's note)

"This offering is the first U.S. title from an award-winning German author and would be a good additional purchase for fans of Cornelia Funke's Inkheart or Kristin Kladstrup's The Book of Story Beginnings." SLJ

Glasgow, Kathleen

  ★ **Girl** in pieces. Kathleen Glasgow. Delacorte Press 2016 416 p.

Grades: 10 11 12

   1. Abandoned children -- Fiction 2. Cutting (Self-mutilation) -- Fiction 3. Emotional problems -- Fiction 4. Homeless persons -- Fiction 5. Sexual abuse -- Fiction 6. Survival -- Fiction 7. Self-harm -- Fiction 8. Survival skills -- Fiction 9. Child sexual abuse -- Fiction

   1101934735; 9781101934715; 9781101934739, $21.99

                 LC 2015044136

This novel, by Kathleen Glasgow, "begins with 17-year-old Charlie in a mental health facility that specializes in the treatment of girls who have self-injury disorders. When Charlie is released prematurely because of a lack of insurance coverage, she must find her own way in a world she is unprepared to deal with. Readers follow her as she struggles to meet the challenges of survival and as she follows the path of least resistance." (School Library Journal)

"This grittily provocative debut explores the horrors of self-harm and the healing power of artistic expression." Kirkus

Gleason, Colleen

The **clockwork** scarab; Colleen Gleason. Chronicle Books 2013 356 p. (Stoker & Holmes) (alk. paper) $17.99

Grades: 7 8 9 10

   1. Mystery fiction 2. Historical fiction 3. Scarabs -- Fiction 4. Time travel -- Fiction 5. Secret societies -- Fiction 6. Detective and mystery stories 7. Mystery and detective stories 8. Great Britain -- History -- 1837-1901 -- Fiction 9. London (England) -- History -- 19th century -- Fiction 10. London (England) -- History -- 19th century

   ISBN 1452110700; 9781452110707

                 LC 2012036578

This is the first book in Colleen Gleason's Stoker and Holmes series. The "narrative switches between two young women living in 1889 London: observant and cerebral Alvermina Holmes (she goes by Mina . . .), the niece of Sherlock Holmes; and Evaline Stoker, the headstrong (and physically strong) younger sister to Bram, and member of a proud line of vampire hunters." They "investigate the connection between the disappearance of a young woman and several recent murders." (Publishers Weekly)

Glewwe, Eleanor

Sparkers. Eleanor Glewwe. Viking, published by the Penguin Group 2014 336 p.

Grades: 5 6 7 8 9

   1. Diseases -- Fiction 2. Fantasy 3. Magic -- Fiction 4. Social classes -- Fiction 5. Fantasy fiction

   0451468767; 9780451468765, $16.99

                 LC 2013038475

In this book, by Eleanor Glewwe, "Marah Levi is ha-lani—one of the lower class, unable to do magic like members of the elite class, the kasiri. . . . When she impulsively saves a young kasir girl, Sarah, from being hurt in a crowd, the girl invites her home, where she finds a kindred spirit in Sarah's brother Azariah. . . . Together they find the cure for a disease. . . . Their work uncovers a sinister plot, however, putting them in grave danger." (Bulletin of the Center for Children's books)

"An unusual protagonist and a South Asian inspired setting make this a promising fantasy debut." Horn Book

Wildings. Eleanor Glewwe. Viking Childrens Books 2016 336 p.

Grades: 5 6 7 8 9

1. Brothers and sisters -- Fiction 2. Fantasy 3. Magic -- Fiction 4. Twins -- Fiction 5. Fantasy fiction
9780698151253, $50.97; 9780451468857, $16.99

LC 2016014413

In this young adult fantasy novel, by Eleanor Glewwe, "Rivka is one of the magical elite and the daughter of an important ambassador. But she harbors a deep secret: She once had a twin brother, Arik. When Arik failed to develop his own magical abilities, the government declared him a wilding, removed him from his home, placed him with non-magical adoptive parents, and forbade him any contact with his birth family. . . . But Rivka refuses to forget her twin brother." (Publisher's note)

"Rivka and her friends are strong-willed, fiercely intelligent, and fearless as they set out to take down the status quo." Pub Wkly

Goeglein, T. M.

Cold fury; T.M. Goeglein. G.P. Putnam's Sons 2012 312 p. (hardcover) $17.99

Grades: 8 9 10 11 12

1. Mafia -- Fiction 2. Chicago (Ill.) -- Fiction 3. Missing persons -- Fiction 4. Violence -- Fiction 5. Secret societies -- Fiction 6. Mystery and detective stories
ISBN 0399257209; 9780399257209

LC 2011025824

This book by T. M. Goeglein follows "Sara Jane Rispoli . . . a normal sixteen-year-old coping with school and a budding romance--until her parents and brother are kidnapped and she discovers her family is deeply embedded in the Chicago Outfit (aka the mob). Now on the run from a masked assassin, rogue cops and her turncoat uncle, Sara Jane is chased and attacked at every turn, fighting back with cold fury as she searches for her family." (Publisher's note)

Goelman, Ari

The **path** of names; by Ari Goelman. Arthur A. Levine Books 2013 352 p. (hard cover: alk. paper) $16.99

Grades: 7 8 9 10

1. Ghost stories 2. Mystery fiction 3. Camps -- Fiction 4. Magic -- Fiction 5. Cabala -- Fiction 6. Labyrinths -- Fiction 7. Magic tricks -- Fiction 8. Camps 9. Brothers and sisters -- Fiction 10. Jews -- United States -- Fiction
ISBN 0545474302; 9780545474306; 9780545474313; 9780545540148

LC 2012030554

This book features Dahlia whom "her parents have sent . . . to Camp Arava. . . . When Dahlia first sees two young girls disappear through the cabin wall, she's convinced it's a great magic trick, but soon she realizes that they're actually ghosts. . . . These strange phenomena begin to converge around a

mysterious garden maze on the campgrounds, a maze that is rumored to be connected to the disappearance of children and that is ferociously guarded by the skulking camp caretaker." (Bulletin of the Center for Children's Books)

"Thirteen-year-old magic nerd Dahlia loathes her Jewish summer camp until she starts dreaming about a Jewish teen in 1940s New York City who seems to be connected to a pair of ghosts haunting the camp. Readers with an interest in Jewish mysticism will enjoy the book's paranormal elements and tweens will appreciate the realistic relationships among the campers." (Horn Book)

Going, K. L.

★ **Fat** kid rules the world. Putnam 2003 187p $17.99; pa $6.99

Grades: 7 8 9 10

1. Obesity -- Fiction 2. Musicians -- Fiction 3. Friendship -- Fiction
ISBN 0-399-23990-1; 0-14-240208-7 pa

LC 2002-67956

Michael L. Printz Award honor book, 2004

Seventeen-year-old Troy, depressed, suicidal, and weighing nearly 300 pounds, gets a new perspective on life when a homeless teenager who is a genius on guitar wants Troy to be the drummer in his rock band

"Going has put together an amazing assortment of characters. . . . This is an impressive debut that offers hope for all kids." Booklist

★ **King** of the screwups. Houghton Mifflin Harcourt 2009 310p $17

Grades: 9 10 11 12

1. Uncles -- Fiction 2. LBGT people -- Fiction 3. Father-son relationship -- Fiction
ISBN 978-0-15-206258-3; 0-15-206258-0

LC 2008-25113

After getting in trouble yet again, popular high school senior Liam, who never seems to live up to his wealthy father's expectations, is sent to live in a trailer park with his gay "glam-rocker" uncle.

"Readers—screwups or not—will empathize as Liam, utterly likable despite his faults, learns to be himself." Publ Wkly

Golden, Christopher

The **sea** wolves; by Christopher Golden & Tim Lebbon; with illustrations by Greg Ruth. Harper 2012 384 p. $16.99

Grades: 7 8 9 10

1. Sea stories 2. Adventure fiction 3. Monsters --Fiction 4. Pirates -- Fiction 5. Supernatural -- Fiction 6. Adventure and adventurers -- Fiction
ISBN 0061863203; 9780061863202; 9780061863219

LC 2011010031

This young adult fantasy adventure novel by Christopher Golden and Tim Lebbon follows "Jack London . . . a writer who lived his own real-life adventures. But . . . even he couldn't set down [all his adventures] in writing. Terrifying, mysterious, bizarre, and magical. . . . Clinging to life after he is captured in an attack by savage pirates, Jack is unprepared for what he faces at the hands of the crew and their charismatic, murderous captain, Ghost. For these mariners are not mortal men but hungry beasts chasing gold and death across the North Pacific. Jack's only hope lies with Sabine—a sad, sultry captive of Ghost's insatiable hunger. But on these waters, nothing is as it seems, and Sabine may be hiding dangerous secrets of her own." (Publisher's note)

The **wild**; by Christopher Golden & Tim Lebbon; with illustrations by Greg Ruth. Harper 2011 348p il (The secret journeys of Jack London) $15.99; lib bdg $16.89

Grades: 7 8 9 10

1. Authors 2. Novelists 3. Adventure fiction 4. Wolves -- Fiction 5. Short story writers 6. Supernatural -- Fiction 7. Wilderness survival -- Fiction 8. Gold mines and mining -- Fiction 9. Yukon River valley (Yukon and Alaska) -- Fiction

ISBN 978-0-06-186317-2; 0-06-186317-3; 978-0-06-186318-9 lib bdg; 0-06-186318-1 lib bdg

LC 2010-07475

Seventeen-year-old Jack London makes the arduous journey to the Yukon's gold fields in 1893, becoming increasingly uneasy about supernatural forces in the wilderness that seem to have taken a special interest in him.

"Golden and Lebbon write with a gritty assurance that brings the fantasy elements . . . down to earth. . . . Occasional sketches add a bit of cinematic drama." Booklist

Gonzalez, Julie

Imaginary enemy. Delacorte Press 2008 241p $15.99; lib bdg $18.99

Grades: 6 7 8 9 10

1. Imaginary playmates -- Fiction

ISBN 978-0-385-73552-0; 0-385-73552-9; 978-0-385-90530-5 lib bdg; 0-385-90530-0 lib bdg

LC 2007-45752

Although her impetuous behavior, smart-mouthed comments, and slacker ways have landed her in trouble over the years, sixteen-year-old Jane has always put the blame on her "imaginary enemy," until a new development forces her to decide whether or not to assume responsibility for her actions.

"Gonzalez has written a witty, realistic novel . . . peppered with funny, authentic dialogue." Booklist

Goo, Maurene

I believe in a thing called love. Maurene Goo. Farrar, Straus & Giroux 2017 325 p.

Grades: 7 8 9 10 11 12

1. Dating (Social customs) -- Fiction; 2. High schools -- Fiction; 3. Korean Americans -- Fiction; 4. Love -- Fiction; 5. Schools -- Fiction

9780374304041, $17.99

LC 2016035865

In this book, by Maurene Goo, "Desi Lee knows how carburetors work. She learned CPR at the age of five. As a high school senior, she has never missed a day of school and never had a B. But in her charmed school life, there's one thing missing?she's never had a boyfriend. In fact, she's a known disaster in romance, a clumsy, stammering humiliation magnet. When the hottest human specimen to have ever lived walks into her life one day, Desi decides it's time to tackle her flirting failures." (Publisher's note)

"Plot-driven as the K dramas Goo's protagonist seeks to emulate, her funny, engaging narrative also delivers powerful messages of inclusion and acceptance." Kirkus

The **way** you make me feel. Maurene Goo. Farrar, Straus & Giroux 2018 336 p.

Grades: 8 9 10 11 12

1. Romance fiction; 2. Dating (Social customs) -- Fiction

9780374304089, $17.99; 9780374304096

LC 2017956980

In this novel, by Maurene Goo, "Clara Shin lives for pranks and disruption. When she takes one joke too far, her dad sentences her to a summer working on his food truck, the KoBra, alongside her uptight classmate Rose Carver. Not the carefree summer Clara had imagined. But maybe Rose isn't so bad. Maybe the boy named Hamlet (yes, Hamlet) crushing on her is pretty cute." (Publisher's note)

Goobie, Beth

Before wings; a novel. Orca Bk. Pubs. 2001 203p hardcover o.p. pa $8.95

Grades: 7 8 9 10

1. Camps -- Fiction 2. Death -- Fiction

ISBN 1-55143-161-0; 1-55143-163-7 pa

LC 00-105582

"Fifteen-year-old Adrien barely survived a brain aneurysm two years earlier, and is haunted by the fact that she could die from another one at any time. In fact, issues of life and death completely fill her world at Camp Lakeshore, owned and operated by her Aunt Erin, a woman with a haunted past of her own. Adrien bonds with Paul, a teen who is convinced that he has dreamt of his own death and that it will happen on his next birthday. She also seems to be experiencing events in the lives of five girls, a group of campers who died long ago in a tragic accident." SLJ

"Full of magic realism and beautifully written, this is a story of good triumphing over evil, life triumphing over death, the power of love, friendship, and the hope for an afterlife." Booklist

Goodman, Alison

The **Dark** Days Club. Alison Goodman. Viking 2016 496 p.

Grades: 8 9 10 11 12

1. Conspiracies -- Fiction 2. Courts and courtiers -- Fiction 3. Secrets -- Fiction 4. Supernatural -- Fiction 5. Charlotte, Queen, consort of George III, King of Great Britain, 1744-1818 -- Fiction 6. Great Britain -- History -- 1800-1837 -- Fiction 7. London (England) -- History -- 19th century -- Fiction 8. London (England) -- Fiction 9. Great Britain -- History -- 1714-1837 -- Fiction

9780670785476, $18.99

LC 2015006792

In this book, by Alison Goodman, "Lady Helen Wrexhall is on the eve of her debut presentation at the royal court of George III. Her life should revolve around gowns, dancing, and securing a suitable marriage. Instead, when one of her family's maids disappears, she is drawn into the shadows of Regency London. There, she meets Lord Carlston, one of the few able to stop the perpetrators: a cabal of demons that has infiltrated all levels of society." (Publisher's note)

"Readers willing to embrace the deep, deliberately paced journey will find the pace and tension increasing until the end leaves them eager for the next volume." Kirkus

★ **Eon**: Dragoneye reborn. Viking 2009 531p $19.99

Grades: 7 8 9 10

    1. Fantasy fiction 2. Magic -- Fiction 3. Dragons -- Fiction 4. Sex role -- Fiction 5. Apprentices -- Fiction
ISBN 978-0-670-06227-0; 0-670-06227-8
                    LC 2008-33223

Sixteen-year-old Eon hopes to become an apprentice to one of the twelve energy dragons of good fortune and learn to be its main interpreter, but to do so will require much, including keeping secret that she is a girl.

"Entangled politics and fierce battle scenes provide a pulse-quickening pace, while the intriguing characters add interest and depth." Booklist

Followed by: Eona: The last Dragoneye (2011)

Eona: the last Dragoneye. Viking 2011 637p il $19.99

Grades: 7 8 9 10

    1. Fantasy fiction 2. Magic -- Fiction 3. Dragons -- Fiction 4. Apprentices -- Fiction
ISBN 978-0-670-06311-6; 0-670-06311-8
                    LC 2011-02997

Sequel to: Eon: Dragoneye reborn (2009)

Eon has been revealed as Eona, the first female Dragoneye in hundreds of years. Along with fellow rebels Ryko and Lady Dela, she is on the run from High Lord Sethon's army. The renegades are on a quest for the black folio, stolen by the drug-riddled Dillon; they must also find Kygo, the young Pearl Emperor, who needs Eona's power and the black folio if he is to wrest back his throne from the self-styled "Emperor" Sethon.

"One of those rare and welcome fantasies that complicate black-and-white morality." Kirkus

Singing the Dogstar blues. Viking 2003 261p $16.99

Grades: 7 8 9 10

    1. Time travel 2. Science fiction
ISBN 0-670-03610-2
                    LC 2002-12161

First published 1998 in Australia

In a future Australia, the saucy eighteen-year-old daughter of a famous newscaster and a sperm donor teams up with a hermaphrodite from the planet Choria in a time travel adventure that may significantly change both of their lives

"This wildly entertaining novel successfully mixes adventure, humor, mystery, and sf into a fast-paced, thrilling story that will apeal to a wide audience." Booklist

Goodman, Shawn

Kindness for weakness; Shawn Goodman. 1st ed. Delacorte Press 2013 272 p. (ebook) $50.97; (library) $19.99; (hardcover) $16.99

Grades: 9 10 11 12

    1. Gangs -- Fiction 2. Juvenile delinquency -- Fiction 3. Brothers -- Fiction 4. Self-esteem -- Fiction 5. Drug

dealers -- Fiction
ISBN 0375991026; 9780307982070; 9780375991028; 9780385743242
                    LC 2012015772

In this book, Shawn Goodman "introduces 15-year-old James, who is caught running drugs for his older brother and sentenced to a year in juvie. Despite a rough initiation to the program, James—inspired by books recommended to him by his English teacher—does his best to stay out of trouble; however, his emotional and physical strength are tested time and again by corrupt, belligerent guards and boys who pressure him into joining a gang." (Publishers Weekly)

Something like hope. Delacorte Press 2011 193p $16.99; lib bdg $19.99

Grades: 9 10 11 12

    1. African Americans -- Fiction 2. Juvenile delinquency -- Fiction
ISBN 978-0-385-73939-9; 978-0-385-90786-6 lib bdg
                    LC 2009-53657

"Smart, angry, and desperate, Shavonne, 17, is in juvenile detention again, and in her present-tense, first-person narrative, she describes the heartbreaking brutality that she suffered before she was locked up, as well as the harsh treatment, and sometimes the kindness, she encounters in juvie." (Booklist)

The author "delivers a gritty, frank tale that doesn't shrink from the harshness of the setting but that also provides a much-needed redemption for both Shavonne and readers." Kirkus

Gorman, Carol

Games. HarperCollinsPublishers 2007 279p $16.99; lib bdg $17.89

Grades: 6 7 8 9

    1. School stories 2. Games -- Fiction
ISBN 978-0-06-057027-9; 0-06-057027-X; 978-0-06-057028-6 lib bdg; 0-06-057028-8 lib bdg
                    LC 2006-31759

When fourteen-year-old rivals Boot Quinn and Mick Sullivan fight once too often, the new principal devises the punishment of having to play games together at his office, where they learn which battles are worth fighting.

"This novel is a great book for middle school students, well scripted, realistic, and entertaining. The characters are true and understandable." Voice Youth Advocates

Goslee, S. J.

★ **Whatever**: a novel. By S.J. Goslee. Roaring Brook Press 2016 266 p.

Grades: 9 10 11 12

    1. Coming out (Sexual orientation) -- Fiction 2. Dating (Social customs) -- Fiction 3. Friendship -- Fiction 4. Gays -- Fiction 5. High schools -- Fiction 6. Humorous stories 7. Schools -- Fiction 8. Humorous fiction
1626723990; 9781626723993, $17.99; 9781626724006, $60
                    LC 2015023376

In this young adult novel, by S. J. Goslee, winner of the 2017 Booklist Youth Editors' Choice award, presents "a hilariously honest view on sex and sexuality, and enough f-bombs to make your mom blush. . . . It's like the apocalypse came, only instead of nuclear bombs and zombies, Mike gets school participation, gay thoughts, and mother-effin' cheerleaders. Junior year is about to start." (Publisher's note)

"A humorous account of a teen's reluctant and awkward journey to acceptance of his emerging bisexuality." Kirkus

Goto, Hiromi

★ **Half** World; illustrations by Jillian Tamaki. Viking 2010 221p il $16.99

Grades: 7 8 9 10

1. Fantasy fiction 2. Mother-daughter relationship -- Fiction

ISBN 978-0-670-01220-6; 0-670-01220-3

"Raised in impoverished circumstances by her single mother, overweight 14-year-old Melanie is the target of ridicule at school and leads a lonely, introverted life. Then an evil being named Mr. Glueskin kidnaps her mother, forcing Melanie to travel to Half World, a colorless land that has been sundered from the realms of flesh and spirit, its deceased inhabitants cursed to relive the most traumatic moments of their lives. . . . Goto writes the hellish Half World as miserably surreal yet horrifyingly believable. . . . It's a fast-moving and provocative journey with cosmically high stakes, and one that should readily appeal to fans of dark, nightmarish fantasy." Publ Wkly

Grace, Amanda

In too deep; Amanda Grace. Flux 2012 228 p. $9.95

Grades: 7 8 9 10 11 12

1. Rape -- Fiction 2. Honesty -- Fiction 3. False accusation -- Fiction 4. High school students -- Fiction 5. Teenagers -- Conduct of life -- Fiction 6. Rumor -- Fiction 7. Schools -- Fiction 8. High schools -- Fiction 9. Conduct of life -- Fiction

ISBN 0738726001; 9780738726007

LC 2011028806

In this young adult novel, a "girl gets caught in a lie she didn't tell but doesn't have the courage to correct. . . . Samantha wants to spark some romantic interest from her best friend and secret heartthrob Nick, so she makes a play for popularity-magnet Carter. He rebuffs her, but someone sees her leaving his bedroom in tears and jumps to the false conclusion that Carter assaulted her. Sam doesn't hear about the resulting rumors until she returns to school. Soon she feels too overwhelmed by social pressure to deny them. Sam finds many opportunities to confess the truth, but she can't bring herself to exonerate Carter. . . . Complicating matters, Sam knows that because of the deception, she's likely to lose Nick, who finally has declared his love for her." (Kirkus)

Graff, Lisa

★ **Lost** in the sun; Lisa Graff. Philomel Books. 2015 289p $16.99

Grades: 4 5 6 7 8 9

1. Brothers -- Fiction 2. Friendship -- Fiction 3. Guilt—Fiction 4. Remarriage -- Fiction 5. Tricks -- Fiction

ISBN: 0399164065; 9780399164064

LC 2014027868

"Trent Zimmerman is consumed by rage. The universe has been manifestly unfair to him and he doesn't know how to handle it. Seven months ago, he struck a hockey puck at a bad angle, sending it like a missile into the chest of a boy with a previously undiagnosed heart ailment. That boy died and Trent feels responsible...Weighty matters deftly handled with humor and grace will give this book wide appeal." SLJ

Gramont, Nina de

Every little thing in the world. Atheneum Books for Young Readers 2010 282p $16.99

Grades: 9 10 11 12

1. Camps -- Fiction 2. Pregnancy -- Fiction 3. Friendship -- Fiction 4. Wilderness areas -- Fiction

ISBN 978-1-4169-8013-1; 1-4169-8013-X

LC 2009-40335

Before she can decide what do about her newly discovered pregnancy, sixteen-year-old Sydney is punished for "borrowing" a car and shipped out, along with best friend Natalia, to a wilderness camp for the next six weeks.

"De Gramont's compelling coming-of-age story, often poetic, compassionately probes the dilemma of and complex choices surrounding Sydney's pregnancy. As told from Sydney's point of view in an authentic adolescent voice, her growing self-awareness of 'what's discovered after losing your way' is both moving and hopeful." Kirkus

Grant, Christopher

Teenie. Alfred A. Knopf 2010 264p $16.99; lib bdg $19.99; ebook $10.99

Grades: 9 10 11 12

1. School stories 2. Family life -- Fiction 3. African Americans -- Fiction 4. Dating (Social customs) -- Fiction 5. Brooklyn (New York, N.Y.) -- Fiction

ISBN 978-0-375-86191-8; 978-0-375-96191-5 lib bdg; 978-0-375-89779-5 ebook

LC 2010-35377

High school freshman Martine, longing to escape Brooklyn and her strict parents, is trying to get into a study-abroad program but when her long-time crush begins to pay attention to her and her best friend starts an online relationship, Teenie's mind is on anything but her grades.

"Realistic descriptions of teenage life and appealing characters make for an enjoyable reading experience." SLJ

Grant, K. M.

Blood red horse. Walker & Co. 2005 277p $16.95; pa $8.99

Grades: 6 7 8 9

1. Horses -- Fiction 2. Crusades -- Fiction 3. Middle Ages -- Fiction

ISBN 0-8027-8960-9; 0-8027-7734-8 pa

LC 2005-42280

First published 2004 in the United Kingdom

A special horse named Hosanna changes the lives of two English brothers and those around them as they fight with King Richard I against Saladin's armies during the Third Crusades.

This "story . . . transcends boundaries of gender and genre, with something to offer fans of equestrian fare, historical fiction, and battlefield drama alike." Booklist

Other titles in this series are:

Green jasper (2006)

Blaze of silver (2007)

Blue flame; book one of the Perfect Fire trilogy. Walker & Co. 2008 246p (Perfect fire trilogy) $16.99

Grades: 7 8 9 10

1. Middle Ages -- Fiction 2. Knights and knighthood -- Fiction 3. France -- History -- 0-1328 -- Fiction

ISBN 978-0-8027-9694-3; 0-8027-9694-X

LC 2007-51384

In 1242 in the restive Languedoc region of France, Parsifal, having been charged as a child to guard an important religious relic, has lived in hiding for much of his life until he befriends a young couple on opposite sides of the escalating conflict between the Catholics and the Cathars.

"Characters are as complex as the moral issues they face, and Grant's nuanced, thought-provoking look at the religious conflicts they face will resonate today." Booklist

Other books in this series are Paradise red (2010)

White heat (2009)

★ **How** the hangman lost his heart. Walker & Co. 2007 244p $16.95

Grades: 7 8 9 10

1. Adventure fiction

ISBN 978-0-8027-9672-1; 0-8027-9672-9

LC 2006-53182

When her Uncle Frank is executed for treason against England's King George in 1746, and his severed head is mounted on a pike for public viewing, daring Alice tries to reclaim the head for a proper burial, finding an unlikely ally in the softhearted executioner, while incurring the wrath of the royal guard.

"The story is filled with action and interesting characters. . . . This is a rousing read." SLJ

Other titles in the series are:

White heat (2009)

Paradise red (2010)

Grant, Michael, 1954-

Eve & Adam; by Michael Grant and Katherine Applegate. Feiwel and Friends 2012 291p. $17.99

Grades: 7 8 9 10

1. Medical genetics 2. Biomedical engineering 3. Mother-daughter relationship -- Fiction

ISBN 0312583516; 9780312583514

In this book by authors Michael Grant and Katherine Applegate, "a run-in with a streetcar left Evening Spiker's body seriously mangled . . . [H]er widowed mother, Terra, insists on moving her from the hospital to . . . [the] biotech company . . . Spiker Biopharmaceuticals. . . . Eve's healing is strangely swift [and] Terra drops a project . . . in her lap: Design a virtual human being from scratch. With help from her feisty, reckless friend Aislin, Eve takes up the challenge." (Kirkus Reviews)

Front Lines. Michael Grant; [edited by] Katherine Tegen. Harpercollins Childrens Books 2016 576 p.

Grades: 9 10 11 12

1. Alternative histories 2. Women soldiers -- Fiction

9780062342157, $18.99; 0062342150

LC 2015939082

This young adult novel, by Michael Grant, edited by Katherine Tegen, "reimagines World War II with girl sol-diers fighting on the front lines. . . . [In] 1942, . . . three girls sign up to fight. . . . Each has her own reasons for volunteering: Rio fights to honor her sister; Frangie needs money for her family; Rainy wants to kill Germans. For the first time they leave behind their homes and families-to go to war." (Publisher's note)

"Bestselling science-fiction author Grant did his research (an extensive bibliography is provided), but the odd and likely unintended consequence of his premise is the erasure of thousands of military women who historically served and fought and died. Still, an engrossing portrayal of ordinary women in extraordinary circumstances." Kirkus

★ **Gone**. HarperTeen 2008 576p $17.99; lib bdg $18.89; pa $9.99

Grades: 7 8 9 10

1. Supernatural -- Fiction 2. Good and evil -- Fiction

ISBN 978-0-06-144876-8; 978-0-06-144877-5 lib bdg; 978-0-06-144878-2 pa

LC 2007-36734

In a small town on the coast of California, everyone over the age of fourteen suddenly disappears, setting up a battle between the remaining town residents and the students from a local private school, as well as those who have "The Power" and are able to perform supernatural feats and those who do not.

"A tour de force that will leave readers dazed, disturbed, and utterly breathless." Booklist

Other titles in this series are:

Hunger (2009)

Lies (2010)

Plague (2011)

Fear (2012)

Messenger of Fear. Michael Grant. Katherine Tegen Books 2014 272 p.

Grades: 9 10 11 12

1. Apprentices -- Fiction 2. Fear -- Fiction 3. Games -- Fiction 4. Good and evil -- Fiction 5. Justice -- Fiction 6. Supernatural -- Fiction

0062207407; 9780062207401, $17.99

LC 2014013832

In this novel by Michael Grant "Mara Todd . . . can't remember who she is or anything about her past. Is it because of the boy that appears? He calls himself the Messenger of Fear. If the world does not bring justice to those who do evil, the Messenger will. He offers the wicked a game. If they win, they go free. If they lose, they will live their greatest fear. Why was Mara chosen to be the Messenger's apprentice?" (Publisher's note)

"Grant explores bullying, family problems, suicide, and more, and several painful passages will have readers cringing, even as they make them think about what they would do in the same situation. This is a solid beginning to a series that is likely to be quite popular with horror and paranormal fans." Booklist

Other titles in the series are: The Tattooed Heart (2015)

Monster. Michael Grant. Katherine Tegen Books 2017 420 p. (Gone)

Grades: 7 8 9 10

1. Extraterrestrial beings -- Fiction; 2. Survival --

Fiction; 3. Virus diseases -- Fiction; 4. Science fiction; 5. Extraterrestrial beings -- Fiction

9780062467867; 0062467840; 9780062467843, $18.99

LC 2017932879

In this book, by Michael Grant, "it's been four years since a meteor hit Perdido Beach and everyone disappeared. Everyone, except the kids trapped in the FAYZ -- an invisible dome that was created by an alien virus. Inside the FAYZ, animals began to mutate and teens developed dangerous powers. The terrifying new world was plagued with hunger, lies, and fear of the unknown." (Publisher's note)

"A bombastic, engaging start to a sequel series full of potential." Kirkus

Another title in this series is: Villain (2018)

★ **Silver** stars. Michael Grant; [edited by] Katherine Tegen. Katherine Tegen Books 2017 576 p. Illustration (A front lines novel)

Grades: 10 11 12

1. Women in combat -- Fiction 2. World War, 1939-1945 -- Campaigns -- Italy -- Sicily -- Fiction 3. World War, 1939-1945 -- Women -- Fiction

9780062342188, $18.99; 9780062342201, $17.99

LC 2016938948

In this book in the Front Lines series, by Michael Grant, edited by Katherine Tegen, it is summer of 1943. Frangie, Rainy, Rio and the rest of the American army are moving on to their next target: the Italian island of Sicily. The women won't conquer Italy alone. They are not heroes for fighting alongside their brothers-they are soldiers. But Frangie, Rainy, Rio, and the millions of brave females fighting for their country have become a symbol in the fight for equality. (Publisher's note)

"This series continues to be a fascinating, stunningly written examination of both war and women's role in it, and this installment only adds to its already considerable depth." Booklist

Includes bibliographical references (pages 546-548).

Gratton, Tessa

The **blood** keeper; Tessa Gratton. Random House Books for Young Readers 2012 432 p. (hardback) $17.99

Grades: 9 10 11 12

1. Love stories 2. Magic -- Fiction 3. Supernatural -- Fiction

ISBN 0375867341; 9780375867347; 9780375897696; 9780375967344

LC 2011049532

This book follows "Mab Prowd, [for whom] the practice of blood magic is as natural as breathing. . . . Growing up on an isolated farm in Kansas with other practitioners may have kept her from making friends her own age, but it has also given her a sense of purpose -- she's connected to the land and protective of the magic. . . . But one morning . . . she encounters Will, a local boy who is trying to exorcise some mundane personal demons." (Publisher's note)

"A perfect book for those who loved Wuthering Heights and are looking for an essentially American gothic." Kirkus

Gratz, Alan

★ **Samurai** shortstop. Dial Books 2006 280p hardcover o.p. pa $7.99

Grades: 7 8 9 10

1. School stories 2. Baseball -- Fiction 3. Tokyo (Japan) -- Fiction 4. Father-son relationship -- Fiction

ISBN 0-8037-3075-6; 978-0-8037-3075-5; 0-14-241099-3 pa; 978-0-14-24099-8 pa

LC 2005-22081

While obtaining a Western education at a prestigious Japanese boarding school in 1890, sixteen-year-old Toyo also receives traditional samurai training which has profound effects on both his baseball game and his relationship with his father. This book features some scenes of graphic violence.

"This is an intense read about a fascinating time and place in world history." Publ Wkly

Graudin, Ryan

★ **Blood** for blood. By Ryan Graudin. Little, Brown & Co. 2016 481 p.

Grades: 9 10 11 12

1. Fantasy 2. Resistance to government -- Fiction 3. Jews -- Fiction 4. Nazis -- Fiction 5. Hitler, Adolf, 1889-1945 -- Fiction 6. Fantasy fiction 7. National socialism -- Fiction

0316405159; 9780316405157, $17.99; 9780316405133, $54

LC 2015043452

This book, by Ryan Graudin, "death camp survivor Yael, who has the power to skinshift, is on the run: the world has just seen her shoot and kill Hitler. But the truth of what happened is far more complicated, and its consequences are deadly. Yael and her unlikely comrades dive into enemy territory to try to turn the tide against the New Order, and there is no alternative but to see their mission through to the end, whatever the cost." (Publisher's note)

"Highly recommended for fans of historical fiction, alternate history, or works of espionage and intrigue." SLJ

Sequel to: Wolf by wolf

Invictus. By Ryan Graudin. Little, Brown & Co. 2017 458 p.

Grades: 9 10 11 12

1. Black market -- Fiction; 2. Gladiators -- Fiction; 3. Thieves -- Fiction; 4. Time travel -- Fiction; 5. Science fiction

9780316503075, $18.99; 9780316503235

LC 2017000174

In this book, by Ryan Graudin, "Farway Gaius McCarthy was born outside of time. The son of a time traveler from 2354 AD and a gladiator living in ancient Rome, Far's very existence defies the laws of nature. All he's ever wanted was to explore history for himself, but after failing his entrance exam into the government program, Far will have to settle for a position on the black market-captaining a time-traveling crew to steal valuables from the past." (Publisher's note)

"A madcap, vivid time-travel tale with a strong ensemble, both indebted and cheekily alluding to Doctor Who and Firefly." Kirkus

The **walled** city. By Ryan Graudin. Little, Brown & Co. 2014 448 p. Illustration

Grades: 9 10 11 12

1. Gangs -- Fiction 2. Sisters -- Fiction 3. Street children -- Fiction 4. Survival -- Fiction 5. Hong Kong (China) -- History -- 20th century -- Fiction 6. Hong Kong (China) -- Fiction 7. Street life -- Fiction
0316405051; 9780316405058, $18

LC 2013044748

In this book, by Ryan Graudin, "Dai, trying to escape a haunting past, traffics drugs for the most ruthless kingpin in the Walled City. . . . Jin hides under the radar, afraid the wild street gangs will discover her biggest secret: Jin passes as a boy to stay safe. Still, every chance she gets, she searches for her lost sister.... Mei Yee has been trapped in a brothel for the past two years, dreaming of getting out while watching the girls who try fail one by one." (Publisher's note)

"Vivid descriptions add color and infuse the story with realism. While there are mature situations dealing with drugs, violence, and rape, they are skillfully relayed without being graphic. This complex, well-written novel is full of tension, twists, and turns, and teens will not be able to put it down." SLJ

Wolf by wolf. By Ryan Graudin. Little, Brown & Co. 2015 400 p.

Grades: 9 10 11 12

1. Resistance to government -- Fiction 2. Motorcycle racing -- Fiction
9780316405126, $18

LC 2014044026

In this book, by Ryan Graudin, "the Axis powers of the Third Reich and Imperial Japan rule. To commemorate their Great Victory, they host the Axis Tour: an annual motorcycle race across their conjoined continents. The prize? An audience with the highly reclusive Adolf Hitler at the Victor's ball in Tokyo. Yael, a former death camp prisoner, has witnessed too much suffering. . . . The resistance has given Yael one goal: Win the race and kill Hitler." (Publisher's note)

"Yael is a compelling protagonist, both strong and flawed, and, even imbued as it is with sci-fi elements, seeing both WWII and the concentration camp experience through her eyes is a terrifying adventure." Booklist

Gray, Claudia
Defy the stars. Claudia Gray. Little, Brown & Co. 2017 503 p.

Grades: 7 8 9 10 11 12

1. Interstellar travel -- Fiction; 2. Orphans -- Fiction; 3. Robots -- Fiction; 4. Science fiction; 5. Soldiers -- Fiction
9780316394062; 9780316394031, $17.99

LC 2016028390

In this novel in the Defy the Stars series, by Claudia Gray, "Noemi and Abel are enemies in an interstellar war, forced by chance to work together as they embark on a daring journey through the stars. Their efforts would end the fighting for good, but they're not without sacrifice. The stakes are even higher than either of them first realized, and the more time they spend together, the more they're forced to question everything they'd been taught was true." (Publisher's note)

"Nuanced philosophical discussions of religion, terrorism, and morality advise and direct the high-stakes action, informing the beautiful, realistic ending. Intelligent and thoughtful, a highly relevant far-off speculative adventure." Kirkus

Another title in this series is: Defy the worlds (2018)

Defy the worlds. Claudia Gray. Little, Brown & Co. 2018 467 p. (Defy the stars)

Grades: 7 8 9 10 11 12

1. Immortality -- Fiction; 2. Interstellar travel -- Fiction; 3. Orphans -- Fiction; 4. Plague -- Fiction; 5. Robots -- Fiction; 6. Science fiction; 7. Soldiers -- Fiction; 8. Interplanetary voyages -- Fiction
9780316394086; 9780316394109, $17.99

LC 2017034001

In this book in the Defy the Stars series, by Claudia Gray, "an outcast from her home -- shunned after a trip through the galaxy with Abel, the most advanced cybernetic man ever created, Noemi Vidal dreams of traveling through the stars one more time. And when a deadly plague arrives on Genesis, Noemi gets her chance. As the only soldier to have ever left the planet, it will be up to her to save its people...if only she wasn't flying straight into a trap." (Publisher's note)

"Romantic and adventurous, this novel contains a plethora of STEM-related content and is a worthy discussion starter for conversations about the ethics of technology." Booklist

Sequel to: Defy the Stars (2017)

Evernight. HarperTeen 2008 327p (Evernight) $16.99; lib bdg $17.89; pa $8.99

Grades: 8 9 10 11 12

1. Horror fiction 2. School stories 3. Vampires -- Fiction
ISBN 978-0-06-128439-7; 0-06-128439-4; 978-0-06-128443-4 lib bdg; 0-06-128443-2 lib bdg; 978-0-06-128444-1 pa; 0-06-128444-0 pa

LC 2007-36733

Bianca has been "uprooted from her small hometown and enrolled at Evernight Academy, an eerie Gothic boarding school where the students are somehow too perfect. . . . Bianca knows she doesn't fit in. Then she meets Lucas. . . . Lucas ignores the rules, stands up to the snobs, and warns Bianca to be careful—even when it comes to caring about him. . . . But the connection between Bianca and Lucas can't be denied. Bianca will risk anything to be with Lucas, but dark secrets are fated to tear them apart." (Publisher's note) "Grades eight to ten." (Bull Cent Child Books)

"Gray's writing hooks readers from the first page and reels them in with surprising plot twists and turns. . . . A must-have for fans of vampire stories." SLJ

Spellcaster; Claudia Gray. HarperTeen 2013 400 p. (hardback) $17.99

Grades: 8 9 10 11 12

1. Occult fiction 2. Witches -- Fiction 3. Love stories 4. Horror stories 5. Magic -- Fiction 6. Schools -- Fiction 7. High schools -- Fiction 8. Rhode Island -- Fiction 9. Blessing and cursing -- Fiction 10. Family life -- Rhode Island -- Fiction
ISBN 0061961205; 9780061961205

LC 2012025331

This young adult paranormal romance story, by Claudia Gray, follows a teenage girl with magical powers. "Descended from witches, Nadia can sense that a spell has been cast over the tiny Rhode Island town--a sickness infecting everyone and everything in it. The magic at work is darker and more powerful than anything she's come across and has sunk its claws most deeply into Mateo . . . her rescuer, her friend, and the guy she yearns to get closer to even as he pushes her away." (Publisher's note)

Steadfast; a Spellcaster novel. Claudia Gray. HarperTeen 2014 352 p. (hardcover bdg.) $17.99
Grades: 8 9 10 11 12

1. Imaginary places 2. Magic -- Fiction 3. Horror stories 4. Schools -- Fiction 5. Witches -- Fiction 6. High schools -- Fiction 7. Rhode Island -- Fiction 8. Blessing and cursing -- Fiction 9. Family life -- Rhode Island -- Fiction
ISBN 0061961221; 9780061961229

LC 2013015445

Sequel to: Spellcaster

"The first barrier between our world and the evil entity known as The One Beneath has been breached and redemption is impossible—unless untrained teen witch Nadia, along with her steadfast Mateo and friend Verlaine, can resist a seemingly invincible sorceress' power and a demon's meddling, all while remaining true to their friendship and ideals...Gray uses unique and lyrical free-verse spells, spoken by both Nadia and the dark sorceress Elizabeth, as inroads to sets of memories—a clever tactic that helps readers understand motivation while providing backstories that make it easy to bond with Nadia and her friends. The ending will provide terrific fodder for book discussions, so make sure you have enough copies to go around." (Booklist)

A **thousand** pieces of you. Claudia Gray. HarperTeen, an imprint of HarperCollinsPublishers 2014 368 p.
Grades: 8 9 10 11

1. Adventure and adventurers -- Fiction 2. Family life -- Fiction 3. Murder -- Fiction 4. Science fiction 5. Space and time -- Fiction 6. Adventure fiction
0062278967; 9780062278968, $17.99

LC 2014001894

This book, by Claudia Gray, is "about a girl who must chase her father's killer through multiple dimensions. Marguerite Caine's physicist parents are known for their groundbreaking achievements. Their most astonishing invention, called the Firebird, allows users to jump into multiple universes. . . . But then Marguerite's father is murdered, and the killer—her parent's handsome, enigmatic assistant Paul—escapes into another dimension before the law can touch him." (Publisher's note)

"Readers will appreciate Marguerite's determination to help her parents, even though she is a misfit, the lone artist in a family of scientific geniuses. The secondary players are equally well rounded, and their various incarnations in each dimension make for intriguing character explorations. In resourceful Marguerite's first-person narration, the story moves quickly, and the science is explained enough to make the plot clear, but not so much as to bog things down." Booklist

Gray, Keith

★ **Ostrich** boys. Random House 2010 297p $17.99; lib bdg $20.99
Grades: 8 9 10 11 12

1. Death -- Fiction 2. Scotland -- Fiction 3. Friendship -- Fiction 4. Great Britain -- Fiction
ISBN 978-0-375-85843-7; 0-375-85843-1; 978-0-375-95843-4 lib bdg; 0-375-95843-6 lib bdg

LC 2008-21729

After their best friend Ross dies, English teenagers Blake, Kenny, and Sim plan a proper memorial by taking his ashes to Ross, Scotland, an adventure-filled journey that tests their loyalty to each other and forces them to question what friendship means.

"Gray's writing is cheeky, crisp, and realistic. He has created funny, bright characters whom readers cannot help but root for." SLJ

Green, John

★ An **abundance** of Katherines. Dutton Books 2006 227p $16.99
Grades: 9 10 11 12

1. Mathematics -- Fiction
ISBN 0-525-47688-1; 978-0-525-47688-7

LC 2006-4191

Michael L. Printz Award honor book, 2007

Having been recently dumped for the nineteenth time by a girl named Katherine, recent high school graduate and former child prodigy Colin sets off on a road trip with his best friend to try to find some new direction in life while also trying to create a mathematical formula to explain his relationships.

This "is an enjoyable, thoughtful novel that will attract readers interested in romance, math, or just good storytelling." Voice Youth Advocates

★ The **fault** in our stars; John Green. Dutton Books 2012 318p
Grades: 9 10 11 12

1. Love stories 2. Cancer -- Patients -- Fiction 3. Terminally ill children -- Fiction 4. Love -- Fiction 5. Cancer -- Fiction
ISBN 9780525478812

LC 2011045783

Odyssey Award Winner (2013)

This book tells the story of "Hazel Lancaster and Augustus Waters [who] are very different: She's a sensitive poetry aficionado; he's a hunky ex-basketball player. But their paths (and stars) cross in a cancer support group for teens. . . . Hazel yearns to travel to Amsterdam to meet her favorite author, and Augustus leaps to help even as their respective cancers threaten to derail her dream." (Washington Post)

★ **Looking** for Alaska. Dutton Books 2005 221p $15.99; pa $7.99
Grades: 9 10 11 12

1. School stories 2. Death -- Fiction 3. Birmingham (Ala.) -- Fiction
ISBN 0-525-47506-0; 0-14-240251-6 pa

LC 2004-10827

Michael L. Printz Award, 2006

Sixteen-year-old Miles' first year at Culver Creek Preparatory School in Alabama includes good friends and great pranks, but is defined by the search for answers about life and death after a fatal car crash.

"The language and sexual situations are aptly and realistically drawn, but sophisticated in nature. Miles's narration is alive with sweet, self-deprecating humor, and his obvious struggle to tell the story truthfully adds to his believability." SLJ

Paper towns. Dutton Books 2008 305p $17.99
Grades: 9 10 11 12
    1. Mystery fiction 2. Florida -- Fiction 3. Missing persons -- Fiction
    ISBN 978-0-525-47818-8; 0-525-47818-3
                    LC 2007-52659

One month before graduating from his Central Florida high school, Quentin "Q" Jacobsen basks in the predictable boringness of his life until the beautiful and exciting Margo Roth Spiegelman, Q's neighbor and classmate, takes him on a midnight adventure and then mysteriously disappears.

"The writing is . . . stellar, with deliciously intelligent dialogue and plenty of mind-twisting insights. . . . Language and sex issues might make this book more appropriate for older teens, but it is still a powerfully great read." Voice Youth Advocates

★ **Turtles** all the way down. John Green. Dutton Books 2017 286 p.
Grades: 9 10 11 12
    1. Anxiety disorders -- Fiction; 2. Teenage girls -- Fiction; 3. Friendship -- Fiction; 4. Obsessive-compulsive disorder -- Fiction; 5. Missing persons -- Fiction
    0525555366; 9780525555353; 9780525555360, $19.99
                    LC 2017299345

In this novel, by John Green, "sixteen-year-old Aza never intended to pursue the mystery of fugitive billionaire Russell Pickett, but there's a hundred-thousand-dollar reward at stake and her Best and Most Fearless Friend, Daisy, is eager to investigate. So together, they navigate the short distance and broad divides that separate them from Russell Pickett's son, Davis." (Publisher's note)

"With its attention to ideas and trademark introspection, it's a challenging but richly rewarding read. It is also the most mature of Green's work to date and deserving of all the accolades that are sure to come its way." Booklist

★ **Will** Grayson, Will Grayson; [by] John Green & David Levithan. Dutton 2010 310p $17.99
Grades: 9 10 11 12
    1. Obesity -- Fiction 2. Theater -- Fiction 3. LGBT youth -- Fiction 4. Chicago (Ill.) -- Fiction 5. Dating (Social customs) -- Fiction
    ISBN 978-0-525-42158-0; 0-525-42158-0
                    LC 2008-48979

When two teens, one gay and one straight, meet accidentally and discover that they share the same name, their lives become intertwined as one begins dating the other's best friend, who produces a play revealing his relationship with them both.

"Each character comes lovingly to life, especially Tiny Cooper, whose linebacker-sized, heart-on-his-sleeve person-

ality could win over the grouchiest of grouches. . . . Their story, along with the rest of the cast's, will have readers simultaneously laughing, crying and singing at the top of their lungs." Kirkus

Green, Sally

Half bad; Sally Green. Viking, published by the Penguin Group 2014 416 p. (hardback) $18.99
Grades: 9 10 11 12
    1. Witches -- Fiction 2. England -- Fiction 3. Prisoners -- Fiction 4. Toleration -- Fiction 5. Good and evil -- Fiction 6. Fathers and sons -- Fiction 7. Family life -- England -- Fiction
    ISBN 0670016780; 9780670016785
                    LC 2013041190

In this book, by Sally Green, "witches live alongside humans: White witches, who are good; Black witches, who are evil; and sixteen-year-old Nathan, who is both. Nathan's father is the world's most powerful and cruel Black witch, and his mother is dead. He is hunted from all sides. Trapped in a cage, beaten and handcuffed, Nathan must escape before his seventeenth birthday, at which point he will receive three gifts from his father and come into his own as a witch--or else he will die." (Publisher's note)

"Told at times in first- and second-person, the story allows unique insights into Nathan's perspectives, including the fast-paced escapes and heart-wrenching torment. An interesting spin on the paranormal that runs adjacent to some important social issues, Half Bad leaves readers questioning if the division between good and evil is ever as simple as black and white." (VOYA)

Half wild. Sally Green. Viking 2015 432 p. (The half bad trilogy)
Grades: 9 10 11 12
    1. Fathers and sons -- Fiction 2. Witches -- Fiction 3. England -- Fiction 4. Father-son relationship -- Fiction
    0670017132; 9780670017133, $18.99
                    LC 2014044805

This book, by Sally Green, takes place in "a modern-day England where two warring factions of witches live amongst humans. . . . Nathan is an abomination, the illegitimate son of the world's most powerful and violent witch. Nathan is hunted from all sides: nowhere is safe and no one can be trusted. Now, Nathan has come into his own unique magical Gift, and he's on the run—but the Hunters are close behind." (Publisher's note)

"The blood and gore, the willingness to endure and survive at any price, and the dichotomies between good and bad, love and hate, wild and civilized-all haunt the reader, climaxing in a tragic ending that portends the horror, violence, and possible relationships in the trilogy's final installment." Booklist

Greenberg, Joanne

I never promised you a rose garden; a novel. Henry Holt 2009 291p pa $15
Grades: 7 8 9 10 11 12 Adult
    1. Mentally ill -- Fiction 2. Psychotherapy -- Fiction
    ISBN 978-0-8050-8926-4; 0-8050-8926-8
                    LC 2010-275768

First published 1964

Chronicles the three-year battle of a mentally ill, but perceptive, teenage girl against a world of her own creation, emphasizing her relationship with the doctor who gave her the ammunition of self-understanding with which to destroy that world of fantasy.

"The hospital world and Deborah's fantasy world are strikingly portrayed, as is the girl's violent struggle between sickness and health, a struggle given added poignancy by youth, wit, and courage." Libr J

Grey, Melissa

The **girl** at midnight. Melissa Grey. Delacorte Press 2015 368 p.

Grades: 9 10 11 12

1. Adopted children 2. Fantasy 3. Fantasy fiction 4. War stories

038574465X; 9780375991790; 9780385744652, $17.99

LC 2014008700

In this book, by Melissa Grey, "[b]eneath the streets of New York City live the Avicen, an ancient race of people with feathers for hair and magic running through their veins. Age-old enchantments keep them hidden from humans. All but one. Echo is a runaway pickpocket who survives by selling stolen treasures on the black market, and the Avicen are the only family she's ever known." (Publisher's note)

"The well-built world, vivid characters, and perfect blend of action and amour should have readers eagerly seeking the sequel." Kirkus

Griffin, Adele

★ **All** you never wanted; Adele Griffin. Alfred A. Knopf 2012 225 p. (hard cover) $16.99

Grades: 9 10 11 12

1. Popularity -- Fiction 2. Self-destructive behavior 3. Sibling rivalry -- Fiction 4. Personal appearance -- Fiction 5. Wealth -- Fiction 6. Sisters -- Fiction

ISBN 9780307974662; 9780375870811; 9780375870828; 9780375970825

LC 2012020504

Author Adele Griffith tells a story of a sibling rivalry. "Alex has it all--brains, beauty, popularity, and a dangerously hot boyfriend. Her little sister Thea wants it all, and she's stepped up her game to get it. Even if it means spinning the truth to win the attention she deserves. Even if it means uncovering a shocking secret her older sister never wanted to share. Even if it means crying wolf. (Publisher's note)

The **Julian** game. G.P. Putnam's Sons 2010 200p $16.99

Grades: 8 9 10 11 12

1. School stories 2. Bullies -- Fiction

ISBN 978-0-399-25460-4; 0-399-25460-9

LC 2010-2281

In an effort to improve her social status, a new scholarship student at an exclusive girls' school uses a fake online profile to help a popular girl get back at her ex-boyfriend, but the consequences are difficult to handle.

This is a "perceptive novel. . . . Canny use of details makes Griffin's characters fully realized and believable. . . . Strong pacing and a sympathetic protagonist ought to keep readers hooked." Publ Wkly

The **unfinished** life of Addison Stone. Adele Griffin. Soho Teen 2014 256 p. Illustration; Color

Grades: 9 10 11 12

1. Artists -- Fiction 2. Celebrities -- Fiction 3. Mystery and detective stories 4. New York (N.Y.) -- Fiction 5. Young adult literature

1616953608; 9781616953607, $17.99

LC 2014009576

In this young adult novel by Adele Griffin, "from the moment she stepped foot in NYC, Addison Stone's subversive street art made her someone to watch, and her violent drowning left her fans and critics craving to know more. [Griffin] conducted interviews with those who knew her best—including close friends, family, teachers, mentors, art dealers, boyfriends, and critics—and retraced the tumultuous path of Addison's life." (Publisher's note)

"This novel is . . . a terrific experiment, something fresh and hard to put down. It gives a sense of both the artistic temperament and the nature of madness-and the sometimes thin line in between." Booklist

Where I want to be. G.P. Putnam's Sons 2005 150p pa $6.99

Grades: 7 8 9 10

1. Death -- Fiction 2. Sisters -- Fiction 3. Rhode Island -- Fiction 4. Mental illness -- Fiction

ISBN 0-399-23783-6; 0-14-240948-0 pa

LC 2004-1887

Two teenaged sisters, separated by death but still connected, work through their feelings of loss over the closeness they shared as children that was later destroyed by one's mental illness, and finally make peace with each other

"Thoughtful, unique, and ultimately life-affirming, this is a fascinating take on the literary device of a main character speaking after death." SLJ

Griffin, Claire J.

Nowhere to run; Claire J. Griffin. 1st ed. Namelos llc 2013 118 p. (hardcover) $18.95

Grades: 7 8 9 10

1. School stories 2. Juvenile delinquency -- Fiction

ISBN 1608981444; 9781608981441; 9781608981458

LC 2012951212

In this novel, by Claire J. Griffin, "Calvin has Deej--and a coach who thinks Calvin can win the championship in the 100-meter dash, a little brother who looks up to him, a boss who trusts him with the keys to the car shop, and Momma, who made him promise to stay in school. And then there's Junior, the girlfriend of Calvin's dreams. . . . But when Calvin and Deej get suspended from school on a trumped-up charge, things start to fall apart." (Publisher's note)

Griffin, Emily Ziff

Light years. Emily Ziff Griffin. Simon Pulse 2017 288 p.

Grades: 7 8 9 10 11

1. Computer programs -- Fiction; 2. Epidemics -- Fiction; 3. Racially mixed people -- Fiction; 4. Synesthesia -- Fiction; 5. Science fiction

1507200056; 9781507200056, $17.99; 9781507200063

LC 2017014940

In this book, by Emily Ziff Griffin, "Luisa is ready for her life to start. Five minutes ago. And she could be on her way, as her extraordinary coding skills have landed her a finalist spot for a fellowship sponsored by Thomas Bell, the world's most brilliant and mercurial tech entrepreneur. Being chosen means funding, mentorship, and most importantly, freedom from her overbearing mother." (Publisher's note)

"A lyrical science fiction novel about a sensitive and creative teenager tasked with saving herself -- and the world." SLJ

Griffin, N.

Just wreck it all. N. Griffin. A Caitlyn Dlouhy Book/Atheneum 2018 336 p.

Grades: 7 8 9 10 11

1. Compulsive eating -- Fiction; 2. Eating disorders -- Fiction; 3. Guilt -- Fiction; 4. High schools -- Fiction; 5. Overweight persons -- Fiction; 6. Schools -- Fiction; 7. Self-mutilation -- Fiction;

9781481465182, $18.99; 9781481465199

LC 2018008167

In this novel, by N. Griffin, "two years ago Bett was athletic, fearless, and prone to daredevil behavior.... But when a dare gone wrong leaves her best friend severely and permanently injured, everything changes. Now, Bett is extremely overweight, depressed, and forbids herself from enjoying anything in life.... But some pluses can't be avoided, and when that happens, Bett punishes herself through binge eating." (Publisher's note)

★ The **whole** stupid way we are; N. Griffin. Atheneum Books for Young Readers 2013 368 p. (hardcover) $16.99

Grades: 9 10 11 12

1. Friendship -- Fiction 2. Dysfunctional families -- Fiction 3. Maine -- Fiction 4. Best friends -- Fiction 5. Family problems -- Fiction

ISBN 1442431555; 9781442431553; 9781442431584

LC 2012002595

In this young adult novel, by N. Griffin, "the friendship between optimistic Dinah Beach and depressed, nihilistic Skint Gilbert is tested. . . . Skint thinks constantly about human cruelty; Dinah wants playful distractions. Skint lives with a father suffering from dementia and a mother who is bitter, angry and occasionally violent; Dinah takes care not to bring up Skint's family . . . ," until one day when she decides to help. (Kirkus Reviews)

Griffin, Paul

Adrift. Paul Griffin. Scholastic Press 2015 228 p.

Grades: 9 10 11 12

1. Sailing -- Fiction 2. Survival -- Fiction 3. Teenagers -- Fiction 4. Survival after airplane accidents, shipwrecks, etc. -- Fiction 5. Sea stories

9780545709392, $17.99; 0545709393; 0545871956; 9780545871952

LC 2015506208

In this young adult novel, by Paul Griffin, "Matt and John are best friends working out in Montauk for the summer. When Driana, JoJo and Stef invite the boys to their Hamptons mansion, Matt and John find themselves in a sticky situation where temptation rivals sensibility. The

newfound friends head out into the Atlantic after midnight in a stolen boat. None of them come back whole, and not all of them come back." (Publisher's note)

"Griffin keeps the pages turning; he has a gift for drawing out the suspense and immersing the reader in the story. At the same time, his characters are complex, unpredictable, and entirely authentic. Dispatches from rescue units heighten the suspense. It's a great summer read-as long as you stay on dry land."

Burning blue; by Paul Griffin. Dial Books 2012 288 p. (hardcover) $17.99

Grades: 9 10 11 12

1. Love stories 2. Accidents -- Fiction 3. Popularity -- Fiction 4. Beauty, Personal -- Fiction 5. Computer hackers -- Fiction 6. Disfigured persons -- Fiction 7. Mystery and detective stories

ISBN 0803738153; 9780803738157

LC 2012003578

Author Paul Griffin's protagonist "Nicole Castro, the most beautiful girl in her wealthy New Jersey high school, is splashed with acid on the left side of her perfect face, [and] the whole world takes notice. But quiet loner Jay Nazarro does more than that--he decides to find out who did it. Jay understands how it feels to be treated like an outsider, and he also has a secret: He's a brilliant hacker. But the deeper he digs, the more danger he's in--and the more he falls for Nicole. Too bad everyone is turning into a suspect, including Nicole herself." (Publisher's note)

★ The **Orange** Houses. Dial Books 2009 147p $16.99

Grades: 9 10 11 12

1. Veterans -- Fiction 2. People with disabilities -- Fiction 3. Illegal aliens -- Fiction 4. Mental illness -- Fiction 5. Bronx (New York, N.Y.) -- Fiction 6. Africans -- United States -- Fiction

ISBN 978-0-8037-3346-6; 0-8037-3346-1

LC 2008-46259

"Tamika, a fifteen-year-old hearing-impaired girl, Jimmi, an eighteen-year-old veteran who stopped taking his antipsychotic medication, and sixteen-year-old Fatima, an illegal immigrant from Africa, meet and connect in their Bronx, New York, neighborhood." (Publisher's note) "Grades eight to twelve." (Bull Cent Child Books)

"Griffin's . . . prose is gorgeous and resonant, and he packs the slim novel with defeats, triumphs, rare moments of beauty and a cast of credible, skillfully drawn characters. A moving story of friendship and hope under harsh conditions." Publ Wkly

★ **Stay** with me. Dial Books for Young Readers 2011 288p il $16.99

Grades: 10 11 12

1. Dogs -- Fiction 2. Family life -- Fiction 3. Restaurants -- Fiction

ISBN 978-0-8037-3448-7

LC 2011001287

Fifteen-year-olds Mack, a high school dropout but a genius with dogs, and Céce, who hopes to use her intelligence to avoid a life like her mother's, meet and fall in love at the restaurant where they both work, but when Mack lands in prison he pushes Céce away and only a one-eared pit-bull can keep them together.

"A stellar story, with genuine dialogue and drama, this is a book that will appeal greatly to teens, especially dog lovers." SLJ

Grimes, Nikki

★ **Bronx** masquerade. Dial Bks. 2002 167p $16.99; pa $5.99
Grades: 7 8 9 10

1. School stories 2. African Americans -- Fiction 3. Bronx (New York, N.Y.) -- Fiction
ISBN 0-8037-2569-8; 0-14-250189-1 pa
LC 00-31701

While studying the Harlem Renaissance, students at a Bronx high school read aloud poems they've written, revealing their innermost thoughts and fears to their formerly clueless classmates

"Funny and painful, awkward and abstract, the poems talk about race, abuse, parental love, neglect, death, and body image. . . . Readers will enjoy the lively, smart voices that talk bravely about real issues and secret fears. A fantastic choice for readers' theater." Booklist

Dark sons. Jump at the Sun 2005 216p $15.99
Grades: 6 7 8 9 10

1. Novels in verse 2. Stepfamilies -- Fiction 3. Father-son relationship -- Fiction
ISBN 0-7868-1888-3
LC 2004-54208

Alternating poems compare and contrast the conflicted feelings of Ishmael, son of the Biblical patriarch Abraham, and Sam, a teenager in New York City, as they try to come to terms with being abandoned by their fathers and with the love they feel for their younger stepbrothers.

"The simple words eloquently reveal what it's like to miss someone. . . . but even more moving is the struggle to forgive and the affection each boy feels for the baby that displaces him. The elemental connections and the hope . . . will speak to a wide audience." Booklist

A **girl** named Mister. Zondervan 2010 223p $15.99
Grades: 8 9 10 11

1. Saints 2. Novels in verse 3. Pregnancy -- Fiction 4. Christian life -- Fiction 5. African Americans -- Fiction
ISBN 978-0-310-72078-2; 0-310-72078-8
LC 2010-10830

A pregnant teenager finds support and forgiveness from God through a book of poetry presented from the Virgin Mary's perspective.

"Writing in lovely prose with lyrical, forthright language that avoids over-moralizing while driving home the big issues of teen pregnancy, award-winning Nikki Grimes just may help a few young women make different choices. At the same time, she effectively makes the case for parents and schools to continue to educate, educate, educate." Voice Youth Advocates

★ **Jazmin's** notebook. Dial Bks. 1998 102p $15.99

Grades: 6 7 8 9

1. Authorship -- Fiction 2. African Americans -- Fiction
ISBN 0-8037-2224-9
LC 97-5850

A Coretta Scott King honor book for text, 1999

Jazmin, an Afro-American fourteen-year-old who lives with her older sister in a small Harlem apartment in the 1960s, finds strength in writing poetry and keeping a record of the events in her sometimes difficult life

"An articulate, admirable heroine, Jazmin leaps over life's hurdles with agility and integrity." Publ Wkly

Grossman, Nancy

A **world** away; Nancy Grossman. Hyperion 2012 394 p. $16.99
Grades: 7 8 9 10

1. Bildungsromans 2. Amish -- Fiction 3. Adolescence -- Fiction 4. Aunts -- Fiction 5. Self-realization -- Fiction
ISBN 1423151534; 9781423151531
LC 2011032890

This book is the story of 16-year-old Eliza, who "feels trapped by the conservative traditions of her Amish community. During her 'rumspringa,' a time when Amish teenagers are allowed to 'step out of the plain world,' she" works as "a nanny . . . . Eliza is thrilled with her new contemporary wardrobe and the modern conveniences available to her, but she didn't anticipate falling in love with a neighbor . . . or discovering secrets that will significantly change her view of her family." (Publishers Weekly)

Groth, Darren

Munro vs. the coyote. Darren Groth. Orca Book Publishers 2017 276 p.
Grades: 7 8 9 10 11 12

1. Australia -- Fiction; 2. Death -- Fiction; 3. Brothers and sisters -- Fiction; 4. Teenage boys -- Fiction
1459814096; 9781459814103; 9781459814097, $19.95; 9781459814110
LC 2017932501

In this book, by Darren Groth, "since the sudden death of his younger sister, Evie, sixteen-year-old Munro Maddux has been having flashbacks and anger-management issues.... And there's a taunting, barking, biting voice he calls 'the Coyote.' Munro...intends to move beyond his troubled past. It is there, at an assisted living residence called Fair Go Community Village, that Munro discovers the Coyote can be silenced." (Publisher's note)

"Characters that will steal readers' hearts with their humor and resilience, smooth writing, and a satisfying and hopeful ending make this a book to enjoy both emotionally and critically." Kirkus

Grove, S. E.

The **crimson** skew. S.E. Grove. Viking, an imprint of Penguin Random House LLC 2016 448 p. Map (Mapmakers)
Grades: 6 7 8 9 10

1. Fantasy 2. Maps -- Fiction 3. Fantasy fiction 4. Magic -- Fiction
9780670785049, $17.99
LC 2015036703

In this book, by S.E. Grove, "Sophia Tims is coming home from a foreign Age. . . . But her homecoming is anything but peaceful. Threatening clouds hang over New Orleans harbor. Sinkholes have been opening in Boston. . . . Rogue weirwinds tear up the Baldlands. Worst of all, New Occident is at war, led by a prime minister who . . . has blackmailed Sophia's beloved uncle Shadrack into drawing the battle maps that will lead countless men and boys . . . to their deaths." (Publisher's note)

"Pirates, sea captains, fortunetellers, a dragon, poisonous red fog, former slave traders, and healers populate a story that may introduce young readers to the old-fashioned pleasure of settling into a long, rich, and complicated tale.A triumphant conclusion to a prodigious feat of storytelling." Kirkus

★ The **glass** sentence; S. E. Grove. Viking 2014 il maps $17.99
Grades: 6 7 8 9 10
  1. Fantasies 2. Kidnapping -- Fiction 3. Maps -- Fiction 4. Historical fiction
ISBN: 0670785024; 9780670785025
                      LC 2013025832
Blue Ribbon Awards (2014)
First volume in the author's Mapmakers trilogy. "In the Great Disruption of 1799, time itself broke apart and fragmented, stranding countries and continents in different time periods, some of them thousands of years apart. Thirteen-year-old Sophia lives with her Uncle Shadrack in New Occident Boston, discovering the magic and science of maps. When her uncle is kidnapped by those seeking a powerful artifact, Sophia must journey through a dangerous, shattered landscape to seek out help and answers." SLJ

"In a world fractured into disparate eras during the Great Disruption, Sophia Tims is entrusted with the Tracing Glass (containing a memory thought to be the cause of the Disruption) when her uncle, the cartographer Shadrack Elli, is kidnapped. An intricate fantasy with a Gilded-Age feel, this solidly constructed quest features maps of all kinds and unusual steampunk-flavored elements." Horn Book

The **golden** specific. S.E. Grove; maps by Dave A. Stevenson. Viking, an imprint of Penguin Group (USA) LLC 2015 528 p. Map (Mapmakers)
Grades: 6 7 8 9 10
  1. Fantasy 2. Maps -- Fiction 3. Missing persons -- Fiction 4. Fantasy fiction
9780670785032, $17.99
                      LC 2014034892
"In the second installment of the Mapmakers trilogy, Sophia Tims goes on a journey in search of her parents in a world broken apart by the Great Disruption of 1799. Sophia's parents are missing, and finding them is no simple task in this new world of 'intermingled futures and pasts,' in which the former United States has splintered—into New Occident, Indian Territories, and the Baldlands—Canada is now Prehistoric Snows, and large pockets of the world are simply 'Unknown.'" (Kirkus Reviews)

"Brilliantly imagined and full of wonder." Kirkus
Includes index.

Guibord, Maurissa
★ **Warped**. Delacorte Press 2011 339p $16.99; lib bdg $19.99
Grades: 7 8 9 10
  1. Magic -- Fiction 2. Tapestry -- Fiction 3. Time travel -- Fiction 4. Great Britain -- History -- 1485-1603, Tudors -- Fiction
ISBN 0-385-73891-9; 0-385-90758-3 lib bdg; 978-0-385-73891-0; 978-0-385-90758-3 lib bdg
                      LC 2009-53654
When seventeen-year-old Tessa Brody comes into possession of an ancient unicorn tapestry, she is thrust into sixteenth-century England, where her life is intertwined with that of a handsome nobleman. "Grades seven to ten." (Bull Cent Child Books)

"This has it all—fantasy, romance, witchcraft, life-threatening situations, detective work, chase scenes, and a smattering of violence. Imaginative and compelling, it's impossible to put down." SLJ

Gurtler, Janet
I'm not her. Sourcebooks Fire 2011 288p pa $9.99
Grades: 7 8 9 10
  1. Cancer -- Fiction 2. Sisters -- Fiction 3. Identity (Psychology) -- Fiction
ISBN 978-1-4022-5636-3; 1-4022-5636-1
Brainy Tess Smith is the younger sibling of the beautiful, popular, volleyball-scholarship-bound Kristina. When Kristina is diagnosed with bone cancer, it drastically changes both sisters' lives.

"This quick and heartbreaking read realistically shows how one person's illness affects an entire community." SLJ

Haas, Abigail
Dangerous girls; by Abigail Haas. Simon Pulse 2013 400 p. (hardback) $16.99
Grades: 10 11 12
  1. Homicide -- Fiction 2. Female friendship -- Fiction 3. Teenagers -- Conduct of life -- Fiction 4. Aruba -- Fiction 5. Murder -- Fiction 6. Friendship -- Fiction 7. Best friends -- Fiction 8. Trials (Murder) -- Fiction 9. Mystery and detective stories
ISBN 1442486597; 9781442486591
                      LC 2013008216
In this book, "an American teen languishes in an Aruba jail, charged with the brutal murder of her best friend. When Anna Chevalier's on-the-rise father moves her . . . to tony Hillcrest Prep, she quickly makes friends with the charismatic Elise. . . .They and their posse of rich and beautiful teens party hard and often; the centerpiece of their senior year is their unsupervised trip to Aruba--where Elise's stabbing death brings their perpetual celebration to a grinding halt." (Kirkus Reviews)

"Anna's wild spring break ends abruptly when her best friend Elise is found murdered. Anna is the primary suspect--she narrates from an Aruban jail, awaiting her trial. Anna's flashbacks reveal additional suspects on the island, but also rivalries, romances, and betrayals among Anna, Elise, and their friends. Anna's riveting unreliable narration will keep readers guessing until the final page." (Horn Book)

Haddix, Margaret Peterson

Full ride; Margaret Peterson Haddix. Simon & Schuster Books for Young Readers 2013 352 p. (hardcover) $16.99

Grades: 6 7 8 9 10 11 12

1. Scholarships -- Fiction 2. Family secrets 3. Ohio -- Fiction 4. Schools -- Fiction 5. Secrets -- Fiction 6. Criminals -- Fiction 7. High schools -- Fiction 8. Mothers and daughters -- Fiction

ISBN 1442442786; 9781442442788; 9781442442795; 9781442442801

LC 2012038146

"Her father in prison for embezzlement, fourteen-year-old Becca and her mother flee to an Ohio suburb to hide from the media and start new lives. Years later, a chain of events reveals layers of secrets behind Becca's father's crimes, his victims, and her mother's motivations. Haddix deftly emphasizes relatable issues: moving, losing faith in a parent, and falling out of economic comfort." (Horn Book)

Just Ella. Simon & Schuster Bks. for Young Readers 1999 185p hardcover o.p. pa $5.99

Grades: 7 8 9 10

1. Sex role -- Fiction 2. Princesses -- Fiction

ISBN 0-689-82186-7; 0-689-83128-5 pa

LC 98-8384

In this continuation of the Cinderella story, fifteen-year-old Ella finds that accepting Prince Charming's proposal ensnares her in a suffocating tangle of palace rules and royal etiquette, so she plots to escape

"In lively prose, with well-developed characters, creative plot twists, wit, and drama, Haddix transforms the Cinderella tale into an insightful coming-of-age story." Booklist

Uprising. Simon & Schuster Books for Young Readers 2007 346p $16.99; pa $7.99

Grades: 6 7 8 9 10

1. Fires -- Fiction 2. Strikes -- Fiction 3. Triangle Shirtwaist Company, Inc. -- Fiction

ISBN 978-1-4169-1171-5; 1-4169-1171-5; 978-1-4169-1172-2 pa; 1-4169-1172-3 pa

LC 2006-34870

In 1927, at the urging of twenty-one-year-old Harriet, Mrs. Livingston reluctantly recalls her experiences at the Triangle Shirtwaist factory, including miserable working conditions that led to a strike, then the fire that took the lives of her two best friends, when Harriet, the boss's daughter, was only five years old. Includes historical notes.

"This deftly crafted historical novel unfolds dramatically with an absorbing story and well-drawn characters who readily evoke empathy and compassion." SLJ

Hahn, Mary Downing, 1937-

Mister Death's blue-eyed girls; Mary Downing Hahn. Clarion Books 2012 330 p. $16.99

Grades: 8 9 10 11 12

1. Mystery fiction 2. Historical fiction 3. Homicide -- Fiction 4. Grief -- Fiction 5. Murder -- Fiction 6. Coming of age -- Fiction 7. Baltimore (Md.) -- History -- 20th century -- Fiction

ISBN 0547760620; 9780547760629

LC 2011025950

In this work of historical fiction, "[t]he high-school year is almost over, there's a party in the park and Mister Death will soon be there, rifle in hand. . . . Two girls, Cheryl and Bobbi Jo, never make it to school the next day, their bloody bodies found in the park where they were shot. [Mary Downing] Hahn's . . . story traces the effects of a crime on everyone involved, including Buddy Novak, accused of a crime he didn't commit." (Kirkus Reviews)

Hahn, Rebecca

A **creature** of moonlight; Rebecca Hahn. Houghton Mifflin Harcourt 2014 224 p. $17.99

Grades: 7 8 9 10 11 12

1. Fantasy fiction 2. Dragons -- Fiction 3. Princesses -- Fiction 4. Fantasy 5. Magic -- Fiction 6. Flowers -- Fiction 7. Identity -- Fiction 8. Forests and forestry -- Fiction

ISBN 054410935X; 9780544109353

LC 2013020188

In this novel, by Rebecca Hahn, "as the only heir to the throne, Marni should have been surrounded by wealth and privilege, not living in exile--but now the time has come when she must choose between claiming her birthright as princess of a realm whose king wants her dead, and life with the father she has never known: a wild dragon who is sending his magical woods to capture her." (Publisher's note)

"Marni lives in a shack at the edge of the woods with her Gramps, where she tends flowers, as she's done for most of her life. Yet change is afoot... This book's greatest strength lies in the vivid woodland scenes and the rich detail that describes the mystical pieces of Marni's tale." (School Library Journal)

★ The **shadow** behind the stars. Rebecca Hahn. Atheneum Books for Young Readers 2015 256 p.

Grades: 7 8 9 10 11 12

1. Fate and fatalism -- Fiction 2. Goddesses, Greek -- Fiction 3. Oracles -- Fiction 4. Prophecies -- Fiction 5. Gods and goddesses -- Fiction 6. Greek mythology -- Fiction

9781481435710, $17.99; 9781481435727

LC 2014026428

In this book, by Rebecca Hahn, "Chloe is the youngest. . . . She and her sisters have been on their isolated Greek island for longer than any mortal can remember. . . . So when a beautiful girl named Aglaia shows up on their doorstep, Chloe tries to make sure her sisters don't become attached. But in seeking to protect them, Chloe discovers the dark power of Aglaia's destiny." (Publisher's note)

"Hahn's lovingly crafted characters and the brief, unexpected pops of violence in an otherwise peaceful narrative enhance yet another explication of the tragedy of humankind, making this an obvious choice for mythology fans (plenty of those around) and teen philosophers alike." Booklist

Haines, Kathryn Miller

★ The **girl** is murder. Roaring Brook Press 2011 352p $16.99

Grades: 7 8 9 10

1. Mystery fiction 2. Social classes -- Fiction 3. Missing persons -- Fiction 4. New York (N.Y.) -- Fiction

5. Father-daughter relationship -- Fiction
ISBN 978-1-59643-609-1; 1-59643-609-3

LC 2010-32935

In 1942 New York City, fifteen-year-old Iris grieves for her mother who committed suicide, and secretly helps her father with his detective business since he, having lost a leg at Pearl Harbor, struggles to make ends meet. "Grades six to ten." (Bull Cent Child Books)

This is "a smart offering that gives both mysteries and historical fiction a good name. . . . The mystery is solid, but what makes this such a standout is the cast. . . . The characters, young and old, leap off the pages." Booklist

The **girl** is trouble; Kathryn Miller Haines. Roaring Brook Press 2012 336p. $17.99

Grades: 6 7 8

1. Mystery fiction 2. Historical fiction 3. Women detectives -- Fiction
ISBN 9781596436107

LC 2011031806

This book is set in "the Fall of 1942 and Iris's world is rapidly changing. Her Pop is back from the war with a missing leg, limiting his ability to do the physically grueling part of his detective work. Iris is dying to help, especially when she discovers that one of Pop's cases involves a boy at her school. Now, instead of sitting at home watching Deanna Durbin movies, Iris is sneaking out of the house, double crossing her friends, and dancing at the Savoy till all hours of the night. There's certainly never a dull moment in the private eye business." (Publisher's note)

Halam, Ann

Snakehead. Wendy Lamb Books 2008 289p il map $16.99; lib bdg $19.99

Grades: 6 7 8 9 10

1. Gods and goddesses -- Fiction 2. Classical mythology -- Fiction 3. Medusa (Greek mythology) -- Fiction 4. Perseus (Greek mythology) -- Fiction
ISBN 978-0-375-84108-8; 978-0-375-94108-5 lib bdg

LC 2007-28318

Compelled by his father Zeus to accept the evil king Polydectes's challenge to bring the head of the monstrous Medusa to the Aegean island of Serifos, Perseus, although questioning the gods' interference in human lives, sets out, accompanied by his beloved Andromeda, a princess with her own harsh destiny to fulfill.

"Mythology buffs will appreciate the plethora of classical figures, while periodic references to contemporary culture (e.g., a band of rich, rowdy teens are dubbed the Yacht Club kids) and occasional slang drive the story home for the target audience without sacrificing its heroic dimensions." Publ Wkly

Hale, Marian

The **goodbye** season. Henry Holt and Co. 2009 271p $16.99

Grades: 7 8 9 10

1. Texas -- Fiction 2. Bereavement -- Fiction 3. Family life -- Fiction 4. Household employees -- Fiction 5. Mother-daughter relationship -- Fiction
ISBN 978-0-8050-8855-7; 0-8050-8855-5

LC 2008-50275

In Canton, Texas, seventeen-year-old Mercy's dreams of a different life than her mother's are postponed by harsh circumstances, including the influenza epidemic of 1918-19, which forces her into doing domestic work for a loving, if troubled, family.

This is a "compelling, tautly written novel." SLJ

Hale, Shannon

★ **Book** of a thousand days; illustrations by James Noel Smith. Bloomsbury Children's Books 2007 305p il $17.95

Grades: 7 8 9 10

1. Love stories 2. Fantasy fiction
ISBN 978-1-59990-051-3; 1-59990-051-3

LC 2006-36999

Fifteen-year-old Dashti, sworn to obey her sixteen-year-old mistress, the Lady Saren, shares Saren's years of punishment locked in a tower, then brings her safely to the lands of her true love, where both must hide who they are as they work as kitchen maids.

This is a "captivating fantasy filled with romance, magic, and strong female characters." Booklist

The **Goose** girl. Bloomsbury Children's Books 2003 383p $17.95; pa $8.99

Grades: 6 7 8 9

1. Fairy tales 2. Princesses -- Fiction
ISBN 1-58234-843-X; 1-58234-990-8 pa

LC 2002-28336

On her way to marry a prince she's never met, Princess Anidori is betrayed by her guards and her lady-in-waiting and must become a goose girl to survive until she can reveal her true identity and reclaim the crown that is rightfully hers

"A fine adventure tale full of danger, suspense, surprising twists, and a satisfying conclusion." Booklist

Other titles in this series are:
Enna burning (2004)
River secrets (2006)
Forest born (2009)

Halpern, Julie

Get well soon. Feiwel & Friends 2007 193p $16.95; pa $8.99

Grades: 7 8 9 10

1. Mental illness -- Fiction 2. Psychiatric hospitals -- Fiction
ISBN 0-312-36795-3; 978-0-312-36795-4; 0-312-58148-3 pa; 978-0-312-58148-0 pa

LC 2006-32358

When her parents confine her to a mental hospital, Anna, an overweight teenage girl who suffers from panic attacks, describes her experiences in a series of letters to a friend.

"Halpern creates a narrative that reflects the changes in Anna with each passing day that includes self-reflection and a good dose of humor." Voice Youth Advocates

Have a nice day; Julie Halpern. Feiwel and Friends 2012 325 p. $16.99

Grades: 7 8 9 10 11 12

1. Mental illness -- Fiction 2. Self-perception 3. Parent-child relationship
ISBN 0312606605; 9780312606602

In author Julie Halpern's book, "Anna Bloom has just come home from a three-week stay in a mental hospital. She feels...okay. It's time to get back to some sort of normal life, whatever that means. She has to go back to school, where teachers and friends are dying to know what happened to her, but are too afraid to ask. And Anna is dying to know what's going on back at the hospital with her crush, Justin, but is too afraid to ask. Meanwhile, Anna's parents aren't getting along, and she wonders if she's the cause of her family's troubles." (Publisher's note)

Into the wild nerd yonder. Feiwel and Friends 2009 247p $16.99

Grades: 9 10 11 12

1. School stories 2. Siblings -- Fiction 3. Friendship -- Fiction 4. Popularity -- Fiction 5. Dungeons & dragons (Game) -- Fiction

ISBN 978-0-312-38252-0; 0-312-38252-9

LC 2008-34751

When high school sophomore Jessie's long-term best friend transforms herself into a punk and goes after Jessie's would-be boyfriend, Jessie decides to visit "the wild nerd yonder" and seek true friends among classmates who play Dungeons and Dragons.

"Descriptions of high school cliques . . . are hilarious and believable. . . . This novel is particularly strong in showing how teen friendships evolve and sometimes die away, and how adolescents redefine themselves." SLJ

Halpin, Brendan

★ **Shutout**. Farrar, Straus and Giroux 2010 183p $16.99

Grades: 6 7 8 9

1. Soccer -- Fiction 2. Friendship -- Fiction

ISBN 978-0-374-36899-9; 0-374-36899-6

LC 2009-32972

Fourteen-year-old Amanda and her best friend Lena start high school looking forward to playing on the varsity soccer team, but when Lena makes varsity and Amanda only makes junior varsity, their long friendship rapidly changes.

"The dialogue is spot-on, and the characters are fully fleshed out. . . . While there is plenty of soccer action for fans of the sport, the book will also appeal to teens looking for a solid friendship story." SLJ

Hamilton, Alwyn

Hero at the fall. Alwyn Hamilton. Viking 2018 452 p. Illustration (Rebel of the sands)

Grades: 9 10 11 12

1. Ability -- Fiction; 2. Deserts -- Fiction; 3. Heads of state -- Fiction; 4. Kidnapping -- Fiction; 5. Revolutions -- Fiction; 6. Shooters of firearms -- Fiction; 7. Sultans -- Fiction; 8. Paranormal fiction; 9. Fantasy fiction; 10. Girls -- Fiction

9780698411715; 9780451477866, $18.99; 0451477863

This book in the Rebel of the Sands series, by Alwyn Hamilton, "when gunslinging Amani Al'Hiza escaped her dead-end town, she never imagined she'd join a revolution, let alone lead one. But after the bloodthirsty Sultan of Miraji imprisoned the Rebel Prince Ahmed in the mythical city of Eremot, she doesn't have a choice. Armed with only her revolver, her wits, and her untameable Demdji powers, Amani

must rally her skeleton crew of rebels for a rescue mission." (Publisher's note)

"Hamilton is a master of twists and unexpected surprises, and she again delivers shocking alliances, reappearances of characters long thought gone, and deadly choices." Booklist

Rebel of the sands. By Alwyn Hamilton. Viking, published by Penguin Group 2016 320 p.

Grades: 9 10 11 12

1. Adventure and adventurers -- Fiction 2. Fantasy 3. Love -- Fiction 4. Shooters of firearms -- Fiction 5. Deserts -- Fiction 6. Romance fiction -- Fiction 7. Fantasy fiction

9780451477538, $18.99

LC 2015026037

In this book, by Alwyn Hamilton, Amani Al'Hiza is a gifted gunslinger with perfect aim, but she can't shoot her way out of Dustwalk, the back-country town where she's destined to wind up wed or dead. Then she meets Jin, a rakish foreigner, in a shooting contest, and sees him as the perfect escape route. But though she's spent years dreaming of leaving Dustwalk, she never imagined she'd gallop away on a mythical horse. (Publisher's note)

"A readable, middle-of-the-pack 'teens save the world' story. Consider for large collections." SLJ

Traitor to the throne. Alwyn Hamilton. Viking 2017 518 p. (Rebel of the sands)

Grades: 9 10 11 12

1. Heads of state -- Fiction; 2. Kidnapping -- Fiction; 3. Adventure fiction; 4. Fantasy fiction; 5. Imaginary wars and battles— Fiction

9780698411708; 9780451477859, $18.99; 9780147519092; 0451477855

LC 2016053384

In this book in the Rebel of the Sands series, by Alwyn Hamilton, "mere months ago, gunslinger Amani al'Hiza fled her dead-end hometown on the back of a mythical horse with the mysterious foreigner Jin, seeking only her own freedom. Now she's fighting to liberate the entire desert nation of Miraji from a bloodthirsty sultan who slew his own father to capture the throne." (Publisher's note)

"Hamilton's strong and exciting sophomore novel is full of compelling twists and turns, and the ending will leave readers highly anticipating the final volume in the Rebel of the Sands trilogy." Booklist

Hamilton, K. R. (Kersten R.)

In the forests of the night; Kersten Hamilton. Clarion Books 2011 295 p. $16.99

Grades: 7 8 9 10

1. Fantasy fiction 2. Goblins -- Fiction 3. Zoos -- Fiction 4. Magic -- Fiction 5. Finn MacCool -- Fiction 6. Irish Americans -- Fiction 7. Imaginary creatures -- Fiction 8. People with mental disabilities -- Fiction

ISBN 0547435606; 9780547435602

LC 2011009846

This book is the second in Kersten Hamilton's Goblin Wars series. Here, "Teagan and her friends must cope with the aftermath of escaping from the Dark Man's forces as well as new dangers. As she picks up the pieces of her life, Teagan begins a tentative relationship with goblin hunter

Finn and struggles with her newly revealed goblin heritage." (School Library Journal)

"In her second book, high schooler Teagan (who found out in Tyger, Tyger that she's half-goblin) is back safely from Mag Mell. While she, her little brother Aiden, and love interest Finn Mac Cumhaill (Finn MacCool from Irish folklore) regroup at home in Chicago, wicked forces track them. Well-incorporated folklore elements blend nicely with everyday concerns (e.g., Teagan's post-high-school plans; best friend/boyfriend rivalry)." (Horn Book)

Tyger tyger; by Kersten Hamilton. Clarion Books 2010 308p (Goblin wars) $17
Grades: 7 8 9 10

    1. Fantasy fiction 2. Magic -- Fiction 3. Goblins -- Fiction 4. Irish Americans -- Fiction 5. Children with mental disabilities -- Fiction

    ISBN 978-0-547-33008-2; 0-547-33008-1

                    LC 2010-01337

Soon after the mysterious and alluring Finn arrives at her family's home, sixteen-year-old Teagan Wylltson and her disabled brother are drawn into the battle Finn's family has fought since the thirteenth century, when Finn MacCumhaill angered the goblin king. "Grades eight to ten." (Bull Cent Child Books)

"Laced with humor, packed with surprises and driven by suspense, the plot grabs readers from the start using the stylistic tactics of the best fantasy writing. Major characters are beautifully drawn, and many of the secondary characters are equally distinct." Kirkus

Followed by: In the forests of the night (2011) and When the Stars Threw Down Their Spears (2013)

When the stars threw down their spears; by Kersten Hamilton. Clarion Books 2013 400 p. (hardback) $16.99
Grades: 7 8 9 10

    1. Love stories 2. Magic -- Fiction 3. Goblins -- Fiction 4. Zoos -- Fiction 5. Finn MacCool -- Fiction 6. Chicago (Ill.) -- Fiction 7. Irish Americans -- Fiction 8. Imaginary creatures -- Fiction 9. People with mental disabilities -- Fiction

    ISBN 0547739648; 9780547739649

                    LC 2012029195

In this novel by Kersten Hamilton "magical creatures are tumbling through mysterious portals from Mag Mell, the world-between-worlds, into the streets of Chicago. Meanwhile, the romance between seventeen-year-old Teagan, who is part goblin, and the alluring bad boy Finn Mac Cumhaill is heating up . . . which is awkward, to say the least, considering he is bound by a family curse to fight goblins his entire life." (Publisher's note)

"In this third book, Teagan and her friends deal with the evil creatures seeping out of Mag Mell and into the streets of Chicago. Teagan and Finn work together to fight the darkness while their love continues to grow, even though it's now forbidden. Fans of fast-paced adventures and Irish folklore will find the two components nicely intertwined." (Horn Book)

Hamley, Dennis

    Without warning; Ellen's story 1914-1918. [by] Dennis Hamley. 1st U.S. ed.; Candlewick Press 2007 326p $17.99
Grades: 6 7 8 9

    1. World War, 1914-1918 -- Fiction

    ISBN 978-0-7636-3338-7; 0-7636-3338-0

                    LC 2007025248

First published 2006 in the United Kingdom with title: Ellen's people

During World War I, an English teenager leaves the safety of home and begins a journey of self-discovery that takes her close to the front lines to pursue her calling as a nurse.

"This intense narrative dramatically offers insight into the effects of World War I on the English home front. . . . This is a highly readable selection with many well-drawn characters." SLJ

Han, Jenny

    The **summer** I turned pretty. Simon & Schuster Books for Young Readers 2009 276p $16.99
Grades: 7 8 9 10

    1. Summer -- Fiction 2. Beaches -- Fiction 3. Vacations -- Fiction 4. Friendship -- Fiction

    ISBN 978-1-4169-6823-8; 1-4169-6823-7

                    LC 2008-27070

Belly spends the summer she turns sixteen at the beach just like every other summer of her life, but this time things are very different.

"Romantic and heartbreakingly real. . . . The novel perfectly blends romance, family drama, and a coming-of-age tale, one that is substantially deeper than most." SLJ

Other titles in this series are:

It's not summer without you (2010)

We'll always have summer (2011)

★ **To** all the boys I've loved before. Jenny Han. Simon & Schuster BFYR 2014 368 p.
Grades: 9 10 11 12

    1. Dating (Social customs) -- Fiction 2. Love -- Fiction 3. Sisters -- Fiction

    1442426705; 9781442426702, $17.99; 9781442426719

                    LC 2013022311

In this book, by Jenny Han, "Lara Jean Song keeps her love letters in a hatbox. . . . They aren't love letters that anyone else wrote for her; these are ones she's written. One for every boy she's ever loved—five in all. When she writes, she pours out her heart and soul and says all the things she would never say in real life, because her letters are for her eyes only. Until the day her secret letters are mailed, and suddenly, Lara Jean's love life goes from imaginary to out of control." (Publisher's note)

"Lara Jean writes letters to boys she's liked without thinking they'll ever be sent. When she discovers that the letters have been mailed, she pretends to date one of those boys to save face in front of another (who also dated her studying-abroad sister). What follows is a sweet, honest, and beautifully written story about sisterly bonds and true first love." Horn Book

Other titles in this series are:

P.S. I still love you (2015)

Always and forever, Lara Jean (2017)

Hand, Cynthia

★ **My** Lady Jane. Cynthia Hand, Brodi Ashton, and Jodi Meadows. Harpercollins Childrens Books 2016 512 p.

Grades: 7 8 9 10 11

1. Kings and rulers -- Fiction 2. Courts and courtiers -- Fiction 3. Grey, Jane, -- Lady, -- 1537-1554 -- Fiction
0062391747; 9780062391742, $17.99

LC 2015948301

In this novel, by Cynthia Hand, Brodi Ashton, and Jodi Meadows, "at sixteen, Lady Jane Grey is about to be married off to a stranger and caught up in a conspiracy to rob her cousin, King Edward, of his throne. But those trifling problems aren't for Jane to worry about. Jane gets to be Queen of England. Like that could go wrong." (Publisher's note)

"Wonky, offbeat, and happily anachronistic-the references run the gamut from Shakespeare to Monty Python, with plenty of nods to The Princess Bride-this fantasy adventure politely tips its hat to history before joyfully punting it out of the way. An utter delight." Booklist

My plain Jane. Cynthia Hand, Brodi Ashton, Jodi Meadows. HarperTeen, an imprint of HarperCollinsPublishers 2018 Xi, 450 p.

Grades: 7 8 9 10 11

1. Eyre, Jane (Fictitious character); 2. Ghost stories; 3. Supernatural -- Fiction; 4. Governesses -- Fiction
9780062652799; 9780062652775, $17.99

LC 2018933339

In this novel, by Cynthia Hand, Brodi Ashton and Jodi Meadows, "you may think you know the story. Penniless orphan Jane Eyre begins a new life as a governess at Thornfield Hall, where she meets one dark, brooding Mr. Rochester -- and, Reader, she marries him. Or does she? Prepare for an adventure of Gothic proportions in this standalone follow-up to 'My Lady Jane.'" (Publisher's note)

"A fun, supernatural mashup of different literary novels that shines on its own merit." Kirkus

Unearthly; [by] Cynthia Hand. HarperTeen 2011 435p $17.99

Grades: 7 8 9 10

1. School stories 2. Angels -- Fiction 3. Moving -- Fiction 4. Wyoming -- Fiction 5. Supernatural -- Fiction
ISBN 978-0-06-199616-0; 0-06-199616-5

LC 2010-17849

Sixteen-year-old Clara Gardner's purpose as an angel-blood begins to manifest itself, forcing her family to pull up stakes and move to Jackson, Wyoming, where she learns that danger and heartbreak come with her powers.

"Hand avoids overt discussion of religion while telling an engaging and romantic tale with a solid backstory. Her characters deal realistically with the uncertainty of being on the cusp of maturity without wrapping themselves in angst." Publ Wkly

Hannan, Peter

My big mouth; 10 songs I wrote that almost got me killed. Scholastic Press 2011 235p il $16.99

Grades: 6 7 8 9

1. School stories 2. Bullies -- Fiction 3. Rock music

-- Fiction 4. Bands (Music) -- Fiction
ISBN 978-0-545-16210-4; 0-545-16210-6

LC 2010034426

"Hannan's abundant cartoons set the tone for the misadventures of Davis Delaware, the new kid in ninth grade. Davis's attempts to blend in quickly land him on the wrong side of school bully Gerald 'the Butcher' when he forms a band with Gerald's cute girlfriend, Molly, and her dweeby friend, Edwin. . . . Hannan's edgy, exaggerated style suits the humor-driven narrative well. Give this to readers who enjoy light, entertaining realistic fiction." SLJ

Handler, Daniel, 1970-

★ **Why** we broke up; art by Maira Kalman. Little, Brown 2012 354p il $19.99

Grades: 8 9 10 11 12

1. Man-woman relationship -- Fiction 2. Breaking up (Interpersonal relations) 3. Letters -- Fiction 4. Dating (Social customs) -- Fiction
ISBN 978-0-316-12725-7

LC 2011009714

Printz Honor Book (2012)

Sixteen-year-old Min Green writes a letter to Ed Slaterton in which she breaks up with him, documenting their relationship and how items in the accompanying box, from bottle caps to a cookbook, foretell the end.

Hardinge, Frances

Cuckoo Song. Frances Hardinge. Amulet Books 2014 416 p.

Grades: 9 10 11 12

1. Families -- England 2. Family life -- England 3. Fantasy 4. Magicians 5. Memory -- Fiction 6. Paranormal fiction 7. Supernatural 8. Great Britain -- History -- George V, 1910-1936 9. Identity (Psychology) -- Fiction 10. Horror fiction
9781419714801, $17.95; 9780330519731; 0330519735; 1419714805

LC 2014045264

In this suspense novel, by Frances Hardinge, "when Triss wakes up after an accident, she knows that something is very wrong. She is insatiably hungry; her sister seems scared of her and her parents whisper behind closed doors. She looks through her diary to try to remember, but the pages have been ripped out. Soon Triss discovers that what happened to her is more strange and terrible than she could ever have imagined, and that she is quite literally not herself." (Publisher's note)

"Nuanced and intense, this painstakingly created tale mimics the Escher-like constructions of its villainous Architect, fooling the eyes and entangling the emotions of readers willing and able to enter into a world like no other." Kirkus

★ A **face** like glass. By Frances Hardinge. Amulet Books 2017 487 p.

Grades: 6 7 8 9 10

1. Underground areas -- Fiction; 2. Masks (Facial) -- Fiction; 3. Emotions -- Fiction; 4. Fantasy fiction
9781683350781; 1419724843; 9781419724848, $19.95

LC 2016037692

In this book, by Frances Hardinge, "in the underground city of Caverna, the world's most skilled craftsmen toil in the darkness to create delicacies beyond compare.... On the surface, the people of Caverna seem ordinary, except for one thing: their faces are as blank as untouched snow.... Into this dark and distrustful world comes Neverfell, a girl with no memory of her past and a face so terrifying to those around her that she must wear a mask at all times. " (Publisher's note)

"Hardinge's characteristically lush and sophisticated language will entrance readers, and she makes wonderful use of her singular setting and wildly eccentric cast to pose haunting questions about reality, artifice, and the things we attempt to conceal." Pub Wkly

Originally published 2013 in the U.K.

★ The **Lie** Tree. Frances Hardinge. Amulet Books 2016 416 p.

Grades: 7 8 9 10 11 12

 1. Murder -- Fiction 2. Secrets -- Fiction 3. Scientists -- Fiction

 1419718959; 9781419718953, $17.95

LC 2015028326

Boston Globe-Horn Book Award: Fiction (2016)

In this book, by Frances Hardinge, "Faith Sunderly leads a double life. To most people, she is . . . a proper young lady. . . . But inside, Faith is full of questions and curiosity, and she cannot resist mysteries. . . . She knows that her family moved to the close-knit island of Vane because her famous scientist father was fleeing a reputation-destroying scandal. And she knows, when her father is discovered dead shortly thereafter, that he was murdered." (Publisher's note)

"Smart, feminist, and shadowy, Hardinge's talents are on full display here." SLJ

Originally published in the United Kingdom by Macmillan Children's Books, 2015

★ A **skinful** of shadows. Frances Hardinge. Amulet Books 2017 415 p.

Grades: 7 8 9 10

 1. Families -- Fiction; 2. Family secrets -- Fiction; 3. Friendship -- Fiction; 4. Girls -- Fiction; 5. Identity (Psychology) -- Fiction; 6. Inheritance and succession -- Fiction; 7. Spirit possession -- Fiction; 8. Great Britain -- History -- Civil War, 1642-1649 -- Fiction; 9. Ghost stories; 10. Fantasy fiction; 11. Horror fiction

 9781419725722, $19.99; 9781683351061

LC 2017039466

This historical fantasy, by Frances Hardinge, is "set in the early part of the English Civil War. Makepeace is an illegitimate daughter of the aristocratic Fellmotte family, and as such, she shares their unique hereditary gift: the capacity to be possessed by ghosts. Reluctant to accept her appointed destiny as vessel for a coterie of her ancestors, she escapes. As she flees the pursuing Fellmottes across war-torn England, she accumulates a motley crew of her own allies." (Publisher's note)

"Hardinge's writing is stunning, and readers will be taken hostage by its intensity, fascinating developments, and the fierce, compassionate girl leading the charge." Booklist

Originally published in hardcover by Macmillan Publishers Limited, United Kingdom, in 2017.

Hardy, Janice

The **shifter**. Balzer + Bray 2009 370p (The Healing Wars) $16.99; pa $7.99

Grades: 7 8 9 10

 1. War stories 2. Fantasy fiction 3. Orphans -- Fiction 4. Sisters -- Fiction

 ISBN 978-0-06-174704-5; 0-06-174704-1; 978-0-06-174708-3 pa; 0-06-174708-4 pa

LC 2008-47673

Nya is an orphan struggling for survival in a city crippled by war. She is also a Taker—with her touch, she can heal injuries, pulling pain from another person into her own body. But unlike her sister, Tali, and the other Takers who become Healers' League apprentices, Nya's skill is flawed: She can't push that pain into pynvium, the enchanted metal used to store it. All she can do is shift it into another person

"The ethical dilemmas raised . . . provide thoughtful discussion material and also make the story accessible to more than just fantasy readers." Booklist

Other titles in this series are:
Blue fire (2010)
Darkfall (2011)

Harland, Richard

Worldshaker. Simon & Schuster Books for Young Readers 2010 388p $16.99

Grades: 6 7 8 9 10

 1. Fantasy fiction 2. Social classes -- Fiction

 ISBN 978-1-4169-9552-4; 1-4169-9552-8

LC 2009-16924

Sixteen-year-old Col Porpentine is being groomed as the next Commander of Worldshaker, a juggernaut where elite families live on the upper decks while the Filthies toil below, but when he meets Riff, a Filthy girl on the run, he discovers how ignorant he is of his home and its residents.

"Harland's steampunk alternate history is filled with oppression, class struggle, and war, showing their devastation on a personal level through Col's privileged eyes. . . . The writing is sharp and the story fast-paced, demonstrating that, despite his elite status, Col may be just as trapped as any Filthy." Publ Wkly

Harmel, Kristin

When you wish; [by] Kristin Harmel. 1st ed.; Delacorte Press 2008 273p $15.99; lib bdg $18.99

Grades: 7 8 9 10

 1. Fame -- Fiction 2. Singers -- Fiction 3. Father-daughter relationship -- Fiction 4. Mother-daughter relationship -- Fiction

 ISBN 978-0-385-73475-2; 0-385-73475-1; 978-0-385-90474-2 lib bdg; 0-385-90474-6 lib bdg

LC 2007020472

When sixteen-year-old pop singing sensation Star Beck learns that her father, who left when she was three, has been writing to her for six years, she disguises herself, leaves her controlling mother and adoring fans behind, and goes to find him—and, perhaps, a normal life—in St. Petersburg, Florida.

"Harmel has created a character and a story that will have wide appeal. There is enough complexity to hold the interest of a more demanding reader, even while remaining basically an entertaining reading experience." KLIATT

Harness, Cheryl

Just for you to know. HarperCollins 2006 308p $16.99; lib bdg $17.89

Grades: 5 6 7 8

　　1. Death -- Fiction 2. Family life -- Fiction

　　ISBN 0-06-078313-3; 0-06-078314-1 lib bdg

　　　　　　　　　　　　　　　　　LC 2006-281855

In Independence, Missouri, in 1963, twelve-year-old Carmen already has her hands full dealing with a dreamy mother, a sometimes reckless father, and five noisy little brothers, but must find a way to hold onto her own dreams when tragedy strikes.

"Carmen's pain and loneliness are brought to life through her narrative. The writing flows nicely." SLJ

Harrington, Hannah

Speechless; Hannah Harrington. Harlequin Teen 2012 268 p. (paperback) $9.99

Grades: 9 10 11 12

　　1. Gossip -- Fiction 2. Bullies -- Fiction 3. Hate crimes -- Fiction 4. Schools -- Fiction 5. Secrets -- Fiction 6. Bullying -- Fiction 7. High schools -- Fiction 8. Interpersonal relations -- Fiction

　　ISBN 0373210523; 9780373210527

　　　　　　　　　　　　　　　　　LC 2012471034

"Chelsea Knot falls from the top of her high school's social ladder to hated loser in one night when she informs the police of an attack on a gay student by a couple of popular basketball players. It's partially her fault she instigated the attack by gossiping about the teen and spreading his secret to the student body. Trapped between guilt and broken pride, Chelsea takes a vow of silence to keep herself from causing any more harm." (Booklist)

Harris, Joanne

Runemarks. Alfred A. Knopf 2008 526p map $18.99; lib bdg $21.99

Grades: 7 8 9 10 11 12

　　1. Fantasy fiction 2. Magic -- Fiction 3. Norse mythology -- Fiction

　　ISBN 978-0-375-84444-7; 978-0-375-94444-4 lib bdg; 0-375-84444-9; 0-375-94444-3 lib bdg

　　　　　　　　　　　　　　　　　LC 2007-28928

Maddy Smith, who bears the mysterious mark of a rune on her hand, learns that she is destined to join the gods of Norse mythology and play a role in the fate of the world.

"Harris demonstrates a knack for moving seamlessly between the serious and comic. . . . She creates a glorious and complex world replete with rune-based magic spells, bickering gods, exciting adventures, and difficult moral issues." Publ Wkly

Harrison, Margot

The killer in me. Margot Harrison. Disney-Hyperion 2016 368 p.

Grades: 9 10 11 12

　　1. Mystery and detective stories 2. Serial murderers -- Fiction 3. Survival -- Fiction 4. Survival skills -- Fiction 5. Serial killers -- Fiction 6. Mystery fiction

　　9781484727997, $17.99; 9781484728512

　　　　　　　　　　　　　　　　　LC 2015030822

"Seventeen-year-old Nina Barrows knows all about the Thief. She's intimately familiar with his hunting methods: how he stalks and kills at random, how he disposes of his victims' bodies in an abandoned mine in the deepest, most desolate part of a desert. Now, for the first time, Nina has the chance to do something about the serial killer that no one else knows exists." (Publisher's note)

"Taut storytelling and believable characters make this a standout mystery, with paranormal notes adding another layer of complexity." Pub Wkly

Harrison, Rory

Looking for group. Rory Harrison. HarperTeen 2017 356 p.

Grades: 9 10 11 12

　　1. Cancer -- Patients -- Fiction; 2. Drug addiction -- Fiction; 3. Gay teenagers -- Fiction; 4. Gender identity -- Fiction; 5. Interpersonal relations -- Fiction; 6. Transgender people -- Fiction; 7. LGBT people -- Fiction; 8. Cancer patients -- Fiction

　　9780062453099; 0062453076; 9780062453075, $17.99

　　　　　　　　　　　　　　　　　LC 2017288674

This book, by Rory Harrison, "recounts one boy's quest to discover a world where he can thrive, one adventure at a time. Dylan doesn't have a lot of experience with comfort.... His only escape has been in the form of his favorite video game -- World of Warcraft -- and the one true friend who makes him feel understood, even if it is just online: Arden. And now that Dylan is suddenly in remission, he wants to take Arden on a real mission, one he never thought he'd live to set out on." (Publisher's note)

"This book is a triumph, allowing honesty, excitement, humor, and heart to step over gender and sexuality constraints and tell a beautiful story." Kirkus

Harstad, Johan

★ **172** hours on the moon; Johan Harstad; translation by Tara F. Chace. Little, Brown and Company 2012 351 p. $17.99

Grades: 9 10 11 12

　　1. Horror fiction 2. Science fiction 3. Moon -- Fiction 4. Astronauts -- Fiction 5. Space flight to the moon -- Fiction 6. United States. National Aeronautics and Space Administration -- Fiction

　　ISBN 0316182885; 9780316182881

　　　　　　　　　　　　　　　　　LC 2011025414

This novel by Johan Harstad tells of "three teenagers [who] join an expedition to the Moon in 2019 and find horror there.... [They are] Mia, a Norwegian punk rocker, Midori, a Japanese girl rebelling against her restrictive culture, and Antoine, a French boy devastated by a broken romance. . . . The group intends to shelter for a week in a previously secret lab that NASA had established on the Moon in the 1970s. As soon as the group arrives, however, things start to go horribly wrong." (Kirkus Reviews)

Hartinger, Brent

Geography Club. HarperTempest 2003 226p hardcover o.p. pa $8.99

Grades: 9 10 11 12

　　1. School stories 2. Clubs -- Fiction 3. LGBT youth

-- Fiction

ISBN 0-06-001221-8; 0-06-001223-4 pa

LC 2001-51736

A group of gay and lesbian teenagers finds mutual support when they form the "Geography Club" at their high school.

"Hartinger grasps the melodrama and teen angst of high school well. . . . Frank language and the intimation of sexual activity might put off some readers." Voice Youth Advocates

Other titles in this series are:

The Order of the Poison Oak (2005)

Split screen (2007)

Project Sweet Life. HarperTeen 2009 282p $16.99

Grades: 6 7 8 9

1. Friendship -- Fiction 2. Summer employment -- Fiction

ISBN 978-0-06-082411-2; 0-06-082411-5

LC 2008-19644

When their fathers insist that they get summer jobs, three fifteen-year-old friends in Tacoma, Washington, dedicate their summer vacation to fooling their parents into thinking that they are working, which proves to be even harder than having real jobs would have been.

This "will keep readers laughing and engaged." SLJ

Three truths and a lie. Brent Hartinger. Simon Pulse 2016 272 p.

Grades: 9 10 11 12

1. Dating (Social customs) -- Fiction 2. Friendship -- Fiction 3. Mystery and detective stories 4. Secrets -- Fiction 5. Psychological fiction 6. Mystery fiction

9781481449601, $17.99; 9781481449618; 9781481449625, $15.99

LC 2015042737

In this psychological thriller, by Brent Hartinger, "a weekend retreat in the woods and an innocent game of three truths and a lie go horribly wrong. . . . Truth #1: Rob is thrilled about the weekend trip. . . . Truth #2: Liam, Rob's boyfriend, is nothing short of perfect. . . . Truth #3: Mia has been Liam's best friend for years...long before Rob came along. . . . Truth #4: Galen, Mia's boyfriend, is sweet, handsome, and incredibly charming. . . . One of these truths is a lie." (Publisher's note)

"The story is suspenseful, with excellent pacing, self-aware humor, and a twist that Hartinger pulls off as well as the best slasher films." Kirkus

Hartley, A. J.

Firebrand. A. J. Hartley. Tor Teen 2017 334 p. (Alternative detective)

Grades: 8 9 10 11 12

1. Conspiracies -- Fiction; 2. Refugees -- Fiction; 3. Thieves -- Fiction; 4. Spies -- Fiction; 5. Politicians -- Fiction

9780765388148; 9780765388131, $17.99; 0765388138

In this novel in the Steeplejack series, by A. J. Hartley, "Anglet has blossomed in this sequel, releasing her previously restrained sharp tongue and expanding her emotional range. Even as she learns to put on a neutral face to be a more effective spy, her empathy for those who are suffering and her relentless search for the truth are her most laudable attributes. Readers who come for the tightly plotted mystery will stay for the heroine who does all she can to resist." (Kirkus Reviews)

"Hartley has composed another electrifying fantasy that buzzes with intrigue and timely political and social issues, making this a must-have addition to any collection." Booklist

Sequel to Steeplejack (2016)

★ **Steeplejack**: A Novel. By A. J. Hartley. St. Martin's Press 2016 336 p.

Grades: 8 9 10 11 12

1. Fantasy fiction 2. Mystery fiction 3. Steampunk fiction

9781466891692, $60; 076538342X; 9780765383426, $17.99

"Seventeen-year-old Anglet Sutonga lives repairing the chimneys, towers, and spires of the city of Bar-Selehm. Dramatically different communities live and work alongside each other. . . . When Ang is supposed to meet her new apprentice Berrit, she finds him dead. That same night, the Beacon, an invaluable historical icon, is stolen." (Publisher's note)

"Hartley's (the Darwen Arkwright series) story is a thought-provoking blend of action and intrigue, with a competent and ethical heroine in Ang and a fully imagined setting whose atmosphere and cultural cues also play important roles. The result is an unforgettable page-turner built on surprises and full of potential." Pub Wkly

Hartman, Rachel

★ **Seraphina**; a novel. by Rachel Hartman. Random House 2012 465 p. (hardcover) $17.99

Grades: 7 8 9 10 11 12

1. Fantasy fiction 2. Dragons -- Fiction 3. Kings and rulers -- Fiction 4. Fantasy 5. Music -- Fiction 6. Secrets -- Fiction 7. Identity -- Fiction 8. Courts and courtiers -- Fiction 9. Self-actualization (Psychology) -- Fiction

ISBN 9780375866562; 9780375896583; 9780375966569; 0375866566

LC 2011003015

William C. Morris Award (2013)

Boston Globe-Horn Book Honor: Fiction (2013).

In this book, "[a]fter 40 years of peace between human and dragon kingdoms, their much-maligned treaty is on the verge of collapse. Tensions are already high with an influx of dragons, reluctantly shifted to human forms, arriving for their ruler Ardmagar Comonot's anniversary. But when Prince Rufus is found murdered in the fashion of dragons--that is, his head has been bitten off--things reach a fever pitch." (Booklist)

★ **Shadow** scale. Rachel Hartman. Random House Books for Young Readers 2015 596 p.

Grades: 9 10 11 12

1. Courts and courtiers -- Fiction 2. Fantasy fiction 3. War stories 4. Dragons -- Fiction 5. Magic -- Fiction

0375966579; 9780375866579; 9780375966576, $21.99

In this sequel to her novel "Seraphina," author Rachel Hartman "continues the adventures of that book's eponymous half-dragon, who is now assigned with finding and uniting her fellow 'ityasaari' before the full-blooded dragons can resolve their civil war and mobilize to wipe out the southern human kingdoms. But some ityasaari don't want to be found, and one, who has the power to enter and control minds, would rather see them united for her own bitter purpose." (Publishers Weekly)

From graceful language to high stakes to daring intrigue, this sequel shines with the same originality, invention, and engagement of feeling that captivated readers in Hartman's debut." Horn Book

Sequel to: Seraphina (2012)

★ **Tess** of the road. Rachel Hartman. Random House 2018 536 p.

Grades: 7 8 9 10 11 12

1. Courts and courtiers -- Fiction; 2. Dragons -- Fiction; 3. Runaway teenagers -- Fiction; 4. Sex role -- Fiction

9781101931301; 9781101931288, $18.99; 9781101931295

LC 2016041764

In this book, by Rachel Hartman, edited by Jenna Lettice, "in the medieval kingdom of Goredd, women are expected to be ladies, men are their protectors, and dragons can be whomever they choose. Tess is none of these things.... So Tess's family decide the only path for her is a nunnery. But on the day she is to join the nuns, Tess chooses a different path for herself. She cuts her hair, pulls on her boots, and sets out on a journey." (Publisher's note)

"Like Tess' journey, surprising, rewarding, and enlightening, both a fantasy adventure and a meta discourse on consent, shame, and female empowerment." Kirkus

Hartnett, Sonya, 1968-
Butterfly. Candlewick Press 2010 232p $16.99

Grades: 7 8 9 10 11 12

1. Australia -- Fiction 2. Family life -- Fiction

ISBN 0-7636-4760-8; 978-0-7636-4760-5

LC 2009046549

In 1980s Australia, nearly fourteen-year-old Ariella "Plum" Coyle fears the disapproval of her friends, feels inferior to her older brothers, and hates her awkward, adolescent body but when her glamorous neighbor befriends her, Plum starts to become what she wants to be—until she discovers her neighbor's ulterior motive.

"The deliberate pacing, insight into teen angst, and masterful word choice make this a captivating read to savor." SLJ

Golden Boys. Sonya Hartnett. Candlewick Press 2016 256 p.

Grades: 10 11 12

1. Neighborhood -- Fiction 2. Father-son relationship -- Fiction 3. Domestic fiction

9780763679491, $17.99; 0763679496

In this novel, by Sonya Hartnett, "Colt Jenson and his younger brother . . . have moved to a new, working-class suburb. . . . Their father, Rex, showers them with gifts . . . and makes them the envy of the neighborhood. To the local kids, the Jensons are a family out of a movie, and Rex a hero. . . . But to Colt he's an impossible figure: unbearable, suffocating. Has Colt got Rex wrong, or has he seen some-

thing in his father that will destroy their fragile new lives?" (Publisher's note)

"The menacing dynamics present in so many of the relationships are persistently disquieting but also authentic, and a tone of dread pervades, though in the end, events are understated. Sophisticated teen readers will be wowed by this gorgeous, tension-filled novel, but its more natural audience may be adults." Kirkus

★ **Surrender.** Candlewick Press 2006 248p $16.99; pa $7.99

Grades: 9 10 11 12

1. Dogs -- Fiction 2. Brothers -- Fiction 3. Family life -- Fiction

ISBN 0-7636-2768-2; 07636-3423-9 pa

LC 2005-54259

Michael L. Printz Award honor book, 2007

As he is dying, a twenty-year-old man known as Gabriel recounts his troubled childhood and his strange relationship with a dangerous counterpart named Finnigan.

"From the gripping cover showing a raging inferno to the blood-chilling revelation of the final chapter, this page-turner is a blistering yet dense psychological thriller." Voice Youth Advocates

Thursday's child. Candlewick Press 2002 261p hardcover o.p. pa $7.99

Grades: 7 8 9 10

1. Poverty -- Fiction 2. Australia -- Fiction 3. Farm life -- Fiction 4. Family life -- Fiction

ISBN 0-7636-1620-6; 0-7636-2203-6 pa

LC 2001-25223

Harper Flute recounts her Australian farm family's poverty during the Depression, her father's cowardice, and her younger brother Tin's obsession for digging tunnels and living underground

"This coming-of-age story with allegorical overtones will burrow into young people's deepest hopes and fears, shining light in the darkest inner rooms." Booklist

What the birds see. Candlewick Press 2003 196p $15.99

Grades: 7 8 9 10

1. Missing children -- Fiction

ISBN 0-7636-2092-0

LC 2002-73717

While the residents of his town concern themselves with the disappearance of three children, a lonely, rejected nine-year-old boy worries that he may inherit his mother's insanity

"Tightly composed and ripe with symbolism, this complex book will offer opportunities for rich discussion." SLJ

Hartzler, Aaron
What we saw. Aaron Hartzler. HarperTeen 2015 336 p.

1. Rape -- Fiction 2. Witnesses -- Fiction 3. Parties -- Fiction

9780062338747, $17.99

LC 2015005619

In this novel, by Aaron Hartzler, "inspired by the events in the Steubenville rape case . . . , The party at John Doone's last Saturday night is a bit of a blur. . . . But when a picture of Stacey passed out over Deacon Mills's shoulder appears online the next morning, [and] . . . Stacey levels charges against four of Kate's classmates, the whole town erupts into controversy." (Publisher's note)

"Even minor characters here are carefully conceived, and every bit of dialogue and social media activity is chillingly note-perfect. Classroom scenes and conversations offer frameworks for understanding what has happened and why, but the touch is so light and the narrative voice so strong that even a two-page passage breaking down the sexism in Grease! avoids seeming didactic. A powerful tale of betrayal and a vital primer on rape culture." Kirkus

Harvey, Alyxandra

Haunting Violet. Walker Books for Young Readers 2011 352p $17.99

Grades: 6 7 8 9

1. Ghost stories 2. Mystery fiction 3. Spiritualism -- Fiction 4. Social classes -- Fiction
ISBN 978-0-8027-9839-8; 0-8027-9839-X

LC 2010-31077

Sixteen-year-old Violet Willoughby has been part of her mother's Spiritualist scam since she was nine, but during an 1872 house party in Hampshire, England, she is horrified to learn that she can actually see ghosts, one of whom wants Violet to solve her murder.

"A well-paced, clever and scary supernatural-suspense story." Kirkus

Hearts at stake. Walker & Co. 2010 248p (The Drake chronicles) $16.99; pa $9.99

Grades: 8 9 10 11 12

1. Siblings -- Fiction 2. Vampires -- Fiction 3. Friendship -- Fiction
ISBN 978-0-8027-9840-4; 0-8027-9840-3; 978-0-8027-2074-0 pa; 0-8027-2074-9 pa

LC 2009-23156

As her momentous sixteenth birthday approaches, Solange Drake, the only born female vampire in 900 years, is protected by her large family of brothers and her human best friend Lucy from increasingly persistent attempts on her life by the powerful vampire queen and her followers.

"Witty, sly, and never disappointing." Booklist

Other titles in this series are:

Blood feud (2010)

Out for blood (2011)

Harvey, Sarah N.

Death benefits. Orca Book Publishers 2010 212p pa $12.95

Grades: 6 7 8 9

1. Old age -- Fiction 2. Grandfathers -- Fiction
ISBN 978-1-55469-226-2 pa; 1-55469-226-1 pa

Royce is pressed into service as a caregiver for his ninety-five-year-old grandfather and gradually comes to appreciate the cantankerous old man.

"Harvey's writing is energetic, and Royce's snarky narration is sure to keep readers' attention." Publ Wkly

Plastic. Orca Book Publishers 2010 120p (Orca soundings) pa $9.95

Grades: 7 8 9 10

1. Friendship -- Fiction 2. Plastic surgery -- Fiction
ISBN 978-1-55469-252-1; 1-55469-252-0

Trying to save his best friend from the horrors of plastic surgery, Jack ends up on the front line of a protest of unscrupulous surgeons.

"This novel is characteristically fast paced and of high interest. Information about both the pros and the cons of plastic surgery is included without detracting from the plot. Plastic does a good job of exploring an important societal issue while telling a timely tale." SLJ

Hassan, Michael

★ **Crash** and Burn; by Michael Hassan. 1st ed. Balzer + Bray 2013 544 p. (hardcover) $14.99

Grades: 9 10 11 12

1. School stories 2. School shootings -- Fiction 3. Schools -- Fiction 4. Violence -- Fiction 5. High schools -- Fiction 6. Emotional problems -- Fiction 7. Interpersonal relations -- Fiction
ISBN 0062112929; 9780062112903

LC 2012004280

In this book, "Steven 'Crash' Crashinsky becomes a hero when he saves more than a thousand people at his high school by confronting his armed and dangerous classmate, David 'Burn' Burnett, during a chilling hostage situation. Crash signs a book deal to write about events leading up to the crisis, his understanding of Burn, and the final secret Burn shared with him that horrible day." (School Library Journal)

Haston, Meg

The **end** of our story. Meg Haston. HarperTeen 2017 280 p.

Grades: 9 10 11 12

1. High school students -- Fiction; 2. Florida -- Fiction; 3. Depression (Psychology) -- Fiction; 4. Mental illness -- Fiction; 5. Interpersonal relations -- Fiction
9780062335791; 9780062335777, $17.99

LC 2016949894

In this book, by Meg Haston, edited by Jennifer Klonsky, "Bridge and Wil have been entangled in each other's lives for years.... But when Bridge betrayed Wil during their junior year, she shattered his heart and their relationship along with it.... When Wil's family suffers a violent loss,... Bridge rushes back to Wil's side. As they struggle to heal old wounds..., Bridge and Wil discover just how much has changed in the past year." (Publisher's note)

Hattemer, Kate

The **vigilante** poets of Selwyn Academy. Alfred A. Knopf 2014 323p $16.99

Grades: 8 9 10 11 12

1. Arts -- Fiction 2. Creative ability -- Fiction 3. Friendship -- Fiction 4. Reality television programs -- Fiction 5. Minnesota -- Fiction 6. Poetry --Fiction 7. School stories
ISBN: 0385753780

LC 2013014325

"Witty, sarcastic Ethan and his three friends decide to take down the reality TV show, 'For Art's Sake,' that is being filmed at their high school, the esteemed Selwyn Arts Academy, where each student is more talented than the next.

While studying Ezra Pound in English class, the friends are inspired to write a vigilante long poem and distribute it to the student body, detailing the evils of 'For Art's Sake.'" (Publisher's note)

"In this place of immense talent, Ethan is immensely relatable as the voice of the average (that is, socially awkward) teen. Hattemer writes with a refreshing narrative style, crafting both believable characters and a cohesive, well-plotted story. Romance, while in the air, takes a sideline to friendship, which proves to be the book's heart and soul. Relying on the passion and ideals that drive adolescence, this has a vibrancy and authenticity that will resonate with anyone who has fought for their beliefs or who has loved a hamster." Booklist

Hautman, Pete

All-in. Simon & Schuster Books for Young Readers 2007 181p hardcover o.p. pa $5.99

Grades: 7 8 9 10

1. Poker -- Fiction 2. Gambling -- Fiction 3. Las Vegas (Nev.) -- Fiction

ISBN 978-1-4169-1325-2; 1-4169-1325-4; 978-1-4169-1326-9 pa; 1-4169-1326-9 pa

LC 2006-23871

Sequel to No limit (2005)

Having won thousands of dollars playing high-stakes poker in Las Vegas, seventeen-year-old Denn Doyle hits a losing streak after falling in love with a young casino card dealer named Cattie Hart.

"Skillfully using the multiple-voice approach, Hautman brings to life the intricacies of poker, crafting a thrilling story of loss, good versus evil, and redemption." Voice Youth Advocates

★ The **big** crunch. Scholastic Press 2011 280p $17.99

Grades: 8 9 10 11 12

1. School stories 2. Dating (Social customs) -- Fiction

ISBN 978-0-545-24075-8; 0-545-24075-1

LC 2010-40011

"Wes Andrews has just ended a suffocating relationship with Izzy. June is new to the school—her sixth in the last four years. Like Wes, she's not looking to get entangled. . . . But in the high-school world of 'users, posers, geeks, skanks, preps, gangstas, macho-morons, punks, burnouts, and so forth,' the two relatively normal, nice kids do find each other . . . eventually. Hautman uses a third-person point of view to weave a humorous and bittersweet tale of romance and the convoluted, uncertain paths that bring two people together. A poignant and quiet tale in which the only special effect is love—refreshing." Kirkus

Blank confession. Simon & Schuster Books for Young Readers 2010 170p $16.99

Grades: 7 8 9 10

1. School stories 2. Bullies -- Fiction 3. Drug traffic -- Fiction

ISBN 978-1-4169-1327-6; 1-4169-1327-0

LC 2009-50169

A new and enigmatic student named Shayne appears at high school one day, befriends the smallest boy in the school, and takes on a notorious drug dealer before turning himself in to the police for killing someone.

"Masterfully written with simple prose, solid dialogue and memorable characters, the tale will grip readers from the start and keep the reading in one big gulp, in the hope of seeing behind Shayne's mask. A sure hit with teen readers." Kirkus

Eden West. Pete Hautman. Candlewick Press 2015 320 p.

Grades: 9 10 11 12

1. Faith --Fiction 3. Cults -- Fiction

0763674184; 9780763674182, $17.99

LC 2014945452

In this book, author Pete Hautman "explores a boy's unraveling allegiance to an insular cult. Twelve square miles of paradise, surrounded by an eight-foot-high chain-link fence: this is Nodd, the land of the Grace. It is all seventeen-year-old Jacob knows. Beyond the fence lies the World, a wicked, terrible place, doomed to destruction. When the Archangel Zerachiel descends from Heaven, only the Grace will be spared the horrors of the Apocalypse. But something is rotten in paradise." (Publisher's note)

"While projecting a unique and expressive voice in Jacob, Hautman sensitively and gracefully explores powerful ideas about faith and church communities, keeping a deft balance between criticism of religious fervor and deep respect for faith and belief. Thought-provoking and quietly captivating." Booklist

★ **Godless.** Simon & Schuster Books for Young Readers 2004 208p $15.95; pa $8.99

Grades: 7 8 9 10

1. Religion -- Fiction

ISBN 0-689-86278-4; 1-4169-0816-1 pa

LC 2003-10468

When sixteen-year-old Jason Bock and his friends create their own religion to worship the town's water tower, what started out as a joke begins to take on a power of its own

"The witty text and provocative subject will make this a supremely enjoyable discussion-starter as well as pleasurable read." Bull Cent Child Books

Hole in the sky. Simon & Schuster Bks. for Young Readers 2001 179p $16; pa $11.95

Grades: 7 8 9 10

1. Science fiction

ISBN 0-689-83118-8; 1-4169-6822-9 pa

LC 00-58324

In a future world ravaged by a mutant virus, sixteen-year-old Ceej and three other teenagers seek to save the Grand Canyon from being flooded, while trying to avoid capture by a band of renegade Survivors

"Readers will appreciate the novel's intense action and fascinating premise." Horn Book Guide

How to steal a car. Scholastic Press 2009 170p $16.99

Grades: 7 8 9 10

1. Theft -- Fiction 2. Family life -- Fiction

ISBN 978-0-545-11318-2; 0-545-11318-0

LC 2008-54146

Fifteen-year-old, suburban high school student Kelleigh, who has her learner's permit, recounts how she began stealing cars one summer, for reasons that seem unclear even to her.

"A sharply observed, subversive coming-of-age tale." Kirkus

★ **Invisible**. Simon & Schuster Books for Young Readers 2005 149p $15.95; pa $7.99
Grades: 7 8 9 10
    1. Friendship -- Fiction 2. Mental illness -- Fiction
ISBN 0-689-86800-6; 0-689-86903-7 pa
                        LC 2004-2484
Doug and Andy are unlikely best friends—one a loner obsessed by his model trains, the other a popular student involved in football and theater—who grew up together and share a bond that nothing can sever

"With its excellent plot development and unforgettable, heartbreaking protagonist, this is a compelling novel of mental illness." SLJ

★ The **obsidian** blade; Pete Hautman. Candlewick Press 2012 308 p. (Klaatu Diskos)
Grades: 7 8 9 10 11 12
    1. Science fiction 2. Uncles -- Fiction 3. Time travel -- Fiction 4. Missing persons -- Fiction 5. Religion -- Fiction 6. Supernatural -- Fiction 8. Space and time -- Fiction
ISBN 9780763654030
                        LC 2011018617
In this book, which is the first in a series, "[o]ne day Tucker sees his father disappear through a strange disk in the air and then come back an hour later changed, . . . but offering no explanation. . . . Tucker . . . realizes that . . . the disks . . . appear to be portals to other times and places. The disks are unpredictable, though, and their passages seem to lead to sites where violent, traumatic events are occurring." (Bulletin of the Center for Children's Books)
    Other titles in this series are:
    The Cydonian pyramid (2013)
    The Klaatu terminus (2014)

Snatched; [by] Pete Hautman and Mary Logue. Putnam 2006 200p (Bloodwater mysteries) $15.99
Grades: 7 8 9 10
    1. Mystery fiction 2. Kidnapping -- Fiction
ISBN 0-399-24377-1
                        LC 2005-28558
Too curious for her own good, Roni, crime reporter for her high school newspaper, teams up with Brian, freshman science geek, to investigate the beating and kidnapping of a classmate.

"Give this solid marks for plotting and characterization, as well as for suspense." Booklist
    Other titles in this series are:
    Skullduggery (2007)
    Doppelganger (2008)

★ **Sweetblood**. Simon & Schuster Bks. for Young Readers 2003 180p $16.95; pa $6.99

Grades: 7 8 9 10
    1. Diabetes -- Fiction
ISBN 0-689-85048-4; 0-689-87324-7 pa
                        LC 2002-11179
"Lucy Szabo has been an insulin-dependent diabetic since she was 6, and now, at age 16, she has developed an interesting theory that links vampirism with diabetic ketoacidosis." SLJ

"Hautman does an outstanding job of making Lucy's theory and her struggle to accept herself credible. . . . Lucy's clever, self-deprecating voice is endlessly original." Booklist

What boys really want? Pete Hautman. Scholastic Press 2012 297 p. (hbk.) $17.99
Grades: 8 9 10 11
    1. Friendship -- Fiction 2. High school students -- Fiction 3. Dating (Social customs) -- Fiction 4. Jealousy -- Fiction 5. Plagiarism -- Fiction 6. Interpersonal relations -- Fiction
ISBN 0545113156; 9780545113151
                        LC 2011278706
In this book, "Lita has never told Adam that she is behind the snarky and irreverent teen advice blog 'Miz Fitz,' or that she has basically sabotaged all of his romantic relationships. . . . Adam hasn't confided the fact that he's getting most of his information for his . . . book on what boys want from girls . . . from the internet, specifically Miz Fitz's blog. As Adam barrels forward with his project, Lita . . . [is] jealous: writing is her territory, not his." (Bulletin of the Center for Children's Books)

"The book moves along at a snappy pace...This is fresh, realistic YA fiction at its best." SLJ

Hawkins, Rachel
    Hex Hall. Disney/Hyperion Books 2010 323p $16.99
Grades: 7 8 9 10
    1. School stories 2. Witches -- Fiction 3. Supernatural -- Fiction
ISBN 1423121309; 9781423121305
When Sophie attracts too much human attention for a prom-night spell gone horribly wrong, she is exiled to Hex Hall, an isolated reform school for witches, faeries, and shapeshifters. "Grades seven to ten." (Bull Cent Child Books)

"Sixteen-year-old Sophie Mercer, whose absentee father is a warlock, discovered both her heritage and her powers at age 13. While at her school prom, Sophie happens upon a miserable girl sobbing in the bathroom and tries to perform a love spell to help her out. It misfires, and Sophie finds herself at Hecate (aka Hex) Hall, a boarding school for delinquent Prodigium (witches, warlocks, faeries, shape-shifters, and the occasional vampire). What makes this fast-paced romp work is Hawkins' wry humor and sharp eye for teen dynamics." Booklist
    Other titles in this series are:
    Demonglass (2101)
    Spell bound (2012)
    School spirits (2013)

Haydu, Corey Ann

★ **OCD** love story; Corey Ann Haydu. Simon Pulse 2013 352 p. (alk. paper) $17.99

Grades: 9 10 11 12

　1. Love stories 2. Obsessive-compulsive disorder -- Fiction 3. Psychotherapy -- Fiction 4. Interpersonal relations -- Fiction

　ISBN 1442457325; 9781442457324

LC 2012021545

In this book, when "Bea kisses a strange boy during a blackout at a school dance, it's clear she's a little eccentric, but it isn't until her therapist slips several pamphlets about OCD into Bea's hands that" her problem becomes clear. "Bea's need to perform certain rituals, even at the risk of alienating those she loves, becomes all-consuming. The one bright spot in Bea's life is a budding romance with Beck, the boy from the school dance, who resurfaces in Bea's group-therapy sessions." (Kirkus Reviews)

"Bea and Beck both have debilitating obsessive-compulsive disorder. As they begin dating, they must navigate their feelings for each other and the complications of their individual compulsions. Thanks to some leaps of faith and a lot of therapy, the teens get a happy ending. Haydu explores a sweet, unconventional romance in this compulsively readable novel." (Horn Book)

Headley, Justina Chen

★ **North** of beautiful. Little, Brown 2009 373p $16.99

Grades: 7 8 9 10 11 12

　1. Aesthetics -- Fiction

　ISBN 978-0-316-02505-8; 0-316-02505-4

LC 2008-09260

Headley's "finely crafted novel traces a teen's uncharted quest to find beauty. Two things block Terra's happiness: a port-wine stain on her face and her verbally abusive father. . . . A car accident brings her together with Jacob, an Asian-born adoptee with unconventional ideas. . . . The author confidently addresses very large, slippery questions about the meaning of art, travel, love and of course, beauty." Publ Wkly

Healey, Karen

Guardian of the dead. Little, Brown 2010 345p $17.99

Grades: 9 10 11 12

　1. School stories 2. Magic -- Fiction 3. Maoris -- Fiction 4. Fairies -- Fiction 5. New Zealand -- Fiction

　ISBN 978-0-316-04430-1

LC 2009-17949

Eighteen-year-old New Zealand boarding school student Ellie Spencer must use her rusty tae kwon do skills and newfound magic to try to stop a fairy-like race of creatures from Maori myth and legend that is plotting to kill millions of humans in order to regain their lost immortality.

"Fast-paced adventure and an unfamiliar, frightening enemy set a new scene for teen urban fantasy." Kirkus

The **shattering**. Little, Brown 2011 311p $17.99

Grades: 7 8 9 10

　1. Mystery fiction 2. Suicide -- Fiction 3. Homicide -- Fiction 4. New Zealand -- Fiction 5. Supernatural

-- Fiction

　ISBN 978-0-316-12572-7; 0-316-12572-5

LC 2010047996

When a rash of suicides disturbs Summerton, an oddly perfect tourist town on the west coast of New Zealand, the younger siblings of the dead boys become suspicious and begin an investigation that reveals dark secrets and puts them in grave danger.

"Juggling multiple viewpoints, Healey skillfully keeps her characters on an emotional roller-coaster even as they deal with physical threats. The climax delivers a gut punch that only underscores the sensitivity of the subject matter (without lessening the thrill at all)." Publ Wkly

When we wake. Little, Brown Books for Young Readers 2013 304 p. (hardcover) $17.99

Grades: 7 8 9 10 11 12

　1. Science fiction 2. Dystopian fiction 3. Australia -- Fiction

　ISBN 031620076X; 9780316200769

LC 2012028739

"Sixteen-year-old Tegan is just like every other girl living in 2027--But on what should have been the best day of Tegan's life, she dies--and wakes up a hundred years in the future, locked in a government facility with no idea what happened. . . . But the future isn't all she hoped it would be, and when . . . secrets come to light, Tegan must make a choice: Does she keep her head down and survive, or fight for a better future?" (Publisher's note)

While we run. Little Brown & Co. 2014 336p $18.00

Grades: 7 8 9 10 11 12

　1. Cryonics -- Fiction 2. Science fiction 3. Australia--Fiction

　ISBN: 031623382X; 9780316233828

LC 2013022281

This is a sequel to When we wake. In the previous installment " Tegan and Abdi revealed the government's plan to populate a new planet with cryogenically frozen slaves. Abdi begins narrating six months after their capture by the government. Like its predecessor, Run succeeds simply as a sci-fi thriller, but it's elevated by its social commentary, emphasizing the importance of fighting for justice in a world that has little of it." Horn Book

Hearn, Julie

Hazel; a novel. Atheneum Books for Young Readers 2009 389p $17.99

Grades: 8 9 10 11

　1. Slavery -- Fiction 2. Social classes -- Fiction 3. Racially mixed people -- Fiction

　ISBN 978-1-4169-2504-0; 1-4169-2504-X

LC 2008-53961

Thirteen-year-old Hazel leaves her comfortable, if somewhat unconventional, London home in 1913 after her father has a breakdown, and goes to live in the Caribbean on her grandparents' sugar plantation where she discovers some shocking family secrets.

"Hearn's characters vividly reveal class distinctions and racial prejudices prevalent in 1913." Voice Youth Advocates

★ **Ivy**; a novel. Atheneum Books for Young Readers 2008 355p $17.99; pa $9.99

Grades: 8 9 10 11 12

1. Artists -- Fiction 2. Criminals -- Fiction 3. Drug abuse -- Fiction 4. London (England) -- Fiction 5. Great Britain -- History -- 19th century -- Fiction

ISBN 978-1-4169-2506-4; 1-4169-2506-6; 978-1-4169-2507-1 pa; 1-4169-2507-4 pa

LC 2007-045463

In mid-nineteenth-century London, young, mistreated, and destitute Ivy, whose main asset is her beautiful red hair, comes to the attention of an aspiring painter of the pre-Raphaelite school of artists who, with the connivance of Ivy's unsavory family, is determined to make her his model and muse.

"Quirky characters, darkly humorous situations, and quick action make this enjoyable historical fiction." SLJ

The **minister's** daughter. Atheneum Books for Young Readers 2005 263p hardcover o.p. pa $7.99

Grades: 7 8 9 10

1. Witchcraft -- Fiction 2. Supernatural -- Fiction 3. Salem (Mass.) -- Fiction 4. Great Britain -- History -- 1642-1660, Civil War and Commonwealth -- Fiction

ISBN 0-689-87690-4; 0-689-87691-2 pa

LC 2004-18324

In 1645 in England, the daughters of the town minister successfully accuse a local healer and her granddaughter of witchcraft to conceal an out-of-wedlock pregnancy, but years later during the 1692 Salem trials their lie has unexpected repercussions.

"With its thought-provoking perceptions about human nature, magic and persecution, this tale will surely cast a spell over readers." Publ Wkly

Heath, Jack

The **Lab**. Scholastic Press 2008 311p $17.99

Grades: 7 8 9 10

1. Science fiction 2. Adventure fiction 3. Spies -- Fiction 4. Genetic engineering -- Fiction

ISBN 978-0-545-06860-4; 0-545-06860-6

"A gritty dystopic world exists under the iron rule of the mega-corporation Chao-Sonic, with only a few vigilante groups around to act as resistance. Six of Hearts is easily the best agent on one such group, the Deck, and he is fiercely dedicated to justice, using his extensive genetic modifications to his advantage. . . . The compelling and memorable protagonist stands out even against the intricately described and disturbing city whose vividness makes the place's questionable fate a suspenseful issue in its own right." Bull Cent Child Books

Followed by: Remote control (2010)

Money run; by Jack Heath. 1st American ed. Scholastic Press 2013 245 p. (hardcover) $17.99

Grades: 8 9 10

1. Crime -- Fiction 2. Adventure fiction 3. Stealing -- Fiction 4. Assassins -- Fiction 5. Theft -- Fiction 6. Thieves -- Fiction 7. Robbers and outlaws -- Fiction

ISBN 0545512662; 9780545512664

LC 2013004005

In this book, "Ashley and Benjamin are two teen partners in crime--real crime, as in major heists--who rely on their youth to avoid suspicion. . . . Their prey today happens to be a billionaire businessman who has sponsored an essay contest with a prize of $10,000 (Ash has won with an essay ghostwritten by Benjamin), but that's peanuts compared to the $2 million they hope to loot." (Kirkus Reviews)

Remote control. Scholastic Press 2010 326p $17.99

Grades: 7 8 9 10

1. Science fiction 2. Adventure fiction 3. Spies -- Fiction 4. Genetic engineering -- Fiction

ISBN 978-0-545-07591-6; 0-545-07591-2

Sequel to: The Lab (2008)

First published 2007 in Australia

Agent Six of Hearts, 16-year-old superhuman, is on a mission. His brother Kyntak has been kidnapped. A strange and sinister new figure is rising in power. Six is suspected of being a double agent. The Deck has been put into lockdown by the Queen of Spades. A mysterious girl has appeared who acts as Six's guardian angel. Who can he trust?

"The technothriller begun in The Lab (2008) takes several intriguing twists . . . on its way to a satisfying, if temporary, resolution." Booklist

Heathfield, Lisa

Seed. Lisa Heathfield. Running Press Teens 2015 336 p.

Grades: 7 8 9 10

1. Teenage girls -- Fiction 2. Communal living -- Fiction 3. Cults -- Fiction 4. Hi-Lo books

9780762456345, $16.95

LC 2014949872

In this young adult novel, by Lisa Heathfield, "Seed is at the center of 15-year-old Pearl's life: it is the isolated family of which she is part . . . and . . . the remote patch of land . . . where she sows and gathers crops. . . . She does not often leave because . . . Seed is pure and leaving risks contact with poisoned Outsiders who may taint Pearl's spiritual core. . . . But when three Outsiders unexpectedly join the family, . . . Pearl's entire reality is challenged." (School Library Journal)

"Well-developed secondary characters and Heathfield's willingness to do serious damage to central ones make this novel a powerful read." Pub Wkly

Hegedus, Bethany

Between us Baxters. WestSide Books 2009 306p $17.95

Grades: 7 8 9 10

1. Friendship -- Fiction 2. Race relations -- Fiction

ISBN 978-1-934813-02-7; 1-934813-02-8

"In 1959, in Holcolm County, GA, there is a palpable tension. Times are slowly changing, causing resentment among some folks and optimism among others. The volatile mix sets the tone for this story of family, friendship, and racial discrimination. . . .When suspicious fires, vandalism, and threats to successful black business owners cause fear and distrust among the townspeople, the strength of Polly and Timbre Ann's bond is tested. . . . The connection between the two girls and their families is beautifully described and believable, and the richness of the characters is apparent.

The pacing of the story is deliberate and suspenseful with twists and turns that add to the bittersweet conclusion." SLJ

Heilig, Heidi

For a muse of fire. By Heidi Heilig. Greenwillow Books, an imprint of HarperCollins Publishers 2018 512 p.

Grades: 9 10 11 12

    1. Fantasy; 2. Magic -- Fiction; 3. Manic-depressive illness -- Fiction; 4. Mental illness -- Fiction; 5. Theater -- Fiction; 6. Fantasy fiction

9780062380814, $17.99

                                 LC 2018008135

In this book, by Heidi Heilig, "Jetta's family is famed as the most talented troupe of shadow players in the land. With Jetta behind the scrim, their puppets seem to move without string or stick.... Her skill and fame are her family's way to earn a spot aboard the royal ship to Aquitan.... But as rebellion seethes and as Jetta meets a young smuggler, she will face truths and decisions that she never imagined -- and safety will never seem so far away." (Publisher's note)

The **Girl** from Everywhere. Heidi Heilig. Harper-collins Childrens Books 2016 464 p.

Grades: 9 10 11 12

    1. Fantasy fiction 2. Sea stories 3. Time travel -- Fiction

0062380753; 9780062380753, $17.99

                                 LC 2015035884

This young adult fantasy novel, by Heidi Heilig, "sweeps from modern-day New York City, to nineteenth-century Hawaii, to places of myth and legend. Sixteen-year-old Nix has sailed across the globe and through centuries aboard her time-traveling father's ship. But when he gambles with her very existence, it all may be about to end." (Publisher's note)

"With time travel, fantasy, Hawaiian history, mythology, cute animals, and a feisty protagonist, romance and fantasy readers will find much to enjoy in this quick read, which features a conclusion suggesting a sequel." Booklist

Another title in this series is:

The Ship Beyond Time (2017)

Hemmings, Kaui Hart

Juniors. Kaui Hart Hemmings. G.P. Putnam's Sons, an imprint of Penguin Group (USA) 2015 320 p.

Grades: 9 10 11 12

    1. Friendship -- Fiction 2. High schools -- Fiction 3. Interpersonal relations -- Fiction 4. Schools -- Fiction 5. Wealth -- Fiction 6. Hawaii -- Fiction 7. School stories

9780399173608, $18.99

                                 LC 2014040377

In this novel, by Kaui Hart Hemmings, "Lea Lane . . . [is] part Hawaiian, part Mainlander. . . . Hanging in the shadow of her actress mother's spotlight. And now: new resident of the prominent West family's guest cottage. Bracing herself for the embarrassment of being her classmates' latest charity case, Lea is surprised when she starts becoming friends with Will and Whitney West insteador in the case of gorgeous, unattainable Will, possibly even more than friends." (Publisher's note)

"Friendship and romance brush cheek to cheek in a story that deals frankly with race, class, and culture while also managing to wonderfully portray the luminous, dreamlike setting of Hawaii. A perfect complement to the shelves of readers who follow Jenny Han and E. Lockhart." Booklist

Hemphill, Stephanie

Hideous love; the story of the girl who wrote Frankenstein. Stephanie Hemphill. Balzer + Bray, an imprint of HarperCollinsPublishers 2013 320 p. (hardcover bdg.) $17.99

Grades: 9 10 11 12

    1. Novels in verse 2. Historical fiction 3. Love -- Fiction 4. Authorship -- Fiction

ISBN 0061853313; 9780061853319

                                 LC 2013000237

This book is a "fictionalized verse biography of" author Mary Shelley. Stephanie Hemphill "explores the particular challenges facing a gifted female artist who allies herself with a renowned male poet. Central to the plot is the parentage of Mary Wollstonecraft Godwin Shelley, daughter of Mary Wollstonecraft, the pioneering feminist philosopher who died days after Mary was born, and William Godwin, a radical political philosopher who espoused free love for all but his daughters." (Kirkus Reviews)

Sisters of glass; Stephanie Hemphill. Alfred A. Knopf 2012 150 p. $16.99

Grades: 7 8 9 10

    1. Love stories 2. Novels in verse 3. Historical fiction 4. Families -- Fiction 5. Family life -- Fiction 6. Venice (Italy) -- Fiction 7. Venice (Italy) 8. Glass blowing and working -- Fiction

ISBN 0375861092; 0375961097; 9780375861093; 9780375961090

                                 LC 2011277551

This book presents "[a] . . . tale of destiny, fidelity, and true love" set in "fourteenth-century Murano, Italy (of glass-making renown) and . . . told through verse. . . . Maria is disdainful of her training to be a society woman and yearns instead to spend her time with her art or in the family's furnaces with Luca, an employee whose skill with glass is the marvel that leads Maria, who once aspired to be a glassblower, to fall in love with him." (Booklist)

★ **Wicked** girls; a novel of the Salem witch trials. Balzer + Bray 2010 408p il $17.99; lib bdg $17.89

Grades: 7 8 9 10 11 12

    1. Novels in verse 2. Trials -- Fiction 3. Witchcraft -- Fiction 4. Salem (Mass.) -- Fiction

ISBN 0-06-185328-3; 0-06-185329-1 lib bdg; 978-0-06-185328-9; 978-0-06-185329-6 lib bdg

                                 LC 2010-9593

This is "a fictionalized account of the Salem witch trials told from the perspectives of three of the real young women living in Salem in 1692. Ann Putnam Jr. plays the queen bee. When her father suggests that a spate of illnesses within the village is the result of witchcraft, Ann . . . puts in motion a chain of events that will change the lives of the people around her forever. Mercy Lewis, the beautiful servant in Ann's house, inspires adulation in some and envy in others.

With a troubled past, she seizes her only chance at safety. Margaret Walcott, Ann's cousin, is desperately in love and consumed with fiery jealousy. She is torn between staying loyal to her friends and pursuing the life she dreams of with her betrothed." (Publisher's note)

"Hemphill's raw, intimate poetry probes behind the abstract facts and creates characters that pulse with complex emotion." Booklist

Includes bibliographical references

Henderson, Jason

The **Triumph** of Death; Jason Henderson. HarperTeen 2012 310 p.

Grades: 8 9 10 11 12

1. Vampires 2. Occult fiction 3. Adventure fiction 4. Horror stories 5. Witches -- Fiction 6. Vampires -- Fiction 7. Supernatural -- Fiction

ISBN 9780061951039

LC 2012004297

This young adult paranormal adventure, by Jason Henderson, is book three of the "Alex Van Helsing" series. "There is a famous painting in Madrid that holds the key to an apocalypse only Alex Van Helsing can stop . . . [and] a newly risen vampire queen threatens the fate of the world. . . . Teaming up with a motorcycle-riding witch, Alex jets between Switzerland, the UK, and Spain in a frantic race to prevent the queen from . . . [plunging] the world into darkness." (Publisher's note)

★ **Vampire** rising. HarperTeen 2010 249p (Alex Van Helsing) $16.99

Grades: 6 7 8 9 10

1. Horror fiction 2. School stories 3. Vampires -- Fiction 4. Supernatural -- Fiction

ISBN 978-0-06-195099-5; 0-06-195099-8

LC 2009-39663

At a boarding school in Switzerland, fourteen-year-old Alex Van Helsing learns that vampires are real, that he has a natural ability to sense them, and that an agency called the Polidorium has been helping his family fight them since 1821.

"Henderson references Mary Shelley's Frankenstein to weave a great story line full of action, suspense, and adventure. The satisfying story captivates readers with a modern-day spin of James Bond meets Dracula." SLJ

Another title about Alex Van Helsing is:
Voice of the undead (2011)
The Triumph of Death (2012)

Henry, April

Torched. G.P. Putnam's Sons 2009 224p $16.99

Grades: 8 9 10 11

1. Terrorism -- Fiction 2. Environmental movement -- Fiction

ISBN 978-0-399-24645-6; 0-399-24645-2

LC 2008-01145

In order to save her parents from going to jail for possession of marijuana, sixteen-year-old Ellie must help the FBI uncover the intentions of a radical environmental group by going undercover.

"The mix of politics and thrilling action will grab teens. . . . This suspenseful story will spark discussion about what it means to fight for right 'by any means necessary.'" Booklist

Henry, Katie

★ **Heretics** Anonymous. Katie Henry. Katherine Tegen Books, an imprint of HarperCollinsPublishers" 2018 336 p.

Grades: 8 9 10 11 12

1. Catholic schools -- Fiction; 2. Conduct of life -- Fiction; 3. Faith -- Fiction; 4. Family problems -- Fiction; 5. Schools -- Fiction; 6. Self-help groups -- Fiction

9780062698872, $17.99

LC 2017034682

In this book, by Katie Henry, "when Michael walks through the doors of Catholic school, things can't get much worse. His dad has just made the family move again, and Michael needs a friend. When a girl challenges their teacher in class, Michael thinks he might have found one, and a fellow atheist at that. Only this girl, Lucy, isn't just Catholic... she wants to be a priest. Lucy introduces Michael to other St. Clare's outcasts, and he officially joins Heretics Anonymous." (Publisher's note)

"The story adeptly asks readers to question what they believe and why, without being preachy, judgmental, or dismissive. Humor interlaced with more serious ideas make for an interesting and enjoyable read." (School Library Journal)

Hensley, Joy N.

Rites of passage. Joy N. Hensley. HarperTeen 2014 416 p.

Grades: 7 8 9 10

1. Bullying -- Fiction 2. Military training -- Fiction 3. Schools -- Fiction 4. Secret societies -- Fiction 5. Sex role -- Fiction 6. Blue Ridge Mountains -- Fiction 7. Bullies -- Fiction 8. School stories

0062295195; 9780062295194, $17.99

LC 2014010022

In this novel by Joy N. Hensley, "sixteen-year-old Sam McKenna discovers that becoming one of the first girls to attend a revered military academy means living with a target on her back. As Sam struggles to prove herself, she learns that a decades-old secret society is alive and active . . . and determined to force her out." (Publisher's note)

"The narrative flows along terrifically as Sam courageously battles to make it even while the forces against her increase. The characters stand out as individual and real; readers will cheer Sam on throughout. Absolutely compelling." Kirkus

Hepler, Heather

The **cupcake** queen. Dutton 2009 242p $16.99; pa $7.99

Grades: 6 7 8 9

1. Baking -- Fiction 2. Moving -- Fiction 3. Family life -- Fiction

ISBN 978-0-525-42157-3; 0-525-42157-2; 978-0-14-241668-6 pa; 0-14-241668-1 pa

LC 2008-48971

While longing to return to life in New York City, thirteen-year-old Penny helps her mother and grandmother run a cupcake bakery in Hog's Hollow, tries to avoid the beastly popular girls, to be a good friend to quirky Tally, and to catch the eye of enigmatic Marcus.

"An endearing and poignant story about standing up to adversity and finding peace in what it is, rather than holding out for what it could be." Publ Wkly

Heppermann, Christine

★ **Ask** Me How I Got Here. Christine Heppermann. Harpercollins Childrens Books 2016 240 p.
Grades: 9 10 11 12
1. Choice (Psychology) -- Fiction 2. Teenage pregnancy -- Fiction 3. Novels in verse 4. Abortion -- Fiction
0062387952; 9780062387950, $17.99

LC 2016004714

In this novel by Christine Heppermann, "Addie is a good student and the star of the cross-country team at her private Catholic school. When she discovers that she is pregnant, she gets an abortion with the support of her boyfriend and parents. Afterward, she struggles with what the pregnancy and her decision mean, both to her self-perception and those around her, leading Addie to discover more surprising things about herself." (School Library Journal)

"Addie has got a great boyfriend, a fantastic cross-country record at her all-girls Catholic high school, and a powerful talent for poetry. When she gets pregnant, she doesn't face terrible strife: her parents are supportive, her boyfriend isn't angry, and it's over in a flash. But in the aftermath, she finds herself reevaluating many of her choices, especially track, and, surprisingly, deeply drawn to a track-star alumna who is taking a break from both running and college. . . . This absorbing book would be an excellent choice for teen book groups." Booklist

Herbach, Geoff

Nothing special; Geoff Herbach. Sourcebooks Inc. 2012 290 p. (paperback) $9.99; (ebook) $9.99
Grades: 6 7 8 9 10
1. Friendship -- Fiction 2. Dysfunctional families -- Fiction 3. Teenagers -- Conduct of life -- Fiction
ISBN 1402265077; 9781402265075; 9781402265099

In this book, author Geoff Herbach tells the story of Felton, a football and track star who deals with his girlfriend Aleah abroad in Germany and "the possibility that his younger brother Andrew could be falling apart. Andrew has convinced their mother to let him go to band camp, but Felton discovers that Andrew, usually the sane member of the family, has in fact run away to Florida. An impromptu road trip with erstwhile best friend Gus turns up surprising reasons for Andrew's escape." (Kirkus Reviews)

Stupid fast. Sourcebooks 2011 311p pa $9.99
Grades: 6 7 8 9 10
1. Boys -- Fiction 2. Football -- Fiction
ISBN 978-1-4022-5630-1; 1-4022-5630-2

"Herbach is at his peak limning the confusion and frustration of a young man who no longer recognizes his own body, and Felton's self-deprecating take on his newly awarded A-list status is funny and compelling." Bull Cent Child Books

Herlong, Madaline

The **great** wide sea; [by] M. H. Herlong. Viking Children's Books 2008 283p $16.99; pa $6.99
Grades: 7 8 9 10
1. Sailing -- Fiction 2. Brothers -- Fiction 3. Bereavement -- Fiction 4. Father-son relationship -- Fiction 5. Survival after airplane accidents, shipwrecks, etc. -- Fiction
ISBN 978-0-670-06330-7; 0-670-06330-4; 978-0-14-241670-9 pa; 0-14-241670-3 pa

LC 2008-08384

Still mourning the death of their mother, three brothers go with their father on an extended sailing trip off the Florida Keys and have an adventure at sea

"Herlong makes the most of the three boys' characters, each exceptionally well developed here, to make this as much a novel of brotherhood as a sea story." Bull Cent Child Books

Hernandez, David

★ **Suckerpunch**. HarperTeen 2008 217p $17.89
Grades: 9 10 11 12
1. Brothers -- Fiction 2. Drug abuse -- Fiction 3. Child abuse -- Fiction 4. Hispanic Americans -- Fiction 5. Father-son relationship -- Fiction
ISBN 978-0-06-117330-1; 0-06-117331-2

Accompanied by two friends, teenage brothers Marcus and Enrique head on a road trip to confront the abusive father who walked out on them a year earlier.

"The author's imagery, sometimes subtle, sometimes searing, invariably hits its mark." Publ Wkly

Herrick, Steven

By the river. Front Street 2006 238p $16.95
Grades: 8 9 10 11 12
1. Death -- Fiction 2. Brothers -- Fiction 3. Australia -- Fiction 4. Single parent family -- Fiction
ISBN 1-932425-72-1

LC 2005-23967

First published 2004 in the United Kingdom

A fourteen-year-old describes, through prose poems, his life in a small Australian town in 1962, where, since their mother's death, he and his brother have been mainly on their own to learn about life, death, and love.

"The poems are simple but potent in their simplicity, blending together in a compelling, evocative story of a gentle, intelligent boy growing up and learning to deal with a sometimes-ugly little world that he . . . will eventually escape." Voice Youth Advocates

The **wolf**. Front Street 2007 214p $17.95
Grades: 8 9 10 11 12
1. Novels in verse 2. Australia -- Fiction 3. Domestic violence -- Fiction 4. Father-daughter relationship -- Fiction
ISBN 978-1-932425-75-8; 1-932425-75-6

LC 2006-12072

Sixteen-year-old Lucy, living in the shadow of her violent father, experiences a night of tenderness, danger and revelation as she and Jake, her fifteen-year-old neighbor, search for a legendary wolf in the Australian outback.

"Herrick's verse style perfectly suits this emotionally taut survival story. . . . Readers will find this novel compelling, its fast-moving narrative rewarding." SLJ

Hesse, Karen

Safekeeping; Karen Hesse. Feiwel and Friends 2012 294 p. ill., map $17.99

Grades: 7 8 9 10 11 12

    1. Alternative histories 2. Revolutions -- Fiction 3. Voyages and travels -- Fiction

    ISBN 1250011345; 9781250011343

LC 2012288414

In this book, a "group of rebels called the American People's Party has taken control" in the U.S. "Radley, an American teenager returning home from doing volunteer work in Haiti, finds her parents gone and her Vermont home abandoned. Not knowing whom to trust or where she'll be safe, she sets out on foot to Canada, befriending a reticent girl along the way. The two form a tentative friendship and manage to cross into Canada." (Publishers Weekly)

Hesse, Monica

Girl in the blue coat. Monica Hesse. Little, Brown & Co. 2016 320 p.

Grades: 9 10 11 12

    1. Black market -- Fiction 2. Holocaust, Jewish (1939-1945) -- Netherlands -- Amsterdam -- Fiction 3. Jews -- Netherlands -- Fiction 4. Missing children -- Fiction 5. Mystery and detective stories 6. World War, 1939-1945 -- Underground movements -- Netherlands -- Fiction 7. Netherlands -- History -- German occupation, 1940-1945 -- Fiction 8. Netherlands -- History -- 1940-1945, German occupation -- Fiction

    9780316260602, $17.99; 0316260606

LC 2015020565

In this novel by Monica Hesse, set "in Nazi-occupied Holland, Hanneke seems like an ordinary . . . [b]ut her Aryan features . . . allow her to work as a courier on the black market smuggling . . . items to paying customers. Her actions are a direct result of the loss of Bas, her boyfriend. When one of her best customers asks for her assistance in finding a Jewish girl she was hiding, Hanneke . . . is drawn into the mysterious disappearance of the girl." (School Library Journal)

"In 1943 Amsterdam, Hanneke nurses a broken heart—her boyfriend has died in the war—while delivering black market goods (foodstuffs, cigarettes, etc.) to her neighbors. One customer, Mrs. Janssen, implores Hanneke to find a missing girl whom the woman had been sheltering, leading to an engaging mystery that shakes Hanneke from her emotional stupor. An author's note includes useful information about the Dutch Resistance." Horn Book

★ The **war** outside. Monica Hesse. Little, Brown & Co. 2018 336 p.

Grades: 8 9 10 11 12

    1. Crystal City Internment Camp (Crystal City, Tex.) -- Fiction; 2. Friendship -- Fiction; 3. German Americans -- Evacuation and relocation, 1941-1948 -- Fiction; 4. Japanese Americans -- Evacuation and relocation, 1942-1945 -- Fiction; 5. World War, 1939-1945 -- United States -- Fiction

    9780316316699, $17.99

LC 2018005733

In this book, by Monica Hesse, "it's 1944, and World War II is raging across Europe and the Pacific.... Haruko and Margot meet at the high school in Crystal City, a 'family internment camp' for those accused of colluding with the enemy.... With everything around them falling apart, Margot and Haruko find solace in their growing, secret friendship. But in a prison the government has deemed full of spies, can they trust anyone -- even each other?" (Publisher's note)

"Interned in a Texas camp during World War II, Japanese-American Haruko and German-American Margot watch their families fall apart and are driven to depend on each other, even if they should not." (Kirkus Reviews)

Hesser, Terry Spencer

Kissing doorknobs. Delacorte Press 1998 149p hardcover o.p. pa $6.50

Grades: 7 8 9 10

    1. Friendship -- Fiction 2. Family life -- Fiction 3. Mental illness -- Fiction 4. Obsessive-compulsive disorder -- Fiction

    ISBN 0-385-32329-8; 0-440-41314-1 pa

LC 97-26937

Fourteen-year-old Tara describes how her increasingly strange compulsions begin to take over her life and affect her relationships with her family and friends

"An honest, fresh, and multilayered story to which readers will instantly relate. . . . The prose is forthright, economical, and peppered with wry humor." SLJ

Hiaasen, Carl

Skink -- no surrender; Carl Hiaasen; Alfred A. Knopf. 2014 281p $18.99

Grades: 9 10 11 12

    1. Missing children -- Fiction 2. Wilderness areas -- Fiction 4. Florida -- Fiction 5. Mystery fiction

    ISBN: 0375870512; 9780375870514; 9780375970511

LC 2014006036

"Richard and his cousin Malley are best friends. But while Richard is pretty levelheaded, Malley tends to get into trouble. So Richard is only mildly surprised to discover that she's run off with a guy she met on the Internet in order to avoid being sent to boarding school in New Hampshire. Richard wants to go find her, and luckily he runs into what may be the perfect person to help him do just that: a ragged, one-eyed ex-governor of Florida named Skink. With Skink at the helm, the two set off across Florida in search of Richard's cousin." Booklist

"A high stakes, action-packed comedy with a lot of heart." VOYA

Higgins, F. E.

The **Eyeball** Collector. Feiwel & Friends 2009 251p $14.99

Grades: 7 8 9 10

    1. Horror fiction 2. Mystery fiction

    ISBN 978-0-312-56681-4; 0-312-56681-6

"In what the author dubs a 'polyquel' that partially bridges her Black Book of Secrets (2007) and its prequel Bone Magician (2008), Higgins sends a suddenly penniless young orphan from the filthy streets of Urbs Umida's South Side to an extravagantly rococo estate house in search of vengeance for his family's ruin. . . . Readers with a taste for lurid prose, macabre twists, riddles, exotic poisons, high-society caricatures, murderous schemes and scenes of stomach-churning degeneracy will find some or all of these in every chapter, and though the author trots in multiple characters and references from previous episodes, this one stands sturdily on its own." Kirkus

Higgins, Jack

★ **Sure** fire; [by] Jack Higgins with Justin Richards. G.P. Putnam's Sons 2007 237p $16.99

Grades: 6 7 8 9

1. Adventure fiction 2. Spies -- Fiction 3. Twins -- Fiction 4. Fathers -- Fiction
ISBN 978-0-399-24784-2; 0-399-24784-X
LC 2007008144

First published 2006 in the United Kingdom

Resentful of having to go and live with their estranged father after the death of their mother, fifteen-year-old twins, Rich and Jade, soon find they have more complicated problems when their father is kidnapped and their attempts to rescue him involve them in a dangerous international plot to control the world's oil.

This is a "standout YA spy novel. . . . Each chapter ends with a cliff-hanger, maintaining the high level of suspense." Publ Wkly

Other titles in this series are:
Death run (2008)
Sharp shot (2009)
First strike (2010)

Higgins, M. G.

Bi-Normal; M. G. Higgins. Saddleback Pub 2013 191 p. (paperback) $9.95

Grades: 7 8 9 10 11 12

1. School stories 2. Gay teenagers -- Fiction
ISBN 1622500040; 9781622500048

In this book, "a teen football player with a girlfriend discovers he has feelings for another boy. When Brett first notices his attraction to Zach, a boy who sits next to him in art class, he wants to push it away Brett and his friends are the kind of guys who ogle girls' bodies and pick on boys they perceive as gay. As his feelings intensify, however, Brett is torn between acting on his attraction and acting out of his denial." (Kirkus Reviews)

Higson, Charles

The **dead**; [by] Charlie Higson. Hyperion 2011 485p map $16.99

Grades: 8 9 10

1. Horror fiction 2. Zombies -- Fiction
ISBN 978-1-4231-3412-1; 1-4231-3412-5

As a disease turns everyone over sixteen into brainless, decomposing, flesh-eating creatures, a group of teenagers head to London. Ed, Jack, Bam and the other students at Rowhurst School learn more about the Disaster, and meet an adult who seems to be immune to the disease.

"With the book's immense cast and substantial body count, it doesn't pay to get too attached to any one character,

while the intense descriptions of violence and sickness will get under readers' skin." Publ Wkly

★ The **enemy**. Hyperion/DBG 2010 440p $16.99; pa $8.99

Grades: 9 10 11 12

1. Horror fiction 2. Zombies -- Fiction 3. London (England) -- Fiction
ISBN 978-1-4231-3175-5; 1-4231-3175-4; 978-1-4231-3312-4 pa; 1-4231-3312-9 pa

First published 2009 in the United Kingdom

"Nearly two years ago, the world changed; everyone over 16 became horrifically ill and began to crave fresh meat. As supplies are exhausted and the vicious grown-ups grow braver, Arrum and Maxie, along with their band of refugees, must embark on a perilous journey across London to reach the safest spot in the city: Buckingham Palace. . . . Intrigue, betrayal and the basic heroic-teens-against-marauding-adults conflict give this work a high place on any beach-reading list." Kirkus

Followed by: The dead (2011)

Hijuelos, Oscar

Dark Dude. Atheneum Books for Young Readers 2008 439p $16.99; pa $9.99

Grades: 7 8 9 10

1. Wisconsin -- Fiction 2. Cuban Americans -- Fiction
ISBN 978-1-4169-4804-9; 1-4169-4804-X; 978-1-4169-4945-9 pa; 1-4169-4945-3 pa
LC 2008-00959

In the 1960s, Rico Fuentes, a pale-skinned Cuban American teenager, abandons drug-infested New York City for the picket fence and apple pie world of Wisconsin, only to discover that he still feels like an outsider and that violent and judgmental people can be found even in the wholesome Midwest.

"Hijuelos weaves a compelling and insightful tale of one outsider's coming-of-age. . . . The resolution is quick and tidy, but the imagery is rich and the content sure to engage teen readers." Voice Youth Advocates

Hill, C. J.

Erasing time; C. J. Hill. Katherine Tegen Books 2012 361 p. $17.99

Grades: 8 9 10 11

1. Secrecy -- Fiction 2. Resistance to government 3. Future life 4. Science fiction 5. Twins -- Fiction 6. Sisters -- Fiction 7. Time travel -- Fiction
ISBN 0062123920; 9780062123923
LC 2011044624

"When twins Sheridan and Taylor wake up 400 years in the future, they find a changed world: domed cities, no animals, and a language that's so different, it barely sounds like English. And the worst news: They can't go back home. The twenty-fifth-century government transported the girls to their city hoping to find a famous scientist to help perfect a devastating new weapon. The same government has implanted tracking devices in the citizens, limiting and examining everything they do. Taylor and Sheridan have to find a way out of the city before the government discovers their secrets." (Publisher's note)

Slayers; friends and traitors. by C. J. Hill. Feiwel & Friends 2013 390 p. $16.99

Grades: 7 8 9 10 11 12

    1. Dragons -- Fiction 2. Teenagers -- Fiction

    ISBN 1250024617; 9781250024619

In this book, by C. J. Hill, "Tori's got a problem. She thought she'd have one more summer to train as a dragon Slayer, but time has run out. When Tori hears the horrifying sound of dragon eggs hatching, she knows the Slayers are in trouble. In less than a year, the dragons will be fully grown and completely lethal. The Slayers are well-prepared, but their group is still not complete, and Tori is determined to track down Ryker--the mysterious missing Slayer." (Publisher's note)

"When Tori breaks the rules that keep the dragon slayers safe, all the slayers are endangered unless they can figure out which one of them is a traitor. A steamy love triangle takes center stage over the dragon-fighting in this installment; though many characters from the first book only show up fleetingly, fans of Slayers will find plenty to entertain them." (Horn Book)

Hill, Will

Department 19. Razorbill 2011 540p

Grades: 10 11 12

    1. Horror fiction 2. Homicide -- Fiction 3. Vampires -- Fiction 4. Supernatural -- Fiction 5. Great Britain -- Fiction

    ISBN 1595144064; 9781595144065

                              LC 2010-54252

After watching his father's murder, sixteen-year-old Jamie Carpenter joins Department 19, a secret government agency, where he learns of the existence of vampires and the history that ties him to the team destined to stop them. "Grades eight to ten." (Bull Cent Child Books)

"This is a nonstop thrill ride right up to the cliffhanger ending. This cinematic adrenaline rush has the makings of a surefire hit." Publ Wkly

The **rising**; Will Hill. Razorbill 2012 576 p.

Grades: 10 11 12

    1. Vampires 2. Supernatural 3. Dracula, Count (Fictional character) 4. Adventure fiction

    ISBN 1595144072; 9781595144072

In this novel, by Will Hill, "Sixteen-year-old Jamie Carpenter's life was violently upended when he was brought into Department 19, a classified government agency of vampire hunters. . . . But being the new recruit at the Department isn't all weapons training and covert missions. Jamie's own mother has been turned into a vampire--and now Jamie will stop at nothing to wreak revenge on her captors." (Publisher's note)

Hills, Lia

★ The **beginner's** guide to living. Farrar, Straus and Giroux 2010 221p il $17.99

Grades: 9 10 11 12

    1. School stories 2. Bereavement -- Fiction

    ISBN 978-0-374-30659-5; 0-374-30659-1

                              LC 2009-19248

Struggling to cope with his mother's sudden death and growing feelings of isolation from his father and brother, seventeen-year-old Will turns to philosophy for answers to life's biggest questions, while finding some solace in a new love.

"Almost nothing escapes Will's notice (though his perceptiveness alone doesn't produce answers), and the mosaic of imagery and musings in his poetic, staccato narration offers thought-provoking ideas about grief and the universal drive to find a purpose. Although this novel begins with a death, it is a celebration of life, companionship, and love." Publ Wkly

Hinton, S. E.

★ The **outsiders**. Viking 1967 188p $17.99; pa $9.99

Grades: 7 8 9 10

    1. Social classes -- Fiction 2. Juvenile delinquency -- Fiction

    ISBN 0-670-53257-6; 0-14-038572-X pa

    ALA YALSA Margaret A. Edwards Award (1988)

"This remarkable novel by a seventeen-year-old girl gives a moving, credible view of the outsiders from the inside—their loyalty to each other, their sensitivity under tough crusts, their understanding of self and society." Horn Book

Hinwood, Christine

The **returning**. Dial Books 2011 302p map $17.99

Grades: 6 7 8 9 10

    1. War stories 2. Villages -- Fiction

    ISBN 978-0-8037-3528-6; 0-8037-3528-6

                              LC 2010-08398

First published 2009 in Australia with title: Bloodflower

When the twelve-year war between the Uplanders and Downlanders is over and Cam returns home to his village, questions dog him, from how he lost an arm to why he was the only one of his fellow soldiers to survive, such that he must leave until his own suspicions are resolved.

"Themes of rebuilding and redemption are powerful, but it is in the small, acutely observed details of debut author Hinwood's world that her story truly shines." Publ Wkly

Hirsch, Jeff

The **eleventh** plague. Scholastic Press 2011 278p $17.99

Grades: 7 8 9 10

    1. Science fiction

    ISBN 978-0-545-29014-2; 0-545-29014-7

                              LC 2010048966

Twenty years after the start of the war that caused the Collapse, fifteen-year-old Stephen, his father, and grandfather travel post-Collapse America scavenging, but when his grandfather dies and his father decides to risk everything to save the lives of two strangers, Stephen's life is turned upside down.

This "novel is an impressive story with strong characters. . . . Hirsch delivers a tight, well-crafted story." Publ Wkly

Hitchcock, Bonnie-Sue

The **smell** of other people's houses. Bonnie-Sue Hitchcock. Wendy Lamb Books 2016 240 p.

Grades: 7 8 9 10

1. Alaska -- History -- 20th century -- Fiction 2. Friendship -- Fiction 3. Alaska -- Fiction 5. Teenagers -- Fiction

9780553497786, $17.99; 9780553497793; 9780553497816

LC 2015011309

Morris Finalist (2017)

"In Alaska, 1970. . . . Ruth has a secret that she can't hide forever. Dora wonders if she can ever truly escape where she comes from, even when good luck strikes. Alyce is trying to reconcile her desire to dance, with the life she's always known on her family's fishing boat. Hank and his brothers decide it's safer to run away than to stay home-until one of them ends up in terrible danger." (Publisher's note)

"Less a narrative and more a series of portraits, this is an exquisitely drawn, deeply heartfelt look at a time and place not often addressed. Hitchcock's measured prose casts a gorgeous, almost otherworldly feel over the text, resulting in a quietly lovely look at the various sides of human nature and growing up in a difficult world." Booklist

Hoban, Russell, 1925-2011

Soonchild; Russell Hoban; illustrated by Alexis Deacon. Candlewick 2012 144 p. (hardback) $15.99

Grades: 9 10 11 12

1. Occult fiction 2. Shamans -- Fiction 3. Arctic regions -- Fiction 4. Inuit -- Fiction 5. Eskimos -- Fiction 6. Pregnancy -- Fiction 7. Supernatural -- Fiction 8. Father and child -- Fiction

ISBN 9780763659202

LC 2011048373

In this book, set "[s]omewhere in the Arctic Circle, Sixteen-Face John, a shaman, learns that his first child, a soonchild, cannot hear the World Songs from her mother's womb. The World Songs are what inspire all newborns to come out into the world, and John must find them for her. But how? The answer takes him through many lifetimes and many shape-shifts, as well as encounters with beasts, demons and a mysterious benevolent owl spirit, Ukpika." (Publisher's note)

Hobbs, Valerie

Sonny's war. Farrar, Straus & Giroux 2002 215p hardcover o.p. pa $7.95

Grades: 7 8 9 10

1. Vietnam War, 1961-1975 -- Fiction

ISBN 0-374-37136-9; 0-374-46970-9 pa

LC 2002-23891

In the late 1960s, fourteen-year-old Cory's life is greatly changed by the sudden death of her father and her brother's tour of duty in Vietnam

"Hobbs writes like a dream . . . but the Cory she conjures up for us is as real as real, completely believable in all her teenage vulnerability and sharp-eyed observation." Horn Book Guide

Hobbs, Will

Beardance. Atheneum Pubs. 1993 197p il pa $5.99

Grades: 7 8 9 10

1. Bears -- Fiction 2. Ute Indians -- Fiction

ISBN 0-689-31867-7; 0-689-87072-8 pa

LC 92-44874

Sequel to Bearstone

While accompanying an elderly rancher on a trip into the San Juan Mountains, Cloyd, a Ute Indian boy, tries to help two orphaned grizzly cubs survive the winter and, at the same time, completes his spirit mission.

"The story offers plenty of action and memorable characters, and the descriptions of Ute rituals and legends, the setting, and Cloyd's first experiences with spirit dreams are particularly well done." Horn Book Guide

Bearstone. Atheneum Pubs. 1989 154p hardcover o.p. pa $4.99

Grades: 7 8 9 10

1. Ute Indians -- Fiction

ISBN 0-689-87071-X pa

LC 89-6641

"The growth and maturity that Cloyd acquires as the summer progresses is juxtaposed poetically against the majestic Colorado landscape. Hobbs has creatively blended myth and reality as Cloyd forges a new identity for himself." Voice Youth Advocates

Followed by Beardance (1993)

Crossing the wire. HarperCollins 2006 216p $15.99; lib bdg $16.89; pa $5.99

Grades: 5 6 7 8

1. Mexicans -- Fiction 2. Illegal aliens -- Fiction

ISBN 978-0-06-074138-9; 0-06-074138-4; 978-0-06-074139-6 lib bdg; 0-06-074139-2 lib bdg; 978-0-06-074140-2 pa; 0-06-074140-6 pa

LC 2005-19697

Fifteen-year-old Victor Flores journeys north in a desperate attempt to cross the Arizona border and find work in the United States to support his family in central Mexico.

This is "an exciting story in a vital contemporary setting." Voice Youth Advocates

Downriver. Atheneum Pubs. 1991 204p hardcover o.p. pa $6.99

Grades: 7 8 9 10

1. White-water canoeing -- Fiction

ISBN 0-689-31690-9; 0-440-22673-2 pa

LC 90-1044

Fifteen-year-old Jessie and the other rebellious teenage members of a wilderness survival school team abandon their adult leader, hijack his boats, and try to run the dangerous white water at the bottom of the Grand Canyon

"The book is exquisitely plotted, with nail-biting suspense and excitement." SLJ

Leaving Protection. HarperCollins 2004 178p il map $15.99; pa $5.99

Grades: 7 8 9 10

1. Alaska -- Fiction 2. Fishing -- Fiction 3. Buried treasure -- Fiction

ISBN 0-688-17475-2; 0-380-73312-9 pa

LC 2003-15545

Sixteen-year-old Robbie Daniels, happy to get a job aboard a troller fishing for king salmon off southeastern Alaska, finds himself in danger when he discovers that his mysterious captain is searching for long-buried Russian plaques that lay claim to Alaska and the Northwest

This "nautical thriller brims with detail about the fishing life and weaves in historical facts as well. . . . Robbie's doubts build to a climactic finale involving a dramatic and fateful storm at sea, grippingly rendered. Fans of maritime tales will relish the atmosphere and the bursts of action." Publ Wkly

★ The **maze**. Morrow Junior Bks. 1998 198p $15.99; pa $5.99

Grades: 7 8 9 10

    1. Condors -- Fiction 2. Runaway teenagers -- Fiction
ISBN 0-688-15092-6; 0-380-72913-X pa

                       LC 98-10791

Rick, a fourteen-year-old foster child, escapes from a juvenile detention facility near Las Vegas and travels to Canyonlands National Park in Utah where he meets a bird biologist working on a project to reintroduce condors to the wild

"Hobbs spins an engrossing yarn, blending adventure with a strong theme, advocating the need for developing personal values." Horn Book Guide

Take me to the river. HarperCollins 2011 184p $15.99; lib bdg $16.89

Grades: 5 6 7 8

    1. Cousins -- Fiction 2. Canoes and canoeing -- Fiction
ISBN 978-0-06-074144-0; 0-06-074144-9; 978-0-06-074145-7 lib bdg; 0-06-074145-7 lib bdg

                       LC 2010003147

When North Carolina fourteen-year-old Dylan Sands joins his fifteen-year-old cousin Rio in running the Rio Grande River, they face a tropical storm and a fugitive kidnapper.

"The story unfolds in a disarming manner. The pace is quick, and the challenges are relentless, but the writing is so grounded in physical details and emotional realism that every turn of events seems convincing within the context of the story." Booklist

Wild Man Island. HarperCollins Pubs. 2002 184p $15.99; lib bdg $16.89; pa $5.99

Grades: 6 7 8 9

    1. Wilderness survival -- Fiction
ISBN 0-688-17473-6; 0-06-029810-3 lib bdg; 0-380-73310-2 pa

                       LC 2001-39818

After fourteen-year-old Andy slips away from his kayaking group to visit the wilderness site of his archaeologist father's death, a storm strands him on Admiralty Island, Alaska, where he manages to survive, encounters unexpected animal and human inhabitants, and looks for traces of the earliest prehistoric immigrants to America

"A well-paced adventure, this novel combines survival saga, mystery, and archaeological expedition." Voice Youth Advocates

Hocking, Amanda

Wake; Amanda Hocking. St. Martin's Griffin 2012 309 p. (hardback) $17.99

Grades: 7 8 9 10

    1. Occult fiction 2. Fantasy fiction 3. Sirens (Mythology) -- Fiction 4. Love -- Fiction 5. Sisters -- Fiction 6. Supernatural -- Fiction 7. Seaside resorts -- Fiction
ISBN 1250008123; 9781250008121; 9781429956581

                       LC 2012014630

This is the first in Amanda Hocking's Watersong series. Here, "Gemma Fisher is happy—she's a star on the swim team, her family is loving and supportive, and the crushworthy boy next door returns her interest. The only downside: three gorgeous but creepy new girls who have her in their sights." These girls ultimately turn out to be Sirens who trick Gemma into drinking potion that turns her into a Siren as well. (Publishers Weekly)

Followed by Lullaby (2012) and Tidal (2013)

Hodge, Rosamund

Crimson bound. Rosamund Hodge. Balzer + Bray 2015 448 p.

Grades: 9 10 11 12

    1. Fantasy 2. Magic -- Fiction 3. Kings and rulers -- Fiction 4. Fantasy fiction
9780062224767, $17.99; 006222476X

                       LC 2014030890

In this novel by Rosamund Hodge "when Rachelle was fifteen she was good—apprenticed to her aunt and in training to protect her village from dark magic. Three years later, Rachelle has given her life to serving the realm, fighting deadly creatures in a vain effort to atone. When the king orders her to guard his son Armand—the man she hates most—Rachelle forces Armand to help her hunt for the legendary sword that might save their world." (Publisher's note)

"Though Rachelle's inner monologue is often bogged down by repetitive moments of self-loathing and doubt, Hodge's writing occasionally glimmers with flashes of brilliance: 'the neckline bared her shoulders and her collarbones like a declaration of war.' Plot twists and romance keep the pages turning in this grim and intricate take on the classic tale." Booklist

Cruel Beauty; Rosamund Hodge. Balzer + Bray, an imprint of HarperCollinsPublishers 2014 352 p. (hardcover) $17.99

Grades: 8 9 10 11 12

    1. Love stories 2. Imaginary places 3. Magic -- Fiction 4. Fantasy
ISBN 0062224735; 9780062224736

                       LC 2013015418

In this book, by Rosamund Hodge, "betrothed to the evil ruler of her kingdom, Nyx has always known her fate was to marry him, kill him, and free her people from his tyranny. On her seventeenth birthday, when she moves into his castle high on the kingdom's mountaintop, nothing is as she expected. Nyx knows she must save her homeland at all costs, yet she can't resist the pull of her sworn enemy--who's gotten in her way by stealing her heart." (Publisher's note)

"Hodge's story infuses elements of Greek mythology and classic fairy tales. The plot moves quickly, and the characters are well formed; their transgressions make them interesting and authentic. The complex relationship between Nyx and Ignifex is especially engaging. An entertaining read for teens who enjoy romantic fantasy." (School Library Journal)

Hodkin, Michelle

The **unbecoming** of Mara Dyer. Simon & Schuster 2011 456p $16.99

Grades: 7 8 9 10 11 12

    1. School stories 2. Family life -- Fiction 3. Supernatural -- Fiction 4. Post-traumatic stress disorder -- Fiction

    ISBN 978-1-4424-2176-9; 1-4424-2176-2

LC 2010050862

Seventeen-year-old Mara cannot remember the accident that took the lives of three of her friends but, after moving from Rhode Island to Florida, finding love with Noah, and more deaths, she realizes uncovering something buried in her memory might save her family and her future.

"The characters are real and wonderful, and the supernatural story is riveting." SLJ

Hoffman, Alice

The **foretelling**. Little, Brown 2005 167p hardcover o.p. pa $7.99

Grades: 7 8 9 10

    1. Amazons -- Fiction 2. Sex role -- Fiction

    ISBN 0-316-01018-9; 0-316-15409-1 pa

LC 2004-25102

Growing up the daughter of an Amazon queen who shuns her, Rain rebels against the ways of her tribe through her sisterlike relationship with Io and her feelings for a boy from a tribe of wanderers.

The "first-person narration is accessible while evoking a sense of otherworldliness. . . . The story unfolds at a measured pace with little dialogue, but the language makes it compulsively readable." SLJ

Green angel. Scholastic Press 2003 116p pa $5.99

Grades: 7 8 9 10

    1. Gardening -- Fiction

    ISBN 0-439-44384-9; 0-545-20411-9 pa

LC 2002-6980

Haunted by grief and by her past after losing her family in a fire, fifteen-year-old Green retreats into her ruined garden as she struggles to survive emotionally and physically on her own

"A powerfully written and thought-provoking selection." SLJ

Green witch. Scholastic Press 2010 135p $17.99

Grades: 7 8 9 10 11 12

    1. Orphans -- Fiction 2. Gardening -- Fiction 3. Bereavement -- Fiction 4. Storytelling -- Fiction 5. Supernatural -- Fiction 6. Missing persons -- Fiction

    ISBN 978-0-545-14195-6; 0-545-14195-8

LC 2009-17606

A year after her world was nearly destroyed, sixteen-year-old Green has become the one villagers turn to for aid, especially to record their stories, but Green will need the

help of other women who, like herself, are believed to be witches if she is to find her best friend and her one true love.

"Haunting, philosophical, and filled with poetic imagery . . . this book will leave an indelible mark." Publ Wkly

★ **Incantation**. Little, Brown 2006 166p hardcover o.p. pa $8.99

Grades: 8 9 10 11 12

    1. Spain -- Fiction 2. Prejudices -- Fiction 3. Inquisition -- Fiction 4. Jews -- Persecutions -- Fiction

    ISBN 978-0-316-01019-1; 0-316-01019-7; 978-0-316-15428-4 pa; 0-316-15428-8 pa

LC 2005-37301

During the Spanish Inquisition, sixteen-year-old Estrella, brought up a Catholic, discovers her family's true Jewish identity, and when their secret is betrayed by Estrella's best friend, the consequences are tragic. Includes some scenes of graphic violence.

"Hoffman's lyrical prose and astute characterization blend to create a riveting, horrific tale that unites despair with elements of hope." SLJ

Hoffman, Mary

★ The **falconer's** knot; a story of friars, flirtation and foul play. Bloomsbury Children's Books 2007 297p $16.95

Grades: 7 8 9 10

    1. Love stories 2. Renaissance -- Fiction 3. Religious life -- Fiction

    ISBN 978-1-59990-056-8; 1-59990-056-4

LC 2006-16365

Silvano and Chiara, teens sent to live in a friary and a nunnery in Renaissance Italy, are drawn to one another and dream of a future together, but when murders are committed in the friary, they must discover who is behind the crimes before they can realize their love.

"Hoffman creates utterly engaging characters and vivid settings, and she skillfully turns up the suspense, wrapping her varied plot threads into a satisfying whole." Booklist

Hoffman, Nina Kiriki

A **stir** of bones. Viking 2003 211p $15.99

Grades: 7 8 9 10

    1. Ghost stories 2. Wife abuse -- Fiction

    ISBN 0-670-03551-3

LC 2003-5029

Fourteen-year-old Susan Blackstrom "begins the painful process of breaking away from her abusive father, with help from allies both human and supernatural. A chance encounter with three classmates leads Susan to an abandoned house that . . . harbors an uncommonly substantial ghost named Nathan. . . . Richly endowed with complex relationships, a strange and subtle brand of magic, evocative language, and suspenseful storytelling, this will draw readers into a world less safe and simple than it seems at first glance." Booklist

Hoffmeister, Peter Brown

This is the part where you laugh. Peter Brown Hoffmeister. Alfred A. Knopf 2016 336 p.

Grades: 9 10 11 12

    1. Basketball -- Fiction 2. Conduct of life -- Fiction 3. Family problems -- Fiction 4. Friendship -- Fiction 5.

Poverty -- Fiction 6. Sick -- Fiction
9780553538106, $17.99; 9780553538113

LC 2015022147

In this book, by Peter Brown Hoffmeister, "Travis is per-petrator, victim, or both. He spends much of the narrative searching for the heroin-addicted mother who abandoned him, and he suffered the depredations of foster care and the juvenile justice system before being taken in by his caring but poverty-stricken grandparents. Basketball provides sol-ace and purpose for his life, but even here his violent nature intrudes." (School Library Journal)

"In this tragicomic YA debut from adult author Hoff-meister (Let Them Be Eaten by Bears), a young man con-tends with anger, family troubles, and romance over a few increasingly chaotic months. Travis's summer goals are simple: improve his basketball skills, stay out of trouble, and try to cheer up his grandmother, who's dying from can-cer. He also hangs out with his best friend Creature, spends time with a mercurial girl named Natalie, and searches for his drug-addicted mother in the homeless camps around the area. . . . The result is a raw, offbeat novel with an abundance of honesty and heart." PW

Hokenson, Terry

The **winter** road; 1st ed.; Front Street 2006 175p $16.95

Grades: 7 8 9 10

1. Survival after airplane accidents, shipwrecks, etc. -- Fiction
ISBN 1-932425-45-4

LC 2005027030

Seventeen-year-old Willa, still grieving over the death of her older brother and the neglect of her father, decides to fly a small plane to fetch her mother from Northern Ontario, but when the plane crashes she is all alone in the snowy wilderness.

"The mortal challenges Willa faces make for a gripping narrative, one sharpened by visceral details." Booklist

Holder, Nancy

Crusade; by Nancy Holder and Debbie Viguie. Simon Pulse 2010 470p $16.99

Grades: 7 8 9 10 11

1. Horror fiction 2. Sisters -- Fiction 3. Vampires -- Fiction 4. Supernatural -- Fiction
ISBN 978-1-4169-9802-0; 1-4169-9802-0

LC 2010-9094

An international team of six teenaged vampire hunters, trained in Salamanca, Spain, goes to New Orleans seeking to rescue team-member Jenn's younger sister as the vampires escalate their efforts to take over the Earth.

"The cinematic writing and apocalyptic scenario should find a ready audience." Publ Wkly

Followed by: Damned (2011)

Damned; by Nancy Holder and Debbie Viguie. Simon Pulse 2011 $16.99; pa $9.99

Grades: 7 8 9 10

1. Horror fiction 2. Vampires -- Fiction 3. Supernatural -- Fiction
ISBN 978-1-4169-9804-4; 1-4169-9804-7; 978-1-4169-9805-1 pa; 1-4169-9805-5 pa

LC 2011005474

As the newly appointed Hunter, teenager Jenn leads the fighting teams who defend against the Cursed Ones--the vampires who are taking over Earth--but an even more sin-ister force now threatens the teams of hunters, with the fate of humanity at stake.

Holland, L. Tam

The **counterfeit** family tree of Vee Crawford-Wong; by L. Tam Holland. 1st ed. Simon & Schuster BFYR 2013 368 p. (hardcover) $17.99

Grades: 9 10 11 12

1. School stories 2. Truthfulness and falsehood -- Fiction 3. China -- Fiction 4. Schools -- Fiction 5. Families -- Fiction 6. High schools -- Fiction 7. Chinese Americans -- Fiction
ISBN 144241264X; 9781442412644; 9781442412651; 9781442412668

LC 2012014542

In this book, Vee has to write an essay on family history, but all he "knows about his Texas grandparents is that their annual Christmas card always makes his mother cry; his father, meanwhile, left China for college and never looked back. Already in trouble for lackluster academics, Vee can't get his parents to talk about their pasts, so he completes the essay by inventing a backstory for his father's family in a fishing village along the Yangtze. After he gets away with that, he's on a roll." (Publishers Weekly)

Holland, Sara

Everless. Sara Holland. HarperTeen 2018 364 p.

Grades: 8 9 10 11 12

1. Social classes -- Fiction; 2. Time -- Fiction; 3. Weddings -- Fiction; 4. Fantasy fiction
9780062653659, $17.99; 9780062653680

LC 2017942898

In this book, by Sara Holland, "in the kingdom of Sem-pera, time is currency.... The rich aristocracy, like the Ger-lings, tax the poor to the hilt, extending their own lives by centuries. No one resents the Gerlings more than Jules Em-ber. A decade ago, she and her father were servants at Ever-less.... until a fateful accident forced them to flee.... When Jules discovers that her father is dying, she knows that she must return to Everless." (Publisher's note)

"Holland's debut is set in an intricate and immersive fan-tasy world, a world she skillfully builds through layers of flashbacks and memories." Booklist

Hooper, Mary

Fallen Grace. Bloomsbury 2011 309p $16.99

Grades: 7 8 9 10

1. Orphans -- Fiction 2. Poverty -- Fiction 3. Sisters -- Fiction 4. London (England) -- Fiction 5. People with mental disabilities -- Fiction 6. Swindlers and swindling -- Fiction 7. Funeral rites and ceremonies -- Fiction 8. Great Britain -- History -- 19th century -- Fiction
ISBN 978-1-59990-564-8; 1-59990-564-7

LC 2010-25498

In Victorian London, impoverished fifteen-year-old orphan Grace takes care of her older but mentally unfit sister Lily, and after enduring many harsh and painful experiences, the two become the victims of a fraud perpetrated by the wealthy owners of several funeral businesses.

Hooper "packs her brisk Dickensian fable with colorful characters and suspenseful, satisfying plot twists. The sobering realities of child poverty and exploitation are vividly conveyed, along with fascinating details of the Victorian funeral trade." Kirkus

Includes bibliographical references

Velvet; by Mary Hooper. 1st U.S. ed. Bloomsbury 2012 323 p. (hardcover) $16.99

Grades: 9 10 11

1. Historical fiction 2. Orphans -- Fiction 3. Spiritualists -- Fiction 4. London (England) -- History -- 19th century -- Fiction 5. Great Britain -- History -- Victoria, 1837-1901 -- Fiction

ISBN 159990912X; 9781599909127

LC 2012005205

In this novel, by Mary Hooper, "Velvet is a laundress in a Victorian steam laundry. . . . The laundry is scalding, back-breaking work and Velvet is desperate to create a better life. Then she is noticed by Madame Savoya, a famed medium, who asks Velvet to come work for her. At first she is dazzled by the young yet beautifully dressed and bejeweled Madame. But Velvet soon realizes that Madame Savoya is not all that she says she is, and Velvet's very life may be in danger." (Publisher's note)

Includes bibliographical references

Hopkins, Ellen

★ **Burned**. Margaret K. McElderry Books 2006 532p $16.95

Grades: 9 10 11 12

1. Novels in verse 2. Mormons -- Fiction 3. Sex role -- Fiction 4. Child abuse -- Fiction 5. Family life -- Fiction

ISBN 1-4169-0354-2; 978-1-4169-0354-3

LC 2005-32461

Seventeen-year-old Pattyn, the eldest daughter in a large Mormon family, is sent to her aunt's Nevada ranch for the summer, where she temporarily escapes her alcoholic, abusive father and finds love and acceptance, only to lose everything when she returns home.

"The free verses, many in the form of concrete poems, create a compressed and intense reading experience with no extraneous dialogue or description. . . . This book will appeal to teens favoring realistic fiction and dramatic interpersonal stories." Voice Youth Advocates

Identical. Margaret K. McElderry Books 2008 565p $17.99

Grades: 10 11 12

1. Novels in verse 2. Twins -- Fiction 3. Sisters -- Fiction 4. Child sexual abuse -- Fiction

ISBN 978-1-4169-5005-9; 1-4169-5005-2

LC 2007-32463

Sixteen-year-old identical twin daughters of a district court judge and a candidate for the United States House of Representatives, Kaeleigh and Raeanne Gardella desperately struggle with secrets that have already torn them and their family apart.

This book "tells the twins' story in intimate and often-graphic detail. Hopkins packs in multiple issues including eating disorders, drug abuse, date rape, alcoholism, sexual abuse, and self-mutilation as she examines a family that 'puts the dys in dysfunction.' . . . Gritty and compelling, this is not a comfortable read, but its keen insights make it hard to put down." SLJ

Rumble; Ellen Hopkins. Margaret K. McElderry Books. 2014 546p $19.99

Grades: 8 9 10 11 12

1. Family problems -- Fiction 2. Grief -- Fiction 3. High schools -- Fiction 4. Novels in verse 5. Suicide -- Fiction

ISBN: 1442482842; 9781442482845

LC 2013037681

In this verse novel, "Matthew Turner doesn't have faith in anything. Not in family--his is a shambles after his younger brother was bullied into suicide. Not in so-called friends who turn their backs when things get tough. Not in some all-powerful creator who lets too much bad stuff happen. . . . No matter what his girlfriend Hayden says about faith and forgiveness, there's no way Matt's letting go of blame." (Publisher's note)

"Matt is a wonderfully faceted character that readers will alternately sympathize with and dislike. His actions are directly related to his emotional turmoil, and teens will understand his pain and admire his intellect, even while shaking their heads over his actions.." SLJ

Smoke; Ellen Hopkins. 1st ed. Margaret K. McElderry Books 2013 560 p. (hardcover) $19.99

Grades: 9 10 11 12

1. Rape -- Fiction 2. Homicide -- Fiction 3. Novels in verse 4. Grief -- Fiction 5. Mormons -- Fiction 6. Sisters -- Fiction 7. Runaways -- Fiction 8. Emotional problems -- Fiction

ISBN 9781416983286; 1416983287

LC 2012038452

Sequel to: Burned

In this sequel to Ellen Hopkins' "Burned," sisters Pattyn and Jackie "wrestle with guilt and fear after one kills the father who battered them." Pattyn stays with a family of farm workers while hiding from police. "Meanwhile, 15-year-old Jackie is stuck at home, narrating her own half of the story. Through free-verse poems . . . , the shooting's details emerge. A schoolmate raped Jackie; blaming Jackie, Dad broke her ribs and loosened her teeth; Pattyn's gun stopped Dad forever." (Kirkus Reviews)

Tricks. Margaret K. McElderry Books 2009 627p $18.99

Grades: 10 11 12

1. Novels in verse 2. Family life -- Fiction 3. Prostitution -- Fiction

ISBN 978-1-4169-5007-3

LC 2009-20297

Five troubled teenagers fall into prostitution as they search for freedom, safety, community, family, and love.

"Hopkins's pithy free verse reveals shards of emotion and quick glimpses of physical detail. It doesn't matter that the first-person voices blur, because the stories are distinct and unmistakable. Graphic sex, rape, drugs, bitter loneliness, despair—and eventually, blessedly, glimmers of hope." Kirkus

★ The **you** I've never known. Ellen Hopkins. Margaret K. McElderry Books 2017 608 p.
Grades: 9 10 11 12

    1. Identity -- Fiction 2. Kidnapping -- Fiction 3. Lesbians -- Fiction 4. Parent and child -- Fiction 5. Psychopaths -- Fiction 6. Sexual orientation -- Fiction 7. Parent-child relationship -- Fiction
9781481442909, $18.99; 9781481442916
LC 2016027736

In this novel, by Ellen Hopkins, "Ariel's mom disappeared when she was a baby. . . . Maya's a teenager who's run from an abusive mother right into the arms of an older man she thinks she can trust. But now she's isolated with a baby on the way, and life's getting more complicated. . . . Ariel and Maya's lives collide unexpectedly when Ariel's mother shows up out of the blue with wild accusations: Ariel wasn't abandoned. Her father kidnapped her fourteen years ago." (Publisher's note)

"Hopkins creates a satisfying and moving story, and her carefully structured poems ensure that each word and phrase is savored." Pub Wkly

Hopkinson, Nalo

The **Chaos**; Nalo Hopkinson. Margaret K. McElderry Books 2012 241p. (hardcover) $16.99
Grades: 7 8 9 10 11 12

    1. Science fiction 2. Toronto (Ont.) -- Fiction 3. Siblings -- Fiction 4. Racially mixed people -- Fiction 5. Canada -- Fiction 6. Identity -- Fiction 7. Supernatural -- Fiction 8. Brothers and sisters -- Fiction 9. Family life -- Canada -- Fiction 10. Interpersonal relations -- Fiction
ISBN 1416954880; 9781416954880; 9781442409552
LC 2011018154

In this young adult science fiction novel, "Scotch's womanly build and mixed heritage (white Jamaican dad, black American mom) made her the target of small-town school bullies. Since moving to Toronto, she's found friends and status. . . . When a giant bubble appears at an open-mic event, Scotch dares her brother, Rich, to touch it. He disappears, a volcano rises from Lake Ontario and chaos ripples across city and world, transforming reality in ways bizarre." (Kirkus Reviews)

Hornby, Nick, 1957-

★ **Slam**. G.P. Putnam's Sons 2007 309p $19.99; (audiobook) $29.95
Grades: 8 9 10 11 12

    1. Skateboarders -- Fiction 2. Skateboarding -- Fiction 3. Teenage fathers -- Fiction
ISBN 9780399250484; 0399250484; 9780143142836
LC 2007-14146

In this book by Nick Hornby, "for 16-year-old Sam, life is about to get extremely complicated. He and his girlfriend--make that ex-girlfriend--Alicia have gotten themselves into a bit of trouble." When she gets pregnant, "Sam is suddenly

forced to grow up and struggle with the familiar fears and inclinations that haunt us all." (Publisher's note)

The author "pens a first novel for teens that is a sweet and funny story about mistakes and choices. . . . Recommend this delightful and poignant novel to older teens who will laugh and weep with Sam." Voice Youth Advocates

Horowitz, Anthony

Raven's gate; book one of the Gatekeepers. [by] Anthony Horowitz. 1st ed; Scholastic Press 2005 254p (Gatekeepers) $17.95; pa $7.99
Grades: 6 7 8 9

    1. Witchcraft -- Fiction 2. Supernatural -- Fiction
ISBN 0-439-67995-8; 0-439-68009-7 pa
LC 2004-21512

Sent to live in a foster home in a remote Yorkshire village, Matt, a troubled fourteen-year-old English boy, uncovers an evil plot involving witchcraft and the site of an ancient stone circle.

"The creepy activities and the overall atmosphere of fear are well defined, and once the action starts, it doesn't let up. . . . This powerful struggle between good and evil is a real page-turner." SLJ

Other titles in the Gatekeepers series are:
Evil star (2006)
Nightrise (2007)
Necropolis (2009)
Oblivion (2013)

★ **Stormbreaker**. Philomel Books 2001 192p (An Alex Rider adventure) $17.99; pa $7.99
Grades: 5 6 7 8

    1. Adventure fiction 2. Spies -- Fiction 3. Orphans -- Fiction 4. Terrorism -- Fiction
ISBN 0-399-23620-1; 0-14-240611-2 pa
LC 00-63683

First published 2000 in the United Kingdom

After the death of the uncle who had been his guardian, fourteen-year-old Alex Rider is coerced to continue his uncle's dangerous work for Britain's intelligence agency, MI6

"Horowitz thoughtfully balances Alex's super-spy finesse with typical teen insecurities to create a likable hero living a fantasy come true. An entertaining, nicely layered novel." Booklist

Other titles about Alex Rider are:
Point blank (2002)
Skeleton key (2003)
Eagle strike (2004)
Scorpia (2005)
Ark angel (2006)
Snakehead (2007)
Crocodile tears (2009)
Scorpia rising (2011)
Russian roulette (2013)
Never say die (2017)

Horvath, Polly

The **Corps** of the Bare-Boned Plane. Farrar, Straus and Giroux 2007 261p $17
Grades: 7 8 9 10 11 12

    1. Death -- Fiction 2. Uncles -- Fiction 3. Cousins -- Fiction 4. Islands -- Fiction 5. Airplanes -- Fiction 6.

Bereavement -- Fiction
ISBN 978-0-374-31553-5; 0-374-31553-1
LC 2006-41281

When their parents are killed in a train accident, cousins Meline and Jocelyn, who have little in common, are sent to live with their wealthy, eccentric, and isolated Uncle Marten on his island off the coast of British Columbia, where they are soon joined by other oddly disconnected and troubled people.

"The savagely dark humor allows Horvath to place her characters in increasingly bizarre psychic positions, building to an almost painful crescendo in a remarkable examination of the extremes of emotional distress." Horn Book

Hough, Robert

Diego's Crossing. By Robert Hough. Firefly Books Ltd 2015 152 p.
Grades: 9 10 11 12JC813/.6
  1. Mexico -- Fiction 2. Drug traffic -- Fiction 3. Mystery fiction 4. Violence -- Fiction
1554517575; 9781554517572, $21.95

In this book, by Robert Hough, "Seventeen-year-old Diego lives in a broken-down town in Mexico, not too far from the U.S. border. The area has been ravaged by drug wars, leaving a trail of dead bodies. To make matters worse, Diego's older brother is a drug dealer with a healthy ego. After his brother is injured during a night of partying, Diego is forced to take his brother's place in the next drug run in order to protect his family." (School Library Journal)

"This short page-turner will appeal to reluctant readers and those looking to read unique, high-stakes YA." SLJ

Houston, Julian

New boy. Houghton Mifflin Co. 2005 282p $16
Grades: 8 9 10 11 12
  1. School stories 2. Prejudices -- Fiction 3. African Americans -- Fiction
ISBN 0-618-43253-1
LC 2004-27207

"As the first black student in an elite Connecticut boarding school in the late 1950s, Rob Garrett, 16, knows he is making history. . . . When his friends in the South plan a sit-in against segregation, he knows he must be part of it. . . . The honest first-person narrative makes stirring drama. . . . This brings up much for discussion about then and now." Booklist

Howard, A. G.

Unhinged: a novel; by A. G. Howard. Amulet Books. 2014 400p $17.95
Grades: 9 10 11 12
  1. Characters in literature -- Fiction 2. Mental illness --Fiction 3. Mother-daughter relationship-- Fiction 4. Supernatural -- Fiction
ISBN: 1419709712; 9781419709715
LC 2013026395

In this sequel to Splintered (2013) Alyssa Gardner, a descendant of Alice Liddell, Lewis Carroll's inspiration for Alice and Wonderland, " has been down the rabbit hole. . . . Now all she has to do is graduate high school. That would be easier without her mother, freshly released from an asylum, acting overly protective and suspicious. It would be much

simpler if the mysterious Morpheus didn't show up for school one day to tempt her with another dangerous quest in the dark, challenging Wonderland." (Publisher's note)

"Alyssa left Wonderland (in Splintered) a year ago, but now her dreams foreshadow new trouble there. When Wonderland's inhabitants enter the human realm, Alyssa's two worlds collide. Though a romantic triangle and Alyssa's identity struggle bog down this second installment, fans will be intrigued by the cliffhanger ending, which hints at future trips to Wonderland--and to "the looking-glass world, Any-Elsewhere." Horn Book

Sequel to: Splintered

Howard, J. J.

That time I joined the circus; J.J. Howard. Point 2013 272 p. (hardcover) $17.99
Grades: 7 8 9 10
  1. Circus -- Fiction 2. Absent mothers -- Fiction 3. Florida -- Fiction 4. Friendship -- Fiction 5. Best friends -- Fiction 6. New York (N.Y.) -- Fiction 7. Mothers and daughters -- Fiction 8. Single-parent families -- Fiction
ISBN 0545433819; 9780545433815
LC 2012016715

In this novel, 17-year-old Lexi lives with her father Gavin, a musician in New York City. Her "long-absent mother . . . has apparently joined the circus. When Gavin dies unexpectedly, leaving his daughter penniless, her only option is to track down her mother in Florida. Failing to find her, Lexi gratefully accepts work with the Circus Europa." (Publishers Weekly)

Howe, Katherine

Conversion; by Katherine Howe. G. P. Putnam's Sons. 2014 432p $18.88
Grades: 7 8 9 10 11 12
  1. Epidemics -- Fiction 2. Friendship -- Fiction 3. High schools -- Fiction 4. Massachusetts -- Fiction 5. Salem (Mass.) -- Fiction 6. Witchcraft -- Fiction
ISBN: 0399167773; 9780399167775
LC 2014000397

When girls start experiencing strange tics and other mysterious symptoms at Colleen's high school, her small town of Danvers, Massachusetts, falls victim to rumors that lead to full-blown panic, and only Colleen connects their fate to the ill-fated Salem Village, where another group of girls suffered from a similarly bizarre epidemic three centuries ago.

"A simmering blend of relatable high-school drama with a persistent pinprick of unearthliness in the background." Booklist

Howell, Simmone

Girl defective. Simmone Howell. Atheneum Books for Young Readers 2014 320 p.
Grades: 9 10 11 12
  1. Coming of age -- Fiction 2. Family life -- Australia -- Fiction 3. Friendship -- Fiction 4. Mystery and detective stories 5. Record stores -- Fiction 6. Australia -- Fiction 7. Saint Kilda (Vic.) -- Fiction 8. Family life -- Fiction 9. Teenage girls -- Fiction
1442497602; 9781442497603, $17.99; 9781442497610
LC 2013032738

This young adult novel by Simmone Howell, with photography by Henry Beer, is "a story about Skylark Martin, who lives with her father and brother in a vintage record shop and is trying to find her place in the world. It's about ten-year-old Super Agent Gully and his case of a lifetime. And about beautiful, reckless, sharp-as-knives Nancy. It's about tragi-hot Luke, and just-plain-tragic Mia Casey. . . . It's about summer, and weirdness, and mystery, and music." (Publisher's note)

"Funny, observant, a relentless critic of the world's (and her own) flaws, Sky is original, thoroughly authentic and great company, decorating her astute, irreverent commentary with vivid Aussie references; chasing these down should provide foreign readers with hours of online fun." Kirkus

"Originally published in 2013 in Australia by Pan Macmillan Australia Pty Limited"—Copyright page.

Howland, Leila

Nantucket blue; Leila Howland. 1st ed. Hyperion 2013 304 p. (reinforced) $16.99

Grades: 8 9 10 11 12

    1. Summer -- Fiction 2. Female friendship -- Fiction 3. Interpersonal relations -- Fiction 4. Grief -- Fiction 5. Divorce -- Fiction 6. Friendship -- Fiction 7. Best friends -- Fiction 8. Dating (Social customs) -- Fiction 9. Nantucket Island (Mass.) -- Fiction

    ISBN 1423160517; 9781423160519

LC 2012035121

"Lacrosse-champ Cricket Thompson has always been welcomed by her best friend Jules's affluent family. But when Nina, Jules's mother, dies suddenly, big changes ensue. Expecting her usual warm reception, Cricket shows up at Jules's family home on Nantucket to find herself shunned. There's some emotional heaviness to the story, but it's also a breezy, beach-ready tale of self-awakening and first love." (Horn Book)

Hrdlitschka, Shelley

Allegra; by Shelley Hrdlitschka. Orca Book Publishers 2013 280 p. (paperback) $12.95; (ebook) $12.99; (ebook) $12.99

Grades: 7 8 9 10

    1. School stories 2. Teacher-student relationship -- Fiction 3. Performing arts high schools -- Fiction 4. Teacher-student relationships -- Fiction

    ISBN 1459801970; 9781459801974; 9781459801981 pdf; 9781459801998

LC 2012952952

In this book, Allegra, daughter of two musicians, is thrilled to be at Deer Lake School for the Fine and Performing Arts. She "has her sights set on becoming a professional dancer. However, her excitement is dimmed by the school's requirement that she take a music-theory class. Despite her initial reluctance, Allegra soon begins to enjoy the class due to the charisma of its young and attractive teacher," Mr. Rocchelli. Is their relationship too close? (School Library Journal)

Sister wife. Orca 2008 269p pa $12.95

Grades: 8 9 10 11 12

    1. Polygamy -- Fiction

    ISBN 978-1-55143-927-3; 1-55143-927-1

In a remote polygamist community, Celeste struggles to accept her destiny while longing to be free to live her life her way.

"This compelling story combines with authentic characters to pique the interest of a wide array of teens and get them talking about faith and free will." Voice Youth Advocates

Hubbard, Amanda

Ripple; [by] Mandy Hubbard. Razorbill 2011 260p $16.99

Grades: 8 9 10 11 12

    1. Love stories 2. Fantasy fiction 3. Sirens (Mythology)

    ISBN 978-1-59514-423-2; 1-59514-423-4

"Lexi, 18, is responsible for the death of Steven, her friend Siena's brother and the only boy she ever loved. That was two years ago, right before discovering that she is a siren, cursed to swim each night and sing out haunting melodies that will lure men to their deaths in the water. She has been protecting herself and those around her by keeping everyone at a distance and swimming in an isolated lake where no one will hear her song. But as the new school year begins, Lexi finds herself pursued by two boys whom she can't ignore. . . . In this new twist on a supernatural romance, Hubbard expands the genre by including both a siren and a nix in among the high school drama. . . . Fans of girl dramas, mysteries, and fantasy romance will devour the story." SLJ

Hubbard, Jennifer R.

Try not to breathe; Jennifer R. Hubbard. Viking 2012 233 p. (hardcover) $16.99

Grades: 10 11 12

    1. Friendship -- Fiction 2. Teenagers -- Suicide -- Fiction 3. Mentally ill -- Institutional care -- Fiction 4. Suicide -- Fiction 5. Interpersonal relations -- Fiction

    ISBN 0670013900; 9780670013906

LC 2011012203

In this book, a "half-hearted suicide attempt lands Ryan at a facility for adolescents with emotional problems. He makes friends and recovers, but now that he's home again, he's not quite sure how to re-enter his life, especially when he meets a girl named Nicki, who keeps pressuring him to share his secrets. . . . He gradually realizes that he has the inner resources to cope with rejection and uncertainty." (Bulletin of the Center for Children's Books)

Hubbard, Jenny

★ **And** we stay; Jenny Hubbard. Delacorte Press 2014 240 p. (hc) $16.99

Grades: 9 10 11 12

    1. High school students -- Fiction 2. Teenagers -- Suicide -- Fiction 3. Poetry -- Fiction 4. Schools -- Fiction 5. Suicide -- Fiction 6. High schools -- Fiction 7. Amherst (Mass.) -- Fiction 8. Boarding schools -- Fiction 9. Interpersonal relations -- Fiction

    ISBN 0385740573; 9780375989551; 9780385740579

LC 2013002236

In this book, by Jenny Hubbard "high school senior Paul Wagoner walks into his school library with a stolen gun, . . . threatens his girlfriend Emily Beam, then takes his own life.

In the wake of the tragedy, an angry and guilt-ridden Emily is shipped off to boarding school in Amherst, Massachusetts, where she encounters a ghostly presence who shares her name. The spirit of Emily Dickinson and two quirky girls offer helping hands, but it is up to Emily to heal her own damaged self." (Publisher's note)

"Budding poets may particularly appreciate Emily's story, but there is certainly something for anyone looking for a good read with a strong, believable female lead who is working her hardest to overcome tragedy." SLJ

★ **Paper** covers rock. Delacorte Press 2011 183p $16.99; lib bdg $19.99; ebook $10.99
Grades: 9 10 11 12
　　1. School stories 2. Death -- Fiction 3. North Carolina -- Fiction 4. Conduct of life -- Fiction
　　ISBN 9781464021572; 9781464021565; 9781464021657; 978-0-385-74055-5; 978-0-375-98954-4 lib bdg; 978-0-375-89942-3 ebook
　　　　　　　　　　　　　　　　　　LC 2010-23462
In this book, set at a "boys' boarding school, 16-year-old Alex is devastated when he fails to save a drowning friend. When questioned, Alex and his friend Glenn, who was also at the river, begin weaving their web of lies. . . . Caught in the web with Alex and Glenn is their English teacher, Miss Dovecott, fresh out of Princeton, who suspects there's more to what happened at the river when she perceives guilt in Alex's writing for class." (Booklist)

This is "a powerful story of how the truth can easily be manipulated, how actions can be misinterpreted, and how fragile adolescent friendships and alliances can be." Voice Youth Advocates

Hubbard, Kirsten

Wanderlove; Kirsten Hubbard. Delacorte Press 2012 338 p. (hc) $17.99
Grades: 10 11 12
　　1. Travel -- Fiction 2. Children -- Travel 3. Central America -- Fiction 4. Love -- Fiction 5. Artists -- Fiction
　　ISBN 0385739370; 9780375897511; 9780385739375; 9780385907859
　　　　　　　　　　　　　　　　　　LC 2011007435
In this book, "Bria decides to do the most un-Bria-like thing she can think of: she signs up alone for a tour to Central America. When she finds out her traveling companions are a group of middle-aged tourists rather than the young, carefree backpackers on the brochure, she's thoroughly disappointed. . . . She breaks from her tour group and joins a girl named Starling and her brother Rowan to pursue what she considers a more authentic traveling experience." (Bulletin of the Center for Children's Books)

"With an extraordinary setting, delicately rendered and well informed by Hubbard's years as a guide to Central American travel on About.com, this becomes a wonderful story of kindred souls in a land of beauty, illuminated by Hubbard's own drawings." Booklist

Hughes, Dean

★ **Four**-Four-Two. Dean Hughes. Atheneum Books for Young Readers 2016 272 p. Illustration

Grades: 7 8 9 10
　　1. United States. Army. Regimental Combat Team, 442nd -- Fiction 2. Japanese Americans -- Evacuation and relocation, 1942-1945 -- Fiction 3. Prejudices -- Fiction 4. Soldiers -- Fiction 5. World War, 1939-1945 -- Fiction
　　9781481462525, $17.99; 9781481462532
　　　　　　　　　　　　　　　　　　LC 2015043700
In this novel, by Dean Hughes, "Yuki Nakahara is an American. But it's the start of World War II, and America doesn't see it that way. . . . But Yuki . . . [is] going to prove it by enlisting in the army to fight for the Allies. When Yuki and his friend Shig ship out, they aren't prepared for the experiences they'll encounter as members of the 'Four-Four-Two,' a segregated regiment made up entirely of Japanese-American soldiers." (Publisher's note)

"Nuanced and riveting in equal parts." Kirkus
Includes bibliographical references

Search and destroy. Atheneum Books for Young Readers 2006 216p $16.95
Grades: 7 8 9 10
　　1. Vietnam War, 1961-1975 -- Fiction
　　ISBN 0-689-87023-X
　　　　　　　　　　　　　　　　　　LC 2005-11255
Recent high school graduate Rick Ward, undecided about his future and eager to escape his unhappy home life, joins the army and experiences the horrors of the war in Vietnam.

"This is a compelling, insightful story about the emotional, physical, and psychological scars that wars leave upon soldiers." Booklist

Humphreys, Chris

The **hunt** of the unicorn. Alfred A. Knopf 2011 345p $16.99; lib bdg $19.99; e-book $16.99
Grades: 6 7 8 9
　　1. Fantasy fiction 2. Unicorns -- Fiction
　　ISBN 978-0-375-85872-7; 0-375-85872-7; 978-0-375-95872-4 lib bdg; 0-375-95872-4; 978-0-375-89624-8 e-book
　　　　　　　　　　　　　　　　　　LC 2010-30852
Despite strange dreams and her ailing father's firm belief in the family lore of a long-ago ancestor's connection to the mythical unicorn, fifteen-year-old New Yorker Elayne remains skeptical until, during a school visit to the unicorn tapestries in the Cloisters, she finds herself entering a tumultuous world where she must fulfill the legacy of her ancestors by taming the unicorn and bringing a tyrant to justice.

"This is wish fulfillment at its finest, with Elayne playing the everyday gal turned spunky heroine. . . . With references to our world's overpopulation and pollution, there is a heady dose of environmentalism here, but it is nicely tempered with a fair amount of humor and adventure." Bull Cent Child Books

Huntley, Amy

The **everafter**. Balzer + Bray 2009 144p $16.99; lib bdg $17.89; pa $8.99
Grades: 7 8 9 10
　　1. Dead -- Fiction 2. Death -- Fiction 3. Friendship

-- Fiction 4. Lost and found possessions -- Fiction
ISBN 978-0-06-177679-3; 0-06-177679-3; 978-0-06-177680-9 lib bdg; 0-06-177680-7 lib bdg; 978-0-06-177681-6 pa; 0-06-177681-5 pa

LC 2008-46149

ALA YALSA Morris Award Finalist, 2010

Madison Stanton doesn't know where she is or how she got there. But she does know this—she is dead. And alone in a vast, dark space. The only company Maddy has in this place are luminescent objects that turn out to be all the things she lost while she was alive. And soon she discovers that, with these artifacts, she can re-experience—and even—change moments from her life.

"This fresh take on a teen's journey of self-exploration is a compelling and highly enjoyable tale. Huntley expertly combines a coming-of-age story with a supernatural mystery that keeps readers engrossed until the climactic ending. This touching story will appeal to those looking for a ghost story, romance, or family drama." SLJ

Hurley, Tonya

★ **Ghostgirl**. Little, Brown 2008 328p $17.99
Grades: 7 8 9 10

1. Ghost stories 2. School stories 3. Death -- Fiction 4. Popularity -- Fiction
ISBN 978-0-316-11357-1; 0-316-11357-3

LC 2007-31541

After dying, high school senior Charlotte Usher is as invisible to nearly everyone as she always felt, but despite what she learns in a sort of alternative high school for dead teens, she clings to life while seeking a way to go to the Fall Ball with the boy of her dreams.

"Hurley combines afterlife antics, gothic gore, and high school hell to produce an original, hilarious satire. . . . Tim Burton and Edgar Allan Poe devotees will die for this fantastic, phantasmal read." SLJ

Other titles in this series are:
Ghostgirl: Homecoming (2009)
Ghostgirl: Lovesick (2010)

Hurwin, Davida

Freaks and revelations; a novel. by Davida Wills Hurwin. Little, Brown and Co. 2009 234p $16.99
Grades: 10 11 12

1. California -- Fiction 2. Drug abuse -- Fiction 3. Prejudices -- Fiction 4. Gay teenagers -- Fiction
ISBN 978-0-316-04996-2; 0-316-04996-4

LC 2008-47384

Tells, in two voices, of events leading up to a 1980 incident in which fourteen-year-old Jason, a gay youth surviving on the streets as a prostitute, and seventeen-year-old Doug, a hate-filled punk rocker, have a fateful meeting in a Los Angeles alley.

"Sympathetic to both characters without shying away from brutality—physical or emotional—the finely crafted story leads to a powerful climax of hope and redemption that will stay with readers." Publ Wkly

Hurwitz, Gregg

The **rains**. By Gregg Hurwitz. SDC Publications 2016 352 p.

Grades: 8 9 10 11

1. Zombies -- Fiction 2. Brothers -- Fiction 3. Paranormal fiction
9781466888517, $60; 9780765382672, $17.99; 0765382679

LC 2016041559

In this novel, by Gregg Hurwitz, "in one terrifying night, the peaceful community of Creek's Cause turns into a war zone. No one under the age of eighteen is safe. Chance Rain and his older brother, Patrick, have already fended off multiple attacks from infected adults by the time they arrive at the school where other young survivors are hiding." (Publisher's note)

"This zombie-esque sci-fi novel will feed the needs of readers looking for a fast-paced, adrenaline-pumping story with elements of horror. " Kirkus

Huser, Glen

Stitches. Groundwood Books 2003 198p hardcover o.p. pa $6.95
Grades: 7 8 9 10

1. Canada -- Fiction 2. Bullies -- Fiction 3. Sex role -- Fiction 4. Puppets and puppet plays -- Fiction
ISBN 0-88899-553-9; 0-88899-578-4 pa

LC 2003-363167

This story of two outsiders who become friends is set in rural Alberta. The protagonists "are Chantelle, who has a limp and a scarred face, and Travis, a boy completely unselfconscious about his love for puppets and sewing. Both kids have ragtaggle families. . . . Chantelle and Travis joined forces back in fifth grade, when she rescued him from the boys who called him 'girlie'; junior high brings new challenges as the teasing gets uglier and, eventually, violent."

"Teachers will use this book in their classrooms, but it will appeal to leisure readers as well." Voice Youth Advocates

Hutchinson, Shaun David

The **apocalypse** of Elena Mendoza. Shaun David Hutchinson. Simon Pulse 2018 438 p.
Grades: 9 10 11 12

1. End of the world -- Fiction; 2. Healers -- Fiction; 3. Miracles -- Fiction; 4. Missing persons -- Fiction; 5. Science fiction; 6. Virgin birth -- Fiction
9781481498548, $17.99; 9781481498562

LC 2017020322

In this book, by Shaun David Hutchinson, "sixteen-year-old Elena Mendoza is the product of a virgin birth. This can be scientifically explained (it's called parthenogenesis), but what can't be explained is how Elena is able to heal Freddie...from a gunshot wound.... As more unbelievable things occur,...the only remaining explanation is... -- that the world is actually coming to an end, and Elena is possibly the only one who can do something about it." (Publisher's note)

"A creative and original tale shot through with quirky humor that entertains while encouraging readers to ponder questions of free will and social responsibility." Kirkus

At the edge of the universe. Shaun David Hutchinson. Simon Pulse 2017 485 p.
Grades: 9 10 11 12

1. Best friends -- Fiction; 2. Gay teenagers -- Fiction; 3. Missing persons -- Fiction; 4. LGBT people -- Fiction; 5.

Interpersonal relations -- Fiction; 6. Gay men -- Fiction
9781481449687; 9781481449663, $17.99

LC 2016956089

In this book, by Shaun David Hutchinson, "Tommy and Ozzie have been best friends since the second grade, and boyfriends since eighth. They spent countless days dreaming of escaping their small town -- and then Tommy...ceased to exist, erased from the minds and memories of everyone who knew him...except Ozzie. Ozzie doesn't know how to navigate life without Tommy, and soon he suspects that something else is going on: that the universe is shrinking." (Publisher's note)

"An earthy, existential coming-of-age gem." Kirkus

The **five** stages of Andrew Brawley. Shaun David Hutchinson; illustrations by Christine Larsen. Simon Pulse 2015 336 p. Illustration
Grades: 9 10 11 12

1. Cartoons and comics -- Fiction 2. Gays -- Fiction 3. Grief -- Fiction 4. Hospitals -- Fiction 5. Orphans -- Fiction 6. Runaways -- Fiction 7. Gay teenagers -- Fiction 8. Bereavement -- Fiction
1481403109; 9781481403108, $17.99

LC 2014022200

In this novel, by Shaun David Hutchinson, with illustrations by Christine Larsen, offers "narrator Andrew is a 17-year-old survivor of a terrible car accident that killed his parents and younger sister. He blames himself . . . , hiding out in a half-finished wing of the hospital where they died. One night, Rusty, another boy his age, arrives in the ER. . . . The boys come to realize a powerful attraction for one another and Andrew begins to open up to love and forgiveness." (School Library Journal)

"Hutchinson's latest is an unflinching look at loss, grief, and recovery. Seventeen-year-old Drew Brawley has been hiding from death for months in the Florida hospital where the rest of his family died. He passes the time working at the cafeteria and making friends with teen patients in the oncology ward. . . . Dark and frequently grim situations are lightened by realistic dialogue and genuineness of feeling. The rapid-fire back-and-forth snark between Drew and his hospital family rings true, and the mystery of Drew's past will keep readers turning the pages. This is a heartbreaking yet ultimately hopeful work from a writer to watch." Booklist

★ **We** are the ants. Shaun David Hutchinson. Simon & Schuster 2016 464 p.

1. Alien abduction -- Fiction 2. Psychological fiction 3. Depression (Psychology) -- Fiction 4. Gay men -- Fiction
148144963X; 9781481449632, $17.99; 9781481475204

LC 2015042594

In this science fiction novel, by Shaun David Hutchinson, "the world will end in 144 days, and all Henry has to do to stop it is push a big red button. . . . But Henry is a scientist first, and facing the question thoroughly and logically, he begins to look for pros and cons. . . . Weighing the pain and the joy that surrounds him, Henry is left with the ultimate choice: push the button and save the planet and everyone on it...or let the world-and his pain-be destroyed forever." (Publisher's note)

"Hutchinson's excellent novel of ideas invites readers to wonder about their place in a world that often seems un-caring and meaningless. The novel is never didactic; on the contrary, it is unfailingly dramatic and crackling with characters who become real upon the page. Will Henry press the button? We all await his decision." Booklist

Hutton, Keely

★ Soldier boy. Keely Hutton ; afterword by Ricky Richard Anywar. Farrar, Straus & Giroux 2017 X, 326 p.
Grades: 8 9 10 11 12

1. Soldiers -- Fiction; 2. Anywar, Ricky Richard; 3. Uganda -- History -- 1979- -- Fiction; 4. Uganda -- Fiction
9780374305642; 9780374305635, $17.99

LC 2016035897

This book, by Keely Hutton, "begins with the story of Ricky Richard Anywar, abducted in 1989 to fight with Joseph Kony's rebel army in the Ugandan civil war (one of Africa's longest running conflicts). Ricky is trained, armed, and forced to fight government soldiers alongside his brutal kidnappers, but never stops dreaming of escape. The story continues twenty years later, with a fictionalized character named Samuel, a boy deathly afraid of trusting anyone ever again." (Publisher's note)

"The novel is a visceral indictment of man's inhumanity to man, while also celebrating human beings' ability to empathize and to rescue those who desperately need saving." Booklist

Hyde, Catherine Ryan

Jumpstart the world. Alfred A. Knopf 2010 186p $16.99; lib bdg $19.99
Grades: 9 10 11 12

1. School stories 2. Moving -- Fiction 3. Transgender people-- Fiction 4. Apartment houses -- Fiction 5. Mother-daughter relationship -- Fiction
ISBN 978-0-375-86665-4; 978-0-375-96665-1 lib bdg; 978-0-375-89677-4 ebook

LC 2010-02511

Sixteen-year-old Elle falls in love with Frank, the neighbor who helps her adjust to being on her own in a big city, but learning that he is transgendered turns her world upside-down.

"For a book loaded with issues—there is even treatment of mental illness—this is a plain good read. These characters are funny, complex, and engaging. . . . There are many teens today who need this book." Voice Youth Advocates

The **year** of my miraculous reappearance. Alfred A. Knopf 2007 228p $15.99; lib bdg $18.99
Grades: 7 8 9 10

1. Siblings -- Fiction 2. Alcoholism -- Fiction 3. Down syndrome -- Fiction
ISBN 978-0-375-83257-4; 978-0-375-93257-1 lib bdg; 0-375-83257-2; 0-375-93257-7 lib bdg

LC 2006-29194

Thirteen-year-old Cynnie has had to deal with her mother's alcoholism and stream of boyfriends all her life, but when her grandparents take custody of her brother, Bill, who has Down Syndrome, Cynnie becomes self-destructive and winds up in court-mandated Alcoholics Anonymous meetings.

"Cynnie's love for and devotion to Bill are wholly believable, as are her attempts to snare a stable adult presence in her life. Secondary characters are multidimensional and well drawn." Booklist

Ibbitson, John

The **Landing**; a novel. KCP Fiction 2008 160p $17.95; pa $7.95

Grades: 7 8 9 10

    1. Canada -- Fiction 2. Uncles -- Fiction 3. Violinists -- Fiction

    ISBN 978-1-55453-234-6; 1-55453-234-5; 978-1-55453-238-4 pa; 1-55453-238-8 pa

Ben thinks he will always be stuck at Cook's Landing, barely making ends meet like his uncle. But when he meets a wealthy widow from New York City, he sees himself there too. When she hires him to play his violin, he realizes his gift could unlock the possibilities of the world. Then, during a stormy night on Lake Muskoka, everything changes.

"With lovely prose, Ibbitson brings to life the rugged beauty and the devastating poverty of the Lake Muskoka region. His characters are as strong and remote as their surroundings." Voice Youth Advocates

Ingold, Jeanette

Hitch. Harcourt, Inc 2005 272p $17; pa $6.95

Grades: 7 8 9 10

    1. Montana -- Fiction 2. Great Depression, 1929-1939 -- Fiction

    ISBN 0-15-204747-6; 0-15-20561-9 pa

                       LC 2004-19447

To help his family during the Depression and avoid becoming a drunk like his father, Moss Trawnley joins the Civilian Conservation Corps, helps build a new camp near Monroe, Montana, and leads the other men in making the camp a success.

This is "a credible, involving story. . . . Both [the author's] writing style and her 1930s setting feels totally true to the time." Booklist

Ireland, Justina

★ **Dread** nation. Justina Ireland. Balzer + Bray 2018 464 p.

Grades: 9 10 11 12

    1. African Americans -- Fiction; 2. Conspiracies -- Fiction; 3. Horror tales; 4. Zombies -- Fiction;

    9780062570604

                      LC 2017943393

"In this alternate-history horror tale, shortly after Jane McKeene was born, the dead rose and attacked the living, effectively ending the Civil War. A reunified army fought the shambling hordes until Congress passed the Negro and Native Reeducation Act, requiring adolescent children of color to train for battle. At age 14, Jane—who is mixed race—enrolled at Miss Preston's School of Combat for Negro Girls, hoping to avoid conscription by becoming a socialite's bodyguard. Three years later, Jane is close to earning her attendant certificate when she, her ex, and her rival stumble across a dastardly plot hatched by Baltimore's elite." (Publishers Weekly)

"This absorbing page-turner works on multiple levels: as unflinching alternate history set in post-Reconstruction-era Maryland and Kansas; as a refreshingly subversive action story starring a badass (and biracial and bisexual) heroine; as zombie fiction suspenseful and gory enough to please any fan of the genre; and as a compelling exhortation to scrutinize the racist underpinnings of contemporary American sociopolitical systems." Kirkus

Isbell, Tom

The **Prey**. Tom Isbell. Harperteen 2015 416 p.

Grades: 7 8 9 10

    1. Orphans -- Fiction 2. Survival -- Fiction 3. Twins -- Fiction 4. Science fiction 5. Dystopian fiction

    0062216015; 9780062216014, $17.99

In this young adult science fiction novel, by Tom Isbell, "orphaned teens, soon to be hunted for sport, must flee their resettlement camps in their fight for survival and a better life. For in the Republic of the True America, it's always hunting season. . . . As unlikely Book and fearless Hope lead their quest for freedom, these teens must find the best in themselves to fight the worst in their enemies." (Publisher's note)

"An electromagnetic pulse followed by radiation-they called it Omega, the end-destroyed civilization as it once existed. The survivors established the Republic of the True America. But the future still looks like a dead end for Book and Hope, two teens who find themselves in the camps that purport to be orphanages...Careful readers will appreciate the irony and subtle, deeper meanings in character and location names as Isbell shapes his own vision of a dark world..." Booklist

Sequel: The Capture (2015)

Iturbe, Antonio

★ The **librarian** of Auschwitz. By Antonio Iturbe ; translated by Lilit Thwaites. Henry Holt & Co. 2017 423 p. Illustration

Grades: 7 8 9 10 11 12

    1. Books and reading -- Fiction; 2. Concentration camps -- Fiction; 3. Holocaust, Jewish (1939-1945) -- Germany -- Fiction; 4. Jews -- Germany -- History -- 1933-1945 -- Fiction; 5. Kraus, Dita, 1929-; 6. Germany -- History -- 1933-1945 -- Fiction; 7. Germany -- History -- 1933-1945 -- Fiction; 8. Jews -- Germany -- Fiction; 9. Auschwitz (Poland: Concentration camp) -- Fiction; 10. Holocaust, 1939-1945 -- Fiction

    9781627796187, $19.99; 9781627796194

                      LC 2017007363

In this book, by Antonio Iturbe, translated by Lilit Thwaites, "[14]-year-old Dita is one of the many imprisoned by the Nazis at Auschwitz. Taken, along with her mother and father, from the Terezín ghetto in Prague, Dita is adjusting to the constant terror that is life in the camp. When Jewish leader Freddy Hirsch asks Dita to take charge of the [8]...volumes the prisoners have managed to sneak past the guards, she agrees. And so Dita becomes the librarian of Auschwitz." (Publisher's note)

"Despite being a fictional retelling of a true story, this novel is one that could easily be recommended or taught alongside Elie Wiesel's Night and The Diary of Anne Frank and a text that, once read, will never be forgotten." SLJ

Includes bibliographical references.

Jae-Jones, S.

★ **Wintersong**: A Novel. S. Jae-Jones. Thomas Dunne Books, St Martin's Press 2016 448 p.

Grades: 9 10 11 12

1. Imaginary places -- Fiction 2. Sisters -- Fiction 3. Imaginary places

9781250079213, $18.99; 9781466892040, $60

LC 2016013865

In this book, by S. Jae-Jones, "all her life, Liesl has heard tales of the beautiful, dangerous Goblin King. They've enraptured her mind, her spirit, and inspired her musical compositions. Now eighteen and helping to run her family's inn, Liesl can't help but feel that her musical dreams and childhood fantasies are slipping away. But when her own sister is taken by the Goblin King, Liesl has no choice but to journey to the Underground to save her." (Publisher's note)

"Give this to readers who want to get lost in a musically deep love story." VOYA

Jackson, Tiffany D.

★ **Allegedly**. Tiffany D. Jackson; [edited by] Benjamin Rosenthal. Katherine Tegen Books 2017 400 p.

Grades: 9 10 11 12

1. African American teenagers -- Fiction; 2. Murder -- Investigation -- Fiction; 3. Teenage pregnancy -- Fiction

9780062422644, $17.99

LC 2016935938

"Mary B. Addison killed a baby. Allegedly. She didn't say much in that first interview with detectives, and the media filled in the only blanks that mattered: a white baby had died while under the care of a churchgoing black woman and her nine-year-old daughter. The public convicted Mary and the jury made it official. But did she do it?" (Publisher's note)

Monday's not coming. Tiffany D. Jackson. Katherine Tegen Books 2018 435 p.

Grades: 8 9 10 11 12

1. Missing persons -- Fiction; 2. Missing persons -- Fiction; 3. High school students -- Fiction; 4. Friendship -- Fiction

9780062422699; 9780062422675, $17.99

LC 2018933268

In this book, by Tiffany D. Jackson, "Monday Charles is missing, and only Claudia seems to notice. Claudia and Monday have always been inseparable -- more sisters than friends. So when Monday doesn't turn up for the first day of school, Claudia's worried. When she doesn't show for the second day, or second week, Claudia knows that something is wrong." (Publisher's note)

"This is a powerful and emotional novel that is gripping and heartbreaking and hits upon serious topics." Booklist

Jacobs, John Hornor

The **Shibboleth** by John Hornor Jacobs. Carolrhoda Lab. 2014 393p $17.95

Grades: 9 10 11 12

1. Ability -- Fiction 2. Bullies -- Fiction 3. Memory -- Fiction 4. Psychiatric hospitals -- Fiction 5.

Supernatural -- Fiction

ISBN: 0761390081; 9780761390084

LC 2013009535

Second title in the author's Twelve-fingered boy trilogy

"Branded a 'candy' dealer for doling out drugs, Shreve is incarcerated in a juvenile detention center at first, but after he frightens a nurse there, he's sent to a mental hospital, where he's drugged for schizophrenia. What his keepers don't know is that he's not schizophrenic at all. Instead, he's a shibboleth, a being that can read minds and possess the bodies of others." (Kirkus Reviews)

"Polydactyl hero Shreve, now sixteen, escapes from Tulaville Psychiatric Hospital to seek Hiram Quincrux--the monster behind an insomnia epidemic causing mayhem in the U.S.--and pit his own "extranatural" powers, his shibboleth, against Quincrux's. The sheer weirdness of it all will captivate readers and involve them in a memorable second installment that nicely sets up what's sure to be a dramatic conclusion." Horn Book

★ The **twelve**-fingered boy; John Hornor Jacobs. Carolrhoda Lab. 2013 264 p. $17.95

Grades: 9 10 11 12

1. Fantasy fiction 2. Teenagers -- Fiction 3. Ability -- Fiction 4. Bullies -- Fiction 5. Supernatural -- Fiction 6. Juvenile detention homes -- Fiction

ISBN 0761390073; 9780761390077

LC 2012015292

This is the first in a trilogy from John Hornor Jacobs about superhuman teens. "Fifteen-year-old Shreve Cannon is passing the time in Pulaski Juvenile Detention Center, . . . when he's assigned a new roommate: Jack Graves, a small, quiet 13-year old with 12 fingers and uncontrollable telekinetic abilities. When a stranger named Mr. Quincrux shows up, sporting nasty mental powers and an uncomfortable interest in Jack, the boys . . . break out of juvie and go on the run." (Publishers Weekly)

Jaden, Denise

Losing Faith. Simon Pulse 2010 381p pa $9.99

Grades: 7 8 9 10 11 12

1. School stories 2. Cults -- Fiction 3. Death -- Fiction 4. Sisters -- Fiction 5. Bereavement -- Fiction 6. Christian life -- Fiction

ISBN 978-1-4169-9609-5; 1-4169-9609-5

LC 2010-7296

Brie tries to cope with her grief over her older sister Faith's sudden death by trying to learn more about the religious "home group" Faith secretly joined and never talked about with Brie or her parents.

"With pitch-perfect portrayals of high school social life and a nuanced view into a variety of Christian experiences of faith, this first novel gives readers much to think about." SLJ

Jaffe, Michele

Bad kitty. HarperCollins Publishers 2006 268p il hardcover o.p. pa $8.99

Grades: 9 10 11 12

1. Mystery fiction 2. Las Vegas (Nev.) -- Fiction

ISBN 0-06-078108-4; 978-0-06-078108-8; 0-06-078110-6 pa; 978-0-06-078110-1 pa

LC 2005-5733

While vacationing with her family in Las Vegas, seventeen-year-old Jasmine stumbles upon a murder mystery that she attempts to solve with the help of her friends, recently arrived from California.

"Readers will likely find themselves quickly clawing their way through this fun novel." Publ Wkly

Followed by: Kitty kitty (2008)

Rosebush. Razorbill 2010 326p $16.99

Grades: 8 9 10 11 12

1. Mystery fiction 2. Traffic accidents -- Fiction

ISBN 978-1-59514-353-2; 1-59514-353-X

Instead of celebrating Memorial Day weekend on the Jersey Shore, Jane is in the hospital surrounded by teddy bears, trying to piece together what happened last night. One minute she was at a party, wearing fairy wings and cuddling with her boyfriend. The next, she was lying near-dead in a rosebush after a hit-and-run.

"Compulsively readable, the novel bristles with red herrings, leading readers down one tempting plot branch after another, each one blooming with plausibility. The characters are skillfully cultivated through flashbacks, and the insecure, people-pleasing Jane grows believably as she takes on the mystery." Booklist

Jägerfeld, Jenny

Me on the Floor, Bleeding. Jenny Jagerfeld; translated by Susan Beard. Stockholm Text 2014 288 p.

Grades: 9 10 11 12

1. High school girls -- Fiction 2. Identity -- Fiction 3. High school students -- Fiction 4. Bildungsromans

917547011X; 9789175470115, $14.95

In this young adult novel by Jenny Jägerfeld, translated by Susan Beard, "High school outsider Maja would never hurt herself on purpose as her dad, teachers, and classmates seem to believe. . . . In this funny and clever coming-of-age novel, seventeen-year-old Maja describes each moment with such bare-bones honesty that one can't help but be drawn into her world." (Publisher's note)

"While the translation from Swedish may account in part for the plodding nature of the narration, Maja's life is plodding, a fact surely understood and appreciated by readers who will come to root for her in her search to understand her parents and thus herself." Booklist

James, Rebecca

Beautiful malice; a novel. Bantam Books 2010 260p $25

Grades: 9 10 11 12

1. Australia -- Fiction 2. Friendship -- Fiction 3. Bereavement -- Fiction

ISBN 978-0-553-80805-6

LC 2010-6255

To escape the media attention generated by her sister's murder, a grieving seventeen-year-old Australian girl moves away and meets a vibrant new friend who harbors a dangerous secret.

This "novel will grab your attention on the first page, and you won't want to turn away even after the last page has been turned." Voice Youth Advocates

Jansen, Hanna

★ **Over** a thousand hills I walk with you; translated from the German by Elizabeth D. Crawford. Carolrhoda Books 2006 342p $16.95

Grades: 7 8 9 10

1. Rwanda -- Fiction

ISBN 1-57505-927-4; 978-1-57505-927-3

LC 2005-21123

Original German edition, 2002

"Eight-year-old Jeanne was the only one of her family to survive the 1994 Rwanda genocide. Then a German family adopted her, and her adoptive mother now tells Jeanne's story in a compelling fictionalized biography that stays true to the traumatized child's bewildered viewpoint." Booklist

Jaramillo, Ann

La linea. Roaring Brook Press 2006 131p $16.95; pa $7.99

Grades: 5 6 7 8

1. Mexicans -- Fiction 2. Siblings -- Fiction 3. Immigrants -- Fiction

ISBN 1-59643-154-7; 0-312-37354-6 pa

LC 2005-20133

When fifteen-year-old Miguel's time finally comes to leave his poor Mexican village, cross the border illegally, and join his parents in California, his younger sister's determination to join him soon imperils them both.

"A gripping contemporary survival adventure, this spare first novel is also a heart-wrenching family story of courage, betrayal, and love." Booklist

Jarzab, Anna

All unquiet things. Delacorte Press 2010 339p $17.99

Grades: 8 9 10 11 12

1. School stories 2. Mystery fiction 3. Homicide -- Fiction 4. California -- Fiction 5. Social classes -- Fiction

ISBN 978-0-385-73835-4; 0-385-73835-8; 978-0-385-90723-1 lib bdg; 0-385-90723-0 lib bdg

LC 2009-11557

After the death of his ex-girlfriend Carly, northern California high school student Neily joins forces with Carly's cousin Audrey to try to solve her murder.

The **opposite** of hallelujah; Anna Jarzab. Delacorte Press 2012 452 p. (hc) $16.99

Grades: 7 8 9 10

1. Ex-nuns -- Fiction 2. Secrets -- Fiction 3. Sisters -- Fiction 4. Nuns -- Fiction 5. Children's secrets -- Fiction

ISBN 0385738366; 9780375894084; 9780385738361; 9780385907248

LC 2012010882

In this book by Anna Jarzab "Caro's parents drop the bombshell news that [her sister] Hannah is returning to live with them. . . . Unable to understand Hannah, Caro resorts to telling lies about her mysterious reappearance. . . . And as she unearths a clue from Hannah's past--one that could save Hannah from the dark secret that possesses her--Caro begins to see her sister in a whole new light." (Publisher's note)

Jaskulka, Marie

The Lost Marble Notebook of Forgotten Girl and Random Boy. Marie Jaskulka. Sky Pony Press 2015 272 p.

Grades: 9 10 11 12

1. Divorce 2. Love stories 3. Novels in verse 4. Poetry -- Authorship 5. Romance fiction 6. Diaries -- Fiction 7. Poetry -- Fiction

1632204266; 9781632204264, $16.99

In this book, by Marie Jaskulka, "Forgotten Girl, a fifteen-year-old poet, is going through the most difficult time of her life—the breakup of her parents, and her mom's resulting depression—when she meets Random Boy, a hot guy who, like her, feels like an outcast and secretly writes poetry to deal with everything going on in his life." (Publisher's note)

"Jaskulka's narrative explores the hows and whys of an abusive teenage relationship with heartbreaking honesty, and her delicate touch renders the dark story even more powerful. Graceful. Searing. Haunting." Kirkus

Jayne, Hannah

Truly, madly, deadly; by Hannah Jayne. Sourcebooks Fire 2013 272 p. (paperback) $9.99

Grades: 9 10 11 12

1. School stories 2. Stalkers -- Fiction 3. Murder -- Fiction 4. Dating violence -- Fiction

ISBN 1402281218; 9781402281211

LC 2012046383

In this book, "high school junior Sawyer Dodd is still reeling from her boyfriend's death in a drunk driving accident when she receives a note from an 'admirer' that simply reads, 'You're welcome.' Meanwhile, Sawyer's former friend Maggie is making her life at school miserable, and her parents want her to attend therapy. When a second person is killed, Sawyer realizes that her admirer/stalker is closer than she suspected and knows everything about her life." (Publishers Weekly)

Jenkins, A. M.

Beating heart; a ghost story. HarperCollins Publishers 2006 244p $15.99; pa $8.99

Grades: 9 10 11 12

1. Ghost stories 2. Moving -- Fiction 3. Divorce -- Fiction

ISBN 0-06-054607-7; 0-06-054609-3 pa

LC 2005-05071

Following his parents' divorce, seventeen-year-old Evan moves with his mother and sister into an old house where the spirit of a teenager who died there awakens and mistakes him for her long-departed lover.

"Both accessible and substantive, this book will be an easy sell to teens." Booklist

Night road. HarperTeen 2008 362p $16.99; lib bdg $17.89; pa $8.99

Grades: 8 9 10 11 12

1. Horror fiction 2. Vampires -- Fiction 3. Automobile travel -- Fiction

ISBN 978-0-06-054604-5; 0-06-054604-2; 978-0-06-054605-2 lib bdg; 0-06-054605-0 lib bdg; 978-0-06-054606-9 pa; 0-06-054606-9 pa

LC 2007-31703

Battling his own memories and fears, Cole, an extraordinarily conscientious vampire, and Sandor, a more impulsive acquaintance, spend a few months on the road, trying to train a young man who recently joined their ranks.

"The real strength of the novel lies in the noirish atmosphere, accessible prose, and crisp, sharp dialogue." Horn Book

Repossessed. HarperTeen 2007 218p $15.99

Grades: 7 8 9 10

1. School stories 2. Devil -- Fiction 3. Demoniac possession -- Fiction

ISBN 978-0-06-083568-2; 0-06-083568-0

LC 2007-09142

Michael L. Printz Award honor book, 2008

A fallen angel, tired of being unappreciated while doing his pointless, demeaning job, leaves Hell, enters the body of a seventeen-year-old boy, and tries to experience the full range of human feelings before being caught and punished, while the boy's family and friends puzzle over his changed behavior.

"Funny and clever. . . . It's a quick, quirky and entertaining read, with some meaty ideas in it, too." Kliatt

Jensen, Cordelia

Skyscraping. Cordelia Jensen. Philomel Books, an imprint of Penguin Group (USA) 2015 352 p.

Grades: 9 10 11 12

1. Fathers and daughters -- Fiction 2. Gay fathers -- Fiction 3. High schools -- Fiction 4. Novels in verse 5. Schools -- Fiction 6. Secrets -- Fiction 7. New York (N.Y.) -- History -- 20th century -- Fiction 8. Father-daughter relationship -- Fiction 9. Adjustment (Psychology) 10. Family secrets -- Fiction

0399167714; 9780399167713, $17.99

LC 2014035150

In Cordelia Jensen's novel "Mira is just beginning her senior year of high school when she discovers her father with his male lover. Unable to comprehend the lies . . . Mira distances herself from her sister and closest friends as a means of coping. A shocking health scare brings to light his battle with HIV. As Mira struggles to make sense of the many fractures in her family's fabric and redefine her wavering sense of self, she must find a way to reconnect with her dad." (Publisher's note)

"Small period details, from Keith Haring's artwork to the emergence of Starbucks to Kurt Cobain's death, layer in historical context naturally, but it's Jensen's stunning ability to bring the raw uncertainty of the AIDS crisis in the 1990s to vivid life that is so exceptional. Illuminating and deeply felt." Booklist

Jeschonek, Robert T.

My favorite band does not exist. Clarion Books 2011 327p $16.99

Grades: 8 9 10 11 12

   1. Fantasy fiction

   ISBN 978-0-547-37027-9; 0-547-37027-X

Sixteen-year-old Idea Deity, who believes that he is a character in a novel who will die in the sixty-fourth chapter, has created a fictional underground rock band on the internet which, it turns out, may actually exist, and whose members are wondering who is broadcasting all their personal information.

"Jeschonek has created a quirky, time and space-bending adventure that might just gather a cult following of its own. . . . Libraries looking for a strong addition to their science-fiction collections will want to invest in this sophisticated novel." SLJ

Jimenez, Francisco

   ★ **Breaking** through. Houghton Mifflin 2001 195p il $15; pa $6.95

Grades: 7 8 9 10 11 12

   1. Migrant labor -- Fiction 2. Mexican Americans -- Fiction

   ISBN 0-618-01173-0; 0-618-34248-6 pa

                 LC 2001-16941

Having come from Mexico to California ten years ago, fourteen-year-old Francisco is still working in the fields but fighting to improve his life and complete his education

"For all its recounting of deprivation, this is a hopeful book, told with rectitude and dignity." Horn Book

   ★ The **circuit** : stories from the life of a migrant child. Houghton Mifflin 1999 $16

Grades: 7 8 9 10 11 12

   1. Family life -- Fiction 2. Migrant labor -- Fiction 3. Mexican Americans -- Fiction

   ISBN 0-395-7902-1; 978-0-395-97902-0

First published 1997 by University of New Mexico Press

The story "begins in Mexico when the author is very young and his parents inform him that they are going on a very long trip to 'El Norte.' What follows is a series of stories of the family's unending migration from one farm to another as they search for the next harvesting job. Each story is told from the point of view of the author as a young child. The simple and direct narrative stays true to this perspective. . . . Lifting the story up from the mundane, Jiménez deftly portrays the strong bonds of love that hold this family together." Publ Wkly

   ★ **Reaching** out. Houghton Mifflin 2008 196p $16; pa $6.99

Grades: 7 8 9 10 11 12

   1. California -- Fiction 2. Mexican Americans -- Fiction 3. Father-son relationship -- Fiction

   ISBN 978-0-618-03851-0; 0-618-03851-5; 978-0-547-25030-4 pa; 0-547-25030-4 pa

   Sequel to: Breaking through (2001)

   A Pura Belpre Author Award honor book, 2009

"Papa's raging depression intensifies young Jiménez's personal guilt and conflict in the 1960s. . . . He is the first in his Mexican American migrant family to attend college in California. . . . Like his other fictionalized autobiographies, The Circuit (1997) and Breaking Through (2001), this sequel tells Jiménez's personal story in self-contained chapters

that join together in a stirring narrative. . . . The spare episodes will draw readers with the quiet daily detail of work, anger, sorrow, and hope." Booklist

Jinks, Catherine

   ★ **Evil** genius. Harcourt 2007 486p $17

Grades: 7 8 9 10

   1. School stories 2. Crime -- Fiction 3. Genius -- Fiction 4. Australia -- Fiction 5. Good and evil -- Fiction

   ISBN 978-0-15-205988-0; 0-15-205988-1

                 LC 2006-14476

   First published 2005 in Australia

Child prodigy Cadel Piggot, an antisocial computer hacker, discovers his true identity when he enrolls as a first-year student at an advanced crime academy.

"Cadel's turnabout is convincingly hampered by his difficulty recognizing appropriate outlets for rage, and Jinks' whiplash-inducing suspense writing will gratify fans of Anthony Horowitz's high-tech spy scenarios." Booklist

   Other titles about Cadel Piggot are:

   Genius squad (2008)

   Genius wars (2010)

   Genius squad. Harcourt 2008 436p $17

Grades: 7 8 9 10

   1. Crime -- Fiction 2. Genius -- Fiction 3. Australia -- Fiction 4. Good and evil -- Fiction

   ISBN 978-0-15-205985-9; 0-15-205985-7

After the Axis Institute is blown up, fifteen-year-old Cadell Piggot is unhappily stuck in foster care with constant police surveillance to protect him from the evil Prosper English until he gets an offer to join a mysterious group called Genius Squad.

"Readers who loved Evil Genius will find this sequel as gripping, devilish and wonderfully dark as its predecessor." Publ Wkly

   The **genius** wars. Harcourt 2010 378p $17

Grades: 7 8 9 10

   1. Science fiction 2. Crime -- Fiction 3. Genius -- Fiction 4. Australia -- Fiction 5. Good and evil -- Fiction

   ISBN 978-0-15-206619-2; 0-15-206619-5

                 LC 2009-49979

Fifteen-year-old genius Cadel Piggot Greenaus sets aside his new, crime-free life when his best friend Sonja is attacked, and he crosses oceans and continents trying to track down his nemesis Prosper English, breaking whatever rules he must.

"The climax is taut, absorbing and tantalizingly ambiguous." Kirkus

   Living hell. Harcourt 2010 256p $17

Grades: 7 8 9 10

   1. Science fiction

   ISBN 978-0-15-206193-7; 0-15-206193-2

                 LC 2009-18938

Chronicles the transformation of a spaceship into a living organism, as seventeen-year-old Cheney leads the hundreds of inhabitants in a fight for survival while machines turn on them, treating all humans as parasites.

"Jinks' well-thought-out environs and rational characters help ground this otherwise out-of-control interstellar thriller." Booklist

Jocelyn, Marthe

A **Big** Dose of Lucky. Marthe Jocelyn. Orca Book Publishers 2015 264 p.

Grades: 7 8 9 10 11 12813; 813/.54

1. Racially mixed people -- Fiction 2. Orphans -- Fiction 3. Teenage girls -- Fiction

1459806689; 9781459806689, $14.95

LC 2015935534

In this novel, by Marthe Jocelyn, "Malou has just turned sixteen . . . and all she knows for sure is that she's of mixed race and that she was left at an orphanage as a newborn. When the orphanage burns to the ground, she finds out that she may have been born in a small town in Ontario. Parry Sound turns out to have quite a few young brown faces, but Malou can't believe they might be related to her. After she finds work . . . an Aboriginal boy . . . helps her find answers to her questions." (Publisher's note)

"Sharp writing keeps this dramatic coming-of-age story from taking a turn toward the saccharine or melodramatic, despite the casual and not-so-casual racism Malou endures outside the sheltered confines of the orphanage. Lovely and easily digestible historical fiction." Booklist

Other titles in series:
Innocent (2015);
Shattered Glass (2015);
My Life Before Me (2015);
Stones on a Grave (2015);
Small Bones (2015)

Folly. Wendy Lamb Books 2010 249p $15.99; lib bdg $18.99

Grades: 8 9 10 11 12

1. London (England) -- Fiction 2. Abandoned children -- Fiction 3. Household employees -- Fiction 4. Foundling Hospital (London, England) -- Fiction 5. Great Britain -- History -- 19th century -- Fiction

ISBN 978-0-385-73846-0; 0-385-73846-3; 978-0-385-90731-6 lib bdg; 0-385-90731-1 lib bdg

LC 2009-23116

In a parallel narrative set in late nineteenth-century England, teenaged country girl Mary Finn relates the unhappy conclusion to her experiences as a young servant in an aristocratic London household while, years later, young James Nelligan describes how he comes to leave his beloved foster family to live and be educated at London's famous Foundling Hospital.

"Mary's spry narration (James's chapters unfold in third-person) combined with the tale's texture and fervent emotion will seduce readers." Horn Book Guide

Would you. Wendy Lamb Books 2008 165p $15.99; lib bdg $18.99; pa $6.50

Grades: 8 9 10 11 12

1. Coma -- Fiction 2. Sisters -- Fiction 3. Family life -- Fiction 4. Medical care -- Fiction 5. Traffic accidents

-- Fiction

ISBN 978-0-375-83703-6; 0-375-83703-5; 978 0 375 93703-3 lib bdg; 0-375-93703-X lib bdg; 978-0-375-83704-3 pa; 0-375-83704-3 pa

LC 2007-18913

When her beloved sister, Claire, steps in front of a car and winds up in a coma, Nat's anticipated summer of working, hanging around with friends, and seeing Claire off to college is transformed into a nightmare of doctors, hospitals, and well-meaning neighbors.

"Jocelyn captures a teen's thoughts and reactions in a time of incredible anguish without making her overly dramatic. Readers will fly through the pages of this book, crying, laughing, and crying some more." SLJ

John, Antony

Five flavors of dumb. Dial Books 2010 337p $16.99

Grades: 7 8 9 10

1. Deaf -- Fiction 2. Rock musicians -- Fiction 3. Seattle (Wash.) -- Fiction

ISBN 978-0-8037-3433-3; 0-8037-3433-6

LC 2009-44449

Eighteen-year-old Piper is profoundly hearing impaired and resents her parent's decision raid her college fund to get cochlear implants for her baby sister. She becomes the manager for her classmates' popular rock band, called Dumb, giving her the chance to prove her capabilities to her parents and others, if only she can get the band members to get along.

"Readers interested in any of the narrative strands . . . will find a solid, satisfyingly complex story here." Bull Cent Child Books

Johnson, Alaya Dawn

★ The **summer** prince; Alaya Dawn Johnson. Arthur A. Levine Books 2013 304 p. (jacketed hardcover: alk. paper) $17.99

Grades: 9 10 11 12

1. Science fiction 2. Artists -- Fiction 3. Resistance to government -- Fiction 4. Love -- Fiction 5. Brazil -- Fiction 6. Kings, queens, rulers, etc. -- Fiction

ISBN 0545417791; 9780545417792; 9780545417808; 9780545520775

LC 2012022236

Rainbow List (2014)
Lambda Literary Awards Finalist (2014)

This speculative fiction novel, by Alaya Dawn Johnson, takes place in "a futuristic Brazil. . . . In the midst of this vibrant metropolis, June Costa creates art that's sure to make her legendary. But her dreams of fame become something more when she meets Enki, the bold new Summer King. . . . Together, June and Enki will stage explosive, dramatic projects that Palmares Tres will never forget. They will add fuel to a growing rebellion against the government's strict limits on new tech." (Publisher's note)

Johnson, Angela, 1691-

★ A **certain** October; Angela Johnson. Simon & Schuster Books For Young Readers 2012 176 p. (hardback) $16.99

Grades: 7 8 9 10 11 12

1. Bildungsromans 2. Death -- Fiction 3. Guilt -- Fiction 4. Teenagers -- Fiction 5. Autism -- Fiction 6. Friendship -- Fiction 7. High schools -- Fiction
ISBN 9781442417267; 9780689865053; 9780689870651

LC 2012001595

In this book, "when a terrible accident occurs, Scotty feels responsible for the loss of someone she hardly knew, and the world goes wrong. She cannot tell what is a dream and what is real. Her friends are having a hard time getting through to her and her family is preoccupied with their own trauma. But the prospect of a boy, a dance, and the possibility that everything can fall back into place soon help Scotty realize that she is capable of adding her own flavor to life." (Publisher's note)

★ The **first** part last. Simon & Schuster Bks. for Young Readers 2003 131p $15.95

Grades: 7 8 9 10

1. Infants -- Fiction 2. Teenage fathers -- Fiction 3. African Americans -- Fiction
ISBN 0-689-84922-2

LC 2002-36512

Michael L. Printz Award, 2004

Bobby's carefree teenage life changes forever when he becomes a father and must care for his adored baby daughter.

"Brief, poetic, and absolutely riveting." SLJ

★ **Heaven**. Simon & Schuster Bks. for Young Readers 1998 138p $16.95; pa $7.99

Grades: 6 7 8 9

1. Parent and child 2. Adoption -- Fiction 3. African Americans -- Fiction
ISBN 0-689-82229-4; 1-4424-0342-X pa

LC 98-3291

Coretta Scott King Award for text, 1999

Fourteen-year-old Marley's seemingly perfect life in the small town of Heaven is disrupted when she discovers that her father and mother are not her real parents

"In spare, often poetic prose . . . Johnson relates Marley's insightful quest into what makes a family." SLJ

Sweet, hereafter; Angela Johnson. 1st ed. Simon and Schuster Books for Young Readers 2010 118 p. (paperback) $7.99; (hardcover) $16.99

Grades: 7 8 9 10

1. Iraq War, 2003-2011 -- Fiction 2. African Americans -- Fiction
ISBN 0689873859; 9780689873867; 9780689873850; 0689873867

LC 2009027618

"Grades seven to ten." (Bull Cent Child Books)

"Johnson concludes the trilogy that began with Heaven (1998) and The First Part Last (2003). . . . Johnson's stripped-down, poetic prose is filled with shattering emotional truths about war's incalculable devastation, love's mysteries, and the bewildering, necessary search for happiness." Booklist

"With heartfelt empathy, we share in Shoogy's personal loss and her need for a new direction. Characters from the two other titles reappear, and we get a glimpse of how their lives are moving forward. This book belongs in all junior and senior high school collections, especially those who already own the first two titles. . . . Johnson now has one more well-woven character development novel to her name." Libr Media Connect

★ **Toning** the sweep. Orchard Bks. 1993 103p hardcover o.p. pa $5.99

Grades: 6 7 8 9

1. Death -- Fiction 2. Family life -- Fiction 3. Grandmothers -- Fiction 4. African Americans -- Fiction
ISBN 0-531-05476-4; 0-531-08626-7 lib bdg; 978-0-590-48142-7 pa; 0-590-48142-8 pa

LC 92-34062

Coretta Scott King Award for text

On a visit to her grandmother Ola, who is dying of cancer in her house in the desert, fourteen-year-old Emmie hears many stories about the past and her family history and comes to a better understanding of relatives both dead and living

"Full of subtle nuance, the novel is overlaid with meaning about the connections of family and the power of friendship." SLJ

Johnson, Harriet McBryde

★ **Accidents** of nature. Holt 2006 229p $16.95

Grades: 9 10 11 12

1. Camps -- Fiction 2. People with disabilities -- Fiction 3. Cerebral palsy -- Fiction
ISBN 0-8050-7634-4; 978-0-8050-7634-9

LC 2005-24598

Having always prided herself on blending in with "normal" people despite her cerebral palsy, seventeen-year-old Jean begins to question her role in the world while attending a summer camp for children with disabilities.

"This book is smart and honest, funny and eye-opening. A must-read." SLJ

Johnson, J. J.

★ The **theory** of everything; by Jen Wichman. Peachtree Publishers 2012 334 p. ill. (hardcover) $16.95

Grades: 7 8 9 10

1. Bereavement -- Fiction 2. Interpersonal relations -- Fiction 3. Grief -- Fiction 4. Friendship -- Fiction 5. Best friends -- Fiction 6. New York (State) -- Fiction 7. Loss (Psychology) -- Fiction 8. Family life -- New York (State) -- Fiction
ISBN 1561456233; 9781561456239

LC 2011020973

In this novel, by J. J. Johnson, "ever since Sarah Jones's best friend Jamie died in a freak accident, life has felt sort of . . . random. Sarah has always followed the rules. . . . Now what? . . . In a last ditch effort to pull it together, Sarah ends up working for Roy, a local eccentric who owns a Christmas tree farm, and who might also be trying to understand the rules, patterns, and connections in life." (Publisher's note)

Johnson, Lindsay Lee

Worlds apart. Front Street 2005 166p il $16.95

Grades: 7 8 9 10

1. Moving -- Fiction 2. Psychiatric hospitals -- Fiction
ISBN 1-932425-28-4

LC 2005-12052

A thirteen-year-old daughter of a surgeon finds herself wrenched away from a comfortable lifestyle to a home on the grounds of a mental hospital, where her father has accepted a five year contract.

"This story brings bias and prejudice to the forefront in a discussable and readable narrative." SLJ

Johnson, LouAnne

Muchacho. Alfred A. Knopf 2009 197p $15.99; lib bdg $18.99

Grades: 8 9 10

1. Bildungsromans 2. Teenagers -- Fiction 3. Mexican Americans -- Fiction 4. School stories 5. New Mexico -- Fiction

ISBN 978-0-375-86117-8; 0-375-86117-3; 978-0-375-96117-5 lib bdg; 0-375-96117-8 lib bdg

LC 2009-1768

Living in a neighborhood of drug dealers and gangs in New Mexico, high school junior Eddie Corazon, a juvenile delinquent-in-training, falls in love with a girl who inspires him to rethink his life and his choices.

"Eddie's first-person narration and street language will hold teenagers' interest. Set in New Mexico, one of the states with the highest dropout rates among Hispanics, this novel unveils the social pressures and struggles of teens living in inner cities." Kirkus

Johnson, Maureen

★ **13** little blue envelopes. HarperCollins Publishers 2005 317p $15.99; pa $8.99

Grades: 8 9 10 11 12

1. Aunts -- Fiction 2. Europe -- Fiction 3. Voyages and travels -- Fiction

ISBN 0-06-054141-5; 0-06-054143-1 pa

LC 2005-02658

When seventeen-year-old Ginny receives a packet of mysterious envelopes from her favorite aunt, she leaves New Jersey to criss-cross Europe on a sort of scavenger hunt that transforms her life.

"Equal parts poignant, funny and inspiring, this tale is sure to spark wanderlust." Publ Wkly

Followed by: The last little blue envelope (2011)

The **madness** underneath; Maureen Johnson. G. P. Putnam's Sons 2013 304 p. (Shades of London) (hardback) $17.99

Grades: 6 7 8 9 10

1. Ghost stories 2. Occult fiction 3. Mystery fiction 4. Murder -- Fiction 5. England -- Fiction 6. Schools -- Fiction 7. Boarding schools -- Fiction 8. London (England) -- Fiction

ISBN 039925661X; 9780399256615

LC 2012026755

This paranormal mystery novel, by Maureen Johnson, is book two of "The Shades of London Trilogy." "After her near-fatal run-in with the Jack the Ripper copycat, Rory Devereaux . . . [has] become a human terminus, with the power to eliminate ghosts on contact. . . . The Ripper may be gone, but now there is a string of new inexplicable deaths threatening London. Rory has evidence that the deaths are

no coincidence. Something much more sinister is going on." (Publisher's note)

★ The **name** of the star. G. P. Putnam's Sons 2011 384p $16.99

Grades: 6 7 8 9 10

1. Ghost stories 2. School stories 3. Homicide -- Fiction 4. Witnesses -- Fiction 5. London (England) -- Fiction

ISBN 978-0-399-25660-8; 0-399-25660-1; 9780399256608; 0399256601

LC 2011009003

"Johnson's trademark sense of humor serves to counterbalance some grisly murders in this page-turner, which opens her Shades of London series. . . . As one mutilated body after another turns up, Johnson . . . amplifies the story's mysteries with smart use of and subtle commentary on modern media shenanigans and London's infamously extensive surveillance network. . . . Readers looking for nonstop fun, action, and a little gore have come to the right place." Publ Wkly

Scarlett fever. Point/Scholastic 2010 336p $16.99

Grades: 7 8 9 10

1. School stories 2. Actors -- Fiction 3. Family life -- Fiction 4. New York (N.Y.) -- Fiction 5. Hotels and motels -- Fiction 6. Dating (Social customs) -- Fiction

ISBN 978-0-439-89928-4; 0-439-89928-1

Sequel to: Suite Scarlett (2008)

Fifteen-year-old Scarlett, who is beginning to get over her breakup with Eric, stays busy as assistant to her theatrical-agent friend who is not only promoting Scarlett's brother Spencer, but also a new client whose bad-boy brother has transferred to Scarlett's school.

"While the novel may be enjoyed for the light if slightly madcap romance that it is, it is notable for its attention to social class and to the Martins' struggles with money." SLJ

The **shadow** cabinet. Maureen Johnson. G. P. Putnam's Sons, an imprint of Penguin Group (USA) 2015 384 p. (Shades of London)

Grades: 9 10 11 12

1. Boarding schools -- Fiction 2. Ghosts -- Fiction 3. Murder -- Fiction 4. Schools -- Fiction 5. England -- Fiction 6. London (England) -- Fiction 7. Ghost stories

0399256628; 9780399256622, $17.99

LC 2014031153

This supernatural novel, by Maureen Johnson, is book three in the "Shades of London" series, "Time is running out as Rory fights to find her friends and the ghost squad struggles to stop Jane from unleashing her spectral nightmare on the entire city. In the process, they'll discover the existence of an organization that underpins London itself . . . and Rory will learn that someone she trusts has been keeping a tremendous secret." (Publisher's note)

"The plot . . . is among Johnson's finest and incorporates creepy bits of backstory, fascinating historical asides, and truly ghoulish side characters-take, for example, a lumpen cemetery ghost that is 'just a glob of people pieces mixed together.' Lots of juicy setup here for the next outing." Booklist

Suite Scarlett. Scholastic Point 2008 353p $16.99

Grades: 6 7 8 9 10

    1. Authorship -- Fiction 2. Family life -- Fiction 3. New York (N.Y.) -- Fiction 4. Hotels and motels -- Fiction

    ISBN 978-0-439-89927-7; 0-439-89927-3

                             LC 2007-041903

Fifteen-year-old Scarlett Marvin is stuck in New York City for the summer working at her quirky family's historic hotel, but her brother's attractive new friend and a seasonal guest who offers her an intriguing and challenging writing project improve her outlook.

    "Utterly winning, madcap Manhattan farce, crafted with a winking, urbane narrative and tight, wry dialogue." Booklist

    Another title about Scarlett is:

    Scarlett fever (2010)

Truly devious: a mystery. Maureen Johnson ; [edited by] Katherine Tegen. Katherine Tegen Books 2018 432 p.

Grades: 8 9 10 11 12

    1. Private schools -- Fiction; 2. Mystery fiction; 3. Cold cases (Criminal investigation) -- Fiction;

    ISBN 9780062338051, $17.99

                             LC 2017951264

"Stevie Bell is a dyed-in-the-wool true-crime buff. And what better place to deepen her understanding than at Ellingham Academy, the Vermont private school founded in the 1930s by wealthy eccentric Albert Ellingham? Partly because the custom courses of study are tailored to students' passion-writing, engineering, film, math-but also because the school was the scene of a notorious crime not long after it opened: Albert Ellingham's wife and daughter were kidnapped, ostensibly for ransom, and a student was killed. His wife's body was found eventually, but his daughter, Alice, never was. Stevie plans to solve the case. But when a classmate is killed, everything changes." (School Library Journal)

    Johnson "deftly twists two mysteries together—Stevie's investigation is interspersed with case files and recollections from the Ellington kidnapping—and the result is a suspenseful, attention-grabbing mystery with no clear solution. Invested readers, never fear-this is just the first in a series." Booklist

    Another title in this series is: The vanishing stair (2019)

Johnson, Varian

Saving Maddie. Delacorte Press 2010 231p $16.99; lib bdg $19.99

Grades: 9 10 11 12

    1. Clergy -- Fiction 2. Religion -- Fiction 3. Family life -- Fiction 4. South Carolina -- Fiction

    ISBN 978-0-385-73804-0; 0-385-73804-8; 978-0-385-90708-8 lib bdg; 0-385-90708-7 lib bdg

                             LC 2010-277721

"Joshua and Maddie, both preacher's kids, were best friends when they were younger, until Maddie's father moved the family to Norfolk. Now Maddie's back in town. Her father, having refused to pay her tuition at Brown, has sent her to an aunt's house to straighten up after years of too much boys and booze. Joshua, PK that he is, is sure he can save Maddie, but angry and hostile, she has resolved to stay the way she is." (Booklist)

Johnston, E. K.

  ★ **Exit**, pursued by a bear. E.K. Johnston. Dutton Books 2016 256 p.

Grades: 9 10 11 12

    1. Best friends -- Fiction 2. Cheerleading -- Fiction 3. Emotional problems -- Fiction 4. Friendship -- Fiction 5. High schools -- Fiction 6. Psychic trauma -- Fiction 7. Rape -- Fiction 8. Rape victims -- Fiction 9. Schools -- Fiction 10. Social isolation -- Fiction 11.Canada -- Fiction 12. Ontario -- Fiction 13. Date rape -- Fiction 14. Teenage girls -- Fiction

    9781101994580, $17.99; 1101994584

                             LC 2015020645

In this novel, by E.K. Johnston, "when Hermione Winters arrives at Camp Manitouwabing for the final pre-season cheer camp of her high school career, she's prepared for intense competition and exhausting practices. Working with her fierce best friend Polly as co-captain, Hermione anticipates athletic challenges and triumphs—not being drugged and raped at a camp dance. . . . When a pregnancy test two weeks later yields a positive result, Hermione knows she has a second chance at justice." (Kirkus)

    "A beautifully written portrait of a young woman facing the unthinkable." SLJ

Prairie fire; E. K. Johnston. Carolrhoda Books. 2015 304p $18.99

Grades: 7 8 9 10

    1. Adventure fiction 2. Bards and bardism -- Fiction 3. Dragons -- Fiction 4. Fame -- Fiction 5. Family life -- Canada -- Fiction 6. High schools -- Fiction 7. Friendship -- Fiction

    ISBN: 146773909X; 9781467739092; 9781467761819; 9781467776790; 9781467776806; 9781467776813

                             LC 2014008995

"Every dragon slayer owes the Oil Watch a period of service, and young Owen was no exception. What made him different was that he did not enlist alone. His two closest friends stood with him shoulder to shoulder. . . . But the arc of history is long and hardened by dragon fire. Try as they might, Owen and his friends could not twist it to their will." (Publisher's note)

    "There is a little something for everyone in this sequel to the acclaimed The Story of Owen. Fantasy fans will love returning to an alternate world in which the armed forces slay dragons...A fantasy YA novel that steers clear of love triangles, teen angst, and a tidy ending is hard to come by; Prairie Fire and its prequel are must-haves." SLJ

The **story** of Owen: dragon slayer of Trondheim; E. K. Johnston. Carolrhoda Lab. 2014 305p $17.95

Grades: 7 8 9 10 11 12

    1. Adventure fiction 2. Bards and bardism -- Fiction 3. Dragons -- Fiction 4. Fame -- Fiction 5. Family life -- Canada -- Fiction 6. High schools -- Fiction 7. Canada

-- Fiction
ISBN: 9781467710664; 1467710660

LC 2013020492

In this book, author E. K. Johnston, "envisions an Earth nearly identical to our own, with one key difference: dragons. . . . After 16-year-old Siobhan McQuaid agrees to become the bard for dragon-slayer-in-training Owen Thorskard, who has moved with his famous dragon-slaying family to her small Ontario town, she winds up at the.center of a grassroots effort to understand an odd spike in dragon numbers." Publishers Weekly

"Humor, pathos and wry social commentary unite in a cleverly drawn, marvelously diverse world. Refreshingly, the focus is on the pair as friends and partners, not on potential romance." Kirkus

That inevitable Victorian thing. E. K. Johnston. Dutton Books for Young Readers 2017 326 p.

Grades: 9 10 11 12

1. Intersex people -- Fiction; 2. Love -- Fiction; 3. Nobility -- Fiction; 4. Princesses -- Fiction; 5. Canada -- Fiction; 6. Toronto (Ont.) -- Fiction
9781101994979, $17.99; 9781101994573

LC 2017010303

In this novel, by E. K. Johnston, "Victoria-Margaret is the crown princess of the empire, a direct descendant of Victoria I, the queen who changed the course of history. The imperial tradition of genetically arranged matchmaking will soon guide Margaret into a politically advantageous marriage. But before she does her duty, she'll have one summer of freedom and privacy.... Posing as a commoner in Toronto, she meets Helena Marcus...and August Callaghan." (Publisher's note)

"A thoughtful exploration of class consciousness, genetics, and politics that doesn't lose track of the human story." Kirkus

A thousand nights. E. K. Johnston. Disney-Hyperion 2015 336 p.

Grades: 7 8 9 10

1. Fairy tales 2. Kings, queens, rulers, etc. -- Fiction 3. Magic -- Fiction 4. Kings and rulers -- Fiction 5. Adventure fiction
9781484722275, $18.99; 1484728475

LC 2014049058

This book, by E.K. Johnston, "explores the setting and central characters from the classic 'Arabian Nights: Tales from One Thousand and One Nights,' adding a mystical backstory for why the Prince kills his 300 wives but spares the Storyteller. In this retelling, the unnamed heroine sacrifices herself for her sister . . . when the Prince comes to claim a new bride. When her sister builds a shrine to make her a small god, the protagonist finds . . . her powers growing unexpectedly strong." (Publisher's note)

"Detailed and quiet, beautifully written with a literary rhythm that evokes a sense of oral tale-telling, this unexpected fantasy should not be missed." Kirkus

Jones, Adam Garnet

Fire   song. Adam Garnet Jones. Annick Press 2018 230 p.

Grades: 9 10 11 12

1. Coming out (Sexual orientation) -- Fiction; 2. Gay teenagers -- Fiction; 3. Indians of North America -- Ontario -- Fiction; 4. Sexual orientation -- Fiction; 5. Ojibwa Indians -- Fiction; 6. Gay teenagers -- Fiction; 7. Suicide -- Fiction
9781554519798;   9781554519774, $9.95; 9781554519781; 1554519772; 1554519780

In this book, by Adam Garnet Jones, "Shane is still reeling from the suicide of his kid sister, Destiny.... What he really wants is to be able to turn to the one person on the rez whom he loves -- his friend, David.... Shane feels that his only chance of a better life is moving to Toronto, but David refuses to join him. When yet another tragedy strikes, the two boys have to make difficult choices about their future together." (Publisher's note)

"A touching story that has been a long time coming for the Indigenous community." Kirkus

"Fire Song by Adam Garnet Jones is based on the film 'Fire Song' produced by Fire Song Films Inc. and Big Soul Productions Inc. and written and directed by Adam Garnet Jones"—Title page verso.

Jones, Kelly

Murder, magic, and what we wore. Kelly Jones. Alfred A. Kn opf 2017 293 p.

Grades: 7 8 9 10 11 12

1. Dressmaking -- Fiction; 2. Murder -- Fiction; 3. Great Britain -- History -- 1800-1837 -- Fiction; 4. London (England) -- History -- 1800-1950 -- Fiction; 5. Spies -- Fiction; 6. Magic -- Fiction; 7. Spy stories
055353520X; 9780553535228; 9780553535204, $17.99

LC 2017297170

In this book, by Kelly Jones, "Annis Whitworth has just learned that her father is dead and all his money is missing.... [So] she decides to become a spy...[and] crafts a new double life for herself.... [Annis] will appear to live a quiet life... with her aunt, and Annis-in-disguise as Madame Martine, glamour artist.... That way she can earn a living, maintain her social standing, and...follow the coded clues her father left behind and unmask his killer." (Publisher's note)

"A cross between Jane Austen dramas and Harriet the Spy, this delightful strong female-led title mixes historical fiction and spy mystery with a touch of magic to produce a story filled with adventure. " SLJ

Jones, Patrick

★ **Bridge**. Patrick Jones. Darby Creek 2014 92 p. (The alternative)

Grades: 6 7 8 9 10 11 12

1. High schools -- Fiction 2. Hispanic Americans -- Fiction 3. Illegal aliens -- Fiction 4. Schools -- Fiction 5. Spanish language -- Fiction 6. Work -- Fiction 7. School stories 8. Family life -- Fiction 9. Unauthorized immigrants -- Fiction
1467744824; 9781467739030; 9781467744829, $7.95

LC 2013041390

"José can't keep up. As the only English speaker in a family of undocumented immigrants, he handles everything from taking family members to the doctor to bargaining with the landlord. Plus he works two jobs. With all this responsibility, he's missing a lot of school. . . . José knows he has to turn things around if he wants to graduate from Rondo Alternative High School. Can he raise his grades enough to have a shot at college and a better life?" (Publisher's note)

"The author's effective use of flashbacks and crisp portraits of positive adult characters add further emotional depth to this emotional glimpse at the high-pressure difficulties facing children in immigrant families. References to O'Brien's book will likely spark the interest of readers in that title as well." PW Reviews

Chasing tail lights. Walker & Co. 2007 294p hardcover o.p. pa $7.99
Grades: 9 10 11 12
    1. Incest -- Fiction 2. Michigan -- Fiction 3. Family life -- Fiction 4. Child sexual abuse -- Fiction
    ISBN 978-0-8027-9628-8; 0-8027-9628-1; 978-0-8027-9762-9 pa; 0-8027-9762-8 pa
                    LC 2006-27657
Seventeen-year-old Christy wants only to finish high school and escape her Flint, Michigan, home, where she cooks, cleans, cares for her niece, and tries to fend off her half-brother, a drug dealer who has been abusing her since she was eleven.

The author "tackles a lot of relevant issues here. . . . His look at teen rebellion and the misunderstandings it can engender is full of hard-to-face truths, and his ultimate faith in teens' ability to survive tough circumstances may inspire readers." Bull Cent Child Books

The **tear** collector. Walker & Company 2009 263p $16.99
Grades: 7 8 9 10
    1. School stories 2. Michigan -- Fiction 3. Family life -- Fiction 4. Supernatural -- Fiction
    ISBN 978-0-8027-8710-1; 0-8027-8710-X
                    LC 2008-55868
As one of an ancient line of creatures who gain energy from human tears, seventeen-year-old Cassandra offers sympathy to anyone at her school or the hospital where she works, but she yearns to be fully human for the boy she loves, even if it means letting her family down.

"Cassandra is a complex character who readers will identify with as she struggles to understand who she really is, where her loyalties lie, and how to take control of her own destiny. Those looking for a new spin on the vampire story should find this one satisfying." SLJ

Jones, Traci L.
Finding my place. Farrar Straus Giroux 2010 181p $16.99
Grades: 6 7 8 9
    1. School stories 2. Moving -- Fiction 3. Friendship -- Fiction 4. Prejudices -- Fiction 5. Race relations -- Fiction 6. African Americans -- Fiction
    ISBN 978-0-374-33573-1; 0-374-33573-7
                    LC 2008-54433
After moving to an affluent suburb of Denver in 1975, ninth-grader Tiphanie feels lonely at her nearly all-white high school until she befriends another "outsider" and discovers that prejudice exists in many forms.

"Tiphanie is refreshingly witty and open-minded. . . . . Jones handles the intricacies of race relations splendidly and excels in the frankness of her prose. . . . This immediate, engaging novel will appeal to readers of all backgrounds." Booklist

Standing against the wind; 1st ed.; Farrar, Straus and Giroux 2006 184p $16
Grades: 6 7 8 9
    1. School stories 2. African Americans -- Fiction 3. City and town life -- Fiction
    ISBN 978-0-374-37174-6; 0-374-37174-1
                    LC 2005-51226
As she tries to escape her poor Chicago neighborhood by winning a scholarship to a prestigious boarding school, shy and studious eighth-grader Patrice discovers that she has more options in life than she previously realized.

"Handled without obscenity, the lively street talk will draw readers to the gripping story of a contemporary kid who works to make her dreams come true." Booklist

Joseph, Lynn
Flowers in the sky; by Lynn Joseph. HarperTeen 2013 240 p. (hardcover) $17.99
Grades: 8 9 10 11 12
    1. Bildungsromans 2. New York (N.Y.) -- Fiction 3. Brothers and sisters -- Fiction 4. Love -- Fiction 5. Immigrants -- Fiction 6. Coming of age -- Fiction 7. Dominican Republic -- Fiction 8. Dominican Americans -- Fiction
    ISBN 0060297948; 9780060297947
                    LC 2012038122
In this novel, by Lynn Joseph, "fifteen-year-old Nina Perez . . . must leave her . . . lush island home in Samana, Dominican Republic, when she's sent . . . to live with her brother, Darrio, in New York, to seek out a better life. . . . But then she meets . . . [a] tall, green-eyed boy . . . , who just might help her learn to see beauty in spite of tragedy." (Publisher's note)

Juby, Susan
Another kind of cowboy. HarperTeen 2007 344p $16.99
Grades: 8 9 10 11 12
    1. Horses -- Fiction 2. Friendship -- Fiction 3. Horsemanship -- Fiction 4. Gay teenagers -- Fiction 5. British Columbia -- Fiction
    ISBN 0-06-076517-8; 978-0-06-076517-0
                    LC 2006-36336
In Vancouver, British Columbia, two teenage dressage riders, one a spoiled rich girl and the other a closeted gay sixteen-year-old boy, come to terms with their identities and learn to accept themselves.

"Wry humor infuses this quiet story with a gentle warmth, and the secondary characters are well developed." Booklist

★ The **fashion** committee: a novel of art, crime and applied design. Susan Juby. Viking 2017 305 p. Illustration
Grades: 7 8 9 10
    1. Competition (Psychology) -- Fiction; 2. Friendship --

Fiction; 3. Fashion -- Fiction

9780451468789, $18.99; 9780698151055; 0451468783

LC 2017014294

In this book, by Susan Juby, "Charlie Dean is a style-obsessed girl who eats, sleeps, and breathes fashion. John Thomas-Smith is a boy who forges metal sculptures in his garage and couldn't care less about clothes. Both are gunning for a scholarship to the private art high school that could make all their dreams come true. Whoever wins the fashion competition will win the scholarship -- and only one can win." (Publisher's note)

"Juby's thoughtful bildungsroman excels in showcasing and normalizing those on society's fringe -- whether it be in her bold portrayal of differing socio-economic class issues or subtle examination of gender identity." Kirkus

Getting the girl; a guide to private investigation, surveillance, and cookery. [by] S. Juby. HarperTeen 2008 341p $16.99; lib bdg $17.89; pa $8.99

Grades: 6 7 8 9 10

1. School stories 2. Mystery fiction 3. Popularity -- Fiction

ISBN 978-0-06-076525-5; 0-06-076525-9; 978-0-06-076527-9 lib bdg; 0-06-076527-5 lib bdg; 978-0-06-076528-6 pa; 0-06-076528-3 pa

LC 2008-00788

Ninth-grader Sherman Mack investigates the "Defilers," a secret group at his British Columbia high school that marks certain female students as pariahs, at first because he is trying to protect the girl he has a crush on, but later as a matter of principle.

Juby "applies her signature brand of humor to a detective novel. . . . [This offers a] strong and memorable female cast. . . . Here's hoping that Juby delivers on the promise of sequels." Horn Book

★ The **Truth** Commission. Susan Juby. Viking, an imprint of Penguin Group (USA) 2015 320 p.

Grades: 9 10 11 12

1. Artists -- Fiction 2. Family problems -- Fiction 3. High schools -- Fiction 4. Schools -- Fiction 5. Sisters -- Fiction 6. Truth -- Fiction

0451468775; 9780451468772, $18.99

LC 2014015259

In this book, by Susan Juby, "open secrets are the heart of gossip—the obvious things that no one is brave or tactless enough to ask. Except for Normandy Pale and her friends. They are juniors at a high school for artists, and have no fear. They are the Truth Commission. Then, one of their truth targets says to Normandy: 'If you want to know about the truth, you might want to look a little closer to home.'" (Publisher's note)

"Best friends and art-school students Normandy (a girl), Dusk (a girl), and Neil (a boy, duh!) form a de facto truth commission: each week, each of them will ask someone to give them the straight truth. The experiment's results will constitute Normandy's creative nonfiction project. The novel, then, is presented as that project, complete with footnotes and the occasional piece of spot art...The problem, as Juby expertly shows, is that truth is messy and sometimes-like a hot potato-hard to handle. Though it comes dangerously close to melodrama by the end, the story is clever, the

characters appealing, and the theme is thought-provoking." Horn Book

Kagawa, Julie

The **Eternity** Cure; Julie Kagawa. Harlequin Books 2013 448 p. (hardcover) $16.99

Grades: 7 8 9 10 11 12

1. Science fiction 2. Vampires -- Fiction 3. Epidemics -- Fiction

ISBN 0373210698; 9780373210695

This vampire novel, by Julie Kagawa, is part of the "Blood of Eden" series. "Allie will follow the call of blood to save her creator, Kanin, from the psychotic vampire Sarren. But when the trail leads to Allie's birthplace in New Covington, what Allie finds there will change the world forever. . . . There's a new plague on the rise, a strain of the Red Lung virus that wiped out most of humanity generations ago--and this strain is deadly to humans and vampires alike." (Publisher's note)

The **forever** song. By Julie Kagawa. Harlequin Books 2014 416 p. (Blood of Eden)

Grades: 7 8 9 10 11 12

1. Fantasy fiction 2. Horror tales 3. Revenge 4. Vampires 5. Vampires -- Fiction

0373211120; 9780373211128, $16.99

In this novel, by Julie Kagawa, "Allie will embrace her cold vampire side to hunt down and end Sarren, the psychopathic vampire who murdered Zeke. But the trail is bloody and long, and Sarren has left many surprises for Allie and her companions—her creator, Kanin, and her blood brother, Jackal. The trail is leading straight to the one place they must protect at any cost—the last vampire-free zone on Earth, Eden. And Sarren has one final, brutal shock in store for Allie." (Publisher's note)

"Stomach-churning gore and heart-pounding action balance the (occasionally repetitive) romantic angst and moral inquiries into the nature of monsters. A bloody good way to end a trilogy."

★ The **immortal** rules; a legend begins. Julie Kagawa. Harlequin Teen 2012 504 p. (Blood of Eden) (hardcover) $18.99

Grades: 7 8 9 10 11 12

1. Love stories 2. Diseases -- Fiction 3. Vampires -- Fiction

ISBN 0373210515; 9780373210510

LC 2011279454

In this book, "[r]abids, vicious hybrid creatures born of the plague, prowl the land beyond the walled vampire cities. . . . When Allie is savagely attacked by a rabid, . . . a mysterious vampire offers her the choice of a human death or 'life' as a vampire. . . . Allie's determination to remain more human than monster is put to the test, particularly when she joins a band of humans on a desperate journey to safety on the island of Eden. Particularly when she falls in love." (Kirkus)

"Kagawa wraps excellent writing and skillful plotting around a well-developed concept and engaging characters, resulting in a fresh and imaginative thrill-ride that deserves a wide audience." Pub Wkly

Shadow of the Fox. Julie Kagawa. Harlequin Teen 2018 416 p.

Grades: 9 10 11 12

1. Ancient scrolls -- Fiction; 2. Dragons -- Fiction; 3. Fantasy; 4. Good and evil -- Fiction; 5. Science fiction
ISBN 1335145168; 9781335145161

"The world of Iwagoto is full of ghosts, kami spirits, shapeshifters, samurai, and blood mages. Yumeko, a half-kitsune (supernatural fox), has lived a sheltered life in a remote monastery. When the leader of the monks informs Yumeko that they protect part of a magical scroll, she is thrust into adventure and danger. A demon attack on the monastery spurs Yumeko into action, and she becomes determined not only to protect the scroll but to set out on a mission to find the next piece." (School Library Journal)

Talon. By Julie Kagawa. Harlequin Books Teen 2014 464 p.

Grades: 8 9 10 11

1. Shapeshifting 2. Fantasy fiction 3. Dragons -- Fiction 4. Brothers and sisters -- Fiction
0373211392; 9780373211395, $17.99

In this book, by Julie Kagawa, "dragons were hunted to near extinction by the Order of St. George, a legendary society of dragon slayers. Hiding in human form and growing their numbers in secret, the dragons of Talon have become strong and cunning. . . . Ember and Dante Hill are the only sister and brother known to dragonkind. Trained to infiltrate society, Ember wants to live the teen experience and enjoy a summer of freedom before taking her destined place in Talon." (Publisher's note)

"Young love, sibling rivalry, rogue dragons, and plots for world domination create an intriguing mix in this new series." Horn Book

Kamata, Suzanne

Gadget Girl; the art of being invisible. Suzanne Kamata. GemmaMedia 2013 256 p. (pbk.) $14.95

Grades: 9 10 11 12

1. Cerebral palsy -- Fiction 2. Mother-daughter relationship -- Fiction 3. France -- Fiction 4. Artists -- Fiction 5. Coming of age -- Fiction 6. Paris (France) -- Fiction 7. Cartoons and comics -- Fiction 8. Mothers and daughters -- Fiction 9. Single-parent families -- Fiction 10. People with disabilities -- Fiction
ISBN 1936846381; 9781936846382

LC 2012051566

Asian/Pacific American Awards for Literature: Young Adult Literature Honor (2014)

In this book by Suzanne Kamata, "Aiko, who has cerebral palsy . . . is the 14-year-old secretive creator of a manga comic starring Lisa Cook as Gadget Girl. Aiko also serves as the reluctant muse to her midwestern American mother, an award-winning sculptor who has been invited to Paris, even as she longs for a connection to her birth father in Japan." (Booklist)

"For Aiko Cassidy, it's hard enough sitting at the "invisible" table and dealing with trespassing geeks. It's harder when her cerebral palsy makes guys notice her in all the wrong ways...Awkwardly and believably, this sensitive novel reveals an artistic teen adapting to family, disability and friendships in all their flawed beauty." (Kirkus)

Kaplan, A. E.

Grendel's guide to love and war: a tale of rivalry, romance, and existential angst. A. E. Kaplan. Alfred A. Knopf 2017 312 p.

Grades: 9 10 11 12

1. Bullying -- Fiction; 2. Emotional problems of children -- Fiction; 3. Friendship -- Fiction; 4. Virginia -- Fiction; 5. Friendship -- Fiction; 6. Bullies -- Fiction
9780399555541, $17.99; 9780399555558; 9780399555565

LC 2016048148

In this book, by A. E. Kaplan, "Tom Grendel lives a quiet life -- writing in his notebooks, mowing lawns for his elderly neighbors, and pining for Willow, a girl next door who rejects the 'manic-pixie-dream' label. But when Willow's brother, Rex (the bro-iest bro ever to don a jockstrap), starts throwing wild parties, the idyllic senior citizens' community where they live is transformed into a war zone." (Publisher's note)

"Deep and uproarious all at once, this doesn't require familiarity with the source material for readers to have a fine time with it. A clever spin on a weighty classic." Kirkus

Kaplan, Ariel

We regret to inform you: an overachiever's guide to college rejection. A.E. Kaplan. Alfred A. Knopf 2018 352 p.

Grades: 9 10 11 12

1. College choice -- Fiction; 2. Friendship -- Fiction; 3. Hackers -- Fiction; 4. High schools -- Fiction; 5. Schools -- Fiction
9781524773700; 9781524773717, $20.99

LC 2018013862

In this novel, by Ariel Kaplan, "Mischa Abramavicius is a walking, talking, top-scoring, perfectly well-rounded college application in human form. So when she's rejected not only by the Ivies, but her loathsome safety school, she is shocked and devastated. All the sacrifices her mother made to send her to prep school, the late nights cramming for tests, the blatantly résumé-padding extracurriculars (read: Students for Sober Driving) ... all that for nothing." (Publisher's note)

Karim, Sheba

Skunk girl. Farrar, Straus & Giroux 2009 231p $16.95

Grades: 8 9 10 11 12

1. School stories 2. Muslims -- Fiction 3. Family life -- Fiction 4. New York (State) -- Fiction 5. Pakistani Americans -- Fiction 6. Dating (Social customs) -- Fiction
ISBN 978-0-374-37011-4; 0-374-37011-7

LC 2008-7482

Nina Khan is not just the only Asian or Muslim student in her small-town high school in upstate New York, she is also faces the legacy of her "Supernerd" older sister, body hair, and the pain of having a crush when her parents forbid her to date.

This novel is "rife with smart, self-deprecating humor." Kirkus

That thing we call a heart. Sheba Karim. Harper-Teen 2017 275 p.

Grades: 9 10 11 12

1. Best friends -- Fiction; 2. Families -- Fiction; 3. Identity (Philosophical concept) -- Fiction; 4. Muslims -- Fiction; 5. Summer -- Fiction; 6. Friendship -- Fiction; 9780062445704, $17.99; 9780062445728

LC 2016949962

In this book, by Sheba Karim, "Shabnam Qureshi is facing a summer of loneliness and boredom until she meets Jamie, who scores her a job at his aunt's pie shack. Shabnam quickly finds herself in love, while her former best friend, Farah, who Shabnam has begun to reconnect with, finds Jamie worrying. In her quest to figure out who she really is and what she really wants, Shabnam looks for help in an unexpected place -- her family, and her father's beloved Urdu poetry." (Publisher's note)

"Funny, fresh, and poignant, Karim's (Skunk Girl, 2009) novel is noteworthy for its authentic depiction of a Pakistani American teen coming of age and falling in love." Booklist

Kaslik, Ibolya

Skinny; [by] Ibi Kaslik. Walker & Company 2006 244p $16.95

Grades: 11 12

1. Sisters -- Fiction 2. Anorexia nervosa -- Fiction 3. Father-daughter relationship -- Fiction

ISBN 978-0-8027-9608-0; 0-8027-9608-7

LC 2006-42140

First published 2004 in Canada

After the death of their father, two sisters struggle with various issues, including their family history, personal relationships, and an extreme eating disorder

"It's refreshing that Gigi's anorexia and briefly described lesbian romance are treated as only parts of a larger story, and the girls' grief following their father's death and the pressures they face growing up with immigrant parents add depth to the novel. . . . This is an ambitious, often moving offering, and older readers will likely connect with the raw emotions and intelligent insights into a family's secrets, pain, and enduring love." Booklist

Katcher, Brian

Almost perfect. Delacorte Press 2009 360p $17.99

Grades: 9 10 11 12

1. School stories 2. Missouri -- Fiction 3. Transgender people -- Fiction 4. Single parent family -- Fiction 5. Dating (Social customs) -- Fiction

ISBN 978-0-385-73664-0; 0-385-73664-9

LC 2008-37659

Stonewall Children's and Young Adult Literature Award, 2011

With his mother working long hours and in pain from a romantic break-up, eighteen-year-old Logan feels alone and unloved until a zany new student arrives at his small-town Missouri high school, keeping a big secret.

"The author tackles issues of homophobia, hate crimes and stereotyping with humor and grace in an accessible tone

that will resonate with teens who may not have encountered the issue of transgender identity before." Kirkus

Deacon Locke went to prom. Brian Katcher. Katherine Tegen Books 2017 389 p.

Grades: 7 8 9 10

1. Grandmothers -- Fiction; 2. Social media -- Fiction; 3. Grandparent and child -- Fiction; 4. Grandmothers -- Fiction; 5. Proms -- Fiction

9780062422545; 9780062422521, $17.99

LC 2016957990

In this novel, by Brian Katcher, edited by Claudia Gabel, "with graduation looming, shy and unusually tall Deacon doesn't think he can get up the nerve to ask anyone to the dance. Especially given all the theatrics. It isn't until Deacon confides in his witty and outgoing best friend Jean that he realizes could be a great person to take.... But when Deacon meets Soraya...he fears he has totally squandered his chances of having a prom he'll never forget." (Publisher's note)

The **improbable** theory of Ana and Zak. Brian Katcher. Katherine Tegen Books, an imprint of HarperCollinsPublishers 2015 336 p.

Grades: 7 8 9 10 11 12

1. Brothers and sisters -- Fiction 2. Contests -- Fiction 3. Genius -- Fiction 4. Schools -- Fiction 5. Science fiction -- Congresses -- Fiction 6. Seattle (Wash.) -- Fiction 7. Teenagers -- Fiction 8. High school students -- Fiction 9. Love -- Fiction

0062272772; 9780062272775, $17.99

LC 2014030718

This book, by Brian Katcher, is a "he said/she said romance about two teens discovering themselves. . . . When Ana Watson's brother ditches a high school trip to run wild at Washingcon, type-A Ana knows that she must find him. . . . In her desperation, she's forced to enlist the last person she'd ever want to spend time with—slacker Zak Duquette—to help find her brother before morning comes." (Publisher's note)

"Type-A Ana and relaxed geek Zak take turns narrating as they spend a night searching for Ana's younger brother at a comic-book convention. The he said/she said romance has been done before, of course, but the unconventional setting, quirky convention-goers, and many over-the-top hijinks (e.g., multiple fights, a sci-fi-themed gay wedding, inadvertent drug-running) give this one a unique twist." Horn Book

Playing with matches. Delacorte Press 2008 294p $15.99; lib bdg $18.99

Grades: 8 9 10 11 12

1. School stories 2. Missouri -- Fiction 3. Burns and scalds -- Fiction 4. Dating (Social customs) -- Fiction

ISBN 978-0-385-73544-5; 0-385-73544-8; 978-0-385-90525-1 lib bdg; 0-385-90525-4 lib bdg

LC 2007-27654

While trying to find a girl who will date him, Missouri high school junior Leon Sanders befriends a lonely, disfigured female classmate.

"This is a strong debut novel with a cast of quirky, multidimensional characters struggling with issues of acceptance, sexuality, identity, and self-worth." SLJ

LIST OF FICTIONAL WORKS
THIRD EDITON

Katsoulis, Gregory Scott

Access restricted. By Gregory Scott Katsoulis. Harlequin Teen 2018 480 p. (Word$)
Grades: 7 8 9 10 11 12
1. Debt -- Fiction; 2. Silence -- Fiction; 3. Freedom of expression -- Fiction
1335016252; 9781335016256, $18.99

"On the day she went silent, Speth never meant for anyone to follow her lead -- or to start a rebellion of Silents. But after taking down the tyrant Silas Rog and freeing the city from his grasp, everyone is looking to Speth for answers she doesn't have. All she wants is to find her parents, who are shackled to a lifetime of servitude in exchange for a debt they can never repay." (Publisher's note)

All rights reserved. Gregory Scott Katsoulis. Harlequin Teen 2017 392 p. Map (Word$)
Grades: 7 8 9 10 11 12
1. Copyright -- Fiction; 2. Dystopias -- Fiction; 3. Manners and customs -- Fiction; 4. Debt -- Fiction; 5. Teenage girls -- Fiction; 6. Families -- Fiction
9780373212446, $18.99; 9781488015472; 0373212445

In this book in the Word$ series, by Gregory Scott Katsoulis, "Speth Jime is anxious to deliver her Last Day speech and celebrate her transition into adulthood. The moment she turns fifteen, Speth must pay for every word she speaks...and even every gesture of affection.... But when Speth's friend Beecher commits suicide..., she can't express her shock and dismay without breaking her Last Day contract and sending her family into Collection." (Publisher's note)
"A fresh and detailed dystopian tale that will capture and make demands upon the attention of its readers, as the genre should, with a conclusion that sets readers up for the sequel." Kirkus
Another title in this series is:
Access restricted (2018)

Kaufman, Amie

★ **Illuminae**. Amie Kaufman; Jay Kristoff. Alfred A. Knopf 2015 608 p. Illustration
Grades: 8 9 10 11 12
1. Artificial intelligence -- Fiction 2. Interplanetary voyages -- Fiction 3. Plague -- Fiction 4. Science fiction
9780553499117, $18.99; 9780553499124; 9780553499148
LC 2014017908
In this young adult novel, by Amie Kaufman and Jay Kristoff, "the year is 2575, and two rival megacorporations are at war over a planet that's little more than an ice-covered speck at the edge of the universe. Too bad nobody thought to warn the people living on it. With enemy fire raining down on them, Kady and Ezra—who are barely even talking to each other—are forced to fight their way onto one of the evacuating fleet, with an enemy warship in hot pursuit." (Publisher's note)

Gemina. Amie Kaufman & Jay Kristoff; journal illustrations by Marie Lu. Knopf Books for Young Readers 2016 672 p. Illustration

Grades: 8 9 10 11 12
1. Artificial intelligence -- Fiction 2. Interplanetary voyages -- Fiction 3. Science fiction 4. Space stations -- Fiction
9780553499155, $19.99; 9780553499162
LC 2015037131
This second book in the Illuminae Files series by Amie Kaufman and Jay Kristoff "describes the experience of Hanna, who lives aboard the Heimdall. . . . Her world unravels when agents attempt to seize control of the space station. . . . Hanna finds an unlikely ally in Nik, an unsavory gang member who deals 'dust' in the space station, as they attempt to defend the Heimdall, save the Hypatia, contain vicious alien creatures, and fix a rip in the space-time continuum." (School Library Journal)
"An action-packed thrill ride and stellar head trip." Kirkus
Sequel to: Illuminae (2015)

Obsidio. Amie Kaufman & Jay Kristoff ; with journal illustrations by Marie Lu. Alfred A. Knopf 2018 624 p.
Grades: 8 9 10 11 12
1. Artificial intelligence -- Fiction; 2. Interplanetary voyages -- Fiction; 3. Science fiction
9780553499193, $19.99; 9780553499209
LC 2017020645
In this book in the Illuminae Files series, by Amie Kaufman and Jay Kristoff, illustrated by Marie Lu, "Kady, Ezra, Hanna, and Nik narrowly escaped with their lives from the attacks on Heimdall station and now find themselves crammed with 2,000 refugees on the container ship, Mao. With the jump station destroyed and their resources scarce, the only option is to return to Kerenza." (Publisher's note)

Kearney, Meg

The **girl** in the mirror; a novel in poems and journal entries. Meg Kearney. Persea Books 2012 168 p. (trade pbk.: alk. paper) $15
Grades: 9 10 11 12
1. Novels in verse 2. Grief -- Fiction 3. Adoptees -- Fiction 4. Identity (Psychology) -- Fiction 5. Adoption -- Fiction
ISBN 0892553855; 9780892553853
LC 2011045052
Sequel to: The secret of me
This book, the sequel to "The Secret of Me," is "told in verse and journal entries." The protagonist's "father passed away on the same day that a letter with non-identifying information about her birth mother arrived from the adoption agency. . . . She . . . joins her older coworkers in late-night partying and drinking. . . . When her change in lifestyle results in losing close friends and a near rape, Lizzie realizes that she no longer recognizes the girl she sees in the mirror." (Kirkus Reviews)
"Kearney tenderly explores Lizzie's anger, sadness, and ambivalence about her identity as she grapples with whether to risk being hurt by the mother she never knew or to approach the future without first claiming her past." Pub Wkly
Includes bibliographical references

Kehoe, Stasia Ward

The sound of letting go; by Stasia Ward Kehoe. Viking 2014 388p $17.99

Grades: 7 8 9 10 11 12

1. Autism -- Fiction 2. Family problems -- Fiction 3. High schools -- Fiction 4. Jazz -- Fiction 5. Novels in verse

ISBN: 0670015539; 9780670015535

LC 2013013098

A novel in verse. "For sixteen years, Daisy has been good. A good daughter, helping out with her autistic younger brother uncomplainingly. A good friend, even when her best friend makes her feel like a third wheel. When her parents announce they're sending her brother to an institution--without consulting her--Daisy's furious, and decides the best way to be a good sister is to start being bad. She quits jazz band and orchestra, slacks in school, and falls for bad-boy Dave." (Publisher's note)

"This painfully honest portrait of a family in crisis raises questions about love, responsibility, and self-sacrifice as it moves gracefully to a difficult but realistic resolution." Pub Wkly

Kelly, Tara

Harmonic feedback. Henry Holt and Company 2010 280p $16.99

Grades: 9 10 11 12

1. Drug abuse -- Fiction 2. Rock music -- Fiction 3. Washington (State) -- Fiction 4. Asperger's syndrome -- Fiction

ISBN 978-0-8050-9010-9; 0-8050-9010-X

LC 2009-24150

When Drea and her mother move in with her grandmother in Bellingham, Washington, the sixteen-year-old finds finds that she can have real friends, in spite of her Asperger's, and that even when you love someone it doesn't make life perfect.

"The novel's strength lies in Drea's dynamic personality: a combination of surprising immaturity, childish wonder, and profound insight. Her search for stability and need to escape being labeled is poignant and convincing." Publ Wkly

Kenneally, Miranda

Coming up for air. Miranda Kenneally. Sourcebooks Fire 2017 288 p. (Hundred oaks)

Grades: 10 11 12

1. Swimming -- Fiction; 2. Schools -- Fiction; 3. Best friends -- Fiction; 4. High schools -- Fiction

9781492630135; 9781492630111, $10.99

LC 2016056048

In this book in the Hundred Oaks series, by Miranda Kenneally, "all of Maggie's focus and free time is spent swimming. She's not only striving to earn scholarships -- she's training to qualify for the Olympics. It helps that her best friend, Levi, is also on the team, and cheers her on. But Levi's already earned an Olympic tryout, so Maggie feels even more pressure to succeed." (Publisher's note)

"Fans of the author's Hundred Oaks series won't be disappointed as they watch Maggie's and Levi's friendship move in a new direction, and the competitive and uncertain element of Maggie's future in swimming makes the page turning all the more enjoyable." Pub Wkly

Racing Savannah; Miranda Kenneally. Sourcebooks Fire 2013 304 p. (tp: alk. paper) $9.99

Grades: 8 9 10 11 12

1. Horsemanship -- Fiction 2. Love -- Fiction 3. Horses -- Fiction 4. Tennessee -- Fiction

ISBN 1402284764; 9781402284762

LC 2013023322

In this book, by Miranda Kenneally, "Savannah has always been much more comfortable around horses than boys. Especially boys like Jack Goodwin. . . . She knows the rules: no mixing between the staff and the Goodwin family. But Jack has no such boundaries. With her dream of becoming a jockey, Savannah isn't exactly one to follow the rules either." (Publisher's note)

"Kenneally (Stealing Parker, 2012) again looks at sports through a female lens, this time tackling male-dominated horse racing, in this fourth Hundred Oaks novel. Savannah, her widowed horse-trainer father, and her father's pregnant girlfriend move to Tennessee's Cedar Hill, a farm that trains horses for races including the Kentucky Derby...The author's knack for weaving forbidden romance, breezy dialogue, and details of this lesser-known sports venue places it in the winner's circle for reluctant readers and chick-lit fans." (Booklist)

Stealing Parker; Miranda Kenneally. Sourcebooks Fire 2012 242 p. (paperback) $8.99; (prebind) $17.99

Grades: 9 10 11 12

1. School stories 2. Children of gay parents -- Fiction

ISBN 1402271875; 9781402271878

In this book, "when Parker's mother comes out, Parker's family falls apart: . . . Parker herself gives up her beloved softball and takes up kissing guys in order to prove that she's nothing like her mother. At the behest of her best friend, Drew, she becomes the manager of the boys' baseball team, where she quickly become attracted to and confused by the good-looking new coach." (Bulletin of the Center for Children's Books)

Kephart, Beth

Going over; Beth Kephart; Chronicle Books. 2014 262p $17.99

Grades: 8 9 10 11 12

1. Berlin Wall (1961-1989) -- Fiction 2. Family life--Germany--Fiction 3. Berlin (Germany)--Fiction 4. Love stories

ISBN: 1452124574; 9781452124575

LC 2012046894

"Ada lives among the rebels, punkers, and immigrants of Kreuzberg in West Berlin. Stefan lives in East Berlin, in a faceless apartment bunker of Friedrichshain. Bound by love and separated by circumstance, their only chance for a life together lies in a high-risk escape. But will Stefan find the courage to leap? Or will forces beyond his control stand in his way?" Publisher's note

"In a present-tense narration alternating between Ada's first-person and Stefan's second-person, the young lovers on opposite sides of the Berlin Wall in 1983 plan for Stefan's escape to the West. Kephart works romantic chemistry into a danger-packed plot with moving results in this captivating glimpse into an underrepresented era that will appeal to older readers with a taste for literary historical fiction." Horn Book

★ The **heart** is not a size. HarperTeen 2010 244p $16.99
Grades: 7 8 9 10
    1. Poverty -- Fiction 2. Friendship -- Fiction 3. Volunteer work -- Fiction
ISBN 978-0-06-147048-6; 0-06-147048-1
                              LC 2008-55721
Fifteen-year-old Georgia learns a great deal about herself and her troubled best friend Riley when they become part of a group of suburban Pennsylvania teenagers that go to Anapra, a squatters village in the border town of Juarez, Mexico, to undertake a community construction project.
    "Kephart's prose is typically poetic. She pens a faster-paced novel that explores teens' inner selves. . . . The writing is vivid, enabling readers to visualize Anapra's desolation and hope." Voice Youth Advocates

House of Dance. HarperTeen 2008 263p $16.99; lib bdg $17.89; pa $10.99
Grades: 7 8 9 10
    1. Death -- Fiction 2. Cancer -- Fiction 3. Dancers -- Fiction 4. Grandfathers -- Fiction 5. Mother-daughter relationship -- Fiction
ISBN 978-0-06-142928-6; 0-06-142928-7; 978-0-06-142929-3 lib bdg; 0-06-142929-5 lib bdg; 978-0-06-142930-9 pa; 0-06-142930-9 pa
                              LC 2007-26011
During one of her daily visits across town to visit her dying grandfather, fifteen-year-old Rosie discovers a dance studio that helps her find a way to bring her family members together.
    This is "distinguished more by its sharp, eloquent prose than by its plot. . . . Poetically expressed memories and moving dialogue both anchor and amplify the characters' emotions." Publ Wkly

One thing stolen. Beth Kephart. Chronicle Books 2015 272 p.
Grades: 9 10 11 12
    1. Dementia -- Fiction 2. Families -- Fiction 3. Family life -- Fiction 4. Kleptomania -- Fiction 5. Florence (Italy) -- Fiction 6. Italy -- Fiction 7. Psychology -- Fiction 8. Theft -- Fiction 12. Romance fiction
9781452128313, $17.99; 1452128316
                              LC 2014005286
In this novel by Beth Kephart, "something very bad is happening to 17-year-old Nadia. Ever since her family relocated to Florence for her father's sabbatical, she's been slipping out at night to steal random objects and then weave them into bizarre nest-shaped forms she hides from her family, and she's losing her ability to speak." (Kirkus Reviews)
    "Fans of Jandy Nelson's dense, unique narratives will lose themselves in Kephart's enigmatic, atmospheric, and beautifully written tale." Booklist

★ **Small** damages; Beth Kephart. Philomel Books 2012 304 p. $17.99
Grades: 10 11 12
    1. Spain -- Fiction 2. Adoption -- Fiction 3. Teenage pregnancy -- Fiction 4. Cooking -- Fiction 5. Pregnancy -- Fiction 6. Ranch life -- Spain -- Fiction 7. Interpersonal relations -- Fiction
ISBN 0399257489; 9780399257483
                              LC 2011020947
As Beth Kephart's character is "provided by her mother with only the barest of details about a couple that wishes to adopt her baby, Kenzie finds herself an unofficial apprentice in the kitchen of the home of a successful bull breeder connected to the prospective adoptive parents. . . . Her initially strained relationship with terse Estela, the marvelous chef charged with her safekeeping, eventually melts into a mutual trust." (Kirkus Reviews)

This is the story of you. Beth Kephart. Chronicle Books Llc 2016 264 p.
Grades: 7 8 9 10 11 12
    1. Hurricanes -- Fiction 2. Islands -- Fiction 3. Survival -- Fiction 4. New Jersey -- Fiction 5. Survival skills -- Fiction
9781452142845, $17.99
                              LC 2015003765
In this book, by Beth Kephart, "on Haven, a six-mile long, half-mile-wide stretch of barrier island, Mira Banul and her Year-Rounder friends have proudly risen to every challenge. But then a superstorm defies all predictions and devastates the island, upending all logic and stranding Mira's mother and brother on the mainland. Nothing will ever be the same." (Publisher's note)
    "At once an exploration of the unrelenting power of nature and a reminder of the one thing in the world that is irreplaceable: family." Booklist

Undercover. HarperTeen 2007 278p $16.99; lib bdg $17.89; pa $8.99
Grades: 8 9 10 11 12
    1. School stories 2. Poetry -- Fiction 3. Family life -- Fiction
ISBN 978-0-06-123893-2; 0-06-123893-7; 978-0-06-123894-9 lib bdg; 0-06-123894-5 lib bdg; 978-0-06-123895-6 pa; 0-06-123895-3 pa
                              LC 2007-2981
High school sophomore Elisa is used to observing while going unnoticed except when classmates ask her to write love notes for them, but a teacher's recognition of her talent, a "client's" desire for her friendship, a love of ice skating, and her parent's marital problems draw her out of herself.
    "Kephart tells a moving story. . . . Readers will fall easily into the compelling premise and Elisa's memorable, graceful voice." Booklist

Keplinger, Kody

A **midsummer's** nightmare; a novel. by Kody Keplinger. Poppy 2012 291 p. $17.99
Grades: 9 10 11 12
    1. Family life 2. Stepfamilies 3. Illinois -- Fiction 4. Remarriage -- Fiction 5. Conduct of life -- Fiction 6. Family problems -- Fiction 7. Fathers and daughters

-- Fiction
ISBN 0316084220; 9780316084222

LC 2011026949

This young adult novel by Kody Keplinger tells how "Whitley Johnson's dream summer with her divorce dad has turned into a nightmare. She's just met his new fiancee and her kids. . . . Worse, she totally doesn't fit in with her dad's perfect new country-club family. So Whitley acts out. . . . It will take all [of her friends and step family] to help Whitley get through her anger and begin to put the pieces of her [life] together." (Publisher's note)

Run. Kody Keplinger. Scholastic Press 2016 295 p.

Grades: 7 8 9 10 11 12

1. Best friends -- Fiction 2. Blind -- Fiction 3. Friendship -- Fiction 4. Fugitives from justice -- Fiction 5. People with disabilities -- Fiction 6. Runaway children -- Fiction 7. Runaways -- Fiction 8. Secrecy -- Fiction 9. Secrets -- Fiction 10. Runaway teenagers -- Fiction

054583113X; 9780545831130, $17.99; 9780545831154, $17.99

LC 2015048824

In this book, by Kody Keplinger, "Bo Dickinson is a girl with a wild reputation, a deadbeat dad, and a mama who's not exactly sober most of the time. . . . Agnes Atwood has never gone on a date, never even stayed out past ten, and never broken any of her parents' overbearing rules. . . . Despite everything, Bo and Agnes become best friends. And it's the sort of friendship that runs truer and deeper than anything else." (Publisher's note)

"A good unlikely friendship story with compelling characters and a nuanced portrait of disability and small-town life." SLJ

That's not what happened. Kody Keplinger. Scholastic Press 2018 336 p.

Grades: 7 8 9 10 11 12

1. Bullying -- Fiction; 2. High schools -- Fiction; 3. Massacre survivors -- Fiction; 4. Rural schools -- Fiction; 5. School shootings -- Fiction; 6. Schools -- Fiction; 7. Secrecy -- Fiction; 8. Secrets -- Fiction; 9. Truth -- Fiction; 10. Truthfulness and falsehood -- Fiction; 11. Truth -- Fiction; 12. Bullies -- Fiction

9781338186529, $18.99

LC 2017060501

In this novel, by Kody Keplinger, "it's been three years since the Virgil County High School Massacre. Three years since my best friend, Sarah, was killed in a bathroom stall during the mass shooting. Everyone knows Sarah's story -- that she died proclaiming her faith. But it's not true. I know because I was with her when she died.... But I'm not the only survivor with a story to tell about what did -- and didn't -- happen that day." (Publisher's note)

Kerbel, Deborah
Mackenzie, lost and found. Dundurn Press 2008 251p pa $12.99

Grades: 7 8 9 10

1. Jerusalem -- Fiction 2. Culture conflict -- Fiction
ISBN 978-1-55002-852-2; 1-55002-852-9

"Fifteen-year-old Mackenzie is uprooted from her native Canada and forced to move to Israel when her archaeologist father takes a visiting professorship at The Hebrew University of Jerusalem. . . . She soon begins to make friends and learn the language, while engaging in a forbidden romance with a Palestinian boy named Nasir. When Mack finds herself in the middle of a plot involving stolen antiquities after Nasir's father enlists his help in illegally digging up and selling artifacts, she must choose between protecting her first real boyfriend and obeying the law. . . . This solid coming-of-age story offers a unique setting and a likeable young heroine." Voice Youth Advocates

Kerr, M. E.
Gentlehands. Harper & Row 1978 183p hardcover o.p. pa $5.99

Grades: 7 8 9 10

1. Criminals -- Fiction 2. Grandfathers -- Fiction 3. Social classes -- Fiction
ISBN 978-0-06-447067-4 pa; 0-06-447067-9 pa

LC 77-11860

ALA YALSA Margaret A. Edwards Award (1993)

"Buddy Boyle falls for Skye and her affluent, breezy way of life. Finding his own parents not 'cultured' enough for this new relationship, Buddy turns to his grandfather, whose love of opera and other refinements make him more suitable to make Skye's acquaintance. A shocking surprise awaits Buddy when Mr. DeLucca, pursuer of an infamous Nazi, finally identifies his quarry." Shapiro. Fic for youth. 3rd edition

If I love you, am I trapped forever? Marshall Cavendish 2008 178p $16.99

Grades: 8 9 10 11 12

1. School stories 2. Newspapers -- Fiction 3. Dating (Social customs) -- Fiction 4. Father-son relationship -- Fiction
ISBN 978-0-7614-5545-5

LC 2007051768

A reissue of the title first published 1973 by Harper & Row

Alan, a popular senior high school student, faces painful changes after a new student, Duncan "Doomed" Stein, comes to town and starts an influential underground newspaper.

"Extremely humorous at times, the story is also occasionally touched with sadness and poignancy." Horn Book Guide

Keyser, Amber J.
★ **Pointe**, claw. By Amber J. Keyser. Carolrhoda Lab 2017 278 p.

Grades: 8 9 10 11 12

1. Ballet dancing -- Fiction; 2. Best friends -- Fiction; 3. Diseases -- Fiction; 4. Friendship -- Fiction; 5. Zoonoses -- Fiction; 6. Ballet dancers -- Fiction

9781512408959; 9781467775915, $18.99

LC 2016006114

In this novel, by Amber J. Keyser, "Jessie Vale dances in an elite ballet program. She has to be perfect to land a spot with the professional company. When Jessie is cast in an animalistic avant-garde production, her careful composure cracks wide open.... Meanwhile, her friend Dawn McCormick's world is full of holes. She wakes in strange places, bruised, battered, and unable to speak. The doctors are out of ideas." (Publisher's note)

"Keyser's writing shimmers with raw emotion and empathy, and her finale, much like in dance, is poetic, bittersweet, and life affirming." Pub Wkly

The **way** back from broken. By Amber J. Keyser. Carolrhoda Lab, a division of Lerner Publishing Group 2015 216 p.
Grades: 9 10 11 12

1. Brothers and sisters -- Fiction 2. Camping -- Fiction 3. Death -- Fiction 4. Grief -- Fiction 5. Racially mixed people -- Fiction 6. Survival -- Fiction 7. Canada -- Fiction 8. Wilderness survival -- Fiction
9781467775908, $18.99; 1467775908

LC 2015001617

In this book, by Amber J. Keyser, "Rakmen Cannon's life is turning out to be one sucker punch after another. His baby sister died in his arms, his parents are on the verge of divorce, and he's flunking out of high school. The only place he fits in is with the other art therapy kids stuck in the basement of Promise House.... When he's shipped off to the Canadian wilderness with ten-year-old Jacey, another member of the support group, and her mom, his summer goes from bad to worse." (Publisher's note)

"With a cast of diverse and well-rounded characters, poignant relationships that never become schmaltzy, and a compelling high-stakes adventure, this vivid, moving exploration of grief and recovery hits all the right notes." Booklist

Khorram, Adib

★ **Darius** the Great is not okay. Adib Khorram. Dial Books 2018 320 p.
Grades: 7 8 9 10 11 12

1. Americans -- Iran -- Fiction; 2. Depression, Mental -- Fiction; 3. Friendship -- Fiction; 4. Grandparents -- Fiction; 5. Iranian Americans -- Fiction; 6. Iran -- Fiction; 7. Depression (Psychology) -- Fiction
9780525552963, $17.99; 9780525552987

LC 2018009825

"Darius has never really fit in at home, and he's sure things are going to be the same in Iran. His clinical depression doesn't exactly help matters.... Then Darius meets Sohrab, the boy next door, and everything changes. Soon, they're spending their days together.... Sohrab calls him Darioush -- the original Persian version of his name -- and Darius has never felt more like himself than he does now that he's Darioush to Sohrab." (Publisher's note)

"Darius is a well-crafted, awkward but endearing character, and his cross-cultural story will inspire reflection about identity and belonging." SLJ

Khoury, Jessica

Origin; Jessica Khoury. Razorbill 2012 393 p. $17.99
Grades: 6 7 8

1. Science fiction 2. Immortality -- Fiction 3. Science -- Experiments -- Fiction 4. Rain forests -- Fiction 5. Indigenous peoples -- Fiction
ISBN 1595145958; 9781595145956

LC 2012014447

In this young adult novel by Jessica Khoury "Pia has grown up in a secret laboratory hidden deep in the Amazon rainforest. She was raised by a team of scientists who have created her to be the start of a new immortal race. But on the night of her seventeenth birthday . . . and sneaks outside the compound for the first time in her life . . . Pia meets Eio, a boy from a nearby village. Together, they embark on a race against time to discover the truth about Pia's origin." (Publisher's note)

Kiely, Brendan

★ The **gospel** of winter; Brendan Kiely. Simon & Schuster 2014 304 p. $17.99
Grades: 9 10 11 12

1. Priests -- Fiction 2. Child sexual abuse -- Fiction
ISBN 1442484896; 9781442484894

Kiely's gutsy debut addresses abuse in the Catholic Church. The year is 2001, the events of 9/11 are only two months old, and 16-year-old Aidan's family is falling apart. Aidan finds comfort in snorting lines of Adderall, swiping drinks from his father's wet bar, and forming a friendship with Father Greg of Most Precious Blood, the town's Catholic church. The scandal among the Boston archdiocese in early 2002 gets Aidan's town's attention, and when it does, Aidan's feelings of rage and denial and fear come to a head. This is challenging, thought-provoking material, presented in beautiful prose that explores the ways in which acts rendered in the name of love can both destroy and heal." (Booklist)

The **last** true love story. Brendan Kiely. Margaret K. McElderry Books 2016 288 p. Map
Grades: 9 10 11 12

1. Alzheimer's disease -- Fiction 2. Grandfathers -- Fiction 3. Love -- Fiction 4. Self-realization -- Fiction 5. Romance fiction
9781481429887, $17.99; 9781481429894; 9781481429900, $15.99

LC 2015036953

In this book, by Brendan Keily, on "one hot July night, Hendrix and Corrina decide to risk everything. They steal a car, spring Gpa from his assisted living facility, stuff, . . . and take off on a cross-country odyssey from LA to NY. With their parents, Gpa's doctors, and the police all hot on their heels, Hendrix and Corrina set off to discover for themselves if what Gpa says is true-that the only stories that last are love stories." (Publisher's note)

"Readers will be swept up in Kiely's musical prose as Teddy learns about love, romance, forgiveness, and reconciliation." Kirkus

Tradition. Brendan Kiely. Margaret K. McElderry Books 2018 339 p.
Grades: 7 8 9 10 11 12

1. Conduct of life -- Fiction; 2. High schools -- Fiction; 3. Preparatory schools -- Fiction; 4. Rape -- Fiction; 5. Schools -- Fiction; 6. Sexism -- Fiction; 7. Wealth -- Fiction; 8. Teenagers -- Sexual behavior -- Fiction
1481480340; 9781481480345, $18.99; 9781481480352; 9781481480369

LC 2017026455

This book, by Brendan Kiely, "explores the insidious nature of tradition at [Fullbrook Academy,] a prestigious boarding school.... When Jamie and Jules meet, they recognize in each other a similar instinct for survival. . . As Jules and Jamie's lives intertwine, and the pressures to play by the rules and remain silent about the school's secrets intensify, they see Fullbrook for what it really is. That tradition, a word Fullbrook hides behind, can be ugly, even violent." (Publisher's note)

"A thoughtfully crafted argument for feminism and allyship." Kirkus

Kiem, Elizabeth

Dancer, daughter, traitor, spy; by Elizabeth Kiem. Soho Teen 2013 288 p. (alk. paper) $17.99
Grades: 9 10 11 12

1. Clairvoyance -- Fiction 2. Russian Americans -- Fiction 3. Soviet Union -- Foreign relations -- United States -- Fiction 4. Spies -- Fiction 5. Soviet Union -- Relations -- United States -- Fiction 6. United States -- Relations -- Soviet Union -- Fiction 7. Brooklyn (New York, N.Y.) -- History -- 20th century -- Fiction
ISBN 1616952636; 9781616952631
LC 2013006502

This book by Elizabeth Kiem is set in "the 'Russia by the Sea' neighborhood of Brighton Beach, Brooklyn. Marina and her father escape there following the State Psychiatric Directorate's institutionalization of her mother, Sveta, a celebrated Bolshoi dancer, who had a vision of a terrible past event the regime must keep hidden. . . . Marina and her father cannot shake the suspicion and danger Sveta's vision put them under." (Publishers Weekly)

"The disappearance of a star ballerina in Soviet Russia shatters the life of her daughter. Bright, 17-year-old Marya is the daughter of the Bolshoi's star ballerina and her scientist husband, and she's a dancer herself...The pacing is somewhat uneven, but there are enough twists to surprise and engage readers to the end. A compelling portrait of a young woman on the verge of adulthood, caught up in the domestic secrets of her parents and the enmity of two countries." (Kirkus)

Kiernan, Celine

Into the grey. Celine Kiernan. Candlewick Press 2014 304 p.
Grades: 9 10 11 12

1. Ghost stories 2. Horror tales 3. Brothers -- Fiction 4. Twins -- Fiction
0763670618; 9780763670610, $16.99
LC 2013952836

In this novel by Celine Kiernan, "after their nan accidentally burns their home down, twin brothers Pat and Dom must move with their parents and baby sister to the seaside cottage they've summered in, now made desolate by the winter wind. It's there that the ghost appears - a strange boy who cries black tears and fears a bad man, a soldier, who is chasing him . . . With white-knuckle pacing and a deft portrayal of family relationships, Celine Kiernan offers a taut psychological thriller that is sure to haunt readers long after the last page is turned." (Publisher's note)

"At its best it is confident, pungent, and poetic. Family love, loyalty, and protectiveness are palpable in a well-drawn cast of characters, and the pace is frequently galva-

nized with energetic drama and dialogue pierced with Irish dialect." Horn Book

Kincaid, S. J.

The diabolic. S. J. Kincaid. Simon & Schuster Books for Young Readers 2016 407 p. (Diabolic trilogy)
Grades: 8 9 10 11 12

1. Courts and courtiers -- Fiction; 2. Science fiction; 3. Bodyguards -- Fiction
9781481472692; 9781481472678, $17.99
LC 2016003698

In this book, by S. J. Kincaid, "Nemesis is a Diabolic, a humanoid teenager created to protect a galactic senator's daughter, Sidonia. . . . When the power-mad Emperor learns Sidonia's father is participating in a rebellion, he summons Sidonia to the Galactic court. She is to serve as a hostage. Now, there is only one way for Nemesis to protect Sidonia. She must become her. Nemesis travels to the court disguised as Sidonia." (Publisher's note)

"Kincaid has crafted incredible characters who readers can relate to and care for even if they range from privileged, bratty children to creations designed to kill. The imagery used in establishing these protagonists and the complex setting will thrill the YA audience." SLJ

The empress. S.J. Kincaid. Simon & Schuster BFYR 2017 378 p. (Diabolic trilogy)
Grades: 8 9 10 11 12

1. Courts and courtiers -- Fiction; 2. Emperors -- Fiction; 3. Empresses -- Fiction; 4. Human beings -- Genetic engineering -- Moral and ethical aspects -- Fiction; 5. Identity (Psychology) -- Fiction; 6. Kings and rulers -- Fiction
1534409920; 9781534409927, $17.99; 9781534409941
LC 2017023825

In this book in The Diabolic series, by S. J. Kincaid, "it's a new day in the Empire. Tyrus has ascended to the throne with Nemesis by his side and now they can find a new way forward.... One where creatures like Nemesis will be given worth and recognition, where science and information can be shared with everyone and not just the elite. But having power isn't the same thing as keeping it, and change isn't always welcome." (Publisher's note)

"Kincaid deftly juggles high-octane action with emotionally devastating punches, and readers will riot for the next installment." Kirkus

Kinch, Michael

The blending time; [by] Michael Kinch. Flux 2010 254p pa $9.95
Grades: 10 11 12

1. Science fiction 2. Africa -- Fiction 3. Violence -- Fiction
ISBN 978-0-7387-2067-8
LC 2010-24149

In the harsh world of 2069, ravaged by plagues and environmental disasters, friends Jaym, Reya, and D'Shay are chosen to help repopulate Africa as their mandatory Global Alliance work, but civil war and mercenaries opposed to the Blending Program separate them and threaten their very lives.

"Determinedly multiethnic, fast-paced, and with plentiful gore and violence, the book will draw reluctant readers who enjoy action and adventure." Booklist

The **fires** of New SUN; a Blending time novel. Michael Kinch. Flux 2012 275 p. (Blending time) $9.95

Grades: 9 10 11 12

    1. Africa -- Fiction 2. Dystopian fiction 3. Deserts -- Fiction 4. Science fiction 5. Survival -- Fiction 6. Violence -- Fiction 7. Friendship -- Fiction

    ISBN 0738730769; 9780738730769

                                LC 2011035527

This dystopian thriller novel, by Michael Kinch, is set "in the harsh African desert. . . . Jaym and D'Shay . . . have helped dozens of Nswibe refugees cross the African desert. . . . They've finally reunited with their friend, Reya, and found safe haven at a New SUN outpost, a cavern fortress hidden in the Blue Mountains. But their troubles are just beginning. . . . As a massive [renegade] attack looms, the three friends are quickly drawn into a deadly battle." (Publisher's note)

The **rebels** of New SUN; a Blending time novel. Michael Kinch. Flux 2013 288 p. (Blending time) $9.99

Grades: 9 10 11 12

    1. Africa -- Fiction 2. Dystopian fiction 3. Deserts -- Fiction 4. Science fiction 5. Survival -- Fiction 6. Violence -- Fiction 7. Friendship -- Fiction

    ISBN 073873151X; 9780738731513

                                LC 2012028409

This dystopian thriller novel, by Michael Kinch, is book three of the "Blending Time" series. "Before the 'gades secure the savannah and wipe out the New SUN resistance, Reya, D'Shay, Jaym, and a handful of other rebels launch a daring mission to infiltrate . . . Chewena's capital city. . . . To free the country from GlobeTran's . . . control, they seek out allies and information that could help the resistance . . . return power to the people of Africa." (Publisher's note)

Kindl, Patrice

Keeping the castle; a tale of romance, riches, and real estate. by Patrice Kindl. Viking Childrens Books 2012 261 p. $16.99; (hardcover) $16.99

Grades: 7 8 9 10 11

    1. Love stories 2. Regency novels 3. Marriage -- Fiction 4. Castles -- Fiction 5. Courtship -- Fiction 6. Social classes -- Fiction 7. Great Britain -- History -- 1789-1820 -- Fiction 8. England -- Social life and customs -- 19th century -- Fiction

    ISBN 0670014389; 9780670014385

                                LC 2011033185

In this book, "[s]eventeen-year-old Althea Crawley is . . . on a quest to marry rich so that she may secure the family's only inheritance, a dilapidated castle on the edge of the North Sea. . . . Marriage prospects in tiny Lesser Hoo are slim, to say the least, until dashing and wealthy Lord Boring arrives on the scene. Matters are further complicated by a revolving cast of potential suitors, including Lord Boring's cousin, Mr. Fredericks." (Booklist)

A **school** for brides: a story of maidens, mystery, and matrimony. By Patrice Kindl. Viking, an imprint of Penguin Group (USA) LLC 2015 272 p.

Grades: 7 8 9 10

    1. Boarding schools -- Fiction 2. Courtship -- Fiction 3. Marriage -- Fiction 4. Mystery and detective stories 5. Schools -- Fiction 6. England -- Social life and customs -- 19th century -- Fiction 7. Great Britain -- History -- 1789-1820 -- Fiction 8. Great Britain -- History -- 1714-1837 -- Fiction 9. School stories

    9780670786084, $17.99

                                LC 2014028087

In this companion novel to "Keeping the Castle," also written by Patrice Kindl, "[t]he Winthrop Hopkins Female Academy of Lesser Hoo, Yorkshire, has one goal: to train its students in the feminine arts with an eye toward getting them married off. This year, there are five girls of marriageable age. There's only one problem: the school is in the middle of nowhere, and there are no men." (Publisher's note)

"This affectionate homage to the genre delivers what's missing: a witty, intelligent plot whose characters-complex, conniving, hypocritical, and hilarious-seek happiness within an ordered world. This airy soufflé of a tale, garnished with quirky charm, is an unmitigated delight from start to finish." Kirkus

Sequel to: Keeping the castle

King, A. S.

★ **Ask** the passengers; a novel. by A.S. King. Little, Brown 2012 304 p. (hardcover) $17.99

Grades: 9 10 11 12

    1. Moving -- Fiction 2. Identity -- Fiction 3. Love stories 4. Love -- Fiction 5. Gossip -- Fiction 6. Schools -- Fiction 7. Lesbians -- Fiction 8. Prejudices -- Fiction 9. High schools -- Fiction 10. Family problems -- Fiction

    ISBN 0316194689; 9780316194686

                                LC 2011053207

This book by A.S. King follows teenage protagonist Astrid, "her closeted BFF, Kristina, and Dee, a star hockey player she met while working for a local catering company. Sparks fly between Astrid and Dee, causing Astrid to feel even more distanced and confused. . . . She's in love with Dee, but she's not sure if she's a lesbian. She's ignoring all of the labels and focusing on what she feels." (Kirkus Reviews)

★ **Everybody** sees the ants; by A.S. King. Little, Brown 2011 282p. $17.99; ebook $9.99

Grades: 9 10 11 12

    1. Family -- Fiction 2. Domestic relations 3. Teenagers -- Fiction 4. Dreams -- Fiction 5. Arizona -- Fiction 6. Bullies -- Fiction 7. Family life -- Fiction 8. Grandfathers -- Fiction 9. Missing persons -- Fiction 10. Vietnam War, 1961-1975 -- Fiction

    ISBN 978-0-316-12928-2; 978-0-316-19181-4 ebook; 9780316129275

                                LC 2010049434

Overburdened by his parents' bickering and a bully's attacks, fifteen-year-old Lucky Linderman begins dreaming of being with his grandfather, who went missing during the Vietnam War, but during a visit to Arizona, his aunt and uncle and their beautiful neighbor, Ginny, help him find a new perspective.

"Blending magic and realism, this is a subtly written, profoundly honest novel about a kid falling through the cracks and pulling himself back up." Booklist

★ **Glory** O'Brien's history of the future: a novel; by A.S. King; Little, Brown & Co. 2014 306p $18.00
Grades: 9 10 11 12
1. Best friends -- Fiction 2. Clairvoyance -- Fiction 3. Eccentrics and eccentricities -- Fiction 4. Father-daughter relationship -- Fiction 5. Friendship -- Fiction 6. Photography -- Fiction 7. Suicide -- Fiction
ISBN: 0316222720; 9780316222723
LC 2013041670

In this novel, the main character Gloria "begins to experience an astonishing new power to see a person's infinite past and future. From ancient ancestors to many generations forward, Glory is bombarded with visions--and what she sees ahead of her is terrifying. . . . Glory makes it her mission to record everything she sees, hoping her notes will somehow make a difference. . . . She may not see a future for herself, but she'll do anything to make sure this one doesn't come to pass." (Publisher's note)

"Imbuing Glory's narrative with a graceful, sometimes dissonant combination of anger, ambivalence, and hopefulness that resists tidy resolution, award-winning King presents another powerful, moving, and compellingly complex coming-of-age story." Booklist

I crawl through it. By A.S. King. Little, Brown & Co. 2015 336 p.
1. Reality -- Fiction 2. Psychological fiction 3. Teenagers -- Fiction
9780316334099, $18
LC 2014036896

In this surrealist novel, by A. S. King, "four teenagers are on the verge of exploding. The anxieties they face at every turn have nearly pushed them to the point of surrender: senseless high-stakes testing, the lingering damage of past trauma, the buried grief and guilt of tragic loss. . . . So they will lie. They will split in two. They will turn inside out. They will even build an invisible helicopter to fly themselves far away . . . but nothing releases the pressure." (Publisher's note)

"Characters unfold like riddles before the reader, while King uses magical realism and a motif of standardized testing to emphasize the flaw in obtaining answers without confronting reality's hard questions. Beautiful prose, poetry, and surreal imagery combine for an utterly original story that urges readers to question, love, and believe-or risk explosion." Booklist

★ **Please** ignore Vera Dietz. Alfred A. Knopf 2010 326p $16.99; lib bdg $19.99; ebook $16.99
Grades: 9 10 11 12
1. Death -- Fiction 2. Friendship -- Fiction
ISBN 978-0-375-86586-2; 978-0-375-96586-9 lib bdg; 978-0-375-89617-0 ebook
LC 2010-12730

A Michael L. Printz honor book, 2011

When her best friend, whom she secretly loves, betrays her and then dies under mysterious circumstances, high school senior Vera Dietz struggles with secrets that could help clear his name.

This "is a gut-wrenching tale about family, friendship, destiny, the meaning of words, and self-discovery." Voice Youth Advocates

Reality Boy; A.S. King. Little, Brown and Co. 2013 368 p. $18
Grades: 10 11 12
1. Special education -- Fiction 2. Reality television programs -- Fiction 3. Fame -- Fiction 4. Family problems -- Fiction 5. Emotional problems -- Fiction 6. Dating (Social customs) -- Fiction 7. Self-actualization (Psychology) -- Fiction
ISBN 0316222704; 9780316222709
LC 2012048432

Author A. S. King's book looks at "a boy saddled with the nickname the Crapper because of his infamous behavior at age five on a reality show, Network Nanny. Now almost 17, Gerald Faust is ostracized by his peers, barely keeping his violent urges at bay, and grateful for his spot in special ed because" it is a safe place for him. Although "the Network Nanny episodes about Gerald's family framed him as the problem child among his siblings, the truth was more disturbing, as King shows in flashbacks." (Publishers Weekly)

"When Gerald was five, TV's Network Nanny came to his house to help solve his behavior problems. Now nearly seventeen, Gerald bears the emotional scars of having his deeply dysfunctional childhood nationally televised. When Gerald meets Hannah, he discovers he's not the only one with a messed-up family. As always, King's societal critique is spot-on and scathing." (Horn Book)

Still life with tornado. By A.S. King. Dutton Books, an imprint of Penguin Random House LLC 2016 304 p.
Grades: 9 10 11 12
1. Family secrets -- Fiction 2. Family violence -- Fiction 3. Domestic violence -- Fiction
9781101994887
LC 2015049462

"Sarah can't draw. This is a problem, because as long as she can remember, she has "done the art." She thinks she's having an existential crisis. And she might be right; she does keep running into past and future versions of herself as she explores the urban ruins of Philadelphia. Or maybe she's finally waking up to the tornado that is her family, the tornado that six years ago sent her once-beloved older brother flying across the country for a reason she can't quite recall. . . . As Sarah herself often observes, nothing about her pain is remotely original -and yet it still hurts." (Publisher's note)

This beautifully written, often surreal narrative will make readers wonder if Sarah is schizophrenic, if she has post-traumatic stress disorder, or if she just needs to take a break from the realities of her life. . . . Sarah's strength, fragility, and ability to survive resonate throughout." SLJ

King, Emily R.
The **hundredth** queen. Emily R. King. Skyscape 2017 287 p. (Hundredth queen series)

Grades: 7 8 9 10

1. Imaginary places -- Fiction; 2. Quests (Expeditions) -- Fiction; 3. Survival -- Fiction; 4. Young women -- Fiction; 5. Fantasy fiction; 6. Orphans -- Fiction; 7. Bildungsromans
9781503943650, $9.99; 1503943658

In this book in the Hundredth Queen Series, by Emily R. King, "an orphan girl blossoms into a warrior, summoning courage and confidence in her fearless quest to upend tradition, overthrow an empire, and reclaim her life as her own.... Eighteen-year-old Kalinda is destined for nothing more than a life of seclusion and prayer.... But a visit from the tyrant Rajah Tarek disrupts Kalinda's life." (Publisher's note)

"Strong characterization, deep worldbuilding, page-turning action scenes and intrigue, as well as social commentary, make this book stand out." Kirkus

Kinsella, Sophie

Finding Audrey. Sophie Kinsella. Delacorte Press 2015 288 p.
Grades: 9 10 11 12

1. Anxiety disorders -- Fiction 2. Anxiety -- Fiction 3. Friendship -- Fiction
9780553536515, $18.99; 0553536516

LC 2014048476

In this novel by Sophie Kinsella, "an anxiety disorder disrupts fourteen-year-old Audrey's daily life. She has been making slow but steady progress with Dr. Sarah, but when Audrey meets Linus, her brother's gaming teammate, she is energized. She connects with him. Audrey can talk through her fears with Linus in a way she's never been able to do with anyone before. As their friendship deepens and her recovery gains momentum, a sweet romantic connection develops." (Publishers Weekly)

"A deep and sensitive portrayal of a British teen's recovery from a traumatic experience. Expect requests!" SLJ

Kirby, Jessi

Golden; Jessi Kirby. 1st ed. Simon & Schuster Books for Young Readers 2013 288 p. (hardcover) $16.99
Grades: 7 8 9 10 11 12

1. Love stories 2. Mystery fiction 3. Diaries -- Fiction 4. Love -- Fiction 5. Choice -- Fiction 6. Family problems -- Fiction 7. Mothers and daughters -- Fiction
ISBN 1442452161; 9781442452169; 9781442452183; 9781442452251

LC 2012042216

In this novel, by Jessi Kirby, "seventeen-year-old Parker Frost has never taken the road less traveled. . . . Julianna Farnetti and Shane Cruz are remembered as the golden couple of Summit Lakes High . . . but Julianna's journal tells . . . . the secrets that were swept away with her the night that Shane's jeep plunged into an icy river. . . . Reading Julianna's journal gives Parker . . . reasons to question what really happened the night of the accident." (Publisher's note)

"Kirby's . . . third novel is inspirational and contemplative in its mood and tone. Multifaceted characters and dashes of mystery and romance come together in a successful me-

diation on the value of taking an active role in one's life." Pub Wkly

Things we know by heart. Jessi Kirby. Harper-Teen, an imprint of HarperCollinsPublishers 2015 304 p.
Grades: 9 10 11 12

1. Grief -- Fiction; 2. Heart -- Transplantation -- Fiction; 3. Love -- Fiction; 4. Transplantation of organs, tissues, etc. -- Fiction;
9780062299437, $17.99

LC 2014038649

In this book, by Jessi Kirby, "it's been 400 days since the death of her beloved long-term boyfriend, Trent, and eighteen-year-old Quinn still hasn't moved on. . . . She illicitly sleuths out the identity of the teenager who received his heart, and she hopes that seeing him . . . will bring closure. Colton doesn't bring closure but complexity, however: Quinn ends up hanging out with him more and more and completely falling for him." (Bulletin of the Center for Children's Books)

Kirby, Matthew J.

★ A **taste** for monsters. Matthew J. Kirby. Scholastic Press 2016 352 p.
Grades: 7 8 9 10

1. Disfigured persons -- Fiction 2. Ghost stories 3. Ghosts -- Fiction 4. Murder -- Fiction 5. Murder -- Investigation -- England -- London -- History -- 19th century -- Fiction 6. Neurofibromatosis -- Fiction 7. Phosphorus -- Physiological effect -- Fiction 8. Serial murderers -- Fiction 9. Serial murders -- England -- London -- History -- 19th century -- Fiction 10. Jack, the Ripper -- Fiction 11. Merrick, Joseph Carey, 1862-1890 -- Fiction 12. Great Britain -- History -- Victoria, 1837-1901 -- Fiction 13. London (England) -- History -- 19th century -- Fiction 14. Jack the Ripper murders, London, England, 1888 -- Fiction
9780545817943, $18.99; 9780545817844, $18.99

LC 2015048826

This novel by Matthew J. Kirby is set in London in 1888, "Jack the Ripper is terrorizing the people of the city. Evelyn, a young woman disfigured by her dangerous work in a matchstick factory . . . [becomes] maid to [Joseph] the Elephant Man in London Hospital, [in whom] . . . she finds a gentle kindred. . . . When the murders begin, however, Joseph and Evelyn are haunted nightly by the ghosts of the Ripper's dead, setting Evelyn on a path to facing her fears." (Publisher's note)

"A lovely, suspenseful, lyrical, imperfect paranormal mystery." Kirkus

Kirkpatrick, Katherine

Between two worlds; by Katherine Kirkpatrick. Wendy Lamb Books. 2014 304p $16.99
Grades: 10 11 12

1. Eskimos -- Fiction 2. Inuit -- Fiction 3. Race relations -- Fiction 4. Peary, Robert E. (Robert Edwin), 1856-1920 -- Fiction 5. Arctic regions -- Exploration

-- Fiction
ISBN: 0385740476; 9780375872211; 9780375989476; 9780385740470

LC 2013014735

"In 1900, sixteen-year-old Greenland Inuit girl Billy Bah sets out to rescue Lieutenant Peary, his ship stuck in the ice during a polar expedition. Though torn between cultures, having spent a year with Peary's family in America, Billy Bah ultimately feels she must risk her life to find him. A compelling tale with enthralling details of the stark, beautiful Greenland landscape." Horn Book Guide

Kisner, Adrienne

Dear Rachel Maddow: a novel. Adrienne Kisner. Feiwel & Friends 2018 272 p.

Grades: 7 8 9 10 11

1. Dating (Social customs) -- Fiction; 2. Drug abuse -- Fiction; 3. E-mail -- Fiction
9781250146014; 9781250146021, $17.99

LC 2017956981

In this book, by Adrienne Kisner, "Brynn Haper's life has one steadying force -- Rachel Maddow. She watches her daily, and after writing to Rachel for a school project... Brynn starts drafting e-mails to Rachel but never sending them.... Then Brynn is confronted with a moral dilemma. One student representative will be allowed to have a voice among the administration in the selection of a new school superintendent.... Brynn feels all students deserve a voice." (Publisher's note)

Kittle, Katrina

Reasons to be happy. Sourcebooks Jabberwocky 2011 281p pa $7.99

Grades: 7 8 9 10

1. School stories 2. Bulimia -- Fiction 3. Popularity -- Fiction 4. Bereavement -- Fiction 5. Personal appearance -- Fiction
ISBN 978-1-4022-6020-9; 1-4022-6020-2

LC 2011020276

Eighth-grader Hannah Carlisle feels unattractive compared to her movie star parents and cliquish Beverly Hills classmates, and when her mother's cancer worsens and her father starts drinking heavily, Hannah's grief and anger turn into bulimia, which only her aunt, a documentary filmmaker, understands.

"Hannah's believability as a character as well as the realistic, painful depiction of bulimia make this a standout." Booklist

Kittredge, Caitlin

The **Iron** Thorn. Delacorte Press 2011 493p (Iron Codex) $17.99; lib bdg $20.99

Grades: 7 8 9 10

1. Fantasy fiction
ISBN 0-385-73829-3; 0-385-90720-6 lib bdg; 978-0-385-73829-3; 978-0-385-90720-0 lib bdg

LC 2010-00972

In an alternate 1950s, mechanically gifted fifteen-year-old Aoife Grayson, whose family has a history of going mad at sixteen, must leave the totalitarian city of Lovecraft and venture into the world of magic to solve the mystery of her brother's disappearance and the mysteries surrounding her father and the Land of Thorn.

"Steampunk fans will delight in this first title in the sure-to-be-popular Iron Codex series. . . . There's plenty of tame but satisfying romance, too, and plot twists galore. Aoife is a caustic-tongued, feisty, and independent young woman, with plenty of nerve and courage." Booklist

The **nightmare** garden; Caitlin Kittredge. Delacorte Press 2012 417 p. (The iron codex) (hardback) $17.99

Grades: 7 8 9 10

1. Fantasy fiction 2. Adventure fiction 3. Steampunk fiction 4. Metaphysics -- Fiction 5. Voyages and travels -- Fiction 6. Fantasy 7. Magic -- Fiction
ISBN 9780375985690; 9780385738316; 9780385907217

LC 2011038306

Sequel to: The Iron Thorn.

This book is the second novel in Caitlin Kittredge's 'Iron Codex' series. "Spoiled, inconsistent, often-thoughtless heroine Aoife Grayson nearly destroyed the world when she broke the Lovecraft Engine and sundered the gates between the worlds of human and Fae. But she's not going to let a little thing like that stop her, so she sets off on an exhausting, somewhat episodic adventure through the steampunk-horror '50s nightmare that is her world . . . . The ending promises even bigger adventures to come." (Kirkus)

Kizer, Amber

A **matter** of days; Amber Kizer. 1st ed. Delacorte Press 2013 288 p. (ebook) $50.97; (hardcover) $16.99; (library) $19.99

Grades: 7 8 9 10

1. Apocalyptic fiction 2. Voyages and travels 3. Science fiction 4. Survival -- Fiction 5. Epidemics -- Fiction 6. Virus diseases -- Fiction 7. Brothers and sisters -- Fiction
ISBN 0385908040; 9780375898259; 9780385739733; 9780385908047

LC 2012012200

In this book, "Nadia and Rabbit's military doctor uncle, Bean, visited them and insisted on injecting them with a vaccine for a 'new bug.' Not long afterward, the disease XRD TB . . . starts ravaging the world, and 16-year-old Nadia and 11-year-old Rabbit are the only survivors in their entire town. With the assorted survival gear their uncle ordered for them, they attempt to make their way from their Seattle suburb to their grandfather in West Virginia." (Publishers Weekly)

"This post-apocalyptic tale is particularly frightening as it doesn't take place in some distant, imagined future. A solid, realistically imagined survival tale with a strong female protagonist." Kirkus

Klages, Ellen

★ Out of left field. Ellen Klages. Viking 2018 320 p.

Grades: 4 5 6 7

1. All-American Girls Professional Baseball League -- Fiction; 2. Baseball -- Fiction; 3. Little League baseball -- Fiction; 4. Sex role -- Fiction; 5. Single-parent families -- Fiction; 6. Women's rights -- Fiction; 7. San Francisco

(Calif.) -- History -- 20th century -- Fiction; 8. Gender role -- Fiction

0425288595; 9780425288597, $16.99

LC 2018009872

In this book, by Ellen Klages, in 1957, "inspired by what...[Katy Gordon is] learning about civil rights in school, she sets out to prove that she's not the only girl who plays baseball. With the help of friendly librarians and some tenacious research skills, Katy discovers the forgotten history of female ball players. Why does no one know about them? Where are they now? And how can one ten-year-old change people's minds about what girls can do?" (Publisher's note)

"The narrative, though rich in details, never gets bogged down. This title also includes substantial back matter, such as a list of female ballplayers, an author's note, a glossary of baseball terms, and further recommended reading. Klages gives Katy a strong voice and helps spotlight the history of marginalized women in sports history. Featuring powerful female characters, this is historical fiction that doesn't drag for a second. A fine purchase." SLJ

Klass, David

Firestorm. Frances Foster Books 2006 289p (The Caretaker trilogy) $17

Grades: 8 9 10 11 12

1. Science fiction

ISBN 0-374-32307-0

LC 2005-52112

After learning that he has been sent from the future for a special purpose, eighteen-year-old Jack receives help from an unusual dog and a shape-shifting female fighter.

"The sobering events and tone are leavened with engaging humor, and the characters are multidimensional. The relentless pace, coupled with issues of ecology, time travel, self-identity, and sexual awakening, makes for a thrilling and memorable read." SLJ

Other books in the Caretaker Trilogy are:

Whirlwind (2008)

Timelock (2009)

★ **You** don't know me; a novel. Foster Bks. 2001 262p $17

Grades: 7 8 9 10

1. School stories 2. Child abuse -- Fiction

ISBN 0-374-38706-0

LC 00-22709

Fourteen-year-old John creates alternative realities in his mind as he tries to deal with his mother's abusive boyfriend, his crush on a beautiful, but shallow classmate and other problems at school

"Klass is effective with John's deliberately distanced voice, his constant dancing with and away from reality, . . . and his brittle and even dorky defenses, and the rising tension is suspenseful." Bull Cent Child Books

Klass, Sheila Solomon

Soldier's secret; the story of Deborah Sampson. Henry Holt 2009 215p $17.95

Grades: 6 7 8 9 10

1. Soldiers 2. Memoirists 3. Soldiers -- Fiction 4. United States -- History -- 1775-1783, Revolution --

Fiction

ISBN 978-0-8050-8200-5; 0-8050-8200-X

LC 2008-36783

During the Revolutionary War, a young woman named Deborah Sampson disguises herself as a man in order to serve in the Continental Army.

In this novel, Sampson "is strong, brave, and witty. . . . Klass doesn't shy away from the horrors of battle; she also is blunt regarding details young readers will wonder about, like how Sampson dealt with bathing, urination, and menstruation. . . . Sampson's romantic yearnings for a fellow soldier . . . is given just the right notes or restraint and realism." Booklist

Klause, Annette Curtis

★ **Blood** and chocolate. Delacorte Press 1997 264p hardcover o.p. pa $6.50

Grades: 7 8 9 10

1. Horror fiction 2. Werewolves -- Fiction

ISBN 0-385-32305-0; 0-440-22668-6 pa

LC 96-35247

Having fallen for a human boy, a beautiful teenage werewolf must battle both her packmates and the fear of the townspeople to decide where she belongs and with whom

"Klause's imagery is magnetic, and her language fierce, rich, and beautiful. . . . Passion and philosophy dovetail superbly in this powerful, unforgettable novel for mature teens." Booklist

★ The **silver** kiss. Delacorte Press 1990 198p hardcover o.p. pa $5.99

Grades: 8 9 10 11 12

1. Death -- Fiction 2. Vampires -- Fiction

ISBN 0-385-30160-X; 0-440-21346-0 pa

LC 89-48880

"One evening, when 17-year-old Zoë is sitting in the park contemplating her mother's imminent death due to cancer, her father's lack of support, and her best friend's move, she meets Simon. Simon is startlingly handsome and strangely compelling. As their friendship grows over time, Simon reveals to Zoë his true identity: he is a vampire, trying to kill his younger vampire brother." SLJ

"There's inherent romantic appeal in the vampire legend, and Klause weaves all the gory details into a poignant love story that becomes both sensuous and suspenseful." Booklist

Klavan, Andrew

MindWar: a novel. Andrew Klavan. Thomas Nelson, Inc. 2014 352 p. (The MindWar Trilogy)

Grades: 7 8 9 10

1. Cyberterrorism -- Prevention -- Fiction 2. Undercover operations -- Fiction 3. Video gamers -- Fiction 4. Video games -- Fiction 5. Virtual reality -- Fiction 6. Teenagers -- Fiction

1401688926; 9781401688929, $15.99

LC 2013050887

In this novel by Andrew Klaven "high school football star Rick Dial . . . immerses himself in video games after a car accident leaves his legs painfully useless. The teen is recruited to fight real life baddies. . . a virtual reality world created by Kurodar, a terrorist out to destroy the free world. He must fight for his life, because what happens to you in this virtual world affects your body in real life." (School Library Journal)

"Edgar Award-winning Klavan's well-orchestrated fantasy thriller features brisk but compelling character development, a touch of wry humor, Christian sensitivity that doesn't proselytize, and an imaginative mix of gaming action with real-life stakes. With just the right cliff-hanger ending, this trilogy opener shows promise." Booklist

Other titles in this series are: Hostage Run (2015)

Klein, Lisa M.

Ophelia. Bloomsbury Children's Books 2006 328p $16.95

Grades: 9 10 11 12

    1. Shakespeare, William, 1564-1616--Adaptations 2. Princes -- Fiction 3. Homicide -- Fiction

    ISBN 978-1-58234-801-8; 1-58234-801-4

                           LC 2005-32601

In a story based on Shakespeare's Hamlet, Ophelia tells of her life in the court at Elsinore, her love for Prince Hamlet, and her escape from the violence in Denmark.

"Teens need not be familiar with Shakespeare's original to enjoy this fresh take—with the added romance and a strong heroine at its center." Publ Wkly

Kluger, Steve

My most excellent year; a novel of love, Mary Poppins, & Fenway Park. Dial Books 2008 403p $16.99; pa $8.99

Grades: 8 9 10 11 12

    1. Friendship -- Fiction 2. Boston (Mass.) -- Fiction

    ISBN 978-0-8037-3227-8; 0-8037-3227-9; 978-0-14-241343-2 pa; 0-14-2413437 pa

                           LC 2007-26651

"Three bright and funny Brookline, MA, eleventh graders look back on their most excellent year—ninth grade—for a school report. Told in alternating chapters by each of them, this enchanting, life-affirming coming-of-age story unfolds through instant messages, emails, memos, diary entries, and letters. . . . This is a rich and humorous novel for older readers." SLJ

Knowles, Jo

Jumping off swings; [by] Jo Knowles. Candlewick Press 2009 230p $16.99

Grades: 10 11 12

    1. Pregnancy -- Fiction

    ISBN 0-7636-3949-4; 978-0-7636-3949-5

                           LC 2009-4587

When Josh 'leads Ellie to the back seat of his van after a party, Ellie gets pregnant and Josh reacts with shame and heartbreak, while their confidantes, Caleb and Corinne grapple with their own complex emotions." (Publisher's note) "Grades seven to ten." (Bull Cent Child Books)

"With so many protagonists in the mix, it is no small feat that each character is fully developed and multidimensional—there are no villains or heroes here, only kids groping their way through a desperate situation. . . . [This is] a moving tale with a realistically unresolved ending." Kirkus

★ **Living** with Jackie Chan; by Jo Knowles. Candlewick Press 2013 384 p. $16.99

Grades: 10 11 12

    1. Teenage fathers 2. Guilt -- Fiction 3. Uncles -- Fiction

    ISBN 0763662801; 9780763662806

                           LC 2012955157

"Overcome with guilt after getting Ellie pregnant (Jumping Off Swings), Josh moves in with his karate-obsessed, incessantly cheerful uncle. He starts senior year at a new school, attends his uncle's karate classes, and makes a new friend-who-might-be-more. Josh is a sensitive guy whose pain is palpable; readers will root for him as he--slowly--conquers the demons of his past." (Horn Book)

Read between the lines. Jo Knowles. Candlewick Press 2015 336 p.

Grades: 9 10 11 12

    1. Cities and towns 2. High school students 3. High school teachers 4. High schools 5. Teenagers -- Fiction 6. School stories

    0763663875; 9780763663872, $16.99

                           LC 2014944796

This novel by Jo Knowles "follows nine teens and one teacher through a seemingly ordinary day. Thanks to a bully in gym class, unpopular Nate suffers a broken finger. Claire envisions herself sitting in an artsy café, filling a journal, but fate has other plans. One cheerleader dates a closeted basketball star; another questions just how, as a 'big girl,' she fits in. These voices and others speak loud and clear about the complex dance that is life in a small town." (Publisher's note)

"Issues of absent parents, conflicted sexuality, eating disorders, and various forms of abuse are dealt with succinctly but tenderly, and some nuances are subtle enough that multiple levels of reading are possible, with a twist at the end so understated you may miss it. This is likely to speak to any teenager in a stage of transition." Booklist

See you at Harry's; Jo Knowles. 1st ed. Candlewick Press 2012 310 p. $16.99

Grades: 6 7 8 9 10 11

    1. Siblings -- Fiction 2. Bereavement -- Fiction 3. Restaurants -- Fiction 4. Gay teenagers -- Fiction 5. Family 6. Grief -- Fiction 7. Family life -- Fiction 8. Homosexuality -- Fiction 9. Family problems -- Fiction 10. Brothers and sisters -- Fiction

    ISBN 9780763654078

                           LC 2011018619

In this children's novel, "seventh grader Fern . . . relates the . . . tragedies of her family. Her high-school-freshman older brother Holden has come to the place in his life where he's acknowledged that he's gay. . . . Fern offers him support and love. . . . And then there's 3-year-old Charlie, always messy, often annoying, but deeply loved. Fern's busy, distracted parents leave all of the kids wanting for more attention--until a tragic accident tears the family apart." (Kirkus Reviews)

Knox, Elizabeth

Dreamhunter; book one of the Dreamhunter duet. Farrar, Straus & Giroux 2006 365p (Dreamhunter duet) $19; pa $8.99

Grades: 7 8 9 10
  1. Fantasy fiction 2. Dreams -- Fiction
  ISBN 0-374-31853-0; 0-312-53571-6 pa
  LC 2005-46366
First published 2005 in the United Kingdom
  In a world where select people can enter "The Place" and find dreams of every kind to share with others for a fee, a fifteen-year-old girl is training to be a dreamhunter when her father disappears, leaving her to carry on his mysterious mission. "Grades nine to twelve." (Bull Cent Child Books)
  This first of a two-book series is "a highly original exploration of the idea of a collective unconscious, mixed with imagery from the raising of Lazarus and with the brave, dark qualities of the psyche of an adolescent female." Horn Book Guide
  Followed by Dreamquake (2007)

Dreamquake; book two of the Dreamhunter duet. Farrar, Straus & Giroux 2007 449p map (Dreamhunter duet) $19
Grades: 7 8 9 10
  1. Fantasy fiction 2. Dreams -- Fiction
  ISBN 978-0-374-31854-3; 0-374-31854-9
  LC 2006-48109
Sequel to Dreamhunter
Michael L. Printz Award honor book, 2008
  Aided by her family and her creation, Nown, Laura investigates the powerful Regulatory Body's involvement in mysterious disappearances and activities and learns, in the process, the true nature of the Place in which dreams are found.
  The author's "haunting, invigorating storytelling will leave readers eager to return to its puzzles—and to reap its rewards." Booklist

Mortal fire; by Elizabeth Knox. 1st ed. Frances Foster Books 2013 448 p. (hardcover) $17.99
Grades: 7 8 9 10 11
  1. Occult fiction 2. Fantasy fiction 3. Magic -- Fiction 4. Identity -- Fiction 5. Stepbrothers -- Fiction 6. Islands of the Pacific -- Fiction
  ISBN 0374388296; 9780374388294
  LC 2012040872
  This novel, set in a fictional area of New Zealand, stars Canny, a "16-year-old Ma'eu, taciturn, antisocial, and exceptionally gifted in math." She has what she calls "Extra," an "ethereal script that Canny alone can see, attached to plants, buildings, or nothing at all." When she and friends "come upon a valley dense with the Extra, Canny realizes that there is more to her visions than her own oddness— there are people, the Zarenes, whose existence is interwoven with this magical language." (Publishers Weekly)

Knudsen, Michelle
  Evil librarian. Michelle Knudsen. Candlewick Press 2014 352 p.
Grades: 9 10 11
  1. Best friends -- Fiction 2. Demonology -- Fiction 3. Friendship -- Fiction 4. High schools -- Fiction 5. Librarians -- Fiction 6. Schools -- Fiction 7. Fantasy

fiction
  0763660388; 9780763660383, $16.99
  LC 2013957277
  In this book, "when Cynthia Rothschild's best friend, Annie, falls head over heels for the new high-school librarian, Cyn can totally see why. He's really young and super cute and thinks Annie would make an excellent library monitor. But after meeting Mr. Gabriel, Cyn realizes something isn't quite right. Maybe it's the creepy look in the librarian's eyes, or the weird feeling Cyn gets whenever she's around him. Before long Cyn realizes that Mr. Gabriel is, in fact . . . a demon." (Publisher's note)
  "There's plenty to like here: a budding will-they-won't-they romance, demonic possession, musical theater references, and more. Knudsen keeps the terror well-tempered with plenty of hilarious situational comedy and touches of the absurd." Booklist

Knutsson, Catherine
  Shadows cast by stars; Catherine Knutsson. 1st ed. Atheneum Books for Young Readers 2012 456 p. (hardcover) $17.99; (paperback) $9.99
Grades: 7 8 9 10
  1. Blood 2. Science fiction 3. Plague -- Fiction 4. Twins -- Fiction 5. Spirits -- Fiction 6. Family life -- Fiction 7. Brothers and sisters -- Fiction 8. Indians of North America -- Fiction
  ISBN 1442401915; 9781442401914; 9781442401938; 9781442401921
  LC 2011038419
  Author Catherine Knutsson tells the story of Native American Cassandra Mercredi. The "sixteen-year-old . . . [may] be immune to Plague, but that doesn't mean she's safe--government forces are searching for those of aboriginal heritage to harvest their blood. When a search threatens Cassandra and her family, they flee to the Island: a mysterious and idyllic territory protected by the Band, a group of guerilla warriors--and by an enigmatic energy barrier that keeps outsiders out and the spirit world in." (Publisher's note)

Koertge, Ronald
  Lies, knives and girls in red dresses; Ron Koertge; illustrated by Andrea Dezso. Candlewick 2012 96 p. ill. (hardcover) $17.99
Grades: 9 10 11
  1. Fairy tales 2. Orphans -- Fiction 3. Princesses -- Fiction 4. Novels in verse
  ISBN 0763644064; 9780763644062
  LC 2011047027
  This illustrated poetry collection "retells 23 classic fairy tales in free verse, written from the perspectives of iconic characters like Little Red Riding Hood, as well as maligned or minor figures such as the Mole from Thumbelina and Cinderella's stepsisters. . . . Several stories trade happily ever after for disappointment and discontent, as with the danger-addicted queen in Rumpelstiltskin." (Publishers Weekly)

  ★ **Margaux** with an X; [by] Ron Koertge. Candlewick Press 2004 165p $15.99; pa $6.99

Grades: 7 8 9 10
  1. Domestic violence -- Fiction
  ISBN 0-7636-2401-2; 0-7636-2679-1 pa
                       LC 2003-65279

Margaux, known as a "tough chick" at her Los Angeles high school, makes a connection with Danny, who, like her, struggles with the emotional impact of family violence and abuse.

This book "excels in character development. It is an intriguing story that constantly provokes readers' curiosity. . . . [The author's] language at times is advanced, an accurate reflection of his characters' intellectual capacity." SLJ

Now playing; Stoner & Spaz II. [by] Ron Koertge. Candlewick Press 2011 208p $16.99
Grades: 8 9 10 11 12
  1. School stories 2. Drug abuse -- Fiction 3. Cerebral palsy -- Fiction 4. Self-acceptance -- Fiction 5. Dating (Social customs) -- Fiction
  ISBN 978-0-7636-5081-0; 0-7636-5081-1
                       LC 2010040151

Sequel to: Stoner & Spaz (2002)

High schooler Ben Bancroft, a budding filmmaker with cerebral palsy, struggles to understand his relationship with drug-addict Colleen while he explores a new friendship with A.J., who shares his obsession with movies and makes a good impression on Ben's grandmother.

"Koertge writes sharp dialogue and vivid scenes." Publ Wkly

★ **Shakespeare** makes the playoffs; [by] Ron Koertge. Candlewick Press 2010 170p lib bdg $15.99; pa $5.99
Grades: 6 7 8 9
  1. Novels in verse 2. Poetry -- Fiction 3. Baseball -- Fiction
  ISBN 978-0-7636-4435-2 lib bdg; 0-7636-4435-8 lib bdg; 978-0-7636-5852-6 pa
                       LC 2009-14519

Fourteen-year-old Kevin Boland, poet and first baseman, is torn between his cute girlfriend Mira and Amy, who is funny, plays Chopin on the piano, and is also a poet.

"The well-crafted poetry is firmly rooted in the experiences of regular teens and addresses subjects that range from breakups to baseball. . . . Appealing and accessible." Booklist

Stoner & Spaz; [by] Ron Koertge. Candlewick Press 2002 169p hardcover o.p. pa $6.99
Grades: 8 9 10 11 12
  1. School stories 2. Cerebral palsy -- Fiction
  ISBN 0-7636-1608-7; 0-7636-2150-1 pa
                       LC 2001-43050

A troubled youth with cerebral palsy struggles toward self-acceptance with the help of a drug-addicted young woman

"Funny, touching, and surprising, it is a hopeful yet realistic view of things as they are and as they could be." Booklist

Followed by: Now Playing: Stoner & Spaz II (2011)

★ **Strays**; [by] Ron Koertge. Candlewick Press 2007 167p $16.99

Grades: 7 8 9 10 11 12
  1. Orphans -- Fiction 2. Foster home care -- Fiction
  ISBN 978-0-7636-2705-8; 0-7636-2705-4
                       LC 2007-24096

After his parents are killed in a car accident, high school senior Sam wonders whether he will ever feel again or if he will remain numbed by grief.

"Though Koertge never soft pedals the horrors faced by some foster children, this thoughtful novel about the lost and abandoned is a hopeful one." Booklist

Koja, Kathe

Buddha boy. Speak 2004 117p pa $5.99
Grades: 7 8 9 10
  1. School stories 2. Artists -- Fiction 3. Buddhism -- Fiction 4. Conduct of life -- Fiction
  ISBN 0-14-240209-5
                       LC 2004041669

First published 2003 by Farrar, Straus & Giroux

Justin spends time with Jinsen, the unusual and artistic new student whom the school bullies torment and call Buddha Boy, and ends up making choices that impact Jinsen, himself, and the entire school.

"A compelling introduction to Buddhism and a credible portrait of how true friendship brings out the best in people." Publ Wkly

Headlong. Farrar, Straus and Giroux 2008 195p $16.95
Grades: 8 9 10 11 12
  1. School stories 2. Orphans -- Fiction 3. Social classes -- Fiction
  ISBN 978-0-374-32912-9; 0-374-32912-5
                       LC 2007-23612

High school sophomore Lily opens herself to new possibilities when, despite warnings, she becomes friends with 'ghetto girl' Hazel, a new student at the private Vaughn School which Lily, following in her elitist mother's footsteps, has attended since preschool.

"Class, identity and friendship are the intersecting subjects of this intelligent novel. . . . [The author] relays this story with her usual insight and, through her lightning-fast characterizations, an ability to project multiple perspectives simultaneously." Publ Wkly

Kissing the bee. Farrar, Straus and Giroux 2007 121p $16
Grades: 8 9 10 11 12
  1. Love stories 2. School stories 3. Bees -- Fiction 4. Friendship -- Fiction
  ISBN 978-0-374-39938-2; 0-374-39938-7
                       LC 2006-37378

While working on a bee project for her advanced biology class, quiet high school senior Dana reflects on her relationship with gorgeous best friend Avra and Avra's boyfriend Emil, whom Dana secretly loves.

The "understated, tightly focused language evokes vivid scenes and heady emotions." Publ Wkly

Kokie, E. M.

Radical. E. M. Kokie. Candlewick Press 2016 448 p.

Grades: 9 10 11 12

 1. Brothers and sisters -- Fiction 2. Survival -- Fiction
3. Survival skills -- Fiction
9780763674144, $17.99; 9780763669621, $17.99
LC 2016944081

In this novel, by E. M. Kokie, "Bex prefers to think of herself as a realist who plans to survive, but regardless of labels, they're all sure of the same thing: a crisis is coming. And when it does, Bex will be ready. . . . When her older brother discovers Clearview, a group that takes survival just as seriously as she does, Bex is intrigued. While outsiders might think they're a delusional doomsday group, she . . . isn't prepared for Lucy, who is soft and beautiful and hates guns." (Publisher's note)

"A hard, cleareyed look at coming of age in a prejudiced world." Kirkus

Konen, Leah

Love & other train wrecks. Leah Konen. Katherine Tegen Books 2018 359 p.

Grades: 7 8 9 10 11

 1. Amtrak -- Fiction; 2. Children of divorced parents -- Fiction; 3. College students -- Fiction; 4. Interpersonal relations -- Fiction; 5. Railroad travel -- Fiction; 6. Strangers -- Fiction; 7. Winter storms -- Fiction; 8. New York (State) -- Fiction
9780062402509, $17.99; 9780062402523
LC 2017938600

In this book, author Leah Konen "spins a charming tale of two people who are meant to be, despite terrible first impressions. Alternating between Ammy and Noah's perspectives, Konen provides rich backstories for both characters while laying groundwork for a realistic love story that, like life, isn't always easy or perfect." (Publishers Weekly)

"An absurdly charming, funny, and romantic odyssey." Kirkus

Konigsberg, Bill

★ **Honestly** Ben. Bill Konigsberg. Arthur A. Levine Books, an imprint of Scholastic Inc. 2017 326 p.

Grades: 7 8 9 10 11 12

 1. Fathers and sons -- Fiction; 2. Homosexuality -- Fiction; 3. Identity -- Fiction; 4. Preparatory schools -- Fiction; 5. Preparatory schools -- Massachusetts -- Fiction; 6. Schools -- Fiction; 7. Sexual orientation -- Fiction; 8. Massachusetts -- Fiction; 9. Identity (Psychology) -- Fiction; 10. Gay teenagers -- Fiction
9780545858267, $17.99; 9780545858311
LC 2016008865

In this book, by Bill Konigsberg, "Ben Carver is back to normal. He's working steadily in his classes at the Natick School. He just got elected captain of the baseball team. He's even won a full scholarship to college, if he can keep up his grades. All that foolishness with Rafe Goldberg the past semester is in the past." (Publisher's note)

"Packed with literary references, pranks, heady conversations, humor, honesty, and tribulation, this is one that will be remembered. A fresh, insightful, inspiring take on what it means to come out." Kirkus

Companion to: Openly straight (2013)

★ **Openly** straight; Bill Konigsberg. Arthur A. Levine Books 2013 336 p. (hard cover: alk. paper) $17.99

Grades: 8 9 10 11

 1. School stories 2. Gay teenagers -- Fiction 3. Schools -- Fiction 4. Identity -- Fiction 5. Homosexuality -- Fiction 6. Massachusetts -- Fiction 7. Preparatory schools -- Fiction 8. Gay teenagers 9. Identity (Psychology) -- Fiction 11. Preparatory schools -- Massachusetts -- Fiction
ISBN 0545509890; 9780545509893; 9780545509909
LC 2012030552

Lambda Literary Awards Finalist (2014)

In this book, "Coloradan Rafe Goldberg has always been the token gay kid. He's been out since eighth grade. His parents and community are totally supportive. . . . On the outside, Rafe seems fine, but on the inside, he's looking for change, which comes with the opportunity to reinvent himself at the prestigious Natick Academy in Massachusetts. There for his junior year, Rafe cloaks his gayness in order to be just like one of the other guys." All is well until he falls for a straight friend. (Kirkus Reviews)

"Rafe is sick of being the poster child for all things gay at his uber-liberal Colorado high school, so when he gets into a Massachusetts boarding school for his junior year, he decides to reboot himself as "openly straight." Konigsberg slyly demonstrates how thoroughly assumptions of straightness are embedded in everyday interactions. For a thought-provoking take on the coming-out story, look no further." (Horn Book)

★ The **porcupine** of truth. Bill Konigsberg. Arthur A. Levine Books, an imprint of Scholastic Inc. 2015 336 p.

Grades: 9 10 11 12

 1. African American teenage girls -- Fiction 2. Alcoholism -- Fiction 3. Children of alcoholics -- Fiction 4. Dysfunctional families -- Fiction 5. Billings (Mont.) -- Fiction 6. Friendship -- Fiction 7. Montana -- Fiction 8. Family secrets -- Fiction
0545648939; 9780545648936, $17.99; 9780545648943; 9780545754927
LC 2014027136

Stonewall Book Award, Young Adult (2016)

In this book, by Bill Konigsberg, "Carson Smith is resigned to spending his summer in Billings, Montana, helping his mom take care of his father, a dying alcoholic he doesn't really know. Then he meets Aisha Stinson, a beautiful girl who has run away from her difficult family, and Pastor John Logan, who's long held a secret regarding Carson's grandfather, who disappeared without warning or explanation thirty years before." (Publisher's note)

"Visiting small-town Montana to care for his long-absent alcoholic father, also the child of estranged parents, Carson becomes obsessed with discovering the reason for his grandfather's abandonment. New friend Aisha, homeless since coming out to her family, joins his cross-country scavenger hunt. Smart-alecky dialogue and quirky roadside characters lighten the commentary on religion, secrets, family, and forgiveness." Horn Book

Konigsburg, E. L.

Silent to the bone. Atheneum Bks. for Young Readers 2000 261p hardcover o.p. pa $5.99

Grades: 7 8 9 10

1. Mystery fiction 2. Siblings -- Fiction
ISBN 0-689-83601-5; 0-689-83602-3 pa

LC 00-20043

When he is wrongly accused of gravely injuring his baby half-sister, thirteen-year-old Branwell loses his power of speech and only his friend Connor is able to reach him and uncover the truth about what really happened

"A compelling mystery that is also a moving story of family, friendship, and seduction." Booklist

Kontis, Alethea

Enchanted; Alethea Kontis. Harcourt 2012 308 p.

Grades: 9 10 11 12

1. Fantasy fiction 2. Frogs -- Fiction 3. Magic -- Fiction 4. Fractured fairy tales 5. Princes 6. Fairy tales
ISBN 0547645708; 9780547645704

LC 2011027317

This young adult fantasy book presents the "fairy-tale mashup" story of the adventures of a girl named Sunday Woodcutter and her six siblings. Sunday becomes friends with the enchanted frog Grumble and unwittingly helps him transform back into Prince Rumbold. Author Alethea Kontis "has . . . woven just about every fairy character tale readers might half-remember into the fabric of her story: the beanstalk, the warrior maiden, Cinderella and Sleeping Beauty and some darker ones, too." (Kirkus)

Korman, Gordon

The Juvie three. Hyperion 2008 249p lib bdg $15.99

Grades: 7 8 9 10

1. Friendship -- Fiction 2. Juvenile delinquency -- Fiction
ISBN 978-1-4231-0158-1; 1-4231-0158-8

LC 2008-19087

Gecko, Arjay, and Terence, all in trouble with the law, must find a way to keep their halfway house open in order to stay out of juvenile detention.

"Korman keeps lots of balls in the air as he handles each boy's distinct voice and character—as well as the increasingly absurd situation—with humor and flashes of sadness." Booklist

Son of the mob. Hyperion Bks. for Children 2002 262p hardcover o.p. pa $7.99

Grades: 7 8 9 10

1. Mafia -- Fiction
ISBN 0-7868-0769-5; 0-7868-1593-0 pa

LC 2002-68672

Seventeen-year-old Vince's life is constantly complicated by the fact that he is the son of a powerful Mafia boss, a relationship that threatens to destroy his romance with the daughter of an FBI agent

"The fast-paced, tightly focused story addresses the problems of being an honest kid in a family of outlaws—and loving them anyway. Korman doesn't ignore the seamier side of mob life, but even when the subject matter gets violent . . . he keeps things light by relating his tale in the first-person voice of a humorously sarcastic yet law-abiding wise guy." Horn Book

Another title about Vince is:
Son of the mob: Hollywood hustle (2004)

Son of the mob: Hollywood hustle. Hyperion 2004 268p $15.99

Grades: 9 10 11 12

1. Mafia -- Fiction 2. California -- Fiction
ISBN 0-7868-0918-3

LC 2004-44181

Sequel to Son of the mob

Eighteen-year-old Vince Luca, son of mob boss Anthony Luca, goes away to college in southern California hoping to escape his past, but soon his brother and a series of "uncles" appear at his dorm, and before long he is caught up in criminal activity once again

"Teens will love this hilarious latest chapter of Vince's life. . . . {This} is a wonderful sauce filled with brilliant characterization, sneaky plot twists, and humor that will make teens fall off their chairs with laughter." Voice Youth Advocates

Kornher-Stace, Nicole

Archivist wasp: a novel. Nicole Kornher-Stace. Big Mouth House 2015 256 p.

Grades: 9 10 11 12

1. Fantasy 2. Ghosts -- Fiction 3. Adventure fiction 4. Dystopian fiction 5. Ghost stories
1618730975; 9781618730978, $14

LC 2014046381

In this young adult novel, by Nicole Kornher-Stace, "Wasp's job is simple. Hunt ghosts. And every year she has to fight to remain Archivist. Desperate and alone, she strikes a bargain with the ghost of a supersoldier. She will go with him on his underworld hunt for the long-long ghost of his partner and in exchange she will find out more about his pre-apocalyptic world than any Archivist before her." (Publisher's note)

"A must-have for dystopian fans who prefer to avoid love stories and pat endings." SLJ

Kositsky, Lynne

The thought of high windows. Kids Can Press 2004 175p hardcover o.p. pa $6.95

Grades: 7 8 9 10

1. Jews -- Fiction 2. Holocaust, 1933-1945 -- Fiction
ISBN 1-55337-621-8; 1-55337-622-6 pa

"Esther describes her life as one of a group of Jewish children taken from Germany to France by the Red Cross during World War II. The novel begins when she is 15 and living in a French castle; her childhood in Berlin is described through flashbacks. . . . Based on true events, this is an immediate, painfully honest story." SLJ

Koss, Amy Goldman

Poison Ivy. Roaring Brook Press 2006 166p $16.96

Grades: 7 8 9 10
1. School stories 2. Bullies -- Fiction
ISBN 1-59643-118-0

LC 2005-17256

In a government class three popular girls undergo a mock trial for their ruthless bullying of a classmate.

"Realistic dialogue and fast-paced action will hold interest, and the final verdict is unsettling, but not unexpected." SLJ

Side effects; 1st ed.; Roaring Brook Press 2006 143p $16.95
Grades: 6 7 8 9
1. Cancer -- Fiction
ISBN 978-1-59643-167-6; 1-59643-167-9

LC 2005-31473

Everything changes for Isabelle, not quite fifteen, when she is diagnosed with lymphoma—but eventually she survives and even thrives.

"Koss refuses to glamorize Issy's illness or treatment. Instead, she settles for an honesty and frankness that will both challenge and enlighten readers." Booklist

Kostick, Conor

★ **Epic**. Viking 2007 364p $17.99
Grades: 7 8 9 10
1. Fantasy fiction 2. Video games -- Fiction
ISBN 0-670-06179-4; 978-0-670-06179-2

LC 2006-19958

On New Earth, a world based on a video role-playing game, fourteen-year-old Erik pursuades his friends to aid him in some unusual gambits in order to save his father from exile and safeguard the futures of each of their families.

"There is intrigue and mystery throughout this captivating page-turner. Veins of moral and ethical social situations and decisions provide some great opportunities for discussion. Well written and engaging." SLJ

Other titles in this series are:
Edda (2011)
Saga (2008)

Kottaras, E. Katherine

The best possible answer. E. Katherine Kottaras. St. Martin's Griffin 2016 272 p.
Grades: 8 9 10 11
1. Perfection -- Fiction 2. Teenage girls -- Fiction
9781250072818, $18.99

LC 2016014556

In this novel, by E. Katherine Kottaras, "super-achiever Viviana Rabinovich-Lowe has never had room to be anything less than perfect. But her quest for perfection is derailed when her boyfriend leaks secret pictures of her to the entire school?pictures no one was ever meant to see. Making matters worse, her parents might be getting divorced and now her perfect family is falling apart. For the first time, Vivi feels like a complete and utter failure." (Publisher's note)

"A sensitive novel about accepting imperfection." Kirkus

Kraus, Daniel

The **death** and life of Zebulon Finch; Volume one: At the edge of empire. As prepared by the esteemed fictionist, Daniel Kraus. Simon & Schuster Books for Young Readers 2015 656 p.
Grades: 9 10 11 12
1. Dead -- Fiction 2. Murder -- Fiction 3. Death -- Fiction
9781481411394, $18.99; 9781481411400

LC 2014039293

In this book, by Daniel Kraus, "Zebulon Finch is gunned down by the shores of Lake Michigan. But after mere minutes in the void, he is mysteriously resurrected. His second life will be nothing like his first. Zebulon's new existence begins as a sideshow attraction in a traveling medicine show. From there he will be poked and prodded by a scientist obsessed with mastering the secrets of death." (Publisher's note)

"A hefty volume for fans of historical fiction with an undead twist." SLJ

Rotters. Delacorte Press 2011 448p $16.99; lib bdg $19.99; ebook $10.99
Grades: 9 10 11 12
1. School stories 2. Iowa -- Fiction 3. Moving -- Fiction 4. Bullies -- Fiction 5. Grave robbing -- Fiction 6. Father-son relationship -- Fiction
ISBN 978-0-385-73857-6; 978-0-385-90737-8 lib bdg; 978-0-375-89558-6 ebook

LC 2010005174

Sixteen-year-old Joey's life takes a very strange turn when his mother's tragic death forces him to move from Chicago to rural Iowa with the father he has never known, and who is the town pariah.

"Disturbing characters and grotesque details make for a tale of death that ultimately exhumes truths about life." Horn Books Guide

Scowler; Daniel Kraus. Delacorte Press 2013 304 p. (glb) $19.99
Grades: 9 10 11 12
1. Horror fiction 2. Meteorites -- Fiction 3. Adult child abuse victims -- Fiction 4. Horror stories 5. Iowa -- Fiction 6. Violence -- Fiction 7. Mentally ill -- Fiction 8. Farm life -- Iowa -- Fiction 9. Family life -- Iowa -- Fiction
ISBN 0375990941; 9780307980878; 9780375990946; 9780385743099

LC 2012005363

Odyssey Award (2014)

"This literary horror novel[, by Daniel Kraus,] gives readers insight into the mind of a controlling homicidal man and the son who must stop him. . . . Nineteen-year-old Ry Burke . . . wishes for anything to distract him from the grim memories of his father's physical and emotional abuse. Then a meteorite falls from the sky, bringing with it not only a fragment from another world but also the arrival of a ruthless man intent on destroying the entire family." (Publisher's note)

"A Midwestern gothic family saga that will hook readers--or scare them away." Kirkus

Kreslehner, Gabi

I Don't Live Here Anymore. Gabi Kreslehner; translated by Shelley Tanaka. Groundwood Books 2015 128 p.

Grades: 7 8 9 10 11 12833/.92; 833

    1. Children of divorced parents -- Fiction 2. Bildungsromans 3. Moving -- Fiction
1554988039; 9781554988037, $16.95

In this novel by Gabi Kreslehner, translated by Shelley Tanaka, "Charlotte's life is changed forever when her parents' marriage breaks up, and Charlotte has to leave her beloved house and her old life behind. Then two very different boys cross her path, and a new emotion creeps into her sadness and anger. As she watches her parents cope, . . . with changes in their own personal lives, and as she deals with a new baby brother, a potential stepfather and unexpected house moves, she realizes that love is a messy business." (Publisher's note)

"It's an immersive, believable portrait of how adolescents cope, or not, with divorce, drawn from an inside view. Powerful and deeply resonant" Kirkus

Kriegman, Mitchell

Being Audrey Hepburn: a novel. Mitchell Kriegman. St. Martin's Griffin 2014 336 p.

Grades: 9 10 11 12

    1. Coming of age -- Fiction 2. Family problems -- Fiction 3. Self-actualization -- Fiction 4. Single-parent families -- Fiction 5. Hepburn, Audrey, 1929-1993 -- Fiction 6. New Jersey -- Fiction 7. Bildungsromans 8. Teenage girls -- Fiction
1250001463; 9781250001467, $18.99

LC 2014027321

This novel by Mitchell Kriegman "tells the story of a 19-year-old girl from Jersey who finds herself thrust into the world of socialites after being seen in Audrey Hepburn's dress from the film 'Breakfast at Tiffany's.' . . . Obsessed with everything Audrey Hepburn, Lisbeth is transformed when she secretly tries on Audrey's iconic Givenchy. She becomes who she wants to be by pretending to be somebody she's not and living among the young and privileged Manhattan elite." (Publisher's note)

"A satisfying ending to this mixture of The Devil Wears Prada and Breakfast at Tiffany's reveals old family secrets and a promising future for the heroine. Probably a read for girls, this is a thoroughly entertaining romp through the world of runways and art openings with great dialogue and characterizations along the way." VOYA

Krokos, Dan

False memory; Dan Krokos. Disney Press 2012 327 p. $17.99

Grades: 6 7 8 9

    1. Secrecy -- Fiction 2. Teenagers -- Fiction 3. Genetic transformation 4. Science fiction 5. Memory -- Fiction 6. Genetic engineering -- Fiction
ISBN 1423149769; 9781423149767

LC 2011053532

In author Dan Krokos' book, "Miranda North wakes up alone on a park bench with no memory. In her panic, she releases a mysterious energy that incites pure terror in everyone around her . . . Miranda discovers she was trained to be a weapon and is part of an elite force of genetically-altered teens who possess flawless combat skills and powers strong enough to destroy a city . . . Then Miranda uncovers a dark truth that sets her team on the run. Suddenly her past doesn't seem to matter when there may not be a future." (Publisher's note)

Krovatin, Christopher

Heavy metal and you. Scholastic 2005 186p $16.95; pa $7.99

Grades: 9 10 11 12

    1. School stories 2. Rock music -- Fiction 3. New York (N.Y.) -- Fiction
ISBN 0-439-73648-X; 0-439-74399-0 pa

LC 2004-23645

High schooler Sam begins losing himself when he falls for a preppy girl who wants him to give up getting wasted with his best friends and even his passion for heavy metal music in order to become a better person.

"From the terrific cover and portrait of selfish love to the clever CD player icons indicating narrative switches . . . this is an authentic portrayal of an obsession with music. Teens don't have to like heavy metal to appreciate this novel, which is guaranteed to attract readers looking for a book to reach their death-metal souls." Booklist

Kuehn, Stephanie

★ Charm & strange; by Stephanie Kuehn. 1st ed. St. Martin's Griffin 2013 224 p. (hardcover) $17.99

Grades: 9 10 11 12

    1. School stories 2. Mystery fiction 3. Sexual abuse -- Fiction 4. Mental illness -- Fiction 5. Psychological abuse -- Fiction
ISBN 1250021944; 9781250021946

LC 2013003247

William C. Morris Award (2014)

This book follows Andrew Winston Winters, known as Win. Present-day "Win is smart, competitive and untrusting, estranged from his former roommate, Lex, his one ally and defender. The reasons for Win's self-loathing and keyed-up anxiety won't be fully revealed until story's end. What exactly does he expect to happen during the full moon? Why has he fallen out with Lex? Win's privileged childhood, when he was known as Drew, is another mystery." (Kirkus Reviews)

"Kuehn . . . keeps us on constant edge regarding exactly what genre of book it is that we're reading." Booklist

Complicit; Stephanie Kuehn. St. Martin's Griffin 2014 256 p. (hardback) $19.99

Grades: 8 9 10 11 12

    1. Orphans -- Fiction 2. Mental illness -- Fiction 3. Private schools -- Fiction 4. Brothers and sisters -- Fiction 5. Amnesia -- Fiction 6. Schools -- Fiction
ISBN 1250044596; 9781250044594

LC 2014008117

"Cate is out of juvie. For her little brother, 17-year-old Jamie, that's bad. It's been two years since Cate horribly injured a rival by setting a barn on fire. This was the last in a long series of tempestuous, violent acts Cate committed since she and Jamie were adopted following the murder of their mother...Her confidence is what's so invigorating: every page shows a firm, surprising choice, whether you like it or not. Cate, naturally, is the main event, the alternatingly irrational, gentle, explosive, and enigmatic center of this fast, black whirlpool of a novel." (Booklist)

Delicate Monsters. Stephanie Kuehn. St. Martin's Press 2015 240 p.
Grades: 10 11 12
1. Psychopaths -- Fiction 2. Secrets -- Fiction
9781250063847, $19.99; 1250063841
LC 2015012473

In this novel, by Stephanie Kuehn, "centers on the convergence of the lives of Sadie, a damaged girl who enjoys causing others pain, and Emerson, a boy who's trying desperately to hide the dysfunction inside his family and himself. The novel follows Sadie as she arrives back in California . . . after being expelled from a series of . . . boarding schools. . . . When a life-or-death crisis occurs, both of them must finally face reality, along with their demons." (School Library Journal)

"Like her previous YA novels, Kuehn's latest benefits from tight construction, expert pacing, and voices that ring especially true for contemporary teenagers, particularly Sadie's entrancing, gleefully acerbic tone. Intelligent, compulsively readable literary fiction with a dark twist." Booklist

When I am through with you. Stephanie Kuehn. Dutton Books 2017 292 p.
Grades: 9 10 11 12
1. Hiking -- Fiction; 2. Survival -- Fiction; 3. Wilderness survival -- Fiction
9781101994740; 9781101994733, $17.99
LC 2016040902

In this novel, by Stephanie Kuehn, "Ben Gibson is many things, but he's not sorry and he's not a liar. He will tell you exactly about what happened on what started as a simple school camping trip in the mountains. About who lived and who died. About who killed and who had the best of intentions. But he's going to tell you in his own time. Because after what happened on that mountain, time is the one thing he has plenty of." (Publisher's note)

"Full of secrets and plot twists, Kuehn's latest is a satisfying, sophisticated study in complicated relationships." Kirkus

Kurti, Richard
Monkey wars. Richard Kurti. Delacorte Press 2015 416 p.
Grades: 7 8 9 10 11 12
1. Langurs -- Fiction 2. Monkeys -- Fiction 3. Rhesus monkey -- Fiction 4. War -- Fiction 5. Human-animal relationships -- Fiction
0385744412; 9780375991653; 9780385744416, $17.99
LC 2014038203

In this novel by Richard Kurti, "when rhesus monkeys are brutally massacred on the dusty streets of Kolkata by a troop of power-hungry langur monkeys, Mico, a privileged langur, becomes entangled in the secrets at the heart of his troop's leadership. He feels compelled to help the few surviving rhesus, especially Papina, a young female he befriends, even though doing so goes against everything he's been taught." (Publisher's note)

"This book will be useful in discussions about apathy versus taking a stand, the domination of one culture over another through time, ethnic cleansing, relocation, boundaries, and genocide." VOYA

Originally published in the United Kingdom by Walker in 2013.

Kwasney, Michelle D.
Blue plate special. Chronicle Books 2009 366p $16.99
Grades: 8 9 10 11 12
1. Forgiveness -- Fiction 2. Mother-daughter relationship -- Fiction
ISBN 978-0-8118-6780-1; 0-8118-6780-3
LC 2009-5322

In alternating chapters, the lives of three teenage girls from three different generations are woven together as each girl learns about forgiveness, empathy, and self-respect.

Kwasney's "protagonists are distinctive and empathetic, her narratives meticulously structured and realistic, exposing the unpredictability—and sometimes unfairness—that life can bring." Publ Wkly

L'Engle, Madeleine
A **wrinkle** in time. Farrar, Straus & Giroux 1962 211p $17; pa $7.99
Grades: 5 6 7 8 9 10
1. Fantasy fiction
ISBN 0-374-38613-7; 0-312-36754-6 pa
ALA YALSA Margaret A. Edwards Award (1998)
Awarded The Newbery Medal, 1963

"A brother and sister, together with a friend, go in search of their scientist father who was lost while engaged in secret work for the government on the tesseract problem. A tesseract is a wrinkle in time. The father is a prisoner on a forbidding planet, and after awesome and terrifying experiences, he is rescued, and the little group returns safely to Earth and home." Child Books Too Good to Miss

This book "makes unusual demands on the imagination and consequently gives great rewards." Horn Book

Other titles in this series are:
A wind in the door (1973)
A swiftly tilting planet (1978)
Many waters (1986)
An acceptable time (1989)

Laban, Elizabeth
The **Tragedy** Paper; Elizabeth LaBan. Alfred A. Knopf 2013 320 p. $17.99
Grades: 7 8 9 10 11 12
1. Love stories 2. School stories 3. Albinos and albinism -- Fiction 4. Schools -- Fiction 5. High schools -- Fiction 6. Boarding schools -- Fiction 7. Dating (Social customs) -- Fiction 8. Interpersonal relations -- Fiction
ISBN 0375870407; 9780375870408; 9780375970405; 9780375989124
LC 2012011294

This novel by Elizabeth Laban "follows the story of Tim Macbeth, a seventeen-year-old albino and a recent transfer to the prestigious Irving School. . . . He finds himself falling for the quintessential 'It' girl, Vanessa Sheller. . . . Vanessa is into him, too, but she can kiss her social status goodbye if anyone ever finds out. Tim and Vanessa begin a clandestine romance, but looming over them is the Tragedy Paper, Irving's version of a senior year thesis." (Publisher's note)

LaCour, Nina

★ The **Disenchantments**; Nina LaCour. Dutton Children's Books 2012 308 p. (hardcover) $16.99
Grades: 9 10 11 12

1. Bildungsromans 2. Teenagers -- Fiction 3. Friendship -- Fiction 4. Bands (Music) -- Fiction 5. Pacific Northwest -- Fiction 6. Artists -- Fiction 7. Secrets -- Fiction 8. Best friends -- Fiction 9. Automobile travel -- Fiction 10. Northwest, Pacific -- Fiction
ISBN 9780525422198

LC 2011021953

In this book, "[a]fter Colby graduates from high school, his . . . plans to spend a year traveling through Europe go up in smoke. . . . He . . . commit[s] himself to playing chauffeur for [his friend] Bev's . . . band . . . on their first . . . summer tour. Chronicling the band's road trip, . . .this . . . coming-of-age story expresses how a teen in limbo learns . . . lessons about disappointment, love, and the pursuit of dreams." (Publishers Weekly)

Everything leads to you; Nina LaCour. Dutton Books 2014 320 p. (hardback) $17.99
Grades: 9 10 11 12

1. Love -- Fiction 2. Summer -- Fiction 3. Secrets -- Fiction 4. Motion picture industry -- Fiction 5. Families -- Fiction 6. Lesbians -- Fiction 7. Set designers -- Fiction
ISBN 0525425888; 9780525425885

LC 2014004799

"Eighteen-year-old production design intern Emi is getting over her first love and trying to establish her place in the Los Angeles film industry...When she and her best friend Charlotte find a letter hidden in the possessions of a recently deceased Hollywood film legend at an estate sale, they begin searching for its intended recipient. Eventually that leads to Ava, a beautiful teen to whom Emi is immediately attracted. ..This one is highly enjoyable and highly recommended." (School Library Journal)

Hold still; with illustrations by Mia Nolting. Dutton 2009 229p il
Grades: 9 10 11 12

1. Suicide -- Fiction 2. Friendship -- Fiction 3. Bereavement -- Fiction
ISBN 0-525-42155-6; 978-0-525-42155-9

LC 2010-275162

Ingrid didn't leave a note. Three months after her best friend's suicide, Caitlin finds what she left instead: a journal, hidden under Caitlin's bed.

"Interspersed with drawings and journal entries, the story of Caitlin's journey through her grief is both heart-wrenching and realistic. . . . LaCour strikes a new path through a familiar story, leading readers with her confident writing and savvy sense of prose." Kirkus

★ **We** Are Okay. Nina LaCour. Dutton Books 2017 240 p.

Grades: 8 9 10 11 12

1. Grief -- Fiction; 2. Friendship -- Fiction
9780399538513; 9780142422939; 9780525425892, $17.99; 0525425896
Printz Award (2018)

This novel, by Nina LaCour, is "about grief and the enduring power of friendship.... Marin hasn't spoken to anyone from her old life since the day she left everything behind. No one knows the truth about those final weeks. Not even her best friend Mabel. But even thousands of miles away from the California coast, at college in New York, Marin still feels the pull of the life and tragedy she's tried to outrun." (Publisher's note)

"Though there's little action, with most of the writing devoted to Marin's memories, thoughts, and musings, the author's nuanced and sensitive depiction of the protagonist's complex and turbulent inner life makes for a rich narrative. Marin is a beautifully crafted character, and her voice is spot-on, conveying isolation, grief, and, eventually, hope." SLJ

You Know Me Well. By David Levithan and Nina LaCour. St. Martin's Press 2016 256 p.
Grades: 9 10 11 12

1. Gay youth -- Fiction
1250098645; 9781250098641, $18.99; 9781250098665, $60

LC 2016001129

In this book, by David Levithan and Nina LaCour, "Mark and Kate have sat next to each other for an entire year. . . . For whatever reason, their paths outside of class have never crossed. That is until Kate spots Mark miles away from home, out in the city for a wild, unexpected night. Kate is lost, having just run away from a chance to finally meet the girl she has been in love with from afar. Mark, meanwhile, is in love with his best friend Ryan, who may or may not feel the same way. " (Publisher's note)

"A once-upon-a-time reminder that life sucks and love stinks-but ain't they grand?" Kirkus

LaFaye, A.

Stella stands alone; [by] A. LaFaye. Simon & Schuster Books for Young Readers 2008 245p map $16.99

Grades: 7 8 9 10

1. Orphans -- Fiction 2. African Americans -- Fiction 3. Swindlers and swindling -- Fiction 4. Reconstruction (1865-1876) -- Fiction
ISBN 978-1-4169-1164-7; 1-4169-1164-2

LC 2007-38725

Fourteen-year-old Stella, orphaned just after the Civil War, fights to keep her family's plantation and fulfill her father's desire to turn land over to the people who have worked on it for generations, but first she must find her father's hidden deed and will.

"Readers will be drawn along by Stella's refusal to act helpless and sweet and her discovery of strength and kindness in unexpected places. The sadness and anger, and the wrenching legacy of slavery are present throughout." Booklist

LaFevers, Robin

★ **Dark** triumph; by Robin LaFevers. Houghton Mifflin Harcourt 2013 400 p. $17.99

Grades: 9 10 11 12

> 1. Fantasy fiction 2. Death -- Fiction 3. Assassins -- Fiction 4. Gods -- Fiction 5. Love -- Fiction 6. Brittany (France) -- History -- 1341-1532 -- Fiction 7. France -- History -- Charles VIII, 1483-1498 -- Fiction

ISBN 0547628382; 9780547628387

LC 2012033555

In this novel, by Robin LaFevers, book 2 of the "His Fair Assassin Trilogy," "Sybella's duty as Death's assassin in 15th-century France forces her return home to the personal hell that she had finally escaped. . . . While Sybella is a weapon of justice wrought by the god of Death himself, He must give her a reason to live. When she discovers an unexpected ally imprisoned in the dungeons, will a daughter of Death find something other than vengeance to live for?" (Publisher's note)

"LaFevers weaves the 'crazed, tangled web' of Sybella's life...with force, suspense and subtle tenderness. The prose's beauty inspires immediate re-reads of many a sentence, but its forward momentum is irresistible. An intricate, masterful page-turner about politics, treachery, religion, love and healing." Kirkus

★ **Grave** mercy; by Robin LaFevers. Houghton Mifflin 2012 549 p.

Grades: 9 10 11 12

> 1. Love stories 2. Historical fiction 3. Executions and executioners -- Fiction 4. Gods -- Fiction 5. Death -- Fiction 6. Assassins -- Fiction 7. Courts and courtiers -- Fiction 8. Brittany (France) -- History -- 1341-1532 -- Fiction 9. France -- History -- Charles VIII, 1483-1498 -- Fiction

ISBN 9780547628349

LC 2011039893

This book is a "historical romance with a . . . recreation of 15th-century Brittany. At its center is 17-year-old Ismae, . . . [who,] fleeing her thuggish husband, is taken in by the convent of St. Mortain. . . . Ismae is trained as an assassin. . . . [and] dispatched to the court of Anne of Brittany to keep track of Duval, the duchess's . . . older brother. Reluctantly, she falls in love with him, knowing . . . that she may someday be called upon to end his life." (Publishers Weekly)

★ **Mortal** heart; by Robin LaFevers . Houghton Mifflin Harcourt. 2014 464p $17.99

Grades: 9 10 11 12

> 1. Assassins -- Fiction 2. Convents -- Fiction 3. Death --Fiction 4. Gods -- Fiction 5. Nuns -- Fiction 6. Brittany (France) -- History -- 1341-1532 -- Fiction 7. France --History -- Charles VIII, 1483-1498 -- Fiction

ISBN: 0547628404; 9780547628400

LC 2014001877

In this book, the conclusion of the His Fair Assassin trilogy, "Annith, overskilled and underused daughter of Mortain, god of Death, rebels against her abbess's decree that she remain immured in the convent as Mortain's seeress. Her rebellious escape to the world of politics, murder, and romance revolutionizes Annith's understanding of her nature and identity and brings about her sexual awakening." (Horn Book Magazine)

"The protagonists' sometimes-contradictory natures enrich their characters, and the intertwined relationships of realistic and Netherworld personages add depth to their personal stories. A plethora of strong females and their romantic relationships will have wide appeal for teens." SLJ

Laidlaw, S. J.

★ **Fifteen** lanes. S.J. Laidlaw. McClelland & Stewart Ltd 2016 304 p.

Grades: 9 10 11 12

> 1. Cyberbullying -- Fiction 2. Teenage girls -- Fiction 3. Friendship -- Fiction

1101917806; 9781101917800, $17.99; 9781101917824, $53.97

LC 2015931503

In this book by S.J. Laidlaw, "Noor has lived all of her . . . years in the fifteen lanes of Mumbai's red light district. Born into a brothel, she is destined for the same fate as her mother. Across the . . . [city] Grace enjoys a life of privilege. Her father, the CEO of one of India's largest international banks. . . . [Grace's] perfect life is shattered when she becomes a victim of a cruel online attack. When their paths intersect, Noor and Grace will be changed forever." (Publisher's note)

"Full of complicated characters from across Mumbai's social classes, the novel challenges readers' expectations." Kirkus

Laird, Elizabeth

The **betrayal** of Maggie Blair. Houghton Mifflin 2011 423p il $16.99

Grades: 7 8 9 10

> 1. Uncles -- Fiction 2. Witchcraft -- Fiction 3. Scotland -- History -- 17th century -- Fiction

ISBN 978-0-547-34126-2; 0-547-34126-1

LC 2010-25120

In seventeenth-century Scotland, sixteen-year-old Maggie Blair is sentenced to be hanged as a witch but escapes to the home of her uncle, placing him and his family in great danger as she risks her life to save them all from the King's men.

"Laird seamlessly weaves a fairly comprehensive history lesson into an engaging, lively story." Bull Cent Child Books

A **little** piece of ground; [by] Elizabeth Laird; with Sonia Nimr. Haymarket Books 2006 216p pa $9.95

Grades: 6 7 8 9 10

> 1. Israel-Arab conflicts -- Fiction

ISBN 978-1-931859-38-7; 1-931859-38-8

LC 2006008707

During the Israeli occupation of Ramallah in the West Bank of Palestine, twelve-year-old Karim and his friends create a secret place for themselves where they can momentarily forget the horrors of war.

"Throughout this powerful narrative, the authors remain true to Karim's character and reactions. He is a typical self-centered adolescent. . . . [This book] deserves serious attention and discussion." SLJ

Lake, Nick

Hostage Three; by Nick Lake. Bloomsbury 2013 320 p. (hardback) $17.99

Grades: 9 10 11 12

1. Pirates -- Fiction 2. Hostages -- Fiction 3. Father-daughter relationship -- Fiction 4. Yachts -- Fiction 5. Survival -- Fiction 6. Fathers and daughters -- Fiction 7. Adventure and adventurers -- Fiction

ISBN 1619631237; 9781619631236

LC 2013002686

"The last way seventeen-year-old Amy wants to spend the summer after high school is sailing around the world with her father and new stepmother. When Somali pirates hijack the family's yacht, the sullen, entitled teen forms a surprising bond with one of their captors. Lake's sensitive character development and sophisticated storytelling (including alternate endings) helps elicit readers' sympathies for his complex characters." (Horn Book)

★ **In** darkness; Nick Lake. Bloomsbury 2012 341 p.

Grades: 8 9 10 11 12

1. Haiti -- Fiction 2. Earthquakes -- Fiction 3. Gangs -- Fiction 4. Survival -- Fiction 5. Violence -- Fiction 6. Haiti Earthquake, Haiti, 2010 -- Fiction 7. Haiti Earthquake, Haiti, 2010

ISBN 9781599907437

LC 2011022350

Michael L. Printz Award (2013)

"This . . . novel, set in Haiti, alternates between the narration of a contemporary fifteen-year-old, trapped in the rubble following the 2010 earthquake, and the story of Toussaint L'Ouverture, the legendary eighteenth-century leader of Haiti's anti-colonial revolution. The two become aware of each other through dreams; Shorty experiences Toussaint's reality while Toussaint perceives the bewildering future setting in which Shorty lives. . . . [B]oth share graphic depictions of the cruelty and violence of the protagonists' lives. Shorty tells of his pre-earthquake life in quick allusions and references that eventually cohere into a complete story." (Bulletin of the Center for Children's Books)

Satellite. Nick Lake. Alfred A. Knopf 2017 453 p.

Grades: 8 9 10 11 12

1. Space stations -- Fiction; 2. Teenagers -- Fiction; 3. Science fiction;

ISBN 9781524713553; 9781524713539; 9781524713546, $20.99

LC 2016056933

"Born and raised on Moon 2, Leo and the twins, Orion and Libra, are finally old enough and strong enough to endure the dangerous trip to Earth. They've been 'parented' by teams of astronauts since birth and have run countless drills to ready themselves for every conceivable difficulty they might face on the flight. But has anything really prepared them for life on terra firma?" (Publisher's note)

"In this free-wheeling sci-fi adventure firmly grounded by its layered characters, Lake . . . explores home, family, and the idea of belonging." Kirkus

Lam, Laura

Pantomime; Laura Lam. Strange Chemistry 2013 394 p. (pbk.) $9.99

Grades: 9 10 11 12

1. Fantasy fiction 2. Magic -- Fiction 3. Circus -- Fiction 4. Fantasy 5. Love stories 6. Love -- Fiction 7. Runaways -- Fiction 8. Circus 9. Runaways

ISBN 190884437X; 9781908844378; 9781908844385

LC 2012540335

"R.H. Ragona's Circus of Magic is the greatest circus of Ellada. Nestled among the glowing blue Penglass -- remnants of a mysterious civilisation long gone -- are wonders beyond the wildest imagination. . . . Iphigenia Laurus, or Gene, the daughter of a noble family, is uncomfortable in corsets and crinoline, and prefers climbing trees to debutante balls. Micah Grey, a runaway living on the streets, joins the circus as an aerialist's apprentice and soon becomes the circus's rising star." (Publisher's note)

"At around page 90 in Lam's impressive debut fantasy novel, there's a reveal so stunning that it makes it difficult to discuss without spoilers... Using a flashback structure to show both why noble-born Iphigenia Laurus runs away and joins the circus and how she changes her identity to become trapeze-artist Micah Grey, Pantomime does feature standard YA elements such as parental estrangement and problematic romance—yet marvelously transfigures them." (Booklist)

Lanagan, Margo

★ The **brides** of Rollrock Island; Margo Lanagan. Alfred A. Knopf 2012 305 p. (hardback) $17.99

Grades: 9 10 11 12

1. Selkies -- Fiction 2. Fantasy fiction 3. Magic -- Fiction 4. Islands -- Fiction 5. Witches -- Fiction

ISBN 0375869190; 9780375869198; 9780375969195; 9780375989308

LC 2011047466

This novel, by Margo Lenagan, takes place around "remote Rollrock Island, [where] men go to sea to make their livings--and to catch their wives. The witch Misskaella knows the way of drawing a girl from the heart of a seal . . . [a]nd for a price a man may buy himself a lovely sea-wife. . . . But from his first look into [her] . . . eyes, he will be just as transformed as she. He will be equally ensnared. And the witch will have her true payment." (Publisher's note)

★ **Tender** morsels. Alfred A. Knopf 2008 436p $16.99; lib bdg $19.99

Grades: 10 11 12

1. Fantasy fiction

ISBN 978-0-375-84811-7; 0-375-84811-8; 978-0-375-94811-4 lib bdg; 0-375-94811-2 lib bdg

LC 2008-04155

Michael L. Printz Award honor book, 2009

A young woman who has endured unspeakable cruelties is magically granted a safe haven apart from the real world and allowed to raise her two daughters in this alternate reality, until the barrier between her world and the real one begins to break down.

The author "touches on nightmarish adult themes, including multiple rape scenarios and borderline human-animal sexual interactions, which reserve this for the most mature readers. . . . Drawing alternate worlds that blur the line between wonder and horror, and characters who traverse the nature of human and beast, this challenging, unforgettable work explores the ramifications of denying the most essential and often savage aspects of life." Booklist

Lancaster, Mike A.

The **future** we left behind; Mike A. Lancaster. Egmont USA 2012 367 p. (hardback) $16.99

Grades: 7 8 9 10

   1. Science fiction 2. Cults -- Fiction 3. England -- Fiction 4. Computer programs -- Fiction 5. Family life -- England -- Fiction 6. Technological innovations -- Fiction

   ISBN 1606844105; 9781606844106; 9781606844113

                       LC 2012003794

Sequel to: Human.4

This sequel to "Human.4" is set in the future. Here, "Peter is the son of the man who saved the world by inventing robot bees. Destined by his wealthy genius father for a future in science, Peter rebels against both by enrolling in a literature class and befriending Alpha, a girl in a wacky religious cult. Alpha is a Strakerite, following the ancient tapes of Kyle Straker. Kyle and his girlfriend Lilly believed humans are regularly upgraded by aliens. Skeptical at first, Peter is soon convinced." (Kirkus)

   ★ **Human.4**. Egmont USA 2011 231p $16.99

Grades: 7 8 9 10

   1. Science fiction 2. Computers -- Fiction 3. Family life -- Fiction

   ISBN 978-1-6068-4099-3; 1-6068-4099-1

                       LC 2010030313

Twenty-first century fourteen-year-old Kyle was hypnotized when humanity was upgraded to 1.0 and he, incompatible with the new technology, exposes its terrifying impact in a tape-recording found by the superhumans of the future.

"Lancaster fashions a fast-paced, upsetting little thriller punctuated by ominous editorial notes that translate Kyle's details for the futuristic audience." Booklist

Landers, Melissa

Starfall. Melissa Landers. Hyperion 2017 361 p. (Starflight)

Grades: 10 11 12

   1. Interplanetary voyages -- Fiction; 2. Love -- Fiction; 3. Princesses -- Fiction; 4. Space ships -- Fiction; 5. Science fiction; 6. Adventure fiction

   9781484785096;   9781484787915;   148475025X; 9781484750254, $17.99

                       LC 2016033382

This Starflight novel, by Melissa Landers, "is a lively tale of romance, space pirates, conspiracy, and made (as opposed to genetic) families. Over the course of the book, all the characters round out nicely, as does the romance... Landers has a firm hand on the plot, which includes a rousing fight scene or two, as well as a nifty twist at the end." (Booklist)

"The strong message of finding a love of equals shines throughout. Landers sets an intergalactic stage that fans of sci-fi, romance, and adventure will devour." SLJ

Sequel to: Starflight (2016)

Landman, Tanya

   ★ **Hell** and high water. Tanya Landman. Candlewick Press 2017 312 p.

Grades: 7 8 9 10

   1. Detective and mystery stories; 2. Historical fiction; 3. Offenses against the person -- Fiction; 4. Racially mixed people -- Fiction

   0763688754; 9780763688752, $17.99; 9780763693824

                       LC 2017942652

This book, by Tanya Landman, is "set in 18th-century England. Fifteen-year-old Caleb Chappell is a mixed-race boy whose life is shrouded in mystery.... His white father -- a talented puppeteer -- is the son of a disgraced earl but never discusses his past. When his father is falsely convicted of theft, Caleb is forced to seek protection from a hitherto-unknown paternal aunt.... [Until] Caleb receives a shock when a body bearing his father's signet ring washes up on the shore." (Kirkus Reviews)

"Murder and mystery abound in this engrossing and atmospheric tale set in 18th-century England." Kirkus

Lane, Andrew

Black ice; Andrew Lane. Farrar Straus Giroux 2013 288 p. (Sherlock Holmes. The legend begins) (hardcover) $17.99

Grades: 5 6 7 8

   1. Mystery fiction 2. Holmes, Sherlock (Fictional character) -- Fiction 3. Murder -- Fiction 4. Mystery and detective stories

   ISBN 0374387699; 9780374387693

                       LC 2012004996

This novel, by Andrew Lane, is the third book of the "Sherlock Holmes: The Legend Begins" series. "When Sherlock and Amyus Crowe, his American tutor, visit Sherlock's brother, Mycroft, in London, all they are expecting is lunch and some polite conversation. What they find shocks both of them to the core: a locked room, a dead body, and Mycroft holding a knife. . . . Threatened with the gallows, Mycroft needs Sherlock to save him." (Publisher's note)

Rebel fire; Andrew Lane. Farrar Straus Giroux 2012 343 p. (Sherlock Holmes. The legend begins) $16.99

Grades: 5 6 7 8

   1. Mystery fiction 2. Holmes, Sherlock (Fictional character) -- Fiction 3. Mystery and detective stories

   ISBN 0374387680; 9780374387686

                       LC 2011000124

This novel, by Andrew Lane, is part of the "Sherlock Holmes: The Legend Begins" series. "Fourteen-year-old Sherlock Holmes knows that Amyus Crowe, his mysterious American tutor, has some dark secrets. But he didn't expect to find John Wilkes Booth, the notorious assassin, apparently alive and well in England--and Crowe somehow mixed up in it. . . . And so begins an adventure that will take Sherlock across the Atlantic, to the center of a deadly web." (Publisher's note)

Includes bibliographical references

Lange, Erin Jade

Butter; Erin Jade Lange. Bloomsbury 2012 296 p. (hardback) $16.99

Grades: 8 9 10 11 12

    1. Eating habits 2. Suicide -- Fiction 3. Teenagers -- Fiction 4. Obesity -- Fiction 5. Eating disorders -- Fiction

    ISBN 1599907801; 9781599907802

LC 2011045509

In author Erin Jade Lange's book, a "lonely obese boy everyone calls 'Butter' is about to make history. He is going to eat himself to death-live on the Internet-and everyone is invited to watch. When he first makes the announcement online to his classmates, Butter expects pity, insults, and possibly sheer indifference. What he gets are morbid cheerleaders rallying around his deadly plan. Yet as their dark encouragement grows, it begins to feel a lot like popularity . . . But what happens when Butter reaches his suicide deadline?" (Publisher's note)

Larbalestier, Justine

How to ditch your fairy. Bloomsbury 2008 307p $16.99

Grades: 6 7 8 9 10

    1. Magic -- Fiction 2. Fairies -- Fiction

    ISBN 978-1-59990-301-9; 1-59990-301-6

LC 2008-02408

In a world in which everyone has a personal fairy who tends to one aspect of daily life, fourteen-year-old Charlie decides she does not want hers—a parking fairy—and embarks on a series of misadventures designed to rid herself of the invisible sprite and replace it with a better one, like her friend Rochelle's shopping fairy.

    "Charlie is totally likable, smart, and sarcastic, a perfectly self-involved, insecure teen. At its core, this is a typical coming-of-age story, but the addition of the fairies, the slightly alternative setting, and the made-up slang make it much more." SLJ

★ **Liar**. Bloomsbury Children's Books 2009 376p $16.99

Grades: 9 10 11 12

    1. Honesty -- Fiction 2. Werewolves -- Fiction

    ISBN 978-1-59990-305-7; 1-59990-305-9

LC 2009-12581

Compulsive liar Micah promises to tell the truth after revealing that her boyfriend has been murdered.

    "Micah's narrative is convincing, and in the end readers will delve into the psyche of a troubled teen and decide for themselves the truths and lies. This one is sure to generate discussion." SLJ

Magic lessons. Razorbill 2006 275p $16.99; pa $7.99

Grades: 8 9 10 11 12

    1. Magic -- Fiction 2. Australia -- Fiction 3. Space and time -- Fiction 4. New York (N.Y.) -- Fiction

    ISBN 1-59514-054-9; 1-59514-124-3 pa

LC 2005-23870

Sequel to Magic or madness (2005)

When fifteen-year-old Reason is pulled through the magical door connecting New York City with the Sydney, Australia, home of her grandmother, she encounters an impossibly ancient man who seems to have some purpose in mind for her.

"Larbalestier creates complex relationships among her characters, and their realistic flaws, combined with the sense of danger throughout, make this a good choice for even reluctant readers." SLJ

Followed by Magic's child (2007)

Magic or madness. Razorbill 2005 288p $16.99; pa $7.99

Grades: 8 9 10 11 12

    1. Magic -- Fiction 2. Australia -- Fiction 3. Grandmothers -- Fiction 4. Space and time -- Fiction 5. New York (N.Y.) -- Fiction

    ISBN 1-59514-022-0; 1-59514-124-3 pa

LC 2004-18263

From the Sydney, Australia home of a grandmother she believes is a witch, fifteen-year-old Reason Cansino is magically transported to New York City, where she discovers that friends and foes can be hard to distinguish

    "Readers looking for layered, understated fantasy will follow the looping paths of Larbalestier's fine writing . . . with gratitude and awe." Booklist

Other titles about Reason Cansino are:

Magic lessons (2006)

Magic's child (2007)

★ **My** sister Rosa. Justine Larbalestier. Soho Teen 2016 320 p.

Grades: 9 10 11 12

    1. Australians -- United States -- Fiction 2. Brothers and sisters -- Fiction 3. Psychopaths -- Fiction 4. New York (N.Y.) -- Fiction 5. Mental illness -- Fiction 6. Children with mental disabilities -- Fiction

    9781616956745

LC 2016006797

"Seventeen-year-old Aussie Che Taylor loves his younger sister, Rosa. But he's also certain that she's a diagnosable psychopath-clinically, threateningly, dangerously. Recently Rosa has been making trouble, hurting things. Che is the only one who knows; he's the only one his sister trusts. Rosa is smart, talented, pretty, and very good at hiding what she is and the violence she's capable of. . . . Alone, Che must balance his desire to protect Rosa from the world with the desperate need to protect the world from her." (Publisher's note)

    "Che knows that his ten-year-old sister Rosa is a ticking bomb. I don't think it matters what you call it: psychopathy, sociopathy, antisocial personality disorder, evil, or the devil within. What matters is to prevent the bomb from exploding. This task falls to Che because his parents don't believe there is anything wrong; they think that she had a problem but that it was merely a phase. He is especially worried now that the family has moved to New York City. What evil could she wreak in such a large city? . . . Che's journey toward self-awareness is at times enlightening, at times devastating, and the threat of violence from Rosa is suspenseful and truly terrifying." Horn Book

Razorhurst. Justine Larbalestier. Soho Teen 2015 309 p. Map

Grades: 9 10 11 12

    1. Criminals -- Fiction 2. Ghost stories -- Fiction 3. Organized crime -- Fiction 4. Australia -- History -- 20th century -- Fiction 5. Sydney (N.S.W.) -- History

-- 20th century -- Fiction 6. Ghost stories 7. Sydney (Australia) -- Fiction

1616955449; 9781616955441, $18.99

LC 2014030128

This young adult historical suspense novel, by Justine Larbalestier, describes "Sydney's deadly Razorhurst neighborhood, 1932. Gloriana Nelson and Mr. Davidson, two ruthless mob bosses, have reached a fragile peace—one maintained by 'razor men.' Kelpie, orphaned and homeless, is blessed (and cursed) with the ability to see Razorhurst's many ghosts. They tell her secrets the living can't know about the cracks already forming in the mobs' truce." (Publisher's note)

"Larbalestier pulls no punches with the gruesome, gory details about the violence of poverty, and the result is a dark, unforgettable and blood-soaked tale of outlaws and masterminds." Kirkus

Originally published in Australia by Allen and Unwin in 2014.

Larson, Kirby

★ **Hattie** Big Sky. Delacorte Press 2006 289p hardcover o.p. pa $6.99

Grades: 6 7 8 9 10

1. Montana -- Fiction 2. Orphans -- Fiction 3. World War, 1914-1918 -- Fiction 4. Frontier and pioneer life -- Fiction

ISBN 0-385-73313-5; 0-385-73595-2 pa

LC 2005-35039

A Newbery Medal honor book, 2007

After inheriting her uncle's homesteading claim in Montana, sixteen-year-old-orphan Hattie Brooks travels from Iowa in 1917 to make a home for herself, befriends a German-American family and encounters some unexpected problems related to the war in Europe. "Grades six to nine." (Bull Cent Child Books)

This is "a richly textured novel full of memorable characters." Booklist

Hattie ever after; Kirby Larson. Delacorte Press 2013 240 p. (hc) $16.99

Grades: 6 7 8 9 10

1. Historical fiction 2. Orphans -- Fiction 3. Reporters and reporting -- Fiction 4. Self-reliance -- Fiction 5. San Francisco (Calif.) -- History -- 20th century -- Fiction

ISBN 0385737467; 9780307979681; 9780385737463; 9780385906685

LC 2012007068

Sequel to: Hattie Big Sky

In this novel, by Newbury Honor award-winning author Kirby Larson, "after leaving Uncle Chester's homestead claim, orphan Hattie Brooks throws a lasso around a new dream, even bigger than the Montana sky. She wants to be a reporter . . . , go to Grand Places, and do Grand Things, like Hattie's hero Nellie Bly. Another girl might be stymied by this, but . . . nothing can squash her desire to write for a big city newspaper." (Publisher's note)

Includes bibliographical references

Laskas, Gretchen Moran

The **miner's** daughter. Simon & Schuster Books for Young Readers 2007 250p $15.99

Grades: 8 9 10 11 12

1. Family life -- Fiction 2. Coal mines and mining -- Fiction 3. Great Depression, 1929-1939 -- Fiction

ISBN 978-1-4169-1262-0; 1-4169-1262-2

LC 2006-00684

Sixteen-year-old Willa, living in a Depression-era West Virginia mining town, works hard to help her family, experiences love and friendship, and finds an outlet for her writing when her family becomes part of the Arthurdale, West Virginia, community supported by Eleanor Roosevelt.

"Richly drawn characters and plot make this an excellent novel that explores the struggles endured by many in America in the 1930s." SLJ

Laskin, Pamela L.

Ronit & Jamil. Pamela L. Laskin. Katherine Tegen Books 2017 183 p.

Grades: 7 8 9 10 11 12

1. Arab-Israeli conflict -- Fiction; 2. Conflict of generations -- Fiction; 3. Families -- Fiction; 4. Israelis -- Fiction; 5. Man-woman relationships -- Fiction; 6. Palestinian Arabs -- Fiction; 7. Gaza -- Fiction; 8. Israel -- Fiction; 9. Romance fiction; 10. Teenagers -- Fiction; 11. Shakespeare, William, 1564-1616 -- Adaptations

9780062458551; 9780062458544, $17.99

LC 2016949687

This book, by Pamela L. Laskin, presents "accessible verse and universal questions about crossing cultural lines [that] make for a quick and powerful read. An obvious choice to pair with Romeo and Juliet in a literature class, this can also open discussion about the Israeli/Palestinian conflict and about bridging cultural boundaries." (School Library Journal)

"At once romantic and revealing, an important window into contemporary conditions in the Middle East." Kirkus

Lasky, Kathryn

★ **Ashes.** Viking 2010 318p $16.99

Grades: 6 7 8 9 10 11 12

1. Germany -- Fiction 2. National socialism -- Fiction

ISBN 978-0-670-01157-5; 0-670-01157-6

LC 2009-33127

In 1932 Berlin, thirteen-year-old Gaby Schramm witnesses the beginning of Hitler's rise to power, as soldiers become ubiquitous, her beloved literature teacher starts wearing a jewelled swastika pin, and the family's dear friend, Albert Einstein, leaves the country while Gaby's parents secretly bury his books and papers in their small yard.

"Gaby's questioning but assertive nature helps form a compelling, readable portrait of pre-WWII Germany." Publ Wkly

Lone wolf. Scholastic Press 2010 219p il map (Wolves of the Beyond) $16.99

Grades: 5 6 7 8

1. Fantasy fiction 2. Wolves -- Fiction

ISBN 978-0-545-09310-1; 0-545-09310-4

LC 2009-17007

Abandoned by his pack, a baby wolf with a mysterious mark on his deformed paw survives and embarks on a journey that will change the world of the wolves of the Beyond.

"Lasky merges anthropomorphic fantasy with realistic details about wolves and bears to produce an almost plausible emotional narrative, complete with dialogue and personalities. . . . The author builds a captivating world of forest, snow and volcanoes populated by intelligent animals and weaves a compelling story sure to bring readers back for the second installment." Kirkus

Other titles in this series are:
Shadow wolf (2010)
Watch wolf (2011)
Frost worlf (2011)

Latham, Jennifer

Scarlett undercover. Jennifer Latham. Little, Brown & Co. 2015 320 p.

Grades: 9 10 11 12

1. Blessing and cursing -- Fiction 2. Genies -- Fiction 3. Mystery and detective stories 4. Private investigators -- Fiction 5. Secrets -- Fiction 6. Supernatural -- Fiction 7. Paranormal fiction 8. Murder -- Fiction 9. Detectives -- Fiction
0316283932; 9780316283939, $18

LC 2014013252

In Jennifer Latham's novel readers "meet Scarlett, a smart, sarcastic fifteen-year-old, ready to take on crime in her hometown. When Scarlett agrees to investigate a local boy's suicide, she figures she's in for an easy case and a quick buck. But it doesn't take long for suicide to start looking a lot like murder. As Scarlett finds herself deep in a world of cults, curses, and the seemingly supernatural, she discovers that her own family secrets may have more to do with the situation than she thinks." (Publisher's note)

"This whip-smart, determined, black Muslim heroine brings a fresh hard-boiled tone to the field of teen mysteries." Kirkus

Lauren, Christina

Autoboyography. Christina Lauren. Simon & Schuster Books for Young Readers 2017 416 p.

Grades: 9 10 11 12

1. Authorship -- Fiction; 2. Bisexuality -- Fiction; 3. Dating (Social customs) -- Fiction; 4. Family life -- Utah -- Fiction; 5. High schools -- Fiction; 6. Mormons -- Fiction; 7. Schools -- Fiction; 8. Utah -- Fiction
ISBN 9781481481687; 9781481481694

LC 2017005047

This book, by Christina Lauren, is "about two boys who fall in love in a writing class—one from a progressive family and the other from a conservative religious community. . . . [W]hen his best friend Autumn dares him to take Provo High's prestigious Seminar . . . Tanner can't resist going. . . . [There, he] notice Sebastian Brother, the Mormon prodigy . . . who now mentors the class. And it takes less than a month for Tanner to fall completely in love with him." (Publisher's note)

"While avoiding any demonizing of any religious groups, this manages to take on the intricacies of sexuality versus organized religion in an intense but ultimately inspirational narrative. Lauren successfully tackles a weighty subject with both ferocity and compassion." Booklist

Laurie, Victoria

Forever, again. Victoria Laurie. Hyperion 2016 368 p.

Grades: 7 8 9 10

1. Love -- Fiction 2. Mystery and detective stories 3. Reincarnation -- Fiction 4. Mystery fiction 5. Romance fiction
9781484700440, $17.99; 1484700090; 9781484700099, $17.99

LC 2015045683

In this novel, by Victoria Laurie, "Lily Bennett is less than thrilled to be the new kid as she starts her junior year in high school. But soon after classes begin, she meets . . . Cole Drepeau, with whom she forms an immediate and intimate bond. As Cole and Lily grow closer, Lily learns about the murder that divided the town more than thirty years before. . . . Lily feels inexplicably linked to Amber, and she can't help but think that there's more to [her tragic story]." (Publisher's note)

"With plot twist after plot twist, the book never dulls, and readers will be totally entertained page after page." VOYA

Lawlor, Laurie

The **two** loves of Will Shakespeare. Holiday House 2006 278p $16.95

Grades: 9 10 11 12

1. Great Britain -- History -- 1485-1603, Tudors -- Fiction 2. Shakespeare, William, 1564-1616 -- Fiction
ISBN 0-8234-1901-0; 978-0-8234-1901-2

LC 2005-52537

After falling in love, eighteen-year-old Will Shakespeare, a bored apprentice in his father's glove business and often in trouble for various misdeeds, vows to live an upstanding life and pursue his passion for writing.

"Quoting lines from Shakespeare's sonnets and highlighting the dismal treatment of women in that brutally repressive society, the author creates both a vivid setting and a feckless protagonist, equally credible as an adolescent and as a product of his times." Booklist

Le Guin, Ursula K.

The **farthest** shore. Pocket Books 2004 259p $15

Grades: 6 7 8 9

1. Fantasy fiction
ISBN 978-1-416-50964-6; 1-416-50964-X

First published 1972 by Atheneum Pubs.

This book continues "the story of Ged and introduces a new hero, Arren, the young prince who travels with the Archmage Ged on his last perilous mission. The writing has, as the concept has, a majestic intricacy; to appreciate it the reader must enjoy ornate language, the grave discussion of life and death and love, and courage, and the tongue-rolling exotic names of a legendary land." Bull Cent Child Books

Gifts. Harcourt 2004 274p $17; $17; pa $7.95

Grades: 7 8 9 10

1. Fantasy fiction
ISBN 9780152051235; 0-15-205123-6; 0-15-205124-4 pa

LC 2003-21449

"Brantors, or chiefs, of the various clans of the Uplands have powers passed down through generations, powers to call animals to the hunt, start fires, cast a wasting disease, or undo the very essence of a life or thing. The clans live isolated from the inhabitants of the Lowland cities in an uneasy truce, where each people's ambitions are kept at bay by fear of the other's vengeance. Two Upland teenagers, Gry and Orrec, have grown from childhood friendship into romance and also into a repudiation of their hereditary powers. . . . Rejecting traditions that bind them to roles unwanted and undesired, Gry and Orrec decide to leave their homes and seek a freer if less privileged life in the Lowlands. . . . Grades seven to twelve." (Bull Cent Child Books)

"Although intriguing as a coming-of-age allegory, Orrec's story is also rich in . . . earthy magic and intelligent plot twists." Booklist

★ The **left** hand of darkness. Ace Books 2000 304p pa $13.95

Grades: 9 10 11 12

1. Science fiction 2. Extrasensory perception -- Fiction
ISBN 0-441-00731-7

A reissue of the title first published 1969 by Walker & Company

ALA YALSA Margaret A. Edwards Award (2004)

"This is a tale of political intrigue and danger on the world of Gethen, the Winter planet. Genly Ai, high official of the Eukeman—the commonwealth of worlds—is on Gethen to convince the royalty to join the Federation. He soon becomes a pawn in Gethen's power struggles, set against the elaborate mores of the Gethenians, a unisex hermaphroditic people whose intricate sexual physiology plays a key role in the conflict. Allied with Estraven, fallen lord, Genly is forced to cross the savage and impassable Gobrin Ice." Shapiro. Fic for Youth. 3d edition

Powers. Harcourt 2007 502p map $17; pa $7.99

Grades: 7 8 9 10

1. Fantasy fiction
ISBN 978-0-15-205770-1; 0-15-205770-6; 978-0-15-206674-1 pa; 0-15-206674-8 pa
LC 2006-13549

Sequel to Voices (2006)

When young Gavir's sister is brutally killed, he escapes from slavery and sets out to explore the world and his own psychic abilities.

"Le Guin uses her own prodigious power as a writer to craft lyrical, precise sentences, evoking a palpable sense of place and believable characters." SLJ

Voices. Harcourt 2006 341p $17

Grades: 7 8 9 10

1. Fantasy fiction
ISBN 978-015-205678-0; 0-15-205678-5
LC 2005020753

Sequel to Gifts (2004)

Young Memer takes on a pivotal role in freeing her war-torn homeland from its oppressive captors.

"While her prose is simple and unadorned, Le Guin's superior narrative voice and storytelling power make even small moments ring with truth, and often with beauty." SLJ

Followed by Powers (2007)

★ A **wizard** of Earthsea; [by] Ursula K. Le Guin; illustrated by Ruth Robbins. Bantam trade pbk. ed.; Bantam Books 2004 182p il pa $15

Grades: 6 7 8 9

1. Fantasy fiction 2. Science fiction 3. Magic -- Fiction
ISBN 0-553-38304-3; 978-0-553-38304-1
LC 2004558962

A reissue of the title first published 1968 by Parnassus Press

ALA YALSA Margaret A. Edwards Award (2004)

A boy grows to manhood while attempting to subdue the evil he unleashed on the world as an apprentice to the Master Wizard.

A "powerful fantasy-allegory. Though set as prose, the rhythms of the langauge are truly and consistently poetical." Read Ladders for Hum Relat. 5th edition

Other titles in this series are:
The Tombs of Atuan (1971)
The farthest shore (1972)
Tehanu (1990)

Leavitt, Lindsey

Going vintage; by Lindsey Leavitt. 1st U.S. ed. Bloomsbury 2013 320 p. (hardcover) $16.99

Grades: 7 8 9 10

1. School stories 2. Sisters -- Fiction 3. Dating (Social customs) -- Fiction 4. Lists -- Fiction 5. Schools -- Fiction 6. California -- Fiction 7. High schools -- Fiction 8. Family life -- California -- Fiction
ISBN 1599907879; 9781599907871
LC 2012023269

In this book, "after discovering her boyfriend has a serious online relationship with another girl, Mallory very publicly dumps him on his social media site. She complicates the situation by deciding to try to fulfill a to-do list her grandmother crafted at the beginning of her junior year of high school in 1962, a time Mallory thinks must have been much simpler than today. . . . She's aided by her loyal younger sister, Ginnie, and the growing affection of her ex's cousin, charming Oliver." (Kirkus)

Sean Griswold's head. Bloomsbury 2011 276p $16.99

Grades: 7 8 9 10

1. School stories 2. Family life -- Fiction 3. Pennsylvania -- Fiction 4. Multiple sclerosis -- Fiction
ISBN 978-1-59990-498-6; 1-59990-498-5
LC 2010-06949

After discovering that her father has multiple sclerosis, fifteen-year-old Payton begins counselling sessions at school, which lead her to become interested in a boy in her biology class, have a falling out with her best friend, develop an interest in bike riding, and eventually allow her to come to terms with life's uncertainties.

"Leavitt capably handles the issues of chronic illness with sensitivity, making this an insightful, humorous, and ultimately uplifting family drama." Bull Cent Child Books

Leavitt, Martine

★ **Calvin**. Martine Leavitt.. Farrar Straus Giroux 2015 192 p.

Grades: 7 8 9 10 11 12

1. Characters in literature -- Fiction 2. High schools -- Fiction 3. Mental illness -- Fiction 4. Schizophrenia -- Fiction 5. Schools -- Fiction 6. Hallucinations and illusions 7. Teenagers -- Fiction

0374380732; 9780374380731, $17.99

LC 2015002574

In Martine Leavitt's novel "Calvin has always known his fate is linked to the comic book character from Calvin & Hobbes. He was born on the day the last strip was published. As a child Calvin played with the toy Hobbes. But now Calvin is a teenager who has been diagnosed with schizophrenia, Hobbes is back—as a delusion—and Calvin can't control him. Calvin decides that if he can convince Bill Watterson to draw one final comic strip, showing a normal teenaged Calvin, he will be cured." (Publisher's note)

"Funny, intellectual, and entertaining, it's a sensitive yet irreverent adventure about a serious subject." Pub Wkly

My book of life by Angel; Martine Leavitt. Farrar, Straus and Giroux Books for Young Readers 2012 252 p. $17.99; (hardback) $17.99; (ebook) $12.95

Grades: 8 9 10 11

1. Novels in verse 2. Runaway teenagers -- Fiction 3. Juvenile prostitution -- Fiction 4. Runaways -- Fiction 5. Drug abuse -- Fiction 6. Prostitution -- Fiction 7. Vancouver (B.C.) -- Fiction

ISBN 0374351236; 9780374351236; 9781554983179

LC 2011044563

This "novel in verse tells the story of 16-year-old Angel, who has been working as a prostitute in Vancouver. . . . After Angel's friend Serena disappears, Angel decides to give up" the drugs her pimp Call feeds her "and try to return home. Angel's withdrawal is severe . . . but it's nothing compared to the pain she feels when Call brings home an 11-year-old girl, Melli, to follow in Angel's footsteps. Angel is determined to keep Melli safe, even while other women continue to disappear." (Publishers Weekly)

Lecesne, James

Absolute brightness. HarperTeen 2008 472p $17.99; lib bdg $18.89

Grades: 7 8 9 10

1. Cousins -- Fiction 2. New Jersey -- Fiction 3. Good and evil -- Fiction

ISBN 978-0-06-125627-1; 0-06-125627-7; 978-0-06-125628-8 lib bdg; 0-06-125628-5 lib bdg

LC 2007-02988

ALA YALSA Morris Award Finalist, 2009

In the beach town of Neptune, New Jersey, Phoebe's life is changed irrevocably when her gay cousin moves into her house and soon goes missing.

"This thoughtful novel is beautifully written; its themes are haunting, and in spite of the central tragedy, it's often laugh-out-loud funny." Kliatt

Lee, Mackenzi

★ The **gentleman's** guide to vice and virtue. Mackenzi Lee. Katherine Tegen Books 2017 513 p.

Grades: 7 8 9 10 11 12

1. Bisexual teenagers -- Fiction; 2. Grand tours (Education) -- Fiction; 3. Hedonism -- Fiction; 4. Self-actualization (Psychology) in adolescence -- Fiction; 5. Young bisexual men -- Fiction; 6. Europe -- History -- 18th century -- Fiction; 7. Europe -- Fiction; 8. Travel -- Fiction; 9. Gay men -- Fiction

9780062382825; 9780062382801, $18.99

LC 2016949692

Stonewall Book Award Honor Book: Children's & Young Adult Literature (2018)

In this book, by Mackenzi Lee, "a young bisexual British lord embarks on an unforgettable Grand Tour of Europe with his best friend.... Henry 'Monty' Montague doesn't care that his roguish passions are far from suitable for the gentleman he was born to be.... So Monty vows to make this yearlong escapade one last hedonistic hurrah and flirt with Percy from Paris to Rome. But...one of Monty's reckless decisions turns their trip abroad into a harrowing manhunt." (Publisher's note)

"Austen, Wilde, and Indiana Jones converge in this deliciously anachronistic bonbon." Kirkus

Other titles in this series:

The Lady's Guide to Petticoats and Piracy (2018)

Lee, Stacey

Outrun the moon. Stacey Lee. G. P. Putnam's Sons 2016 400 p.

Grades: 7 8 9 10

1. Chinese Americans -- Fiction; 2. Earthquakes -- Fiction; 3. Private schools -- Fiction

ISBN 9780399175411, $17.99

LC 2015032478

"San Francisco, 1906: Fifteen-year-old Mercy Wong is determined to [gain] . . . an education at St. Clare's School for Girls. . . . Mercy gains admittance through a mix of cunning and a little bribery, only to discover that getting in was the easiest part. . . . On April 18, a historic earthquake rocks San Francisco, destroying Mercy's home and school. Now she's forced to wait with her classmates for their families in a temporary park encampment." (Publisher's note)

Under a painted sky. Stacey Lee. G. P. Putnam's Sons 2015 374 p.

Grades: 9 10 11 12

1. Adventure and adventurers -- Fiction 2. African Americans -- Fiction 3. Chinese Americans -- Fiction 4. Runaways -- Fiction 5. Sex role -- Fiction 6. Slavery -- Fiction 7. Oregon National Historic Trail -- Fiction 8. West (U.S.) -- History -- 1848-1860 -- Fiction 9. Oregon Trail -- Fiction 10. Fugitive slaves -- Fiction

0399168036; 9780399168031, $16.99

LC 2014015976

In this book by Stacey Lee, "it's 1849 in Missouri and Chinese American Samantha is in trouble. Her father's shop burned down, he died in the blaze, and she is wanted for murder after killing a man who tried to rape her. Luckily, plucky Annamae, a slave, helps her escape. A runaway slave and a Chinese girl would stick out like a sore thumb on the Oregon Trail, so they disguise themselves as boys—Andy and Sammy—and try to lie low as they make their way to California." (Booklist)

"Lee packs the plot with plenty of peril and Wild West excitement, and Sammy's fixation on fate, luck, and the Chinese zodiac adds a unique flavor. A great fit for fans of historical adventure with a touch of romance." Booklist

Lee, Tanith

Piratica; being a daring tale of a singular girl's adventure upon the high seas. Presented most handsomely by the notorious Tanith Lee. Dutton Children's Books 2004 288p $17.99

Grades: 6 7 8 9

1. Adventure fiction 2. Pirates -- Fiction 3. Sex role -- Fiction

ISBN 0-525-47324-6

First published 2003 in the United Kingdom

A bump on the head restores Art's memories of her mother and the exciting life they led, so the sixteen-year-old leaves Angels Academy for Young Maidens, seeks out the pirates who were her family before her mother's death, and leads them back to adventure on the high seas.

"Piratica is a refreshing, tongue-in-cheek, tangled tale that will entice readers who crave adventure and fantasy." SLJ

Piratica II: return to Parrot Island; being the return of a most intrepid heroine to sea and secrets. Dutton Children's Books 2006 320p $17.99

Grades: 6 7 8 9

1. Adventure fiction 2. Pirates -- Fiction 3. Sex role -- Fiction

ISBN 0-525-47769-1

Art Blastside is bored with life ashore, so she jumps at the chance to return to sea.

"Lee's writing is complex, and she uses her skill to craft subtle pundit humor and lush description." Voice Youth Advocates

Lee, Ying S.

A **spy** in the house. Candlewick Press 2010 335p (The Agency) $16.99

Grades: 8 9 10 11 12

1. Mystery fiction 2. Orphans -- Fiction 3. Household employees -- Fiction 4. Swindlers and swindling -- Fiction 5. Great Britain -- History -- 19th century -- Fiction

ISBN 978-0-7636-4067-5; 0-7636-4067-0

LC 2009-32736

Rescued from the gallows in 1850s London, young orphan and thief Mary Quinn is offered a place at Miss Scrimshaw's Academy for Girls where she is trained to be part of an all-female investigative unit called The Agency and, at age seventeen, she infiltrates a rich merchant's home in hopes of tracing his missing cargo ships.

"Lee fills the story with classic elements of Victorian mystery and melodrama. Class differences, love gone awry, racial discrimination, London's growing pains in the 1850s, and the status of women in society are all addressed. Historical details are woven seamlessly into the plot, and descriptive writing allows readers to be part of each scene." SLJ

Other titles in this series are:
The body at the tower (2010)
The traitor in the tunnel (2012)

LeFlore, Lyah

The **world** is mine; [by] Lyah B. LeFlore; with illustrations by DL Warfield. Simon Pulse 2009 269p il (Come up) pa $8.99

Grades: 7 8 9 10

1. School stories 2. Maryland -- Fiction 3. Family life -- Fiction 4. Music industry -- Fiction 5. African Americans -- Fiction

ISBN 978-1-4169-7963-0; 1-4169-7963-8

LC 2009-6900

Maryland high school juniors and best friends Blue Reynolds and Collin Andrews seem to have it all, and when they decide to become party promoters, anything can happen—including being pitted against parents, jealous girlfriends, and even one another.

"Teens, especially the hip-hop obsessed, will relate to the characters' stratospheric aspirations, their struggles to balance their passions with parental demands, as well as the sharp dialogue and narration." Publ Wkly

Legrand, Claire

Furyborn. Claire Legrand. Sourcebooks Fire 2018 512 p. Illustration; Map (Empirium trilogy)

Grades: 9 10 11 12

1. Fantasy; 2. Magic -- Juvenile fiction; 3. Prophecies -- Juvenile fiction; 4. Quests (Expeditions) -- Juvenile fiction

ISBN 9781492656623

LC 2017034431

"When assassins ambush her best friend, Rielle Dardenne risks everything to save him, exposing herself as one of a pair of prophesied queens: a queen of light, and a queen of blood. To prove she is the Sun Queen, Rielle must endure seven elemental magic trials. If she fails, she will be executed... unless the trials kill her first. One thousand years later, the legend of Queen Rielle is a fairy tale to Eliana Ferracora. A bounty hunter for the Undying Empire, Eliana believes herself untouchable—until her mother vanishes. To find her, Eliana joins a rebel captain and discovers that the evil at the empire's heart is more terrible than she ever imagined." (Publisher's note)

"Legrand excels at world building, deftly integrating the religion and history of this imaginary world into a dark yet rousing adventure story that combines passion and danger at every turn." Booklist

★ **Sawkill** girls. Claire Legrand. Katherine Tegen Books 2018 464 p.

Grades: 9 10 11 12

1. Horror fiction; 2. Female friendship -- Fiction; 3. Fantasy fiction

ISBN 9780062696601, $17.99

LC 2018943193

Author Claire Legrand's "atmospheric, Gothic-flavored chiller, which mingles elements of dark fairy tales and outright horror... includes an asexual character and a beautifully wrought queer romance, [and] focuses on the power of female friendship and what it means to pit women against one another in fiction and in life." (Publishers Weekly)

"Through this dank, atmospheric, and genuinely frightening narrative, Legrand weaves powerful threads about the dangerous journey of growing up female. In a world where monsters linger at the edges, this is an intensely character-driven story about girls who support each other, girls who betray each other, and girls who love each other in many complicated ways. Strange, eerie, and unforgettable." Booklist

Leitch, Will

Catch. Razorbill 2005 288p pa $7.99

Grades: 9 10 11 12

    1. Illinois -- Fiction

    ISBN 1-59514-069-7

                                LC 2005-08146

Teenager Tim Temples must decide if he wants to leave his comfortable life in a small town and go to college.

"This substantive title will entice both male and female YA readers with its thoughtful, authentic, and romantic young man's voice." Booklist

Lennon, Tom

When love comes to town; Tom Lennon. Albert Whitman 2013 304 p. (reinforced) $15.99

Grades: 8 9 10 11 12

    1. Historical fiction 2. Gay teenagers -- Fiction 3. Gays -- Fiction 4. Ireland -- Fiction 5. Coming out (Sexual orientation) -- Fiction

    ISBN 0807589160; 9780807589168

                                LC 2012020160

In this novel, by Tom Lennon, "the year is 1990, and in his hometown of Dublin, Ireland, Neil Byrne plays rugby, keeps up with the in-crowd at his school, and is just a regular guy. A guy who's gay. It's a secret he keeps from the wider world as he explores the city at night and struggles to figure out how to reveal his real self--and to whom." (Publisher's note)

Leno, Katrina

The **lost** & found. Katrina Leno. HarperTeen, an imprint of HarperCollinsPublishers 2016 352 p.

Grades: 7 8 9 10 11

    1. Loss (Psychology) -- Fiction 2. Automobile travel -- Fiction 3. Post-traumatic stress disorder -- Fiction 4. Brothers and sisters -- Fiction

    9780062231208

                                LC 2015038550

"Forging a friendship through an online support group, Frannie and Louis, teens whose losses are tied to mysterious disappearances, search for answers during a road trip to Austin, where they find magical things that the other has lost." (Publisher's note)

"This is a beautiful exploration of loss in many forms and the emotional toll it can take on those who are affected. . . . An emotional journey that's well worth the ride." SLJ

Leonard, Julia Platt

Cold case. Aladdin 2011 281p $15.99

Grades: 6 7 8 9

    1. Mystery fiction 2. Spies -- Fiction 3. Brothers -- Fiction 4. Homicide -- Fiction 5. Family life -- Fiction 6. Restaurants -- Fiction

    ISBN 978-1-4424-2009-0; 1-4424-2009-X

                                LC 2010041854

When thirteen-year-old Oz Keillor finds a dead body in his family's Santa Fe, New Mexico, restaurant, he is deter-

mined to solve the mystery in which his older brother is implicated, but which also involves their long-dead father, who was accused of being a spy.

"The well-plotted double mystery is propped up by a few choice details about restaurant life, some sly red herrings, and a cast of nicely rounded characters." Booklist

Les Becquets, Diane

★ **Season** of ice. Bloomsbury U.S.A. Children's Books 2008 281p $16.95

Grades: 8 9 10 11 12

    1. Lakes -- Fiction 2. Maine -- Fiction 3. Stepfamilies -- Fiction 4. Missing persons -- Fiction 5. Father-daughter relationship -- Fiction

    ISBN 978-1-59990-063-6; 1-59990-063-7

                                LC 2007-30845

When seventeen-year-old Genesis Sommer's father disappears on Moosehead Lake near their small-town Maine home in mid-November, she must cope with the pressure of keeping her family together, even while rumors about the event plague her.

This is "a heartbreaking story from the very beginning, but Les Becquets turns it into something well beyond a mere tearjerker. . . . It's a tender story of a tough, smart, loving girl who finds that she can rise to the challenge of what she's lost because of what she's gained. Readers will understand her and admire her, and find her difficult indeed to forget." Bull Cent Child Books

Leslea, Newman

October mourning; a song for Matthew Shepard. Lesléa Newman. Candlewick 2012 xi, 111 p.p

Grades: 10 11 12

    1. Poetry -- Collections 2. Gays -- Fiction 3. Novels in verse 4. Murder -- Fiction 5. Hate crimes -- Fiction 6. Laramie (Wyo.) -- Fiction

    ISBN 0763658073; 9780763658076

                                LC 2011048358

Stonewall Honor Book (2013)

In this book "lesbian literary icon [Lesléa] Newman offers a 68-poem tribute to Matthew Shepard, . . . [who was] lured from a bar by two men who drove him to the outskirts of town, beat him mercilessly, tied him to a fence and left him to die. This cycle of poems, meant to be read sequentially as a whole, incorporates Newman's reflections on Shepard's killing and its aftermath, using a number of . . . literary devices to portray. . . that fateful night and the trial that followed." (Kirkus Reviews)

Includes bibliographical references.

Lester, Joan Steinau

Black, white, other. Zondervan 2011 222p $15.99

Grades: 7 8 9 10

    1. Divorce -- Fiction 2. Slavery -- Fiction 3. California -- Fiction 4. Family life -- Fiction 5. Grandmothers -- Fiction 6. Race relations -- Fiction 7. Racially mixed people -- Fiction

    ISBN 978-0-310-72763-7; 0-310-72763-4

                                LC 2011015208

Twenty miles from Oakland, California, where fires have led to racial tension, multi-racial fifteen-year-old Nina faces the bigotry of long-time friends, her parents' divorce, and her brother's misbehavior, while learning of her great-great grandmother Sarah's escape from slavery.

"Lester . . . conjures a credible plot and complications; divorce is a fact of life and racially mixed heritage is conspicuously becoming one. The simple contrapuntal narrative of Sarah Armstrong's escaping slavery distinguishes the book emotionally and psychologically, raising it above other issue-oriented YA novels. Lester writes with social sensitivity and an ear for teen language and concerns. This is engaging treatment of a challenging subject that comes with little precedent." Publ Wkly

Includes bibliographical references

Lester, Julius

★ **Day** of tears; a novel in dialogue. Hyperion 2005 177p hardcover o.p. pa $7.99

Grades: 7 8 9 10

1. Slavery -- Fiction 2. African Americans -- Fiction
ISBN 0-7868-0490-4; 1-42310-409-9 pa

Coretta Scott King Award for text

Emma has taken care of the Butler children since Sarah and Frances's mother, Fanny, left. Emma wants to raise the girls to have good hearts, as a rift over slavery has ripped the Butler household apart. Now, to pay off debts, Pierce Butler wants to cash in his slave "assets", possibly including Emma.

"The horror of the auction and its aftermath is unforgettable. . . . The racism is virulent (there's widespread use of the n-word). The personal voices make this a stirring text for group discussion." Booklist

★ **Guardian**. Amistad/HarperTeen 2008 129p $16.99; lib bdg $17.89

Grades: 7 8 9 10

1. Lynching -- Fiction 2. Race relations -- Fiction 3. Southern States -- Fiction 4. African Americans -- Fiction
ISBN 978-0-06-155890-0; 0-06-155890-7; 978-0-06-155891-7 lib bdg; 0-06-155891-5 lib bdg

LC 2008-14251

In a rural southern town in 1946, a white man and his son witness the lynching of an innocent black man. Includes historical note on lynching.

"The author's understated, haunting prose is as compelling as it is dark; . . . [the story] leaves a deep impression." Publ Wkly

Includes bibliographical references

Time's memory. Farrar, Straus & Giroux 2006 230p $17

Grades: 8 9 10 11 12

1. Slavery -- Fiction 2. African Americans -- Fiction
ISBN 0-374-37178-4; 978-0-374-37178-4

LC 2005-47716

Ekundayo, a Dogon spirit brought to America from Africa, inhabits the body of a young African American slave on a Virginia plantation, where he experiences loss, sorrow, and reconciliation in the months preceding the Civil War.

"More than a picture of slavery through the eyes of those enslaved or their captors, Lester's narrative evokes spiritual images of Mali's Dogon people." SLJ

Levenseller, Tricia

Daughter of the pirate king. Tricia Levenseller. Feiwel & Friends 2017 320 p.

Grades: 8 9 10 11

1. Love -- Fiction 2. Pirates -- Fiction 3. Princesses -- Fiction
9781250095961; 9781250095978

LC 2016009251

"Sent on a mission to retrieve an ancient hidden map—the key to a legendary treasure trove--seventeen-year-old pirate captain Alosa deliberately allows herself to be captured by her enemies, giving her the perfect opportunity to search their ship. More than a match for the ruthless pirate crew, Alosa has only one thing standing between her and the map: her captor, the unexpectedly clever and unfairly attractive first mate Riden." (Publisher's note)

Levine, Ellen, 1939-2012

In trouble. Carolrhoda Lab 2011 200p $17.95

Grades: 7 8 9 10

1. Rape -- Fiction 2. Abortion -- Fiction 3. Pregnancy -- Fiction 4. Family life -- Fiction 5. New York (State) -- Fiction
ISBN 978-0-7613-6558-7; 0-7613-6558-3; 9780761365587; 0761365583

LC 2010051448

In 1950s New York, sixteen-year-old Jamie's life is unsettled since her father returned from serving time in prison for refusing to name people as Communists, when her best friend turns to Jamie for help with an unplanned pregnancy.

"The author's notes and acknowledgments draw together the past and present, making the book a good choice for required reading in sociology or advanced American history classes. In Trouble should be available in every library serving young adults." SLJ

Levine, Kristin

★ The **best** bad luck I ever had. Putnam 2009 266p $16.99

Grades: 6 7 8 9

1. Friendship -- Fiction 2. Prejudices -- Fiction 3. Family life -- Fiction 4. Country life -- Fiction 5. Race relations -- Fiction
ISBN 978-0-399-25090-3; 0-399-25090-5

LC 2008-11570

In Moundville, Alabama, in 1917, twelve-year-old Dit hopes the new postmaster will have a son his age, but instead he meets Emma, who is black, and their friendship challenges accepted ways of thinking and leads them to save the life of a condemned man.

"Tension builds just below the surface of this energetic, seamlessly narrated . . . novel. . . . Levine handles the setting with grace and nuance." Publ Wkly

Levithan, David

★ **Boy** meets boy. David Levithan. Alfred A. Knopf 2003 208p.

Grades: 9 10 11 12

1. Teenage boys -- Fiction; 2. Gay teenagers -- Fiction
ISBN 0-375-82400-6; 9780375832994; 0-375-83299-8, $8.95

LC 2002-73154

"Somewhere on the eastern coast of the US that's home to Francesca Lia Block's Los Angeles is a town where six-foot-five drag queens play high-school football, kindergarten teachers write comments like 'Definitely gay and has a very good sense of self' on student report cards, quiz-bowl teams are as important as football teams, and cheerleaders ride Harleys. Paul and his friends go to high school in this town. Paul meets Noah, falls for him, does something dumb, and loses him. The last half of the story is about Paul working to get Noah back." (Kirkus)

★ **Every** day; by David Levithan. Alfred A. Knopf 2012 336 p. (hard cover) $16.99

Grades: 9 10 11 12

1. Love stories 2. Occult fiction 3. Teenagers -- Fiction 4. Love -- Fiction 5. Interpersonal relations -- Fiction
ISBN 0307931889; 9780307931887; 9780307931894; 9780307975638; 9780375971112

LC 2012004173

This book follows A, "who takes over the body of a different person each day at midnight. Right around A's 6,000th day on the planet, A meets Rhiannon—girlfriend of current host body Justin—and falls in love. A is careful not to disrupt the lives of the bodies he/she inhabits (A doesn't identify as male or female), but that starts to change as A pursues Rhiannon." (Publishers Weekly)

"Levithan's self-conscious, analytical style marries perfectly with the plot...Readers will devour his trademark poetic wordplay and cadences that feel as fresh as they were when he wrote Boy Meets Boy (2003)." Kirkus

Hold me closer: the Tiny Cooper story. By David Levithan. Dutton Books 2015 208 p.

Grades: 9 10 11 12

1. Dating (Social customs) -- Fiction 2. Gays -- Fiction 3. Love -- Fiction 4. Musicals -- Fiction 5. Gay teenagers -- Fiction
0525428844; 9780525428848, $17.99

LC 2014039368

This book by David Levithan presents the "autobiographical musical extravaganza" composed by the character Tiny Cooper in the book "Will Grayson, Will Grayson". "The musical traces Tiny's life from birth through age sixteen. . . . Tiny . . . delivers extensive stage directions that tell some of the story behind the story, indicating tone, mood, and what other musicals he's channeling so that readers will be able to visualize the production." (Bulletin of the Center for Children's Books)

Companion book to: Will Grayson, Will Grayson by John Green and David Levithan.

Love is the higher law. Alfred A. Knopf 2009 167p $15.99; lib bdg $18.99

Grades: 8 9 10 11 12

1. LGBT youth -- Fiction 2. New York (N.Y.) -- Fiction 3. September 11 terrorist attacks, 2001 -- Fiction
ISBN 978-0-375-83468-4; 0-375-83468-0; 978-0-375-93468-1 lib bdg; 0-375-93468-5 lib bdg

LC 2008-40886

Three New York City teens express their reactions to the bombing of the World Trade Center on September 11, 2001, and its impact on their lives and the world.

"The author's prose has never been deeper in thought or feeling. His writing here is especially pure—unsentimental, restrained, and full of love for his characters and setting. . . . Levithan captures the mood of post-9/11 New York exquisitely, slashed open to reveal a deep heart." SLJ

★ **Two** boys kissing; by David Levithan. Alfred A. Knopf 2013 208 p. (hardcover library binding) $19.99

Grades: 8 9 10 11 12

1. School stories 2. Gay teenagers -- Fiction 3. Gays -- Fiction 4. Love -- Fiction 5. Homosexuality -- Fiction 6. Social change -- Fiction
ISBN 0307931900; 0375971122; 9780307931900; 9780307931917; 9780375971129

LC 2012047089

Stonewall Honor Book: Children and Young Adult (2014)

Lambda Literary Awards - LGBT Children's/YA (2014)

In this book, students Craig and Henry are trying to set a world record for the longest kiss They "are no longer dating, throwing an element of uncertainty into an act that's romantic, political, and personal. Neil and Peter have been dating for a year and are beginning to wonder what's next. Avery, 'born a boy that the rest of the world saw as a girl,' and Ryan are caught up in the dizzying excitement of meeting someone new. And Cooper is rapidly losing himself into a digital oblivion." (Publishers Weekly)

"Craig and Harry attempt to break the world record for longest kiss, which, in turn, affects the lives of the people around them. Narrated by a ghostly chorus of past generations of gay men who died of AIDS, Levithan's latest novel weaves together an informed (sometimes melodramatic) perspective on the past with the present-day stories of seven boys constructing their own sexual identities." (Horn Book)

Levitin, Sonia

Strange relations. Alfred A. Knopf 2007 298p hardcover o.p. pa $6.50

Grades: 7 8 9 10

1. Jews -- Fiction 2. Hawaii -- Fiction 3. Cousins -- Fiction 4. Religion -- Fiction
ISBN 978-0-375-83751-7; 0-375-83751-5; 978-0-440-23963-5 pa; 0-440-23963-X pa

LC 2006-33275

Fifteen-year-old Marne is excited to be able to spend her summer vacation in Hawaii, not realizing the change in her lifestyle it would bring staying with her aunt, seven cousins, and uncle who is a Chasidic rabbi.

"It's rare to find such well-developed characters, empathetic and sensitive religious treatment, and carefully crafted plotlines in one novel." SLJ

Lewis, Stewart

The **secret** ingredient; Stewart Lewis. Delacorte Press 2013 256 p. (hc) $17.99

Grades: 7 8 9 10

1. Cooking -- Fiction 2. Mothers -- Fiction 3. Interpersonal relations -- Fiction 4. Self-realization -- Fiction 5. Los Angeles (Calif.) -- Fiction
ISBN 0385743319; 9780375991066; 9780385743310

LC 2012027203

This novel by Stewart Lewis is a "journey of family, food, romance, and self-discovery as Olivia, a teen chef living in L.A., finds a vintage cookbook and begins a search for her birthmother that will change her life forever. A new job leads Olivia to a gorgeous, mysterious boy named Theo. And as Olivia cooks the recipes from a vintage cookbook she stumbles upon, she begins to wonder if the mother she's never known might be the secret ingredient she's been lacking." (Publisher's note)

"Adopted by two dads, Olivia begins to sense a void in her life. Serendipitously, Olivia finds her supposedly "nameless" birth mother but quickly realizes that maybe the secret ingredient to a fulfilled life is appreciating what one already has. Lewis's mature protagonist adapts remarkably well to her nontraditional life in this story that limns themes of adolescence, adoption, illness, and financial instability." (Horn Book)

Lieberman, Leanne

Lauren Yanofsky hates the Holocaust; Leanne Lieberman. Orca Book Publishers 2013 240 p. (paperback) $12.95; (ebook) $12.99

Grades: 7 8 9 10

1. Jews -- Fiction 2. Holocaust, 1939-1945 -- Fiction
ISBN 1459801091; 9781459801097; 9781459801103 pdf; 9781459801110

LC 2012952950

In this novel, by Leanne Lieberman, "Lauren Yanofsky doesn't want to be Jewish anymore. Her father, a noted Holocaust historian, keeps giving her Holocaust memoirs to read, and her mother doesn't understand why Lauren hates the idea of Jewish youth camps and family vacations to Holocaust memorials. But when Lauren sees some of her friends . . . playing Nazi war games, she is faced with a terrible choice: betray her friends or betray her heritage." (Publisher's note)

"Lieberman . . . smoothly weaves humor and knowledge about Judaism through Lauren's story. Lauren's narration is contemplative and from the heart, and readers should relate to her attempts to identify her beliefs and tackle life's big questions." Pub Wkly

Off pointe. Leanne Lieberman. Orca Book Publishers 2015 128 p. (Orca limelights)

Grades: 6 7 8 9

1. Ballet dancers -- Fiction 2. Camps -- Fiction 3. Dancers -- Fiction 4. Ballet -- Fiction 5. Hi-Lo books 6. Friendship -- Fiction
1459802802; 9781459802803, $9.95; 9781459802810; 9781459802827

LC 2014935396

In this novel by Leanne Lieberman "Meg's summer ballet program is canceled and her ballet teacher suggests she attend Camp Dance to learn new dance styles. At camp, Meg struggles to learn contemporary dance. A girl named Logan, who is jealous of Meg's ballet technique and her friendship with Nio . . . makes Meg's life even more difficult. When Meg, Nio and Logan have to work together to create a piece for the final show, arguments threaten to ruin their dance. " (Publisher's note)

Lindstrom, Eric

Not if I see you first. Eric Lindstrom. Little, Brown & Co. 2016 320 p.

Grades: 9 10 11 12

1. Blind -- Fiction 2. Dating (Social customs) -- Fiction 3. Friendship -- Fiction 4. High schools -- Fiction 5. Orphans -- Fiction 6. People with disabilities -- Fiction 7. Schools -- Fiction 8. School stories 9. Teenage girls -- Fiction
9780316259859, $18

LC 2014037483

This novel, by Eric Lindstrom, follows a blind teenage girl. "Parker Grant doesn't need 20/20 vision to see right through you. . . . Just ask Scott Kilpatrick, the boy who broke her heart. When Scott suddenly reappears in her life after being gone for years, . . . avoiding her past quickly proves impossible, and the more Parker learns about what really happened—both with Scott, and her dad—the more she starts to question if things are always as they seem." (Publisher's Note)

"While Lindstrom's debut understandably contains plenty of melancholy, angst, and self-doubt, it also possesses crackling wit, intense teen drama, and a lively pace that pulls readers in, as do the everyday details of Parker's world: spoken-word texts, clever methods of finding her way, and a guide runner who helps Parker when she considers joining the school track team. This unique coming-of-age tale is off and running from the start." Booklist

Linn, Laurent

★ **Draw** the line. Laurent Linn. Margaret K. McElderry Books 2016 528 p. Illustration

Grades: 9 10 11 12

1. Artists -- Fiction 2. Gays -- Fiction 3. Hate crimes -- Fiction 4. High schools -- Fiction 5. Schools -- Fiction 6. Gay teenagers -- Fiction 7. High school students -- Fiction
9781481452809, $17.99; 9781481452816; 1481452800

LC 2015029314

In this novel, by Laurent Linn, "Adrian Piper is used to blending into the background. He may be a talented artist, a sci-fi geek, and gay, but at his Texas high school those traits would only bring him the worst kind of attention. The only place he feels free . . . is at his drawing table, crafting a secret world through his own Renaissance-art-inspired superhero, Graphite. When a shocking hate crime flips his world upside down, Adrian must decide what kind of person he wants to be." (Publisher's note)

"At the risk of revealing his closeted sexuality and artistic talent, a Texas wallflower combats small minds. Adrian Piper dresses to hide. Innocuous palette, faded jeans, a hoodie: disappearing = safety at Rock Hollow High, where Bubbas with a penchant for pickups and longnecks are the dominant species. Adrian's escape from aggressive heteronormativity is "the feel of a 3B pencil skimming across the paper's surface." The result of said skimming: a gay superhero named Graphite with a flair for Renaissance couture and a longing for love. . . . A definite draw for comic-book fans, it will resonate with anyone struggling with a concealed or revealed identity. More defiant than its superhero's diaphanous costume portends. Bravo." Kirkus

Lippert-Martin, Kristen

Tabula rasa. Kristen Lippert-Martin. Egmont USA 2014 335 p.

Grades: 7 8 9 10

1. Adventure and adventurers -- Fiction 2. Memory -- Fiction 3. Science fiction 4. Hospitals -- Fiction 5. Adventure fiction

1606845187; 9781606845189, $17.99

LC 2013030315

In this book, by Kristen Lippert-Martin, "Sarah starts a crazy battle for her life within the walls of her hospital-turned-prison when a procedure to eliminate her memory goes awry and she starts to remember snatches of her past. Was she an urban terrorist or vigilante? Has the procedure been her salvation or her destruction? The answers lie trapped within her mind. To access them, she'll need the help of the teen computer hacker who's trying to bring the hospital down for his own reasons." (Publisher's note)

"Mysteries stack upon mysteries in this gripping, multi-faceted thriller." Horn Book

Lipsyte, Robert

★ The **contender**. Harper & Row 1967 182p hardcover o.p. pa $5.99

Grades: 7 8 9 10

1. Boxing -- Fiction 2. African Americans -- Fiction 3. Harlem (New York, N.Y.) -- Fiction

ISBN 0-06-447039-3

ALA YALSA Margaret A. Edwards Award (2001)

"After a street fight in which he is the chief target, Alfred wanders into a gym in his neighborhood. He decides not only to improve his physical condition but also to become a boxer. Because of this interest Alfred's life is completely changed. He assumes a more positive outlook on his immediate future, even within the confines of a black ghetto." Shapiro. Fic for Youth. 3d edition

Followed by The brave (1991) and The chief (1993)

Raiders night. HarperTempest 2006 232p hardcover o.p. pa $6.99

Grades: 9 10 11 12

1. Rape -- Fiction 2. Football -- Fiction 3. Drug abuse -- Fiction

ISBN 978-0-06-059946-1; 0-06-059946-4; 978-0-06-059948-5 pa; 0-06-059948-0 pa

LC 2005-17865

Matt Rydeck, co-captain of his high school football team, endures a traumatic season as he witnesses the rape of a rookie player by teammates and grapples with his own use of performance-enhancing drugs.

This is "is a riveting and chilling look inside contemporary high school football." Publ Wkly

Littlefield, Sophie

Infected. Sophie Littlefield. Delacorte Press 2015 256 p.

Grades: 7 8 9 10

1. Dating (Social customs) -- Fiction 2. Spies -- Fiction 3. Survival -- Fiction 4. National security -- United States 5. Conspiracies -- Fiction 6. Family secrets

-- Fiction

0385741065; 9780375989834; 9780385741064, $17.99

LC 2013046923

"Carina's senior year is spiraling downward. Fast. Both her mother and her uncle, the only two family members she's ever known, are dead. Their deaths were accidents, unfortunate results of the highly confidential research they performed for a national security organization. The people Carina loved kept dangerous secrets. Secrets that make her question the life she's been living up to now." (Publisher's note)

"Nail-biting action with a scientifically and technologically involved plotline gives this novel an edge, and, moreover, the character development is surprisingly rich given the fast pace of the narrative. The weight of the themes also keeps the story from reading like a movie script. Red herrings keep the reader guessing until the end." Booklist

Littman, Sarah

Backlash. Sarah Darer Littman. Scholastic Press 2015 325 p.

Grades: 7 8 9

1. Bullying -- Fiction 2. Cyberbullying -- Fiction 3. Families -- Fiction 4. Family life -- Fiction 5. Friendship -- Fiction 6. Neighbors -- Fiction 7. Sisters -- Fiction 8. Suicidal behavior -- Fiction 9. Suicide -- Fiction 10. Bullies -- Fiction

0545651263; 9780545651264, $17.99; 9780545651271; 9780545755023

LC 2014020226

In this book, by Sarah Darer Littman, "Lara just got told off on Facebook. She thought that Christian liked her, that he was finally going to ask her to his school's homecoming dance. It's been a long time since Lara's felt this bad, this depressed. . . . Bree used to be BBFs with overweight, depressed Lara in middle school, but constantly listening to Lara's problems got to be too much. Bree's secretly glad that Christian's pointed out Lara's flaws to the world." (Publisher's note)

"The depression and bullying are handled realistically without sugarcoating, and fortunately, consequences are applied. An excellent choice for any antibullying campaign." Booklist

Life, after; [by] Sarah Darer Littman. Scholastic Press 2010 281p $17.99

Grades: 7 8 9 10 11 12

1. Terrorism -- Fiction 2. Immigrants -- Fiction

ISBN 978-0-545-15144-3; 0-545-15144-9

After a terrorist attack kills Dani's aunt and unborn cousin, life in Argentina—private school, a boyfriend, a loving family—crumbles quickly. In order to escape a country that is sinking under their feet, Dani and her family move to the United States.

The author "weaves sensitively articulated themes . . . and credible teen banter into an emotionally complex tale." Booklist

Liu, Jennie

Girls on the line. By Jennie Liu. Carolrhoda Lab 2018 232 p.

Grades: 10 11 12

1. Factories -- Fiction; 2. Missing persons -- Fiction; 3. Orphans -- Fiction; 4. Pregnancy -- Fiction; 5. China -- Fiction

9781512459388, $18.99

LC 2017031554

In this book, by Jennie Liu, "Yun loves...her factory job.... and Yong, her new boyfriend.... Some people say... [Yong is] a bride trafficker.... Yun.... discovers she's pregnant the same day she gets fired from her job. If she can't... terminate the pregnancy, she'll face a huge fine for having an unauthorized child. [Her friend] Luli wants to help..., but she's worried about what Yong might do...especially when Yun disappears." (Publisher's note)

Lloyd, Saci

★ The **carbon** diaries 2015. Holiday House 2009 330p il map $17.95

Grades: 8 9 10 11 12

1. Science fiction 2. Family life -- Fiction 3. Great Britain -- Fiction 4. Conservation of natural resources -- Fiction

ISBN 978-0-8234-2190-9; 0-8234-2190-2

LC 2008-19712

First published 2008 in the United Kingdom

In 2015, when England becomes the first nation to introduce carbon dioxide rationing in a drastic bid to combat climate change, sixteen-year-old Laura documents the first year of rationing as her family spirals out of control.

"Deeply compulsive and urgently compulsory reading." Booklist

Includes bibliographical references

Followed by The carbon diaries 2017 (2010)

The **carbon** diaries 2017. Holiday House 2010 326p il map $17.95

Grades: 8 9 10 11 12

1. Science fiction 2. College students -- Fiction 3. London (England) -- Fiction 4. Conservation of natural resources -- Fiction

ISBN 978-0-8234-2260-9; 0-8234-2260-7

Sequel to: The carbon diaries 2015 (2009)

First published 2009 in the United Kingdom

Two years after England introduces carbon dioxide rationing to combat climatic change, eighteen-year-old Laura chronicles her first year at a London university as natural disasters and political upheaval disrupt her studies.

"The friction of living life in times of radical upheaval remains potent, sobering, and awfully exciting." Booklist

Lloyd-Jones, Emily

Illusive. Emily Lloyd-Jones. Little, Brown & Co. 2014 416 p.

Grades: 7 8 9 10 11 12

1. Adventure and adventurers -- Fiction 2. Organized crime -- Fiction 3. Robbers and outlaws -- Fiction 4. Science fiction 5. Superheroes -- Fiction 6. Vaccines -- Fiction 7. Dystopian fiction

0316254568; 9780316254564, $18

LC 2013025295

In this young adult science fiction novel by Emily Lloyd-Jones, "When the MK virus swept across the planet, a vaccine was created to stop the epidemic, but it came with some unexpected side effects. A small percentage of the population developed superhero-like powers. Seventeen-year-old Ciere Giba has the handy ability to change her appearance at will. She's what's known as an illusionist...She's also a thief." (Publisher's note)

"Ciere, a teenage career criminal with the ability to create illusions, lives in a dystopian future where a vaccine gone wrong created a feared minority of people with superpowers. Her latest job pulls her and her Dickensian gang of misfit allies into a power struggle involving the future of the vaccine. Innovative world-building and a scrappy protagonist strengthen this high-stakes caper." Horn Book

Sequel: Deceptive (2015)

Lo, Malinda

Adaptation; Malinda Lo. Little, Brown Books for Young Readers 2012 400 p. (hardcover) $17.99

Grades: 9 10 11 12

1. Mystery fiction 2. Secrecy -- Fiction 3. Lesbians -- Fiction 4. Love -- Fiction 5. Science fiction 6. Conspiracies -- Fiction 7. Sexual orientation -- Fiction 8. Genetic engineering -- Fiction 9. Extraterrestrial beings -- Fiction

ISBN 0316197963; 9780316197960

LC 2012005489

Author Malinda Lo tells the story of "Reese and David, traveling home after a disastrous debate tournament, [who] are in a near-fatal car accident near a mysterious government facility. The tension is relentless until the teens make it safely back to San Francisco, at which point romantic entanglements (Reese falls for Amber, but maybe she likes David too) detract from the strange abilities Reese and David are developing and the conspiracies they begin to unravel (with lots of men in black after the)." (Kirkus)

★ **Ash**. Little, Brown and Co. 2009 264p $16.99; pa $8.99

Grades: 8 9 10 11

1. Fairy tales 2. Love stories 3. Fairies -- Fiction 4. Stepfamilies -- Fiction

ISBN 978-0-316-04009-9; 0-316-04009-6; 978-0-316-04010-5 pa; 0-316-04010-X pa

LC 2009-17471

ALA YALSA Morris Award Finalist, 2010

In this variation on the Cinderella story, Ash grows up believing in the fairy realm that the king and his philosophers have sought to suppress, until one day she must choose between a handsome fairy cursed to love her and the King's Huntress whom she loves.

"Part heart-pounding lesbian romance and part universal coming-of-age story, Lo's powerful tale is richly embroidered with folklore and glittering fairy magic that will draw fans of Sharon Shinn's earthy, herb-laced fantasies." Booklist

Followed by Huntress (2011)

Huntress. Little, Brown 2011 371p map $17.99

Grades: 9 10 11 12

1. Fairy tales 2. Love stories 3. Fairies -- Fiction 4. Lesbians -- Fiction 5. Voyages and travels -- Fiction

ISBN 978-0-316-04007-5; 0-316-04007-X

LC 2010-38827

"A 'Tam Lin'-inspired rendition of fairy society blends nicely with the author's Chinese and I Ching-inspired human society, creating a delicate, unusual setting; and although the expeditionary plot has an overly deliberate pace, the episodes are varied and emotional enough to retain interest. Most notably, the inclusion of gay characters in a young adult fantasy, and the natural unfolding of their relationship, comes as a refreshing change." Horn Book

Inheritance; by Malinda Lo. Little, Brown and Co. 2013 470 p. $18

Grades: 9 10 11 12

1. Love stories 2. Teenagers -- Fiction 3. Human-alien encounters -- Fiction 4. Love -- Fiction 5. Science fiction 6. Kidnapping -- Fiction 7. Conspiracies -- Fiction 8. Sexual orientation -- Fiction 9. Genetic engineering -- Fiction 10. Extraterrestrial beings -- Fiction

ISBN 0316198005; 9780316198004

LC 2012048433

Sequel to: Adaptation

In this book, by Malinda Lo, "after a car accident, mortally injured Reese and David are revived by an injection of alien DNA that has given the teens special abilities. They are kidnapped by brutal government forces. . . . Returned home, Reese and David are caught in a web of intrigue and lies. . . . The fate of the world seems to be at risk as the government, a secret faction of the government, and the aliens square off at the United Nations." (School Library Journal)

"Reese (Adaptation) juggles her discovery that the government has been working for decades with aliens called the Imria and her feelings for her Imrian ex and her new guy. When huge secrets are revealed, romantic alliances get back-burnered as Reese tries to understand what's next for Earth. Clever plot and strong world-building are this sequel's strengths." (Horn Book)

A **line** in the dark. By Malinda Lo. Dutton Books 2017 281 p.

Grades: 8 9 10 11

1. Best friends -- Fiction; 2. Chinese Americans -- Fiction; 3. Dating (Social customs) -- Fiction; 4. Friendship -- Fiction; 5. Lesbians -- Fction; 6. Murder -- Fiction; 7. Social classes -- Fiction; 8. Massachusetts -- Fiction

9780735227422, $17.99; 9780735227446

LC 2017003862

In this book, by Malinda Lo, "Jess Wong is Angie Redmond's best friend. And that's the most important thing.... But when Angie...fall[s] for Margot Adams, a girl from the nearby boarding school, Jess can see it coming a mile away.... As Angie drags Jess further into Margot's circle, Jess discovers...[that s]ecrets and cruelty lie just beneath the...world of wealth and privilege, and...Jess knows [that] Angie won't be able to handle the consequences." (Publisher's note)

"In this unusually structured murder mystery, Lo (Inheritance) explores the knotty jealousies, romantic longings, and class disparities among students at a pair of Massachusetts high schools." Pub Wkly

Lockhart, E.

The **boy** book; a study of habits and behaviors, plus techniques for taming them. Delacorte Press 2006 193p $15.95; lib bdg $17.99

Grades: 8 9 10 11 12

1. School stories 2. Friendship -- Fiction 3. Dating (Social customs) -- Fiction

ISBN 978-0-385-73208-6; 0-385-73208-2; 978-0-385-90239-7 lib bdg; 0-385-90239-5 lib bdg

LC 2006-4601

A high school junior continues her quest for relevant data on the male species, while enjoying her freedom as a newly licensed driver and examining her friendship with a clean-living vegetarian classmate.

"Lockhart achieves the perfect balance of self-deprecating humor and self-pity in Ruby, and thus imbues her with such realism that she seems almost to fly off the page." Voice Youth Advocates

The **boyfriend** list; (15 guys, 11 shrink appointments, 4 ceramic frogs, and me, Ruby Oliver) Delacorte Press 2005 240p hardcover o.p. pa $8.95

Grades: 9 10 11 12

1. School stories 2. Washington (State) -- Fiction 3. Dating (Social customs) -- Fiction

ISBN 0-385-73206-6; 0-385-73207-4 pa

LC 2004-6691

A Seattle fifteen-year-old explains some of the reasons for her recent panic attacks, including breaking up with her boyfriend, losing all her girlfriends, tensions between her performance-artist mother and her father, and more.

"Readers will find many of Ruby's experiences familiar, and they'll appreciate the story as a lively, often entertaining read." Booklist

Other titles about Ruby Oliver are:

The boy book (2006)

Real live boyfriends (2010)

The treasure map of boys (2009)

Dramarama. Hyperion 2007 311p $15.99

Grades: 7 8 9 10 11 12

1. School stories 2. Actors -- Fiction 3. Friendship -- Fiction

ISBN 0-7868-3815-9; 978-0-7868-3815-8

LC 2006-49599

Spending their summer at Wildewood Academy, an elite boarding school for the performing arts, tests the bond between best friends Sadye and Demi.

"Teens will identify strongly with both the heartbreak and the humor in this authentic portrayal of friendships maturing and decaying." SLJ

★ The **disreputable** history of Frankie Landau-Banks. Hyperion 2008 352p $16.99; pa $8.99

Grades: 7 8 9 10 11 12

1. School stories

ISBN 0-7868-3818-3; 0-7868-3819-1 pa; 978-0-7868-3818-9; 978-0-7868-3819-6 pa

Michael L. Printz Award honor book, 2009

"On her return to Alabaster Prep . . . [Frankie] attracts the attention of gorgeous Matthew . . . [who] is a member of the Loyal Order of the Basset Hounds, an all-male Alabaster secret society. . . . Frankie engineers her own guerilla membership by assuming a false online identity. . . . Lockhart creates a unique, indelible character. . . . Teens will be galvanized." Booklist

★ **Genuine** fraud. E. Lockhart. Delacorte Press 2017 272 p.

Grades: 7 8 9 10 11 12

    1. Psychological fiction; 2. Deception -- Fiction; 3. Best friends -- Fiction

9781471406638; 9780375991844; 9780385744775, $18.99; 9781524770679

                  LC 2017009709

In this book, by E. Lockhart, "Jule West Williams is 18, white, and an orphan, all of which she has in common with her best friend, heiress Imogen Sokoloff -- or does she? Jule, an impulsive, complicated protagonist like no other, tells her story as though she were living in an adventure movie.... She's proud of her strength and fighting ability, her talents for disguises and imitating accents." (Kirkus Reviews)

"This quietly unsettling, cinematic novel is deliciously suspenseful, and while it's slim, it packs a real punch." (Booklist)

How to be bad; [by] E. Lockhart, Sarah Mlynowski [and] Lauren Myracle. HarperTeen 2008 325p $16.99; lib bdg $17.89

Grades: 9 10 11 12

    1. Friendship -- Fiction 2. Automobile travel -- Fiction

ISBN 978-0-06-128422-9; 0-06-128422-X; 978-0-06-128423-6 lib bdg; 0-06-128423-8 lib bdg

                  LC 2007-52946

Told in alternating voices, Jesse, Vicks, and Mel, hoping to leave all their worries and woes behind, escape their small town by taking a road trip to Miami.

"Whip-smart dialogue and a fast-moving, picaresque plot that zooms from lump-in-the-throat moments to all-out giddiness will keep readers going, and it's a testimony to how real these girls seem that the final chapters are profoundly satisfying rather than tidy." Publ Wkly

Real live boyfriends; yes, boyfriends, plural, if my life weren't complicated I wouldn't be Ruby Oliver. Delacorte Press 2010 224p $16.99; lib bdg $19.99

Grades: 8 9 10 11

    1. School stories 2. Seattle (Wash.) -- Fiction 3. Dating (Social customs) -- Fiction

ISBN 978-0-385-73428-8; 0-385-73428-X; 978-0-385-90438-4 lib bdg; 0-385-90438-X lib bdg

                  LC 2009-41988

Now a senior at her Seattle prep school, Ruby continues her angst-filled days coping with the dilemmas of boyfriends, college applications, her parents' squabbling, and realizing that her "deranged" persona may no longer apply.

The treasure map of boys; Noel, Jackson, Finn, Hutch, Gideon--and me, Ruby Oliver. Delacorte Press 2009 244p $15.99; lib bdg $18.99

Grades: 8 9 10 11 12

    1. School stories 2. Friendship -- Fiction 3. Seattle

(Wash.) -- Fiction 4. Dating (Social customs) -- Fiction

ISBN 978-0-385-73426-4; 0-385-73426-3; 978-0-385-90437-7 lib bdg; 0-385-90437-1 lib bdg

                  LC 2008-33062

A Seattle sixteen-year-old juggles therapy, running a school bake sale, coping with her performance artist mother, growing distant from an old friend, and conflicting feelings about her ex-boyfriend and potential new boyfriends.

"Replete with wordplay, footnotes and . . . lots of laugh-out-loud moments, this is a worthy follow-up." Kirkus

★ **We** were liars; E. Lockhart. Delacorte Press 2014 240 p. (hardback) $17.99

Grades: 7 8 9 10 11 12

    1. Summer -- Fiction 2. Wealth -- Fiction 3. Love -- Fiction 4. Amnesia -- Fiction 5. Families -- Fiction 6. Friendship -- Fiction

ISBN 038574126X; 9780375989940; 9780385741262

                  LC 2013042127

"Cadence Sinclair Easton comes from an old-money family, headed by a patriarch who owns a private island off of Cape Cod. Each summer, the extended family gathers at the various houses on the island, and Cadence, her cousins Johnny and Mirren, and friend Gat (the four "Liars"), have been inseparable since age eight....The story, while lightly touching on issues of class and race, more fully focuses on dysfunctional family drama, a heart-wrenching romance between Cadence and Gat, and, ultimately, the suspense of what happened during that fateful summer. The ending is a stunner that will haunt readers for a long time to come." (School Library Journal)

London, Alex

Black wings beating. Alex London. Farrar, Straus & Giroux 2018 432 p.

Grades: 8 9 10 11 12

    1. Brothers and sisters -- Fiction; 2. Falconry -- Fiction; 3. Fantasy; 4. Twins -- Fiction; 5. Fantasy fiction

9780374306823, $17.99

                  LC 2018001439

In this book in the Skybound Saga, by Alex London, "the people of Uztar have long looked to the sky with hope and wonder. Nothing in their world is more revered than the birds of prey and no one more honored than the falconers who call them to their fists. Brysen strives to be a great falconer -- while his twin sister, Kylee, rejects her ancient gifts for the sport.... Together the twins must journey into the treacherous mountains to trap the Ghost Eagle." (Publisher's note)

Guardian; Alex London. Philomel Books. 2014 340p $17.99

Grades: 7 8 9

    1. Epidemics -- Fiction 2. Gays -- Fiction 3. Science fiction 4. Social classes -- Fiction 5. Dystopian fiction

ISBN: 0399165762; 9780399165764

                  LC 2013025938

"It's a grave new world when the revolution a reluctant hero inspired could mean the death of everyone he tried to save, including himself. In this sequel to Proxy (2013), radical groups form in the wake of the Jubilee. The Reconciliation staunchly endorses tech-free purity, while Machinists demand a renaissance of the networks. Reluctant 16-year-old hero Syd is paraded as a political puppet, labeled a savior by supporters and marked a target by the opposition. His importance as a mascot for the Reconciliation necessitates a bodyguard, 17-year-old Liam. Liam is strong (he has a killer metal hand), silent (too shy for vocal eloquence) and will do anything to remain near Syd for reasons other than professional integrity. Amid political upheaval, an illness begins to spread, rendering victims' blue blood black and diminishing their mental faculties. Syd has been a hesitant political figure but knows he is the only hope for ending the illness." (Kirkus)

"Nonstop action and breakneck pace characterize this exceptional thriller. London provides his audience with an intricate plot, enriched by fine world-building and believable characters. The ample backstory will enable readers to enjoy Guardian without having read Proxy, although most will want to read these in sequence. This thought-provoking and breathtaking novel belongs in all collections serving young adults." VOYA

Proxy. Alex London. Philomel 2013 379 p.
Grades: 7 8 9 10

1. Gays -- Fiction; 2. Science fiction; 3. Social classes -- Fiction; 4. Dystopian fiction
ISBN 0399257764; 9780399257766, $17.99
LC 2012039704

In this book, "Knox is a 'patron,' a privileged and wealthy citizen of Mountain City. His only concerns are hacking, scoring with girls, and causing trouble while angering his bigwig dad. His proxy, a person who is contractually obligated to serve out Knox's punishments, is a gay teen. In exchange for working as a proxy, Syd is able to pay off his debts. When Knox accidentally kills a girl, 16 years at the Old Sterling Work Colony is too great a punishment for Syd to bear, so he escapes." (School Library Journal)

Long, Hayley

Sophie someone. Hayley Long. Candlewick Press 2017 258 p.
Grades: 6 7 8 9

1. Family secrets -- Fiction; 2. Teenagers -- Fiction; 3. Domestic fiction
0763689955; 9780763689957, $16.99
LC 2017933643

In this novel, by Hayley Long, "Sophie and her circle of family and friends are sympathetic and appealing in all their flawed humanity. Her peculiar way of speech soon reads as clearly as plain English and perfectly mirrors her internal turmoil as she navigates her parents' shift from just mambo and don to people with a past she never imagined -- which, to some extent, is a transformation every young person will understand." (Kirkus Reviews)

Longshore, Katherine

Brazen. By Katherine Longshore. Viking, published by Penguin Group 2014 528 p.
Grades: 9 10 11 12

1. Courts and courtiers -- Fiction 2. Kings, queens, rulers, etc. -- Fiction 3. Howard, Mary, Lady, 1519-1557 -- Fiction 4. Richmond and Somerset, Mary Fitzroy, Duchess of, 1519-1557 -- Fiction 5. Great Britain -- History -- Henry VIII, 1509-1547 -- Fiction 6.

Romance fiction
067001401X; 9780670014019, $17.99
LC 2013026557

In this young adult romance novel by Katherine Longshore, "Mary Howard has always lived in the shadow of her powerful family. But when she's married off to Henry Fitzroy, King Henry VIII's illegitimate son, she rockets into the Tudor court's inner circle. Mary and 'Fitz' join a tight clique of rebels who test the boundaries of court's strict rules with their games, dares, and flirtations." (Publisher's note)

"At age fourteen, Mary Howard and Henry FitzRoy (an illegitimate son of King Henry VIII) were married but forbidden to consummate the relationship. From this thin skein of historic fact, Longshore weaves a tale of love growing amid the corruption, ambition, and betrayals of the Tudor court. Detailed research and a deftly composed heroine make this hefty historical romance novel satisfying." Horn Book

Lowitz, Leza

Jet Black and the ninja wind; Leza Lowitz, Shogo Oketani. Tuttle Publishing 2013 319 p. $17.99
Grades: 9 10 11 12

1. Ninja -- Fiction 2. Family secrets -- Fiction 3. Japan -- Fiction 4. Secrets -- Fiction 5. Buried treasure -- Fiction 6. Family life -- Japan -- Fiction 7. Adventure and adventurers -- Fiction
ISBN 480531284X; 9784805312841
LC 2013023578

Asian/Pacific American Awards for Literature: Young Adult Lit (2014)

In this book, by Leza Lowitz and Shogo Oketani, "Seventeen-year-old Jet Black is a ninja. There's only one problem—she doesn't know it. Others do, however, and they're scheming to capture her and uncover her secrets. When her mother dies, Jet knows only that she must go to Japan to protect a family treasure hidden in her ancestral land. . . . Stalked by bounty hunters and desperately in love with the man who's been sent to kill her, Jet must be strong enough to protect the treasure." (Publisher's note)

"At her mother's insistence, Rika Kuroi, nicknamed Jet Black, has spent her young life training in the art of combat and ninja techniques-with no idea why. Her mother dies before explaining, and when Jet travels to her family's village in Japan to lay her mother's ashes to rest, she is plunged into a complicated web of ancient mysteries and family secrets... Give this book to anime fans or anyone seeking an engaging and thought-provoking read." (School Library Journal)

Lowry, Lois, 1937-

Gathering blue. Houghton Mifflin 2000 215p $16; pa $8.95
Grades: 5 6 7 8

1. Artists 2. Orphans 3. Science fiction 4. People with physical disabilities
ISBN 0-618-05581-9; 0-385-73256-2 pa
LC 00-24359

Lame and suddenly orphaned, Kira is mysteriously removed from her squalid village to live in the palatial Council Edifice, where she is expected to use her gifts as a weaver to do the bidding of the all-powerful Guardians

"Lowry has once again created a fully realized world full of drama, suspense, and even humor." SLJ

★ The **giver**. Houghton Mifflin 1993 180p
$17; pa $8.95

Grades: 6 7 8 9 10

1. Science fiction

ISBN 0-395-64566-2; 0-385-73255-4 pa

LC 92-15034

Awarded the Newbery Medal, 1994

Given his lifetime assignment at the Ceremony of Twelve, Jonas becomes the receiver of memories shared by only one other in his community and discovers the terrible truth about the society in which he lives.

"A riveting, chilling story that inspires a new appreciation for diversity, love, and even pain. Truly memorable." SLJ

★ **Son**; by Lois Lowry. Houghton Mifflin 2012 393 p. $17.99

Grades: 6 7 8 9 10 11 12

1. Science fiction 2. Dystopian fiction 3. Amnesia -- Fiction 4. Mothers -- Fiction 5. Secrecy -- Fiction 6. Identity -- Fiction 7. Mother-child relationship -- Fiction 8. Mother and child -- Fiction 9. Separation (Psychology) -- Fiction

ISBN 0547887205; 9780547887203

LC 2012014034

Author Lois Lowry tells the story of "14-year-old Claire, [who] has no contact with her baby Gabe until she surreptitiously bonds with him in the community Nurturing Center. . . . After living for years with Alys, a childless healer, Claire's memory returns. Intent on finding Gabe, she . . . encounters the sinister Trademaster and exchanges her youth for his help in finding her child, now living in the same village as middle-aged Jonas and his wife Kira. Elderly and failing, Claire reveals her identity to Gabe, who must use his unique talent to save the village." (Kirkus Reviews)

Lu, Marie

Batman: Nightwalker. Marie Lu. Random House 2018 252 p. (DC icons)

Grades: 7 8 9 10

1. Community service (Punishment) -- Fiction; 2. Teenagers -- Fiction; 3. Batman (Fictional character) — Juvenile fiction; 4. Mystery fiction

9780399549779, $21.99; 9780399549786; 9780399549793

LC 2017021544

In this book, in the DC Icons Series, by Marie Lu, "the Nightwalkers are terrorizing Gotham City.... The city's elites are being taken out one by one.... Meanwhile, Bruce is about to become eighteen and inherit his family's fortune.... But on the way home from his birthday party, he makes an impulsive choice and is sentenced to community service at Arkham Asylum,...[a] prison that holds...nefarious criminals." (Publisher's note)

"A fast-paced story line, action-packed fight sequences, and hi-tech gadgetry expected from any Batman story make this a fun read with wide appeal." SLJ

★ **Champion**; a Legend novel. Marie Lu. G.P. Putnam's Sons, an imprint of Penguin Group (USA) 2013 384 p. (hardback) $18.99

Grades: 8 9 10 11 12

1. Love -- Fiction 2. Dystopian fiction 3. Plague --

Fiction 4. Science fiction

ISBN 0399256776; 9780399256776

LC 2013028221

In this novel, by Marie Lu, "June and Day have sacrificed so much for the people of the Republic—and each other—and now their country is on the brink of a new existence. June is back in the good graces of the Republic, working within the government's elite circles as Princeps Elect while Day has been assigned a high level military position. But neither could have predicted the circumstances that will reunite them once again." (Publisher's note)

"Having been diagnosed with a terminal illness, Day (Legend; Prodigy) takes care of his brother, Eden, victim of the Republic's experiments in biological warfare. International diplomacy raises the stakes in this final volume of the trilogy, but readers will likely care more about whether Day and June (the Republic's prodigy) can repair their passionate romance. Lu's storytelling is compulsively readable." (Horn Book)

★ **Legend**. G. P. Putnam's Sons 2011 305p $17.99

Grades: 8 9 10 11 12

1. War stories 2. Science fiction 3. Plague -- Fiction 4. Siblings -- Fiction 5. Soldiers -- Fiction 6. Criminals -- Fiction 7. Resistance to government -- Fiction

ISBN 978-0-399-25675-2; 0-399-25675-X

LC 2011002003

"What was once the western United States is now home to the Republic, a nation perpetually at war with its neighbors. Born into an elite family in one of the Republic's wealthiest districts, fifteen-year-old June is a prodigy being groomed for success in the Republic's highest military circles. Born into the slums, fifteen-year-old Day is the country's most wanted criminal. But his motives may not be as malicious as they seem." Publisher's note

"The characters are likable, the plot moves at a good pace, and the adventure is solid." SLJ

★ **Prodigy**; a Legend novel. Marie Lu. G. P. Putnam's Sons 2012 384 p. (Legend) $17.99

Grades: 8 9 10 11 12

1. Science fiction 2. Dystopian fiction 3. Fugitives from justice -- Fiction 4. Resistance to government -- Fiction 5. War -- Fiction 6. Soldiers -- Fiction 7. Criminals -- Fiction 8. Assassination -- Fiction 9. Government, Resistance to -- Fiction

ISBN 0399256768; 9780399256769

LC 2012003773

This young adult science fiction adventure novel, by Marie Lu, is the sequel to her novel "Legend." "Injured and on the run, it has been seven days since June and Day barely escaped Los Angeles and the Republic with their lives. Day is believed dead. . . . June is now the Republic's most wanted traitor. Desperate for help, they turn to the Patriots--a vigilante rebel group sworn to bring down the Republic. But can they trust them?" (Publisher's note)

"This is a well-molded mixture of intrigue, romance, and action, where things can change with almost any turn of the page, and frequently do." Booklist

The **Rose** Society. Marie Lu. Penguin Group USA 2015 416 p. Map

Grades: 9 10 11 12

>1. Revenge -- Fiction 2. Fantasy fiction

>9780399167843, $18.99; 0399167846

LC 2015954795

In this fantasy novel, by Marie Lu, book two of the "Young Elites" series, "Adelina Amouteru . . . , now known and feared as the White Wolf, . . . and her sister flee Kenettra to find other Young Elites in the hopes of building her own army of allies. Her goal: to strike down the Inquisition Axis, the white-cloaked soldiers who nearly killed her. But Adelina is no heroine. Her powers, fed only by fear and hate, have started to grow beyond her control." (Publisher's note)

"The Young Elites was both an instant best-seller and critically acclaimed, and the success is sure to hop to this even-stronger sequel." Booklist

★ **Warcross**. Marie Lu. Putnam Publishing Group 2017 368 p.

Grades: 8 9 10 11 12

>1. Children's stories; 2. Computer hackers -- Fiction; 3. Internet games -- Fiction

>0399547967; 9780399547966, $18.99; 9780399547980, $56.97

LC 2017016555

In this book, by Marie Lu, "teenage hacker Emika Chen works as a bounty hunter, tracking down Warcross players who bet on the game illegally. But the bounty-hunting world is a competitive one, and survival has not been easy. To make some quick cash, Emika takes a risk and hacks into the opening game of the international Warcross Championships -- only to accidentally glitch herself into the action and become an overnight sensation." (Publisher's note)

"Readers will move effortlessly through Lu's fantastic writing, and they will enjoy getting to know this international cast of characters. The author adeptly weaves together exciting video games scenes, virtual reality, and romance." (SLJ)

Another title in this series is: Wildcard (2018)

Wildcard. Marie Lu. G.P. Putnam's Sons 2018 352 p. (Warcross)

Grades: 8 9 10 11 12

>1. Bounty hunters -- Fiction; 2. Computer crimes -- Fiction; 3. Hackers -- Fiction; 4. Internet games -- Fiction; 5. Spies -- Fiction; 6. Computer hackers -- Fiction

>9780399547997, $18.99

LC 2018011748

"Emika Chen barely made it out of the Warcross Championships alive. Now that she knows the truth behind Hideo's new NeuroLink algorithm, she can no longer trust the one person she's always looked up to. . . . Determined to put a stop to Hideo's grim plans, Emika and the Phoenix Riders band together, only to find a new threat lurking on the neon-lit streets of Tokyo." (Publisher's note)

"The plotting is exquisite, with tiny details connecting back to the first book, big twists that never feel forced, and emotional power drawn from character growth." Kirkus

The **Young** Elites. Marie Lu. Putnam Publishing Group 2014 368 p. Map

Grades: 8 9 10 11 12

>1. Ability -- Fiction 2. Adventure and adventurers -- Fiction 3. Secret societies -- Fiction 4. Supernatural -- Fiction 5. Fantasy fiction

>0399167838; 9780399167836, $18.99

LC 2014025732

In this fantasy novel, by Marie Lu, "Adelina Amouteru is a survivor of the blood fever. . . . But some of the fever's survivors are rumored to possess . . . mysterious and powerful gifts, and though their identities remain secret, they have come to be called the Young Elites. . . . Teren Santoro . . . , as Leader of the Inquisition Axis, it is his job to seek out the Young Elites. . . . Enzo Valenciano is a member of . . . [a] secret sect of Young Elites [that] seeks out others like them before the Inquisition Axis can." (Publisher's note)

"In a gorgeously constructed world that somewhat resembles Renaissance Italy but with its own pantheon, geography and fauna, the multiethnic and multisexual Young Elites offer a cinematically perfect ensemble of gorgeous-but-unusual illusionists, animal speakers, fire summoners and wind callers. A must for fans of Kristin Cashore's Fire (2009) and other totally immersive fantasies." Kirkus

Lubar, David

★ **Character**, driven. David Lubar. Tor Teen 2016 304 p.

Grades: 8 9 10 11 12

>1. Fathers and sons -- Fiction 2. Sex -- Fiction 3. Teenagers -- Fiction 4. High school students -- Fiction

>9780765316332, $17.99; 0765316331

LC 2015032626

In this novel, by David Lubar, "with only one year left of high school, seventeen-year-old Cliff Sparks is desperate to find a girlfriend. But he's never had much luck with girls. At the same time, Cliff has to figure out what to do with the rest of his life, since he's pretty sure his unemployed father plans to kick him out of the house the minute he turns eighteen. Time is running out. Cliff is at the edge, on the verge, dangling—and holding on for dear life." (Publisher's note)

"With high-school graduation drawing near, Cliff stands at the precipice of his future, uncertain which way to jump. Yet he knows he has to do two things before the end of his senior year: lose his virginity and get Jillian, the new girl, to notice him. But that's not everything crowding his proverbial plate because life isn't that simple. His unemployed father threatens to kick him out when he turns 18 unless he contributes to the household, so Cliff works two part-time jobs and shelves the idea of college for the time being. His only havens are his closest friends, books, and art. However, one day he's forced to dial 911, and life as he knows it changes. . . . It wouldn't be fair to reveal whether he gets the girl, but readers will certainly fall for Cliff and find support in his trials and tribulations." Booklist

Includes bibliographical references and index; A Tom Doherty Associates book.

Sleeping freshmen never lie. Dutton Books 2005 279p $16.99; pa $6.99

Grades: 7 8 9 10

1. School stories 2. Authorship -- Fiction
ISBN 0-525-47311-4; 0-14-240780-1 pa

LC 2004-23067

While navigating his first year of high school and await-ing the birth of his new baby brother, Scott loses old friends and gains some unlikely new ones as he hones his skills as a writer

"The plot is framed by Scott's journal of advice for the unborn baby. The novel's absurd, comical mood is evident in its entries. . . . The author brings the protagonist to three-dimensional life by combining these introspective musings with active, hilarious narration." SLJ

Lucier, Makiia

A **death**-struck year; Makiia Lucier. Houghton Mifflin Harcourt 2014 288 p. (hardback) $17.99
Grades: 9 10 11 12

1. Nurses -- Fiction 2. Epidemics -- Fiction 3. Influenza -- Fiction 4. Portland (Or.) -- Fiction 5. Influenza Epidemic, 1918-1919 -- Fiction 6. Portland (Or.) -- History -- 20th century -- Fiction
ISBN 0544164504; 9780544164505

LC 2013037482

In this novel, by Makiia Lucier, "the Spanish influenza is devastating the East Coast–but Cleo Berry knows it is a world away from the safety of her home in Portland, Ore-gon. Then the flu moves into the Pacific Northwest. Schools, churches, and theaters are shut down. The entire city is thrust into survival mode–and into a panic. Seventeen-year-old Cleo is told to stay put in her quarantined boarding school, but when the Red Cross pleads for volunteers, she cannot ignore the call for help." (Publisher's note)

"A teen girl struggles to survive the Spanish influenza pandemic of 1918...Readers will be swept up in the story as Cleo builds friendships and manages to find hope amid disease and death. A notable debut." (Kirkus)

Includes bibliographical references

★ **Isle** of blood and stone. Makiia Lucier. Hough-ton Mifflin Harcourt 2018 390 p.
Grades: 7 8 9 10 11 12

1. Cartographers -- Fiction; 2. Kings and rulers -- Fiction; 3. Maps -- Fiction; 4. Missing persons -- Fiction; 5. Secrecy -- Fiction; 6. Voyages and travels -- Fiction; 7. Missing children -- Fiction; 8. Secrets -- Fiction
9780544968578, $17.99; 9780544968608

LC 2017015656

In this book, by Makiia Lucier, "eighteen years ago two princes of the island kingdom of St. John del Mar were kidnapped and murdered.... Everyone knows the story, but for Elias, Mercedes, and Ulises, the aftermath of that tragic day is deeply personal.... Now, the three friends just want to move on with their lives. But when two maps surface..., troubling questions arise." (Publisher's note)

"A romantic maritime epic and a charming tribute to mapmakers, calligraphers, and explorers." Kirkus

Luedeke, Lisa

Smashed; Lisa Luedeke. Margaret K. McElderry Books 2012 323 p.

Grades: 9 10 11 12

1. Alcoholism -- Fiction 2. Field hockey players -- Fiction 3. Teenagers -- Alcohol use -- Fiction 4. High schools -- Fiction 5. Emotional problems -- Fiction
ISBN 1442427795; 9781442427792; 9781442427952

LC 2011030515

In this novel by Lisa Luedeke "Katie Martin is a field hockey star on the fast track to a college scholarship. Her relationship with alcohol has always been a little question-able, but things get bleak really quickly when she takes up with bad boy Alec Osborne.... On a rain-soaked, alcohol-drenched night, one impulsive decision threatens Katie's dreams, leaving her indebted to Alec in the worst possible way." (Author's note)

Lundin, Britta

Ship it. Britta Lundin. Freeform Books 2018 384 p. Illustration
Grades: 7 8 9 10 11 12

1. Actors and actresses -- Fiction; 2. Blogs -- Fiction; 3. Fan fiction -- Fiction; 4. Homosexuality -- Fiction; 5. Popularity -- Fiction; 6. Television -- Production and direction -- Fiction; 7. Fan fiction; 8. Actors -- Fiction; 9781368003131, $17.99

LC 2017034202

"Claire, a teen fan fiction author, is beyond thrilled when the stars of her favorite TV show, Demon Heart, come to nearby Boise, ID, for a convention. But when she asks For-rest, the show's star, about the possibility that his character is gay, he calls her 'crazy,' and she leaves the room in tears. In an effort to repair this publicity nightmare, the show sends Claire on the rest of the convention tour, where she goes to increasingly desperate lengths to make her "ship" a reality. The book alternates between Forrest and Claire's perspec-tives, as Forrest confronts some internalized homopho-bia and Claire begins to explore her own queer identity." (School Library Journal)

Luper, Eric

Bug boy. Farrar, Straus and Giroux 2009 248p $16.99

Grades: 7 8 9 10

1. Gambling -- Fiction 2. Horse racing -- Fiction 3. New York (State) -- Fiction 4. Father-son relationship -- Fiction 5. Swindlers and swindling -- Fiction
ISBN 978-0-374-31000-4; 0-374-31000-9

LC 2008-26730

In 1934 Saratoga, New York, just as fifteen-year-old Jack Walsh finally realizes his dream of becoming a jockey, complications arise in the form of a female bookie, an un-expected visit from his father, and a man who wants him to "fix" a race.

"This well-written, engaging story effectively captures the desperate times of the Depression and the hard-edged world of horse racing." SLJ

Seth Baumgartner's love manifesto. Balzer + Bray 2010 293p $16.99
Grades: 8 9 10 11 12

1. Golf -- Fiction 2. Love -- Fiction 3. Dating (Social

customs) -- Fiction 4. Father-son relationship -- Fiction
ISBN 978-0-06-182753-2; 0-06-182753-3

LC 2009-29706

After his girlfriend breaks up with him and he sees his father out with another woman, high school senior Seth Baumgartner, who has a summer job at the country club and is preparing for a father-son golf tournament, launches a podcast in which he explores the mysteries of love.

"Luper weaves together many themes—trust and secrets, lies and truth, love, lust and, of course, golf—in a way that even the most introspection-hating male reader will eat with a spoon." Kirkus

Lupica, Mike

The **batboy**. Philomel Books 2010 247p $17.99

Grades: 5 6 7 8

1. Baseball -- Fiction 2. Mother-son relationship -- Fiction
ISBN 978-0-399-25000-2; 0-399-25000-X

LC 2009015067

Even though his mother feels baseball ruined her marriage to his father, she allows fourteen-year-old Brian to become a bat boy for the Detroit Tigers, who have just drafted his favorite player back onto the team.

Lupica gives "his readers a behind-the-scenes look at major league sports. In this novel, he adds genuine insights into family dynamics and the emotional state of his hero." Booklist

The **big** field. Philomel Books 2008 243p $17.99

Grades: 5 6 7 8

1. Baseball -- Fiction 2. Father-son relationship -- Fiction
ISBN 978-0-399-24625-8; 0-399-24625-8

LC 2007-23647

When fourteen-year-old baseball player Hutch feels threatened by the arrival of a new teammate named Darryl, he tries to work through his insecurities about both Darryl and his remote and silent father, who was once a great ballplayer too.

"Writing in typically fluid prose and laying in a strong supporting lineup, Lupica strikes the right balance between personal issues and game action." Booklist

Hero. Philomel Books 2010 289p $17.99

Grades: 6 7 8 9

1. Adventure fiction 2. Death -- Fiction 3. Politics -- Fiction 4. Family life -- Fiction 5. Superheroes -- Fiction 6. Father-son relationship -- Fiction
ISBN 978-0-399-25283-9; 0-399-25283-5

LC 2010-01772

Fourteen-year-old Zach learns he has the same special abilities as his father, who was the President's globe-trotting troubleshooter until "the Bads" killed him, and now Zach must decide whether to use his powers in the same way at the risk of his own life.

"Lupica effectively unfolds this high-adventure story." Booklist

Miracle on 49th Street. Philomel Books 2006 246p $17.99; pa $7.99

Grades: 5 6 7 8

1. Basketball -- Fiction 2. Father-daughter relationship -- Fiction
ISBN 0-399-24488-3; 0-14-240942-1 pa

LC 2005-32648

After her mother's death, twelve-year-old Molly learns that her father is a basketball star for the Boston Celtics.

"Lupica creates intriguing, complex characters . . . and he paces his story well, with enough twists and cliff-hangers to keep the pages turning." SLJ

Summer ball; [by] Mike Lupica. Philomel Books 2007 244p $17.99

Grades: 6 7 8 9

1. Camps -- Fiction 2. Basketball -- Fiction
ISBN 978-0-399-24487-2

LC 2006021781

Thirteen-year-old Danny must prove himself all over again for a disapproving coach and against new rivals at a summer basketball camp.

"Lupica breathes life into both characters and story. Danny is . . . sympathetic and engaging. He is surrounded by a cast of supporting characters who add humor and whose interactions ring true." SLJ

Lurie, April

The **latent** powers of Dylan Fontaine. Delacorte Press 2008 208p $15.99; lib bdg $18.99

Grades: 8 9 10 11 12

1. Family life -- Fiction 2. New York (N.Y.) -- Fiction
ISBN 978-0-385-73125-6; 978-0-385-90153-6 lib bdg

LC 2007-32313

Fifteen-year-old Dylan's friend Angie is making a film about him while he is busy trying to keep his older brother from getting caught with drugs, to deal with his mother having left the family, and to figure out how to get Angie to think of him as more than just a friend.

"This is a story about guys, primarily . . . brothers; fathers and sons; lonely young men who are feeling somewhat lost. Any reader will care for each one of them. Lurie does a wonderful job of making them real." KLIATT

Lyga, Barry

★ The **astonishing** adventures of Fanboy & Goth Girl. Houghton Mifflin 2006 311p $16.95

Grades: 8 9 10 11 12

1. School stories 2. Friendship -- Fiction 3. Cartoons and caricatures -- Fiction
ISBN 0-618-72392-7

LC 2005-33259

A fifteen-year-old "geek" who keeps a list of the high school jocks and others who torment him, and pours his energy into creating a great graphic novel, encounters Kyra, Goth Girl, who helps change his outlook on almost everything, including himself.

"This engaging first novel has good characterization with genuine voices. . . . The book is compulsively readable." Voice Youth Advocates

Followed by: Goth Girl rising (2009)

★ **Bang**. By Barry Lyga. Little, Brown & Co. 2017 295 p.

Grades: 9 10 11 12

1. Family problems -- Fiction; 2. Friendship -- Fiction; 3. Guilt -- Fiction; 4. Single-parent families -- Fiction; 5. YouTube (Electronic resource) -- Fiction
9780316315524; 9780316315500, $17.99

LC 2016019843

In this book, by Barry Lyga, "Sebastian Cody did something horrible, something no one -- not even Sebastian himself -- can forgive. At the age of four, he accidentally shot and killed his infant sister with his father's gun. Now, ten years later, Sebastian has lived with the guilt and horror for his entire life. With his best friend away for the summer, Sebastian has only a new friend, Aneesa, to distract him from his darkest thoughts. But even this relationship cannot blunt the pain of his past." (Publisher's note)

"It's a raw exploration of persistent social stigmas, a beautiful study of forgiveness, and an unflinching portrait of a parent's worst nightmare." Pub Wkly

Boy toy. Houghton Mifflin 2007 410p $16.95
Grades: 10 11 12

1. School stories 2. Child sexual abuse -- Fiction
ISBN 978-0-618-72393-5; 0-618-72393-5

LC 2006-39840

After five years of fighting his way past flickers of memory about the teacher who molested him and the incident that brought the crime to light, eighteen-year-old Josh gets help in coping with his molestor's release from prison when he finally tells his best friends the whole truth.

The author "tackles this incredibly sensitive story with boldness and confidence. He does not shy away from graphic descriptions of Josh's past and even makes the audacious choice of showing young Josh enjoying the attention . . . [Josh] works hard at healing himself and moving into healthy adulthood, and by the end of this well-written, challenging novel, the reader has high hopes that he will make it." Voice Youth Advocates

Goth girl rising. Houghton Mifflin Harcourt 2009 390p $17
Grades: 8 9 10 11 12

1. School stories 2. Psychotherapy -- Fiction
ISBN 978-0-547-07664-5; 0-547-07664-9

Sequel to: The astonishing adventures of Fanboy and Goth Girl (2006)

"After six months in a mental hospital, Kyra, the newly shaven-headed heroine of The Astonishing Adventures of Fan Boy and Goth Girl (2006), has only one plan: to exact embarrassing revenge on sweet, loyal Fan Boy for not contacting her while she was away. . . . Goth teens and fans of the first novel will be drawn into the darkness that is her life." Kirkus

Hero-type. Houghton Mifflin Co. 2008 295p $16
Grades: 7 8 9 10

1. School stories 2. Maryland -- Fiction 3. Patriotism -- Fiction 4. Heroes and heroines -- Fiction
ISBN 978-0-547-07663-8; 0-547-07663-0

LC 2008-7276

Feeling awkward and ugly is only one reason sixteen-year-old Kevin is uncomfortable with the publicity surrounding his act of accidental heroism, but when a reporter photographs him apparently being unpatriotic, he steps into the limelight to encourage people to think about what the symbols of freedom really mean.

"Leavened by much humor . . . this neatly plotted look at what real patriotism and heroism mean will get readers thinking." KLIATT

★ **I** hunt killers; by Barry Lyga. Little, Brown 2012 359 p.
Grades: 10 11 12

1. Mystery fiction 2. Serial killers -- Fiction 3. Father-son relationship -- Fiction 4. Teenagers -- Conduct of life -- Fiction 5. Murder -- Fiction 6. Psychopaths -- Fiction 7. Conduct of life -- Fiction 8. Fathers and sons -- Fiction
ISBN 9780316125840

LC 2011025418

This book tells the story of Jasper, a 17-year-old boy whose father "is the most notorious serial killer of the 21st century" and who has found that "having a normal life is a struggle. . . . Now living with his Gramma, Jasper finds himself investigating another serial killer with help from his best friend Howie." (Kirkus Reviews)

Followed by: Game (2013)

Lynch, Chris, 1962-

★ **Angry** young man. Simon & Schuster BFYR 2011 167p $16.99
Grades: 7 8 9 10

1. Brothers -- Fiction 2. Conduct of life -- Fiction 3. Single parent family -- Fiction 4. Mother-son relationship -- Fiction
ISBN 0-689-84790-4; 978-0-689-84790-5

LC 2009-52832

Eighteen-year-old Robert tries to help his half-brother Xan, a seventeen-year-old misfit, to make better choices as he becomes increasingly attracted to a variety of protesters, anarchists, and the like.

"For those who wonder about the roots of homegrown terror and extremism, . . . Lynch pushes the spotlight from the individual to society in a story that can be brutal and ugly, yet isn't devoid of hope." Publ Wkly

Hit count: a novel. By Chris Lynch. Algonquin Young Readers 2015 368 p.
Grades: 8 9 10 11 12

1. Football -- Fiction 2. Sports injuries -- Fiction 3. Wounds and injuries -- Fiction 4. High school students -- Fiction
1616202505; 9781616202507, $17.95

LC 2014043009

In this young adult novel by Chris Lynch, "Arlo Brodie loves being at the heart of the action on the football field, getting hit hard and hitting back harder. . . . Arlo's girlfriend tries to make him see how dangerously he's playing; when that doesn't work, she calls time out on their relationship. Even Arlo's coaches begin to track his hit count, ready to pull him off the field when he nears the limit." (Publisher's note)

"This intense, timely story provides incredible insight into the reasons why knowledge of football's potential danger is not enough to keep young players from taking the field." Kirkus

Hothouse. HarperTeen 2010 198p $16.99
Grades: 8 9 10 11 12
  1. Death -- Fiction 2. Friendship -- Fiction 3. Bereavement -- Fiction 4. Fire fighters -- Fiction 5. Father-son relationship -- Fiction
ISBN 978-0-06-167379-5; 0-06-167379-X
LC 2010-3145
Teens D.J. and Russell, life-long friends and neighbors, had drifted apart but when their firefighter fathers are both killed, they try to help one another come to terms with the tragedy and its aftermath.

"Lynch fully commits to the first-person voice, giving into Russ' second-by-second conflicts and contradictions. The author also has a strong grasp of the garrulous slaps and punches that make up many male relationships. Russ' friendships are so real they hurt. The story hurts, too, but that's how it should be." Booklist

★ **Inexcusable**. Atheneum Books for Young Readers 2005 165p $16.95; pa $6.99
Grades: 8 9 10 11 12
  1. School stories 2. Rape -- Fiction 3. Football -- Fiction
ISBN 0-689-84789-0; 1-416-93972-5 pa
LC 2004-30874
High school senior and football player Keir sets out to enjoy himself on graduation night, but when he attempts to comfort a friend whose date has left her stranded, things go terribly wrong

"This finely crafted and thought-provoking page-turner carefully conveys that it is simply inexcusable to whitewash wrongs, and that those responsible should (and hopefully will) pay the price." SLJ

Pieces; Chris Lynch. Simon & Schuster Books for Young Readers 2013 176 p. (hardcover) $16.99
Grades: 7 8 9 10 11 12
  1. Bereavement -- Fiction 2. Death -- Fiction 3. Grief -- Fiction 4. Brothers -- Fiction 5. Interpersonal relations -- Fiction 6. Donation of organs, tissues, etc. -- Fiction
ISBN 1416927034; 9781416927037; 9781442453111
LC 2011042049
In this book, "a year after his 20-year-old brother Duane died in a diving accident, 18-year-old Eric still can't seem to move forward. In an attempt to keep the 'nothingness that is filling the Duane space' from taking hold, he reaches out to three of the donors who received his brother's 'pieces.' After meeting shy, redheaded Phil, brassy Barry and sweet single mom Melinda, Eric finds himself constantly asking the questions, 'Who are these people? Who are they, to me? Who am I, to them?'" (Kirkus Reviews)

Lynch, Janet Nichols

My beautiful hippie; Janet Nichols Lynch. Holiday House 2013 186 p. (hardcover) $16.95
Grades: 10 11 12
  1. Bildungsromans 2. Hippies -- Fiction 3. Historical fiction 4. Feminism -- Fiction 5. Pianists -- Fiction 6.

Coming of age -- Fiction 7. Vietnam War, 1961-1975 -- Fiction 8. Family life -- California -- Fiction 9. San Francisco (Calif.) -- History -- 20th century -- Fiction
ISBN 0823426033; 9780823426034
LC 2012016563
In this novel, by Janet Nichols Lynch, "it's 1967 and Joanne's San Francisco neighborhood has become inundated with hippies . . . , which thrills her but appalls the rest of her family. In the midst of preparations for her sister's wedding, Joanne meets Martin . . . and begins to see him secretly. Over the course of the next year, Joanne discovers a world of drugs, anti-war demonstrations, and psychedelic dances that both fascinates and frightens her." (Publisher's note)

Lyne, Jennifer H.

Catch rider; by Jennifer H. Lyne. Clarion Books 2013 288 p. (hardcover) $16.99
Grades: 9 10 11 12
  1. Poor -- Fiction 2. Horses -- Fiction 3. Uncles -- Fiction 4. Virginia -- Fiction 5. Horse shows -- Fiction 6. Horsemanship -- Fiction 7. Social classes -- Fiction 8. Single-parent families -- Fiction 9. Family life -- Virginia -- Fiction
ISBN 0547868715; 9780547868714
LC 2012022616
In this book, "Sidney Criser might still be 14, but that doesn't stop her from driving the junk car her uncle gave her an hour over mountains to clean stalls at a rich woman's barn. Sid grew up tough, and she can ride anything, but times are desperate: Since her father's death, her mother has taken up with a no-good abuser who threatens to move them to California. Her mother's lost her job, and . . . her uncle Wayne, who's long been Sidney's mainstay, is just about to drink himself to death." (Kirkus)

Lyons, Mary E.

Letters from a slave boy; the story of Joseph Jacobs. Atheneum Books for Young Readers 2007 197p il map $15.99; pa $5.99
Grades: 6 7 8 9
  1. Letters -- Fiction 2. Slavery -- Fiction 3. African Americans -- Fiction
ISBN 978-0-689-87867-1; 0-689-87867-2; 978-0-689-87868-8 pa; 0-689-87868-0 pa
LC 2006-01277
A fictionalized look at the life of Joseph Jacobs, son of a slave, told in the form of letters that he might have written during his life in pre-Civil War North Carolina, on a whaling expedition, in New York, New England, and finally in California during the Gold Rush.

"The 'letters' are short and the pace is quick. The dialect and spelling give authenticity without making the text difficult to read and understand. . . . This title stands on its own, but children who appreciated the forthright perspective of the first book will want to read this one as well." SLJ

★ **Letters** from a slave girl; the story of Harriet Jacobs. Scribner 1992 146p il hardcover o.p. pa $5.99; pa $5.99
Grades: 6 7 8 9
  1. Slaves 2. Letters -- Fiction 3. African Americans

-- Fiction
ISBN 0-684-19446-5; 1-4169-3637-8 pa;
9781416936374 pa

LC 91-45778

This is a fictionalized version of the life of Harriet Jacobs, told in the form of letters that she might have written during her slavery in North Carolina and as she prepared for escape to the North in 1842. Glossary. Bibliography.

This "is historical fiction at its best. . . . Mary Lyons has remained faithful to Jacobs's actual autobiography throughout her readable, compelling novel. . . . Her observations of the horrors of slavery are concise and lucid. The letters are written in dialect, based on Jacobs's own writing and on other slave narrations of the period." Horn Book

Maas, Sarah J.

Catwoman: soulstealer. Sarah J. Maas. Random House 2018 384 p.

Grades: 7 8 9 10

1. Criminals -- Fiction; 2. Friendship -- Fiction; 3. Catwoman (Fictional character)
9780399549694, $18.99; 9780399549700

LC 2017051966

In this book in the DC Icons Series, by Sarah J. Maas, "two years after escaping Gotham City's slums, Selina Kyle returns as the mysterious and wealthy Holly Vanderhees. She quickly discovers that with Batman off on a vital mission, Gotham City looks ripe for the taking.... Selina is playing a desperate game of cat and mouse, forming unexpected friendships and entangling herself with Batwing by night and her devilishly handsome neighbor Luke Fox by day." (Publisher's note)

DC Comics.

A **court** of thorns and roses. By Sarah J. Maas. Bloomsbury 2015 432 p. Map

Grades: 9 10 11 12

1. Blessing and cursing -- Fiction 2. Fairies -- Fiction 3. Fantasy 4. Love -- Fiction 5. Fantasy fiction
1619634449; 9781619634442, $18.99

LC 2014020071

In this fantasy novel, by Sarah J. Maas, "when nineteen-year-old huntress Feyre kills a wolf in the woods, a beast-like creature arrives to demand retribution for it. Dragged to a treacherous magical land she only knows about from legends, Feyre discovers that her captor is not an animal, but Tamlin—one of the lethal, immortal faeries who once ruled their world." (Publisher's note)

Other titles in this series:
A Court of Mist and Fury (2016)
A Court of Wings and Ruin (2017)
A Court of Frost and Starlight (2018)

★ **Throne** of glass; Sarah J. Maas. Bloomsbury 2012 406 p. (hardback) $17.99

Grades: 10 11 12

1. Fantasy fiction 2. Contests -- Fiction 3. Assassins -- Fiction 4. Fantasy 5. Princes -- Fiction 6. Prisoners -- Fiction 7. Courts and courtiers -- Fiction
ISBN 1599906953; 9781599906959

LC 2012011229

An assassin whose work "has landed her in a slave-labor prison no one has ever survived. A year into her sentence, the Crown Prince offers to sponsor Celaena in a competition with 23 other criminals and murderers that, should she win, will result in her freedom. The only catch? She'll become the king's personal assassin for four years, the same dark-hearted king who sentenced her to imprisonment." (Kirkus Reviews)

Other titles in this series:
Crown of Midnight (2013)
Heir of Fire (2014)
Queen of Shadows (2015)
Empire of Storms (2016)
Tower of Dawn (2017)
Kingdom of Ash (2018)

Maberry, Jonathan

★ **Rot** & ruin. Simon & Schuster Books for Young Readers 2010 458p $17.99

Grades: 9 10 11 12

1. Horror fiction 2. Zombies -- Fiction 3. Brothers -- Fiction
ISBN 978-1-4424-0232-4; 1-4424-0232-6

LC 2009-46041

In a post-apocalyptic world where fences and border patrols guard the few people left from the zombies that have overtaken civilization, fifteen-year-old Benny Imura is finally convinced that he must follow in his older brother's footsteps and become a bounty hunter.

"In turns mythic and down-to-earth, this intense novel combines adventure and philosophy to tell a truly memorable zombie story." Publ Wkly

Other titles in this series:
Dust & decay (2011)
Flesh & Bone (2012)
Fire & Ash (2013)
Bits & Pieces (2015)

Mabry, Samantha

All the wind in the world. Samantha Mabry. Algonquin Young Readers 2017 264 p.

Grades: 9 10 11 12

1. Ranch life -- Southwestern States -- Fiction; 2. Southwestern States -- Fiction; 3. Love -- Fiction; 4. Ranch life -- Fiction; 5. Secrecy -- Fiction
9781616207595; 1616206667; 9781616206666, $17.95

LC 2017020570

In this book, by Samantha Mabry, "Sarah Jac Crow and James Holt have fallen in love working in the endless fields that span a bone-dry Southwest in the near future.... To protect themselves, they've learned to work hard and...keep their love hidden from the people who might use it against them. Then, just when...[they] have settled in and begun saving money for the home they dream of near the coast, a horrible accident sends them on the run." (Publisher's note)

"A gripping, fablelike story of a love ferocious enough to destroy and a world prepared to burn with it." Booklist

Mac, Carrie

★ **10** things I can see from here. Carrie Mac. Alfred A. Knopf 2017 312 p.

Grades: 7 8 9 10 11 12

1. Anxiety disorders -- Fiction; 2. Fathers and daughters -- Fiction; 3. Lesbians -- Fiction; 4. Love -- Fiction; 5. Anxiety -- Fiction; 6. Lesbian teenagers -- Fiction
9780399556258; 9780399556258; 9780399556272; 9780399556265, $20.99

LC 2015046690

In this young adult novel, by Carrie Mac, "Maeve has... been struggling with severe anxiety for a long time, and as much as she wishes it was something she could just talk herself out of, it's not.... But Maeve finds brief moments of calm...with Salix, a local girl who doesn't seem to worry about anything. Between her dad's wavering sobriety...and her bumbling courtship with Salix, this summer brings more catastrophes than even Maeve could have foreseen." (Publisher's note)

"With Maeve, Mac delivers a character who's heart-warmingly real and sympathetic, and her story provides a much needed mirror for anxious queer girls everywhere." Kirkus

Ten things I can see from here

MacColl, Michaela

Nobody's secret; by Michaela MacColl. Chronicle Books 2013 288 p. (reinforced) $16.99
Grades: 7 8 9 10

1. Mystery fiction 2. Historical fiction 3. Poets -- Fiction 4. Amherst (Mass.) -- History -- 19th century -- Fiction 5. Women poets, American -- 19th century
ISBN 1452108609; 9781452108605

LC 2012030364

In this book, when "15-year-old Emily Dickinson meets and flirts with a handsome stranger, she feels the first flicker of romance. Then the young man is found dead in her family's pond, and the budding poet is sure that he was a victim of foul play. Determined to see that justice is done, she and her younger sister, Vinnie, investigate and discover that he is James Wentworth, heir to a fortune from which his aunt and uncle have defrauded him. Suspecting murder, Emily sets out to solve the case." (School Library Journal)

Promise the night. Chronicle Books 2011 $16.99
Grades: 6 7 8 9

1. Women air pilots -- Fiction
ISBN 978-0-8118-7625-4; 0-8118-7625-X

LC 2011010938

This novel explores the early life of Beryl Markham, who grew up on a farm in Kenya, and became the first person to fly solo across the Atlantic from east to west.

"MacColl vividly portrays her headstrong protagonist . . . with fierce, exuberant spirit." Booklist

The **revelation** of Louisa May: a novel of intrigue and romance. By Michaela MacColl. Chronicle Books LLC 2015 272 p.
Grades: 7 8 9 10

1. Families -- Massachusetts -- Concord -- Fiction 2. Family life -- Massachusetts -- Concord -- Fiction 3. Fugitive slaves -- Fiction 4. Fugitive slaves -- United States -- History -- 19th century -- Fiction 5. Murder -- Fiction 6. Murder -- Massachusetts -- Concord -- Fiction 7. Slavery -- Fiction 8. Underground Railroad -- Fiction 9. Underground Railroad -- Massachusetts -- Fiction 10. Alcott, Louisa May, 1832-1888 -- Fiction 11. Concord (Mass.) -- History -- 19th century -- Fiction
9781452133577, $16.99

LC 2014028073

In this book, by Michaela MacColl, "Louisa May Alcott can't believe it-her mother is leaving for the summer to earn money for the family and Louisa is to be in charge of the household. How will she find the time to write her stories, much less have any adventures of her own? But before long, Louisa finds herself juggling her temperamental father, a mysterious murder, a fugitive seeking refuge along the Underground Railroad, and blossoming love." (Publisher's note)

"Based on the life of Louisa May Alcott, MacColl's latest seamlessly weaves fact and fiction together, and she handles many challenging issues, such as the conflict between philosophical principles and the obligations of supporting a family, with deft and grace. Fans of historical fiction will relish this glimpse into the storied life of the pioneering author." Booklist

Includes bibliographical references.

MacCready, Robin Merrow

Buried. Dutton Books 2006 198p $16.99; pa $6.99

Grades: 8 9 10 11 12

1. Children of alcoholics -- Fiction 2. Mother-daughter relationship -- Fiction 3. Obsessive-compulsive disorder -- Fiction
ISBN 978-0-525-47724-2; 0-525-47724-1; 978-0-14-241141-4 pa; 0-14-241141-8 pa

LC 2006-03870

When her alcoholic mother goes missing, seventeen-year-old Claudine begins to spin out of control, despite her attempts to impose order on every aspect of her life.

"Readers who came for the issues may find themselves reaching for the tissues as Claudine finally finds closure with her mother." Bull Cent Child Books

MacCullough, Carolyn

Always a witch. Clarion Books 2011 276p $16.99

Grades: 8 9 10 11 12

1. Witches -- Fiction 2. Time travel -- Fiction 3. Good and evil -- Fiction
ISBN 978-0-547-22485-5; 0-547-22485-0

LC 2011008148

Haunted by her grandmother's prophecy that she will soon be forced to make a terrible decision, witch Tamsin Greene risks everything to travel back in time to 1887 New York to confront the enemy that wants to destroy her family.

This is "an enjoyable magical adventure." Kirkus

Once a witch. Clarion Books 2009 292p $16
Grades: 8 9 10 11 12

1. Sisters -- Fiction 2. Witches -- Fiction 3. Time travel -- Fiction 4. Good and evil -- Fiction 5. New York (N.Y.) -- Fiction
ISBN 978-0-547-22399-5; 0-547-22399-4

LC 2008-49234

Born into a family of witches, seventeen-year-old Tamsin is raised believing that she alone lacks a magical "Talent," but when her beautiful and powerful sister is taken by an age-old rival of the family in an attempt to change the balance of power, Tamsin discovers her true destiny.

"The book will appeal to teen readers who enjoy stories with romance, magic, or time travel, along with hardcore fantasy aficionados, and it is appropriate for all young adult collections." Voice Youth Advocates

Followed by: Always a witch (2011)

Stealing Henry. Roaring Brook Press 2005 196p $16.95

Grades: 9 10 11 12

    1. Siblings -- Fiction 2. Child abuse -- Fiction 3. Runaway teenagers -- Fiction 4. Mother-daughter relationship -- Fiction

    ISBN 1-596-43045-1

                       LC 2004-17550

The experiences of high-schooler Savannah, following her decision to take her eight-year-old half brother from his abusive father and their oblivious mother, are interspersed with the earlier story of her mother, Alice, as she meets Savannah's father and unexpectedly becomes pregnant.

"Young adult readers will find this [book] fascinating and appealing." Libr Media Connect

Macdonald, Maryann

Odette's secrets; by Maryann Macdonald. Bloomsbury 2013 240 p. (hardback) $16.99

Grades: 6 7 8 9

    1. Novels in verse 2. Hidden children (Holocaust) 3. France -- History -- 1940-1945, German occupation -- Fiction 4. Identity -- Fiction 5. Jews -- France -- Fiction 6. Holocaust, Jewish (1939-1945) -- Fiction 7. World War, 1939-1945 -- France -- Fiction

    ISBN 159990750X; 9781599907505

                       LC 2012015549

This biographical story-in-verse, by Maryann Macdonald, takes place in Nazi-occupied France. "Odette is a young Jewish girl living in Paris during a dangerous time. . . . After Odette's father enlists in the French army and her mother joins the Resistance, Odette is sent to the countryside until it is safe to return. On the surface, she leads the life of a regular girl . . . but inside, she is burning with secrets about the life she left behind and her true identity." (Publisher's note)

MacHale, D. J.

The **merchant** of death. Aladdin 2002 375p. (Pendragon)

Grades: 7 8 9 10

    1. Adventure fiction; 2. Fantasy fiction

    ISBN 978-1-4169-3625-1, $17.99; 1-4169-3625-4; 978-0-7434-3731-8 (pa), $8.99; 0-7434-3731-4 (pa)

                       LC 2002101645

The soldiers of Halla Bobby Pendragon is a seemingly normal fourteen-year-old boy. He has a family, a home, and even Marley, his beloved dog. But there is something very special about Bobby. He is going to save the world. . . . Before he can object, he is swept off to an alternate dimension known as Denduron, a territory inhabited by strange beings, ruled by a magical tyrant, and plagued by dangerous revolution.

Other titles in this series are:
The lost city of Faar (2003)
The never war (2003)
The reality bug (2003)
Black water (2004)
The rivers of Zadaa (2005)
Quillan games (2006)
The pilgrims of Rayne (2007)
Raven rise (2008)

★ The **pilgrims** of Rayne. Simon & Schuster Books for Young Readers 2007 547p (Pendragon) $16.99; pa $8.99

Grades: 7 8 9 10

    1. Fantasy fiction 2. Adventure fiction

    ISBN 978-1-4169-1416-7; 1-4169-1416-1; 978-1-4169-1417-4 pa; 1-4169-1417-X pa

                       LC 2006038131

With Saint Dane seemingly on the verge of toppling all of the territories, Pendragon and Courtney set out to rescue Mark and find themselves traveling—and battling—their way through different worlds as they try to save all of Halla.

This is "packed . . . with nonstop action, mind-boggling plot twists, and well-imagined locales." Voice Youth Advocates

Other titles in this series are:
The merchant of death (2002)
The lost city of Faar (2003)
The never war (2003)
The reality bug (2003)
Black water (2004)
The rivers of Zadaa (2005)
Quillan games (2006)
Raven rise (2008)
The soldiers of Halla (2009)

SYLO; by D.J. MacHale. Penguin Group USA 2013 416 p. (hardcover) $17.99

Grades: 5 6 7 8 9

    1. Dystopian fiction 2. Adventure fiction

    ISBN 1595146652; 9781595146656

This is the first book in a proposed trilogy from D.J. MacHale. Here, Tucker Pierce has a small but satisfying life on a small island. But when the island is quarantined by the U.S. Navy, things start to fall apart. . . . People start dying. The girl he wants to get to know a whole lot better, Tori, is captured along with Tucker and imprisoned behind barbed wire." They must escape to the mainland and try to figure out what this SYLO organization that is imprisoning them is. (Kirkus Reviews)

Maciel, Amanda

Tease. Amanda Maciel; Balzer + Bray. 2014 328p $17.99

Grades: 9 10 11 12

    1. Bullying -- Fiction 2. High schools -- Fiction 3. Suicide

    ISBN: 0062305301; 9780062305305

                       LC 2013043067

"Sara is climbing the high school social ladder when a new girl, Emma, steals her spotlight. Sara and her friends retaliate with pranks, rumors, and social media warfare, but all are shocked when Emma commits suicide. Sara is a fragile, conflicted narrator struggling to understand her role in Emma's death. A complex and thought-provoking examination of modern teen bullying." Horn Book

Mackall, Dandi Daley

★ **Eva** underground. Harcourt 2006 239p $17

Grades: 9 10 11 12

1. Poland -- Fiction 2. Communism -- Fiction 3. Father-daughter relationship -- Fiction

ISBN 0-15-205462-6; 978-0-15-205462-5

LC 2005-04195

In 1978, a high school senior is forced by her widowed father to move from their comfortable Chicago suburb to help with an underground education movement in communist Poland.

"Poland behind the Iron Curtain is rarely found in modern young adult literature, and Mackall has done a superb job in captivating high reader interest in this unique setting." Libr Media Connect

Mackel, Kathy

★ **Boost**. Dial Books 2008 248p $16.99; pa $7.99

Grades: 6 7 8 9

1. Steroids -- Fiction 2. Basketball -- Fiction

ISBN 978-0-8037-3240-7; 0-8037-3240-6; 978-0-14-241539-9 pa; 0-14-241539-1 pa

LC 2007-49441

Thirteen-year-old Savvy's dreams of starting for her elite basketball team are in danger when she is accused of taking steroids

"Mackel has turned a tough subject in the world of teen competitive sports into a highly readable blend of intense action, interfamily relationships, and intrigue." SLJ

Mackey, Weezie Kerr

Throwing like a girl; [by] Weezie Kerr Mackey. Marshall Cavendish 2007 271p $16.99

Grades: 6 7 8 9

1. School stories 2. Softball -- Fiction 3. Family life -- Fiction

ISBN 978-0-7614-5342-0

LC 2006030233

After moving from Chicago to Dallas in the spring of her sophomore year, fifteen-year-old Ella finds that joining the softball team at her private school not only helps her make friends, it also provides unexpected opportunities to learn and grow.

"Readers will be delighted with how well the athletics and the girly stuff work in tandem." Booklist

Mackler, Carolyn

★ The **earth,** my butt, and other big, round things. Candlewick Press 2003 246p $15.99; pa $8.99

Grades: 7 8 9 10

1. School stories 2. Obesity -- Fiction 3. Family life

-- Fiction 4. New York (N.Y.) -- Fiction

ISBN 0-7636-1958-2; 0-7636-2091-2 pa

LC 2002-73921

Michael L. Printz Award honor book, 2004

Sequel: The Universe Is Expanding and So Am I (2018)

Feeling like she does not fit in with the other members of her family, who are all thin, brilliant, and good-looking, fifteen-year-old Virginia tries to deal with her self-image, her first physical relationship, and her disillusionment with some of the people closest to her

"The e-mails [Virginia] exchanges . . . and the lists she makes (e.g., 'The Fat Girl Code of Conduct') add both realism and insight to her character. The heroine's transformation into someone who finds her own style and speaks her own mind is believable—and worthy of applause." Publ Wkly

Guyaholic; a story of finding, flirting, forgetting . . . and the boy who changes everything. Candlewick Press 2007 176p $16.99; pa $7.99

Grades: 9 10 11 12

1. Dating (Social customs) -- Fiction

ISBN 978-0-7636-2537-5; 0-7636-2537-X; 978-0-7636-280107 pa; 0-7636-2801-8 pa

LC 2007-24098

Sequel to Vegan virgin Valentine (2004)

V is "still living with her grandparents and still sleeping around. Then a hockey puck hits her in the head, and she literally falls into the arms of Sam Almond. . . . V comes across as an engaging character whose struggles seem very real. The details of her road trip are written with humor and verve, and the sex, while prevalent, is not graphic. There's also a sweetness here that makes V and Sam worth rooting for." Booklist

★ **Infinite** in Between. Carolyn Mackler. Harpercollins Childrens Books 2015 480 p.

Grades: 9 10 11 12

1. High school students -- Fiction 2. School stories

0061731072; 9780061731075, $17.99

This novel, by Carolyn Mackler, "chronicles the lives of five teenagers through the thrills, heartbreaks, and joys of their four years in high school. . . . Zoe, Jake, Mia, Gregor, and Whitney meet at freshman orientation. At the end of that first day, they make a promise to reunite after graduation. So much can happen in those in-between years." (Publisher's note)

"Things happen, for the most part, no more dramatically than they do in high schools every day. A clear, true portrait of life as it is for many teenagers." Booklist

Vegan virgin Valentine. Candlewick Press 2004 228p $16.99; pa $8.99

Grades: 9 10 11 12

1. School stories 2. Aunts -- Fiction

ISBN 0-7636-2155-2; 0-7636-2613-9 pa

LC 2004-45774

Mara's niece, who is only one-year-younger, moves in bringing conflict between the two teenagers because of their opposite personalities

"Racily narrated by likeable Mara, this fast-paced coming-of-age story is charged with sarcasm, angst, honesty, and hope. Many teen girls will recognize parts of themselves within its pages." Voice Youth Advocates

Followed by Guyaholic (2007)

MacLean, Jill

Nix Minus One; by Jill Maclean. Pajama Press 2013 296 p. (hardcover) $21.95

Grades: 7 8 9 10

1. School stories 2. Novels in verse
ISBN 192748524X; 9781927485248

This novel in verse focuses on 15-year-old Nix. "Formerly known as 'Fatty Humbolt,' he is struggling with his crush on Loren Cody, the girlfriend of the best player on the hockey team, and his love-hate relationship with his older sister, Roxy." Nix is shy while Roxy is the opposite. "Then Roxy falls for Bryan Sykes, a popular but notorious cad and politician's son, and Nix is forced to come out of his shell and find his voice." (School Library Journal)

Macvie, Meagan

The **ocean** in my ears. Meagan Macvie. Ooligan Press, Portland State University 2017 285 p.

Grades: 10 11 12

1. Coming of age -- Fiction; 2. Dating (Social customs) -- Fiction; 3. Family life -- Alaska -- Fiction; 4. Friendship -- Fiction; 5. Grief -- Fiction; 6. High schools -- Fiction; 7. Schools -- Fiction; 8. Alaska -- Fiction; 9. Family life -- Fiction
9781932010947, $16; 9781932010954

LC 2017005062

This novel, by Meagan Macvie, "set in the early 1990s, follows 17-year-old Meri Miller during her last year of high school in (very) small-town Soldotna, Alaska, yet the year turns out to be anything but uneventful. As she seeks a way to leave Alaska for college, she navigates her first sexual encounter, the loss of her grandmother, a friend who drifts away, and the stifling rules of her religious parents." (Publishers Weekly)

"An unforgettable journey to adulthood." Kirkus

Madigan, L. K.

★ **Flash** burnout; a novel. Houghton Mifflin 2009 332p $16

Grades: 9 10 11 12

1. School stories 2. Friendship -- Fiction 3. Photographers -- Fiction 4. Dating (Social customs) -- Fiction
ISBN 978-0-547-19489-9; 0-547-19489-7

LC 2010-278252

ALA YALSA The William C. Morris YA Debut Award (2010)

"When he snapped a picture of a street person for his photography homework, Blake never dreamed that the woman in the photo was his friend Marissa's long-lost meth addicted mom. Blake's participation in the ensuing drama opens up a world of trouble, both for him and for Marissa." Publisher's note

"This rich romance explores the complexities of friendship and love, and the all-too-human limitations of both. It's a sobering, compelling, and satisfying read for teens." Booklist

Madison, Bennett

★ **September** Girls; Bennett Madison. Harpercollins Childrens Books 2013 352 p. (hardcover) $17.99

Grades: 9 10 11 12

1. Love stories 2. Summer -- Fiction 3. Mermaids and mermen -- Fiction
ISBN 0061255637; 9780061255632

In this young adult, magical realist novel, by Bennett Madison, "Sam is spending the summer in a beach town filled with beautiful blond girls. . . . Sam finds himself in an unexpected summer romance when he falls for one of the Girls, DeeDee. But as they get closer, she pulls away without explanation. Sam knows that if he is going to win her back, he'll have to learn the Girls' secret." (Publisher's note)

Maetani, Valynne E.

Ink & ashes. Valynne E. Maetani. Tu Books, an imprint of Lee & Low Books, Inc. 2015 368 p.

Grades: 7 8 9 10

1. Fathers -- Fiction 2. Japanese Americans -- Fiction 3. Love -- Fiction 4. Mystery and detective stories 5. Organized crime -- Fiction 6. Mystery fiction
9781620142110, $19.95

LC 2015006632

In this mystery novel by Valynne E. Maetani, "Claire Takata has never known much about her father. . . . But on the anniversary of his death, she finds a letter from her deceased father to her stepfather. . . . Struggling to understand why her parents kept this surprising history hidden, Claire combs through anything that might give her information about her father . . . until she discovers that he was a member of the yakuza, a Japanese organized crime syndicate." (Publisher's note)

"Maetani's fast-paced debut will appeal to readers who like their intrigue with a generous helping of romance." Booklist

Mafi, Tahereh

★ **Shatter** me. Tahereh Mafi. HarperTeen 2011 338 p

Grades: 8 9 10 11 12

1. Ability -- Fiction; 2. Love stories; 3. Science fiction; 4. Soldiers -- Fiction; 5. Romance fiction
ISBN 9780062085481, $17.99

LC 2011019370

"Juliette knows that she is a monster; her touch is fatal. She has been living in a cell in a mental institution for 264 days, all alone. When a boy is brought in as her cell mate, his arrival sparks an explosion of events that changes her life as well as the world. Shatter Me takes place in a future time in which a lack of resources has so frightened the citizens that they have handed over all of their basic rights to a totalitarian government. The regime has plans for Juliette, but she finds the strength to resist the powers that be and joins in a rebel movement, becoming the central figure that everyone is fighting to possess." (School Library Journal)

Other titles in this series are: Unravel me (2013); Ignite me (2014); Restore me (2018); Defy me (2019)

★ A **very** large expanse of sea. Tahereh Mafi. HarperTeen 2018 320 p.

Grades: 8 9 10 11 12

1. Prejudices -- Fiction; 2. Romance fiction; 3. Muslims -- Fiction

9780062866561, $18.99

LC 2018945999

In this book, by Tahereh Mafi, "it's 2002, a year after 9/11. It's an extremely turbulent time politically, but especially so for someone like Shirin, a sixteen-year-old Muslim girl who's tired of being stereotyped.... So she's built up protective walls and refuses to let anyone close enough to hurt her.... But then she meets Ocean James. He's the first person...who really seems to want to get to know...[her.]" (Publisher's note)

Magnin, Joyce

Carrying Mason; [by] Joyce Magnin. Zonderkidz 2011 153p $14.99

Grades: 5 6 7 8

1. Family life -- Fiction 2. Country life -- Fiction 3. People with mental disabilities -- Fiction

ISBN 978-0-310-72681-4; 0-310-72681-6

LC 2011014462

In rural Pennsylvania in 1958, when thirteen-year-old Luna's best friend Mason dies, she decides to move in with his mentally disabled mother and care for her as Mason did.

"Gently, deliberately paced, Luna's first-person tale provides a fresh look at mental disabilities and the additional burden of negative attitudes. While Ruby's disability is apparent, this effort also celebrates her capabilities. Although the primary focus is Luna, her quirky father, supportive mother and boy-crazy older sister are also sufficiently developed to provide additional depth. A quiet coming-of-age tale with heart offers a fresh look at mentally disabled adults." Kirkus

Magoon, Kekla

37 things I love (in no particular order) Kekla Magoon. Henry Holt 2012 218 p. (hc) $16.99

Grades: 9 10 11 12

1. Girls -- Fiction 2. Family life -- Fiction 3. Coma -- Fiction 4. Grief -- Fiction 5. Schools -- Fiction 6. High schools -- Fiction 7. Interpersonal relations -- Fiction 8. Self-actualization (Psychology) -- Fiction

ISBN 0805094652; 9780805094657

LC 2011031998

This young adult novel by Kekla Magoon follows Ellis, who "only has four days of her sophomore year left. . . . Her father has been in a coma for years, . . . and her already-fragile relationship with her mother is strained over whether or not to remove him from life support. Her best friend fails even to notice that anything is wrong and Ellis feels like her world is falling apart. But when all seems bleak, Ellis finds comfort in the most unexpected places." (Publisher's note)

Camo girl. Aladdin 2010 218p $16.99

Grades: 5 6 7 8

1. Friendship -- Fiction 2. Prejudices -- Fiction 3. Racially mixed people -- Fiction

ISBN 978-1-4169-7804-6; 1-4169-7804-6

A novel about a biracial girl living in the suburbs of Las Vegas examines the friendships that grow out of, and despite, her race.

"Magoon . . . offers a sensitive and articulate portrayal of a pair of middle-school outsiders. . . . This poetic and nuanced story addresses the courage it takes to truly know and support someone, as well as the difficult choices that come with growing up." Publ Wkly

Fire in the streets; by Kekla Magoon. 1st Aladdin hardcover ed. Aladdin 2012 336 p. $15.99

Grades: 7 8 9 10

1. Historical fiction 2. Black nationalism -- Fiction 3. African Americans -- Civil rights -- Fiction 4. Racism -- Fiction 5. African Americans -- Fiction 6. Black Panther Party -- Fiction 7. Brothers and sisters -- Fiction 8. Civil rights movements -- Fiction 9. United States -- History -- 20th century -- Fiction 10. Chicago (Ill.) -- History -- 20th century -- Fiction

ISBN 1442422300; 9781442422308

LC 2011039129

Sequel to: The rock and the river

This historical novel by Kekla Magoon, is set "in the sweltering Chicago summer of 1968. [Maxie] is a Black Panther--or at least she wants to be one. . . . At fourteen, she's allowed to help out in the office, but she certainly can't help patrol the streets. Then Maxie realizes that there is a traitor in their midst, and if she can figure out who it is, it may be her ticket to becoming a real Panther. But when she learns the truth, the knowledge threatens to destroy her world." (Publisher's note)

★ **How** it went down; Kekla Magoon, Henry Holt & Co. 2014 336p $17.99

Grades: 9 10 11 12

1. African Americans -- Fiction 2. Death -- Fiction 3. Race relations -- Fiction 4. Witnesses -- Fiction 5. United States -- Race relations -- Fiction 6. Murder -- Fiction

ISBN: 0805098690; 9780805098693; 9781250068231

LC 2014027402

Coretta Scott King Author Award Honor Book (2015)

"When 16-year-old Tariq, a black teen, is shot and killed by a white man, every witness has a slightly different perception of the chain of events leading up to the murder. Family, friends, gang members, neighbors, and a well-meaning but self-serving minster make up the broad cast of characters... With a great hook and relatable characters, this will be popular for fans of realistic fiction. The unique storytelling style and thematic relevance will make it a potentially intriguing pick for classroom discussion." SLJ

The **rock** and the river. Aladdin 2009 290p $15.99

Grades: 7 8 9 10

1. Brothers -- Fiction 2. Chicago (Ill.) -- Fiction 3. African Americans -- Fiction 4. Black Panther Party -- Fiction

ISBN 978-1-4169-7582-3; 1-4169-7582-9

LC 2008-29170

ALA EMIERT Coretta Scott King John Steptoe New Talent Award (2010)

In 1968 Chicago, fourteen-year-old Sam Childs is caught in a conflict between his father's nonviolent approach to seeking civil rights for African Americans and his older brother, who has joined the Black Panther Party.

This "novel will make readers feel what it was like to be young, black, and militant 40 years ago, including the seething fury and desperation over the daily discrimination that drove the oppressed to fight back." Booklist

Maguire, Gregory

Egg & spoon; Gregory Maguire; Candlewick Press. 2014 475p $17.99

Grades: 7 8 9 10 11 12

1. Baba Yaga (Legendary Character) --Fiction 2. Mistaken identity --Fiction 3. Monks --Fiction 4. Princes --Fiction 5. Teenage girls --Fiction 6. Poor -- Fiction 7. Girls —Fiction 8. Russia -- Fiction

ISBN: 0763672203; 9780763672201

LC 2014931834

Boston Globe-Horn Book Honor: Fiction (2015)

"With one brother conscripted into the Tsar's army and another bound to serve a local landowner, Elena is left alone to care for her widowed and ailing mother in early 20th-century Russia. When an elegant train bearing a noble her age rolls through their barren village, Elena and her counterpart, Cat, accidentally swap places. . . . The author weaves a lyrical tale full of magic and promise, yet checkered with the desperation of poverty and the treacherous prospect of a world gone completely awry. Egg and Spoon is a beautiful reminder that fairy tales are at their best when they illuminate the precarious balance between lighthearted childhood and the darkness and danger of adulthood." SLJ

Mahoney, Karen

The **iron** witch. Flux 2011 299p $9.95

Grades: 6 7 8 9 10

1. Magic -- Fiction 2. Alchemy -- Fiction 3. Orphans -- Fiction 4. Kidnapping -- Fiction

ISBN 0-7387-2582-X; 978-0-7387-2582-6

LC 2010037692

Seventeen-year-old Donna Underwood is considered a freak, cursed by the magical heritage that destroyed her alchemist parents, but when vicious wood elves abduct her best friend Navin, Donna must betray all her parents fought for and join the battle between the humans and the fey.

"Adventurous, dark and dangerous. The Iron Witch will have teen readers clamoring for more." Libr Media Connect

Maldonado, Torrey

Secret Saturdays. G.P. Putnam's Sons 2010 195p $16.99

Grades: 6 7 8 9

1. School stories 2. African Americans -- Fiction 3. Single parent family -- Fiction 4. Racially mixed people -- Fiction

ISBN 978-0-399-25158-0; 0-399-25158-8

LC 2009-10361

Twelve-year-old boys living in a rough part of New York confront questions about what it means to be a friend, a father, and a man.

"Maldonado convincingly portrays roughneck playgrounds where boys are expected to be 'hard' and . . . Justin's narration resonates with the authenticity of a preteen doing his best in an urban landscape that has taught him all he knows. . . . The book remains a moving portrayal of the hope to be found through honest relationships." Publ Wkly

Malley, Gemma

The **Declaration**. Bloomsbury 2007 300p $16.95

Grades: 7 8 9 10

1. Science fiction 2. Immortality -- Fiction 3. Great Britain -- Fiction

ISBN 978-1-59990-119-0; 1-59990-119-6

LC 2006-102138

In 2140 England, where drugs enable people to live forever and children are illegal, teenaged Anna, an obedient "Surplus" training to become a house servant, discovers that her birth parents are trying to find her.

This is "gripping. . . . The indoctrinated teen's awakening to massive injustice makes compulsive reading." Booklist

Other titles in this series are:

The legacy (2011)

The resistance (2008)

Maniscalco, Kerri

Stalking Jack the Ripper. Kerri Maniscalco. JIM-MY Patterson Books/Little, Brown & Co. 2016 336 p. Illustration

Grades: 10 11 12

1. Mystery and detective stories 2. Serial murderers -- Fiction 3. Jack, the Ripper -- Fiction 4. Great Britain -- History -- Victoria, 1837-1901 -- Fiction 5. London (England) -- History -- 19th century -- Fiction 6. Serial killers -- Fiction 7. Mystery fiction 8. London (England) -- Fiction

9780316317313, $57; 9780316273497, $18.99

LC 2016006139

In this book, by Kerri Maniscalco, "seventeen-year-old Audrey Rose Wadsworth was born a lord's daughter. . . . . Against her stern father's wishes and society's expectations, Audrey often slips away to her uncle's laboratory to study the gruesome practice of forensic medicine. When her work on a string of savagely killed corpses drags Audrey into the investigation of a serial murderer, her search for answers brings her close to her own sheltered world." (Publisher's note)

"An entertaining debut full of twists and turns, perfect for fans of historical fiction and mystery." SLJ

Other titles in this series:

Hunting Prince Dracula (2017)

Escaping from Houdini (2018)

Manivong, Laura

Escaping the tiger. Harper 2010 216p il $15.99

Grades: 6 7 8 9

1. Refugees -- Fiction 2. Family life -- Fiction

ISBN 978-0-06-166177-8; 0-06-166177-5

LC 2009-24095

In 1982, twelve-year-old Vonlai, his parents, and sister, Dalah, escape from Laos to a Thai refugee camp, where they spend four long years struggling to survive in hopes on one day reaching America.

"This compelling novel offers significant historical background. This is certainly a book to prompt purposeful discussion to increase historical and multicultural awareness." SLJ

Mankell, Henning

★ A **bridge** to the stars. Delacorte Press 2007 164p $15.99; lib bdg $18.99; pa $8.99

Grades: 6 7 8 9

1. Father-son relationship -- Fiction

ISBN 978-0-385-73495-0; 0-385-73495-6; 978-0-385-90489-6 lib bdg; 0-385-90489-4 lib bdg; 978-0-440-24042-6 pa; 0-440-24042-5 pa

LC 2006-26901

In Sweden in 1956, eleven-year-old Joel and his father, a logger who was once a sailor, live alone with their secrets, including Joel's secret society that meets at night and his father's new romantic interest.

This is a "quiet but deeply satisfying coming-of-age story. . . . Those who welcome character-driven fiction will treasure this beautifully realized novel." Booklist

Other titles in this series are:
Shadows in the twilight (2008)
When the snow fell (2009)

Shadow of the leopard; [translated from the Swedish by Anna Paterson] Annick Press; Distributed in the U.S.A. by Firefly Books 2009 177p $19.95; pa $10.95

Grades: 10 11 12

1. Adultery -- Fiction 2. Amputees -- Fiction 3. Mozambique -- Fiction 4. Family life -- Fiction

ISBN 978-1-55451-200-3; 978-1-55451-199-0 pa

Sequel to Secrets of the fire (2003)

First published in Australia with title: The fury in the fire

Sofia, who lost her legs as a child, is now grown up with children in Mozambique, but when she discovers that Armando, the father of her children, is cheating on her, she leaves him, igniting his terrible rage.

"Readers will remember the indomitable Sofia—whose tale is based on real events—long after they close the book." Kirkus

Mantchev, Lisa

Eyes like stars. Feiwel and Friends 2009 356p $16.99

Grades: 8 9 10 11 12

1. Magic -- Fiction 2. Actors -- Fiction 3. Orphans -- Fiction 4. Theater -- Fiction 5. Books and reading -- Fiction

ISBN 978-0-312-38096-0; 0-312-38096-8

LC 2008-15317

Thirteen-year-old Bertie strives to save Theater Illuminata, the only home she has ever known, but is hindered by the Players who magically live on there, especially Ariel, who is willing to destroy the Book at the center of the magic in order to escape into the outside world.

"The story contains enough mystery and mayhem to keep readers engaged, even as they analyze." Voice Youth Advocates

Other titles in this series include:
Perchance to dream (2010)
So silver bright (2011)

Manzano, Sonia

★ The **revolution** of Evelyn Serrano; Sonia Manzano. Scholastic 2012 205 p. $17.99

Grades: 6 7 8 9 10

1. Historical fiction 2. Puerto Ricans -- Fiction 3. Identity -- Fiction 4. Grandmothers -- Fiction 5. New York (N.Y.) -- History -- 20th century -- Fiction 6. East Harlem (New York, N.Y.) 7. Protest movements -- New York (State) -- New York

ISBN 0545325056; 9780545325059; 9780545325066

LC 2012009240

Pura Belpré Author Honor Book (2013)

This novel, by Sonia Manzano, is set "in New York's El Barrio in 1969. . . . The Young Lords, a Puerto Rican activist group, dump garbage in the street and set it on fire, igniting a powerful protest. When Abuela steps in to take charge, Evelyn is thrust into the action. . . . Evelyn learns important truths about her Latino heritage and the history makers who shaped a nation." (Publisher's note)

Includes bibliographical references

Marchetta, Melina

★ **Finnikin** of the rock. Candlewick Press 2010 399p map $18.99

Grades: 8 9 10 11 12

1. Fantasy fiction

ISBN 0-7636-4361-0; 978-0-7636-4361-4

LC 2009-28046

In this fantasy novel, "Finnikin was only a child during the five days of the unspeakable, when the royal family of Lumatere were brutally murdered, and an imposter seized the throne. . . . Finnikin, now on the cusp of manhood, is compelled to join forces with an arrogant and enigmatic young novice named Evanjalin, who claims that her dark dreams will lead the exiles to a surviving royal child and a way to pierce the cursed barrier and regain the land of Lumatere." (Publisher's note)

"The skillful world building includes just enough detail to create a vivid sense of place, and Marchetta maintains suspense with unexpected story arcs. It is the achingly real characters, though, and the relationships that emerge through the captivating dialogue that drive the story. Filled with questions about the impact of exile and the human need to belong, this standout fantasy quickly reveals that its real magic lies in its accomplished writing." Booklist

★ **Froi** of the exiles. Candlewick 2012 608 p.

Grades: 8 9 10 11 12

1. Exiles 2. War stories 3. Fantasy fiction

ISBN 9780763647599

In this fantasy book, "Froi, a former street thief who has started a new life in Lumatere, is sent to Charyn in disguise to assassinate its king, but his worldview is shaken by revelations about his own unknown past. Tensions between the two kingdoms ratchet up, and Froi's loyalties are tested as he becomes entrenched in the chaotic political situation in Charyn and is drawn to its unpredictable princess, Quintana, who has been horribly abused in an attempt to break Charyn's curse." (Publishers Weekly)

★ **Jellicoe** Road. HarperTeen 2008 419p $17.99; lib bdg $18.89

Grades: 9 10 11 12

1. School stories 2. Australia -- Fiction 3. Abandoned

children -- Fiction 4. Identity (Psychology) -- Fiction
ISBN 978-0-06-143183-8; 0-06-143183-4; 978-0-06-143184-5 lib bdg; 0-06-143184-2 lib bdg

LC 2008-00760

First published 2006 in Australia with title: On the Jellicoe Road

Michael L. Printz Award, 2009

Abandoned by her drug-addicted mother at the age of eleven, high school student Taylor Markham struggles with her identity and family history at a boarding school in Australia.

"Readers may feel dizzied and disoriented, but as they puzzle out exactly how Hannah's narrative connects with Taylor's current reality, they will find themselves ensnared in the story's fascinating, intricate structure. A beautifully rendered mystery." Kirkus

The **piper's** son. Candlewick Press 2011 328p $17.99

Grades: 9 10 11 12

1. Australia -- Fiction 2. Musicians -- Fiction 3. Bereavement -- Fiction 4. Family life -- Fiction
ISBN 978-0-7636-4758-2; 0-7636-4758-6

LC 2010-39168

"Award-winning author Melina Marchetta reopens the story of the group of friends from her acclaimed novel Saving Francesca - but five years have passed, and now it's Thomas Mackee who needs saving. After his favorite uncle was blown to bits on his way to work in a foreign city, Tom watched his family implode. He quit school and turned his back on his music and everyone that mattered, including the girl he can't forget...An unflinching look at family, forgiveness, and the fierce inner workings of love and friendship, The Piper's Son redefines what it means to go home again." Publisher's Note

"A memorable portrait of first love, surviving grief, and the messy contradictions and fierce bonds that hold friends and family together." Booklist

★ **Quintana** of Charyn; Melina Marchetta. Candlewick Press 2013 528 p. (Lumatere chronicles) $18.99

Grades: 8 9 10 11 12

1. War stories 2. Fantasy fiction
ISBN 0763658359; 9780763658359

LC 2012955120

This is the conclusion of Melina Marchetta's trilogy which began with "Finnikin of the Rock." Here, "the kingdoms of Lumatere and Charyn attempt to bridge past atrocities through a new generation of leaders. Although tragedies arise, unity and healing are core themes, compared to the horrors of the previous books. As the title suggests, Quintana--the rightful ruler of Charyn, hidden following the uprising in the kingdom in Froi of the Exiles--is at the center of this final book." (Publishers Weekly)

Saving Francesca. Knopf 2004 243p hardcover o.p. pa $8.95

Grades: 9 10 11 12

1. School stories 2. Australia -- Fiction 3. Mental illness -- Fiction 4. Mother-daughter relationship --

Fiction
ISBN 0-375-82982-2; 0-375-82983-0 pa

LC 2004-3926

Sixteen-year-old Francesca could use her outspoken mother's help with the problems of being one of a handful of girls at a parochial school that has just turned co-ed, but her mother has suddenly become severely depressed

This book "has great characterizations, witty dialogue, a terrific relationship between Francesca and her younger brother, and a sweet romance. Teens will relate to this tender novel and will take to heart its solid messages and realistic treatment of a very real problem." SLJ

Followed by The piper's son (2011)

Marcus, Kimberly

Exposed. Random House 2011 260p $16.99; lib bdg $19.99

Grades: 8 9 10

1. School stories 2. Novels in verse 3. Rape -- Fiction 4. Guilt -- Fiction 5. Friendship -- Fiction 6. Photography -- Fiction
ISBN 0-375-86693-0; 0-375-96693-5 lib bdg; 978-0-375-86693-7; 978-0-375-89724-5 e-book; 978-0-375-96693-4 lib bdg

LC 2009-51545

High school senior Liz, a gifted photographer, can no longer see things clearly after her best friend accuses Liz's older brother of a terrible crime.

"The narrative largely zooms in on Liz's pain and her struggle to ground herself in her photography and gain admission to art school as events swirl around her. As a result of tethering the narrative to Liz's perspective, the ongoing discussion of Kate's rape and ensuing trial are not heavy-handed or gratuitous. In Liz, Marcus has created a sympathetic lead. A worthy addition to any collection." SLJ

Marillier, Juliet

Cybele's secret. Alfred A. Knopf 2008 432p $17.99; lib bdg $20.99

Grades: 7 8 9 10

1. Magic -- Fiction 2. Turkey -- Fiction 3. Sisters -- Fiction 4. Supernatural -- Fiction
ISBN 978-0-375-83365-6; 0-375-83365-X; 978-0-375-93365-3 lib bdg; 0-375-93365-4 lib bdg

LC 2008-4758

Scholarly eighteen-year-old Paula and her merchant father journey from Transylvania to Istanbul to buy an ancient pagan artifact rumored to be charmed, but others, including a handsome Portuguese pirate and an envoy from the magical Wildwood, want to acquire the item, as well.

This is a "honeyed draught of a [novel]. . . . Marillier embroiders Ottoman Empire cultural details into every fold and drape of her story." Booklist

Raven flight; a Shadowfell novel. Juliet Marillier. Alfred A. Knopf 2013 416 p.

Grades: 7 8 9 10

1. Occult fiction 2. Fantasy fiction 3. Fantasy 4. Magic -- Fiction 5. Orphans -- Fiction 6. Insurgency -- Fiction 7. Voyages and travels -- Fiction
ISBN 9780375869556; 9780375969553

LC 2012039483

This is the second volume of Juliet Marillier's Shadowfell series. Here, "Neryn's time among the rebels has left her stronger and healthier but no closer to grasping her power and becoming a true Caller. When a potential ally sets a time limit for rebelling against tyrannical King Keldec, Neryn can no longer hide and sets off to find the Hag of the Isles and the Lord of the North." (Kirkus Reviews)

Shadowfell; Juliet Marillier. Alfred A. Knopf 2012 410 p. map (trade) $16.99

Grades: 7 8 9 10 11 12

1. Fantasy fiction 2. Magic -- Fiction 3. Adventure fiction 4. Fantasy 5. Orphans -- Fiction 6. Insurgency -- Fiction 7. Voyages and travels -- Fiction
ISBN 0375869549; 9780375869549; 9780375969546; 9780375983665

LC 2011041050

Originally published: Sydney, N.S.W.: Pan Macmillan, 2012.

In this novel by Juliet Marillier "Fifteen-year-old Neryn is alone in the land of Alban, where the oppressive king has ordered anyone with magical strengths captured and brought before him. Eager to hide her own canny skill--a uniquely powerful ability to communicate with the fairy-like Good Folk--Neryn sets out for the legendary Shadowfell, a home and training ground for a secret rebel group determined to overthrow the evil King Keldec." (Publisher's note)

Wildwood dancing. Knopf 2007 416p $16.99; lib bdg $18.99

Grades: 7 8 9 10

1. Magic -- Fiction 2. Sisters -- Fiction 3. Supernatural -- Fiction
ISBN 0-375-83364-1; 0-375-93364-6 lib bdg

LC 2006-16075

Five sisters who live with their merchant father in Transylvania use a hidden portal in their home to cross over into a magical world, the Wildwood.

This is told "with a striking sense of place, magical elements, beautifully portrayed characters, strong heroines, and an emotional core that touches the heart." Voice Youth Advocates

Followed by: Cybele's secret (2008)

Mariz, Rae

The **Unidentified**. Balzer + Bray 2010 296p $16.99

Grades: 7 8 9 10

1. School stories 2. Science fiction
ISBN 978-0-06-180208-9; 0-06-180208-5

LC 2009-54254

In a futuristic alternative school set in a shopping mall where video game-playing students are observed and used by corporate sponsors for market research, Katey "Kid" Dade struggles to figure out where she fits in and whether she even wants to.

"An all-too-logical extrapolation of today's trends, this story of conformity, rebellion, and seeking one's identity is evocative of Scott Westerfeld and Cory Doctorow, injecting a dystopian setting with an optimistic, antiestablishment undercurrent." Publ Wkly

Marquardt, Marie F.

Dream Things True. Marie Marquardt. St. Martin's Press 2015 352 p.

Grades: 9 10 11 12

1. Love -- Fiction 2. Unauthorized immigrants -- Fiction
1250070457; 9781250070456, $18.99

LC 2015019022

In this novel, by Marie Marquardt, "the nephew of a senator, Evan seems to have it all - except a functional family. Alma has lived in Georgia since she was two, surrounded by a large (sometimes smothering) Mexican family. They both want out of this town. When they fall in love, they fall hard, trying to ignore their differences. Then Immigration and Customs Enforcement begins raids in their town, and Alma knows that she needs to share her secret. But how will she tell her country-club boyfriend that she and almost everyone she's close to are undocumented immigrants?" (Publisher's note)

"A debut romance for libraries looking to diversify their offerings." SLJ

★ The **radius** of us. Marie Marquardt ; illustrations by Carlos Alfredo Morataya. St. Martin's Griffin 2017 295 p. Illustration

Grades: 9 10 11 12

1. Brothers -- Fiction; 2. Emigration and immigration -- Fiction; 3. Mugging victims -- Fiction; 4. Panic attacks -- Fiction; 5. Victims of crimes -- Fiction; 6. Gangs -- Fiction; 7. Immigration and emigration -- Fiction
9781250096906; 9781250096890, $18.99; 1250096898

LC 2016036416

This young adult novel, by Marie Marquardt, "told in alternating first person points of view,...is a story of love, sacrifice, and the journey from victim to survivor. It offers an intimate glimpse into the causes and devastating impact of Latino gang violence, both in the U.S. and in Central America, and explores the risks that victims take when they try to start over." (Publisher's note)

"Tackling the issues of gang violence, immigration, mental health, and cultural bias, this is a compelling story that delivers profound messages through engaging, accessible prose." SLJ

Marr, Melissa

Wicked lovely. HarperTeen 2007 328p il $16.99; lib bdg $17.89

Grades: 8 9 10 11 12

1. Fantasy fiction 2. Fairies -- Fiction 3. Kings and rulers -- Fiction
ISBN 978-0-06-121465-3; 0-06-121465-5; 978-0-06-121466-0 lib bdg; 0-06-121466-3 lib bdg

LC 2007-09143

Seventeen-year-old Aislinn, who has the rare ability to see faeries, is drawn against her will into a centuries-old battle between the Summer King and the Winter Queen, and the survival of her life, her love, and summer all hang in the balance.

"This story explores the themes of love, commitment, and what it really means to give of oneself for the greater good to save everyone else. It is the unusual combination of past legends and modern-day life that gives a unique twist to this 'fairy' tale." SLJ

Other titles in this series are:
Darkest mercy (2011)
Fragile eternity (2009)
Ink exchange (2008)
Radiant shadows (2010)

Marsden, Carolyn, 1950-

My Own Revolution; Carolyn Marsden. Candlewick Press 2012 174 p. $16.99

Grades: 7 8 9 10 11 12

1. Czechoslovakia -- Fiction 2. Communist countries -- Fiction 3. Resistance to government -- Fiction

ISBN 0763653950; 9780763653958

LC 2012942296

This novel takes place "in 1960s Czechoslovakia, [where] . . . fourteen-year-old Patrik rebels against the communist regime in small ways whenever he gets the chance. . . . But anti-Party sentiment is risky, and when party interference cuts a little too close to home, Patrik and his family find themselves faced with a decision . . . that will change everything." (Publisher's note)

Sahwira; an African friendship. [by] Carolyn Marsden and Philip Matzigkeit. Candlewick Press 2009 189p $15.99

Grades: 5 6 7 8

1. Clergy -- Fiction 2. Friendship -- Fiction 3. Race relations -- Fiction

ISBN 978-0-7636-3575-6; 0-7636-3575-8

The strong friendship between two boys, one black and one white, who live on a mission in Rhodesia, begins to unravel as protests against white colonial rule intensify in 1964.

"The book looks beyond race to examine questions about the meaning of being Christian, fear of Communism, family loyalty, and ethical choices. Marsden and Matzigkeit . . . deftly navigate the dynamic forces at play in the two boys' lives. . . . The story crosses genres to bring in elements of historical fiction, intrigue, and mystery." Bull Cent Child Books

Marsden, John, 1950-

Hamlet: a novel. Candlewick Press 2009 229p $16.99

Grades: 10 11 12

1. Shakespeare, William, 1564-1616 -- Adaptations 2. Denmark -- Fiction 3. Princes -- Fiction 4. Homicide -- Fiction

ISBN 978-0-7636-4451-2; 0-7636-4451-X

LC 2009-7331

This is a retelling of Shakespeare's play. Grieving for the recent death of his beloved father and appalled by his mother's quick remarriage to his uncle, Hamlet, heir to the Danish throne, struggles with conflicting emotions, particularly after his father's ghost appeals to him to avenge his death.

"The setting is contemporary, but feels timeless. Marsden stays true to Shakespeare's text, while modernizing the dialogue. He makes the prince a sympathetic teen who is struggling with his hormones, his grief, and the fact that his uncle is now his stepfather. . . . This is a wonderful treatment of the play: engaging, gripping, dark, and lovely." SLJ

Tomorrow, when the war began. Houghton Mifflin 1995 286p pa $9.99

Grades: 7 8 9 10

1. War stories 2. Australia -- Fiction

ISBN 9780439829106; 0395706734

LC 94-29299

First published 1993 in Australia

"Australian teenager Ellie and six of her friends return from a winter break camping trip to find their homes burned or deserted, their families imprisoned, and their country occupied by a foreign military force in league with a band of disaffected Australians. As their shock wears off, the seven decide they must stick together if they are to survive. After a life-threatening skirmish with the occupiers, the teens retreat to their isolated campsite in the bush country and make plans to fight a guerilla war against the invaders. . . . " (SLJ)

Other titles in this series:
The Dead of Night (1994)
A Killing Frost (1995)
Darkness Be My Friend (1996)
Burning for Revenge (1997)
The Night is for Hunting (1998)
The Other Side of Dawn (1999)

While I live. Scholastic 2007 299p (The Ellie chronicles) $16.99

Grades: 7 8 9 10

1. War stories 2. Australia -- Fiction

ISBN 978-0-439-78318-7; 0-439-78318-6

Officially the war is over, but Ellie can not seem to escape it and resume a normal life especially after her parents are murdered and she becomes the ward of an unscrupulous lawyer who wants to acquire her family's property.

"Fans of 16-year-old Ellie Linton . . . will be overjoyed that she's back in an exciting series of her own. The realistic and shocking war-related violence that characterized the earlier titles is just as prevalent here." SLJ

Other titles about Ellie Linton are:
Circle of flight (2009)
Incurable (2008)

Marsh, Katherine

Jepp, who defied the stars; Katherine Marsh. Hyperion 2012 385 p. (hardback) $16.99

Grades: 6 7 8 9 10

1. Bildungsromans 2. Dwarfs -- Fiction 3. Historical fiction 4. Renaissance -- Fiction 5. Voyages and travels -- Fiction 6. Courts and courtiers -- Fiction 7. Europe -- History -- 16th century -- Fiction

ISBN 1423135008; 9781423135005

LC 2011053065

This book tells the story of "a 15-year-old dwarf named Jepp. . . . The first of the book's three sections finds a battered and beaten Jepp being transported ignobly in a cage to an unknown destination; along the way, he recalls the events that led him there, from his humble upbringing in an inn to becoming a court dwarf in Brussels. . . . Jepp's fortunes continue to wax and wane in the later sections, as he arrives at the island castle of astronomer Tycho Brahe." (Publishers Weekly)

The **night** tourist; [by] Katherine Marsh. 1st ed.; Hyperion Books for Children 2007 232p $17.99

Grades: 6 7 8 9

1. Death -- Fiction 2. Classical mythology -- Fiction
ISBN 978-1-4231-0689-0; 1-4231-0689-X

LC 2007013311

After fourteen-year-old classics prodigy Jack Perdu has a near fatal accident he meets Euri, a young ghost who introduces him to New York's Underworld, where those who died in New York reside until they are ready to move on, and Jack vows to find his dead mother there.

"Mixing numerous references to mythology and classical literature with deft touches of humor and extensive historical details . . . this intelligent and self-assured debut will compel readers from its outset and leave them satisfied." Publ Wkly

Marshall, Catherine

Christy. Avon Books 2006 576p pa $6.99

Grades: 9 10 11 12

1. Teachers -- Fiction 2. Appalachian region -- Fiction
ISBN 0-380-00141-1

A reissue of the title first published 1967 by McGraw-Hill

"A spirited young woman leaves the security of her home to become a teacher in Cutter Gap, Kentucky. It is 1912 and the needs of the Appalachian people are great. Christy learns much from the poverty and superstition of the mountain folk. Marshall's Christian faith and ideals are intertwined in the plot, which includes a love story." Shapiro. Fic for Youth. 3d edition

Marshall, Kate

I am still alive. Kate Alice Marshall. Penguin Group USA 2018 336 p.

Grades: 8 9 10 11

1. Revenge -- Fiction; 2. Survival skills -- Fiction; 3. Father-daughter relationship -- Fiction
0425290980; 9780425290989, $17.99

In this book, by Kate Alice Marshall, "Jess hadn't seen her survivalist, off-the-grid dad in over a decade. But after a car crash killed her mother and left her injured, she was forced to move to his cabin in the remote Canadian wilderness. Just as Jess was beginning to get to know him, a secret from his past paid them a visit, leaving her father dead and Jess stranded.... Jess will survive. She has to. She knows who killed her father...and she wants revenge." (Publisher's note)

Martin, C. K. Kelly

★ **I** know it's over. Random House 2008 244p $16.99; lib bdg $19.99

Grades: 9 10 11 12

1. Love stories 2. School stories 3. Canada -- Fiction
4. Pregnancy -- Fiction
ISBN 978-0-375-84566-6; 978-0-375-94566-3 lib bdg

LC 2007-29180

Sixteen-year-old Nick, still trying to come to terms with his parents' divorce, experiences exhilaration and despair in his relationship with his girlfriend Sasha especially when, after instigating a trial separation, she announces that she is pregnant.

"This measured but heartbreaking rendering of an all-too-common situation would be a great choice for mixed-gender book groups." Bull Cent Child Books

The **lighter** side of life and death. Random House Children's Books 2010 231p $16.99; lib bdg $19.99

Grades: 9 10 11 12

1. School stories 2. Theater -- Fiction 3. Remarriage -- Fiction
ISBN 978-0-375-84588-8; 0-375-84588-7; 978-0-375-95588-4 lib bdg; 0-375-95588-7 lib bdg

LC 2009-15608

After the last, triumphant night of the school play, fifteen-year-old Mason loses his virginity to his good friend and secret crush, Kat Medina, which leads to enormous complications at school just as his home life is thrown into turmoil by his father's marriage to a woman with two children.

"This is not your ordinary teen romance. It's heavy on the sex but carefully nuanced. . . . The layers of emotion, so rarely evoked by young men in YA novels, give a depth and authenticity to Mason's personality that expose his naïveté and occasional bewilderment. The book's other characters are equally complex. . . . A more genuine representation of teen life would be hard to find." Booklist

Yesterday; C.K. Kelly Martin. Random House 2012 368 p. (hardcover library binding) $19.99

Grades: 9 10 11 12

1. Occult fiction 2. Mystery fiction 3. Interpersonal relations -- Fiction 4. Science fiction 5. Memory -- Fiction 6. Schools -- Fiction 7. Identity -- Fiction 8. High schools -- Fiction 9. Family life -- Canada -- Fiction 10. Canada -- History -- 20th century -- Fiction
ISBN 0375866507; 0375966501; 9780375866500; 9780375896446; 9780375966507

LC 2011023994

In this book, "[h]er father's recent death and the move from New Zealand to Toronto with her mother and sister in 1985 have left Freya Kallas seriously disoriented and plagued by headaches. Worse, her memories have puzzling gaps. . . . What do Freya's dreams of living another life mean? . . . Freya is sure the boy she spots on a school field trip has the answers she needs. Though she doesn't know his name and he doesn't recognize her, Freya, increasingly desperate, can't let him go." (Kirkus)

Martin, T. Michael

The **end** games; T. Michael Martin. Balzer + Bray 2013 384 p. (hardcover) $17.99

Grades: 9 10 11 12

1. Science fiction 2. Zombies -- Fiction 3. Brothers -- Fiction 4. Survival -- Fiction 5. West Virginia -- Fiction
ISBN 0062201808; 9780062201805

LC 2012038108

This novel, by T. Michael Martin, "takes place in rural West Virginia after a zombie apocalypse. Seventeen-year-old Michael and his baby brother . . . have managed to stay alive by following the Instructions of a mysterious Games Master. They spend their nights fighting the Bellows, grotesque, flesh-eating creatures. But the brothers may not survive much longer. The Bellows are evolving. And the others in The Game don't always follow the rules." (Publisher's note)

Martinez, Claudia Guadalupe

Pig Park. By Claudia Guadalupe Martinez. Cinco Puntos Press 2014 248 p. Illustration

Grades: 8 9 10 11

1. Bakers and bakeries -- Fiction 2. Building -- Fiction 3. Family life -- Illinois -- Chicago -- Fiction 4. Hispanic Americans -- Fiction 5. Neighborhoods -- Fiction 6. Community life 7. Ghost towns

1935955764; 9781935955764, $15.95; 9781935955771

LC 2013040645

In this novel by Claudia Guadalupe Martinez "Masi Burciaga hauls bricks to help build a giant pyramid in her neighborhood park. Her neighborhood is becoming more of a ghost town each day since the lard company moved away. As a last resort, the neighborhood grown-ups enlist all the remaining able-bodied boys and girls into this scheme in hopes of luring visitors. But something's not right about the entrepreneur behind it all." (Publisher's note)

"Martinez uses nicely specific physical details to relate Masi's experiences, and the moments in the bakery seem particularly authentic and are suffused with love. The warm, diverse community setting and the realistic family interactions help overcome the somewhat jumbled plotlines." Kirkus

Martinez, Jessica

Kiss kill vanish. By Jessica Martinez. Katherine Tegen Books, an imprint of HarperCollinsPublishers 2014 432 p.

Grades: 9 10 11 12

1. Organized crime -- Fiction 2. Family secrets -- Fiction 3. Runaway children -- Fiction

006227449X; 9780062274496, $17.99

LC 2013043192

In this novel by Jessica Martinez "Valentina is living a charmed, glittering life in Miami . . . when one shocking moment shatters everything she thought she knew about herself, her boyfriend, and her world. With no one left to trust, Valentina sheds her identity and flees to Montreal. [Her] new life comes crashing down when someone from her past resurfaces, putting her safety in question and her heart on the line." (Publisher's note)

"Valentina's decision making is sometimes opaque, but her strong voice, full of sensory imagery, and her exquisitely drawn relationships with Emilio, Marcel, and her father make this a memorable thriller." Publishers Weekly

Virtuosity. Simon Pulse 2011 294p $16.99

Grades: 8 9 10 11 12

1. Musicians -- Fiction 2. Drug abuse -- Fiction 3. Violinists -- Fiction 4. Chicago (Ill.) -- Fiction 5. Mother-daughter relationship -- Fiction

ISBN 978-1-4424-2052-6; 1-4424-2052-9

LC 2010042513

This is a "riveting novel. . . . The portrayal of Carmen's world . . . is unique and convincing. . . . Even readers without much interest in music will enjoy this exceptional novel." SLJ

Martinez, Victor

★ **Parrot** in the oven; a novel. Cotler Bks. 1996 216p $19.99; pa $5.99

Grades: 7 8 9 10

1. Family life -- Fiction 2. Mexican Americans -- Fiction

ISBN 0-06-026704-6; 0-06-447186-1 pa

LC 96-2119

Manny relates his coming of age experiences as a member of a poor Mexican American family in which the alcoholic father only adds to everyone's struggle

The author "maintains the authenticity of his setting and characterizations through a razor-sharp combination of tense dialogue, coursing narrative and startlingly elegant imagery." Publ Wkly

Mary-Todd, Jonathan

Shot down; Jonathan Mary-Todd. Darby Creek 2012 92 p. (lib. bdg. : alk. paper) $27.93

Grades: 7 8 9 10 11 12

1. Adventure fiction 2. Apocalyptic fiction 3. Survival skills -- Fiction 4. Survival after airplane accidents, shipwrecks, etc. -- Fiction 5. Science fiction 6. Hunting -- Fiction 7. Kentucky -- Fiction 8. Survival -- Fiction

ISBN 0761383298; 9780761383291

LC 2012006864

This young adult novel, by Jonathan Mary-Todd, is a post-apocalyptic adventure story. "When a bullet knocks Malik and the Captain's hot-air balloon out of the sky, Malik goes into wilderness survival mode. . . . Whatever the crisis, he's always counted on the Gene Matterhorn Wilderness Survival Guidebook when things got crazy. Now he and the Captain are in the middle of miles of Kentucky wilderness, being chased by manhunters." (Publisher's note)

Mason, Prue

Camel rider; [by] Prue Mason. 1st U.S. ed.; Charlesbridge 2007 204p $15.95

Grades: 6 7 8 9

1. War stories 2. Deserts -- Fiction 3. Wilderness survival -- Fiction

ISBN 978-1-58089-314-5; 1-58089-314-7

LC 2006034125

Two expatriates living in a Middle Eastern country, twelve-year-old Adam from Australia and Walid from Bangladesh, must rely on one another when war breaks out and they find themselves in the desert, both trying to reach the same city with no water, little food, and no common language.

"The suspense is sustained and the wildly improbable happy ending is very satisfying." SLJ

Mason, Simon

Running girl. Simon Mason. David Fickling Books/Scholastic Inc. 2016 432 p.

Grades: 9 10 11 12

1. Detective and mystery stories 2. Genius -- Fiction 3. Gifted boys -- Fiction 4. Juvenile delinquency -- England -- Fiction 5. Juvenile delinquency -- Fiction 6. Murder -- Fiction 7. Murder -- Investigation -- England -- Fiction 8. Mystery and detective stories 9. Secrets -- Fiction 10. Teenage girls -- Crimes against

-- England -- Fiction 11. England -- Fiction 12. Murder -- Investigation -- Fiction 13. Mystery fiction
9781338036435, $18.99; 1338036424; 9781338036428, $18.99

LC 2016005739

In this novel, by Simon Mason, "Garvie Smith is a whip-smart and drolly cool high school slacker who spends his free time mulling over mathematical riddles and solving imaginary crimes. When . . . Chloe Dow, is found murdered, Garvie applies his skills to solving a real-life homicide. . . . Garvie forges a strained partnership with the detective on the case, an observant Sikh named Raminder Singh. (School Library Journal)

"Mason (Moon Pie) grounds the story in reality as Garvie grows to better understand that actions have real and sometimes permanent consequences, seamlessly melding British teen drama with a believable and suspenseful plot full of well-executed twists. " Pub Wkly

"First published in the United Kingdom in 2014 by David Fickling Books"—Copyright page.

Mass, Wendy

Heaven looks a lot like the mall; a novel. Little, Brown 2007 251p $16.99

Grades: 8 9 10 11 12

1. School stories 2. Coma -- Fiction 3. Shopping centers and malls -- Fiction
ISBN 978-0-316-05851-3; 0-316-05851-3

LC 2007-12333

When high school junior Tessa Reynolds falls into a coma after getting hit in the head during gym class, she experiences heaven as the mall where her parents work, and she revisits key events from her life, causing her to reevaluate herself and how she wants to live.

"Tessa's journey and authentic voice is one that readers will appreciate. . . . Funny, thought-provoking, and at times heartbreaking, this story will entertain and inspire readers." SLJ

A **mango**-shaped space; a novel. Little, Brown 2003 220p $16.95

Grades: 5 6 7 8

1. School stories 2. Synesthesia -- Fiction
ISBN 0-316-52388-7

LC 2002-72989

Afraid that she is crazy, thirteen-year-old Mia, who sees a special color with every letter, number, and sound, keeps this a secret until she becomes overwhelmed by school, changing relationships, and the loss of something important to her

"Mass skillfully conveys Mia's emotions, and readers will be intrigued with this fictional depiction of an actual, and fascinating, condition." Horn Book Guide

Massey, David

Torn; David Massey. Scholastic 2013 288 p. $17.99

Grades: 9 10 11 12

1. Missing children -- Fiction 2. Afghan War, 2001- -- Fiction 3. War -- Fiction 4. Soldiers -- Fiction 5.

Afghanistan -- Fiction 6. Medical care -- Fiction
ISBN 0545496454; 9780545496452

LC 2012024405

In this novel by David Massey, set "in war-torn Afghanistan, a girl walks right into a hail of bullets: Elinor watches it with her own eyes. The young British army medic risks the line of fire to rescue her, only to realize the girl is gone. To find the missing, mysterious child, Elinor enlists the help of an American Navy SEAL. But in all the confusion, with coalition troops fighting every day to maintain a fragile peace, does Ben have something to hide?" (Publisher's note)

Massey, a former counter-terrorism consultant, brings an air of authenticity to this intense novel that explores the power of friendships formed in combat as well as war's effect on one young woman's idealism." (Horn Book)

Masson, Sophie

Snow, fire, sword; 1st American ed.; Eos 2006 359p $15.99; lib bdg $16.89

Grades: 6 7 8 9

1. Fantasy fiction 2. Magic -- Fiction
ISBN 978-0-06-079091-2; 0-06-079091-1; 978-0-06-079092-9 lib bdg; 0-06-079092-X lib bdg

LC 2005-18149

In the mythical, Indonesia-like country of Jayangan, a village girl and an apprentice swordmaker embark on a magical journey to defeat a hidden evil that threatens their land.

"The sense of a permeable membrane between spirit worlds and contemporary reality will fascinate many readers, as will the shifting images of water buffaloes and motorbikes, villages and cities, and sacred and secular ways." Booklist

The **madman** of Venice. Delacorte Press 2010 276p $17.99; lib bdg $20.99

Grades: 6 7 8 9

1. Missing persons -- Fiction
ISBN 978-0-385-73843-9; 0-385-73843-9; 978-0-385-90729-3 lib bdg; 0-385-90729-X lib bdg

LC 2009022369

First published 2009 in the United Kingdom

"An exotic setting and delicious intrigue combine to make intense historical fiction in this tale of missing persons, murder, and, of course, romance. English merchant Master Ashby heads to Venice in 1602 to investigate the murder of his agent Salerio and the strange disappearance of a young Jewish girl accused of witchcraft by the cruel, conniving wife of the Count of Montemaro. . . . Ashby and his alchemist friend Dr. Leone soon find themselves entangled in a morass that involves Venetian pirates, mistaken identities, and the poisoning of the Count." SLJ

Master, Irfan

★ A **beautiful** lie; by Irfan Master. Albert Whitman 2012 301 p. (hardcover) $16.99

Grades: 7 8 9 10

1. Deception -- Fiction 2. India -- History -- Fiction 3. Father-son relationship -- Fiction 4. Honesty -- Fiction 5. Terminally ill -- Fiction 6. Fathers and sons -- Fiction 7. India -- History -- Partition, 1947 -- Fiction

8. Pakistan -- History -- 20th century -- Fiction
ISBN 0807505978; 9780807505977

LC 2011051132

In this book by Irfan Master, set "in India in 1947, the country is coming apart -- and so is thirteen-year-old Bilal's life. He is determined to protect his dying father from the news of Partition, news that he knows will break his father's heart. With spirit and determination, and with the help of his good friends, Bilal builds an elaborate deception, even printing false pages of the local newspaper to hide the signs of national unrest." (Publisher's note)

Matas, Carol
After the war. Simon & Schuster Bks. for Young Readers 1996 116p map hardcover o.p. pa $4.99
Grades: 7 8 9 10
1. Jews -- Fiction 2. Holocaust, 1933-1945 -- Fiction
ISBN 0-689-80350-8; 0-689-80722-8

LC 95-43613

After being released from Buchenwald at the end of World War II, fifteen-year-old Ruth risks her life to lead a group of children across Europe to Palestine

"Rich in texture and simple in its honesty, this story resonates with feeling." Voice Youth Advocates

The **whirlwind**. Orca 2007 128p pa $8.95
Grades: 6 7 8 9
1. Jews -- Fiction 2. Immigrants -- Fiction 3. World War, 1939-1945 -- Fiction
ISBN 978-1-55143-703-3 pa; 1-55143-703-1 pa

"Benjamin Friedman, a 15-year-old Jewish boy, fears for his life in Nazi Germany. Fortunately, his family is able to escape Hitler, arriving in Seattle in the summer of 1941. Ben is relieved to be there but is upset and confused by his experiences. . . . This unique and thought-provoking story shows what prejudice and indifference to suffering and wrongdoing can lead to. It imparts an understanding of the Holocaust and World War II." SLJ

Mathieu, Jennifer
★ **Moxie**: a novel. Jennifer Mathieu. Roaring Brook Press 2017 330 p.
Grades: 8 9 10 11 12
1. Feminism -- Fiction; 2. High schools -- Fiction; 3. Mothers and daughters -- Fiction; 4. Schools -- Fiction; 5. Sexism -- Fiction; 6. Zines -- Fiction; 7. Texas -- Fiction; 8. Fanzines -- Fiction
9781250104267, $9.99; 9781626726352, $17.99

LC 2016057288

In this book, by Jennifer Mathieu, "Vivian Carter is fed up...with an administration at her high school that thinks the football team can do no wrong. Fed up with sexist dress codes, hallway harassment, and gross comments from guys.... But most of all,...fed up with always following the rules.... [She] creates a feminist zine that she distributes anonymously to her classmates. . . [and] realizes that what she has started is nothing short of a girl revolution." (Publisher's note)

Matson, Morgan
Amy & Roger's epic detour. Simon and Schuster Books for Young Readers 2010 343p il $16.99

Grades: 9 10 11 12
1. Death -- Fiction 2. Guilt -- Fiction 3. Fathers -- Fiction 4. Bereavement -- Fiction 5. Automobile travel -- Fiction
ISBN 978-1-4169-9065-9; 1-4169-9065-8

LC 2009-49988

After the death of her father, Amy, a high school student, and Roger, a college freshman, set out on a carefully planned road trip from California to Connecticut. "Grades eight to twelve." (Bull Cent Child Books)

"This entertaining and thoughtful summertime road trip serves up slices of America with a big scoop of romance on the side." Kirkus

Since you've been gone; Morgan Matson; Simon & Schuster Books for Young Readers. 2014 464p $17.99

Grades: 7 8 9 10
1. Best friends -- Fiction 2. Dating (Social customs) -- Fiction 3. Family life -- Connecticut -- Fiction 4. Friendship -- Fiction 5. Self-reliance -- Fiction 6. Connecticut -- Fiction
ISBN: 1442435003; 9781442435001; 9781442435018

LC 2013041617

"Emily feels lost when her best friend, Sloane, disappears without explanation. But Sloane left Emily a daunting to-do list (with items like 'kiss a stranger'), and Emily bravely takes on each task, finding new friends, confidence, and a crush along the way. A perfectly awkward protagonist; well-rounded, quirky supporting characters; and spot-on dialogue make this novel of self-discovery stand out." Horn Book

Mattison, Booker T.
Unsigned hype; a novel. Revell 2009 207p pa $9.99

Grades: 7 8 9 10
1. Rap music -- Fiction 2. Christian life -- Fiction 3. African Americans -- Fiction
ISBN 978-0-8007-3380-3; 0-8007-3380-0

LC 2008-54966

Fifteen-year-old Tory Tyson dreams of producing hip hop records, and as he rapidly begins to experience success doing just that, he finds that he must make choices between the way he has been raised by his single, God-fearing mother and the folks he meets in the music world.

This "novel has an authentic voice, taking readers into the world of New York City hip-hop through the wide eyes of a kid who's still refreshingly innocent." Publ Wkly

Maxwell, Lisa
The **last** magician. By Lisa Maxwell. Simon Pulse 2017 500 p. (Last Magician)
Grades: 10 11 12
1. Gangs -- Fiction; 2. Time travel -- Fiction; 3. New York (N.Y.) -- History -- 20th century -- Young adult fiction; 4. Time travel -- Fiction; 5. Magic -- Fiction; 6. Magicians -- Fiction
9781481432092; 9781481432078, $18.99

LC 2016052609

In this book in the Last Magician series, by Lisa Maxwell, "in modern-day New York, magic is all but extinct. The remaining few who have an affinity for magic -- the Mageus -- live in the shadows.... Any Mageus who enters Manhattan becomes trapped by the Brink, a dark energy barrier that confines them to the island.... Esta is a talented thief, and she's been raised to steal magical artifacts from the sinister Order that created the Brink." (Publisher's note)

Mayhew, Julie

The **Big** Lie. Julie Mayhew. Hot Key Books 2015 368 p.

Grades: 9 10 11 12

1. Friendship -- Fiction 2. England -- Fiction 3. National socialism -- Fiction

1471404706; 9781471404702, $6.45

In this book, by Julie Mayhew, "Jessika Keller is a good girl: she obeys her father, does her best to impress Herr Fisher at the Bund Deutscher Mädel meetings and is set to be a world champion ice skater. Her neighbour Clementine is not so submissive. Outspoken and radical, Clem is delectably dangerous and rebellious. And the regime has noticed. Jess cannot keep both her perfect life and her dearest friend. But which can she live without?" (Publisher's note)

Red ink. Julie Mayhew. Candlewick Press 2015 297 p.

Grades: 9 10 11 12

1. London (England) -- Fiction 2. Mother-daughter relationship -- Fiction 3. Grief -- Fiction

0763677310; 9780763677312, $16.99

LC 2014957107

In this book, by Julie Mayhew, "when her mother is knocked down and killed by a London bus, fifteen-year-old Melon Fouraki is left with no family worth mentioning. Her mother, Maria, never did introduce her to a living, breathing father. The indomitable Auntie Aphrodite, meanwhile, is hundreds of miles away on a farm in Crete, and she is not likely to jump on a plane to come to East Finchley anytime soon. But at least Melon has . . . the Fouraki family fairy tale." (Publisher's note)

"Melon tells her own story interspersed with her mother's in fractured, chaotic vignettes that circle the day of the accident: 17 days since, 3 days since, 6 years before. As a narrator, she is harsh and abrasive but always sympathetic. Gritty and sad as this may be, it certainly rings true." Booklist

Mazer, Harry

A **boy** at war; a novel of Pearl Harbor. Simon & Schuster Bks. for Young Readers 2001 104p il hardcover o.p. pa $4.99

Grades: 7 8 9 10

1. Pearl Harbor (Oahu, Hawaii), Attack on, 1941 -- Fiction

ISBN 0-689-84161-2; 0-689-84160-4 pa

LC 00-49687

While fishing with his friends off Honolulu on December 7, 1941, teenaged Adam is caught in the midst of the Japanese attack and through the chaos of the subsequent days tries to find his father, a naval officer who was serving on the U.S.S. Arizona when the bombs fell

"Mazer's graphic, sensory descriptions give the narrative immediacy, putting readers alongside Adam, watching

with him as 'pieces of the ship and pieces of men rained down around him.' . . . This is a thought-provoking, sobering account of the human costs of war." Horn Book Guide

Other titles in this series are:

A boy no more (2004)

Heroes don't run (2005)

The **last** mission. Dell 1981 188p pa $5.99

Grades: 7 8 9 10

1. Jews -- Fiction 2. Prisoners of war -- Fiction 3. World War, 1939-1945 -- Fiction

ISBN 0-440-94797-9

First published 1979 by Delacorte Press

In 1944 a 15-year-old Jewish boy tells his family he will travel in the West but instead, enlists in the United States Air Corps and is subsequently taken prisoner by the Germans.

"Told in a rapid journalistic style, occasionally peppered with barrack-room vulgarities, the story is a vivid and moving account of a boy's experience during World War II as well as a skillful, convincing portrayal of his misgivings as a Jew on enemy soil and of his ability to size up—in mature human fashion—the misery around him." Horn Book

★ **Snow** bound. Delacorte Press 1973 146p hardcover o.p. pa $5.99

Grades: 7 8 9 10

1. Runaway children -- Fiction 2. Wilderness survival -- Fiction

ISBN 0-440-96134-3

LC 72-7958

"Tony Laporte is angry when his parents will not allow him to keep a stray dog, so he takes off in his mother's old car. Driving without a license in the middle of a snowstorm that soon becomes a blizzard, Tony picks up a hitchhiker, Cindy Reichert. Trying to impress the slightly older girl with his driving skill, Tony wrecks the car, leaving the two stranded in a desolate area far from a main highway, with little likelihood of rescue for days." Shapiro. Fic for Youth. 3d edition

Mazer, Norma Fox

After the rain. Morrow 1987 291p hardcover o.p. pa $5.99

Grades: 6 7 8 9

1. Death -- Fiction 2. Grandfathers -- Fiction

ISBN 0-688-06867-7; 0-380-75025-2 pa

LC 86-33270

A Newbery Medal honor book, 1988

After discovering her grandfather is dying, fifteen-year-old Rachel gets to know him better than ever before and finds the experience bittersweet

"A powerful book, dealing with death and dying and the strength of family affection." Horn Book

★ The **missing** girl. HarperTeen 2008 288p $16.99; lib bdg $17.89

Grades: 7 8 9 10

1. Sisters -- Fiction 2. Kidnapping -- Fiction 3. New York (State) -- Fiction 4. Child sexual abuse -- Fiction

ISBN 978-0-06-623776-3; 978-0-06-623777-0 lib bdg

LC 2007-09136

In Mallory, New York, as five sisters, aged eleven to seventeen, deal with assorted problems, conflicts, fears, and yearnings, a mysterious middle-aged man watches them, fascinated, deciding which one he likes the best.

"Fans of . . . classic tales of high-tension peril will appreciate the way this successfully plays on their deepest fears." Bull Cent Child Books

McBay, Bruce

Waiting for Sarah; {by} Bruce McBay & James Heneghan. Orca Book Publishers 2003 170p pa $7.95

Grades: 9 10 11 12

1. Canada -- Fiction 2. Orphans -- Fiction 3. People with physical disabilities -- Fiction
ISBN 1-55143-270-6

LC 2002-117768

After Mike loses his family and is severely injured in a car accident, he withdraws until he meets mysterious Sarah, a girl who is not who she seems

"This is a well-developed novel that shatters the teen perceptions of invincibility, as well as dealing with loss, handicaps, and positive ways to break through grief." Lib Media Connect

McBride, Lish

Hold me closer, necromancer. Henry Holt 2010 342p $16.99

Grades: 9 10 11 12

1. Dead -- Fiction 2. Magic -- Fiction 3. Werewolves -- Fiction 4. Supernatural -- Fiction 5. Seattle (Wash.) -- Fiction
ISBN 978-0-8050-9098-7; 0-8050-9098-3

LC 2009-50768

Sam LaCroix, a Seattle fast-food worker and college dropout, discovers that he is a necromancer, part of a world of harbingers, werewolves, satyrs, and one particular necromancer who sees Sam as a threat to his lucrative business of raising the dead.

"With fine writing, tight plotting, a unique and uniquely odd cast of teens, adults, and children, and a pace that smashes through any curtain of disbelief, this sardonic and outrageous story's only problem is that it must, like all good things, come to an end." Booklist

McCafferty, Megan

Bumped. Balzer + Bray 2011 323p $16.99

Grades: 9 10 11 12

1. Twins -- Fiction 2. Sisters -- Fiction 3. Viruses -- Fiction 4. Pregnancy -- Fiction 5. New Jersey -- Fiction
ISBN 978-0-06-196274-5; 0-06-196274-0

LC 2010-30704

In 2036 New Jersey, when teens are expected to become fanatically religious wives and mothers or high-priced Surrogettes for couples made infertile by a widespread virus, sixteen-year-old identical twins Melody and Harmony find in one another the courage to believe they have choices.

"The book's carefree sexuality and exploitation makes it uncomfortable, scandalous, and not easily forgotten—

there's little doubt that's exactly what McCafferty is going for." Publ Wkly

Sloppy Firsts Crown Publishers 2001 280p $13.99

Grades 9 10 11 12

1. High school students -- Fiction. 2. Teenage girls -- Fiction. 3. Bildungsromans. 4. New Jersey -- Fiction.
ISBN 0609807900

"When her best friend, Hope, moves away after Jess's brother dies of a drug overdose, sixteen-year-old Jess copes with loss of the only friend who understands her. Diary entries and monthly letters to Hope reflect Jess's longing for love but refusal to settle for just anyone, and reveal her rivalry with her perfect, engaged sister...The author shines with painfully honest portrayals of a variety of relationships, from simple best-friend pacts to complex family interactions in a house where the death of the only son is never mentioned. Ultimately, the author exposes the harm teens do to themselves and to one another, and juxtaposes their resilience alongside their destruction." VOYA

Other titles about Jessica Darling are:
Second Helpings (2003)
Charmed Thirds (2006)
Fourth Comings (2007)
Perfect Fifths (2009)

Thumped; Megan McCafferty. Balzer + Bray 2012 290 p. (hardback) $17.99

Grades: 9 10 11 12

1. Science fiction 2. Dystopian fiction 3. Teenage mothers -- Fiction 4. Teenage pregnancy -- Fiction 5. Twins -- Fiction 6. Honesty -- Fiction 7. Pregnancy -- Fiction 9. Infertility -- Fiction
ISBN 0061962767; 9780061962769

LC 2011042149

This book is the sequel to Megan McCafferty's science fiction novel 'Bumped' about the pregnancies of teenage twin girls twins Melody and Harmony in a future dystopian United States. "After a virus destroyed the ability of anyone over the age of 18 to reproduce, teen pregnancy became big business. . . . [T]his book . . . makes the deliberate point that teenage pregnancy and sex without love can seriously damage both the teens and society." (Kirkus Reviews)

"The well-paced plot and the twins' alternating narratives will keep readers engaged... A worthwhile read for teens beginning to think about their personal reproductive choices." LJ

McCaffrey, Anne

Dragon's kin; {by} Anne McCaffrey, Todd McCaffrey. Del Rey 2003 304p $24.95

Grades: 9 10 11 12

1. Fantasy fiction
ISBN 0-345-46198-3

"On the planet Pern, the colonists prepare for the return of the Red Star and the deadly fall of Thread, which consumes any organic matter it touches. When the mines that provide the planet with minerals for metalworking and coal for heat play out, a pair of young people discover a heretofore hidden power of the watchwhers, the lowly kin of dragonkind, and learn a new way to provide assistance for the people of Pern. . . . Personable characters and superb storytelling make this an excellent choice for sf collections and essential for Pern fans of all ages. Highly recommended." Libr J

Dragonflight; volume 1 of The Dragonriders of Pern. Ballantine Bks. 1978 337p il (Dragonriders of Pern) hardcover o.p. pa $12.95

Grades: 8 9 10 11 12 Adult

    1. Fantasy fiction 2. Science fiction 3. Dragons -- Fiction

ISBN 0-345-27749-X; 0-345-48426-6 pa

                        LC 78-16707

First published 1968 in paperback. Based on two award winning stories entitled: Weyr search and Dragonrider. Many titles co-written by Todd McCaffrey

ALA YALSA Margaret A. Edwards Award (1999)

The planet Pern, originally colonized from Earth but long out of contact with it, has been periodically threatened by the deadly silver Threads which fall from the wandering Red Star. To combat them a life form on the planet was developed into winged, fire-breathing dragons. Humans with a high degree of empathy and telepathic power are needed to train and preserve these creatures. As the story begins, Pern has fallen into decay, the threat of the Red Star has been forgotten, the Dragonriders and dragons are reduced in number and in disrepute, and the evil Lord Fax has begun conquering neighboring holds.

    Fantasy titles set on Pern include:

    All the Weyrs of Pern (1991)

    The chronicles of Pern: first fall (1993)

    Dragon Harper (2007)

    Dragon's fire (2006)

    Dragon's kin (2003)

    Dragon's time (2011)

    Dragondrums (1979)

    Dragonquest (1971)

    Dragonsdawn (1988)

    Dragonseye (1997)

    Dragonsinger (1977)

    Dragonsong (1976)

    The masterharper of Pern (1998)

    Morets: Dragonlady of Pern (1983)

    Nerilka's story (1986)

    The Renegades of Pern (1989)

    The skies of Pern (2001)

    White dragon (1978)

McCaffrey, Todd J.

Dragongirl; [by] Todd McCaffrey. Del Rey-Ballantine Books 2010 482p map (Dragonriders of Pern) $26; ebook $26

Grades: 9 10 11 12 Adult

    1. Fantasy fiction 2. Dragons -- Fiction

ISBN 978-0-345-49116-9; 978-0-345-52191-0 ebook

                LC 2010-14672

Sequel to Dragonheart (2008)

"Once again, the Red Star appears in the skies over Pern, triggering the fall of Thread, a corrosive and deadly spaceborn spore that comes in Passes that last approximately 50 years. This time, however, the dragons bred by the colonists of Pern to fight Thread are dying from a mysterious plague,

and the population of Pern faces extinction. While gold-dragon rider Fiona concentrates on learning to heal sick and injured dragons and their riders, the harper Kindan and ex-dragon rider Lorana search for a cure." Libr J

McCahan, Erin

The **lake** effect. By Erin McCahan. Dial Books, an imprint of Penguin Random House LLC 2017 391 p.

Grades: 7 8 9 10 11 12

    1. Dating (Social customs) -- Fiction; 2. Family problems -- Fiction; 3. Old age -- Fiction; 4. Serbian Americans -- Fiction; 5. Summer employment -- Fiction; 6. Michigan, Lake -- Fiction; 7. Bildungsromans; 8. Romance fiction

9781101625989; 9780803740525, $17.99

              LC 2016047984

In this coming-of-age novel, by Erin McCahan, "it's the summer after senior year, and Briggs Henry is out the door. He's leaving behind his ex-girlfriend and his parents' money troubles for Lake Michigan and its miles of sandy beaches, working a summer job as a personal assistant, and living in a gorgeous Victorian on the shore.... [But when] he gets there...his eighty-four-year-old boss tells him to put on a suit for her funeral." (Publisher's note)

"Observant, sarcastic, compelling, and very funny, narrator Briggs is entirely convincing and -- ably abetted by an abundance of diverse characters -- never less than good company." Kirkus

Love and other foreign words. By Erin McCahan. Dial Books, an imprint of Penguin Group (USA) Inc. 2014 336 p.

Grades: 8 9 10 11 12

    1. Best friends -- Fiction 2. Friendship -- Fiction 3. Interpersonal communication -- Fiction 4. Love -- Fiction 5. Sisters -- Fiction 6. Interpersonal relations -- Fiction 7. Romance fiction

0803740514; 9780803740518, $17.99

              LC 2013027095

In this book, by Erin McCahan, "[s]ixteen-year-old Josie lives her life in translation. She speaks High School, College, Friends, Boyfriends, Break-ups, and even the language of Beautiful Girls. But none of these is her native tongue—the only people who speak that are her best friend Stu and her sister Kate. So when Kate gets engaged to an epically insufferable guy, how can Josie see it as anything but the mistake of a lifetime?" (Publisher's note)

"Josie doesn't like change. So when her sister Kate announces she's going to marry Geoff, Josie immediately tries everything to alienate him. But she also becomes curious about the nature of love and, with the help of her friends and family, tries to understand it. The highlight of this effectively drawn, often funny novel is its smart, precocious, and irrepressibly inquisitive protagonist." Horn Book

McCall, Guadalupe Garcia

All the stars denied. By Guadalupe García McCall. Tu Books, an imprint of Lee & Low Books Inc. 2018 336 p.

Grades: 6 7 8 9 10

    1. Deportation -- Fiction; 2. Depressions -- 1929 -- Fiction; 3. Family life -- Texas -- Fiction; 4. Mexican

Americans -- Fiction; 5. Race relations -- Fiction; 6. Texas -- History -- 20th century -- Fiction
9781620142813, $19.95; 9781620142837

LC 2017058034

In this book, by Guadalupe García McCall, "when Estrella organizes a protest against the treatment of tejanos in their town of Monteseco, Texas, her whole family becomes a target of repatriation efforts to send Mexicans back to Mexico whether they were ever Mexican citizens or not. Dumped across the border and separated from half her family, Estrella must figure out a way to survive and care for her mother and baby brother." (Publisher's note)

Shame the Stars. By Guadalupe Garcia McCall. Lee & Low Books 2016 320 p. Illustration
Grades: 6 7 8 9

1. Historical fiction 2. Texas -- Fiction
1620142783; 9781620142783, $19.95

LC 2016031436

In this book, by Guadalupe Garcia McCall, "eighteen-year-old Joaquin del Toro's future looks bright. With his older brother in the priesthood, he s set to inherit his family s Texas ranch. He s in love with Dulcena and she s in love with him. But it s 1915, and trouble has been brewing along the US-Mexico border. On one side, the Mexican Revolution is taking hold; on the other, Texas Rangers fight Tejano insurgents, and ordinary citizens are caught in the middle." (Publisher's note)

"Pura Belpré winner McCall delivers an ambitious, sardonically relevant historical novel-a must-read, complex twist on a political Shakespearean tragedy." Kirkus

Includes bibliographical references.

★ **Under** the mesquite. Lee & Low Books 2011 224p $17.95
Grades: 7 8 9 10 11 12

1. Texas -- Fiction 2. Cancer -- Fiction 3. Family life -- Fiction 4. Mexican Americans -- Fiction
ISBN 978-1-60060-429-4; 1-60060-429-3; 978-1-60060-875-9 ebook

LC 2010052567

Throughout her high school years, as her mother battles cancer, Lupita takes on more responsibility for her house and seven younger siblings, while finding refuge in acting and writing poetry. Includes glossary of Spanish terms.

"With poignant imagery and well-placed Spanish, the author effectively captures the complex lives of teenagers in many Latino and/or immigrant families." Kirkus

McCarry, Sarah

About a girl. Sarah McCarry. St. Martin's Griffin 2015 260 p.

1. Bisexuality -- Fiction 2. Identity -- Fiction 3. Love -- Fiction 4. Supernatural -- Fiction 5. Teenage girls -- Fiction
1250068622; 9781250068620, $21.99

LC 2015016090

In this young adult novel, by Sarah McCarry, "eighteen-year-old Tally is . . . sure of everything. . . . There's no room in her tidy world for . . . the . . . mother who abandoned her soon after she was born. But when a sudden discovery upends her fiercely ordered world, Tally sets out on an un-

expected quest to seek out the reclusive musician who may hold the key to her past?and instead finds Maddy, an enigmatic and beautiful girl who will unlock the door to her future." (Publisher's note)

"As in other books in the trilogy, McCarry inflects the Pacific Northwest setting with Greek mythology, weaving ancient magic throughout Tally's story and adding an enchanting dose of magic realism. Tally's imagistic, melodic narrative roils with urgent emotion, and readers who loved the first two installments in the series will be richly rewarded by this series ender." Booklist

Sequel to: All our pretty songs

All our pretty songs; by Sarah McCarry. 1st ed. St. Martin's Griffin 2013 234 p. (paperback) $9.99; (hardcover) $18.99
Grades: 9 10 11 12

1. Music -- Fiction 2. Supernatural -- Fiction 3. Triangles (Interpersonal relations) -- Fiction 4. Love -- Fiction 5. Musicians -- Fiction 6. Friendship -- Fiction 7. Best friends -- Fiction
ISBN 1250040884; 9781250027085; 9781250040886

LC 2013003451

This novel by Sarah McCarry is about "two best friends who grew up like sisters: charismatic, mercurial, and beautiful Aurora, and the devoted, watchful narrator. Their unbreakable bond is challenged when a mysterious and gifted musician named Jack comes between them. They're not the only ones who have noticed Jack's gift; his music has awakened an ancient evil--and a world both above and below which may not be mythical at all." (Publisher's note)

"Art and music run rampant through an unnamed narrator's journey with her best friend, strikingly beautiful Aurora, as frightening and elusive strangers promise drugs, fame, and love. The writing is rich and lush, yet conveys immediacy and is comprehensible even when the events are not...The descent into the underworld is riveting as the heroine tries to fight for her loved ones' fates. Raw sex and foul language accompany the shadow world that promises fame and one's heart's desire, and only faith in the narrator makes the journey endurable. Brilliant in concept and execution." (School Library Journal)

Dirty wings. Sarah McCarry. St. Martin's Griffin 2014 288 p.
Grades: 9 10 11 12

1. Friendship -- Fiction 2. Love -- Fiction 3. Supernatural -- Fiction 4. Teenage girls -- Fiction 5. Musicians -- Fiction
1250049385; 9781250049384, $19.99

LC 2014000136

"In 'Dirty Wings' by Sarah McCarry, Maia is a teenage piano prodigy and dutiful daughter, imprisoned in the oppressive silence of her adoptive parents' house like a princess in an ivory tower. Cass is a street rat, witch, and runaway, scraping by with her wits and her knack for a five-fingered discount. When a chance encounter brings the two girls together, an unlikely friendship blossoms that will soon change the course of both their lives." (Publisher's note)

"The mothers of the girls featured in All Our Pretty Songs (2013) receive their own girlhood story in this beautifully constructed and grim tale...Identity, musical talent, and poisonous relationships between parents and children are depicted in a bravura retelling of a classic myth." Booklist

Prequel to: All our pretty songs.

McCarthy, Andrew

Just fly away. Andrew McCarthy. Algonquin Young Readers 2017 260 p.

Grades: 7 8 9 10 11 12

    1. Brothers and sisters -- Fiction; 2. Families -- Fiction; 3. Family secrets -- Fiction; 4. Fathers and daughters -- Fiction; 5. Secrecy -- Fiction; 6. Father-daughter relationship -- Fiction

    9781616207113; 9781616206291, $17.95

LC 2016038077

In this novel, by Andrew McCarthy, "when 15-year-old Lucy Willows discovers that her father has a child from a brief affair,...she begins to question everything she thinks she knows about her home and her life.... Lucy grows more and more isolated from her friends, her family, and even her boyfriend, Simon.... When Lucy escapes to Maine, the home of her mysteriously estranged grandfather, she finally begins to get to the bottom of her family's secrets and lies." (Publisher's note)

"This is a moving coming-of-age story for young adults who enjoy calm, character-driven reading." VOYA

McCarthy, Maureen

Rose by any other name. Roaring Brook Press 2008 336p $17.95

Grades: 9 10 11 12

    1. Australia -- Fiction 2. Family life -- Fiction 3. Automobile travel -- Fiction

    ISBN 978-1-59643-372-4; 1-59643-372-8

LC 2007-18406

First published 2006 in Australia

During a road trip with her mother from Melbourne to Fairy Point, Australia, to see her dying grandmother, nineteen-year-old Rose gains a new perspective on events of the previous year, when family problems, the end of a long-term friendship, and bad personal choices dramatically transformed her near-perfect life.

"This complex coming-of-age novel, which explores both universal self-destructive tendencies and resilience, will resonate with teen readers as well as many adults." Booklist

McCarthy, Susan Carol

True fires. Bantam Books 2004 306p hardcover o.p. pa $13

Grades: 9 10 11 12

    1. Florida -- Fiction 2. Race relations -- Fiction 3. Segregation in education -- Fiction

    ISBN 0-553-80170-8; 0-553-38104-0 pa

LC 2003-70885

"Recently widowed, Franklin Dare moves his family to Florida to start a new life in the lush citrus groves. But his young children catch the eye of a corrupt sheriff, K.A. De-Luth, who proclaims Daniel's hair too 'kinked' and Rebecca's nose too wide and bans them from Lake Esther Elementary (according to Florida law, any child deemed one-eighth black or more cannot attend an all-white school). Only unimpeachable evidence that Franklin has no black blood—in fact, he is part Croatan Indian—will result in the children's readmittance. . . . The ending may present more questions than answers, but it doesn't take away from McCarthy's flawless dialogue, warm characters and compassionate wit, all of which service a moving story about the powers of love and justice." Publ Wkly

McCaughrean, Geraldine

★ The **death** -defying Pepper Roux. Harper 2010 328p $16.99; lib bdg $17.89

Grades: 5 6 7 8

    1. Adventure fiction 2. Fate and fatalism -- Fiction

    ISBN 978-0-06-183665-7; 0-06-183665-6; 978-0-06-183666-4 lib bdg; 0-06-183666-4 lib bdg

LC 2009-39665

Having been raised believing he will die before he reaches the age of fourteen, Pepper Roux runs away on his fourteenth birthday in an attempt to elude his fate, assumes another identity, and continues to try to outrun death, no matter the consequences.

"McCaughrean's exuberant prose and whirling humor animate an unforgettable cast of characters." Booklist

The **glorious** adventures of the Sunshine Queen. Harper 2011 325p $16.99

Grades: 5 6 7 8

    1. Adventure fiction 2. Theater -- Fiction

    ISBN 978-0-06-200806-0; 0-06-200806-4

LC 2010021958

When a diphtheria outbreak forces twelve-year-old Cissy to leave her Oklahoma hometown in the 1890s, she and her two classmates embark on a wild adventure down the Missouri River with a team of traveling actors who are living on a dilapidated paddle steamer.

"McCaughrean invests her characters with humanity and shows a farcical sense for dialogue, while her arch narrative voice, includes the theatrical and clever turns of phrase." Booklist

★ The **kite** rider; a novel. HarperCollins Pubs. 2002 272p maps hardcover o.p. pa $6.99

Grades: 5 6 7 8

    1. Kites -- Fiction 2. China -- History -- Yüan dynasty, 1260-1368

    ISBN 0-06-623874-9; 0-06-441091-9 pa

LC 2001-39522

In thirteenth-century China, after trying to save his widowed mother from a horrendous second marriage, twelve-year-old Haoyou has life-changing adventures when he takes to the sky as a circus kite rider and ends up meeting the great Mongol ruler Kublai Khan

"The story is a genuine page-turner. . . . McCaughrean fully immerses her memorable characters in the culture and lore of the ancient Chinese and Mongols, which make this not only a solid adventure story but also a window to a fascinating time and place." Booklist

★ The **white** darkness. HarperTempest 2007 384p hardcover o.p. pa $8.99

260

Grades: 8 9 10 11 12

    1. Antarctica -- Fiction 2. Wilderness survival -- Fiction
ISBN 978-0-06-089035-3; 0-06-089035-5; 978-0-06-089037-7 pa; 0-06-089037-1 pa

        LC 2006-02503

First published 2005 in the United Kingdom

Michael L. Printz Award, 2008

Taken to Antarctica by the man she thinks of as her uncle for what she believes to be a vacation, Symone—a troubled fourteen year old—discovers that he is dangerously obsessed with seeking Symme's Hole, an opening that supposedly leads into the center of a hollow Earth.

    "McCaughrean's lyrical language actively engages the senses, plunging readers into a captivating landscape that challenges the boundaries of reality." Booklist

McClintock, Norah, d. 2017

About that night. Norah McClintock. Orca Book Publishers 2014 248 p.

Grades: 7 8 9 10

    1. Detective and mystery stories 2. Murder -- Fiction 3. Missing persons -- Fiction 4. High school students -- Fiction 5. Triangles (Interpersonal relations) -- Fiction
1459805941; 9781459805941, $12.95;
9781459805958; 9781459805965

        LC 2014935377

"Derek is staying with his new girlfriend and her parents while his family is out of town. He can't believe his luck—Jordie is the hottest girl in school, and he's going out with her. When Ronan, school bad boy and Jordie's ex-boyfriend, shows up, Jordie decides that maybe Derek isn't the one after all. But before she can end it with him, Derek disappears. Did he run away? Or did something happen to him?" (Publisher's note)

"Mystery fans will appreciate the thoughtful plotting, the complex characters, and an ambiguous ending that guarantees readers will be mulling over the story long after they finish. Of special note are the descriptions of landscape and weather: cold, forbidding, and characters in themselves, with their own secrets and dangers." Booklist

Masked; written by Norah McClintock. Orca Book Publishers 2010 108p (Orca soundings) pa $9.95

Grades: 7 8 9 10

    1. Mystery fiction
ISBN 978-1-55469-364-1; 1-55469-364-0

Rosie walks in on an armed robbery in her father's convienence store. Who is that masked man? And why is the loser from school there?

"Tight plotting, swift pacing, and tension that intensifies with each page mark this entry in the always-reliable Orca Soundings series for reluctant readers." Booklist

Out of tune. Norah McClintock. Orca Book Publishers 2017 222 p. (Riley Donovan mystery)

Grades: 7 8 9 10

    1. High school students -- Fiction; 2. Musicians -- Fiction; 3. Mystery fiction; 4. Murder -- Investigation -- Fiction
9781459814677; 9781459814660; 9781459814653,

$10.95

        LC 2017933015

In this book, by Norah McClintock, "when Alicia, a talented violinist at Riley Donovan's high school, is found bludgeoned to death in a field on the outskirts of town, suspicion immediately falls on Carrie, the teen's musical rival. But Riley isn't convinced of Carrie's guilt, and even though her police-officer aunt tells her to stay out of it, Riley goes searching for the truth. Did Carrie really kill Alicia in a fit of jealous rage, or is there another explanation for Alicia's death?" (Publisher's note)

"The plot is complex and tightly woven, the reveal is both surprising and satisfying, the violence is prominent but tastefully presented, and Riley continues to be a strong and relatable protagonist with good moral fiber." Booklist

Taken. Orca Book Publishers 2009 166p pa $12.95

Grades: 7 8 9 10

    1. Kidnapping -- Fiction 2. Wilderness survival -- Fiction
ISBN 978-1-55469-152-4; 1-55469-152-4

"After two girls from a nearby town go missing everyone goes on high alert, suspecting a serial killer, and while walking home, Stephanie is grabbed from behind and injected with a drug that knocks her out. She awakens hours later to find herself tied up in an abandoned cabin deep in a densely wooded area. . . . Her harrowing journey back to safety propels this plot-driven, fast-paced tale forward. . . . Told in the first person, this suspenseful survival story is sure to have strong appeal." Kirkus

McCormick, Patricia, 1956-

★ **Cut**. Front St. 2000 168p $16.95

Grades: 7 8 9 10

    1. Self-mutilation -- Fiction 2. Psychiatric hospitals -- Fiction
ISBN 1-88691-061-8

        LC 00-34840

While confined to a mental hospital, thirteen-year-old Callie slowly comes to understand some of the reasons behind her self-mutilation, and gradually starts to get better

"Realistic, sensitive, and heartfelt." Voice Youth Advocates

My brother's keeper. Hyperion Books for Children 2004 187p $15.99

Grades: 7 8 9 10

    1. Baseball -- Fiction 2. Brothers -- Fiction 3. Drug abuse -- Fiction
ISBN 0-7868-5173-2

        LC 2004-55233

Thirteen-year-old Toby, a prematurely gray-haired Pittsburgh Pirates fan and baseball card collector, tries to cope with his brother's drug use, his father's absence, and his mother dating Stanley the Food King.

"This is a clever and believable first-person narrative by a responsible, caring, and appealing kid who is doing his utmost to hold together people he loves." Booklist

Never fall down; a novel. Patricia McCormick. Balzer + Bray 2012 216 p.

Grades: 9 10 11 12

1. Genocide -- Fiction 2. Musicians -- Fiction 3. Human rights -- Fiction 4. Cambodian refugees -- Fiction 5. Cambodia -- History -- 1975- -- Fiction 6. Soldiers -- Fiction 7. Party of Democratic Kampuchea -- Fiction

ISBN 0061730939; 9780061730931

LC 2011052211

In this book, "drawing on hundreds of hours of interviews with Arn Chorn-Pond, who was eleven in 1975 when the Khmer Rouge gained control of Cambodia, [author Patricia] McCormick creates a . . . portrait of genocide as seen through a boy's eyes. . . . He becomes a motivating force for fellow prisoners such as Mek, the music teacher enlisted to teach the boys how to play patriotic songs on traditional instruments. . . . Mek wants to die, too, but Arn won't let him." (Horn Book Magazine)

Includes bibliographical references and index

Purple Heart. Balzer + Bray 2009 198p $16.99; lib bdg $17.89; pa $8.99

Grades: 7 8 9 10

1. Memory -- Fiction 2. Soldiers -- Fiction 3. Hospitals -- Fiction 4. Iraq War, 2003-2011 -- Fiction 5. Brain -- Wounds and injuries -- Fiction

ISBN 978-0-06-173090-0; 0-06-173090-4; 978-0-06-173091-7 lib bdg; 0-06-173091-2 lib bdg; 978-0-06-173092-4 pa; 0-06-173092-0 pa

LC 2009-1757

While recuperating in a Baghdad hospital from a traumatic brain injury sustained during the Iraq War, eighteen-year-old soldier Matt Duffy struggles to recall what happened to him and how it relates to his ten-year-old friend, Ali.

"Strong characters heighten the drama. . . . McCormick raises moral questions without judgment and will have readers examining not only this conflict but the nature of heroism and war." Publ Wkly

★ **Sold**. Hyperion 2006 263p $15.99

Grades: 9 10 11 12

1. Nepal -- Fiction 2. Slavery -- Fiction 3. Prostitution -- Fiction

ISBN 0-7868-5171-6; 978-0-7868-5171-3

LC 2006-49594

Thirteen-year-old Lakshmi leaves her poor mountain home in Nepal thinking that she is to work in the city as a maid only to find that she has been sold into the sex slave trade in India and that there is no hope of escape.

"In beautiful clear prose and free verse that remains true to the child's viewpoint, first-person, present-tense vignettes fill in Lakshmi's story. The brutality and cruelty are ever present ('I have been beaten here, / locked away, / violated a hundred times / and a hundred times more'), but not sensationalized. . . . An unforgettable account of sexual slavery as it exists now." Booklist

McCoy, Chris

The **prom** goer's interstellar excursion. By Chris McCoy. Alfred A. Knopf 2015 304 p.

Grades: 8 9 10 11 12

1. Adventure and adventurers -- Fiction 2. Alien abduction -- Fiction 3. Bands (Music) -- Fiction 4. Dating (Social customs) -- Fiction 5. Extraterrestrial beings -- Fiction 6. Humorous stories 7. Interplanetary voyages -- Fiction 8. Adventure fiction 9. Science fiction

9780375855993, $17.99; 9780375955990

LC 2013045875

In this book, by Chris McCoy, "Bennett pulls off something he never imagined possible: his dream girl, Sophie, agrees to be his date [to the prom]. Moments afterward, however, he watches Sophie get abducted by aliens in the middle of the New Mexico desert. Faced with a dateless prom (and likely kidnapping charges), Bennett does the only thing he can think of: he catches a ride into outer space with a band of extraterrestrial musicians to bring her back." (Publisher's note)

"Readers will root for Bennett to get the girl and even for crusty band member Skark to accomplish his dream of becoming better than the one billionth and sixteenth band in the universe. The book's ending is a nicely placed, realistic surprise. Witty and action-packed, the plot boldly glazes over science-fiction details in favor of well-wrought characters." SLJ

McCoy, Mary

Camp So-and-So. Mary McCoy. Carolrhoda Lab 2017 413 p.

Grades: 9 10 11 12

1. Camps -- Fiction; 2. Friendship -- Fiction; 3. Summer -- Fiction; 4. Suspense fiction

9781512415971, $18.99; 9781512434293; 9781512426939

LC 2016006371

In this book, by Mary McCoy, "the letters went out in mid-February. Each letter invited its recipient to spend a week at Camp So-and-So, a lakeside retreat for girls.... By the end of the month, twenty-five applications had been... mailed.... Had any of these girls tried to...visit the camp for themselves on that day in February, they would have discovered that there was no such town and...that no one...had ever heard of Camp So-and-So." (Publisher's note)

"All the world's a stage in this clever compendium of horror and fantasy tropes, set at an Appalachian summer camp for girls." Booklist

McCreight, Kimberly

The **scattering**. Kimberly McCreight. Harper, an imprint of HarperCollinsPublishers 2017 300 p. (Outliers trilogy)

Grades: 9 10 11 12

1. Emotion recognition -- Fiction; 2. Emotional intelligence -- Fiction; 3. Friendship -- Fiction; 4. Friendship in adolescence -- Fiction; 5. Psychic ability -- Fiction; 6. Teenagers -- Fiction; 7. Emotions -- Fiction

9780062359131; 9780062359124, $18.99; 9780062359148; 0062359126

LC 2016950348

In this book in the Outliers series, by Kimberly McCreight, "Wylie may have escaped the camp in Maine, but she is far from safe. The best way for her to protect herself is to understand her ability, fast. But after spending a lifetime trying to ignore her own feelings, giving in to her ability to read other peoples' emotions is as difficult as it is dangerous." (Publisher's note)

"Another twisty-turny psychological thriller from a master." Booklist

McDonald, Abby

The **anti**-prom. Candlewick Press 2011 280p $16.99

Grades: 8 9 10 11

    1. School stories

    ISBN 978-0-7636-4956-2; 0-7636-4956-2

LC 2010-39170

On prom night, Bliss, Jolene, and Meg, students from the same high school who barely know one another, band together to get revenge against Bliss's boyfriend and her best friend, whom she caught together in the limousine they rented.

"McDonald instills more intelligence than you'd expect from such a plot while not skimping on the simple pleasures, either." Booklist

Boys, bears, and a serious pair of hiking boots. Candlewick Press 2010 293p $16.99

Grades: 9 10 11 12

    1. Canada -- Fiction 2. Social action -- Fiction 3. Self-perception -- Fiction 4. Wilderness areas -- Fiction 5. Environmental protection -- Fiction

    ISBN 978-0-7636-4382-9; 0-7636-4382-3

LC 2009-26015

Seventeen-year-old Jenna, an ardent vegetarian and environmentalist, is thrilled to be spending the summer communing with nature in rural Canada, until she discovers that not all of the rugged residents there share her beliefs.

McDonald "composes a fun summer read, closely examining the conflict between sticking to one's beliefs and learning the art of compromise." Publ Wkly

McDonald, Ian

Be my enemy; by Ian McDonald. Pyr 2012 280 p. (hardcover) $16.95

Grades: 7 8 9 10

    1. Science fiction 2. Kidnapping -- Fiction 3. Technology -- Fiction 4. Father-son relationship -- Fiction

    ISBN 1616146788; 9781616146788

LC 2012018572

Sequel to: Planesrunner (2011)

This book by Ian McDonald is the second in the Everness Series. "Everett Singh has escaped with the Infundibulum from the clutches of Charlotte Villiers and the Order, but at a terrible price. His father is missing, banished to one of the billions of parallel universes of the Panoply of All Worlds, and Everett and the crew of the airship Everness have taken a wild Heisenberg jump to a random parallel plane." (Publisher's note)

Empress of the sun; by Ian McDonald. Pyr 2014 290 p. (Everness) (hardback) $17.99

Grades: 7 8 9 10

    1. War stories 2. Airships -- Fiction 3. Human-alien encounters -- Fiction 4. Science fiction 5. Adventure and adventurers -- Fiction

    ISBN 1616148659; 9781616148652

LC 2013036315

In this book by Ian McDonald, "the The airship Everness [enters an] . . . alternate Earth unlike any her crew has ever seen. Everett, Sen, and the crew find themselves above a plain that goes on forever in every direction without any horizon. There they find an Alderson Disc, an astronomical megastructure of incredibly strong material. Then they meet the Jiju, the dominant species on a plane where the dinosaurs didn't die out. War between their kingdoms is inevitable, total and terrible." (Publisher's note)

"The marvelous Everness series takes readers to a world with highly evolved dinosaurs in this third voyage through parallel universes...Fans might wish for more focus on the original Everett, but eventually, the three storylines weave themselves together nicely, setting up another sequel with hints of forthcoming romance. Endlessly fascinating and fun." (Kirkus)

★ **Planesrunner**. Pyr 2011 (Everness) 269p $16.95

Grades: 6 7 8 9

    1. Science fiction

    ISBN 978-1-61614-541-5; 1-61614-541-2

LC 2011032751

When fourteen-year-old Everett Singh's scientist father is kidnapped from the streets of London, he leaves a mysterious app on Everett's computer giving him access to the Infundibulum—a map of parallel earths—which is being sought by technologically advanced dark powers that Everett must somehow elude while he tries to rescue his father.

"McDonald writes with scientific and literary sophistication, as well as a wicked sense of humor. Add nonstop action, eccentric characters, and expert universe building, and this first volume of the Everness series is a winner." Publ Wkly

McDonald, Janet

Chill wind. Farrar, Straus & Giroux 2002 134p hardcover o.p. pa $6.95

Grades: 7 8 9 10

    1. Public welfare -- Fiction 2. New York (N.Y.) -- Fiction 3. Teenage mothers -- Fiction 4. African Americans -- Fiction

    ISBN 0-374-39958-1; 0-374-41183-2 pa

LC 2001-54785

Afraid that she will have nowhere to go when her welfare checks are stopped, nineteen-year-old high school dropout Aisha tries to figure out how she can support herself and her two young children in New York City

"McDonald writes with such honesty, wit, and insight that you want to quote from every page and read the story aloud to share the laughter and anguish, fury and tenderness." Booklist

Harlem Hustle. Frances Foster Books 2006 182p $16

Grades: 8 9 10 11

    1. Rap music -- Fiction 2. African Americans -- Fiction 3. Harlem (New York, N.Y.) -- Fiction

    ISBN 978-0-374-37184-5; 0-374-37184-9

LC 2005-52108

Eric "Hustle" Samson, a smart and streetwise seventeen-year-old dropout from Harlem, aspires to rap stardom, a dream he naively believes is about to come true.

"The author nails the hip-hop lingo and the street slang, and her characters strike just the right attitude. . . . Young adults will love this book." SLJ

Off-color. Farrar, Straus and Giroux 2007 163p $16

Grades: 7 8 9 10 11 12

1. Single parent family -- Fiction 2. Racially mixed people -- Fiction 3. Brooklyn (New York, N.Y.) -- Fiction 4. Mother-daughter relationship -- Fiction
ISBN 0-374-37196-2

LC 2006-47334

Fifteen-year-old Cameron living with her single mother in Brooklyn finds her search for identity further challenged when she discovers that she is the product of a biracial relationship.

"McDonald dramatizes the big issues from the inside, showing the hard times and the joy in fast-talking dialogue that is honest, insulting, angry, tender, and very funny." Booklist

McEntire, Myra

Hourglass. Egmont USA 2011 390p $17.99

Grades: 7 8 9 10

1. Science fiction 2. Orphans -- Fiction 3. Homicide -- Fiction 4. Siblings -- Fiction 5. Parapsychology -- Fiction 6. Space and time -- Fiction
ISBN 1-60684-144-0; 978-1-60684-144-0

LC 2010-43618

Seventeen-year-old Emerson uses her power to manipulate time to help Michael, a consultant hired by her brother, to prevent a murder that happened six months ago. "Grades seven to ten." (Bull Cent Child Books)

"Em is an entertainingly cheeky narrator and appealingly resilient heroine. . . . McEntire deftly juggles plot, characters and dialogue; her portrait of grief is particularly poignant." Kirkus

McGarry, Katie

★ **Dare** You to; by Katie McGarry. Harlequin Books 2013 480 p. (hardcover) $17.99

Grades: 9 10 11 12

1. Love stories 2. Dysfunctional families -- Fiction 3. Man-woman relationship -- Fiction
ISBN 0373210639; 9780373210633

This book is a "coming-of-age love story" which follows "tattooed, pierced 'skater girl' Beth and high school baseball star Ryan. . . . Raised on opposite sides of the tracks, both teens contend with selfish, manipulative parents who use their children to satisfy their own desires; both also have mentors and family members offering guidance and support. . . . Beth's compulsive efforts to rescue her drug-addicted mother . . . captures their greatest obstacle." (Publishers Weekly)

Only a breath apart. Katie McGarry. Tor Teen 2019 368 p.

Grades: 8 9 10 11 12

1. Best friends -- Fiction; 2. Family problems -- Fiction;

3. Farms -- Fiction; 4. Friendship -- Fiction; 5. Love -- Fiction
ISBN 9781250193858, $17.99

LC 2018044554

In this novel, by Katie McGarry, "the only curse Jesse Lachlin believes in is is his grandmother's will: in order to inherit his family farm he must win the approval of his childhood best friend, the girl he froze out his freshman year. A fortuneteller tells Scarlett she's psychic, but what is real is Scarlett's father's controlling attitude and the dark secrets at home. She may be able to escape, but only if she can rely on the one boy who broke her heart." (Publisher's note)

"The novel manages to tackle domestic violence in a way that never feels clichéd, and the romance is sure to win over even the most cynical reader." Booklist

Pushing the limits. Harlequin Teen 2012 403 p.

Grades: 9 10 11 12

1. Love stories
ISBN 0373210493; 9780373210497

LC 2011287989

In this young adult novel by Katie McGarry "[n]o one knows what happened the night Echo Emerson went from popular girl with jock boyfriend to gossiped-about outsider with 'freaky' scars on her arms. . . . [W]hen Noah Hutchins, the smoking-hot, girl-using loner in the black leather jacket, explodes into her life with his tough attitude and surprising understanding, Echo's world shifts in ways she could never have imagined." (Author's note)

McGhee, Alison

★ **What** I leave behind. Alison McGhee. Atheneum 2018 202 p.

Grades: 9 10 11 12

1. Fathers and sons -- Fiction; 2. Rape -- Fiction; 3. Single-parent families -- Fiction; 4. Stores, Retail -- Fiction; 5. Suicide -- Fiction; 6. Father-son relationship -- Fiction; 7. Grief -- Fiction
9781481476584; 9781481476560, $17.99; 9781481476577

LC 2017001373

In this book, by Alison McGhee, "after his dad commits suicide, Will tries to overcome his own misery by secretly helping the people around him.... Will started walking after his father committed suicide, and three years later he hasn't stopped. But there are some places Will can't walk by: The blessings store with the chest of 100 Chinese blessings in the back, the bridge on Fourth Street where his father died, and his childhood friend Playa's house." (Publisher's note)

"McGhee skillfully evokes sense memory, as Will attempts to find solace in his nighttime wanderings. Ultimately, the piercing narrative offers an affirmation of remaining connected to others through loss as Will embraces his relationships and begins to heal." Pub Wkly

A Caitlyn Dlouhy Book.

McGinnis, Mindy

★ The **female** of the species. Mindy McGinnis; [edited by] Ben Rosenthal. Katherine Tegen Books 2016 352 p.

Grades: 10 11 12

1. Adventure fiction 2. Revenge -- Fiction 3. Friendship

-- Fiction
9780062320896

LC 2016932089

"Living a life in the shadows after violently retaliating against the killer who walked free after murdering her sister, Alex unexpectedly befriends guilt-ridden athlete Jack and defiant preacher's kid Peekay, who must navigate Alex's darker nature throughout their senior year." (Publisher's note)

"What would you do if your sister were raped and murdered, but the killer went free? Alex delivers her own brand of swift, ferocious justice for her sister Anna, and then hides in plain sight from the close-knit, rural Ohio town where everyone thinks they know everything. The community is surrounded by woods that serve as a great place to party-or, in her case, run-from her mother, her memories, and the fellow classmates she can't trust herself to be around. While volunteering at the local animal shelter, she meets Claire, known as Peekay (preacher's kid), who becomes her first friend, and as a result, Alex begins to participate in senior-year activities. . . . Whether a catcall, an unwelcome touch, or more, sexual aggression towards females happens daily; McGinnis explores how one teen uses violence for justice in this gripping story that should be read and discussed by teens, as well as those who work with them." Booklist

A **madness** so discreet. Mindy McGinnis. Katherine Tegen Books 2015 384 p.
Grades: 9 10 11 12
  1. Criminal investigation -- Fiction 2. Ohio -- History -- 19th century -- Fiction 3. Physicians -- Fiction 4. Mystery fiction 5. Mentally ill -- Fiction
9780062320865, $17.99

LC 2014041255

In this novel, by Mindy McGinnis, "Grace Mae is already familiar with madness when family secrets and the bulge in her belly send her to an insane asylum—but . . . when a visiting doctor interested in criminal psychology recognizes Grace's brilliant mind beneath her rage, he recruits her as his assistant. Continuing to operate under the cloak of madness at crime scenes allows her to gather clues from bystanders who believe her less than human." (Publisher's note)

"Readers will wish they could watch [Grace] and Thornhollow solve murders for pages and pages more. A dark study of the effects of power in the wrong hands, buoyed by a tenacious heroine and her colorful companions." Kirkus

McGovern, Cammie
  Say what you will. Cammie McGovern; [edited by] Tara Weikum. HarperTeen 2014 352 p.
Grades: 9 10 11 12
  1. Cerebral palsy -- Fiction 2. Obsessive-compulsive disorder -- Fiction 3. Teenagers with disabilities -- Fiction
0062271105; 9780062271105, $17.99

LC 2013958343

In this young adult novel by Cammie McGovern, "Born with cerebral palsy, Amy can't walk without a walker, talk without a voice box, or even fully control her facial expressions. Plagued by obsessive-compulsive disorder, Matthew is consumed with repeated thoughts, neurotic rituals, and crippling fear. Both in desperate need of someone to help

them reach out to the world, Amy and Matthew are more alike than either ever realized." (Publisher's note)

"Amy, who has cerebral palsy, convinces her parents to hire a peer helper, Matthew (who has a severe anxiety disorder), so she can learn to socialize before college. The two develop a significant friendship—and a confusing mutual attraction. This book moves beyond the typical concerns people with disabilities encounter to present an honest portrayal of the lives of these particular characters." Horn Book

★ A **step** toward falling. Cammie McGovern; [edited by] Tara Weikum. HarperTeen 2015 384 p.
  1. People with disabilities -- Fiction 2. Teenagers -- Conduct of life -- Fiction
9780062271136, $17.99

LC 2015946375

"Emily has always been the kind of girl who tries to do the right thing-until one night when she . . . sees Belinda, a classmate with developmental disabilities, being attacked. Inexplicably, she does nothing at all. . . . When their high school finds out what happened, Emily and Lucas, a football player who was also there that night, are required to perform community service at a center for disabled people." (Publisher's note)

"No mere empathy builder for Emily and Lucas, Belinda is a fully developed character—good at some things (better than Emily and Lucas, in fact), bad at others. Without evading or sugarcoating difficult topics, McGovern . . . shows that disabled and able aren't binary states but part of a continuum—a human one." Pub Wkly

McGowan, Anthony
  The **knife** that killed me. Delacorte Press 2010 216p $16.99
Grades: 10 11 12
  1. School stories 2. Gangs -- Fiction 3. Bullies -- Fiction 4. Homicide -- Fiction 5. Friendship -- Fiction 6. Great Britain -- Fiction
ISBN 978-0-385-73822-4; 0-385-73822-6

LC 2009-11662

Paul Varderman, a secondary student in an English Catholic School, is a loner until, just as he is becoming friends with 'the freaks,' the school bully encourages Paul to join his gang and gives him a knife to carry as an incentive.

"Depicting brutality without a hint of glamour, this tale of alienation and reaction cuts deeply into school culture and the teenage mind." Kirkus

McGuigan, Mary Ann
  Morning in a different place. Front Street 2009 195p $17.95
Grades: 7 8 9 10
  1. Friendship -- Fiction 2. Race relations -- Fiction 3. African Americans -- Fiction 4. Bronx (New York, N.Y.) -- Fiction
ISBN 978-1-59078-551-5; 1-59078-551-7

LC 2007-17547

In 1963 in the Bronx, New York, eighth-graders Fiona and Yolanda help one another face hard decisions at home despite family and social opposition to their interracial friendship, but Fiona is on her own when popular classmates start paying attention to her and give her a glimpse of both a different way of life and a new kind of hatefulness.

This book is "never didactic. McGuigan's writing is spare and low-key, and her metaphors are acute." Booklist

McKay, Hilary

★ **Saffy's** angel. Margaret K. McElderry Bks. 2002 152p $16; pa $4.99

Grades: 5 6 7 8

    1. Adoption -- Fiction 5. Family life -- Fiction
    ISBN 0-689-84933-8; 0-689-84934-6 pa

                      LC 2001-44110

First published 2001 in the United Kingdom

After learning that she was adopted, thirteen-year-old Saffron's relationship with her eccentric, artistic family changes, until they help her go back to Italy where she was born to find a special momento of her past

"Like the Casson household itself, the plot is a chaotic whirl that careens off in several directions simultaneously. But McKay always skillfully draws each clearly defined character back into the story with witty, well-edited details; rapid dialogue; and fine pacing." Booklist

Other titles in this series are:

Indigo's star (2004)

Permanent Rose (2005)

Caddy ever after (2006)

Forever Rose (2008)

McKay, Sharon E.

Enemy territory; Sharon McKay. Annick Press 2012 184 p. $21.95

Grades: 6 7 8 9 10 11 12

    1. Toleration -- Fiction 2. Friendship 3. Israel-Arab conflicts -- Fiction
    ISBN 1554514312; 9781554514311

In author Sharon E. McKay's book, "Sam, an Israeli teen whose leg may have to be amputated, and Yusuf, a Palestinian teen who has lost his left eye, find themselves uneasy roommates in a Jerusalem hospital. One night, the boys decide to slip away while the nurses aren't looking and go on an adventure to the Old City. . . . They band together to find their way home and to defend themselves against unfriendly locals, arrest by the military police, and an encounter with a deadly desert snake." (Publisher's note)

Thunder over Kandahar; photographs by Rafal Gerszak. Annick Press 2010 260p il $21.95; pa $12.95

Grades: 7 8 9 10 11 12

    1. Afghanistan -- Fiction 2. Afghan War, 2001- -- Fiction
    ISBN 978-1-55451-267-6; 1-55451-267-0; 978-1-55451-266-9 pa; 1-55451-266-2 pa

"When her British and American-educated parents' return to Afghanistan is cut short by a terrible attack, 14-year-old Yasmine is sent to Kandahar for safety. Instead, the driver abandons her and her friend Tamanna along the way, and they must travel on their own through Taliban-controlled mountains. . . . In spite of unrelenting violence, along with grinding poverty, restrictive customs, and the horrors of war, what shines through this sad narrative is the love Afghans have for their country. . . . [The author] traveled to Afghanistan and provides numerous credits for this gripping tale." SLJ

McKenzie, Paige

The **sacrifice** of Sunshine Girl. Paige McKenzie with Nancy Ohlin ; story by Nick Hagen & Nancy Ohlin ; based on the web series created by Nick Hagen ; illustrations by Paige McKenzie. Weinstein Books 2017 322 p. (Haunting of Sunshine girl)

Grades: 7 8 9

    1. Teenage girls -- Fiction; 2. Ghost stories; 3. Paranormal fiction
    9781602865501; 9781602863354; 9781602862982, $17.99; 1602862982

                      LC 2017288568

In this book in the Haunting of Sunshine Girl Series, by Paige McKenzie with Nancy Ohlin, "Sunshine's powers are unique. She doesn't just help humans transition to the afterlife; her empathy allows her to feel connections to their whole lived experience, a power that proves both dangerous and useful... Sunshine continues to be a likable protagonist who strives to grow into herself and her unusual role in life. A cliff-hanger ending will have fans clamoring for the third installment." (Booklist)

McKernan, Victoria

Shackleton's stowaway. Knopf 2005 336p $15.95; lib bdg $17.99

Grades: 7 8 9 10

    1. Explorers 2. Adventure fiction 3. Survival after airplane accidents, shipwrecks, etc. -- Fiction
    ISBN 0-375-82691-2; 0-375-92691-7 lib bdg

                      LC 2004-10313

A fictionalized account of the adventures of eighteen-year-old Perce Blackborow, who stowed away for the 1914 Shackleton Antarctic expedition and, after their ship Endurance was crushed by ice, endured many hardships, including the loss of the toes of his left foot to frostbite, during the nearly two-year return journey across sea and ice

"This book provides historical information for history and geography classes who are interested in exploration, the Antarctic, and early history of great sea voyages." Libr Media Connect

McKinley, Robin

★ **Beauty**; a retelling of the story of Beauty & the beast. Harper & Row 1978 247p $15.99; pa $5.99

Grades: 7 8 9 10

    1. Fairy tales
    ISBN 0-06-024149-7; 0-06-440477-3 pa

                      LC 77-25636

"McKinley's version of this folktale is embellished with rich descriptions and settings and detailed characterizations. The author has not modernized the story but varied the traditional version to attract modern readers. The values of love, honor, and beauty are placed in a magical setting that will please the reader of fantasy." Shapiro. Fic for Youth. 3d edition

The **blue** sword. Greenwillow Bks. 1982 272p $17.99; pa $6.99

Grades: 7 8 9 10

    1. Fantasy fiction

    ISBN 0-688-00938-7; 0-441-06880-4 pa

                          LC 82-2895

A Newbery Medal honor book, 1983

Harry, bored with her sheltered life in the remote orange-growing colony of Daria, discovers magic in herself when she is kidnapped by a native king with mysterious powers.

"This is a zesty, romantic, heroic fantasy with an appealing stalwart heroine, a finely realixed mythical kingdom, and a grounding in reality." Booklist

The **hero** and the crown. Greenwillow Bks. 1985 246p lib bdg $16.99

Grades: 6 7 8 9

    1. Fantasy fiction

    ISBN 0-688-02593-5

                          LC 84-4074

Awarded the Newbery Medal, 1985

"A prequel rather than sequel to 'The Blue Sword' [1982], McKinley's second novel set in the . . . mythical kingdom of Damar centers on Aerin, daughter of a Damarian king and his second wife, a witchwoman from the feared, demon-ridden North. The narrative follows Aerin as she seeks her birthright, becoming first a dragon killer and eventually the savior of the kingdom." Booklist

The author "has in this suspenseful prequel . . . created an utterly engrossing fantasy, replete with a fairly mature romantic subplot as well as adventure." N Y Times Book Rev

Chalice. G.P. Putnam's Sons 2008 263p $18.99

Grades: 7 8 9 10 11 12

    1. Fantasy fiction 2. Bees -- Fiction

    ISBN 978-0-399-24676-0; 0-399-24676-2

                          LC 2008-704

A beekeeper by trade, Mirasol's life changes completely when she is named the new Chalice, the most important advisor to the new Master, a former priest of fire.

"The fantasy realm is evoked in thorough and telling detail. . . . A lavish and lasting treat." Publ Wkly

Dragonhaven. G.P. Putnam's Sons 2007 342p $17.99

Grades: 7 8 9 10 11 12

    1. Fantasy fiction 2. Dragons -- Fiction

    ISBN 978-0-399-24675-3; 0-399-24675-4

                          LC 2007-8197

When Jake Mendoza, who lives in the Smokehill National Park where his father runs the Makepeace Institute of Integrated Dragon Studies, goes on his first solo overnight in the park, he finds an infant dragon whose mother has been killed by a poacher.

Readers "will be engaged by McKinley's well-drawn characters and want to root for the Smokehill community's fight to save the ultimate endangered species." SLJ

Pegasus. G.P. Putnam's Sons 2010 404p $18.99

Grades: 8 9 10 11 12

    1. Fantasy fiction 2. Magic -- Fiction 3. Princesses --

Fiction 4. Pegasus (Greek mythology) -- Fiction

    ISBN 0-399-24677-0; 978-0-399-24677-7

                        LC 2010-2279

Because of a thousand-year-old alliance between humans and pegasi, Princess Sylvi is ceremonially bound to Ebon, her own pegasus, on her twelfth birthday, but the closeness of their bond becomes a threat to the status quo and possibly to the safety of their two nations.

"McKinley's storytelling is to be savored. She lavishes page after page upon rituals and ceremonies, basks in the awe of her intricately constructed world, and displays a masterful sense of pegasi physicality and mannerisms." Booklist

McKissack, Fredrick, Jr.

Shooting star. Atheneum Books for Young Readers 2009 273p $16.99

Grades: 8 9 10 11 12

    1. School stories 2. Football -- Fiction 3. Steroids -- Fiction 4. African Americans -- Fiction

    ISBN 978-1-4169-4745-5; 1-4169-4745-0

                        LC 2008-55525

Jomo Rogers, a naturally talented athlete, starts taking performance enhancing drugs in order to be an even better high school football player, but finds his life spinning out of control as his game improves.

"Profane and scatological language abounds, but it is not outside the realm of what one could hear any day in a school locker room. Top-notch sports fiction." SLJ

McLaughlin, Lauren

The **Free**. Lauren McLaughlin.. Soho Teen 2017 278 p.

Grades: 8 9 10 11 12

    1. Criminals -- Fiction; 2. Dysfunctional families -- Fiction; 3. Families -- Fiction; 4. Secrecy -- Fiction; 5. Juvenile delinquency -- Fiction; 6. Family problems -- Fiction; 7. Secrets -- Fiction; 8. Brothers and sisters -- Fiction

    9781616957322; 161695731X; 9781616957315, $18.99

                        LC 2016020652

In this book, by Lauren McLaughlin, "Isaac West stole to give his younger sister, Janelle, little things: a new sweater, a scarf, just things that made her look less like a charity case whose mother spent money on booze and more like the prep school girls he's seen on the way to school. But when his biggest job to date, a car theft, goes wrong, Isaac chooses to take the full rap himself, and he's cut off from helping Janelle." (Publisher's note)

"Compassionate, compelling, gritty, and redeeming, this story's broad appeal will hit the mark with mystery or realistic fiction fans and those who care about social justice." Booklist

Scored. Random House 2011 226p $17.99; lib bdg $20.99

Grades: 6 7 8 9 10

    1. Science fiction

    ISBN 978-0-375-86820-7; 978-0-375-96820-4 lib bdg

                        LC 2010028113

In the not-so-distant future, teenaged Imani must struggle within a world where a monolithic corporation assigns young people a score that will determine the rest of their lives.

"The bold, aggressive narrative condemns both No Child Left Behind–style testing and current financial policies, cautioning about what could happen to social mobility in the face of stark inequity." Kirkus

McLemore, Anna-Marie

Blanca & Roja. Anna-Marie McLemore. Feiwel and Friends 2018 384 p.

Grades: 8 9 10 11

1. Sisters -- Fiction; 2. Swans -- Fiction; 3. Blessing and cursing -- Fiction
9781250162700; 9781250162717, $17.99

LC 2018936436

In this book, by Anna-Marie McLemore, "the del Cisne girls [Blanca and Roja] have never just been sisters; they're also rivals.... They know that, because of a generations-old spell,...[that] one day, the swans will pull them into a dangerous game that will leave one of them a girl, and trap the other in the body of a swan. But when two local boys become drawn into the game, the swans' spell intertwines with the strange and unpredictable magic lacing the woods." (Publisher's note)

The **weight** of feathers. Anna-Marie McLemore. St. Martin's Press 2015 320 p.

Grades: 9 10 11 12

1. Performing arts -- Fiction 2. Vendetta -- Fiction 3. Romance fiction
1250058651; 9781250058652, $18.99

LC 2015019216

William C. Morris Award Finalist (2016)

"Lace Paloma may be new to her family's show, but she knows as well as anyone that the Corbeaus are pure magia negra, black magic from the devil himself . . . and she's been taught from birth to keep away. But when disaster strikes the small town where both families are performing, it's a Corbeau boy, Cluck, who saves Lace's life." (Publisher's note)

★ **When** the moon was ours: A Novel. Anna-Marie McLemore. Thomas Dunne Books, St. Martin's Griffin 2016 288 p.

Grades: 9 10 11 12

1. Magic -- Fiction 2. Fantasy fiction
9781466873247, $60; 9781250058669, $18.99

LC 2016016411

Stonewall Book Award Honor Book, Youth (2017)

In this book, by Anna-Marie McLemore, "best friends Miel and Sam are as strange as they are inseparable. Roses grow out of Miel's wrist, and rumors say that she spilled out of a water tower when she was five. Sam is known for the moons he paints and hangs in the trees. . . . But as odd as everyone considers Miel and Sam, even they stay away from the Bonner girls, four beautiful sisters rumored to be witches." (Publisher's note)

"Readers who stick with this novel will be rewarded with a love story that is as endearingly old-fashioned as it is modern and as fantastical as it is real." SLJ

Wild beauty. Anna-Marie McLemore. Feiwel and Friends 2017 339 p.

Grades: 9 10 11 12

1. Families -- Fiction; 2. Gardens -- Fiction; 3. Magic -- Fiction
9781250124555; 9781250124562

LC 2016058771

In this book, by Anna-Marie McLemore, "For nearly a century the Nomeolvides women have tended the grounds and lush estate gardens of La Pradera. They have a tragic legacy: if they fall in love too deeply, their lovers vanish. When a strange boy appears in the gardens, he is a mystery to Estrella and to her family, but he's even more a mystery to himself. He knows nothing more about who he is or where he came from than his first name. As Estrella tries to help Fel piece together his unknown past, they uncover secrets as dangerous as they are magical." (Publisher's note)

"This is not only a powerful exploration of truth and family...but also gender identity, sexuality...and love itself. Sheer magic: fierce, bright, and blazing with possibility." Booklist

McLoughlin, Jane

At Yellow Lake. Frances Lincoln Children's Books 2012 358 p. (paperback) $8.99

Grades: 7 8 9 10

1. Mystery fiction 2. Teenagers -- Fiction 3. Native Americans -- Fiction
ISBN 1847802877; 9781847802873

In this book by Jane McLoughlin, "Etta, Peter and Jonah all find themselves at a cabin by the shore of Yellow Lake. . . . Jonah has come to Yellow Lake to try to get in touch with his Ojibwe roots. Peter is there to bury a lock of his mother's hair -- her final request. Etta is on the run from her mother's creepy boyfriend. . . . But as the three take shelter in the cabin . . . they soon realise that they have inadvertently stumbled onto the scene of a horrifying crime." (Publisher's note)

McMann, Lisa

Wake. Simon Pulse 2008 210p $15.99; pa $8.99

Grades: 7 8 9 10

1. School stories 2. Dreams -- Fiction
ISBN 978-1-4169-5357-9; 1-4169-5357-4; 978-1-4169-7447-5 pa; 1-4169-7447-4 pa

LC 2007036267

Ever since she was eight years old, high school student Janie Hannagan has been uncontrollably drawn into other people's dreams, but it is not until she befriends an elderly nursing home patient and becomes involved with an enigmatic fellow-student that she discovers her true power.

"A fast pace, a great mix of teen angst and supernatural experiences, and an eerie, attention-grabbing cover will make this a hit." Booklist

Other titles in this series are:
Fade (2009)
Gone (2010)

McMullan, Margaret

Cashay. Houghton Mifflin Harcourt 2009 166p $15

Grades: 7 8 9 10

1. Anger -- Fiction 2. Mentoring -- Fiction 3. Bereavement -- Fiction 4. Racially mixed people --

Fiction
ISBN 978-0-547-07656-0; 0-547-07656-8

LC 2008-36111

When her world is turned upside down by her sister's death, a mentor is assigned to fourteen-year-old Cashay to help her through her anger and grief.

"Cashay's spirited voice and non-frothy prose will draw both confirmed and newer fans of inner-city drama." Kirkus

★ **Sources** of light. Houghton Mifflin 2010 233p $15

Grades: 6 7 8 9

1. Photography -- Fiction 2. Race relations -- Fiction 3. African Americans -- Civil rights -- Fiction
ISBN 978-0-547-07659-1; 0-547-07659-2

LC 2009-49708

"When 14-year-old Samantha Thomas moves to Jackson, Miss., in 1962, following her father's death in Vietnam, she learns about love and hate all in the same year. Her mother meets Perry Walker, a photographer who teaches Sam about taking photographs and seeing the world in new ways, but what she begins seeing and pondering is the racial situation in Jackson—lunch-counter sit-ins, voter-registration protests and the violent reprisals of many in the white community, including the father of the boy she begins to like. . . . This offers a superb portrait of a place and time and a memorable character trying to make sense of a world both ugly and beautiful." Kirkus

McNab, Andy

Traitor; [by] Andy McNab and Robert Rigby. G.P. Putnam's Sons 2005 265p $15.99

Grades: 7 8 9 10

1. Spies -- Fiction 2. Orphans -- Fiction 3. Grandfathers -- Fiction
ISBN 0-399-24464-6

LC 2005-6701

"Orphaned Londoner Danny Watts wants nothing to do with his estranged grandfather, a traitor who went MIA years ago, until the British military offers Danny a proposition: find his grandfather and he'll receive a scholarship. . . . With help from his best friend, Elena, he sets off to find his relative and the truth. . . . The well-crafted language includes a few coarse phrases. . . . With its brisk plot and unpredictable characters, this story of intrigue rises above many standard adventure stories." Booklist

Other titles in this series are:
Payback (2006)
Avenger (2007)
Meltdown (2008)

McNally, Janet

Girls in the moon. Janet McNalley; [edited by] Kristin Pettit. HarperTeen 2016 352 p.

Grades: 8 9 10 11

1. Family life -- Fiction 2. Musicians -- Fiction 3. Love -- Fiction 4. Sisters -- Fiction
9780062436269, $16.99; 9780062436245, $17.99

LC 2016949903

In this novel, by Janet McNally, "Phoebe, a budding poet in search of an identity to call her own, is tired of half-truths and vague explanations. When she visits [her sister,] Luna

in New York, she's determined to find out how she fits in to this family of storytellers, and maybe even to continue her own tale—the one with the musician boy she's been secretly writing for months." (Publisher's note)

"McNally is a polished storyteller, her prose alive with vivid descriptions, the excitement of romance, and an artist's yearning to create." Pub Wkly

The **looking** glass. Janet McNally. HarperTeen 2018 336 p.

Grades: 7 8 9 10

1. Ballet dancing -- Fiction; 2. Runaways -- Fiction; 3. Sisters -- Fiction; 4. Supernatural -- Fiction; 5. Ballet -- Fiction
9780062436276, $17.99

LC 2017034545

In this book, by Janet McNally, "GIRLS IN TROUBLE. That's what Sylvie Blake's older sister Julia renamed their favorite fairy tale book, way back when they were just girls themselves. Now Julia has disappeared -- and no one knows for sure if she wants to be away, or if she's the one in trouble. Then a copy of their old storybook arrives with a mysterious list inside, and Sylvie begins to see signs of her sister, and their favorite fairy tales, everywhere she goes." (Publisher's note)

McNamee, Eoin

The **Navigator**. Wendy Lamb Books 2007 342p il (Navigator trilogy) $15.99; pa $6.99

Grades: 6 7 8 9

1. Fantasy fiction 2. Time -- Fiction
ISBN 978-0-375-83910-8; 0-375-83910-0; 978-0-385-73554-4 pa; 0-385-73554-5 pa

LC 2006-26691

Owen has always been different, and not only because his father committed suicide, but he is not prepared for the knowledge that he has a mission to help the Wakeful—the custodians of time—to stop the Harsh from reversing the flow of time.

McNamee "shows a deft hand in writing for children. Excellent world-building, a thrilling and propulsive plot, internal consistency and a multitude of child heroes guarantee a following for this exciting fantasy." Kirkus

Other titles in this series are:
City of Time (2008)
The Frost Child (2009)

McNamee, Graham

★ **Acceleration**. Wendy Lamb Bks. 2003 210p hardcover o.p. pa $6.99

Grades: 8 9 10 11 12

1. Mystery fiction 2. Canada -- Fiction 3. Homicide -- Fiction
ISBN 0-385-73119-1; 0-440-23836-6 pa

LC 2003-3708

Stuck working in the Lost and Found of the Toronto Transit Authority for the summer, seventeen-year-old Duncan finds the diary of a serial killer and sets out to stop him

"Never overexploits the sensational potential of the subject and builds suspense layer upon layer, while injecting some surprising comedy relief." Booklist

Beyond; a ghost story. by Graham McNamee. Wendy Lamb Books 2012 226 p. (trade) $15.99
Grades: 9 10 11 12

1. Supernatural -- Fiction 2. Shades and shadows -- Fiction 3. Near-death experiences -- Fiction 4. Ghosts -- Fiction
ISBN 0385737750; 9780375851650; 9780375897597; 9780385737753; 9780385906876

LC 2011043610

This book by Graham McNamee follows "Jane, [who is] no stranger to near-death experiences. Her shadow has forced her to drink drain cleaner and held her down on a train track as a speeding train approached. After a recent nail-gun 'accident' to the skull causes her to flat-line, Jane returns to the living with her shadow even more determined to kill her." (Kirkus Reviews)

McNaughton, Janet
An **earthly** knight. HarperCollins Publishers 2004 261p $15.99; lib bdg $16.89
Grades: 7 8 9 10

1. Fantasy fiction
ISBN 0-06-008992-X; 0-06-008993-8 lib bdg

LC 2003-9561

First published 2003 in Canada

In 1162 in Scotland, sixteen-year-old Jenny Avenel falls in love with the mysterious Tam Lin while being courted by the king's brother and must navigate the tides of tradition and the power of ancient magic to define her own destiny.

"The author does an excellent job of interweaving legend and history to create an exciting and engaging tale." SLJ

McNeal, Laura
Dark water. Alfred A. Knopf 2010 287p $16.99; lib bdg $19.99
Grades: 7 8 9 10

1. Fires -- Fiction 2. Divorce -- Fiction 3. California -- Fiction 4. Family life -- Fiction 5. Illegal aliens -- Fiction 6. Homeless persons -- Fiction
ISBN 978-0-375-84973-2; 0-375-84973-4; 978-0-375-94973-9 lib bdg; 0-375-94973-9 lib bdg

LC 2009-43249

Living in a cottage on her uncle's southern California avocado ranch since her parent's messy divorce, fifteen-year-old Pearl Dewitt meets and falls in love with an illegal migrant worker, and is trapped with him when wildfires approach his makeshift forest home.

"Notable for well-drawn characters, an engaging plot and, especially, hauntingly beautiful language, this is an outstanding book." Kirkus

Zipped; [by] Laura and Tom McNeal. Knopf 2003 283p hardcover o.p. pa $7.99
Grades: 9 10 11 12

1. Stepfamilies -- Fiction
ISBN 0-375-81491-4; 0-375-83098-7 pa

LC 2002-2781

At the end of their sophomore year in high school, the lives of four teenagers are woven together as they start a tough new job, face family problems, deal with changing friendships, and find love

"There's a realism here that takes the narrative beyond the problem novel and into one of relationships, their difficult demands in the face of human complexity and frailty, and their nonetheless often satisfying rewards. The book never loses sight of the kids at the heart of this, however, which keeps this accessible to the teens it's about." Bull Cent Child Books

McNeal, Tom
★ **Far** far away; by Tom McNeal. 1st ed. Alfred A. Knopf Books for Young Readers 2013 371 p. (hardcover) $17.99; (ebook) $53.97; (library) $20.99
Grades: 7 8 9 10

1. Occult fiction 2. Fantasy fiction 3. Ghosts -- Fiction 4. Friendship -- Fiction 5. Supernatural -- Fiction 6. Missing persons -- Fiction
ISBN 0375849726; 9780375849725; 9780375896989; 9780375949722

LC 2012020603

Parents' Choice: Gold Medal Fiction (2013)

This book "is narrated by the ghost of Jacob Grimm . . . , unhappily caught in the Zwischenraum (a plane of existence between life and death). For now, he is the nearly constant companion of Jeremy Johnson," who hears voices. This ability "has made him an object of derision for many in his little town, though—thrillingly—not to the electrifyingly vibrant Ginger Boultinghouse, who is more than happy to lure Jeremy into more trouble than he's ever encountered." (School Library Journal)

McNeil, Gretchen
I'm not your manic pixie dream girl. Gretchen McNeil. Balzer + Bray 2016 352 p.
Grades: 8 9 10 11

1. Bullying -- Fiction 2. Dating (Social customs) -- Fiction 3. Dating (Social customs) -- Fiction 4. Revenge -- Fiction 5. High school students -- Fiction 6. Bullies -- Fiction 7. Romance fiction -- Fiction
9780062409133, $16.99; 9780062409119, $17.99

LC 2016013283

In this novel, by Gretchen McNeil, "Beatrice Maria Estrella Giovannini has life all figured out. She's starting senior year at the top of her class, she's a shoo-in for a scholarship to M.I.T., and she's got a new boyfriend. . . The only problem: . . . Bea and her best friends Spencer and Gabe have been the targets of horrific bullying. So Bea uses her math skills to come up with The Formula, a 100% mathematically guaranteed path to social happiness in high school." (Publisher's note)

"The love rhombus crafted here is a tad predictable, but the excitement's in the execution: the author's strong characterizations and smart humor put this above most similar titles." Kirkus

McNicoll, Sylvia
Last chance for Paris. Fitzhenry & Whiteside 2008 204p pa $11.95
Grades: 6 7 8 9

1. Twins -- Fiction 2. Wolves -- Fiction 3. Siblings -- Fiction
ISBN 978-1-5545-5061-6 pa; 1-5545-5061-0 pa

Fourteen-year-old Zanna goes to the Alberta ice fields with her father and twin brother, Martin, where they find a wolf pup which they name Paris. When Martin is lost, Paris helps find him.

"Written with elements of wry humor and romance, this Canadian novel features a narrator whose disarmingly candid opinions make her an appealing guide for readers who usually veer away from backwoods or survival stories." Booklist

McPhee, Peter

New blood. James Lorimer 2008 167p pa $8.95

Grades: 6 7 8 9 10

1. School stories 2. Canada -- Fiction 3. Bullies -- Fiction

ISBN 978-1-55028-996-1; 1-55028-996-9

When his family moves from the tough streets of Glasgow to Winnipeg, Canada, Callum finds that his high school days of dealing with bullies are far from over.

"The Scottish culture, which becomes a colorful character, adds to the fullness of the story. The writing, rich in dialogue, does not waste words and keeps the reader involved and cheering for this gutsy hero who fights his fear to stand against abuse aimed at himself and others." Voice Youth Advocates

McQuein, Josin L.

Arclight; Josin L. McQuein. 1st ed. Greenwillow Books, an imprint of HarperCollins Publishers 2013 416 p. (hardcover) $17.99

Grades: 8 9 10 11 12

1. Orphans 2. Fantasy fiction 3. Science fiction 4. Amnesia -- Fiction 5. Identity -- Fiction

ISBN 0062130145; 9780062130143

LC 2013002929

In this book, "Marina was pulled from the Dark at the cost of nine lives, and she is paying the price. Ostracized and abused by those whose parents died for her sake, Marina is all but alone in the Arclight, a safe zone where it is never dark. The Fade live in the Dark—chameleons, they steal humans from the light to an unknown fate. Marina dreams of their voices and frets that she has no memory of her life before her rescue." She seeks answers about her past. (Publishers Weekly)

McQuerry, Maureen Doyle

The **Peculiars**; a novel. Maureen Doyle McQuerry. Amulet Books 2012 359 p. (hardback) $16.95

Grades: 7 8 9 10 11 12

1. Fantasy fiction 2. Voyages and travels -- Fiction 3. Father-daughter relationship -- Fiction 4. Goblins -- Fiction 5. Identity -- Fiction 6. Abnormalities, Human -- Fiction 7. Adventure and adventurers -- Fiction

ISBN 1419701789; 9781419701788

LC 2012000844

This is the story of Lena Mattacascar, who at age 18 "travel[s] to Scree, an uncharted wilderness of 'indigenous folks' and deported convicts," sitting on the train with young librarian "Jimson Quiggley," with "marshal Thomas Saltre" watching them. "Lena cannot stop thinking about her mysterious father" or the possibility that she's part Pecu-

liar (goblin). "Scree is the place where Lena's questions might be answered, but arriving there just multiplies them." (Publishers Weekly)

McStay, Moriah

Everything that makes you. Moriah McStay. Katherine Tegen Books, an imprint of HarperCollins Children's Books 2015 346 p.

Grades: 8 9 10 11

1. Disfigured persons -- Fiction 2. Family life -- Fiction 3. Interpersonal relations -- Fiction 4. Self-confidence -- Fiction 5. Accidents -- Fiction

0062295489; 9780062295484, $17.99

LC 2014005864

In this book, by Moriah McStay, "Fiona Doyle's face was horribly scarred as a child. She writes about her frustrations and dreams in notebooks, penning song lyrics. But she'd never be brave enough to sing those songs in public. Fi Doyle . . . [is] the best lacrosse player in the state and can't be distracted by her friend who wants to be more than that. But then her luck on the field goes south. Alternating chapters between Fiona and Fi tell two stories about the same girl." (Publisher's note)

"Entertaining and intellectually stimulating, the novel invites discussion about how much of a person's life is determined by events and whether some tendencies are inborn." Publishers Weekly

McVoy, Terra Elan

Pure. Simon Pulse 2009 330p $16.99

Grades: 8 9 10 11 12

1. Friendship -- Fiction 2. Christian life -- Fiction 3. Dating (Social customs) -- Fiction

ISBN 978-1-4169-7872-5; 1-4169-7872-0

LC 2008-33404

Fifteen-year-old Tabitha and her four best friends all wear purity rings to symbolize their pledge to remain virgins until they marry, but when one admits that she has broken the pledge each girl must reexamine her faith, friendships, and what it means to be pure.

"Tabitha's blooming romance with Jake and her positive relationship with her supportive, if somewhat quirky, parents add pleasant undercurrents to a book that girls of a spiritual bent will enjoy." SLJ

McWilliams, Kelly

Doormat; a novel. Delacorte Press 2004 131p $15.95; lib bdg $17.99

Grades: 6 7 8 9

1. Theater -- Fiction 2. Pregnancy -- Fiction 3. Friendship -- Fiction

ISBN 0-385-73168-X; 0-385-90204-2 lib bdg

LC 2003-19675

Fourteen-year-old Jaime has always been a doormat, but her diary reveals how getting the lead in a school play, finding her first boyfriend, discovering her dream, and helping her best friend cope with being pregnant transform her life.

"McWilliams' first-person, present-tense vignettes are taut, funny, and touching, the dialogue is authentic, and both the teen and adult characters ring true." Booklist

Meaker, Marijane

Night kites. Harper & Row 1986 216p.

Grades: 7 8 9 10

1. AIDS (Disease) -- Fiction; 2. Brothers -- Fiction; 3. Homosexuality -- Fiction

0-06-023253-6; 0-06-447035-0, $5.99

LC 85-45386

ALA YALSA Margaret A. Edwards Award (1993)

"Erick is comfortable with his senior crowd, delighted with his girl Dill and his best friend Jack. But Jack falls for Nicki, an insecure fashion-plate who wants only what she can't have. Erick tries to steer Jack clear of such a troublemaker, so Nicki sets her sights on him next. Complicating his guilt for betraying Jack and Dill by seeing Nicki is Erick's misery over learning that his beloved older brother Pete has AIDS. Thus the horrified family finds out about Pete's imminent death at the same time they find out about his life style. . . . Grade seven and up." (SLJ)

Mead, Alice

Dawn and dusk. Farrar, Straus and Giroux 2007 151p $16

Grades: 6 7 8 9

1. Refugees -- Fiction 2. Iran-Iraq War, 1980-1988 -- Fiction

ISBN 0-374-31708-9; 978-0-374-31708-9

LC 2006-40850

As thirteen-year-old Azad tries desperately to cling to the life he has known, the political situation in Iran during the war with Iraq finally forces his family to flee their home and seek safety elsewhere.

"Azad is an appealing protagonist, and it is his simple and direct story that will draw readers through the complexities of a multinational ethnic longing for self-determination that remains at the heart of an international tinderbox." SLJ

★ **Swimming** to America; Alice Mead. 1st ed; Farrar, Straus and Giroux 2005 153p $16

Grades: 6 7 8 9

1. Immigrants -- Fiction

ISBN 0-374-38047-3

LC 2004-53249

Eighth grader Linda Berati struggles to understand who she is within the context of her mother's secrecy about the family background, her discomfort with her old girlfriends, her involvement with the family problems of her Cuban-American friend Ramon, and an opportunity to attend a school for "free spirits" like herself.

Written with "sensitivity and optimism. . . . [This is] an informative, empathetic, contemporary portrait of the immigrant experience." SLJ

Mebus, Scott

Gods of Manhattan. Dutton Children's Books 2008 372p (Gods of Manhattan) $17.99

Grades: 6 7 8 9

1. Fantasy fiction 2. Adventure fiction 3. Space and time -- Fiction 4. Gods and goddesses -- Fiction

ISBN 978-0-525-47955-0; 0-525-47955-4

LC 2007-18113

"Rory, 13, and his sister Bridget, 9, live in present-day New York City unaware of the spirits from Manhattan's or 'Mannahatta's' past that coexist alongside them. Rory has a gift for seeing this other world but has repressed this ability until the day he notices a cockroach riding a rat, an ancient Indian warrior, a papier-mâché boy, and other oddities. . . . The use of real historical figures and events lends authenticity to this compulsively readable and fast-paced fantasy." SLJ

Other titles in this series are:

Spirits in the park (2009)

The sorcerer's secret (2010)

Medina, Meg

★ **Burn** Baby Burn. Meg Medina. Candlewick Press 2016 320 p.

Grades: 9 10 11 12

1. Teenage girls -- Fiction 2. Bildungsromans 3. New York (N.Y.) -- Fiction

0763674672; 9780763674670, $17.99

LC 2015954454

In this novel, by Meg Medina, "Nora Lopez is seventeen during the infamous New York summer of 1977, when the city is besieged by arson, a massive blackout, and a serial killer named Son of Sam who shoots young women on the streets. Nora's family life isn't going so well either. All Nora wants is to turn eighteen and be on her own. And while there is a cute new guy who started working with her at the deli, is dating even worth the risk when the killer likes picking off couples who stay out too late? " (Publisher's note)

"Powerfully moving, this stellar piece of historical fiction emphasizes the timeless concerns of family loyalty and personal strength while highlighting important issues that still resonate today." Booklist

★ **Milagros**; girl from Away. Henry Holt and Co. 2008 279p $17.89

Grades: 6 7 8 9

1. Magic -- Fiction 2. Islands -- Fiction 3. Rays (Fishes) -- Fiction 4. Mother-daughter relationship -- Fiction

ISBN 978-0-8050-8230-2; 0-8050-8230-1

LC 2007-46939

Twelve-year-old Milagros barely survives an invasion of her tiny, Caribbean island home, escapes with the help of mysterious sea creatures, reunites briefly with her pirate-father, and learns about a mother's love when cast ashore on another island.

"Medina's use of magical realism keeps readers tantalizingly off-balance as she navigates among settings. . . . [This] haunting tale . . . will remain with readers." Horn Book

★ **Yaqui** Delgado wants to kick your ass; Meg Medina. Candlewick Press 2013 272 p. (reinforced) $16.99

Grades: 9 10 11 12

1. School stories 2. Bullies -- Fiction

ISBN 0763658596; 9780763658595

LC 2012943645

Pura Belpre Author Award (2014)

In this novel, by Meg Medina, "a Latina teen is targeted by a bully at her new school--and must discover resources she never knew she had. One morning before school, some girl tells Piddy Sanchez that Yaqui Delgado hates her and wants to . . . [beat her up.] . . . As the harassment escalates, avoiding Yaqui and her gang starts to take over Piddy's life. Is there any way for Piddy to survive without closing herself off or running away?" (Publisher's note)

Meehan, Kierin

★ **Hannah's** winter. Kane/Miller Book Publishers 2009 212p $15.95

Grades: 5 6 7 8

1. Adventure fiction
ISBN 978-1-933605-98-2; 1-933605-98-7
First published 2001 in Australia

Hannah would much rather be back in Australia, starting high school with her friends. But Japan turns out to be nothing like she'd imagined. When Hannah and her new friend Miki find an ancient message in the stationery shop, they are drawn into involving a mysterious riddle.

"Meehan utilizes beautifully crafted similes and metaphors as she creates a loving and detailed portrayal of Japan and its people. . . . The tale remains so grounded in reality that it never defies belief. A fine fantasy." Kirkus

Meehl, Brian

Suck it up. Delacorte Press 2008 323p $15.99; pa $8.99

Grades: 8 9 10 11

1. Vampires -- Fiction
ISBN 978-0-385-73300-7; 0-385-73300-3; 978-0-440-42091-0 pa; 0-440-42091-1 pa

LC 2007-27995

After graduating from the International Vampire League, a scrawny, teenaged vampire named Morning is given the chance to fulfill his childhood dream of becoming a superhero when he embarks on a League mission to become the first vampire to reveal his identity to humans and to demonstrate how peacefully-evolved, blood-substitute-drinking vampires can use their powers to help humanity.

This "an original and light variation on the current trend in brooding teen vampire protagonists. . . . Puns abound in this lengthy, complicated romp. . . . Teens will find it delightful." Booklist

You don't know about me. Delacorte Press 2011 406p $17.99; ebook $10.99; lib bdg $20.99

Grades: 9 10 11 12

1. LGBT people -- Fiction 2. Christian life -- Fiction 3. Automobile travel -- Fiction 4. Father-son relationship -- Fiction 5. Mother-son relationship -- Fiction
ISBN 978-0-385-73909-2; 978-0-375-89715-3 ebook; 978-0-385-90771-2 lib bdg

LC 2010-17101

Billy has spent his almost-sixteen years with four cardinal points—Mother, Christ, Bible, and Home-school—but when he sets off on a wild road trip to find the father he thought was dead, he learns much about himself and life.

"The humor, action, and edgy social commentary make this a book a mature reader, with knowledge and interest of the works of Mark Twain, might enjoy." Voice Youth Advocates

Meldrum, Christina

★ **Madapple**. Alfred A. Knopf 2008 410p il $16.99; lib bdg $19.99

Grades: 9 10 11 12

1. Trials -- Fiction 2. Miracles -- Fiction 3. Mother-daughter relationship -- Fiction
ISBN 978-0-375-85176-6; 978-0-375-95176-3 lib bdg

LC 2007-49653

ALA YALSA Morris Award finalist, 2009

A girl who has been brought up in near isolation is thrown into a twisted web of family secrets and religious fundamentalism when her mother dies and she goes to live with relatives she never knew she had.

"A markedly intelligent offering mixing lush descriptions of plants, history, science and religion, this should surely spark interest among a wide array of readers." Kirkus

Include bibliographical references

Melling, O. R.

The **book** of dreams. Amulet Books 2009 698p map (Chronicles of Faerie) $19.95

Grades: 7 8 9 10

1. Magic -- Fiction 2. Canada -- Fiction 3. Fairies -- Fiction 4. Native Americans -- Fiction 5. Voyages and travels -- Fiction
ISBN 978-0-8109-8346-5; 0-8109-8346-X

LC 2008-24689

Sequel to The Light-Bearer's daughter (2007)

Now thirteen and depressed, Dana has been living with her father and his new wife in Canada for two years, and when she finds that her gateway to the land of Faerie has been mysteriously shattered, she must travel the length and breadth of Canada to find the secret that will re-open the Faerie world.

"The author's exploration of folk traditions across cultures makes the book unique." Voice Youth Advocates

The **Hunter's** Moon. Amulet Books 2005 284p (Chronicles of Faerie) $16.95; pa $7.95

Grades: 7 8 9 10

1. Magic -- Fiction 2. Ireland -- Fiction
ISBN 0-8109-5857-0; 0-8109-9214-0 pa

LC 2004-22216

First published 1992 in Ireland

Two teenage cousins, one Irish, the other from the United States, set out to find a magic doorway to the Faraway Country, where humans must bow to the little people.

"This novel is a compelling blend of Irish mythology and geography. Characters that breathe and connect with readers, and a picturesque landscape that shifts between the present and the past, bring readers into the experience." SLJ

Other available titles in this series are:
The book of dreams (2009)
The Light-Bearer's daughter (2007)
The Summer King (2006)

The **Light-**Bearer's daughter. Amulet Books 2007 348p map (Chronicles of Faerie) hardcover o.p. pa $7.95

Grades: 7 8 9 10 11

1. Magic -- Fiction 2. Ireland -- Fiction
ISBN 978-0-8109-0781-2; 0-8109-0781-X; 978-0-8109-7123-3 pa; 0-8109-7123-2 pa

LC 2006-33517

Sequel to The Summer King (2006)

In exchange for the granting of her heart's desire, twelve-year-old Dana agrees to make an arduous journey to Lugnaquillia through the land of Faerie in order to warn King Lugh, second in command to the High King, that an evil destroyer has entered the Mountain Kingdom.

"The richly integrated, vivid fantasy scenes balance the strident calls for environmental protection and world peace, and the characters' private passages through 'layers of storied memory' will bring the issues home for readers." Booklist

Followed by The book of dreams (2009)

The **Summer** King. Amulet Books 2006 359p map (Chronicles of Faerie) $16.95

Grades: 7 8 9 10

1. Magic -- Fiction 2. Ireland -- Fiction
ISBN 0-8109-5969-0

LC 2005-15083

Seventeen-year-old Laurel returns to her grandparents' home in Ireland, where she encounters the roly-poly man, a cluricaun who sets Laurel on a quest to free her twin sister, thought to be dead, to live with her lover in the legendary world of Faerie.

"Fans of Melling's first title in the Chronicles of Faerie, The Hunter's Moon (2005), will recognize similarly thrilling action, fascinating Irish mythology, and magnificently detailed magic." Booklist

Meloy, Maile

★ The **apothecary**. G. P. Putnam's Sons 2011 353p $16.99

Grades: 6 7 8 9

1. Adventure fiction 2. Alchemy -- Fiction 3. Cold war -- Fiction
ISBN 978-0-399-25627-1; 0-399-25627-X

LC 2010045003

This novel follows a fourteen-year-old American girl whose life unexpectedly changes when she moves to London in 1952 and gets swept up in a race to save the world from nuclear war

"With evocative, confident prose and equally atmospheric spot art from Schoenherr, adult author Meloy's first book for young readers is an auspicious one." Publ Wkly

The **apprentices**; by Maile Meloy; illustrated by Ian Schoenherr. G.P. Putnam's Sons, an imprint of Penguin Group (USA) Inc. 2013 432 p. (hardcover) $16.99

Grades: 6 7 8 9

1. Magic -- Fiction 2. Alchemy -- Fiction 3. Voyages and travels -- Fiction 4. Adventure and adventurers -- Fiction 5. Southeast Asia -- History -- 1945- -- Fiction
ISBN 9780399162459

LC 2012048715

"Janie, now 16, is alone at an elite American boarding school, unaware of the whereabouts of her first boyfriend, Benjamin, and his apothecary father. After she is wrongly expelled, she realizes she is the victim of a nefarious scheme, which again poses a threat to world peace. The . . . plot spans the globe as the heroes find their way back to each other." (Publishers Weekly)

Meminger, Neesha

Shine, coconut moon. Margaret K. McElderry Books 2009 256p $16.99; pa $8.99

Grades: 7 8 9 10

1. School stories 2. Prejudices -- Fiction 3. East Indian Americans -- Fiction 4. September 11 terrorist attacks, 2001 -- Fiction
ISBN 978-1-4169-5495-8; 1-4169-5495-3; 978-1-4424-0305-5 pa; 1-4424-0305-5 pa

LC 2008-9836

In the days and weeks following the terrorist attacks on September 11, 2001, Samar, who is of Punjabi heritage but has been raised with no knowledge of her past by her single mother, wants to learn about her family's history and to get in touch with the grandparents her mother shuns.

"Meminger's debut book is a beautiful and sensitive portrait of a young woman's journey from self-absorbed navet to selfless, unified awareness." SLJ

Menon, Sandhya

★ **From** Twinkle, with love. Sandhya Menon. Simon Pulse 2018 330 p.

Grades: 7 8 9 10 11

1. Brothers -- Fiction; 2. Dating (Social customs) -- Fiction; 3. East Indian Americans -- Fiction; 4. Letters -- Fiction; 5. Producers and directors -- Fiction; 6. Twins -- Fiction
9781481495424; 9781481495400, $18.99

LC 2017048138

In this book, by Sandhya Menon, aspiring filmmaker and wallflower Twinkle Mehra has stories she wants to tell.... So when fellow film geek Sahil Roy approaches her to direct a movie for the...Summer Festival, Twinkle is all over it.... When mystery man 'N' begins emailing her, Twinkle is sure it's Neil, [Sahil's twin brother] finally ready to begin their happily-ever-after. The only...problem is that,...she's fallen madly in love with...Sahil." (Publisher's note)

"This is an often laugh-out-loud funny journey through the tribulations of high school that's tempered by Twinkle's very real feelings of isolation...A charming addition to the rom-com canon." Booklist

When Dimple met Rishi. Sandhya Menon. Simon Pulse 2017 380 p.

Grades: 7 8 9 10

1. Arranged marriage -- Fiction; 2. Dating (Social customs) -- Fiction; 3. East Indian Americans -- Fiction; 4. Family life -- Fiction
9781481478687, $17.99; 9781481478700

LC 2016023129

This novel, by Sandhya Menon, is "about two Indian-American teens whose parents conspire to arrange their marriage. Dimple Shah...[is] more than ready for a break from her family, from Mamma's inexplicable obsession with her finding the 'Ideal Indian Husband.'...Rishi Patel is a hopeless romantic. So when his parents tell him that his future wife will be attending the same summer program as him -- wherein he'll have to woo her -- he's totally on board." (Publisher's note)

"The strength of the story comes from its blending of Indian culture and values into a modern-day romance that scores of readers can enjoy. This novel touches on issues of identity while remaining light and fun." SLJ

Mesrobian, Carrie

Cut both ways. Carrie Mesrobian. HarperTeen 2015 352 p.

Grades: 10 11 12

> 1. Bisexual people -- Fiction 2. Friendship -- Fiction 3. Gays -- Fiction 4. Interpersonal relations -- Fiction 5. Sex -- Fiction 6. School stories

9780062349880, $17.99

LC 2014047809

This novel, by Carrie Mesrobian, follows "a high school senior who must come to terms with his attraction to both his girlfriend and his male best friend. It took Will Caynes seventeen years to have his first kiss. He should be ecstatic . . . except that it was shared with his best friend, Angus, while they were both drunk and stoned." (Publisher's note)

"Intense, honestly described, and sometimes awkward sexual encounters will ring true for teen readers, and many will identify with the family strife, too. Pitch perfect, raw, and moving." Kirkus

★ **Just** a girl. Carrier Mesrobian. Harper, an imprint of HarperCollinsPublishers 2017 293 p.

Grades: 9 10 11 12

> 1. Divorced parents -- Fiction; 2. Families -- Fiction; 3. High schools -- Fiction; 4. Schools -- Fiction; 5. Minnesota -- Fiction; 6. Children of divorced parents -- Fiction; 7. High school students -- Fiction; 8. Family life -- Fiction

9780062349934; 9780062349910, $17.99

LC 2016957936

In this book, by Carrie Mesrobian, "in small-town Wereford, [Minnesota,] high school senior Rianne has a reputation as an easy hookup.... As graduation nears, Rianne finds herself with a steady boyfriend, a mother who has basically washed her hands of her, a father suddenly back in the picture, and no plans for what's next." (Publishers Weekly)

"Rianne's rich inner life, especially when it's at odds with what's expected of her, is captivatingly full of meaningful, compelling drama, and Mesrobian's frank, realistic depiction of teenage sexuality is a particular bright spot." Booklist

Sex and violence; by Carrie Mesrobian. Carolrhoda Lab 2013 304 p. (reinforced) $17.95

Grades: 10 11 12

> 1. School stories 2. Violence -- Fiction 3. Sex -- Fiction 4. Psychotherapy -- Fiction 5. Emotional problems -- Fiction 6. Interpersonal relations -- Fiction

ISBN 1467705977; 9781467705974

LC 2012047181

William C. Morris Honor Book (2014)

In this book, a teen boy "is brutally beaten in a communal shower by two classmates after he hooks up with one of their former girlfriends, setting the stage for a difficult recovery. After the assault that leaves Evan in the hospital, his father whisks him off to his own boyhood home in Minnesota, where he's uneasily sucked into a tightknit group spending their last summer at home getting high and hanging out before going off to college." (Kirkus Reviews)

"The absence of sentimentality and melodrama in favor of frank dialogue and bruising honesty is a gasp of fresh air." Booklist

Metzger, Lois

A trick of the light; by Lois Metzger. 1st ed. Balzer + Bray 2013 208 p. (hardcover) $17.99

Grades: 9 10 11 12

> 1. Family life -- Fiction 2. Anorexia nervosa -- Fiction 3. Schools -- Fiction 4. High schools -- Fiction 5. Family problems -- Fiction 6. Eating disorders -- Fiction

ISBN 006213308X; 9780062133083

LC 2012019039

In this book by Lois Metzger, "[t]he story of 15-year-old Mike Welles's descent into anorexia is narrated by the disease itself, the insidious voice inside his head preying on his every vulnerability. The voice waits patiently for an opening, which comes in the form of Mike's parents' marital crisis and his insecurity around a new crush, pushing Mike to exercise, coaching him to subsist on next to nothing, and encouraging a friendship with Amber, who is also anorexic." (Publishers Weekly)

"This is a somewhat familiar story told in a new way. . . . A chilling, straightforward novel written with depth and understanding." SLJ

Meyer, Carolyn

Beware, Princess Elizabeth. Harcourt 2001 214p (Young royals) hardcover o.p. pa $5.95

Grades: 7 8 9 10

> 1. Elizabeth I, Queen of England, 1533-1603 -- Childhood and youth --Fiction; 2. Mary I, Queen of England, 1516-1558 -- Fiction

ISBN 0-15-202659-2; 0-15-204556-2 pa

LC 00-11700

After the death of her father, King Henry VIII, in 1547, thirteen-year-old Elizabeth must endure the political intrigues and dangers of the reigns of her half-brother Edward and her half-sister Mary before finally becoming Queen of England eleven years later

"The story moves along swiftly with hints of romance, life-and-death plots, and snippets of everyday life." Book Rep

Cleopatra confesses. Simon & Schuster Books for Young Readers 2011 289p $16.99

Grades: 6 7 8 9

> 1. Queens -- Fiction 2. Princesses -- Fiction; 3. Cleopatra, Queen of Egypt, -30 B.C. -- Childhood and youth - Fiction

ISBN 978-1-4169-8727-7; 1-4169-8727-4

LC 2010025989

Princess Cleopatra, the third (and favorite) daughter of King Ptolemy XII, comes of age in ancient Egypt, accumulating power and discovering love.

Meyer's "lush, detail-rich prose ably evokes Cleopatra's life as a young princess, beginning at age 10 and continuing on until she turns 22. . . . Narrating with the poise and confidence of a born leader, this Cleopatra should win readers over." Publ Wkly

Includes bibliographical references

Duchessina; a novel of Catherine de' Medici. Harcourt 2007 261p (Young royals) $17

Grades: 7 8 9 10

1. Catherine de Médicis, Queen, consort of Henry II, King of France, 1519-1589 -- Childhood and youth -- Fiction; 2. Italy -- Fiction 4. Queens -- Fiction 5. Orphans -- Fiction

ISBN 978-0-15-205588-2; 0-15-205588-6

LC 2006028876

While her tyrannical family is out of favor in Italy, young Catherine de Medici is raised in convents, then in 1533, when she is fourteen, her uncle, Pope Clement VII, arranges for her marriage to prince Henri of France, who is destined to become king.

"With meticulous historical detail, sensitive characterizations, and Catherine's strong narration, Meyer's memorable story of a fascinating young woman who relies on her intelligence, rather than her beauty, will hit home with many teens." Booklist

The true adventures of Charley Darwin. Harcourt 2009 321p il $17

Grades: 7 8 9 10

1. Natural history -- Fiction 2. Voyages around the world -- Fiction 3. Beagle Expedition (1831-1836) -- Fiction; 4. Darwin, Charles, 1809-1882 -- Fiction

ISBN 978-0-15-206194-4; 0-15-206194-0

LC 2008-17451

In nineteenth-century England, young Charles Darwin rejects the more traditional careers of physician and clergyman, choosing instead to embark on a dangerous five-year journey by ship to explore the natural world.

"Meyer's writing has a light touch that capitalizes on the humorous, romantic, and exciting events in the man's life while introducing his scientific pursuits and the beliefs of his time. . . . This novel paints a readable and detailed portrait of the young Charles Darwin." SLJ

Includes bibliographical references

Meyer, L. A.

Bloody Jack; being an account of the curious adventures of Mary Jacky Faber, ship's boy. Harcourt 2002 278p hardcover o.p. pa $6.95

Grades: 7 8 9 10

1. Adventure fiction 2. Orphans -- Fiction 3. Pirates -- Fiction 4. Sex role -- Fiction 5. Seafaring life -- Fiction

ISBN 0-15-216731-5; 0-15-205085-X pa

LC 2002-759

Reduced to begging and thievery in the streets of 18th-century London, a thirteen-year-old orphan disguises herself as a boy and connives her way onto a British warship set for high sea adventure in search of pirates

"From shooting a pirate in battle to foiling a shipmate's sexual attack to surviving when stranded alone on a Caribbean island, the action in Jacky's tale will entertain readers with a taste for adventure." Booklist

Other titles in this series are:

Curse of the blue tattoo (2004)

In the belly of The Bloodhound (2006)

The mark of the golden dragon (2011)

Mississippi Jack (2007)

My bonny light horseman (2008)

Rapture of the deep (2009)

Under the Jolly Roger (2005)

The wake of the Lorelei Lee (2010)

Viva Jacquelina! being an account of the further adventures of Jacky Faber, over the hills and far away. written by L.A. Meyer. Harcourt 2012 p. cm. $16.99

Grades: 7 8 9 10

1. Spain -- History -- Fiction 2. Adventure fiction 3. Historical fiction 4. Spies -- Fiction 5. Sex role -- Fiction 6. Seafaring life -- Fiction 7. Europe -- History -- 1789-1815 -- Fiction 8. Great Britain -- History -- George III, 1760-1820 -- Fiction

ISBN 9780547763507

LC 2011041931

This young adult adventure novel, by L. A. Meyer, continues the "Bloody Jack Adventures" series. "Once again under the thumb of British Intelligence, Jacky is sent to Spain to spy for the Crown during the early days of the nineteenth-century Peninsular War. She finds herself in the company of guerilla freedom fighters, poses for the famous artist Goya, runs with the bulls, is kidnapped by the Spanish Inquisition, and travels with a caravan of gypsies." (Publisher's note)

Meyer, Marissa, 1984-

★ **Cinder**; Marissa Meyer. Feiwel & Friends 2012 320 p. $17.99

Grades: 7 8 9 10 11 12

1. Fairy tales 2. Science fiction 3. Robots -- Fiction

ISBN 9780312641894

LC 2011036123

In this book, "as plague ravages the overcrowded Earth, observed by a ruthless lunar people, Cinder, a gifted mechanic and cyborg, becomes involved with handsome Prince Kai and must uncover secrets about her past in order to protect the world in this futuristic take on the Cinderella story." (Publisher's note)

Followed by: Scarlet (2013)

★ **Cress**; Marissa Meyer. Feiwel & Friends 2014 560 p. $18.99

Grades: 7 8 9 10 11 12

1. Fugitives from justice -- Fiction 2. Human-alien encounters -- Fiction

ISBN 0312642970; 9780312642976

In this book by Marissa Meyer, third in her Lunar Chronicles series, "Cinder and Captain Thorne are fugitives on the run, now with Scarlet and Wolf in tow. Together, they're plotting to overthrow Queen Levana and prevent her army from invading Earth. Their best hope lies with Cress, a girl trapped on a satellite since childhood. When a daring rescue of Cress goes awry, the group is splintered. Meanwhile, Queen Levana will let nothing prevent her marriage to Emperor Kai." (Publisher's note)

"Cress fills in more historical details about Earth and Luna's relationship—most of which will be of no surprise to the reader—and Cinder's rebirth as a cyborg. Fans of Scarlet and Wolf may be disappointed that their relationship takes a backseat to the newly introduced pairing. As always, Meyer excels at interweaving new characters that extend beyond the archetypes of their fairy tale into the main story. Readers will eagerly await the final installment of this highly appealing and well-constructed series." (School Library Journal)

Heartless. Marissa Meyer. Feiwel & Friends 2016 464 p.

Grades: 7 8 9 10

1. Characters in literature -- Fiction; 2. Love -- Fiction; 3. Fantasy fiction

1250044650; 9781250044655, $19.99; 9781250080271, $60

LC 2015021393

In this book, by Marissa Meyer, "Catherine may be one of the most desired girls in Wonderland, and a favorite of the unmarried King of Hearts, but her interests lie elsewhere. A talented baker, all she wants is to open a shop with her best friend. But according to her mother, such a goal is unthinkable for the young woman who could be the next queen. Then Cath meets Jest, the handsome and mysterious court joker." (Publisher's note)

"If you only read one fractured fairy tale this year, make it Heartless. A must-have title." SLJ

Renegades. Marissa Meyer. Feiwel & Friends 2017 556 p. (Renegades)

Grades: 8 9 10 11 12

1. Good and evil -- Fiction; 2. Heroes -- Fiction; 3. Interpersonal relations -- Fiction; 4. Revenge -- Fiction; 5. Superheroes -- Fiction; 6. Supervillains -- Fiction; 7. Science fiction; 8. Superheroes -- Fiction

1250044669; 9781250044662, $19.99; 9781250164070

LC 2017902456

In this novel, by Marissa Meyer, "the Renegades are a syndicate of prodigies...who emerged from the ruins of a crumbled society and established peace and order where chaos reigned.... Nova has a reason to hate the Renegades, and she is on a mission for vengeance. As she gets closer to her target, she meets Adrian, a Renegade boy who believes in justice -- and in Nova. But Nova's allegiance is to the villains who have the power to end them both." (Publisher's note)

"Fans of Marissa Meyer and teens who enjoy a deep storyline will be more than satisfied with all the clever details, plot twists, and thought-provoking dilemmas that fill the pages of this first book in a new series." VOYA

★ **Scarlet**; Marissa Meyer. Feiwel and Friends 2013 464 p. $17.99

Grades: 7 8 9 10 11 12

1. Science fiction 2. Fractured fairy tales 3. Cyborgs -- Fiction 4. Missing persons -- Fiction 5. Extraterrestrial beings -- Fiction

ISBN 0312642962; 9780312642969

LC 2012034060

This novel, by Marissa Meyer, is the second book of the "Lunar Chronicles" series. "Cinder, the cyborg mechanic, . . . [is] trying to break out of prison. . . . [Meanwhile,] Scarlet Benoit's grandmother is missing. . . . When Scarlet encounters Wolf, a street fighter who may have information . . . , she is loath to trust this stranger. . . . As Scarlet and Wolf unravel one mystery, they encounter another when they meet Cinder." (Publisher's note)

★ **Winter**. Marissa Meyer. Feiwel & Friends 2015 827 p.

Grades: 7 8 9 10 11 12

1. Princesses -- Fiction 2. Revolutions -- Fiction

0312642989; 9780312642983, $22.99

In this novel by Marissa Meyer "Winter despises her stepmother, and knows Levana won't approve of her feelings for her childhood friend—the handsome palace guard, Jacin. But Winter isn't as weak as Levana believes her to be and she's been undermining her stepmother's wishes for years. Together with the cyborg mechanic, Cinder, and her allies, Winter might even have the power to launch a revolution and win a war that's been raging for far too long." (Publisher's note)

"Like the previous entries in this widely appealing series, this title features strong heroines taking control of their destinies set against a fully developed and imaginative world." SLJ

Meyer, Stephenie

★ **Twilight**. Little, Brown and Co. 2005 498p $17.99; pa $8.99

Grades: 8 9 10 11 12

1. School stories 2. Vampires -- Fiction 3. Washington (State) -- Fiction

ISBN 0-316-16017-2; 0-316-01584-9 pa

LC 2004-24730

When seventeen-year-old Bella leaves Phoenix to live with her father in Forks, Washington, she meets an exquisitely handsome boy at school for whom she feels an overwhelming attraction and who she comes to realize is not wholly human.

"Realistic, subtle, succinct, and easy to follow, . . . [this book] will have readers dying to sink their teeth into it." SLJ

Other titles in this series are:

Breaking dawn (2008)

Eclipse (2007)

New moon (2006)

Meyerhoff, Jenny

Queen of secrets. Farrar, Straus and Giroux 2010 230p $16.99

Grades: 8 9 10 11 12

1. School stories 2. Cousins -- Fiction 3. Orphans -- Fiction 4. Grandparents -- Fiction 5. Jews -- United States -- Fiction

ISBN 978-0-374-32628-9; 0-374-32628-2

LC 2008-55561

Fifteen-year-old Essie Green, an orphan who has been raised by her secular Jewish grandparents in Michigan, experiences conflicting loyalties and confusing emotions when her aunt, uncle, and cousin move back from New York, and her very religious cousin tries to fit in with the other football players at Essie's high school, one of whom is Essie's popular new boyfriend.

"Compelling characters, dramatic tension, and thoughtful exploration of how teenagers create their own identity amid familial and cultural influences should give this story wide appeal." Publ Wkly

Michael, Jan

★ **City** boy. Clarion Books 2009 186p $16

Grades: 5 6 7 8

1. Orphans -- Fiction 2. Country life -- Fiction
ISBN 978-0-547-22310-0; 0-547-22310-2

LC 2008-37418

First published in the United Kingdom with title:
Leaving home

In the southern African country of Malawi, after the
AIDS-related deaths of both of his parents, a boy leaves his
affluent life in the city to live in a rural village, sharing a one-
roomed hut with his aunt, his cousins, and other orphans.

"This is a powerful portrait of poverty and hardship,
evenly balanced with shades of hope. Michael's simple
prose subtly layers detail, building full-bodied descriptions
of landscapes and characters, leaving no room for shortcuts.
. . . A stoic tale of surviving life's uncertainties." Kirkus

Michaelis, Antonia

Tiger moon; translated from the German by
Anthea Bell. Amulet Books 2008 453p pa $9.95;
$19.95

Grades: 8 9 10 11 12

1. India -- Fiction 2. Tigers -- Fiction 3. Thieves
-- Fiction 4. Princesses -- Fiction 5. Storytelling --
Fiction
ISBN 0-8109-4499-5 pa; 0-8109-9481-X; 978-0-
8109-4499-2 pa; 978-0-8109-9481-2

LC 2007-22823

Sold to be the eighth wife of a rich and cruel merchant,
Safia, also called Raka, tries to escape her fate by telling stories of Farhad the thief, his companion Nitish the white tiger,
and their travels across India to retrieve a famous jewel that
will save a kidnapped princess from becoming the bride of a
demon king. "Grades eight to ten." (Bull Cent Child Books)

"The plot is fast paced and exciting, and the story gives
an excellent overview of the conflicts of India at the time
of British occupation, and of Hindu religious beliefs." SLJ

Mieville, China

★ **Railsea**; China Mieville. Del Rey/Ballantine
Books 2012 424 p. ill. (hbk. : alk. paper) $18.00
Grades: 7 8 9 10

1. Adventure fiction 2. Steampunk fiction 3. Railroads
-- Fiction 4. Imaginary places -- Fiction
ISBN 0345524527; 9780345524522; 9780345524546

LC 2012009516

This book presents "a steampunk spin on 'Moby-Dick'
. . . . Instead of chasing whales on the sea, the crew of the
diesel train Medes hunt moldywarpes—enormous, man-
eating, molelike creatures who are only one of the countless
menacing species who burrow in the perilous earth beneath
a tangled ocean of train tracks. And it is one moldywarpe
in particular, the great Mocker-Jack, that Captain Naphi is
after—it's trendy for any captain worth her iron to have such
a defining obsession, and she is fully aware that they hunt
metaphor in beast form. Aboard for the grand adventure is
your hero, young Sham (don't call him Ishmael)." (Booklist)

★ **Un** Lun Dun. Ballantine Books 2007 432p il
hardcover o.p. pa $9

Grades: 5 6 7 8 9

1. Fantasy fiction
ISBN 978-0-345-49516-7; 0-345-49516-0; 978-0-345-
45844-5 pa; 0-345-45844-3 pa

LC 2007-296921

When 12-year-old Zanna and her friend Deeba find a
secret entrance leading out of London and into the strange
city of Un Lun Dun, it appears that an ancient prophesy is
coming true at last

"Miéville's fantastical city is vivid and splendidly crafted. . . . The story is exceptional and the action moves along
at a quick pace." SLJ

Miklowitz, Gloria D.

The **enemy** has a face. Eerdmans Bks. for Young
Readers 2003 139p $16; pa $8

Grades: 7 8 9 10

1. Missing persons 2. Palestinian Arabs 3. Arab-Israeli
conflict 4. Jews -- United States 5. Missing persons
-- Fiction
ISBN 0-8028-5243-2; 0-8028-5261-0 pa

LC 2002-9233

Netta and her family have relocated temporarily from Israel to Los Angeles, and when her seventeen-year-old brother mysteriously disappears, she becomes convinced that he
has been abducted by Palestinian terrorists

"Almost unbearably suspenseful, the plot will keep
readers turning pages as fast as they can. Nicely interspersed
with the events is a thoughtful examination of some of the
reasons behind the age-old strife between Palestinians and
Israelis. Readers come away with a greater understanding of
the conflict, and Netta is given the opportunity to modify her
attitude about her former enemies." SLJ

Milan, Maura

Ignite the stars. By Maura Milan. Albert Whitman & Co. 2018 400 p.

Grades: 7 8 9 10

1. Criminals -- Fiction; 2. Loyalty -- Fiction; 3. Science
fiction
9780807536254, $17.99

LC 2017061615

In this book, by Maura Milan, "everyone in the universe
fears him. But no one realizes that notorious outlaw Ia C?cha
is a seventeen-year-old girl. A criminal mastermind..., Ia has
spent her life terrorizing the Olympus Commonwealth, the
imperialist nation that destroyed her home. When the Commonwealth captures her and her true identity is exposed,
they see Ia...as an opportunity: by forcing her to serve them,
they will prove that no one is beyond their control." (Publisher's note)

Milford, Kate

The **Boneshaker**; [illustrations by Andrea Offer-
mann] Clarion Books 2010 372p il $17

Grades: 5 6 7 8 9

1. Bicycles -- Fiction 2. Missouri -- Fiction 3.
Demonology -- Fiction 4. Supernatural -- Fiction
ISBN 978-0-547-24187-6; 0-547-24187-9

LC 2009-45350

When Jake Limberleg brings his traveling medicine
show to a small Missouri town in 1913, thirteen-year-old

Natalie senses that something is wrong and, after investigating, learns that her love of automata and other machines make her the only one who can set things right.

"Natalie is a well-drawn protagonist with sturdy supporting characters around her. The tension built into the solidly constructed plot is complemented by themes that explore the literal and metaphorical role of crossroads and that thin line between good and evil." Kirkus

The **Broken** Lands; by Kate Milford; with illustrations by Andrea Offermann. Clarion Books 2012 455 p. ill. (hardback) $16.99
Grades: 5 6 7 8 9 10

1. Bridges -- Fiction 2. Supernatural -- Fiction 3. New York (N.Y.) -- Fiction 4. New York (N.Y.) -- History -- 1865-1898 -- Fiction 5. Coney Island (New York, N.Y.) -- History -- 19th century -- Fiction
ISBN 0547739664; 9780547739663
LC 2011049466

This book, a prequel to "Kate Milford's 'The Boneshaker,' [is] set in . . . nineteenth-century Coney Island and New York City. Few crossroads compare to the one being formed by the Brooklyn Bridge and the East River, and as the bridge's construction progresses, forces of unimaginable evil seek to bend that power to their advantage. . . . Can the teenagers Sam, a card sharp, and Jin, a fireworks expert, stop them before it's too late?" (Publisher's note)

Miller, Ashley Edward
Colin Fischer; Ashley Edward Miller & Zack Stentz. Razorbill 2012 228 p. (hardcover) $17.99
Grades: 9 10 11

1. Mystery fiction 2. Bullies -- Fiction 3. Schools -- Fiction 4. High schools -- Fiction 5. Mystery and detective stories 6. Asperger's syndrome -- Fiction
ISBN 1595145788; 9781595145789
LC 2012014274

This book focuses on Colin Fischer, "whose Asperger's means he has difficulty reading social cues despite his high intelligence. When a melee breaks out in the [school] cafeteria one day, culminating in a gun's going off, Colin is convinced that as the nearest person to the gun he's likely to be suspected of being the shooter. He therefore decides to bring his inquisitive nature and love of logic to the problem and solve the mystery himself." (Bulletin of the Center for Children's Books)

Miller, Kirsten
All you desire; can you trust your heart? Razorbill 2011 423p $17.99
Grades: 6 7 8 9 10

1. Love stories 2. Reincarnation -- Fiction 3. Fate and fatalism -- Fiction
ISBN 978-1-59514-323-5; 1-59514-323-8

Haven Moore and Iain Morrow have been living a blissful life in Rome, an ocean way from the Ouroboros Society and its diabolical leader. But paradise is not to last. The mysterious disappearance of Haven's best friend, Beau, sends the pair running back to New York, where they encounter the Horae, an underground group of women who have spent centuries scheming to destroy Adam Rosier.

"A multi-layered mystery with (mostly) rounded characters." Kirkus

The **eternal** ones. Razorbill 2010 411p $17.99
Grades: 6 7 8 9 10

1. Love stories 2. Faith -- Fiction 3. Tennessee -- Fiction 4. Reincarnation -- Fiction 5. New York (N.Y.) -- Fiction 6. Fate and fatalism -- Fiction
ISBN 978-1-59514-308-2; 1-59514-308-4
LC 2010-22775

Seventeen-year-old Haven Moore leaves East Tennessee to attend the Fashion Institute of Technology in New York City, where she meets playboy Iain Morrow, whose fate may be tied to hers through a series of past lives.

"Miller's writing elevates the supernatural romance well beyond typical fare, and Haven's mix of naïveté and determination makes her a solid, credible heroine." Publ Wkly
Followed by: All you desire (2011)

How to lead a life of crime; Kirsten Miller. Razorbill 2013 358 p. (hardcover) $18.99
Grades: 9 10 11 12

1. School stories 2. Criminals -- Fiction 3. Ghosts -- Fiction 4. Schools -- Fiction 5. Survival -- Fiction
ISBN 1595145184; 9781595145185
LC 2012031576

In this young adult novel, by Kirsten Miller, "the Mandel Academy . . . has been training young criminals for over a century. Only the most ruthless . . . graduate. The rest disappear. Flick . . . has risen to the top of his class. But then Mandel recruits a fierce new competitor who also happens to be Flick's old flame. They've been told only one of them will make it out of the Mandel Academy. Will they find a way to save each other--or will the school destroy them both?" (Publisher's note)

Miller, Michael
Shadow run. AdriAnne Strickland & Michael Miller. Delacorte Press 2017 390 p.
Grades: 7 8 9 10 11 12

1. Families -- Fiction; 2. Princes -- Fiction; 3. Science fiction; 4. Adventure fiction
9780399552533, $17.99; 9780399552557; 9780399552540
LC 2015044876

In this novel, by Michael Miller and AdriAnne Strickland, "Nev has just joined the crew of the starship Kaitan Heritage as the cargo loader. His captain, Qole, is the youngest-ever person to command her own ship, but she brooks no argument from her crew of orphans, fugitives, and con men.... As for Nev, he's a prince, in hiding on the ship. He believes Qole holds the key to changing galactic civilization, and...[he'll] get her to his home planet by any means necessary." (Publisher's note)

"The world-building is excellent, with a convincingly unique source of cosmic energy that has the potential for extraordinary power. The writing is accomplished; the plot, though familiar, has good twists; and the pace is appropriately fast." SLJ

Miller, Sam J.

The **art** of starving. Sam J. Miller. HarperTeen 2017 372 p.

Grades: 9 10 11 12

1. Bullying -- Fiction; 2. Families -- Fiction; 3. Gay teenagers -- Fiction; 4. Psychic ability -- Fiction; 5. Self-acceptance -- Fiction; 6. Starvation -- Fiction; 7. Victims of bullying -- Fiction; 8. Friendship -- Fiction; 9. Eating disorders -- Fiction; 10. Love -- Fiction; 11. Body image -- Fiction

9780062456731; 9780062456717, $17.99

LC 2016958596

In this book, by Sam J. Miller, "Matt hasn't eaten in days. His stomach stabs and twists inside, pleading for a meal, but Matt won't give in. The hunger clears his mind, keeps him sharp -- and he needs to be as sharp as possible if he's going to find out just how Tariq and his band of high school bullies drove his sister, Maya, away." (Publisher's note)

"A dark and lovely tale of supernatural vengeance and self-destruction." Kirkus

Miller, Samuel

A **lite** too bright. Samuel Miller. Katherine Tegen Books 2018 465 p.

Grades: 9 10 11 12

1. Alzheimer's disease -- Fiction; 2. Diaries -- Fiction; 3. Grandfathers -- Fiction; 4. Railroad travel -- Fiction

9780062662026; 9780062662002, $17.99

LC 2018933385

In this novel, by Samuel Miller, Arthur Louis Pullman the Third's "been stripped of his college scholarship...and has been sent away to live with his aunt and uncle. It's there that Arthur discovers a journal written by his grandfather, the first Arthur Louis Pullman, an iconic...author who went missing the last week of his life and died hundreds of miles away from...home.... Arthur embarks on a cross-country train ride to relive his grandfather's last week." (Publisher's note)

"Beautifully conceived and executed, it has an irresistible premise; an ingenious plot tinged with mystery; compelling, multidimensional characters; and a haunting ethos that will linger in readers' minds long after they have finished." Booklist

Miller, Sarah

The **lost** crown. Atheneum Books for Young Readers 2011 412p $17.99

Grades: 8 9 10 11 12

1. Emperors 2. Sisters -- Fiction 3. Kings and rulers -- Fiction 4. World War, 1914-1918 -- Fiction 5. Russia -- History -- 1905, Revolution -- Fiction

ISBN 978-1-4169-8340-8; 1-4169-8340-6

LC 2010037001

In alternating chapters, Grand Duchesses Olga, Tatiana, Maria, and Anastasia tell how their privileged lives as the daughters of the tsar in early twentieth-century Russia are transformed by world war and revolution.

"Each Grand Duchess comes across as a unique personality. . . . Like the best historical novels, this allows modern-day teens to see themselves in very different people." Booklist

Miss Spitfire; reaching Helen Keller. Atheneum Books for Young Readers 2007 208p $16.99

Grades: 7 8 9 10 11

1. Deaf -- Fiction; 2. Blind -- Fiction; 3. Teachers -- Fiction; 4. Sullivan, Annie, 1866-1936 -- Fiction; 5. Keller, Helen, 1880-1968 -- Fiction

ISBN 978-1-4169-2542-2; 1-4169-2542-2

LC 2006014738

At age twenty-one, partially-blind, lonely but spirited Annie Sullivan travels from Massachusetts to Alabama to try and teach six-year-old Helen Keller, deaf and blind since age two, self-discipline and communication skills. Includes historical notes and timeline.

"This excellent novel is compelling reading even for those familiar with the Keller/Sullivan experience." SLJ

Includes bibliographical references

Miller-Lachmann, Lyn

Gringolandia; a novel. Curbstone Press 2009 279p $16.95

Grades: 9 10 11 12

1. Chile -- Fiction 2. Wisconsin -- Fiction 3. Political activists -- Fiction 4. Father-son relationship -- Fiction 5. Post-traumatic stress disorder -- Fiction

ISBN 978-1-931896-49-8; 1-931896-49-6

LC 2008-36990

In 1986, when seventeen-year-old Daniel's father arrives in Madison, Wisconsin, after five years of torture as a political prisoner in Chile, Daniel and his eighteen-year-old "gringa" girlfriend, Courtney, use different methods to help this bitter, self-destructive stranger who yearns to return home and continue his work.

"This poignant, often surprising and essential novel illuminates too-often ignored political aspects of many South Americans' migration to the United States." Kirkus

Mills, Emma

First & then. Emma Mills. Henry Holt & Co. 2015 272 p.

Grades: 8 9 10 11 12

1. Cousins -- Fiction; 2. Cousins -- Juvenile fiction; 3. Dating (Social customs) -- Fiction; 4. Dating (Social customs) -- Juvenile fiction; 5. Families -- Florida -- Juvenile fiction; 6. Family life -- Florida -- Fiction; 7. Football players -- Juvenile fiction; 8. High schools -- Fiction; 9. High schools -- Florida -- Juvenile fiction; 10. Schools -- Fiction; 11. Florida -- Fiction; 12. Florida -- Juvenile fiction; 13. School stories

ISBN 9781627792356, $17.99

LC 2014043456

In this novel, by Emma Mills, "Devon Tennyson . . . [is] happy watching Friday night games from the bleachers, silently crushing on best friend Cas, and blissfully ignoring the future after high school. . . . [Until] Devon's cousin Foster, an unrepentant social outlier with a surprising talent for football, and the obnoxiously superior and maddeningly attractive star running back, Ezra, [arrive] . . . first into her P.E. class and then into every other aspect of her life." (Publisher's note)

"With sporadic references to Jane Austen's famous characters and wickedly inventive language, Mills closely observes the social milieu of an American high school obsessed with our favorite sport and makes readers care what happens." Kirkus

This adventure ends. Emma Mills. Henry Holt & Co. 2016 320 p.

Grades: 8 9 10 11

    1. Dating (Social customs) -- Fiction 2. Friendship -- Fiction 3. High schools -- Fiction 4. Moving, Household -- Fiction 5. Schools -- Fiction 6. Florida -- Fiction 7. School stories 8. Florida -- Fiction

9781627799362, $60; 9781627799355, $17.99

LC 2016001536

In this novel, by Emma Mills, "Sloane isn't expecting to fall in with a group of friends when she moves from New York to Florida?especially not a group of friends so intense, so in love, so all-consuming. Yet that's exactly what happens. Sloane becomes closest to Vera, a social-media star who lights up any room, and Gabe, Vera's twin brother and the most serious person Sloane's ever met." (Publisher's note)

"Mild in every way but language, this tale of privileged teens offers a fairly satisfying glimpse of an almost alternate universe in which mundane life can be ignored." Kirkus

Mills, Wendy

    All we have left. By Wendy Mills. Bloomsbury 2016 368 p.

Grades: 8 9 10 11 12

    1. Conduct of life -- Fiction 2. Interpersonal relations -- Fiction 3. Love -- Fiction 4. Muslims -- Fiction 5. September 11 Terrorist Attacks, 2001 -- Fiction 6. Romance fiction

9781619633438, $17.99; 9781619633445, $42

LC 2015037717

This coming-of-age story by Wendy Mills "traces the lives of two girls whose worlds intersect on September 11, 2001. Chapters alternate between the present-day story of Jesse, whose brother died on that fateful day, and . . . of Muslim teen Alia's experience inside one of the beleaguered Twin Towers. . . . Jesse's journey to discover why Travis was at the Twin Towers . . . eventually leads her to a search for Alia, the girl Travis was with when the planes hit." (School Library Journal)

"This outstanding, touching look at a national tragedy promotes healing and understanding and belongs in every library." SLJ

Minchin, Adele

    ★ The **beat** goes on. Simon & Schuster Books for Young Readers 2004 212p hardcover o.p. pa $11.95

Grades: 9 10 11 12

    1. Cousins -- Fiction 2. Great Britain -- Fiction 3. AIDS (Disease) -- Fiction

ISBN 0-689-86611-9; 1-4169-6755-9 pa

First published 2001 in the United Kingdom

"Fifteen-year-old Leyla must keep her cousin's secret: Emma is HIV positive, and only her mother and Leyla know. The secret becomes a burden, especially when Leyla must lie to her parents in order to work with Emma's support group on their special project—to teach other HIV-positive teens how to play the drums. In spite of its heavy Briticisms and a

didactic tone, this is one of the better YA books about HIV. The facts of transmission and symptoms are clearly presented, as are Emma's struggles to lead a normal, healthy life. . . . . Minchin educates young readers while telling a gripping story that will keep personal tragedy aficionados turning the pages to the hopeful yet realistic conclusion." Booklist

Miranda, Megan

    Hysteria; by Megan Miranda. Walker 2013 336 p. (hardback) $17.99

Grades: 9 10 11 12

    1. School stories 2. Memory -- Fiction 3. Homicide -- Fiction 4. Boarding schools -- Fiction

ISBN 0802723101; 9780802723109

LC 2012015780

In this novel, by Megan Miranda, "Mallory killed her boyfriend, Brian. She can't remember the details . . . but everyone knows it was self-defense, so she isn't charged. . . . In desperate need of a fresh start, Mallory is sent to . . . a fancy prep school where no one knows her. . . . Then, one of her new classmates turns up dead. As suspicion falls on Mallory, she must find a way to remember the details of both deadly nights so she can prove her innocence." (Publisher's note)

    Soulprint. By Megan Miranda. Bloomsbury/ Walker 2015 368 p.

Grades: 7 8 9 10

    1. Conduct of life -- Fiction 2. Fugitives from justice -- Fiction 3. Guilt -- Fiction 4. Prisoners -- Fiction 5. Reincarnation -- Fiction 6. Science fiction 7. Soul -- Fiction

0802737749; 9780802737748, $17.99

LC 2014009921

This novel by Megan Miranda is set "in a future where reincarnation can be scientifically tracked. . . .17-year-old half-Hispanic Alina Chase has spent her life isolated, allegedly for her own protection. She carries within her the soul of a charismatic and destructive whistleblower turned blackmailer, June Calahan. Broken out of confinement by a daring trio barely older than she is, Alina finds she still cannot escape June's shadow." (Publishers Weekly)

"A unique spin on recent dystopian reads featuring genetic heritability . . . [Soulprint] will fascinate teens already enthralled with questions about what they might do with their lives. A surprising new sf thriller with just enough of a touch of romance." Booklist

Mitchard, Jacquelyn

    ★ **All** we know of heaven; a novel. HarperTeen 2008 312p $16.99; lib bdg $17.89

Grades: 7 8 9 10 11 12

    1. Death -- Fiction 2. Bereavement -- Fiction 3. Traffic accidents -- Fiction

ISBN 978-0-06-134578-4; 0-06-134578-4; 978-0-06-134579-1 lib bdg; 0-06-134579-2 lib bdg

When Maureen and Bridget, two sixteen-year-old best friends who look like sisters, are in a terrible car accident and one of them dies, they are at first incorrectly identified at the hospital, and then, as Maureen achieves a remarkable recovery, she must deal with the repercussions of the accident, the mixup, and some choices she made while she was getting better.

"Riveting, compassionate and psychologically nuanced. . . . Utterly gripping." Publ Wkly

The **midnight** twins. Razorbill 2008 235p $16.99; pa $8.99

Grades: 6 7 8 9

    1. Twins -- Fiction 2. Telepathy -- Fiction 3. Clairvoyance -- Fiction

ISBN 978-1-59514-160-6; 1-59514-160-X; 978-1-59514-226-9 pa; 1-59514-226-6 pa

                    LC 2007-31139

Identical twins Meredith and Mallory Brynn have always shared one another's thoughts, even as they dream, but their connection diminishes as they approach their thirteenth birthday, and one begins to see the future, the other the past, leading them to discover that a high school student they know is doing horrible things that place the twins, and others, in grave danger.

"The plot moves quickly, propelled by the mysteries of the sisters' relationship. . . . The girls' supernatural knowledge is a delicious bonus." Publ Wkly

    Other titles about Meredith and Mallory are:

Look both ways (2009)

Watch for me by moonlight (2010)

Mitchell, Saundra

All out: the no-longer-secret stories of queer teens throughout the ages. Edited by Saundra Mitchell. Harlequin Books 2018 353 p.

Grades: 9 10 11 12

    1. Asexual people -- Fiction; 2. Gays -- Fiction; 3. Lesbians -- Fiction; 4. Teenagers -- Fiction; 5. Transgender people -- Fiction; 6. Identity (Psychology) -- Fiction

9781335470454, $18.99; 9781488030451; 133547045X

In this book, edited by Saundra Mitchell, "seventeen young adult authors across the queer spectrum have come together to create a collection of beautifully written diverse historical fiction for teens.... 'All Out' tells a diverse range of stories across cultures, time periods and identities, shedding light on an area of history often ignored or forgotten." (Publisher's note)

"LGBTQIA story collections are scarce, but even if they weren't, this one would be essential." Booklist

The **vespertine**. Harcourt 2011 296p $16.99

Grades: 8 9 10 11 12

    1. Clairvoyance -- Fiction 2. Baltimore (Md.) -- Fiction

ISBN 978-0-547-48247-7; 0-547-48247-7

It's the summer of 1889, and Amelia van den Broek is new to Baltimore and eager to take in all the pleasures the city has to offer. But her gaiety is interrupted by disturbing, dreamlike visions she has only at sunset—visions that offer glimpses of the future. Soon, friends and strangers alike call on Amelia to hear her prophecies. However, a forbidden romance with Nathaniel, an artist, threatens the new life Amelia is building in Baltimore.

"Nathaniel's forbidden charms will most certainly have readers swooning. . . . There's . . . considerable fun to be had here, and Amelia's supernatural power is believably portrayed." Bull Cent Child Books

Mitchell, Todd

The **secret** to lying. Candlewick Press 2010 328p $17.99

Grades: 9 10 11 12

    1. School stories

ISBN 978-0-7636-4084-2

                    LC 2009032484

Fifteen-year-old James lies about himself to be considered "cool" when he gets into an exclusive boarding school. "Grades nine to twelve." (Bull Cent Child Books)

"Mitchell paints a vivid picture of teenage social and mental health issues, neither overdramatizing nor understating their impact, and the result is a great read." Publ Wkly

Mlawski, Shana

Hammer of witches; by Shana Mlawski. Tu Books 2013 400 p. (reinforced) $18.95

Grades: 6 7 8 9

    1. Fantasy fiction 2. Storytelling -- Fiction 3. America -- Exploration -- Fiction 4. Magic -- Fiction 5. Wizards -- Fiction 6. Explorers -- Fiction 7. America -- Discovery and exploration -- Spanish -- Fiction

ISBN 1600609872; 9781600609879

                    LC 2012048627

In this novel, by Shana Mlawski, "Baltasar Infante . . . encounters a monster straight out of stories one night . . . . Captured by . . . a mysterious witch-hunting arm of the Spanish Inquisition, . . . the Inquisitor demands he reveal the whereabouts of Amir al-Katib, a legendary Moorish sorcerer who can bring myths and the creatures within them to life. Now Baltasar must escape, find al-Katib, and defeat a dreadful power that may destroy the world." (Publisher's note)

"Newcomer Mlawski delivers a fast-paced coming-of-age adventure, respectfully evoking the complexities and cultural landscape of the period. She draws from a variety of sources, including Jewish and Biblical myth, offering an accessible, attention-grabbing story that seamlessly inserts its magical elements into historical fact." Pub Wkly

Mlynowski, Sarah

Don't even think about it; Sarah Mlynowski. Delacorte Press. 2014 336p $17.99

Grades: 7 8 9 10

    1. Extrasensory perception -- Fiction 2. High schools -- Fiction 3. New York (N.Y.) -- Fiction 5. Telepathy -- Fiction

ISBN: 0385737386; 9780385737388; 9780385906623

                    LC 2012050777

"When a group of Manhattan 10th graders inadvertently receives telepathic abilities from tainted flu shots, things rapidly get chaotic (and noisy). Finding out too much information dramatically upends family relationships, friendships, and romances. . . . Filled with heartbreak, hilarity, and some brutal truths, Mlynowski's novel will leave readers thinking about the gaps between our private and public selves and the lies we tell others and ourselves." Pub Wkly

Gimme a call. Delacorte Press 2010 301p $17.99; lib bdg $20.99

Grades: 7 8 9 10

1. School stories 2. Time travel -- Fiction
ISBN 978-0-385-73588-9; 0-385-73588-X; 978-0-385-90574-9 lib bdg; 0-385-90574-2 lib bdg

LC 2009-20020

"When Devi's high-school sweetheart breaks up with her right before their senior prom, she is devastated. Not only is she dateless but she is also friendless and relegated to a mediocre college because she has concentrated on her boyfriend instead of academics. . . . In a fresh twist on time travel, she contacts her freshman self via cell phone and proceeds to change their future. Of course, one small change leads to others, and both girls begin to wonder about the wisdom of this collaboration. Mlynowski has given herself a complicated, challenging story, and she is particularly effective in conveying the differences in maturity and perspective between a freshman and a senior." Booklist

Ten things we did (and probably shouldn't have) HarperTeen 2011 357p $16.99; ebook $9.99
Grades: 7 8 9 10

1. Friendship -- Fiction 2. Connecticut -- Fiction
ISBN 978-0-06-170124-5; 0-06-170124-6; 978-0-06-208461-3 ebook; 0-06-208461-5 ebook

LC 2010-45556

Sixteen-year-old April, a high school junior, and her friend Vi, a senior, get a crash course in reality as the list of things they should not do becomes a list of things they did while living parent-free in Westport, Connecticut, for the semester.

"With wit, energy, and an uncanny understanding of teenage logic, Mlynowski . . . weighs the pros and cons of independence in this modern cautionary tale. . . . Mlynowski avoids sermonizing, offering 10 madcap and remarkably tense escapades that will have readers laughing, cringing, and guessing how April will get out of the next pickle." Publ Wkly

Mochizuki, Ken

Beacon Hill boys. Scholastic Press 2002 201p $16.95; pa $5.99
Grades: 7 8 9 10

1. Japanese Americans -- Fiction
ISBN 0-439-26749-8; 0-439-24906-6 pa

LC 2002-2343

In 1972 in Seattle, a teenager in a Japanese American family struggles for his own identity, along with a group of three friends who share his anger and confusion

"The author nicely balances universal experiences of male adolescence . . . with scenes that bring readers right into the complicated era, and his important, thought-provoking story asks tough questions about racial and cultural identity, prejudice, and family." Booklist

Molloy, Michael

Peter Raven under fire. Scholastic 2005 502p il maps $17.95
Grades: 6 7 8 9

1. Sea stories 2. Adventure fiction
ISBN 0-439-72454-6

"In 1800, continuous war has depleted France's treasury, but Napoleon still wants to expand his empire. To this end, he needs money to defeat the superior British Navy and to exploit Louisiana for the greatest gain. In England, midshipman Peter Raven, 13, is assigned to HMS Torren. When powerful, sadistic pirates murder everyone on the ship except Peter and jack-of-all-trades Matthew Book, the protagonist finds himself apprenticed to a British spy. . . . Fast paced with multiple plot twists. . . . Molloy's writing is intelligent and engaging." SLJ

Moloney, James

Black taxi. HarperCollins Publishers 2005 264p hardcover o.p. lib bdg $16.89
Grades: 9 10 11 12

1. Mystery fiction 2. Crime -- Fiction 3. Automobiles -- Fiction 4. Great Britain -- Fiction
ISBN 0-06-055937-3; 0-06-055938-1 lib bdg

LC 2003-27848

When Rosie agrees to take care of her grandfather's Mercedes while he is in jail, she gets more than she bargained for, including being thrust into the middle of a jewel heist mystery and being attracted to a dangerous boy.

"Love and larceny are center stage in this British import, which is best suited to older readers even though it has no explicit language or dicey situations. Only the main characters are developed, but the story is entertaining enough to appeal to fans of lightweight mystery who also relish a hint of romance." Booklist

The **Book** of Lies. HarperCollinsPublishers 2007 360p $16.99; lib bdg $17.89
Grades: 5 6 7 8

1. Fantasy fiction 2. Magic -- Fiction 3. Orphans -- Fiction
ISBN 978-0-06-057842-8; 0-06-057842-4; 978-0-06-057843-5 lib bdg; 0-06-057843-2 lib bdg

LC 2006-29874

On the night he was brought to an orphanage, Marcel's memories were taken by a sorceror and replaced with new ones by his Book of Lies, but Bea, a girl with the ability to make herself invisible, was watching and is determined to help him discover his true identity.

"Readers who enjoy the mixture of mystery, riddles, action, and camaraderie will be pleased that the open-ended conclusion leads to a planned sequel." Booklist

Molope, Kagiso Lesego

This book betrays my brother. Kagiso Lesego Molope. Mawenzi House Publishers Ltd. 2018 192 p.
Grades: 8 9 10 11 12

1. Rape -- Fiction; 2. Siblings -- Fiction; 3. Teenage girls -- Fiction
1988449294; 9781988449296, $15

In this novel, by Kagiso Lesego Molope, "all her life, Naledi has been in awe of Basi, her charming and outgoing older brother. They've shared their childhood, with its jokes and secrets, the alliances and stories about the community. Having reached thirteen, she is preparing to go to the school dance. Then she sees Basi commit an act that violates everything she believes about him. How will she live her life now?" (Publisher's note)

Monaghan, Annabel

A **girl** named Digit; by Annabel Monaghan. Houghton Mifflin Harcourt 2012 187 p. $16.99; $16.99

Grades: 7 8 9

1. School stories 2. Terrorism -- Fiction 3. Cryptography -- Fiction 4. Kidnapping -- Fiction 5. Interpersonal relations -- Fiction 6. Adventure and adventurers -- Fiction

ISBN 054766852X; 9780547668529; 9780544022485

LC 2011012239

In this book, "saddled with the nickname Digit, Farrah resolved to fit in once she reached high school by hiding her math skills. Then Farrah stumbles upon an eco-terrorist organization after their suicide bomb attack on JFK Airport, and the terrorists want her dead. . . . Farrah's FBI protector, the cute, young rookie agent John Bennett, . . . works with Farrah to uncover a blackmail scheme involving the attack's bomber." (Kirkus Reviews)

Monir, Alexandra

The **girl** in the picture. Alexandra Monir. Delacorte Press 2016 272 p.

Grades: 7 8 9 10

1. Disfigured persons -- Fiction 2. High schools -- Fiction 3. Murder -- Fiction 4. Mystery and detective stories 5. Schools -- Fiction 6. Secrets -- Fiction 7. Mystery fiction

9780375991370; 9780385743907, $17.99; 9780385372527

LC 2015042550

In this book, by Alexandra Monir, "Nicole Morgan has been labeled many things—the geeky music girl, the shy sidekick of Miss Popularity, and the girl with the scar. . . . After heartthrob Chace Porter is found dead . . . , the police search for the girl snuggled up next to him in a picture discovered among his personal effects. A girl no one knew was even close to him—and whose best friend, Lana Rivera, was his girlfriend. Nicole is . . . the primary suspect in his murder." (Publisher's note)

"Teens will enjoy the cleverly crafted ride of this whodunit." SLJ

Monninger, Joseph

★ **Finding** somewhere. Delacorte Press 2011 $17.99; lib bdg $20.99; e-book $17.99

Grades: 7 8 9 10

1. Horses -- Fiction 2. Friendship -- Fiction 3. Automobile travel -- Fiction

ISBN 978-0-385-73942-9; 978-0-385-90789-7 lib bdg; 978-0-375-86214-4 e-book

LC 2010053551

Sixteen-year-old Hattie and eighteen-year-old Delores set off on a road trip that takes unexpected turns as they discover the healing power of friendship and confront what each of them is fleeing from.

"Monninger's writing is delicious, evocative and, especially during horse-focused scenes, moving. Horse story, road trip, coming-of-age tale: It's any and all of these, but mostly a tender and authentic voyage into the mind of a wise, funny and wholly likable protagonist." Kirkus

★ **Hippie** chick. Front Street 2008 156p $16.95

Grades: 8 9 10 11 12

1. Manatees -- Fiction 2. Shipwrecks -- Fiction 3. Survival after airplane accidents, shipwrecks, etc. -- Fiction

ISBN 978-1-59078-598-0; 1-59078-598-3

LC 2007-51976

After her sailboat capsizes, fifteen-year-old Lolly Emmerson is rescued by manatees and taken to a mangrove key in the Everglades, where she forms a bond with her aquatic companions while struggling to survive.

"It's an affecting account, beautifully told." SLJ

Whippoorwill. By Joseph Monninger. Houghton Mifflin Harcourt 2015 288 p.

Grades: 7 8 9 10

1. Animals -- Treatment -- Fiction 2. Dating (Social customs) -- Fiction 3. Dogs -- Training -- Fiction 4. Fathers and daughters -- Fiction 5. Labrador retriever -- Fiction 6. Neighborhoods -- Fiction 7. Single-parent families -- Fiction 8. Neighbors -- Fiction 9. Dogs -- Fiction 10. Father-daughter relationship -- Fiction

9780544531239, $17.99

LC 2014046833

In this young adult novel, by Joseph Monninger, "Sixteen-year-old Clair Taylor has neighbors who are what locals call whippoorwills, the kind of people who fill their yards with rusty junk. Clair tries to ignore her surroundings, choosing instead to dream of a future beyond her rural New Hampshire town. But, when a black dog named Wally is chained up to a pole next door, Clair can't look the other way." (Publisher's note)

"Monninger revitalizes the boy-and-his-dog trope in this sweet novel." SLJ

Wish. Delacorte Press 2010 193p $17.99; lib bdg $20.99

Grades: 6 7 8 9 10

1. Sharks -- Fiction 2. Wishes -- Fiction 3. Siblings -- Fiction 4. Cystic fibrosis -- Fiction

ISBN 978-0-385-73941-2; 0-385-73941-9; 978-0-385-90788-0 lib bdg; 0-385-90788-5 lib bdg

LC 2010-09958

Bee's brother, Tommy, knows everything there is to know about sharks. He also knows that his life will be cut short by cystic fibrosis. And so does Bee. That's why she wants to make his wish-foundation-sponsored trip to swim with a great white shark an unforgettable memory. Only when Bee takes Tommy to meet a famous shark attack survivor and hard-core surfer does Tommy have the chance to live one day to the fullest.

"Fans of Monninger's other works will recognize the fluid, thoughtful writing and vivid characters, and this could be an eye-opener for shark aficionados looking to take their interest beyond the glitz of shark week." Bull Cent Child Books

Mont, Eve Marie

A **breath** of Eyre. Kensington/Kteen 2012 342 p.

Grades: 9 10 11 12

1. Love stories 2. Fantasy fiction 3. Supernatural --

Fiction 4. Eyre, Jane (Fictional character)
ISBN 9780758269485

In this book, "Emma Townsend has always believed in stories. . . . Perhaps it's because she feels like an outsider at her . . . school, or because her stepmother doesn't come close to filling the void left by her mother's death. And her only romantic prospect . . . is . . . a long-time friend who just adds to Emma's confusion. But escape soon arrives in a . . . copy of 'Jane Eyre.'. . . Reading of Jane's isolation sparks a deep sense of kinship. Then . . . a lightning storm catapults Emma right into Jane's body and her nineteenth-century world. . . . Emma has a sense of belonging she's never known"and an attraction to the brooding Mr. Rochester. Now, moving between her two realities and uncovering secrets in both, Emma must decide . . . [where] her destiny lies." (Publisher's note)

Moon, Sarah

Sparrow. Sarah Moon. Arthur A. Levine Books, an imprint of Scholastic Inc. 2017 264 p.
Grades: 7 8 9 10 11

> 1. African American girls -- Fiction; 2. African Americans -- Fiction; 3. Grief -- Fiction; 4. Librarians -- Fiction; 4. Mothers and daughters -- Fiction; 5. Psychotherapy -- Fiction; 6. Suicide -- Fiction; 7. Brooklyn (New York, N.Y.) -- Fiction; 8. African American teenage girls -- Fiction
> 1338032585; 9781338032581, $18.99; 9781338032598
> LC 2017017322

In this book, by Sarah Moon, "Sparrow has always had a difficult time making friends.... And that's made school a lonely experience for her.... But when the one teacher who really understood her -- Mrs. Wexler, the school librarian,... is killed in a freak car accident, Sparrow's world unravels.... With the help of an insightful therapist, Sparrow finally reveals the truth of her inner life. And it's here that she discovers an outlet in rock & roll music." (Publisher's note)

"An elegantly told and important novel about learning to cope, live, and be happy with depression and anxiety." Booklist

Moore, Carley

The **stalker** chronicles; Carley Moore. Farrar Straus Giroux 2012 230 p. (hardcover) $16.99
Grades: 8 9 10 11 12

> 1. School stories 2. Divorce -- Fiction 3. Interpersonal relations -- Fiction 4. Best friends -- Fiction 5. New York (State) -- Fiction 6. Family life -- New York (State) -- Fiction
> ISBN 9780374371807; 9781429961752
> LC 2011013093

This book features "Cammie, a high-school sophomore, whose history has involved such intense interest in guys . . . that she's now known around school as a stalker. When cute new guy Toby turns up in her small town, Cammie's determined that she'll change her ways, . . . and finally get the relationship she's been longing for. . . . The dissolution of Cammie's parents' marriage . . . brings her dysfunctional patterns into sharp relief." (Bulletin of the Center for Children's Books)

Moore, Derrick

Always upbeat / All that; Stephanie Perry Moore; All that / Stephanie Perry Moore & Derrick Moore. Saddleback 2012 314 p. $14.95
Grades: 7 8 9 10 11 12

> 1. Football players 2. Cheerleading -- Fiction 3. High school students -- Fiction
> ISBN 1616518847; 9781616518844

This book by Stephanie Perry Moore and Derrick Moore "deliver[s] a pair of intersecting but distinct stories from the points of view of a cheerleader and a quarterback at a predominantly African-American Atlanta high school. Spoiled, confident Charli Black and driven athlete Blake Strong have been together for two years. Now, at the start of their junior year, they are growing apart. Blake wants to 'take [their] relationship to the next level,' but Charli wants to wait." (Kirkus Reviews)

Moore, Kelly

★ **Amber** House; by Kelly Moore, Tucker Reed, and Larkin Reed. Arthur A. Levine Books 2012 349 p. (hardback) $17.99
Grades: 9 10 11 12

> 1. Death -- Fiction 2. Friendship -- Fiction 3. Grandmothers -- Fiction 4. Family secrets -- Fiction 5. Haunted houses -- Fiction 6. Visions -- Fiction 7. Maryland -- Fiction 8. Psychic ability -- Fiction 9. Mystery and detective stories 10. Brothers and sisters -- Fiction
> ISBN 0545434165; 9780545434164; 9780545434171; 9780545469739
> LC 2012014729

In this first title of the authors' proposed trilogy, protagonist "Sarah Parsons has never seen Amber House, the grand Maryland estate that's been in her family for three centuries. She's never walked its hedge maze nor found its secret chambers; she's never glimpsed the shades that haunt it, nor hunted for lost diamonds in its walls. But all of that is about to change. After her grandmother passes away, Sarah and her friend Jackson decide to search for the diamonds, and the house comes alive." (Publisher's note)

Neverwas; by Kelly Moore, Tucker Reed, and Larkin Reed. Arthur A. Levine Books 2014 320 p. (Amber House trilogy) (hardback) $17.99
Grades: 9 10 11 12

> 1. Historical fiction 2. Alternative histories 3. Love -- Fiction 4. Visions -- Fiction 5. Maryland -- Fiction 6. Dwellings -- Fiction 7. Supernatural -- Fiction 8. Psychic ability -- Fiction 9. Family life -- Maryland -- Fiction
> ISBN 0545434181; 9780545434188; 9780545434195
> LC 2013020546

This second title in the authors' Amber House trilogy "presents a stark departure from the preceding volume; gone are the creepy ghost children and specters in mirrors, now replaced by Sarah's confident knowledge that these ghosts are there to guide her. The authors' vision of this alternate, broken United States slowly comes into focus, rather as a ghost might materialize in the background. Sure, ghosts are scary, but a world where the Holocaust lasted for 75 years and may continue? That's inconceivably frightening. A wild ride that leaves its readers breathless for the final installment." (Kirkus)

Moore, Lisa

★ **Flannery**. Lisa Moore. Groundwood Books 2016 256 p.

Grades: 9 10 11 12

1. Teenage girls -- Fiction 2. Romance fiction 3. High school students -- Fiction 4. Love -- Fiction
1554980763; 9781554980765, $16.95

LC 20159046068

In this novel, by Lisa Moore, Flannery is "in love with Tyrone O'Rourke. Tyrone has grown from a dorky kid into an outlaw graffiti artist. Which is a problem, since he and Flannery are partners for the entrepreneurship class that she needs to graduate. And Tyrone's vanishing act may have darker causes than she realizes. When Flannery decides to make a love potion for her entrepreneurship project, rumors that it actually works go viral, and she suddenly has a hot commodity on her hands." (Publisher's note)

"An engaging story and strong purchase with some valuable lessons about love, friendship, and growing up." SLJ

Moore, Perry

Hero. Hyperion 2007 428p $16.99

Grades: 7 8 9 10 11 12

1. Science fiction 2. Superheroes -- Fiction 3. Gay teenagers -- Fiction 5. Father-son relationship -- Fiction
ISBN 978-1-4231-0195-6; 1-4231-0195-2

Thom Creed, the gay son of a disowned superhero, finds that he, too, has special powers and is asked to join the very League that rejected his father, and it is there that Thom finds other misfits whom he can finally trust.

"The combination of mystery, fantasy, thriller, and romance create a delightful and compelling read." Voice Youth Advocates

Moore, Peter

Red moon rising. Hyperion 2011 328p $16.99

Grades: 7 8 9 10

1. Vampires -- Fiction 2. Werewolves -- Fiction
ISBN 978-1-4231-1665-3; 1-4231-1665-8

LC 2009-40375

In a world where vampires dominate and werewolves are despised, a teenaged half-vampire discovers his recessive werewolf genes are developing with the approaching full moon.

"The details are imaginative and believable, as are the social interactions at school and in Danny's home." Booklist

V is for villain; Peter Moore. Hyperion. 2014 336p $17.99

Grades: 7 8 9 10

1. Ability -- Fiction 2. Brothers -- Fiction 3. Good and evil -- Fiction 4. Superheroes -- Fiction 5. Adventure fiction
ISBN: 1423157494; 9781423157496

LC 2013026304

"When Brad makes friends who are more into political action than weight lifting, he's happy to join a new crew—especially since it means spending more time with Layla, a girl who may or may not have a totally illegal, totally secret super-power. And with her help, Brad begins to hone a dangerous new power of his own." (Publisher's note)

"Some of the characterizations in this quasi-dystopian novel can be a little heavy-handed, but with plenty of plot twists, dastardly conspiracies, and a snarky narrator, the latest from Moore . . . has lots of sparkle." Booklist

Moracho, Cristina

Althea and Oliver. Cristina Moracho. Viking, an imprint of Penguin Group (USA) 2014 384 p.

Grades: 9 10 11 12

1. Best friends -- Fiction 2. Coming of age -- Fiction 3. Friendship -- Fiction 4. High schools -- Fiction 5. Schools -- Fiction 6. Single-parent families -- Fiction 7. Sleep disorders -- Fiction
0670785393; 9780670785391, $17.99

LC 2013041135

In this young adult novel by Cristina Moracho, "Althea Carter and Oliver McKinley have been best friends since they were six. . . . Their journey will take them from . . . their North Carolina hometown to . . . New York City before they once more stand together and face their chances. Set in the DIY, mix tape, and zine culture of the mid-1990s, Cristina Moracho's . . . debut is [a] story about identity, illness, and love—and why bad decisions sometimes feel so good." (Publisher's note)

"Prickly teenager Althea's more passive best friend Oliver develops a sleeping disorder. While she desires a romantic relationship with him, Oliver just wants everything to return to normal. This culturally rich novel set in mid-1990s North Carolina and New York City explores the duo's complex coming-of-age—full of bad decisions and secrets—and the undoing of their friendship. An ambitious, noteworthy, well-written debut." Horn Book

A **good** idea. Cristina Moracho. Viking 2017 357 p.

Grades: 9 10 11 12

1. Mystery and detective stories; 2. Revenge -- Fiction; 3. Revenge -- Fiction; 4. Mystery fiction; 5. Best friends -- Fiction
9780451476241, $18.99; 9780698198593

LC 2016020075

In this book, by Cristina Moracho, "Finley and Betty's close friendship survived Fin's ninth-grade move from their coastal Maine town to Manhattan. Calls, letters, and summer visits continued to bind them together.... Then Betty disappears. Her ex-boyfriend Calder admits to drowning her, but his confession is thrown out.... Fin knows the truth, and she returns to Williston for one final summer, determined to get justice for her friend." (Publisher's note)

"Edgy, atmospheric, and sometimes steamy, this is a thoughtful portrait of grief and an engaging examination of the risks we take for the ones we love. Ideal for mystery enthusiasts and noir newcomers." Booklist

Moran, Katy

Bloodline. Candlewick Press 2009 297p il map $16.99

Grades: 7 8 9 10

1. War stories 2. Adventure fiction 3. Middle Ages

-- Fiction 4. Great Britain -- History -- 0-1066 -- Fiction
ISBN 978-07636-4083-5; 0-7636-4083-2

LC 2008-21413

While traveling through early seventh-century Britain trying to stop an impending war, Essa, who bears the blood of native British tribes and of the invading Anglish, makes discoveries that divide his loyalties.

"Essa is a complex, sympathetic protagonist: prickly and quick of temper, but also clever, determined and of unflinching integrity. If his struggle is authentically gory and ultimately tragic, it is not without glimpses of love and hope." Kirkus

Followed by: Bloodline rising (2011)

Bloodline rising. Candlewick Press 2011 328p map $16.99

Grades: 7 8 9 10

1. Slaves -- Fiction 2. Criminals -- Fiction 3. Middle Ages -- Fiction 4. Great Britain -- History -- 0-1066 -- Fiction
ISBN 978-0-7636-4508-3; 0-7636-4508-7

LC 2010-46692

Sequel to: Bloodline (2009)

Cai, a thief in seventh-century Constantinople, finds himself held captive on a trading ship bound for Britain—the home his father, a ruthless barbarian assassin, fled long ago—where he discovers that his Anglish captors know more about the secrets of his family than he does.

"At its heart, this is the story of a boy's turbulent relationship with his father, torn between resentment and admiration, rivalry and respect, which renders the tale both as intimate as heartbreak and universal as hope. Grim, lyrical and unforgettable." Kirkus

Morgan, Page

The **beautiful** and the cursed; by Page Morgan. 1st ed. Delacorte Press 2013 352 p. (library) $21.99; (hardcover) $18.99

Grades: 7 8 9 10 11 12

1. Love stories 2. Gargoyles -- Fiction 3. Brothers and sisters -- Fiction 4. Sisters -- Fiction 5. Supernatural -- Fiction 6. Paris (France) -- History -- 1870-1940 -- Fiction 7. France -- History -- Third Republic, 1870-1940 -- Fiction
ISBN 0385743114; 9780375990953; 9780385743112

LC 2012022378

In this book by Page Morgan, "Ingrid, her sister Gabby, and their mom arrive at the abandoned abbey that they plan to turn into an art gallery. Grayson, Ingrid's twin brother, had procured the place and was supposed to meet them there. Grayson, however, does not show up and the girls are surprised to learn that he has actually been missing for several days. . . . [Ingrid] and Gabby . . .discover a world of living gargoyles that can transform into humans." (Children's Literature)

Moriarty, Jaclyn

★ A **corner** of white; Jaclyn Moriarty. Arthur A. Levine Books 2013 384 p. (Colors of Madeleine trilogy) (hardcover) $17.99

Grades: 7 8 9 10 11 12

1. Fantasy fiction 2. Epistolary fiction 3. Color --

Fiction 4. Magic -- Fiction 5. England -- Fiction 6. Princesses -- Fiction 7. Missing persons -- Fiction 8. Cambridge (England) -- Fiction 9. Interpersonal relations -- Fiction
ISBN 0545397367; 9780545397360

LC 2012016582

Boston Globe-Horn Book Honor: Fiction (2013).

This opening volume of a fantasy series from Jaclyn Moriarty focuses on 14-year-old Madeleine, who "lives in Cambridge, England, with her zany mother in uncertain circumstances, having run away from their fabulously privileged international existence. Meanwhile, Elliot lives in Bonfire, The Farms, Cello, a parallel reality. . . . Through a crack between their worlds, they begin exchanging letters." (Kirkus Reviews)

"Australian writer Moriarty's marvelously original fantasy is quirky and clever... [she] captures the proud iconoclasm of many homeschoolers and does not shy away from tenderness and poignancy." BookList

★ The **cracks** in the kingdom; Jaclyn Moriarty. Arthur A. Levine Books, an imprint of Scholastic Inc. 2014 480 p. (The colors of Madeleine) (hardcover : alk. paper) $18.99

Grades: 7 8 9 10 11 12

1. Princesses -- Fiction; 2. Fantasy fiction; 3. Color -- Fiction; 4. Magic -- Fiction; 5. England -- Fiction; 6. Missing persons -- Fiction; 7. Cambridge (England) -- Fiction; 8. Interpersonal relations -- Fiction
ISBN 0545397383; 9780545397384; 9780545397391

LC 2013022827

"In this lively follow-up to A Corner of White (Scholastic, 2013), Moriarty chronicles the ever-intertwining lives of Cambridge resident Madeline Tully and her secret correspondent Elliot Baranski, a quick-witted farm boy from the Kingdom of Cello...The RYA's work around Cello expands an already complex and intricately drawn world. Readers will be clamoring for the next title after the thrilling yet satisfying conclusion." (School Library Journal)

Feeling sorry for Celia St. Martin's Press 2001 276p $9.27

Grades 7 8 9 10 11 12

1. Teenage girls -- Fiction 2. Epistolary fiction 3. Bildungsromans 4. Australia -- Fiction

"Life is pretty complicated for Elizabeth Clarry. Her best friend Celia keeps disappearing, her absent father suddenly reappears, and her communication with her mother consists entirely of wacky notes left on the fridge...But Elizabeth is on the verge of some major changes. She may lose her best friend, find a wonderful new friend, kiss the sexiest guy alive, and run in a marathon. So much can happen in the time it takes to write a letter..." (Publisher's Note)

The **ghosts** of Ashbury High. Arthur A. Levine Books 2010 480p $18.99

Grades: 8 9 10 11 12

1. School stories 2. Australia -- Fiction
ISBN 978-0-545-06972-4; 0-545-06972-6

LC 2009-32651

Student essays, scholarship committee members' notes, and other writings reveal interactions between a group of modern-day students at an exclusive New South Wales high school and their strange connection to a young Irishman transported to Australia in the early 1800s.

"The off-the-rails zaniness . . . is . . . satisfying, and in between all the irreverence, Moriarty slips in plenty of sharp-eyed, poignant observations." SLJ

A **tangle** of gold. Jaclyn Moriarty. Arthur A. Levine Books, an imprint of Scholastic Inc. 2016 480 p. (Colors of Madeleine)

Grades: 9 10 11 12

    1. Color -- Fiction 2. Colors -- Fiction 3. Interpersonal relations -- Fiction 4. Kings, queens, rulers, etc. -- Fiction 5. Magic -- Fiction 6. Missing persons -- Fiction 7. Royal houses -- Fiction 8. Cambridge (England) -- Fiction 9. England -- Fiction 10. England -- Fiction 11. Kings and rulers -- Fiction

9780545397407, $18.99

LC 2015027754

In this book, by Jaclyn Moriarty, "Cello is in crisis. Princess Ko's deception of her people has emerged and the Kingdom is outraged; the Jagged Edge Elite have taken control, placing the Princess and two members of the Royal Youth Alliance under arrest and ordering their execution; the King's attempts to negotiate their release have failed; Color storms are rampant; and nobody has heard the Cello wind blowing in months." (Publisher's note)

"Readers may find themselves slowing down to savor Moriarty's distinctive language and humor in this final outing. This remains a series unlike any other, with frequent pockets of beautiful imagery and a unique rhythm all its own." Booklist

Moriarty, Laura

The **center** of everything. Hyperion 2003 291p $22.95; pa $14

Grades: 9 10 11 12

    1. Kansas -- Fiction 2. Single parent family -- Fiction 3. Mother-daughter relationship -- Fiction

ISBN 1-401-30031-6; 0-7868-8845-8 pa

LC 2002-32898

"Any map clearly shows that Kansas is the center of everything. Ten-year-old Evelyn Bucknow notices it on every map that she sees and truly believes that is where she belongs—in the center. Unfortunately, Evelyn is forced to parent her mother, a flighty, unrealistically romantic woman who is having an affair with her married boss. . . . Fortunately, Evelyn takes the events of her life and her mother's life and learns her lessons, with a few glitches along the way. Young people will find Evelyn appealing and real despite the book's setting in the age of Ronald Reagan and big hair, and they will respond positively to her determination." Voice Youth Advocates

Morpurgo, Michael

An **elephant** in the garden. Feiwel and Friends 2011 199p $16.99

Grades: 6 7 8 9

    1. Zoos -- Fiction 2. Elephants -- Fiction 3. World War, 1939-1945 -- Fiction

ISBN 978-0-312-59369-8; 0-312-59369-4

Lizzie and Karl's mother is a zoo keeper; the family has become attached to an orphaned elephant named Marlene, who will be destroyed as a precautionary measure so she and the other animals don't run wild should the zoo be hit by bombs. The family persuades the zoo director to let Marlene stay in their garden instead. When the city is bombed, the family flees with thousands of others, but how can they walk the same route when they have an elephant in tow, and keep themselves safe?

"This well-paced, heartwarming narrative by a master storyteller will appeal to readers on several levels—as a tale of adventure and suspense, as a commentary on human trauma and animal welfare during war, as a perspective on the hardships facing the German people in the final months of World War II, and as a tribute to the rich memories and experiences of an older generation." SLJ

Half a man; Michael Morpurgo, illustrated by Gemma O'Callaghan. Candlewick Press. 2015 64p $16.99

Grades: 7 8 9 10

    1. Grandparent and child -- Fiction 2. Veterans -- Fiction 3. World War, 1939-1945 -- Fiction 4. Grandfathers -- Fiction

ISBN: 0763677477; 9780763677473

LC 2014939339

In this book, "author Michael Morpurgo evokes the postwar Britain of his childhood. . . . From a young age, Michael was both fascinated by and afraid of his grandfather. Grandpa's ship was torpedoed during the Second World War, leaving him with terrible burns. . . . As he grows older, Michael stays with his grandfather during the summer holidays and learns the story behind Grandpa's injuries, finally getting to know the real man behind the solemn figure from his childhood." (Publisher's note)

"Morpurgo has penned an extraordinary little book of pain and triumph. It is a fictionalized tale but is based on the heroic work of Dr. McIndoe, a pioneering plastic surgeon who treated severely burned soldiers during World War II... This title will resonate with a variety of readers . . . and is an outstanding choice for reluctant readers. With our returning wounded warriors of today, this is a timely and superb addition to all collections and not to be missed." SLJ

Listen to the Moon. By Michael Morpurgo. Feiwel & Friends 2015 352 p.

Grades: 5 6 7 8 9

    1. Girls -- Fiction 2. England -- Fiction 3. World War, 1914-1918 -- Fiction 4. Father-son relationship -- Fiction

1250042046; 9781250042040, $16.99

"In May 1915 a fisherman and his son, Alfie, from the Scilly Isles west of Great Britain, find a little girl near death on a deserted island, take her home, and care for her. She does not speak but clings to a teddy bear and a blanket with a German name sewn on it. Naming her Lucy Lost, Alfie and his parents and a kindly and wise doctor nurture her with love, music from a gramophone, and drawing material. Months go by, and still no one can uncover any details about her life. But World War I is raging, the British harbor fierce anti-German sentiments, and when news of the name on her blanket spreads, the family is shunned." (Kirkus)

"A framing device, built around the research of Lucy's future grandson, allows Morpurgo to shift among multiple narrators as he unspools the mystery of where she came from. Along the way, Morpurgo offers powerful descriptions of shipwreck, mass drowning, and devastation, as well as healing and growth." Pub Wkly

★ **Private** Peaceful. Scholastic Press 2004 202p $16.95; pa $5.99
Grades: 7 8 9 10
 1. Great Britain -- Fiction 2. World War, 1914-1918 -- Fiction
 ISBN 0-439-63648-5; 0-439-63653-1 pa
           LC 2003-65347
First published 2003 in the United Kingdom
When Thomas Peaceful's older brother is forced to join the British Army, Thomas decides to sign up as well, although he is only fourteen years old, to prove himself to his country, his family, his childhood love, Molly, and himself
"In this World War I story, the terse and beautiful narrative of a young English soldier is as compelling about the world left behind as about the horrific daily details of trench warfare. . . . Suspense builds right to the end, which is shocking, honest, and unforgettable." Booklist

Morris, Gerald
 ★ The **squire's** tale. Houghton Mifflin 1998 212p (The squire's tales) $15; pa $5.50
Grades: 6 7 8 9
 1. Magic -- Fiction 2. Knights and knighthood -- Fiction 3. Gawain (Legendary character) -- Fiction
 ISBN 0-395-86959-5; 0-440-22823-9 pa
           LC 97-12447
In medieval England, fourteen-year-old Terence finds his tranquil existence suddenly changed when he becomes the squire of the young Gawain of Orkney and accompanies him on a long quest, proving Gawain's worth as a knight and revealing an important secret about his own true identity
"Well-drawn characters, excellent, snappy dialogue, detailed descriptions of medieval life, and a dry wit put a new spin on this engaging tale of the characters and events of King Arthur's time." Booklist
 Other titles in this series are:
 The squire, his knight, & his lady (1999)
 The savage damsel and the dwarf (2000)
 Parsifal's page (2001)
 The ballad of Sir Dinadan (2003)
 The princess, the crone, and the dung-cart knight (2004)
 The lionness & her knight (2005)
 The quest of the Fair Unknown (2006)
 The squire's quest (2009)
 The legend of the king (2010)

Morton-Shaw, Christine
 The **riddles** of Epsilon. Katherine Tegen Books 2005 375p $16.99; lib bdg $17.89
Grades: 7 8 9 10
 1. Supernatural -- Fiction
 ISBN 0-06-072819-1; 0-06-072820-5 lib bdg
           LC 2004-14641
After moving with her parents to a remote English island, fourteen-year-old Jess attempts to dispel an ancient curse by solving a series of riddles, aided by Epsilon, a supernatural being.

Moses, Shelia P.
 Joseph. Margaret K. McElderry Books 2008 174p $16.99; pa $8.99
Grades: 7 8 9 10
 1. Drug abuse -- Fiction 2. African Americans -- Fiction 3. Mother-son relationship -- Fiction
 ISBN 978-1-4169-1752-6; 1-4169-1752-7; 978-4169-9442-8 pa; 1-4169-9442-4 pa
Fourteen-year-old Joseph tries to avoid trouble and keep in touch with his father, who is serving in Iraq, as he and his alcoholic, drug-addicted mother move from one homeless shelter to another.
"Moses creates a compelling character in Joseph. His struggle to survive his current situation intact is fascinating to read. . . . Negative influences such as drug dealers and users are described in a clear, cold light. Education and hard work are praised for their positive influences. Middle school and junior high teens will enjoy this story." Voice Youth Advocates

 The **legend** of Buddy Bush. Margaret K. McElderry Books 2004 216p $15.95
Grades: 6 7 8 9
 1. Race relations 2. African Americans -- Fiction 3. Family life -- North Carolina
 ISBN 0-689-85839-6
           LC 2003-8024
In 1947, twelve-year-old Pattie Mae is sustained by her dreams of escaping Rich Square, North Carolina, and moving to Harlem when her Uncle Buddy is arrested for attempted rape of a white woman and her grandfather is diagnosed with a terminal brain tumor.
"Patti Mae's first-person voice, steeped in the inflections of the South, rings true, and her observations richly evoke a time, place, and a resilient African American community." Booklist
 Another title about Buddy Bush is:
 The return of Buddy Bush (2005)

Moskowitz, Hannah
 Gone, gone, gone. Pulse/Simon & Schuster 2012 251 p.
Grades: 9 10 11 12
 1. Love stories 2. September 11 Terrorist Attacks, 2001 -- Fiction 3. Grief -- Fiction 4. Bereavement -- Fiction 5. Gay teenagers -- Fiction
 9781442453128, $16.99; 1442453125; 9781442407534
           LC 2011935726
Stonewall Honor Book (2013)
This book presents the story of the relationship between two 15-year-old boys, Craig and Lio, as they search for Craig's missing pets in the fall of 2002. Craig and Lio explore their feelings about the 2011 World Trade Center and Pentagon terrorist attacks and other current events as they look for the animals, relating these tragedies to losses in their own lives. "The Beltway sniper shootings and the attacks of 9/11 become the crucible for this exploration of teenage grief and love." (Kirkus Reviews)

"First-person narratives alternate in this raw, immediate love story set outside DC during the 2002 Beltway sniper attacks." Horn Book

★ **Teeth**; Hannah Moskowitz. Simon Pulse 2013 242 p. $17.99

Grades: 9 10 11 12

    1. Fantasy fiction 2. Mermaids and mermen -- Fiction 3. Mermen -- Fiction 4. Islands -- Fiction 5. Brothers -- Fiction 6. Loneliness -- Fiction 7. Supernatural -- Fiction 8. Cystic fibrosis -- Fiction

    ISBN 1442465328; 9781442449466; 9781442465329

                  LC 2012019114

This novel, by Hannah Moskowitz, offers a "gritty, romantic modern fairy tale. . . . Rudy's . . . family moves to a remote island in a last attempt to save his sick younger brother. . . . Then he meets Diana, who makes him wonder what he even knows about love, and Teeth, who makes him question what he knows about anything. . . . He soon learns that Teeth has terrible secrets . . . that will force Rudy to choose between his own happiness and his brother's life." (Publisher's note)

Mosley, Walter

    47. Little, Brown 2005 232p $16.99

Grades: 7 8 9 10

    1. Magic -- Fiction 2. Slavery -- Fiction 3. African Americans -- Fiction

    ISBN 0-316-11035-3

                  LC 2004-12500

Number 47, a fourteen-year-old slave boy growing up under the watchful eye of a brutal master in 1832, meets the mysterious Tall John, who introduces him to a magical science and also teaches him the meaning of freedom.

    "Time travel, shape-shifting, and intergalactic conflict add unusual, provocative elements to this story. And yet, well-drawn characters; lively dialogue filled with gritty, regional dialect; vivid descriptions; and poignant reflections ground it in harsh reality." SLJ

Moulton, Courtney Allison

    Angelfire; 1st ed. Katherine Tegen Books 2011 453 p. (trade bdg.) $17.99

Grades: 7 8 9 10

    1. Horror fiction 2. Horror stories 3. Souls -- Fiction 4. Youths' writings 5. Angels -- Fiction 6. Monsters -- Fiction 7. Reincarnation -- Fiction

    ISBN 9780062002327; 9780062002341

                  LC 2010012821

A seventeen-year-old girl discovers that she has the reincarnated soul of an ancient warrior destined to battle the reapers --creatures who devour humans and send their souls to Hell. --Grades nine to twelve. -- (Bull Cent Child Books)

    "The author has introduced a dark and compelling world of action and intrigue, albeit with enough 'normal' drama and humor sprinkled throughout to lighten it. . . . Older junior and senior high school readers will find themselves engrossed in the story until its powerful conclusion— then anxiously awaiting the second installment." Voice Youth Advocates

Mourlevat, Jean-Claude

    ★ **Winter's** end; translated by Anthea Bell. Candlewick Press 2009 415p lib bdg $21.99

Grades: 8 9 10 11 12

    1. Fantasy fiction 2. Adventure fiction 3. Orphans -- Fiction 4. Despotism -- Fiction 5. Resistance to government -- Fiction

    ISBN 978-0-7636-4450-5; 0-7636-4450-1

                  LC 2009-8456

Fleeing across icy mountains from a pack of terrifying dog-men sent to hunt them down, four teenagers escape from their prison-like boarding schools to take up the fight against the tyrannical government that murdered their parents fifteen years earlier.

    "Teeming with heroic acts, heartbreaking instances of sacrifice and intriguing characters . . . the book will keep readers absorbed and set imaginations spinning." Publ Wkly

Mowll, Joshua

    Operation Red Jericho; [illustrated by Benjamin Mowll, Julek Heller, Niroot Puttapipat] Candlewick Press 2005 271p il map (The Guild of Specialists) hardcover o.p. pa $8.99

Grades: 9 10 11 12

    1. Adventure fiction 2. Uncles -- Fiction 3. Siblings -- Fiction

    ISBN 0-7636-2634-1; 0-7636-3475-1 pa

                  LC 2005-45382

The posthumous papers of Rebecca MacKenzie document her adventures, along with her brother Doug, in 1920s China as the teenaged siblings are sent to live aboard their uncle's ship where they become involved in the dangerous activities of a mysterious secret society called the Honourable Guild of Specialists.

    "Some readers may pore over the details in this novel; others will simply appreciate the comic adventure." SLJ

    Operation Storm City. Candlewick Press 2009 273p il (The Guild of Specialists) $16.99

Grades: 7 8 9 10

    1. Adventure fiction 2. China -- Fiction 3. Siblings -- Fiction

    ISBN 978-0-7636-4224-2; 0-7636-4224-X

                  LC 2008-19703

Siblings Becca and Doug discover important clues to their missing parents' expedition route and the location of Ur-Can, the fabled Storm City, and they embark on a perilous journey to the Takla Makan desert, racing against their Guild enemies by steam train, riverboat, and airship across the Himalayas, trying to save not only their parents, but the entire planet.

    "For readers who love adventure stories and can handle a greater level of complexity, this whirlwind of travel, fighting, and impending disaster is a great trip." Voice Youth Advocates

    Operation typhoon shore. Candlewick Press 2006 272p il map (The Guild of Specialists) $15.99

Grades: 7 8 9 10

    1. Adventure fiction 2. China -- Fiction 3. Ships --

Fiction 4. Uncles -- Fiction 5. Siblings -- Fiction
ISBN 978-0-7636-3122-2; 0-7636-3122-1

LC 2006-47481

Sequel to Operation Red Jericho (2005)

In the spring of 1920, teenaged siblings Rebecca and Doug MacKenzie continue their adventures on their uncle's ship, sailing through a typhoon into the Celebes Sea in pursuit of a missing "gyrolabe" which may be connected to the disappearance of their parents.

"This book rolls along with plenty of action and fun. Readers will be captivated by the story line, but also will be intrigued by all of the sketches, photographs, newspaper clippings, and foldout information on technology." SLJ

Mukherjee, Sonya

Gemini. Sonya Mukherjee. Simon & Schuster Books for Young Readers 2016 326 p.

Grades: 8 9 10 11 12

1. Conjoined twins -- Fiction 2. Bildungsromans 3. Sisters -- Fiction

1481456776; 9781481456777, $17.99

LC 2015019774

In this novel by Sonya Mukherjee, "conjoined twins Clara and Hailey have lived in the same small town their entire lives . . . but there are cracks in their quiet existence. . . . Clara wants to stay close to home, avoid all attention, and study the night sky. Hailey wants to travel the world, learn from great artists, and dance with mysterious boys. . . . Each twin must untangle her dreams from her sister's and figure out what it means to be her own person." (Publisher's note)

"Even for sisters, Clara and Hailey are close. They have to be—they're conjoined twins attached at the spine. . . . [T]his debut is a well-researched and particularly heartfelt account of a rare medical condition and the people it affects. Though they share a body, Clara and Hailey are two very different people with different dreams, and their fight for a normal life will resonate with many." Booklist

Mulder, Michelle

Out of the box. Orca Book Publishers 2011 150p pa $9.95

Grades: 6 7 8 9

1. Aunts -- Fiction 2. Family life -- Fiction 3. Mother-daughter relationship -- Fiction

ISBN 978-1-55469-328-3 pa; 1-55469-328-4 pa

Ellie's passion for tango music leads to an interest in Argentine history and a desire to separate herself from her parents' problems.

"Ellie's narration authentically conveys her gradual growth, the insecurities that surround her developing friendships, her role in a dysfunctional family, and the pleasure she takes in music. Adults and their relationships are portrayed credibly. . . . A bit of Argentine history rounds out the believable plot." SLJ

Mulligan, Andy

Trash. David Fickling Books 2010 232p $16.99; lib bdg $19.99

Grades: 6 7 8 9

1. Mystery fiction 2. Poverty -- Fiction 3. Political corruption -- Fiction 4. Refuse and refuse disposal --

Fiction

ISBN 978-0-385-75214-5; 0-385-75214-8; 978-0-385-75215-2 lib bdg; 0-385-75215-6 lib bdg

LC 2010-15940

Fourteen-year-olds Raphael and Gardo team up with a younger boy, Rat, to figure out the mysteries surrounding a bag Raphael finds during their daily life of sorting through trash in a third-world country's dump.

"While on the surface the book reads like a fast-paced adventure title, it also makes a larger statement about the horrors of poverty and injustice in the world. . . . Trash is a compelling read." SLJ

Mullin, Mike

Ashfall. Tanglewood 2011 466p $16.99

Grades: 9 10 11 12

1. Science fiction 2. Volcanoes -- Fiction 3. Wilderness survival -- Fiction

ISBN 978-1-933718-55-2

LC 2011007133

"Mullin puts his characters through hell, depicting numerous deaths in detail. . . . There's also cannibalism and a rape before the novel comes to a believable ending. . . . The book is well written and its protagonists are well-drawn, particularly the nontraditional and mechanically inclined Darla. Although more appropriate for older teens due to its violence, this is a riveting tale of survival." Publ Wkly

Sunrise; Mike Mullin. Tanglewood Publishing. 2014 546p $17.99

Grades: 9 10 11 12

1. Science fiction 2. Volcanoes -- Fiction 3. Wilderness survival -- Fiction

ISBN: 1939100011; 9781939100016

LC 2013050876

In this final book of the Ashfall Trilogy, "the Yellowstone supervolcano nearly wiped out the human race. Now, almost a year after the eruption, the survivors seem determined to finish the job. Communities wage war on each other, gangs of cannibals roam the countryside, and what little government survived the eruption has collapsed completely. The ham radio has gone silent. Sickness, cold, and starvation are the survivors' constant companions." (Publisher's note)

"The writing, even in transitory moments of peace, never lets readers forget that potential catastrophe lurks around every corner. A story about how hope is earned, as heart-pounding as it is heart-wrenching." Kirkus

Murdoch, Emily

★ **If** you find me; Emily Murdoch. St. Martin's Griffin 2013 256 p. (hardback) $17.99

Grades: 9 10 11 12

1. Abandoned children -- Fiction 2. Children of drug addicts -- Fiction 3. Sisters -- Fiction 4. Foundlings -- Fiction 5. Family secrets -- Fiction 6. Abused children -- Fiction

ISBN 1250021529; 9781250021526

LC 2013002656

This is the story of "14-year-old Carey and her younger sister, Nessa, [who] were kidnapped, hidden in the backwoods of Tennessee, and raised apart from society by their meth-addicted mother. After having abandoned the girls for months, she contacts the girls' father, who rescues them from the trailer where they've been living on their own, whisking them away to his gorgeous home, his understanding new wife, and her less understanding daughter." (Publishers Weekly)

Murdock, Catherine Gilbert

★ **Dairy** Queen; a novel. Houghton Mifflin 2006 275p $16

Grades: 7 8 9 10

1. Football -- Fiction 2. Farm life -- Fiction

ISBN 0-618-68307-0

LC 2005-19077

After spending her summer running the family farm and training the quarterback for her school's rival football team, sixteen-year-old D.J. decides to go out for the sport herself, not anticipating the reactions of those around her.

"D. J.'s voice is funny, frank, and intelligent, and her story is not easily pigeonholed." Voice Youth Advocates

Front and center. Houghton Mifflin 2009 256p (The dairy queen trilogy) $16

Grades: 7 8 9 10

1. Farm life -- Fiction 2. Basketball -- Fiction

ISBN 978-0-618-95982-2; 0-618-95982-3

LC 2009-24167

Sequel to: The off season (2007)

"In the third and final book . . . about farm girl, linebacker, and basketball star D.J. Schwenk, the self-aggrandizing heroine must decide her future: is she up to playing basketball for the Big Ten schools that are starting to recruit her, or should she choose a smaller college, where the game is less brutal but also less challenging? . . . D.J.'s voice is intimate and compelling, her story both universal and unique, familiar and eye-opening." Horn Book

The off season. Houghton Mifflin 2007 277p $16

Grades: 7 8 9 10

1. Football -- Fiction 2. Farm life -- Fiction

ISBN 978-0-618-68695-7; 0-618-68695-9

LC 2006029278

Sequel to: Dairy Queen (2006)

High school junior D.J. staggers under the weight of caring for her badly injured brother, her responsibilities on the dairy farm, a changing relationship with her friend Brian, and her own athletic aspirations.

This "depicts a believably maturing D.J., a young woman whose character shines through even as she struggles to find her voice. Readers will root for her at every tragicomic turn." SLJ

Followed by: Front and center (2009)

Princess Ben; being a wholly truthful account of her various discoveries and misadventures, recounted to the best of her recollection, in four parts. written by Catherine Gilbert Murdock. Houghton Mifflin 2008 344p $16; pa $8.99

Grades: 7 8 9 10

1. Fairy tales 2. Magic -- Fiction 3. Princesses --

Fiction 4. Courts and courtiers -- Fiction

ISBN 978-0-618-95971-6; 0-618-95971-8; 978-0-547-22325-4 pa; 0-547-22325-0 pa

LC 2007-34300

A girl is transformed, through instruction in life at court, determination, and magic, from sullen, pudgy, graceless Ben into Crown Princess Benevolence, a fit ruler of the kindgom of Montagne as it faces war with neighboring Drachensbett.

"Murdock's prose sweeps the reader up and never falters, blending a formal syntax and vocabulary with an intimate tone that bonds the reader with Ben." Horn Book

Wisdom's kiss; a thrilling and romantic adventure, incorporating magic, villany and a cat. written by Catherine Gilbert Murdock. Houghton Mifflin 2011 284p $16.99

Grades: 7 8 9 10

1. Fairy tales 2. Cats -- Fiction 3. Orphans -- Fiction 4. Soldiers -- Fiction 5. Princesses -- Fiction 6. Supernatural -- Fiction 7. Household employees -- Fiction

ISBN 978-0-547-56687-0; 0-547-56687-5

LC 2011003708

Princess Wisdom, who yearns for a life of adventure beyond the kingdom of Montagne, Tips, a soldier keeping his true life secret from his family, Fortitude, an orphaned maid who longs for Tips, and Magic the cat form an uneasy alliance as they try to save the kingdom from certain destruction. Told through diaries, memoirs, encyclopedia entries, letters, biographies, and a stage play.

"Packed with double entendres, humorous dialogue and situations, and a black cat that will capture the reader's imagination, this is a joyful, timeless fantasy that teens will savor." Booklist

Murphy, Julie

Dumplin'. Julie Murphy. Balzer + Bray, an imprint of HarperCollins Publishers 2015 384 p.

Grades: 8 9 10 11 12

1. Beauty contests -- Fiction 2. Dating (Social customs) -- Fiction 3. Friendship -- Fiction 4. Overweight persons -- Fiction 5. Self-esteem -- Fiction 6. Texas -- Fiction

9780062327185, $17.99

LC 2014041047

This novel, by Julie Murphy, follows an overweight teen girl. "Dubbed 'Dumplin'' by her former beauty queen mom, Willowdean has always been at home in her own skin . . . until she meets Private School Bo, a hot former jock. . . . Instead of finding new heights of self-assurance in her relationship with Bo, Will starts to doubt herself. So she sets out to take back her confidence by doing the most horrifying thing she can imagine: entering the Miss Teen Blue Bonnet Pageant." (Publisher's note)

"The story's set piece is the beauty contest, which Will and several other misfits decide to enter, ready to take the ridicule in trade for their right to the spotlight, but there are also splendid subplots involving friendships, the push-pull of the mother-daughter relationship, and the kindness of strangers, including an encouraging drag queen." Booklist

★ **Ramona** Blue. Julie Murphy. Balzer + Bray 2017 408 p.

Grades: 8 9 10 11

1. Interpersonal relations -- Fiction; 2. Sexual orientation -- Fiction; 3. Bildungsromans; 4. Lesbians -- Fiction
9780062418371; 9780062418357, $17.99

LC 2016950250

In this young adult novel, by Julie Murphy, "Ramona was only five years old when Hurricane Katrina changed her life forever. Since then, it's been Ramona and her family against the world. Standing over six feet tall with unmistakable blue hair, Ramona is sure of three things: she likes girls, she's fiercely devoted to her family, and she knows she's destined for something bigger than the trailer she calls home in Eulogy, Mississippi." (Publisher's note)

"An exquisite, thoughtful exploration of the ties that bind and the fluidity of relationships, sexuality, and life." Kirkus

Mussi, Sarah

★ The **door** of no return. Margaret K. McElderry Books 2008 394p $17.99; pa $8.99

Grades: 8 9 10 11 12

1. Adventure fiction 2. Ghana -- Fiction 3. Blacks -- Fiction 4. Homicide -- Fiction 5. Great Britain -- Fiction 6. Buried treasure -- Fiction
ISBN 978-1-4169-1550-8; 1-4169-1550-8; 978-1-4169-6825-2 pa; 1-4169-6825-3 pa

LC 2007-18670

Sixteen-year-old Zac never believed his grandfather's tales about their enslaved ancestors being descended from an African king, but when his grandfather is murdered and the villains come after Zac, he sets out for Ghana to find King Baktu's long-lost treasure before the murderers do.

"This exciting narrative takes place in England and Africa; in jungles, dark caves, and on the sea. . . . Overall, this is a complex, masterful story for confident readers." SLJ

Myers, Walter Dean, 1937-2014

All the right stuff; by Walter Dean Myers. HarperTeen 2012 213 p.

Grades: 8 9 10 11 12

1. Bildungsromans 2. Mentoring -- Fiction 3. Soup kitchens -- Fiction 4. Social contract -- Fiction 5. African Americans -- Harlem (New York, N.Y.) -- Fiction 6. Coming of age -- Fiction 7. Conduct of life -- Fiction 8. African Americans -- Fiction 9. Harlem (New York, N.Y.) -- Fiction
ISBN 9780061960871; 9780061960888

LC 2011024251

This novel tells the story of Paul DuPree, a 16-year-old boy who "has taken on two jobs: work in a soup kitchen and the required mentoring of a young basketball player. At the soup kitchen, he meets Elijah Jones, the project's driving force and resident philosopher," who helps Paul understand "how one person's decisions and actions might affect the entire community" as he mentors teenage mother Keisha and comes to terms with the death of his father." (Kirkus)

Amiri & Odette; a love story. a poem by Walter Dean Myers; paintings by Javaka Steptoe. Scholastic Press 2009 un il $17.99

Grades: 7 8 9 10

1. Fairy tales; 2. Love stories; 3. Novels in verse; 4. African Americans -- Fiction
0-590-68041-7; 0-590-68041-2

LC 2008-11563

Presents a modern, urban retelling in verse of the ballet in which brave Amiri falls in love with beautiful Odette and fights evil Big Red for her on the streets of the Swan Lake Projects.

"Myers's verse is almost overwrought—as it should be to suit the story, and the intensity of teenage love. The melodrama combines with an energy and beat that—heightened by dynamic text design—makes this ideal for performance. Steptoe's collage-on-cinderblock illustrations have a roughness, darkness, and density that suit the tone." SLJ

Carmen; an urban adaptation of the opera. Egmont USA 2011 various pagings $16.99

Grades: 8 9 10 11 12

1. Love -- Fiction 2. Hispanic Americans -- Fiction
ISBN 978-1-60684-115-0; 1-60684-115-7; 978-1-60684-199-0 e-book

LC 2011002491

A policeman's obsessive love for a tempestuous wig factory worker ends in tragedy in this updated version of Bizet's Carmen, set in Spanish Harlem, and told in screenplay format.

"Myers seamlessly pulls off the drama's transportation to a contemporary urban setting and, true to form, renders it accessible to today's teens. . . . An excellent choice for reluctant readers, urban or otherwise." SLJ

★ The **Cruisers**; Walter Dean Myers. Scholastic Press 2010 126 p. $15.99

Grades: 6 7 8 9

1. Schools -- Fiction 2. Newspapers -- Fiction 3. Middle schools -- Fiction 4. Race relations -- Fiction 5. African Americans -- Fiction 6. Freedom of speech -- Fiction
ISBN 978-0-439-91626-4; 0-439-91626-7; 9780439916264

LC 2009052426

Friends Zander, Kambui, LaShonda, and Bobbi, caught in the middle of a mock Civil War at DaVinci Academy, learn the true cost of freedom of speech when they use their alternative newspaper, The Cruiser, to try to make peace.

"A finely crafted look at smart, urban underachievers. . . . [The book offers] fleet pacing, a spot-on voice, good characters, great dialogue, smart ideas, and an unusual story that can maneuver whip-quick from light to heavy and right back again." Booklist

Another title in this series is:
The Cruisers: checkmate (2011)

★ **Darius** & Twig; Walter Dean Myers. 1st ed. Harper, an imprint of HarperCollinsPublishers 2013 208 p. (hardcover) $17.99

Grades: 8 9 10 11 12

1. Friendship -- Fiction 2. Harlem (New York, N.Y.) -- Fiction 3. Running -- Fiction 4. Authorship -- Fiction 5. Best friends -- Fiction 6. New York (N.Y.) -- Fiction 7. African Americans -- Fiction 8. Dominican

Americans -- Fiction
ISBN 0061728233; 9780061728235; 9780061728242
LC 2012050678

Coretta Scott King Honor Book: Author (2014)

In this book by Walter Dean Myers, "Harlem teenager Darius, a writer, wants to get out of his neighborhood and make it to college, but his grades aren't good enough. He's hoping that if he can get a story published, he might nab a college scholarship. His best friend Twig is a track star, and sees athletics as his escape. Both are skeptical of the hype they are fed about how hard work pays off, and they face obstacles ranging from school bullies . . . to indifferent educators." (Publishers Weekly)

"This encouraging text may inspire teens who feel trapped by their surroundings...Told in Darius's voice, the prose is poetic but concise. This would be a worthwhile addition to any middle or high school media center or public library shelf and would make a valuable book for discussion in a middle school classroom." VOYA

Dope sick. HarperTeen/Amistad 2009 186p $16.99; lib bdg $17.89

Grades: 8 9 10 11 12

1. Drug abuse -- Fiction 2. Supernatural -- Fiction 3. African Americans -- Fiction 4. Harlem (New York, N.Y.) -- Fiction
ISBN 978-0-06-121477-6; 0-06-121477-9; 978-0-06-121478-3 lib bdg; 0-06-121478-7 lib bdg
LC 2008-10568

Seeing no way out of his difficult life in Harlem, seventeen-year-old Jeremy "Lil J" Dance flees into a house after a drug deal goes awry and meets a weird man who shows different turning points in Lil J's life when he could have made better choices.

"Myers uses street-style lingo to cover Lil J's sorry history of drug use, jail time, irresponsible fatherhood and his own childhood grief. A didn't-see-that-coming ending wraps up the story on a note of well-earned hope and will leave readers with plenty to think about." Publ Wkly

★ **Fallen** angels; Walter Dean Myers. Scholastic Paperbacks 2008 336 p. hardcover o.p. (pbk.) $7.99

Grades: 8 9 10 11 12

1. Vietnam War, 1961-1975 -- Fiction 2. African American soldiers -- Fiction
ISBN 9780545055765; 0545055768
First published 1988

ALA YALSA Margaret A. Edwards Award (1994)

"Black, seventeen, perceptive and sensitive, Richie (the narrator) has enlisted and been sent to Vietnam; in telling the story of his year of active service, Richie is candid about the horror of killing and the fear of being killed, the fear and bravery and confusion and tragedy of the war." Bull Cent Child Books

"Except for occasional outbursts, the narration is remarkably direct and understated; and the dialogue, with morbid humor sometimes adding comic relief, is steeped in natural vulgarity, without which verisimilitude would be unthinkable. In fact, the foul talk, which serves as the story's linguistic setting, is not nearly as obscene as the events." Horn Book

Game. HarperTeen 2008 218p $16.99; lib bdg $17.89

Grades: 8 9 10 11 12

1. School stories 2. Basketball -- Fiction 3. Czech Americans -- Fiction 4. African Americans -- Fiction 5. Harlem (New York, N.Y.) -- Fiction
ISBN 978-0-06-058294-4; 978-0-06-058295-1 lib bdg
LC 2007-18370

If Harlem high school senior Drew Lawson is going to realize his dream of playing college, then professional, basketball, he will have to improve at being coached and being a team player, especially after a new—white—student threatens to take the scouts' attention away from him.

"Basketball fans will love the long passages of detailed court action. . . . The authentic thoughts of a strong, likable, African American teen whose anxieties, sharp insights, and belief in his own abilities will captivate readers of all backgrounds." Booklist

Harlem summer. Scholastic Press 2007 176p il $16.99

Grades: 6 7 8 9

1. African Americans -- Fiction 2. Harlem Renaissance -- Fiction
ISBN 978-0-439-36843-8; 0-439-36843-X
LC 2006-46812

In 1920s Harlem, sixteen-year-old Mark Purvis, an aspiring jazz saxophonist, gets a summer job as an errand boy for the publishers of the groundbreaking African American magazine, "The Crisis," but soon finds himself on the enemy list of mobster Dutch Shultz.

"Readers will be delighted to accompany the teen on his action-packed adventures." Booklist

★ **Hoops**; a novel. Delacorte Press 1981 183p hardcover o.p. pa $5.99

Grades: 7 8 9 10

1. Basketball -- Fiction 2. African Americans -- Fiction
ISBN 0-440-93884-8 pa
LC 81-65497

ALA YALSA Margaret A. Edwards Award (1994)

"This story offers the reader some fast, descriptive basketball action, a love story between Lonnie and girlfriend Mary-Ann, peer friendship problems, and gangster intrigues. Most importantly, however, it portrays the growth of a trusting and deeply caring father-son relationship between [the coach] Cal and [fatherless] Lonnie." Voice Youth Advocates

Invasion! Walter Dean Myers. Scholastic Press 2013 224 p. $17.99

Grades: 7 8 9 10

1. Friendship -- Fiction; 2. African American soldiers -- Fiction; 3. Normandy (France), Attack on, 1944 -- Fiction; 4. War -- Fiction; 5. Soldiers -- Fiction
ISBN 0545384281; 9780545384285; 9780545384292; 9780545576598
LC 2013005595

In this book by Walter Dean Myers, "old friends Josiah 'Woody' Wedgewood and Marcus Perry see each other in England prior to the invasion of Normandy. Woody is with the 29th Infantry, and Marcus, who's black, is with the Transportation Corps, the segregation of their Virginia hometown following them right into wartime. Their friendship frames the story, as the two occasionally encounter each other in the horrific days ahead." (Kirkus Reviews)

"Myers eloquently conveys how exhausting war is physically and emotionally. . . . [T]his novel can be hard to read, but it is also hard to put down." SLJ

Juba!. Walter Dean Myers. HarperTeen 2015 208 p. Illustration
Grades: 7 8 9 10

    1. African Americans -- New York (State) -- New York -- Fiction 2. Dancers -- Fiction 3. Prejudices -- Fiction 4. Lane, William Henry, approximately 1825-1852 -- Fiction 5. Five Points (New York, N.Y.) -- History -- 19th century -- Fiction 6. Great Britain -- History -- Victoria, 1837-1901 -- Fiction 7. London (England) -- History -- 19th century -- Fiction 8. New York (N.Y.) -- History -- 19th century -- Fiction 9. African American dancers
9780062112712, $17.99; 0062112716

                                            LC 2014042527

This historical novel by Walter Dean Myers "is based on the true story of the meteoric rise of an immensely talented young black dancer, William Henry Lane, who influenced today's tap, jazz, and step dancing. . . . The novel includes photographs, maps, and other images from Juba's time and an afterword from Walter Dean Myers's wife about the writing process." (Publisher's note)

"Juba is presented as a thoughtful, proud young man who means well and works hard; Myers gives him a direct and sympathetic voice, depicting the struggles and successes of his short life in the Five Points neighborhood of New York City, and later in London, with warmth and convincing detail." Pub Wkly

Kick; [by] Walter Dean Myers and Ross Workman. HarperTeen 2011 197p $16.99; lib bdg $17.89
Grades: 7 8 9 10

    1. Police -- Fiction 2. Soccer -- Fiction 3. Mentoring -- Fiction 4. New Jersey -- Fiction 5. Family life -- Fiction 6. Criminal investigation -- Fiction
ISBN 978-0-06-200489-5; 0-06-200489-1; 978-0-06-200490-1 lib bdg; 0-06-200490-5 lib bdg

                                            LC 2010-18441

Told in their separate voices, thirteen-year-old soccer star Kevin and police sergeant Brown, who knew his father, try to keep Kevin out of juvenile hall after he is arrested on very serious charges.

"Workman is a genuine talent, writing short, declarative sentences that move that narrative forward with assurance and a page-turning tempo. Myers, of course, is a master. . . . The respective voices and characters play off each other as successfully as a high-stakes soccer match." Booklist

Lockdown. Amistad 2010 247p $16.99; lib bdg $17.89
Grades: 8 9 10 11 12

    1. Old age -- Fiction 2. Friendship -- Fiction 3. African Americans -- Fiction 4. Juvenile delinquency -- Fiction
ISBN 978-0-06-121480-6; 0-06-121480-9; 978-0-06-121481-3 lib bdg; 0-06-121481-7 lib bdg

                                            LC 2009-7287

Coretta Scott King Author Award honor book, 2011

Teenage Reese, serving time at a juvenile detention facility, gets a lesson in making it through hard times from an unlikely friend with a harrowing past.

"Reese's first-person narration rings with authenticity. . . . Myers' storytelling skills ensure that the messages he offers are never heavy-handed." Booklist

★ **Monster**; illustrations by Christopher Myers. HarperCollins Pubs. 1999 281p il $14.95; lib bdg $14.89; pa $8.99
Grades: 7 8 9 10

    1. Trials -- Fiction 2. African Americans -- Fiction
ISBN 0-06-028077-8; 0-06-028078-6 lib bdg; 0-06-440731-4 pa

                                            LC 98-40958

Michael L. Printz Award, 2000

While on trial as an accomplice to a murder, sixteen-year-old Steve Harmon records his experiences in prison and in the courtroom in the form of a film script as he tries to come to terms with the course his life has taken.

"Balancing courtroom drama and a sordid jailhouse setting with flashbacks to the crime, Myers adeptly allows each character to speak for him or herself, leaving readers to judge for themselves the truthfulness of the defendants, witnesses, lawyers, and, most compellingly, Steve himself." Horn Book Guide

Oh, Snap! by Walter Dean Myers. Scholastic 2013 128 p. (hardcover) $17.99
Grades: 6 7 8 9

    1. Theft -- Fiction 2. Journalists -- Fiction
ISBN 0439916291; 9780439916295

This is the fourth book in Walter Dean Myers's Cruisers series. Here, the "four budding urban journalists are psyched that their underground publication, 'The Cruiser,' was named the third-best school newspaper in the city, an honor that doesn't sit well with the official school newspaper, which ups its game. This pushes narrator Zander to hastily get involved with the case of Phat Tony, a wannabe rapper classmate who may be involved in a robbery." (Booklist)

On a clear day. Walter Dean Myers. Crown Books for Young Readers, an imprint of Random House Children's Books 2014 256 p.
Grades: 6 7 8 9 10

    1. Interpersonal relations -- Fiction 2. Science fiction 3. Social action -- Fiction 4. England -- Fiction 5. Dystopian fiction 6. Teenagers -- Fiction;
0385387539; 9780385387538, $17.99; 9780385387545

                                            LC 2013046708

In this book, by Walter Dean Myers, "[y]oung heroes decide that they are not too young or too powerless to change their world. . . . It is 2035. Teens, armed only with their ideals, must wage war on the power elite. Dahlia is a Low Gater. . . . The Gaters live in closed safe communities, protected from the Sturmers, mercenary thugs. And the C-8, a consortium of giant companies, control global access to finance, media, food, water, and energy resources." (Publisher's note)

"Readers are left to question what actions are possible, what actions are needed and what actions are right in a world where inaction is an impossibility. A clarion call from a beloved, much-missed master." Kirkus

★ **Riot**. Egmont 2009 164p $16.99; lib bdg $19.99; pa $8.99

Grades: 7 8 9 10 11 12

1. Riots -- Fiction 2. Race relations -- Fiction 3. Irish Americans -- Fiction 4. African Americans -- Fiction 5. Racially mixed people -- Fiction

ISBN 978-1-60684-000-9; 1-60684-000-2; 978-1-60684-042-9 lib bdg; 1-60684-042-8 lib bdg; 978-1-60684-209-6 pa; 1-60684-209-9 pa

LC 2009-14638

In 1863, fifteen-year-old Claire, the daughter of an Irish mother and a black father, faces ugly truths and great danger when Irish immigrants, enraged by the Civil War and a federal draft, lash out against blacks and wealthy "swells" of New York City.

"In this fast, dramatic novel told in screenplay format, Myers takes on a controversial historical conflict that is seldom written about. . . . There are no easy resolutions, idealized characters, or stereotypes, and the conflicts are unforgettable." Booklist

Scorpions. Harper & Row 1988 216p $16.99; lib bdg $16.89; pa $5.99

Grades: 6 7 8 9

1. African Americans -- Fiction 2. Juvenile delinquency -- Fiction

ISBN 0-06-024364-3; 0-06-024365-1 lib bdg; 0-06-447066-0 pa

LC 85-45815

A Newbery Medal honor book, 1989

Set in Harlem, this "story presents a brutally honest picture of the tragic influence of gang membership and pressures on a young black adolescent. Jamal Hicks, age twelve, reluctantly follows the orders of his older brother, now serving time in prison for robbery, and takes his place as leader of the Scorpions. When Jamal's leadership is challenged, disaster follows and Jamal learns some tragic lessons about friendship and owning a gun." Child Book Rev Serv

★ **Slam!** Scholastic Press 1996 266p hardcover o.p. pa $5.99

Grades: 7 8 9 10

1. School stories 2. Basketball -- Fiction 3. African Americans -- Fiction

ISBN 0-590-48667-5; 0-590-48668-3 pa

LC 95-46647

Coretta Scott King Award for text

Seventeen-year-old "Slam" Harris is counting on his noteworthy basketball talents to get him out of the inner city and give him a chance to succeed in life, but his coach sees things differently

Myers "descriptions of Slam on the court . . . use crisp details, not flowery language, to achieve their muscular poetry, and Myers is equally vivid in relating the torment Slam feels as he stares at a page of indecipherable algebra formulas. . . . [This is an] admirably realistic coming-of-age novel." Booklist

A **star** is born; Walter Dean Myers. Scholastic 2012 176 p. (Cruisers) (ebook) $17.99; (hardcover) $17.99

Grades: 6 7 8 9

1. School stories 2. Autism -- Fiction 3. Siblings -- Fiction 4. Gifted children -- Fiction 5. Theater -- Fiction 6. Middle schools -- Fiction 7. African Americans -- Fiction 8. Brothers and sisters -- Fiction 9. Harlem (New York, N.Y.) -- Fiction

ISBN 9780545512688; 9780439916288

LC 2011030333

This book is the third in the Cruisers series. "For 14-year-old LaShonda Powell, real life is a lot tougher than solving for x and y in algebra class. She's been offered a full scholarship to the Virginia Woolf Society Program for Young Ladies, thanks to her costume designs for the recent class play, and if she completes the program, she'll qualify for future college scholarships. The problem is that LaShonda lives in a group home with her autistic brother, Chris, and the two are inseparable." (Kirkus)

Street love. Amistad/Harper Tempest 2006 134p $15.99; lib bdg $16.89

Grades: 8 9 10 11 12

1. Novels in verse 2. Love -- Fiction 3. African Americans -- Fiction

ISBN 978-0-06-028079-6; 0-06-028079-4; 978-0-06-028080-2 lib bdg; 0-06-028080-8 lib bdg

LC 2006-02457

This story told in free verse is set against a background of street gangs and poverty in Harlem in which seventeen-year-old African American Damien takes a bold step to ensure that he and his new love will not be separated.

"The realistic drama on the street and at home tells a gripping story." Booklist

★ **Sunrise** over Fallujah. Scholastic Press 2008 290p $17.99

Grades: 8 9 10 11 12

1. Iraq War, 2003-2011 -- Fiction 2. African Americans -- Fiction

ISBN 978-0-439-91624-0; 0-439-91624-0

LC 2007-25444

"Instead of heading to college as his father wishes, Robin leaves Harlem and joins the army to stand up for his country after 9/11. While stationed in Iraq with a war looming that he hopes will be averted, he begins writing letters home to his parents and to his Uncle Richie. . . . Myers brilliantly freeze-frames the opening months of the current Iraq War by realistically capturing its pivotal moments in 2003 and creating a vivid setting. Memorable characters share instances of wry levity that balance the story without deflecting its serious tone." SLJ

Myracle, Lauren, 1969-

★ **Bliss**. Amulet Books 2008 444p $16.95

Grades: 9 10 11 12

1. Horror fiction 2. School stories 3. Occultism -- Fiction 4. Atlanta (Ga.) -- Fiction

ISBN 978-0-8109-7071-7; 0-8109-7071-6

LC 2007-50036

Having grown up in a California commune, Bliss sees her aloof grandmother's Atlanta world as a foreign country, but she is determined to be nice as a freshman at an elite high school, which makes her the perfect target for Sandy, a girl obsessed with the occult.

"Catering to teens with a taste for horror, this carefully plotted occult thriller set in 1969-1970 combines genre staples with creepy period particulars." Publ Wkly

The **infinite** moment of us; by Lauren Myracle. Amulet Books 2013 336 p. (hardback) $17.95
Grades: 9 10 11 12

    1. Love stories 2. Foster children -- Fiction 3. Love -- Fiction 4. Atlanta (Ga.) -- Fiction 5. Family life -- Georgia -- Fiction 6. Dating (Social customs) -- Fiction 7. Assertiveness (Psychology) -- Fiction
    ISBN 1419707930; 9781419707933
                    LC 2013017135

This book is a love story between two high school graduates. "Poised and accomplished, Wren has always done what her parents have expected of her, while Charlie is a foster child, self-conscious about his often unpleasant upbringing, but fiercely protective of his current family." The story is an "account of two young people whose insecurities and personal histories weigh on the romance they work to build with each other." (Publishers Weekly)

Peace, love, and baby ducks. Dutton Children's Books 2009 292p $16.99; pa $8.99
Grades: 8 9 10 11 12

    1. Sisters -- Fiction 2. Atlanta (Ga.) -- Fiction
    ISBN 978-0-525-47743-3; 0-525-47743-8; 978-0-14-241527-6 pa; 0-14-241527-8 pa
                    LC 2008-34221

Fifteen-year-old Carly's summer volunteer experience makes her feel more real than her life of privilege in Atlanta ever did, but her younger sister starts high school pretending to be what she is not, and both find their relationships suffering.

"Myracle empathetically explores issues of socioeconomic class, sibling rivalry, and parental influence in a story that is deeper and more nuanced than the title and cutesy cover." Booklist

Shine. Amulet Books 2011 359p $16.95
Grades: 10 11 12

    1. Friendship -- Fiction 2. Hate crimes -- Fiction 3. LGBT youth -- Fiction 4. North Carolina -- Fiction
    ISBN 0-8109-8417-2; 978-0-8109-8417-2
                    LC 2010-45017

When her best friend falls victim to a vicious hate crime, sixteen-year-old Cat sets out to discover the culprits in her small North Carolina town.

"Readers will find themselves thinking about Cat's complicated rural community long after the mystery has been solved." Publ Wkly

ttyl Harry N Abrams 2014 182p $8.95
Grades: 7 8 9 10 11 12

    1. Friendship -- Fiction 2. Interpersonal relations -- Fiction 3. High Schools -- Fiction

"It's time for a new generation of readers to discover the phenomenally bestselling and beloved series, told entirely in messages and texts. With a fresh look and updated cultural references, the notorious list-topping series is ready for the iPhone generation. First published in 2004 (holy moly!), ttyl and its sequels follow the ups and downs of high school for the winsome threesome, three very different but very close friends: wild Maddie (mad maddie), bubbly Angela (SnowAngel), and reserved Zoe (zoegirl)..." (Publisher's Note)

"Told entirely in instant messages, this modern epistolary tale prompts both tears and LOL (laughing out loud). Best buds SnowAngel (Angela), zoegirl (Zoe), and mad maddie (Maddie) IM with one another constantly when not in school. Tenth grade is tough, with obnoxious trendy classmates, unfair parents, and sex. Friends can help each other get through the year, but only if they manage to stay together...But best friends are always there for each other, and a series of emergencies pushes them further apart and then brings them back together, closer than ever." Kirkus

    Other titles in the series are:
    ttfn (2006)
    l8r, g8r (2007)
    yolo (2014)

Yolo. Lauren Myracle. Amulet Books 2014 208 p.
Grades: 9 10 11 12

    1. Best friends -- Fiction 2. Colleges and universities -- Fiction 3. Friendship -- Fiction 4. Instant messaging -- Fiction 5. Interpersonal relations -- Fiction 6. Teenage girls -- Fiction
    1419708716; 9781419708718, $16.95
                    LC 2014014986

"It's freshman year of college for the winsome threesome, and *everything* is different. For one, the best friends are facing their first semester apart. Way, way apart. Maddie's in California, Zoe's in Ohio, and Angela's back in Georgia." (Publisher's note)

"The story, which can stand independently from the rest of the Internet Girls series, offers readers realistic, engaging, and provocative perspectives on scary first semesters away from home and sage advice about drinking, partying, and shutting down socially, all without ever leaving the perfectly crafted text-message flow." Booklist

Na, An

    ★ A **step** from heaven. Front St. 2000 156p $15.95
Grades: 7 8 9 10

    1. Family life -- Fiction 2. Korean Americans -- Fiction
    ISBN 1-88691-058-8
                    LC 00-41083

Michael L. Printz Award, 2002

A young Korean girl and her family find it difficult to learn English and adjust to life in America

"This isn't a quick read, especially at the beginning when the child is trying to decipher American words and customs, but the coming-of-age drama will grab teens and make them think of their own conflicts between home and outside. As in the best writing, the particulars make the story universal." Booklist

★ **Wait** for me. Putnam 2006 169p hardcover o.p. pa $7.99

Grades: 8 9 10 11 12

    1. Deaf -- Fiction 2. Sisters -- Fiction 3. Korean Americans -- Fiction 4. Mother-daughter relationship -- Fiction

ISBN 0-399-24275-9; 0-14-240918-9 pa

LC 2005-30931

As her senior year in high school approaches, Mina yearns to find her own path in life but working at the family business, taking care of her little sister, and dealing with her mother's impossible expectations are as stifling as the southern California heat, until she falls in love with a man who offers a way out.

"This is a well-crafted tale, sensitively told. . . . The mother-daughter conflict will resonate with teens of any culture who have wrestled parents for the right to choose their own paths." Bull Cent Child Books

Nader, Elisa

Escape from Eden; Elisa Nader. Adams Media Corp 2013 272 p. $17.95

Grades: 9 10 11 12

    1. Cults -- Fiction 2. Escapes -- Fiction 3. Christian fundamentalism -- Fiction

ISBN 1440563926; 9781440563928

"At 16, Mia is disenchanted with Edenton, the religious cult compound in the South American jungle where she has lived for six years. She learns to hide her disloyal thoughts from the Reverend and his potential spies, but it is difficult to avoid Edenton's subtle influence on her mind. Only when Mia is called to the community's "Prayer Circle"—actually a forced prostitution scheme perpetrated by the so-called spiritual leader—does she grasp the truth about their commune...The brutal, horrific climactic scene is far less credible as those building up to it. Still, many readers will find Mia's first-person narrative a riveting read, from the slow burn of her growing sexual awareness to the many fast-paced action scenes." (Booklist)

Nadin, Joanna

Wonderland. Candlewick Press 2011 208p $16.99

Grades: 9 10 11 12

    1. Friendship -- Fiction 2. Bereavement -- Fiction 3. Great Britain -- Fiction 4. Conduct of life -- Fiction 5. Father-daughter relationship -- Fiction

ISBN 978-0-7636-4846-6; 0-7636-4846-9

LC 2010-38715

Sixteen-year-old Jude hopes to finally become who she wants to be, away from tiny Churchtown and the father who cannot get over her mother's death, by joining a prestigious drama program in London until Stella, her wild childhood friend, returns and causes Jude to wonder if she really wants to be the center of attention, after all.

"This is more of a psychological thriller than a book about bad girls. Once they reach this surprising disclosure, teens will think about the book differently and maybe even read it again." SLJ

Nadol, Jen

The **mark**. Bloomsbury 2010 228p $16.99

Grades: 9 10 11 12

    1. Death -- Fiction 2. Kansas -- Fiction 3. Orphans -- Fiction 4. Clairvoyance -- Fiction 5. Fate and fatalism -- Fiction

ISBN 978-1-59990-431-3; 1-59990-431-4

LC 2009-16974

While in Kansas living with an aunt she never knew existed and taking a course in philosophy, sixteen-year-old Cass struggles to learn what, if anything, she should do with her ability to see people marked to die within a day's time.

"Nadol's story is more than a modern take on the Cassandra story of Greek myth, and the author uses her protagonist's moral torment (and a philosophy course she takes) to touch on schools of philosophical thought, from Aristotle to Plato. As in life, there are no tidy endings, but the engrossing narration and realistic characters create a deep, lingering story." Publ Wkly

Followed by The vision (2011)

The **vision**. Bloomsbury Children's Books 2011 232p $16.99

Grades: 9 10 11 12

    1. Death -- Fiction 2. Orphans -- Fiction 3. Illinois -- Fiction 4. Clairvoyance -- Fiction 5. Fate and fatalism -- Fiction 6. Undertakers and undertaking -- Fiction

ISBN 978-1-59990-597-6

LC 2011004927

Sequel to The mark (2010)

Seventeen-year-old Cassie, now working in a funeral home on the outskirts of Chicago, continues to try to learn about death and her ability to identify people who will soon die, but her efforts to get help from others like herself only prove that she is on her own.

"For those willing to ponder difficult questions and appreciate the opportunity to come to their own conclusions, Cassie's visions will resonate long after the last page is turned." Kirkus

Naidoo, Beverley

★ **Burn** my heart. HarperCollins 2009 209p $15.99; lib bdg $16.89

Grades: 7 8 9 10 11 12

    1. Kenya -- Fiction 2. Friendship -- Fiction 3. Race relations -- Fiction

ISBN 978-0-06-143297-2; 0-06-143297-0; 978-0-06-143298-9 lib bdg; 0-06-143298-9 lib bdg

LC 2008-928322

First published 2007 in the United Kingdom

This "is an interesting story of which few people will be aware but might wish to know more. This solid novel would be a good multicultural addition to a teen collection." Voice Youth Advocates

Namioka, Lensey

Mismatch; a novel. Delacorte Press 2006 217p $15.95; lib bdg $17.99

Grades: 7 8 9 10

    1. Prejudices -- Fiction 2. Chinese Americans -- Fiction 3. Japanese Americans -- Fiction 4. Dating (Social customs) -- Fiction

ISBN 0-385-73183-3; 0-385-90220-4 lib bdg

Their families clash when Andy, a Japanese-American teenaged boy, starts dating Sue, a Chinese-American teenaged girl.

"A story that is current, relevant, and upbeat." SLJ

Nance, Andrew

Daemon Hall; [by] Andrew Nance; with illustrations by Coleman Polhemus. Henry Holt 2007 259p $16.95

Grades: 7 8 9 10

1. Horror fiction 2. Authorship -- Fiction

ISBN 978-0-8050-8171-8; 0-8050-8171-2

LC 2006-31044

Famous horror story writer R. U. Tremblin comes to the town of Maplewood to hold a short story writing contest, offering the five finalists the chance to spend what turns out to be a terrifying—and deadly—night with him in a haunted house.

"Readers looking for creepy chills and thrills will find plenty of satisfaction in this fast-paced book." Booklist

Return to Daemon Hall: evil roots; with illustrations by Coleman Polhemus. Henry Holt 2011 240p il $16.99

Grades: 7 8 9 10

1. Horror fiction 2. Authors -- Fiction 3. Contests -- Fiction 4. Authorship -- Fiction 5. Storytelling -- Fiction

ISBN 978-0-8050-8748-2; 0-8050-8748-6

LC 2010048609

Sequel to: Daemon Hall (2007)

Wade and Demarius go to author Ian Tremblin's home as judges of the second writing contest but soon are mysteriously transported to Daemon Hall, where they and the three finalists must tell—and act out—the stories each has written.

"Polhemus' stark artwork builds the mood, with heavy lines and crosshatching complementing the campfire nature of the tales." Kirkus

Nanji, Shenaaz

Child of dandelions. Front Street 2008 214p $17.95

Grades: 7 8 9 10 11 12

1. Generals 2. Presidents 3. Uganda -- Fiction 4. Family life -- Fiction 5. East Indians -- Fiction

ISBN 978-1-93242-593-2; 1-93242-593-4

LC 2007-31576

In Uganda in 1972, fifteen-year-old Sabine and her family, wealthy citizens of Indian descent, try to preserve their normal life during the ninety days allowed by President Idi Amin for all foreign Indians to leave the country, while soldiers and others terrorize them and people disappear.

"This is an absorbing story rich with historical detail and human dynamics." Bull Cent Child Books

Napoli, Donna Jo

Alligator bayou. Wendy Lamb Books 2009 280p $16.99; lib bdg $19.99

Grades: 6 7 8 9 10

1. Uncles -- Fiction 2. Prejudices -- Fiction 3. Country

life -- Fiction 4. Italian Americans -- Fiction

ISBN 978-0-385-74654-0; 0-385-74654-7; 978-0-385-90891-7 lib bdg; 0-385-90891-1 lib bdg

LC 2008-14504

Fourteen-year-old Calogero Scalise and his Sicilian uncles and cousin live in small-town Louisiana in 1898, when Jim Crow laws rule and anti-immigration sentiment is strong, so despite his attempts to be polite and to follow American customs, disaster dogs his family at every turn.

"Napoli's skillful pacing and fascinating detail combine in a gripping story that sheds cold, new light on Southern history and on the nature of racial prejudice." Booklist

Beast. Atheneum Bks. for Young Readers 2000 260p hardcover o.p. pa $8

Grades: 7 8 9 10

1. Fairy tales 2. Iran -- Fiction

ISBN 0-689-83589-2; 0-689-87005-1 pa

LC 99-89923

"The reader is immersed in the imagery and spirituality of ancient Persia. . . . Although Napoli uses Farsi (Persian) and Arabic words in the text (there is a glossary), this only adds to the texture and richness of her remarkable piece of writing." Book Rep

★ **Bound**. Atheneum Books for Young Readers 2004 186p hardcover o.p. pa $5.99

Grades: 8 9 10 11 12

1. China -- Fiction 2. Sex role -- Fiction

ISBN 0-689-86175-3; 0-689-86178-8 pa

LC 2004-365

In a novel based on Chinese Cinderella tales, fourteen-year-old stepchild Xing-Xing endures a life of neglect and servitude, as her stepmother cruelly mutilates her own child's feet so that she alone might marry well

The author "fleshes out and enriches the story with well-rounded characters and with accurate information about a specific time and place in Chinese history; the result is a dramatic and masterful retelling." SLJ

The **great** god Pan. Wendy Lamb Bks. 2003 149p $15.95; lib bdg $17.99

Grades: 7 8 9 10

1. Pan (Greek deity) -- Fiction 2. Classical mythology -- Fiction

ISBN 0-385-32777-3; 0-385-90120-8 lib bdg

LC 2002-13139

A retelling of the Greek myths about Pan, both goat and god, whose reed flute frolicking leads him to a meeting with Iphigenia, a human raised as the daughter of King Agamemnon and Queen Clytemnestra

"Filling in gaps that appear in other myths about Pan and Iphigenia, Napoli creates a novel filled with breathtaking language about nature, music, and desire. Teen readers will swoon." Booklist

Hush; an Irish princess' tale. Atheneum Books for Young Readers 2007 308p $16.99

Grades: 8 9 10 11 12

1. Ireland -- Fiction 2. Slavery -- Fiction 3. Princesses

-- Fiction 4. Middle Ages -- Fiction

ISBN 978-0-689-86176-5; 0-689-86176-1

LC 2007-2676

Fifteen-year-old Melkorka, an Irish princess, is kidnapped by Russian slave traders and not only learns how to survive but to challenge some of the brutality of her captors, who are fascinated by her apparent muteness and the possibility that she is enchanted.

This is a "powerful survival story. . . . Napoli does not shy from detailing practices that will make readers wince . . . and the Russian crew repeatedly gang-rapes an older captive. . . . The tension over Mel's hopes for escape paces this story like a thriller." Publ Wkly

The magic circle. Dutton Children's Bks. 1993 118p hardcover o.p. pa $4.99

Grades: 9 10 11 12

1. Fairy tales 2. Witchcraft -- Fiction

ISBN 0-525-45127-7; 0-14-037439-6 pa

LC 92-27008

After learning sorcery to become a healer, a good-hearted woman is turned into a witch by evil spirits and she fights their power until her encounter with Hansel and Gretel years later

"The strength of Napoli's writing and the clarity of her vision make this story fresh and absorbing. A brilliantly conceived and beautifully executed novel that is sure to be appreciated by thoughtful readers." SLJ

The smile. Dutton Children's Books 2008 260p $17.99

Grades: 7 8 9 10

1. Artists -- Fiction 2. Renaissance -- Fiction

ISBN 978-0-525-47999-4; 0-525-47999-6

LC 2007-48522

In Renaissance Italy, Elisabetta longs for romance, and when Leonardo da Vinci introduces her to Guiliano de Medici, whose family rules Florence but is about to be deposed, she has no inkling of the romance—and sorrow—that will ensue.

"Napoli skillfully draws readers into the vibrant settings . . . with tangible, sensory details that enliven the novel's intriguing references to history and art. Elisabetta's strength and individuality . . . will captivate readers." Booklist

Storm; Donna Jo Napoli. Simon & Schuster. 2014 350p $17.99

Grades: 8 9 10 11 12

1. Animals -- Fiction 2. Floods -- Fiction 3. Noah's ark -- Fiction 4. Survival after airplane accidents, shipwrecks, etc. -- Fiction

ISBN: 1481403028; 9781481403023

LC 2013026808

National Jewish Book Award: Children's and Young Adult (2014)

This young adult novel, by Donna Jo Napoli, is a re-imagining of the Noah flood myth. "After days of downpour, her family lost, Sebah . . . is tempted just to die in the flames rather than succumb to a slow, watery death. Instead, she and her companion, a boy named Aban, build a raft. What they find on the stormy seas is beyond imagining: a gigantic

ark. But Sebah does not know what she'll find on board, and Aban is too weak to leave their raft." (Publisher's note)

"Exhausted and grief-stricken, Sebah finds herself in a cage with a pair of bonobos, with whom she soon bonds. The characters that Napoli creates to flesh out her retelling of the classic story add both veracity and depth.." Horn Book

The wager. Henry Holt 2010 262p il $16.99

Grades: 8 9 10 11 12

1. Fairy tales 2. Devil -- Fiction

ISBN 978-0-8050-8781-9; 0-8050-8781-8

LC 2009-23436

Having lost everything in a tidal wave in 1169 Sicily, nineteen-year-old Don Giovanni makes a simple-sounding wager with a stranger he recognizes as the devil but, while desperate enough to surrender his pride and good looks for three years, he is not willing to give up his soul.

"Evocative of Hermann Hesse's Siddhartha, this marvelous story is well told, and the rich, sophisticated language will grip skilled readers." SLJ

Nayeri, Daniel

Another Faust; [by] Daniel & Dina Nayeri. Candlewick Press 2009 387p $16.99

Grades: 9 10 11 12

1. School stories 2. Devil -- Fiction 3. Supernatural -- Fiction 4. New York (N.Y.) -- Fiction

ISBN 978-0-7636-3707-1; 0-7636-3707-6

LC 2008-940873

Years after vanishing, five teens reappear with a strange governess, and when they enter New York City's most prestigious high school, they soar to suspicious heights with the help of their benefactor's extraordinary "gifts."

"The writing is clever and stylish . . . It's an absorbing, imaginative read, with a tense climax." Publ Wkly

Followed by Another Pan (2010)

Another Pan; [by] Daniel & Dina Nayeri. Candlewick Press 2010 393p $16.99

Grades: 9 10 11 12

1. Fantasy fiction 2. Peter Pan (Fictional character)

ISBN 978-0-7636-3712-5

LC 2010-6606

Companion volume to Another Faust (2009)

While attending an elite prep school where their father is a professor, Wendy and John Darling discover a book which opens the door to other worlds, to Egyptian myths long thought impossible, and to the home of an age-old darkness.

"Teens who like their fantasy layered and with multifaceted characters will enjoy this thought-provoking read." SLJ

Naylor, Phyllis Reynolds

Alice in April. Atheneum Pubs. 1993 164p hardcover o.p. pa $5.99

Grades: 5 6 7 8

1. School stories 2. Family life -- Fiction

ISBN 0-689-31805-7; 978-1-442-42757-0 pa; 1-442-42757-4 pa

LC 92-17016

While trying to survive seventh grade, Alice discovers that turning thirteen will make her the Woman of the House at home, so she starts a campaign to get more appreciated for taking care of her father and older brother

"Deftly written dialogue and an empathetic tone neatly balance substantial themes with plain good fun." Publ Wkly

Alice in rapture, sort of. Atheneum Pubs. 1989 166p hardcover o.p. pa $5.99

Grades: 5 6 7 8

    1. Family life -- Fiction

    ISBN 0-689-31466-3; 1-442-42362-5 pa

                                         LC 88-8174

The summer before she enters the seventh grade becomes the summer of Alice's first boyfriend, and she discovers that love is about the most mixed-up thing that can possibly happen to you, especially since she has no mother to go to for advice

"A book that is wise, perceptive, and hilarious." SLJ

Faith, hope, and Ivy June. Delacorte Press 2009 280p $16.99; lib bdg $19.99

Grades: 5 6 7 8

    1. School stories

    ISBN 978-0-385-73615-2; 0-385-73615-0; 978-0-385-90588-6 lib bdg; 0-385-90588-2 lib bdg

                                LC 2008-19625

During a student exchange program, seventh-graders Ivy June and Catherine share their lives, homes, and communities, and find that although their lifestyles are total opposites they have a lot in common.

"This finely crafted novel . . . depicts a deep friendship growing slowly through understanding. As both girls wait out tragedies at the book's end, they cling to hope—and each other—in a thoroughly real and unaffected way. Naylor depicts Appalachia with sympathetic realism." Kirkus

Incredibly Alice. Atheneum Books for Young Readers 2011 278p $16.99

Grades: 7 8 9 10

    1. School stories 2. Theater -- Fiction 3. Family life -- Fiction 4. Dating (Social customs) -- Fiction

    ISBN 978-1-4169-7553-3; 1-4169-7553-5

                              LC 2010036982

Maryland teenager Alice McKinley spends her last semester of high school performing in the school play, working on the student paper, worrying about being away from her boyfriend, who will be studying in Spain, and anticipating her future in college.

"Realistic and satisfying, Alice and friends' bittersweet senior year's ending and their preparations for adulthood's exciting and intimidating world will resonate with any high school female." Voice Youth Advocates

Intensely Alice. Atheneum Books for Young Readers 2009 269p $16.99; pa $6.99

Grades: 7 8 9 10

    1. Summer -- Fiction 2. Maryland -- Fiction

    ISBN 978-1-4169-7551-9; 1-4169-7551-9; 978-1-4169-7554-0 pa; 1-4169-7554-3 pa

                              LC 2008-49047

During the summer between her junior and senior years of high school, Maryland teenager Alice McKinley volunteers at a local soup kitchen, tries to do "something wild"

without getting arrested, and wonders if her trip to Chicago to visit boyfriend Patrick will result in a sleepover.

"As candid, funny, and touching as the rest of the series." Booklist

★ **Reluctantly** Alice. Atheneum Pubs. 1991 182p $16; pa $4.99

Grades: 7 8 9 10

    1. School stories 2. Family life -- Fiction

    ISBN 0-689-31681-X; 0-689-81688-X pa

                              LC 90-37956

Alice experiences the joys and embarrassments of seventh grade while advising her father and older brother on their love lives

"Naylor combines laugh-out-loud scenes with moments of sudden gentleness. . . . The characters are complex, the dialogue is droll, the junior high world authentic." Booklist

    Other titles about Alice are:

    Achingly Alice (1998)

    Alice alone (2001)

    Alice in-between (1994)

    Alice in lace (1996)

    Alice in the know (2006)

    Alice on her way (2005)

    Alice on the outside (1999)

    Alice the brave (1995)

    All but Alice (1992)

    Almost Alice (2008)

    Intensely Alice (2009)

    Dangerously Alice (2007)

    The grooming of Alice (2000)

    Including Alice (2004)

    Outrageously Alice (1997)

    Patiently Alice (2003)

    Simply Alice (2002)

Neff, Henry H.

The **hound** of Rowan. Random House 2007 414p il (The tapestry) $17.99; lib bdg $20.99; pa $6.99

Grades: 6 7 8 9

    1. School stories 2. Magic -- Fiction

    ISBN 978-0-375-83894-1; 0-375-83894-5; 978-0-375-93894-8 lib bdg; 0-375-93894-4 lib bdg; 978-0-375-83895-8 pa; 0-375-83895-3 pa

                              LC 2006-20970

After glimpsing a hint of his destiny in a mysterious tapestry, twelve-year-old Max McDaniels becomes a student at Rowan Academy, where he trains in "mystics and combat" in preparation for war with an ancient enemy that has been kidnapping children like him.

"Max's intelligence and goodhearted nature give the story a solid emotional core even as the surprising twists and turns keep the pages turning." Voice Youth Advocates

    Other titles in this series are:

    The second siege (2008)

    The fiend and the forge (2011)

Nelson, Blake

Destroy all cars. Scholastic Press 2009 218p $17.99

Grades: 7 8 9 10

1. School stories 2. Ecology -- Fiction 3. Social action -- Fiction

ISBN 978-0-545-10474-6; 0-545-10474-2

LC 2008-34850

Through assignments for English class, seventeen-year-old James Hoff rants against consumerism and his classmates' apathy, puzzles over his feelings for his ex-girlfriend, and expresses disdain for his emotionally-distant parents.

Nelson "offers an elegant and bittersweet story of a teenager who is finding his voice and trying to make meaning in a world he often finds hopeless." Publ Wkly

Recovery Road. Scholastic Press 2011 310p $17.99

Grades: 9 10 11 12

1. Alcoholism -- Fiction 2. Drug abuse -- Fiction 3. Drug addicts -- Rehabilitation -- Fiction

ISBN 978-0-545-10729-7; 0-545-10729-6

LC 2010-31288

"Madeline is sent away to Spring Meadows to help with a drinking and rage problem she has. It's a pretty intense place, but there is the weekly movie night in town--where Madeline meets Stewart, who's at another rehab place nearby. They fall for each other during a really crazy time in their lives. Madeline gets out and tries to get back on her feet, waiting for Stewart to join her. When he does, though, it's not the ideal recovery world Madeline dreamed of." (Publisher's note)

The author "gives a hard, honest appraisal of addiction, its often-fatal consequences, and the high probability of relapse. This is an important story that pulls no punches." Publ Wkly

Rock star, superstar; by Blake Nelson. Viking 2004 229p hardcover o.p. pa $6.99

Grades: 9 10 11 12

1. Musicians -- Fiction 2. Rock music -- Fiction

ISBN 0-670-05933-1; 0-14-240574-4 pa

LC 2003-27556

When Pete, a talented bass player, moves from playing in the school jazz band to playing in a popular rock group, he finds the experience exhilarating even as his new fame jeopardizes his relationship with girlfriend Margaret.

"A brilliant, tender, funny, and utterly believable novel about music and relationships. . . . Pete is one of the best male protagonists in recent YA fiction and the other characters are equally strong." SLJ

They came from below. Tor 2007 299p $17.95

Grades: 7 8 9 10

1. Beaches -- Fiction 2. Supernatural -- Fiction 3. Marine pollution -- Fiction

ISBN 978-0-7653-1423-9; 0-7653-1423-1

LC 2007-09542

While vacationing on Cape Cod, best friends Emily, age sixteen, and Reese, seventeen, meet Steve and Dave, who seem too good to be true, and whose presence turns out to be related to a dire threat of global pollution.

"Offering wittiness, suspense and ideologies borrowed from Eastern religions, Nelson reaches a new level of depth and creativity with this intriguing depiction of one very weird summer." Publ Wkly

Nelson, James

On the volcano. G.P. Putnam's Sons 2011 275p $16.99

Grades: 7 8 9 10

1. Violence -- Fiction 2. Volcanoes -- Fiction 3. Wilderness areas -- Fiction 4. Frontier and pioneer life -- Fiction

ISBN 978-0-399-25282-2; 0-399-25282-7

LC 2008-53557

In the 1870s, sixteen-year-old Katie has grown up in a remote cabin on the edge of a volcano with her father and their friend Lorraine, the only people she has ever seen, but, after eagerly anticipating it for so long, her first trip into a town ultimately brings tragedy into their lives.

"Nelson has created a moving tale of frontier life. Katie shows tremendous fighting spirit as she deal with the trials in her life. . . . [This] is perfect for historical fiction fans." Voice Youth Advocates

Nelson, Jandy

★ **I'll** give you the sun. Jandy Nelson. Dial Books for Young Readers. 2014 384p $17.99

Grades: 9 10 11 12

1. Artists -- Fiction 2. Death -- Fiction 3. Gays -- Fiction 4. Grief -- Fiction 5. Twins -- Fiction 6. California -- Fiction 7. Love stories

ISBN: 0803734964; 9780803734968

LC 2014001596

Michael L. Printz Award (2015)

Stonewall Honor Book: Children's & Young Adult Literature (2015)

In this novel by Jandy Nelson, "Jude and her twin brother, Noah, are incredibly close. At thirteen, isolated Noah draws constantly and is falling in love with the charismatic boy next door, while daredevil Jude cliff-dives and wears red-red lipstick and does the talking for both of them. But three years later, Jude and Noah are barely speaking. Something has happened to wreck the twins in different and dramatic ways." Publisher's note

"Nelson's prose is replete with moments of stunning emotional clarity, and her characters are as irresistible to the reader as they are to each other," Bulletin Center Child Books

★ **The sky** is everywhere. Dial Books 2010 275p il $17.99

Grades: 9 10 11 12

1. Sisters -- Fiction 2. Musicians -- Fiction 3. Bereavement -- Fiction

ISBN 978-0-8037-3495-1; 0-8037-3495-6

LC 2009-22809

In the months after her sister dies, seventeen-year-old Lennie falls into a love triangle and discovers the strength to follow her dream of becoming a musician.

"This is a heartfelt and appealing tale. Girls who gobble up romantic and/or weep-over fiction will undoubtedly flock to this realistic, sometimes funny, and heartbreaking story." SLJ

"Nelson's prose is replete with moments of stunning emotional clarity, and her characters are as irresistible to the reader as they are to each other," Bulletin Center Child Books

Nelson, Marilyn

American ace. Marilyn Nelson. Dial Books 2016 128 p. Illustration

Grades: 8 9 10 11 12

1. United States. Army Air Forces. Bombardment Group, 477th -- Fiction 2. Family life -- Fiction 3. Fathers and sons -- Fiction 4. Identity -- Fiction 5. Novels in verse 6. Racially mixed people -- Fiction 7. Fathers -- Fiction 8. Family secrets -- Fiction

9780803733053, $17.99; 0803733054

LC 2015000851

In this novel, by Marilyn Nelson, "Connor's grandmother leaves his dad a letter when she dies, and the letter's confession shakes their tight-knit Italian-American family: The man who raised Dad is not his birth father. But the only clues to this birth father's identity are a class ring and a pair of pilot's wings. And so Connor takes it upon himself to investigate. What Connor discovers will lead him and his father to a new, richer understanding of race, identity, and each other." (Publisher's note)

"The author's meticulous verse is the perfect vehicle to convey the devastating fragility of racial and familial identity in an America where interracial love is still divided through the problem of the color line. Readers will join Nelson's protagonist in quietly hoping for that healing, too." Kirkus

Nelson, Vaunda Micheaux

No crystal stair; a documentary novel of the life and work of Lewis Michaux, Harlem bookseller. by Vaunda Micheaux Nelson; art work by R. Gregory Christie. Carolrhoda Lab 2012 188p. ill.

Grades: 6 7 8 9 10 11 12

1. Harlem (New York, N.Y.) 2. African American authors 3. Booksellers and bookselling 4. African Americans -- Books and reading 5. Bookstores -- New York (State) -- New York

ISBN 9780761361695

LC 2011021251

Coretta Scott King Author Honor Book (2013)

This "biographical novel presents the life and work of a man whose Harlem bookstore became an intellectual, literary haven for African Americans from 1939 until 1975. [The book proceeds t]hrough alternating voices of actual family members, acquaintances, journalists, and the subject himself, [Lewis] Michaux. . . . Influenced by the nationalism of Marcus Garvey and the intellect of Frederick Douglass, he believed that black people needed to educate themselves . . . [and h]e opened the National Memorial African Bookstore. . . . He accumulated works by black writers and talked to customers and passersby about cultural awareness and self-improvement. His bookstore attracted Harlem residents; civil-rights activists, including Malcolm X and Muhammad Ali; and political attention." (School Libr J)

Neri, G.

Knockout Games. By G. Neri. Carolrhoda Lab 2014 304 p.

Grades: 7 8 9 10

1. Gangs -- Fiction 2. Violence -- Fiction 3. Teenagers -- Fiction

1467732699; 9781467732697, $17.95

LC 2013036855

In this young adult novel by G. Neri, "for Kalvin Barnes, the only thing that comes close to the rush of playing the knockout game is watching videos of the knockout game . . . For a while, Kalvin's knockouts are strangers. For a while, Erica can ignore their suffering in the rush of creativity and Kalvin's attention. Then comes the KO that forces her eyes open, that makes her see what's really happening. No one wins the knockout game." (Publisher's note)

"Kalvin may seem like every parent's worst nightmare for their daughter, but the author draws him with a complexity that helps illustrate the larger themes being explored. Neri's main concern is the 'post-racial' urban landscape, raising many talking points while letting readers come to their own conclusions. Harsh and relentless, a tough but worthy read." Kirkus

Ness, Patrick, 1971-

★ **And** the ocean was our sky. Patrick Ness ; illustrated by Rovina Cai. HarperTeen 2018 160 p. Illustration; Color

Grades: 7 8 9 10 11 12

1. Ships -- Fiction; 2. Human-animal relationships -- Fiction; 3. Whales -- Fiction

9780062860729, $19.99

LC 2018938254

This book, by Patrick Ness, illustrated by Rovina Cia, "asks harrowing questions about power, loyalty, obsession, and the monsters we make of others. With harpoons strapped to their backs, the proud whales of Bathsheba's pod live for the hunt, fighting in the ongoing war against the world of men. When they attack a ship bobbing on the surface of the Abyss, they expect to find easy prey. Instead, they find the trail of a myth, a monster, perhaps the devil himself." (Publisher's note)

Ness "mines Moby-Dick for incidents and motifs, pitting men against whales in a futuristic alternate world.... The story, though far shorter than its progenitor, conjures similar allegorical weight by pairing the narrative's rolling cadences with powerful, shadowy illustrations featuring looming whales, an upside-down ship in full sail, and swarms of red-eyed sharks, all amid dense swirls of water and blood." Kirkus

The **Ask** and the Answer; a novel. Candlewick Press 2009 519p (Chaos walking) $18.99

Grades: 8 9 10 11 12

1. Science fiction 2. Telepathy -- Fiction 3. Space colonies -- Fiction 4. Social problems -- Fiction

ISBN 978-0-7636-4490-1; 0-7636-4490-0

LC 2009-7329

Sequel to: The knife of never letting go (2008)

Alternate chapters follow teenagers Todd and Viola, who become separated as the Mayor's oppressive new regime takes power in New Prentisstown, a space colony where residents can hear each other's thoughts.

"Provocative questions about gender bias, racism, the meaning of war and the price of peace are thoughtfully threaded throughout a breathless, often violent plot peopled with heartbreakingly real characters." Kirkus

Followed by: Monsters of men (2010)

★ The **knife** of never letting go. Candlewick Press 2008 479p (Chaos walking) $18.99

Grades: 8 9 10 11 12

1. Boys -- Fiction 2. Science fiction 3. Dystopian fiction 4. Psychics -- Fiction 5. Telepathy -- Fiction 6. Space colonies -- Fiction

ISBN 978-0-7636-3931-0; 0-7636-3931-1

LC 2007-52334

Pursued by power-hungry Prentiss and mad minister Aaron, young Todd and Viola set out across New World searching for answers about his colony's true past and seeking a way to warn the ship bringing hopeful settlers from Old World.

"This troubling, unforgettable opener to the Chaos Walking trilogy is a penetrating look at the ways in which we reveal ourselves to one another, and what it takes to be a man in a society gone horribly wrong." Booklist

Monsters of men. Candlewick Press 2010 603p (Chaos walking) $18.99; pa $9.99

Grades: 8 9 10 11 12

1. War stories 2. Science fiction 3. Telepathy -- Fiction 4. Space colonies -- Fiction 5. Social problems -- Fiction

ISBN 978-0-7636-4751-3; 0-7636-4751-9; 978-0-7636-5665-2 pa; 0-7636-5665-8 pa

Sequel to: The Ask and the Answer (2009)

As a world-ending war surges to life around them, Todd and Viola face monstrous decisions, questioning all they have ever known as they try to step back from the darkness and find the best way to achieve peace.

"The Chaos Walking trilogy comes to a powerful conclusion in this grueling but triumphant tale." Publ Wkly

★ A **monster** calls; a novel. Candlewick Press 2011 204p il $15.99

Grades: 6 7 8 9 10

1. School stories 2. Cancer -- Fiction 3. Monsters -- Fiction 4. Great Britain -- Fiction 5. Loss (Psychology) -- Fiction 6. Mother-son relationship -- Fiction

ISBN 978-0-7636-5559-4; 0-7636-5559-7

LC 2010040741

"Conor O'Malley is struggling with his mother's illness and terrorized by nightmares which seem to come to life. The monster who visits him tells Conor three allegorical stories, each time instructing Conor that he will have to tell his own truth in the fourth and final story. Conor's daily life and "truth" are even more haunting than the monster." (Library Media Connection)

This is a "profoundly moving, expertly crafted tale of unaccountable loss. . . . A singular masterpiece, exceptionally well-served by Kay's atmospheric and ominous illustrations." Publ Wkly

More than this; Patrick Ness. Candlewick Press 2013 480 p. $19.99

Grades: 9 10 11 12

1. Death -- Fiction 2. Dystopian fiction

ISBN 0763662585; 9780763662585

LC 2013943065

In this book, "teenage Seth is experiencing his own death in painful detail. In the next chapter, he wakes up physically weak, covered in bandages and strange wounds, and wonders if he is in Hell or the future or somewhere else entirely. . . . He is plagued by intense flashbacks of his life before he died. . . . Upon discovering two other young people . . . Seth begins to learn the Matrix-like truth about what has happened to the rest of humanity." (School Library Journal)

★ **Release**. Patrick Ness. HarperTeen 2017 277 p.

Grades: 9 10 11 12

1. Gay teenagers -- Fiction; 2. Interpersonal relations -- Fiction; 3. Self-acceptance -- Fiction; 4. Bildungsromans

9780062403216; 9780062403193, $17.99

LC 2017934821

In this novel, by Patrick Ness, "Adam Thorn doesn't know it yet, but today will change his life. Between his religious family, a deeply unpleasant ultimatum from his boss, and his own unrequited love for his sort-of ex, Enzo, it seems as though Adam's life is falling apart. At least he has two people to keep him sane: his new boyfriend . . .and his best friend, Angela.... [A] raw, darkly funny, and deeply affecting story about the courage it takes to live your truth." (Publisher's note)

"Part character study, part reckoning, this is a painful, magical gem of a novel that, even when it perplexes, will rip the hearts right out of its readers." Booklist

★ The **rest** of us just live here. Patrick Ness. HarperTeen 2015 336 p.

Grades: 9 10 11 12

1. Teenagers -- Fiction 2. High schools -- Fiction 3. Zombies -- Fiction

0062403168; 9780062403162, $17.99

LC 2014959934

This young adult novel, by Patrick Ness, "reminds us that there are many different types of remarkable. What if you aren't the Chosen One? The one who's supposed to fight the zombies, or the soul-eating ghosts, or whatever the heck this new thing is, with the blue lights and the death? What if you're like Mikey? Who just wants to graduate and go to prom and maybe finally work up the courage to ask Henna out before someone goes and blows up the high school." (Publisher's note)

"The diverse cast of characters is multidimensional and memorable, and the depiction of teen sexuality is refreshingly matter-of-fact. Magical pillars of light and zombie deer may occasionally drive the action here, but ultimately this novel celebrates the everyday heroism of teens doing the hard work of growing up." Kirkus

Neumeier, Rachel

The **City** in the Lake. Alfred A. Knopf 2008 304p $15.99; lib bdg $18.99

LIST OF FICTIONAL WORKS

Grades: 8 9 10 11 12

    1. Fantasy fiction 2. Magic -- Fiction
ISBN 978-0-375-84704-2; 0-375-84704-9; 978-0-375-94704-9 lib bdg; 0-375-94704-3 lib bdg

                    LC 2008-08941

Seventeen-year-old Timou, who is learning to be a mage, must save her mysterious, magical homeland, The Kingdom, from a powerful force that is trying to control it.

    "Neumeier structures her story around archetypal fantasy elements. . . . It's the poetic, shimmering language and fascinating unfolding of worlds that elevates this engrossing story beyond its formula." Booklist

The **keeper** of the mist. Rachel Neumeier. Alfred A. Knopf 2016 400 p.

Grades: 7 8 9 10 11 12

    1. Fantasy 2. Kings, queens, rulers, etc. -- Fiction 3. Magic -- Fiction 4. Kings and rulers -- Fiction 5. Fantasy fiction
9780553509281; 9780553509298, $20.99

                    LC 2015000547

In this book, by Rachel Neumeier, "Keri has been struggling to run her family bakery since her mother passed away. Now the father she barely knew—the Lord of Nimmira—has died, and ancient magic has decreed that she will take his place as the new Lady. The position has never been so dangerous: the mists that hide Nimmira from its vicious, land-hungry neighbors have failed, and Keri's people are visible to strangers for the first time since the mists were put in place generations ago." (Publisher's note)

    "This is a beautifully written story that emphasizes intelligence and diplomacy. Recommend to fans of Patricia Wrede and Tamora Pierce, as well as lovers of traditional fantasy." SLJ

★ The **white** road of the moon. Rachel Neumeier. Alfred A. Knopf 2017 376 p. Map

Grades: 7 8 9 10 11 12

    1. Psychic ability -- Fiction; 2. Ghost stories; 3. Runaway teenagers -- Fiction; 4. Aunts -- Fiction
0553509322; 9780553509342; 9780553509328, $17.99

                    LC 2017288569

In this novel, by Rachel Neumeier, "imagine you live with your aunt, who hates you so much she's going to sell you into a dreadful apprenticeship. Imagine you run away before that can happen. Imagine that you can see ghosts -- and talk with the dead. People like you are feared, even shunned. Now imagine...the first people you encounter after your escape are a mysterious stranger and a ghost boy, who seem to need you desperately." (Publisher's note)

    "A richly rewarding stand-alone story evoking far more color than its titular tint might suggest." Kirkus

Nicholson, William

    Seeker. Harcourt 2006 413p (Noble warriors) $17; pa $7.95

Grades: 7 8 9 10

    1. Fantasy fiction
ISBN 978-0-15-205768-8; 0-15-205768-4; 978-0-15-205866-1 pa; 0-15-205866-4 pa
    LC 2005-17171

"Seeker, Morning Star, and Wildman are three teens who hope to join the Nomana, a society of noble warriors and worshippers of the All and Only (the god who makes all things). . . . Conjuring up a plan to prove their worth, this motley trio plays a key role in foiling the murderous plans of the royalty in a nearby town." Bull Cent Child Books

    "The classic coming-of-age tale is combined with a rich setting of cold villains, strange powers, and disturbing warriors." Voice Youth Advocates

    Other titles in this series are:
Jango (2007)
Noman (2008)

Nielsen, Susin

    ★ **Optimists** die first. Susin Nielsen. Wendy Lamb Books 2017 228 p.

Grades: 7 8 9 10 11 12

    1. Art therapy -- Fiction; 2. Emotional problems of teenagers -- Fiction; 3. Fear -- Fiction; 4. Friendship -- Fiction; 5. High school students -- Fiction; 6. Love in adolescence -- Fiction; 7. Sisters -- Death -- Fiction; 8. Romance fiction
9780553496901; 9780553496918, $20.99; 9780553496932; 9780553496925

                    LC 2016014407

In this book, by Susin Nielsen, "sixteen-year-old Petula de Wilde is anything but wild. A former crafting fiend with a happy life, Petula shut herself off from the world after a family tragedy. She sees danger in all the ordinary things.... She knows: life is out to get you. The worst part of her week is her comically lame mandatory art therapy class with a small group of fellow misfits. Then a new boy, Jacob, appears at school and in her therapy group." (Publisher's note)

    "Heartbreaking and hopeful, this is a solid choice for readers looking for a book to make them cry and laugh at the same time." Booklist

The **reluctant** journal of Henry K. Larsen; Susin Nielsen. Tundra Books of Northern New York 2012 243 p. (hardcover) $17.95

Grades: 7 8 9 10 11 12

    1. Bullies 2. Grief 3. Diaries
ISBN 1770493727; 9781770493728

                    LC 2011938782

In this novel, by Susin Nielsen, "thirteen-year-old Henry's happy life abruptly ends when his older brother kills the boy who bullied him in school and then takes his own life. Henry refers to this tragedy as 'IT.' He moves to a new city . . . for a fresh start. To help him cope with IT, Henry's therapist recommends he keep a journal. Henry hates the suggestion but soon finds himself recording his thoughts and feelings constantly, even updating it multiple times per day." (Kirkus Reviews)

We are all made of molecules. By Susin Nielsen. Wendy Lamb Books, an imprint of Random House Children's Books 2015 256 p.

Grades: 9 10 11 12

    1. Bullies -- Fiction 2. Dating (Social customs) -- Fiction 3. Family problems -- Fiction 4. Gay fathers -- Fiction 5. High schools -- Fiction 6. Interpersonal relations -- Fiction 7. Moving, Household -- Fiction 8.

Schools -- Fiction 9. Moving -- Fiction 10. Children of gay parents -- Fiction 11. Family life -- Fiction
0553496875; 9780553496864; 9780553496871, $19.99; 9780553496895

LC 2014017652

In this book, by Susin Nielsen, "Stewart and Ashley are having a tough time adjusting to their new, blended family. Stewart is a highly gifted, socially awkward geek, whereas Ashley deems herself a fashion-conscious, popular girl. . . . Their comfortable lives are thrust together after the death of Stewart's mother and the coming out of Ashley's gay father. All of a sudden, Stewart and his dad must get used to sharing space with Ashley and her mother." (Voice of Youth Advocates)

Niven, Jennifer

All the bright places. Jennifer Niven. Alfred A. Knopf 2015 400 p.

Grades: 9 10 11 12

1. Emotional problems -- Fiction 2. Friendship -- Fiction 3. Suicide -- Fiction 4. Indiana -- Fiction 5. Emotions -- Fiction
0385755880; 9780385755894; 9780385755887, $17.99

LC 2014002238

In this book, by Jennifer Niven, "Theodore Finch is fascinated by death, and he constantly thinks of ways he might kill himself. But each time, something good, no matter how small, stops him. Violet Markey lives for the future, counting the days until graduation, when she can escape her Indiana town and her aching grief in the wake of her sister's recent death. When Finch and Violet meet on the ledge of the bell tower at school, it's unclear who saves whom." (Publisher's note)

"The journey to, through, and past tragedy is romantic and heartbreaking, as characters and readers confront darkness, joy, and the possibilities—and limits—of love in the face of mental illness." Pub Wkly

Includes bibliographical references

★ **Holding** up the universe. Jennifer Niven. Alfred A. Knopf 2016 400 p.

Grades: 9 10 11 12

1. Brain -- Wounds and injuries -- Fiction 2. Love -- Fiction 3. Obesity -- Fiction 4. Prosopagnosia -- Fiction 5. Romance fiction
9780385755924, $17.99

LC 2016003865

In this novel, by Jennifer Niven, "Libby Strout is used to being alone. After her mother's unexpected death, she had eaten her grief away to the point of morbid obesity. . . . Now she is entering high school after years of homeschooling and a medical surgery. . . . Jack Masselin is the resident bad boy . . . [but he] has prosopagnosia, a neurological condition that causes facial blindness. . . . Libby's and Jack's worlds eventually collide after a bullying incident." (Publisher's note)

"More a story about falling in love with yourself than with a romantic interest, this novel will resonate with all readers who've struggled to love themselves." Kirkus

Nix, Garth, 1963-

Clariel: the lost Abhorsen. Garth Nix. HarperCollins. 2014 400p $18.99

Grades: 7 8 9 10

1. Magic -- Fiction 2. Fantasy fiction
ISBN: 006156155X; 9780061561559

LC 2013047958

In this title, part of the author's Old Kingdom fantasy series, "Clariel is the daughter of one of the most notable families in the Old Kingdom, with blood relations to the Abhorsen and, most important, to the King. She dreams of living a simple life but discovers this is hard to achieve when a dangerous Free Magic creature is loose in the city, her parents want to marry her off to a killer, and there is a plot brewing against the old and withdrawn King Orrikan." (Publisher's note)

"Nix's intricate world building reveals more Old Kingdom history and its ever-shifting alliance between the political and magical. Themes of freedom and destiny underpin Clariel's harrowing, bittersweet story, and readers will delight in the telling." Booklist

A confusion of princes; by Garth Nix. HarperTeen 2012 337 p.

Grades: 8 9 10 11 12

1. Science fiction 2. Adventure fiction 3. Inheritance and succession -- Fiction 4. Princes -- Fiction 5. Adventure and adventurers -- Fiction
ISBN 9780060096946; 9780060096953

LC 2011042308

This book tells the story of "a vast empire of 10 million biologically and mechanically augmented princes," where prince "Khemri discovers that--assassination attempts and imperial interference aside--royal life isn't what he'd been led to believe. While on a secret mission, he meets Raine, a young woman who changes his perspective and Khemri begins trying to fulfill his true potential. Aurealis Award-winning author [Garth] Nix develops an empire . . . with an emphasis on house loyalty and political machinations." (Booklist)

Frogkisser! Garth Nix. Scholastic Press 2017 372 p.

Grades: 8 9 10

1. Dogs -- Fiction; 2. Magic -- Fiction; 3. Princesses -- Fiction; 4. Sisters -- Fiction; 5. Wizards -- Fiction
9781338052107; 9781338052084, $18.99

LC 2016026559

Kirkus: Best Books (2016)

In this book, by Garth Nix, "poor Princess Anya. Forced to live with her evil stepmother's new husband, her evil stepstepfather. Plagued with an unfortunate ability to break curses with a magic-assisted kiss. And forced to go on the run when her stepstepfather decides to make the kingdom entirely his own. Aided by a loyal talking dog...and some extraordinarily mischievous wizards, Anya sets off on a Quest that, if she plays it right, will ultimately free her land." (Publisher's note)

"Well-developed characters, an unfailing sense of humor, and polished prose make Nix's uproarious adventure a pleasure to read." Pub Wkly

Goldenhand. Garth Nix. Katherine Tegen Books 2016 368 p. Map (Old Kingdom series)

Grades: 7 8 9 10

1. Fantasy and magic 2. Magic -- Fiction 3. Adventure fiction

9780061561580, $19.99; 9780062216786, $18.99

LC 2016935936

In this book, in the Old Kingdom series by Garth Nix, Lirael lost one of her hands in the binding of Orannis, but now she has a new hand, one of gilded steel and Charter Magic. . . . Lirael returns to her . . . home, the Clayr's Glacier, where she was once a Second Assistant Librarian. There, a young woman from the distant North brings her a message from her long-dead mother. . . . It is a warning about the Witch with No Face. But who is the Witch, and what is she planning? (Publisher's note)

"A masterfully spun tale well worth the yearslong wait." Kirkus

Mister Monday; Keys to the kingdom, book one. Scholastic 2003 361p (Keys to the kingdom) $15.99; pa $5.99

Grades: 6 7 8 9

1. Fantasy fiction

ISBN 0-439-70370-0; 0-439-55123-4 pa

LC 2004-540574

Arthur Penhaligon is supposed to die at a young age, but is saved by a key that is shaped like the minute hand of a clock. The key causes bizarre creatures to come from another realm, bringing with them a plague. A man named Mister Monday will stop at nothing to get the key back. Arthur goes to a mysterious house that only he can see, so that he can learn the truth about himself and the key

"The first in a seven part series for middle graders is every bit as exciting and suspenseful as the author's previous young adult novels." SLJ

Other titles in the Keys to the Kingdom series are:

Grim Tuesday (2004)
Drowned Wednesday (2005)
Sir Thursday (2006)
Lady Friday (2007)
Superior Saturday (2008)
Lord Sunday (2010)

★ **Sabriel.** HarperCollins Pubs. 1996 292p hardcover o.p. pa $7.99

Grades: 7 8 9 10

1. Fantasy fiction

ISBN 0-06-027322-4; 0-06-447183-7 pa

LC 96-1295

First published 1995 in Australia

Sabriel, daughter of the necromancer Abhorsen, must journey into the mysterious and magical Old Kingdom to rescue her father from the Land of the Dead.

"The final battle is gripping, and the bloody cost of combat is forcefully presented. The story is remarkable for the level of originality of the fantastic elements . . . and for the subtle presentation, which leaves readers to explore for themselves the complex structure and significance of the magic elements." Horn Book

Other titles in this series are:

Abhorsen (2003)
Across the wall (2005)
Clariel (2014)

Goldenhand (2016)
Lirael, daughter of the Clayr (2001)
To hold the bridge (2015)

Shade's children. HarperCollins Pubs. 1997 310p $18.99; pa $6.99

Grades: 7 8 9 10

1. Science fiction

ISBN 0-06-027324-0; 0-06-447196-9 pa

LC 97-3841

In a savage postnuclear world, four young fugitives attempt to overthrow the bloodthirsty rule of the Overlords with the help of Shade, their mysterious mentor

"Grim, unusual, and fascinating." Horn Book

★ **To** Hold the Bridge. By Garth Nix. Harpercollins Childrens Books 2015 416 p.

Grades: 6 7 8 9 10 11 12

1. Fantasy fiction 2. Detectives -- Fiction 3. Short stories -- Collections 4. Spirits -- Fiction 5. Vampires -- Fiction

ISBN 0062292528; 9780062292520, $17.99

This book, by Garth Nix, "offers nineteen short stories from every genre of literature including science fiction, paranormal, realistic fiction, mystery, and adventure. Whether writing about vampires, detectives, ancient spirits, or odd jobs, Garth Nix's ability to pull his readers into new worlds is extraordinary." (Publisher's note)

"This anthology's titular novella is a suspenseful prequel to The Old Kingdom Chronicles. Eighteen other tales are organized by theme, with a satisfying variety of genres and tones. Some pay homage to famous speculative fiction (Hellboy; John Carter of Mars), others are companion pieces to Nix's own work; the majority stand alone. Nix's superb world-building and tight plotting are evident here." Horn Book

Noël, Alyson

Radiance. Square Fish 2010 183p pa $7.99

Grades: 5 6 7 8

1. Ghost stories 2. Dead -- Fiction 3. Future life -- Fiction

ISBN 978-0-312-62917-5; 0-312-62917-6

LC 2010015840

After crossing the bridge into the afterlife, a place called Here where the time is always Now, Riley's existence continues in much the same way as when she was alive until she is given the job of Soul Catcher and, together with her teacher Bodhi, returns to earth for her first assignment, a ghost called the Radiant Boy who has been haunting an English castle for centuries and resisted all previous attempts to get him across the bridge.

"Narrating in a contemporary voice with an honest and comfortable cadence, Riley is imperfect, but always likable. . . . In the midst of this wildly fanciful setting, Noël is able to capture with nail-on-the-head accuracy common worries and concerns of today's tweens." SLJ

Other titles in this series are:

Dreamland (2011)
Shimmer (2011)

Unrivaled. By Alyson Noël. Harpercollins Childrens Books 2016 432 p. (A beautiful idols novel)

Grades: 9 10 11 12

1. Fame -- Fiction

0062324527; 9780062324528, $17.99; 9780062324542, $9.99

LC 2015046273

In this book, by Alyson Noel, "Layla Harrison wants to be a reporter. Aster Amirpour wants to be an actress. Tommy Phillips wants to be a guitar hero. But Madison Brooks took destiny and made it her own a long time ago. She's Hollywood's hottest starlet, and the things she did . . . are merely a stain on the pavement. . . . That is, until Layla, Aster, and Tommy find themselves with a VIP invite to . . . Los Angeles . . . and lured into a competition where Madison . . . is the target." (Publisher's note)

"This is a suspenseful, scandalous, and consumable novel that is sure to gain instant fandom and leave readers eagerly awaiting the next installment." SLJ

Other titles in the series are:

Blacklist (2017)

Infamous (2018)

Nolan, Han

Crazy. Harcourt 2010 348p $17

Grades: 7 8 9 10

1. School stories 2. Friendship -- Fiction 3. Bereavement -- Fiction 4. Mental illness -- Fiction 5. Father-son relationship -- Fiction

ISBN 978-0-15-205109-9; 0-15-205109-0

LC 2009-49969

Fifteen-year-old loner Jason struggles to hide father's declining mental condition after his mother's death, but when his father disappears he must confide in the other members of a therapy group he has been forced to join at school.

"Nolan leavens this haunting but hopeful story with spot-on humor and a well-developed cast of characters." Booklist

North, Phoebe

Starglass; by Phoebe North. 1st ed. Simon & Schuster Books for Young Readers 2013 448 p. (hardcover) $17.99

Grades: 7 8 9 10

1. Jews -- Fiction 2. Underground movements -- Fiction 3. Interplanetary voyages -- Fiction 4. Science fiction 5. Insurgency -- Fiction 6. Fathers and daughters -- Fiction

ISBN 1442459530; 9781442459533; 9781442459557

LC 2012021171

In this book by Phoebe North, "[o]n a generation ship that left Earth 500 years ago, a teenager grapples with disillusionment and emotional isolation as her society nears the planet it intends to land on. Terra lives with her harsh, alcoholic father and awaits her adult job assignment . . . from the strict ruling Council." She "discovers a secret rebellion aboard the Asherah." (Kirkus Reviews)

Northrop, Michael

Gentlemen. Scholastic Press 2009 234p $16.99

Grades: 8 9 10

1. School stories 2. Crime -- Fiction 3. Guilt -- Fiction

4. Teachers -- Fiction 5. Missing persons -- Fiction

ISBN 978-0-545-09749-9; 0-545-09749-5

LC 2008-38971

When three teenaged boys suspect that their English teacher is responsible for their friend's disappearance, they must navigate a maze of assorted clues, fraying friendships, violence, and Dostoevsky's "Crime and Punishment" before learning the truth.

"The brutal narration, friendships put through the wringer and the sense of dread that permeates the novel will keep readers hooked through the violent climax and its aftermath." Publ Wkly

Trapped. Scholastic Press 2011 225p $17.99

Grades: 7 8 9 10

1. School stories 2. Blizzards -- Fiction

ISBN 978-0-545-21012-6; 0-545-21012-7

LC 2010-36595

Seven high school students are stranded at their New England high school during a week-long blizzard that shuts down the power and heat, freezes the pipes, and leaves them wondering if they will survive.

"Northrop is cooly brilliant in his setup, amassing the tension along with the snow, shrewdly observing the shifting social dynamics within the group." Bull Cent Child Books

Nowlin, Laura

If he had been with me; Laura Nowlin. Sourcebooks Fire 2013 336 p. (tp : alk. paper) $9.99

Grades: 9 10 11 12

1. Love stories 2. Friendship -- Fiction 3. Love -- Fiction

ISBN 1402277822; 9781402277825

LC 2012041338

In this book by Laura Nowlin, "in eighth grade, Autumn and Finny stop being friends due to an unexpected kiss. They drift apart and find new friends, but their friendship keeps asserting itself at parties, shared holiday gatherings and random encounters. In the summer after graduation, Autumn and Finny reconnect and are finally ready to be more than friends. But on August 8, everything changes, and Autumn has to rely on all her strength to move on." (Kirkus Reviews)

Nuzum, K. A.

A **small** white scar; [by] K.A. Nuzum. 1st ed.; Joanna Cotler Books 2006 180p $15.99; lib bdg $16.89

Grades: 6 7 8 9

1. Twins -- Fiction 2. Brothers -- Fiction 3. Cowhands -- Fiction 4. People with mental disabilities-- Fiction

ISBN 978-0-06-075639-0; 0-06-075639-X; 978-0-06-075640-6 lib bdg; 0-06-075640-3 lib bdg

LC 2005017721

While trying to live his dream of crossing the plains to La Junta to become the radio champoin, Will Bennon must face troubling past issues when his twin brother, Denny, comes along for the adventure and acts as a constant reminder of Will's past. (Publisher's Note)

"The images of the stark 1940s Colorado countryside suffering from drought, and the wild animals that populate it, are clearly drawn with poetic turns of phrase. Characters, plot, and theme all combine to make a compelling story." SLJ

Nwaubani, Adaobi Tricia

Buried beneath the baobab tree. Adaobi Tricia Nwaubani. Katherine Tegen Books 2018 336 p.
Grades: 9 10 11 12

    1. Kidnapping -- Fiction; 2. Women -- Nigeria -- Fiction; 3. Prejudices -- Fiction
9780062696724, $17.99

                                LC 2018933386

"This poignant novel by Adaobi Tricia Nwaubani tells the timely story of one girl who was taken from her home in Nigeria and her harrowing fight for survival.... [S]he is taken with other girls and women into the forest where she is forced to follow her captors' radical beliefs and watch as her best friend slowly accepts everything she's been told. Still, the girl defends her existence. As impossible as escape may seem, her life -- her future -- is hers to fight for." (Publisher's note)

Nye, Naomi Shihab

Going going. Greenwillow Books 2005 232p il $15.99; lib bdg $16.89
Grades: 7 8 9 10

    1. Small business -- Fiction 2. Political activists -- Fiction
ISBN 0-688-16185-5; 0-06-029366-7 lib bdg

                                LC 2004-10146

In San Antonio, Texas, sixteen-year-old Florrie leads her friends and a new boyfriend in a campaign which supports small businesses and protests the effects of chain stores.

The "novel's strong message belongs honestly to Florrie, whose vivid individualism will engage readers. Nye evokes history through small details, inviting readers to view their own cities and towns with a new perspective." Horn Book Guide

★ **Habibi**. Simon & Schuster Bks. for Young Readers 1997 259p $16; pa $5.99
Grades: 7 8 9 10

    1. Jewish-Arab relations -- Fiction
ISBN 0-689-80149-1; 0-689-82523-4 pa

                                LC 97-10943

When fourteen-year-old Liyanne Abboud, her younger brother, and her parents move from St. Louis to a new home between Jerusalem and the Palestinian village where her father was born, they face many changes and must deal with the tensions between Jews and Palestinians

"Poetically imaged and leavened with humor, the story renders layered and complex history understandable through character and incident." SLJ

O'Brien, Annemarie

Lara's gift; by Annemarie O'Brien. Alfred A. Knopf 2013 176 p. (hardcover) $16.99; (ebook) $50.97; (library binding) 19.99
Grades: 5 6 7 8 9

    1. Historical fiction 2. Dogs -- Fiction 3. Borzoi -- Fiction 4. Visions -- Fiction 5. Sex role -- Fiction 6. Family life -- Russia -- Fiction 7. Fathers and daughters -- Fiction 8. Russia -- History -- 1904-1914 -- Fiction
ISBN 0307931749; 9780307931740; 9780307975485; 9780375971051

                                LC 2012034070

In this book, on "a remote estate in 1910s Russia, Lara must prove herself capable of following in her father's footsteps as the head of a prestigious borzoi breeding kennel. There are so many things between her and the realization of her dream. That she is female is the biggest obstacle, but she must also hide the fact that she has visions of future occurrences that involve the dogs and the dangerous wolves that populate the estate." (Kirkus Reviews)

O'Brien, Caragh M.

Birthmarked. Roaring Brook Press 2010 362p map $16.99
Grades: 6 7 8 9 10

    1. Science fiction 2. Midwives -- Fiction 3. Genetic engineering -- Fiction
ISBN 978-1-59643-569-8; 1-59643-569-0

                                LC 2010-281716

In a future world baked dry by the sun and divided into those who live inside the wall and those who live outside it, sixteen-year-old midwife Gaia Stone is forced into a difficult choice when her parents are arrested and taken into the city.

"Readers who enjoy adventures with a strong heroine standing up to authority against the odds will enjoy this compelling tale." SLJ

The **vault** of dreamers. Caragh M. O'Brien. Roaring Brook Press 2014 432 p. Illustration
Grades: 8 9 10 11

    1. Dreams -- Fiction 2. High schools -- Fiction 3. Reality television programs -- Fiction 4. Schools -- Fiction 5. Science fiction
1596439386; 9781596439382, $17.99; 9781596439399

                                LC 2014013322

In this novel, by Caragh M. O'Brien, "the Forge School is the most prestigious arts school in the country. The secret to its success: every moment of the students' lives is televised as part of the insanely popular Forge Show, and the students' schedule includes twelve hours of induced sleep meant to enhance creativity. But when first year student Rosie Sinclair skips her sleeping pill, she discovers there is something off about Forge." (Publisher's note)

"Like O'Brien's Birthmarked trilogy, this dystopian, sci-fi, psychological-thriller hybrid raises ethical and moral questions about science. This might have been a difficult story to pull off, given the environment, but with a likable narrator who is thoroughly unimpressed with herself, it works. The end is abrupt, hinting at a sequel, and there is a good measure of predictability." Booklist

O'Brien, Johnny

Day of the assassins; a Jack Christie novel. [illustrated by Nick Hardcastle] Templar Books 2009 211p il $15.99
Grades: 5 6 7 8

    1. Princes 2. Science fiction 3. Adventure fiction 4. Time travel -- Fiction 5. World War, 1914-1918 --

Fiction
ISBN 978-0-7636-4595-3; 0-7636-4595-8

LC 2009023630

Fifteen-year-old Jack is sent to 1914 Europe as a pawn in the battle between his long-lost father, who has built a time machine, and a secret network of scientists who want to prevent him from trying to use it to change history for the better.

"From an explosive escape out of captivity to a much-anticipated scene that decides the fate of World War I, the end of the book has plenty of action. Historical information and photographs about the events and people central to the period enhance this title even more." SLJ

Another title about Jack is:
Day of deliverance (2010)

O'Brien, Robert C.

★ **Z** for Zachariah. Atheneum Pubs. 1975 246p hardcover o.p. pa $7.99

Grades: 7 8 9 10

1. Science fiction
ISBN 0-689-30442-0; 1-416-93921-0 pa

Seemingly the only person left alive after a nuclear war, a sixteen-year-old girl is relieved to see a man arrive into her valley until she realizes that he is a tyrant and she must somehow escape.

"The journal form is used by O'Brien very effectively, with no lack of drama and contrast, and the pace and suspense of the story are adroitly maintained until the dramatic and surprising ending." Bull Cent Child Books

O'Connell, Mary

★ The **sharp** time; Mary O'Connell. 1st ed. Delacorte Press 2011 229 p.

Grades: 9 10 11 12

1. Dropouts -- Fiction 2. Orphans -- Fiction 3. Bereavement -- Fiction 4. Grief -- Fiction 5. Revenge -- Fiction 6. High schools -- Fiction 7. Vintage clothing -- Fiction 8. Interpersonal relations -- Fiction 9. Teacher-student relationships -- Fiction
ISBN 9780375899294; 9780375989483; 9780385740487

LC 2010044170

In this book, "[a]fter algebra teacher Mrs. Bennett inappropriately chides ADD-suffering Sandinista Jones . . . for not paying attention in class, the 18-year-old, whose single mother has recently died, gives up on school and life. . . . To fill her days, the teen quickly finds a job at the Pale Circus, a vintage clothing store, a companion in heartache with co-worker and 'druggie Robin Hood' Bradley and in possession of a handgun. . . . It takes a village, or at least a street full of eclectic shop workers in her rundown Kansas City neighborhood, to raise Sandinista out of despair. From her newfound community, comprised of the HIV-positive Pale Circus owner, Erika of Erika's Erotic Confections, a sympathetic pawn-shop owner and friendly Trappist monks, she finds faith, the will to go on in and unexpected beauty in an often cruel world." (Kirkus)

O'Connor, Heather M.

Betting Game. Heather M. O'Connor. Orca Book Publishers 2015 216 p.

Grades: 7 8 9 10

1. Sports betting 2. Brothers -- Fiction 3. Hi-Lo books 4. Soccer -- Fiction
1459809300; 9781459809307, $9.95

LC 2015935527

In this novel, by Heather O'Connor, "Jack's a star player on an elite soccer team along with his brother. The Lancers are . . . favored to win the National Championship. A slick bookie wins Jack's friendship and introduces him to illegal betting. Before long, Jack is hooked. An ever-widening rift is forming between the two brothers. Suddenly, Jack's . . . luck runs out. When he can't pay, the bookie gives Jack one way out. But can he betray his brother, his team and himself?" (Publisher's note)

"The fast-paced writing has enough soccer action to keep reluctant readers turning the pages, and the gambling intrigue, along with a side plot involving a new player on Jack's team, adds to the increasing conflict. . . . A solid pick for high/low sports fiction." Booklist

O'Connor, Sheila

★ **Sparrow** Road. G. P. Putnam's Sons 2011 247p $16.99

Grades: 5 6 7 8

1. Artists -- Fiction
ISBN 978-0-399-25458-1; 0-399-25458-7

LC 2010-28290

Twelve-year-old Raine spends the summer at a mysterious artists colony and discovers a secret about her past.

This is a "beautifully written novel. . . . Readers finding themselves in this quiet world will find plenty of space to imagine and dream for themselves." Kirkus

O'Dell, Scott

★ **Island** of the Blue Dolphins; illustrated by Ted Lewin. 50th anniversary ed.; Houghton Mifflin Books for Children 2010 177p il $22

Grades: 5 6 7 8

1. Native Americans -- Fiction 2. Wilderness survival -- Fiction
ISBN 978-0-547-42483-5; 0-547-42483-3

A reissue of the newly illustrated edition published 1990; first published 1960

Awarded the Newbery Medal, 1961

Left alone on a beautiful but isolated island off the coast of California, a young Indian girl spends eighteen years, not only merely surviving through her enormous courage and self-reliance, but also finding a measure of happiness in her solitary life.

The edition illustrated by Ted Lewin "features twelve full-page, full-color watercolors in purple and blue hues that are appropriate to the island setting. This handsome gift-edition version includes a new introduction by Lois Lowry to commemorate the book's fiftieth anniversary." Horn Book Guide

Sing down the moon. Houghton Mifflin 1970 137p hardcover o.p. pa $6.99

Grades: 5 6 7 8

1. Navajo Indians -- Fiction
ISBN 0-395-10919-1; 978-0-547-40632-9 pa; 0-547-40632-0 pa

A Newbery Medal honor book, 1971

A young Navajo girl recounts the events of 1864 when her tribe was forced to march to Fort Sumner as prisoners of the white soldiers.

"There is a poetic sonority of style, a sense of identification, and a note of indomitable courage and stoicism that is touching and impressive." Saturday Rev

Streams to the river, river to the sea; a novel of Sacagawea. Houghton Mifflin 1986 191p hardcover o.p. pa $6.99

Grades: 5 6 7 8

1. Interpreters 2. Guides (Persons) 3. Native Americans -- Fiction
ISBN 0-395-40430-4; 0-618-96642-0 pa

LC 86-936

A young Indian woman, accompanied by her infant and cruel husband, experiences joy and heartbreak when she joins the Lewis and Clark Expedition seeking a way to the Pacific.

"An informative and involving choice for American history students and pioneer-adventure readers." Bull Cent Child Books

Thunder rolling in the mountains; [by] Scott O'Dell and Elizabeth Hall. Houghton Mifflin 1992 128p map $17

Grades: 5 6 7 8

1. Nez Perce Indians -- Fiction
ISBN 0-395-59966-0

LC 91-15961

This account of the defeat of the Nez Perce Indians in 1877 by the United States Army is narrated by Chief Joseph's daughter.

"This is a sad, dark-hued story told in Mr. O'Dell's lean, affecting prose." Child Book Rev Serv

O'Guilin, Peadar

The **call**. Peadar O'Guilin. David Fickling Books/Scholastic Inc. 2016 307 p.

Grades: 9 10 11 12

1. Fairies -- Fiction 2. Good and evil -- Fiction 3. Mythology, Celtic -- Fiction 4. People with disabilities -- Fiction 5. Survival -- Fiction 6. Ireland -- Fiction 7. Survival skills -- Fiction
9781338048063, $18.99; 133804561X; 9781338045611, $18.99

LC 2016012970

Written by Peadar O'Guilin, the book examines the possibility of "waking up alone in a horrible land. A horn sounds. The Call has begun.Could you survive the Call . . . Nessa will be Called soon. No one thinks she has any chance to survive. But she's determined to prove them wrong . . . A genre-changing blend of fantasy, horror, and folkore, The Call won't ever leave your mind from the moment you choose to answer it." (Publisher's note)

"This is a bleak, gripping story, one where only the most muted of happy endings is possible." Pub Wkly

First published in the United Kingdom in 2016 by David Fickling Books.

O'Neill, Louise

★ **Asking** for it. Louise O'Neill. Quercus 2016 304 p.

Grades: 9 10 11 12

1. Ireland -- Fiction 2. Rape -- Fiction
1681445379; 9781681445373, $16.99

LC 2016930915

Printz Honor Book (2017)

In this book by Louise O'Neill, "Emma O'Donovan is eighteen, beautiful, and fearless. It's . . . summer in a quiet Irish town and . . . everyone is at the party, and all eyes are on Emma. The next morning Emma's parents discover her collapsed on the doorstop of their home, unconscious. She is disheveled, bleeding, and disoriented, looking as if she had been dumped there. . . . To her distress, Emma can't remember what happened the night before." (Publisher's note)

"O'Neill's treatment of how communities mishandle sexual assault and victimize its victims is unforgiving, and readers will despair to see Emma helpless in the face of injustice. It's a brutal, hard-to-forget portrait of human cruelty that makes disturbingly clear the way women and girls internalize sexist societal attitudes and unwarranted guilt." Pub Wkly

O'Sullivan, Joanne

★ Between Two Skies. By Joanne O'Sullivan. Candlewick Press 2017 267 p.

Grades: 7 8 9 10 11 12

1. Fishing -- Fiction; 2. Hurricane Katrina, 2005 -- Fiction; 3. Teenage girls -- Fiction
9780763690342, $16.99; 9780763693862; 0763690341

LC 2017935665

In this book, by Joanne O'Sullivan, "Bayou Perdu,... Louisiana, is home to sixteen-year-old Evangeline Riley. She has her best friends;...her wise, beloved Mamere; and back-to-back titles in the under-sixteen fishing rodeo. But, dearest to her heart, she has the peace that only comes when she takes her skiff out to where there is nothing but sky and air and water and wings. It's a small life, but it is Evangeline's. And then the storm comes, and everything changes." (Publisher's note)

"Told in a strong, purposeful voice filled with controlled emotion and hope, the impact of Katrina on families is as compelling as Evangeline's drive to regain her sense of self and belonging." Booklist

Oakes, Stephanie

The **arsonist**. Stephanie Oakes. Dial Books 2017 493 p.

Grades: 7 8 9

1. Epilepsy -- Fiction; 2. Identity (Philosophical concept) -- Fiction; 3. Kuwaiti Americans -- Fiction; 4. Mothers and daughters -- Fiction; 5. People with disabilities -- Fiction; 6. Germany (East) -- History -- 20th century -- Fiction; 7. Mother-daughter relationship -- Fiction; 8. Identity (Psychology) -- Fiction
9781101633724; 9780803740716, $17.99

LC 2016032499

In this novel, by Stephanie Oakes, Molly Mavity and Pepper Al-Yusef are dealing with their own personal tragedies "when Molly gets a package leading her to Pepper, they're tasked with solving a decades-old mystery: find out who killed Ava [Dreyman], back in 1989. Using Ava's diary for clues, Molly and Pepper realize there's more to her life -- and death -- than meets the eye. Someone is lying to them. And someone out there is guiding them along, desperate for answers." (Publisher's note)

"Packed with dynamic characters, thoughtful writing, and a decades-spanning mystery, this will appeal to readers looking for something off the beaten path." Booklist

★ The **sacred** lies of Minnow Bly. By Stephanie Oakes. Dial Books 2015 400 p.
1. African Americans -- Fiction 2. Amputees -- Fiction 3. Cults -- Fiction 4. Juvenile detention homes -- Fiction 5. Murder -- Fiction 6. People with disabilities -- Fiction
9780803740709, $17.99; 0803740700
LC 2014033187
William C. Morris Award Finalist (2016)
In this novel, by Stephanie Oakes, "Minnow Bly survives when her hands are chopped off as punishment for refusing to wed the self-proclaimed 'Kevinian' Prophet, leader of an oppressive, polygamous Montana wilderness cult in which she was raised.... Furious, frightened, and heartbroken, she lashes out and commits a hideous random assault, Imprisoned for this crime in a juvenile detention facility until age 18, Minnow is coaxed to reveal the truth about the demise of the Community." (School Library Journal)

"Dark and not just a little sensational but hugely involving nevertheless." Kirkus

Oates, Joyce Carol, 1938-
★ **Big** Mouth & Ugly Girl. HarperCollins Pubs. 2002 265p hardcover o.p. pa $7.99
Grades: 7 8 9 10
1. School stories 2. Friendship -- Fiction
ISBN 0-06-623756-4; 0-06-447347-3 pa
LC 2001-24601
When sixteen-year-old Matt is falsely accused of threatening to blow up his high school and his friends turn against him, an unlikely classmate comes to his aid.

"Readers will be propelled through these pages by an intense curiosity to learn how events will play out. Oates has written a fast-moving, timely, compelling story." SLJ

★ **Freaky** green eyes. Harper Tempest 2003 341p hardcover o.p. pa $6.99
Grades: 7 8 9 10
1. Domestic violence -- Fiction
ISBN 0-06-623757-2 lib bdg; 0-06-447348-1 pa
LC 2002-32868
Fifteen-year-old Frankie relates the events of the year leading up to her mother's mysterious disappearance and her own struggle to discover and accept the truth about her parents' relationship.

"Oates pulls readers into a fast-paced, first-person thriller.... An absorbing page-turner." Booklist

Two or three things I forgot to tell you; Joyce Carol Oates. HarperTeen 2012 277 p. (trade bdg.) $17.99
Grades: 9 10 11 12
1. School stories 2. Secrecy -- Fiction 3. Teenagers --

Suicide -- Fiction 4. Secrets -- Fiction 5. Friendship -- Fiction 6. Self-esteem -- Fiction 7. Preparatory schools -- Fiction 8. Cutting (Self-mutilation) -- Fiction
ISBN 0062110470; 9780062110473
LC 2012009699
This novel, by Joyce Carol Oates, tells a "story of three teenage girls in crisis.... In part one, Merissa ... secretly embraces cutting. Part two flashes back to 15 months earlier, when ... Tink, a former child star, transfers into their junior class and changes everything. Part three picks back up in the winter of their senior year and focuses on Nadia, who falls prey to sexts and cyberbullying." (Kirkus)

Ockler, Sarah
The **Book** of Broken Hearts; by Sarah Ockler. 1st Simon Pulse hardcover ed. Simon Pulse 2013 368 p. (hardcover) $16.99
Grades: 9 10 11 12
1. Love stories 2. Family life -- Fiction 3. Argentine Americans -- Fiction
ISBN 1442430389; 9781442430389
LC 2012033041
In this romance novel, by Sarah Ockler, "Jude has learned a lot from her older sisters, but the most important thing is this: The Vargas brothers are notorious heartbreakers.... Now Jude is the only sister still living at home, and she's spending the summer helping her ailing father restore his vintage motorcycle--which means hiring a mechanic to help out. Is it Jude's fault he happens to be cute? And surprisingly sweet? And a Vargas?" (Publisher's note)

Fixing Delilah. Little, Brown 2010 308p $16.99
Grades: 8 9 10 11 12
1. Vermont -- Fiction 2. Bereavement -- Fiction 3. Single parent family -- Fiction 4. Depression (Psychology) -- Fiction
ISBN 978-0-316-05209-2; 0-316-05209-4
LC 2010-08631
Delilah Hannaford "used to be a good student, but she can't seem to keep it together anymore. Her 'boyfriend' isn't much of a boyfriend. And her mother refuses to discuss the fight that divided their family eight years ago. Falling apart, it seems, is a Hannaford tradition. Over a summer of new friendships, unexpected romance, and moments that test the complex bonds between mothers and daughters, Delilah must face her family's painful past." (Publisher's note)

Delilah "tells her own story in a lyrical and authentic voice; the thoughtful reader will get lost in her anguish, her triumphs, and her eventual resolution." Voice Youth Advocates

Oelke, Lianne
Nice try, Jane Sinner. Lianne Oelke. Clarion Books, Houghton Mifflin Harcourt 2018 420 p.
Grades: 9 10 11 12
1. Community college students -- Fiction; 2. Diaries -- Fiction; 3. High school dropouts -- Fiction; 4. Internet television -- Fiction; 5. Reality television programs -- Fiction; 6. Teenage girls -- Fiction; 7. Dropouts -- Fiction
9780544867857, $17.99; 9781328828842
LC 2016035569

In this novel, by Lianne Oelke, "the only thing 17-year-old Jane Sinner hates more than failure is pity. After a personal crisis and her subsequent expulsion from high school, she's going nowhere fast. Jane's...parents push her to attend a high school completion program at...Elbow River Community College, and she agrees, on one condition: she gets to move out. Jane tackles her housing problem by signing up for...a student-run reality show." (Publisher's note)

"Character-driven, humorous, and deceptively profound." Kirkus

Okorafor, Nnedi

Akata warrior. Nnedi Okorafor. Viking 2017 477 p.

Grades: 6 7 8 9 10

1. Albinos and albinism -- Fiction; 2. Blacks -- Nigeria -- Fiction; 3. Magic -- Fiction; 4. Secret societies -- Fiction; 5. Supernatural -- Fiction; 6. Nigeria -- Fiction

067078561X; 9780670785612, $18.99; 9781101598986

LC 2016055398

In this book, by Nnedi Okorafor, "a year ago, Sunny Nwazue, an American-born girl Nigerian girl, was inducted into the secret Leopard Society. As she began to develop her magical powers, Sunny learned that she had been chosen to lead a dangerous mission to avert an apocalypse, brought about by the terrifying masquerade, Ekwensu. Now, stronger, feistier, and a bit older, Sunny is studying with her mentor Sugar Cream and struggling to unlock the secrets in her strange Nsibidi book." (Publisher's note)

"Okorafor's novel will ensnare readers and keep them turning pages until the very end to see if and how Sunny fulfills the tremendous destiny that awaits her." Booklist

Sequel to: Akata witch (2011)

Akata witch. Viking 2011 349p $16.99

Grades: 6 7 8 9

1. Fantasy fiction 2. Witchcraft -- Fiction 3. Albinos and albinism -- Fiction

ISBN 978-0-670-01196-4; 0-670-01196-7

"Although 12-year-old Sunny is Nigerian, she was born in America, and her Nigerian classmates see her as an outsider. Worse, she's an albino, an obvious target for bullies and suspected of being a ghost or a witch. Things change, however, when she has a vision of impending nuclear war. Then her classmate Orlu and his friend Chichi turn out to be Leopard People—witches—and insist that she is, too. . . . This tale is filled with marvels and is sure to appeal to teens whose interest in fantasy goes beyond dwarves and fairies." Publ Wkly

The **shadow** speaker; [by] Nnedi Okorafor-Mbachu. Jump at the Sun/Hyperion Books for Children 2007 336p hardcover o.p. pa $8.99

Grades: 7 8 9 10

1. Fantasy fiction 2. Science fiction 3. West Africa -- Fiction 4. Sahara Desert -- Fiction

ISBN 978-1-4231-0033-1; 1-4231-0033-6; 978-1-4231-0036-2 pa; 1-4231-0036-0 pa

LC 2007-13313

In West Africa in 2070, after fifteen-year-old "shadow speaker" Ejii witnesses her father's beheading, she embarks on a dangerous journey across the Sahara to find Jaa, her

father's killer, and upon finding her, she also discovers a greater purpose to her life and to the mystical powers she possesses.

"Okorafor-Mbachu does an excellent job of combining both science fiction and fantasy elements into this novel. . . . The action moves along at a quick pace and will keep most readers on their toes and wanting more at the end of the novel." Voice Youth Advocates

Older, Daniel José

★ **Shadowhouse** fall. Daniel Jose Older. Arthur A. Levine Books, an imprint of Scholastic Inc. 2017 358 p. (Shadowshaper cypher)

Grades: 9 10 11 12

1. Magic -- Fiction; 2. Magic -- Fiction; 3. Occultism -- Fiction; 4. Paranormal fiction; 5. Puerto Rican families -- Fiction; 6. Puerto Rican youth -- New York (State) -- New York -- Fiction; 7. Puerto Ricans -- New York (State) -- New York -- Fiction; 8. Brooklyn (New York, N.Y.) -- Fiction; 9. Puerto Ricans -- Fiction

9780545952835; 0545952824; 9780545952828, $18.99

LC 2017016620

In this novel in the Shadowshaper Cypher series, by Daniel José Older, "Sierra and her friends love their new lives as shadowshapers, making art and creating change with the spirits of Brooklyn. Then Sierra receives a strange card depicting a beast called the Hound of Light.... Thrust into an ancient struggle..., Sierra and Shadowhouse are determined to win.... Sierra must take down the Hound and master the Deck of Worlds...or risk losing them all." (Publisher's note)

"The expanding cast of well-rounded characters, clearly choreographed action, and foreshadowing of installments to come will have fantasy fans eagerly awaiting more of this dynamic, smart series." Booklist

Sequel to: Shadowshaper (2015)

★ **Shadowshaper**. Daniel Jose Older. Arthur A. Levine Books, an imprint of Scholastic Inc. 2015 304 p.

Grades: 9 10 11 12

1. Magic -- Fiction 2. Paranormal fiction 3. Puerto Rican families -- Fiction 4. Brooklyn (New York, N.Y.) -- Fiction 5. Art -- Fiction 6. Family secrets -- Fiction

0545591619; 9780545591614, $17.99

LC 2014032311

In this book by Daniel José Older, "Sierra finally learns the truth: her grandfather was a powerful shadowshaper, able to animate art with the spirit of a departed soul, and now an interloper, anthropologist Dr. Wick, is trying to steal these powers for himself. As Sierra investigates the shadowshapers, she discovers her own shockingly powerful role in the disappearing community." (Booklist)

"Excellent diverse genre fiction in an appealing package." SLJ

Oliver, Jana

The **demon** trapper's daughter; a demon trapper novel. [by] Jana Oliver. St. Martin's Griffin 2011 355p pa $9.99

Grades: 7 8 9 10

1. Demonology -- Fiction 2. Apprentices -- Fiction 3. Supernatural -- Fiction 4. Atlanta (Ga.) -- Fiction 5.

Father-daughter relationship -- Fiction
ISBN 978-0-312-61478-2; 0-312-61478-0

LC 2010-38860

In 2018 Atlanta, Georgia, after a demon threatens seventeen-year-old Riley Blackthorne's life and murders her father, a legendary demon trapper to whom she was apprenticed, her father's partner, Beck, steps in to care for her, knowing she hates him.

"With a strong female heroine, a fascinating setting, and a complex, thrill-soaked story, this series is off to a strong start." Publ Wkly

Followed by Soul thief (2011)

Soul thief; [by] Jana Oliver. St. Martin's Griffin 2011 339p (A demon trappers novel) pa $9.99
Grades: 7 8 9 10

1. Orphans -- Fiction 2. Demonology -- Fiction 3. Apprentices -- Fiction 4. Supernatural -- Fiction 5. Atlanta (Ga.) -- Fiction
ISBN 978-0-312-61479-9

LC 2011019930

Sequel to The demon trapper's daughter (2011)

In 2018 Atlanta, Georgia, seventeen-year-old apprentice Demon Trapper Riley Blackthorne must deal with unwanted fame, an unofficial bodyguard, an overprotective friend, the Vatican's own Demon Trappers, and an extremely powerful Grade Five demon who is stalking her.

Oliver, Lauren

Before I fall. The Bowen Press 2010 470p $17.99

Grades: 9 10 11 12

1. School stories 2. Dead -- Fiction 3. Popularity -- Fiction 4. Self-perception -- Fiction
ISBN 006172680X; 9780061726804; 978-0-06-172680-4; 0-06-172680-X

LC 2009-7288

After she dies in a car crash, teenage Samantha relives the day of her death over and over again until, on the seventh day, she finally discovers a way to save herself.

"This is a compelling book with a powerful message that will strike a chord with many teens." Booklist

★ **Delirium.** HarperCollins 2011 441p $17.99
Grades: 8 9 10 11

1. Science fiction 2. Love -- Fiction 3. Maine -- Fiction 4. Resistance to government -- Fiction
ISBN 978-0-06-172682-8; 0-06-172682-6

LC 2010-17839

Lena looks forward to receiving the government-mandated cure that prevents the delirium of love and leads to a safe, predictable, and happy life, until ninety-five days before her eighteenth birthday and her treatment, she falls in love.

This book is a "deft blend of realism and fantasy. . . . The story bogs down as it revels in romance—Alex is standard-issue perfection—but the book never loses its A Clockwork Orange–style bite regarding safety versus choice." Booklist

Pandemonium; Lauren Oliver. 1st ed.; Harper-CollinsPublishers 2012 375p $17.99

Grades: 8 9 10 11

1. Science fiction 2. Love -- Fiction 3. Resistance to government -- Fiction
ISBN 978-0-06-197806-7

LC 2011024241

Sequel to Delirium (2011)

After falling in love, Lena and Alex flee their oppressive society where love is outlawed and everyone must receive "the cure"—an operation that makes them immune to the delirium of love—but Lena alone manages to find her way to a community of resistance fighters, and although she is bereft without the boy she loves, her struggles seem to be leading her toward a new love.

Panic; Lauren Oliver. Harper, an imprint of HarperCollinsPublishers 2014 416 p. (hardcover bdg.) $17.99

Grades: 9 10 11 12

1. City and town life -- Fiction 2. Games -- Fiction 3. Risk-taking (Psychology) -- Fiction
ISBN 0062014552; 9780062014559

LC 2013008472

Written by Lauren Oliver, this young adult novel describes how "Heather never thought she would compete in Panic, a legendary game played by graduating seniors, where the stakes are high and the payoff is even higher. . . . Dodge has never been afraid of Panic. . . . For Heather and Dodge, the game will bring new alliances, unexpected revelations, and the possibility of first love for each of them." (Publisher's note)

"There's not much to do in tiny Carp, New York, so a group of teenagers take it upon themselves to create their own excitement through Panic, a risky game with potentially deadly sets of challenges... The bleak setting, tenacious characters, and anxiety-filled atmosphere will draw readers right into this unique story. Oliver's powerful return to a contemporary realistic setting will find wide a readership with this fast-paced and captivating book." (School Library Journal)

Requiem; Lauren Oliver. Harper 2013 432 p. (hardcover) $18.99

Grades: 8 9 10 11 12

1. Science fiction 2. Resistance to government -- Fiction 3. Love -- Fiction 4. Maine -- Fiction 5. Marriage -- Fiction 6. Friendship -- Fiction 7. Best friends -- Fiction
ISBN 0062014536; 9780062014535

LC 2012030236

Sequel to: Pandemonium

This young adult novel, by Lauren Oliver, is the conclusion to the "Delirium" trilogy. "The nascent rebellion . . . has ignited into an all-out revolution . . . , and Lena is at the center of the fight. After rescuing Julian from a death sentence, Lena and her friends fled to the Wilds. But the Wilds are no longer a safe haven. . . . As Lena navigates the increasingly dangerous terrain of the Wilds, her best friend, Hana, lives a safe, loveless life in Portland." (Publisher's note)

Vanishing girls. By Lauren Oliver. Harper 2015 357 p. Illustration

Grades: 9 10 11 12

1. Dissociative disorders -- Fiction 2. Missing children

-- Fiction 3. Sisters -- Fiction 4. Accidents -- Fiction
0062224107; 9780062224101, $18.99

LC 2014028437

In this book, by Lauren Oliver, "Dara and Nick used to be inseparable, but that was before the accident that left Dara's beautiful face scarred and the two sisters totally estranged. When Dara vanishes on her birthday, Nick thinks Dara is just playing around. But another girl, nine-year-old Madeline Snow, has vanished, too, and Nick becomes increasingly convinced that the two disappearances are linked. Now Nick has to find her sister, before it's too late." (Publisher's note)

"Perfect for readers who devoured We Were Liars, it's the sort of novel that readers will race to finish, then return to the beginning to marvel at how it was constructed—and at everything they missed." Publishers Weekly

Omololu, Cynthia Jaynes

Dirty little secrets; [by] C.J. Omololu. Walker & Co. 2010 212p $16.99

Grades: 8 9 10 11 12

1. School stories 2. Death -- Fiction 3. Compulsive behavior -- Fiction 4. Mother-daughter relationship -- Fiction

ISBN 978-0-8027-8660-9; 0-8027-8660-X

LC 2009-22461

When her unstable mother dies unexpectedly, sixteen-year-old Lucy must take control and find a way to keep the long-held secret of her mother's compulsive hoarding from being revealed to friends, neighbors, and especially the media.

"As a valuable new addition to heartbreaking but honest books about teens immersed in emotionally distressed families, . . . this potent and creatively woven page-turner brings a traumatic situation front and center." SLJ

Oppegaard, David

The **Firebug** of Balrog County. By David Oppegaard. Llewellyn Worldwide Ltd 2015 312 p.

Grades: 9 10 11 12

1. Pyromania 2. High school students -- Fiction 3. Country life -- Fiction

073874543X; 9780738745435, $11.99

LC 2015014186

In this book, by David Oppegaard, "Dark times have fallen on remote Balrog County, and Mack Druneswald, a high school senior with a love of arson, is doing his best to deal. While his family is haunted by his mother's recent death, Mack spends his nights roaming the countryside, looking for something new to burn. When he encounters Katrina, a college girl with her own baggage, Mack sets out on a path of pyromania the likes of which sleepy Balrog County has never seen before." (Publisher's note)

"Drinking, F-bombs, and humor abound, but so does a genuine sense of mourning and growth, even if Mack's narrative sometimes smacks of adult understanding." Kirkus

Oppel, Kenneth

Airborn. Eos 2004 355p $16.99; lib bdg $17.89

Grades: 7 8 9 10

1. Fantasy fiction 2. Airships -- Fiction 3. Imaginary creatures

ISBN 0-06-053180-0; 0-06-053181-9 lib bdg

LC 2003-15642

Michael L. Printz Award honor book, 2005

Matt, a young cabin boy aboard an airship, and Kate, a wealthy young girl traveling with her chaperone, team up to search for the existence of mysterious winged creatures reportedly living hundreds of feet above the Earth's surface.

"This rousing adventure has something for everyone: appealing and enterprising characters, nasty villains, and a little romance." SLJ

Other titles in this series are:
Skybreaker (2005)
Starclimber (2009)

Every hidden thing. Kenneth Oppel. Simon & Schuster Books for Young Readers 2016 368 p.

Grades: 9 10 11 12

1. Dinosaurs -- Fiction 2. Families -- Fiction 3. Fossils -- Fiction 4. Love -- Fiction 5. Paleontology -- Fiction 6. Tyrannosaurus rex -- Fiction 7. Romance fiction

9781481464161, $17.99; 9781481464185, $12.99

LC 2015045436

In this novel by Kenneth Oppel, "Rachel and Samuel both lost their mothers at a young age and have fathers obsessed with dinosaur fossils, but the similarities in their upbringing end there. Rachel grew up in relative luxury . . . [while] Samuel and his father, a self-taught paleontologist without official credentials, can barely make ends meet. However, they all end up on the same train headed out west in a race to be the first to find the fossil of a T. rex." (School Library Journal)

"Suspense, romance, and the excitement of discovery make this Western thoroughly enjoyable." Kirkus

Half brother. Scholastic Press 2010 375p $17.99

Grades: 7 8 9 10

1. Canada -- Fiction 2. Research -- Fiction 3. Chimpanzees -- Fiction 4. Family life -- Fiction

ISBN 978-0-545-22925-8; 0-545-22925-1

LC 2010-2696

In 1973, when a renowned Canadian behavioral psychologist pursues his latest research project—an experiment to determine whether chimpanzees can acquire advanced language skills—he brings home a baby chimp named Zan and asks his thirteen-year-old son to treat Zan like a little brother.

"Oppel has taken a fascinating subject and molded it into a topnotch read. Deftly integrating family dynamics, animal-rights issues, and the painful lessons of growing up, Half Brother draws readers in from the beginning and doesn't let go." SLJ

Skybreaker. Eos 2005 369p il hardcover o.p. lib bdg $17.89; pa $6.99

Grades: 7 8 9 10

1. Fantasy fiction 2. Airships -- Fiction

ISBN 0-06-053227-0; 0-06-053228-9 lib bdg; 0-06-053229-7 pa

LC 2005-08386

Matt Cruse, a student at the Airship Academy, and Kate de Vries, a young heiress, team up with a gypsy and a daring captain, to find a long-lost airship, rumored to carry a treasure beyond imagination.

This "starts with a bang and doesn't let up until the satisfying ending. . . . This worthy companion to Airborn maintains its roller-coaster thrills in true swashbuckling style." SLJ

Starclimber. Eos 2009 390p $17.99; lib bdg $18.89
Grades: 7 8 9 10
    1. Fantasy fiction 2. Airships -- Fiction 3. Outer space -- Exploration -- Fiction
    ISBN 978-0-06-085057-9; 0-06-085057-4; 978-0-06-085058-6 lib bdg; 0-06-085058-2 lib bdg
                      LC 2008019747
As members of the first crew of astralnauts, Matt Cruse and Kate De Vries journey into outer space on the Starclimber and face a series of catastrophes that threaten the survival of all on board.

This "is a thrilling roller-coaster ride of a book, full of humor and derring-do and guaranteed to keep readers up long past midnight." SLJ

Such wicked intent; Kenneth Oppel. Simon & Schuster Books For Young Readers 2012 320 p. (hardback) $16.99; (paperback) $9.99
Grades: 7 8 9 10
    1. Love stories 2. Death -- Fiction 3. Friendship -- Fiction 4. Horror stories 5. Dead -- Fiction 6. Twins -- Fiction 7. Alchemy -- Fiction 8. Brothers -- Fiction 9. Supernatural -- Fiction 10. Geneva (Republic) -- History -- 18th century -- Fiction
    ISBN 1442403187; 9781442403185; 9781442403208; 9781442403192
                      LC 2011042843
This book by Kenneth Oppel is part of the "Apprenticeship of Victor Frankenstein" series. "[T]hree weeks after [his twin] Konrad's death, Victor plucks a mysterious box from the still-warm ashes of the books of the Dark Library. Demonstrating tremendous hubris, Victor aims to return Konrad to the living world and still win Elizabeth, Konrad's grief-stricken love and the boys' childhood friend." (Kirkus Reviews)

This dark endeavor; the apprenticeship of Victor Frankenstein. Simon & Schuster Books for Young Readers 2011 298p $17.99
Grades: 7 8 9 10
    1. Horror fiction 2. Twins -- Fiction 3. Alchemy -- Fiction 4. Brothers -- Fiction
    ISBN 1-4424-0315-2; 1-4424-0317-9 ebook; 978-1-4424-0315-4; 978-1-4424-0317-8 ebook
                      LC 2011016974
When his twin brother falls ill in the family's chateau in the independent republic of Geneva in the eighteenth century, sixteen-year-old Victor Frankenstein embarks on a dangerous and uncertain quest to create the forbidden Elixir of Life described in an ancient text in the family's secret Biblioteka Obscura.

"Written in a readable approximation of early 19th-century style, Oppel's . . . tale is melodramatic, exciting, disquieting, and intentionally over the top." Publ Wkly

Ormsbee, Kathryn

Tash hearts Tolstoy. Kathryn Ormsbee. Salaam Reads/Simon & Schuster 2017 372 p.
Grades: 9 10 11 12
    1. Asexuality (Sexual orientation) -- Fiction; 2. Dating (Social customs) -- Fiction; 3. Internet television -- Production and direction -- Fiction; 4. Tolstoy, Leo, graf, 1828-1910 -- Fiction; 5. Fame -- Fiction
    9781481489355; 9781481489331, $18.99; 9781481489348
                      LC 2016032661
In this book, by Kathryn Ormsbee, "after a shout-out from one of the Internet's superstar vloggers, Natasha 'Tash' Zelenka suddenly finds herself and her obscure, amateur web series, Unhappy Families, thrust in the limelight.... Her show is a modern adaption of Anna Karenina -- written by Tash's literary love Count Lev Nikolayevich 'Leo' Tolstoy. Tash is a fan of the 40,000 new subscribers.... Not so much the pressure to deliver the best web series ever." (Publisher's note)

"Whip-smart, funny, flawed, and compassionate, these are characters readers will want to know and cheer for. A clever, thoroughly enjoyable addition to the growing body of diverse teen literature." Kirkus

Oron, Judie

Cry of the giraffe; based on a true story. Annick Press 2010 193p map $21.95; pa $12.95
Grades: 8 9 10 11 12
    1. Jews -- Ethiopia -- Fiction 2. Jews -- Persecutions -- Fiction
    ISBN 978-1-55451-272-0; 978-1-55451-271-3 pa
Labeled outcasts by their Ethiopian neighbors because of their Jewish faith, 13-year-old Wuditu and her family make the arduous trek on foot to Sudan in the hope of being transported to Yerusalem and its promise of a better life. Based on real events.

"Oron's novel shows with brutal, unflinching detail the horrors of refugee life and child slavery and the shocking vulnerability of young females in the developing world, and she offers a sobering introduction to a community and historical episodes rarely covered in books for youth." Booklist

Ortiz Cofer, Judith

Call me Maria; a novel. Orchard Books 2004 127p $16.95
Grades: 7 8 9 10
    1. Identity 2. Puerto Ricans -- Fiction
    ISBN 0-439-38577-6
                      LC 2004-2674
Fifteen-year-old Maria leaves her mother and their Puerto Rican home to live in the barrio of New York with her father, feeling torn between the two cultures in which she has been raised.

"Through a mixture of poems, letters, and prose, María gradually reveals herself as a true student of language and life. . . . Understated but with a brilliant combination of all the right words to convey events, Cofer aptly relates the complexities of María's two homes, her parents' lives, and the difficulty of her choice between them." SLJ

If I could fly. Farrar Straus & Giroux 2011 195p $16.99

Grades: 8 9 10 11 12

1. Pigeons -- Fiction 2. Singers -- Fiction 3. Family life -- Fiction 4. Puerto Ricans -- Fiction
ISBN 978-0-374-33517-5; 0-374-33517-6

LC 2010022309

When fifteen-year-old Doris's mother, a professional singer, returns to Puerto Rico and her father finds a girl-friend, Doris cares for a neighbor's pigeons and relies on friends as she begins to find her own voice and wings.

"A familiar story of mother/daughter relationships delivered lyrically, simply and inspirationally." Kirkus

Oseman, Alice

Solitaire. Alice Oseman. HarperTeen 2015 357 p.
Grades: 9 10 11 12

1. High schools -- Fiction 2. Love -- Fiction 3. Practical jokes -- Fiction 4. Schools -- Fiction 5. Friendship -- Fiction 6. High school students -- Fiction
0062335685; 9780062335685, $17.99

LC 2014026695

"Sixteen-year-old Victoria 'Tori' Spring is the personification of angst. Her best friend has become preoccupied with boys; her brother, Charlie, is recovering from an episode of mental illness and attempted suicide; a former childhood friend has suddenly resurfaced with expectations that she can't fulfill. Then, there's Michael Holden, the crazy new student. He forces himself into her life at the same time as a bizarre prank is unleashed to instigate rebellion among the students at Higgs." (School Library Journal)

"The obvious nod to The Catcher in the Rye provides another pull to readers who will enjoy parsing the parallels." Booklist

Oshiro, Mark

Anger is a gift: a novel. Mark Oshiro. St. Martin's Press 2018 464 p.
Grades: 8 9 10 11 12

1. Teenagers -- Fiction; 2. Anxiety -- Fiction; 3. Anger -- Fiction
1250167027; 9781250167026, $17.99

In this book by Mark Oshiro, "Moss [Jeffries]...and his friends are subject to the lack of funds and crumbling infrastructure at West Oakland High, as well as constant intimidation by the resource officer stationed in their halls. That was even before the new regulations -- it seems sometimes that the students are treated more like criminals. Something will have to change -- but who will listen to a group of teens?" (Publisher's note)

Osterlund, Anne

Aurelia. Speak 2008 246p pa $8.99
Grades: 8 9 10 11

1. Mystery fiction 2. Princesses -- Fiction
ISBN 978-0-14-240579-6; 0-14-240579-5

LC 2007-36074

The king sends for Robert, whose father was a trusted spy, when someone tries to assassinate Aurelia, the stubborn and feisty crown princess of Tyralt.

"Osterlund's characters are both believable, relatable, and enviable, which makes this book enjoyable to read. Even though the book might seem to fit the mold of a quint-essential princess fairy tale, Aurelia's spitfire attitude and her resulting actions lend the story a unique twist." Voice Youth Advocates

Followed by: Exile (2011)

Exile. Speak 2011 295p pa $8.99
Grades: 8 9 10 11

1. Princesses -- Fiction 2. Voyages and travels -- Fiction
ISBN 978-0-14-241739-3; 0-14-241739-4

LC 2010009645

Sequel to Aurelia (2008)

In exile, Princess Aurelia is free of responsibilities, able to travel the country and meet the people of Tyralt, but when her journey erupts in a fiery conflagration that puts the fate of the kingdom in peril, she and her companion Robert must determine whether they have the strength and the will to complete their mission.

Ostlere, Cathy

★ Karma; a novel in verse. Razorbill 2011 517p map $18.99
Grades: 7 8 9 10 11 12

1. Novels in verse 2. India -- Fiction 3. Violence -- Fiction 4. Culture conflict -- Fiction
ISBN 978-1-59514-338-9; 1-59514-338-6

"The novel's pace and tension will compel readers to read at a gallop, but then stop again and again to turn a finely crafted phrase, whether to appreciate the richness of the language and imagery or to reconsider the layers beneath a thought. This is a book in which readers will consider the roots and realities of destiny and chance. Karma is a spectacular, sophisticated tale that will stick with readers long after they're done considering its last lines." SLJ

Ostow, Micol

The devil and Winnie Flynn. By Micol Ostow and David Ostow. Soho Teen 2015 336 p. Illustration
Grades: 9 10 11 12

1. Mystery and detective stories 2. Psychic ability -- Fiction 3. Supernatural -- Fiction 4. Television programs -- Production and direction -- Fiction 5. Mystery fiction 6. Television programs -- Fiction
9781616955977, $18.99

LC 2015009878

In this book, by Micol Ostow and David Ostow, Winnie Flynn doesn't believe in ghosts. . . . When her mysterious aunt Maggie . . . recruits Winnie to spend a summer working as a production assistant on her current reality hit, Fantastic, Fearsome, she suddenly finds herself in . . . New Jersey. New Jersey's famous Devil makes perfect fodder for Maggie's show. But as the filming progresses, Winnie sees and hears things that make her think that the Devil might not be totally fake." (Publisher's note)

"This stylish novel is both a celebration of horror as a genre and chilling in its own right." Kirkus

Emily Goldberg learns to salsa. Razorbill 2006 200p $16.99
Grades: 7 8 9 10

1. Jews -- Fiction 2. Family life -- Fiction 3. Puerto Ricans -- Fiction 4. Racially mixed people -- Fiction
ISBN 1-59514-081-6

LC 2006-14651

Forced to stay with her mother in Puerto Rico for weeks after her grandmother's funeral, half-Jewish Emily, who has just graduated from a Westchester, New York high school, does not find it easy to connect with her Puerto Rican heritage and relatives she had never met.

This is "a moving story that has a solid plotline and plenty of family secrets." Booklist

★ **So** punk rock (and other ways to disappoint your mother) a novel. with art by David Ostow. Flux 2009 246p il pa $9.95

Grades: 8 9 10 11 12

1. School stories 2. New Jersey -- Fiction 3. Rock music -- Fiction 4. Bands (Music) -- Fiction 5. Jews -- United States -- Fiction

ISBN 978-0-7387-1471-4; 0-7387-1471-2

LC 2009-8216

Four suburban New Jersey students from the Leo R. Gittleman Jewish Day School form a rock band that becomes inexplicably popular, creating exhiliration, friction, confrontation, and soul-searching among its members.

The "comic-strip-style illustrations are true show-stoppers. . . . A rollicking, witty, and ultra-contemporary book that drums on the funny bone and reverberates through the heart." Booklist

Ostrovski, Emil

Away we go. By Emil Ostrovski. Harpercollins Childrens Books 2016 288 p.

Grades: 9 10 11 12

1. School stories 2. Death -- Fiction

9780062238559, $17.99; 0062238558

LC 2015035883

In this novel, by Emil Ostrovski, "Westing is not your typical school. For starters, you have to have one very important quality in order to be admitted—you have to be dying. Every student at Westing has been diagnosed with PPV, or the Peter Pan Virus, and no one is expected to live to graduation. What do you do when you go to a high school where no one has a future or any clue how to find meaning in their remaining days?" (Publisher's note)

"Noah's snarky repartee and constant jokes belie the depth of his struggle, and the oscillation between his heartfelt interior thoughts and sometimes careless actions and words is both moving and infuriating-in other words, vividly human. An intelligent, thought-provoking exploration of living in spite of futility." Booklist

Owen, James A.

Here, there be dragons; written and illustrated by James A. Owen. Simon & Schuster Books for Young Readers 2006 326p il (The Chronicles of the Imaginarium Geographica) $17.95

Grades: 8 9 10 11 12

1. Poets 2. Fantasy fiction

ISBN 978-1-4169-1227-9; 1-4169-1227-4

LC 2005-30486

Three young men are entrusted with the Imaginarium Geographica, an atlas of fantastical places to which they travel in hopes of defeating the Winter King whose bid for power is related to the First World War raging in the Real World.

"From the arresting prologue, the reader is gripped by a finely crafted fantasy tale and compelled to continue. . . . This superb saga has interesting characters and plenty of action." Voice Youth Advocates

Other titles in this series are:

The search for the Red Dragon (2007)

The indigo king (2008)

The shadow dragons (2009)

The dragon's apprentice (2010)

Padian, Maria

Jersey tomatoes are the best. Alfred A. Knopf 2011 344p $16.99; lib bdg $19.99

Grades: 7 8 9 10

1. Camps -- Fiction 2. Ballet -- Fiction 3. Tennis -- Fiction 4. Friendship -- Fiction 5. Anorexia nervosa -- Fiction

ISBN 978-0-375-86579-4; 0-375-86579-9; 978-0-375-96579-1 lib bdg; 0-375-96579-3 lib bdg

LC 2010-11827

When fifteen-year-old best friends Henry and Eve leave New Jersey, one for tennis camp in Florida and one for ballet camp in New York, each faces challenges that put her long-cherished dreams of the future to the test.

"Padian's writing and plotting are clean and clear, and her handling of the duo's dilemmas never stoops to melodrama. An excellent read for sports lovers who desire some meaty beefsteak in their stories." Booklist

★ **Wrecked**. By Maria Padian. Algonquin Young Readers 2016 357 p.

Grades: 9 10 11 12

1. Rape -- Investigation -- Fiction 2. Universities and colleges -- Fiction 3. College students -- Fiction 4. Date rape -- Fiction

9781616206604, $17.95; 1616206241; 9781616206246, $17.95

LC 2016020315

In this novel, by Maria Padian, "when Jenny accuses Jordan of rape, Haley and Richard are pushed to opposite sides of the school's investigation. Now conflicting versions of the story may make bringing the truth to light nearly impossible—especially when reputations, relationships, and whole futures are riding on the verdict." (Publisher's note)

"All characters are realistically flawed and human as they struggle to do what's right. In the face of recent college rape trials, readers will be rapt and emotionally spent by the end." Kirkus

Published simultaneously in Canada by Thomas Allen & Son Limited.

Palmer, Robin

The **Corner** of Bitter and Sweet; by Robin Palmer. Penguin Group USA 2013 400 p. $9.99

Grades: 7 8 9 10 11 12

1. Children of alcoholics -- Fiction 2. Television personalities -- Fiction 3. Mother-daughter relationship -- Fiction

ISBN 0142412503; 9780142412503

In this book by Robin Palmer, "a teenage girl and her showbiz mom are forced to re-evaluate their relationship after rehab. . . . To learn how to cope, Annabelle joins Alateen.

But when Janie scores a role in a new movie with hot young superstar Billy Barrett, Annabelle frets that if anything goes wrong, it could put her mom right back on the bottle. Fortunately she's distracted by her own crush on small-town boy Matt and the lure of a college photography fellowship." (Kirkus Reviews)

Geek charming. Speak 2009 338p pa $7.99

Grades: 7 8 9 10

1. School stories 2. Popularity -- Fiction
ISBN 0-14-241122-1; 978-0-14-241122-3

LC 2008-25918

Rich, spoiled, and popular high school senior Dylan is coerced into doing a documentary film with Josh, one of the school's geeks, who leads her to realize that the world does not revolve around her.

This is "a lighthearted contemporary novel filled with snappy dialogue. . . . Rather than following the predictable route of having opposites fall in love, Palmer . . . offers a slightly more original and plausible alternative." Publ Wkly

Paolini, Christopher

★ **Eragon**. Knopf 2003 509p (Inheritance) $18.95; lib bdg $20.99; pa $6.99

Grades: 7 8 9 10

1. Fantasy fiction 2. Dragons -- Fiction
ISBN 0-375-82668-8; 0-375-92668-2 lib bdg; 0-440-23848-X pa

LC 2003-47481

First published 2002 in different form by Paolini International

In Alagaesia, a fifteen-year-old boy of unknown lineage called Eragon finds a mysterious stone that weaves his life into an intricate tapestry of destiny, magic, and power, peopled with dragons, elves, and monsters

"This unusual, powerful tale . . . is the first book in the planned Inheritance trilogy. . . . The telling remains constantly fresh and fluid, and [the author] has done a fine job of creating an appealing and convincing relationship between the youth and the dragon." Booklist

Other titles in this series are:
Eldest (2005)
Brisingr (2008)
Inheritance (2011)

Papademetriou, Lisa

Drop. Alfred A. Knopf 2008 169p $15.99; lib bdg $18.99

Grades: 8 9 10 11 12

1. Gambling -- Fiction
ISBN 978-0-375-84244-3; 0-375-84244-6; 978-0-375-94244-0 lib bdg; 0-375-94244-0 lib bdg

LC 2008-02568

Sixteen-year-old math prodigy Jerrica discovers she has the ability to predict outcomes in blackjack and roulette, and joins forces with Sanjay and Kat to develop her theories while helping them get the money they desperately need.

"The characters are well drawn and the excitement of the gambling scenes is well executed. Additionally, some surprising details about the teens turn the story upside down, unraveling everything that readers thought they knew about them. A page-turner." SLJ

Park, Linda Sue, 1960-

Click; [by] Linda Sue Park [et al.] Arthur A. Levine Books 2007 217p $16.99

Grades: 7 8 9 10

1. Adventure fiction 2. Photojournalism -- Fiction
ISBN 0-439-41138-6; 978-0-439-41138-7

LC 2006-100069

"Ten distinguished authors each write a chapter of this intriguing novel of mystery and family, which examines the lives touched by a photojournalist George Keane, aka Gee. . . . The authors' distinctive styles remain evident; although readers expecting a more straightforward or linear story may find the leaps through time and place challenging, the thematic currents help the chapters gel into a cohesive whole." Publ Wkly

A **long** walk to water; based on a true story. Clarion Books 2010 121p map $16

Grades: 6 7 8 9 10

1. Refugees 2. Relief workers 3. Water -- Fiction 4. Africans -- Fiction 5. Refugees -- Fiction 6. Sudan -- History -- Civil War, 1983-2005 -- Fiction
ISBN 0-547-25127-0; 978-0-547-25127-1

LC 2009-48857

When the Sudanese civil war reaches his village in 1985, eleven-year-old Salva becomes separated from his family and must walk with other Dinka tribe members through southern Sudan, Ethiopia, and Kenya in search of safe haven. Based on the life of Salva Dut, who, after emigrating to America in 1996, began a project to dig water wells in Sudan.

This is a "spare, immediate account. . . . Young readers will be stunned by the triumphant climax of the former refugee who makes a difference." Booklist

Parker, Amy Christine

Astray. Amy Christine Parker. Random House 2014 343 p.

Grades: 9 10 11 12

1. Charisma (Personality trait) -- Fiction 2. Cults -- Fiction 3. Religious leaders -- Fiction 4. Survival -- Fiction 5. Utopias -- Fiction 6. Utopian fiction 7. Religious life -- Fiction 8. Brainwashing -- Fiction 9. Survival skills -- Fiction
0449816028; 9780449816028, $17.99; 9780449816035

LC 2013034047

This book, by Amy Christine Parker, is a "contemporary young adult thriller. . . . Lyla Hamilton almost died escaping the Community. In her new life, the outsiders call the Community a cult. . . . The Community is willing to do terrible things to bring her back to the fold. The members are still preaching Pioneer's twisted message that the end of the world is near. Pulled in two directions and unsure which way to turn, Lyla risks everything to follow her heart." (Publisher's note)

"As a brainwashed teen, Lyla's first-person narration is unreliable and emotional, scared yet resilient. This is a creepy, compelling, and enjoyable read." Horn Book

Sequel to: Gated (2013)

★ **Gated**; by Amy Christine Parker. 1st ed. Random House Inc 2013 339 p. (hardcover) $17.99; (library) $20.99

Grades: 9 10 11 12

    1. Love stories 2. Cults -- Fiction 3. Utopias -- Fiction 4. Survival -- Fiction 5. Religious leaders -- Fiction

    ISBN 0449815978; 9780449815977; 9780449815984

                      LC 2012048123

In this book, 17-year-old "Lyla is part of the Community, a group of families led by the charismatic Pioneer, who has secluded them from the outside world in anticipation of the imminent apocalypse. With Pioneer's prophesied deadline fast approaching, Lyla struggles with her faith and resolve. A chance encounter with Cody, a boy from the outside, further tempts her away from the way of the Community, but when events escalate," she may have to make a difficult choice. (Publishers Weekly)

"Part of a select few who will survive the end of the world, Lyla and her family live in the Community, led by prophet Pioneer, and she can barely remember her old life. Then an outsider raises questions she shouldn't be asking, and Pioneer does not appreciate questions. Slowly mounting action builds suspense in this coming-of-age story and examination of cult mentality." (Horn Book)

Parker, S. M.

The rattled bones. By S.M. Parker. Simon Pulse 2017 370 p.

Grades: 10 11 12

    1. Archaeology -- Fiction; 2. Islands -- Fiction; 3. Lobster fishers -- Fiction; 4. Racism -- Fiction; 5. Maine -- Fiction; 6. Fishers -- Fiction; 7. Ghost stories -- Fiction; 8. Archeology -- Fiction

    9781481482066; 9781481482042, $17.99

                      LC 2016056047

In this novel, by S.M. Parker, "Maine-bred, independent Rilla Brae...knows the rhythms of hard work and harder seas. But when she experiences the sudden death of her father, the veil between the living and the dead blurs and she begins to be haunted by a girl on a nearby, uninhabited island.... Then Rilla meets Sam, a University of Southern Maine archeology student tasked with excavating the very island where the ghostly girl has appeared." (Publisher's note)

"Parker's vivid descriptions of life on Maine's coast and the lobstering business ground a haunting and atmospheric tale about the sea and reckoning with a community's past." Pub Wkly

Includes bibliographical references and index

Parkinson, Siobhán

Long story short. Roaring Brook Press 2011 160p $16.99

Grades: 6 7 8 9 10

    1. Ireland -- Fiction 2. Siblings -- Fiction 3. Runaway children -- Fiction

    ISBN 978-1-59643-647-3; 1-59643-647-6

                      LC 2010-29023

Fourteen-year-old Jono and his eight-year-old sister Julie run away when, soon after their grandmother's death, their alcoholic mother hits Julie, but when the police find them in Galway, Jono learns he is in big trouble.

"A deeply affecting story about what can go wrong when adults fail children and the choices available to them are all bad." Publ Wkly

Parks, Kathy

Notes from my captivity. Kathy Parks, edited by Claudia Gabel. Katherine Tegen Books 2018 352 p.

Grades: 9 10 11 12

    1. Siberia (Russia) -- Fiction; 2. Family life -- Fiction; 3. Wilderness survival -- Fiction

    9780062394002, $17.99

                      LC 2017962569

In this book, by Kathy Parks, edited by Claudia Gabel, "Adrienne Cahill cares about three things: getting into a great college; becoming a revered journalist...and making her late father proud of her. So when Adrienne is offered the chance to write an article that will get her into her dream school and debunk her foolish stepfather's belief that a legendary family of hermits is living in the Siberian wilderness, there's no question that she's going to fly across the world." (Publisher's note)

Patel, Sonia

Rani Patel in full effect. By Sonia Patel. Cinco Puntos Press 2016 224 p.

Grades: 9 10 11 12

    1. East Indian Americans -- Fiction 2. Family life -- Hawaii -- Fiction 3. Hip-hop -- Fiction 4. Immigrants -- Fiction 5. Self-esteem -- Fiction 6. Sexual abuse -- Fiction 7. Molokai (Hawaii) -- Fiction 8. Sex crimes -- Fiction

    9781941026519, $11.99; 1941026494; 9781941026496, $16.95; 9781941026502

                      LC 2016013016

Morris Finalist (2017)

In this young adult novel by Sonia Patel, "Rani Patel . . . [is a] nobody who lives with her Gujarati immigrant parents on the remote Hawaiian island of Moloka'i, isolated from her high school peers by the unsettling norms of Indian culture where 'husband is God.' . . . Her sexy bald head and hard-driving rhyming skills attract the attention of Mark, . . . [who] is closer in age to her dad than to her. . . . [Mark] leads Rani into . . . things she's never done." (Publisher's note)

"Vivid, bold, and passionate." Booklist

Patrick, Cat

Forgotten; a novel. Little, Brown 2011 288p $17.99

Grades: 7 8 9 10 11

    1. School stories 2. Memory -- Fiction 3. Family life -- Fiction 4. Dating (Social customs) -- Fiction

    ISBN 978-0-316-09461-0; 0-316-09461-7

                      LC 2010-43032

Sixteen-year-old London Lane forgets everything each night and must use notes to struggle through the day, even to recall her wonderful boyfriend, but she "remembers" future events and as her "flashforwards" become more disturbing she realizes she must learn more about the past lest it destroy her future.

"Patrick raises philosophical issues of real interest. . . . Thoughtful readers will enjoy the mind games, romance readers will enjoy the relationship dynamics, and all readers will find themselves inexorably pulled into a logical yet surprising and compelling finish." Booklist

The Originals; Cat Patrick. 1st ed. Little, Brown and Co. 2013 304 p. (hardcover) $18
Grades: 8 9 10 11 12
    1. Sisters -- Fiction 2. Human cloning -- Fiction 3. Dating (Social customs) -- Fiction 4. Cloning -- Fiction 5. Individuality -- Fiction 6. Single-parent families -- Fiction
ISBN 0316219436; 9780316219433
                         LC 2012029853
In this novel, by Cat Patrick, "17-year-olds Lizzie, Ella, and Betsey Best grew up as identical triplets . . . until they discovered a shocking family secret. They're actually closer than sisters, they're clones . . . , hiding from a government agency that would expose them. . . . Then Lizzie meets Sean Kelly. . . . As their relationship develops, Lizzie realizes that she's not a carbon copy of her sisters; she's an individual with unique dreams and desires." (Publisher's note)

Revived; by Cat Patrick. 1st ed. Little, Brown & Co. 2012 336 p. (hardcover) $17.99; (paperback) $8.99
Grades: 7 8 9 10 11 12
    1. Drugs -- Testing 2. Secrecy -- Fiction 3. Science -- Experiments -- Fiction 4. Death -- Fiction 5. Drugs -- Fiction 6. High schools -- Fiction 7. Moving, Household -- Fiction
ISBN 0316094625; 9780316094627; 9780316094634
                         LC 2011026950
This book, by Cat Patrick, follows Daisy, who since the age of five has been "part of a top-secret clinical trial for a drug called Revive that can bring the deceased back to life. . . . Daisy uncovers some secrets within the program: a mysterious extra case file, a new test batch of Revive, some unexplained car crashes, and the erratic behavior of the mysterious man at the top, nicknamed God." (Bulletin of the Center for Children's Books)

Patrick, Denise Lewis
    A **matter** of souls. Denise Lewis Patrick. Carolrhoda Lab. 2014 186p $16.95
Grades: 7 8 9 10 11 12
    1. African Americans -- Southern States -- Fiction 2. Race relations -- Fiction 3. Southern States -- History -- Fiction 4. American short stories 5. African Americans -- History 6. Southern States -- Fiction
ISBN: 0761392807; 9780761392804
                         LC 2013017597
Through a series of vignettes the author "considers the souls of black men and women across centuries and continents. In each, she takes the measure of their dignity, describes their dreams, and catalogs their fears. Brutality, beauty, laughter, rage, and love all take their turns in each story, but the final impression is of indomitable, luminous, and connected souls." (Publisher's note)
"Eight short stories with long memory cut to the quick- all the more as they could be true. Patrick's tales from the distant and not-so-distant past shed fresh light on interracial and intraracial conflicts that shape and often distort the realities of African-Americans. . . . The plots and characters

change from one story to the next, but each one artfully tells a poignant truth without flinching. Shocking, informative and powerful, this volume offers spectacular literary snapshots of black history and culture." Kirkus

Patterson, James
    Homeroom diaries. by James Patterson & Lisa Papademetriou ; illustrated by Keino. Little, Brown and Co. 2014 246p $18.00
Grades: 7 8 9 10
    1. Diaries -- Fiction 2. Foster home care -- Fiction 3. Friendship -- Fiction 4. High schools -- Fiction 5. Teenage girls —Fiction
ISBN: 0316207624; 9780316207621
                         LC 2013016061
"Margaret 'Cuckoo' Clarke recently had a brief stay in a mental institution following an emotional breakdown, but she's turning over a new leaf with her 'Operation Happiness.' She's determined to beat down the bad vibes of the Haters, the Terror Teachers, and all of the trials and tribulations of high school by writing and drawing in her diary." (Publisher's note)
"Cuckoo is a well-developed and accessible protagonist. She is introspective and she copes with life's difficulties by spending a lot of time in her head and writing alternative endings to movies in her journal. Despite the fact that serious issues (a negligent mother, an attempted sexual assault, and an incident of cyberbullying) are at play, the lighthearted tone adds levity to the work." SLJ

    Maximum Ride: the angel experiment. Little, Brown 2005 422p (Maximum Ride) $16.99
Grades: 7 8 9 10
    1. Science fiction 2. Genetic engineering -- Fiction
ISBN 0-316-15556-X
                         LC 2004-18623
After the mutant Erasers abduct the youngest member of their group, the "bird kids," who are the result of genetic experimentation, take off in pursuit and find themselves struggling to understand their own origins and purpose.
"Smart-mouthed sympathetic characters and copious butt-kicking make this fast read pure escapist pleasure." Horn Book Guide
    Other titles in this series are:
    School's out - forever (2006)
    Saving the world and other extreme sports (2007)
    Final warning (2008)
    Max (2009)
    Fang (2010)
    Angel (2011)

Pattou, Edith
    East. Harcourt 2003 498p hardcover o.p. pa $8.95
Grades: 7 8 9 10
    1. Fairy tales 2. Bears -- Fiction
ISBN 0-15-204563-5; 0-15-205221-6 pa
                         LC 2003-2338
A young woman journeys to a distant castle on the back of a great white bear who is the victim of a cruel enchantment

"Readers with a taste for fantasy and folklore will embrace Pattou's . . . lushly rendered retelling of 'East of the Sun and West of the Moon'." Publ Wkly

Ghosting. Edith Pattou. Skyscape 2014 423 p.
Grades: 9 10 11 12
　　1. Firearms accidents -- Fiction 2. Teenagers -- Fiction 3. Practical jokes -- Fiction 4. Violence -- Fiction
147784774X; 9781477847749, $16.99; 9781477847893
　　　　　　　　　　　　　　　　LC 2014933207
In this young adult novel by Edith Pattou, "on a hot summer night in a midwestern town, a high school teenage prank goes horrifically awry. Alcohol, guns, and a dare. Within minutes, as events collide, innocents becomes victims—with tragic outcomes altering lives forever, a grisly and unfortunate scenario all too familiar from current real-life headlines. But victims can also become survivors, and . . . we see how . . . they can reach out to one another . . . and survive." (Publisher's note)
"Pattou's deliberate attentiveness to character maturation, along with familial ties that bind and strain, strengthen this skillful portrayal of teen wrongheadedness at a most vulnerable moment." Booklist

Paulsen, Gary
　　Crush; the theory, practice, and destructive properties of love. Gary Paulsen. Wendy Lamb Books 2012 136 p.
Grades: 5 6 7 8
　　1. Love -- Fiction 2. Humorous fiction 3. Crushes -- Fiction 4. High school students -- Fiction 5. Dating (Social customs) -- Fiction 6. Humorous stories 7. Interpersonal relations -- Fiction
ISBN 0385742304; 9780307974532; 9780375990540; 9780385742306; 9780385742313
　　　　　　　　　　　　　　　　LC 2011028915
In this book, "Tina, aka the most beautiful girl he's ever seen, has stolen Kevin's heart, although she's blissfully oblivious to the effect she has on him. . . . Rather than reveal his ardor outright, Kevin decides it's safer to first make a scientific study of just how love works by setting up romantic opportunities for his victims (otherwise known as study subjects). He starts by trying to create a candlelit dinner for his parents, although he accidentally causes a fire." (Kirkus Reviews)

　　Nightjohn. Delacorte Press 1993 92p $15.95; pa $5.99
Grades: 7 8 9 10
　　1. Reading -- Fiction 2. Slavery -- Fiction 3. African Americans -- Fiction
ISBN 0-385-30838-8; 0-440-21936-1 pa
　　　　　　　　　　　　　　　　LC 92-1222
Twelve-year-old Sarny's brutal life as a slave becomes even more dangerous when a newly arrived slave offers to teach her how to read
"Paulsen is at his best here: the writing is stark and bare-boned, without stylistic pretensions of any kind. The narrator's voice is strong and true, the violence real but stylized with an almost mythic tone. . . . The simplicity of the text will make the book ideal for older reluctant readers who can handle violence but can't or won't handle fancy writing in

long books. Best of all, the metaphor of reading as an act of freedom speaks for itself through striking action unembroidered by didactic messages." Bull Cent Child Books

★ **Woods** runner. Wendy Lamb Books 2010 164p $15.99; lib bdg $18.99
Grades: 6 7 8 9
　　1. Spies -- Fiction 2. Soldiers -- Fiction 3. Kidnapping -- Fiction 4. Native Americans -- Fiction 5. Frontier and pioneer life -- Fiction
ISBN 978-0-385-73884-2; 0-385-73884-6; 978-0-385-90751-4 lib bdg; 0-385-90751-6 lib bdg
　　　　　　　　　　　　　　　　LC 2009-27397
From his 1776 Pennsylvania homestead, thirteen-year-old Samuel, who is a highly-skilled woodsman, sets out toward New York City to rescue his parents from the band of British soldiers and Indians who kidnapped them after slaughtering most of their community. Includes historical notes.
"Paulsen fortifies this illuminating and gripping story with interspersed historical sections that offer details about frontier life and the war (such as technology, alliances, and other period information), helping place Sam's struggles in context." Publ Wkly

Peacock, Shane
　　Eye of the crow. Tundra Books 2007 264p (The boy Sherlock Holmes) $24.99; pa $9.95
Grades: 6 7 8 9 10
　　1. Mystery fiction 2. Great Britain -- History -- 19th century -- Fiction
ISBN 978-0-88776-850-7; 0-88776-850-4; 978-0-88776-919-1 pa; 0-88776-919-5 pa
"A young woman is brutally murdered in a dark back street of Whitechapel; a young Arab is discovered with the bloody murder weapon; and a thirteen-year-old Sherlock Holmes, who was seen speaking with the alleged killer as he was hauled into jail, is suspected to be his accomplice. . . . Although imaginative reconstruction of Holmes childhood has been the subject of literary and cinematic endeavors, Peacock's take ranks among the most successful." Bull Cent Child Books
　　Other titles in this series are:
　　Death in the air (2008)
　　The dragon turn (2011)
　　The secret fiend (2010)
　　Vanishing girl (2009)

Pearce, Jackson
　　As you wish. HarperTeen 2009 298p $16.99
Grades: 6 7 8 9
　　1. School stories 2. Wishes -- Fiction 3. Artists -- Fiction 4. Popularity -- Fiction 5. Gay teenagers -- Fiction
ISBN 006166152X; 0061661538; 0061661546; 9780061661525; 9780061661532; 9780061661549
　　　　　　　　　　　　　　　　LC 2008-44033
When a genie arrives to grant sixteen-year-old Viola's wish to feel she belongs, as she did before her best friend/boyfriend announced that he is gay, her delay in making wishes gives her and the mysterious Jinn time to fall in love.

"Written in alternating chapters between Jinn and Viola, the story unfolds to rapidly change from the regular 'genie in the bottle' saga to a poignant tale of love and sacrifices made in the name of love. . . . The result is a fabulous fantasy from a first time author." Voice Youth Advocates

Sisters red. Little, Brown 2010 328p $16.99
Grades: 9 10 11 12
    1. Sisters -- Fiction 2. Werewolves -- Fiction 3. Supernatural -- Fiction
    ISBN 978-0-316-06868-0
                      LC 2009-44734
After a Fenris, or werewolf, killed their grandmother and almost killed them, sisters Scarlett and Rosie March devote themselves to hunting and killing the beasts that prey on teenaged girls, learning how to lure them with red cloaks and occasionally using the help of their old friend, Silas, the woodsman's son.

"Told by the sisters in alternating chapters, this well-written, high-action adventure grabs readers and never lets go." SLJ

Pearson, Joanna
    The **rites** & wrongs of Janice Wills. Arthur A. Levine Books 2011 218p $16.99
Grades: 8 9 10 11 12
    1. School stories 2. Anthropology -- Fiction 3. North Carolina -- Fiction
    ISBN 978-0-545-19773-1; 0-545-19773-2
                      LC 2010029348
Aspiring anthropologist Janice Wills reports on the sociocultural ordeals of being an almost-seventeen-year-old in Melva, North Carolina, including "Beautiful Rich Girls," parties, and the Miss Livermush pageant.

"This anthropological observation-style novel is unique and provides a great social commentary on the life of teenagers. It is a cute story that includes mentions of bisexuality, some strong language, and the hint that the Hot Theater Guy might push Janice too far, but it remains a fun look at life in small town Southern society." Voice Youth Advocates

Pearson, Mary E.
    ★ The **adoration** of Jenna Fox; [by] Mary E. Pearson. Henry Holt and Co. 2008 272p $16.95; pa $8.99
Grades: 7 8 9 10 11 12
    1. Science fiction 2. Bioethics -- Fiction
    ISBN 978-0-8050-7668-4; 0-8050-7668-9; 978-0-312-59441-1 pa; 0-312-59441-0 pa
                      LC 2007-27314
In the not-too-distant future, when biotechnological advances have made synthetic bodies and brains possible but illegal, a seventeen-year-old girl, recovering from a serious accident and suffering from memory lapses, learns a startling secret about her existence.

"The science . . . and the science fiction are fascinating, but what will hold readers most are the moral issues of betrayal, loyalty, sacrifice, and survival." Booklist
Followed by The Fox inheritance (2011)

Dance of thieves. Mary E. Pearson. Henry Holt & Co. 2018 512 p.

Grades: 8 9 10 11 12
    1. Criminals -- Fiction; 2. Romance fiction; 3. Thieves -- Fiction
    9781250159014, $18.99; 9781250159021
                      LC 2017957735
In this book, by Mary E. Pearson "a formidable outlaw family that claims to be the first among nations. A son destined to lead, thrust suddenly into power. Three fierce young women of the Rahtan, the queen's premier guard. A legendary street thief leading a mission.... When outlaw leader meets reformed thief, a cat-and-mouse game of false moves ensues, bringing them intimately together in a battle that may cost them their lives -- and their hearts." (Publisher's note)

Fox forever; Mary E. Pearson. Henry Holt and Company 2013 304 p. (hardcover) $17.99
Grades: 7 8 9 10 11 12
    1. Science fiction 2. Dystopian fiction 3. Bioethics -- Fiction 4. Biotechnology -- Fiction 5. Medical ethics -- Fiction 6. Government, resistance to -- Fiction
    ISBN 0805094342; 9780805094343
                      LC 2012027677
This young adult novel, by Mary E. Pearson, is the conclusion to the "Jenna Fox Chronicles." "After . . . 260 years as a disembodied mind in a little black box, [Lock Jenkins] has a . . . body. But . . . he'll have to return the Favor he accepted from the . . . Network. Locke must infiltrate the home of a government official by gaining the trust of his daughter, seventeen-year-old Raine, and he soon finds himself pulled deep into the world of the resistance--and into Raine's life." (Publisher's note)

The **Fox** Inheritance; [by] Mary E. Pearson. Henry Holt 2011 384p $16.99
Grades: 7 8 9 10 11 12
    1. Science fiction 2. Bioethics -- Fiction
    ISBN 0805088296; 9780805088298
                      LC 2011004800
Sequel to: The adoration of Jenna Fox (2008)
Two-hundred-sixty years after a terrible accident destroyed their bodies, sixteen-year-old Locke and seventeen-year-old Kara have been brought back to life in newly bioengineered bodies, with many questions about the world they find themselves in and more than two centuries of horrible memories of being trapped in a digital netherworld wondering what would become of them.

"Pearson delivers another spellbinding thriller. . . . A dazzling blend of science fiction, mystery, and teen friendship drama." Publ Wkly

The **kiss** of deception. Mary E. Pearson. Henry Holt Books for Young Readers 2014 496 p. (The Remnant Chronicles)
Grades: 9 10 11 12
    1. Deception -- Fiction 2. Fantasy 3. Love -- Fiction 4. Princesses -- Fiction
    0805099239; 9780805099232, $17.99
                      LC 2014005163
In this novel by Mary E. Pearson, "Princess Lia's life follows a preordained course. As First Daughter, she is expected to have the revered gift of sight—but she doesn't—and she knows her parents are perpetrating a sham when they

arrange her marriage to secure an alliance with a neighboring kingdom—to a prince she has never met. On the morning of her wedding, Lia flees to a distant village. She settles into a new life, hopeful when two mysterious and handsome strangers arrive—and unaware that one is the jilted prince and the other an assassin sent to kill her. Deception abounds, and Lia finds herself on the brink of unlocking perilous secrets—even as she finds herself falling in love." (Publisher's note)

"This has the sweep of an epic tale, told with some twists; it's a book that almost doesn't need a sequel, but readers will be thrilled that it continues on." Booklist

Other titles in the series are: The Heart of Betrayal (2015)

★ The **miles** between; [by] Mary E. Pearson. Henry Holt 2009 266p $16.99

Grades: 9 10 11 12

1. School stories 2. Friendship -- Fiction

ISBN 978-0-8050-8828-1; 0-8050-8828-8

LC 2008-50277

Seventeen-year-old Destiny keeps a painful childhood secret all to herself until she and three classmates from her exclusive boarding school take off on an unauthorized road trip in search of "one fair day."

"Pearson skillfully separates truth from illusion and offers an uplifting book, in which grace and redemption are never left to chance." Booklist

A **room** on Lorelei Street; [by] Mary E. Pearson. Henry Holt 2005 266p $16.95

Grades: 9 10 11 12

1. Texas -- Fiction 2. Alcoholism -- Fiction 3. Family life -- Fiction

ISBN 0-8050-7667-0

LC 2004-54015

To escape a miserable existence taking care of her alcoholic mother, seventeen-year-old Zoe rents a room from an eccentric woman, but her earnings as a waitress after school are minimal and she must go to extremes to cover expenses.

"Readers drawn to rescue dramas may particularly appreciate this story of a girl who's trying against odds to rescue herself." Bull Cent Child Books

Peck, Dale

Sprout. Bloomsbury 2009 277p $16.99

Grades: 9 10 11 12

1. Kansas -- Fiction 2. Friendship -- Fiction 3. Gay teenagers -- Fiction 4. Father-son relationship -- Fiction

ISBN 978-1-59990-160-2; 1-59990-160-9

LC 2008-40922

ALA GLBTRT Stonewall Book Award Honor Book (2010)

Moving from Long Island to Kansas after his mother dies, a teenaged boy nicknamed Sprout is surprised to find new friends, a fascinating landscape, and romantic love.

"Sharply witty and bittersweet, this story . . . is a stellar step ahead for young adult literature's traditional examination of the life of the heroic antihero. Finely honed characters and an engaging voice make it an easy book for teen readers who like emotional challenges as well as word tricks to love." Voice Youth Advocates

Peck, Richard

The **river** between us. Dial Bks. 2003 164p $16.99; pa $6.99

Grades: 7 8 9 10

1. Race relations -- Fiction 2. Racially mixed people -- Fiction

ISBN 0-8037-2735-6; 0-14-240310-5 pa

LC 2002-34815

During the early days of the Civil War, the Pruitt family takes in two mysterious young ladies who have fled New Orleans to come north to Illinois

"The harsh realities of war are brutally related in a complex, always surprising plot that resonates on mutiple levels." Horn Book Guide

Peck, Robert Newton

★ A **day** no pigs would die. Knopf 1973 150p $25; pa $5.50

Grades: 6 7 8 9

1. Pigs -- Fiction 2. Shakers -- Fiction 3. Family life -- Fiction 4. Autobiographical stories 5. Father-son relationship -- Fiction

ISBN 0-394-48235-2; 0-679-85306-5 pa

"Rob lives a rigorous life on a Shaker farm in Vermont in the 1920s. Since farm life is earthy, this book is filled with Yankee humor and explicit descriptions of animals mating. A painful incident that involves the slaughter of Rob's beloved pet pig is instrumental in urging him toward adulthood. The death of his father completes the process of his accepting responsibility." Shapiro. Fic for Youth. 3d edition

Peet, Mal

Beck. Mal Peet ; with Meg Rosoff. Candlewick Press 2017 261 p.

Grades: 10 11 12

1. Orphans -- Fiction; 2. Bildungsromans; 3. Depressions -- 1929 -- Fiction

0763678422; 9780763678425, $17.99; 9780763687175

LC 2017933647

This final novel from Mal Peet, completed by Meg Rosoff, "is a not-quite-YA, not-quite-adult historical fiction story of hardship after hardship...The book itself is incredibly ambitious, as was Rosoff's task of finishing it. Beck is a passive character in his own life, but in the moments when he pushes himself to take action, readers will finally get some satisfaction. A heartbreaking, painful work that gives hope to the restorative power of true human connection." (School Library Journal)

"Harrowing but hopeful, it's a memorable portrait of a boy struggling to love, be loved, and find his way against overwhelming odds." Pub Wkly

Includes bibliographical references (page 266)

★ **Life**; an exploded diagram. Candlewick Press 2011 385p il $17.99

Grades: 9 10 11 12

1. War stories 2. Family life -- Fiction 3. Great Britain -- Fiction 4. Social classes -- Fiction

ISBN 978-0-7636-5227-2; 978-0-7636-5631-7 ebook

LC 2010042742

In 1960s Norfolk, England, seventeen-year-old Clem Ackroyd lives with his mother and grandmother in a tiny cottage, but his life is transformed when he falls in love with the daughter of a wealthy farmer in this tale that flashes back through the stories of three generations.

"This [book] is mesmerizing through the sheer force and liveliness of its prose, as well as its unpredictable, inexorable plot. . . . Peet's subtle, literary play with narrative voice, style, and chronology make this a satisfyingly sophisticated teen novel. Outstanding." Horn Book

★ **Tamar**. Candlewick Press 2007 424p $17.99
Grades: 8 9 10 11 12
1. Netherlands -- Fiction 2. Grandfathers -- Fiction 3. World War, 1939-1945 -- Fiction
ISBN 978-0-7636-3488-9; 0-7636-3488-3
LC 2006-51837

In 1995, 15-year-old Tamar inherits a box containing a series of coded messages from his late grandfather. The messages show Tamar the life that his grandfather lived during World War II the life of an Allied undercover operative in Nazi-occupied Holland.

"Peet's plot is tightly constructed, and striking, descriptive language, full of metaphor, grounds the story." Booklist

Peevyhouse, Parker
Where futures end. Parker Peevyhouse. Kathy Dawson Books 2016 304 p.
Grades: 9 10 11 12S C; Fic
1. Science fiction 2. Short stories
9780803741607, $17.99; 080374160X
LC 2015022984

This book, by Parker Peevyhouse, "is a collection of five time-spanning, interconnected novellas that weave a subtly science-fictional web stretching out from the present into the future, presenting eerily plausible possibilities for social media, corporate sponsorship, and humanity, as our world collides with a mysterious alternate universe." (Publisher's note)

Perera, Anna
★ **Guantanamo** boy. Albert Whitman 2011 339p $17.99
Grades: 7 8 9 10 11 12
1. Cousins -- Fiction 2. Muslims -- Fiction 3. Torture -- Fiction 4. Prisoners -- Fiction 5. Prejudices -- Fiction 6. Guantanamo Bay Naval Base (Cuba) -- Detention Camp -- Fiction
ISBN 978-0-8075-3077-1; 0-8075-3077-8
LC 2010048016

Six months after the events of September 11, 2001, Khalid, a Muslim fifteen-year-old boy from England is kidnapped during a family trip to Pakistan and imprisoned in Guantanamo Bay, Cuba, where he is held for two years suffering interrogations, water-boarding, isolation, and more for reasons unknown to him.

"Readers will feel every ounce of Khalid's terror, frustration, and helplessness in this disturbing look at a sad, ongoing chapter in contemporary history." Publ Wkly

Perez, Ashley Hope
The **knife** and the butterfly; Ashley Hope Pérez. Carolrhoda Lab 2012 209 p.

Grades: 9 10 11 12
1. Gangs -- Fiction 2. Juvenile delinquency -- Fiction 3. Salvadoran Americans -- Fiction 4. Juvenile detention homes -- Fiction
ISBN 0761361561; 9780761361565
LC 2011021236

"Fifteen-year-old Salvadoran Martín 'Azael' Arevalo awakens in a cell remembering bits and pieces of a fight in a Houston park between his gang, Mara Salvatrucha or MS-13, and Crazy Crew. Yet he cannot recall how the fight ended or why he is behind bars again. . . . Azael finds himself assigned to the secret observation of a white 17-year-old girl named Alexis 'Lexi' Allen, although he fails to see any connection the two might have had on the outside. While Azael hates Lexi at the beginning, he finds himself beginning to empathize with the struggles she has faced over her life." (Kirkus)

★ **Out** of darkness. By Ashley Hope Perez. Carolrhoda Lab 2015 408 p. Illustration
Grades: 9 10 11 12
1. African Americans -- Fiction 2. Explosions -- Fiction 3. Mexican Americans -- Fiction 4. Race relations -- Fiction 5. Schools -- Fiction 6. New London (Tex.) -- History -- 20th century -- Fiction 7. School stories 8. Historical fiction
9781467742023, $18.99; 9781467761796; 9781467776783; 9781467776776; 9781467776769
LC 2014023837

Printz Award Honor Book (2016)

In this book, author "Ashley Hope Perez takes the facts of the 1937 New London school explosion the worst school disaster in American history as a backdrop for a . . . novel about segregation, love, family, and the forces that destroy people. . . . Naomi Vargas and Wash Fuller know about the lines in East Texas as well as anyone. . . . But sometimes the attraction between two people is so powerful it breaks through even the most entrenched color lines." (Publisher's note)

"Elegant prose and gently escalating action will leave readers gasping for breath at the tragic climax and moving conclusion." Booklist

What can(t) wait. Carolrhoda 2011 234p $17.95
Grades: 7 8 9 10
1. Family life -- Fiction 2. Mexican Americans -- Fiction
ISBN 978-0-7613-6155-8; 0-7613-6155-3
LC 2010-28175

"Pérez fills a hole in YA lit by giving Marisa an authentic voice that smoothly blends Spanish phrases into dialogue and captures the pressures of both Latina life and being caught between two cultures." Kirkus

Perez, Marlene
Dead is a battlefield; Marlene Perez. Graphia 2012 227 p.
Grades: 7 8 9 10
1. Zombies -- Fiction 2. Perfumes -- Fiction 3. Supernatural -- Fiction 4. Female friendship -- Fiction 5. High school students -- Fiction 6. High schools --

Fiction 7. Interpersonal relations -- Fiction
ISBN 0547607342; 9780547607344

LC 2011031489

In this young adult novel, a "high-school freshman learns that she's one of a group of women who fight evil beasties in her supernatural town of Nightshade, Calif. In this sixth installment of the "Dead Is . . ." series, Jessica discovers to her dismay that she's a "virago," a woman warrior destined to fight paranormal baddies. Jessica worries, too, about her very best friend in the whole world, Eva, who's been acting strangely since she discovered a new perfume. . . . Jessica also finds herself attracted to Dominic . . . while she's juggling dates with Connor. . . . Meanwhile, Eva joins the groupies hanging around creepy Edgar and becomes ever more hostile toward Jessica, even trying to bite her. It seems that Edgar's perfume turns girls into zombies. Now Jessica has to find a cure and drive Edgar out of town." (Kirkus)

Dead is a killer tune; Marlene Perez. Graphia 2012 204 p. (paperback) $7.99

Grades: 8 9 10 11 12

1. Accidents -- Fiction 2. Bands (Music) -- Fiction 3. Mystery fiction 4. Music -- Fiction 5. High schools -- Fiction 6. Supernatural -- Fiction 7. Interpersonal relations -- Fiction
ISBN 0547608349; 9780547608341

LC 2012014798

Author Marlene Perez tells the story of a Battle of the Bands competition. "Jessica's romance with Dominic hasn't exactly progressed smoothly . . . Dominic's band, Side Effects May Vary, finds competition in an out-of-town act followed by a large entourage of obsessed fans--Hamlin, fronted by Brett Piper. When the most competitive bands start losing members to recklessness and bizarre accidents, Jessica must not only get to the bottom of the mystery, but also step into the spotlight as a musician herself." (Kirkus)

Dead is just a dream; by Marlene Perez. Houghton Mifflin Harcourt 2013 164 p. (Dead is) (hardback) $16.99

Grades: 8 9 10

1. Fantasy fiction 2. Clowns -- Fiction 3. Homicide -- Fiction 4. Murder -- Fiction 5. Schools -- Fiction 6. Nightmares -- Fiction 7. High schools -- Fiction 8. Supernatural -- Fiction 9. Psychic ability -- Fiction 10. Interpersonal relations -- Fiction
ISBN 0544102622; 9780544102620

LC 2013003883

"Jessica and her virago friends are back in this latest Dead Is series entry. This time they're in the midst of four murders, all seemingly connected to creepy paintings being installed in the homes of Nightshade's most influential citizens. Just when the girls think they've solved the mystery, a bloody clown begins to stalk Jessica, confounding their original suspicions...Girl drama, sweet romance, and murder—what more could young teens want in a breezy read?" Booklist

Dead is the new black. Harcourt 2008 190p pa $7.95

Grades: 7 8 9 10

1. School stories 2. Cheerleading -- Fiction 3.

Supernatural -- Fiction 4. Extrasensory perception -- Fiction
ISBN 978-0-15-206408-2; 0-15-206408-7

LC 2007027677

While dealing with her first boyfriend and suddenly being pressed into service as a substitute cheerleader, seventeen-year-old Daisy Giordano, daughter and sister of psychics but herself a 'normal', attempts to help her mother discover who is behind a series of bizarre attacks on teenage girls in their little town of Nightshade, California.

"This is the witty and humorous first installment in a series; it provides romance, mystery, friendship, adventure, and the supernatural all rolled up in a fast-paced, plot-twisting story." SLJ

Other titles in this series are:
Dead is a state of mind (2009)
Dead is so last year (2009)
Dead is just a rumor (2010)
Dead is not an option (2011)

Perez, Rene S., II

Seeing off the Johns. By Rene S. Perez II. Cinco Puntos Press 2015 256 p.

Grades: 9 10 11 12813/.6; 813

1. City and town life -- Fiction 2. High school students -- Fiction 3. Athletes -- Fiction 4. Texas -- Fiction
9781941026113, $16.95; 9781941026120

LC 2014032016

"People in the small town of Greenton mark their lives from that day in late summer when crowds lined the streets to see off high school athletic stars John Robison and John Mijias. That was the day the Johns, . . . left for state college, and never made it there-or back. . . . For Concepcion 'Chon' Gonzales, the days that the Johns headed out and didn't return was the first day of his new life." (Publisher's note)

"An atmospheric, refreshing read that will resonate with readers from towns both small and large." Kirkus

Perkins, Lynne Rae

★ **As** easy as falling off the face of the earth. Greenwillow Books 2010 352p il $16.99

Grades: 8 9 10 11 12

1. Adventure fiction 2. Chance -- Fiction 3. Accidents -- Fiction
ISBN 978-0-06-187090-3; 0-06-187090-0

LC 2009-42524

A teenaged boy encounters one comedic calamity after another when his train strands him in the middle of nowhere, and everything comes down to luck.

"The real pleasure is Perkins' relentlessly entertaining writing. . . . Wallowing in the wry humor, small but potent truths, and cheerful implausibility is an absolute delight." Booklist

★ **Criss** cross. Greenwillow Books 2005 337p $16.99; lib bdg $17.89; pa $6.99

Grades: 6 7 8 9

1. Nineteen sixties -- Fiction
ISBN 0-06-009272-6; 0-06-009273-4 lib bdg; 0-06-009274-2 pa

LC 2004-54023

Awarded the Newbery Medal, 2006

Teenagers in a small town in the 1960s experience new thoughts and feelings, question their identities, connect, and disconnect as they search for the meaning of life and love.

"Debbie . . . and Hector . . . narrate most of the novel. Both are 14 years old. Hector is a fabulous character with a wry humor and an appealing sense of self-awareness. . . . The descriptive, measured writing includes poems, prose, haiku, and question-and-answer formats. There is a great deal of humor in this gentle story." SLJ

Perkins, Mitali

Secret keeper. Delacorte Press 2009 225p $16.99; lib bdg $19.99

Grades: 7 8 9 10

1. India -- Fiction 2. Sisters -- Fiction 3. Family life -- Fiction

ISBN 978-0-385-73340-3; 0-385-73340-2; 978-0-385-90356-1 lib bdg; 0-385-90356-1 lib bdg

LC 2008-21475

In 1974 when her father leaves New Delhi, India, to seek a job in New York, Ashi, a tomboy at the advanced age of sixteen, feels thwarted in the home of her extended family in Calcutta where she, her mother, and sister must stay, and when her father dies before he can send for them, they must remain with their relatives and observe the old-fashioned traditions that Ashi hates.

"The plot is full of surprising secrets rooted in the characters' conflicts and deep connections with each other. The two sisters and their mutual sacrifices are both heartbreaking and hopeful." Booklist

★ **You** bring the distant near. Mitali Perkins. Farrar, Straus & Giroux 2017 303 p.

Grades: 9 10 11 12

1. East Indian Americans -- Fiction; 2. Family life -- New York (State) -- Fiction; 3. Immigrants -- Fiction; 4. New York (N.Y.) -- Fiction; 5. New York (N.Y.) -- Fiction; 6. Family life -- Fiction

9780374304904, $17.99; 9780374304911

LC 2016057822

This book, by Mitali Perkins, "explores sisterhood, first loves, friendship, and the inheritance of culture -- for better or worse. Ranee, worried that her children are losing their Indian culture; Sonia, wrapped up in a forbidden biracial love affair; Tara, seeking the limelight to hide her true self; Shanti, desperately trying to make peace in the family; Anna, fighting to preserve Bengal tigers and her Bengali identity." (Publisher's note)

"Full of sisterhood, diversity, and complex, strong women, this book will speak to readers as they will undoubtedly find a kindred spirit in at least one of the Das women." Booklist

Perkins, Stephanie

Anna and the French kiss. Dutton 2010 372p $16.99

Grades: 7 8 9 10

1. School stories 2. France -- Fiction 3. Foreign study -- Fiction 4. Paris (France) -- Fiction

ISBN 978-0-525-42327-0; 0-525-42327-3

LC 2009-53290

"Perkin's debut surpasses the usual chick-lit fare with smart dialogue, fresh characters and plenty of tingly interactions, all set amid pastries, parks and walks along the Seine in arguably the most romantic city in the world." Kirkus

Isla and the happily ever after: a novel. Stephanie Perkins. Dutton Books 2014 352 p.

Grades: 9 10 11 12

1. Boarding schools -- Fiction 2. Foreign study -- Fiction 3. Love -- Fiction 4. Schools -- Fiction 5. France -- Fiction 6. Paris (France) -- Fiction 7. Romance fiction 8. Americans -- France -- Fiction

0525425632; 9780525425632, $17.99

LC 2014020689

In this novel by Stephanie Perkins "Isla has had a crush on . . . Josh since their first year at the School of America in Paris. And after a chance encounter in Manhattan over the summer, romance might be closer than Isla imagined. But as they begin their senior year back in France, Isla and Josh are forced to confront the challenges every young couple must face, including family drama, uncertainty about their college futures, and the very real possibility of being apart." (Publisher's note)

"These choppy waters of neurosis will snag the soaring hearts of readers who have been there (and who hasn't?), and they'll ache upon Isla and Josh's rite-of-passage first doubts about their relationship. Fans of literary heart flutters will love it." Booklist

Lola and the boy next door. Dutton Books 2011 338p $16.99

Grades: 9 10 11 12

1. Costume -- Fiction 2. San Francisco (Calif.) -- Fiction 3. Dating (Social customs) -- Fiction 4. Father-daughter relationship -- Fiction

ISBN 978-0-525-42328-7

LC 2011015533

"Perkins's novel goes a bit deeper than standard chick-lit fare, and Lola is a sympathetic protagonist even when readers disagree with her decisions. . . . Step back—it's going to fly off the shelves." SLJ

Peterfreund, Diana

Across a star-swept sea; Diana Peterfreund. Balzer + Bray, an imprint of HarperCollinsPublishers 2013 464 p. (hardcover bdg.) $17.99

Grades: 9 10 11 12

1. Spy stories 2. Science fiction 3. Spies -- Fiction 4. Social classes -- Fiction 5. Government, Resistance to -- Fiction

ISBN 0062006169; 9780062006165

LC 2013003082

This book, a retelling of "The Scarlet Pimpernel," is a follow-up to Diana Peterfreund's "For Darkness Shows the Stars." Here, on "a Pacific island in a high-tech future, 16-year-old Persis Blake seems the epitome of a lady: beautiful, charming, stylish . . . shallow and stupid. The Wild Poppy, her alter ego, is clever, courageous and noble, crossing the sea to rescue aristos imprisoned by the tyrannical revolution." (Kirkus Reviews)

For darkness shows the stars; by Diana Peterfreund. Balzer + Bray 2012 407 p. (hardback) $17.99

Grades: 9 10 11 12

1. Science fiction 2. Farmers -- Fiction 3. Apocalyptic fiction 4. Man-woman relationship -- Fiction 5. Love -- Fiction 6. Social classes -- Fiction 7. Family problems -- Fiction

ISBN 0062006142; 9780062006141

LC 2011042126

Elliot North fights to save her family's land and her own heart in this post-apocalyptic reimaging of Jane Austen's 'Persuasion.'

"The story stands on its own, a richly envisioned portrait of a society in flux, a steely yet vulnerable heroine, and a young man who does some growing up." Publ Wkly

Peters, Julie Anne, 1952-

Between Mom and Jo. Little, Brown 2006 232p $16.99

Grades: 7 8 9 10

1. Lesbians -- Fiction 2. Prejudices -- Fiction 3. Family life -- Fiction 4. Mother-son relationship -- Fiction

ISBN 0-316-73906-5

LC 2005-22012

Fourteen-year-old Nick has a three-legged dog named Lucky 2, some pet fish, and two mothers, whose relationship complicates his entire life as they face prejudice, work problems, alcoholism, cancer, and finally separation.

"A powerful, moving examination of the relationships we forge within the family we are given." Horn Book Guide

By the time you read this, I'll be dead. Disney/ Hyperion Books 2010 200p $16.99

Grades: 8 9 10 11 12

1. Bullies -- Fiction 2. Obesity -- Fiction 3. Suicide -- Fiction 4. Depression (Psychology) -- Fiction

ISBN 1-4231-1618-6; 978-1-4231-1618-9

LC 2009-8315

High school student Daelyn Rice, who has been bullied throughout her school career and has more than once attempted suicide, again makes plans to kill herself, in spite of the persistent attempts of an unusual boy to draw her out.

"Powerfully portrayed in the first person, the protagonist's account offers compelling insight into just how spiritually and emotionally devastating bullying can be." Voice Youth Advocates

Define normal; a novel. Little, Brown 2000 196p $14.95; pa $5.95

Grades: 7 8 9 10

1. Friendship 2. School stories 3. Peer counseling 4. Family problems 5. Parent and child

ISBN 0-316-70631-0; 0-316-73489-6 pa

LC 99-42774

When she agrees to meet with Jasmine as a peer counselor at their middle school, Antonia never dreams that this girl with the black lipstick and pierced eyebrow will end up helping her deal with the serious problems she faces at home and become a good friend

"Readers who are looking for believable characters and a good story about friendship, being different, and growing wiser will appreciate Define 'Normal'" Voice Youth Advocates

It's our prom (so deal with it) a novel. by Julie Anne Peters. 1st ed. Little, Brown 2012 342 p. (paperback) $8.99; (hardcover) $17.99

Grades: 9 10 11 12

1. Lesbians -- Fiction 2. Bisexual people -- Fiction 3. High school students -- Fiction 4. Interpersonal relations -- Fiction 5. Proms -- Fiction 6. Popularity -- Fiction 7. Bisexuality -- Fiction 8. High schools -- Fiction 9. Family problems -- Fiction

ISBN 9780316131445; 031613158X; 9780316131582

LC 2011031756

This novel, by Julie Anne Peters, describes what happens when "Azure's principal gives her the chance to turn the school's traditional (and boring) senior prom into an event that will appeal to everyone. . . . Soon Azure manages to convince her best friends . . . to join . . . as well. . . . [T]he three friends are . . . determined to succeed—if Luke's and Azure's secret crushes on Radhika don't push the committee members, and their friendships, to the breaking point first." (Publisher's note)

★ **Luna**; a novel. Little, Brown 2003 248p hardcover o.p. pa $7.99

Grades: 9 10 11 12

1. Siblings -- Fiction 2. Transgender youth -- Fiction

ISBN 0-316-73369-5; 0-316-01127-4 pa

LC 2003-58913

Regan's brother Liam can't stand the person he is during the day... His true self, Luna, only reveals herself at night. In the secrecy of his basement bedroom Liam transforms himself into the beautiful girl he longs to be, with help from his sister's clothes and make up...But are Liam's family and friends ready to welcome Luna into their lives. Compelling and provoactive, this is an unforgettable novel about a transgender teen's struggle for self-identity and acceptance. (Publisher's note)

"The author gradually reveals the issues facing a transgender teen, educating readers without feeling too instructional (Luna and Regan discuss lingo, hormones and even sex change operations). Flashbacks throughout help round out the story, explaining Liam/Luna's longtime struggle with a dual existence, and funny, sarcastic-but-strong Regan narrates with an authentic voice that will draw readers into this new territory." Publ Wkly

Rage; a love story. Alfred A. Knopf 2009 293p $16.99; lib bdg $19.99

Grades: 9 10 11 12

1. Sisters -- Fiction 2. Lesbians -- Fiction 3. Child abuse -- Fiction 4. Abused women -- Fiction

ISBN 978-0-375-85209-1; 0-375-85209-3; 978-0-375-95209-8 lib bdg; 0-375-95209-8 lib bdg

LC 2008-33500

At the end of high school, Johanna finally begins dating the girl she has loved from afar, but Reeve is as much trouble as she claims to be as she and her twin brother damage Johanna's self-esteem, friendships, and already precarious relationship with her sister.

"The appeal of Johanna and Reeve's romance is its edgy, tragic drama, and Johanna's take on things offers keen insight into why kind, sane people allow themselves to be hit and then make excuses for their abusers. . . . The issues raised here are important and thought-provoking while never overpowering the appeal of the story itself." Bull Cent Child Books

She loves you, she loves you not-- Little, Brown 2011 278p $17.99
Grades: 9 10 11 12
    1. Mothers -- Fiction 2. Colorado -- Fiction 3. Lesbians -- Fiction 4. Family life -- Fiction
    ISBN 978-0-316-07874-0; 0-316-07874-3
                     LC 2010-22853
The author "skillfully depicts the self-obsessed, tumultuous life of a heartbroken teenager, adding just enough action to draw along a plot that might otherwise be tepid. While the book alludes to the girls' sexual relations, the descriptions are not graphic and should not deter high school libraries from adding this title to their LGBTQ collection." Libr Media Connect

Peterson, Lois J.
Beyond repair; [by] Lois Peterson. Orca Book Publishers 2011 121p (Orca currents) pa $9.95
Grades: 6 7 8 9
    1. Bereavement -- Fiction
    ISBN 978-1-55469-816-5; 1-55469-816-2
Cam, still grieving over the death of his father, is worried that he is being stalked.
"Compact, dialogue driven writing keeps the atmosphere tense as Cam races toward a confrontation with his father's killer. . . . A resonant, quick read from a reliable reluctant reader series." Booklist

Silver rain; [by] Lois Peterson. Orca Book Publishers 2010 181p pa $9.95
Grades: 6 7 8 9
    1. Missing persons -- Fiction 2. Great Depression, 1929-1939 -- Fiction
    ISBN 978-1-55469-280-4; 1-55469-280-6
Elsie's father has disappeared and, as the Depression wears on, the family becomes desperate for money.
"Terse, grim, and funny, the plainspoken narrative from Elsie's viewpoint beautifully conveys a child's sense of the times." Booklist

Peterson, Will
Triskellion; [by] Will Peterson. Candlewick Press 2008 365p $16.99
Grades: 6 7 8 9
    1. Twins -- Fiction 2. Siblings -- Fiction 3. Supernatural -- Fiction
    ISBN 978-0-7636-3971-6; 0-7636-3971-0
After their parents' divorce, Rachel and Adam are sent to live with their grandmother in the English village of Triskellion, where they find danger and paranormal activity as they discover hidden secrets that some will kill to keep buried.

"The plot moves along at a brisk pace, and there's plenty of adventure, dark and creepy atmosphere, and a touch of the paranormal." SLJ

Triskellion 2: The burning. Candlewick Press 2009 461p $16.99
Grades: 6 7 8 9
    1. Twins -- Fiction 2. Siblings -- Fiction 3. Archeology -- Fiction 4. Supernatural -- Fiction
    ISBN 978-0-7636-4223-5; 0-7636-4223-1
                     LC 2009006657
Fourteen-year-old twins Adam and Rachel, pursued by both their former 'Hope Project' benefactors and followers of a zombie-like figure, flee London for Paris, Seville, and finally Morocco, where they unearth an ancient secret more startling than the first.
This is an "action-packed sequel. . . . [It is] imaginative and centered on two likable teens." SLJ

Petrucha, Stefan
The **Rule** of Won. Walker & Co. 2008 227p $16.99
Grades: 8 9 10 11 12
    1. School stories 2. Clubs -- Fiction 3. Supernatural -- Fiction 4. Books and reading -- Fiction
    ISBN 978-0-8027-9651-6; 0-8027-9651-6
                     LC 2008-00255
Caleb Dunne, the quintessential slacker, is pressured by his girlfriend to join a high school club based on The Rule of Won, which promises to fulfill members' every "crave," but when nonbelievers start being ostracized and even hurt, Caleb must act.
"The book is fast paced and gripping enough to draw in reluctant readers. . . . Raising questions about issues such as personal responsibility, freedom of speech and the press, and standing up for unpopular beliefs, this novel would be a terrific choice for book-group and class discussions." SLJ

★ **Teen,** Inc. [by] Stefan Petrucha. Walker 2007 244p $16.95
Grades: 8 9 10 11 12
    1. Orphans -- Fiction 2. Pollution -- Fiction 3. Business ethics -- Fiction
    ISBN 978-0-8027-9650-9; 0-8027-9650-8
                     LC 2007-2368
Fourteen-year-old Jaiden has been raised by NECorp. since his parents were killed when he was a baby, so when he discovers that the corporation has been lying about producing illegal levels of mercury emissions, he and his two friends decide to try to do something about it.
"Witty and provocative without being preachy, this novel has both daring characters and a heady plot." Booklist

Petty, Heather W.
Lock & Mori. Heather Petty. SSBFYR Teen 2015 256 p.
Grades: 9 10 11 12
    1. Characters in literature -- Fiction 2. Family problems -- Fiction 3. Love -- Fiction 4. Mystery and detective stories 5. England -- Fiction 6. London (England) --

Fiction 7. Mystery fiction
9781481423038, $17.99; 9781481423045

LC 2014028105

"In modern-day London, two brilliant high school students—one Sherlock Holmes and a Miss James 'Mori' Moriarty—meet. A murder will bring them together. The truth very well might drive them apart. . . . [They] should be hitting the books on a school night. Instead, they are out crashing a crime scene. . . . Lock has challenged Mori to solve the case before he does." (Publisher's note)

Pfeffer, Susan Beth

Blood wounds. Harcourt 2011 248p $16.99
Grades: 7 8 9 10

1. Homicide -- Fiction 2. Family life -- Fiction 3. Stepfamilies -- Fiction 4. Self-mutilation -- Fiction
ISBN 978-0-547-49638-2

LC 2011009602

Willa seems to have a perfect life as a member of a loving blended family until the estranged father she barely remembers murders his wife and children, then heads toward Willa and her mother.

"This intense psychological drama, showing the brightest and darkest sides of humanity, offers remarkable acts of courage and disturbing images of domestic violence. Willa's frankly portrayed grief, confusion, and uncertainties will have a strong impact on readers." Publ Wkly

Life as we knew it. Harcourt 2006 337p $17
Grades: 7 8 9 10

1. Science fiction 2. Family life -- Fiction 3. Natural disasters -- Fiction
ISBN 0-15-205826-5; 978-0-15-205826-5

LC 2005-36321

Through journal entries sixteen-year-old Miranda describes her family's struggle to survive after a meteor hits the moon, causing worldwide tsunamis, earthquakes, and volcanic eruptions.

"Each page is filled with events both wearying and terrifying and infused with honest emotions. Pfeffer brings cataclysmic tragedy very close." Booklist

Other titles in this series are:
The dead & gone (2008)
This world we live in (2010)
The shade of the moon (2013)

Philbin, Joanna

The **daughters**. Little, Brown 2010 275p il $16.99
Grades: 6 7 8 9

1. School stories 2. Fame -- Fiction 3. Wealth -- Fiction 4. Friendship -- Fiction
ISBN 978-0-316-04900-9; 0-316-04900-X

In New York City, three fourteen-year-old best friends who are all daughters of celebrities watch out for each other as they try to strike a balance between ordinary high school events, such as finding a date for the homecoming dance, and family functions like walking the red carpet with their famous parents.

This is a "fun, quick read. . . . Readers will be intrigued by the well-drawn characters and their growth over the course of several months." SLJ

Other titles in this series are:
The daughters break the rules (2010)
The daughters take the stage (2011)

Philbrick, W. R.

★ The **last** book in the universe; by Rodman Philbrick. Blue Sky Press (NY) 2001 223p hardcover o.p. pa $5.99
Grades: 9 10 11 12

1. Science fiction 2. Epilepsy -- Fiction
ISBN 0-439-08758-9; 0-439-08759-7 pa

LC 99-59878

Expanded from a short story in Tomorrowland edited by Michael Cart, published 1999 by Scholastic Press

After an earthquake has destroyed much of the planet, an epileptic teenager nicknamed Spaz begins the heroic fight to bring human intelligence back to the Earth of a distant future

"Enthralling, thought-provoking, and unsettling." Voice Youth Advocates

Philpot, Chelsey

Even in paradise. Chelsey Philpot. HarperCollins Childrens Books 2014 368 p.
Grades: 9 10 11 12

1. Artists -- Fiction 2. Boarding schools -- Fiction 3. Friendship -- Fiction 4. Schools -- Fiction 5. Private schools -- Fiction 6. School stories
0062293699; 9780062293695, $17.99

LC 2013047956

In this book, by Chelsey Philpot, "Julia Buchanan enrolls at St. Anne's . . . [and] Charlotte Ryder already knows all about her. . . . Charlotte certainly never expects she'll be Julia's friend. But almost immediately, she dives headfirst into the larger-than-life new girl's world . . . a world of midnight rendezvous, dazzling parties, palatial vacation homes, and fizzy champagne cocktails. And then Charlotte meets, and begins falling for, Julia's handsome older brother, Sebastian." (Publisher's note)

"There is nothing in this Gatsbyesque world we haven't seen before, but Philpot knows that and happily hands over the tragic goods: disaffected, charming, well-drawn characters; gauzy tuxedo-and-gown parties; and a wistful, melancholy tone that makes it all seem achingly fleeting." Booklist

Pierce, Tamora

Alanna: the first adventure. Atheneum 2014 249p (Song of the Lioness) $19.99
Grades: 7 8 9 10

1. Fantasy fiction 2. Knights and knighthood -- Fiction 3. Gender role -- Fiction
ISBN 9781481439589; 1481439588
First published 1983

"Neither Alanna nor her twin brother Thom were happy with their father's decision to send Alanna to a convent and Thom to court. The two decide to switch places and Alanna posing as 'Alan' becomes a page at court while Tom goes to the convent to learn sorcery. Alanna finds life as a page hard, particularly as she is lighter and smaller than the other pages, but she struggles hard to overcome these disadvantages. She makes many friends at court, including . . . Prince Jonathan whose life she saves using her magical gift of healing." (Voice of Youth Advocates)

Other titles in this series are:
In the hand of the goddess (1984)
The woman who rides like a man (1986)
Lioness rampant (1988)

Bloodhound. Random House 2009 551p il (Beka Cooper) $18.99; lib bdg $21.99; pa $10.99
Grades: 7 8 9 10

    1. Fantasy fiction 2. Police -- Fiction 3. Counterfeits and counterfeiting -- Fiction
ISBN 978-0-375-81469-3; 0-375-81469-8; 978-0-375-91469-0 lib bdg; 0-375-91469-2 lib bdg; 978-0-375-83817-0 pa; 0-375-83817-1 pa

                              LC 2008025838

Sequel to Terrier (2006)

Having been promoted from "Puppy" to "Dog," Beka, now a full-fledged member of the Provost's Guard, and her former partner head to a neighboring port city to investigate a case of counterfeit coins.

    "Quirky, endearing characters save the story." Booklist
Followed by Mastiff (2011)

★ **First** test. Random House 1999 216p (Protector of the small) hardcover o.p. pa $5.99
Grades: 6 7 8 9

    1. Fantasy fiction 2. Sex role -- Fiction 3. Knights and knighthood -- Fiction
ISBN 0-679-88914-0; 0-679-98914-5 lib bdg; 0-679-88917-5 pa

                              LC 98-30903

First title in the Protector of the small series. Ten-year-old Keladry of Mindalen, daughter of nobles, serves as a page but must prove herself to the males around her if she is ever to fulfill her dream of becoming a knight

    "Pierce spins a whopping good yarn, her plot balanced on a solid base of action and characterization." Bull Cent Child Books

Other titles in this series are:
Page (2001)
Squire (2002)
Lady knight (2002)

Mastiff. Random House 2011 593p (Beka Cooper) $18.99; lib bdg $21.99; e-book $10.99
Grades: 7 8 9 10

    1. Fantasy fiction 2. Police -- Fiction 3. Kidnapping -- Fiction 4. Kings and rulers -- Fiction
ISBN 978-0-375-81470-9; 978-0-375-91470-6 lib bdg; 978-0-375-89328-5 e-book

                              LC 2011024152

Sequel to Bloodhound (2009)

Beka, having just lost her fiance in a slaver's raid, is able to distract herself by going with her team on an important hunt at the queen's request, unaware that the throne of Tortall depends on their success.

    "This novel provides both crackerjack storytelling and an endearingly complex protagonist." Kirkus

★ **Melting** stones. Scholastic Press 2008 312p $17.99

Grades: 8 9 10 11 12

    1. Fantasy fiction 2. Magic -- Fiction
ISBN 978-0-545-05264-1; 0-545-05264-5

                              LC 2007045036

Residents of the island of Starns send for help from Winding Circle temple, and when prickly green mage Rosethorn and young stone mage trainee Evvy respond, Evvy finds that the problem is with a long-dormant volcano and tries to use her talents to avert the looming destruction.

    This "is a riveting story that has many inventive and exciting plot twists and turns. . . . The story features excellent character development." SLJ

★ **Sandry's** book. Scholastic Press 1997 252p (Circle of magic) hardcover o.p. pa $6.99
Grades: 6 7 8 9

    1. Fantasy fiction 2. Magic -- Fiction
ISBN 0-590-55356-9; 0-590-55408-5 pa

                              LC 95-39540

Four young misfits find themselves living in a strictly disciplined temple community where they become friends while also learning to do crafts and to use their powers, especially magic

    "Pierce has created an excellent new world where magic is a science and utterly believable and populated it with a cast of well-developed characters." Booklist

Other available titles in this series are:
Tris's book (1998)
Daja's book (1998)
Briar's book (1999)

Terrier. Random House 2006 581p il map (Beka Cooper) hardcover o.p. pa $9.99
Grades: 7 8 9 10

    1. Fantasy fiction 2. Magic -- Fiction 3. Police -- Fiction
ISBN 978-0-375-81468-6; 0-375-81468-X; 978-0-375-83816-3 pa; 0-375-83816-3 pa

                              LC 2006-14834

When sixteen-year-old Beka becomes "Puppy" to a pair of "Dogs," as the Provost's Guards are called, she uses her police training, natural abilities and a touch of magic to help them solve the case of a murdered baby in Tortall's Lower City.

    "Pierce deftly handles the novel's journal structure, and her clear homage to the police-procedural genre applies a welcome twist to the girl-legend-in-the-making story line." Booklist

Other titles featuring Beka Cooper are:
Bloodhound (2009)
Mastiff (2011)

★ **Trickster's** choice. Random House 2003 422p $17.95; pa $8.95
Grades: 7 8 9 10

    1. Fantasy fiction
ISBN 0-375-81466-3; 0-375-82879-6 pa

                              LC 2003-5202

Alianne must call forth her mother Alanna's courage and her father's wit in order to survive on the Copper Isles in a royal court rife with political intrigue and murderous conspiracy

"This series opener is packed with Pierce's alluring mix of fantasy, adventure, romance, and humor, making the book an essential purchase for school and public libraries." Voice Youth Advocates

Another title in this series is:
Trickster's queen (2004)

Wild magic. Atheneum 2015 (The immortals) $19.99

Grades: 7 8 9 10

1. Fantasy fiction 2. Magic -- Fiction 3. Human-animal communication -- Fiction
ISBN 9781481440233; 1481440233
First published 1992

"Thirteen-year-old Daine has always had a special connection with animals, but only when she's forced to leave home does she realize it's more than a knack--it's magic. With this wild magic, not only can Daine speak to animals, but she can also make them obey her. Daine takes a job handling horses for the Queen's Riders, where she meets the master mage Numair and becomes his student. Under Numair's guidance, Daine explores the scope of her magic." (Publisher's note)

Other titles in this series are:
Wolf-speaker (1994)
Emperor mage (1995)
The realms of the gods (1996)

The **will** of the empress. Scholastic Press 2005 550p $17.99; pa $8.99

Grades: 8 9 10 11 12

1. Fantasy fiction
ISBN 0-439-44171-4; 0-439-44172-2 pa
LC 2005-02874

On visit to Namorn to visit her vast landholdings and her devious cousin, Empress Berenene, eighteen-year-old Sandry must rely on her childhood friends and fellow mages, Daja, Tris, and Briar, despite the distance that has grown between them

"This novel begins two years after the Circle of Magic and The Circle Opens series. . . . Readers will enjoy being reacquainted with these older but still very well-developed characters." SLJ

Pierson, D. C.

Crap kingdom; by DC Pierson. Viking 2013 368 p. (hardcover) $17.99

Grades: 7 8 9 10 11 12

1. Fantasy fiction 2. Humorous fiction 3. Heroes -- Fiction
ISBN 067001432X; 9780670014323
LC 2012015578

In this comic novel, by D. C. Pierson, "with [a] . . . mysterious yet oddly ordinary-looking prophecy, Tom's fate is sealed: he's . . . whisked away to a magical kingdom to be its Chosen One. There's just one problem: The kingdom is mostly made of garbage from Earth. . . . When Tom turns down the job of Chosen One, he thinks he's making a smart decision. But when Tom discovers he's been replaced by his best friend Kyle, . . . Tom wants Crap Kingdom back--at any cost." (Publisher's note)

Pike, Aprilynne

Earthbound. Penguin Group USA 2013 352 p. $17.99

Grades: 7 8 9 10

1. Occult fiction 2. Science fiction
ISBN 1595146504; 9781595146502

This is the first book in a series from Aprilynne Pike. Here, plane crash survivor Tavia "is in rehab and finishing her senior year online. She has time to look at the world with attentive eyes, and what she sees is often unnerving: glowing triangles on the historic houses of Portsmouth, N.H., or pedestrians who flicker. She tries to attribute these visions to the brain injury she sustained in the crash, but she can't dismiss the stalker with a blond ponytail so easily." (Publishers Weekly)

"The characters are well developed and the narrative is easy to follow... Pike does take a while to get to the heart of the matter, but overall the story is compelling. Readers of supernatural romances will be clamoring." SLJ

★ **Glitter.** Aprilynne Pike. Random House Inc 2016 384 p. Illustration

Grades: 8 9 10 11

1. Adventure and adventurers -- Fiction 2. Courts and courtiers -- Fiction 3. Drug dealers -- Fiction 4. Science fiction 5. Versailles (France) -- 18th century -- Fiction
9781101933701, $17.99; 9781101933718
LC 2015039116

In this novel by Aprilynne Pike, it's the twenty-first century, but at the palace of Versailles everyone "acts like it's the eighteenth century. . . . When Danica witnesses an act of murder by the young king, her mother makes a cruel power play . . . blackmailing the king into making Dani his queen. . . . She has six months to escape her . . . destiny. . . . Her ticket out? Glitter. A drug so powerful that a tiny pinch . . . can make the wearer hopelessly addicted." (Publisher's note)

"Poufy gowns and corsets in a futuristic setting make for an interesting spin on a perennially popular genre." Kirkus

Wings. HarperTeen 2009 294p $16.99; lib bdg $17.89; pa $8.99

Grades: 7 8 9 10

1. Fantasy fiction 2. Plants -- Fiction 3. Trolls -- Fiction 4. Fairies -- Fiction
ISBN 978-0-06-166803-6; 0-06-166803-6; 978-0-06-166804-3 lib bdg; 0-06-166804-4 lib bdg; 978-0-06-166805-0 pa; 0-06-166805-2 pa
LC 2008-24653

When a plant blooms out of fifteen-year-old Laurel's back, it leads her to discover the fact that she is a faerie and that she has a crucial role to play in keeping the world safe from the encroaching enemy trolls.

"Replete with budding romance, teen heroics, a good smattering of evil individuals, and an ending that serves up a ready sequel, this novel nonetheless provides an unusual approach to middle level fantasy through its startlingly creative premise that faeries are of the plant world and not the animal world. . . . Both male and female fantasy readers will enjoy this fast-paced action fantasy." Voice Youth Advocates

Other titles in this series are:
Illusions (2011)
Spells (2010)

Pink, Randi

★ **Into** white. Randi Pink. Feiwel & Friends 2016 288 p.

Grades: 8 9 10 11

1. Alabama -- Fiction 2. High school students -- Fiction 3. Discrimination -- Fiction
9781250070210, $17.99; 9781250086907

LC 2016937797

In this novel, by Randi Pink, "LaToya Williams lives in Montgomery, Alabama, and attends a mostly white high school. It seems as if her only friend is her older brother, Alex. Toya doesn't know where she fits in, but after a run-in with another student, she wonders if life would be different if she were . . . different. And then a higher power answers her prayer: to be 'anything but black.' Toya is suddenly white, blond, and popular. Now what?" (Publisher's note)

"This debut ought to inspire readers to have conversations among themselves about family, empathy, community, and respect for others." Booklist

Pitcher, Annabel

★ **Ketchup** clouds; a novel. by Annabel Pitcher. Little, Brown and Company 2013 272 p. $18

Grades: 8 9 10 11 12

1. Grief -- Fiction 2. Guilt -- Fiction 3. Secrets -- Fiction 4. England -- Fiction 5. Epistolary fiction 6. Letters -- Fiction 7. Bath (England) -- Fiction 8. Family life -- England -- Fiction
ISBN 031624676X; 9780316246767

LC 2012044116

In this book, by Annabel Pitcher, "Zoe has an unconventional pen pal—Mr. Stuart Harris, a Texas Death Row inmate and convicted murderer. But then again, Zoe has an unconventional story to tell. A story about how she fell for two boys, betrayed one of them, and killed the other." (Publisher's note)

"Guilt-ridden British teen Zoe feels responsible for the fates of two brothers--Max, the hot guy with whom she's been making out; and Aaron, with whom she's in love. Zoe's original turns of phrase and sprightly narrative style give her story quick, light momentum and moments of lyricism. Sharp, articulate perceptions and a measure of suspense make this an engaging read." (Horn Book)

My sister lives on the mantelpiece; a novel. Annabel Pitcher. 1st US ed. Little, Brown & Co. 2012 214 p. (hardcover) $17.99

Grades: 6 7 8 9 10

1. Grief -- Fiction 2. England -- Fiction 3. Family problems -- Fiction
ISBN 0316176907; 9780316176903

LC 2011027350

In this book, Annabel Pitcher tells a story about "grief, prejudice, religion, bullying, and familial instability. . . . Jamie and his family are still dealing with his sister Rose's death in a terrorist bombing five years earlier. . . . The family falls apart--their mother runs off with another man, and their alcoholic father moves from London to the Lake District with the children, where he lavishes attention on Rose's urn. . . . Jamie's pivotal friendship with a Muslim girl, Sunya, is a standout." (Publishers Weekly)

Silence is goldfish: a novel. By Annabel Pitcher. Little, Brown & Co. 2016 352 p.

Grades: 7 8 9 10

1. Fathers -- Fiction 2. Identity -- Fiction 3. Selective mutism -- Fiction 4. Manchester (England) -- Ficition 5. Identity (Psychology) -- Fiction
9780316370752, $17.99

LC 2015024312

In this young adult novel, by Annabel Pitcher, "fifteen-year-old Tess doesn't mean to become mute. At first, she's just too shocked to speak. . . . Reeling from her family's betrayal, Tess sets out to discover the identity of her real father. . . . Tess continues to investigate, uncovering a secret that could ruin multiple lives. It all may be too much for Tess to handle, but how can she ask for help when she's forgotten how to use her voice?" (Publisher's note)

"Tess, fifteen, is an offbeat English introvert with a highly involved dad. After she discovers his startling blog post recounting her own birth ('It wasn't my daughter. It was... some sperm donor's'), her anger emboldens her to stand up against Dad's expectations. Her rebellion of choice is silence, but her narrative voice speaks loudly—Tess is a witty and appealing protagonist." Horn Book

"Originally published in Great Britain in 2015 by Orion Publishing Group"—Copyright page.

Pixley, Marcella

Ready to fall. Marcella Pixley. Farrar, Straus & Giroux 2017 362 p.

Grades: 9 10 11 12

1. Friendship -- Fiction; 2. Grief -- Fiction; 3. High schools -- Fiction; 4. Jews -- United States -- Fiction; 5. Schools -- Fiction; 6. Theater -- Fiction
9780374303594; 0374303584; 9780374303587, $17.99

LC 2016058779

In this book, by Marcella Pixley, "when Max Friedman's mother dies of cancer, instead of facing his loss, Max imagines that her tumor has taken up residence in his brain. It's a terrible tenant?isolating him from family, distracting him in school, and taunting him mercilessly about his manhood.... Finally, Max is sent to the artsy, off-beat Baldwin School to regain his footing. He joins a group of theater misfits in a steam-punk production of Hamlet." (Publisher's note)

". . . this work is ultimately an affecting novel about parental relationships, grieving, and recovery." SLJ

Plum, Amy

Die for me. HarperTeen 2011 344p $17.99

Grades: 8 9 10 11

1. Love stories 2. Dead -- Fiction 3. Sisters -- Fiction 4. Bereavement -- Fiction 5. Supernatural -- Fiction
ISBN 978-0-06-200401-7; 0-06-200401-8

LC 2010-30785

After their parents are killed in a car accident, sixteen-year-old Kate Mercier and her older sister Georgia, each grieving in her own way, move to Paris to live with their grandparents and Kate finds herself powerfully drawn to the handsome but elusive Vincent who seems to harbor a mysterious and dangerous secret.

"Plum deftly navigates the real world and the fantastical. Her characters are authentic, and their romances are believable. Plum introduces a world and a story that are sure to intrigue teen readers and will easily attract fans of the Twilight series." Booklist

Plum-Ucci, Carol

Fire will fall. Harcourt 2010 485p $18

Grades: 8 9 10 11

1. Spies -- Fiction 2. Diseases -- Fiction 3. Terrorism -- Fiction 4. New Jersey -- Fiction 5. Supernatural -- Fiction

ISBN 978-0-15-216562-8; 0-15-216562-2

LC 2009-23854

Sequel to: Stream of Babel (2008)

Moved to a mansion in the South Jersey Pine Barrens, four teenagers, trying to recover from being poisoned by terrorists, struggle with health issues, personal demons, and supernatural events, as operatives try to track down the terror cell.

"The compelling characters, dramatic situations, and page-turning pace of this thriller will keep readers enthralled right up to the climax." SLJ

Streams of Babel. Harcourt 2008 424p $17

Grades: 8 9 10 11

1. Spies -- Fiction 2. Computers -- Fiction 3. Terrorism -- Fiction 4. New Jersey -- Fiction

ISBN 978-0-15-216556-7; 0-15-216556-8

LC 2007-26503

Six teens face a bioterrorist attack on American soil as four are infected with a mysterious disease affecting their small New Jersey neighborhood and two others, both brilliant computer hackers, assist the United States Intelligence Coalition in tracking the perpetrators.

The "story's threads are brought together in ways designed to keep readers on the edge of their seats. . . . Fans of suspense will discover a thrilling ride." Voice Youth Advocates

Followed by: Fire will fall (2010)

Polisner, Gae

In sight of stars. Gae Polisner. Wednesday Books 2018 246 p.

Grades: 10 11 12

1. Children of gay parents -- Fiction; 2. Fathers -- Death -- Fiction; 3. Loss (Psychology) -- Fiction; 4. Psychiatric hospital patients -- Fiction; 5. Psychotherapy patients -- Fiction; 6. New York (N.Y.) -- Fiction; 7. Suicide -- Fiction; 8. Loss (Psychology) -- Fiction

9781250143839, $18.99; 9781250143853

LC 2018931153

In this book, by Gae Polisner, "seventeen-year-old Klee's father was the center of his life.... Until his death. Now, forced to live...with his mom, Klee can't help but feel he's lost all the identifying parts of himself.... That is until he meets...Sarah in art class.... Suddenly it seems as if she's the only thing that makes him happy. But when an act of betrayal sends him reeling, Klee lands in...a psychiatric hospital for teens in Northhollow." (Publisher's note)

"An intense, sometimes graphic, totally heartbreaking portrait of a character who will keep pages turning." Booklist

The **memory** of things. Gae Polisner. St. Martin's Press 2016 288 p.

Grades: 9 10 11 12

1. September 11 terrorist attacks, 2001 -- Fiction 2. Memory -- Fiction 3. Friendship -- Fiction

1250095522; 9781250095534, $60; 9781250095527, $18.99

LC 2016016274

In this novel, by Gae Polisner, "on the morning of September 11, 2001, sixteen-year-old Kyle Donohue watches the first twin tower come down from the window of Stuyvesant High School. Moments later, terrified and fleeing home to safety across the Brooklyn Bridge, he stumbles across a girl . . . covered in ash, and wearing a pair of costume wings. With his mother and sister in California and unable to reach his father, a NYC detective, . . . Kyle . . . bring[s] the girl home." (Publisher's note)

"Overall, a touching look at the power of selflessness, memory, and hope in the face of tragedy." Booklist

Pollock, Tom

★ The **city's** son; Tom Pollock. Flux 2012 460p $16.99

Grades: 6 7 8

1. London (England) -- Fiction 2. Magic -- Fiction 3. Supernatural -- Fiction 4. Family problems -- Fiction

ISBN 9780738734309

LC 2012010589

This novel, by Tom Pollock, follows "teenage graffiti artist Beth Bradley . . . [and] Filius, the ragged crown prince of London's underworld. . . . Reach, the malign god of demolition, is on a rampage . . . to lay claim to the skyscraper throne. Caught up in helping Filius raise an alleyway army to battle Reach, Beth soon forgets her old life. But when the enemy claims her best friend, Beth must choose between the acceptance she finds in the streets and the life she left behind." (Publisher's note)

Pon, Cindy

Fury of the phoenix. Greenwillow Books 2011 362p $17.99

Grades: 9 10 11 12

1. China -- Fiction 2. Supernatural -- Fiction 3. Voyages and travels -- Fiction 4. Father-son relationship -- Fiction

ISBN 978-0-06-173025-2

LC 2010-11700

Sequel to Silver phoenix (2009)

When Ai Ling leaves her home and family to accompany Chen Yong on his quest to find his father, haunted by the ancient evil she thought she had banished to the underworld, she must use her growing supernatural powers to save Chen Yong from the curses that follow her.

Serpentine. Cindy Pon. Month9Books, LLC 2015 300 p.

Grades: 9 10 11 12

1. Bildungsromans 2. Self-acceptance 3. China -- History -- Fiction

1942664338; 9781942664338, $14.99

This novel by Cindy Pon is "set in the ancient Kingdom of Xia and tells the coming of age story of Skybright, a young girl who worries about her growing otherness. As she turns 16, Skybright notices troubling changes. By day, she is a companion and handmaid to the youngest daughter of a very wealthy family. But nighttime brings with it a darkness. Skybright learns that despite a dark destiny, she must struggle to retain her sense of self—even as she falls in love for the first time." (Publisher's note)

"A fast-paced and engrossing read for anyone weary of the same old hackneyed storylines." Kirkus

★ **Silver** phoenix; beyond the kingdom of Xia. Greenwillow Books 2009 338p $17.99; lib bdg $18.89; pa $8.99

Grades: 9 10 11 12

1. China -- Fiction 2. Supernatural -- Fiction 3. Voyages and travels -- Fiction 4. Father-daughter relationship -- Fiction

ISBN 978-0-06-173021-4; 0-06-173021-1; 978-0-06-178033-2 lib bdg; 0-06-178033-2 lib bdg; 978-0-06-173024-5 pa; 0-06-173024-6 pa

LC 2008-29149

With her father long overdue from his journey and a lecherous merchant blackmailing her into marriage, seventeen-year-old Ai Ling becomes aware of a strange power within her as she goes in search of her parent.

"Pon's writing, both fluid and exhilarating, shines whether she's describing a dinner delicacy or what it feels like to stab an evil spirit in the gut. There's a bit of sex here, including a near rape, but it's all integral to a saga that spins and slashes as its heroine tries to find her way home." Booklist

Followed by Fury of the phoenix (2011)

Porter, Sarah

Lost voices. Houghton Mifflin Harcourt 2011 291p $16.99

Grades: 7 8 9 10

1. Singing -- Fiction 2. Supernatural -- Fiction 3. Mermaids and mermen -- Fiction

ISBN 978-0-547-48250-7; 0-547-48250-7

LC 2011008438

Assaulted and left on the cliffs outside of her grim Alaskan fishing village by her abusive, alcoholic uncle, fourteen-year-old Luce expects to die when she tumbles into the icy waters below, but when she instead transforms into a mermaid she is faced with struggles and choices she could never have imagined.

"Porter's writing is expressive and graceful. . . . A captivatingly different story." Booklist

★ **Vassa** in the Night: A Novel. Sarah Porter. St. Martin's Press 2016 304 p.

Grades: 9 10 11 12

1. Baba Yaga (Fictional character) -- Fiction 2. Magic -- Fiction 3. Fantasy fiction

9780765380548; 0765380544

LC 2016288285

This book by Sarah Porter, "inspired by the Russian folktale classic 'Vassilissa the Beautiful,' a modern fairy tale finds a girl from a working-class section of a magical Brooklyn tapping the powers of her dead mother's protective doll to defend against the evil of a murderous owner of a local convenience store." (Publisher's note)

"Sixteen-year-old Vassa Lisa Lowenstein's mother is dead, and her father is gone. She has a stepmother and two stepsisters. It's an odd living arrangement but no more peculiar than a lot of things in her working-class Brooklyn neighborhood. The nights have been especially strange, growing longer and longer. When her stepsister sends Vassa out in the middle of the night for lightbulbs, the only store that's still open is the local BY's. Everyone knows about BY's, and its owner Babs Yagg, but people do tend to remember a store that dances around on chicken legs and has a habit of decapitating shoplifters. . . . A deliberate lack of romantic tension makes this a refreshing read, and elements of traditional horror blend well with high-concept fantasy in this surprising and engaging tale. A must-have for YA urban fantasy collections." SLJ

When I Cast Your Shadow. By Sarah Porter. Tor Teen 2017 383 p.

Grades: 9 10 11 12

1. Brothers -- Death -- Fiction; 2. Families -- Fiction; 3. Spirits -- Fiction; 4. Twins -- Fiction; 5. Fantasy fiction; 6. Horror fiction; 7. Brothers and sisters -- Fiction

ISBN 9780765397560; 9780765380562, $17.99; 0765380560

LC 2017288859

In this novel, by Sarah Porter, "haunted by her dead brother, unable to let him go, Ruby must figure out whether his nightly appearances in her dreams are the answer to her prayers?or a nightmare come true.... He's always been jealous of his dashing older brother. Now Everett must do everything he can to save his twin sister Ruby from his clutches." (Publisher's note)

"A wildly innovative, whip-smart, and utterly spellbinding testament to family, memory, and love -- and the messes and miracles of each -- poised to possess legions of readers." Booklist

Porter, Tracey

Lark. HarperTeen 2011 183p $15.99

Grades: 8 9 10 11 12

1. Homicide -- Fiction 2. Virginia -- Fiction 3. Bereavement -- Fiction 4. Supernatural -- Fiction

ISBN 978-0-06-112287-3; 0-06-112287-4

LC 2010021959

"When sixteen-year-old Lark is raped and murdered, her two friends Nyetta and Eve must deal with the aftermath. Nyetta is being haunted by Lark, who wants someone to acknowledge her pain before she becomes trapped in the tree where she died. Eve, who has been estranged from Lark ever since she left the swimming team after an assistant coach fondled her, must process her long-repressed feelings as she falls in love with Ian, a boy Lark also admired. Unable to face her fears, Nyetta falls further into her own emotional darkness until she connects with Eve, and together the girls are able to free Lark's soul." (VOYA)

"The concise narrative holds deep and honest emotions as the characters go through the stages of dealing with Lark's untimely and gruesome death. An excellent addition to YA collections." SLJ

Portes, Andrea

Anatomy of a misfit. Andrea Portes. HarperTeen, an imprint of HarperCollinsPublishers 2014 336 p.

Grades: 9 10 11 12

    1. Dating (Social customs) -- Fiction 2. High schools -- Fiction 3. Popularity -- Fiction 4. Schools -- Fiction 5. School stories

    0062313649; 9780062313645, $17.99

LC 2014008722

In this young adult novel by Andrea Portes, "narrator Anika Dragomir is the third most popular girl at Pound High School. But inside, she knows she's a freak; she can't stop thinking about former loner Logan McDonough, who showed up on the first day of tenth grade hotter, bolder, and more mysterious than ever. . . . So Anika must choose—ignore her feelings and keep her social status? Or follow her heart and risk becoming a pariah." (Publisher's note)

    "Anika Dragomir looks like the All-American girl-next-door, but 'nobody knows that on the inside I am spider soup.' 'Nerd-ball turned goth romance hero' Logan McDonough and God's-gift-to-Nebraska, Jared Kline, vie for her affections. A dramatic climax is foreshadowed by sections in italics that hint at tragedy. Anika's observations are razor-sharp, especially when she's describing other people (and especially when she's ragging on her family)." Horn Book

Portman, Frank

    Andromeda Klein. Delacorte Press 2009 424p $17.99; lib bdg $20.99

Grades: 8 9 10 11 12

    1. Deaf -- Fiction 2. Tarot -- Fiction 3. Libraries -- Fiction 4. Occultism -- Fiction 5. People with disabilities -- Fiction 6. Books and reading -- Fiction

    ISBN 978-0-385-73525-4; 0-385-73525-1; 978-0-385-90512-1 lib bdg; 0-385-90512-2 lib bdg

LC 2009-15879

High school sophomore Andromeda, an outcast because she studies the occult and has a hearing impairment and other disabilities, overcomes grief over terrible losses by enlisting others' help in her plan to save library books—and finds a kindred spirit along the way.

    "Andromeda is a compelling character, whose reclaiming of misheard words and misspelled text messages gives her unique and likable flavor. . . . For readers who are occult fans, this quirky text will be a self-satisfied joy." Kirkus

    ★ **King** Dork. Delacorte Press 2006 344p il hardcover o.p. pa $8.99

Grades: 10 11 12

    1. School stories 2. Fathers -- Fiction 3. Short story writers

    ISBN 0-385-73291-0; 978-0-385-73291-8; 0-385-73450-6 pa; 978-0-385-73450-9 pa

LC 2005-12556

High school loser Tom Henderson discovers that "The Catcher in the Rye" may hold the clues to the many mysteries in his life.

    "Mature situations, casual sexual experiences, and allusions to Salinger suggest an older teen audience, who will also best appreciate the appended bandography and the very funny glossary." Booklist

    King Dork Approximately. Frank Portman. Delacorte Press 2014 368 p. Illustration

Grades: 9 10 11 12

    1. High schools -- Fiction 2. Interpersonal relations -- Fiction 3. Schools -- Fiction 4. Interpersonal relations 5. High school students -- Fiction

    0385736185; 9780385736183, $17.99; 9780385905916

LC 2013042885

In Frank Portman's novel "high school sophomore, aspiring rock star, and self-proclaimed outsider Tom Henderson is back in the [sequel] to 'King Dork.' The book opens with Tom being sent to a new school in the wake of the shutdown of his old school. New horizons provide more humorous opportunities for Tom to cast a snarky eye over all he sees." (School Library Journal)

    "Because the novel is packed with music, book, and movie references, readers' cultural literacy will get a definite boost. Utterly enjoyable, this book's culture-meets-romantic-confusion focus makes it a teen take on Nick Hornby's High Fidelity (1995), and it should hit home with social misfits and 'subnormals.'" Booklist

    Sequel to: King Dork

Potter, Ryan

    Exit strategy. Flux 2010 303p pa $9.95

Grades: 8 9 10 11 12

    1. Summer -- Fiction 2. Michigan -- Fiction 3. Steroids -- Fiction 4. Friendship -- Fiction

    ISBN 978-0-7387-1573-5; 0-7387-1573-5

LC 2009-27697

Seventeen-year-old Zach, his best friend (and state wrestling champion) Tank, and Tank's twin sister Sarah, an Ivy League-bound scholar, are desperate to leave their depressing hometown of Blaine, Michigan, after next year's graduation, but plans go awry when Zach uncovers a steroid scandal and falls in love with Sarah.

    "Packed with suspense and drama, with some romance and a fight, this book is bound to be popular among the male crowd. Just make sure you get it into the right hands; mature themes exist, including extramarital affairs, underage drinking, and anger management." Libr Media Connect

Poulsen, David A.

    ★ **And** Then the Sky Exploded. David A. Poulsen. Ingram Pub Services 2016 208 p.

Grades: 7 8 9 10

    1. Atomic bomb -- Fiction 2. Manhattan Project (U.S.) -- Fiction 3. Teenagers -- Fiction

    1459736370; 9781459736375, $12.99; 9781459736382; 9781459736399

In this novel, by David A. Poulsen, "ninth-grader Christian Larkin learns that the man he loved and respected was a member of the Manhattan Project, the team that designed and created the atomic bombs dropped on Japan during the Second World War. On a school trip to Japan, Chris meets . . . Yuko, who was eleven when the first bomb exploded over Hiroshima, horribly injuring her. Christian is determined to do something to make up for what his great-grandfather did." (Publisher's note)

    "Yuko's story and her meeting with Christian are worth reading and can start the conversation with young readers about Hiroshima and Nagasaki." Kirkus

Powell, Kelley

The **Merit** Birds. By Kelley Powell. Dundurn 2015 240 p.

Grades: 9 10 11 12

    1. Mother-son relationship -- Fiction 2. Laos -- Fiction 3. Culture conflict -- Fiction

    1459729315; 9781459729315, $14.99

In this book, by Kelley Powell, "Cam's mood is further worsened when he is torn away from his friends, school, and basket-ball team and must contend with the 'Dark Ages' quality of life in Laos, its slow pace, and his inability to communicate. Things don't really get better for Cam in Laos. Sure, he meets a girl and develops a friendship, but when tragedy strikes, Cam's situation becomes much worse than he could have imagined." (Quill & Quire)

A "thought-provoking story that will appeal to older teens willing to expand their worldview." SLJ

Powell, Laura

The **game** of triumphs. Alfred A. Knopf 2011 269p $16.99; lib bdg $19.99; ebook $10.99

Grades: 7 8 9 10

    1. Games -- Fiction 2. Tarot -- Fiction 3. Supernatural -- Fiction 4. Space and time -- Fiction 5. London (England) -- Fiction

    ISBN 978-0-375-86587-9; 0-375-86587-X; 978-0-375-96587-6 lib bdg; 0-375-96587-4 lib bdg; 978-0-375-89774-0 ebook

                    LC 2010021813

Fifteen-year-old Cat and three other London teens are drawn into a dangerous game in which Tarot cards open doorways into a different dimension and while there is everything to win, losing can be fatal.

"Original and engrossing." Kirkus

The **Master** of Misrule; Laura Powell. Alfred A. Knopf 2012 363 p. (trade hardcover) $16.99

Grades: 7 8 9 10 11 12

    1. Games -- Fiction 2. Tarot -- Fiction 3. Supernatural -- Fiction 4. Role playing -- Fiction 5. Space and time -- Fiction 6. London (England) -- Fiction

    ISBN 0375865888; 9780375865664; 9780375865886; 9780375897849; 9780375965883

                    LC 2011021135

Sequel to: The Game of Triumphs

In this book, "despite holding the Triumphs that promise answers to their various back stories (including the murder of Cat's parents, Blaine's abusive stepfather and Flora's comatose sister, all related to the Game of Triumphs), resolution eludes Cat and her friends. They must fight the Fool, now the Master of Misrule, whom they released in the first volume, not only for their own success, but to save the world." (Kirkus Reviews)

"This fast-paced novel mixes fantasy and reality in an intricately described setting... Packed with mystery, action, and even a hint of romance, The Master of Misrule will appeal to fans of role-playing games or anyone seeking an adventurous read." VOYA

Powell, William Campbell

Expiration day; William Campbell Powell. Tor Teen 2014 336 p. (hardback) $17.99

Grades: 8 9 10 11 12

    1. Bildungsromans 2. Science fiction 3. Robots -- Fiction 4. Diaries -- Fiction 5. England -- Fiction 6. Coming of age -- Fiction

    ISBN 0765338289; 9780765338280

                    LC 2013025453

In this book, by William Campbell Powell, "it is the year 2049, and humanity is on the brink of extinction. . . . Tania Deeley has always been told that she's a rarity: a human child in a world where most children are sophisticated androids manufactured by Oxted Corporation. . . . Though she has always been aware of the existence of teknoids, it is not until her first day at The Lady Maud High School for Girls that Tania realizes that her best friend, Siân, may be one." (Publisher's note)

"The author pays homage to the genre's giants while combining realistic characters (both human and android) and detailed worldbuilding with an unpredictably optimistic conclusion." (Kirkus)

Pratchett, Terry

★ The **amazing** Maurice and his educated rodents. HarperCollins Pubs. 2001 241p hardcover o.p. pa $6.99

Grades: 7 8 9 10

    1. Fantasy fiction 2. Cats -- Fiction 3. Rats -- Fiction

    ISBN 0-06-001233-1; 0-06-001235-8 pa

                    LC 2001-42411

A talking cat, intelligent rats, and a strange boy cooperate in a Pied Piper scam until they try to con the wrong town and are confronted by a deadly evil rat king

"In this laugh-out-loud fantasy, his first 'Discworld' novel for younger readers, Pratchett rethinks a classic story and comes up with a winner." SLJ

★ **Dodger**; by Terry Pratchett. HarperCollins 2012 360 p. (hardback) $17.99

Grades: 7 8 9 10

    1. Lifesaving 2. Love stories 3. Historical fiction 4. Humorous fiction 5. Conduct of life -- Fiction 6. Adventure and adventurers -- Fiction 7. Todd, Sweeney (Legendary character) -- Fiction 8. London (England) -- History -- 19th century -- Fiction 9. Great Britain -- History -- Victoria, 1837-1901 -- Fiction

    ISBN 0062009494; 9780062009494; 9780062009500

                    LC 2012022155

Michael L. Printz Honor Book (2013)

Author Terry Pratchett presents a story of historical fiction. "Dodger is a guttersnipe and a tosher . . . [and] a petty criminal but also (generally) one of the good guys. One night he rescues a beautiful young woman and finds himself hobnobbing quite literally with the likes of Charlie Dickens . . . and Ben Disraeli . . . And when he attempts to smarten himself up to impress the damsel in distress, he unexpectedly comes face to face with . . . Sweeney Todd." (Kirkus)

I shall wear midnight. Harper 2010 355p $16.99

Grades: 7 8 9 10

    1. Ghost stories 2. Fantasy fiction 3. Fairies -- Fiction 4. Witches -- Fiction

    ISBN 978-0-06-143304-7; 0-06-143304-7

                    LC 2010-24442

Sequel to: Wintersmith (2006)

Fifteen-year-old Tiffany Aching, the witch of the Chalk, seeks her place amid a troublesome populace and tries to control the ill-behaved, six-inch-high Wee Free Men who follow her as she faces an ancient evil that agitates against witches.

"The final adventure in Pratchett's Tiffany Aching series brings this subset of Discworld novels to a moving and highly satisfactory conclusion." Publ Wkly

★ **Nation**. HarperCollins 2008 367p $16.99; lib bdg $17.89; pa $8.99

Grades: 7 8 9 10 11 12

  1. Islands -- Fiction 2. Tsunamis -- Fiction 3. Survival after airplane accidents, shipwrecks, etc. -- Fiction
  ISBN 978-0-06-143301-6; 0-06-143301-2; 978-0-06-143302-3 lib bdg; 0-06-143302-0 lib bdg; 978-0-06-143303-0 pa; 0-06-143303-9 pa

LC 2008-20211

Boston Globe-Horn Book Award: Fiction (2009)

After a devastating tsunami destroys all that they have ever known, Mau, an island boy, and Daphne, an aristocratic English girl, together with a small band of refugees, set about rebuilding their community and all the things that are important in their lives.

"Quirky wit and broad vision make this a fascinating survival story on many levels." Booklist

★ **Only** you can save mankind. HarperCollins 2005 207p hardcover o.p. lib bdg $16.89; pa $6.99

Grades: 5 6 7 8

  1. War stories 2. Computer games -- Fiction
  ISBN 0-06-054185-7; 0-06-054186-5 lib bdg; 0-06-054187-3 pa

First published 1992 in the United Kingdom

Twelve-year-old Johnny endures tensions between his parents, watches television coverage of the Gulf War, and plays a computer game called Only You Can Save Mankind, in which he is increasingly drawn into the reality of the alien ScreeWee

This is "a wild ride, full of Pratchett's trademark humor; digs at primitive, low-resolution games . . . ; and some not-so-subtle philosophy about war and peace." Booklist

  Other titles in this trilogy are:
  Johnny and the dead (2006)
  Johnny and the bomb (2006)

The **shepherd's** crown. Terry Pratchett; [edited by] Kathrine Tegen. HarperCollins 2015 276 p. (Discworld series)

Grades: 6 7 8 9 10

  1. Witches -- Fiction 2. Fairies -- Fiction 3. Fantasy fiction
  9780062429971, $18.99; 9780062430557

LC 2015943558

In this book, by Terry Pratchett, "Deep in the Chalk, something is stirring. The owls and the foxes can sense it, and Tiffany Aching feels it in her boots. An old enemy is gathering strength. This is a time of endings and beginnings, old friends and new, a blurring of edges and a shifting of power. Now Tiffany stands between the light and the dark, the good and the bad. As the fairy horde prepares for in-vasion, Tiffany must summon all the witches to stand with her." (Publisher's Note)

"Readers young and old will savor this tale that emphasizes the values of hard work and standing firm in the face of evil. An exceptionally crafted finale from one of the greats." SLJ

★ The **Wee** Free Men. HarperCollins Pubs. 2003 263p hardcover o.p. pa $9.99

Grades: 7 8 9 10

  1. Fantasy fiction 2. Witches -- Fiction
  ISBN 0-06-001236-6; 0-06-201217-7 pa

LC 2002-15396

A young witch-to-be named Tiffany teams up with the Wee Free Men, a clan of six-inch-high blue men, to rescue her baby brother and ward off a sinister invasion from Fairyland

"Pratchett invites readers into his well-established realm of Discworld where action, magic, and characters are firmly rooted in literary reality. Humor ripples throughout, making tense, dangerous moments stand out in stark contrast." Bull Cent Child Books

  Other titles about Tiffany are:
  A hat full of sky (2004)
  Wintersmith (2006)
  I shall wear midnight (2010)
  The Shepherd's crown (2015)

Preus, Margi

Enchantment Lake: a Northwoods mystery. By Margi Preus. University of Minnesota Press 2015 200 p.

Grades: 6 7 8 9 10

  1. Buried treasure -- Fiction 2. Great-aunts -- Fiction 3. Lakes -- Fiction 4. Mystery and detective stories 5. Swindlers and swindling -- Fiction 6. Minnesota -- Fiction 7. Mystery fiction 8. Aunts -- Fiction
  0816683026; 9780816683024, $16.95

LC 2014042651

In this book, by Margi Preus, a "call from her great aunts Astrid and Jeannette sends seventeen-year-old Francie far from her new home in New York into a tangle of mysteries. Ditching an audition in a Manhattan theater, Francie travels to . . . the shores of Enchantment Lake in the woods of northern Minnesota, [where] something ominous is afoot, and as Francie begins to investigate, the mysteries multiply." (Publisher's note)

Preus "offers intriguing characters, suspenseful moments, and a love interest—plenty to keep readers involved." Booklist

★ **Heart** of a samurai; based on the true story of Nakahama Manjiro. Abrams/Amulet 2010 301p il $15.95

Grades: 7 8 9 10 11 12

  1. Interpreters 2. Japanese -- United States -- Fiction 3. Survival after airplane accidents, shipwrecks, etc. -- Fiction
  ISBN 978-0-8109-8981-8; 0-8109-8981-6

LC 2009-51634

A Newbery Medal honor book, 2011

In 1841, rescued by an American whaler after a terrible shipwreck leaves him and his four companions castaways on a remote island, fourteen-year-old Manjiro, who dreams of becoming a samurai, learns new laws and customs as he becomes the first Japanese person to set foot in the United States.

The author "mixes fact with fiction in a tale that is at once adventurous, heartwarming, sprawling, and nerve-racking in its depictions of early anti-Asian sentiment. She succeeds in making readers feel every bit as 'other' as Manjiro, while showing America at its best and worst through his eyes." Publ Wkly

Includes bibliographical references

Price, Charlie

★ **Dead** connection. Roaring Brook Press 2006 225p $16.95

Grades: 8 9 10 11 12

1. Ghost stories 2. Homicide -- Fiction
ISBN 1-59643-114-8; 978-1-59643-114-0

LC 2005-17138

A loner who communes with the dead in the town cemetery hears the voice of a murdered cheerleader and tries to convince the adults that he knows what happened to her

"Readers will like the edginess and be intrigued by the extrasensory elements as well as the darker turns the mystery takes. This is something different." Booklist

The **interrogation** of Gabriel James. Farrar Straus Giroux 2010 170p $16.99

Grades: 9 10 11 12

1. Montana -- Fiction 2. Homicide -- Fiction 3. Criminal investigation -- Fiction
ISBN 978-0-374-33545-8; 0-374-33545-1

LC 2009-37309

As an eyewitness to two murders, a Montana teenager relates the shocking story behind the crimes in a police interrogation interspersed with flashbacks.

"The author writes intriguing and believable characters and keeps a stream of realism moving through the story even when neither readers nor Gabriel are really sure what's going on. Patience from readers won't be required, though, as plenty of action keeps the narrative moving while the plot details unfold. The result is not only suspense but a memorable and believable characterization. Top notch." Kirkus

Price, Lissa

Enders; by Lissa Price. Delacorte Press 2014 288 p. (hc : alk. paper) $17.99

Grades: 7 8 9 10

1. Brainwashing 2. Teenagers -- Fiction 3. Science -- Experiments -- Fiction 4. Science fiction
ISBN 0385742495; 9780375990618; 9780385742498

LC 2013011679

Sequel to: Starters

In this book by Lissa Price, the conclusion to her Starters series, "someone is after Starters like Callie and Michael-teens with chips in their brains. They want to experiment on anyone left over from Prime Destinations--Starters who can be controlled and manipulated. With the body bank destroyed, Callie no longer has to rent herself out to creepy Enders. But Enders can still get inside her mind and make her do things she doesn't want to do." (Publisher's note)

"Some glossed-over twists stretch believability, though the threat (and villain's secret plan), smaller-scale than in Starters, is personal in a creepy way. Metals can be controlled remotely, and Callie's modified chip keeps her awake and aware, leading to a delightfully disturbing climax. It's not as intense as Starters, but it offers some answers and a solid conclusion that will repay readers." (Kirkus)

Starters; Lissa Price. Delacorte Press 2012 336 p. (paperback) $9.99; (ebook) $53.97; (glb) $20.99; (hardcover) $17.99

Grades: 7 8 9 10

1. Science fiction 2. Orphans -- Fiction 3. Intergenerational relations -- Fiction 4. Brothers and sisters -- Fiction
ISBN 9780385742481; 0385742371; 9780307975232; 9780375990601; 9780385742375

LC 2011040820

In this book, "[w]hen a deadly virus wipes out the entire population of the U.S. save the elderly and the young, . . . the result is a dysfunctional society polarized between young 'Starters' and the increasingly long-lived 'Enders.' Children who are unclaimed by surviving relatives are institutionalized, and many -- like Callie and her little brother, Tyler -- learn to fend for themselves in virtual hiding from the law to escape that fate." (Bulletin of the Center for Children's Books)

Price, Nora

Zoe letting go; Nora Price. Razorbill 2012 279 p. $17.99

Grades: 8 9 10 11 12

1. Rehabilitation -- Fiction 2. Eating disorders -- Fiction 3. Diaries -- Fiction 4. Letters -- Fiction 5. Friendship -- Fiction 6. Anorexia nervosa -- Fiction 7. Emotional problems -- Fiction
ISBN 1595144668; 9781595144669

LC 2012012257

This book tells the story of 16-year-old Zoe, who "finds herself in a small rehabilitation center for girls with eating disorders," which she feels "must be some kind of mistake" because "she feels in control of her cautious dietary habits. Through letters to her mysteriously silent best friend, Elise, as well as a personal journal," it becomes clear that Zoe is in denial and "that she is, in fact, a girl with a disorder that is spiraling out of control." (School Library Journal)

Priest, Cherie

★ **I** Am Princess X. Cherie Priest; with comic art by Kali Ciesemier. Scholastic Inc. 2015 240 p.

Grades: 7 8 9 10 11 12

1. Best friends -- Fiction 2. Missing children -- Fiction 3. Webcomics -- Fiction 4. Female friendship -- Fiction 5. Comic books, strips, etc. -- Fiction
0545620856; 9780545620857, $18.99

LC 2015003694

In this novel, by Cherie Priest, with comic art by Kali Ciesemier, "two best friends created a princess together . . . and their heroine, Princess X, slayed all the dragons and scaled all the mountains their imaginations could conjure.

Once upon a few years later, . . . Libby passed away, and Princess X died with her. Once upon a now: May is sixteen and lonely, wandering the streets of Seattle, when she sees a sticker slapped in a corner window. Princess X?" (Publisher's note)

"May and Libby created Princess X on the day they met in fifth grade. That was before Libby and her mother died in a car crash. Now May is 16 and looking at another long, lonely summer in Seattle when she spots a Princess X sticker on the corner of a store window. Suddenly she starts seeing Princess X everywhere, including in a webcomic at IAmPrincessX.com, where the princess story is eerily similar to Libby's. . . . An excellent book with loads of cross-genre and cross-format appeal." SLJ

Proimos, James
12 things to do before you crash and burn. Roaring Brook Press 2011 121p $14.99
Grades: 7 8 9 10
    1. Uncles -- Fiction 2. Bereavement -- Fiction 3. Father-son relationship -- Fiction
    ISBN 978-1-59643-595-7; 1-59643-595-X
                              LC 2010043935
Sixteen-year-old James 'Hercules' Martino completes twelve tasks while spending two weeks in Baltimore with his Uncle Anthony, and gains insights into himself, his uncle, and his recently deceased father, a self-help author and daytime talk show host who was beloved by the public but a terrible father.

"Proimos fully inhabits the mind and voice of his hero, whose almost mythic journey offers moments hilarious, heartbreaking, and triumphant." Publ Wkly

Prose, Francine
After. HarperCollins Pubs. 2003 330p $15.99; lib bdg $16.89
Grades: 7 8 9 10
    1. School stories 2. Conspiracies -- Fiction 3. School violence -- Fiction
    ISBN 0-06-008081-7; 0-06-008082-5 lib bdg
                              LC 2002-14386
In the aftermath of a nearby school shooting, a grief and crisis counselor takes over Central High School and enacts increasingly harsh measures to control students, while those who do not comply disappear

"This drama raises all-too-relevant questions about the fine line between safety as a means of protection versus encroachment on individual rights and free will. Sure to spur heated discussions." Publ Wkly

Touch. HarperTeen 2009 262p $16.99; lib bdg $17.89
Grades: 7 8 9 10
    1. School stories 2. Friendship -- Fiction 3. Family life -- Fiction 4. Stepmothers -- Fiction
    ISBN 978-0-06-137517-0; 0-06-137517-9; 978-0-06-137518-7 lib bdg; 0-06-137518-7 lib bdg
                              LC 2008-20208
Ninth-grader Maisie's concepts of friendship, loyalty, self-acceptance, and truth are tested to their limit after a schoolbus incident with the three boys who have been her best friends since early childhood.

"Readers will be fascinated by this convincing tale and the questions that it raises, from its gripping first chapter to its poignant and surprising conclusion." Voice Youth Advocates

The **turning**; by Francine Prose. HarperTeen 2012 256 p. (hardcover) $17.99
Grades: 7 8 9 10
    1. Ghost stories 2. Horror fiction 3. Babysitters -- Fiction 4. Ghosts -- Fiction
    ISBN 0061999660; 9780061999666
                              LC 2012019090
This book by Francine Prose is an "epistolary retelling of Henry James's 'The Turn of the Screw' [which] traces a contemporary babysitter's supernatural encounters. The protagonist, Jack, is hoping to earn some money for college when he agrees to care for orphan siblings on Crackstone's Landing, a remote island without phones, Internet, or TV. . . . Jack is spooked by two ethereal figures, perhaps the ghosts of the children's former governess and her beau." (Publishers Weekly)

Pullman, Philip, 1946-
★ The **golden** compass; his dark materials book I. [appendix illustrations by Ian Beck] Deluxe 10th anniversary ed.; Alfred A. Knopf 2006 399p il $22.95
Grades: 7 8 9 10 11 12
    1. Fantasy fiction
    ISBN 978-0-375-83830-9; 0-375-83830-9
                              LC 2005-32556
First published 1995 in the United Kingdom with title: Northern lights

This first title in a fantasy trilogy "introduces the characters and sets up the basic conflict, namely, a race to unlock the mystery of a newly discovered type of charged particles simply called 'dust' that may be a bridge to an alternate universe. The action follows 11-year-old protagonist Lyra Belacqua from her home at Oxford University to the frozen wastes of the North on a quest to save dozens of kidnapped children from the evil 'Gobblers,' who are using them as part of a sinister experiment involving dust." Libr J [review of 1996 edition]

Other titles in the His dark materials series are:
The amber spyglass (2000)
The subtle knife (1997)

★ **La** Belle Sauvage. Philip Pullman. Alfred A. Knopf 2017 449 p. Color; Illustration (Book of dust)
Grades: 8 9 10 11 12
    1. Belacqua, Lyra (Fictitious character) -- Fiction; 2. Familiars (Spirits) -- Fiction; 3. Spies -- Fiction; 4. Friendship -- Fiction; 5. England -- Fiction
    9780375815300, $22.99; 0375815309; 9780553510737
                              LC 2017478729
In this novel in the Book of Dust series, by Philip Pullman, "Malcolm Polstead is the kind of boy who notices everything but is not much noticed himself.... He finds a secret message inquiring about a dangerous substance called Dust -- and the spy it was intended for finds him.... He sees suspicious characters everywhere.... All are asking about...a girl -- just a baby -- named Lyra.... And Malcolm will brave

any danger...to bring her safely through the storm." (Publisher's note)

"Magisterial storytelling will sweep readers along; the cast is as vividly drawn as ever; and big themes running beneath the surface invite profound responses and reflection." Kirkus

Once upon a time in the North; illustrated by John Lawrence. Knopf 2008 95p il $12.99

Grades: 7 8 9 10 11 12

    1. Fantasy fiction

    ISBN 978-0-375-84510-9; 0-375-84510-0

                        LC 2007-43993

Prequel to: The golden compass

In a time before Lyra Silvertongue was born, the tough American balloonist Lee Scoresby and the great armoured bear Iorek Byrnison meet when Lee and his hare daemon Hester crash-land their trading balloon onto a port in the far Arctic North and find themselves right in the middle of a political powder keg.

"The precise narrative prose is spiced up with Lee's flights of 'oratorical flamboyancy,' and the sardonic banter between Lee and his daemon Hester is as amusing as ever. [Illustrated with] engraved spot illustrations and 'reproduced' documents." Horn Book

Pung, Alice

★ **Lucy** and Linh. Alice Pung. Alfred A. Knopf 2016 352 p.

Grades: 9 10 11 12

    1. Asians -- Australia -- Fiction 2. Cliques (Sociology) -- Fiction 3. High schools -- Fiction 4. Immigrants -- Fiction 5. Letters -- Fiction 6. Schools -- Fiction 7. Australia -- Fiction

    9780399550485, $17.99; 9780399550492; 9780399550508, $53.97

                        LC 2015024300

In this book, by Alice Pung, "Lucy is a bit of a pushover, but she's ambitious and smart, and she has just received the opportunity of a lifetime: a scholarship to a prestigious school, and a ticket out of her broken-down suburb. Though she's worried she will stick out like badly cut bangs among the razor-straight students, she is soon welcomed into the Cabinet, the supremely popular trio who wield influence over classmates and teachers alike." (Publisher's note)

"A bracing, enthralling gut-punch and an essential read for teens, teachers, and parents alike." Kirkus

Originally published in Australia by Black Inc. in 2014 under title: Laurinda.

Purcell, Kim

Trafficked; by Kim Purcell. Viking 2012 384 p.

Grades: 9 10 11 12

    1. Slavery -- Fiction 2. Immigrants -- United States -- Fiction 3. Juvenile prostitution -- Fiction 4. Human trafficking -- Fiction 5. Los Angeles (Calif.) -- Fiction 6. Moldovans -- United States -- Fiction

    ISBN 0670012807; 9780670012800

                        LC 2011011530

In this young adult novel by Kim Purcell, "[w]hen Hannah's parents are killed in an explosion in a café in the breakaway republic of Transnistria, she and her grandmother are

hard pressed to make ends meet in their Moldovan home. . . . Hannah decides to take an offer to go to America as a nanny for a Russian family. . . . What she finds in America is a harsh reality check; yes, she is a nanny to a reasonably wealthy family, but the family confiscates her return ticket, she is forbidden to leave the house or even speak English, and no money is forthcoming. She is also under threat from a family friend to . . . [who] imports Russian girls as prostitutes. . . . Hannah is constantly worried about what will happen to her." (Bulletin of the Center for Children's Books)

Qamar, Amjed

★ **Beneath** my mother's feet. Atheneum Books for Young Readers 2008 198p $16.99

Grades: 7 8 9 10

    1. Poverty -- Fiction 2. Pakistan -- Fiction 3. Sex role -- Fiction 4. Household employees -- Fiction

    ISBN 978-1-4169-4728-8; 1-4169-4728-0

                        LC 2007-19001

When her father is injured, fourteen-year-old Nazia is pulled away from school, her friends, and her preparations for an arranged marriage, to help her mother clean houses in a wealthy part of Karachi, Pakistan, where she finally rebels against the destiny that is planned for her.

This novel "provides a fascinating glimpse into a world remarkably distant from that of most American teens, and would be an excellent suggestion for readers who want to know about how other young people live." SLJ

Quick, Matthew

Boy21; by Matthew Quick. Little, Brown and Co. 2012 250 p.

Grades: 8 9 10 11 12

    1. Basketball -- Fiction 2. Friendship -- Fiction 3. Race relations -- Fiction 4. Boys -- Psychology -- Fiction 5. High school students -- Fiction 6. Violence -- Fiction 7. High schools -- Fiction 8. Pennsylvania -- Fiction 9. African Americans -- Fiction

    ISBN 0316127973; 9780316127974

                        LC 2010047995

In this book, high school basketball player "Finley . . . take[s] under his wing Russell Washington, the . . . son of a family friend. Boy21, as Russell now calls himself, was a phenom . . . until his parents were killed and he withdrew into an outer-space obsession and refused to play ball. . . . Just as Boy21 begins to get his life back together, Finley's goes into a tailspin when [his girlfriend] Erin is run down by an enemy of her brother." (Bulletin of the Center for Children's Books)

Every exquisite thing. By Matthew Quick. Little, Brown & Co. 2016 272 p.

Grades: 9 10 11 12

    1. Authors -- Fiction 2. Books and reading -- Fiction 3. Self-realization -- Fiction 4. Teacher-student relationships -- Fiction 5. Teachers -- Fiction 6. High school students -- Fiction

    9780316379595

                        LC 2015011641

"Nanette O'Hare is an unassuming teen who has played the role of dutiful daughter, hardworking student, and star athlete for as long as she can remember. But when a beloved teacher gives her his worn copy of The Bugglegum Reaper—a mysterious, out-of-print cult classic—the rebel within Nanette awakens. As she befriends the reclusive author, falls in love with a young but troubled poet, and attempts to insert her true self into the world with wild abandon, Nanette learns the hard way that rebellion sometimes comes at a high price." (Publisher's note)

"Conventional high-schooler Nanette's life changes after she befriends Nigel Booker, elderly author of a classic cult novel about nonconformity. Booker sets her up with fellow teen fan Alex, a poet with a troubled, violent past. This is an ode to revolutionary literature—its power to inspire change and incite action (positive and otherwise); it's also an engaging bildungsroman as Nanette comes into her own." Horn Book

Forgive me, Leonard Peacock; by Matthew Quick. Little, Brown and Co. 2013 288 p. $18
Grades: 9 10 11 12
1. School stories 2. Suicide -- Fiction 3. School shootings -- Fiction
ISBN 0316221333; 9780316221337
LC 2012031410

This book by Matthew Quick follows "Leonard Peacock . . . a teenager who feels let down by adults and out of step with his sheeplike classmates. Foreseeing only more unhappiness and disappointment in life (and harboring a secret that's destroying him), Leonard packs up his grandfather's WWII handgun and heads to school, intending to kill his former best friend and then himself. First, though, he will visit the important people in his life." (Publishers Weekly)

"Eighteen-year-old Leonard Peacock is packing a handgun and planning to kill his former best friend, then himself. Over the course of one intense day (with flashbacks), Leonard's existential crisis is delineated through an engaging first-person narrative supplemented with letters from the future that urge Leonard to believe in a "life beyond the bermorons" at school. Complicated characters and ideas mark this memorable story." (Horn Book)

Sorta like a rockstar; a novel. Little, Brown 2010 355p $16.99; pa $8.99
Grades: 7 8 9 10 11
1. School stories 2. Homeless persons -- Fiction 3. Depression (Psychology) -- Fiction
ISBN 978-0-316-04352-6; 0-316-04352-4; 978-0-316-04353-3 pa; 0-316-04353-2 pa
LC 2008-46746

Although seventeen-year-old Amber Appleton is homeless, living in a school bus with her unfit mother, she is a relentless optimist who visits the elderly at a nursing home, teaches English to Korean Catholic women with the use of rhythm and blues music, and befriends a solitary Vietnam veteran and his dog, but eventually she experiences one burden more than she can bear and slips into a deep depression.

"This book is the answer to all those angst-ridden and painfully grim novels in the shortcut lingo of short attention-span theater. Hugely enjoyable." SLJ

Quigley, Dawn

Apple in the middle. Dawn Quigley. North Dakota State University Press 2018 264 p.

Grades: 6 7 8 9 10
1. Stepfamilies -- Fiction; 2. Native Americans -- Fiction; 3. Teenage girls -- Fiction
9781946163073, $25.95
LC 2018941180

In this book in the Contemporary Voice of Indigenous Peoples, by Dawn Quigley, "Apple Starkington turned her back on her Native American heritage the moment she was called a racial slur for someone of white and Indian descent, not that she really even knew how to be an Indian in the first place. Too bad the white world doesn't accept her either. And so begins her quirky habits to gain acceptance." (Publisher's note)

Quintero, Isabel

★ **Gabi,** a girl in pieces. Isabel Quintero. Cinco Puntos Press. 2014 208p $17.95
Grades: 9 10 11 12
1. Family problems -- Fiction 2. Gays -- Fiction 3. High schools -- Fiction 4. Mexican Americans -- Fiction 5. Pregnancy -- Fiction 6. Diaries--Fiction
ISBN: 1935955942; 9781935955948; 9781935955955
LC 2014007658

William C. Morris Award (2015)

"Sixteen-year-old Gabi Hernandez has a lot to deal with during her senior year. Her best friend Cindy is pregnant; her other best friend Sebastian just got kicked out of his house for coming out to his strict parents; her meth addict dad is trying to quit, again; and her super religious Tía Bertha is constantly putting a damper on Gabi's love life. In lyrical diary entries peppered with the burgeoning poet's writing, Spanglish, and phone conversations, Quintero gives voice to a complex, not always likable but totally believable teen who struggles to figure out her own place in the world. Believing she's not Mexican enough for her family and not white enough for Berkeley, Gabi still meets every challenge head-on with vulgar humor and raw honesty." Booklist

Quintero, Sofia

★ **Efrain's** secret. Alfred A. Knopf 2010 265p $16.99; lib bdg $19.99
Grades: 8 9 10 11 12
1. School stories 2. Violence -- Fiction 3. Drug traffic -- Fiction 4. Hispanic Americans -- Fiction 5. Bronx (New York, N.Y.) -- Fiction
ISBN 978-0-375-84706-6; 0-375-84706-5; 978-0-375-94706-3 lib bdg; 0-375-94706-X lib bdg
LC 2009-8493

Ambitious high school senior and honor student Efrain Rodriguez makes some questionable choices in pursuit of his dream to escape the South Bronx and attend an Ivy League college.

"Quintero imbues her characters with unexpected grace and charm. . . . Mostly, though, it is Quintero's effortless grasp of teen slang that gives her first-person story its heart." Booklist

Rabb, Margo

★ **Kissing** in America. Margo Rabb. Harpercollins Childrens Books 2015 400 p.
Grades: 9 10 11 12
1. Automobile travel -- Fiction 2. Best friends -- Fiction

3. Teenage girls -- Fiction 4. Romance fiction 5. Grief -- Fiction 6. Travel -- Fiction
0062322370; 9780062322371, $17.99

"In the two years since her father died, sixteen-year-old Eva has found comfort in reading romance novels. Her romantic fantasies become a reality when she meets Will, who understands Eva's grief. Unfortunately . . . he picks up and moves to California without any warning. Not wanting to lose the only person who has been able to pull her out of sadness . . . Eva and her best friend, Annie, concoct a plan to travel to the West Coast to see Will again." (Publisher's note)

"A lineup of friends and meddling relatives adds humor and depth beyond the romance plot, giving Eva a chance to repair her relationships." Horn Book

Raf, Mindy

The **symptoms** of my insanity; Mindy Raf. Dial 2013 384 p. (hardcover) $17.99
Grades: 8 9 10 11 12

1. School stories 2. Puberty -- Fiction 3. Teenage girls -- Fiction 4. Mothers -- Fiction 5. High schools -- Fiction 6. Hypochondria -- Fiction
ISBN 0803732414; 9780803732414

LC 2012024708

"Izzy is running out of time to complete her art portfolio, her ever-expanding chest is the brunt of ogling and inappropriate jokes, and her mother's rare stomach cancer has probably returned. Naturally, the high school sophomore assumes that her body's idiosyncrasies must be a sign of a developing disease. There's still some hope for Izzy when popular basketball player Blake shows an interest in her. His affection is a ruse for a hazing prank, however, and when a cellphone photo of Izzy's bare breast goes viral, she becomes known as 'Boobgirl' around school." Kirkus

"While the plot is predictable . . . Izzy's self-deprecating humor and wry observations bring fresh air to tired tropes. Raf's background in comedy serves her well and gives her protagonist an authenticity that will make readers feel invested in her story. A fairly standard contribution to the genre, but a solid one." SLJ

Raina, Arushi

★ **When** morning comes. By Arushi Raina. Tradewind Books 2017 221 p.
Grades: 8 9 10 11 12

1. Anti-apartheid movements -- South Africa -- Fiction; 2. Government, Resistance to -- Fiction; 3. High school students -- Fiction; 4. Race relations -- Fiction; 5. Apartheid; 6. South Africa -- Race relations -- Fiction; 7. South Africa -- Fiction
9781926890739; 9781896580692, $18.95; 1896580696

In this book, by Arushi Raina, "Zanele is skipping school and secretly plotting against the apartheid government.... Her best friend Thabo, schoolboy turned gang member, can tell she's up to something. But he has troubles of his own -- a deal gone wrong and some powerful enemies. Across the bridge, in the wealthy white suburbs, Jack plans to spend his last days in Johannesburg burning miles on his beat-up Mustang." (Publisher's note)

"A sophisticated political thriller that challenges readers and offers no pat endings. The appended historical note and glossary are essential." Booklist

Rainfield, Cheryl

★ **Scars**; Cheryl Rainfield. WestSide Books 2010 248p. $16.95
Grades: 9 10 11 12

1. Memory -- Fiction 2. Lesbians -- Fiction 3. Self-mutilation -- Fiction 4. Child sexual abuse -- Fiction 5. Artists -- Fiction 6. Emotional problems -- Fiction 7. Cutting (Self-mutilation) -- Fiction
ISBN 9781934813324

LC 2009052076

This novel tells the story of "Kendra, fifteen, [who] hasn't felt safe since she began to recall devastating memories of childhood sexual abuse—especially because she still can't remember the most important detail—her abuser's identity. Frightened, Kendra believes someone is always watching and following her, leaving menacing messages only she understands. . . . To relieve the pressure, Kendra cuts; aside from her brilliantly expressive artwork, it's her only way of coping. Since her own mother is too self-absorbed to hear her cries for help, Kendra finds support in others instead: from her therapist and her art teacher, from Sandy, the close family friend who encourages her artwork, and from Meghan, the classmate who's becoming a friend and maybe more." (Publisher's note)

"The excellent resource section covers widely respected books, Web sites, organizations, and help lines for youth seeking information on extreme abuse, cutting, same-sex attraction, and dissociation. This book will be a particular comfort and source of insight for teens facing any of these challenges, but whatever their life experience, they will be on the edge of their seats, rooting for Kendra to unravel the mystery that shadows her life. This is one heck of a good book!" SLJ

Stained; by Cheryl Rainfield. Harcourt, Houghton Mifflin Harcourt 2013 304 p. $16.99
Grades: 9 10 11 12

1. Kidnapping -- Fiction 2. Survival skills -- Fiction 3. Birthmarks -- Fiction 4. Body image -- Fiction 5. Psychopaths -- Fiction 6. Sexual abuse -- Fiction 7. Beauty, Personal -- Fiction
ISBN 0547942087; 9780547942087

LC 2012047540

In this book by Cheryl Rainfield, "Sarah Meadows longs for 'normal.' Born with a port wine stain covering half her face, all her life she's been plagued by stares, giggles, bullying, and disgust. But when she's abducted on the way home from school, Sarah is forced to uncover the courage she never knew she had, become a hero rather than a victim, and learn to look beyond her face to find the beauty and strength she has inside. It's that—or succumb to a killer." (Publisher's note)

Randall, Thomas

Dreams of the dead. Bloomsbury Children's Books 2009 276p (The waking) pa $8.99
Grades: 8 9 10 11 12

1. School stories 2. Death -- Fiction 3. Japan -- Fiction 4. Supernatural -- Fiction
ISBN 978-1-59990-250-0; 1-59990-250-8

LC 2008-30844

After her mother dies, sixteen-year-old Kara and her father move to Japan, where he teaches and she attends school, but she is haunted by a series of frightening nightmares and deaths that might be revenge—or something worse

"The story has suspense, mystery, and horror. It will be a great hit with fans of manga, anime, or Japanese culture." SLJ

Followed by: Spirits of the Noh (2011)

Spirits of the Noh. Bloomsbury U.S.A. Children's Books 2010 264p (The waking) $8.99

Grades: 8 9 10 11 12

1. Horror fiction 2. School stories 3. Japan -- Fiction 4. Monsters -- Fiction 5. Supernatural -- Fiction

ISBN 978-1-59990-251-7; 1-59990-251-6

LC 2009018251

Sequel to: Dreams of the dead (2009)

Just as Kara and her friends at the Monju-no-Chie school in Japan are beginning to get over the horrifying deaths of two students, another monster emerges to terrorize the school.

"Using all the usual horror elements, Randall constructs a fine teen chiller complete with mean-girl drama, a dash of romance and the angst of teens who believe that adults do not understand them." Kirkus

Rapp, Adam

The **children** and the wolves; Adam Rapp. Candlewick Press 2011 152 p. $16.99

Grades: 8 9 10

1. Kidnapping -- Fiction 2. Psychological fiction 3. Juvenile delinquency -- Fiction 4. Drug abuse -- Fiction 5. Single parent family -- Fiction

ISBN 0763653373; 9780763653378

LC 2011013676

This book by Printz Honor-winning author Adam Rapp presents a story "about three disaffected teens and a kidnapped child. Three teenagers—a sharp, well-to-do girl named Bounce and two struggling boys named Wiggins and Orange—are holding a four-year old girl hostage in Orange's basement. The little girl answers to 'the Frog' and seems content to play a video game about wolves all day long, a game that parallels the reality around her. As the stakes grow higher and the guilt and tension mount, Wiggins cracks and finally brings Frog to a trusted adult." (Publisher's note)

★ **Punkzilla**. Candlewick Press 2009 244p $16.99

Grades: 10 11 12

1. Brothers -- Fiction 2. Drug abuse -- Fiction 3. Runaway teenagers -- Fiction

ISBN 978-0-7636-3031-7; 0-7636-3031-4

LC 2008-935655

ALA YALSA Printz Award Honor Book (2010)

"Punkzilla" is on a mission to see his older brother "P", before "P" dies of cancer. Still buzzing from his last hit of meth, he embarks on a days-long trip from Portland, Ore. to Memphis, Tenn., writing letters to his family and friends. Along the way, he sees a sketchier side of America and worries if he will make it to see his brother in time.

★ **Under** the wolf, under the dog. Candlewick Press 2004 310p $16.99

Grades: 9 10 11 12

1. Suicide -- Fiction 2. Illinois -- Fiction 3. Family life -- Fiction

ISBN 0-7636-1818-7

LC 2004-50255

"Steve currently resides in a facility for troubled youth, but most are here for drug abuse or suicidal tendencies, and he doesn't really fit in either category. What's led him here, as he describes in his journal, is a series of life depredations that have sent him reeling into irrationality: his mother's long, horrible, and unsuccessful bout with cancer, his father's concomitant catatonic depression, his brother's drug-induced haze and subsequent suicide, and his own unintentional self-woundings along the way, from a lacerated leg to an injury that eventually results in blindness in one eye." Bull Cent Child Books

Redgate, Riley

Final draft. Riley Redgate. Amulet Books 2018 272 p.

Grades: 9 10 11 12

1. Authorship -- Fiction; 2. Creative ability -- Fiction; 3. Racially mixed people -- Fiction

9781419728723, $17.99

LC 2017057158

In this book, by Riley Redgate, "The only sort of risk 18-year-old Laila Piedra enjoys is the peril she writes for the characters in her stories: epic sci-fi worlds full of quests, forbidden love, and robots. Her creative writing teacher has always told her she has a special talent. But three months before her graduation, he's suddenly replaced -- by Nadiya Nazarenko, a Pulitzer Prize-winning novelist who is sadistically critical and perpetually unimpressed." (Publisher's note)

★ **Noteworthy**. Riley Redgate. Amulet Books 2017 384 p.

Grades: 9 10 11 12

1. Disguise -- Fiction; 2. Women singers -- Fiction; 3. Private schools -- Fiction

9781683350699; 9781419723735, $17.95

LC 2016045116

In this novel, by Riley Redgate, "it's the start of Jordan Sun's junior year at the Kensington-Blaine Boarding School for the Performing Arts. Unfortunately, she's an Alto 2,... [and] nobody's falling over themselves to express their appreciation.... But then the school gets a mass email: A spot has opened up in the Sharpshooters, Kensington's elite a cappella octet. Worshiped..., revered..., [and] all male." (Publisher's note)

"A heart song for all readers who have ever felt like strangers in their own skins." Kirkus

Redwine, C. J.

The **wish** granter: a Ravenspire novel. C. J. Redwine. Balzer + Bray 2017 423 p. Color; Map (Ravenspire)

Grades: 9 10 11 12

1. Illegitimate children of royalty -- Fiction; 2. Mothers -- Death -- Fiction; 3. Twins -- Fiction; 4. Rumpelstiltskin

(Folk tale) -- Adaptations; 5. Princesses -- Fiction; 6. Fantasy fiction; 7. Teenage girls -- Fiction
9780062360304; 9780062360274, $17.99

LC 2016949521

In this novel in the Ravenspire series, by C. J. Redwine, "the world has turned upside down for Thad and Ari Glavan, the bastard twins of Súndraille's king. Their mother was murdered. The royal family died mysteriously. And now Thad sits on the throne of a kingdom whose streets are suddenly overrun with violence he can't stop." (Publisher's note)

"A cast of interesting and complex characters, an unconventional attraction, several fascinating plot threads, and an effective conclusion should endear this to Redwine's fans and beyond. " Booklist

Reed, Amy

★ The **Nowhere** Girls. By Amy Reed. Simon Pulse 2017 404 p.

Grades: 9 10 11 12

    1. Conduct of life -- Fiction; 2. Family life -- Oregon -- Fiction; 3. High schools -- Fiction; 4. Rape -- Fiction; 5. Schools -- Fiction; 6. Sex -- Fiction; 7. Oregon -- Fiction; 8. Family life -- Fiction
9781481481755; 1481481738; 9781481481731, $17.99; 9781481481748

LC 2016044338

In this book, by Amy Reed, "three misfits come together to avenge the rape of a fellow classmate and in the process trigger a change in the misogynist culture at their high school transforming the lives of everyone around them in this searing and timely story. Who are the Nowhere Girls? They're everygirl. But they start with just three." (Publisher's note)

". . . a highly nuanced and self-reflective narrative that captures rape culture's ubiquitous harm without swerving into didactic, one-size-fits-all solutions or relying on false notions of homogenous young womanhood. Scandal, justice, romance, sex positivity, subversive anti-sexism -- just try to put it down." Kirkus

Over you; by Amy Reed. 1st Simon Pulse hardcover ed. Simon Pulse 2013 299 p. (hardcover) $16.99

Grades: 9 10 11 12

    1. Communal living -- Fiction 2. Female friendship -- Fiction 3. Nebraska -- Fiction 4. Friendship -- Fiction 5. Family problems -- Fiction 6. Farm life -- Nebraska -- Fiction 7. Mothers and daughters -- Fiction
ISBN 1442456965; 9781442456969

LC 2012023492

In this book, 17-year-old friends Max and Sadie spend a summer on a communal farm. "Max welcomes the hippie residents (which include Sadie's absentee mother), yurts, and grueling farm work, but Sadie--volatile, self-absorbed, and always the center of attention--quickly grows bored and irate. After Sadie is quarantined with mono, Max has even more freedom to explore her own thoughts, interests, and desires--including a love/hate crush on a surly older boy that surprises even Max." (Publishers Weekly)

Reeve, Philip, 1966-

★ **Fever** Crumb. Scholastic Press 2010 325p $17.99

Grades: 6 7 8 9 10

    1. Science fiction 2. Orphans -- Fiction 3. Sex role -- Fiction 4. London (England) -- Fiction
ISBN 978-0-545-20719-5; 0-545-20719-3

LC 2009-15457

Prequel to: The Hungry City Chronicles series

Foundling Fever Crumb has been raised as an engineer although females in the future London, England, are not believed capable of rational thought, but at age fourteen she leaves her sheltered world and begins to learn startling truths about her past while facing danger in the present.

"Reeve's captivating flights of imagination play as vital a role in the story as his endearing heroine, hiss-worthy villains, and nifty array of supporting characters." Booklist

Followed by A web of air (2011)

★ **Here** lies Arthur. Scholastic Press 2008 339p $16.99

Grades: 7 8 9 10

    1. Kings 2. Magic -- Fiction 3. Great Britain -- History -- 0-1066 -- Fiction
ISBN 978-0-545-09334-7; 0-545-09334-1

LC 2008-05787

When her village is attacked and burned, Gwyna seeks protection from the bard Myrddin, who uses Gwyna in his plan to transform young Arthur into the heroic King Arthur.

"Powerfully inventive. . . . Events rush headlong toward the inevitable ending, but Gwyna's observations illuminate them in a new way." Booklist

Scrivener's moon; the third book in the Fever Crumb series. Philip Reeve. Scholastic Press 2012 341 p. (Fever Crumb series) (hardcover) $17.99

Grades: 6 7 8 9 10

    1. Steampunk fiction 2. Technology -- Fiction 3. Science fiction 4. England -- Fiction 5. Identity -- Fiction 6. London (England) -- Fiction 7. Dystopias 8. Mutation (Biology) -- Fiction
ISBN 0545222184; 9780545222181

LC 2012008124

This young adult steampunk adventure novel, by Philip Reeve, is the conclusion to the "Fever Crumb" trilogy. "The Scriven people are brilliant, mad--and dead. All except one, whose monstrous creation is nearly complete--a giant city on wheels. New London terrifies the rest of the world, and an army of mammoth-riders gathers to fight it. Meanwhile, young Fever Crumb begins a hunt for Ancient technology in the icy strongholds of the north." (Publisher's note)

A **Web** of Air. Scholastic Press 2011 293p $17.99

Grades: 6 7 8 9 10

    1. Science fiction 2. Flight -- Fiction 3. Orphans -- Fiction
ISBN 0-545-22216-8; 978-0-545-22216-7

LC 2010043341

Sequel to: Fever Crumb (2010)

Two years ago, Fever Crumb escaped the wartorn city of London in a traveling theater. Now, she arrives in the extraordinary city of Mayda, where buildings ascend the cliffs on funicular rails, and a mysterious recluse is building a machine that can fly.

"It's clear that Reeve . . . is building toward an epic, and his remarkable storytelling gifts, coupled with a trenchant understanding of human nature, make these projected volumes worth the wait." Horn Book

Reichs, Brendan

★ **Nemesis**. Brendan Reichs. G. P. Putnam's Sons 2017 443 p.

Grades: 8 9 10 11 12

1. Asteroids -- Collisions with Earth -- Fiction; 2. Conspiracies -- Fiction; 3. Science fiction; 4. Survival -- Fiction; 5. Asteroids -- Fiction

0399544933; 9780399544934, $17.99; 9780399544958

LC 2016021737

In this book, by Brendan Reichs, "it's been happening since Min was eight. Every two years, on her birthday, a strange man finds her and murders her in cold blood. But hours later, she wakes up in a clearing just outside her tiny Idaho hometown -- alone, unhurt, and with all evidence of the horrifying crime erased. Across the valley, Noah just wants to be like everyone else. But he's not. Nightmares of murder and death plague him, though he does his best to hide the signs." (Publisher's note)

"Reichs's new novel offers readers a glimpse into the final moments of a preapocalyptic world, as seen through the eyes of two radically different teens." SLJ

Reinhardt, Dana

★ **How** to build a house; a novel. Wendy Lamb Books 2008 227p $15.99; lib bdg $18.99

Grades: 8 9 10 11 12

1. Divorce -- Fiction 2. Building -- Fiction 3. Tennessee -- Fiction 4. Stepfamilies -- Fiction 5. Volunteer work -- Fiction

ISBN 978-0-375-84453-9; 0-375-84453-8; 978-0-375-94454-3 lib bdg; 0-375-94454-0 lib bdg

LC 2007-33403

Seventeen-year-old Harper Evans hopes to escape the effects of her father's divorce on her family and friendships by volunteering her summer to build a house in a small Tennessee town devastated by a tornado.

"This meticulously crafted book illustrates how both homes and relationships can be resurrected through hard work, hope and teamwork." Publ Wkly

★ **Tell** us something true. Dana Reinhardt. Wendy Lamb Books 2016 208 p.

Grades: 9 10 11 12

1. Dating (Social customs) -- Fiction 2. Honesty -- Fiction 3. Interpersonal relations -- Fiction 4. Self-help groups -- Fiction

9780307975829, $53.97; 9780375990663; 9780385742597, $17.99

LC 2015026155

In this book, by Dana Reinhardt, "seventeen-year-old River doesn't know what to do with himself when Penny, the girl he adores, breaks up with him. . . . He stumbles upon a support group for teens with various addictions. He fakes his way into the meetings, and begins to connect with the

other kids, especially an amazing girl. River wants to tell the truth, but he can't stop lying, and his tangle of deception may unravel." (Publisher's note)

"Reinhardt constructs a character who, haltingly, rebuilds himself in believable ways as he confronts family trauma, lost love, and growing up." Booklist

★ The **things** a brother knows. Wendy Lamb Books 2010 245p $16.99; lib bdg $19.99

Grades: 7 8 9 10 11 12

1. Brothers -- Fiction 2. Soldiers -- Fiction 3. Family life -- Fiction 4. Boston (Mass.) -- Fiction 5. Jews -- United States -- Fiction

ISBN 978-0-375-84455-3; 0-375-84455-4; 978-0-375-94455-9 lib bdg; 0-375-94455-9 lib bdg

Although they have never gotten along well, seventeen-year-old Levi follows his older brother Boaz, an ex-Marine, on a walking trip from Boston to Washington, D.C. in hopes of learning why Boaz is completely withdrawn.

"Reinhardt's poignant story of a soldier coping with survivor's guilt and trauma, and his Israeli American family's struggle to understand and help, is timely and honest." Booklist

We are the Goldens. by Dana Reinhardt. Wendy Lamb Books.. 2014 197p $16.99

Grades: 9 10 11 12

1. Divorce -- Fiction 2. High schools -- Fiction 3. Sexual abuse -- Fiction 4. Sisters -- Fiction 5. Teacher-student relationship -- Fiction

ISBN: 0385742576; 9780375990656; 9780385742573; 9780385742580

LC 2013023351

"Reinhardt plunges into the dilemmas of sibling affection and loyalty. High schooler Nell's equilibrium shatters when she realizes that her sister Layla is having an affair with a teacher. Nell's narrative (directly addressed to Layla as "you") explains how she arrived at the difficult decision to tell their parents. Nell's voice is engaging, clever, and colloquial, making this a speedy, engrossing read." Horn Book

Renn, Diana

Latitude zero. By Diana Renn. Viking, published by Penguin Group 2014 448 p.

Grades: 7 8 9 10

1. Bicycle racing -- Fiction 2. Bicycles and bicycling -- Fiction 3. Investigative journalists -- Fiction 4. Murder -- Fiction 5. Mystery and detective stories 6. Organized crime -- Fiction 7. Reporters and reporting -- Fiction 8. Ecuador -- Fiction 9. Mystery fiction 10. Journalists -- Fiction 11. Bicycles -- Fiction

067001558X; 9780670015580, $17.99

LC 2013043837

In this book, by Diana Renn, "[w]hen star cyclist Juan Carlos Macias-Leon is murdered during the course of a charity bicycle race, Tess, one of the last to see him alive, finds herself involved and, as she begins to investigate, in jeopardy. Determined, nevertheless, to find the truth, she travels to Juan Carlos' native country, Ecuador (the latitude zero of the title). There, she discovers that danger has pursued her, and the more she investigates, the more questions she has." (Booklist)

"Renn has constructed a salient Whodunit totally upon the sport of professional bike racing, injecting the plot with adrenaline at every twist, and throwing the reader in tandem with the characters. Furthermore, this diverse array of talented teen characters makes Latitude Zero an inspiring read for the adolescent reader." VOYA

Rennison, Louise

★ **Angus,** thongs and full-frontal snogging; confessions of Georgia Nicolson. HarperCollins Pubs. 2000 247p hardcover o.p. pa $6.95
Grades: 7 8 9 10
    1. Great Britain -- Fiction
    ISBN 0-06-028814-0; 0-06-447227-2 pa
                        LC 99-40591
First published 1999 in the United Kingdom
Michael L. Printz Award honor book, 2001
Presents the humorous journal of a year in the life of Georgia, a fourteen-year-old British girl who tries to reduce the size of her nose, stop her mad cat from terrorizing the neighborhood animals, and win the love of handsome hunk Robbie.
"Georgia is a wonderful character whose misadventures are not only hysterically funny but universally recognizable." Booklist
    Other titles about Georgia are:
    Are these my basoomas I see before me? (2009)
    Away laughing on a fast camel (2004)
    Dancing in my nuddy-pants (2003)
    Knocked out by my nunga-nungas (2002)
    Love is a many trousered thing (2007)
    On the bright side, I'm now the girlfriend of a sex god (2001)
    Startled by his furry shorts (2006)
    Stop in the name of pants (2008)
    Then he ate my boy entrancers (2005)

Are these my basoomas I see before me? final confessions of Georgia Nicolson. HarperTeen 2009 310p $16.99; lib bdg $17.89
Grades: 7 8 9 10
    1. Diaries -- Fiction 2. Theater -- Fiction 3. Great Britain -- Fiction 4. Dating (Social customs) -- Fiction
    ISBN 978-0-06-145935-1; 0-06-145935-6; 978-0-06-145936-8 lib bdg; 0-06-145936-4 lib bdg
                       LC 2009-25449
British teenager Georgia Nicolson's humorous diary entries reveal the results as she finally chooses between potential boyfriends, but then becomes involved in a play with the one not chosen, further complicating her love life.

Stop in the name of pants! HarperTeen 2008 310p $16.99; lib bdg $17.89
Grades: 7 8 9 10
    1. Diaries -- Fiction 2. Great Britain -- Fiction 3. Dating (Social customs) -- Fiction
    ISBN 978-0-06-145932-0; 0-06-145932-1; 978-0-06-145933-7 lib bdg; 0-06-145933-X lib bdg
                       LC 2008-14686
In a series of humorous diary entries, British teenager Georgia Nicolson tries to decide between two potential boy-

friends—Masimo from Pizzagogoland (Italy) or local boy Dave the Laugh.

The **taming** of the tights; Louise Rennison. HarperTeen 2013 306 p. (trade bdg.) $17.99
Grades: 7 8 9 10 11 12
    1. Love stories 2. School stories 3. Actresses -- Fiction 4. Teenagers -- Fiction 5. Humorous stories 6. England -- Fiction 7. High schools -- Fiction 8. Performing arts -- Fiction 9. Yorkshire (England) -- Fiction 10. Dating (Social customs) -- Fiction
    ISBN 0062226207; 9780062226204
                       LC 2013021359
Sequel to: A midsummer tights dream
"Tallulah (A Midsummer Tights Dream) and the Tree Sisters are back for another term at performing arts college where they comically reinterpret another Shakespeare play. But drama follows Tallulah offstage as she debates who is better boyfriend material: Cain or Charlie. Though the book is light on plot, readers will welcome the return of Tallulah's humorous musings and this distinctly British, quirky cast of characters." (Horn Book)

Withering tights. HarperTeen 2011 274p (Misadventures of Tallulah Casey) $16.99
Grades: 7 8 9 10
    1. Camps -- Fiction 2. Acting -- Fiction
    ISBN 0-06-179931-9; 978-0-06-179931-0
                       LC 2010045552
Self-conscious about her knobby knees but confident in her acting ability, fourteen-year-old Tallulah spends the summer at a Yorkshire performing arts camp that, she is surprised to learn, is for girls only.
"Tallulah is a vivacious and hilarious character who will speak to every girl." SLJ

Rens, Kristin

Even the darkest stars. Heather Fawcett. Balzer + Bray 2017 427 p.
Grades: 8 9 10 11 12
    1. Imaginary places -- Fiction; 2. Magic -- Fiction; 3. Mountaineering -- Fiction; 4. Fantasy fiction
    9780062463388, $17.99; 9780062463401
                       LC 2017932797
In this novel by Heather Fawcett, "Kamzin has always dreamed of becoming one of the Emperor's...elite climbers.... [Explorer] River Shara,...hire[s] Kamzin...for his next expedition. The challenges of climbing Raksha are unlike anything Kamzin expected.... And as dark secrets are revealed, Kamzin must unravel the truth of their mission and of her companions -- while surviving the deadliest climb she has ever faced." (Publisher's note)
"Add in a detailed, well-realized setting, an unsettling villain that lingers just off the page, and buckets of danger to result in an utterly inventive and wholly original debut." Booklist
Followed by: All the wandering light (2018)

Resau, Laura

The **indigo** notebook. Delacorte Press 2009 324p $16.99; lib bdg $19.99; pa $9.99

Grades: 7 8 9 10 11 12

1. Ecuador -- Fiction 2. Fathers -- Fiction 3. Single parent family -- Fiction 4. Mother-daughter relationship -- Fiction

ISBN 978-0-385-73652-7; 0-385-73652-5; 978-0-385-90614-2 lib bdg; 0-385-90614-5 lib bdg; 978-0-375-84524-6 pa; 0-375-84524-0 pa

LC 2008-40519

Fifteen-year-old Zeeta comes to terms with her flighty mother and their itinerant life when, soon after moving to Ecuador, she helps an American teenager find his birth father in a nearby village

"Observant, aware, and occasionally wry, Zeeta's first-person narration will attract readers and hold them." Booklist

Followed by: The ruby notebook (2010)

The **jade** notebook; Laura Resau. Delacorte Press 2012 365 p. (hc) $16.99

Grades: 9 10 11 12

1. Mexico -- Fiction 2. Fathers -- Fiction 3. Missing persons -- Fiction 4. Mother-daughter relationship -- Fiction 5. Secrets -- Fiction 6. Mazunte (Mexico) -- Fiction 7. Single-parent families -- Fiction

ISBN 0385740530; 9780375899416; 9780375989537; 9780385740531

LC 2011034861

Sequel to: The ruby notebook

This book is the "third in a series of novels focusing on Zeeta and her wanderlust-stricken mother. . . . Zeeta's decision to find her mom a job in Mazunte was no accident. Newly armed with a slew of hints about her father's background . . . she is madly hoping that it might be his hometown. . . . With her boyfriend, Wendell, by her side, she begins to fit together the pieces of the puzzle. Yet each answer uncovered seems to create more questions about her father's complex past." (Kirkus Reviews)

"The lush descriptions, intermittent action sequences, and sprinkling of fantasy all come together to form an engaging reading experience that will delight teens looking for a more mature story." SLJ

Red glass. Delacorte Press 2007 275p $15.99; lib bdg $18.99

Grades: 7 8 9 10

1. Mexico -- Fiction 2. Orphans -- Fiction 3. Guatemala -- Fiction 4. Family life -- Fiction 5. Automobile travel -- Fiction

ISBN 978-0-385-73466-0; 0-385-73466-2; 978-0-385-90464-3 lib bdg; 0-385-90464-9 lib bdg

LC 2007-02408

Sixteen-year-old Sophie has been frail and delicate since her premature birth, but discovers her true strength during a journey through Mexico, where the six-year-old orphan her family hopes to adopt was born, and to Guatemala, where her would-be boyfriend hopes to find his mother and plans to remain.

"The vivid characters, the fine imagery, and the satisfying story arc make this a rewarding novel." Booklist

The **ruby** notebook. Delacorte Press 2010 373p $16.99; lib bdg $19.99

Grades: 7 8 9 10

1. France -- Fiction 2. Single parent family -- Fiction 3. Mother-daughter relationship -- Fiction

ISBN 978-0-385-73653-4; 0-385-73653-3; 978-0-385-90615-9 lib bdg; 0-385-90615-3 lib bdg

LC 2009-51965

Sequel to: The indigo notebook (2009)

When sixteen-year-old Zeeta and her itinerant mother move to Aix-en-Provence, France, Zeeta is haunted by a mysterious admirer who keeps leaving mementoes for her, and when her Ecuadorian boyfriend comes to visit, their relationship seems to have changed.

"Weaving bits of magic, city lore and bittersweet romance into each of the many plot lines, Resau has again crafted a complex and satisfying novel. . . . Characters are rich and vibrant." Kirkus

Restrepo, Bettina

Illegal. Katherine Tegen Books 2011 251p $16.99

Grades: 7 8 9 10

1. Texas -- Fiction 2. Mexicans -- Fiction 3. Illegal aliens -- Fiction

ISBN 978-0-06-195342-2; 0-06-195342-3

LC 2010-19451

Nora, a fifteen-year-old Mexican girl, faces the challenges of being an illegal immigrant in Texas when she and her mother cross the border in search of Nora's father.

"Restrepo's novel offers an unsparing immigrant story that is both gritty and redemptive. . . . This is urban realism meets quest tale, told with great emotional immediacy, and it will appeal to many teen readers." Bull Cent Child Books

Revis, Beth

Across the universe. Razorbill 2011 398p $17.99

Grades: 7 8 9 10

1. Science fiction 2. Dictators -- Fiction 3. Space vehicles -- Fiction

ISBN 978-1-59514-397-6; 1-59514-397-1

LC 2010-51834

Amy, a cryogenically frozen passenger aboard the vast spaceship Godspeed, is nearly killed when her cyro chamber is unplugged fifty years before Godspeed's scheduled landing. All she knows is that she must race to unlock Godspeed's hidden secrets before whoever woke her tries to kill again—and she doesn't know who she can trust on a ship ruled by a tyrant.

"Revis's tale hits all of the standard dystopian notes, while presenting a believable romance and a series of tantalizing mysteries that will hold readers' attention." Publ Wkly

A **million** suns. Razorbill 2012 400 p.

Grades: 9 10 11 12

1. Science fiction 2. Homicide -- Fiction 3. Space flight -- Fiction 4. Interplanetary voyages -- Fiction

ISBN 9781101552247; 9781595143983; 9781595145376

This book follows a girl named Amy, who has been cryogenically frozen and placed "aboard the spaceship Godspeed" along with over two-thousand others. She and "16-year-old leader Elder . . . deal with two puzzles: who is killing members of the ship, and where are the hidden clues left behind by the murderer Orion leading?" (Booklist) "Since Elder demanded that the tranquilizing drug Phydus be removed from the water supply, people have awakened to their real emotions, and many are violent, angry, or depressed. Elder is faced with the very real possibility of rebellion, which he doesn't have time for because he's desperately trying to figure out what has gone wrong with the ship's engines. Also, food supplies are running low and the ship is beginning to break down." (School Libr J)

Shades of Earth; An Across the Universe Novel. Beth Revis. Penguin Group USA 2013 400 p. $18.99

Grades: 9 10 11 12

1. Science fiction 2. Space colonies -- Fiction 3. Life on other planets -- Fiction
ISBN 1595143998; 9781595143990

This young adult science fiction adventure story, by Beth Revis, is the conclusion to the "Across the Universe" trilogy. "Amy and Elder have finally left the oppressive walls of the spaceship Godspeed behind. They're ready to start life afresh . . . on Centauri-Earth, the planet that Amy has traveled 25 trillion miles across the universe to experience. But this new Earth isn't the paradise Amy had been hoping for. . . . And if they're going to stay, they'll have to fight." (Publisher's note)

Rex, Adam

Fat vampire; a never coming of age story. Balzer + Bray 2010 324p $16.99

Grades: 9 10 11 12

1. School stories 2. Obesity -- Fiction 3. Vampires -- Fiction 4. Television programs -- Fiction
ISBN 978-0-06-192090-5
LC 2010-9616

After being bitten by a vampire, not only is fifteen-year-old Doug doomed eternally to be fat, but now he must also save himself from the desperate host of a public-access-cable vampire-hunting television show that is on the verge of cancellation.

"Rex successfully sustains the wonderfully dry humor and calculated silliness and then surprises the reader with a thoughtful, poignant, ambiguous ending that is bound to inspire discussion." Booklist

Reynolds, Jason

★ **All** American Boys. By Jason Reynolds and Brendan Kiely. Simon & Schuster 2015 320 p.

Grades: 9 10 11 12

1. Racism -- Fiction 2. Police brutality -- Fiction 3. Teenagers -- Fiction 4. Race relations -- Fiction
1481463330; 9781481463331, $17.99
Coretta Scott King Author Award, Honor Book (2016)

In this book, by Jason Reynolds and Brendan Kiely, "two teens—one black, one white—grapple with the repercussions of a single violent act that leaves their school, their community, and, ultimately, the country bitterly divided by racial tension. . . . [It] shares the alternating perspectives of Rashad and Quinn as the complications from that single violent moment, the type taken from the headlines, unfold

and reverberate to highlight an unwelcome truth." (Publisher's note)

★ **Boy** in the black suit. Jason Reynolds. Atheneum Books for Young Readers 2015 272 p.

Grades: 7 8 9 10

1. African Americans -- Fiction 2. Family life -- New York (State) -- Brooklyn -- Fiction 3. Funeral homes -- Fiction 4. Funeral rites and ceremonies -- Fiction 5. Grief -- Fiction 6. Brooklyn (New York, N.Y.) -- Fiction 7. Undertakers and undertaking -- Fiction
1442459506; 9781442459502, $17.99; 9781442459519
LC 2014001493
Coretta Scott King Author Award, Honor Book (2016)

In this teen novel, by Jason Reynolds, "with his mother newly dead, a job in a funeral home somehow becomes the perfect way for Matthew to deal with his crushing grief. Initially skeptical, he plans to use his early-release senior year program to work at a fried-chicken joint that's staffed by an entrancing girl with whom he eventually develops a . . . relationship. But the funerals intrigue him and then become deeply satisfying; Matthew finds solace in seeing others experiencing his pain." (Kirkus Reviews)

"High-school senior Matt has a job at Mr. Ray's funeral home, but he's also in mourning, for his mother who died and his long-on-the-wagon father who's returned to drink. While all this sounds like heavy problem-novel territory, it isn't. Reynolds writes about urban African American kids in a warm and empathetic way that the late Walter Dean Myers would have applauded." Horn Book

★ **Long** way down. Jason Reynolds.. Atheneum 2017 320 p.

Grades: 6 7 8 9 10 11 12

1. Brothers -- Fiction; 2. Conduct of life -- Fiction; 3. Ghosts -- Fiction; 4. Murder -- Fiction; 5. Novels in verse; 6. Revenge -- Fiction
1481438255; 9781481438254, $17.99; 9781481438261
LC 2017001395
Newbery Honor Book (2018); Coretta Scott King Author Award Honor Book (2018); Printz Honor Book (2018); LA Times Book Prize: Young Adult Literature (2017)

This book, by Jason Reynolds, "takes place in sixty potent seconds -- the time it takes a kid to decide whether or not he's going to murder the guy who killed his brother.... Revenge. That's where Will's now heading, with that gun shoved in the back waistband of his jeans, the gun that was his brother's gun. He gets on the elevator, seventh floor, stoked. He knows who he's after. Or does he?" (Publisher's note)

"Teens are left with an unresolved ending that goes beyond the simple question of whether Will will seek revenge. Told in verse, this title is fabulistic in its simplicity and begs to be discussed." SLJ

A Caitlyn Dlouhy Book.

Miles Morales: Spider-Man. Jason Reynolds. Marvel Press 2017 272 p.

Grades: 7 8 9 10 11 12

1. Superheroes -- Fiction; 2. Spider-Man (Fictional

character)
9781484787489, $17.99

LC 2017000504

In this book by Jason Reynolds, "Miles Morales is just your average teenager. Dinner every Sunday with his parents, chilling out playing old-school video games with his best friend, Ganke, crushing on brainy, beautiful poet Alicia. He's even got a scholarship spot at the prestigious Brooklyn Visions Academy. Oh yeah, and he's Spider Man.... When a misunderstanding leads to his suspension from school, Miles begins to question his abilities. After all, his dad and uncle were Brooklyn jack-boys with criminal records. Maybe kids like Miles aren't meant to be superheroes. Maybe Miles should take his dad's advice and focus on saving himself." (Publisher's note)

"Reynolds builds on a comic book plot and neatly ties in Miles' Marvel Universe background, but he focuses more on his 16-year-old protagonist's struggle with self-doubt in a vividly rendered urban setting stocked with engaging supporting characters." Booklist

When I was the greatest; Jason Reynolds. Atheneum Books for Young Readers 2014 240 p. (hardcover) $17.99

Grades: 9 10 11 12

1. Street life 2. Teenagers -- Fiction 3. Neighborhoods -- Fiction 4. Brothers and sisters -- Fiction 5. Brooklyn (New York, N.Y.) -- Fiction 6. Family life -- New York (State) -- Brooklyn -- Fiction
ISBN 1442459476; 9781442459472

LC 2012045734

In this book by Jason Reynolds "Ali lives . . . in the Bed-Stuy neighborhood of Brooklyn and spends all of his free time with best friends Noodles and Needles. Needles was born with Tourette's syndrome . . . [and the] teens hang out on the stoop and streets, living life and getting in just a touch of mischief. When their friend Tasha gets them into a party-and not just any party, an exclusive, adults-only party-trouble escalates." (School Library Journal)

"Sixteen-year-old Ali is a walking contradiction. He's a lauded boxer-in-training who's afraid of stepping into the ring; a straight-laced, head-down kind of kid on a bad block in Bed-Stuy, a neighborhood rife with drugs and violence... With fresh, fast-paced dialogue, Reynolds' debut novel chronicles Ali's friendship with next-door brothers Needles and Noodles, flawed but unforgettable characters all their own, as the three prepare for the party of a lifetime—and pay the consequences for thrusting themselves into a more sordid encounter than any of them could have envisioned. When I Was the Greatest is urban fiction with heart, a meditation on the meaning of family, the power of friendship, and the value of loyalty." (Booklist)

Rice-Gonzalez, Charles

Chulito; Charles Rice-González. 1st Magnus Books ed. Magnus Books 2011 317 p. (paperback) $14.95

Grades: 10 11 12

1. School stories 2. Gay teenagers -- Fiction 3. Gay youth -- Fiction 4. Bronx (New York, N.Y.) -- Fiction 5. Coming out (Sexual orientation) -- Fiction 6. Latin

Americans -- New York (State) -- New York -- Fiction
ISBN 1936833034; 9781936833030

LC 2011279750

In this book, "Chulito is a 15-year-old Puerto Rican high school dropout, who is right at home among the hip-hop-loving, macho, 'anything to survive' neighbors in a tough section of the Bronx. Growing up, he is close to Carlos, who—like Chulito—lived with a single mother in the same building. But the boys grow apart when Carlos finishes high school and goes to Long Island to attend college—primarily because he is perceived as being gay." Chulito falls in love with Carlos. (Echo Magazine)

Richards, Jame

Three rivers rising; a novel of the Johnstown flood. Alfred A. Knopf 2010 293p $16.99; lib bdg $19.99

Grades: 6 7 8 9 10

1. Novels in verse 2. Floods -- Fiction 3. Pennsylvania -- Fiction 4. Social classes -- Fiction
ISBN 978-0-375-85885-7; 0-375-85885-7; 978-0-375-95885-4 lib bdg; 0-375-95885-1 lib bdg

LC 2009-4251

Sixteen-year-old Celestia is a wealthy member of the South Fork Fishing and Hunting Club, where she meets and falls in love with Peter, a hired hand who lives in the valley below, and by the time of the torrential rains that lead to the disastrous Johnstown flood of 1889, she has been disowned by her family and is staying with him in Johnstown. Includes an author's note and historical timeline.

This is a "striking novel in verse. . . . Richards builds strong characters with few words and artfully interweaves the lives of these independent thinkers." Publ Wkly

Includes bibliographical references

Richards, Natalie D.

Six months later; by Natalie D. Richards. Sourcebooks Fire 2013 336 p. (tp : alk. paper) $9.99

Grades: 9 10 11 12

1. School stories 2. Memory -- Fiction 3. Secrets -- Fiction 4. High schools -- Fiction
ISBN 1402285515; 9781402285516

LC 2013012470

In this book, by Natalie Richards, "Chloe, an average student with a bit of a rebellious streak, wakes up in study hall one day not remembering the past six months. But suddenly she's popular, dating her longtime crush, being recruited by Ivy League colleges because of top SAT scores, and her best friend is no longer speaking to her. As Chloe tries to unravel her memories, she begins to uncover secrets more dangerous than she ever thought possible." (Publisher's note)

Richmond, Peter

Always a catch. Peter Richmond. Philomel Books, An Imprint of Penguin Group (USA) 2014 288 p.

Grades: 9 10 11 12

1. Boarding schools -- Fiction 2. Football -- Fiction 3. Pianists -- Fiction 4. Schools -- Fiction 5. Self-realization -- Fiction 6. High school students -- Fiction
0399250557; 9780399250552, $17.99

LC 2013045424

In this young adult novel by Peter Richmond, "Oakhurst is more than an escape—it's a chance for Jack to do something new, to try out for the football team. Once Jack makes the team, he's thrust into a foreign world—one of intense hazing, vitamin supplements, monkey hormones and steroids. Jack has to decide how far he's willing to go to fit in—and how much he's willing to compromise himself to be the man his team wants him to be." (Publisher's note)

"Jack treads the line between letting down his team and being honest with himself in a way that feels honest and tense without a false note of hope tacked on." Horn Book

Riggs, Ransom

Hollow city. By Ransom Riggs. Quirk Books 2014 399 p. (Novel of Miss Peregrine's Peculiar Children)
Grades: 6 7 8 9 10

1. Escapes -- Fiction 2. Orphanages -- Fiction 3. Supernatural -- Fiction 4. London (England) -- Fiction
1594746125; 9781594746123, $17.99

"Having escaped Miss Peregrine's island by the skin of their teeth, Jacob and his new friends must journey to London, the peculiar capital of the world. Along the way, they encounter new allies, a menagerie of peculiar animals, and other unexpected surprises." (Publisher's note)

"Like the first volume, this one is generously illustrated with peculiar period photographs that capture and enhance the eerie mood and mode." Booklist

Library of souls. Ransom Riggs. Quirk Books 2015 458 p. Illustration; Portrait
Grades: 6 7 8 9 10

1. Rescue work -- Fiction 2. Paranormal fiction
9781594747588, $18.99; 159474758X

LC 2015939051

"Time is running out for the Peculiar Children. With a dangerous madman on the loose and their beloved Miss Peregrine still in danger, Jacob Portman and Emma Bloom are forced to stage the most daring of rescue missions. They'll travel through a war-torn landscape, meet new allies, and face greater dangers than ever." (Publisher's Note)

Miss Peregrine's home for peculiar children. Quirk Books 2011 352p il $17.99
Grades: 6 7 8 9

1. Ghost stories
ISBN 978-1-59474-476-1; 1-59474-476-9

"When Jacob's grandfather, Abe, a WWII veteran, is savagely murdered, Jacob has a nervous breakdown, in part because he believes that his grandfather was killed by a monster that only they could see. On his psychiatrist's advice, Jacob and his father travel from their home in Florida to Cairnholm Island off the coast of Wales, which, during the war, housed Miss Peregrine's Home for Peculiar Children. . . . Nearly 50 unsettling vintage photographs appear throughout, forming the framework of this dark but empowering tale, as Riggs creates supernatural backstories and identities for those pictured in them. . . . It's an enjoyable, eccentric read, distinguished by well-developed characters, a believable Welsh setting, and some very creepy monsters." Publ Wkly

Rinaldi, Ann

The **redheaded** princess. HarperCollinsPublishers 2008 214p $15.99; lib bdg $16.89
Grades: 6 7 8 9

1. Queens 2. Elizabeth I, Queen of England, 1533-1603 -- Childhood and youth -- Fiction
ISBN 978-0-06-073374-2; 0-06-073374-8; 978-0-06-073375-9 lib bdg; 0-06-073375-6 lib bdg

LC 2007-18577

In 1542, nine-year-old Lady Elizabeth lives on an estate near London, striving to get back into the good graces of her father, King Henry VIII, and as the years pass she faces his death and those of other close relatives until she finds herself next in line to ascend the throne of England in 1558.

"The rich scene-setting and believable, appealing heroine will satisfy Rinaldi's many fans." Booklist

Ritter, William

Beastly bones: a Jackaby novel. William Ritter. Algonquin Young Readers 2015 304 p.
Grades: 7 8 9 10

1. Imaginary creatures -- Fiction 2. Monsters -- Fiction 3. Mystery and detective stories 4. Supernatural -- Fiction 5. New England -- History -- 19th century -- Fiction 6. Private investigators -- Fiction
1616203544; 9781616203542, $17.95

LC 2015010990

In this novel by William Ritter, set "in 1892, New Fiddleham, New England, things are never quite what they seem, especially when Abigail Rook and her eccentric employer, R. F. Jackaby, are called upon to investigate the supernatural. Policeman Charlie Cane, exiled from New Fiddleham to the valley, calls on Abigail for help, and soon Abigail and Jackaby are on the hunt for a thief, a monster, and a murderer." (Publisher's note)

"With one case closed but two unsolved, the well-matched, well-written duo will undoubtedly return to fight a more fearsome foe. A witty and weird adventure equal parts Sherlock and Three Stooges." Kirkus

Sequel to: Jackaby

The **dire** king. William Ritter. Algonquin Young Readers 2017 344 p. (Jackaby series)
Grades: 7 8 9 10

1. Animals, Mythical -- Fiction; 2. Private investigators -- Fiction; 3. Zombies -- Fiction; 4. New England -- Social life and customs -- 19th century -- Fiction; 5. Supernatural -- Fiction; 6. Magic -- Fiction; 7. New England -- Fiction
9781616207625; 9781616206703, $17.95

LC 2017002941

In this book, by William Ritter, "the fate of the world is in the hands of detective of the supernatural R. F. Jackaby and his...assistant, Abigail Rook. An evil king is turning ancient tensions into modern strife, using a blend of magic and technology to push Earth and the Otherworld into a mortal competition. Jackaby and Abigail are caught in the middle as they continue to solve the daily mysteries of New Fiddleham, New England." (Publisher's note)

"A humorous, energetic, action-packed, and magical conclusion." Kirkus

Rivers, Karen

Love, Ish. Karen Rivers. Algonquin Young Readers 2017 279 p.

Grades: 6 7 8 9

> 1. Ambition -- Fiction; 2. Best friends -- Fiction; 3. Brain -- Tumors -- Fiction; 4. Cancer -- Fiction; 5. Friendship -- Fiction; 6. Mars (Planet) -- Fiction;
> 9781616205706, $16.95

LC 2016038086

In this novel, by Karen Rivers, "Ish, who is determined to be among the first settlers on Mars, goes on a different and unexpected journey after she is diagnosed with a malignant brain tumor. She's prone to long stream-of-consciousness monologues anyway, but after discovery of the tumor that she imagines as a sort of Brussels sprout and starting on chemotherapy and radiation treatments, many of her dreams (and nightmares) focus on her imagined life in a Mars colony." (Kirkus Reviews)

Roat, Sharon Huss

How to Disappear. By Sharon Huss Roat. HarperTeen 2017 377 p.

Grades: 7 8 9 10 11 12

> 1. High school girls -- Fiction; 2. Introverts -- Fiction; 3. Social media -- Fiction; 4. Emotions -- Fiction; 5. Girls -- Fiction; 6. Popularity -- Fiction; 7. Friendship -- Fiction
> 0062291750; 9780062291752, $17.99; 9780062291776

In this book, by Sharon Huss Roat, "Vicky Decker's social anxiety has helped her to master the art of hiding in plain sight, appearing only to her best friend, Jenna. But when Jenna moves away, Vicky's isolation becomes unbearable. So she decides to invent a social life by Photoshopping herself into other people's photos and posting them on Instagram under the screen name Vicurious." (Publisher's note)

"This is a witty, hard-to-put-down novel that's appropriate for younger teens. However, the lack of grittiness won't deter older teens, who will be carried along by familiar lingo and references to social networks and celebrities." SLJ

Robert, Na'ima B.

Boy vs. girl. Frances Lincoln Children's Books 2011 260p $15.95

Grades: 6 7 8 9 10

> 1. Twins -- Fiction 2. Muslims -- Fiction 3. Ramadan -- Fiction 4. Siblings -- Fiction 5. Great Britain -- Fiction 6. Pakistanis -- Great Britain -- Fiction
> ISBN 978-1-84780-150-0; 1-84780-150-1

"Twins Farhana and Faraz determine to fast during Ramadan now that they are 16. . . . As first-generation Brits, they must respond to the demands of their Pakistani family, their secular schools, and their friends. . . . The characters are realistic. . . . A well-balanced chord is struck here between storytelling and exploring the complex and sometimes conflicting pulls of tradition, family, friends, and lifestyle." Booklist

From Somalia with love; [by] Na'ima B. Robert. Frances Lincoln Children's Books 2008 159p $15.95; pa $7.95

Grades: 7 8 9 10

> 1. Muslims -- Fiction 2. Father-daughter relationship

-- Fiction

> ISBN 978-1-84507-831-7; 1-84507-831-4; 978-1-84507-832-4 pa; 1-84507-832-2 pa

"Safia has grown up believing her father died in the fighting in Somalia. When she finds out that he is alive and on his way to London to join the family, she is apprehensive about the difference his presence will make in her life. . . . This is a unique title that will be popular in regions that have large Somali populations or where Randa Abdel-Fattah's books are popular." SLJ

Includes glossary

She wore red trainers: A Muslim Love Story. By Na'ima B. Robert. Kube Publishing Ltd 2014 261 p.

Grades: 9 10 11 12

> 1. Courtship -- Fiction 2. Dating (Social customs) -- Religious aspects -- Fiction 3. Loss (Psychology) -- Fiction 4. Marriage -- Fiction 5. Muslims -- Fiction 6. Love -- Fiction
> 1847740650; 9781847740656, $12.95

In this book, by Na'ima B. Robert, "[w]hen Ali first meets Amirah, he notices everything about her—her hijab, her long eyelashes and her red trainers-in the time it takes to have one look, before lowering his gaze. And, although Ali is still coming to terms with the loss of his mother and exploring his identity as a Muslim, and although Amirah has sworn never to get married, they can't stop thinking about each other. Can Ali and Amirah ever have a halal 'happily ever after'?" (Publisher's note)

"Eighteen-year-old Muslim neighbors Ali and Amirah surprise themselves and each other by falling in love at first sight. . . . Alternating between Amirah and Ali's perspectives, Robert (Black Sheep) teases out the subtleties of young romance and the confounding pull of mutual attraction. While the story takes some melodramatic turns, it speaks vividly to conflicts of freedom, temptation, and faith." PW

Rocco, John

Swim that rock. John Rocco & Jay Primiano. Candlewick Press 2014 293p $16.99

Grades: 7 8 9 10

> 1. Fishing -- Fiction 2. Rhode Island -- Fiction 3. Family life -- Fiction 4. Bildungsromans
> ISBN: 0763669059; 9780763669058

LC 2013952797

In this book, by John Rocco and Jay Primiano, "a young working-class teen fights to save his family's diner after his father is lost in a fishing-boat accident. . . . In Narragansett Bay, scrabbling out a living as a quahogger isn't easy, but with the help of some local clammers, Jake is determined to work hard and earn enough money to ensure his family's security and save the diner in time." (Publisher's note)

"With a lushly detailed sense of place and character, the story examines a boy coming to terms with his situation." Horn Book

Roe, Robin

★ A **list** of cages. Robin Roe. Hyperion 2017 320 p.

Grades: 8 9 10 11

    1. Child abuse -- Fiction 2. Friendship -- Fiction
9781484763803, $17.99; 9781484781098, $17.99

                    LC 2015045422

In this novel, by Robin Roe, "when Adam Blake lands the best elective ever in his senior year, serving as an aide to the school psychologist, he thinks he's got it made. Sure, it means a lot of sitting around, which isn't easy for a guy with ADHD. . . . Then the doctor asks him to track down the troubled freshman who keeps dodging her, and Adam discovers that the boy is Julian—the foster brother he hasn't seen in five years." (Publisher's note)

"A triumphant story about the power of friendship and of truly being seen." Kirkus

Roecker, Lisa

The **Liar** Society; by Lisa and Laura Roecker. Sourcebooks Fire 2011 361p pa $9.99

Grades: 7 8 9 10

    1. School stories 2. Mystery fiction 3. Secret societies -- Fiction

ISBN 978-1-4022-5633-2; 1-4022-5633-7

When Kate receives a mysterious e-mail from her dead friend Grace, she must prove that Grace's death was not an accident, but finds that her elite private school holds secrets so big people are willing to kill to protect them.

This is a "smartly paced and plotted first novel, full of twists, clues, and sleuthing. Add this to your go-to list of mysteries." Booklist

The **lies** that bind; Lisa and Laura Roecker. Sourcebooks Fire 2012 314 p. (The Liar Society) (tp : alk. paper) $9.99

Grades: 7 8 9 10

    1. School stories 2. Missing persons -- Fiction 3. Secret societies -- Fiction 4. High schools -- Fiction

ISBN 1402270240; 9781402270246

                    LC 2012035855

This young adult school mystery, by Lisa and Laura Roecker, is part of "The Liar Society" series. "Kate has heard of messages from beyond the grave, but she never expected to find one in a fortune cookie. Especially from her best friend, Grace--who's supposed to be dead. At the elite Pemberly Brown Academy, . . . a popular girl has gone missing, and Kate owes it to Grace's memory to find out what happened. But in a school ruled by secret societies, who can she trust?" (Publisher's note)

Rogerson, Margaret

An **enchantment** of ravens. Margaret Rogerson. Margaret K. McElderry Books 2017 300 p.

Grades: 7 8 9 10

    1. Princes -- Fiction; 2. Fairies -- Fiction; 3. Painters -- Fiction; 4. Fantasy fiction

9781481497596; 9781481497589, $17.99

                    LC 2017297177

In this novel, by Margaret Rogerson, "Isobel is a prodigy portrait artist with a dangerous set of clients: the sinister fair folk, immortal creatures who cannot bake bread, weave cloth, or put a pen to paper without crumbling to dust.... But when she receives her first royal patron -- Rook, the autumn prince -- she makes a terrible mistake. She paints mortal sorrow in his eyes -- a weakness that could cost him his life." (Publisher's note)

"Rogerson ably builds this fantasy world through canny details and contemporary dialogue, allowing for an enjoyable read by fantasy and non-fantasy readers alike. She also craftily depicts the power imbalance between Isobel and Rook, offering a refreshing dynamic in which Isobel often comes out on top." SLJ.

Rorby, Ginny

Lost in the river of grass. Carolrhoda Lab 2011 255p $17.95

Grades: 7 8 9 10

    1. Wilderness survival -- Fiction

ISBN 978-0-7613-5685-1; 0-7613-5685-1

                    LC 2009-53999

"In this authentic survival adventure, Sarah, a 13-year-old scholarship student, leaves her preppy classmates on a weekend trip to the Everglades and takes off with Andy, 15 . . . who offers her a brief guided tour in his airboat. After the boat sinks, they walk for three days through the swamp . . . until, finally, helicopters rescue them. What comes through best here is not only the teens' courage and mutual support but also the realism of their fights and weaknesses." Booklist

The **outside** of a horse; a novel. Dial Books for Young Readers 2010 343p $16.99

Grades: 7 8 9 10

    1. Horses -- Fiction 2. Amputees -- Fiction 3. Veterans -- Fiction 4. Father-daughter relationship -- Fiction

ISBN 978-0-8037-3478-4; 0-8037-3478-6

                    LC 2009-25101

When her father returns from the Iraq War as an amputee with post-traumatic stress disorder, Hannah escapes by volunteering to work with rescued horses, never thinking that the abused horses could also help her father recover.

Hannah "comes across as a believable teen. As a backdrop to the story, Rorby has interwoven a good deal of disturbing information about animal cruelty. Horse lovers and most others will saddle up right away with this poignant tale." Booklist

Rosen, Renee

★ **Every** crooked pot. St. Martin's Griffin 2007 227p pa $8.95

Grades: 7 8 9 10

    1. Birth defects -- Fiction 2. Father-daughter relationship -- Fiction

ISBN 978-0-312-36543-1; 0-312-36543-8

                    LC 2007-10457

"Rosen looks back at the life of Nina Goldman, whose growing up is tied to two pillars: a port-wine stain around her eye and her inimitable father, Artie. The birthmark, she hates; her father, she loves. Both shape her in ways that merit Rosen's minute investigation. . . . There's real power in the writing." Booklist

Rosenfield, Kat

Amelia Anne is dead and gone; Kat Rosenfield. Dutton Books 2012 304 p. (hardcover) $17.99

Grades: 9 10 11 12

    1. Mystery fiction 2. Homicide -- Fiction 3. Young

women -- Fiction 4. Murder -- Fiction 5. Community life -- Fiction 6. Summer resorts -- Fiction 7. Dating violence -- Fiction 8. Mystery and detective stories 9. Dating (Social customs) -- Fiction
ISBN 9780525423898

LC 2011029958

In this book, "[t]he lives of two girls on the cusp of something bigger intertwine on a dusty road in a small, dead-end New England town. Amelia has just finished college and is on her way to a summer beach rental with her boyfriend before going to acting school. Becca, just graduated from high school, is looking forward to college. . . . Just hours before Amelia is beaten and left for dead, Becca's boyfriend breaks up with her--right after they have sex in the bed of his pickup." (Kirkus Reivews)

Inland. By Kat Rosenfield. Dutton Books 2014 400 p.

Grades: 9 10 11 12

1. Families -- Fiction 2. Ocean -- Fiction 3. Psychic trauma -- Fiction 4. Secrets -- Fiction 5. Single-parent families -- Fiction 6. Supernatural -- Fiction 7. Psychological fiction
0525426485; 9780525426486, $17.99

LC 2014004800

In this young adult novel by Kat Rosenfield, "Callie Morgan has long lived choked by the failure of her own lungs, the result of an elusive pulmonary illness that has plagued her since childhood. A childhood marked early by the drowning death of her mother—a death to which Callie was the sole witness. Her father has moved them inland, away from the memories of the California coast her mother loved so much and toward promises of recovery . . . in arid, landlocked air." (Publisher's note)

" The delicious confusion between fantasy and madness finds perfect expression in Rosenfield's hypnotic prose and upside-down chapter construction; which direction is up is never clear. Combine Margo Lanagan's The Brides of Rollrock Island (2012) with Hannah Moskowitz's Teeth (2013), chum it with the remains of John Ajvide Lindqvist's Let Me In (2007), and you'll get something close to this sinister, salt-water sonata." Booklist

Roskos, Evan

★ **Dr.** Bird's advice for sad poets; Evan Roskos. Houghton Mifflin Harcourt 2013 320 p. $16.99

Grades: 9 10 11 12

1. Poetry -- Fiction 2. Siblings -- Fiction 3. Depression (Psychology) -- Fiction 4. Family problems -- Fiction 5. Depression, Mental -- Fiction
ISBN 054792853X; 9780547928531

LC 2012033315

William C. Morris Honor Book (2014)

This novel "portrays the struggle of 16-year-old James Whitman to overcome anxiety and depression. James blames himself for his older sister's expulsion from their home and estrangement from their bullying parents. [Evan] Roskos . . . sketches James as a boy who is far more comfortable inside his own head than in connecting with others (case in point, he hugs trees to make himself feel better and seeks advice from Dr. Bird, an imaginary pigeon therapist)." (Publishers Weekly)

"Author Roskos's strength lies in his refusal to tidy up the mess in James's life and in his relentless honesty about surviving with depression and anxiety." Horn Book

Rosoff, Meg

How I Live Now Wendy Lamb Books 2004 194p $16.95

Grades: 7 8 9 10

1. Cousins -- Fiction 2. War stories 3. Great Britain -- Fiction
ISBN 0385746776

To get away from her pregnant stepmother in New York City, fifteen-year-old Daisy goes to England to stay with her aunt and cousins, with whom she instantly bonds, but soon war breaks out and rips apart the family while devastating the land.

"Teens may feel that they have experienced a war themselves as they vicariously witness Daisy's worst nightmares. Like the heroine, readers will emerge from the rubble much shaken, a little wiser and with perhaps a greater sense of humanity." Publ Wkly

★ **Picture** me gone; by Meg Rosoff. G.P. Putnam's Sons 2013 256 p. $17.99

Grades: 7 8 9

1. Missing persons -- Fiction 2. Parent-child relationship -- Fiction 3. Coming of age -- Fiction 4. Mystery and detective stories 5. Fathers and daughters -- Fiction
ISBN 0399257659; 9780399257650

LC 2012048974

"Sensitive Londoner Mila, twelve, travels with her father, Gil, to upstate New York to search for Gil's boyhood friend, who has inexplicably disappeared. The subject of this road-trip novel--how much guilt and tragedy can a person bear before he gives up on life?--is adult, but the writing is up to Rosoff's usual standards of originality, depth, wit, and insight." (Horn Book)

★ **There** is no dog; Meg Rosoff. G. P. Putnam's Sons 2011 243p. $17.99

Grades: 7 8 9

1. Love stories 2. God -- Fiction 3. Man-woman relationship -- Fiction
ISBN 9780399257643

LC 2011020651

This book "looks at the world's natural disasters, injustices, and chaos and presents a[n] . . . explanation: God is a horny teenage boy. According to this . . . account, God, aka 'Bob,' was given Earth by his mother, who won the planet in a poker game. Bob showed flashes of brilliance during Creation, but he feels little responsibility for the planet. When he falls head-over-heels in lust with a beautiful zoo employee, Lucy, Bob's passion and growing anger toward those who would keep them apart is manifested through wildly fluctuating weather and rampant flooding." (Publishers Weekly)

Ross, Elizabeth

Belle epoque; Elizabeth Ross. Delacorte Press 2013 336 p. (ebook) $53.97; (library) $20.99; (hardcover) $17.99

Grades: 7 8 9 10 11 12

1. Love stories 2. Historical fiction 3. Female friendship

-- Fiction 4. Runaways -- Fiction 5. Social classes -- Fiction 6. Conduct of life -- Fiction 7. Beauty, Personal -- Fiction 8. Interpersonal relations -- Fiction 9. Paris (France) -- History -- 1870-1940 -- Fiction 10. France -- History -- Third Republic, 1870-1940 -- Fiction
ISBN 0375990054; 9780375985270; 9780375990052; 9780385741460

LC 2012034694

William C. Morris Honor Book (2014)

In this book, "sixteen-year-old runaway Maude Pichon is ugly—so much so that she lands a job as a 'repoussoir,' an unattractive girl paid to be seen with a lovelier girl to make her appear even more beautiful by comparison . . . . Maude is humiliated by the idea, but her poverty leaves her few options." Then "chance sends a dashing composer Maude's way, and a countess hires her to befriend her independent-minded daughter, Isabelle." (Publishers Weekly)

"Ross models her plot on an 1866 story by Zola, "Les Repoussoirs," expanding its focus to highlight Maude's plight and using that to illuminate the chasm that existed between the wealthy and the poor... A refreshingly relevant and inspiring historical venture." Kirkus

Rossetti, Rinsai

The **girl** with borrowed wings; by Rinsai Rossetti. Dial Books 2012 300 p. (hardcover) $17.99

Grades: 7 8 9 10 11 12

1. Cats -- Fiction 2. Voyages and travels -- Fiction 3. Father-daughter relationship -- Fiction 4. Love -- Fiction 5. Flying -- Fiction 6. Deserts -- Fiction 7. Shapeshifting -- Fiction
ISBN 0803735669; 9780803735668

LC 2011027164

This is Rinsai Rossetti's debut, a coming-of-age novel. Of "Thai descent, 17-year-old Frenenqer Paje has grown up" with "her coldly overbearing father . . . . [S]he disobeys her father by rescuing a mistreated cat" who "is actually a shape-shifting 'Free person' named Sangris . . . . By night, he flies Frenenqer around the world to places both real and magical, slowly chipping away at the defenses she has built up to withstand her father's callous cruelty." (Publishers Weekly)

Rossi, Veronica

Under the never sky; Veronica Rossi. Harper-Collins 2012 376 p. (hardback) $17.99

Grades: 6 7 8 9 10 11 12

1. Science fiction 2. Apocalyptic fiction 3. Cannibalism -- Fiction 4. Man-woman relationship -- Fiction
ISBN 9780062072030

LC 2011044631

This book tells the story of "Aria [who] knows her chances of surviving in the outer wasteland--known as The Death Shop--are slim. . . . Then Aria meets an Outsider named Perry. He's wild--a savage--and her only hope of staying alive. A hunter for his tribe in a merciless landscape, Perry views Aria as sheltered and fragile--everything he would expect from a Dweller. . . . Opposites in nearly every way, Aria and Perry must accept each other to survive." (Publisher's note)

Roth, Veronica

Allegiant; Veronica Roth; [edited by] Molly O'Neill. Katherine Tegen Books 2013 544 p. (hardcover bdg.) $19.99

Grades: 9 10 11 12

1. Love stories 2. Dystopian fiction 3. Science fiction 4. Loyalty -- Fiction 5. Social classes -- Fiction 6. Courage 7. Families -- Fiction 8. Social classes -- Fiction 9. Identity (Philosophical concept) -- Fiction
ISBN 006202406X; 9780062024060

LC 2013941315

Sequel to: Insurgent

Author Veronica Roth presents the conclusion to her dystopian Divergent trilogy. "Tris and Tobias conarrate their adventures and attempt to understand their surroundings. As their true love relationship plays out, they venture beyond war-torn Chicago, only to uncover a new network of conspiracies and key revelations about eugenics, authority, and social duty." (Bookmarks)

"Roth shakes up her storytelling (and will do the same to some readers) in this highly anticipated, largely satisfying wrap-up to the Divergent trilogy...for those who have faithfully followed these five factions, and especially the Dauntless duo who stole hearts two books ago, this final installment will capture and hold attention until the divisive final battle has been waged." (Publishers Weekly)

Carve the mark. Veronica Roth. Katherine Tegen Books 2017 468 p. Map (Carve the mark)

Grades: 8 9 10 11 12

1. Ability -- Fiction; 2. Brothers and sisters -- Fiction; 3. Survival -- Fiction; 4. Dystopian fiction; 5. Science fiction; 6. Imaginary places -- Fiction
9780062348630, $22.99; 9780062348654

LC 2016949683

In this novel in the Carve the Mark series, by Veronica Roth, "Cyra Noavek and Akos Kereseth have grown up in enemy countries locked in a long-standing fight for dominance over their shared planet.... When Akos and Cyra are caught in the middle of a raging rebellion, everything they've been led to believe about their world and themselves must be called into question. But fighting for what's right might mean betraying their countries, their families, and each other." (Publisher's note)

"Roth offers a richly imagined, often-brutal world of political intrigue and adventure, with a slow-burning romance at its core." Booklist

Another title in this series is: The fates divide (2018)

★ **Divergent**. Katherine Tegen Books 2011 487p $17.99; ebook $9.99

Grades: 9 10 11 12

1. Science fiction 2. Courage -- Fiction 3. Family life -- Fiction 4. Social classes -- Fiction 5. Identity (Psychology) -- Fiction
ISBN 978-0-06-202402-2; 0-06-202402-7; 978-0-06-207701-1 ebook; 0-06-207701-5 ebook

LC 2010-40579

"Roth's nonstop action, excellent voice, and simple yet accessible writing style will draw in many new readers to the genre. The themes are particularly poignant for young adults trying to identify their place in the world—having the choice to follow in your parents' footsteps or do something new... This is a fast-paced and fun read." Voice Youth Advocates

Other books in the Divergent Trilogy are:
Insurgent (2012)
Allegiant (2013)

The fates divide. Veronica Roth. Katherine Tegen Books, an imprint of HarperCollinsPublishers 2018 X, 443 p. (Carve the mark)
Grades: 8 9 10 11 12
1. Ability -- Fiction; 2. Imaginary places -- Fiction; 3. Science fiction; 4. Survival -- Fiction; 5. Fantasy fiction
ISBN 0008192200; 0062426958; 0062842382; 9780008192204; 9780062426956, $21.99; 9780062842381
LC 2018932646

In this book in the Carve the Mark series, by Veronica Roth, "the lives of Cyra Noavek and Akos Kereseth are ruled by their fates, spoken by the oracles at their births. The fates, once determined, are inescapable. Akos is in love with Cyra, in spite of his fate: He will die in service to Cyra's family. And when Cyra's father, Lazmet Noavek -- a soulless tyrant, thought to be dead -- reclaims the Shotet throne, Akos believes his end is closer than ever." (Publisher's note)

Sequel to: Carve the mark

Insurgent; Veronica Roth. Katherine Tegen Books 2012 525 p.
Grades: 9 10 11 12
1. Science fiction 2. Courage -- Fiction 3. Apocalyptic fiction 4. Personality -- Fiction 5. Social classes -- Fiction 6. Families -- Fiction 7. Identity -- Fiction
ISBN 0062024043; 9780062024046
LC 2011053287

Sequel to: Divergent

In this "sequel to . . . 'Divergent' . . . a bleak post-apocalyptic Chicago ruled by 'factions' exemplifying different personality traits collapses into all-out civil war. With both the Dauntless and Abnegation factions shattered by the Erudite attack, Tris and her companions seek refuge with Amity and Candor, and even among the factionless. But the Erudite search for 'Divergents' continues relentlessly." (Kirkus Reviews)

Roux, Madeleine

House of furies. Madeleine Roux. HarperTeen 2017 407 p. Illustration; Color (House of furies)
Grades: 9 10 11 12
1. Horror tales; 2. Paranormal fiction; 3. Hotels and motels -- Fiction; 4. Teenage girls -- Fiction; 5. Household employees -- Fiction
9780062498601; 9780062498618, $17.99
LC 2016960403

In this book, by Madeleine Roux, "seventeen-year-old Louisa Ditton is thrilled to find employment as a maid at a boarding house. But soon after her arrival at Coldthistle House, Louisa begins to realize that the house's mysterious owner, Mr. Morningside, is providing much more than lodging for his guests. Far from a place of rest, the house is a place of judgment, and Mr. Morningside and his unusual staff are meant to execute their own justice on those who are past being saved." (Publisher's note)

"Atmospheric and troubling, this series starter will sink its hooks into readers as surely as it frightens them." Booklist

Rowell, Rainbow

★ **Carry** on: a novel. By Rainbow Rowell. St. Martin's Griffin 2015 528 p. Illustration
Grades: 9 10 11 12
1. Boarding schools -- Fiction 2. Dating (Social customs) -- Fiction 3. Magic -- Fiction 4. Monsters -- Fiction 5. Schools -- Fiction 6. Private schools -- Fiction
1250049555; 9781250049551, $19.99
LC 2015029653

"Simon Snow is the worst Chosen One who's ever been chosen. That's what his roommate, Baz, says. And Baz might be evil and a vampire and a complete git, but he's probably right. Half the time, Simon can't even make his wand work, and the other half, he starts something on fire. His mentor's avoiding him, his girlfriend broke up with him, and there's a magic-eating monster running around, wearing Simon's face." (Publisher's note)

"The novel playfully twists genre conventions—there are plenty of wink-wink, nudge-nudge moments to satisfy faithful fantasy readers—but it also stands alone as a modern bildungsroman." Kirkus

★ **Eleanor** & Park; Rainbow Rowell. St. Martin's Griffin 2013 320 p. (hardcover) $18.99
Grades: 9 10 11 12
1. Love stories 2. School stories 3. Bullies -- Fiction 4. Love -- Fiction 5. Schools -- Fiction 6. High schools -- Fiction 7. Dating (Social customs) -- Fiction
ISBN 1250012570; 9781250012579; 9781250031211
LC 2012042136

Printz Honor Book (2014)
Boston Globe-Horn Book Award: Fiction (2013).
Odyssey Honor Recording (2014)

This book tells the story of the friendship between half-Korean sophomore Park Sheridan and the new girl Eleanor. "Tall, with bright red hair and a dress code all her own, [Eleanor is] an instant target. Too nice not to let her sit next to him, Park is alternately resentful and guilty for not being kinder to her. When he realizes she's reading his comics over his shoulder, a silent friendship is born" that will become something more. (Publishers Weekly)

"Through Eleanor and Park's alternating voices, readers glimpse the swoon-inducing, often hilarious aspects of first love... Funny, hopeful, foulmouthed, sexy and tear-jerking, this winning romance will captivate teen and adult readers alike." Kirkus

★ **Fangirl**; by Rainbow Rowell. St. Martin's Griffin 2013 448 p. (hardcover) $18.99
Grades: 9 10 11 12
1. Fan fiction 2. School stories 3. Characters and characteristics in literature
ISBN 1250030951; 9781250030955
LC 2013013842

"Change-resistant college freshman Cather holes up in her dorm room, writing fantasy fanfiction. But as the year progresses, she is pushed outside her comfort zone by her snarky roommate, Reagan; by Levi, Reagan's ex-boyfriend (and eventually Cath's first love interest); and by her manic but well-meaning father. Rowell transitions seamlessly between Cath's strong interior voice and clever dialogue in this sophisticated coming-of-age novel." (Horn Book)

Rowling, J. K., 1965-

★ **Harry** Potter and the Sorcerer's Stone; illustrations by Mary Grandpré. Arthur A. Levine Bks. 1998 309p il $22.99; pa $8.99

Grades: 4 5 6 7 8 9 10

1. Fantasy fiction 2. Witches -- Fiction
ISBN 0-590-35340-3; 0-590-35342-X pa

LC 97-39059

First published 1997 in the United Kingdom with title: Harry Potter and the Philosopher's Stone

Rescued from the outrageous neglect of his aunt and uncle, a young boy with a great destiny proves his worth while attending Hogwarts School for Witchcraft and Wizardry.

This "is a brilliantly imagined and beautifully written fantasy." Booklist

Other titles in this series are:
Harry Potter and the Chamber of Secrets (1999)
Harry Potter and the Deathly Hallows (2007)
Harry Potter and the Goblet of Fire (2000)
Harry Potter and the Half-Blood Prince (2005)
Harry Potter and the Order of the Phoenix (2003)
Harry Potter and the prisoner of Azkaban (1999)

Roy, Jennifer Rozines

★ **Mindblind**; [by] Jennifer Roy. Marshall Cavendish 2010 248p il $15.99

Grades: 7 8 9 10 11

1. Genius -- Fiction 2. Bands (Music) -- Fiction 3. Asperger's syndrome -- Fiction
ISBN 978-0-7614-5716-9; 0-7614-5716-X

LC 2010-6966

Fourteen-year-old Nathaniel Clark, who has Asperger's Syndrome, tries to prove that he is a genius by writing songs for his rock band, so that he can become a member of the prestigious Aldus Institute, the premier organization for the profoundly gifted.

"Mature readers will empathize with Nathaniel as his friends, Jessa and Cooper, do. This book is for teens who appreciate a story about self-discovery, dreams, and friendship." Voice Youth Advocates

Rubens, Michael

The **bad** decisions playlist. Michael Rubens. Clarion Books, an imprint of Houghton Mifflin Harcourt 2016 304 p.

Grades: 9 10 11 12

1. Decision making -- Fiction 2. Fathers and sons -- Fiction 3. Love -- Fiction 4. Musicians -- Fiction 5. Rock music -- Fiction 6. Father-son relationship -- Fiction
9780544098855, $16.99; 9780544096677, $17.99

LC 2015028509

In this book, by Michael Rubens, "sixteen-year-old Austin is always messing up and then joking his way out of tough spots. The sudden appearance of his allegedly dead father, who happens to be the very-much-alive rock star Shane Tyler, stops him cold. Austin-a talented musician himself-is

sucked into his newfound father's alluring music-biz orbit, pulling his true love, Josephine, along with him." (Publisher's note)

"Funny and painful, it's a sharply etched portrait of fallible human beings living, loving, screwing up, and making do-and a fine look at the Twin Cities music scene." Pub Wkly

Sons of the 613; Mike Rubens. Clarion Books 2012 305 p. (hardcover) $16.99

Grades: 7 8 9 10

1. Brothers -- Fiction 2. Bar mitzvah -- Fiction 3. Masculinity -- Fiction 4. Minnesota -- Fiction 5. Coming of age -- Fiction 6. Junior high schools -- Fiction 7. Jews -- United States -- Fiction 8. Family life -- Minnesota -- Fiction
ISBN 0547612168; 9780547612164

LC 2011044352

In this book by Michael Rubens, "Isaac's parents have abandoned him for a trip to Italy in the final days before his bar mitzvah. And even worse, his hotheaded older brother, Josh, has been left in charge. . . . When Josh declares that there is more to becoming a man than memorization, the mad 'quest' begins for Isaac. . . . But when Isaac begins to fall for Josh's girlfriend, Leslie, the challenges escalate from bad to worse." (Publisher's note)

Rubin, Lance

Denton Little's deathdate: a novel. By Lance Rubin. Alfred A. Knopf 2015 352 p.

Grades: 9 10 11 12

1. Identity -- Fiction 2. Science fiction
0553496964; 9780553496963, $17.99; 9780553496970; 9780553496994

LC 2014008677

This book, by Lance Rubin, "takes place in a world exactly like our own except that everyone knows the day on which they will die. For Denton, that's in just two days—the day of his senior prom. Despite his early deathdate, Denton has always wanted to live a normal life, but his final days are filled with dramatic firsts. First hangover. First sex. First love triangle—as the first sex seems to have happened not with his adoring girlfriend, but with his best friend's hostile sister." (Publisher's note)

Denton Little's still not dead. Lance Rubin. Alfred A. Knopf 2017 345 p. (Denton Little)

Grades: 9 10 11 12

1. Death -- Fiction; 2. Death -- Fiction; 3. Humorous fiction; 4. Teenagers -- Fiction
9780553497007, $17.99; 9780553497021; 0553497006

LC 2017289020

In this novel, by Lance Rubin, "Denton Little lives in a world exactly like our own except that everyone knows the day on which they will die. The good news: Denton has lived through his deathdate. Yay! The bad news: He's being chased by the DIA (Death Investigation Agency), he can never see his family again, and he may now die anytime. Huh. Cheating death isn't quite as awesome as Denton would have thought." (Publisher's note)

"Denton and his quirky friends are laugh-out-loud funny, even as their riotous adventures raise deeper questions about science, government control, life, and death." SLJ

Sequel to: Denton Little's Deathdate (2015)

Ruby, Laura

★ **Bad** apple. HarperTeen 2009 247p $16.99; pa $8.99

Grades: 8 9 10 11 12

1. School stories 2. Bullies -- Fiction 3. Divorce -- Fiction 4. Teacher-student relationship -- Fiction
ISBN 978-0-06-124330-1; 0-06-124330-2; 978-0-06-124333-2 pa; 0-06-124333-7 pa

LC 2009-1409

Tola Riley, a high school junior, struggles to tell the truth when she and her art teacher are accused of having an affair.

"Tola and her family are fascinating, quirky-yet-believable, and wholly likable. Ruby works in traditional fairy-tale elements . . . with wry humor." Booklist

★ **Bone** Gap. Laura Ruby. Balzer + Bray, an imprint of HarperCollinsPublishers 2015 345 p.

Grades: 9 10 11 12

1. Brothers -- Fiction 2. Bullying -- Fiction 3. Face perception -- Fiction 4. Interpersonal relations -- Fiction 5. Kidnapping -- Fiction
0062317601; 9780062317605, $17.99

LC 2014013676

National Book Award Finalist: Young People's Literature (2015); Printz Award (2016)

In this book by Laura Ruby, "Bone Gap is the small Illinois town where seventeen-year-old Finn has lived with his older brother, Sean, since their mother left them for a brand-new life with her brand-new husband two years ago. Now Finn's devastated by a new loss: Roza, the beautiful young Polish woman who turned up on Finn and Sean's farm from out of nowhere . . . was abducted one night, but nobody believes Finn's account of her departure." (Bulletin of the Center for Children's Books)

"In Ruby's refined and delicately crafty hand, reality and fantasy don't fall neatly into place. She compellingly muddles the two together right through to the end. Even then, after she reveals many secrets, magic still seems to linger in the real parts of Bone Gap, and the magical elements retain their frightening reality. Wonder, beauty, imperfection, cruelty, love, and pain are all inextricably linked but bewitchingly so." Booklist

Rudnick, Paul, 1957-

Gorgeous; by Paul Rudnick. 1st ed. Scholastic 2013 336 p. (hardcover) $18.99

Grades: 9 10 11 12

1. Fame -- Fiction 2. Magic -- Fiction 3. Princes -- Fiction 4. Identity -- Fiction 5. Beauty, Personal -- Fiction
ISBN 0545464269; 9780545464260

LC 2012046062

In this satirical modern fairy tale, Becky, a teenage girl from a trailer park, "receives three dresses from reclusive super-designer Tom Kelly, who knew Becky's late mother. The ensembles transform Becky into nothing less than the most beautiful woman in the world . . . with a couple catches." Suddenly she's "on the cover of 'Vogue,' dating a Hollywood hunk, and possibly in line to be the next queen of England." (Publishers Weekly)

Ruiz Zafon, Carlos, 1964-

Marina. Carlos Ruiz Zafon; translated by Lucia Graves. Little, Brown & Co. 2014 336 p.

Grades: 8 9 10 11 12

1. Love -- Fiction 2. Mystery and detective stories 3. Supernatural -- Fiction 4. Spain -- History -- 20th century -- Fiction 5. Suspense fiction 6. Young adult literature 7. Barcelona (Spain) -- Fiction
0316044717; 9780316044714, $19

LC 2013016666

In this novel by Carlos Ruiz Zafón, "15-year-old Oscar Drai suddenly vanishes from his boarding school in the old quarter of Barcelona. For seven days and nights no one knows his whereabouts. . . . His story begins in the heart of old Barcelona when he meets Marina and her father German Blau, a portrait painter." (Publisher's note)

"Set in Barcelona, Spain from late 1979 to May 1980, this gothic novel centers around 15-year-old boarding school student Oscar Drai. Instead of studying during his free time, the teen explores the city, and one day ends up in an area that seems deserted. Drawn in by music coming from an old dilapidated house, Oscar is given a scare by the owner, an eccentric and haunted German artist...With elements of romance, mystery, and horror, none of them overwhelming the other, this complex volume that hints at Mary Shelley's Frankenstein manages to weave together three separate stories for a cohesive and eerie result." SLJ

Originally published in Spanish in Barcelona by Edebé, 1999.

The **Prince** of Mist; translated by Lucia Graves. Little, Brown 2010 320p $17.99

Grades: 6 7 8 9 10

1. Dead -- Fiction 2. Magic -- Fiction 3. Siblings -- Fiction 4. Shipwrecks -- Fiction 5. Supernatural -- Fiction 6. Europe -- History -- 1918-1945 -- Fiction
ISBN 978-0-316-04477-6; 0-316-04477-6

LC 2009-51256

In 1943, in a seaside town where their family has gone to be safe from war, thirteen-year-old Max Carver and sister, fifteen-year-old Alicia, with new friend Roland, face off against an evil magician who is striving to complete a bargain made before he died.

"Zafon is a master storyteller. From the first page, the reader is drawn into the mystery and suspense that the young people encounter when they move into the Fleischmann house. . . . This book can be read and enjoyed by every level of reader." Voice Youth Advocates

Runyon, Brent

Surface tension; a novel in four summers. Alfred A. Knopf 2009 197p $16.99; lib bdg $19.99

Grades: 8 9 10 11

1. Vacations -- Fiction 2. Family life -- Fiction 3. New York (State) -- Fiction
ISBN 978-0-375-84446-1; 0-375-84446-5; 978-0-375-94446-8 lib bdg; 0-375-94446-X lib bdg

LC 2008-9193

During the summer vacations of his thirteenth through his sixteenth year at the family's lake cottage, Luke realizes that although some things stay the same over the years that many more change.

"With sensitivity and candor, Runyon reveals how life changes us all and how these unavoidable changes can be full of both turmoil and wonder." Kirkus

Rupp, Rebecca

After Eli; Rebecca Rupp. 1st ed. Candlewick 2012 245 p. (hardcover) $15.99; (ebook) $15.99
Grades: 7 8 9 10
    1. Bildungsromans 2. Family -- Fiction 3. Brothers -- Fiction 4. Bereavement -- Fiction 5. Death -- Fiction 6. Books and reading -- Fiction 7. Interpersonal relations -- Fiction
    ISBN 0763658103; 9780763658106; 9780763661946
    LC 2011048344
In this book, "Daniel, a wry and thoughtful narrator, looks back on the summer when he was 14, three years after his older brother, Eli, died in Iraq at age 22." Daniel's "memories of larger-than-life Eli and his lingering anger about his death" are interwoven with "Daniel's day-to-day challenges, including his dysfunctional family . . . ; his frustrations with his . . . friends; his attraction to Isabelle, a . . . newcomer to town; and his nascent friendship with school outcast Walter." (Publishers Weekly)

Rush, Jennifer

Altered; by Jennifer Rush. 1st ed. Little, Brown and Co. 2013 336 p. (hardcover) $17.99
Grades: 7 8 9 10 11 12
    1. Science fiction 2. Runaway teenagers -- Fiction 3. Memory -- Fiction 4. Identity -- Fiction 5. Runaways -- Fiction 6. Genetic engineering -- Fiction 7. Fathers and daughters -- Fiction
    ISBN 0316197084; 9780316197083
    LC 2012007545
This is the debut novel in a series from Jennifer Rush. Here, "homeschooled 18-year-old Anna Mason has a life ruled by secrecy. Her widower father works for a clandestine organization called the Branch, and four gorgeous genetically altered teenage boys live in the basement laboratory of their New York State farmhouse. . . . When the Branch tries to collect 'the units,' chaos erupts, and Sam, Anna, and the others take off on the run." (Publishers Weekly)

"[T]his debut's strengths--pacing and plot twists, especially--outweigh the deficits. Riveting." Kirkus

Russell, Chris

Songs about a girl. Chris Russell. Flatiron Books 2017 362 p.
Grades: 7 8 9 10
    1. Bands (Music) -- Fiction; 2. Bullying -- Fiction; 3. Fame -- Fiction; 4. Photography -- Fiction; 5. Popular music -- Fiction; 6. Single-parent families -- Fiction
    1250095166; 9781250095169, $10.99; 9781250095152
    LC 2017003061
In this book, by Chris Russell, "when former classmate Olly Samson... ask[ed Charlie Bloom]...to take backstage pictures of his new band, she takes him up on it.... But Olly's band, Fire&Lights, isn't playing ordinary gigs. They're stars on the rise.... As the boys' rivalry threatens to tear the band apart, Charlie stumbles on a secret about the band -- and herself -- hidden within the lyrics of their new #1 single." (Publisher's note)

Russo, Meredith

★ **If** I Was Your Girl. Meredith Russo. St. Martin's Press 2016 288 p.
Grades: 9 10 11 12
    1. Transgender people -- Fiction 2. Gender identity -- Fiction 3. Romance fiction
    1250078407; 9781250078407, $17.99
    LC 2016001596
Stonewall Book Award, Young Adult (2017)
In this young adult novel, by Meredith Russo, "Amanda Hardy is the new girl in school. . . . But when she meets sweet, easygoing Grant, Amanda can't help but start to let him into her life. . . . She finds herself yearning to share with Grant everything about herself, including her past. But Amanda's terrified that once she tells him the truth, . . . that at her old school, she used to be Andrew . . . , the truth cost Amanda her new life, and her new love." (Publisher's note)

"Though she's determined to lie low while finishing high school, she finds unexpected friendships with a trio of churchgoing Baptist girls and with art classmate Bee, a bisexual girl secretly in a relationship with one of them. Even more unexpected is her blossoming relationship with tender and respectful Grant, who has a complicated past of his own. . . . Flashbacks to Amanda's life pre-, during, and post-suicide attempt and subsequent transition are interspersed throughout the narrative. There is no gratuitous trauma, and Amanda's story is neither overly sentimental nor didactic. Russo, herself a trans woman living in Tennessee, crafts a thoughtful, truthful, and much needed coming-of-age tale." Horn Book

Rutkoski, Marie

The **shadow** society; Marie Rutkoski. Farrar, Straus and Giroux 2012 408 p. $17.99
Grades: 7 8 9 10 11 12
    1. Science fiction 2. Alternative histories 3. Supernatural -- Fiction 4. Identity -- Fiction 5. Illinois -- Fiction 6. High schools -- Fiction 7. Foster home care -- Fiction
    ISBN 0374349053; 9780374349059
    LC 2011033158
In this novel by Marie Rutkoski "Darcy Jones doesn't remember anything before the day she was abandoned as a child outside a Chicago firehouse. . . . But she couldn't have guessed that she comes from an alternate world where the Great Chicago Fire didn't happen and deadly creatures called Shades terrorize the human population. Memories begin to haunt Darcy when a new boy arrives at her high school, and he makes her feel both desire and desired in a way she hadn't thought possible." (Publisher's note)

The **winner's** crime. Marie Rutkoski. Farrar Straus & Giroux 2015 416 p. (The winner's trilogy)
Grades: 9 10 11 12
    1. Fantasy -- Fiction 2. Love -- Fiction 3. Secrets -- Fiction 4. Romance fiction 5. Fantasy fiction 6. Weddings -- Fiction
    0374384703; 9780374384708, $17.99
    LC 2014025185
"Lady Kestrel has successfully bargained for limited independence for the Herrani people, but only at the price of her own freedom. Now betrothed to the feckless Impe-

rial heir, she risks even more as a spy, while managing to convince everyone—most particularly Arin, once her slave, then her captor, now governor of Herran—of her ruthless devotion to tyrannical Valorian dominion." (Kirkus Reviews)

"A rich and complex story of political intrigue, missed opportunities, and thwarted trust fill the pages of this sequel to The Winner's Curse (2014). Rutkoski's world is splendid in its cruelty and beauty, with characters that continue to claim our hearts." Booklist

★ The **winner's** curse. Marie Rutkoski. Farrar Straus & Giroux 2014 368 p. (The winner's trilogy)
Grades: 7 8 9 10 11 12
1. Love -- Fiction 2. Slavery -- Fiction 3. Imperialism -- Fiction
0374384673; 9780374384678, $17.99

LC 2013000312

In this book, by Marie Rutkoski, "winning what you want may cost you everything you love. As a general's daughter in a vast empire that revels in war and enslaves those it conquers, seventeen-year-old Kestrel has two choices: she can join the military or get married. But Kestrel has other intentions. One day, she is startled to find a kindred spirit in a young slave up for auction. Arin's eyes seem to defy everything and everyone. Following her instinct, Kestrel buys him." (Publisher's note)

Full-bodied characters explore issues of loyalty, class, and values (for example, arts versus military strengths), without sacrificing any of the relationship-related tension that is a hallmark of this kind of story.

Other titles in this series are:
The winner's crime (2015)
The winner's kiss (2016)

Ryan, Amy Kathleen

Flame; a Sky Chasers novel. Amy Kathleen Ryan. St. Martin's Griffin 2014 336 p. (Sky Chasers) (hardback) $18.99
Grades: 8 9 10 11 12
1. War stories 2. Airships -- Fiction 3. Science fiction
ISBN 0312621361; 9780312621360

LC 2013039416

"When this meaty, harrowing conclusion to the Sky Chasers series opens, the inhabitants of the vessel Empyrean are fleeing their destroyed spacecraft to join their former enemies on board the New Horizon. Action begins immediately, and the story shifts mainly among the points of view of Waverly, Kieran and Seth...The pace is at times methodical, and much of the suspense comes from characters' and readers' uncertainty as to whom to trust. Stakes are high, however, and readers witness graphic (though generally not gory) violence and bodily harm as the three teens work to both overthrow and defend Pastor Anne Mather, the New Horizon's leader. It all comes to a head in a climax that is tense and viscerally frightening. Detailed and gripping, with a thorough and satisfying resolution." (Kirkus)

Glow. St. Martin's Griffin 2011 307p (Sky chasers) $17.99

Grades: 8 9 10 11 12
1. Science fiction
ISBN 978-0-312-59056-7; 0-312-59056-3

LC 2011020385

Part of the first generation to be conceived in deep space, fifteen-year-old Waverly is expected to marry young and have children to populate a new planet, but a violent betrayal by the dogmatic leader of their sister ship could have devastating consequences.

"The themes of survival, morality, religion, and power are well developed, and the characters are equally complex. The author has also created a unique and vivid outer-space setting that is exciting and easy to imagine." SLJ

Spark; a Sky chasers novel. Amy Kathleen Ryan. 1st ed. St. Martin's Press 2012 309 p. (hardcover) $17.99; (paperback) $9.99
Grades: 8 9 10 11 12
1. Mystery fiction 2. Friendship -- Fiction 3. Parent-child relationship -- Fiction 4. Science fiction
ISBN 0312621353; 9780312621353; 9781250014160; 9781250031952

LC 2012004631

Author Amy Kathleen Ryan's character "Waverly Marshall has endured and committed terrible acts aboard the 'New Horizon.' . . . [Kieran] delivers sermons designed to promote both unity and loyalty. . . . Meanwhile, Seth . . . escapes the brig under mysterious circumstances and discovers a major threat to the ship. As Waverly, Kieran, [and] Seth . . . work . . . to keep the peace, secure the ship and rescue their parents from the 'New Horizon,' . . . political and moral questions arise." (Kirkus Reviews)

Ryan, Carrie

★ The **Forest** of Hands and Teeth. Delacorte Press 2009 310p
Grades: 9 10 11 12
1. Horror fiction 2. Orphans -- Fiction 3. Zombies -- Fiction
ISBN 978-0-385-73681-7; 978-0-385-90631-9 lib bdg

LC 2008-06494

Through twists and turns of fate, orphaned Mary seeks knowledge of life, love, and especially what lies beyond her walled village and the surrounding forest, where dwell the Unconsecrated, aggressive flesh-eating people who were once dead.

"Mary's observant, careful narration pulls readers into a bleak but gripping story of survival and the endless capacity of humanity to persevere. . . . Fresh and riveting." Publ Wkly

Other titles in this series are:
The dark and hollow places (2011)
The dead-tossed waves (2010)

Ryan, Sara

Empress of the world. Viking 2001 213p $15.99
Grades: 9 10 11 12
1. Lesbians 2. Bisexual people -- Fiction 3. Schools 4. LGBT youth -- Fiction
ISBN 0-670-89688-8

LC 00-52758

Lambda Literary Awards Children's and Teen Finalist (2002)

"At a summer institute for gifted high-school students, Nicola finds herself attracted to another girl. Nic's uncertainty about whether she's either lesbian or bisexual is believably conveyed, and the dialogue is convincingly realistic. Despite a flimsily constructed conflict, YA readers are sure to embrace the believable passions in this summer romance." (Horn Book)

Sachar, Louis

The **cardturner**; a novel about a king, a queen, and a joker. Delacorte Press 2010 336p $17.99; lib bdg $20.99

Grades: 8 9 10 11 12

1. Uncles -- Fiction 2. Family life -- Fiction 3. Bridge (Game) -- Fiction
ISBN 978-0-385-73662-6; 0-385-73662-2; 978-0-385-90619-7 lib bdg; 0-385-90619-6 lib bdg

LC 2009-27585

"Alton gets roped into serving as a card turner for his great-uncle, Lester Trapp, a bridge whizz who recently lost his eyesight. . . . To Alton's surprise, he becomes enamored of the game and begins to bond with his crusty uncle. . . . With dry, understated humor, Alton makes the intricacies of bridge accessible, while his relationships with and observations about family members and friends . . . form a portrait of a reflective teenager whose life is infinitely enriched by connections he never expected to make." Publ Wkly

Saeed, Aisha

Written in the stars. By Aisha Saeed. Nancy Paulsen Books 2015 284 p.

Grades: 9 10 11 12

1. Dating (Social customs) -- Fiction 2. Forced marriage -- Fiction 3. Love -- Fiction 4. Pakistani American teenage girls 5. Pakistani Americans -- Fiction 6. Pakistan -- Fiction 7. Arranged marriage -- Fiction
0399171703; 9780399171703, $17.99

LC 2014019860

In this book, by Aisha Saeed, "Naila's conservative immigrant parents have always said the same thing: She may choose what to study, how to wear her hair, and what to be when she grows up—but they will choose her husband. . . . And until then, dating—even friendship with a boy—is forbidden. When Naila breaks their rule by falling in love with Saif, her parents are livid. Convinced she has forgotten who she truly is, they travel to Pakistan to visit relatives and explore their roots." (Publisher's note)

"Naila's harrowing story is compellingly told, and Saeed includes an afterword about the problem of forced marriages not only in Pakistan but among immigrant communities in the U.S. Stirring, haunting, and ultimately hopeful." Booklist

Includes bibliographical references

Sáenz, Benjamin Alire

★ **Aristotle** and Dante discover the secrets of the universe; Benjamin Alire Sáenz. Simon & Schuster Books for Young Readers 2012 359 p. (hardcover) $16.99

Grades: 9 10 11 12

1. Bildungsromans 2. Friendship -- Fiction 3. Gay teenagers -- Fiction 4. Mexican Americans -- Fiction

5. Families -- Fiction 6. Coming of age -- Fiction 7. Mexican-Americans -- Fiction
ISBN 1442408928; 9781442408920

LC 2010033649

Michael L. Printz Honor Book (2013)

This book follows "fifteen-year-old Ari [who] is restless and bored when a boy named Dante offers to teach him to swim. . . . When Dante is almost hit by a car, Ari risks his life to save him and then pulls back emotionally from Dante's effusive gratitude, but it isn't until Dante moves away for the school year and begins experimenting with his sexuality . . . that Ari really has to confront the secrets of his own universe." (Bulletin of the Center for Children's Books)

He forgot to say good-bye. Simon & Schuster 2008 321p $16.99

Grades: 8 9 10 11

1. Drug abuse -- Fiction 2. Mexican Americans -- Fiction
ISBN 978-1-4169-4963-3; 1-4169-4963-1

LC 2007-21959

Two teenaged boys with very different lives find that they share a common bond—fathers they have never met who left when they were small boys—and in spite of their differences, they become close when they each need someone who understands.

"The affirming and hopeful ending is well-earned for the characters and a great payoff for the reader. . . . Characters are well-developed and complex. . . . Overall it is a strong novel with broad teenage appeal." Voice Youth Advocates

★ The **inexplicable** logic of my life. By Benjamin Alire Sáenz. Clarion Books, Houghton Mifflin Harcourt 2017 445 p.

Grades: 8 9 10 11 12

1. Adoption -- Fiction; 2. Children of gay parents -- Fiction; 3. Death -- Fiction; 4. Families -- Fiction; 5. Friendship -- Fiction; 6. High school students -- Fiction; 7. Identity -- Fiction; 8. Mexican Americans -- Fiction
9780544586505, $17.99; 9780544583528

LC 2016001079

In this young adult novel by Benjamin Alire Saenz, "Sal used to know his place with his adoptive gay father, their loving Mexican American family, and his best friend, Samantha. But it's senior year, and suddenly Sal is throwing punches, questioning everything, and realizing he no longer knows himself. If Sal's not who he thought he was, who is he?" (Publisher's note)

"The themes of love, social responsibility, death, and redemption are expertly intertwined with well-developed characters and a compelling story line. This complex, sensitive, and profoundly moving book is beautifully written and will stay with readers." SLJ

★ **Last** night I sang to the monster; a novel. Cinco Puntos Press 2009 239p $16.95

Grades: 9 10 11 12

1. Alcoholism -- Fiction 2. Family life -- Fiction 3. Psychotherapy -- Fiction
ISBN 978-1-933693-58-3; 1-933693-58-4

LC 2009-15833

Eighteen-year-old Zach does not remember how he came to be in a treatment center for alcoholics. Through therapy and and the help of friends such as Rafael, his amnesia fades and he begins to heal. "Grades nine to twelve." (Bull Cent Child Books)

"Saenz' poetic narrative will captivate readers from the first sentence to the last paragraph of this beautifully written novel, which explores the painful journey of an adolescent through the labyrinth of addiction and alcoholism. It is also a celebration of life and a song of hope in celebration of family and friendship, one that will resonate loud and long with teens." Kirkus

★ **Sammy** and Juliana in Hollywood; by Benjamin Alire Saenz. Cinco Puntos Press 2004 294p hardcover o.p. pa $11.95

Grades: 9 10 11 12

1. Violence -- Fiction 2. New Mexico -- Fiction 3. Mexican Americans -- Fiction

ISBN 0-938317-81-4; 1-933693-99-1 pa

LC 2004-2414

As a Chicano boy living in the unglamorous town of Hollywood, New Mexico, and a member of the graduating class of 1969, Sammy Santos faces the challenges of "gringo" racism, unpopular dress codes, the Vietnam War, barrio violence, and poverty

Safi, Aminah Mae

Not the girls you're looking for. Aminah Mae Safi. Feiwel and Friends 2018 336 p.

Grades: 9 10 11 12

1. Teenage girls -- Fiction; 2. Female friendship -- Fiction; 3. Arab Americans -- Fiction

9781250151803; 9781250151810, $17.99

LC 2017956992

In this book, by Aminah Mae Safi, "Lulu Saad doesn't need your advice.... She's got her three best friends.... Sure, for half a minute she thought she'd nearly drowned a cute guy at a party.... And...she caused a scene during Ramadan.... Except maybe this time she's done a little more damage than she realizes. And if Lulu can't find her way out of this mess soon, she'll have to do more than repair friendships, family alliances, and wet clothing." (Publisher's note)

Saldana, Rene

A **good** long way; by Rene Saldana, Jr. Piñata Books 2010 103p pa $10.95

Grades: 8 9 10 11

1. School stories 2. Texas -- Fiction 3. Brothers -- Fiction 4. Mexican Americans -- Fiction 5. Runaway teenagers -- Fiction

ISBN 978-1-55885-607-3; 1-55885-607-2

LC 2010-32989

Three Mexican American teenagers in a small-town in Texas struggle with difficulties at home and at school as they try to attain the elusive status of adulthood.

"This fast-paced novel will make readers think about their own lives and responsibilities." SLJ

Sales, Leila

This song will save your life; Leila Sales. Farrar Straus & Giroux 2013 288 p. (hard) $17.99

Grades: 8 9 10 11 12

1. Bullies -- Fiction 2. Disc jockeys -- Fiction 3. Suicide -- Fiction 4. Popularity -- Fiction 5. High schools -- Fiction 6. Interpersonal relations -- Fiction

ISBN 0374351384; 9780374351380

LC 2012050408

In this book, "Elise has endured a lifetime of social isolation and bullying at school. Walking alone one night soon after a halfhearted suicide attempt, the 16-year-old inadvertently ends up at an underground nightclub. There, an aspiring musician befriends her, and she catches the eye of Char, a cute DJ who agrees to teach her to mix music. But as talented, driven Elise spends more nights sneaking out to learn how to DJ (and kiss Char), her double life spins out of control." (Publishers Weekly)

Tonight the streets are ours. Leila Sales. Farrar, Straus & Giroux 2015 352 p.

Grades: 7 8 9 10 11 12

1. Authors -- Fiction 2. Blogs -- Fiction 3. Conduct of life -- Fiction 4. Family problems -- Fiction 5. High schools -- Fiction 6. Interpersonal relations -- Fiction 7. Schools -- Fiction 8. New York (N.Y.) -- Fiction 9. New York (N.Y.) -- Fiction 10. Self-realization -- Fiction

9780374376659, $17.99; 0374376654

LC 2015003571

"Taking care of her loved ones is what gives Arden purpose in her life and makes her feel like she matters. But lately she's grown resentful of everyone—including her needy best friend and her absent mom—taking her loyalty for granted.Then Arden stumbles upon a website called Tonight the Streets Are Ours, the musings of a young New York City writer named Peter, who gives voice to feelings that Arden has never known how to express. He seems to get her in a way that no one else does, and he hasn't even met her. Until Arden sets out on a road trip to find him." (Publisher's note)

"This book will resonate with any reader who has experienced disappointments in romantic love or with any loved ones. Themes of recklessness, disregard for others, and dishonesty are thoughtfully explored." VOYA

Salisbury, Graham

★ **Eyes** of the emperor. Wendy Lamb Books 2005 228p hardcover o.p. pa $6.99

Grades: 7 8 9 10

1. Japanese Americans -- Fiction 2. World War, 1939-1945 -- Fiction

ISBN 0-385-72971-5; 0-440-22956-1 pa

LC 2004-15142

Following orders from the United States Army, several young Japanese American men train K-9 units to hunt Asians during World War II.

"Based on the experiences of 26 Hawaiian-Americans of Japanese ancestry, this novel tells an uncomfortable story. Yet it tells of belief in honor, respect, and love of country." Libr Media Connect

Hunt for the bamboo rat. By Graham Salisbury. Wendy Lamb Books, an imprint of Random House Children's Books 2014 336 p. Illustration

Grades: 6 7 8 9 10

1. Japanese Americans -- Fiction 2. Prisoners of war -- Fiction 3. Spies -- Fiction 4. Survival -- Fiction 5. World War, 1939-1945 -- Philippines -- Fiction 6. Philippines -- History -- Japanese occupation, 1942-1945 -- Fiction 7. Spy stories 8. World War, 1939-1945 -- Fiction

0375842667; 9780375842665, $16.99; 9780375940705

LC 2014005743

This book by Graham Salisbury is set "in August 1941. . . . Seventeen-year-old Zenji Watanabe . . . is Nisei, speaks perfect English and Japanese, and is recruited by the U.S. Army as a special undercover intelligence agent working in Manila, code name: Bamboo Rat. It's a dangerous assignment to be in the Philippines on the eve of Japanese invasion and imminent American involvement. He's American, but looks Japanese, and soon finds himself caught in the middle." (Horn Book Magazine)

"Written in short, rapid-fire paragraphs that move the plot along at a brisk pace, the story will leave readers spellbound. A gripping saga of wartime survival. (maps, author's note, glossary, resources)" Kirkus

★ **Under** the blood-red sun. Delacorte Press 1994 246p hardcover o.p. pa $5.99

Grades: 5 6 7 8 9 10

1. Hawaii -- Fiction 2. Japanese Americans -- Fiction 3. World War, 1939-1945 -- Fiction 4. Pearl Harbor (Oahu, Hawaii), Attack on, 1941 -- Fiction

ISBN 0-385-32099-X; 0-440-41139-4 pa

LC 94-444

Tomikazu Nakaji's biggest concerns are baseball, homework, and a local bully, until life with his Japanese family in Hawaii changes drastically after the bombing of Pearl Harbor in December 1941

"Character development of major figures is good, the setting is warmly realized, and the pace of the story moves gently though inexorably forward." SLJ

Followed by: House of the red fish (2006)

Salisbury, Melinda

The **Sin** Eater's daughter. Melinda Salisbury. Scholastic Press, an imprint of Scholastic Inc. 2015 320 p.

Grades: 9 10 11 12

1. Bodyguards -- Fiction 2. Death -- Fiction 3. Executions and executioners -- Fiction 4. Goddesses -- Fiction 5. Kings, queens, rulers, etc. -- Fiction 6. Love -- Fiction 7. Poisons -- Fiction 8. Princes -- Fiction 9. Trust -- Fiction 10. Fantasy fiction 11. Queens -- Fiction 12. Romance fiction

0545810620; 9780545810623, $17.99

LC 2014038970

In this book by Melinda Salisbury, "seventeen-year-old Twylla has a gift and a curse as the embodiment of a goddess on Earth: she is worshipped and she can kill men in seconds with the briefest of touches. Twylla's mother is a Sin Eater, one who eats symbolic foods of the deceased person's sins at their grave site; Twylla is set to pursue this path until the Queen of Lormere takes her from her home to become the goddess Daunen Embodied." (School Library Journal)

"Salisbury weaves a complex tale of romance, religion, fairy tales and politics. A slow but satisfying read with impressive depth and emotion." Kirkus

Salomon, Peter Adam

All those broken angels. Peter Adam Salomon. Flux 2014 240 p.

Grades: 9 10 11 12

1. Best friends -- Fiction 2. Friendship -- Fiction 3. Ghosts -- Fiction 4. Missing children -- Fiction 5. Mystery and detective stories 6. Savannah (Ga.) -- Fiction 7. Mystery fiction 8. Ghost stories 9. Savannah (Ga.) -- Fiction

0738740799; 9780738740799, $9.99

LC 2014014104

In this book, by Peter Adam Salomon, "Richard Harrison was the last person to see his friend Melanie alive. She vanished when they were six, and while the police never found her, a part of her remained - a living shadow that became Richard's closest friend. For ten years, Richard has never questioned the shadow that keeps him company . . . until a new girl moves to town, claiming to be Melanie." (Publisher's note)

"It has been 10 years since Richard's best friend, Melanie, vanished during their game of hide-and-seek, but over the subsequent decade, he has been comforted by the presence of her ghost: a silent, willful shadow figure, the single strong constant in his otherwise cowering life...An overly rationalized climax undercuts this accomplishment a bit, but that doesn't erase the effect of the book's dreadful, inching progress; startling, evolving relationships; and pervading sense of shuddery doom." Booklist

Sanchez, Alex

Bait. Simon & Schuster Books for Young Readers 2009 239p $16.99

Grades: 7 8 9 10

1. Stepfathers -- Fiction 2. Mexican Americans -- Fiction 3. Child sexual abuse -- Fiction

ISBN 978-1-4169-3772-2; 1-4169-3772-2

LC 2008-38815

Diego keeps getting into trouble because of his explosive temper until he finally finds a probation officer who helps him get to the root of his anger so that he can stop running from his past.

"This groundbreaking novel brings to life an appealing young man who is neither totally a victim nor a victimizer, one who struggles to handle conflicts that derail many young lives. . . . High interest and accessible, this coming-of-age story belongs in every collection." SLJ

Getting it. Simon & Schuster 2006 210p $16.95; pa $8.99

Grades: 9 10 11 12

1. School stories 2. Friendship -- Fiction 3. Gay teenagers -- Fiction 4. Mexican Americans -- Fiction

ISBN 978-1-4169-0896-8; 1-4169-0896-X; 978-1-4169-0898-2 pa; 1-4169-0898-6 pa

LC 2005-29905

Hoping to impress a sexy female classmate, fifteen-year-old Carlos secretly hires gay student Sal to give him an image makeover, in exchange for Carlos's help in forming a Gay-Straight Alliance at their Texas high school.

"This title's sexual frankness may make it a controversial choice, particularly for school libraries in more conservative communities, but its themes, appeal, and readability make it a nearly essential purchase." Voice Youth Advocates

Rainbow boys. Simon & Schuster 2001 233p hardcover o.p. pa $8.99

Grades: 10 11 12

1. School stories 2. Gay teenagers -- Fiction
ISBN 0-689-84100-0; 0-689-85770-5 pa
LC 2001-20952

Three high school seniors, a jock with a girlfriend and an alcoholic father, a closeted gay, and a flamboyant gay rights advocate, struggle with family issues, gay bashers, first sex, and conflicting feelings about each other.

"Some of the language and sexual situations may be too mature for some readers, but overall there's enough conflict, humor and tenderness to make this story believable—and touching." Publ Wkly

Other titles featuring Nelson, Kyle, and Jason are:
Rainbow High (2004)
Rainbow road (2005)

Rainbow High. Simon & Schuster Books for Young Readers 2004 247p $16.95; pa $8.99

Grades: 10 11 12

1. School stories 2. Gay teenagers -- Fiction
ISBN 0-689-85477-3; 0-689-85478-1 pa
LC 2003-8252

Sequel to Rainbow boys (2001)

Follows three gay high school seniors as they struggle with issues of coming out, safe sex, homophobia, being in love, and college choices.

Followed by Rainbow road (2005)

Rainbow road. Simon & Schuster 2005 243p $16.95; pa $8.99

Grades: 10 11 12

1. Gay teenagers -- Fiction 2. Automobile travel -- Fiction
ISBN 0-689-86565-1; 1-4169-1191-X pa
LC 2004-25980

Sequel to Rainbow high (2003)

While driving across the United States during the summer after high school graduation, three young gay men encounter various bisexual and homosexual people and make some decisions about their own relationships and lives.

"Some mature romance scenes, occasional frank language, and an inclusion of transgender/transsexual/bisexual story lines translate into a tender book that will likely be appreciated and embraced by young adult readers." SLJ

So hard to say; Alex Sanchez. 1st ed; Simon & Schuster Books for Young Readers 2004 230p $14.95

Grades: 6 7 8 9

1. LGBT youth 2. Mexican Americans -- Fiction
ISBN 0-689-86564-3
LC 2003-21128

Thirteen-year-old Xio, a Mexican American girl, and Frederick, who has just moved to California from Wisconsin, quickly become close friends, but when Xio starts thinking of Frederick as her boyfriend, he must confront his feelings of confusion and face the fear that he might be gay.

"Adventurous, multifaceted, funny, and unpredictably insightful, Sanchez's novel . . . gels well-rounded characterizations with the universal excitement of first love." SLJ

Sanchez, Erika L.

I Am Not Your Perfect Mexican Daughter. Erika L. Sánchez. Alfred A. Knopf 2017 344 p.

Grades: 9 10 11 12

1. Mexican American families -- Fiction; 2. Mexican Americans -- Fiction; 3. Mothers and daughters -- Fiction; 4. Sisters -- Death -- Fiction; 5. Chicago (Ill.) -- Fiction; 6. Sisters -- Fiction; 7. Mother-daughter relationship -- Fiction; 8. Grief -- Fiction; 9. Secrecy -- Fiction
1524700495; 9781524700508; 9781524700492, $20.99; 9781524700485
LC 2017297201

National Book Award Finalist: Young People's Literature (2017)

In this book, by Erika L. Sánchez, "Julia is not your perfect Mexican daughter. That was Olga's role. Then a tragic accident on the busiest street in Chicago leaves Olga dead and Julia left behind to reassemble the shattered pieces of her family.... But it's not long before Julia discovers that Olga might not have been as perfect as everyone thought.... Was Olga really what she seemed? Or was there more to her sister's story?" (Publisher's note)

"The depiction of Julia as she processes her losses is hauntingly memorable and noteworthy in its authentic representation of culture and experience too rarely written." Horn Book

Sanders, Shelly

Rachel's secret. Second Story Press 2012 248 p. $12.95

Grades: 6 7 8 9 10

1. Historical fiction 2. Antisemitism -- Fiction 3. Judaism -- Relations -- Christianity -- Fiction
ISBN 1926920376; 9781926920375

This book follows "14-year-old Rachel . . . living under Russian rule in Kishinev in 1903, [she] was one of the last people to see her Christian friend Mikhail alive when she witnessed his murder at the hands of disgruntled relatives who stood to lose out on an inheritance. His death is blamed on Jews, however, and a vicious pogrom is unleashed on the city. Rachel's anguish about knowing what happened stems from a justified fear of not being believed if she comes forward, thus evoking more turmoil. She also harbors guilt that her somewhat risky friendship with a non-Jewish boy somehow triggered the calamity.... [W]hile Rachel does act courageously and courtroom justice is meted out, virulent anti-Semitism still rules the day." (Booklist)

Sanderson, Brandon

The **Rithmatist**; Brandon Sanderson. Tor Teen 2013 384 p. ill. (hardcover) $17.99

Grades: 7 8 9 10
>   1. Fantasy fiction 2. Magic -- Fiction 3. Fantasy
> ISBN 0765320320; 9780765320322

LC 2012043417

In this young adult fantasy novel, by Brandon Sanderson, "Joel wants to be a Rithmatist. Chosen by the Master in a mysterious inception ceremony, Rithmatists have the power to infuse life into two-dimensional figures known as Chalklings. Rithmatists are humanity's only defense against the Wild Chalklings--merciless creatures that leave mangled corpses in their wake. Having nearly overrun the territory of Nebrask, the Wild Chalklings now threaten all of the American Isles." (Publisher's note)

Sandler, Karen

Rebellion. Karen Sandler. Tu Books 2014 396 p. Map (Tankborn)

Grades: 7 8 9 10
>   1. Genetic engineering -- Fiction 2. Kidnapping -- Fiction 3. Science fiction 4. Terrorism -- Fiction
> 9781600609848, $19.95; 1600609848

LC 2014002775

In this young adult science fiction novel by Karen Sandler, part of the Tankborn Trilogy series, "Kayla is a GEN—a genetically engineered nonhuman—in a world torn apart by castes separating GENs from 'real' humans. In the wake of a devastating bomb blast, Kayla finds herself at the headquarters of the organization that planted the bomb—and many others like it in GEN food warehouses and homes." (Publisher's note)

"Sandler tackles caste systems, slavery and terrorism (including its muddled logic) head-on. . . . With rebellions, ideological questions and a nonwhite, not-entirely-heterosexual cast, this series is a strong addition to the genre." Kirkus

Sequel to: Awakening

Tankborn. Tu Books 2011 373p map $17.95
Grades: 7 8 9 10
>   1. Science fiction 2. Genetic engineering -- Fiction
> ISBN 978-1-60060-662-5; 1-60060-662-8

LC 2011014589

Kayla and Mishalla, two genetically engineered nonhuman slaves (GENs), fall in love with higher-status boys, discover deep secrets about the creation of GENs, and in the process find out what it means to be human.

"Sandler has created a fascinating dystopian world. . . . The author's speculative vision of the darker side of future possibilities in genetic engineering and mind control is both chilling and thought-provoking." SLJ

Sangster, Caitlin

Last star burning. By Caitlin Sangster. Simon Pulse 2017 396 p.
Grades: 7 8 9 10 11 12
>   1. Epidemics -- Fiction; 2. Fugitives from justice -- Fiction; 3. Survival -- Fiction; 4. Adventure fiction; 5. Runaway teenagers -- Fiction
> 9781481486132, $18.99; 9781481486156

LC 2016046285

In this novel, by Caitlin Sangster, "when the government blames Sev for a horrific bombing, she must escape the city or face the chopping block.... Sev's only hope of survival lies with the most unlikely person -- Howl, the chairman's son. Though he promises to lead her to safety, Howl has secrets, and Sev can't help but wonder if he knows more about her past...than he lets on." (Publisher's note)

"Brimming with rich detail in an Asian-inflected alternative world that's lightly touched with Maoist terminology and concepts and helmed by achingly real characters, Sevvy's story is thrilling to get lost in.... Incredibly immersive and tightly plotted." Kirkus

Other titles in this series are: Shatters the sun (2018)

Sattar, Arshia

Ramayana: an illustrated retelling. By Arshia Sattar, illustrated by Sonali Zohra. Restless Books 2018 192 p.

Grades: 5 6 7 8 9
>   1. Rama (Hindu deity) -- Fiction; 2. Sita (Hindu deity) -- Fiction; 3. Hindu mythology -- Fiction
> 9781632061775, $19.99

LC 2017944635

In this retelling of the Indian epic Ramayana, by Arshia Sattar, illustrated by Sonali Zohra, "Rama is a brave young prince who is forced into exile. His brother Lakshmana and his wife,...princess Sita, loyally follow him into the depths of the mysterious forest.... Ravana, the ten-headed demon king...kidnaps Sita.... To rescue her, Rama enlists the help of hundreds of thousands of magical monkeys and bears to fight the demon army and win her back." (Publisher's note)

Savage, Kim

★ **Beautiful** broken girls. Kim Savage. Farrar, Straus & Giroux 2017 320 p.
Grades: 9 10 11 12
>   1. Death -- Fiction; 2. Mystery and detective stories; 3. Sisters -- Fiction; 4. Mystery fiction
> 9780374300586; 9780374300593, $17.99

LC 2016001909

In this book, by Kim Savage, "Mira and Francesca Cillo were beautiful, overprotected by their father, and, frankly, odd. To the neighborhood boys they seemed untouchable. But one boy, Ben, touched seven parts of Mira: her palm, hair, chest, cheek, lips, throat, and heart. After the sisters drown themselves in the quarry lake, a post-mortem letter from Mira arrives in Ben's mailbox. The letter sends Ben on a quest to find notes in the places where they touched." (Publisher's note)

"Even though the truth can be seen before it's revealed, the girls' secrets pack a gut punch that lingers. Haunting and mesmerizing." Kirkus

Savit, Gavriel

Anna and the Swallow Man. Gavriel Savit. Alfred A. Knopf 2016 240 p. Illustration
Grades: 8 9 10 11 12
>   1. Survival -- Fiction 2. World War, 1939-1945 -- Poland -- Fiction 3. Poland -- History -- Occupation, 1939-1945 -- Fiction 4. World War, 1939-1945 -- Fiction 5. Survival skills -- Fiction 6. Poland -- Fiction
> 9780553513349, $17.99; 9780553522068

LC 2014034472

This novel, by Gavriel Savit, is "set in Poland during the Second World War. . . . Anna Lania is just seven years old when the Germans take her father, a linguistics professor, during their purge of intellectuals in Poland. She's alone. And then Anna meets the Swallow Man. He is a mystery, strange and tall, a skilled deceiver with more than a little magic up his sleeve. And when the soldiers in the streets look at him, they see what he wants them to see." (Publisher's note)

"Full of sophisticated questions and advanced vocabulary, Savit's debut occasionally feels like an adult novel, but young readers with the patience for his gauzy pacing and oblique plot turns will be rewarded by a moving, thought-provoking story about coming-of-age in the midst of trauma." Booklist

Sax, Aline

★ The **war** within these walls; by Aline Sax; illustrated by Caryl Strzelecki; translated from the Dutch by Laura Watkinson. Eerdmans Books for Young Readers 2013 176 p. $17

Grades: 9 10 11 12

1. Jewish ghettos 2. World War, 1939-1945 -- Fiction 3. Jews -- Poland -- Fiction 4. Holocaust, Jewish (1939-1945) -- Poland -- Fiction 5. Poland -- History -- Occupation, 1939-1945 -- Fiction 6. Holocaust, Jewish (1939-1945) -- Poland 7. Warsaw (Poland) -- History -- Warsaw Ghetto Uprising, 1943 -- Fiction

ISBN 0802854281; 9780802854285

LC 2013005663

Mildred L. Batchelder Honor Book (2014)

National Jewish Book Award: Winner, Children's and Young Adult (2013)

"The narrator lives with his parents and sister in what becomes the Warsaw Ghetto. He finds a secret escape from the ghetto and begins smuggling food, eventually joining with Mordechai Anielewicz's organized Resistance. The prose is spare; the book's format, with text on black or white pages and plentiful ink and wash illustrations, is dramatic and will grab young readers." (Horn Book)

Scelsa, Kate

Fans of the impossible life. Kate Scelsa. Balzer + Bray, an imprint of HarperCollins Publishers 2015 368 p.

Grades: 9 10 11 12

1. Best friends -- Fiction 2. Bullying -- Fiction 3. Family problems -- Fiction 4. Foster home care -- Fiction 5. Friendship -- Fiction 6. Gays -- Fiction 7. Mental illness -- Fiction 8. School stories

0062331752; 9780062331755, $17.99

LC 2015005754

In this novel, by Kate Scelsa, "Mira is starting over at Saint Francis Prep. . . . Jeremy is the painfully shy art nerd at Saint Francis who's been in self-imposed isolation after an incident that ruined his last year of school. . . . Sebby, Mira's gay best friend, is a boy who seems to carry sunlight around with him. . . . As Jeremy finds himself drawn into Sebby and Mira's world, he begins to understand the secrets that they hide in order to protect themselves." (Publisher's note)

"So much more than a love triangle novel, Scelsa's debut is filled with teens discovering how to handle life's situations." SLJ

Schantz, Sarah Elizabeth

Fig. Sarah Elizabeth Schantz. Margaret K. McElderry Books 2015 352 p.

Grades: 9 10 11 12

1. Family life -- Kansas -- Fiction 2. Farm life -- Kansas -- Fiction 3. Mental illness -- Fiction 4. Mothers and daughters -- Fiction 5. Schizophrenia -- Fiction 6. Schools -- Fiction 7. Self-destructive behavior -- Fiction 8. Kansas -- History -- 20th century -- Fiction 9. Mother-daughter relationship -- Fiction

1481423584; 9781481423588, $17.99; 9781481423595

LC 2014025394

In this novel, by Sarah Elizabeth Schantz, "love and sacrifice intertwine in this . . . [story] about a girl dealing with her mother's schizophrenia and her own mental illness. . . . Spanning the course of Fig's childhood from age six to nineteen, this . . . novel is more than a portrait of a mother, a daughter, and the struggle that comes with all-consuming love. It is an acutely honest and often painful portrayal of life with mental illness." (Publisher's note)

"Though some readers may be frustrated by the meandering pace of Fig's story, patient readers who appreciate melancholic, lyrical narratives will likely be moved by Fig's heartbreaking tale." Booklist

Scheidt, Erica Lorraine

★ **Uses** for boys; Erica Lorraine Scheidt. St. Martin's Press 2013 240 p. $9.99

Grades: 9 10 11 12

1. Love stories 2. Dating (Social customs) -- Fiction 3. Teenagers -- Conduct of life -- Fiction

ISBN 1250007119; 9781250007117

In this novel by Erica Lorraine Scheidt "Anna learns that if you give boys what they want, you can get what you need. But the price is high--the other kids make fun of her; the girls call her a slut. . . . Then comes Sam. When Anna actually meets a boy who is more than just useful, whose family eats dinner together, laughs, and tells stories, the truth about love becomes clear. And she finally learns how it feels to have something to lose--and something to offer." (Publisher's note)

Schlitz, Laura Amy

★ The **hired** girl. Laura Amy Schlitz. Candlewick Press 2015 400 p.

Grades: 7 8 9 10

1. Diaries -- Fiction 2. Household employees -- Fiction 3. Young women -- Fiction

9780763678180, $17.99

LC 2014955411

Boston Globe-Horn Book Fiction Honor Book (2016)

In this book, by Laura Amy Schlitz, "Joan Skraggs . . . yearns for real life and true love. But what hope is there for adventure, beauty, or art on a hardscrabble farm in Pennsylvania where the work never ends? Over the summer of 1911, Joan pours her heart out into her diary as she seeks a new, better life for herself-because maybe, just maybe, a hired girl cleaning and cooking for six dollars a week can become what a farm girl could only dream of-a woman with a future." (Publisher's note)

"A wonderful look into the life of strong girl who learns that she needs the love of others to truly grow up." SLJ

Schmatz, Pat
★ **Bluefish**. Candlewick Press 2011 226p $15.99

Grades: 7 8 9 10

1. School stories 2. Literacy -- Fiction 3. Teachers -- Fiction

ISBN 978-0-7636-5334-7; 0-7636-5334-9

LC 2010044815

Everything changes for thirteen-year-old Travis, a new student who is trying to hide a learning disability, when he meets a remarkable teacher and Velveeta, a sassy classmate with her own secrets.

"A cast of richly developed characters peoples this work of contemporary fiction, told in the third person from Travis' point of view, with first-person vignettes from Velveeta's perspective peppered throughout. . . . A story rife with unusual honesty and hope." Kirkus

Lizard radio. Pat Schmatz. Candlewick Press 2015 288 p.

Grades: 9 10 11 12

1. Gender role -- Fiction 2. Future life -- Fiction

0763676357; 9780763676353, $16.99

LC 2014960012

In this novel, by Pat Schmatz, "fifteen-year-old bender Kivali has had a rough time in a gender-rigid culture. Abandoned as a baby . . . Kivali has always been surrounded by uncertainty. Where did she come from? Now she's in Crop-Camp, with all of its schedules and regs, and the first real friends she's ever had. Strange occurrences and complicated relationships raise questions. But she has . . . the power to enter a trancelike state to harness the 'knowings' inside her." (Publisher's note)

"An entertaining and thought-provoking read, this title will be a big hit for those who want something deeper from their dystopian fiction." SLJ

Schmidt, Gary D.
★ **Lizzie** Bright and the Buckminster boy. Clarion Books 2004 219p $15; pa $6.99

Grades: 7 8 9 10

1. Race relations -- Fiction

ISBN 0-618-43929-3; 0-553-49495-3 pa

LC 2003-20967

A Newbery Medal honor book, 2005

In 1911, Turner Buckminster hates his new home of Phippsburg, Maine, but things improve when he meets Lizzie Bright Griffin, a girl from a poor, nearby island community founded by former slaves that the town fathers—and Turner's—want to change into a tourist spot

"Although the story is hauntingly sad, there is much humor, too. Schmidt's writing is infused with feeling and rich in imagery. With fully developed, memorable characters and a fascinating, little-known piece of history, this novel will leave a powerful impression on readers." SLJ

★ **Orbiting** Jupiter. Gary D. Schmidt. Clarion Books, Houghton Mifflin Harcourt 2015 192 p.

Grades: 6 7 8 9

1. Child abuse -- Fiction 2. Emotional problems -- Fiction 3. Foster home care -- Fiction 4. Friendship -- Fiction 5. Teenage fathers -- Fiction

9780544462229, $17.99

LC 2015001338

This young adult novel, by Gary D. Schmidt, tells the "story of Joseph, 14, who joins his family as a foster child. Damaged in prison, Joseph wants nothing more than to find his baby daughter, Jupiter, whom he has never seen. When Joseph has begun to believe he'll have a future, he is confronted by demons from his past that force a tragic sacrifice." (Publisher's note)

"The matter-of-fact narrative voice ensures that the tragic plot never overwhelms this wrenching tale of growth and loss." SLJ

★ **Trouble**. Clarion Books 2008 297p $16

Grades: 6 7 8 9 10

1. Death -- Fiction 2. Prejudices -- Fiction 3. Family life -- Fiction 4. Traffic accidents -- Fiction 5. Cambodian Americans -- Fiction

ISBN 978-0-618-92766-1; 0-618-92766-2

LC 2007-40104

Fourteen-year-old Henry, wishing to honor his brother Franklin's dying wish, sets out to hike Maine's Mount Katahdin with his best friend and dog, but fate adds another companion—the Cambodian refugee accused of fatally injuring Franklin—and reveals troubles that predate the accident.

"Schmidt creates a rich and credible world peopled with fully developed characters who have a lot of complex reckoning to do. . . . [The author's prose] is flawless, and Henry's odyssey of growth and understanding is pitch-perfect and deeply satisfying." Bull Cent Child Books

★ The **Wednesday** wars. Clarion Books 2007 264p pa $6.99; $16

Grades: 5 6 7 8

1. School stories

ISBN 054723760X; 0618724834; 9780547237602; 9780618724833

LC 2006-23660

A Newbery Medal honor book, 2008

During the 1967 school year, on Wednesday afternoons when all his classmates go to either Catechism or Hebrew school, seventh-grader Holling Hoodhound stays in Mrs. Baker's classroom where they read the plays of William Shakespeare and Holling learns something of value about the world he lives in.

"The serious issues are leavened with ample humor, and the supporting cast . . . is fully dimensional. Best of all is the hero." Publ Wkly

Schneider, Robyn
★ The **beginning** of everything; by Robyn Schneider. 1st ed. Katherine Tegen Books 2013 336 p. (hardcover) $17.99

Grades: 9 10 11 12

1. School stories 2. Popularity -- Fiction 3. California -- Fiction 4. High schools -- Fiction 5. Debates and

debating -- Fiction 6. Interpersonal relations -- Fiction 7. People with disabilities -- Fiction 8. Family life -- California -- Fiction

ISBN 0062217135; 9780062217134

LC 2012030976

In this book, after "finding his vapid girlfriend going down on another guy, Ezra Faulkner is seriously injured in a hit-and-run accident, leaving him out of the loop with the jock-and-cheerleader set. When senior year begins, he gravitates toward his old friend Toby, no stranger to tragedy himself. Toby and his debate team welcome Ezra to their lunch table when they find out that the prom king is as smart and funny as they are." (Kirkus Reviews)

Schoenherr, Ian

The **speaker**. Traci Chee. G.P. Putnam's Sons 2017 487 p. Map (Sea of ink and gold)

Grades: 8 9 10 11 12

1. Books and reading -- Fiction; 2. Kidnapping -- Fiction; 3. Nightmares -- Fiction; 4. Orphans -- Fiction; 5. Fantasy fiction

9780698410633; 0399176780; 9780399176784, $19.99

LC 2017016556

In this book, by Traci Chee, "having barely escaped the clutches of the Guard, Sefia and Archer are back on the run, slipping into the safety of the forest to tend to their wounds and plan their next move. Haunted by painful memories, Archer struggles to overcome the trauma of his past with the impressors, whose cruelty plagues him whenever he closes his eyes. But when Sefia and Archer happen upon a crew of impressors in the wilderness, Archer finally finds a way to combat his nightmares." (Publisher's note)

"Filled with even more magic and intrigue than its predecessor, this is a gripping follow-up that will leave readers speculating and wanting more." Kirkus

Schrefer, Eliot

The **deadly** sister. Scholastic Press 2010 310p $17.99

Grades: 8 9 10 11 12

1. Mystery fiction 2. Sisters -- Fiction 3. Homicide -- Fiction

ISBN 978-0-545-16574-7; 0-545-16574-1

LC 2010-281733

Abby Goodwin has always covered for her sister, Maya, but now Maya has been accused of murder, and Abby's not sure she'll be able to cover for her sister anymore. Abby helps Maya escape. But when Abby begins investigating the death, she find that you can't trust anyone, not even the people you think you know.

"Well-drawn characters, realistic dialogue, and suspenseful twists and turns add to the appeal. Teens crave mystery, and this book will suit them just fine." SLJ

★ **Endangered**; Eliot Schrefer. Scholastic Press 2012 264 p. (reinforced) $17.99

Grades: 7 8 9 10 11 12

1. Animal sanctuaries -- Fiction 2. Wildlife conservation -- Fiction 3. Congo (Democratic Republic) -- Fiction 4. Apes -- Fiction 5. Bonobo -- Fiction 6. Divorce -- Fiction 7. Wildlife rescue -- Fiction 8. Racially mixed people -- Fiction 9. Blacks -- Congo (Democratic Republic) -- Fiction

ISBN 0545165768; 9780545165761

LC 2012030877

This book by Eliot Schrefer was a 2012 National Book Award Finalist for Young People's Literature. "When one girl has to follow her mother to her sanctuary for bonobos, she's not thrilled to be there. It's her mother's passion, and she'd rather have nothing to do with it. But when revolution breaks out and their sanctuary is attacked, she must rescue the bonobos and hide in the jungle. Together, they will fight to keep safe, to eat, and to survive." (Publisher's note)

★ **Threatened**; Eliot Schrefer. Scholastic Press 2014 288 p. (jacketed hardcover) $17.99

Grades: 7 8 9 10 11 12

1. Gabon -- Fiction 2. Adventure stories 3. Chimpanzees -- Fiction 4. Animal rescue -- Fiction 5. Orphans -- Gabon -- Fiction 6. Wildlife rescue -- Fiction

ISBN 0545551439; 9780545551434

LC 2013018599

"Luc and Prof head into the rough, dangerous jungle in order to study the elusive chimpanzees. There, Luc finally finds a new family--and must act when that family comes under attack. . . . [It] is the story of a boy fleeing his present, a man fleeing his past, and a trio of chimpanzees who are struggling not to flee at all." (Publisher's note)

"After the death of his mother and sister, Luc is left in the hands of a moneylender, Monsieur Tatagani. One of many orphans forced to do Tatagani's bidding, Luc has found a way to be useful and earn a few coins wiping glasses in a bar in Gabon...There are times when Luc's voice as an uneducated orphan adolescent seems vivid and real, at other times less so. Still, the valor and soul of Luc is captivating. Fascinating and sure to lead to discussion." (School Library Journal)

Schreiber, Joe

Au revoir, crazy European chick. Houghton Mifflin 2011 190p $16.99

Grades: 9 10 11 12

1. Adventure fiction 2. New York (N.Y.) -- Fiction

ISBN 978-0-547-57738-8

LC 2011009845

Perry's parents insist that he take Gobi, their quiet, Lithuanian exchange student, to senior prom but after an incident at the dance he learns that Gobi is actually a trained assassin who needs him as a henchman, behind the wheel of his father's precious Jaguar, on a mission in Manhattan.

"Perfect for action adventure junkies who will enjoy the car chases, thugs, graphic killing scenes, explosions, and a random bear fight, Schreiber's debut novel also contains enough humor, sexual tension, distinctive language, and character development to make this more than just a quick thrill read." Horn Book

★ **Perry's** killer playlist; by Joe Schreiber. Houghton Mifflin 2012 209 p. $16.99

Grades: 9 10 11 12

1. Adventure fiction 2. Europe -- Fiction 3. Assassins -- Fiction 4. Adventure and adventurers -- Fiction

ISBN 0547601174; 9780547601175

LC 2011041392

Sequel to: Au revoir, crazy European chick

This novel, by Joe Schreiber, is the sequel to the young adult adventure "Au Revoir, Crazy European Chick." "The last time [Perry] saw Gobi, five people were assassinated one crazy night in New York City. Well . . . Gobi shows up, and once again Perry is roped into a wild, nonstop thrill ride with a body count. Double crossings, kidnappings, CIA agents, arms dealers, boat chases in Venetian canals, and a shootout in the middle of a Santa Claus convention ensue." (Publisher's note)

Schröder, Monika

My brother's shadow. Farrar Straus Giroux 2011 217p $16.99

Grades: 6 7 8 9 10

1. Germany -- Fiction 2. Journalism -- Fiction 3. Family life -- Fiction 4. Political activists -- Fiction 5. World War, 1914-1918 -- Fiction

ISBN 978-0-374-35122-9; 0-374-35122-8

LC 2010033107

In 1918 Berlin, Germany, sixteen-year-old Moritz struggles to do what is right on his newspaper job, in his relationship with his mother and sister who are outspoken socialists, and with his brother, who returns from the war physically and emotionally scarred.

"In this nuanced and realistic work of historical fiction, Schröder . . . immerses readers in her setting with meticulous details and dynamic characters that contribute to a palpable sense of tension." Publ Wkly

Schroeder, Lisa

Chasing Brooklyn. Simon Pulse 2010 412p $15.99

Grades: 7 8 9 10

1. Novels in verse 2. Dreams -- Fiction 3. Bereavement -- Fiction

ISBN 978-1-4169-9168-7; 1-4169-9168-9

LC 2009-19442

As teenagers Brooklyn and Nico work to help each other recover from the deaths of Brooklyn's boyfriend—Nico's brother Lucca—and their friend Gabe, the two begin to rediscover their passion for life, and a newly blossoming passion for one another.

"Chasing Brooklyn is told in a verse format that enables the author to cut right to the emotional quick. The short sentences and minimal dialogue keep the focus on the pain and fear of the two main characters. . . . While the wrenching impact will leave readers raw, the ultimately hopeful ending is comforting. A quick read, but one with substance." SLJ

Far from you. Simon Pulse 2009 355p $15.99

Grades: 7 8 9 10

1. Novels in verse 2. Snow -- Fiction 3. Stepfamilies -- Fiction

ISBN 978-1-4169-7506-9; 1-4169-7506-3

LC 2008-25268

A novel-in-verse about sixteen-year-old Ali's reluctant road trip with her stepmother and new baby sister, and the terror that ensues after they end up lost in the snow-covered woods.

"Schroeder weaves Alice in Wonderland . . . references throughout the book to echo the topsy-turvy nature of her protagonist's life. It is this roller coaster of emotions to which many teen readers will relate. A quick, yet satisfying, novel in verse." SLJ

Schumacher, Julie

★ **Black** box; a novel. Delacorte Press 2008 168p $15.99; lib bdg $18.99

Grades: 8 9 10 11 12

1. School stories 2. Sisters -- Fiction 3. Family life -- Fiction 4. Depression (Psychology) -- Fiction

ISBN 978-0-385-73542-1; 0-385-73542-1; 978-0-385-90523-7 lib bdg; 0-385-90523-8 lib bdg

LC 2007-45774

When her sixteen-year-old sister is hospitalized for depression and her parents want to keep it a secret, fourteen-year-old Elena tries to cope with her own anxiety and feelings of guilt that she is determined to conceal from outsiders.

"The writing is spare, direct, and honest. Written in the first person, this is a readable, ultimately uplifting book about a difficult subject." SLJ

Schwab, Victoria

The **Near** Witch. Hyperion Books 2011 282p $16.99

Grades: 7 8 9 10

1. Witches -- Fiction 2. Villages -- Fiction 3. Supernatural -- Fiction

ISBN 978-1-4231-3787-0; 1-4231-3787-6

LC 2010036289

Sixteen-year-old Lexi, who lives on an enchanted moor at the edge of the village of Near, must solve the mystery when, the day after a mysterious boy appears in town, children start disappearing.

"Part fairy tale, part legend with a little romance, this well-written mystery will capture the attention of teens." SLJ

Our Dark Duet. By Victoria Schwab. Greenwillow Books 2017 Ii, 510 p. (Monsters of Verity)

Grades: 9 10 11 12

1. Fantasy -- Fiction; 2. Fantasy fiction; 3. Monsters -- Fiction

9780062380883, $17.99; 9780062380906; 0062380885

In this book, by Victoria Schwab, part of the series "This Savage Song," "Kate Harker is a girl who isn't afraid of the dark. She's a girl who hunts monsters. And she's good at it. August Flynn is a monster who can never be human. No matter how much he once yearned for it. He has a part to play. And he will play it, no matter the cost. Nearly six months after Kate and August were first thrown together, the war between the monsters and the humans is a terrifying reality." (Publisher's note)

"Masterly writing, a fast-moving plot, and just the right amount of bittersweet romance make this book hard to put down." SLJ

★ **This** Savage Song. Harpercollins Childrens Books 2016 464 p. (Monsters of Verity)

Grades: 9 10 11 12

1. Fantasy fiction

9780062380876, $16.99; 0062380850; 9780062380852, $17.99

LC 2016005221

In this book, by Victoria Schwab, "a young woman and a young man must choose whether to become heroes or villains—and friends or enemies—with the future of their home at stake. Kate Harker and August Flynn are the heirs to a divided city. All Kate wants is to be as ruthless as her father, who lets the monsters roam free and makes the humans pay for his protection. All August wants is to be human, as good-hearted as his own father, to play a bigger role in protecting the innocent-but he's one of the monsters." (Publisher's note)

"Crackling with energy, just the ticket for an all-night read." Kirkus

Schwartz, Ellen

Cellular; written by Ellen Schwartz. Orca Book Publishers 2010 115p (Orca soundings) pa $9.95
Grades: 7 8 9 10

    1. Leukemia -- Fiction 2. Friendship -- Fiction
    ISBN 978-1-55469-296-5; 1-55469-296-2

When Brendan is diagnosed with leukemia, his life is turned upside down. With smothering family, and distant friends, all seems hopeless until he meets Lark, terminally ill, and yet full of life.

"In this emotional entry in the Orca Soundings series, Lark's sweetness and wisdom spin out on a trajectory that readers just know will not end happily for her, even though Brendan realizes she has touched his life mightily." Booklist

Schwartz, Virginia Frances

Send one angel down. Holiday House 2000 163p $15.95

    1. Cousins -- Fiction 2. Slavery -- Fiction 3. African Americans -- Fiction 4. Racially mixed people -- Fiction
    ISBN 0-8234-1484-1

                              LC 99-52818

Abram, a young slave tries to hide the horrors of slavery from his younger cousin Eliza, a light-skinned slave who is the daughter of the plantation owner

"Schwartz's well-developed characters are full of humanity and personality, and the story vividly acknowledges the sustaining power of music . . . in the lives of the slaves. This is a profoundly moving tale that is ultimately hopeful but never glosses over the horrific treatment of slaves." Booklist

Scieszka, Jon, 1954-

Who done it? an investigation of murder most foul. conducted by Jon Scieszka and you, the reader. Soho Teen, an imprint of Soho Press, Inc. 2013 373 p. (hardcover) $17.99
Grades: 9 10 11 12

    1. Mystery fiction 2. Humorous fiction 3. Authors -- Fiction 4. Humorous stories 5. Authorship -- Fiction
    ISBN 1616951524; 9781616951528

                         LC 2012033468

In this juvenile mystery, by Jon Scieszka, "the most cantankerous book editor alive . . . is Herman Mildew. The anthology opens with an invitation to a party, care of this . . . monster, where more than 80 of the most . . . recognizable names in . . . fiction learn that they are suspects in his murder. All must provide alibis in brief first-person entries. The problem is that all of them are liars, all of them are fabulists, and all have something to hide." (Publisher's note)

Scott, Elizabeth

Between here and forever. Simon Pulse 2011 250p $16.99; ebook $9.99
Grades: 9 10 11 12

    1. Coma -- Fiction 2. Sisters -- Fiction
    ISBN 978-1-4169-9484-8; 978-1-4169-9486-2 ebook

                         LC 2010051366

When her older, "perfect" sister Tess has a car accident that puts her in a coma, seventeen-year-old Abby, who has always felt unseen in Tess's shadow, plans to bring her back with the help of Eli, a gorgeous boy she has met at the hospital, but her plans go awry when she learns some secrets about both Tess and Eli, enabling her to make some decisions about her own life.

"Abby's emotional growth from her experiences, conversations and introspection emerges ever so slowly but will satisfy many teen readers. Leisurely but gratifying." Kirkus

★ **Living** dead girl. Simon Pulse 2008 170p $16.99; pa $8.99
Grades: 9 10 11 12

    1. Kidnapping -- Fiction 2. Child sexual abuse -- Fiction
    ISBN 978-1-4169-6059-1; 1-4169-6059-7; 978-1-4169-6060-7 pa; 1-4169-6060-0 pa

                         LC 2007-943736

A novel about a 15-year-old girl who has spent the last five years being abused by a kidnapper named Ray and is kept powerless by Ray's promise to harm her family if she makes one false move.

"Scott's prose is spare and damning, relying on suggestive details and their impact on Alice to convey the unimaginable violence she repeatedly experiences. Disturbing but fascinating, the book exerts an inescapable grip on readers—like Alice, they have virtually no choice but to continue until the conclusion sets them free." Publ Wkly

Love you hate you miss you. HarperTeen 2009 276p $16.99; lib bdg $17.89; pa $8.99
Grades: 9 10 11 12

    1. School stories 2. Death -- Fiction 3. Guilt -- Fiction 4. Alcoholism -- Fiction 5. Friendship -- Fiction
    ISBN 978-0-06-112283-5; 0-06-112283-1; 978-0-06-112284-2 lib bdg; 0-06-112284-X lib bdg; 978-0-06-112285-9 pa; 0-06-112285-8 pa

                         LC 2008-31420

After coming out of alcohol rehabilitation, sixteen-year-old Amy sorts out conflicting emotions about her best friend Julia's death in a car accident for which she feels responsible.

"The pain, confusion, insights, and hope Amy expresses will speak to teen readers. The issue of binge drinking is handled clearly and bluntly, and without preaching: readers understand why Amy drinks and why she stops." Voice Youth Advocates

Miracle; Elizabeth Scott. Simon Pulse 2012 217 p. (hbk.) $16.99
Grades: 9 10 11 12

    1. Aircraft accidents -- Fiction 2. Interpersonal relations -- Fiction 3. Post-traumatic stress disorder -- Fiction 4.

Survival -- Fiction 5. Family life -- Fiction
ISBN 1442417064; 9781442417069

LC 2011008655

This book's main character, Megan, is the sole survivor of a plane crash, and is hailed as a miracle. "However, when Megan returns to her small, rural hometown, she feels overwhelmed by both the onslaught of well-wishers and the slowly returning memories of the crash and its victims. Megan is most challenged by her parents, who are unable to see beyond her miraculous escape and fail to recognize that she is suffering from post-traumatic stress disorder (PTSD) and seriously needs help." (Kirkus Reviews)

Scott, Michael

★ The **alchemyst**. Delacorte Press 2007 375p
(The secrets of the immortal Nicholas Flammel)
$16.99; lib bdg $19.99
Grades: 7 8 9 10

1. Magic -- Fiction 2. Twins -- Fiction 3. Alchemy -- Fiction 4. Writers on science 5. Siblings -- Fiction
ISBN 978-0-385-73357-1; 0-385-73357-7; 978-0-385-90372-1 lib bdg; 0-385-90372-3 lib bdg

LC 2006-24417

While working at pleasant but mundane summer jobs in San Francisco, fifteen-year-old twins, Sophie and Josh, suddenly find themselves caught up in the deadly, centuries-old struggle between rival alchemists, Nicholas Flamel and John Dee, over the possession of an ancient and powerful book holding the secret formulas for alchemy and everlasting life.

"Scott uses a gigantic canvas for this riveting fantasy. . . . A fabulous read." SLJ

Other titles in this series are:
The magician (2008)
The sorceress (2009)
The necromancer (2010)
The warlock (2011)

The **enchantress**; Michael Scott. Delacorte Press 2012 517 p. $18.99
Grades: 7 8 9 10

1. Atlantis -- Fiction 2. Monsters -- Fiction 3. Time travel -- Fiction 4. Flamel, Nicolas, d. 1418 -- Fiction 5. Magic -- Fiction 6. Twins -- Fiction 7. Alchemists -- Fiction 8. Supernatural -- Fiction 9. Brothers and sisters -- Fiction
ISBN 0385735359; 9780385735353

LC 2012006497

In this book, the final installment of the "Secrets of the Immortal Nicholas Flamel" series, "Nicholas Flamel and his beloved wife, Perenelle, are making a final stand to save San Francisco from an attack of monsters large and small, launched from Alcatraz Island by Quetzalcoatl. Twins Josh (Gold) and Sophie (Silver) are being staged to take power from Aten and become rulers of an overthrown Danu Talis 10,000 years earlier." (Booklist)

"[Scott] fully fleshes out his main characters in their final roles, realistically and sometimes surprisingly melding their lives, their deaths, and their futures. This is a powerful and tidy conclusion to [the] series." Booklist

Scott, Victoria

Violet Grenade. Victoria Scott. Entangled Publishing 2017 366 p.
Grades: 9 10 11 12

1. Brothels -- Fiction; 2. Bullying -- Fiction; 3. Prostitution -- Fiction; 4. Secrecy -- Fiction; 5. Texas -- Fiction; 6. Bullies -- Fiction; 7. Juvenile prostitution -- Fiction; 8. Secrets -- Fiction
9781633756878, $17.99; 9781633756885; 1633756874

In this book, by Victoria Scott, "her name is Domino Ray. But the voice inside her head has a different name. When the mysterious Ms. Karina finds Domino in an alleyway, she offers her a position at her girls' home in secluded West Texas.... It isn't long before she is fighting her way up the ranks to gain the woman's approval...and falling for Cain, the mysterious boy living in the basement. But the home has horrible secrets. So do the girls living there." (Publisher's note)

Seamon, Hollis

★ **Somebody** up there hates you; a novel. by Hollis Seamon. 1st ed. Algonquin 2013 256 p. (hardcover) $16.95
Grades: 9 10 11 12

1. Cancer -- Fiction 2. Parties -- Fiction 3. Terminally ill children -- Fiction 4. Terminally ill -- Fiction 5. Hospices (Terminal care) -- Fiction
ISBN 1616202602; 9781616202606

LC 2013008476

This book follows Richie, a 17-year-old with terminal cancer. "Richie's uncle takes him out for a night of partying; girls start paying attention to him (and not just Sylvie, the 15-year-old across the hall); there are pranks and fistfights; and Richie gets a chance to be a normal teenager—or as normal as possible, given that he's surrounded by nurses, never knows how he'll feel next, and the annoying harpist in the lobby just keeps playing." (Publishers Weekly)

Sedgwick, Marcus

★ The **ghosts** of heaven. Marcus Sedgwick. Roaring Brook Press 2015 336 p.
Grades: 9 10 11 12S C

1. Science fiction 2. Space and time -- Fiction
1626721254; 9781250073679; 9781626721258, $17.99

LC 2014040471

Printz Award Honor Book (2016)

This collection of linked short stories, by Marcus Sedgwick, "range chronologically from the prehistoric past; to rural Britain at the end of the witch hunts in the eighteenth century; to the early twentieth century, at an insane asylum on Long Island; and finally to a spacecraft in deep space and the distant future." (Horn Book)

"What openly draws these stories together is a spiral and spinning symbolism that presents itself through vivid details, from the seemingly mundane to literary references. Individually they conform to conventions; together they defy expectations as they raise questions about humanity and its connections to the universe and one another." Kirkus

First published in the United Kingdom in 2014 by Orion Children's Books, London.

★ **Midwinterblood**. Marcus Sedgwick. Roaring Brook Press 2013 272 p.

Grades: 7 8 9 10 11 12

1. Islands -- Fiction 2. Love -- Fiction 3. Reincarnation -- Fiction 4. Scandinavia -- Fiction 5. Romance fiction

1596438002; 9781596438002, $17.99

LC 2012013302

Printz Award Winner (2014)

Author Marcus Sedgwick presents seven stories about "an archaeologist who unearths a mysterious artifact, an airman who finds himself far from home, a painter, a ghost, a vampire, and a Viking." The stories "take place on the remote Scandinavian island of Blessed where a curiously powerful plant that resembles a dragon grows. . . . What secrets lurk beneath the surface of this idyllic countryside? And what might be powerful enough to break the cycle of midwinterblood?" (Publisher's note)

My swordhand is singing. Wendy Lamb Books 2007 205p hardcover o.p. pa $6.99

Grades: 7 8 9 10

1. Horror fiction 2. Gypsies -- Fiction 3. Vampires -- Fiction 4. Supernatural -- Fiction

ISBN 978-0-375-84689-2; 978-0-375-84690-8 pa

LC 2007-07051

In the dangerous dark of winter in an Eastern European village during the early seventeenth century, Peter learns from a gypsy girl that the Shadow Queen is behind the recent murders and reanimations, and his father's secret past may hold the key to stopping her.

"Sedgwick writes a compellingly fresh vampire story, combining elements from ancient myths and legends to create a believable and frightening tale." Voice Youth Advocates

★ **Revolver**. Roaring Brook Press 2010 204p $16.99

Grades: 7 8 9 10

1. Death -- Fiction 2. Siblings -- Fiction 3. Arctic regions -- Fiction 4. Alaska -- Gold discoveries -- Fiction

ISBN 978-1-59643-592-6; 1-59643-592-5

First published 2009 in the United Kingdom

A Michael L. Printz honor book, 2011

In an isolated cabin, fourteen-year-old Sig is alone with a corpse: his father, who has fallen through the ice and frozen to death only hours earlier. Then comes a stranger claiming that Sig's father owes him a share of a horde of stolen gold. Sig's only protection is a loaded Colt revolver hidden in the cabin's storeroom.

"Tight plotting and a wealth of moral concerns—good versus evil; faith, love, and hope; the presence of God; survival in a bleak landscape; trusting the lessons parents teach—make this a memorable tale." Horn Book

★ **Saint** death. Marcus Sedgwick. Roaring Brook Press 2017 227 p.

Grades: 9 10 11 12

1. Drug traffic -- Fiction; 2. Human trafficking -- Fiction; 3. Mexican-American Border Region -- Fiction; 4. Smuggling -- Fiction; 5. Mexico -- Fiction; 6. Organized crime -- Mexico -- Fiction

9781626725492, $17.99; 9781626725508

LC 2016035286

This novel, by Marcus Sedgwick, is "set in the grimly violent world of the human and drug trade on the US-Mexican border. On the outskirts of Juarez, Arturo scrapes together a living working odd jobs and staying out of sight. But his friend Faustino is in trouble: he's stolen money from the narcos to smuggle his girlfriend and her baby into the US, and needs Arturo's help to get it back." (Publisher's note)

"This well-researched novel is an absorbing, heart-rending read and a scathing indictment of the conditions that have allowed the drug trade and human trafficking to flourish in Mexico." SLJ

"First published in the United Kingdom in 2016 by Orion Children's Books, London " -- Title page verso.

★ **She** is not invisible; Marcus Sedgwick. Roaring Brook Press 2014 224 p. (hardback) $16.99

Grades: 7 8 9 10 11 12

1. Mystery fiction 2. Missing persons 3. Brothers and sisters 4. Blind -- Fiction 5. Fathers -- Fiction 6. Missing persons -- Fiction 7. Mystery and detective stories 8. Brothers and sisters -- Fiction 9. People with disabilities -- Fiction

ISBN 1596438010; 9781596438019

LC 2013029561

"Laureth is sixteen, smart, self-doubting, and blind. She is also desperate to find her missing famous writer father -- desperate enough to boost her mother's credit card to buy two plane tickets from London to New York City, forge travel documents, and "abduct" her beloved seven-year-old brother in order to disguise her blindness... Laureth herself is worth the journey. The tricks she uses to negotiate in a sighted world.. her determination to fight the tendency of sighted people to treat blind people as stupid or deaf or, most insidiously, invisible -- all are presented matter-of-factly and sympathetically. Readers will applaud Laureth's believable evolution into a more confident -- and definitely more visible -- young woman." (Horn Book)

★ **White** crow. Roaring Brook Press 2011 234p $15.99

Grades: 8 9 10 11 12

1. Horror fiction 2. Villages -- Fiction 3. Friendship -- Fiction 4. Good and evil -- Fiction 5. Great Britain -- Fiction

ISBN 978-1-59643-594-0; 1-59643-594-1

LC 2010034053

Sixteen-year-old Rebecca moves with her father from London to a small, seaside village, where she befriends another motherless girl and they spend the summer together exploring the village's sinister history.

"Showing his customary skill with a gothic setting and morally troubled characters, Sedgwick keeps readers guessing to the very end." Publ Wkly

Selfors, Suzanne

Mad love. Walker Books for Young Readers 2011 323p $16.99

Grades: 7 8 9 10

1. Love stories 2. Authorship -- Fiction 3. Eros (Greek

deity) -- Fiction 4. Manic-depressive illness -- Fiction 5. Mother-daughter relationship -- Fiction
ISBN 978-0-8027-8450-6; 0-8027-8450-X

LC 2010-23261

When her famous romance-novelist mother is secretly hospitalized in an expensive mental facility, sixteen-year-old Alice tries to fulfill her mother's contract with her publisher by writing a love story—with the help of Cupid.

"There's a bit of mythology, a bit of romance, a bit of the paranormal, and some real-life problems, but Selfors juggles them all assuredly. Serious ideas are handled carefully, while real humor is spread throughout the whole book. This book has real charm with great depth." Voice Youth Advocates

The **sweetest** spell; Suzanne Selfors. Walker & Co. 2012 404 p. (hardback) $16.99
Grades: 7 8 9 10 11 12
   1. Love stories 2. Fantasy fiction 3. People with physical disabilities -- Fiction 4. Fantasy 5. Magic -- Fiction 6. Chocolate -- Fiction 7. Prejudices -- Fiction 8. People with disabilities -- Fiction
ISBN 0802723764; 9780802723765

LC 2011034591

This book follows "Emmeline . . . an outcast among her people, the Kell. When the king enslaves the men and her village is destroyed in a flood, Emmeline is taken in by Owen Oak and his family. She discovers that she can churn butter into chocolate -- a food that's been lost for years in the land of Anglund. Romance blossoms, but the two are separated when the girl is kidnapped for her magical abilities." (School Library Journal)

"Selfors's story line initially comes across as chaotic, but the pacing is strong, and the elements of her tale fall into place in a logical and entirely satisfying manner. An exhilarating, romantic, and frequently funny story of self-discovery." Pub Wkly

Selzer, Adam
How to get suspended and influence people; a novel. Delacorte Press 2007 183p $15.99; lib bdg $18.99
Grades: 6 7 8 9
   1. School stories 2. Censorship -- Fiction 3. Motion pictures -- Fiction
ISBN 978-0-385-73369-4; 978-0-385-90384-4 lib bdg

LC 2006-20438

Gifted eighth-grader Leon Harris becomes an instant celebrity when the film he makes for a class project sends him to in-school suspension.

"This funny, fast-paced novel is filled with characters who epitomize the middle school experience, and it presents a lesson or two about free speech as well." SLJ

Another title about Leon is:
Pirates of the retail wasteland (2008)

Sepetys, Ruta
   ★ **Between** shades of gray; Ruta Sepetys. Philomel Books 2011 344p map $17.99
Grades: 8 9 10 11 12
   1. Lithuania -- Fiction 2. Soviet Union -- Fiction
ISBN 978-0-399-25412-3; 0-399-25412-9

LC 2009-50092

In this novel by Ruta Sepetys, "Fifteen-year-old Lina is a Lithuanian girl living an ordinary life--until Soviet officers invade her home and tear her family apart. Separated from her father and forced onto a crowded train, Lina, her mother, and her young brother make their way to a Siberian work camp, where they are forced to fight for their lives." (Publisher's note)

"A harrowing page-turner, made all the more so for its basis in historical fact, the novel illuminates the persecution suffered by Stalin's victims (20 million were killed), while presenting memorable characters who retain their will to survive even after more than a decade in exile." Publ Wkly

   ★ **Out** of the Easy; Ruta Sepetys. Philomel Books 2013 352 p. $17.99
Grades: 9 10 11 12
   1. Mystery fiction 2. Historical fiction 3. Prostitution -- Fiction 4. New Orleans (La.) -- Fiction 5. Murder -- Fiction 6. Conduct of life -- Fiction 7. Mothers and daughters -- Fiction 8. New Orleans (La.) -- History -- 20th century -- Fiction
ISBN 039925692X; 9780399256929

LC 2012016062

This book, by Ruta Sepetys, is set in "1950 [in] . . . the French Quarter of New Orleans. . . . Known among locals as the daughter of a brothel prostitute, Josie Moraine wants more out of life than the Big Easy has to offer. She devises a plan get out, but a mysterious death in the Quarter leaves Josie tangled in an investigation that will challenge her allegiance to her mother, her conscience, and Willie Woodley, the brusque madam on Conti Street." (Publisher's note)

   ★ **Salt** to the sea: a novel. Ruta Sepetys. Philomel Books 2016 400 p. Map
Grades: 8 9 10 11 12
   1. Refugees -- Fiction 2. World War, 1939-1945 -- Fiction 3. Prussia -- Fiction
0399160302; 9780399160301, $18.99

LC 2015009057

In this novel, by Ruta Sepetys, "World War II is drawing to a close in East Prussia and thousands of refugees are on a desperate trek toward freedom, many with something to hide. Among them are Joana, Emilia, and Florian, whose paths converge en route to the ship that promises salvation, the Wilhelm Gustloff. Forced by circumstance to unite, the three find their strength, courage, and trust in each other tested with each step closer to safety." (Publisher's note)

Sepetys "describes an almost unknown maritime disaster whose nearly 9,000 casualties dwarfed those of both the Titanic and the Lusitania. Told alternately from the perspective of each of the main characters, the novel also highlights the struggle and sacrifices that ordinary people—children—were forced to make. At once beautiful and heart-wrenching, this title will remind readers that there are far more casualties of war than are recorded in history books." LJ

Shabazz, Ilyasah
   ★ **X**: a novel. Ilyasah Shabazz, Kekla Magoon. Candlewick Press 2015 384 p.
Grades: 8 9 10 11 12
   1. Black muslims -- Fiction 2. Poor -- Fiction 3. Racism -- Fiction 4. X, Malcolm, 1925-1965 -- Childhood and

youth -- Fiction 5. African Americans -- Biography
0763669679; 9780763669676, $16.99

LC 2014931838

Coretta Scott King Author Award, Honor Book (2016);
NAACP Image Award: Outstanding Literary Work- Youth/
Teens (2016)

This novel, by Ilyasah Shabazz and Kekla Magoon,
"follows the formative years of [Malcolm X]. . . . Malcolm
Little's parents have always told him that he can achieve
anything, but from what he can tell, that's a pack of lies—after all, his father's been murdered, his mother's been taken
away, and his dreams of becoming a lawyer have gotten him
laughed out of school." (Publisher's note)

"Malcolm X was born Malcolm Little. The story opens
with his departure from Michigan as a teen, though there are
flashbacks to his younger years. It follows Malcolm through
his time in Boston and Harlem, culminating with his conversion to Islam and his decision to change his name while
in prison in 1948. . . . The author's honesty about his early
troubles serves to convey that it is possible to rise through
adversity to make a positive difference in this world." SLJ

Shan, Darren

The **thin** executioner. Little, Brown 2010 483p
map $17.99

Grades: 10 11 12

    1. Slavery -- Fiction 2. Conduct of life -- Fiction 3.
Capital punishment -- Fiction 4. Voyages and travels
-- Fiction

ISBN 978-0-316-07865-8; 0-316-07865-4

LC 2009-45606

In a nation of warriors where weakness is shunned and
all crimes, no matter how minor, are punishable by beheading, young Jebel Rum, along with a slave who is fated to be
sacrificed, sets forth on a quest to petition the Fire God for
invincibility, but when the long and arduous journey is over,
Jebel has learned much about fairness and the value of life.

"Readers will hate the villains, feel sorry for the innocent, and root for Tel Hesani and Jebel to complete their
mission. This is a must-read for thrill seekers with a strong
stomach looking for an action-packed adventure with a host
of fantastical creatures." Voice Youth Advocates

Sharenow, Rob

The **Berlin** Boxing Club. HarperTeen 2011
404p il $17.99

Grades: 7 8 9 10

    1. Boxers (Persons) 2. Boxing -- Fiction 3. Family
life -- Fiction 4. Jews -- Germany -- Fiction 5. Berlin
(Germany) -- Fiction 6. National socialism -- Fiction 7.
Holocaust, 1933-1945 -- Fiction 8. Germany -- History
-- 1933-1945 -- Fiction

ISBN 978-0-06-157968-4; 0-06-157968-8

LC 2010024446

In 1936 Berlin, fourteen-year-old Karl Stern, considered
Jewish despite a non-religious upbringing, learns to box
from the legendary Max Schmeling while struggling with
the realities of the Holocaust.

"Readers will be drawn by the sports detail and by the
close-up narrative of the daily oppression." Booklist

Sharpe, Tess

Far from you. Tess Sharpe. Hyperion Books 2014
352 p.

Grades: 9 10 11 12

    1. Best friends -- Fiction 2. Drug abuse -- Fiction 3.
Friendship -- Fiction 4. Murder -- Fiction 5. Mystery
and detective stories 6. Bisexual people -- Fiction

1423184629; 9781423184621, $17.99

LC 2013037960

In this young adult novel by Tess Sharpe, "Sophie Winters nearly died. Twice. The first time, she's fourteen, and
escapes a near-fatal car accident with . . . an addiction to Oxy
that'll take years to kick. The second time, she's seventeen,
and . . . Sophie and her best friend Mina are confronted by
a masked man in the woods. Sophie survives, but Mina is
not so lucky. . . . No one is looking in the right places and
Sophie must search for Mina's murderer on her own." (Publisher's note)

"Sophie was there when her best friend, Mina, was murdered, but she doesn't know by whom, or why. So Sophie
launches her own investigation, knowing that Mina's death
isn't related to Sophie's painkiller addiction, as everyone
else seems to think. This tense, tragic page-turner has plenty
of chills, but just as compelling is the depth of Sophie's
physical and emotional pain." Horn Book

Shaw, Susan

Safe. Dutton Books 2007 168p $16.99

Grades: 7 8 9 10

    1. Rape -- Fiction 2. Mothers -- Fiction

ISBN 978-0-525-47829-4; 0-525-47829-9

LC 2006-36428

When thirteen-year-old Tracy, whose mother died when
she was three years old, is raped and beaten on the last day
of school, all her feelings of security disappear and she does
not know how to cope with the fear and dread that engulf her.

This is an "extraordinarily tender novel. . . . Intimate,
first-person narrative honestly expresses Tracy's full range
of emotions." Publ Wkly

Tunnel vision. Margaret K. McElderry Books
2011 272p $16.99

Grades: 7 8 9 10

    1. Crime -- Fiction 2. Homicide -- Fiction 3. Witnesses
-- Fiction 4. Organized crime -- Fiction

ISBN 978-1-4424-0839-5; 1-4424-0839-1

LC 2010036306

After witnessing her mother's murder, sixteen-year-old
high school student Liza Wellington and her father go into
the witness protection program.

"The author creates a completely believable character in
Liza, who often reverts to childlike emotions only to learn
the hard way that cold reality takes precedence over even
dearly held wishes. Kudos for the unexpected double ending,
both illusory and realistic, giving readers a choice." Kirkus

Sheinmel, Courtney

Positively. Simon & Schuster Books for Young
Readers 2009 216p $15.99

Grades: 6 7 8 9 10

    1. Camps -- Fiction 2. Death -- Fiction 3. Friendship
-- Fiction 4. Bereavement -- Fiction 5. Stepfamilies

-- Fiction 6. AIDS (Disease) -- Fiction
ISBN 978-1-4169-7169-6; 1-4169-7169-6

LC 2008-35447

Thirteen-year-old Emmy, grieving over her mother who died of AIDS, resentful of having to live with her father and pregnant stepmother, and despairing about her future, finds hope at a summer camp for HIV-positive girls like herself. Includes facts about Elizabeth Glaser, one of the founders of the Pediatric AIDS Foundation.

"This valuable story discusses uncertainty, very human fears, and most important, hope. . . . It is a terrific introduction to a complex and important topic." Voice Youth Advocates

Shepard, Sara

The **amateurs**. Sara Shepard. Freeform Books 2016 307 p.

Grades: 9 10 11 12

1. Love -- Fiction 2. Murder -- Fiction 3. Mystery and detective stories 4. Mystery fiction
9781484747353, $17.99; 1484742273; 9781484742273, $17.99

LC 2015044197

In this book, by Sara Shepard, "as soon as Seneca Frazier sees the post on the Case Not Closed website about Helena Kelly, she's hooked. Helena's high-profile disappearance five years earlier is the one that originally got Seneca addicted to true crime. It's the reason she's a member of the site in the first place. So when Maddy Wright, her best friend from the CNC site, invites Seneca to spend spring break in Connecticut looking into the cold case, she immediately packs her bag." (Publisher's note)

"A twisty and ultimately satisfying romantic whodunit." Kirkus

The **lying** game. HarperTeen 2010 307p $16.99

Grades: 9 10 11 12

1. Mystery fiction 2. Dead -- Fiction 3. Twins -- Fiction 4. Sisters -- Fiction 5. Homicide -- Fiction
ISBN 978-0-06-186970-9; 0-06-186970-8

LC 2010-40332

Seventeen-year-old Emma Paxton steps into the life of her long-lost twin Sutton to solve her murder, while Sutton looks on from her afterlife.

"Shepard keeps the action rolling and the clues confusing as she spends this installment uncovering the twins' characters but not solving the murder yet. Naturally, boys and fashion also figure into the story, fleshing out a distinctive scenario that should appeal to many teen girls." Kirkus

Shepherd, Megan

Her Dark Curiosity. Harpercollins Childrens Books 2014 432 p. $17.99

Grades: 9 10 11 12

1. Murder -- Fiction 2. Father-daughter relationship -- Fiction
ISBN 0062128051; 9780062128058

This sequel to The madman's daughter "continues with Juliet's return to London after her escape from her father's island. Life is somewhat easier for Juliet now that she is back—a former colleague of her father's has taken her under his wing so that she does not want for anything, she has a job developing grafted rose bushes, and her friend Lucy has welcomed her with open arms. But not all is well...While the novel can be read independently of the first title, as enough of the backstory is given to make what is happening clear, readers will have a more satisfying experience if familiar with the previous installment. The psychological questions that Prince/Jekyll raises as to evil, desire, and nature vs. nurture add a depth of richness not often seen in young adult literature." (School Library Journal)

The **madman's** daughter; Megan Shepherd. Balzer + Bray 2013 432 p. (trade bdg.) $17.99

Grades: 9 10 11 12

1. Mental illness -- Fiction 2. Science -- Experiments -- Fiction 3. Father-daughter relationship -- Fiction 4. Science fiction 5. Fathers and daughters -- Fiction 6. Characters in literature -- Fiction
ISBN 0062128027; 9780062128027

LC 2012004281

This book by Megan Shepherd follows the events of "H.G. Wells' 'The Island of Doctor Moreau,' as seen through the eyes of the doctor's daughter. . . . When she learns that her father inhabits an island far, far away, where he performs horrific experiments on animals via vivisection, Juliet makes her way there along with Montgomery, her father's assistant, and Edward Prince, a castaway they meet along the way." (Kirkus Reviews)

Other titles in this series are:
Her dark curiosity (2014)
A cold legacy (2015)

Sherman, Delia

★ The **freedom** maze. Big Mouth House 2011 267p $16.95

Grades: 7 8 9 10

1. Slavery -- Fiction 2. Time travel -- Fiction 3. Race relations -- Fiction 4. Plantation life -- Fiction
ISBN 978-1-931520-30-0; 1-931520-30-5

"It's 1960, but on the decayed Fairchild sugar plantation in rural Louisiana, vestiges of a grimmer past remain—the old cottage, overgrown garden maze, relations between white and black races. Stuck for the summer in the family ancestral home under the thumb of her cranky, imperious grandmother, Sophie, 13, makes a reckless wish that lands her in 1860, enslaved-by her own ancestors. . . . Plantation life for whites and blacks unfolds in compelling, often excruciating detail. . . . Multilayered, compassionate and thought-provoking." Kirkus

Sheth, Kashmira

Keeping corner. Hyperion 2007 281p hardcover o.p. pa $5.99

Grades: 7 8 9 10 11 12

1. Gandhi, Mahatma, 1869-1948 -- Fiction; 2. India -- Fiction; 3. Political leaders; 4. Widows -- Fiction; 5. Women's rights -- Fiction
ISBN 978-0-7868-3859-2; 0-7868-3859-0; 978-0-7868-3860-8 pa; 0-7868-3860-4 pa

LC 2007-15314

In India in the 1940s, twelve-year-old Leela's happy, spoiled childhood ends when her husband since age nine, whom she barely knows, dies, leaving her a widow whose only hope of happiness could come from Mahatma Ghandi's social and political reforms.

Sheth "sets up a thrilling premise in which politics become achingly personal." Booklist

Shinn, Sharon

Gateway. Viking 2009 280p $17.99

Grades: 6 7 8 9 10

1. Space and time -- Fiction 2. Chinese Americans -- Fiction

ISBN 978-0-670-01178-0; 0-670-01178-9

LC 2009-14002

While passing through the Arch in St. Louis, Missouri, a Chinese American teenager is transported to a parallel world where she is given a dangerous assignment.

The author's "fantasy finds the right balance between adventure and romance, while illuminating how seductive evil can be and that sometimes the best weapon one can possess is a skeptical mind." Publ Wkly

Shirvington, Jessica

Embrace. Sourcebooks, Inc. 2012 397p

Grades: 10 11 12

1. Fantasy fiction 2. Angels -- Fiction 3. Teenagers -- Fiction

ISBN 9781402271250; 9781402268403

This book follows "seventeen-year-old Violet Eden, [whose] mother died in childbirth, leaving her to be raised by her detached, workaholic father. If it weren't for her best friend Steph and her trainer (and secret love) Lincoln, Violet would be very much alone. But on her 17th birthday, everything changes. Though finally being kissed by Lincoln is a dream come true, Violet learns that their romantic involvement is forbidden because he and Violet are both Grigori--half angel and half human. They're destined to be eternal partners in the battle against exiled angels on Earth, and romance would make things far too complicated. Furious with Lincoln for keeping this secret, Violet pushes him away, making room for the dark and seductive Phoenix to take hold of her heart." (Kirkus)

Other titles in this series are:
Enticed
Emblaze
Endless
Empower

Showalter, Gena

Intertwined. Harlequin Teen 2009 440p $15.99

Grades: 7 8 9 10

1. Vampires -- Fiction 2. Werewolves -- Fiction 3. Supernatural -- Fiction

ISBN 978-0-373-21002-2; 0-373-21002-7

"Most sixteen-year-olds have friends. Aden Stone has four human souls living inside him: one can time travel, one can raise the dead, one can tell the future, and one can possess another human, and then he meets a girl who quiets the voices." Publisher's note

"This fast-paced, action-driven plot has many unexpected twists and turns. Well written, with a unique story line and strong characters." SLJ

Other titles in this series are:
Unraveled (2010)
Twisted (2011)

Shreve, Susan

The lovely shoes; [by] Susan Shreve. Arthur A. Levine Books 2011 252p $16.99

Grades: 6 7 8 9

1. Shoemakers -- Fiction 2. School stories 3. Birth defects -- Fiction 4. Mother-daughter relationship -- Fiction

ISBN 978-0-439-68049-3; 0-439-68049-2

LC 2010027937

In 1950s Ohio, ninth-grader Franny feels isolated and self-conscious at high school because of her deformed leg and feet, but her irrepressibly high-spirited mother is determined to find shoes for Franny to wear at the school dances.

"Celebrating the rewards of determination and a positive attitude, this atmospheric novel credibly depicts Franny's internal growth and changing attitude. The contrast between smalltown Ohio and splendorous Florence provides an intriguing framework for the book's classic themes." Publ Wkly

Shukert, Rachel, 1980-

Love me; Rachel Shukert. Delacorte Press. 2014 325p $17.99

Grades: 9 10 11 12

1. Actors and actresses -- Fiction 2. Fame -- Fiction 3. Hollywood (Los Angeles, Calif.) -- History -- 20th century -- Fiction 4. Actresses -- Fiction

ISBN: 0385741103; 9780375989858; 9780385741101

LC 2012047071

"Actresses Margo, Gabby, and Amanda return for another soap about making it big--and staying big--in late-1930s Tinseltown. Much of the focus is on each girl's heartache at the hands of the domineering men in their lives, both lovers and movie-studio bigwigs. This sequel to Starstruck is rife with far-fetched coincidences and melodrama, but it's all deliciously entertaining." Horn Book

Starstruck; by Rachel Shukert. Delacorte Press 2013 352 p. (ebook) $53.97; (library) $20.99; (hardcover) $17.99; (paperback) $9.99

Grades: 9 10 11 12

1. Fame -- Fiction 2. Actresses -- Fiction 3. Actors and actresses -- Fiction 4. Hollywood (Los Angeles, Calif.) -- History -- 20th century -- Fiction

ISBN 0375989846; 9780375984259; 9780375989841; 9780385741088; 9780385741095

LC 2012015771

This novel, by Rachel Shukert, follows a girl trying to become a star. When "Margaret . . . [is] discovered by a powerful agent, she can barely believe her luck. She's more than ready to escape her snobby private school and conservative Pasadena family for a chance to light up the silver screen. . . . Set in Old Hollywood, [the story] follows the lives of three teen girls as they live, love, and claw their way to the top in a world where being a star is all that matters." (Publisher's note)

Shulman, Mark

Scrawl. Roaring Brook Press 2010 234p $16.99

Grades: 6 7 8 9 10

1. School stories 2. Bullies -- Fiction 3. Diaries -- Fiction 4. Poverty -- Fiction 5. Self-perception --

Fiction

ISBN 978-1-59643-417-2; 1-59643-417-1

LC 2010-10521

When eighth-grade school bully Tod and his friends get caught committing a crime on school property, his penalty—staying after school and writing in a journal under the eye of the school guidance counsellor—reveals aspects of himself that he prefers to keep hidden.

"Blackmail, cliques, and a sense of hopelessness from both students and teachers sets up an unexpected ending that will leave readers with a new appreciation for how difficult high school can be. With the potential to occupy the rarified air of titles like S.E. Hinton's The Outsiders and Chris Crutcher's Staying Fat for Sarah Byrnes . . ., Scrawl paints the stereotypical school bully in a different, poignant light." Voice Youth Advocates

Shulman, Polly

Enthusiasm. G. P. Putnam's Sons 2006 198p hardcover o.p. pa $7.99

Grades: 7 8 9 10

1. School stories

ISBN 0-399-24389-5; 0-14-240935-9 pa

LC 2005-13490

Julie and Ashleigh, high school sophomores and Jane Austen fans, seem to fall for the same Mr. Darcy-like boy and struggle to hide their true feelings from one another while rehearsing for a school musical.

"While familiarity with Austen's world through her books or, more likely, the movie renditions will deepen readers' appreciation for Shulman's impressive . . . novel, it is by no means a prerequisite to enjoying this involving and often amusing narrative of friendship, courtship, and (of course) true love." Booklist

Shusterman, Neal, 1962-

★ **Antsy** does time. Dutton Children's Books 2008 247p $16.99

Grades: 7 8 9 10

1. School stories 2. Death -- Fiction

ISBN 978-0-525-47825-6; 0-525-47825-6

LC 2008-00459

Fourteen-year-old Anthony "Antsy" Bonano learns about life, death, and a lot more when he tries to help a friend with a terminal illness feel hopeful about the future.

"Featuring a terrific supporting cast led by Antsy's wise, acerbic mother, an expert blend of comedy and near tragedy, and the wry observations of a narrator . . . this will keep tween readers hooked from start to finish." Booklist

Bruiser. HarperTeen 2010 328p $16.99; lib bdg $17.89

Grades: 8 9 10 11 12

1. Twins -- Fiction 2. Siblings -- Fiction 3. Child abuse -- Fiction 4. Supernatural -- Fiction

ISBN 978-0-06-113408-1; 0-06-113408-2; 978-0-06-113409-8 lib bdg; 0-06-113409-0 lib bdg

LC 2009-30930

Inexplicable events start to occur when sixteen-year-old twins Tennyson and Bronte befriend a troubled and misunderstood outcast, aptly nicknamed Bruiser, and his little brother, Cody.

"Narrated in turns by Tennyson, Bronte, Bruiser, and Bruiser's little brother, Cody, the story is a fascinating study in the art of self-deception and the way our best intentions for others are often based in the selfish desires of our deepest selves. . . . This eloquent and thoughtful story will most certainly leave its mark." Bull Cent Child Books

★ **Challenger** deep. Neal Shusterman. Harper-Collins 2015 320 p. Illustration

Grades: 9 10 11 12

1. Schizophrenia -- Fiction

0061134112; 9780061134111, $17.99

LC 2014009664

Boston Globe-Horn Book Honor: Fiction (2015);
National Book Award: Young People's Literature (2015)

In this novel about a schizophrenic teenager by Neal Shusterman, illustrated by Brendan Shusterman, "Caden Bosch is a brilliant high school student whose friends are starting to notice his odd behavior. . . . Caden Bosch pretends to join the school track team but spends his days walking for miles, absorbed by the thoughts in his head." (Publisher's note)

"This novel is a challenge to the reader from its first lines: author Shusterman takes us into the seemingly random, rambling, and surreal fantasies of fifteen-year-old Caden Bosch (yes, it makes sense to associate him with artist Hieronymus) as mental illness increasingly governs his consciousness. . . . Clearly written with love, the novel is moving; but it's also funny, with dry, insightful humor. Illustrations by the author's son Brendan, drawn during his own time in the depths of mental illness, haunt the story with scrambling, rambling lines, tremulousness, and intensity." Horn Book

Downsiders. Simon & Schuster Bks. for Young Readers 1999 246p hardcover o.p. pa $8.99

Grades: 9 10 11 12

1. Subways -- Fiction 2. New York (N.Y.) -- Fiction

ISBN 0-689-80375-3; 1-4169-9747-4 pa

LC 98-38555

When fourteen-year-old Lindsay meets Talon and discovers the Downsiders world which had evolved from the subway built in New York in 1867 by Alfred Ely Beach, she and her new friend experience the clash of their two cultures.

"Shusterman has invented an alternate world in the Downside that is both original and humorous." Voice Youth Advocates

Dry. Neal Shusterman and Jarrod Shusterman. Simon & Schuster Books for Young Readers 2018 400 p.

Grades: 7 8 9 10 11 12

1. Brothers and sisters -- Fiction; 2. Conduct of life -- Fiction; 3. Droughts -- Fiction; 4. Survival -- Fiction; 5. California -- Fiction; 6. Siblings -- Fiction

9781481481960, $18.99; 9781481481977

LC 2018008928

In this book, by Neal Shusterman and Jarrod Shusterman, "the drought -- or the Tap-Out... -- has been going on for a while now.... Until the taps run dry. Suddenly, Alyssa's quiet suburban street spirals into a warzone of desperation; neighbors and families turned against each other on the hunt for water. And when her parents don't return and her life

-- and the life of her brother -- is threatened, Alyssa has to make impossible choices if she's going to survive." (Publisher's note)

★ **Everlost**. Simon & Schuster Books for Young Readers 2006 313p (The Skinjacker trilogy) $16.95; pa $8.99

Grades: 8 9 10 11 12
    1. Death -- Fiction 2. Future life -- Fiction 3. Traffic accidents -- Fiction
    ISBN 978-0-689-87237-2; 0-689-87237-2; 978-1-4169-9749-8 pa; 1-4169-9749-0 pa
                                            LC 2005-32244

When Nick and Allie are killed in a car crash, they end up in Everlost, or limbo for lost souls, where although Nick is satisfied, Allie will stop at nothing—even skinjacking—to break free.

"Shusterman has reimagined what happens after death and questions power and the meaning of charity. While all this is going on, he has also managed to write a rip-roaring adventure complete with monsters, blimps, and high-diving horses." SLJ

Other titles in this series are:
Everfound (2011)
Everwild (2009)

Full tilt; a novel. Simon & Schuster Bks. for Young Readers 2003 201p $16.95; pa $8.99

Grades: 7 8 9 10
    1. Horror fiction 2. Brothers -- Fiction 3. Amusement parks -- Fiction
    ISBN 0-689-80374-5; 1-4169-9748-2 pa
                                            LC 2002-13867

When sixteen-year-old Blake goes to a mysterious, by-invitation-only carnival he somehow knows that it could save his comatose brother, but soon learns that much more is at stake if he fails to meet the challenge presented there by the beautiful Cassandra.

"Shusterman has created a surreal, scary fantasy, packed with suspenseful psychological drama." Booklist

The **Schwa** was here; [by] Neal Shusterman. 1st ed; Dutton Children's Books 2004 228p $15.99

Grades: 7 8 9 10
    1. Friendship -- Fiction
    ISBN 0-525-47182-0
                                            LC 2004-45072

A Brooklyn eighth-grader nicknamed Antsy befriends the Schwa, an "invisible-ish" boy who is tired of blending into his surroundings and going unnoticed by nearly everyone.

"Antsy is one funny narrator. . . . Shusterman has created yet another very readable and refreshingly different story." Voice Youth Advocates

★ **Scythe**. Neal Shusterman. Simon & Schuster Books for Young Readers 2016 448 p.

Grades: 8 9 10 11 12
    1. Death -- Fiction 2. Murder -- Fiction 3. Science fiction
    1442472421; 144247243X; 9781442472426, $18.99; 9781442472433
                                            LC 2016006502

Printz Honor Book (2017)

This book, by Neal Shusterman, takes place in "a world with no hunger, no disease, no war, no misery: humanity has conquered all those things, and has even conquered death. Now Scythes are the only ones who can end life—and they are commanded to do so, in order to keep the size of the population under control. Citra and Rowan are chosen to apprentice to a scythe—a role that neither wants." (Publisher's note)

"Elegant and elegiac, brooding but imbued with gallows humor, Shusterman's dark tale thrusts realistic, likable teens into a surreal situation and raises deep philosophic questions." Kirkus

★ **Thunderhead**. Neal Shusterman. Simon & Schuster Books for Young Readers 2018 512 p.

Grades: 8 9 10 11 12
    1. Death -- Fiction; 2. Murder -- Fiction; 3. Science fiction
    9781442472457, $18.99; 9781442472464
                                            LC 2017040210

In this book in the Arc of a Scythe series, by Neal Shusterman, "a year has passed since Rowan had gone off grid. Since then, he has become an urban legend.... As Scythe Anastasia, Citra gleans with compassion and openly challenges the ideals of the 'new order.' But when her life is threatened and her methods questioned, it becomes clear that not everyone is open to the change. Will the Thunderhead intervene? Or will it simply watch as this perfect world begins to unravel?" (Publisher's note)

UnDivided. Neal Shusterman. Simon & Schuster Books for Young Readers 2014 384 p. (Unwind dystology)

Grades: 6 7 8 9 10 11 12
    1. Fugitives from justice -- Fiction 2. Revolutionaries -- Fiction 3. Science fiction
    1481409751; 9781481409759, $18.99
                                            LC 2014003060

In this novel, by Neal Shusterman, "Proactive Citizenry, the company that created Cam from the parts of unwound teens, has a plan: to mass produce rewound teens like Cam for military purposes. And . . . Proactive Citizenry has been suppressing technology that could make unwinding completely unnecessary. As Conner, Risa, and Lev uncover these startling secrets, enraged teens begin to march on Washington to demand justice and a better future." (Publisher's note)

UnSouled; Neal Shusterman. Simon & Schuster Books for Young Readers 2013 416 p. (Unwind trilogy) (hardback) $17.99

Grades: 6 7 8 9 10 11 12
    1. Science fiction 2. Traffic accidents 3. Travel -- Fiction 4. Identity -- Fiction 5. Survival -- Fiction 6. Revolutionaries -- Fiction 7. Fugitives from justice -- Fiction
    ISBN 1442423692; 9781442423695
                                            LC 2013022703

In this book, the third in author Neal Shusterman's UnWholly series, "Lev and Connor are on the road again. Their destination is back to Ohio where Sonia, an antiques dealer with an important past, will help them end Unwinding once and for all. After a bizarre car accident . . . they wind up on a Native American reservation. Here, readers learn a lot more about Lev's past, and Connor meets up with Cam, the one and only Rewind." (School Library Journal)

"In the third of his projected four-volume Unwind 'dystology' Shusterman brings most of his central cast of teenage fugitives together and introduces an important new character, who is exempt from being unwound (legally disassembled for body parts) because she has a mild spectrum disorder. Frequent references to events in previous episodes slow the pace somewhat but the present-tense tale remains suspenseful, the overall premise is as hauntingly plausible as ever, and an electrifying revelation at the end points the way to a possible resolution." (Booklist)

UnWholly; Neal Shusterman. Simon & Schuster Books For Young Readers 2012 402 p. (hardback) $17.99

Grades: 6 7 8 9 10 11 12

1. Science fiction 2. Identity -- Fiction 3. Survival skills -- Fiction 4. Survival -- Fiction 5. Revolutionaries -- Fiction 6. Fugitives from justice -- Fiction

ISBN 1442423668; 9781442423664; 9781442423688

LC 2012002729

Sequel to: Unwind

This sequel to Neal Shusterman's book "Unwind" follows "Cam . . . a product of unwinding; made entirely out of the parts of other unwinds, he is a teen who does not technically exist. A futuristic Frankenstein, Cam struggles with a search for identity and meaning. . . . And when the actions of a sadistic bounty hunter cause Cam's fate to become inextricably bound with the fates of Connor, Risa, and Lev, he'll have to question humanity itself." (Publisher's note)

Unwind. Simon & Schuster Books for Young Readers 2007 335p $17.99

Grades: 6 7 8 9 10 11 12

1. Science fiction

ISBN 1-4169-1204-5; 1-4169-1205-3 pa; 978-1-4169-1204-0; 978-1-4169-1205-7 pa

LC 2006032689

In a future world where those between the ages of thirteen and eighteen can have their lives "unwound" and their body parts harvested for use by others, three teens go to extreme lengths to uphold their beliefs—and, perhaps, save their own lives. "Grades eight to ten." (Bull Cent Child Books)

"Poignant, compelling, and ultimately terrifying." Voice Youth Advocates

Silbert, Leslie

★ The **intelligencer**. Atria Bks. 2004 335p hardcover o.p. pa $14

Grades: 9 10 11 12

1. Marlowe, Christopher, 1564-1593 -- Fiction; 2. Mystery fiction 3. Great Britain -- History -- 1485-1603, Tudors -- Fiction

ISBN 0-7434-3292-4; 0-7434-3293-2 pa

LC 2004-298225

This mystery "alternates between the present and the England of Elizabeth I and Christopher Marlowe. In addition to being a skilled and popular playwright, Marlowe was a spy, or intelligencer, for both Cecil and Essex, rivals for the favor of the Queen. Kate Morgan, a present-day Renaissance scholar working as a PI for a former agent still working clandestinely for the government, takes on a case involving a bound collection of coded reports of intelligencers gathered by an employee of Cecil, Essex, and others. The trail of the manuscript and its codes intersects with modern investigations involving murders, a crooked but charming art dealer, a charming but devious entrepreneur, a captured spy, Iranian prisons, Kate's father, a U.S. senator, and the current CIA director. There are a lot of strands, but the pace is quick and the action fascinating." SLJ

Silver, Eve

Rush; Eve Silver. Katherine Tegen Books 2013 368 p. (The game) (hardcover) $17.99

Grades: 9 10 11 12

1. Science fiction 2. Violence -- Fiction 3. Extraterrestrial beings -- Fiction 4. Combat -- Fiction 5. Interpersonal relations -- Fiction

ISBN 0062192132; 9780062192134

LC 2012025496

This young adult novel, by Eve Silver, is the first entry in "The Game" series. "Seventeen-year-old Miki Jones . . . wakes up . . . in a place called the lobby--pulled from her life, pulled through time and space into some kind of game in which she and a team of other teens are sent on missions to eliminate the Drau, terrifying and beautiful alien creatures." (Publisher's note)

Silvera, Adam

★ **History** is all you left me. Adam Silvera. Soho Teen 2017 294 p.

Grades: 9 10 11 12

1. Gay teenagers -- Fiction; 2. Gays -- Fiction; 3. Obsessive-compulsive disorder -- Fiction; 4. LGBT people -- Fiction; 5. Grief -- Fiction; 6. Love -- Fiction

9781616956936; 9781616956929, $18.99

LC 2016020598

In this book, by Adam Silvera, "when Griffin's first love and ex-boyfriend, Theo, dies in a drowning accident, his universe implodes. Even though Theo had moved to California for college and started seeing Jackson, Griffin never doubted Theo would come back to him when the time was right. But now, the future he's been imagining for himself has gone far off course.... If Griffin is ever to rebuild his future, he must first confront his history." (Publisher's note)

"The talented author of More Happy than Not (2015) returns with a moving novel that explores friendship, grief, and trust among four young men." Kirkus

★ **More** happy than not. Adam Silvera. Soho Teen 2015 304 p. Illustration

Grades: 9 10 11 12

1. Coming out (Sexual orientation) -- Fiction 2. Dating (Social customs) -- Fiction 3. Gays -- Fiction 4. Memory -- Fiction 5. Single-parent families -- Fiction 6. Bronx (New York, N.Y.) -- Fiction 7. New York (N.Y.) -- Fiction 8. Grief -- Fiction 9. Gay teenagers -- Fiction

ISBN 9781616955601, $18.99

LC 2014044586

In this novel, by Adam Silvera, "Aaron struggles to find happiness despite the presence of his mother, older brother, and girlfriend, as well as a set of childhood buddies and a new, intriguing friend, Thomas. He is haunted by painful physical and emotional scars: the memory of his father's suicide in their home, his own similar failed attempt with its resulting smiley face scar, not to mention his family's poverty and his personal angst at an increasingly strong attraction for Thomas." (School Library Journal)

"Silvera pulls no punches in this portrait of a boy struggling with who he is in the face of immense cultural and societal pressure to be somebody else." Pub Wkly

★ **They** both die at the end. Adam Silvera. Harper Teen 2017 373 p.

Grades: 9 10 11 12

1. Action and adventure fiction; 2. Death -- Fiction; 3. Friendship -- Fiction; 4. Gay men -- Fiction; 5. Gay teenagers -- Fiction; 6. Hispanic Americans -- Fiction; 7. Love -- Fiction; 8. Romance fiction; 9. New York (N.Y.) -- Fiction

9780062457790, $17.99; 9780062457813

LC 2016053514

In this book, by Adam Silvera, "Death-Cast calls Mateo Torrez and Rufus Emeterio to give them some bad news: They're going to die today. Mateo and Rufus are total strangers, but...they're both looking to make a new friend on their End Day. The good news: There's an app for that. It's called the Last Friend, and through it, Rufus and Mateo are about to meet up for one last great adventure -- to live a lifetime in a single day." (Publisher's note)

"Engrossing, contemplative, and as heart-wrenching as the title promises." Kirkus

Silvey, Craig

★ **Jasper** Jones; a novel. Alfred A. Knopf 2011 312p $16.99

Grades: 6 7 8 9 10

1. Mystery fiction 2. Homicide -- Fiction 3. Australia -- Fiction 4. Family life -- Fiction

ISBN 0-375-86666-3; 0-375-96666-8 lib bdg; 978-0-375-86666-1; 978-0-375-96666-8 lib bdg

LC 2010-9364

In small-town Australia, teens Jasper and Charlie form an unlikely friendship when one asks the other to help him cover up a murder until they can prove who is responsible.

"Silvey infuses his prose with a musician's sensibility—Charlie's pounding heart is echoed in the terse staccato sentences of the opening scenes, alternating with legato phrases laden with meaning. The author's keen ear for dialogue is evident in the humorous verbal sparring between Charlie and Jeffrey, typical of smart 13-year-old boys. . . . A richly rewarding exploration of truth and lies by a masterful storyteller." Kirkus

Simmons, Kristen

Article 5; Kristen Simmons. Tor Teen 2012 364 p.

Grades: 9 10 11

1. Science fiction 2. Dystopian fiction 3. Mother-daughter relationship -- Fiction 4. Soldiers -- Fiction 5.

Government, Resistance to -- Fiction

ISBN 0765329581; 9780765329585

LC 2011035411

This young adult dystopian novel, by Kristen Simmons, is set where "The Bill of Rights has been revoked, and replaced with the Moral Statutes. There are no more police--instead, there are soldiers. . . . Ember Miller . . . has perfected the art of keeping a low profile. . . . That is, until her mother is arrested for noncompliance with Article 5 of the Moral Statutes. And one of the arresting officers is none other than Chase Jennings . . . the only boy Ember has ever loved." (Publisher's note)

Three. Kristen Simmons. Tor. 2014 382p $17.99

Grades: 9 10 11 12

1. Fugitives from justice -- Fiction 2. Science fiction 3. Dystopian fiction 4. Resistance to government -- Fiction

ISBN: 0765329603; 9780765329608; 9781429948036

LC 2013026344

Conclusion of the author's dystopian trilogy which began with Article 5 (2012) and Breaking point (2013). "When the book opens, Ember is sleeping in what remains of a destroyed resistance safe house along with the boy she loves, Chase, and a handful of others. As they continue to travel underground, they encounter the legendary resistance group, Three. This is a war story: Ember and her friends continually flee, camp out, strategize and fight, often at a moment's notice. Where earlier volumes' action sequences felt repetitive, these are suspenseful and immediate. Whom to trust and how far are rarely clear. Some interesting moral questions about pragmatism and violence arise, and no easy answers are given. Ember and Chase's relationship, including a gentle and warmly presented sex scene, gives the story both hope and warmth." Kirkus

Simner, Janni Lee

Bones of Faerie. Random House 2009 247p $16.99; lib bdg $19.99

Grades: 7 8 9 10

1. Fantasy fiction 2. Magic -- Fiction 3. Fairies -- Fiction

ISBN 978-0-375-84563-5; 978-0-375-94563-2 lib bdg

LC 2008-2022

Fifteen-year-old Liza travels through war-ravaged territory, accompanied by two companions, in a struggle to bridge the faerie and human worlds and to bring back her mother while learning of her own powers and that magic can be controlled.

This is a "compelling developed, highly vulnerable trio whose resolute defiance against the status quo will resonate with readers long after specific details of the story may be forgotten." Bull Cent Child Books

Followed by: Faerie winter (2011)

Faerie after; Janni Lee Simner. Random House Inc. 2013 272 p. (ebook) $50.97; (hardcover) $16.99; (library) $19.99

Grades: 7 8 9 10

1. Occult fiction 2. Fantasy fiction 3. Fairies -- Fiction

4. Magic -- Fiction 5. Coming of age -- Fiction
ISBN 0375870695; 9780307974556; 9780375870699; 9780375970696

LC 2012006430

Sequel to: Faerie winter

This is the third book in Janni Lee's Bones of Faerie trilogy. "Relative peace has descended upon Liza's town, where she practices her summoner magic and waits for her half-faerie baby sister to be born. But the forest is showing new dangers, though subtle ones," particularly a strange dust. "Liza's quest to find out what's wrong reveals fresh disasters." (Kirkus)

Faerie winter. Random House Children's Books 2011 270p $16.99; lib bdg $19.99

Grades: 7 8 9 10

1. Magic -- Fiction 2. Fairies -- Fiction 3. Mother-daughter relationship -- Fiction
ISBN 978-0-375-86671-5; 0-375-86671-X; 978-0-375-96671-2 lib bdg; 0-375-96671-4 lib bdg

LC 2010014250

Unable to get answers from her mother, sixteen-year-old Liza learns from Karin that while her own actions may have doomed the fairy and human worlds, she may be able to save them with more training, if the Faerie Queen can first be stopped.

"Simner tells a more streamlined story this time around and keeps up the dark atmospherics of her high-appeal blend of unsettling speculative-fiction scenarios." Booklist

Simone, Ni-Ni

Upgrade U; Ni-Ni Simone. Dafina Books 2011 viii, 276 p.p $9.95

Grades: 10 11 12

1. Love stories 2. Friendship -- Fiction 3. College students -- Fiction 4. College basketball -- Fiction 5. African Americans -- Fiction 6. Basketball players -- Fiction 7. Dating (Social customs) -- Fiction 8. Interpersonal relations -- Fiction
ISBN 0758241917; 9780758241917

LC 2011282065

In this novel, "Seven McKnight, introduced in 'Shortie Like Mine' (2008), moves from Newark, N.J., to New Orleans, La., to join her best friend Shae and boyfriend Josiah at Stiles University. . . . Problem is, Josiah hasn't returned any of Seven's many texts or phone calls, and Seven is afraid. . . . As Seven and Josiah cycle through fighting and making up, Seven finds support in her band of new and old friends: insightful Shae; bold, flirtatious and social-networking-obsessed Khya; and boa-clad next-door neighbor Courtney, who inserts himself into practically every conversation and outing. When Seven meets Zaire, a seemingly forthright, sophisticated New Orleans native, a love triangle develops--or is that a love quadrangle?" (Kirkus)

Simukka, Salla

As Red As Blood. Salla Simukka, translated by Owen Witesman. Skyscape 2014 272 p.

Grades: 9 10 11 12

1. Art students -- Finland 2. Suspense fiction 3. Young adult fiction 4. Crime -- Fiction 5. Murder -- Fiction

6. Mystery fiction
1477847715; 9781477847718, $9.99

In this crime novel by Salla Simukka, translated by Owen Witesman, part of the Snow White Trilogy, "seventeen-year-old Lumikki Andersson walks into her school's dark room and finds a stash of wet, crimson-colored money. Thousands of Euros left to dry—splattered with someone's blood. . . . Suddenly, Lumikki is swept into a whirlpool of events as she finds herself helping to trace the origins of the money." (Publisher's note)

"The starkly powerful opening paragraph of the Grimms' Snow White provides the narrative frame, and it's no flimsy high concept-rather, Simukka's onto something: Fairy tales, like mysteries, present uncompromising moral imperatives-no soft, comforting shades of gray for even the youngest readers.Limned in stark red, white and black, this cold, delicate snowflake of a tale sparkles with icy magic." Kirkus

Other titles in the series are:

As White as Snow (2015)

As Black as Ebony (2015)

Sitomer, Alan Lawrence

The **secret** story of Sonia Rodriguez. Jump at the Sun/Hyperion Books For Children 2008 312p lib bdg $17.99

Grades: 7 8 9 10

1. Family life -- Fiction 2. Mexican Americans -- Fiction
ISBN 978-1-4231-1072-9; 1-4231-1072-2

LC 2007-45265

Tenth-grader Sonia reveals secrets about her life and her Hispanic family as she studies hard to become the first Rodriguez to finish high school.

"Sonia's immediate voice will hold teens with its mix of anger, sorrow, tenderness, and humor." Booklist

Skilton, Sarah

Bruised; by Sarah Skilton. Amulet Books 2013 288 p. $16.95

Grades: 9 10 11 12

1. Bildungsromans 2. Martial arts -- Fiction 3. Tae kwon do -- Fiction 4. Self-perception -- Fiction
ISBN 1419703870; 9781419703874

LC 2012042801

This book follows sixteen-year-old Imogen, a martial artist who "can break boards with her feet and toss a man twice her size, but when her skills are tested during a diner holdup, she cowers rather than acts, and a man dies. Having lost her confidence and her pride, Imogen is ready to give up martial arts until Ricky—another witness of the holdup—asks her to teach him how to throw a punch. While working with Ricky, Imogen makes discoveries about her passions and fears." (Publishers Weekly)

Skurzynski, Gloria

The **Virtual** War. Simon & Schuster Bks. for Young Readers 1997 152p hardcover o.p. pa $10.95

Grades: 6 7 8 9

1. Science fiction 2. Virtual reality -- Fiction
ISBN 0-689-81374-0; 1-4169-7577-2 pa

LC 96-35346

In a future world where global contamination has necessitated limited human contact, three young people with unique genetically engineered abilities are teamed up to wage a war in virtual reality

"Skurzynski's anti-war message is clear yet never didactic; her characters are complex and fully realized, the pacing brisk, and the story compelling." Bull Cent Child Books

Other titles in this series are:

The choice (2006)

The clones (2002)

The revolt (2005)

Skuse, C. J.

Rockoholic; C.J. Skuse. Scholastic 2012 358 p. (reinforced) $18.99

Grades: 9 10 11 12

1. Teenagers -- Fiction 2. Kidnapping -- Fiction 3. Rock musicians -- Fiction 4. Fame -- Fiction 5. Wales -- Fiction 6. Musicians -- Fiction 7. Friendship -- Fiction 8. Rock music -- Fiction 9. Best friends -- Fiction

ISBN 0545429609; 9780545429603

LC 2011046582

In this young adult novel, by C. J. Skuse, "Jody's addicted to Jackson Gatlin, frontman of The Regulators, and . . . she's front and center at his sold-out concert. But when she gets mashed in the moshpit . . . and bodysurfs backstage, she ends up with more than a mild concussion to deal with. By the next morning, the strung-out rock star is coming down in her garage. Jody . . . kind of kidnapped him. By accident. And now he doesn't want to leave." (Publisher's note)

Sleator, William

★ The **duplicate**. Dutton 1988 154p hardcover o.p. pa $5.99

Grades: 7 8 9 10

1. Science fiction

ISBN 0-14-130431-6

LC 87-30562

Sixteen-year-old David, finding a strange machine that creates replicas of living organisms, duplicates himself and suffers the horrible consequences when the duplicate turns against him

"There are some points in the story when the roles of the clones (referred to as Duplicates A and B) become congested to the detriment of the book's pace, but fantasy fans will doubtless find the concept fresh enough and eerie enough to compensate for this, and Sleator is, as always, economical in casting and structuring his story." Bull Cent Child Books

Sloan, Brian

★ A **tale** of two summers. Simon & Schuster Books for Young Readers 2006 241p $15.95

Grades: 9 10 11 12

1. Theater -- Fiction 2. Friendship -- Fiction 3. Gay teenagers -- Fiction

ISBN 978-0-689-87439-0; 0-689-87439-1

LC 2005-20697

Even though Hal is gay and Chuck is straight, the two fifteen-year-olds are best friends and set up a blog where Hal records his budding romance with a young Frenchman and Chuck falls for a summer theater camp diva.

"This book is for readers mature enough to handle some very direct, realistic, and often-humorous entries about heterosexuality, homosexuality, masturbation, and alcohol and marijuana use. This title would be ideal for discussion within Gay/Straight Alliance groups." Voice Youth Advocates

Sloan, Holly Goldberg

★ **I'll** be there. Little, Brown 2011 392p $17.99

Grades: 7 8 9 10

1. Brothers -- Fiction 2. Family life -- Fiction 3. Mental illness -- Fiction 4. Father-son relationship -- Fiction

ISBN 978-0-316-12279-5; 0-316-12279-3

LC 2010-42994

Raised by an unstable father who keeps constantly on the move, Sam Border has long been the voice of his younger brother, Riddle, but everything changes when Sam meets Emily Bell and, welcomed by her family, the brothers are faced with normalcy for the first time.

"This riveting story will keep readers interested and guessing until the end." SLJ

Smith, Alexander Gordon

The **Devil's** engine: Hellraisers. Alexander Gordon Smith. Farrar, Straus & Giroux 2015 352 p.

Grades: 9 10 11 12

1. Adventure and adventurers -- Fiction 2. Adventure stories 3. Demonology -- Fiction 4. High schools -- Fiction 6. Monsters -- Fiction 7. Schools -- Fiction 8. Science fiction 9. New York (N.Y.) -- Fiction 10. Paranormal fiction 11. Adventure fiction

9780374301699, $17.99

LC 2015007190

In this novel, by Alexander Gordon Smith, "when a sixteen-year-old troublemaker named Marlow Green is trapped in a surreal firefight against nightmarish creatures in . . . New York City neighborhood, he unwittingly finds himself amid a squad of secret soldiers dedicated to battling the legions of the devil himself. Powering this army of young misfits is . . . the devil's engine, it can make any wish come true-as long as you are willing to put your life on the line." (Publisher's note)

"Marlow is a likable, flawed underdog of a hero, and his many comrades in arms gradually gain dimension as the plot progresses. First in a planned trilogy, Smith's latest is largely going to appeal to readers in it for the gritty action and horror." Booklist

Lockdown. Farrar, Straus and Giroux 2009 273p (Escape from Furnace) $14.99

Grades: 7 8 9 10

1. Science fiction 2. Escapes -- Fiction 3. Prisoners -- Fiction

ISBN 978-0-374-32491-9; 0-374-32491-3

LC 2008-43439

When fourteen-year-old Alex is framed for murder, he becomes an inmate in the Furnace Penitentiary, where brutal inmates and sadistic guards reign, boys who disappear in the middle of the night sometimes return weirdly altered, and escape might just be possible.

"Once a plot is hatched, readers will be turning pages without pause, and the cliffhanger ending will have them anticipating the next installment. Most appealing is Smith's flowing writing style, filled with kid-speak, colorful adjectives, and amusing analogies." SLJ

Other titles in this series are:
Death sentence (2011)
Solitary (2010)

Smith, Andrew, 1959-

★ The **Alex** Crow: a novel. By Andrew Smith. Dutton Books, an imprint of Penguin Group (USA) LLC 2015 304 p.
Grades: 9 10 11 12
1. Adoption -- Fiction 2. Death -- Fiction 3. Science fiction
0525426531; 9780525426530, $18.99
LC 2014039366

In this novel, author Andrew Smith "chronicles the story of Ariel, a refugee who is the sole survivor of an attack on his small village. Now living with an adoptive family in Sunday, West Virginia, Ariel's story is juxtaposed against those of a schizophrenic bomber and the diaries of a failed arctic expedition from the late nineteenth century . . . and a depressed, bionic reincarnated crow." (Publisher's note)

"Anchored by Smith's reliably strong prose with a distinct teenage-boy sensibility, the whole is a smartly cohesive exploration of survival and extinction, and the control humans have (or shouldn't have) over such matters." Horn Book

★ **Ghost** medicine. Feiwel & Friends 2008 357p $17.95
Grades: 8 9 10 11 12
1. Death -- Fiction 2. Friendship -- Fiction 3. Ranch life -- Fiction 4. West (U.S.) -- Fiction
ISBN 978-0-312-37557-7; 0-312-37557-3

Still mourning the recent death of his mother, seventeen-year-old Troy Stotts relates the events of the previous year when he and his two closest friends try to retaliate against the sheriff's son, who has been bullying them for years.

This novel "defies expectations via its sublime imagery and its elliptical narrative structure." Publ Wkly

Grasshopper jungle; by Andrew Smith. Dutton Juvenile 2014 432 p. (hardback) $18.99
Grades: 9 10 11 12
1. Praying mantis 2. Apocalyptic fiction 3. Iowa -- Fiction 4. Science fiction 5. Humorous fiction 6. Insects -- Fiction 7. Survival -- Fiction 8. Friendship -- Fiction 9. Gender identity -- Fiction 10. Family life -- Iowa -- Fiction
ISBN 0525426035; 9780525426035
LC 2013030265

Boston Globe-Horn Book Award: Fiction (2014)

Author Andrew Smith presents a "novel of the apocalypse [featuring] a (dead) mad scientist, a fabulous underground bunker, voracious giant praying mantises and gobs of messy violence. Narrated by hapless Polish-Iowan sophomore Austin Szerba, [it describes] the dead-end town of Ealing, Iowa; his girlfriend, Shann Collins, . . . and most importantly, his gay best friend, Robby Brees, to whom he finds himself as attracted as he is to Shann." (Kirkus)

"Award-winning author Smith has cleverly used a B movie science fiction plot to explore the intricacies of teen-age sexuality, love, and friendship. Austin's desires might garner buzz and controversy among adults but not among the teenage boys who can identify with his internal struggles. This novel is proof that when an author creates solely for himself—as Smith notes in the acknowledgments section-the result is an original, honest, and extraordinary work that speaks directly to teens as it pushes the boundaries of young adult literature." (School Library Journal)

The **Marbury** lens. Feiwel and Friends 2010 358p $17.99
Grades: 10 11 12
1. Horror fiction 2. Kidnapping -- Fiction 3. London (England) -- Fiction
ISBN 978-0-312-61342-6; 0-312-61342-3
LC 2010-13007

After being kidnapped and barely escaping, sixteen-year-old Jack goes to London with his best friend Connor, where someone gives him a pair of glasses that send him to an alternate universe where war is raging, he is responsible for the survival of two younger boys, and Connor is trying to kill them all.

"This bloody and genuinely upsetting book packs an enormous emotional punch. Smith's characters are very well developed and the ruined alternate universe they travel through is both surreal and believable." Publ Wkly

★ **Passenger**; Andrew Smith. Feiwel and Friends 2012 465 p. $17.99
Grades: 9 10 11 12
1. Horror fiction 2. Occult fiction 3. Fantasy fiction 4. Survival -- Fiction 5. Kidnapping -- Fiction 6. London (England) -- Fiction
ISBN 125000487X; 9781250004871
LC 2012288522

This horror fantasy novel, by Andrew Smith, is the sequel to "The Marbury Lens." "Best friends Jack and Conner can't stay away from Marbury. It's partly because of their obsession with this alternate world and the unresolved war that still wages there. . . . The boys try to destroy the lens that transports them to Marbury. But that dark world is not so easily reckoned with." (Publisher's note)

★ 100 **sideways** miles. Andrew Smith. Simon & Schuster Books for Young Readers. 2014 288p
Grades: 9 10 11 12
1. Authors -- Fiction 2. Best friends -- Fiction 3. Dating (Social customs) -- Fiction 4. Epilepsy -- Fiction 5. Father-son relationship -- Fiction 6. Friendship -- Fiction 7. California -- Fiction 8. Boys -- Fiction
ISBN: 1442444959; 9781442444959
LC 2013030326

"Finn Easton has lived his life in the shadow of a book. As a child, Finn was severely injured and his mother killed in a freak accident: a dead horse landed on them when it fell off a truck that was traveling over a bridge. After the accident, his father took many of Finn's unique characteristics (his name, heterochromatic eyes, propensity to measure time in miles traveled by the Earth in orbit, struggle with epilepsy, and a particular scar along his back) and made them into a character in a Robert Heinlein-esque novel, The Lazarus Door...This will appeal to teens who like novels with a bit

of an absurdist edge, such as Libba Bray's Going Bovine..."
(School Library Journal)

★ **Stand-off**. Andrew Smith. Simon & Schuster Books for Young Readers 2015 416 p. Illustration
Grades: 9 10 11 12

1. Boarding schools -- Fiction 2. High schools -- Fiction 3. Interpersonal relations -- Fiction 4. Rugby football -- Fiction 5. Schools -- Fiction 6. School stories 7. Private schools -- Fiction
9781481418294, $17.99; 9781481418300

LC 2015002163

In this novel, by Andrew Smith, "it's his last year at Pine Mountain, and Ryan Dean should be focused on his future, but instead, he's haunted by his past. His rugby coach expects him to fill the roles once played by his lost friend, Joey, as the rugby team's stand-off and new captain. And somehow he's stuck rooming with twelve-year-old freshman Sam Abernathy, a cooking whiz with extreme claustrophobia and a serious crush on Annie Altman-aka Ryan Dean's girlfriend, for now, anyway." (Publisher's note)

"A brave, wickedly funny novel about grief and finding a way to live with it, with sweetly realistic first sexual experiences." Kirkus
Sequel to Winger

Stick. Feiwel and Friends 2011 292p $17.99; ebook $9.99

Grades: 9 10 11 12

1. Brothers -- Fiction 2. Child abuse -- Fiction 3. Birth defects -- Fiction 4. Gay teenagers -- Fiction 5. Runaway teenagers -- Fiction
ISBN 978-0-312-61341-9; 978-1-4299-9537-5 ebook

LC 2011023541

"Thirteen-year-old Stick was born with only one ear and secretly sadistic parents; for the slightest infraction, Stick s father will beat him and his older brother Bosten. After Dad finds out Bosten is gay, both boys, separately, run away." (Horn Book)

"Dark, painful, but ultimately hopeful, this is not a book for everyone, but in the right reader's hands, it will be treasured." Voice Youth Advocates

★ **Winger**; Andrew Smith. 1st ed. Simon & Schuster Books for Young Readers 2013 448 p. (hardcover) $16.99

Grades: 9 10 11 12

1. School stories 2. Rugby football -- Fiction 3. High schools -- Fiction 4. Boarding schools -- Fiction 5. Interpersonal relations -- Fiction
ISBN 1442444924; 9781442444928; 9781442444942

LC 2011052750

In this novel, by Andrew Smith, "Ryan Dean West is a fourteen-year-old junior at a boarding school for rich kids. He's living in . . . the dorm for troublemakers, and rooming with the biggest bully on the rugby team. And he's madly in love with his best friend Annie, who thinks of him as a little boy. With the help of his . . . humor, rugby buddies, and his penchant for doodling comics, Ryan Dean manages to survive life's complications and even find some happiness along the way." (Publisher's note)

"Smith deftly builds characters--readers will suddenly realize they've effortlessly fallen in love with them--and he laces meaning and poignantly real dialogue into uproariously funny scatological and hormonally charged humor, somehow creating a balance between the two that seems to intensify both extremes. Bawdily comic but ultimately devastating, this is unforgettable." Kirkus

Smith, Cynthia Leitich

Blessed. Candlewick Press 2011 462p $17.99

Grades: 9 10 11 12

1. Texas -- Fiction 2. Orphans -- Fiction 3. Vampires -- Fiction 4. Werewolves -- Fiction 5. Restaurants -- Fiction 6. Supernatural -- Fiction
ISBN 978-0-7636-4326-3

LC 2010-38697

Even as teenaged Quincie Morris adjusts to her appetites as a neophyte vampire, she must clear her true love, the hybrid-werewolf Kieren, of murder charges; thwart the apocalyptic ambitions of Bradley Sanguini, the vampire-chef who "blessed" her; and keep her dead parents' restaurant up and running before she loses her own soul.

"A satisfying blend of excitement and intrigue, Blessed provides a fun and entertaining read. Appealing to high schoolers with a flair for fantasy, this book provides a twist on life as an 'eternal.'" Voice Youth Advocates

Eternal. Candlewick Press 2009 307p $17.99

Grades: 8 9 10 11

1. Angels -- Fiction 2. Vampires -- Fiction
ISBN 978-0-7636-3573-2

LC 2008-27658

When Miranda's guardian angel Zachary recklessly saves her from falling into an open grave and dying, the result is that she turns into a vampire and he is left to try to reinstate his reputation by finally doing the right thing.

"Readers should be hooked by this fully formed world, up through the action-packed finale." Publ Wkly

Feral curse. Cynthia Leitich Smith. Candlewick Press. 2014 272p $17.99

Grades: 9 10 11 12

1. Adopted children -- Fiction 2. Shapeshifting -- Fiction 3. Curses -- Fiction 4. Fantasy fiction
ISBN: 076365910X; 9780763659103

LC 2013946609

Second title in the author's Feral fantasy series. This "installment begins in the small town of Pine Ridge, Texas. Kayla is a teenage werecat adopted at birth and raised by loving human parents. Isolated from the shifter world, she has hidden her inner cat from those she cares about. Driven by her love for Benjamin and an attempt to be open and honest, she reveals her true nature. The result is disastrous, ending in betrayal, regret, and rejection. Determined to "save" Kayla, Ben unleashes a mystical curse that ensnares shifters and ties them to enchanted carousel animals while causing his untimely death." SLJ

"Debut character Kayla--level-headed, religious, but also quietly proud of her shifter nature--holds her own. Witty banter keeps the tone light even as the stakes ramp up." Horn Book

Feral nights; Cynthia Leitich Smith. Candlewick Press 2013 304 p. $17.99

Grades: 9 10 11 12

    1. Shapeshifting --Fiction 2. Fantasy fiction

    ISBN 0763659096; 9780763659097

                         LC 2012942377

This young adult paranormal fantasy story, by Cynthia Leitich Smith, is the first entry in the series "Feral." "When sexy, free-spirited werecat Yoshi tracks his sister, Ruby, to Austin, he discovers that she is not only MIA, but also the key suspect in a murder investigation. Meanwhile, werepossum Clyde and human Aimee have set out to do a little detective work of their own, sworn to avenge the brutal killing of werearmadillo pal Travis." (Publisher's note)

Rain is not my Indian name. HarperCollins Pubs. 2001 135p $15.99; lib bdg $16.89

Grades: 6 7 8 9

    1. Death -- Fiction 2. Photography -- Fiction 3. Native Americans -- Fiction

    ISBN 0-688-17397-7; 0-06-029504-X lib bdg

                         LC 00-59705

Tired of staying in seclusion since the death of her best friend, a fourteen-year-old Native American girl takes on a photographic assignment with her local newspaper to cover events at the Native American summer youth camp

"The engaging first-person narrative convincingly portrays Rain's grieving process and addresses the varying degrees of prejudice she encounters." Horn Book Guide

Tantalize. Candlewick Press 2007 310p $16.99; pa $8.99

Grades: 9 10 11 12

    1. Texas -- Fiction 2. Vampires -- Fiction 3. Werewolves -- Fiction 4. Restaurants -- Fiction 5. Supernatural -- Fiction

    ISBN 0-7636-2791-7; 978-0-7636-2791-1; 0-7636-4059-X pa; 978-0-7636-4059-0 pa

                         LC 2005-58124

When multiple murders in Austin, Texas, threaten the grand reopening of her family's vampire-themed restaurant, seventeen-year-old, orphaned Quincie worries that her best friend-turned-love interest, Kieren, a werewolf-in-training, may be the prime suspect.

"Horror fans will be hooked by Kieren's quiet, hirsute hunkiness, and Texans by the premise that nearly everybody in their capitol is a shapeshifter." Publ Wkly

Followed by Blessed (2011)

Smith, Emily Wing

Back when you were easier to love. Dutton Books 2011 296p $16.99

Grades: 8 9 10 11 12

    1. Love stories 2. Mormons -- Fiction 3. Automobile travel -- Fiction

    ISBN 978-0-525-42199-3; 0-525-42199-8

                         LC 2010-13469

When her boyfriend Zan leaves high school in Utah a year early to attend Pitzer College, a broken-hearted Joy and Zan's best friend Noah take off on a road trip to California seeking "closure."

Smith "effectively reconstructs Zan and Joy's relationship. . . . Joy's voice is sturdy, and her articulations about loss and belief are thoughtful and often moving. Self-acceptance and both the comforts and restrictions of the Mormon religion and identity are central themes in this sweet story." Publ Wkly

★ The **way** he lived; [by] Emily Wing Smith. 1st ed.; Flux 2008 232p pa $9.95

Grades: 8 9 10 11 12

    1. Death -- Fiction 2. Mormons -- Fiction

    ISBN 978-0-7387-1404-2 pa

                         LC 2008024416

"Besides living in the same Mormon community in Utah, Tabbatha, Adlen, Miles, Claire, Norah and Lissa have something else in common: each had a special connection to Joel Espen, who died of dehydration after giving away his water during a badly planned Boy Scout expedition. In vignettes showing the six teens differing points of view, first-time author Smith probes into the psychologies of the survivors to demonstrate Joel's effect on their lives and their attempts to make sense of his death. . . . The author preserves each narrator's complexity. . . It's a testimony to Smith's skills that although her central character speaks only through other people's recollections, his identity emerges distinctly by the end of the novel." Publ Wkly

Smith, Hilary T.

A **Sense** of the Infinite. Hilary T. Smith. Katherine Tegen Books 2015 400 p.

Grades: 9 10 11 12

    1. Bildungsromans 2. School stories 3. Female friendship -- Fiction

    0062184717; 9780062184719, $17.99

                         LC 2014952736

In this coming of age novel by Hilary T. Smith, "it's senior year of high school, and Annabeth is ready—ready for everything she and her best friend, Noe, have been planning and dreaming. But there are some things Annabeth isn't prepared for, like the constant presence of Noe's new boyfriend. Like how her relationship with her mom is wearing and fraying. And like the way the secret she's been keeping hidden deep inside her for years has started clawing at her insides." (Publisher's note)

"Smith's prose is knock-down gorgeous. A fearless writer ably tackles a difficult story." Kirkus

Wild awake; Hilary T. Smith. 1st ed. Katherine Tegen Books, an imprint of HarperCollinsPublishers 2013 375 p. (hardcover) $17.99

Grades: 9 10 11 12

    1. Bereavement -- Fiction 2. Dating (Social customs) -- Fiction 3. Secrets -- Fiction 4. Sisters -- Fiction 5. Mental illness -- Fiction

    ISBN 0062184687; 9780062184689

                         LC 2012045524

In this young adult novel, by Hilary T. Smith, "Kiri Byrd . . . intends to devote herself to her music and win the Battle of the Bands with her bandmate and best friend, Lukas. Perhaps then . . . he will finally realize she's the girl of his dreams. But a phone call from a stranger shatters Kiri's plans. He says he has her sister Suki's stuff--her sister Suki, who died five years ago. This call throws Kiri into a spiral of chaos that opens old wounds and new mysteries." (Publisher's note)

Smith, Jennifer E.

The **comeback** season. Simon & Schuster Books for Young Readers 2008 246p $15.99

Grades: 6 7 8 9 10

    1. Baseball -- Fiction 2. Bereavement -- Fiction 3. Family life -- Fiction 4. Chicago (Ill.) -- Fiction 5. Father-daughter relationship -- Fiction

ISBN 978-1-4169-3847-7; 1-4169-3847-8

LC 2007-17067

High school freshman Ryan Walsh, a Chicago Cubs fan, meets Nick when they both skip school on opening day, and their blossoming relationship becomes difficult for Ryan when she discovers that Nick is seriously ill and she again feels the pain of losing her father five years earlier.

"Smith deftly twines strands of grief, romance, baseball, family, and friendships lost and regained into this tale. . . . The present-tense narrative has an immediacy that will engage readers and the supporting cast is unusually vivid." Booklist

The **geography** of you and me. Jennifer E. Smith. Little, Brown & Co. 2014 352p $18.00

Grades: 7 8 9 10 11 12

    1. Electric power failures -- Fiction 2. Love -- Fiction 3. Social classes -- Fiction 4. Voyages and travels -- Fiction 5. New York (N.Y.) -- Fiction

ISBN: 0316254770; 9780316254779

LC 2013022845

"Owen and Lucy meet during a citywide blackout in New York and spend a memorable (chaste) night together. Soon afterward, Lucy's parents take her to Europe, and Owen and his dad move to San Francisco, but even on opposite sides of the world, they think about each other. Smith's fans will recognize the alternating narration; reflective, deliberate writing style; and serendipitous coincidences." Horn Book

Hello, goodbye, and everything in between. Jennifer E. Smith. Little, Brown & Co. 2015 256 p.

Grades: 9 10 11 12

    1. Dating (Social customs) -- Fiction 2. Love -- Fiction 3. Breaking up (Interpersonal relations) -- Fiction

9780316334426, $18

LC 2014043210

In this young adult novel, by Jennifer E. Smith, "on the night before they leave for college, Clare and Aidan only have one thing left to do: figure out whether they should stay together or break up. Over the course of twelve hours, they'll retrace the steps of their relationship, trying to find something in their past that might help them decide what their future should be." (Publisher's note)

"Students approaching the college transition, those who have already experienced it, and fans of romantic, realistic fiction will most enjoy this relatable, emotive story." SLJ

The **statistical** probability of love at first sight; Jennifer E. Smith. 1st ed. Little, Brown 2012 236 p.

Grades: 9 10 11 12

    1. Love stories 2. Weddings -- Fiction 3. Air travel -- Fiction 4. Love -- Fiction 5. England -- Fiction 6. Remarriage -- Fiction 7. London (England) -- Fiction 8. Fate and fatalism -- Fiction 9. Funeral rites and ceremonies -- Fiction

ISBN 9780316122382

LC 2010048704

In this book, "[a]lthough her mother has made peace with the situation, Hadley is still angry and hurt that her father left them for an Englishwoman. Rebooked on the next flight after missing her plane to London, where she's to be a bridesmaid in their wedding, Hadley is seated next to the English boy who helped her in the terminal. He comes to her rescue again after she confesses she suffers from claustrophobia. A good-looking Yale student, Oliver is smart, funny and thoughtful, though evasive about the purpose of his trip. Their mutual attraction is heightened by the limbo of air travel, but on arrival, they're separated. With just minutes to get to the wedding, Hadley . . . makes her way to the church and the father she's avoided seeing for a year." (Kirkus)

This is what happy looks like; Jennifer E. Smith. 1st ed. Poppy 2013 416 p. (hardcover) $17.99

Grades: 9 10 11

    1. Love stories 2. Online dating -- Fiction 3. Teenage girls -- Fiction 4. Love -- Fiction 5. Maine -- Fiction 6. Actors and actresses -- Fiction

ISBN 0316212822; 9780316212823

LC 2012028755

In this novel, by Jennifer E. Smith, "when teenage movie star Graham Larkin accidentally sends small town girl Ellie O'Neill an email about his pet pig, the two seventeen-year-olds strike up a witty and unforgettable correspondence, discussing everything . . . except for their names or backgrounds. Then Graham finds out that Ellie's Maine hometown is the perfect location for his latest film, and he decides to take their relationship from online to in-person." (Publisher's note)

Windfall. Jennifer E. Smith. Delacorte Press 2017 417 p.

Grades: 9 10 11 12

    1. Friendship -- Fiction; 2. Lotteries -- Fiction; 3. Love -- Fiction; 4. Luck -- Fiction; 5. Orphans -- Fiction; 6. Wealth -- Fiction; 7. Romance fiction

ISBN 0399559396; 9780399559372; 9780399559396, $21.99; 9780399559389

LC 2016034305

In this novel, by Jennifer E. Smith, "Alice doesn't believe in luck -- at least, not the good kind. But she does believe in love, and for some time now, she's been pining for her best friend, Teddy. On his eighteenth birthday...she buys him a lottery ticket on a lark. To their astonishment, he wins $140 million, and in an instant, everything changes." (Publisher's note)

"A story that could have easily skimmed the surface of emotions plunges head-on into the complexities of grief, loss, and love." SLJ

Smith, Lindsay

Dreamstrider. Lindsay Smith. Roaring Brook Press 2015 400 p. Map

Grades: 9 10 11 12
1. Dreams -- Fiction 2. Fantasy 3. Spy stories
1626720428; 9781626720428, $17.99

LC 2015011848

In this novel, by Lindsay Smith, "Livia . . . can inhabit a subject's body while they are sleeping and, for a short time, move around in their skin. She uses her talent to work as a spy for the Barstadt Empire. But her partner, Brandt, has lately become distant, and when Marez comes to join their team from a neighboring kingdom, he offers Livia the option of a life she had never dared to imagine. So only she understands the stakes when a plot against the Empire emerges that threatens to consume both the dreaming world and the waking one." (Publisher's note)

"An engaging stand-alone fantasy spy thriller." SLJ

Sekret; Lindsay Smith. Roaring Brook Press. 2014 345p $17.99

Grades: 8 9 10 11 12
1. KGB -- Fiction 2. Psychic ability -- Fiction 3. Spies -- Fiction 4. Soviet Union -- History -- 1953-1985 -- Fiction
ISBN: 1596438924; 9781596438927

LC 2013027913

"Yulia's father always taught her to hide her thoughts and control her emotions to survive the harsh realities of Soviet Russia. But when she's captured by the KGB and forced to work as a psychic spy with a mission to undermine the U.S. space program, she's thrust into a world of suspicion, deceit, and horrifying power." (Publisher's note)

"We the Living meets Genius Squad, this novel follows the misfortunes of Yulia, one of a group of psychic teens pressed into the service of the 1960s KGB. The concept is ambitious and the heroine fiery, but there is a surfeit of plot elements (including a hokey love triangle) and the writing is frequently turgid." Horn Book

Smith, Roland

The **edge**. By Roland Smith. Houghton Mifflin Harcourt 2015 240 p.

Grades: 6 7 8 9 10
1. Leopard -- Fiction 2. Mountaineering -- Fiction 3. Mountaineering -- Hindu Kush Mountains (Afghanistan and Pakistan) -- Fiction 4. Snow leopard -- Fiction 5. Survival -- Fiction 6. Hindu Kush Mountains (Afghanistan and Pakistan) -- Fiction 7. Wilderness survival -- Fiction
ISBN 9780544341227, $17.99

LC 2014044086

"The International Peace Ascent is the brainchild of billionaire Sebastian Plank: Recruit a global team of young climbers and film an inspiring, world-uniting documentary. The adventure begins when fifteen-year-old Peak Marcello and his mountaineer mother are helicptered to . . . the Hindu Kush Mountains on the Afghanistan-Pakistan border. When the camp is attacked and his mother taken, Peak has no choice but to track down the perpetrators." (Publisher's note)

Sequel to: Peak

Elephant run. Hyperion Books for Children 2007 318p $15.99

Grades: 6 7 8 9 10 11 12
1. Elephants -- Fiction 2. Prisoners of war -- Fiction 3. World War, 1939-1945 -- Fiction
ISBN 978-1-4231-0402-5; 1-4231-0402-1

LC 2007-13310

Nick endures servitude, beatings, and more after his British father's plantation in Burma is invaded by the Japanese in 1941.

"The Burmese setting and the role of elephants in the lumbering industry are exceptionally well integrated into this wartime adventure tale." Bull Cent Child Books

★ **Peak**. Harcourt 2007 246p $17

Grades: 7 8 9 10
1. Mountaineering -- Fiction 2. Fathers and sons -- Fiction 3. Father-son relationship -- Fiction
ISBN 978-0-15-202417-8

LC 2006024325

After fourteen-year-old Peak Marcello is arrested for scaling a New York City skyscraper, he is sent to live with his long-lost father, who wants him to be the youngest person to reach the Everest summit.

"This is a thrilling, multifaceted adventure story. Smith includes plenty of mountaineering facts told in vivid detail. . . . But he also explores other issues, such as the selfishness that nearly always accompanies the intensely single-minded." Booklist

Smith, Sarah

The **other** side of dark. Atheneum Books for Young Readers 2010 312p $16.99

Grades: 6 7 8 9 10
1. Ghost stories 2. Orphans -- Fiction 3. Supernatural -- Fiction 4. Boston (Mass.) -- Fiction 5. Race relations -- Fiction 6. African Americans -- Fiction
ISBN 978-1-4424-0280-5; 1-4424-0280-6

LC 2010-14690

Since losing both of her parents, fifteen-year-old Katie can see and talk to ghosts, which makes her a loner until fellow student Law sees her drawing of a historic house and together they seek a treasure rumored to be hidden there by illegal slave-traders.

The author "weaves complicated racial issues into a romantic, mysterious novel." Booklist

Smith, Sherri L.

★ **Flygirl**. G.P. Putnam's Sons 2009 275p $16.99

Grades: 7 8 9 10
1. Air pilots -- Fiction 2. Women air pilots -- Fiction 3. African Americans -- Fiction 4. World War, 1939-1945 -- Fiction
ISBN 978-0-399-24709-5; 0-399-24709-2

LC 2008-25407

During World War II, a light-skinned African American girl "passes" for white in order to join the Women Airforce Service Pilots.

"The details about navigation are exciting, but tougher than any flight maneuver are Ida Mae's loneliness, shame, and fear that she will be thrown out of the the military, feelings that culminate in an unforgettable climax." Booklist

Orleans; Sherri L. Smith. G.P. Putnam's Sons 2013 324 p. (hardcover) $17.99

Grades: 9 10 11 12

1. Science fiction 2. Viruses -- Fiction 3. New Orleans (La.) -- Fiction 4. Virus diseases -- Fiction

ISBN 0399252940; 9780399252945

LC 2012009634

This novel, by Sherri L. Smith, describes a dystopian New Orleans. "After a . . . severe outbreak of Delta Fever, the Gulf Coast has been quarantined. Years later, residents of the Outer States are under the assumption that life in the Delta is all but extinct . . . but in reality, a new primitive society has been born. Fen de la Guerre . . . , left with her tribe leader's newborn, . . . is determined to get the baby to a better life over the wall." (Publisher's note)

Smith-Ready, Jeri

Shade. Simon Pulse 2010 309p $17.99

Grades: 9 10 11 12

1. Ghost stories 2. Trials -- Fiction 3. Musicians -- Fiction 4. Supernatural -- Fiction 5. Baltimore (Md.) -- Fiction

ISBN 978-1-4169-9406-0

LC 2009-39487

Sixteen-year-old Aura of Baltimore, Maryland, reluctantly works at her aunt's law firm helping ghosts with wrongful death cases file suits in hopes of moving on, but it becomes personal when her boyfriend, a promising musician, dies and persistently haunts her.

Although "Smith-Ready's occasionally racy . . . [book] resolves almost none of the issues surrounding the Shift, leaving the door open for future books, it is a fully satisfying read on its own, with well-developed, believable characters. . . . Perhaps even more impressive is the understatement of the paranormal premise—Smith-Ready changes the world completely by simply changing our ability to see." Publ Wkly

Followed by Shift (2011)

Shift. Simon Pulse 2011 367p $17.99

Grades: 9 10 11 12

1. Ghost stories 2. Musicians -- Fiction 3. Supernatural -- Fiction 4. Baltimore (Md.) -- Fiction

ISBN 978-1-4169-9408-4

LC 2010036784

Sequel to Shade (2011)

Logan returns as a ghost, complicating sixteen-year-old Aura's budding relationship with Zachary, especially when they discover that Logan might be able to become solid again.

"Smith-Ready's strengths are well-developed core characters, dialogue, and the clever narrative tone. Mature language and content make this better suited for older teens." SLJ

This side of salvation. Jeri Smith-Ready. Simon Pulse. 2014 384p $17.99

Grades: 9 10 11 12

1. Cults -- Fiction 2. End of the world -- Fiction 3. Grief -- Fiction 4. Missing persons -- Fiction 5. Schools --

Fiction 6. Family life -- Fiction

ISBN: 1442439483; 9781442439481

LC 2013019948

"Following the death of his soldier brother, David's grief-stricken parents have turned to religion--specifically a fundamentalist cult--for solace. His recovering-alcoholic father speaks only in Bible verses; his mother is fixated on the upcoming Rapture, or Rush. When his parents disappear, David must untangle the mystery. Chapter flashbacks to "Before the Rush" alternate with "Now" in this nuanced study of relationships, religion, and faith." Horn Book

Smythe, J. P.

Way down dark. J.P. Smythe. Quercus. Distributed in the United States and Canada by Hachette Book Group. 2016 288 p. (The Australia trilogy)

Grades: 10 11 12

1. Science fiction 2. Space ships -- Fiction 3. Survival -- Fiction 4. Violence -- Fiction 5. Survival skills -- Fiction 6. Space vehicles -- Fiction

9781681443843; 9781681443850, $16.99; 9781681443829, $51

LC 2016030129

"Seventeen-year-old Chan's ancestors left a dying Earth hundreds of years ago, in search of a new home. Generations later, they are still searching . . . Every day aboard the interstellar transport ship Australia is a kind of hell, where no one is safe, no one can hide. Indeed, the only life Chan's ever known is one of endless violence. . . . Fiercely independent and entirely self-sufficient, she has learned to keep her head down as much as possible." (Publisher's note)

"Young adults will be drawn to Chan's realistic persona and addicted to a tale that leaves them wanting to know more." SLJ

Somper, Justin

Demons of the ocean. Little, Brown 2006 330p (Vampirates) $15.99

Grades: 6 7 8 9

1. Adventure fiction 2. Twins -- Fiction 3. Pirates -- Fiction 4. Vampires -- Fiction

ISBN 0-316-01373-0

When twins Connor and Grace's ship is wrecked in a storm and Connor is rescued by pirates, he believes that Grace has been taken aboard the mythical Vampirate's ship, and he is determined to find her.

"This winning fantasy features both pirates and vampires with adventure, bloodcurling action, and sinister characters." Voice Youth Advocates

Other titles in this series are:

Tide of terror (2007)

Blood Captain (2008)

Black heart (2009)

Empire of night (2010)

Sones, Sonya

One of those hideous books where the mother dies. Simon & Schuster Books for Young Readers 2004 268p $15.95; pa $6.99

Grades: 7 8 9 10

1. Actors -- Fiction 2. Bereavement -- Fiction 3.

Father-daughter relationship -- Fiction
ISBN 0-689-85820-5; 1-416-90788-2 pa

LC 2003-9355

Fifteen-year-old Ruby Milliken leaves her best friend, her boyfriend, her aunt, and her mother's grave in Boston and reluctantly flies to Los Angeles to live with her father, a famous movie star who divorced her mother before Ruby was born

"Ruby's affable personality is evident in her humorous quips and clever wordplays. Her depth of character is revealed through her honest admissions, poignant revelations, and sensitive insights. . . . Ruby's story is gripping, enjoyable, and memorable." SLJ

What my girlfriend doesn't know. Simon & Schuster Books for Young Readers 2007 291p $16.99

Grades: 7 8 9 10

1. School stories 2. Artists -- Fiction 3. Boston (Mass.) -- Fiction 4. Dating (Social customs) -- Fiction
ISBN 978-0-689-87602-8; 0-689-87602-5

LC 2006-14682

Sequel to What my mother doesn't know (2001)

Fourteen-year-old Robin Murphy is so unpopular at high school that his name is slang for "loser," and so when he begins dating the beautiful and popular Sophie her reputation plummets, but he finds acceptance as a student in a drawing class at Harvard.

"Robin's believable voice is distinctive, and Sones uses her spare words (and a few drawings) to expert effect." Booklist

What my mother doesn't know. Simon & Schuster Bks. for Young Readers 2001 259p hardcover o.p. pa $7.99

Grades: 7 8 9 10

1. Novels in verse 2. Dating (Social customs) -- Fiction
ISBN 0-689-84114-0; 0-689-85553-2 pa

LC 00-52634

Sophie describes her relationships with a series of boys as she searches for Mr. Right

This is "a fast, funny, touching book. . . . The very short, sometimes rhythmic lines make each page fly. Sophie's voice is colloquial and intimate." Booklist

Followed by What my girlfriend doesn't know (2007)

Sonnenblick, Jordan

★ **After** ever after. Scholastic Press 2010 260p $16.99

Grades: 5 6 7 8

1. School stories 2. Cancer -- Fiction 3. Friendship -- Fiction 4. Family life -- Fiction
ISBN 978-0-439-83706-4; 0-439-83706-5

Jeffrey's cancer is in remission but the chemotherapy and radiation treatments have left him with concentration problems, and he worries about school work, his friends, his family, and a girl who likes him

"Sonnenblick imbues Jeffrey with a smooth, likable, and unaffected voice. . . . As hilarious as it is tragic, and as honest as it is hopeful . . . [this book is] irresistable reading." Booklist

Drums, girls, & dangerous pie. Scholastic Press 2005 273p $16.99

Grades: 5 6 7 8

1. Brothers -- Fiction 2. Leukemia -- Fiction
ISBN 0-439-75519-0

LC 2004-62563

First published 2004 by Turning Tide Press

When his younger brother is diagnosed with leukemia, thirteen-year-old Steven tries to deal with his complicated emotions, his school life, and his desire to support his family.

"A story that could have morphed into melodrama is saved by reality, rawness, and the wit Sonnenblick infuses into Steven's first-person voice." Booklist

Falling over sideways. Jordan Sonnenblick. Scholastic Press 2016 272 p.

Grades: 7 8 9 10

1. Brothers and sisters -- Fiction 2. Cerebrovascular disease -- Fiction 3. Family life -- Fiction 4. Fathers and daughters -- Fiction 5. Mothers and daughters -- Fiction 6. Schools -- Fiction 7. Stroke -- Fiction 8. Children of parents with disabilities -- Fiction
9780545863247
LC 2016022926

"The butt of jokes in her school and at home, awkward Claire is forced to confront more serious aspects of her life in the wake of her father's medical emergency, which challenges Claire to bring laughter back into the lives of those she loves." (Publisher's note)

"In Claire, Sonnenblick crafts a convincing, lightly sardonic narrator, and her bittersweet and hopeful story will likely stay with readers for some time." Horn Book

Notes from the midnight driver. Scholastic Press 2006 265p $16.99

Grades: 8 9 10 11 12

1. Old age -- Fiction 2. Musicians -- Fiction 3. Friendship -- Fiction
ISBN 0-439-75779-7

LC 2005-27972

After being assigned to perform community service at a nursing home, sixteen-year-old Alex befriends a cantankerous old man who has some lessons to impart about jazz guitar playing, love, and forgiveness.

The author "deftly infiltrates the teenage mind to produce a first-person narrative riddled with enough hapless confusion, mulish equivocation, and beleaguered deadpan humor to have readers nodding with recognition, sighing with sympathy, and gasping with laughter—often on the same page." Horn Book

★ **Zen** and the art of faking it. Scholastic Press 2007 264p $16.99; pa $7.99

Grades: 5 6 7 8

1. School stories 2. Zen Buddhism -- Fiction 3. Asian Americans -- Fiction
ISBN 978-0-439-83707-1; 0-439-83707-3; 978-0-439-83709-5 pa; 0-439-83709-X pa

LC 2006-28841

When thirteen-year-old San Lee moves to a new town and school for the umpteenth time, he is looking for a way to stand out when his knowledge of Zen Buddhism, gained in his previous school, provides the answer—and the need to quickly become a convincing Zen master.

The author gives readers "plenty to laugh at. . . . Mixed with more serious scenes, . . . lighter moments take a basic message about the importance of honesty and forgiveness and treat it with panache." Publ Wkly

Sorosiak, Carlie

Wild blue wonder. Carlie Sorosiak. Harpercollins Childrens Books 2018 368 p.

Grades: 7 8 9 10 11

1. Nineteen sixties -- Fiction; 2. War correspondents -- Fiction; 3. Friendship -- Fiction; 4. Family life -- Fiction; 5. Grief -- Fiction

0062563998; 9780062563996, $17.99

In this book, by Carlie Sorosiak, "last June, the summer camp Quinn's family owns in Winship, Maine, was still a magical place.... [It was where] Quinn fell in love with her best friend, Dylan. Then the accident happened. Now it's winter, the magic has drained from Quinn's life.... But the new boy in town, Alexander, doesn't see her as the monster she believes herself to be.... [S]he begins to understand the truth about love, loss, and monsters -- real and imagined." (Publisher's note)

Soto, Gary

★ **Buried** onions. Harcourt Brace & Co. 1997 149p hardcover o.p. pa $6.95

Grades: 8 9 10 11 12

1. Violence -- Fiction 2. Mexican Americans -- Fiction

ISBN 0-15-201333-4; 0-15-206265-3 pa

LC 96-53112

When nineteen-year-old Eddie drops out of college, he struggles to find a place for himself as a Mexican American living in a violence-infested neighborhood of Fresno, California.

"Soto has created a beautiful, touching, and truthful story. . . . The lyrical language and Spanish phrases add to the immediacy of setting and to the sensitivity the author brings to his character's life." Voice Youth Advocates

★ **Taking** sides. Harcourt Brace Jovanovich 1991 138p hardcover o.p. pa $5.95

Grades: 5 6 7 8

1. Basketball -- Fiction 2. Hispanic Americans -- Fiction

ISBN 0-15-284076-1; 0-15-204694-1 pa

LC 91-11082

Fourteen-year-old Lincoln Mendoza, an aspiring basketball player, must come to terms with his divided loyalties when he moves from the Hispanic inner city to a white suburban neighborhood

This is a "light but appealing story. . . . Because of its subject matter and its clear, straightforward prose, it will be especially good for reluctant readers." SLJ

Includes glossary

Spangler, Brie

Beast. Brie Spangler. Alfred A. Knopf 2016 330 p.

Grades: 9 10 11 12

1. Dating (Social customs) -- Fiction 2. Interpersonal relations -- Fiction 3. Self-help groups -- Fiction 4.

Transgender people -- Fiction

1101937165; 9781101937167, $17.99; 9781101937181; 9781101937174, $53.97

LC 2015048797

In this book, by Brie Spangler, "Dylan doesn't look like your average fifteen-year-old, so, naturally, high school has not been kind to him. To make matters worse, on the day his school bans hats (his preferred camouflage), Dylan goes up on his roof only to fall and wake up in the hospital with a broken leg-and a mandate to attend group therapy for self-harmers. Dylan vows to say nothing and zones out at therapy-until he meets Jamie." (Publisher's note)

"Very lightly borrowing on the classic fairy tale, she allows them to fail and succeed without resorting to paper villains or violent plot points to manipulate compassion. A believable and beautiful human story." Kirkus

Speare, Elizabeth George

★ The **witch** of Blackbird Pond. Houghton Mifflin 1958 249p $17

Grades: 6 7 8 9

1. Puritans -- Fiction 2. Witchcraft -- Fiction

ISBN 0-395-07114-3

LC 58-11063

Awarded the Newbery Medal, 1959

"Headstrong and undisciplined, Barbados-bred Kit Tyler is an embarrassment to her Puritan relatives, and her sincere attempts to aid a reputed witch soon bring her to trial as a suspect." Child Books Too Good to Miss

Spears, Kat

Breakaway: a novel. Kat Spears. St. Martin's Griffin 2015 304 p.

Grades: 10 11 12

1. Grief -- Fiction 2. Friendship -- Fiction 3. Love -- Fiction

9781250065513, $18.99

LC 2015019024

In this novel, by Kat Spears, "[w]hen Jason Marshall's younger sister passes away, he knows he can count on his three best friends and soccer teammates?Mario, Jordie, and Chick?to be there for him. With a grief-crippled mother and a father who's not in the picture, he needs them more than ever. . . . Then Jason meets Raine, a girl he thinks is out of his league but who sees him for everything he wants to be." (Publisher's note)

"Readers will be hard-pressed to find a more realistic portrait of friends finding themselves while losing one another. A rare study of growing pains that gives equal weight to humor and hardship." Kirkus

Sway. By Kat Spears. St. Martin's Press 2014 320 p.

Grades: 9 10 11 12

1. High school students 2. Interpersonal relations 3. Love stories 4. Teenagers -- Fiction 5. High schools -- Fiction 6. Interpersonal relations -- Fiction

1250051436; 9781250051431, $18.99

In this book, by Kat Spears, "high school senior Jesse Alderman, or 'Sway,' as he's known, . . . specializes in getting things people want—-term papers, a date with the prom queen, fake IDs. . . . But when Ken Foster, captain of the football team, leading candidate for homecoming king, and all-around jerk, hires Jesse to help him win the heart of the angelic Bridget Smalley, Jesse finds himself feeling all sorts of things." (Publisher's note)

"Spears develops Jesse's character so thoroughly readers will believe they know him. Despite his ill egality and immorality, he remains sympathetic, revealing his hidden emotions as he forms real friendships with Pete and with an elderly man he meets while spying on Bridget. A compelling debut told with swagger and real depth." Kirkus

Spinelli, Jerry

Smiles to go. Joanna Cotler Books 2008 248p $16.99; lib bdg $17.89; pa $6.99

Grades: 6 7 8 9 10

1. School stories 2. Siblings -- Fiction 3. Friendship -- Fiction 4. Family life -- Fiction
ISBN 978-0-06-028133-5; 0-06-028133-2; 978-0-06-028134-2 lib bdg; 0-06-028134-0 lib bdg; 978-0-06-447197-8 pa; 0-06-447197-7 pa

LC 2007-29563

Will Tuppence's life has always been ruled by science and common sense but in ninth grade, shaken up by the discovery that protons decay, he begins to see the entire world differently and gains new perspective on his relationships with his little sister and two closest friends.

"What makes a Spinelli novel isn't plotting so much as character, dialogue, voice and humor. The Spinelli touch remains true in this funny and thoroughly enjoyable read." Publ Wkly

★ **Stargirl**. Knopf 2000 186p $15.95; lib bdg $17.99; pa $8.95

Grades: 7 8 9 10

1. School stories
ISBN 0-679-88637-0; 0-679-98637-5 lib bdg; 0-375-82233-X pa

LC 99-87944

In this story about the perils of popularity, the courage of nonconformity, and the thrill of first love, an eccentric student named Stargirl changes Mica High School forever

"As always respectful of his audience, Spinelli poses searching questions about loyalty to one's friends and oneself and leaves readers to form their own answers." Publ Wkly

Another title about Stargirl is:
Love, Stargirl (2007)

St. Crow, Lili

Strange angels. Razorbill 2009 293p pa $9.99

Grades: 8 9 10 11 12

1. Orphans -- Fiction 2. Vampires -- Fiction 3. Werewolves -- Fiction 4. Supernatural -- Fiction 5. Extrasensory perception -- Fiction
ISBN 978-1-59514-251-1; 1-59514-251-7

LC 2008-39720

Sixteen-year-old Dru's psychic abilities helped her father battle zombies and other creatures of the "Real World," but now she must rely on herself, a "werwulf"-bitten friend, and a half-human vampire hunter to learn who murdered her parents, and why.

"The book grabs readers by the throat, sets hearts beating loudly and never lets go." Kirkus

Other titles in this series are:
Betrayals (2009)
Defiance (2011)
Jealousy (2010)

St. James, James

Freak show. Dutton Children's Books 2007 297p $18.99

Grades: 8 9 10 11 12

1. School stories 2. Florida -- Fiction 3. Prejudices -- Fiction 4. Gay teenagers -- Fiction 5. Drag culture -- Fiction
ISBN 978-0-525-47799-0; 0-525-47799-3

LC 2006-29716

Having faced teasing that turned into a brutal attack, Christianity expressed as persecution, and the loss of his only real friend when he could no longer keep his crush under wraps, seventeen-year-old Billy Bloom, a drag queen, decides the only to become fabulous again is to run for Homecoming Queen at his elite, private school near Fort Lauderdale, Florida.

Stamper, Vesper

What the night sings. Vesper Stamper. Alfred A. Knopf 2018 266 p. Illustration

Grades: 9 10 11 12

1. Holocaust, Jewish (1939-1945) -- Fiction; 2. Jews -- Fiction; 3. Musicians -- Fiction; 4. Refugees -- Fiction; 5. Survival -- Fiction; 6. Germany -- History -- 1945-1955 -- Fiction; 7. Holocaust survivors -- Fiction; 8. Holocaust, 1939-1945 -- Fiction
9781524700409; 9781524700386, $19.99; 9781524700393

LC 2017020646

In this novel about a teen Holocaust survivor, by Vesper Stamper, "after losing her family and everything she knew in the Nazi concentration camps, Gerta is finally liberated, only to find herself completely alone.... In the displaced persons camp..., Gerta meets Lev, a fellow teen survivor.... With a newfound Jewish identity she never knew she had, and a return to the life of music she thought she lost forever, Gerta must choose how to build a new future." (Publisher's note)

"A well-researched, elegant, and fittingly melodic exploration of reclaiming one's voice -- and the many kinds of faith it can spark." Booklist

Includes bibliographical references (pages 262-263).

Standiford, Natalie

★ **Confessions** of the Sullivan sisters. Scholastic Press 2010 313p

Grades: 9 10 11 12

1. Sisters -- Fiction 2. Family life -- Fiction 3. Grandmothers -- Fiction 4. Baltimore (Md.) -- Fiction 5. Conduct of life -- Fiction 6. Inheritance and succession -- Fiction
ISBN 9780545107105

LC 2010014512

Upon learning on Christmas Day that their rich and imperious grandmother may soon die and disown the family unless the one who offended her deeply will confess, each of the three Sullivan sisters sets down her offenses on paper. "High school." (Horn Book)

"A step above most books about rich girls, their boys, and their toys in both style and substance." Booklist

★ **How** to say goodbye in Robot. Scholastic 2009 276p $17.99; pa $8.99

Grades: 9 10 11 12

    1. Death -- Fiction 2. Friendship -- Fiction 3. Family life -- Fiction 4. Baltimore (Md.) -- Fiction

    ISBN 978-0-545-10708-2; 0-545-10708-3; 978-0-545-10709-9 pa; 0-545-10709-1 pa

                    LC 2009-5256

After moving to Baltimore and enrolling in a private school, high school senior Beatrice befriends a quiet loner with a troubled family history.

"This is an honest and complex depiction of a meaningful platonic friendship and doesn't gloss over troubling issues. The minor characters, particularly the talk-show regulars, are quirky and depicted with sly humor. . . . An outstanding choice for a book discussion group." SLJ

Staples, Suzanne Fisher

★ **Shabanu**; daughter of the wind. Knopf 1989 240p hardcover o.p. pa $6.50

Grades: 8 9 10 11 12

    1. Pakistan -- Fiction 2. Sex role -- Fiction

    ISBN 0-394-84815-2; 0-440-23856-0 pa

                    LC 89-2714

A Newbery Medal honor book, 1990

When eleven-year-old Shabanu, the daughter of a nomad in the Cholistan Desert of present-day Pakistan, is pledged in marriage to an older man whose money will bring prestige to the family, she must either accept the decision, as is the custom, or risk the consequences of defying her father's wishes

"Interspersing native words throughout adds realism, but may trip up readers, who must be patient enough to find meaning through context. This use of language is, however, an important element in helping Staples paint an evocative picture of life in the desert that includes references to the hard facts of reality." Booklist

Other titles in this series are:

Haveli (1993)

The house of djinn (2008)

★ **Under** the Persimmon tree. Farrar, Straus & Giroux 2005 275p $17

Grades: 78 9 10

    1. Afghanistan – Fiction 2. Pakistan -- Fiction

    ISBN 0-374-38025-2

During the 2001 Afghan War, the lives of Najmal, a young refugee from Kunduz, Afghanistan, and Nusrat, an American-Muslim teacher who is awaiting her huband's return from Mazar-i-Sharif, intersect at a school in Peshawar, Pakistan.

"Staples weaves a lot of history and politics into her story. . . . But . . . it's the personal story . . . that compels as it takes readers beyond the modern stereotypes of Muslims as fundamentalist fanatics. There are no sweet reunions, but there's hope in heartbreaking scenes of kindness and courage." Booklist

Starmer, Aaron

Spontaneous. By Aaron Starmer. Penguin Group USA 2016 368 p.

Grades: 9 10 11 12

    1. Death -- Fiction 2. Identity (Psychology) -- Fiction 3. Friendship -- Fiction 4. High schools -- Fiction

    9780698408081, $53.97; 0525429743; 9780525429746, $17.99

This book, by Aaron Starmer, is a "tale of identity, friendship, love, lust, and gory, grisly death. Covington High is facing a unique crisis: one by one, members of the senior class are spontaneously combusting, inexplicably blowing up in a mess of blood and guts. As the body count increases and the government gets involved, 12th grader Mara Carlyle attempts to figure out what's going on, with the help of her best friend Tess and an FBI agent." (Publisher's note)

"A blood-soaked, laugh-filled, tear-drenched, endlessly compelling read." Kirkus

Steiger, A. J.

When my heart joins the thousand. A.J. Steiger. HarperTeen 2018 338 p.

Grades: 9 10 11 12

    1. Osteogenesis imperfecta -- Patients -- Fiction; 2. Teenagers -- Sexual behavior -- Fiction; 3. Youth with autism spectrum disorders -- Fiction; 4. Mental illness -- Fiction; 5. Asperger's syndrome -- Fiction; 6. Romance fiction

    9780062656490; 9780062656476, $17.99

                    LC 2017938997

This novel, by A.J. Steiger, features "a neuroatypical girl with a tragic history and the chronically ill boy trying to break the vault encasing her heart. Alvie Fitz doesn't fit in, and she doesn't care. She's spent years swallowing meds and bad advice from doctors and social workers.... If she can make it to her eighteenth birthday without...mishaps, she'll be legally emancipated. Free. But if she fails, she'll become a ward of the state." (Publisher's note)

"A gorgeous love story of depth and raw emotion that beautifully dismantles the ugly perceptions of autism." Kirkus

Stevenson, Sarah Jamila

The **Latte** Rebellion. Flux 2011 328p pa $9.95

Grades: 8 9 10 11 12

    1. School stories 2. Clubs -- Fiction 3. California -- Fiction 4. Family life -- Fiction 5. Racially mixed people -- Fiction

    ISBN 978-0-7387-2278-8; 0-7387-2278-2

                    LC 2010-35002

When high school senior Asha Jamison is called a "towel head" at a pool party, she and her best friend Carey start a club to raise awareness of mixed-race students that soon sweeps the country, but the hubbub puts her Ivy League dreams, friendship, and beliefs to the test.

"The novel speaks directly to teenagers who are beginning to find their place in their world and figuring out how to make the world a better place for others. . . . This coming-of-age story is craftily written, fast paced and delivers a message of doing the right thing under difficult circumstances." Voice Youth Advocates

Stewart, Martin

Riverkeep. Martin Stewart. Viking, an imprint of Penguin Random House LLC 2016 416 p. Map
Grades: 6 7 8 9 10
    1. Fantasy 2. Father-son relationship -- Fiction 3. Fantasy fiction 4. Rivers -- Fiction 5. Sea monsters -- Fiction
9781101998298, $17.99

LC 2015028442

In this novel by Martin Stewart, "Wulliam's father, the current Riverkeep, is proud of this work. Wull dreads it. . . . Then the unthinkable happens. While recovering a drowned man, Wull's father is pulled under-and when he emerges, he is no longer himself. A dark spirit possesses him, devouring him from the inside. . . . When he hears that a cure for his father lurks in the belly of a great sea-dwelling beast known as the mormorach, he embarks on an epic journey." (Publisher's note)

"Filled with wild adventure and hilarious dialogue (Tillinghast has a particularly saucy mouth), this vivid, engrossing fantasy will delight readers, even those who occasionally find the dialect tricky to navigate." Pub Wkly

The **sacrifice** box. Martin Stewart. Penguin Group USA 2018 368 p.
Grades: 8 9 10 11 12
    1. Supernatural beings -- Fiction; 2. Friendship -- Fiction; 3. Blessing and cursing -- Fiction; 4. Horror fiction
0425289532; 9780425289532, $17.99

In this book, by Martin Stewart, "in the summer of 1982, five friends discover an ancient stone box hidden deep in the woods. They seal inside of it treasured objects from their childhoods, and they make a vow: Never come to the box alone. Never open it after dark. Never take back your sacrifice. Four years later, a series of strange and terrifying events begin to unfold.... Someone broke the rules of the box, and now everyone has to pay." (Publisher's note)

Stiefvater, Maggie

All the crooked saints. Maggie Stiefvater. Scholastic 2017 311 p.
Grades: 9 10 11 12
    1. Cousins -- Fiction; 2. Mexican American teenagers -- Fiction; 3. Pirate radio broadcasting -- Fiction; 4. Colorado -- Fiction; 4. Miracles -- Fiction; 6. Magic -- Fiction; 7. Families -- Fiction
9780545930826; 9780545930802, $18.99; 0545930804

LC 2017046317

In this book, by Maggie Stiefvater, "at the heart of...[Bicho Raro, Colorado] you will find the Soria family, who all have the ability to perform unusual miracles. And at the heart of this family are three cousins longing to change its future: Beatriz, the girl without feelings,...; Daniel, the Saint of Bicho Raro, who performs miracles for everyone but himself; and Joaquin, who spends his nights running a renegade radio station under the name Diablo Diablo." (Publisher's note)

"True history blends with traditional and fanciful folklore as fallen saints find salvation in the lyrical power of family, community, and rock-'n'-roll." Kirkus

Ballad; a gathering of faerie. Flux 2009 353p pa $9.95
Grades: 8 9 10 11 12
    1. School stories 2. Magic -- Fiction 3. Fairies -- Fiction 4. Musicians -- Fiction 5. Supernatural -- Fiction
ISBN 978-0-7387-1484-4 pa; 0-7387-1484-4 pa

LC 2009-19393

Sequel to: Lament: the faerie queen's deception (2008)

When music prodigy James Morgan and his best friend, Deirdre, join a private conservatory for musicians, his talent attracts Nuala, a faerie muse who fosters and feeds on creative energies, but soon he finds himself battling the Queen of the Fey for the very lives of Deirdre and Nuala.

"The themes of music, faerie, and romance combined with a smart male voice wil satisfy realistic fantasy readers as well as existing and new readers of the series." Libr Media Connect

★ **Blue** Lily, Lily Blue; Maggie Stiefvater. Scholastic Press; 2014 400p $18.99
Grades: 9 10 11 12
    1. Magic--Fiction 2.Occultism--Fiction 3. Dreams--Fiction 4. Family secrets--Fiction
ISBN: 9780545424967; 0545424968

LC 2014947741

In this third title in the author's Raven Cycle, "Blue Sargent has found things. For the first time in her life, she has friends she can trust, a group to which she can belong. The Raven Boys have taken her in as one of their own. Their problems have become hers, and her problems have become theirs. The trick with found things, though, is how easily they can be lost. Friends can betray. Mothers can disappear. Visions can mislead. Certainties can unravel." (Publisher's note)

"This atmospheric fantasy is far more character driven than the former book, with increased and especially satisfying interactions among players. . . . The book's luminous and lively prose takes unanticipated paths, some new and surprising, with others connecting to previous events, demonstrating meticulous plot design." VOYA

★ The **dream** thieves; Maggie Stiefvater. Scholastic 2013 416 p. (Raven cycle) (jacketed hardcover) $18.99
Grades: 8 9 10 11 12
    1. Occult fiction 2. Fantasy fiction 3. Magic -- Fiction 4. Dreams -- Fiction 5. Paranormal fiction 6. Secrets -- Fiction
ISBN 0545424941; 9780545424943

LC 2013018731

This is the second book in Maggie Stiefvater's Raven Cycle series. Here, after "the transformative events at Cabeswater . . . , the context in which Gansey, Blue, Adam, Ronan, and Noah operate is further altered by the arrival of the Gray Man, a self-described hit man. . . . The Gray Man brings with him the machinations of larger, previously unknown forces as he takes orders from a voice on the phone to hunt the Greywaren, the identity of which is revealed early on." (Publishers Weekly)

"In this darker second book (The Raven Boys), Gansey, Blue, and the search for Glendower take a backseat to the exploration of Ronan's and Adam's tortured personalities. Stiefvater's descriptive prose reveals a complicated plot, multiple viewpoints, and detailed backstories. Many mysteries remain, but the cliffhanger ending makes it clear that Glendower will resurface as the main focus of book three." (Horn Book)

Forever. Scholastic Press 2011 390p $17.99
Grades: 9 10 11 12
　　1. Love stories 2. Werewolves -- Fiction 3. Supernatural -- Fiction
ISBN 978-0-545-25908-8
　　　　　　　　　　　　　　　　　LC 2011023889
Sequel to Linger (2010)
A human girl and her werewolf boyfriend must fight for their love as death comes closing in.

"Stiefvater's emotional prose is rich without being melodramatic, and she clearly shares her fans' love of these characters." Booklist

Linger. Scholastic 2010 362p $17.99
Grades: 8 9 10 11 12
　　1. Werewolves -- Fiction 2. Supernatural -- Fiction
ISBN 978-0-545-12328-0; 0-545-12328-3
　　　　　　　　　　　　　　　　　LC 2009-39500
Sequel to Shiver (2009)
As Grace hides the vast depth of her love for Sam from her parents and Sam struggles to release his werewolf past and claim a human future, a new wolf named Cole wins Isabel's heart but his own past threatens to destroy the whole pack.

"This riveting narrative, impossible to put down, is not only an excellent addition to the current fangs and fur craze but is also a beautifully written romance that, along with Shiver, will have teens clamoring for the third and final entry." Voice Youth Advocates

Followed by Forever (2011)

★ The **Raven** Boys; Maggie Stiefvater. Scholastic Press 2012 409 p. (hardcover) $18.99
Grades: 8 9 10 11 12
　　1. Magic -- Fiction 2. Supernatural -- Fiction 3. Paranormal fiction 4. Occultism -- Fiction 5. Clairvoyance -- Fiction
ISBN 0545424925; 9780545424929
　　　　　　　　　　　　　　　　　LC 2012030880
This book is the first in Maggie Stiefvater's series the "Raven Cycle". It follows "16-year-old Blue Sargent, daughter of a small-town psychic, [who] has lived her whole life under a prophecy: If she kisses her true love, he will die. . . . She sees a vision of a dying Raven boy named Gansey. The Raven Boys--students at Aglionby, a nearby prep school, so-called because of the ravens on their school crest--soon encounter Blue in person." (Kirkus Reviews)

★ The **Raven** King. By Maggie Stiefvater. Scholastic Inc. 2016 400 p. (Raven Cycle)
Grades: 8 9 10 11 12
　　1. Bildungsromans 2. Love -- Fiction 3. Magic -- Fiction 4. Teenagers -- Fiction
0545424984; 9780545424981, $18.99
"This [final] installment finds the world of the Raven Boys (Gansey, Ronan, Adam, and Noah) and their best friend Blue in considerable and dangerous disarray. As strange, in-

creasingly sinister things begin happening in Henrietta and the magic forest of Cabeswater, the search for sleeping king Owen Glendower becomes more imperative, as it becomes apparent that something wicked this way comes." (Booklist)

"Stiefvater excels at building an intricately layered narrative with twisting, unpredictable turns, and her ability to introduce new, complex characters and storylines while also tying up previous loose ends is remarkable." VOYA

★ The **Scorpio** Races. Scholastic Press 2011 409p $17.99
Grades: 8 9 10 11 12
　　1. Love stories 2. Fantasy fiction 3. Horses -- Fiction 4. Racing -- Fiction 5. Orphans -- Fiction
ISBN 978-0-545-22490-1; 0-545-22490-X
　　　　　　　　　　　　　　　　　LC 2011015775
"Stiefvater's narration is as much about atmospherics as it is about event, and the water horses are the environment in which Sean and Puck move, allies and rivals to the end. It's not a feel-good story—dread, loss, and hard choices are the islanders' lot. As a study of courage and loyalty tested, however, it is an utterly compelling read." Publ Wkly

★ **Shiver**. Scholastic 2009 392p $17.99; pa $8.99
Grades: 9 10 11 12
　　1. Werewolves -- Fiction 2. Supernatural -- Fiction
ISBN 978-0-545-12326-6; 0-545-12326-7; 978-0-545-12327-3 pa; 0-545-12327-5 pa
　　　　　　　　　　　　　　　　　LC 2009-5257
In all the years she has watched the wolves in the woods behind her house, Grace has been particularly drawn to an unusual yellow-eyed wolf who, in his turn, has been watching her with increasing intensity.

"Stiefvater skillfully increases the tension throughout; her take on werewolves is interesting and original while her characters are refreshingly willing to use their brains to deal with the challenges they face." Publ Wkly

Other titles featuring the wolves of Mercy Falls are:
Forever (2011)
Linger (2010)

Sinner. Maggie Stiefvater. Scholastic Press 2014 368 p.
Grades: 9 10 11 12
　　1. Human-animal relationships -- Fiction; 2. Metamorphosis -- Fiction; 3. Paranormal fiction; 4. Wolves -- Fiction; 5. Romance fiction; 6. Los Angeles (Calif.) -- Fiction
0545654572; 9780545654579, $18.99
　　　　　　　　　　　　　　　　　LC 2014937299
In this young adult novel by Maggie Stiefvater, part of the Shiver series, "Cole St. Clair has come to California for one reason: to get back Isabel Culpeper. She fled from his damaged, drained life, and damaged and drained it even more. He doesn't just want her. He needs her. . . . Cole and Isabel share a past that never seemed to have a future. They have the power to love each other and the power to tear each other apart." (Publisher's note)

"The relationship between the richly drawn characters is the heart of the book-it is light on paranormal and wolf action. Cole and Isabel are both jerks, but they are jerks with hearts, and they keep up with each other's witty banter. The ending wraps up a bit too neatly, but getting there is an absolute delight.A spectacularly messy, emotionally oh-so-human romance." Kirkus

Stirling, Tricia

When my heart was wicked. Tricia Stirling. Scholastic Press 2015 192 p.

Grades: 9 10 11 12Fic; 813.6

1. Choice -- Fiction 2. Magic -- Fiction 3. Mothers and daughters -- Fiction 4. Stepmothers -- Fiction 5. Botany 6. Mother-daughter relationship -- Fiction
0545695732; 9780545695732, $17.99

LC 2014021741

In this book, by Tricia Stirling, "after a childhood bouncing between her mother, possibly a witch and probably unstable, and her father, whose presence made it possible for Lacy to see magic and beauty everywhere, Lacy's mother, Cheyenne, disappeared. Her mother's influence gone, Lacy's darkness blossomed into light and kindness. But her father has died, and although stepmother Anna wants to keep her, Cheyenne returns to drag Lacy back to Sacramento." (Kirkus Reviews)

"Stirling does a wonderful job of making the reader care for Lacy, who is not beyond casting spells herself. Her Northern California world of idiosyncratic personalities and oddball beauty is memorable and will be sure to appeal to teens who like their realism tempered with the otherworldly." Booklist

Stohl, Margaret

Black Widow: forever red. By Margaret Stohl. Marvel 2015 416 p.

Grades: 7 8 9 10 11 12

1. Adventure stories 2. Superheroes -- Fiction 3. Avengers (Fictional characters) 4. Secret societies -- Fiction 5. Assassins -- Fiction 6. Black Widow (Fictional character)
9781484726433, $17.99; 148472643X

LC 2015020692

This is a prose novel about the Marvel character. "Natasha Romanoff is one of the world's most lethal assassins. . . . Natasha was given the title of Black Widow by Ivan Somodorov, her brutal teacher at the Red Room, Moscow's infamous academy for operatives. Ava Orlova is just trying to fit in as an average Brooklyn teenager. . . . The daughter of a missing Russian quantum physicist, Ava was once subjected to a series of ruthless military experiments-until she was rescued by Black Widow." (Publisher's note)

"Great fight sequences, plenty of action, twists in the plot, and characters motivated by strong emotions will keep readers engaged and entertained." SLJ

Stokes, Paula

Girl against the universe. Paula Stokes; [edited by] Karen Chaplin. HarperTeen 2016 400 p.

Grades: 8 9 10 11

1. Fortune -- Fiction 2. Luck -- Fiction 3. Romance fiction -- Fiction 4. Teenagers -- Fiction 5. Tennis players -- Fiction
9780062379962, $17.99

LC 2015961051

In this novel by Paula Stokes, "no matter how many charms she buys off the internet or good luck rituals she performs each morning, horrible things happen when Maguire is around. Like that time her brother, father, and uncle were all killed in a car crash—and Maguire walked away with barely a scratch. But then on her way out of her therapist's office, she meets Jordy, an aspiring tennis star, who wants to help Maguire break her unlucky streak." (Publisher's note)

"Stokes' engaging prose and sympathetic characters serve up great lessons in acceptance for teens dealing with trauma." Kirkus

Stone, Nic

★ **Dear** Martin. Nic Stone. Crown Books for Young Readers 2017 224 p.

Grades: 9 10 11 12

1. African Americans -- Fiction; 2. Letters -- Fiction; 3. Police brutality -- Fiction; 4. Race relations -- Fiction; 5. Racial profiling in law enforcement -- Fiction; 6. Racism -- Fiction; 7. King, Martin Luther, Jr., 1929-1968 -- Fiction
1101939494; 9781101939499, $17.99; 9781101939505; 9781101939529

LC 2016058582

William C. Morris Honor Book (2018)

In this book, by Nic Stone, "Justyce McAllister is top of his class and set for the Ivy League -- but none of that matters to the police officer who just put him in handcuffs. And despite leaving his rough neighborhood behind, he can't escape the scorn of his former peers or the ridicule of his new classmates. Justyce looks to the teachings of Dr. Martin Luther King Jr. for answers. But do they hold up anymore? He starts a journal to Dr. King to find out." (Publisher's note)

"Stone's debut confronts the reality of police brutality, misconduct, and fatal shootings in the U.S., using an authentic voice to accurately portray the struggle of self-exploration teens like Justyce experience every day." (Booklist)

Stone, Tamara Ireland

Little do we know. Tamara Ireland Stone. Hyperion 2018 416 p.

Grades: 9 10 11 12

1. Best friends -- Fiction; 2. Dating (Social customs) -- Fiction; 3. Family problems -- Fiction; 4. Friendship -- Fiction; 5. Secrets -- Fiction
9781484768211, $17.99

LC 2018004933

In this book, by Tamara Ireland Stone, "next-door neighbors and ex-best friends Hannah and Emory haven't spoken in months.... Now, Emory is fine-tuning her UCLA performing arts application.... Meanwhile, Hannah's strong faith is shaken when her family's financial problems come to light.... No matter how much Hannah and Emory desperately want to bridge the thirty-six steps between their bedroom windows, they can't. Not anymore." (Publisher's note)

Time between us; Tamara Ireland Stone. Hyperion 2012 384 p. (hardcover) $17.99

Grades: 7 8 9 10

1. Love stories 2. Time travel -- Fiction 3. Love -- Fiction 4. Illinois -- Fiction 5. High schools -- Fiction 6. Space and time -- Fiction 7. Family life -- Illinois

-- Fiction
ISBN 142315956X; 9781423159568

LC 2011053368

This book by Tamara Ireland Stone follows "Anna and Bennett," a couple who "were never supposed to meet: she lives in 1995 Chicago and he lives in 2012 San Francisco. But Bennett's unique ability to travel through time and space brings him into Anna's life, and with him, a new world of adventure and possibility. As their relationship deepens, they face the reality that time might knock Bennett back where he belongs." (Publisher's note)

Stone, Tanya Lee

★ A **bad** boy can be good for a girl. Wendy Lamb Books 2006 228p hardcover o.p. pa $7.99

Grades: 9 10 11 12

1. School stories
ISBN 0-385-74702-0; 978-0-385-74702-8; 0-553-49509-7 pa; 978-0-553-49509-6 pa

LC 2006-272453

Josie, Nicolette, and Aviva all get mixed up with a senior boy who can talk them into doing almost anything he wants. In a blur of high school hormones and personal doubt, each girl struggles with how much to give up and what ultimately to keep for herself.

"The language is realistic and frank, and, while not graphic, it is filled with descriptions of the teens and their sexuality. This is not a book that will sit quietly on any shelf; it will be passed from girl to girl to girl." SLJ

Stork, Francisco X.

Disappeared. Francisco X. Stork. Arthur A. Levine Books, an imprint of Scholastic Inc. 2017 326 p.

Grades: 7 8 9 10

1. Brothers and sisters -- Fiction; 2. Brothers and sisters -- Mexico -- Ciudad Juárez -- Fiction; 3. Crime -- Mexico -- Ciudad Juárez -- Fiction; 4. Kidnapping -- Fiction; 5. Kidnapping -- Mexico -- Ciudad Juárez -- Fiction; 6. Reporters and reporting -- Fiction; 7. Reporters and reporting -- Mexico -- Ciudad Juárez -- Fiction; 8. Women -- Violence against -- Mexico -- Ciudad Juárez -- Fiction; 9. Ciudad Juárez (Mexico) -- Fiction; 10. Mexico -- Fiction

9780545945844; 9780545944472, $17.99

LC 2017017320

In this book, by Francisco X. Stork, "Sara Zapata's best friend disappeared, kidnapped by the web of criminals who terrorize Juarez.... Emiliano Zapata fell in love with Perla Rubi, who will never be his so long as he's poor.... In the next four days, Sara and Emiliano will each face impossible choices.... But when the web closes in on Sara, only one path remains for the siblings: the way across the desert to the United States." (Publisher's note)

"Stork (The Memory of Light) crafts a narrative that is both riveting and eye-opening. Part thriller, part sociological study, the novel sheds light on poverty, corruption, and greed while bringing readers intimately close to the plight of those who illegally cross borders with the hope of a brighter future." Pub Wkly

★ The **last** summer of the death warriors. Arthur A. Levine Books 2010 344p $17.99

Grades: 8 9 10 11 12

1. Death -- Fiction 2. Orphans -- Fiction 3. New Mexico -- Fiction 4. Mexican Americans -- Fiction
ISBN 978-0-545-15133-7; 0-545-15133-3

LC 2009-19853

"Seventeen-year-old Pancho Sanchez is sent to a Catholic orphanage after his father and sister die in the span of a few months. Though the cause of his sister's death is technically 'undetermined,' Pancho plans to kill the man he believes responsible. . . . When D.Q., a fellow resident dying from brain cancer, asks Pancho to accompany him to Albuquerque for experimental treatments, Pancho agrees—he'll get paid and it's where his sister's killer lives." Publ Wkly

"This novel, in the way of the best literary fiction, is an invitation to careful reading that rewards serious analysis and discussion. Thoughtful readers will be delighted by both the challenge and Stork's respect for their abilities." Booklist

★ **Marcelo** in the real world. Arthur A. Levine Books 2009 312p $17.99

Grades: 8 9 10 11 12

1. Autism -- Fiction 2. Asperger's syndrome -- Fiction
ISBN 0-545-05474-5; 978-0-545-05474-4

LC 2008-14729

ALA Schneider Family Book Award Honor Book (2010)

This book features "Marcelo Sandoval [who] is a 17-year-old looking forward to his senior year in high school. Living with something akin to Asperger's syndrome, Marcelo has spent his life learning step by step how to do things that many people learn intuitively. . . . Marcelo's father makes a deal with him: if he will spend the summer working at his father's law firm and successfully follow the rules of the real world, he can choose where he will spend his senior year." (Christian Century)

"Stork introduces ethical dilemmas, the possibility of love, and other 'real world' conflicts, all the while preserving the integrity of his characterizations and intensifying the novel's psychological and emotional stakes." Publ Wkly

★ The **memory** of light. Francisco X. Stork. Arthur A. Levine Books, an imprint of Scholastic Inc. 2016 325 p.

Grades: 9 10 11 12

1. Depression, Mental -- Fiction 2. Families -- Texas -- Fiction 3. Family life -- Texas -- Fiction 4. Friendship -- Fiction 5. Mexican Americans -- Fiction 5. Psychotherapy -- Fiction 6. Psychotherapy patients -- Fiction 7. Suicide -- Fiction 8. Texas -- Fiction 9. Depression (Psychology) -- Fiction

0545474329; 0545474337; 9780545474320, $17.99

LC 2014044136

In this book, by Francisco X. Stork, "When Vicky Cruz wakes up in the Lakeview Hospital Mental Disorders ward, she knows one thing: She can't even commit suicide right. But there she meets Mona, the live wire; Gabriel, the saint; E.M., always angry; and Dr. Desai, a quiet force. With stories and honesty, kindness and hard work, they push her to reconsider her life before Lakeview, and offer her an acceptance she's never had." (Publisher's note)

"Stork remains loyal to his characters, their moments of weakness, and their pragmatic views, and he does not shy away from such topics as domestic violence, social-class struggles, theology, and philosophy." Kirkus

Strasser, Todd

Boot camp. Simon & Schuster Books for Young Readers 2007 238p hardcover o.p. pa $6.99

Grades: 8 9 10 11 12

    1. Torture -- Fiction 2. Juvenile delinquency -- Fiction

ISBN 978-1-4169-0848-7; 1-4169-0848-X; 978-1-4169-5942-7 pa; 1-4169-5942-4 pa

                        LC 2006-13634

After ignoring several warnings to stop dating his former teacher, Garrett is sent to Lake Harmony, a boot camp that uses brutal methods to train students to obey their parents.

"The ending is both realistic and disturbing. . . . Writing in the teen's mature and perceptive voice, Strasser creates characters who will provoke strong reactions from readers. . . . [This is a] fast-paced and revealing story." SLJ

Can't get there from here. Simon & Schuster Books for Young Readers 2004 198p $15.95

Grades: 7 8 9 10

    1. Homeless persons -- Fiction 2. Runaway teenagers -- Fiction

ISBN 0-689-84169-8

                        LC 2003-170

Tired of being hungry, cold, and dirty from living on the streets of New York City with a tribe of other homeless teenagers who are dying, one by one, a girl named Maybe ponders her future and longs for someone to care about her

"While the events described in this cautionary tale are shocking, the language is not, making these all-too-real problems accessible to a wide readership." SLJ

Famous. Simon & Schuster Books for Young Readers 2011 257p $15.99

Grades: 7 8 9 10

    1. Fame -- Fiction 2. Actors -- Fiction 3. Celebrities -- Fiction 4. Hollywood (Calif.) -- Fiction

ISBN 978-1-4169-7511-3; 1-4169-7511-X

                        LC 2009-48163

Sixteen-year-old Jamie Gordon had a taste of praise and recognition at age fourteen when her unflattering photograph of an actress was published, but as she pursues her dream of being a celebrity photographer, she becomes immersed in the dark side of fame.

"The book makes some astute observations about America's reality-television culture and its obsession with fame. . . . This well-crafted novel clearly belongs in all public, junior high, and high school libraries." Voice Youth Advocates

★ **Give** a boy a gun. Simon & Schuster Bks. for Young Readers 2000 146p hardcover o.p. pa $5.99

Grades: 9 10 11 12

    1. School stories 2. Violence -- Fiction

ISBN 0-689-81112-8; 0-689-84893-5 pa

"Statistics, quotes, and facts related to actual incidents of school violence appear in dark print at the bottom of the pages. An appendix includes a chronology of school shootings in the United States, the author's own treatise on gun control, and places to get more information." SLJ

If I grow up. Simon & Schuster Books for Young Readers 2009 222p $16.99

Grades: 7 8 9 10

    1. Gangs -- Fiction 2. Poverty -- Fiction 3. Violence -- Fiction 4. African Americans -- Fiction

ISBN 978-1-4169-2523-1; 1-4169-2523-6

                        LC 2008-00655

Growing up in the inner-city projects, DeShawn is reluctantly forced into the gang world by circumstances beyond his control.

"Strasser's writing puts the reader in the midst of the projects and offers totally real characters." Voice Youth Advocates

Includes bibliographical references

No place; Todd Strasser. Simon & Schuster Books for Young Readers 2014 272 p. (hardcover) $17.99

Grades: 7 8 9 10

    1. Homelessness -- Fiction 2. Homeless persons -- Fiction 3. Poverty -- Fiction

ISBN 144245721X; 9781442457218

                        LC 2012043701

In this novel, by Todd Strasser, "It seems like Dan has it all. . . . Then his family loses their home. Forced to move into the town's Tent City, Dan feels his world shifting. . . . As Dan struggles to adjust to his new life, he gets involved with the people who are fighting for better conditions and services for the residents of Tent City. But someone wants Tent City gone, and will stop at nothing until it's destroyed." (Publisher's note)

"High school senior Dan Halprin is the star pitcher on the baseball team, has been offered a scholarship to Rice University, and is dating wealthy Talia. When his parents lose their jobs as a stockbroker and youth athletics coach, and then their home, the family is forced to move into Dignityville, a tent community in the center of town. Humiliated and angry, Dan struggles to maintain his self-confidence, relationships, and aspirations...Coping with their personal financial catastrophe, wanting to stay in their familiar town, finding work, accepting charity, and maintaining self-respect are issues that weigh heavily on Dan and his parents. Readers will be drawn into this contemporary story." (School Library Journal)

Price of duty. Todd Strasser. Simon & Shuster Books for Young Readers 2018 192 p.

Grades: 8 9 10 11

    1. Dating (Social customs) -- Fiction; 2. Duty -- Fiction; 3. Family life -- Fiction; 4. Heroes -- Fiction; 5. Post-traumatic stress disorder -- Fiction; 6. Soldiers -- Fiction; 7. War -- Fiction

148149709X; 1481497103; 9781481497091, $17.99; 9781481497107

                        LC 2017025647

In this novel, by Todd Strasser, "Jake Liddell is a war hero. The military is considering awarding him a Silver Star, a huge honor for any soldier -- especially for the son of a military family. Only Jake's questioning everything his family brought him up to believe. Now at home, recovering from his physical wounds, the memories of what he experienced 'over there' haunt him." (Publisher's note)

Wish you were dead. Egmont USA 2009 236p
Grades: 8 9 10 11 12
    1. School stories 2. Weblogs -- Fiction 3. Kidnapping -- Fiction 4. Missing persons -- Fiction 5. New York (State) -- Fiction
ISBN 160684007X; 1606840495; 9781606840078; 9781606840498
                    LC 2009-14641
Madison, a senior at a suburban New York high school, tries to uncover who is responsible for the disappearance of her friends, popular students mentioned in the posts of an anonymous blogger, while she, herself, is being stalked online and in-person.

    "The themes of bullying, tolerance, and friendship are issues to which readers can relate, as well as the inclusion of the IMing, blogging, texting, and social networking. This thriller will be popular and passed from one reader to another." Voice Youth Advocates

Stratton, Allan

    ★ **Borderline**. HarperTeen 2010 298p $16.99; lib bdg $17.89
Grades: 6 7 8 9 10
    1. Muslims -- Fiction 2. Terrorism -- Fiction 3. Friendship -- Fiction 4. Prejudices -- Fiction 5. Father-son relationship -- Fiction
ISBN 978-0-06-145111-9; 0-06-145111-8; 978-0-06-145112-6 lib bdg; 0-06-145112-6 lib bdg
                    LC 2009-5241
Despite the strained relationship between them, teenaged Sami Sabiri risks his life to uncover the truth when his father is implicated in a terrorist plot.

    This is "a powerful story and excellent resource for teaching tolerance, with a message that extends well beyond the timely subject matter." Publ Wkly

    ★ **Chanda's** secrets. Annick Press 2004 193p $19.95; pa $8.95
Grades: 7 8 9 10
    1. Africa -- Fiction 2. AIDS (Disease) -- Fiction
ISBN 1-55037-835-X; 1-55037-834-1 pa
Michael L. Printz Award honor book, 2005
    "The details of sub-Saharan African life are convincing and smoothly woven into this moving story of poverty and courage, but the real insight for readers will be the appalling treatment of the AIDS victims. Strong language and frank description are appropriate to the subject matter." SLJ
    Another title about Chanda is:
    Chanda's war (2007)

Chanda's wars; with an afterword by Roméo Dallaire. HarperCollinsPublishers 2008 384p $17.99; lib bdg $18.89; pa $8.99
Grades: 8 9 10 11 12
    1. War stories 2. Africa -- Fiction 3. Orphans -- Fiction

    4. Kidnapping -- Fiction
ISBN 978-0-06-087262-5; 0-06-087262-4; 978-0-06-087264-9 lib bdg; 0-06-087264-0 lib bdg; 978-0-06-087265-6 pa; 0-06-087265-9 pa
                    LC 2007-10829
Sequel to: Chanda's secrets (2004)
    Chanda Kabelo, a teenaged African girl, must save her younger siblings after they are kidnapped and forced to serve as child soldiers in General Mandiki's rebel army.

    "The characters are drawn without sentimentality, and the story is a moving portrayal of betrayal and love. The army's brutality and the traumas of the child soldiers are graphic and disturbing." Booklist

Strauss, Victoria

Passion blue; by Victoria Strauss. Marshall Cavendish Children 2012 346 p. (hardcover) $17.99
Grades: 7 8 9 10 11 12
    1. Historical fiction 2. Convents -- Fiction 3. Women artists -- Fiction 4. Self-realization -- Fiction 5. Nuns -- Fiction 6. Magic -- Fiction 7. Artists -- Fiction 8. Talismans -- Fiction 9. Italy -- History -- 15th century -- Fiction
ISBN 0761462309; 9780761462309; 9780761462316
                    LC 2011040133
In this book by Victoria Strauss, when "Giulia is forced into a convent . . . she is surprised to learn of the beauty within, and that nuns and novices have vocations. . . . Her world expands as she learns the tools, materials, and techniques of great Renaissance painters. By chance, she meets a young male artisan repairing a convent masterpiece. They begin a clandestine romance. Her two desires -- painting and a husband -- war within as she contemplates her future." (School Library Journal)

Strohmeyer, Sarah

Smart girls get what they want; by Sarah Strohmeyer. 1st ed. Harpercollins Childrens Books 2012 348 p. (tr. bdg.) $17.99; (paperback) $9.99
Grades: 7 8 9 10 11 12
    1. Female friendship -- Fiction 2. Grading and marking (Education) 3. High school students -- Fiction 4. Friendship -- Fiction 5. Best friends -- Fiction 6. High schools -- Fiction 7. Interpersonal relations -- Fiction
ISBN 0061953407; 9780061953408; 9780061953415
                    LC 2011026094
Author Sarah Strohmeyer tells the story of Gigi, Neerja, and Bea, three friends who "stumble upon . . . [Neerja's sister] Parad's signature-less yearbook, making them think that maybe studying isn't everything. . . . When Gigi is accused of cheating on the AP Chemistry midterm along with Mike, a Man Clan wannabe who calls her 'Einstein,' the girls launch into action. Gigi finds herself running for student rep against Will, the new guy from California. . . . Neerja tries out for the lead in Romeo and Juliet and Bea convinces Gigi to join the ski team with her." (Kirkus Reviews)

Stroud, Jonathan

The **Amulet** of Samarkand. Hyperion Bks. for Children 2003 462p (Bartimaeus trilogy) $17.95; pa $7.99

Grades: 7 8 9 10
1. Fantasy fiction
ISBN 0-7868-1859-X; 0-7868-5255-0 pa
LC 2003-49904

Nathaniel, a magician's apprentice, summons up the djinni Bartimaeus and instructs him to steal the Amulet of Samarkand from the powerful magician Simon Lovelace.

"There is plenty of action, mystery, and humor to keep readers turning the pages. This title, the first in a trilogy, is a must for fantasy fans." SLJ

Other titles in this series are:
The golem's eye (2004)
Ptolemy's gate (2006)

★ **Heroes** of the valley. Hyperion Books for Children 2009 483p $17.99
Grades: 7 8 9 10
1. Adventure fiction 2. Middle Ages -- Fiction
ISBN 978-1-4231-0966-2; 1-4231-0966-X

"Twelve Houses control sections of a valley. Halli Sveinsson—at 15, the youngest child of the rulers of the House of Svein—goes against tradition when he sets out to avenge the death of his murdered uncle, and his actions result in warfare among Houses for the first time in generations. . . . Smart, funny dialogue and prose, revealing passages about the exploits of the hero Svein, bouts of action and a touch of romance briskly move the story along." Publ Wkly

The **ring** of Solomon; a Bartimaeus novel. Disney/Hyperion Books 2010 398p $17.99
Grades: 7 8 9 10
1. Fantasy fiction 2. Kings 3. Magic -- Fiction 4. Jerusalem -- Fiction 5. Witchcraft -- Fiction
ISBN 978-1-4231-2372-9; 1-4231-2372-7
LC 2010015468

Wise-cracking djinni Bartimaeus finds himself at the court of King Solomon with an unpleasant master, a sinister servant, and King Solomon's magic ring.

"In this exciting prequel set in ancient Israel, Stroud presents an early adventure of his sharp-tongued djinn, Bartimaeus. . . . This is a superior fantasy that should have fans racing back to those books." Publ Wkly

Stuber, Barbara

★ **Crossing** the tracks. Margarert K. McElderry Books 2010 258p $16.99
Grades: 6 7 8 9
1. Household employees -- Fiction 2. Father-daughter relationship -- Fiction
ISBN 978-1-4169-9703-0; 1-4169-9703-2
LC 2009-42672

In Missouri in 1926, fifteen-year-old Iris Baldwin discovers what family truly means when her father hires her out for the summer as a companion to a country doctor's invalid mother.

"Thought-provoking and tenderhearted, Iris's story is one of a mature young woman who faces life with courage and common sense. . . . This thoughtful novel offers strong character development and an engaging protagonist." SLJ

Sturtevant, Katherine

A **true** and faithful narrative. Farrar, Straus & Giroux 2006 247p $17
Grades: 6 7 8 9
1. London (England)--Fiction
ISBN 0-374-37809-6
LC 2005046922

In London in the 1680s, Meg—now sixteen years old—tries to decide whether to marry either of the two men who court her, taking into account both love and her writing ambitions.

The author "offers readers a story depicted with great clarity and many vivid details of everyday life. Written in the first-person, the narrative reveals Meg as a strong-willed yet vulnerable young woman who emerges as a well-rounded, convincing individual." Booklist

Sugiura, Misa

It's not like it's a secret. Misa Sugiura. HarperTeen 2017 394 p.
Grades: 7 8 9 10 11
1. Adultery -- Fiction; 2. Fathers and daughters -- Fiction; 3. Japanese Americans -- Fiction; 4. Lesbian teenagers -- Fiction; 5. Teenage girls -- Fiction; 6. California -- Fiction; 7. Romance fiction; 8. Lesbians -- Fiction; 9. Bildungsromans
9780062473431; 9780062473417, $17.99
LC 2016961849

In this book, by Misa Sugiura, edited by Jennifer Klonsky, "Sana is a fully realized protagonist with faults and unacknowledged privilege alongside her nuanced experience of identity and 'model minority' racism. Sugiura thoughtfully explores intersecting issues of race, immigrant-family relationships, queer romance, and, less explicitly, class dynamics without implying the significance of one over the others. Well-paced, brimming with drama, and utterly vital." (Kirkus Reviews)

Includes bibliographical references (pages 389-390).

Sullivan, Tara

★ The **Bitter** Side of Sweet. Tara Sullivan. Penguin Group USA 2016 320 p.
Grades: 9 10 11 12
1. Slavery -- Fiction 2. Child labor -- Fiction
9780399173073, $17.99; 0399173072
LC 2015038251

In this novel, by Tara Sullivan, "two young boys must escape a life of slavery in modern-day Ivory Coast. . . . The boys only wanted to make some money during the dry season to help their impoverished family. Instead they were tricked into forced labor on a plantation in the Ivory Coast; they spend day after day living on little food and harvesting beans in the hot sun-dangerous, backbreaking work." (Publisher's note)

"There are so few stories for teenagers that provide a glimpse into the complex global systems, such as cocoa production, that they unwittingly participate in every day and likely take for granted. An author's note, glossary, and source material provide further context to engage readers and teachers. Absorbing and important." Booklist

Golden boy; Tara Sullivan. G.P. Putnam's Sons, an imprint of Penguin Group (USA) Inc. 2013 368 p. (hardcover) $16.99

Grades: 7 8 9 10 11 12

1. Voyages and travels -- Fiction 2. Albinos and albinism -- Fiction 3. Survival -- Fiction 4. Tanzania -- Fiction 5. Human rights -- Fiction 6. Human skin color -- Fiction

ISBN 0399161120; 9780399161124

LC 2012043310

In this book, an albino boy named Habo does not fit in with his Tanzanian family, who shun him. "Only Habo's sister, Asu, protects and nurtures him. Poverty forces the family from their rural home near Arusha to Mwanza, hundreds of miles away, to stay with relatives. After their bus fare runs out, they hitch a ride across the Serengeti with an ivory poacher who sees opportunity in Habo. Forced to flee for his life, the boy eventually becomes an apprentice to Kweli, a wise, blind carver." (Kirkus)

Sullivan, Tricia

Shadowboxer. Tricia Sullivan. Ravenstone 2014 288 p.

Grades: 9 10 11 12

1. Mixed martial arts 2. Paranormal fiction 3. Thailand 4. Immortality -- Fiction 5. Boxers (Sports) -- Fiction

1781082820; 9781781082829, $9.99

In Tricia Sullivan's novel "after she has a confrontation with a Hollywood martial arts star that threatens her gym's reputation, Jade's coach sends her to a training camp in Thailand for an attitude adjustment. Hoping to discover herself, she instead uncovers a shocking conspiracy. In a world just beyond our own, a man is stealing the souls of children to try and live forever." (Publisher's note)

"SF author Sullivan (Lightborn) spins a kinetic, violent, and magical tale that makes excellent use of Jade's hard-edged voice. Sullivan brings to life the beauty of Thailand and the sweat and blood of the gym, infusing them with magic and danger." Publishers Weekly

Suma, Nova Ren

17 & gone; Nova Ren Suma. 1st ed. Dutton 2013 320 p. (hardcover) $17.99

Grades: 9 10 11 12

1. Occult fiction 2. Schizophrenia -- Fiction 3. Missing persons -- Fiction 4. Supernatural -- Fiction 5. Mental illness -- Fiction 6. Missing children -- Fiction 7. Psychiatric hospitals -- Fiction

ISBN 0525423400; 9780525423409

LC 2012029324

In this novel, by Nova Ren Suma, "seventeen-year-old Lauren is having visions of girls who have gone missing. And all these girls have just one thing in common--they are 17 and gone without a trace. As Lauren struggles to shake these waking nightmares, impossible questions demand urgent answers: Why are the girls speaking to Lauren? How can she help them? And . . . is she next?" (Publisher's note)

"Mature without being graphic, with a complex and intriguing plot, this novel should have no trouble finding readers." SLJ

Imaginary girls. Dutton 2011 348p $17.99

Grades: 9 10 11 12

1. Dead -- Fiction 2. Sisters -- Fiction 3. Supernatural -- Fiction 4. New York (State) -- Fiction

ISBN 978-0-525-42338-6; 0-525-42338-9

LC 2010-42758

Two years after sixteen-year-old Chloe discovered classmate London's dead body floating in a Hudson Valley reservoir, she returns home to be with her devoted older sister Ruby, a town favorite, and finds that London is alive and well, and that Ruby may somehow have brought her back to life and persuaded everyone that nothing is amiss.

The author "uses the story's supernatural, horror movie-ready elements in the best of ways; beneath all the strangeness lies beauty, along with a powerful statement about the devotion between sisters. Not your average paranormal novel." Publ Wkly

★ The **walls** around us: a novel. By Nova Ren Suma. Algonquin Young Readers 2015 336 p.

Grades: 9 10 11 12

1. Ballet dancers -- Fiction 2. Juvenile detention homes -- Fiction 3. Supernatural -- Fiction 4. Murder -- Fiction 5. Juvenile delinquency -- Fiction

1616203722; 9781616203726, $17.95

LC 2014031972

In this novel, by Nova Ren Suma, "Orianna and Violet are ballet dancers and best friends, but when the ballerinas who have been harassing Violet are murdered, Orianna is accused of the crime and sent to a juvenile detention center where she meets Amber and they experience supernatural events linking the girls together." (Publisher's note)

"This haunting and evocative tale of magical realism immerses readers in two settings that seem worlds apart. The book is told in alternating first-person voices from the perspective of two teenagers: lonely Amber, who at age 13 was convicted of murdering her abusive stepfather and sent to Aurora Hills, a juvenile detention facility, and Vee, an insecure yet ruthlessly ambitious Julliard-bound ballerina. . . . A powerful story that will linger with readers." SLJ

Summers, Courtney

All the rage. By Courtney Summers. St. Martin's Griffin 2015 336 p.

Grades: 9 10 11 12

1. Bullying -- Fiction 2. Conduct of life -- Fiction 3. Interpersonal relations -- Fiction 4. Missing persons -- Fiction 5. Rape -- Fiction

125002191X; 9781250021915, $18.99

LC 2014040846

In this novel, by Courtney Summers, "the sheriff's son, Kellan Turner, is not the golden boy everyone thinks he is, and Romy Grey knows that for a fact. . . . But when a girl with ties to both Romy and Kellan goes missing after a party, and news of him assaulting another girl in a town close by gets out, Romy must decide whether she wants to fight or carry the burden of knowing more girls could get hurt if she doesn't speak up." (Publisher's note)

"Summers takes victim-shaming to task in this timely story, and the cruelties not only of Romy's classmates but also the adults she should be able to trust come heartbreakingly to the fore. Romy's breathy internal monologue is filled with bitter indignation, and while the narrative style may require some patience, older teens who like gritty realism will find plenty to ponder." Booklist

Fall for anything. St. Martin's Griffin 2011 230p pa $9.99

Grades: 9 10 11 12

1. Mystery fiction 2. Suicide -- Fiction 3. Bereavement -- Fiction 4. Father-daughter relationship -- Fiction
ISBN 978-0-312-65673-7

LC 2010-37873

As she searches for clues that would explain the suicide of her successful photographer father, Eddie Reeves meets the strangely compelling Culler Evans who seems to know a great deal about her father and could hold the key to the mystery surrounding his death.

"Readers may find the book fascinating or mesmerizingly melancholy depending on their moods, but there is no denying that Summers has brought Eddie's intense experience into the world of her readers. An unusual, bold effort that deserves attention." Kirkus

Some girls are. St. Martin's Griffin 2010 245p pa $9.99

Grades: 9 10 11 12

1. School stories 2. Bullies -- Fiction
ISBN 978-0-312-57380-5

LC 2009-33859

Regina, a high school senior in the popular—and feared—crowd, suddenly falls out of favor and becomes the object of the same sort of vicious bullying that she used to inflict on others, until she finds solace with one of her former victims.

"Regina's every emotion is palpable, and it's impossible not to feel every punch—physical or emotional—she takes." Publ Wkly

This is not a test; Courtney Summers. St. Martin's Griffin 2012 336 p. $9.99; (pbk.) $9.99

Grades: 7 8 9 10 11 12

1. Adventure fiction 2. Zombies -- Fiction 3. Child abuse -- Fiction 4. Horror stories 5. Survival -- Fiction 6. High schools -- Fiction 7. Family problems -- Fiction
ISBN 0312656742; 9780312656744; 9781250011817

LC 2012004633

In this book, "six teens who barely know or like each other seek refuge in their high school while the undead hordes lurk outside. . . . The end of the world unfolds through the eyes of high school junior Sloane Price, who has been contemplating suicide since her older sister ran away six months earlier, leaving Sloane with their physically abusive father. But these worries are pushed aside as Sloane tries to keep her fellow students alive." (Publishers Weekly)

Sun, Amanda

Ink; Amanda Sun. Harlequin Books 2013 304 p. (paperback) $9.99

Grades: 7 8 9 10 11 12

1. Love stories 2. Fantasy fiction 3. Japan -- Fiction
ISBN 037321071X; 9780373210718

In this teen romance novel, by Amanda Sun, part of "The Paper Gods" series, "Katie Greene must move halfway across the world. Stuck with her aunt in Shizuoka, Japan,

Katie feels lost. Alone. . . . When Katie meets aloof but gorgeous Tomohiro, the star of the school's kendo team, she is intrigued by him. . . . Somehow Tomo is connected to the kami, powerful ancient beings who once ruled Japan--and as feelings develop between Katie and Tomo, things begin to spiral out of control." (Publisher's note)

"Katie's tendency to jump to conclusions, cry, and act before she thinks is frustrating, but it leaves plenty of room for growth. The descriptions of life in Japan—particularly teen life—create a strong sense of place, and set a vivid backdrop for this intriguing series opener by a debut author." BookList

Supplee, Suzanne

Somebody everybody listens to. Dutton 2010 245p $16.99

Grades: 7 8 9 10 11 12

1. Singers -- Fiction 2. Country music -- Fiction 3. Nashville (Tenn.) -- Fiction
ISBN 978-0-525-42242-6; 0-525-42242-0

LC 2009-25089

Retta Lee Jones is blessed with a beautiful voice and has big dreams of leaving her tiny Tennessee hometown. With a beaten down car, a pocketful of hard-earned waitressing money, and stars in her eyes, Retta sets out to make it big in Nashville.

"While a must read for country music lovers, . . . [this book] will appeal to a wide audience, especially those who long to pursue a dream against the odds." Publ Wkly

Sutton, Kelsey

Some quiet place; by Kelsey Sutton. 1st ed. Flux 2013 336 p. (paperback) $9.99

Grades: 7 8 9 10

1. Occult fiction 2. School stories 3. Fear -- Fiction 4. Emotions -- Fiction 5. Wisconsin -- Fiction 6. High schools -- Fiction 7. Supernatural -- Fiction 8. Family problems -- Fiction 9. Farm life -- Wisconsin -- Fiction
ISBN 0738736430; 9780738736433

LC 2013005021

In this book, "Elizabeth Caldwell's best friend is dying of cancer, one of the cutest boys in school loves her, and her alcoholic father beats her—but Elizabeth doesn't care about any of it. Her only meaningful interactions are with the Emotions, immortal personifications of the feelings she can't experience. With them, she does not have to pretend, as she must when she tries to muster believable social responses." The book explores the reasons behind Elizabeth's coldness. (Publishers Weekly)

"Haunting, chilling and achingly romantic, Sutton's debut novel for teens will keep readers up until the wee hours, unable to tear themselves away from this strange and beautifully crafted story. Elizabeth Caldwell can't feel emotions, yet she sees them everywhere, human in appearance, standing alongside their "summons."...Chills and goose bumps of the very best kind accompany this haunting, memorable achievement." (Kirkus)

Sweeney, Diana

The **minnow**. Diana Sweeney. Text Publishing Co. 2015 263 p.

Grades: 8 9 10 11 12

1. Bildungsromans 2. Coming of age -- Fiction 3. Grief

-- Fiction 4. Loss (Psychology) -- Fiction 5. Teenage pregnancy -- Fiction 6. Teenage mothers -- Fiction
192218201X; 9781922182012, $9.95

LC 2015376822

In this book, by Diana Sweeney, "Tom survived a devastating flood that claimed the lives of her sister and parents. Now she lives with Bill in his old shed by the lake. But it's time to move out—Tom is pregnant. . . . In her longing for what is lost, Tom talks to fish: Oscar the carp in the pet shop, little Sarah catfish who might be her sister, an unhelpful turtle in a tank at the maternity ward. And the Minnow." (Publisher's note)

"Readers who can accept the ambiguous chronology and Tom's glib ability to communicate beyond worlds will be rewarded: the universe into which Minnow is born and will undoubtedly thrive is engaging and extraordinary. A promising and welcome debut." Booklist

Tahir, Sabaa

An **ember** in the ashes: a novel. By Sabaa Tahir. Razorbill 2015 464 p.

Grades: 9 10 11 12

1. Brothers and sisters -- Fiction 2. Fantasy 3. Love -- Fiction 4. Undercover operations -- Fiction 5. Slaves -- Fiction 6. Fantasy fiction
1595148035; 9781595148032, $19.95

LC 2014029687

In this book, by Sabaa Tahir, "Laia is a member of the conquered Scholars, who have lived under the rule of the oppressive Martial Empire for 500 years. Elias is on the winning side, close to graduating from a harsh program that produces Masks . . . a fate he feels trapped by. The two stumble into each other because Laia, a slave in the household, is attempting to spy on the Commandant, Elias' mother." (Bulletin of the Center for Children's Books)

"This epic debut, set in a fantasy empire with nods to ancient Rome and Egypt, relates the intersecting struggles of Elias, an elite enforcer, and Laia, a Resistance spy. Nuanced, multileveled world-building provides a dynamic backdrop for an often brutal exploration of moral ambiguity and the power of empathy. A compelling emergent romance is only one reason among many to anticipate the sequel." Horn Book

Sequel: A Torch Against the Night (2016)

A **reaper** at the gates. Sabaa Tahir. Penguin Group USA 2018 464 p.

Grades: 9 10 11 12

1. Sisters -- Fiction; 2. Insurgency -- Fiction
0448494507; 9780448494500, $19.95

In this novel in the series An Ember in the Ashes, by Sabaa Tahir, "beyond the Empire and within it, the threat of war looms ever larger. The Blood Shrike, Helene Aquilla, is assailed on all sides. Emperor Marcus...grows increasingly unstable, while the Commandant capitalizes on his madness to bolster her own power. As Helene searches for a way to hold back the approaching darkness, her sister's life and the lives of all those in the Empire hang in the balance." (Publisher's note)

A **Torch** Against the Night. Sabaa Tahir. Penguin Group USA 2016 464 pp.

Grades: 9 10 11 12

1. Brothers and sisters -- Fiction 2. Fugitives from justice -- Fiction 3. Fantasy fiction
1101998873; 9781101998878, $19.95

In this second book of the series by Sabaa Tahir, "Elias and Laia are running for their lives. Following the events of the Fourth Trial, an army led by Masks hunts the two fugitives. . . . Elias and Laia will have to fight every step of the way if they're going to outsmart their enemies: the bloodthirsty Emperor Marcus, the merciless Commandant, the sadistic Warden of Kauf, and, . . . Helene-Elias's former friend." (Publisher's note)

"Infusing her story with magic, Tahir proves to be a master of suspense and a canny practitioner of the cliff-hanger, riveting readers' attention throughout." Booklist

Tal, Eve

Cursing Columbus. Cinco Puntos Press 2009 248p $17.95

Grades: 7 8 9 10

1. Jews -- Fiction 2. Immigrants -- Fiction 3. Family life -- Fiction 4. New York (N.Y.) -- Fiction 5. Russian Americans -- Fiction
ISBN 978-1-933693-59-0; 1-933693-59-2

LC 2009-15834

Sequel to: Double crossing (2005)

In 1907, fourteen-year-old Raizel, who has lived in New York City for three years, and her brother Lemmel, newly-arrived, respond very differently to the challenges of living as Ukrainian Jews in the Lower East Side as Raizel works toward fitting in and getting ahead, while Lemmel joins a gang and lives on the streets

"The story offers a realistic and poignant picture of a bygone time." SLJ

Double crossing. Cinco Puntos Press 2005 261p $16.95

Grades: 7 8 9 10

1. Jews -- Fiction 2. Immigrants -- Fiction
ISBN 0-938317-94-6

LC 2005-8188

In 1905, as life becomes increasingly difficult for Jews in Ukraine, eleven-year-old Raizel and her father flee to America in hopes of earning money to bring the rest of the family there, but her father's health and Orthodox faith become barriers.

"Tal's fictionalized account of her grandfather's journey to America is fast paced, full of suspense, and highly readable." SLJ

Followed by: Cursing Columbus (2009)

Talley, Robin

Our own private universe. Robin Talley. Harlequin Teen 2017 376 p.

Grades: 7 8 9 10 11 12

1. Americans -- Mexico -- Fiction; 2. Bisexual high school students -- Fiction; 3. Bisexual teenagers -- Fiction; 4. Church group work -- Fiction; 5. High school students -- Fiction; 6. Teenagers -- Fiction; 7. High school students -- Fiction; 8. Romance fiction; 9.

Lesbians -- Fiction
9781488015274; 9780373211982, $18.99; 0373211988
LC 2017296952

In this book, by Robin Talley, "Aki Simon has a theory, and it's mostly about sex.... Aki already knows she's bisexual -- even if, until now, it's mostly been in the hypothetical sense.... Her best friend, Lori, is the only person who knows she likes girls, too. Aki's theory is that she's got only one shot at living an interesting life -- and that means she's got to stop sitting around and thinking so much. It's time for her to actually do something. Or at least try." (Publisher's note)

"An important and heartfelt contribution to contemporary teen lit about queer women: hopeful, realistic, and romantic, Talley's newest is sure to satisfy." Kirkus

Pulp. Robin Talley. Harlequin Books 2018 416 p.
Grades: 8 9 10 11 12
 1. Lesbianism -- Fiction; 2. Lesbians -- Fiction; 3. Lesbian teenagers -- Fiction
1335012907; 9781335012906, $18.99

"In this novel told in dual narratives, 'New York Times' bestselling author Robin Talley weaves together the lives of two young women connected across generations through the power of words. A stunning story of bravery, love, how far we've come and how much farther we have to go." (Publisher's note)

"Two Washington, D.C., lesbian teens, 62 years apart, each discover classic lesbian pulp fiction -- late midcentury paperbacks depicting a shadowy world of forbidden love." (Kirkus)

What We Left Behind. By Robin Talley. Harlequin Books 2015 416 p.
Grades: 9 10 11 12
 1. Lesbian teenagers -- Fiction 2. Self realization -- Fiction 3. College students -- Fiction 4. Gender identity -- Fiction 5. Transgender people -- Fiction 6. Dating (Social customs) -- Fiction 7. LGBT youth -- Fiction
0373211759; 9780373211753, $18.99
LC 2016297369

In this book, by Robin Talley, "Toni and Gretchen are the couple everyone envied in high school. They've been together forever. They never fight. They're deeply, hopelessly in love. When they separate for their first year at college—Toni to Harvard and Gretchen to NYU—they're sure they'll be fine. Where other long-distance relationships have fallen apart, theirs is bound to stay rock-solid. The reality of being apart, though, is very different than they expected." (Publisher's note)

"High school's perfect queer couple, Toni and Gretchen, navigate changes in their relationship freshman year as they attend separate colleges and form new friendships. A group of transgender upperclassmen at Harvard befriend Toni, who identifies as genderqueer, and offer support to explore questions of gender identity despite roommate drama and family strife. At NYU, Gretchen quickly forms a close friendship with Carroll, a freshman eager to experience gay life in the big city. . . . Recommended for all collections trying to fill a gap in the representation of transgender voices in teen fiction." SLJ

Tamani, Liara

Calling my name. Liara Tamani. Greenwillow Books, an imprint of HarperCollinsPublishers 2017 310 p.
Grades: 9 10 11 12
 1. African Americans -- Fiction; 2. Families -- Texas -- Fiction; 3. Texas -- Fiction; 4. Families -- Fiction; 5. Bildungsromans; 6. African Americans -- Fiction
9780062656865, $17.99; 9780062656889; 0062656864
LC 2017029705

This book, by Liara Tamani, "tells a universal coming-of-age story about Taja Brown, a young African American girl growing up in Houston, Texas, and it deftly and beautifully explores the universal struggles of growing up, battling family expectations, discovering a sense of self, and finding a unique voice and purpose. Told in fifty-three short, episodic, moving, and iridescent chapters, Calling My Name follows Taja on her journey from middle school to high school." (Publisher's note)

"An excellent portrayal of African American culture, gorgeous lyrical prose, strong characters, and societal critique make Tamani's debut a must-read." Booklist

Tan, Shaun

★ Tales from the inner city. Shaun Tan. Arthur A. Levine Books, an imprint of Scholastic Inc. 2018 224 p.
Grades: 7 8 9 10 11 12
 1. Animal behavior -- Fiction; 2. Animals -- Habits and behavior -- Fiction; 3. City and town life -- Fiction; 4. Human-animal relationships -- Fiction; 5. Short stories; 6. Urban animals -- Fiction; 7. Animal behavior -- Fiction
9781338298406, $24.99
LC 2018017790

This book, written and illustrated by Shaun Tan, "is a collection of strikingly original stories about the relationship between animals and human beings. By turns moving, shocking, hilarious, and surreal, Tan's stories place frogs in a corporate boardroom, bears in the legal system, horses on the highway, and more. Each tale is accompanied by the author's luminous paintings, windows upon a hidden world of truth and feeling beneath the surface of our everyday lives." (Publisher's note)

"In contrast to the neighborhood settings of Tales from Outer Suburbia (2009), this collection of 25 illustrated poems and stories explores the dynamics between animals and humans amid breathtakingly imaginative scenes in skyscrapers and gutters." (Kirkus Reviews)

Tash, Sarvenaz

The geek's guide to unrequited love. Sarvenaz Tash. Simon & Schuster Books for Young Readers 2016 256 p.
Grades: 9 10 11 12
 1. Friendship -- Fiction 2. Love -- Fiction
9781481456555, $12.99; 9781481456531, $17.99; 9781481456548
LC 2015033511

In this book, by Sarvenaz Tash, "Graham met his best friend, Roxana, when he moved into her neighborhood eight years ago. . . . Graham has been in love with her ever since. . . . When Graham learns that the creator of their favorite comic, The Chronicles of Althena, is making a rare appearance at this year's New York Comic Con, he knows he must score tickets. And the event inspires Graham to come up with the perfect plan to tell Roxy how he really feels about her." (Publisher's note)

"As Tash introduces a cast of charming, goofy, and diverse characters, she uses the hopeful voice of a young man in the throes of first love to gently poke fun at fandom while celebrating the passion and camaraderie of the community." Pub Wkly

Tashjian, Janet

The **gospel** according to Larry. Holt & Co. 2001 227p il $16.95; pa $5.99

Grades: 7 8 9 10

1. Fame -- Fiction 2. Identity -- Fiction 3. Coming of age -- Fiction 4. Web sites -- Fiction
ISBN 0-8050-6378-1; 0-440-23792-0 pa

LC 2001-24568

Seventeen-year-old Josh, a loner-philosopher who wants to make a difference in the world, tries to maintain his secret identity as the author of a web site that is receiving national attention

"Tashjian fabricates a cleverly constructed scenario and expertly carries it out to the bittersweet end." Horn Book Guide

Other titles about Larry are:
Vote for Larry (2004)
Larry and the meaning of life (2008)

Tayleur, Karen

Chasing boys. Walker & Co. 2009 244p $16.99
Grades: 7 8 9 10 11

1. School stories 2. Fathers -- Fiction
ISBN 978-0-8027-9830-5; 0-8027-9830-6

LC 2008-23241

First published 2007 by Black Dog Books

With her father gone and her family dealing with financial problems, El transfers to a new school, where she falls for one of the popular boys and then must decide whether to remain true to herself or become like the girls she scorns.

"All the ingredients of El's life are blended seamlessly, never downplaying the audience's intelligence, as Tayleur captures the all-consuming nature of a teenage crush without making El ridiculous. Moody, poetic, and intimate, this book is billed as the 'romance for girls who don't like pink,' but is much more than that." Booklist

Taylor, Greg

Killer Pizza. Feiwel and Friends 2009 346p $16.99

Grades: 6 7 8 9

1. Horror fiction 2. Monsters -- Fiction
ISBN 978-0-312-37379-5; 0-312-37379-1

LC 2008028543

While working as summer employees in a local pizza parlor, three teenagers are recruited by an underground organization of monster hunters.

"Toby is an easygoing and relatable young adult, and young teens will enjoy the fun, slightly scary read." Voice Youth Advocates

Killer Pizza: the slice. Feiwel and Friends 2011 341p $16.99

Grades: 6 7 8 9

1. Horror fiction 2. Adventure fiction 3. Monsters -- Fiction
ISBN 978-0-312-58088-9; 0-312-58088-6

LC 2010048928

Having passed the tests to become Monster Combat Officers, teens Toby, Annabel, and Strobe are sent on a secret mission to deliver to the Monster Protection Program a beautiful fourteen-year-old monster who wants to defect, regardless of the considerable dangers this poses.

Taylor, Laini

Blackbringer. G. P. Putnam's Sons 2007 437p (Faeries of Dreamdark) $17.99

Grades: 6 7 8 9

1. Fantasy fiction 2. Magic -- Fiction 3. Fairies -- Fiction
ISBN 978-0-399-24630-2; 0-399-24630-4

LC 2006026540

Magpie Windwitch, faerie, devil hunter, and granddaughter of the West Wind, must defeat an ancient evil creature, the Blackbringer, who has escaped from his bottle and threatens to unmake all of creation.

"Taylor drives the story forward by slowly teasing the reader with twists and turns in the plot. . . . Teen readers will identify with this faerie's humanness." Voice Youth Advocates

★ **Daughter** of smoke and bone. Little, Brown 2011 418p $18.99

Grades: 8 9 10 11 12

1. Love stories 2. Occult fiction 3. Fantasy fiction 4. School stories 5. Angels -- Fiction 6. Artists -- Fiction 7. Supernatural -- Fiction 8. Classical mythology -- Fiction
ISBN 978-0-316-13402-6; 0-316-13402-3; 9780316196192

LC 2010045802

Seventeen-year-old Karou, a lovely, enigmatic art student in a Prague boarding school, carries a sketchbook of hideous, frightening monsters—the chimaerae who form the only family she has ever known.

Taylor "again weaves a masterful mix of reality and fantasy with cross-genre appeal. Exquisitely written and beautifully paced." Publ Wkly

★ **Days** of blood & starlight; Laini Taylor. 1st ed. Little, Brown Books for Young Readers 2012 528 p. maps (Daughter of smoke and bone trilogy) (hardcover) $18.99

Grades: 9 10 11 12

1. Occult fiction 2. Fantasy fiction 3. Angels -- Fiction 4. Demonology -- Fiction 5. Supernatural -- Fiction 6. Czech Republic -- Fiction 7. Mythology, Greek -- Fiction 8. Prague (Czech Republic) -- Fiction 9. Chimera (Greek mythology) -- Fiction
ISBN 0316133973; 9780316133975

LC 2012028752

Sequel to: Daughter of smoke and bone

In this fantasy sequel to "Daughter of Smoke and Bone," "Karou . . . has taken up the resurrection work . . . under the direction of the dangerous chimaera leader, Thiago. . . . The angel army is menacing the countryside in an attempt to kill the remaining chimaera, so she is designing and resurrecting stronger, more effective winged warriors to protect her people." (Bulletin of the Center for Children's Books)

Dreams of gods & monsters; by Laini Taylor. Little, Brown and Co. 2014 624 p. (hardback) $19
Grades: 8 9 10 11 12

1. Angels -- Fiction 2. Supernatural -- Fiction 3. Good and evil -- Fiction 4. Greek mythology -- Fiction 5. Demonology -- Fiction 6. Chimera (Greek mythology) -- Fiction
ISBN 0316134074; 9780316134071
LC 2014003645

"In Taylor's third and final installment in her Daughter of Smoke and Bone trilogy, Karou and Akiva's dream of peace and a life together comes tantalizingly close, only to be repeatedly thwarted by their peoples' separate and conflicting histories, both mystical and real. Joined by angels and chimaera, Karou and Akiva lead their armies and fight side by side to prevent the apocalypse by banishing Jael, captain of the Dominion of Seraphim, from the earth he is determined to destroy." (Booklist)

Dreams of gods and monsters

Silksinger; illustrations by Jim Di Bartolo. G.P. Putnam's Sons 2009 449p il (Dreamdark) $18.99
Grades: 6 7 8 9

1. Fantasy fiction 2. Fairies -- Fiction 3. Mercenary soldiers -- Fiction 4. Good and evil -- Fiction
ISBN 978-0-399-24631-9; 0-399-24631-2
LC 2008047981

While journeying by dragonfly caravan over the Sayash Mountains, warrior-faerie Whisper Silksinger, hunted by devils, meets a young mercenary with an ancient scimitar and secrets of his own.

"With excellent world-building and deft pacing, this story is difficult to put down. The characters are well developed, and their close relationships and rapid-fire dialogue enhance the story." SLJ

★ **Strange** the Dreamer. Little, Brown & Co. 2017 544 p.
Grades: 9 10 11 12

0316341681; 9780316341684

In this novel, by Laini Taylor, "the dream chooses the dreamer, not the other way around--and Lazlo Strange, war orphan and junior librarian, has always feared that his dream chose poorly. Since he was five years old he's been obsessed with the mythic lost city of Weep, but it would take someone bolder than he to cross half the world in search of it. Then a stunning opportunity presents itself, in the person of a hero called the Godslayer and a band of legendary warriors." (Publisher's note)

Taylor, Mildred D.

★ The **land**. Phyllis Fogelman Bks. 2001 375p $17.99; pa $6.99

Grades: 7 8 9 10

1. Race relations -- Fiction 2. African Americans -- Fiction 3. Racially mixed people -- Fiction
ISBN 0-8037-1950-7; 0-14-250146-8 pa
LC 00-39329

Prequel to Roll of Thunder, Hear My Cry
Coretta Scott King Award for text

After the Civil War Paul-Edward Logan, the son of a white father and a black mother, finds himself caught between the two worlds of colored folks and white folks as he pursues his dream of owning land of his own.

"Taylor masterfully uses harsh historical realities to frame a powerful coming-of-age story that stands on its own merits." Horn Book Guide

★ **Roll** of thunder, hear my cry; 40th anniversary edition. By Mildred Taylor; illustrated by Kadir Nelson. Dial Books for Younger Readers. 2016 276p il $19.99

Grades: 4 5 6 7 8 9

1. African Americans -- Fiction 2. Mississippi -- Fiction 3. Racism -- Fiction
ISBN 9781101993880
Newbery Medal (1977)
40th Anniversary edition

Why is the land so important to Cassie's family? It takes the events of one turbulent year--the year of the night riders and the burnings, the year a white girl humiliates Cassie in public simply because she is black--to show Cassie that having a place of their own is the Logan family's lifeblood. It is the land that gives the Logans their courage and pride, for no matter how others may degrade them, the Logans possess something no one can take away." (Publisher's note)

Teller, Janne

★ **Nothing**; translated from the Danish by Martin Aitken. Atheneum Books for Young Readers 2010 227p $16.99
Grades: 7 8 9 10 11 12

1. School stories 2. Meaning (Philosophy) -- Fiction
ISBN 978-1-4169-8579-2; 1-4169-8579-4
LC 2009-19784

Michael J. Printz honor book, 2011

When thirteen-year-old Pierre Anthon leaves school to sit in a plum tree and train for becoming part of nothing, his seventh grade classmates set out on a desperate quest for the meaning of life.

"Indelible, elusive, and timeless, this uncompromising novel has all the marks of a classic." Booklist

Temblador, Alex

Secrets of the Casa Rosada. By Alex Temblador. Pinata Books, an imprint of Arte Publico Press 2018 160 p.
Grades: 8 9 10 11 12

1. Blessing and cursing -- Fiction; 2. Family life -- Texas -- Fiction; 3. Grandmothers -- Fiction; 4. Healers -- Fiction; 5. Mexican Americans -- Fiction; 6. Secrets -- Fiction; 7. Texas -- History -- 20th century -- Fiction
1558858709; 9781558858701, $12.95
LC 2018029355

This novel, by Alex Temblador, presents "a magical story about a girl who awakens to her potential when her vagabond mother abandons her at her grandmother's home in Laredo, Texas. Kept in the dark her entire life, 16-year-old Martha discovers that everything she thinks she knows about herself is a lie.... As Martha endeavors to learn the language of her long-lost family, she discovers that her grandmother is a curandera with healing powers." (Kirkus Reviews)

Templeman, McCormick

The **glass** casket; McCormick Templeman. Delacorte Press 2014 352 p. (hc) $17.99

Grades: 9 10 11 12

1. Villages -- Fiction 2. Supernatural -- Fiction 3. Fairy tales 4. Love -- Fiction 5. Murder -- Fiction 6. Witches -- Fiction 7. Community life -- Fiction

ISBN 0385743459; 9780375991134; 9780385743457

LC 2013001970

In this young adult fantasy novel, by McCormick Templeman, "one bleak morning, . . . five horses and their riders thunder into [Rowan's] village and through the forest, disappearing into the hills. Days later, the riders' bodies are found. . . . Something has followed the path those riders made and has come down from the hills, through the forest, and into the village. Beast or man, it has brought death to Rowan's door." (Publisher's note)

"Templeman pulls a 180 from her incisive contemporary debut, The Little Woods (2012), with a fantasy involving witches, magic, and monsters...The story doesn't always fire, but, in fact, Templeman is at her best when leaving plot behind, as when one character's death acts as a sort of forbidden fruit leading to unleashed sexual passion—it's challenging, dizzying material. The legion of Maggie Stiefvater fans out there ought to look this way." (Booklist)

Terrill, Cristin

All our yesterdays; Cristin Terrill. Hyperion 2013 368 p. (hardback) $17.99

Grades: 7 8 9 10 11 12

1. Science fiction 2. Time travel -- Fiction 3. Love -- Fiction 4. Murder -- Fiction

ISBN 1423176375; 9781423176374

LC 2013008007

In this book, narrator "Em and her boyfriend, Finn, escape from their totalitarian future, time traveling back four years to commit a heart-wrenching assassination of a loved one in order to prevent time travel from being invented and the future from turning so wrong. . . . The other side of the storyline, taking place in the past that Em and Finn travel to and starring their past selves, is narrated by Marina" and talks about her best friend and crush, James. (Kirkus Reviews)

Terry, Teri

Fractured; Teri Terry. Nancy Paulsen Books 2013 336 p. (Slated trilogy) $17.99

Grades: 7 8 9 10

1. Dystopian fiction 2. Memory -- Fiction 3. Science fiction 4. England -- Fiction 5. Identity -- Fiction 6. Terrorism -- Fiction 7. High schools -- Fiction 8. Identity (Psychology)

ISBN 0399161732; 9780399161735

LC 2012044317

Author Teri Terry presents the "second installment of the Slated trilogy . . . set in a future where violent teens have their memory erased as an alternative to jail. Kyla has been Slated--her personality wiped blank, her memories lost to her forever. Or so she thought. When a mysterious man from her past comes back into her life and wants her help, she thinks she's on her way to finding the truth." (Publisher's note)

"Kyla's memories, wiped by the government in Slated, are slowly returning; she's been found by an anti-government group that claims she's a member and wants her to complete one last mission. Kyla's struggles to uncover her identity and think through the consequences of her actions are realistic and add an emotional backbone to this fast-paced middle volume of the trilogy." (Horn Book)

Slated; Teri Terry. Nancy Paulsen Books 2013 346 p. (hardcover) $17.99

Grades: 7 8 9 10

1. Science fiction 2. Memory -- Fiction 3. Identity -- Fiction 4. High schools -- Fiction 5. Family life -- England -- Fiction

ISBN 0399161724; 9780399161728

LC 2012020873

In this novel, by Teri Terry, "Kyla has been Slated--her memory and personality erased as punishment for committing a crime she can't remember. The government has taught her how to walk and talk again, given her a new identity and a new family, and told her to be grateful for this second chance that she doesn't deserve. It's also her last chance--because they'll be watching to make sure she plays by their rules." (Publisher's note)

Other titles in this series are:
Fractured (2013)
Shattered (2014)

Tharp, Tim

Badd. Alfred A. Knopf 2011 308p $16.99; lib bdg $19.99; ebook $10.99

Grades: 9 10 11 12

1. Siblings -- Fiction 2. Iraq War, 2003-2011 -- Fiction 3. Post-traumatic stress disorder -- Fiction

ISBN 978-0-375-86444-5; 978-0-375-96444-2 lib bdg; 978-0-375-89579-1 ebook

LC 2010-12732

A teenaged girl's beloved brother returns home from the Iraq War completely unlike the person she remembers.

"With convincing three-dimensional characters, Tharp paints a sympathetic portrait of the constraints of small town life, the struggles of PTSD, and the challenges of faith." Publ Wkly

Knights of the hill country. Alfred A. Knopf 2006 233p hardcover o.p. pa $6.99

Grades: 8 9 10 11 12

1. School stories 2. Football -- Fiction 3. Oklahoma -- Fiction

ISBN 978-0-375-83653-4; 0-375-83653-5; 978-0-553-49513-3 pa; 0-553-49513-5 pa

LC 2005-33279

In his senior year, high school star linebacker Hampton Greene finally begins to think for himself and discovers that he might be interested in more than just football.

"Taut scenes on the football field and the dilemmas about choosing what feels right over what's expected are all made memorable by Hamp's unforgettable, colloquial voice." Booklist

Mojo; Tim Tharp. Knopf Books for Young Readers 2013 288 p. (hardcover) $16.99; (ebook) $50.97; (library) $19.99
Grades: 7 8 9 10 11 12
    1. School stories 2. Mystery fiction 3. High schools -- Fiction 4. Missing children -- Fiction 5. Secret societies -- Fiction 6. Self-realization -- Fiction 7. Mystery and detective stories
ISBN 0375864458; 9780375864452; 9780375895807; 9780375964459
                         LC 2012023886
In this novel, by Tim Tharp, "all Dylan wants is mojo. What is mojo? . . . It's everything Dylan doesn't have. . . . So when Dylan hears about a missing rich girl from the other side of town, he jumps at the chance to dive into this mystery. . . . His investigation takes him into the world of an elite private high school and an underground club called Gangland." (Publisher's note)

    ★ The **spectacular** now. Alfred A. Knopf 2008 294p $16.99; lib bdg $19.99
Grades: 9 10 11 12
    1. School stories 2. Oklahoma -- Fiction 3. Alcoholism -- Fiction 4. Stepfamilies -- Fiction 5. Dating (Social customs) -- Fiction
ISBN 978-0-375-85179-7; 0-375-85179-7; 978-0-375-95179-4 lib bdg; 0-375-95179-2 lib bdg
                         LC 2008-03544
In the last months of high school, charismatic eighteen-year-old Sutter Keely lives in the present, staying drunk or high most of the time, but that could change when he starts working to boost the self-confidence of a classmate, Aimee.
    "Tharp offers a poignant, funny book about a teen who sees his life as livable only when his senses are dulled by drink . . . . Sutter is an authentic character [who] . . . will strike a chord with teen readers." Booklist

Thomas, Angie, ca. 1988-
    ★ The **hate** u give. Angie Thomas. Balzer + Bray 2017 464 p.
Grades: 8 9 10 11 12
    1. Police shootings -- Fiction; 2. African Americans -- Fiction
0062498533; 9780062498533, $17.99
                         LC 2016950333
Kirkus Prize Finalist: Young Readers' Literature (2017); Coretta Scott King Author Award Honor Book (2018); William C. Morris Award (2018); Printz Honor Book (2018)
    "Sixteen-year-old Starr Carter moves between two worlds: the poor neighborhood where she lives and the fancy suburban prep school she attends. The uneasy balance between these worlds is shattered when Starr witnesses the fatal shooting of her childhood best friend Khalil at the hands of a police officer. Khalil was unarmed. Soon afterward, his death is a national headline." (Publisher's note)
    "With smooth but powerful prose delivered in Starr's natural, emphatic voice, finely nuanced characters, and in-

tricate and realistic relationship dynamics, this novel will have readers rooting for Starr and opening their hearts to her friends and family." Kirkus

Thomas, Erin
    Boarder patrol; written by Erin Thomas. Orca Book Publishers 2010 170p (Orca sports) pa $9.95
Grades: 6 7 8 9
    1. Mystery fiction 2. Skiing -- Fiction 3. Cousins -- Fiction 4. Snowboarding -- Fiction
ISBN 978-1-55469-294-1 pa; 1-55469-294-6 pa
    "Ryan, 16, works as a Junior Ski Patrol volunteer in order to earn a free lift pass. His dream is to pursue snowboarding professionally. His cousin, Kevin, who works at the lifts, starts acting strangely, especially when Ryan begins investigating the disappearance of some ski equipment, including his own, on the mountain. . . . The story includes vivid descriptions of snowboarding and mountain rescue, and the mystery is involving." SLJ

Thomas, Kara
    The **darkest** corners. Kara Thomas. Delacorte Press 2016 336 p.
Grades: 9 10 11 12
    1. Detective and mystery stories 2. Friendship -- Fiction 3. Murder -- Fiction 4. Mystery and detective stories 5. Secrets -- Fiction 6. Serial murderers -- Fiction 7. Sisters -- Fiction 8. Pennsylvania -- Fiction 9. Mystery fiction
9780553521450, $17.99; 9780553521467
                         LC 2015004181
In this book, by Kara Thomas, "there are secrets around every corner in Fayette, Pennsylvania. Tessa left when she was nine and has been trying ever since not to think about what happened there that last summer. She and her childhood best friend Callie never talked about what they saw. Not before the trial. And certainly not after. But ever since she left, Tessa has had questions. Things have never quite added up." (Publisher's note)
    "Equally concerned with a quest for the truth and the powerful motivation of guilt, this compelling novel won't linger on the shelf." Booklist

    Little monsters. Kara Thomas. Delacorte Press 2017 324 p.
    Grades: 10 11 12
    1. Betrayal -- Fiction; 2. Friendship -- Fiction; 3. Missing children -- Fiction; 4. Moving, Household -- Fiction
9780553521511;   9780553521498, $17.99; 9780553521504
                         LC 2016032457
In this novel, by Kara Thomas, "Kacey is the new girl in Broken Falls. When she moved in with her father, she stepped into a brand-new life.... And everyone is so nice in Broken Falls -- she's even been welcomed into a tight new circle of friends.... Which is why it's so odd when they start acting distant.... Suddenly, Broken Falls doesn't seem so welcoming after all." (Publisher's note)

Thomas, Leah
    Nowhere near you. By Leah Thomas. Bloomsbury 2017 389 p.

Grades: 9 10 11 12

> 1. Blind -- Fiction; 2. Epilepsy -- Fiction; 3. Friendship -- Fiction; 4. Letters -- Fiction; 5. People with disabilities -- Fiction; 6. Science fiction
>
> 9781681191799; 9781681191782, $17.99

LC 2016022577

In this book, by Leah Thomas, "Ollie and Moritz might never meet, but their friendship knows no bounds.... Along the way they meet other teens like them, other products of strange science who lead seemingly normal lives in ways Ollie and Moritz never imagined possible.... But even as Ollie and Moritz dare to enjoy life, they can't escape their past, which threatens to destroy any progress they've made." (Publisher's note)

"A fantastic novel that will be especially resonant for readers who struggle with being or feeling outside of 'normal.'" Booklist

Sequel to: Because you'll never meet me (2015)

Thomas, Rhiannon

Long may she reign. Rhiannon Thomas. Harper-Teen 2017 422 p.

Grades: 7 8 9 10 11 12

> 1. Courts and courtiers -- Fiction; 2. Fathers and daughters -- Fiction; 3. Murder -- Investigation -- Fiction; 4. Poisons and poisoning -- Fiction; 5. Queens -- Fiction
>
> 978006241808; 9780062418685, $17.99

LC 2016952956

In this novel, by Rhiannon Thomas, "Freya was never meant to be queen. Twenty-third in line to the throne, she never dreamed of a life in the palace, and would much rather research in her laboratory than participate in the intrigues of the court. However, when an extravagant banquet turns deadly and the king and those closest to him are poisoned, Freya suddenly finds herself on the throne." (Publisher's note)

"A clever, absorbing mystery of court intrigue, intense friendships, and newfound courage." Booklist

Thomas, Rob

Rats saw God. Simon & Schuster Bks. for Young Readers 1996 219p hardcover o.p. pa $6.99

Grades: 7 8 9 10

> 1. School stories 2. Father-son relationship -- Fiction
>
> ISBN 0-689-80207-2; 1-4169-3897-4 pa

LC 95-43548

"High-school senior Steve York isn't doing well. The former straight-A student is flunking, and his new friends are dopers. . . . A counselor steps in and suggests Steve can write something to bring up his failing English grade. So Steve writes his story, and as the action flips between his former life in Texas and the present in California, readers will learn about Steve's cold war with his astronaut father, his dabbling with dadaism, and, most of all, his heavenly-hellish experience with first love." Booklist

"The sharp descriptions of cliques, clubs and annoying authority figures will strike a familiar chord. The dialogue is fresh and Steve's intelligent banter and introspective musings never sound wiser than his years." Publ Wkly

Thomas, Sherry

The **burning** sky; by Sherry Thomas. Balzer + Bray 2013 480 p. (hardcover bdg.) $17.99

Grades: 7 8 9 10 11 12

> 1. Fantasy fiction 2. Magic -- Fiction 3. Fantasy
>
> ISBN 0062207296; 9780062207296

LC 2013014504

This book, by author Sherry Thomas presents "the story of a girl who fooled a thousand boys, a boy who fooled an entire country, a partnership that would change the fate of realms, and a power to challenge the greatest tyrant the world had ever known." (Publisher's note)

"When sixteen-year-old elemental mage Iolanthe summons a lightning bolt, she draws the unwelcome attention of the Inquisitor of Atlantis. She also draws the eye of resistance fighter Prince Titus, who rescues her and disguises her as a boy. Heightened action combined with Scarlet Pimpernel-esque cleverness will keep readers eagerly turning pages, while the romantic tension adds juiciness to the fantasy plot." (Horn Book)

> Other titles in the series are:
> The Perilous Sea (2014)
> The Immortal Heights (2015)

Thompson, Holly

The **language** inside; Holly Thompson. 1st ed. Delacorte Press 2013 528 p. (hardcover) $17.99

Grades: 7 8 9 10 11 12

> 1. Novels in verse 2. Moving -- Fiction 3. Interpersonal relations -- Fiction 4. Japan -- Fiction 5. Cancer -- Fiction 6. Tsunamis -- Fiction 7. Massachusetts -- Fiction 8. Moving, Household -- Fiction 9. Family life -- Massachusetts -- Fiction
>
> ISBN 0385739796; 9780375898358; 9780385739795; 9780385908078

LC 2012030596

In this novel in verse, by Holly Thompson, "Emma's family moves to a town outside Lowell, Massachusetts, to stay with Emma's grandmother while her mom undergoes treatment. Emma feels out of place in the United States. She begins to have migraines, and longs to be back in Japan. At her grandmother's urging, she volunteers in a long-term care center to help Zena, a patient with locked-in syndrome, write down her poems." (Publisher's note)

Orchards. Delacorte Press 2011 327p il $17.99; lib bdg $20.99

Grades: 7 8 9 10

> 1. Novels in verse 2. Japan -- Fiction 3. Suicide -- Fiction 4. Bereavement -- Fiction 5. Family life -- Fiction 6. Racially mixed people -- Fiction
>
> ISBN 978-0-385-73977-1; 0-385-73977-X; 978-0-385-90806-1 lib bdg; 0-385-90806-7 lib bdg

LC 2010-23724

"After a classmate commits suicide, Kana, a half-Japanese, half-Jewish American eighth grader, is sent to her maternal grandmother's farm in rural Japan for personal reflection. Kana tells her story in poignantly straightforward verse directed at the deceased classmate as she struggles with blame and regret, wondering if she and her friends are responsible because they took part in ostracizing the girl. She struggles, too, with her biracial, bicultural identity, feeling isolated in her new surroundings." (School Library Journal)

"Kanako's urgent teen voice, written in rapid free verse and illustrated with occasional black-and-white sketches, will hold readers with its nonreverential family story." Booklist

Thompson, Kate

★ **Creature** of the night. Roaring Brook Press 2008 250p $17.95

Grades: 9 10 11 12

1. Ireland -- Fiction 2. Homicide -- Fiction 3. Juvenile delinquency -- Fiction

ISBN 978-1-59643-511-7; 1-59643-511-9

Bobby lives a reckless life smoking, drinking, and stealing cars in Dublin. So his mother moves the family to the country. But Bobby suspects their cottage might not be as quaint as it seems. And spooky details of the history of their little cottage gradually turn Bobby into a detective of night creatures real and imagined.

"A unique blend of subtlety and brashness, this is an honest coming-of-age novel in the guise of a gripping YA thriller." Booklist

★ The **new** policeman. Greenwillow Books 2007 442p hardcover o.p. pa $8.99

Grades: 7 8 9 10

1. Fantasy fiction 2. Music -- Fiction 3. Fairies -- Fiction 4. Ireland -- Fiction 5. Space and time -- Fiction

ISBN 978-0-06-117427-8; 0-06-117427-0; 978-0-06-117429-2 pa; 0-06-117429-7 pa

LC 2006-8246

First published 2005 in the United Kingdom

Irish teenager JJ Liddy discovers that time is leaking from his world into Tir na nOg, the land of the fairies, and when he attempts to stop the leak he finds out a lot about his family history, the music that he loves, and a crime his great-grandfather may or may not have committed.

"Mesmerizing and captivating, this book is guaranteed to charm fantasy fans." Voice Youth Advocates

Other titles in this series are:

The last of the High Kings (2008)

The white horse trick (2010)

Thompson, Mary G.

Amy Chelsea Stacie Dee. Mary G. Thompson. G.P. Putnam's 2016 304 p.

Grades: 9 10 11 12

1. Cousins -- Fiction 2. Friendship -- Fiction 3. Guilt -- Fiction 4. Kidnapping -- Fiction 5. Secrets -- Fiction 6. Psychological fiction

9781101996805, $17.99

LC 2016008732

In this story of loss, love, and survival by Mary G. Thompson, Amy can't tell her family "where she's been since she and her best friend, her cousin Dee, were kidnapped six years ago—who stole them from their families or what's become of Dee. . . . She's a stranger in her own family, and the guilt that she's the one who returned is insurmountable. Amy soon realizes that keeping secrets won't change what's happened, and they may end up hurting those she loves the most." (Publisher's note)

"Thompson expertly builds the novel's tension to an unbearable pitch as she guides readers to a bittersweet, satisfying conclusion." Pub Wkly

Thor, Annika

Deep sea. Annika Thor; translated from the Swedish by Linda Schenck. Delacorte Press 2015 240 p.

Grades: 7 8 9 10 11 12

1. Friendship -- Fiction 2. Jews -- Sweden -- Fiction 3. Refugees -- Fiction 4. Schools -- Fiction 5. Sisters -- Fiction 6. World War, 1939-1945 -- Refugees -- Fiction 7. Sweden -- History -- Gustav V, 1907-1950 -- Fiction 8. Jews -- Fiction 9. Sweden -- Fiction

0385743858; 9780375991325; 9780385743853, $17.99

LC 2014005586

In this book, by Annika Thor, "Stephie and her younger sister, Nellie, escaped the Nazis in Vienna and fled to an island in Sweden, where they were taken in by different families. . . . Nellie wants to be adopted by her foster family. Stephie, on the other hand, can't stop thinking about her parents, who are in a Nazi camp in Austria." (Publisher's note)

"This novel about coming of age during a complicated, tragic time in history is both delicate and poignant, as when Stephie and Nellie sit on the dock, remembering a lullaby their mother sang. Thor's novel capably demonstrates the loneliness, powerlessness, and prejudice Stephie faces, as well as her growing inner strength." Pub Wkly

Originally published 1998 in Sweden; Sequel to The Lily Pond

★ A **thousand** beginnings and endings: 15 retellings of Asian myths and legends. Edited by Ellen Oh and Elsie Chapman. Greenwillow Books 2018 328 p.

Grades: 6 7 8 9 10 11 12

1. Mythology, Asian -- Fiction; 2. Tales -- Asia -- Fiction; 3. Short stories; 4. Anthologies; 5. Folklore

9780062671158, $17.99; 9780062671172; 0062671154

LC 2018020967

This collection, edited by Ellen Oh and Elsie Chapman, presents short stories about "star-crossed lovers, meddling immortals, feigned identities, battles of wits, and dire warnings.... Fifteen bestselling and acclaimed authors reimagine the folklore and mythology of East and South Asia in...stories that are by turns enchanting, heartbreaking, romantic, and passionate." (Publisher's note)

"A marvelous anthology of retold Asian myths and legends tying the traditional and modern together and accessible to all teens of all backgrounds." Kirkus

Tibensky, Arlaina

And then things fall apart. Simon Pulse 2011 254p pa $9.99; ebook $9.99

Grades: 9 10 11 12

1. Poets 2. Authors 3. Novelists 4. Divorce -- Fiction 5. Chicago (Ill.) -- Fiction 6. Dating (Social customs) -- Fiction

ISBN 978-1-4424-1323-8 pa; 978-1-4424-1324-5 ebook

LC 2010044631

Devastated by her parents' decision to split up, pressured by her boyfriend to have sex, and saddled with a case of chicken pox, fifteen-year-old Keek finds consolation in her beloved, well-worn copy of Sylvia Plath's "The Bell Jar."

This "is a short, intoxicating, bouncy, lustful, stream-of-consciousness narrative. . . . Keek's poetry—not bad, either—punctuates the diary entries and offers more catnip to Plathians." Booklist

Tiernan, Cate

★ **Balefire**. Razorbill 2011 974p pa $8.99
Grades: 8 9 10 11 12

1. Twins -- Fiction 2. Sisters -- Fiction 3. Witchcraft -- Fiction 4. New Orleans (La.) -- Fiction
ISBN 978-1-59514-411-9

An omnibus edition of four titles previously published separately, the first three of which were first published 2005. The last, A necklace of water, was first published 2006

Separated since birth, seventeen-year-old twins Thais and Clio unexpectedly meet in New Orleans where they seem to be pursued by a coven of witches who want to harness the twins' magical powers for its own ends.

Immortal beloved. Little, Brown and Company 2010 407p $16.99
Grades: 8 9 10 11 12

1. Fantasy fiction 2. Magic -- Fiction 3. Immortality -- Fiction 4. Massachusetts -- Fiction 5. Conduct of life -- Fiction
ISBN 978-0-316-03592-7; 0-316-03592-0
LC 2010-06884

After seeing her best friend, a Dark Immortal called Incy, torture a human with magick, Nastasya, a spoiled party girl, enters a home for wayword immortals and finally begins to deal with life, even as she learns that someone wants her dead.

"Humor overlies serious issues of identity and personal responsibility explored within the story, and readers who enjoy character-driven works of romantic fantasy will flock to this book." Voice Youth Advocates

Tingle, Tim

House of purple cedar. By Tim Tingle. Cinco Puntos Press 2014 192 p.
Grades: 10 11 12

1. Choctaw Indians -- Oklahoma -- Fiction 2. Oklahoma -- History -- Land Rush, 1893 -- Fiction 3. Choctaw Indians -- Fiction 4. Oklahoma -- Fiction
1935955241; 9781935955245, $16.95; 9781935955696
LC 2013010570

This book, by Tim Tingle, is "Rose Goode's story of . . . growing up in Indian Territory in pre-statehood Oklahoma. Skullyville, a once-thriving Choctaw community, was destroyed by land-grabbers, culminating in the arson on New Year's Eve, 1896, of New Hope Academy for Girls. Twenty Choctaw girls died, but Rose escaped. She is blessed by the presence of her grandmother Pokoni and her grandfather Amafo, both respected elders who understand the old ways." (Publisher's note)

"In 1896, as white settlers hungry for land flooded into Indian territory in what is now Oklahoma, a boarding school for Indian girls called the New Hope Academy was burned to the ground with a severe loss of life. It presaged the de-struction of the Choctaw community, related here by fire survivor Rose Goode in measured but heartfelt language." LJ

Tintera, Amy

Reboot; Amy Tintera. 1st ed. HarperTeen, an imprint of HarperCollinsPublishers 2013 384 p. (hardcover) $17.99
Grades: 9 10 11 12

1. Dead -- Fiction 2. Science fiction 3. Soldiers -- Fiction 4. Adventure and adventurers -- Fiction
ISBN 0062217070; 9780062217073
LC 2012051741

In this dystopian novel, by Any Tintera, "a seventeen-year-old girl rises from the dead as a Reboot and is trained as an elite crime-fighting soldier. . . . Wren 178 [is] the deadliest Reboot in the Republic of Texas. Callum 22, on the other hand, is practically still human. . . . When Callum fails to measure up to Reboot standards, Wren is told to eliminate him. Wren has never disobeyed before, but she'll do whatever it takes to save Callum's life." (Publisher's note)

Torres Sanchez, Jenny

Death, Dickinson, and the demented life of Frenchie Garcia; by Jenny Torres Sanchez. Running Press 2013 272 p. (paperback) $9.95
Grades: 9 10 11 12

1. Grief -- Fiction 2. Suicide -- Fiction
ISBN 0762446803; 9780762446803
LC 2013934992

In this book, "Frenchie is in the limbo of what-comes-next. She's finished high school but has been rejected by art school. She is sullen and anxious and can't seem to get her life moving. Gradually, what happened that night with Andy and its lingering impact on Frenchie are revealed. It was the same night that Andy ended his own life. No one even knows that she liked Andy, let alone about the time they spent together, so Frenchie keeps her guilt and confusion to herself." (Kirkus Reviews)

Toten, Teresa

Beware that girl. Teresa Toten. Delacorte Press 2016 336 p.
Grades: 9 10 11 12

1. Friendship -- Fiction 2. Mental illness -- Fiction 3. Psychopaths -- Fiction 4. Secrets -- Fiction 5. Teacher-student relationships -- Fiction 6. Secrecy -- Fiction 7. Teacher-student relationship -- Fiction
9780553507904; 9780553507911, $20.99; 9780553507928, $53.97
LC 2015028074

In this novel by Teresa Toten, "Kate is an admitted liar. . . . As a new scholarship student at the prestigious Waverly School in New York, she relies heavily on her smarts, good looks, and experience to get by. Kate searches for a target, . . . [and] spots Olivia, a beautiful and rich girl. . . . [Their] friendship blossoms, until a mysterious man, Mark Redkin, enters their lives. The handsome Mark charms Olivia, but Kate senses that there is something terribly wrong." (School Library Journal)

"Complete with a disturbing yet satisfying conclusion, this is a must-have for teen fans of psychological thrillers such as Gillian Flynn's Gone Girl." SLJ

Townley, Roderick

Sky; a novel in three sets and an encore. by Roderick Townley. 1st ed; Atheneum Books for Young Readers 2004 265p $16.95

Grades: 7 8 9 10

    1.. Jazz musicians -- Fiction 2. New York (N.Y.) -- History -- 20th century

    ISBN 0-689-85712-8

                    LC 2003-11354

In New York City in 1959, fifteen-year-old Alec Schuyler, at odds with his widowed father over his love of music, finds a mentor and friend in a blind, black jazz musician.

"Townley presents a compassionate portrait of a young man who is battling for his own place in life and sets the story in the exciting time of the beat poets and the explosive development of jazz music." SLJ

Tregay, Sarah

Love & leftovers; a novel in verse. Sarah Tregay. 1st ed. Katherine Tegen Books 2011 432 p. (hardcover) $17.99

Grades: 8 9 10 11

    1. Love stories 2. Novels in verse 3. Teenagers -- Fiction 4. Children of gay parents -- Fiction 5. Iowa -- Fiction 6. Moving -- Fiction 7. Bisexuality -- Fiction 8. Family life -- Fiction 9. New Hampshire -- Fiction

    ISBN 0062023586; 9780062023582

                    LC 2011019367

In this verse novel, "[s]ophomore Marcie Foster unwillingly moves from Idaho to her mother's childhood home in New Hampshire after her father leaves her mother for a male bartender. Marcie is resentful until she realizes the move could be a chance to remake herself." A heated relationship with "popular athlete J.D.," makes her question "her nonphysical relationship with Linus," her boyfriend in Idaho. "Seven months later Marcie returns to Idaho, and things are more confusing than ever." (Publishers Weekly)

Treggiari, Jo

Ashes, ashes. Scholastic Press 2011 360p $17.99

Grades: 7 8 9 10

    1. Science fiction 2. Dogs -- Fiction 3. Epidemics -- Fiction 4. New York (N.Y.) -- Fiction

    ISBN 978-0-545-25563-9; 0-545-25563-5

                    LC 2010032398

In a future Manhattan devastated by environmental catastrophes and epidemics, sixteen-year-old Lucy survives alone until vicious hounds target her and force her to join Aidan and his band, but soon they learn that she is the target of Sweepers, who kidnap and infect people with plague.

"The tense plot, cinematic moments, and highly capable protagonists make this a fast, gripping read." Publ Wkly

Treichel, Eliot

A **series** of small maneuvers. Eliot Treichel. Ooligan Press 2015 300 p.

Grades: 8 9 10 11

    1. Fathers and daughters -- Fiction 2. Grief -- Fiction 3.

Father-daughter relationship -- Fiction

9781932010794, $14.95

                    LC 2015020922

In this book, by Eliot Treichel, "Emma's growing up and feels isolated from her friends and family. Things go from bad to unfathomably worse when Emma inadvertently causes an accident that kills her increasingly distant father on a spring break canoe trip meant to bring them closer together. Suddenly, Emma's efforts to reconcile with her father as a parent and a person have to happen without him, and she must confront her guilt and her grief to begin moving forward." (Publisher's note)

"Dad's overbearing manner and the heavy factual overlay about rivers, canoeing, and all things outdoorsy may put some readers off, but this is a strong, coming-of-age tale, especially for those teens who would rather be adventuring in the great outdoors than doing anything else." Booklist

Trigiani, Adriana

Viola in reel life. HarperTeen 2009 282p $16.99

Grades: 7 8 9 10

    1. Ghost stories 2. School stories 3. Video recording -- Fiction 4. Dating (Social customs) -- Fiction

    ISBN 978-0-06-145102-7; 0-06-145102-9

                    LC 2009-14269

When fourteen-year-old Viola is sent from her beloved Brooklyn to boarding school in Indiana for ninth grade, she overcomes her initial reservations as she makes friends with her roommates, goes on a real date, and uses the unsettling ghost she keeps seeing as the subject of a short film—her first.

This "is a sweet, character-driven story. Viola is very real, as are her feelings, hopes, desires, and dreams." SLJ

Viola in the spotlight. HarperTeen 2011 283p $16.99

Grades: 7 8 9 10

    1. Theater -- Fiction 2. Family life -- Fiction 3. Dating (Social customs) -- Fiction

    ISBN 978-0-06-145105-8; 0-06-145105-3

                    LC 2010045553

Back home in Brooklyn, fifteen-year-old Viola has big summer plans but with one best friend going to camp and the other not only working but experiencing her first crush, Viola is glad to be overworked as an unpaid lighting intern when her grandmother's play goes to Broadway.

"An equally enjoyable follow-up to Viola in Reel Life." Booklist

Tripp, Ben

The **accidental** highwayman: being the tale of Kit Bristol, his horse Midnight, a mysterious princess, and sundry magical persons besides. Ben Tripp. Tor Teen 2014 304 p. Illustration

Grades: 7 8 9 10

    1. Adventure and adventurers -- Fiction 2. Fairies -- Fiction 3. Fate and fatalism -- Fiction 4. Magic -- Fiction 5. Princesses -- Fiction 6. Robbers and outlaws -- Fiction 7. Great Britain -- History -- George III, 1760-1820 -- Fiction 8. Great Britain -- Fiction 9. Adventure

fiction
0765335492; 9780765335494, $17.99

LC 2014033724

In this book, by Ben Tripp, "Christopher 'Kit' Bristol is the unwitting servant of notorious highwayman Whistling Jack. One dark night, Kit finds his master bleeding from a mortal wound, dons the man's riding cloak to seek help, and changes the course of his life forever. Mistaken for Whistling Jack and on the run from redcoats, . . . Kit takes up his master's quest to rescue a rebellious fairy princess from an arranged marriage to King George III of England." (Publisher's note)

"Readers will root for star-crossed lovers, Kit and Morgana, and delight in their 'opposites attract' romance, drawn onward by a rollicking plot . . . Fantasy readers, especially fans of Cathrynne Valente's work, will enjoy the author's elegant turns of phrase. A first purchase for all fantasy collections." SLJ

Tromly, Stephanie

Trouble is a friend of mine. By Stephanie Tromly. Kathy Dawson Books, an imprint of Penguin Group (USA) LLC 2015 336 p.

Grades: 9 10 11 12

1. Divorce -- Fiction 2. High schools -- Fiction 3. Missing children -- Fiction 4. Moving, Household -- Fiction 5. Mystery and detective stories 6. Schools -- Fiction 7. Moving -- Fiction 8. Mystery fiction

9780525428404, $17.99

LC 2014040605

In this book, by Stephanie Tromly, "when Philip Digby first shows up on her doorstep, Zoe Webster is not impressed. He's rude and he treats her like a book he's already read and knows the ending to. But before she knows it, Digby—annoying, brilliant and somehow attractive?—has dragged her into a series of hilarious and dangerous situations all related to an investigation into the kidnapping of a local teenage girl." (Publisher's note)

Trueman, Terry

★ **Cruise** control; 1st ed; HarperTempest 2004 149p $15.99; lib bdg $16.89; pa $8.99

Grades: 7 8 9 10

1. Brothers -- Fiction 2. Basketball -- Fiction 3. People with disabilities 4. Cerebral palsy -- Fiction 5. Father-son relationship -- Fiction

ISBN 0-06-623960-5; 0-06-623961-3 lib bdg; 0-06-447377-5 pa

LC 2003-19822

A talented basketball player struggles to deal with the helplessness and anger that come with having a brother rendered completely dysfunctional by severe cerebral palsy and a father who deserted the family.

"This powerful tale is extremely well written and will give readers an understanding of what it's like to have a challenged sibling." SLJ

★ **Inside** out. HarperTempest 2003 117p hardcover o.p. pa $8.99

Grades: 7 8 9 10

1. Suicide -- Fiction 2. Hostages -- Fiction 3. Mentally ill -- Fiction 4. Schizophrenia -- Fiction 5. Juvenile

delinquency -- Fiction
ISBN 0-06-623962-1; 0-06-447376-7 pa

LC 2002-151604

A sixteen-year-old with schizophrenia is caught up in the events surrounding an attempted robbery by two other teens who eventually hold him hostage.

"Trueman sometimes captures moments of heartbreaking truth, and his swift, suspenseful plot will have particular appeal to reluctant readers." Booklist

Life happens next; a novel. Terry Trueman. HarperTeen 2012 132 p. (trade bdg.) $17.99

Grades: 7 8 9 10

1. Love stories 2. Down syndrome -- Fiction 3. Cerebral palsy -- Fiction 4. Dogs -- Fiction 5. Communication -- Fiction 6. Seattle (Wash.) -- Fiction 7. Special education -- Fiction 8. People with disabilities -- Fiction 9. Family life -- Washington (State) -- Seattle -- Fiction

ISBN 0062028030; 9780062028037; 9780062028051

LC 2011044627

Sequel to: Stuck in neutral

This book is the sequel to author Terry Trueman's "Stuck in Neutral." Here, Shawn McDaniel, who has cerebral palsy, "fantasizes about his sister's best friend, Ally, and what it would be like if he ever got up the courage to tell her how he felt about her." He is also dealing with "Debi, [who] moves in with them. . . . Debi has Down's syndrome and is often disruptive, but . . . she becomes the first person to connect with Shawn on more than a surface level." (Voice of Youth Advocates)

★ **Stuck** in neutral. HarperCollins Pubs. 2000 114p $14.95; lib bdg $16.89; pa $6.99

Grades: 7 8 9 10

1. Euthanasia -- Fiction 2. People with disabilities 3. Cerebral palsy -- Fiction 4. Father-son relationship -- Fiction

ISBN 0-06-028519-2; 0-06-028518-4 lib bdg; 0-06-447213-2 pa

LC 99-37098

Michael L. Printz Award honor book, 2001

Fourteen-year-old Shawn McDaniel, who suffers from severe cerebral palsy and cannot function, relates his perceptions of his life, his family, and his condition, especially as he believes his father is planning to kill him.

"Trueman has created a compelling novel that poses questions about ability and existence while fostering sympathy for people with severe physical limitations." Bull Cent Child Books

Tubb, Kristin O'Donnell

The **13th** sign; Kristin O'Donnell Tubb. Feiwel and Friends 2013 272 p. $16.99

Grades: 6 7 8 9

1. Astrology -- Fiction 2. Occult fiction 3. Zodiac -- Fiction 4. Supernatural -- Fiction 5. Books and reading -- Fiction 6. New Orleans (La.) -- Fiction 7. Adventure and adventurers -- Fiction

ISBN 0312583524; 9780312583521

LC 2012034058

In this fantasy novel, by Kristin O'Donnell Tubb, "when a teen accidentally unlocks the lost 13th zodiac sign, everyone's personality shifts, and she must confront 12 Keepers of the zodiac to restore global order. . . . Unless she can find and restore Ophiuchus to the heavens within 23 hours, all personality changes will be permanent. To do this, Jalen must destroy 12 Keepers who protect Ophiuchus." (Kirkus Reviews)

Tucholke, April Genevieve

Between the devil and the deep blue sea; by April Genevieve Tucholke. Dial Books 2013 368 p. (hardcover) $17.99

Grades: 9 10 11

1. Horror fiction 2. Mystery fiction

ISBN 0803738897; 9780803738898

LC 2012035586

In this horror novel, "Violet White and her 17-year-old twin brother are living in the dilapidated glory of their family's coastal estate while their parents traipse Europe. To help pay the bills, Violet places an ad for a boarder for their guesthouse; it's quickly answered by River West, a mysterious boy who cannily avoids giving straight answers about his past. Violet doesn't typically pay boys much mind, but she's soon spending the night with River, both drawn to and wary of him." (Publishers Weekly)

"It's no coincidence that when the alluring River West shows up to rent the guesthouse of Violet's dilapidated seaside mansion, eerie and brutal things begin to happen in town. Yet love-struck Violet finds herself powerless to act, or really care. A highly atmospheric and unreliable narrative wends its way between scenes alternately homey and macabre to a twisty ending." (Horn Book)

Between the spark and the burn. April Genevieve Tucholke. Dial Books 2014 368 p.

Grades: 7 8 9 10

1. Good and evil -- Fiction 2. Love -- Fiction 3. Trust -- Fiction 4. Adventure fiction 5. Gothic romances

0803740476; 9780803740471, $17.99

LC 2013048697

"The crooked-smiling liar River West Redding, who drove into Violet's life one summer day and shook her world to pieces, is gone. Violet and Neely, River's other brother, are left to worry—until they catch a two a.m. radio program about strange events in a distant mountain town." (Publisher's note)

"The faded opulence of the setting is an ideal backdrop for this lushly atmospheric gothic thriller, which, happily, comes with a satisfying conclusion.Darkly romantic and evocative." Kirkus

Sequel to: Between the devil and the deep blue sea (2013)

Turner, Megan Whalen

★ **Thick** as thieves. Megan Whalen Turner. Greenwillow Books, an imprint of HarperCollins Publishers 2017 336 p. Map (Queen's thief)

Grades: 7 8 9 10 11 12

1. Adventure and adventurers -- Fiction; 2. Fantasy; 3. Kings, queens, rulers, etc. -- Fiction; 4. Secretaries -- Fiction; 5. Slavery -- Fiction

0062568248; 9780062568243, $17.99

LC 2016047028

In this book in the Queen's Thief series, by Megan Whalen Turner, "Kamet, a secretary and slave to his Mede master, has the ambition and the means to become one of the most powerful people in the Empire. But with a whispered warning the future he envisioned is wrenched away, and he is forced onto a very different path. Set in the world of the Queen's Thief, this epic adventure sees an ordinary hero take on an extraordinary mission." (Publisher's note)

"This series fifth can stand alone without reading the rest of the books.... This invites an older audience, but...offer[s] more teen appeal than the political drama of earlier Queen's Thief novels." Kirkus.

★ The **thief**. Greenwillow Bks. 1996 219p $17.99; pa $6.99

Grades: 7 8 9 10

1. Adventure fiction 2. Thieves -- Fiction

ISBN 0-688-14627-9; 0-06-082497-2 pa

LC 95-41040

A Newbery Medal honor book, 1997

"Gen languishes in prison for boasting of his skill as a thief. The magus—the king's powerful advisor—needing a clever thief to find an ancient ring that gives the owner the right to rule a neighboring country, bails Gen out. Their journey toward the treasure is marked by danger and political intrigue, and features a motley cast, tales of old gods, and the revelation of Gen's true identity." Publisher's note

"A tantalizing, suspenseful, exceptionally clever novel. . . . The author's characterization of Gen is simply superb." Horn Book

Other titles in this series are:

The Queen of Attolia (2000)

The King of Attolia (2006)

A conspiracy of kings (2010)

Thick as thieves (2017)

Turrisi, Kim

Just a normal Tuesday. Kim Turrisi. Kids Can Press 2017 252 p.

Grades: 7 8 9 10

1. Death -- Fiction; 2. Grief -- Fiction; 3. Death -- Fiction; 4. Teenagers -- Suicide -- Fiction

9781771387934, $17.95; 9781771388634; 1771387939

In this book, by Kim Turrisi, "what begins as just a normal Tuesday becomes a day that will shatter sixteen-year-old Kai's life forever. All it takes is a letter.... from Kai's older sister, Jen.... Jen has committed suicide.... Kai is heartbroken and furious, and soon she's caught in a vicious downward spiral.... That's when her parents shock her: they're sending her to the Tree House, a summer camp for grieving teens." (Publisher's note)

"A nuanced tale about grief in the aftermath of suicide." SLJ

Turtschaninoff, Maria

★ **Maresi**. Maria Turtschaninoff ; translated by A. A. Prime. Harry N Abrams Inc 2017 256 p. Illustration (The Red Abbey chronicles)

Grades: 8 9 10 11

1. Fantasy fiction; 2. Abbeys -- Fiction

1419722697; 9781419722691, $17.95; 9781613129746,

$15.54

LC 2016054460

In this book in the Red Abbey Chronicles series, by Maria Turtschaninoff, "the Red Abbey [is] a haven from abuse and oppression. Maresi, a thirteen-year-old novice there, arrived in the hunger winter and now lives a happy life in the Abbey.... Into this idyllic existence comes Jai, a girl with a dark past.... Soon the dangers of the outside world follow Jai into the sacred space of the Abbey, and Maresi can no longer hide in books and words but must become one who acts." (Publisher's note)

"Utterly satisfying and completely different from standard YA fantasy, this Finnish import seems primed to win over American readers." Booklist

"Originally published in 2014 in Finland under the title Maresi by Schildts & Socerstrom" -- Title page verso.; Another title in this series is: Naondel (2018)

Naondel. By Maria Turtschaninoff ; translated by A.A. Prime. Amulet Books 2018 375 p. (Red Abbey chronicles)

Grades: 8 9 10 11

1. Abused women -- Fiction; 2. Sex crimes -- Fiction; 3. Fantasy fiction; 4. Escapes -- Fiction; 5. Abused women -- Fiction

9781683351412; 9781419725555, $18.99

LC 2017011854

This book in The Red Abbey Chronicles series, by Maria Turtschaninoff, translated by A.A. Prime, "tells the story of the First Sisters -- the founders of the female utopia the Red Abbey. Imprisoned in a harem by a dangerous man with a dark magic that grants him power over life and death, the First Sisters must overcome their mistrust of one another in order to escape. But they can only do so at a great cost, both for those who leave and for those left behind." (Publisher's note)

"This is not an easy story, with its perpetual backdrop of sexual violence, but in the foreground is a fierce, slow-burning exposition of female courage and resilience." Horn Book

Originally published in Sweden by Berghs in 2016 under title: Naondel : krönikor från Röda klostret.

Uehashi, Nahoko

★ **Moribito**; Guardian of the Spirit. [by] Nahoko Uehashi; translated by Cathy Hirano; illustrated by Yuko Shimizu. Arthur A. Levine Books 2008 248p il $17.99

Grades: 6 7 8 9

1. Fantasy fiction 2. Martial arts -- Fiction
ISBN 978-0-5450-0542-5; 0-5450-0542-6

The wandering warrior Balsa is hired to protect Prince Chagum from both a mysterious monster and the prince's father, the Mikado.

"This book is first in a series of ten that have garnered literary and popular success in Japan. . . . Balsa and Chagum's story is brought to America with a strong translation. . . . Readers who are fans of action manga, especially with strong female characters, will enjoy the ninja-like fighting scenes. . . . The exciting premise, combined with an attractive cover, should insure that this title will circulate well." Voice Youth Advocates

Moribito II; Guardian of the Darkness. by Nahoko Uehashi; translated by Cathy Hirano; illustrated by Yuko Shimizu. Arthur A. Levine Books 2009 245p il $17.99

Grades: 6 7 8 9

1. Fantasy fiction
ISBN 978-0-545-10295-7; 0-545-10295-2

LC 2008-37444

ALA ALSC Batchelder Award Honor Book (2010)

The wandering female bodyguard Balsa returns to her native country of Kanbal, where she uncovers a conspiracy to frame her mentor and herself.

"Once again, Uehashi immerses readers in the culture, traditions, mythology–even diet–of the populace, creating a full, captivating world. . . . This growing series has something for everyone." Publ Wkly

Umminger, Alison

★ **American** Girls: A Novel. Alison Umminger. St. Martin's Press 2016 304 p.

Grades: 8 9 10 11

1. Motion picture industry -- Fiction 2. Self-realization -- Fiction 3. Runaway teenagers -- Fiction 4. Los Angeles (Calif.) -- Fiction 5. Stepsisters -- Fiction
1250075009; 9781250075000, $17.99; 9781250075024

In this novel by Alison Umminger, "Anna is a fifteen-year-old girl . . . [who] 'borrows' her stepmom's credit card and runs away to Los Angeles, where her half-sister takes her in. But LA isn't quite the glamorous escape Anna had imagined. As Anna spends her days on TV and movie sets, she engrosses herself in a project researching the murderous Manson girls?and . . . begins to notice the parallels between herself and the lost girls of LA, and of America, past and present." (Publisher's note)

"An insightful, original take on the coming-of-age story, this novel plumbs the depths of American culture to arrive at a poignant emotional truth." Kirkus

Unsworth, Tania

The **one** safe place: a novel; by Tania Unsworth. Algonquin Young Readers. 2014 304p $15.95

Grades: 6 7 8 9 10

1. Abandoned children -- Fiction 2. Orphans -- Fiction 3. Science fiction 4. Survival -- Fiction 5. Dystopian fiction
ISBN: 1616203293; 9781616203290

LC 2013043145

"Orphaned twelve-year-old Devin is invited to live at the paradisaical Home for Childhood, but something terrifying is happening to the children there. Devin's synesthesia, which makes him interesting to the Home's sinister Administrator, may provide the key to their escape. Set in a world of post climate change desperation, Unsworth's story thoughtfully explores the theme of adults' nostalgia for childhood." Horn Book

Vail, Rachel

Lucky. HarperTeen 2008 233p $16.99; lib bdg $17.89

Grades: 7 8 9 10

1. School stories 2. Wealth -- Fiction 3. Friendship

-- Fiction

ISBN 978-0-06-089043-8; 978-0-06-089044-5 lib bdg

As Phoebe and her clique of privileged girlfriends get ready to graduate from eighth grade, a financial scandal threatens her family's security—as well as Phoebe's social status—but ultimately it teaches her the real meaning of friendship.

"Vail's insightful characterizations of teen girls and their shifting loyalties is right on target." Booklist

Other titles in this series are:

Gorgeous (2009)

Brilliant (2010)

Unfriended. Rachel Vail. Viking, published by Penguin Group 2014 288 p.

Grades: 6 7 8 9

1. Friendship -- Fiction 2. Middle schools -- Fiction 3. Popularity -- Fiction 4. Schools -- Fiction 5. Social media -- Fiction 6. Social media

0670013072; 9780670013074, $16.99

LC 2014006247

In this young adult novel by Rachel Vail, "when Truly is invited to sit at the Popular Table with the group she has dreamed of joining, she can hardly believe her luck. Everyone seems so nice, so kind to one another. But all is not as it seems with her new friends, and soon she's caught in a maelstrom of lies, misunderstandings, accusations and counter-accusations, all happening very publicly in the relentless, hyperconnected social media world from which there is no escape." (Publisher's note)

"The points of view allow the reader to be drawn into the teens' motivations and illustrate the importance of clear communication, the dangers of online bullying, and the universal struggles teens face. Mean girls, misunderstood girls, awkward boys, friendship, popularity, social misfits, all play into this book that epitomizes the roller coaster that is middle school." Lib Med Con

Valentine, Allyson

How (not) to find a boyfriend; by Allyson Valentine. Philomel Books 2013 304 p. (hardcover) $16.99

Grades: 7 8 9 10

1. School stories 2. Popularity -- Fiction 3. Genius -- Fiction 4. Cheerleading -- Fiction 5. High schools -- Fiction 6. Dating (Social customs) -- Fiction

ISBN 0399257713; 9780399257711

LC 2012019316

In this book, former nerd Nora Fulbright has worked hard to shed her geeky image since starting high school. "As sophomore year begins, she's made the cheerleading squad, and it looks like the handsome fullback is taking notice of her. . . . Worried that the cheer captain will mock her for taking AP classes, she switches her schedule, then has to switch it back so she'll have classes with Adam, the brainy and adorable new boy in school." (Publishers Weekly)

Valentine, Jenny

Double; Jenny Valentine. Disney-Hyperion 2012 246 p. (alk. paper) $16.99

Grades: 7 8 9 10 11 12

1. Mystery fiction 2. Identity -- Fiction 3. Homeless persons -- Fiction 4. London (England) -- Fiction 5. Missing children -- Fiction 6. England -- Fiction 7. Impersonation -- Fiction

ISBN 1423147146; 9781423147145

LC 2011010027

In this book, "[w]hat starts as a case of mistaken identity turns into a . . . mystery. . . . Homeless, 16-year-old Chap is . . . presented with . . . [the]opportunity of a lifetime: if he pretends to be Cassiel Roadnight, a teen who has been missing for two years and who looks just like Chap, Chap can have the life and family he's always dreamed of. As he tries to pass in his new identity . . . Chap begins to suspect that there's more to Cassiel's disappearance than meets the eye." (Publishers Weekly)

★ **Fire** color one. Jenny Valentine. Philomel Books 2017 228 p.

Grades: 9 10 11 12

1. Arson -- Fiction; 2. Fathers and daughters -- Fiction; 3. Mothers and daughters -- Fiction; 4. Terminally ill -- Fiction; 5. Wealth -- Fiction; 6. Father-daughter relationship -- Fiction

9780399546921, $17.99; 9780399546938

LC 2016006188

In this novel, by Jenny Valentine, "sixteen-year-old Iris itches constantly for the strike of a match. But when she's caught setting one too many fires, she's dragged away to London before she can get arrested. At least, that's the story her mother tells. Soon Iris finds herself in the English countryside, where her millionaire father -- a man she's never met -- lives. Though not for very much longer." (Publisher's note)

"This is a quiet, reflective novel that blooms into a thrilling mystery, and its complex family dynamics will appeal to fans of Jenny Downham's Unbecoming (2016)." Booklist

★ **Me**, the missing, and the dead. HarperTeen 2008 201p $16.99; lib bdg $17.89

Grades: 8 9 10 11

1. Death -- Fiction 2. Fathers -- Fiction 3. Missing persons -- Fiction 4. London (England) -- Fiction 5. Single parent family -- Fiction

ISBN 978-0-06-085068-5; 0-06-085068-X; 978-0-06-085069-2 lib bdg; 0-06-085069-8 lib bdg

LC 2007-14476

First published 2007 in the United Kingdom with title: Finding Violet Park

ALA YALSA Morris Award finalist, 2009

When a series of chance events leaves him in possession of an urn with ashes, sixteen-year-old Londoner Lucas Swain becomes convinced that its occupant, Violet Park, is communicating with him, initiating a voyage of self-discovery that forces him to finally confront the events surrounding his father's sudden disappearance.

"Part mystery, part magical realism, part story of personal growth, and in large part simply about a funny teenager making light of his and his family's pain, this short novel is engaging from start to finish." SLJ

Van de Ruit, John

Spud. Razorbill 2007 331p hardcover o.p. pa $9.99

Grades: 6 7 8 9 10

1. School stories 2. South Africa -- Fiction
ISBN 978-1-59514-170-5; 0-14-302484-1; 978-1-59514-187-3 pa; 1-59514-187-1 pa

LC 2007-6065

In 1990, thirteen-year-old John "Spud" Milton, a prepubescent choirboy, keeps a diary of his first year at an elite, boys-only boarding school in South Africa.

"This raucous autobiographical novel about a scholarship boy in an elite boys' boarding school in 1990 is mainly farce but also part coming-of-age tale." Booklist

Followed by Spud the madness continues... (2008)

Van Diepen, Allison

Takedown; Allison van Diepen. Simon Pulse 2013 288 p. (hardcover edition : alk. paper) $16.99
Grades: 9 10 11 12

1. Hostages 2. Adventure fiction 3. Vendetta -- Fiction 4. Drug traffic -- Fiction 5. African Americans -- Fiction 6. Criminal investigation -- Fiction
ISBN 1442463112; 9781442463110; 9781442463127

LC 2012039237

In this book, "Joe is hosting a party in honor of his favorite weekly wrestling show when a college student-turned-murderer crashes the get-together and holds the 13-year-olds hostage. As the terrifying ordeal continues, Joe thinks back about how he met each friend, their history together, and problems they are facing in their lives." (School Library Journal)

Van Draanen, Wendelin

Flipped. Knopf 2001 212p $14.95
Grades: 6 7 8 9

1. Family life 2. Conduct of life 3. Self-perception 4. Interpersonal relations
ISBN 9780375811746; 0-375-81174-5; 0-375-82544-4 pa

LC 2001-29238

In alternating chapters, two teenagers describe how their feelings about themselves, each other, and their families have changed over the years.

"There"s lots of laugh-out-loud egg puns and humor in this novel. There"s also, however, a substantial amount of serious social commentary woven in, as well as an exploration of the importance of perspective in relationships." SLJ

Runaway. Knopf 2006 250p $15.95; lib bdg $17.99
Grades: 6 7 8 9

1. Orphans -- Fiction 2. Homeless persons -- Fiction 3. Runaway children -- Fiction
ISBN 0-375-83522-9; 0-375-93522-3 lib bdg

LC 2005-33276

After running away from her fifth foster home, Holly, a twelve-year-old orphan, travels across the country, keeping a journal of her experiences and struggle to survive.

"The ending of this taut, powerful story seems possible and deeply hopeful." Booklist

The **running** dream. Alfred A. Knopf 2011 336p $16.99; lib bdg $19.99

Grades: 7 8 9 10 11 12

1. School stories 2. Running -- Fiction 3. Amputees -- Fiction 4. People with disabilities -- Fiction
ISBN 978-0-375-86667-8; 0-375-86667-1; 978-0-375-96667-5 lib bdg; 0-375-96667-6 lib bdg

LC 2010-07072

When a school bus accident leaves sixteen-year-old Jessica an amputee, she returns to school with a prosthetic limb and her track team finds a wonderful way to help rekindle her dream of running again

"It's a classic problem novel in a lot of ways. . . . Overall, though, this is a tremendously upbeat book. . . . Van Draanen's extensive research into both running and amputees pays dividends." Booklist

Vande Velde, Vivian

★ The **book** of Mordred; [illustrations by Justin Gerard] Houghton Mifflin 2005 342p hardcover o.p. pa $8.99
Grades: 8 9 10 11 12

1. Kings 2. Knights and knighthood -- Fiction 3. Mordred (Legendary character) -- Fiction 4. Great Britain -- History -- 0-1066 -- Fiction
ISBN 0-618-50754-X; 0-618-80916-3 pa

LC 2004-28223

As the peaceful King Arthur reigns, the five-year-old daughter of Lady Alayna, newly widowed of the village-wizard Toland, is abducted by knights who leave their barn burning and their only servant dead.

"All of the characters are well developed and have a strong presence throughout. . . . [This] provides an intriguing counterpoint to anyone who is interested in Arthurian legend." SLJ

Heir apparent. Harcourt 2002 315p $17; pa $6.95
Grades: 6 7 8 9

1. Science fiction 2. Virtual reality -- Fiction
ISBN 0-15-204560-0; 0-15-205125-2 pa

LC 2002-2441

While playing a total immersion virtual reality game of kings and intrigue, fourteen-year-old Giannine learns that demonstrators have damaged the equipment to which she is connected, and she must win the game quickly or be damaged herself

"This adventure includes a cast of intriguing characters and personalities. The feisty heroine has a funny, sarcastic sense of humor and succeeds because of her ingenuity and determination." SLJ

Magic can be murder. Harcourt 2000 197p hardcover o.p. pa $6.99
Grades: 6 7 8 9

1. Witchcraft 2. Mystery fiction 3. Murder
ISBN 0-15-202665-7; 0-547-25872-0 pa

LC 00-8595

Nola and her mother have unusual abilities that have always set them apart from others, but when Nola sees a murder using her power to call up images using water and a person's hair, she finds herself in the worst danger ever

"The well-developed characters provide entertaining reading." SLJ

Vanhee, Jason

Engines of the broken world; Jason Vanhee. Henry Holt and Company 2013 272 p. (hardcover) $16.99

Grades: 8 9 10 11 12

   1. Supernatural -- Fiction 2. Brothers and sisters -- Fiction 3. Science fiction

   ISBN 0805096299; 9780805096293

                        LC 2013026768

"For siblings Merciful and Gospel Truth, it's the end of the world as they know it. But it's hardly fine when their recently deceased mother refuses to stay dead, and their "minister" (present in the form of an unsettling feline) can't be trusted. The real problem in this apocalyptic debut novel, however, is the fog devouring the world. Unlike most action-packed dystopias, the story's slower pace (almost too slow in some parts) allows readers to feel the fog encroaching on Merciful and Gospel's rustic home, and hear every scratch of their dead mother's awkward movements upon the cellar stairs." (Booklist)

Vaughn, Carrie

Steel. HarperTeen 2011 294p $16.99; lib bdg $17.89

Grades: 7 8 9 10

   1. Fencing -- Fiction 2. Pirates -- Fiction 3. Time travel -- Fiction

   ISBN 978-0-06-154791-1; 0-06-154791-3; 978-0-06-195648-5 lib bdg; 0-06-195648-1 lib bdg

                        LC 2010012631

When Jill, a competitive high school fencer, goes with her family on vacation to the Bahamas, she is magically transported to an early-eighteenth-century pirate ship in the middle of the ocean.

This is "thoroughly enjoyable. . . . Through her assertive, appealing protagonist and a satisfying plot that sheds light on lesser-known aspects of pirate life, Vaughn introduces readers to an intriguing sport with an ancient pedigree." Kirkus

Voices of dragons. HarperTeen 2010 309p $16.99

Grades: 7 8 9 10

   1. Fantasy fiction 2. Dragons -- Fiction

   ISBN 978-0-06-179894-8; 0-06-179894-0

                        LC 2009-11604

In a parallel world where humans and dragons live in a state of cold war, seventeen-year-old Kay and her dragon friend, Artegal, struggle to find a way to show that dragons and humans can coexist.

"Vaughn's story is charming and fast paced with a strong, likable heroine." Publ Wkly

Vaught, Susan

Freaks like us; by Susan Vaught. Bloomsbury 2012 240 p. (hardcover) $16.99

Grades: 7 8 9 10 11 12

   1. Friendship -- Fiction 2. Schizophrenia -- Fiction 3. Mental illness -- Fiction 4. Missing persons -- Fiction 5. Love -- Fiction 6. Missing children -- Fiction 7. Mystery and detective stories

   ISBN 1599908727; 9781599908724

                        LC 2012004227

This is the story of Jason, whose selectively mute friend Sunshine has "vanished, and Jason, whose schizophrenia has shaped his life, is a suspect in her disappearance. Seniors Jason, Drip and Sunshine have ridden the short bus and gone through school labeled SED--that's 'Severely Emotionally Disturbed.' Bullying at the hands of kids with behavioral disabilities goes unreported and unpunished, but the trio's alliance made life bearable in their catchall special ed program . . . . As the FBI investigates, Jason's always-shaky world threatens to come apart. Not taking "fuzzy pills" keeps his brain sharp, but the voices plaguing him grow louder. Jason carries Sunshine's secrets--should he break his promise not to tell?" (Kirkus)

Vawter, Vince

Copyboy. By Vince Vawter ; illustrated by Alessia Trunfio. Capstone Editions 2018 240 p.

Grades: 7 8 9 10

   1. Automobile travel -- Fiction; 2. Family life -- Tennessee -- Fiction; 3. Interpersonal relations -- Fiction; 4. Newspaper employees -- Fiction; 5. Self-esteem -- Fiction; 6. Stuttering -- Fiction; 7. Memphis (Tenn.) -- History -- 20th century -- Fiction

   9781630791056, $15.95

                        LC 2018001840

In this book, by Vince Vawter, illustrated by Alessia Trunfio, "Victor Vollmer isn't a paperboy anymore. He's a copyboy now, but his duties at the newspaper get interrupted by a last request from Mr. Spiro, the old man who became Victor's mentor and helped him take on his stutter.... Victor takes off on a journey that sends him hundreds of miles from home -- toward the teeth of a gathering storm." (Publisher's note)

Sequel to: Paperboy

Venkatraman, Padma

★ **Climbing** the stairs. G.P. Putnam's Sons 2008 247p $16.99

Grades: 6 7 8 9 10

   1. Prejudices -- Fiction 2. Family life -- Fiction 3. Brain -- Wounds and injuries -- Fiction 4. India -- History -- 1765-1947, British occupation -- Fiction

   ISBN 978-0-399-24746-0; 0-399-24746-7

                        LC 2007-21757

In India, in 1941, when her father becomes brain-damaged in a non-violent protest march, fifteen-year-old Vidya and her family are forced to move in with her father's extended family and become accustomed to a totally different way of life.

"Venkatraman paints an intricate and convincing backdrop of a conservative Brahmin home in a time of change. . . . . The striking cover art . . . will draw readers to this vividly told story." Booklist

★ **Island's** end. G.P. Putnam's Sons 2011 240p $16.99

Grades: 5 6 7 8 9

   1. Islands -- Fiction 2. Apprentices -- Fiction

   ISBN 978-0-399-25099-6; 0-399-25099-9

                        LC 2010036298

"Uido's clear, intelligent, present-tense voice consistently engrosses as she pushes through doubt and loss to find the right path. The beach, jungle and cliff settings are palpable. . . . There is very little information known about Andaman Islanders, making it hard to gauge the authenticity of this portrayal; the author's note indicates a respectful and diligent approach to her subject. . . . Refreshingly hopeful and beautifully written." Kirku

★ A **time** to dance. Padma Venkatraman. Nancy Paulsen Books, an imprint of Penguin Group (USA) Inc. 2014 320p $17.99

Grades: 8 9 10 11 12

1. Amputees -- Fiction 2. Dance -- Fiction 3. Novels in verse 4. People with disabilities -- Fiction 5. India -- Fiction

ISBN: 0399257101; 9780399257100

LC 2013024244

"This free-verse novel set in contemporary India stars Veda, a teenage Bharatanatyam dancer. After a tragic accident, one of Veda's legs must be amputated below the knee. Veda tries a series of customized prosthetic legs, determined to return to dancing as soon as possible. Brief lines, powerful images, and motifs of sound communicate Veda's struggle to accept her changed body." Horn Book

Verday, Jessica

The **Hollow**. Simon Pulse 2009 515p $17.99

Grades: 7 8 9 10 11 12

1. Ghost stories 2. School stories 3. Bereavement -- Fiction 4. Supernatural -- Fiction

ISBN 1-4169-7893-3; 978-1-4169-7893-0

LC 2008042817

High-school junior Abbey struggles with the loss of her best friend Kristen, who vanished on a legendary bridge, but her grief is eased by Caspian, an attractive and mysterious stranger she meets in the Sleepy Hollow cemetery.

"Abbey's narration is heartfelt and authentically written." SLJ

Vigan, Delphine de

No and me; translated by George Miller. Bloomsbury Children's Books 2010 244p $16.99

Grades: 9 10 11 12

1. Family life -- Fiction 2. Paris (France) -- Fiction 3. Gifted children -- Fiction 4. Homeless persons -- Fiction

ISBN 978-1-59990-479-5

LC 2009-36897

Original French edition, 2007

Precocious thirteen-year-old Lou meets a homeless eighteen-year-old girl on the streets of Paris and Lou's life is forever changed.

"Subtle, authentic details; memorable characters . . . and realistic ambiguities in each scene ground the story's weighty themes, and teens will easily recognize Lou's fragile shifts between heartbreak, bitter disillusionment, and quiet, miraculous hope." Booklist

Villareal, Ray

Body slammed! by Ray Villareal. Piñata Books 2012 194 p. (alk. paper) $11.95

Grades: 7 8 9 10

1. Wrestling -- Fiction 2. Father-son relationship 3.

Choice -- Fiction 4. High schools -- Fiction 5. Fathers and sons -- Fiction 6. Mexican Americans -- Fiction 7. San Antonio (Tex.) -- Fiction

ISBN 1558857494; 9781558857490

LC 2012003181

Sequel to: My father, the Angel of Death

This novel, by Ray Villareal, follows "[s]ixteen-year-old Jesse Baron . . . [who] is fed up with being cut down and dismissed, whether by the coach or his friends. . . . But it's through his dad that Jesse meets TJ Masters, a brash, new wrestling talent who's over 21, . . . TJ makes Jesse feel tough and confident. . . . But will Jesse listen to his family and friends when they warn him about hanging out with someone who's often reckless and irresponsible?" (Publisher's note)

Vivian, Siobhan

The **list**; Siobhan Vivian. Scholastic 2012 333 p. (hardcover : alk. paper) $17.99

Grades: 7 8 9 10 11 12

1. Female friendship 2. Self-perception -- Fiction 3. Personal appearance -- Fiction 4. High school students -- Fiction 5. Identity (Psychology) -- Fiction 6. Friendship -- Fiction 7. Self-esteem -- Fiction 8. High schools -- Fiction

ISBN 0545169178; 9780545169172

LC 2012004248

This young adult novel presents an "exploration of physical appearance and the status it confers. . . . Every year during homecoming week, a list is posted anonymously at Mount Washington High naming the prettiest and ugliest girls in each class. . . . The list confers instant status, transforming formerly homeschooled sophomore Lauren from geeky to hot while consigning her counterpart . . . Candace, to pariah. But what the label mainly confers is anxiety. Prettiest junior Bridget despairs that she'll ever be thin enough to merit her title. . . . Jennifer, four-time 'ugliest' winner, tries to relish the notoriety. . . . Whether clued in or clueless to the intricate social complexities, boyfriends reinforce the status quo, while moms carry scars of their own past physical insecurities." (Kirkus)

Not that kind of girl. PUSH/Scholastic 2010 322p $17.99

Grades: 9 10 11 12

1. School stories 2. Dating (Social customs) -- Fiction

ISBN 978-0-545-16915-8; 0-545-16915-1

LC 2010-13806

High school senior and student body president, Natalie likes to have everything under control, but when she becomes attracted to one of the senior boys and her best friend starts keeping secrets from her, Natalie does not know how to act.

The author "challenges the assumptions about sex being rampant in high school and sends a positive message about acceptance, forgiveness, and love." Booklist

Vizzini, Ned, 1981-2013

★ **It's** kind of a funny story. Miramax Books/ Hyperion Books For Children 2006 444p hardcover o.p. pa $9.99

Grades: 9 10 11 12

1. New York (N.Y.) -- Fiction 2. Psychiatric hospitals

-- Fiction 3. Depression (Psychology) -- Fiction
ISBN 0-7868-5196-1; 1-4231-4191-1 pa

LC 2005-52670

A humorous account of a New York City teenager's battle with depression and his time spent in a psychiatric hospital.

"What's terrific about the book is Craig's voice—intimate, real, funny, ironic, and one kids will come closer to hear." Booklist

Vlahos, Len

★ **Life** in a fishbowl. By Len Vlahos. Bloomsbury 2017 336 p.

Grades: 7 8 9 10

1. Brain -- Tumors -- Fiction 2. Cancer -- Fiction 3. Family problems -- Fiction 4. Reality television programs -- Fiction 5. Terminally ill -- Fiction
9781681190358, $17.99

LC 2016022364

In this book, by Len Vlahos, "when Jackie discovers that her father has been diagnosed with a terminal brain tumor, her whole world starts to crumble. . . . In a desperate act to secure his family's future, Jackie's father . . . puts his life up for auction on eBay. . . . Jackie can do nothing but watch and wait, . . . no one can predict how the auction will finally end, or any of the very public fallout that ensues. Life as Jackie knows it is about to change forever." (Publisher's note)

"From page one, it's evident that the ending will not be a happy one, but numerous laugh-out-loud moments and beautifully drawn characters make for a powerful journey that will leave a lasting imprint on readers." Pub Wkly

The **Scar** Boys: a novel. Len Vlahos. Egmont USA. 2014 256p $17.99

Grades: 9 10 11 12

1. Bands (Music) -- Fiction 2. Disfigured persons -- Fiction 3. Family life -- Fiction 4. Friendship -- Fiction 5. Near-death experiences -- Fiction 6. New York (State) -- Fiction 7. Bullies -- Fiction
ISBN: 9781606844397; 1606844393

LC 2013018265

William C. Morris Finalist (2015)

In this book, by Len Vlahos, "Harry is used to making people squirm. When others see his badly scarred face, there is an inevitable reaction that ranges from forced kindness to primal cruelty. In this first-person tale written as an extended college entrance essay, . . . he recounts the trauma of his young life spent recuperating from the act of childhood bullying that left him a burn victim. In middle school, he meets Johnny McKenna, the first person to seem to offer him genuine friendship." (Kirkus Reviews)

"Harry's obsession with punk music will appeal to music lovers, while his journey to accept himself for who he is--scarred face and all--is one that will likely resonate with any teen trying to find his way in the world." Booklist

Voigt, Cynthia

★ **Homecoming**. Atheneum Pubs. 1981 312p $18.95; pa $6.99

Grades: 6 7 8 9

1. Siblings -- Fiction 2. Abandoned children -- Fiction
ISBN 0-689-30833-7; 0-689-86361-6 pa

LC 80-36723

ALA YALSA Margaret A. Edwards Award (1995)

Abandoned by their mother, four children begin a search for a home and an identity.

"The characterizations of the children are original and intriguing, and there are a number of interesting minor characters encountered in their travels." SLJ

Other books about the Tillermans are:

Dicey's Song
A Solitary Blue
The Runner
Come a Stranger
Sons from Afar
Seventeen Against the Dealer

★ **Izzy,** willy-nilly; Rev. format ed.; Atheneum Books for Young Readers 2005 327p $17.95; pa $6.99

Grades: 7 8 9 10

1. Amputees -- Fiction 2. Friendship -- Fiction 3. Drunk driving -- Fiction
ISBN 978-1-4169-0340-6; 1-4169-0340-2; 978-1-4169-0339-0 pa; 1-4169-0339-9 pa

LC 2005299062

A reissue of the title first published 1986
ALA YALSA Margaret A. Edwards Award (1995)

A car accident causes fifteen-year-old Izzy to lose one leg and face the need to start building a new life as an amputee.

"Voigt shows unusual insight into the workings of a 15-year-old girl's mind. . . . Just as Voigt's perceptive empathy brings Izzy to life, other characterizations are memorable, whether of Izzy's shallow former friends or of her egocentric 10-year-old sister." Pub Wkly [review of 1986 edition]

Volponi, Paul

Black and white. Viking 2005 185p $15.99; pa $6.99

Grades: 7 8 9 10

1. Basketball -- Fiction 2. Race relations -- Fiction 3. African Americans -- Fiction
ISBN 0-670-06006-2; 0-14-240692-9 pa

LC 2004-24543

Two star high school basketball players, one black and one white, experience the justice system differently after committing a crime together and getting caught.

"These complex characters share a mutual respect and struggle with issues of loyalty, honesty, and courage. Social conflicts, basketball fervor, and tough personal choices make this title a gripping story." SLJ

The **Final** Four; by Paul Volponi. Viking 2012 244 p.

Grades: 9 10 11 12

1. Athletes -- Conduct of life -- Fiction 2. College basketball -- Fiction 3. Sports tournaments -- Fiction 4. African American youth -- Fiction 5. Immigrants -- United States -- Fiction 6. Conduct of life -- Fiction
ISBN 9780670012640

LC 2011011587

In this book by Paul "Volponi, . . . basketball's March Madness draws down toward the championship game with a match-up between the Michigan State Spartans and the Troy

University (Alabama) Trojans, to see who will take on Duke or North Carolina for the national title. Spartans are led by Malcolm McBride, a . . . freshman who's headed directly to the NBA and is more than willing to spout his views to sports reporters concerning the inequity of unpaid college athletics. The Trojans boast Roko Bacic, a towering immigrant from war-torn Croatia who treasures his opportunity to play the game he loves and get a free college education into the bargain." (Bulletin of the Center for Children's Books)

★ The **hand** you're dealt. Atheneum Books for Young Readers 2008 176p $16.99

Grades: 8 9 10 11

1. School stories 2. Poker -- Fiction 3. Teachers -- Fiction

ISBN 978-1-4169-3989-4; 1-4169-3989-X

LC 2007-22988

When seventeen-year-old Huck's vindictive math teacher wins the town poker tournament and takes the winner's watch away from Huck's father while he is in a coma, Huck vows to get even with him no matter what it takes.

"The varied characters are unique and add to the book's interest quotient." Voice Youth Advocates

★ **Hurricane** song; a novel of New Orleans. Viking Childrens Books 2008 144p $15.99

Grades: 7 8 9 10 11 12

1. Jazz music -- Fiction 2. New Orleans (La.) -- Fiction 3. Father-son relationship -- Fiction 4. Hurricane Katrina, 2005 -- Fiction

ISBN 978-0-670-06160-0; 0-670-06160-3

LC 2007-38215

Twelve-year-old Miles Shaw goes to live with his father, a jazz musician, in New Orleans, and together they survive the horrors of Hurricane Katrina in the Superdome, learning about each other and growing closer through their painful experiences.

"A brilliant blend of reality and fiction, this novel hits every chord just right." Voice Youth Advocates

Voorhees, Coert

★ The **brothers** Torres. Hyperion Books for Children 2008 316p hardcover o.p. pa $8.99

Grades: 9 10 11 12

1. School stories 2. Gangs -- Fiction 3. Brothers -- Fiction 4. Racially mixed people -- Fiction 5. Dating (Social customs) -- Fiction

ISBN 978-1-4231-0304-2; 1-4231-0304-1; 978-1-4231-0306-6 pa; 1-4231-0306-8 pa

LC 2007-15152

Sophomore Frankie finally finds the courage to ask his long-term friend, Julianne, to the Homecoming dance, which ultimately leads to a face-off between a tough senior whose family owns most of their small, New Mexico town, and Frankie's soccer-star older brother and his gang-member friends.

This "novel is solidly plotted and exceptionally well paced; escalating tension keeps the pages flying, while narrator Frankie's self-deprecating humor prevents the action from devolving into Southwestside Story melodrama." Bull Cent Child Books

Vrettos, Adrienne Maria

★ **Skin**. Margaret K. McElderry Books 2006 227p $16.95

Grades: 7 8 9 10

1. Siblings -- Fiction 2. Anorexia nervosa -- Fiction

ISBN 1-4169-0655-X

LC 2005001119

When his parents decide to separate, eighth-grader Donnie watches with horror as the physical condition of his sixteen-year old sister, Karen, deteriorates due to an eating disorder.

"The overwhelming alienation Donnie endures will speak to many teens, while his honest perspective will be welcomed by boys." Booklist

Wagner, Laura Rose

Hold tight, don't let go. By Laura Rose Wagner. Amulet Books 2015 272 p.

Grades: 9 10 11 12

1. Cousins -- Fiction 2. Earthquakes -- Fiction 3. Haiti Earthquake, Haiti, 2010 -- Fiction 4. Refugee camps -- Fiction 5. Separation (Psychology) -- Fiction 6. Haiti -- Fiction 7. Port-au-Prince (Haiti) -- Fiction 8. Refugees

1419712047; 9781419712043, $17.95

LC 2014019622

Author Laura Rose Wagner's novel "follows the vivid story of two teenage cousins, raised as sisters, who survive the devastating 2010 earthquake in Haiti. After losing the woman who raised them in the tragedy, Magdalie and Nadine must fend for themselves in the aftermath of the quake. The girls are inseparable . . . until Nadine, whose father lives in Miami, sends for her but not Magdalie." (Publisher's note)

"Wagner breaks away from stereotypes of an abject Haiti, giving us complex characters who connect with and care for one another, economies that rebuild, and environments that recover. By the end, readers will be buoyed by the hopeful future the author imagines for Magdalie and for Haiti." Booklist

Wakefield, Vikki

Friday never leaving; Vikki Wakefield. Simon & Schuster Books for Young Readers 2013 336 p. (hardcover) $16.99

Grades: 9 10 11 12

1. Runaway teenagers -- Fiction 2. Teenagers -- Conduct of life 3. Australia -- Fiction 4. Coming of age -- Fiction

ISBN 144248652X; 9781442486522; 9781442486539

LC 2012036386

This book by Vikki Wakefield follows "Friday Brown, [who] has never had a home. She and her mother live on the road, running away from the past. . . . So when her mom succumbs to cancer, the only thing Friday can do is keep moving. Her journey takes her to an abandoned house where a bunch of street kids are squatting, and an intimidating girl named Arden holds court. Friday gets initiated into the group, but her relationship with Arden is precarious." (Publisher's note)

Waldorf, Heather

Tripping. Red Deer Press 2008 342p pa $12.95

Grades: 8 9 10 11 12

   1. Canada -- Fiction 2. Amputees -- Fiction 3. Voyages and travels -- Fiction 4. Wilderness survival -- Fiction

ISBN 978-0-88995-426-7; 0-88995-426-7

"Rainey and five other teens begin an eight-week school-sponsored educational/survival trek across Canada. . . . Rainey's challenge is heightened because she has an artificial leg and she learns that her mother, who abandoned her as a baby, lives near one of their stops and wants to meet her. As the trip progresses, the individuals bond and become part of a team. . . . Waldorf has written a unique story in which six very different young people are united in a common cause. Told with wit and humor, this fast-paced novel has character development that is extraordinary." SLJ

Walker, Brian F.

Black boy/white school; Brian F. Walker. HarperTeen 2012 246p (trade bdg.) $17.99

Grades: 9 10 11 12

   1. Scholarships 2. Private schools -- Fiction 3. High school students -- Fiction 4. Maine -- Fiction 5. Schools -- Fiction 6. Identity -- Fiction 7. Race relations -- Fiction 8. African Americans -- Fiction 9. Preparatory schools -- Fiction

ISBN 9780061914836; 9780061914843

LC 2011016608

This book tells the story of "Anthony 'Ant' Jones [who] has never been outside his rough East Cleveland neighborhood when he's given a scholarship to Belton Academy, an elite prep school in Maine. But at Belton things are far from perfect. Everyone calls him 'Tony,' assumes he's from Brooklyn, expects him to play basketball, and yet acts shocked when he fights back. As Anthony tries to adapt to a world that will never fully accept him, he's in for a rude awakening: Home is becoming a place where he no longer belongs." (Publisher's note)

Wallace, Rich

Perpetual check. Alfred A. Knopf 2009 112p $15.99; lib bdg $18.99

Grades: 8 9 10 11

   1. Chess -- Fiction 2. Brothers -- Fiction 3. Father-son relationship -- Fiction

ISBN 978-0-375-84058-6; 0-375-84058-3; 978-0-375-94058-3 lib bdg; 0-375-94058-8 lib bdg

LC 2008-04159

Brothers Zeke and Randy participate in an important chess tournament, playing against each other while also trying to deal with their father's intensely competitive tendencies.

"Wallace cleverly positions Randy and Zeke for a win-win conclusion in this satisfying, engaging, and deceptively simple story." SLJ

★ **Wrestling** Sturbridge. Knopf 1996 135p hardcover o.p. pa $4.99

Grades: 7 8 9 10

   1. Wrestling -- Fiction 2. Friendship -- Fiction

ISBN 0-679-87803-3; 0-679-88555-2 pa

LC 95-20468

Stuck in a small town where no one ever leaves and relegated by his wrestling coach to sit on the bench while his best friend becomes state champion, Ben decides he can't let his last high school wrestling season slip by without challenging his friend and the future.

"The wresting scenes are thrilling. . . . Like Ben, whose voice is so strong and clear here, Wallace weighs his words carefully, making every one count in this excellent, understated first novel." Booklist

Wallace, Sandra Neil

Muckers; Sandra Neil Wallace. Alfred A. Knopf 2013 288 p. (hardback) $16.99

Grades: 7 8 9 10

   1. Historical fiction 2. Grief -- Fiction 3. Schools -- Fiction 4. Football -- Fiction 5. High schools -- Fiction 6. Race relations -- Fiction 7. Mexican Americans -- Fiction 8. Copper mines and mining -- Fiction 9. Arizona -- History -- 20th century -- Fiction

ISBN 0375867546; 9780375867545; 9780375967542

LC 2013003537

In this book, "Felix 'Red' O'Sullivan is the best hope to lead his team to a statewide football championship. Unlike other teams in 1950 in Arizona, whites and Latinos play together on the Hartley Muckers. Nevertheless, both groups are aware of the dividing lines." Red must also deal with an alcoholic father and a mother grieving for Red's older brother, killed in World War II. "For Red, this season will be his last chance to return glory to 'Bobby's school.'" (Kirkus Reviews)

Wallach, Tommy

Thanks for the trouble. Tommy Wallach. Simon & Schuster Books for Young Readers 2016 288 p.

Grades: 9 10 11 12

   1. Death -- Fiction 2. Love -- Fiction 3. Selective mutism -- Fiction 4. Romance fiction

9781481418805, $17.99; 9781481418812

LC 2015013388

"Parker Santé hasn't spoken a word in five years. While his classmates plan for bright futures, he skips school to hang out in hotels, killing time by watching the guests. But when he meets a silver-haired girl named Zelda Toth, a girl who claims to be quite a bit older than she looks, he'll discover there just might be a few things left worth living for." (Publisher's note)

"Bittersweet moments intersect with the intricate fairy tales Parker writes, compelling readers to judge what is real and what is make-believe." Pub Wkly

We all looked up. Tommy Wallach. Simon & Schuster Books for Young Readers 2015 384 p.

Grades: 9 10 11 12

   1. Friendship -- Fiction 2. High schools -- Fiction 3. Meteors -- Fiction 4. Schools -- Fiction 5. Self-realization -- Fiction 6. High school students -- Fiction

1481418777; 9781481418775, $17.99; 9781481418782

LC 2014004565

In this book, by Tommy Wallach, "[f]our high school seniors put their hopes, hearts, and humanity on the line as an asteroid hurtles toward Earth. . . . As these four seniors—along with the rest of the planet—wait to see what damage an asteroid will cause, they must abandon all thoughts of the future and decide how they're going to spend what remains of the present." (Publisher's note)

"Debut novelist Wallach increases the tension among characters throughout, ending in a shocking climax that resonates with religious symbolism. Stark scenes alternating between anarchy and police states are counterbalanced by deepening emotional ties and ethical dilemmas, creating a novel that asks far bigger questions than it answers." Publishers Weekly

Wallenfels, Stephen

POD. Namelos 2009 212p $18.95; pa $9.95
Grades: 7 8 9 10
1. Science fiction 2. Extraterrestrial beings -- Fiction
ISBN 978-1-60898-011-6; 1-60898-011-1; 978-1-60898-010-9 pa; 1-60898-010-3 pa
LC 2008-29721

As alien spacecrafts fill the sky and zap up any human being who dares to go outside, fifteen-year-old Josh and twelve-year-old Megs, living in different cities, describe what could be their last days on Earth.

"The dire circumstances don't negate the humor, the hormones, or the humanity found in the young narrators. This is solid, straightforward sci-fi." Booklist

Waller, Sharon Biggs

The **Forbidden** Orchid. By Sharon Biggs Waller. Penguin Group USA 2016 416 p. Map
Grades: 7 8 9 10 11 12
1. Father-daughter relationship -- Fiction 2. Historical fiction
9780451474117, $18.99; 0451474112
LC 2015039617

In this novel, by Sharon Biggs Waller, "Elodie Buchanan is the eldest of ten sisters growing up in a small English market town in 1861. The girls barely know their father, a plant hunter usually off adventuring through China.... Then disaster strikes: Mr. Buchanan reneges on his contract to collect an extremely rare and valuable orchid.... Elodie can't stand by and see her family destroyed, so she persuades her father to return to China once more to try to hunt down the flower." (Publisher's note)

"Historical details, including the liberal prescription of morphine and Britain's patriarchal economy, lend rich, textural background. Well-researched and filled with adventure, romance, and lots of tension-this work of historical fiction has all the elements of an intriguing read." Kirkus

A **mad**, wicked folly. Sharon Biggs Waller. Viking, published by the Penguin Group. 2014 448p $17.99
Grades: 8 9 10 11 12
1. Artists -- Fiction 2. Love -- Fiction 3. Sex role --Fiction 4. Great Britain -- History -- Edward VII, 1901-1910 -- Fiction 5. London (England)
ISBN: 0670014680; 9780670014682
LC 2013029858

A novel "about a young English woman who is talented, beautiful, passionate, and wealthy. Despite these advantages, Victoria Darling struggles with the harsh limitations imposed upon women prior to and during the Edwardian era of 1901-1910, which curtail her attempts to attend art school. While Victoria does not initially associate with the Suffragette Movement, she ultimately discovers that her fate is intertwined with the cause." (SLJ)

"Victoria's dream of becoming an artist leads her naively into scandals, tempts her into a convenient marriage, and drives her to join the Women's Social and Political Union. Persistence eventually triumphs, and friendships, love, and art lessons are her rewards. Sound historical research provides the backbone for this warm novel about the development of women's opportunities in Edwardian London." Horn Book

Walrath, Dana

★ **Like** water on stone. Dana Walrath. Delacorte Press 2014 368 p.
Grades: 8 9 10 11 12
1. Armenian massacres, 1915-1923 -- Fiction 2. Armenians -- Turkey -- Fiction 3. Brothers and sisters -- Fiction 4. Genocide -- Fiction 5. Novels in verse 6. Turkey -- History -- Ottoman Empire, 1288-1918 -- Fiction 7. Orphans -- Fiction
0385743971; 9780375991424; 9780385743976, $16.99
LC 2013026323

"Shahen Donabedian dreams of going to New York. Sosi, his twin sister, never wants to leave her home, especially now that she is in love. But when the Ottoman pashas set in motion their plans to eliminate all Armenians, neither twin has a choice. They flee into the mountains . . . [b]ut the children are not alone. An eagle watches over them as they run at night and hide each day, making their way across mountain ridges and rivers red with blood." (Publisher's note)

"This beautiful, yet at times brutally vivid, historical verse novel will bring this horrifying, tragic period to life for astute, mature readers.... A cast of characters, and author note with historical background are thoughtfully included." SLJ

Walsh, Alice

A **Long** Way from Home. Orca Book Pub 2012 232 p. (paperback) $11.95
Grades: 7 8 9 10
1. Immigrants -- Fiction 2. Prejudices -- Fiction 3. September 11 terrorist attacks, 2001 -- Fiction
ISBN 1926920791; 9781926920795

In this book by Alice Walsh, "thirteen-year-old Rabia, along with her mother and younger brother, flees Afghanistan.... They take part in a program that is relocating refugee widows and orphans to America.... After the terrorist attack on the World Trade Center in New York City, their plane is diverted to Gander, Newfoundland. Also on the plane is a boy named Colin, who struggles with his prejudices against Rabia and her family." (Publisher's note)

Walter, Jon

My name is not Friday. By Jon Walter. David Fickling Books/Scholastic Inc. 2016 384 p.
Grades: 7 8 9 10Fic; 813.6
1. African Americans -- Fiction 2. Brothers -- Fiction 3. Orphans -- Fiction 4. Slavery -- Fiction 5. United States -- History -- Civil War, 1861-1865 -- Fiction 6. Slavery -- United States -- Fiction
9780545855228, $18.99
LC 2015035464

In this novel, by Jon Walter, "well-mannered Samuel and his mischievous younger brother Joshua are free black boys living in an orphanage during the end of the Civil War. Samuel takes the blame for Joshua's latest prank, and the consequence is worse than he could ever imagine. He's taken from the orphanage to the South, given a new name—Friday—and sold into slavery." (Publisher's note)

"While readers on the young end of the age range and those unfamiliar with religious concepts may find the opening chapters somewhat confusing, Samuel's endearing, immersive narration makes the novel a fascinating and unforgettable account of a brutal and shameful chapter in America's history. A heartbreaking story about family, justice, and the resilience of the human spirit." Kirkus

First published in the United Kingdom in 2015.

Waltman, Kevin

Slump. By Kevin Waltman. Cinco Puntos Press 2014 216 p. (D-Bow's high school hoops)
Grades: 9 10 11 12
1. African Americans -- Fiction 2. Basketball -- Fiction 3. High schools -- Fiction 4. Schools -- Fiction 5. School stories
1941026001; 9781941026007, $16.95; 9781941026014
LC 2014007657

In this book, by Kevin Waltman, "Derrick Bowen's sophomore year is a grind. He's been looking forward to the basketball season all summer, but his girlfriend Jasmine leaves him for putting too much focus on basketball. The promise his Marion East basketball team showed at the end of last season isn't materializing. . . . When Derrick's father is severely injured in a car crash, Derrick is faced with a new reality where basketball can't be his only priority." (Publisher's note)

"All-star point guard Derrick "D-Bow" Bowen's (Next) sophomore year isn't turning out how he expected. He's having problems with his girlfriend, his team is struggling to click, and then an accident leaves his father injured and his family straining to make ends meet. Once again, Waltman skillfully blends play-by-play basketball action and strong character development; readers are left anticipating another book." Horn Book

Walton, Julia

Words on bathroom walls. Julia Walton. Random House 2017 294 p.
Grades: 7 8 9 10 11 12
1. Dating (Social customs) -- Fiction; 2. Hallucinations and illusions -- Fiction; 3. Mental illness -- Treatment -- Fiction; 4. Schizophrenia in adolescence -- Fiction; 5. Secrecy -- Fiction; 6. Schizophrenia -- Fiction; 7. Mental illness -- Fiction
9780399550904; 9780399550881, $17.99; 9780399550898
LC 2016017419

In this book, by Julia Walton, "Adam has just been diagnosed with schizophrenia. He sees and hears people who aren't there.... Still, there's hope. As Adam starts fresh at a new school, he begins a drug trial that helps him ignore his visions.... When he meets Maya, a fiercely intelligent girl, he desperately wants to be the great guy that she thinks he is. But then the...drug begins to fail, and Adam will do anything to keep Maya from discovering his secret." (Publisher's note)

"First-time author Walton creates a psychologically tense story with sympathetic characters while dispelling myths about a much-feared condition." Pub Wkly

Walton, Leslye

The **Strange** and beautiful sorrows of Ava Lavender; Leslye Walton. Candlewick Press 2014 320 p. $17.99
Grades: 9 10 11 12
1. Love stories 2. Teenagers -- Fiction 3. Supernatural -- Fiction
ISBN 0763665665; 9780763665661
LC 2013946615

In this book, by Leslye Walton, "Ava -- in all other ways a normal girl -- is born with the wings of a bird. . . . sixteen-year old Ava ventures into the wider world, ill-prepared for what she might discover and naive to the twisted motives of others. Others like the pious Nathaniel Sorrows, who mistakes Ava for an angel and whose obsession with her grows until the night of the summer solstice celebration." (Publisher's note)

"Ava Lavender, a typical girl in every respect except for the fact that she was born with wings, sits upon a family tree of doomed lovers...here are many sorrows in Walton's debut, and most of them are Ava's through inheritance. Readers should prepare themselves for a tale where myth and reality, lust and love, the corporal and the ghostly, are interchangeable and surprising." (Booklist)

Wang, Corrie

The **takedown**. Corrie Wang. Freeform 2017 369 p.
Grades: 7 8 9 10
1. Cyberbullying -- Fiction; 2. High schools -- Fiction; 3. Popularity -- Fiction; 4. Racially mixed people -- Fiction; 5. Schools -- Fiction; 6. Social media -- Fiction; 7. Brooklyn (New York, N.Y.) -- Fiction
9781484757420, $17.99; 1484757424
LC 2016028339

In this novel, by Corrie Wang, "a week before college applications are due, a video of Kyla 'doing it' with her crush-worthy English teacher is uploaded to her school's website. It instantly goes viral, but here's the thing: it's not Kyla in the video. With time running out, Kyla delves into a world of hackers, haters and creepy stalkers in an attempt to do the impossible-take something off the internet-all while dealing with the fallout from her own karmic footprint." (Publisher's note)

"A thought-provoking, entertaining read, Wang's debut illustrates a future that is easily conceivable." Kirkus

Ward, Rachel

The **Chaos**. Chicken House 2011 339p $17.99
Grades: 8 9 10 11 12
1. Science fiction 2. Death -- Fiction 3. Orphans -- Fiction 4. London (England) -- Fiction 5. Blacks -- Great Britain -- Fiction 7. Extrasensory perception -- Fiction
ISBN 978-0-545-24269-1; 0-545-24269-X
Sequel to: Numbers (2010)

When rising flood waters force him and his grandmother to evacuate their coastal home and return to London, sixteen-year-old Adam, who has inherited his mother's curse of being able to see the day that someone will die when he looks into their eyes, becomes disturbed when he begins to see January 1, 2027, a date six months into the future, in nearly everyone around him.

"In this sequel to Numbers a fascinating premise is again worked out through gripping episodes and a lightly handled metaphysical dilemma." Horn Book

Infinity; Rachel Ward. Chicken House/Scholastic 2012 249 p. (Numbers) $17.99

Grades: 8 9 10 11 12

1. Death -- Fiction 2. England -- Fiction 3. Psychic ability -- Fiction 4. London (England) -- Fiction 5. Interpersonal relations -- Fiction 6. Blacks -- England -- London -- Fiction

ISBN 0545350921; 9780545350921; 9780545381918

LC 2011032709

This novel, by Rachel Ward, is the conclusion to the "Numbers" trilogy. "Sarah loves Adam, but can't bear the thought that every time he looks in her eyes, he can see her dying; can see her last day. It's 2029. Two years since the Chaos. . . . Little Mia was supposed to die that New Year's Day. The numbers don't lie. But somehow she changed her date. Mia's just a baby, oblivious to her special power. But ruthless people are hunting her down, determined to steal her secret." (Publisher's note)

Num8ers. Chicken House/Scholastic 2010 325p $17.99

Grades: 8 9 10 11 12

1. Science fiction 2. Death -- Fiction 3. Runaway teenagers -- Fiction 4. Blacks -- Great Britain -- Fiction 5. Extrasensory perception -- Fiction

ISBN 978-0-545-14299-1; 0-545-14299-7

LC 2008-55440

Fifteen-year-old Jem knows when she looks at someone the exact date they will die, so she avoids relationships and tries to keep out of the way, but when she meets a boy named Spider and they plan a day out together, they become more involved than either of them had planned.

"Ward's debut novel is gritty, bold, and utterly unique. Jem's isolation and pain, hidden beneath a veneer of toughness, are palpable, and the ending is a real shocker." SLJ

Followed by: The Chaos (2011)

Warman, Janice

The **world** beneath: one South African boy's struggle to be free. Janice Warman. Candlewick Press 2015 176 p.

Grades: 8 9 10 11

1. Historical fiction 2. South Africa -- Race relations -- Fiction 3. Bildungsromans

9780763680572, $16.99; 9780763678562, $16.99; 0763678562

LC 2015931429

This novel, by Janice Warman, is set in "South Africa, 1976. Joshua lives with his mother in the maid's room, in the backyard of their wealthy white employers' house in the city by the sea. He doesn't quite understand the events going on around him. But when he rescues a stranger and riots begin to sweep the country, Joshua has to face the world beneath the world deep inside him—to make heartbreaking choices that will change his life forever." (Publisher's note)

"A good complement to nonfiction about apartheid South Africa, a little-explored place and period in children's literature." Kirkus

Warman, Jessica

Between. Walker 2011 454p $17.99

Grades: 10 11 12

1. Dead -- Fiction 2. Family life -- Fiction 3. Future life -- Fiction

ISBN 978-0-8027-2182-2

LC 2010-40986

"Liz runs the gamut of strong emotion throughout this compelling backtrack of a short life punctuated by early grief, parental failings, and honest, flawed love; her journey offers insight into the effects all of these things can have on an ordinary life." Bull Cent Child Books

Where the truth lies. Walker & Co. 2010 308p $16.99

Grades: 9 10 11 12

1. School stories 2. Dreams -- Fiction 3. Memory -- Fiction 4. Connecticut -- Fiction 5. Family life -- Fiction 6. Dating (Social customs) -- Fiction

ISBN 978-0-8027-2078-8; 0-8027-2078-1

LC 2010-00782

Emily, whose father is headmaster of a Connecticut boarding school, suffers from nightmares, and when she meets and falls in love with the handsome Del Sugar, pieces of her traumatic past start falling into place.

"Emily's unflinching, multilayered narration and realistic dialogue capture the wishes and fears that drive teens. A page-turner to the bittersweet ending." Kirkus

Wasserman, Robin

The **book** of blood and shadow; by Robin Wasserman. Alfred A. Knopf 2012 352p. $17.99

Grades: 7 8 9

1. Mystery fiction 2. Suspense fiction 3. Homicide -- Fiction 4. Prague (Czech Republic) -- Fiction

ISBN 9780375868764; 9780375872778; 9780375899614; 9780375968761

LC 2011003920

In this book, "Nora . . . help[s] an eccentric professor translate a sixteenth-century book by a notable alchemist (and the letters left by his daughter, Elizabeth), . . . spending more time with her best friend, Chris, and his roommate, Max, who are also working on the project. Just as quickly as Nora becomes invested in Elizabeth"s life, Max transforms from a slightly creepy tagalong to a sweet, solicitous boyfriend. Then Chris is brutally murdered, his girlfriend Adriane is left without memory of the night, and Max (the main suspect in the crime) disappears. . . . Nora . . . continu[es] her translation of the secrets encrypted in Elizabeth"s . . . communications and uncovering conspiracies . . . in which she herself is . . . a key figure." (Bulletin of the Center for Children"s Books)

The **waking** dark; Robin Wasserman. Alfred A. Knopf 2013 464 p. $17.99

Grades: 9 10 11 12

1. Horror fiction 2. Homicide -- Fiction 3. Science fiction 4. Death -- Fiction 5. Kansas -- Fiction 6. Murder -- Fiction 7. City and town life -- Kansas -- Fiction

ISBN 0375868771; 9780375868771; 9780375968778

LC 2012032802

In this horror novel set in a small Kansas town, "five people suddenly go on murder sprees, with four of them committing suicide. A year later, five survivors are united when a storm (and later, soldiers) isolate the town: loner Daniel, closeted jock West, newly evangelical Ellie, outcast Jule, and Cassie—the one remaining murderer, who has no recollection of what she did or why. As the days pass, the five grow increasingly aware that everyone else in Oleander is starting to act strange." (Publishers Weekly)

Watkins, Steve

Great Falls. Steve Watkins. Candlewick Press 2016 256 p.

Grades: 8 9 10 11

1. Brothers -- Fiction 2. Veterans -- Fiction 3. Post-traumatic stress disorder -- Fiction

076367155X; 9780763671556, $17.99

"Shane has always worshiped his big brother, Jeremy. But three tours in Iraq and Afghanistan have taken their toll, and the easy-go-lucky brother Shane knew has been replaced by a surly drunk. When Jeremy . . . offers to take him to the family cabin overnight, Shane goes along. But as the camping trip turns into a days-long canoe trip . . . Shane realizes he . . . has no idea how to persuade Jeremy to return home and get the help he needs." (Publisher's note)

"Watkins (Juvie) delivers a powerful, emotionally raw tale, heartbreaking in its portrayal of damaged veterans, the price some pay to serve, and the toll it takes on their friends and family. It's also a raw coming-of-age journey for Shane as he struggles with his own feelings, especially toward 'the Colonel,' the brothers' emotionally abusive, micromanaging, ex-military stepfather." Pub Wkly

Juvie; by Steve Watkins. Candlewick Press 2013 320 p. $17.99

Grades: 9 10 11 12

1. Sisters -- Fiction 2. Juvenile delinquency -- Fiction

ISBN 0763655090; 9780763655099

LC 2012955219

This book, by Steve Watkins, "tells the story of two sisters grappling with accountability [and] sacrifice. Sadie Windas has always been the responsible one . . . not like her older sister, Carla, who leaves her three-year-old daughter, Lulu, with Aunt Sadie while she parties and gets high. But when both sisters are caught up in a drug deal—wrong place, wrong time—it falls to Sadie to confess to a crime she didn't commit to keep Carla out of jail and Lulu out of foster care." (Publisher's note)

"When seventeen-year-old Sadie and her sister, Carla, are caught participating (unintentionally) in a drug deal, Sadie takes the blame to protect her family; her punishment is a six-month sentence in a juvenile corrections facility. The novel is bleak and brutal--which, of course, is the point-

-making Sadie's loyalty to Carla and resolve to survive all the more powerful." (Horn Book)

What comes after. Candlewick Press 2011 334p $16.99

Grades: 8 9 10 11 12

1. Moving -- Fiction 2. Farm life -- Fiction 3. Bereavement -- Fiction 4. Child abuse -- Fiction 5. North Carolina -- Fiction 6. Domestic animals -- Fiction

ISBN 0-7636-4250-9; 978-0-7636-4250-1

LC 2010-38711

When her veterinarian father dies, sixteen-year-old Iris Wight must move from Maine to North Carolina where her Aunt Sue spends Iris's small inheritance while abusing her physically and emotionally, but the hardest to take is her mistreatment of the farm animals.

"This is the kind of book where readers will likely literally sigh with relief when Iris finally catches a break—while there is no rainbows-and-clouds-parting happy ending for a life this hard, it is enough that she is, for the moment, loved by a few fiercely loyal allies, beginning to face her demons, and wielding a bit more control over her own life." Bull Cent Child Books

Watkins, Yoko Kawashima

★ **My** brother, my sister, and I. Bradbury Press 1994 275p hardcover o.p. pa $5.99

Grades: 6 7 8 9

1. World War, 1939-1945 -- Fiction

ISBN 0-02-792526-9; 0-689-80656-6 pa

LC 93-23535

Living as refugees in Japan in 1947 while trying to locate their missing father, thirteen-year-old Yoko and her older brother and sister must endure a bad fire, injury, and false charges of arson, theft, and murder.

"Watkins's first-person narrative is beautifully direct and emotionally honest." Publ Wkly

★ **So** far from the bamboo grove. Lothrop, Lee & Shepard Bks. 1986 183p map hardcover o.p. pa $5.99

Grades: 6 7 8 9

1. World War, 1939-1945 -- Fiction

ISBN 0-688-13115-8 pa

LC 85-15939

A fictionalized autobiography in which eight-year-old Yoko escapes from Korea to Japan with her mother and sister at the end of World War II

"An admirably told and absorbing novel." Horn Book

Watson, Renée

★ **Piecing** me together. Renée Watson. Bloomsbury 2017 264 p.

Grades: 7 8 9 10 11 12

1. African Americans -- Fiction; 2. High schools -- Fiction; 3. Mentoring -- Fiction; 4. Schools -- Fiction; 5. School stories

9781681191065; 9781681191058, $17.99

LC 2016023127

Newbery Honor Book (2018); Coretta Scott King Author Award (2018)

In this book, by Renée Watson, "Jade believes she must get out of her poor neighborhood if she's ever going to succeed. Her mother tells her to take advantage of every opportunity that comes her way.... She accepted...an invitation to join...a mentorship program for 'at-risk' girls. Except really, it's for black girls. From 'bad' neighborhoods. And just because Maxine, her college-graduate mentor, is black doesn't mean she understands Jade." (Publisher's note)

"A timely, nuanced, and unforgettable story about the power of art, community, and friendship." Kirkus

This side of home. By Renée Watson. Bloomsbury 2015 326 p.

Grades: 9 10 11 12

1. Best friends -- Fiction 2. Dating (Social customs) -- Fiction 3. Friendship -- Fiction 4. Neighborhoods -- Fiction 5. Sisters -- Fiction 6. Twins -- Fiction 7. Urban renewal -- Fiction 8. Portland (Or.) -- Fiction 9. Neighborhood -- Fiction

1599906686; 9781599906683, $17.99

LC 2014013743

In this novel, by Renée Watson, "identical twins Nikki and Maya have been on the same page for everything.... But as their neighborhood goes from rough-and-tumble to up-and-coming, . . . Nikki is thrilled while Maya feels like their home is slipping away. Suddenly, the sisters . . . must confront their dissenting feelings on the importance of their ethnic and cultural identities and, in the process, learn to separate themselves from the long shadow of their identity as twins." (Publisher's note)

"Readers may be surprised to find this multicultural story set in Portland, Oregon, but that just adds to its distinctive appeal. Here's hoping Watson's teen debut will be followed by many more." Kirkus

Weatherford, Carole Boston

★ **Becoming** Billie Holiday; art by Floyd Cooper. Wordsong 2008 116p il $19.95

Grades: 7 8 9 10

1. Novels in verse; 2. Singers -- Fiction; 3. Jazz music -- Fiction; 4. African Americans -- Fiction; 5. Holiday, Billie, 1915-1959 -- Fiction

ISBN 978-1-59078-507-2; 1-59078-507-X

LC 2007-51214

Coretta Scott King honor book for text, 2009

Jazz vocalist Billie Holiday looks back on her early years in this fictional memoir written in verse.

"This captivating title places readers solidly into Holiday's world, and is suitable for independent reading as well as a variety of classroom uses." SLJ

Includes bibliographical references

Weaver, Will

Saturday night dirt. Farrar, Straus and Giroux 2008 163p $14.95; pa $7.99

Grades: 8 9 10 11

1. Minnesota -- Fiction 2. Automobile racing -- Fiction

ISBN 978-0-374-35060-4; 0-374-35060-4; 978-0-312-56131-4 pa; 0-312-56131-8 pa

LC 2007-6988

In a small town in northern Minnesota, the much-anticipated Saturday night dirt-track race at the old-fashioned, barely viable, Headwaters Speedway becomes, in many ways, an important life-changing event for all the participants on and off the track.

"Weaver presents compelling character studies. . . . Young racing fans . . . will find much that rings true here." Booklist

Other titles in this series are:

Checkered flag cheater (2010)

Super stock rookie (2009)

Webber, Katherine

The **heartbeats** of Wing Jones. Katherine Webber. Delacorte Press 2017 328 p.

Grades: 7 8 9 10 11 12

1. Brothers and sisters -- Fiction; 2. Coma -- Patients -- Fiction; 3. Emotional problems of teenagers -- Fiction; 4. Racially mixed people -- Fiction; 5. Running -- Fiction; 6. Emotional problems -- Fiction; 7. Traffic accidents -- Fiction

9780399555022, $17.99; 9780399555046; 9780399555039

LC 2016005580

In this novel, by Katherine Webber, "Wing Jones, like everyone else in her town, has worshipped her older brother for as long as she can remember.... Marcus is everything his sister is not. Until...Marcus, drunk at the wheel after a party, kills two people and barely survives himself. With Marcus now in a coma, Wing is crushed, confused, and angry. She is tormented at school for Marcus's mistake, haunted at home by her mother and grandmothers' grief." (Publisher's note)

"Written in Wing's believable first-person voice, the novel conveys the teen's perspective of the changing world around her as the plot moves quickly along. Recommend this to fans of Jandy Nelson's and Stephanie Perkins's books." SLJ

Wegelius, Jakob

★ The **murderer's** ape. Jakob Wegelius; translated from the Swedish by Peter Graves. Delacorte Press 2017 624 p. Illustration; Color; Map

Grades: 7 8 9 10

1. Adventure and adventurers -- Fiction 2. Friendship -- Fiction 3. Gorilla -- Fiction 4. Human-animal relationships -- Fiction 5. Mystery and detective stories 6. Mystery fiction -- Fiction

9781101931776, $53.97; 9781101931752, $17.99; 9781101931769

LC 2016010508

Mildred L. Batchelder Award (2018)

This novel, by Jakob Wegelius, translated by Peter Graves, is a "quirky mystery featuring a gorilla named Sally Jones. . . . While carrying what they think is a crate of tiles, Sally Jones and the Chief are attacked by robbers, and [their] ship is sunk. Things go from bad to worse when the Chief is shortly thereafter arrested for the murder of the man who hired them to transport the cargo. . . . Jones forges a new life but is determined to prove the Chief's innocence." (School Library Journal)

"While the sheer length and thoughtful pace of Sally Jones' journey might discourage some, those who persevere will have a richly imagined and thoroughly unique adventure in store." Booklist

Maps on lining papers.

Weil, Cynthia

I'm glad I did. Cynthia Weil. Soho Teen 2015 272 p.

Grades: 8 9 10 11 12

1. Composers -- Fiction 2. Love -- Fiction 3. Popular music -- Fiction 4. Secrets -- Fiction 5. Songwriters and songwriting 6. Nineteen sixties 7. Rock music -- Fiction

161695356X; 9781616953560, $18.99

LC 2014025047

In this novel by Cynthia Weil "it's the summer of 1963 and JJ Green is a born songwriter . . . [and] she takes an internship at the Brill Building, the epicenter of a new sound called rock and roll. She even finds herself a writing partner in Luke Silver, a boy . . . who seems to connect instantly with her music. Best of all, they'll be cutting their first demo with legendary singer Dulcie Brown. But Dulcie's past is a tangle of secrets." (Publisher's note)

"Grammy-winning songwriter Weil makes an impressive YA debut with this period novel set against the rapidly changing music industry of the early 1960s. . . [s]howing both the bright and the dark sides of the music business, Weil crafts an enticing tale of a sheltered teenager's induction into a world where ambitions and morals are repeatedly tested." PW

Wein, Elizabeth

★ **Black** dove, white raven. Elizabeth Wein. Disney-Hyperion 2015 368 p.

Grades: 8 9 10 11 12

1. Adoption -- Fiction 2. Adventure and adventurers -- Fiction 3. Americans -- Ethiopia -- Fiction 4. Brothers and sisters -- Fiction 5. Race relations -- Fiction 6. Ethiopia -- History -- 1889-1974 -- Fiction 7. Italo-Ethiopian War, 1935-1936 -- Fiction 8. Air pilots -- Fiction

142318310X; 9781423183105, $17.99

LC 2014044446

In this book, by Elizabeth Wein, "Emilia and Teo's lives changed in a fiery, terrifying instant when a bird strike brought down the plane their stunt pilot mothers were flying. Teo's mother died immediately, but Em's survived, determined to raise Teo according to his late mother's wishes. . . . But in 1930s America, a white woman raising a black adoptive son alongside a white daughter is too often seen as a threat." (Publisher's note)

"The intellectual, psychological, and emotional substance of this story is formidable, and Wein makes it all approachable and engaging." Horn Book

★ **Code** name Verity; Elizabeth Wein. Hyperion Books 2012 343 p.

Grades: 9 10 11 12 Adult

1. Historical fiction 2. Prisoners of war -- Fiction 3. Women air pilots -- Fiction 4. Female friendship -- Fiction 5. France -- History -- 1940-1945, German occupation -- Fiction 6. Nazis -- Fiction 7. Espionage -- Fiction 8. Air pilots -- Fiction 9. Friendship -- Fiction 10. Insurgency -- Fiction 11. World War, 1939-1945 -- Fiction 12. Great Britain -- History -- 1936-

1945 -- Fiction
ISBN 1423152190; 9781423152194

LC 2011024857

Michael L. Printz Honor Book (2013)

This young adult historical fiction novel presents a "tale of friendship during World War II. In a cell in Nazi-occupied France, a young woman writes. Like Scheherazade, to whom she is compared by the SS officer in charge of her case, she dribbles out information . . . in exchange for time and a reprieve from torture. . . . [S]he describes her friendship with Maddie, the pilot who flew them to France. . . . She also describes . . . her unbearable current situation." (Kirkus Reviews)

The **empty** kingdom. Viking 2008 217p (Mark of Solomon) $16.99

Grades: 7 8 9 10

1. Princes -- Fiction
ISBN 978-0-670-06273-7; 0-670-06273-1

LC 2007-29082

Telemakos, imprisoned on the upper levels of Abreha's, ruler of Himyar, twelve-story palace and lacking any way to communicate his predicament to his family in faraway Aksum, tries to find a subtle and effective way to regain his freedom.

"Wein deftly balances the political with the personal. . . . A unique, epic journey into adulthood." Horn Book

★ The **lion** hunter. Viking 2007 223p (Mark of Solomon) $16.99

Grades: 7 8 9 10

1. Kings 2. Princes -- Fiction
ISBN 978-0-670-06163-1; 0-670-03638-2

Still recovering from his ordeal as a government spy, twelve-year-old Telemakos, the half-Ethiopian grandson of King Artos of Britain, is sent with his sister to live with Abreha, the ruler of Himyar. His Aunt Goewin warns him that Abreha is a dangerous man, but just how dangerous remains to be seen.

"The vividly evoked setting provides a lush backdrop for the story's seemingly casual permutations, and readers' sympathies toward the embattled, wounded hero will draw them on willingly while Wein weaves her web of loyalty and intrigue." Horn Book

★ The **pearl** thief. By Elizabeth Wein. Hyperion 2017 325 p. Map

Grades: 8 9 10 11

1. Friendship -- Fiction; 2. Mystery and detective stories; 3. Prejudices -- Fiction; 4. Scottish Travellers (Nomadic people) -- Fiction; 5. Scotland -- History -- 20th century -- Fiction

9781484719510; 1484717163; 9781484717165, $18.99

LC 2016041527

In this novel, by Elizabeth Wein, "fifteen-year-old Julia Beaufort-Stuart.... begins to realize that her injury might not have been an accident. One of her family's employees... disappeared on the...day she landed in the hospital.... She befriends Euan McEwen,...[a] Scottish Traveller.... As Julie grows closer to this family, she witnesses...some of the prejudices they've grown used to...and finds herself exploring... new experiences...." (Publisher's note)

"A finely crafted book that brings one girl's coming-of-age story to life, especially poignant for those who already know her fate." Booklist

Includes bibliographical references.; Prequel to: Code name Verity (2012)

★ **Rose** under fire; by Elizabeth Wein. 1st ed. Hyperion 2013 368 p. (hardcover) $17.99
Grades: 9 10 11 12
  1. Historical fiction 2. World War, 1939-1945 -- Fiction 3. Diaries -- Fiction 4. Air pilots -- Fiction 5. Prisoners of war -- Fiction 6. Ravensbruck (Concentration camp) -- Fiction 7. World War, 1939-1945 -- Prisoners and prisons, German -- Fiction
ISBN 1423183096; 9781423183099
LC 2013010337
Schneider Family Book Award: Teen (2014)
Boston Globe-Horn Book Honor: Fiction (2014)

This historical novel chronicles the experiences of American pilot Rose in a Polish concentration camp. "After being brutally punished for her refusal to make fuses for flying bombs . . . , Rose is befriended by Polish 'Rabbits,' victims of horrific medical experimentation. She uses 'counting-out rhymes' to preserve her sanity and as a way to memorize the names of the Rabbits. Rose's poetry . . . is at the heart of the story, revealing her growing understanding of what's happening around her." (Kirkus Reviews)

"Wein excels at weaving research seamlessly into narrative and has crafted another indelible story about friendship borne out of unimaginable adversity." (Pub Wkly)

Wells, Dan
  Bluescreen. Dan Wells. Balzer + Bray 2016 352 p.
Grades: 7 8 9 10
  1. Future life -- Fiction 2. Internet industry -- Fiction 3. Drugs -- Fiction
006234787X; 9780062347879, $17.99
LC 2015943608

In this novel, by Dan Wells, "Los Angeles in 2050 is a city of open doors, as long as you have the right connections. That connection is a djinni—a smart device implanted right in a person's head. In a world where virtually everyone is online twenty-four hours a day, Anja . . . gets her hands on . . . a virtual drug that plugs right into a person's djinni and delivers a . . . safe high. But . . . Mari and her friends soon find themselves in the middle of a conspiracy." (Publisher's note)

"Wells' thrilling tale makes great use of its setting, and its diverse cast of characters is well suited for the futuristic L.A. demographic. Though it might hold special appeal for gamers, this is a great fit for readers who fancy noir thrillers and realistically flawed characters." Booklist

  Fragments; Dan Wells. Balzer + Bray 2013 576 p. (hardcover bdg.) $17.99
Grades: 9 10 11 12
  1. Survival skills -- Fiction 2. Genetic engineering -- Fiction 3. Identity (Psychology) -- Fiction 4. Science fiction 5. Robots -- Fiction 6. Identity -- Fiction 7. Survival -- Fiction 8. Medical care -- Fiction
ISBN 0062071076; 9780062071071
LC 2012038107

"In this second book in the saga, set in a postapocalyptic U.S. in 2076, Kira is struggling to accept the fact that she is a genetically enhanced human known as a Partial. She makes her way on foot from East Meadow, New York, to the company headquarters of ParaGen in Manhattan in search of a way to cure the RM virus that kills newborns and to stop the expiration of Partials at age 20. Kira allies herself with the last human in Manhattan . . . who may be able to help her." (School Library Journal)

  Partials; Dan Wells. 1st ed. Balzer + Bray 2012 470 p. (paperback) $9.99; (hbk : trade bdg.) $17.99
Grades: 9 10 11 12
  1. Science fiction 2. Genetic engineering -- Fiction 3. Communicable diseases -- Fiction 4. Robots -- Fiction 5. Diseases -- Fiction 6. Survival -- Fiction 7. Medical care -- Fiction 8. Medicine -- Research -- Fiction
ISBN 9780062071057; 0062071041; 9780062071040; 9780062135698
LC 2011042146

In this work of speculative fiction by Dan Wells, "after a virus released by the Partials (genetically engineered supersoldiers) . . . topples human civilization . . . [the] government . . . mandates pregnancy for every woman older than eighteen. . . . Kira Walker . . . has an alternative plan: since the Partials were immune to the virus, why not leave the safety of the island, capture a Partial, and bring it back to be studied?" (Bulletin of the Center for Children's Books)

  Ruins; Dan Wells; [edited by] Jordan Brown. Balzer + Bray 2014 464 p. (hardcover) $17.99
Grades: 9 10 11 12
  1. Science fiction 2. Robots -- Fiction 3. Apocalyptic fiction
ISBN 0062071106; 9780062071101
LC 2013953788

The conclusion of the author's Partial sequence trilogy. "As the clock ticks closer and closer to the final Partial expiration date, humans and Partials stand on the brink of war. Caught in the middle . . . are Samm and Kira: Samm, who is trapped on the far side of the continent beyond the vast toxic wasteland of the American Midwest; and Kira, now in the hands of Dr. Morgan, who is hell-bent on saving what's left of the Partials." (Publisher's note)

"Wells concludes his post-apocalyptic, action-packed trilogy with a literal bang and a lot of blood. Believable characters face tough moral choices, and though the end is tidy, the twists and treachery that get readers there are all the fun. It's enjoyable alone but best read after the first two. Science (fiction) at the end of the world done right." (Kirkus)

Wells, Martha
  Emilie & the hollow world; by Martha Wells. Strange Chemistry 2013 301 p. (paperback) $9.99
Grades: 9 10 11 12
  1. Fantasy fiction 2. Runaway teenagers -- Fiction 3. Missing persons -- Fiction 4. Runaway children -- Fiction
ISBN 1908844493; 9781908844491
LC 2012277394

In this book, Emilie is trying to run away. "After spending too much on snacks, [she] can't afford the ferry ticket to reach her cousin's home. There's only one logical thing to do: jump off the docks, swim to the nearest boat and hope for the best. After boarding what she hopes is the right ship, she witnesses a pirate attack, saves a scaled man and watches as a merging of magic and science transports the ship to a legendary world within a world." (Kirkus Reviews)

Wells, Robison E.

Feedback; Robison Wells. HarperTeen 2012 312 p. (hardback) $17.99

Grades: 7 8 9 10

    1. Private schools -- Fiction 2. School stories 3. Mystery fiction 4. Science fiction 5. Robots -- Fiction 6. Survival -- Fiction

    ISBN 0062026100; 9780062026101; 9780062228307

                      LC 2012004296

Sequel to: Variant

In author Robison Wells' story, "Benson Fisher escaped from Maxfield Academy's deadly rules and brutal gangs. The worst was over. Or so he thought. But now he's trapped on the other side of the wall, in a different kind of prison. . . . [His friends] are all pawns in the school's twisted experiment, held captive and controlled by an unseen force. And while Benson struggles to figure out who, if anyone, can be trusted, he discovers that Maxfield Academy's plans are darker than anything he imagined--and they may be impossible to stop." (Publisher's note)

Variant. HarperTeen 2011 376p $17.99

Grades: 7 8 9 10

    1. School stories 2. Science fiction

    ISBN 978-0-06-202608-8; 0-06-202608-9

                      LC 2010042661

After years in foster homes, seventeen-year-old Benson Fisher applies to New Mexico's Maxfield Academy in hopes of securing a brighter future, but instead he finds that the school is a prison and no one is what he or she seems.

"Hard to put down from the very first page, this fast-paced novel with Stepford overtones answers only some of the questions it poses, holding some of the most tantalizing open for the next installment in a series that is anything but ordinary." Kirkus

Wells, Rosemary

  ★ **Red** moon at Sharpsburg. Viking 2007 236p $16.99; pa $7.99

Grades: 6 7 8 9 10

    1. United States -- History -- 1861-1865, Civil War -- Fiction

    ISBN 0-670-03638-2; 978-0-670-03638-7; 0-14-241205-8 pa; 978-0-14-241205-3 pa

As the Civil War breaks out, India, a young Southern girl, summons her sharp intelligence and the courage she didn't know she had to survive the war that threatens to destroy her family, her Virginia home and the only life she has ever known.

"This powerful novel is unflinching in its depiction of war and the devastation it causes, yet shows the resilience and hope that can follow such a tragedy. India is a memorable, thoroughly believable character." SLJ

Wendig, Chuck

Under the Empyrean Sky. Amazon Childrens Pub 2013 368 p. $17.99

Grades: 7 8 9 10

    1. Science fiction 2. Apocalyptic fiction

    ISBN 1477817204; 9781477817209

In this first book in Chuck Wendig's Heartland Trilogy, "the haves hover above ruined Earth in luxurious flotillas and the have-nots toil below in the Heartland, [are] told whom to marry and what to grow. . . . When Cael and his friends discover a trail of precious, prohibited vegetables growing deep in the corn, they stumble on a secret that may save them—or get them killed." (Kirkus Reviews)

Other titles in this series are:
Blightborn (2014)
The Harvest (2015)

Werlin, Nancy

  ★ **Double** helix. Dial Books 2004 252p hardcover o.p. pa $6.99

Grades: 7 8 9 10

    1. Science fiction 2. Bioethics -- Fiction 3. Genetic engineering -- Fiction

    ISBN 0-8037-2606-6; 0-14-240327-X pa

                      LC 2003-12269

Eighteen-year-old Eli discovers a shocking secret about his life and his family while working for a Nobel Prizewinning scientist whose specialty is genetic engineering.

"Werlin clearly and dramatically raises fundamental bioethical issues for teens to ponder. She also creates a riveting story with sharply etched characters and complex relationships that will stick with readers long after the book is closed." SLJ

Impossible; a novel. Dial Books 2008 376p $17.99

Grades: 7 8 9 10

    1. Magic -- Fiction 2. Pregnancy -- Fiction 3. Teenage mothers -- Fiction

    ISBN 978-0-8037-3002-1; 0-8037-3002-0

                      LC 2008-06633

When seventeen-year-old Lucy discovers her family is under an ancient curse by an evil Elfin Knight, she realizes to break the curse she must perform three impossible tasks before her daughter is born in order to save them both.

"Werlin earns high marks for the tale's graceful interplay between wild magic and contemporary reality." Booklist

  ★ The **rules** of survival. Dial Books 2006 259p $16.99

Grades: 8 9 10 11 12

    1. Siblings -- Fiction 2. Child abuse -- Fiction

    ISBN 0-8037-3001-2

                      LC 2006-1675

Seventeen-year-old Matthew recounts his attempts, starting at a young age, to free himself and his sisters from the grip of their emotionally and physically abusive mother.

The author "tackles the topic of child abuse with grace and insight. . . . Teens will empathize with these siblings and the secrets they keep in this psychological horror story." SLJ

West, Kasie

Pivot point; Kasie West. HarperTeen 2013 352 p. (hardback) $17.99

Grades: 7 8 9 10

    1. Love stories 2. Occult fiction 3. Divorce -- Fiction 4. Love -- Fiction 5. Schools -- Fiction 6. High schools -- Fiction 7. Choice (Psychology) -- Fiction

    ISBN 0062117378; 9780062117373

                  LC 2012019089

This book tells the story of Addie Coleman, who has the ability to see into the future and choose between the better of two options. "She is a Searcher living in the Compound, the southern Texas home of the most gifted individuals in the county. When her parents decide to divorce, with her mother staying in the Compound, and her father opting to live in the normal world, she decides to use her ability to help her chose with whom to live." (Booklist)

Split second; Kasie West. HarperTeen, an imprint of HarperCollinsPublishers 2014 368 p. (hardcover bdg.) $17.99

Grades: 7 8 9 10

    1. Love stories 2. Memory -- Fiction 3. Psychics -- Fiction 4. Love -- Fiction 5. Schools -- Fiction 6. Family life -- Fiction 7. High schools -- Fiction 8. Psychic ability -- Fiction 9. Choice (Psychology) -- Fiction

    ISBN 0062117386; 9780062117380

                  LC 2013008053

"In this follow-up to Pivot Point (HarperCollins, 2013), Addie leaves the Compound after a bad breakup. As a Searcher, Addie can see two possible futures, and she finds it hard to believe this is the one she chose, the one in which she is betrayed by her best friend and her boyfriend... In this fast-paced fantasy, the plot is slow to begin but takes off after the first few chapters. Recommended for readers who love dystopian stories with a bit of romance." (School Library Journal)

Westerfeld, Scott

Afterworlds; by Scott Westerfeld. Simon Pulse. 2014 608p $19.99

Grades: 9 10 11 12

    1. Dead -- Fiction 2. East Indian Americans -- Fiction 3. Ghosts -- Fiction 4. Lesbians -- Fiction 5. Love -- Fiction 6. New York (N.Y.) -- Fiction;) 7. Authors -- Fiction

                  LC 2014006852

Rainbow List (2015)

"Eighteen-year-old Darcy drops her college plans and moves to New York to revise her soon-to-be-published novel and start the second one. Meanwhile, in chapters that alternate with Darcy's NYC adventures, her fictional protagonist, Lizzie, survives a near-death experience to find she has become a psychopomp, responsible for guiding souls to the afterlife." Booklist

"Readers who pay attention will see how Darcy's learning curve plays out and how she incorporates and transmutes her real-world experiences into her novel.Watching Darcy's story play off Darcy's novel will fascinate readers as well as writers." Kirkus

Blue noon; [by] Scott Westerfeld. 1st ed.; Eos 2006 378p (Midnighters) $15.99; lib bdg $16.89

Grades: 7 8 9 10

    1. Science fiction

    ISBN 0-06-051957-6; 0-06-051958-4 lib bdg

                  LC 2005017597

The five midnighters from Bixby discover that the secret hour is starting to invade the daylight world, and if they cannot stop it, the darklings will soon be free to hunt again.

"The plot maintains an exciting pace. . . . This is fun recreational reading." SLJ

Extras. Simon Pulse 2011 399p $17.99; pa $9.99

Grades: 7 8 9 10

    1. Science fiction

    ISBN 978-1-4424-3007-5; 978-1-4424-1978-0 pa

    Sequel to Specials (2006)

    First published 2007

Aya is "an 'extra' (face rank stuck in the mid-400,000s) in a city run on a 'reputation economy.' If Aya can win fame as a 'kicker,' reporting with her trusty hovercam on a story that captures the city's imagination, her face rank will soar. . . . Westerfeld shows he has a finger on the pulse of our reputation economy, alchemizing the cult of celebrity, advertising's constant competition for consumer attention." Horn Book

★ **Leviathan**; written by Scott Westerfeld; illustrated by Keith Thompson. Simon Pulse 2009 440p il map $19.99; pa $9.99

Grades: 7 8 9 10

    1. War stories 2. Science fiction 3. Princes -- Fiction 4. Mythical animals -- Fiction 5. Genetic engineering -- Fiction

    ISBN 978-1-4169-7173-3; 1-4169-7173-4; 978-1-4169-7174-0 pa; 1-4169-7174-2 pa

                  LC 2009-881

In an alternate 1914 Europe, fifteen-year-old Austrian Prince Alek, on the run from the Clanker Powers who are attempting to take over the globe using mechanical machinery, forms an uneasy alliance with Deryn who, disguised as a boy to join the British Air Service, is learning to fly genetically-engineered beasts.

"The protagonists' stories are equally gripping and keep the story moving, and Thompson's detail-rich panels bring Westerfeld's unusual creations to life." Publ Wkly

    Other titles in this series are:

    Behemoth (2010)

    Goliath (2011)

★ **Peeps**. Razorbill 2005 312p hardcover o.p. pa $8.99

Grades: 9 10 11 12

    1. Vampires -- Fiction

    ISBN 1-59514-031-X; 1-59514-083-2 pa

                  LC 2005-8151

Cal Thompson is a carrier of a parasite that causes vampirism, and must hunt down all of the girlfriends he has unknowingly infected.

"This innovative and original vampire story, full of engaging characters and just enough horror without any gore, will appeal to a wide audience." SLJ

Followed by The last days (2006)

Pretties. Simon Pulse 2011 348p $17.99; pa $9.99

Grades: 7 8 9 10

  1. Science fiction

  ISBN 978-1-4169-3639-8; 978-1-4424-1980-3 pa

Sequel to Uglies

First published 2005

Tally's transformation to perfect and popular including her totally hot boyfriend is everything she always wanted. But beneath the fun and freedom something is wrong and now Tally has to fight for her life because what she knows has put her in danger with the authorities.

"Riveting and compulsively readable, this action-packed sequel does not disappoint." Booklist

Followed by Specials

★ **So** yesterday; a novel. Razorbill 2004 225p $16.99; pa $7.99

Grades: 7 8 9 10

  1. Mystery fiction 2. Missing persons -- Fiction

  ISBN 1-59514-000-X; 1-59514-032-8 pa

                      LC 2004-2302

Hunter Braque, a New York City teenager who is paid by corporations to spot what is "cool," combines his analytical skills with girlfriend Jen's creative talents to find a missing person and thwart a conspiracy directed at the heart of consumer culture

"This hip, fascinating thriller aggressively questions consumer culture. . . . Teens will inhale this wholly entertaining, thought-provoking look at a system fueled by their purchasing power. " Booklist

Specials. Simon Pulse 2011 350p $17.99; pa $9.99

Grades: 7 8 9 10

  1. Science fiction

  ISBN 978-1-4424-3008-2; 978-1-4424-1979-7 pa

Sequel to Pretties

First published 2006

Tally has been transformed from a repellent ugly to supermodel pretty. Now she's a super-amped fighting machine. Her mission is to keep the uglies down and the pretties stupid. But Tally's never been good at playing by the rules.

"Readers who enjoyed Uglies and Pretties . . . will not want to miss Specials. . . . Westerfeld's themes include vanity, environmental conservation, Utopian idealism, fascism, violence, and love." SLJ

Followed by Extras

Uglies. Simon Pulse 2005 425p rpt $17.99

Grades: 7 8 9 10

  1. Science fiction

  ISBN 9781416936381

"Tally is an ugly, waiting eagerly for her sixteenth birthday, when surgery will make her into a Pretty and she can join her old friend Peris in the life of the beautiful in New Pretty Town. In the meantime, she revels in hoverboard-ing and pulling tricks with her rebellious friend, Shay, who doesn't share Tally's anticipation for joining the Pretty world. When Shay runs away to join dissidents outside the city, Tally is blackmailed by the city's Special Circumstances unit into following Shay and uncovering the location of the anti-establishment rebels, a task that becomes more difficult when Tally's sympathies begin to skew toward the rebels, especially their charismatic leader, David. . . . Grades six to ten." (Bull Cent Child Books)

"Fifteen-year-old Tally's eerily harmonious, postapocalyptic society gives extreme makeovers to teens on their sixteenth birthdays. . . . When a top-secret agency threatens to leave Tally ugly forever unless she spies on runaway teens, she agrees to infiltrate the Smoke, a shadowy colony of refugees from the 'tyranny of physical perfection.'" Booklist

Zeroes. By Scott Westerfeld, Margo Lanagan, and Deborah Biancotti. Simon Pulse 2015 546 p.

Grades: 8 9 10 11

  1. California -- Fiction 2. Superheroes -- Fiction 3. Teenagers -- Fiction

  9781481443371; 1481443372; 1481443364; 9781481443364, $19.99

                      LC 2015001667

In this book, "X-Men meets Heroes when New York Times bestselling author Scott Westerfeld teams up with award-winning authors Margo Lanagan and Deborah Biancotti to create a sizzling new series filled with action and adventure. Don't call them heroes. But these six Californian teens have powers that set them apart." (Publisher's note)

"A powerful tale with an emotional rawness that will resonate with readers." Booklist

Weston, Carol

  Speed of life. Carol Weston. Sourcebooks Jabberwocky 2017 329 p.

Grades: 7 8 9 10

  1. Advice columnists -- Fiction; 2. Grief -- Fiction; 3. Spanish Americans -- Fiction; 4. New York (N.Y.) -- Fiction; 5. Advice columns

  1492654493; 9781492654490, $16.99

                      LC 2016051104

In this book, by Carol Weston, "Sofia lost her mother eight months ago, and her friends were 100% there for her. Now it's a new year and they're ready for Sofia to move on. Problem is, Sofia can't bounce back, can't recharge like a cellphone. She decides to write Dear Kate, an advice columnist for Fifteen Magazine, and is surprised to receive a fast reply. Soon the two are exchanging emails, and Sofia opens up and spills all." (Publisher's note)

Weston, Robert Paul

  Blues for Zoey. Robert Paul Weston. Flux 2015 304 p.

Grades: 9 10 11 12

  1. Bildungsromans 2. Coming of age -- Fiction 3. Fund-raising -- Fiction 4. Racially mixed people -- Fiction 5. Musicians -- Fiction 6. Romance fiction

  0738743402; 9780738743400, $9.99

                      LC 2014037101

In this book by Robert Paul Weston, "from his first glimpse, 16-year-old Kaz Barrett is hypnotized by Zoey, a mysterious street performer with pink dreadlocks and an enormous crucifix-shaped musical instrument. While they explore their frenetic romantic connection, Kaz is also pre-occupied with his mother's immobilizing sleep disorder, a job at the local Laundromat, and untangling the lies and deceptions of the con artists and vagrants he tends to associate with." (Publishers Weekly)

"Weston effectively drops hints about Zoey's mysterious past, and it won't be too difficult for astute readers to put the pieces together a step or two ahead of Kaz. This isn't necessarily a criticism; rather, it's entirely believable that Kaz's obsessive love for Zoey would blind him to the truth. Fortunately, the novel's journey is suitably winding to keep the reader intrigued." Quill & Quire

Wettersten, Laura

My faire lady. Laura Wettersten. Simon & Schuster 2014 352 p.
Grades: 7 8 9 10 11 12
    1. Dating (Social customs) -- Fiction 2. Love -- Fiction 3. Renaissance fairs -- Fiction 4. Summer employment -- Fiction 5. Teenage girls -- Fiction 6. Historical reenactments
    1442489332; 9781442489332, $17.99
LC 2013021542

In this young adult novel by Laura Wettersten, "Rowena Duncan is a thoroughly modern girl with big plans for her summer . . . until she catches her boyfriend making out with another girl. Heartbroken, she applies to an out-of-town job posting and finds herself somewhere she never expected: the Renaissance Faire. As a face-painter doubling as a serving wench, Ro is thrown headfirst into a vibrant community of artists and performers." (Publisher's note)

"Sharp, funny dialogue is mixed with thoughtful resolutions of relevant teenage topics-love and lust, admitting fault, the mettle it takes to pursue a passion. The rich backdrop of the fair, with its vivid description and appealing characters, is icing on the cake.Verily, fine fare." Kirkus

Whaley, John Corey

★ **Highly** illogical behavior. John Corey Whaley. Dial Books 2016 256 p.
Grades: 9 10 11 12
    1. Agoraphobia -- Fiction 2. Friendship -- Fiction 3. Gays -- Fiction 4. Panic attacks -- Fiction 5. Gay teenagers -- Fiction
    9780525428183
LC 2015025530

In this novel by John Corey Whaley, "sixteen-year-old Solomon is agoraphobic. He hasn't left the house in three years, which is fine by him. . . . Ambitious Lisa desperately wants to get into the second-best psychiatry program for college. . . . But how can she prove she deserves a spot there? Solomon is the answer. Determined to 'fix' Sol, Lisa thrusts herself into his life." (Publisher's note)

"Solomon Reed, 16, has not left his house in three years. Regular panic attacks keep him from handling the outside. Yet he is a smart and resourceful teenager with a love for Star Trek, gratifying hobbies, and a supportive family. Solomon is being educated online and doesn't feel that any social life he might be missing is worth the mental anguish that daily life causes him to endure. However, he knows he can't live like this forever. Then Lisa Praytor, a vivacious and take-charge extrovert appears, wanting to be his friend. Lisa is convinced that she can treat Solomon's agoraphobia and get him outside. . . . What looks like a typical friendship story is blended with issues of trust, vulnerability, and identity. Solomon's agoraphobia is not the only thing that defines him, which speaks to the larger message about those living with mental illness. Each character has an authentic voice and temperament that feel realistic, and the alternating narratives capture the perspective of the bright, witty, and decidedly quirky protagonists. The spare writing makes this a taut, tender, and appealing read." SLJ

Noggin; by John Corey Whaley. Atheneum Books for Young Readers 2014 352 p. (hardback) $17.99
Grades: 9 10 11 12
    1. Cryonics 2. Medical novels 3. Teenagers -- Fiction 4. Science fiction 5. Death -- Fiction 6. Identity -- Fiction 7. Interpersonal relations -- Fiction 8. Family life -- Missouri -- Kansas City -- Fiction 9. Transplantation of organs, tissues, etc. -- Fiction
    ISBN 1442458720; 9781442458727; 9781442458734
LC 2013020137

"Losing his battle to terminal cancer, sixteen-year-old Travis opts to have his head surgically removed, stored cryogenically, and restored to life at some point in the distant future when medical technology is able to attach it to a new body...Readers will find it easy to become invested in Travis's second coming-of age -- brimming with humor, pathos, and angst -- and root for him to make peace with his new life." (Horn Book)

★ **Where** things come back. Atheneum Books for Young Readers 2011 228p. $16.99
Grades: 9 10 11 12
    1. Birds -- Fiction 2. Arkansas -- Fiction 3. Friendship -- Fiction 4. Family life -- Fiction 5. Missing persons -- Fiction
    ISBN 978-1-4424-1333-7; 1-4424-1333-6
LC 201024836
Michael L. Printz Award (2012)
William C. Morris YA Debut Award (2012)

Seventeen-year-old Cullen's summer in Lily, Arkansas, is marked by his cousin's death by overdose, an alleged spotting of a woodpecker thought to be extinct, failed romances, and his younger brother's sudden disappearance.

"The realistic characters and fascinating mix of mundane with life changing and tragic events create a memorable story most young adult readers will connect to." Libr Media Connect

Whelan, Gloria

★ **Homeless** bird. HarperCollins Pubs. 2000 216p hardcover o.p. pa $5.99
Grades: 6 7 8 9 10
    1. India -- Fiction 2. Women -- India -- Fiction
    ISBN 0-06-028454-4; 0-06-440819-1 pa
LC 99-33241
When thirteen-year-old Koly enters into an ill-fated arranged marriage, she must either suffer a destiny dictated by India's tradition or find the courage to oppose it.

"This beautifully told, inspiring story takes readers on a fascinating journey through modern India and the universal intricacies of a young woman's heart." Booklist

See what I see. HarperTeen 2011 199p $16.99
Grades: 7 8 9 10 11 12
    1. Sick -- Fiction 2. Artists -- Fiction 3. Detroit (Mich.) -- Fiction 4. Father-daughter relationship -- Fiction
ISBN 978-0-06-125545-8; 0-06-125545-9
                    LC 2010-03094
When eighteen-year-old Kate arrives on the Detroit doorstep of her long-estranged father, a famous painter, she is shocked to learn that he is dying and does not want to support her efforts to attend the local art school.

"With elegant prose, Whelan portrays a gradually developing and complex relationship built on guilt, curiosity, love, and a passion for art." Booklist

Whitaker, Alecia
Wildflower. By Alecia Whitaker. Little, Brown and Co. 2014 320 p. Illustration
Grades: 7 8 9 10
    1. Country music -- Fiction 2. Dating (Social customs) -- Fiction 3. Fame -- Fiction 4. Family life -- Fiction 5. Musicians -- Fiction 6. Nashville (Tenn.) -- Fiction 7. Women musicians
0316251380; 9780316251365; 9780316251389, $18
                    LC 2013023693
In this young adult novel by Alecia Whitaker, "Bird Barrett has grown up on the road, singing backup in her family's bluegrass band and playing everywhere from Nashville, Tennessee, to Nowhere, Oklahoma. But one fateful night, when Bird fills in for her dad by singing lead, a scout in the audience offers her a spotlight all her own. . . . With Bird's star on the rise, though, the rest of her life falls into chaos as tradition and ambition collide." (Publisher's note)

"Genuine dialogue, a quick pace and a plot that strikes the right balance between realistic and fantastic make for an engaging read. The lyrics and sheet music for one of Bird's songs are appended.This tender introduction to a newly minted country superstar sets the stage for a compelling series." Kirkus

Whitcomb, Laura
A **certain** slant of light. Graphia 2005 282p $8.99
Grades: 9 10 11 12
    1. Ghost stories 2. Future life -- Fiction
ISBN 0-618-58532-X pa
                    LC 2004-27208
After benignly haunting a series of people for 130 years, Helen meets a teenage boy who can see her and together they unlock the mysteries of their pasts.

The author "creatively pulls together a dramatic and compelling plot that cleverly grants rebellious teen romance a timeless grandeur." Bull Cent Child Books

White, Andrea
Surviving Antarctica; reality TV 2083. HarperCollins Publishers 2005 327p hardcover o.p. pa $6.99

Grades: 7 8 9 10
    1. Science fiction 2. Antarctica -- Fiction
ISBN 0-06-055454-1; 0-06-055456-8 pa
                    LC 2004-6249
In the year 2083, five fourteen-year-olds who were deprived by chance of the opportunity to continue their educations reenact Scott's 1910-1913 expedition to the South Pole as contestants on a reality television show, secretly aided by a Department of Entertainment employee

"A real page-turner, this novel will give readers pause as they ponder the ethics of teens risking their lives in adult-contrived situations for the entertainment of the masses." Booklist

White, Ellen Emerson
Long may she reign. Feiwel and Friends 2007 708p $15.95
Grades: 6 7 8 9 10
    1. School stories 2. Presidents -- Fiction 3. Post-traumatic stress disorder -- Fiction
ISBN 978-0-312-36767-1; 0-312-36767-8
                    LC 2007-32635
Meg Powers, daughter of the president of the United States, is recovering from a brutal kidnapping, and in an effort to deal with her horrific experience and her anger at her mother—the president—for not negotiating for her release, Meg decides to go away for her second semester of college, where she encounters even more challenges.

"The hip dialogue will hook teens. . . . Beneath its chick-lit veneer, this book is a thought-provoking read." Voice Youth Advocates

The **President's** daughter. Feiwel and Friends 2008 304p pa $9.99
Grades: 7 8 9 10
    1. Moving -- Fiction 2. Politics -- Fiction 3. Washington (D.C.) -- Fiction 4. Mother-daughter relationship -- Fiction
ISBN 0-312-37488-7; 978-0-312-37488-4
                    LC 2008-6888
First published 1984
Sixteen-year-old Meghan Powers' happy life in Massachusetts changes drastically when her mother, one of the most prestigious senators in the country, becomes the front-runner in the race for United States President.

"Besides offering a solid look at the political system, this [book] has very strong characterizations." Booklist
Other titles about Meg are:
White House autumn (2008)
Long live the queen (2008)
Long may she reign (2007)

A **season** of daring greatly. Ellen Emerson White. Greenwillow Books, an imprint of HarperCollinsPublishers 2017 420 p.
Grades: 8 9 10 11 12
    1. Major League Baseball (Organization) -- Fiction; 2. Role models -- Fiction; 3. Self-perception in women -- Fiction; 4. Sex discrimination in sports -- Fiction; 5. Women baseball players -- Fiction; 6. Women athletes

-- Fiction; 7. Sex discrimination -- Fiction
9780062463210, $17.99; 9780062463234; 0062463217

LC 2016036667

In this novel by Ellen Emerson White, "on top of the pressure heaped on every pitcher, Jill must deal with defying conventions and living up to impossible expectations, all while living away from home for the first time. She'll go head-to-head against those who are determined to keep baseball an all-male sport." (Publisher's note)

"White (the President's Daughter series) offers a credible portrait of a young woman breaking traditional gender boundaries while being scrutinized by the entire nation." Pub Wkly

White, Kiersten

And I darken. Kiersten White. Delacorte Press 2016 496 p.

Grades: 9 10 11 12

1. Good and evil -- Fiction 2. Princesses -- Fiction 3. Princesses -- Romania -- Transylvania -- Fiction 4. Transylvania (Romania) -- History -- 15th century -- Fiction

9780553522310, $18.99; 9780553522327, $21.99

LC 2015020681

In this novel, by Kiersten White, "ever since Lada Dragwlya and her brother, Radu, were wrenched from their homeland of Wallachia and abandoned by their father to be raised in the Ottoman courts, Lada has known that being ruthless is the key to survival, and when she meets Mehmed, the heir to the very empire that Lada has sworn to fight against, complications arise as Lada, Radu and Mehmed form a toxic triangle that strains the bonds of love and loyalty to the breaking point." (Publisher's note)

Now I rise. Kiersten White. Delacorte Press 2017 470 p. Illustration

Grades: 10 11 12

1. Good and evil -- Fiction; 2. Princesses -- Fiction; 3. Istanbul (Turkey) -- History -- 15th century -- Fiction; 4. Transylvania (Romania) -- History -- 15th century -- Fiction; 5. Turkey -- History -- Mehmed II, 1451-1481 -- Fiction; 6. Istanbul (Turkey) -- Fiction

9780553522372; 9780553522358, $18.99; 9780553522365

LC 2016038757

In this book, by Kiersten White, "Lada Dracul has no allies. No crown. All she has is what she's always had: herself. After failing to secure the Wallachian throne, Lada is out to punish anyone who dares cross her. She storms the countryside with her men, but brute force isn't getting Lada what she wants. And thinking of Mehmed, the defiant Ottoman sultan, brings little comfort to her thorny heart. There's no time to wonder whether he still thinks about her." (Publisher's note)

"In this sequel to And I Darken, White continues to weave a dramatic tapestry of espionage, passion, and conquest." SLJ

Sequel to: And I darken (2016)

White, Ruth

★ A **month** of Sundays. Margaret Ferguson Books/Farrar Straus Giroux 2011 168p $16.99

Grades: 6 7 8 9

1. Sick -- Fiction 2. Family life -- Fiction 3. Country life -- Fiction 4. Christian life -- Fiction

ISBN 978-0-374-39912-2; 0-374-39912-3

LC 2010036311

In the summer of 1956 while her mother is in Florida searching for a job, fourteen-year-old April Garnet Rose, who has never met her father, stays with her terminally ill aunt in Virginia and accompanies her as she visits different churches, looking for God.

"White captures life in small-town America. . . . This heartwarming story has more than a touch of wonder. Expanding one's emotional life . . . is beautifully captured here." Booklist

Whitley, David

Midnight charter. Roaring Brook Press 2009 319p $17.99

Grades: 7 8 9 10

1. Science fiction

ISBN 978-1-59643-381-6; 1-59643-381-7

"Deft world-building and crafty plotting combine for a zinger of an ending that will leave readers poised for book two. Surprisingly sophisticated upper-middle-grade fare, with enough meat to satisfy older readers as well." Kirkus

Followed by: The children of the lost (2011)

Whitman, Emily

Wildwing. Greenwillow Books 2010 359p $16.99

Grades: 7 8 9 10

1. Falcons -- Fiction 2. Time travel -- Fiction 3. Social classes -- Fiction 4. Great Britain -- History -- 1066-1154, Norman period -- Fiction

ISBN 978-0-06-172452-7; 0-06-172452-1

LC 2009-44189

In 1913 London, fifteen-year-old Addy is a lowly servant, but when she gets inside an elevator car in her employer's study, she is suddenly transported to a castle in 1240 and discovers that she is mistaken for the lord's intended bride.

"Whitman populates both of her worlds with vivid, believable characters. . . . This historical novel with a time-travel twist of sci-fi will find an avid readership." SLJ

Whitman, Sylvia

The **milk** of birds; by Sylvia Whitman. 1st ed. Atheneum Books for Young Readers 2013 384 p. (hardcover) $16.99; (paperback) $9.99

Grades: 9 10 11 12

1. Pen pals -- Fiction 2. Friendship -- Fiction 3. Sudan -- History -- Darfur conflict, 2003- -- Fiction 4. Sudan -- Fiction 5. Letters -- Fiction 6. Genocide -- Fiction 7. Refugees -- Fiction 8. Darfur (Sudan) -- Fiction

ISBN 144244682X; 9781442446823; 9781442446830; 9781442446847

LC 2012005594

In this book, "an American teen from Richmond, Va., and a Sudanese teen in Darfur exchange letters. . . . Fourteen-year-old Nawra has been raped, her family murdered and her village burned in Darfur's genocidal war. . . . Nonprofit Save the Girls matches Nawra with American pen pal K.C. Cannelli, an unconventional 14-year-old with an undiagnosed learning disability. . . . As K.C. discovers everything Nawra has endured, she becomes an advocate and fundraiser for Darfur's refugees." (Kirkus Reviews)

Whitney, Daisy

The **Mockingbirds**. Little, Brown 2010 339p $16.99

Grades: 10 11 12

    1. School stories 2. Rape -- Fiction 3. Sisters -- Fiction 4. Secret societies -- Fiction

    ISBN 978-0-316-09053-7; 0-316-09053-0

                      LC 2009-51257

When Alex, a junior at an elite preparatory school, realizes that she may have been the victim of date rape, she confides in her roommates and sister who convince her to seek help from a secret society, the Mockingbirds.

"Authentic and illuminating, this strong . . . [title] explores vital teen topics of sex and violence; crime and punishment; ineffectual authority; and the immeasurable, healing influence of friendship and love." Booklist

Whitney, Kim Ablon

The **perfect** distance. Knopf 2005 256p hardcover o.p. pa $5.99

Grades: 9 10 11 12

    1. Horsemanship -- Fiction 2. Mexican Americans -- Fiction

    ISBN 0-375-83243-2; 0-553-49467-8 pa

                      LC 2005-40726

While competing in the three junior national equitation championships, seventeen-year-old Francie Martinez learns to believe in herself and makes some decisions about the type of person she wants to be

The author "inhabits Francie's character wholly and convincingly and gets the universals of serious competition just right—any athlete will recognize the imperious, unfeeling coach; the snotty front-runner; and the unparalleled thrill of hitting the zone." Booklist

Wiggins, Bethany

Cured. by Bethany Wiggins. Bloomsbury/Walker. 2014 320p $17.99

Grades: 7 8 9 10 11 12

    1. Brothers and sisters -- Fiction 2. Science fiction 3. Survival -- Fiction 4. Twins -- Fiction 5. Voyages and travels -- Fiction

    ISBN: 0802734200; 9780802734204

                      LC 2013024935

This sequel to Stung is a "reimagining of our world after an environmental catastrophe. . . . Now that Fiona Tarsis and her twin brother, Jonah, are no longer beasts, they set out to find their mother. . . . Heading for a safe settlement rumored to be in Wyoming . . . they are attacked by raiders. Luckily, they find a new ally in Kevin, who saves them and leads them to safety in his underground shelter. But the more they get to know Kevin, the more they suspect he has ties to the raiders." (Publisher's note)

"While the Mad Max–esque raiders and zombielike beasts (children transformed into murderous monsters by their vaccines against the bee flu) seem to be standard post-

apocalyptic fare, Wiggins poignantly raises issues of transformation and redemption." Kirkus

Stung; Bethany Wiggins. Walker & Company 2013 304 p. (hardcover) $17.99

Grades: 7 8 9 10 11 12

    1. Science fiction 2. Epidemics -- Fiction 3. Survival -- Fiction

    ISBN 0802734189; 9780802734181

                      LC 2012027183

In this novel, by Bethany Wiggins, "a worldwide pandemic occurred and the government tried to bio-engineer a cure. Only the solution was deadlier than the original problem-the vaccination turned people into ferocious, deadly beasts who were branded as a warning to un-vaccinated survivors. Key people needed to rebuild society are protected from disease and beasts inside a fortress-like wall. But Fiona has awakened branded, alone-and on the wrong side of the wall." (Publisher's note)

"Wiggins. . . muses on the dangers of science and medicine and deftly maps out the chain of events that has led to catastrophe, creating a violent world vastly different from ours but still recognizable. With a stirring conclusion and space for a sequel, it's an altogether captivating story." Kirkus

Wilkinson, Lili

Pink. HarperTeen 2011 310p $16.99

Grades: 7 8 9 10 11 12

    1. School stories 2. Theater -- Fiction 3. Australia -- Fiction 4. LGBT youth -- Fiction 5. Identity (Psychology) -- Fiction

    ISBN 978-0-06-192653-2; 0-06-192653-1

                      LC 2010-9389

Sixteen-year-old Ava does not know who she is or where she belongs, but when she tries out a new personality—and sexual orientation—at a different school, her edgy girlfriend, potential boyfriend, and others are hurt by her lack of honesty.

"The novel is in turn laugh-out-loud funny, endearing, and heartbreaking as Ava repeatedly steps into teenage social land mines—with unexpected results. Because Wilkinson doesn't rely on stereotypes, the characters are well-developed, and interactions between them feel genuine." Voice Youth Advocates

Wilkinson, Sheena

Taking Flight. By Sheena Wilkinson. Midpoint Trade Books Inc 2014 310 p.

Grades: 7 8 9 10 11 12

    1. Horsemanship -- Fiction 2. Courage -- Fiction 3. Belfast (Northern Ireland) -- Fiction

    1554553288; 9781554553280, $12.95

    Children's Books Ireland: Book of the Year (2014)

This book, by Sheena Wilkinson, "is a . . . story of courage overcoming jealousy. The only riding fifteen-year-old Declan has ever done is joyriding. When he's forced to stay with his snobby cousin 'Princess' Vicky, he's shocked to find himself falling in love with horses. Vicky would do anything to keep this grubby hood away from her precious showjumper." (Publisher's note)

Recommended for general purchase, this title should appeal to fans of horse stories." SLJ

Sequel: Grounded

Willey, Margaret

Beetle Boy; by Margaret Willey. Carolrhoda Lab. 2014 208p $17.95

Grades: 8 9 10 11

1. Dating (Social customs) -- Fiction 2. Emotional problems -- Fiction 3. Family problems -- Fiction 4. Father-son relationship -- Fiction 5. Child authors -- Fiction

ISBN: 1467726397; 9781467726399

LC 2013036853

Charlie Porter "didn't intend to become famous, but at age seven, Charlie began telling a story about a talking beetle in order to stop his father from crying. Soon the story becomes a book, which becomes a long series of events, festivals, and marketing campaigns. . . . Now 18, Charlie is forced to reconcile his traumatic past and forge ahead building normal relationships." SLJ

"Willey takes readers along on Charlie's painful journey back to physical and emotional health via a meandering timeline of flashbacks, dreams and wrenching conversations, skillfully weaving together the bits and pieces of his life. Innovative use of type brings an immediacy to Charlie's struggles as he slowly looks the truth--and his brother--squarely in the face." Kirkus

Williams, Carol Lynch

The chosen one. St. Martin's Griffin 2009 213p $16.95

Grades: 7 8 9 10

1. Cults -- Fiction 2. Polygamy -- Fiction 3. Family life -- Fiction

ISBN 978-0-312-55511-5; 0-312-55511-3

LC 2009-4800

In a polygamous cult in the desert, Kyra, not yet fourteen, sees being chosen to be the seventh wife of her uncle as just punishment for having read books and kissed a boy, in violation of Prophet Childs' teachings, and is torn between facing her fate and running away from all that she knows and loves.

"This book is a highly emotional, terrifying read. It is not measured or objective. Physical abuse, fear, and even murder are constants. It is a girl-in-peril story, and as such, it is impossible to put down and holds tremendous teen appeal." Voice Youth Advocates

Glimpse. Simon & Schuster Books for Young Readers 2010 484p $16.99

Grades: 7 8 9 10

1. Novels in verse 2. Sisters -- Fiction 3. Suicide -- Fiction 4. Child sexual abuse -- Fiction 5. Mother-daughter relationship -- Fiction

ISBN 978-1-4169-9730-6; 1-4169-9730-X

LC 2009-41147

Living with their mother who earns money as a prostitute, two sisters take care of each other and when the older one attempts suicide, the younger one tries to uncover the reason.

"Williams leans hard on her free-verse line breaks for drama . . . and it works. A page-turner for Ellen Hopkins fans." Kirkus

Miles from ordinary; a novel. St. Martin's Press 2011 197p $16.99

Grades: 7 8 9 10

1. Family life -- Fiction 2. Mental illness -- Fiction 3. Mother-daughter relationship -- Fiction

ISBN 978-0-312-55512-2; 0-312-55512-1

LC 2010-40324

As her mother's mental illness spins terrifyingly out of control, thirteen-year-old Lacey must face the truth of what life with her mother means for both of them.

"The author has crafted both a riveting, unusual suspense tale and an absolutely convincing character in Lacey. The book truly is miles from ordinary, in the very best way. Outstanding." Kirkus

Waiting; Carol Lynch Williams. Simon and Schuster Books For Young Readers 2012 335 p.

Grades: 9 10 11 12

1. Siblings -- Fiction 2. Bereavement -- Fiction 3. Grief -- Fiction 4. Family problems -- Fiction 5. Brothers and sisters -- Fiction

ISBN 1442443537; 9781442443532; 9781442443556

LC 2011043898

This young adult novel by Carol Lynch Williams portrays "a teen [who] struggles to rediscover love and find redemption . . . [a]fter her brother's death. . . . Growing up, London and Zach were as close as could be. And then Zach dies, and the family is gutted. London's father is distant. Her mother won't speak. The days are filled with what-ifs and whispers: Was it London's fault? Alone and adrift, London finds herself torn between her brother's best friend and the handsome new boy in town as she struggles to find herself—and ultimately redemption." (Publisher's note)

Williams, Gabrielle

★ **Beetle** meets Destiny. Marshall Cavendish 2010 342p $17.99

Grades: 8 9 10 11 12

1. Love stories 2. Twins -- Fiction 3. Siblings -- Fiction 4. Australia -- Fiction 5. Family life -- Fiction 6. Dating (Social customs) -- Fiction

ISBN 978-0-7614-5723-7

When superstitious eighteen-year-old John "Beetle" Lennon, who is dating the best friend of his twin sister, meets Destiny McCartney, their instant rapport and shared quirkiness make it seem that their fate is written in the stars.

"Clever, amusing, yet surprisingly thoughtful, the book will appeal to readers looking for something a little different." Publ Wkly

Williams, Ismee

Water in May. Ismee Williams. Amulet Books 2017 309 p.

Grades: 7 8 9 10 11 12

1. Dominican Americans -- Fiction; 2. Family problems -- Fiction; 3. Friendship -- Fiction; 4. Heart --

Abnormalities -- Fiction; 5. Pregnancy -- Fiction
9781419725395, $17.99; 9781683351344

LC 2017008518

In this book, by Ismee Williams, "fifteen-year-old Mari Pujols believes that the baby she's carrying will finally mean she'll have a family member who will love her deeply and won't ever leave her -- not like her mama,...or her papi,...or her abuela.... But when doctors discover a potentially fatal heart defect in the fetus, Mari faces choices she never could have imagined." (Publisher's note)

"Debut author Williams creates an unforgettable young character who will make readers reconsider their assumptions about teen moms, in particular Latina teen moms." Kirkus

Williams, Kathryn

Pizza, love, and other stuff that made me famous; Kathryn Williams. Henry Holt 2012 231 p. (hc) $16.99

Grades: 7 8 9 10

1. Cooking -- Fiction 2. Reality television programs -- Fiction 3. Restaurants -- Fiction 4. Interpersonal relations -- Fiction 5. Competition (Psychology) -- Fiction 6. Television -- Production and direction -- Fiction
ISBN 0805092854; 9780805092851

LC 2011034053

"Sixteen-year-old Sophie Nicolaides . . . audition[s] for a new reality show, 'Teen Test Kitchen.'. . . [T]he prize includes a full scholarship to one of America's finest culinary schools and a summer in Napa, California, not to mention fame. Once on set, Sophie immediately finds herself in the thick of the drama -- including a secret burn book, cutthroat celebrity judges, and a very cute French chef." (Publisher's note)

Williams, Katie

Absent; by Katie Williams. Chronicle Books 2013 288 p. (hardcover) $16.99

Grades: 9 10 11 12

1. Ghost stories 2. Suicide -- Fiction 3. High school students -- Fiction 4. Drug abuse -- Fiction 5. High schools -- Fiction
ISBN 0811871509; 9780811871501

LC 2012033600

In this novel, by Katie Williams, "when seventeen-year-old Paige dies in a freak fall from the roof . . . , her spirit is bound to the grounds of her high school. . . . But when Paige hears the rumor that her death wasn't an accident--that she supposedly jumped on purpose--she can't bear it. Then Paige discovers . . . she can possess living people when they think of her. . . . Maybe . . . she can get to the most popular girl in school and stop the rumors once and for all." (Publisher's note)

"The mystery is solid, but it is complicated; funny Paige herself sets the story apart." Booklist

Williams, Lori Aurelia

★ **When** Kambia Elaine flew in from Neptune. Simon & Schuster 2000 246p hardcover o.p. pa $10

Grades: 7 8 9 10

1. Houston (Tex.) -- Fiction 2. African Americans -- Fiction
ISBN 0-689-82468-8; 0-689-84593-6 pa

LC 99-65154

"Shayla Dubois lives in a Houston neighborhood known as the Bottom, where life is colorful but never easy. She wants only two things out of life: to become a writer and to have a nice, peaceful home. Instead, her life has been turned upside down. Shayla's mama kicked her sister, Tia, out of the house for messing around with an older guy, and months later Tia still hasn't come home. Shayla's father, Mr. Anderson Fox, has rolled back into town and has been spending a lot of time at the house with Mama. And Shayla still doesn't know what to make of her strange new neighbor, Kambia Elaine." Publisher's note

"This is a strong and disturbing novel, told in beautiful language. Teens will find it engrossing." SLJ

Williams, Michael

Diamond boy. Michael Williams. Little, Brown & Co. 2014 400 p. Map

Grades: 7 8 9 10

1. Blacks -- Zimbabwe -- Fiction 2. Diamond mines and mining -- Fiction 3. Shona (African people) -- Fiction 4. Survival -- Fiction 5. Zimbabwe -- Fiction 6. Blacks -- Fiction 7. Survival skills -- Fiction 8. Mines and mineral resources -- Fiction
0316320692; 9780316320672; 9780316320696, $18

LC 2013042071

"Patson Moyo's life is perfectly ordinary. . . . His father, a teacher, is often a little dreamy but a wonderful storyteller. . . . Patson never would have guessed that his smart, university-graduate father . . . can barely make ends meet, due to government corruption and the massive devaluation of the Zimbabwean dollar. Egged on by Patson's stepmother, Sylvia, the Moyos decide to improve their situation by traveling to Marage." (School Library Journal)

"Written in diary format, the story brings the reader into the mind and soul of a young refugee suffering in a hell created by the greed and violence of powerful adults. More than simply a good read, Diamond Boy is a multilayered, teachable novel with a variety of approaches and is highly recommended for middle and high school collections." VOYA

Now is the time for running. Little, Brown 2011 233p $17.99

Grades: 6 7 8 9 10

1. Soccer -- Fiction 2. Brothers -- Fiction 3. Refugees -- Fiction 4. Zimbabwe -- Fiction 5. Homeless persons -- Fiction 6. People with mental disabilites -- Fiction
ISBN 978-0-316-07790-3; 0-316-07790-9

LC 2010043460

"There is plenty of material to captivate readers: fast-paced soccer matches every bit as tough as the players; the determination of Deo and his fellow refugees to survive unthinkably harsh conditions; and raw depictions of violence. . . . But it's the tender relationship between Deo and Innocent, along with some heartbreaking twists of fate, that will endure in readers' minds." Publ Wkly

Williams, Sarah DeFord

★ **Palace** beautiful. G.P. Putnam's Sons 2010 232p $16.99

Grades: 6 7 8 9

> 1. Moving -- Fiction 2. Diaries -- Fiction 3. Influenza -- Fiction 4. Family life -- Fiction

ISBN 978-0-399-25298-3; 0-399-25298-3

LC 2009-03213

After her move in 1985 to Salt Lake City, thirteen-year-old Sadie finds a journal in a hidey-hole in the attic, and along with her sister and new friend she reads about the influenza epidemic of 1918.

"Williams does a super job with the characters in this beautifully written book, and it is satisfying to see how they develop." SLJ

Williams, Sean

Twinmaker; by Sean Williams. HarperCollins 2013 352 p. (hardcover bdg.) $17.99

Grades: 9 10 11 12

> 1. Fantasy fiction 2. Conspiracies -- Fiction 3. Teleportation -- Fiction 4. Science fiction 5. Friendship -- Fiction 6. Best friends -- Fiction 7. Space and time -- Fiction

ISBN 0062203215; 9780062203212

LC 2012043498

In this book, "thanks to D-mat technology, teen Clair" and her friends "can jump around the globe in a matter of minutes simply by entering a booth. . . . They initially dismiss Improvement, a way to transform yourself through a series of jumps, but then Libby uses Improvement to remove her permanent birthmark, and as the disturbing consequences roll out, Clair digs for answers." (Booklist)

Williams-Garcia, Rita

★ **Jumped**. HarperTeen 2009 169p $16.99; lib bdg $17.89

Grades: 8 9 10 11 12

> 1. School stories 2. Bullies -- Fiction

ISBN 978-0-06-076091-5; 0-06-076091-5; 978-0-06-076092-2 lib bdg; 0-06-076092-3 lib bdg

LC 2008-22381

The lives of Leticia, Dominique, and Trina are irrevocably intertwined through the course of one day in an urban high school after Leticia overhears Dominique's plans to beat up Trina and must decide whether or not to get involved.

"In alternating chapters narrated by Leticia, Trina, and Dominique, Williams-Garcia has given her characters strong, individual voices that ring true to teenage speech, and she lets them make their choices without judgment or moralizing." SLJ

★ **Like** sisters on the homefront. Lodestar Bks. 1995 165p hardcover o.p. pa $5.99

Grades: 7 8 9 10

> 1. Family life -- Fiction 2. Teenage mothers -- Fiction 3. African Americans -- Fiction

ISBN 0-525-67465-9; 0-14-038561-4 pa

LC 95-3690

"It's bad enough that 14-year-old Gayle has one baby, but when she becomes pregnant again by another boy, Mama's had enough. She takes Gayle for an abortion and then

ships her and her baby south to stay with religious relatives. . . . With the help of her dying great-grandmother, who leaves Gayle the family's African-American oral tradition, she begins to mature and understand her place in the family and her future." Child Book Rev Serv

"Beautifully written, the text captures the cadence and rhythm of New York street talk and the dilemma of being poor, black, and uneducated. This is a gritty, realistic, well-told story." SLJ

Wilson, Diane L.

Firehorse. Margaret K. McElderry Books 2006 325p $16.95

Grades: 7 8 9 10

> 1. Arson -- Fiction 2. Horses -- Fiction 3. Sex role -- Fiction 4. Family life -- Fiction 5. Boston (Mass.) -- Fiction 6. Veterinary medicine -- Fiction

ISBN 1-4169-1551-6; 978-1-4169-1551-5

LC 2005-30785

Spirited fifteen-year-old horse lover Rachel Selby determines to become a veterinarian, despite the opposition of her rigid father, her proper mother, and the norms of Boston in 1872, while that city faces a serial arsonist and an epidemic spreading through its firehorse population.

"Wilson paces the story well, with tension building. . . . The novel's finest achievement, though, is the convincing depiction of family dynamics in an era when men ruled the household and and women, who had few opportunities, folded their dreams and put them away with the linens they embroidered." Booklist

Wilson, John

And in the morning. Kids Can Press 2003 198p $16.95

Grades: 7 8 9 10

> 1. World War, 1914-1918 -- Fiction

ISBN 1-55337-400-2

"Jim Hay, 16, is caught up in the patriotic fervor sweeping across Scotland as the British troops prepare to enter World War I. . . . His father is killed in action and 10 days later his mother dies from shock and grief. Within weeks, Jim has signed up and is soon in the trenches. . . . A compelling, fascinating, and ultimately disturbing book that is not to be missed." SLJ

Wilson, Martin

★ **What** they always tell us. Delacorte Press 2008 293p $15.99; lib bdg $18.99

Grades: 9 10 11 12

> 1. School stories 2. Alabama -- Fiction 3. Brothers -- Fiction 4. Gay teenagers -- Fiction

ISBN 978-0-385-73507-0; 0-385-73507-3; 978-0-385-90500-8 lib bdg; 0-385-90500-9 lib bdg

LC 2007-30269

Sixteen-year-old Alex feels so disconnected from his friends that he starts his junior year at a Tuscaloosa, Alabama, high school by attempting suicide, but soon, a friend of his older brother draws him into cross-country running and a new understanding of himself.

This "novel does an excellent job of showing the tension with which siblings deal on a daily basis. He also does a great job of exploring controversial issues, such as suicide and homosexuality. . . . Public and school libraries should seriously consider adding this book to their shelves." Voice Youth Advocates

Winfrey, Kerry

Things Jolie needs to do before she bites it. Kerry Winfrey. Feiwel and Friends 2018 288 p.

Grades: 8 9 10 11

1. Teeth -- Fiction; 2. Self-acceptance -- Fiction; 3. Teenagers -- Fiction

9781250119544, $17.99; 9781250119551

LC 2017957509

In this novel, by Kerry Winfrey, "[Jolie] has mandibular prognathism, which is the medical term for underbite. Chewing is a pain, headaches are a common occurrence, and she's never been kissed. She's months out from having a procedure to correct her underbite, and she cannot wait to be fixed.... She and her best friends, Evelyn and Derek, decide to make a 'Things Jolie Needs to Do Before She Bites It' [list].... But since when did everything ever go exactly to plan?" (Publisher's note)

Winston, Sherri

The **Kayla** chronicles; a novel. Little, Brown 2007 188p hardcover o.p. pa $7.99

Grades: 6 7 8 9 10

1. School stories 2. Dancers -- Fiction 3. Journalism -- Fiction 4. African Americans -- Fiction

ISBN 978-0-316-11430-1; 0-316-11430-8; 978-0-316-11431-8 pa; 0-316-11431-6 pa

LC 2006-933219

Kayla transforms herself from mild-mannered journalist to hot-trotting dance diva in order to properly investigate her high school's dance team, and has a hard time remaining true to her real self while in the role.

"Few recent novels for younger YAs mesh levity and substance this successfully." Booklist

Winters, Cat

★ **In** the shadow of blackbirds; Cat Winters. Amulet Books 2013 400 p. $16.95

Grades: 8 9 10 11 12

1. Occult fiction 2. Historical fiction 3. Ghosts -- Fiction 4. Spiritualism -- Fiction 5. World War, 1914-1918 -- Fiction 6. Influenza Epidemic, 1918-1919 -- Fiction 7. San Diego (Calif.) -- History -- 20th century -- Fiction

ISBN 141970530X; 9781419705304

LC 2012039262

William C. Morris Honor Book (2014)

In this book, sixteen-year-old Mary Shelley Black lives in 1918. "With WWI raging on and Mary's father on trial for treason, she goes to live with her Aunt Eva in San Diego, Calif. . . . Grieving for her childhood beau Stephen, who died while fighting overseas with the Army, Mary goes outside during a thunderstorm and is struck dead by lightning—for a few minutes. When Mary comes to, she discovers she can communicate with the dead, including Stephen." (Publishers Weekly)

"Winters strikes just the right balance between history and ghost story . . . . Vintage photographs contribute

to the authenticity of the atmospheric and nicely paced storytelling." Kirkus

Odd & true. By Cat Winters. Amulet Books 2017 358 p.

Grades: 8 9 10 11 12

1. Missing persons -- Fiction; 2. Monsters -- Fiction; 3. People with disabilities -- Fiction; 4. Poliomyelitis -- Fiction; 5. Historical fiction; 6. Sisters -- Fiction

9781419723100, $17.99; 9781683351443

LC 2017009966

In this book, by Cat Winters, "Trudchen grew up hearing Odette's stories of their monster-slaying mother and a magician's curse. But now that Tru's older, she's starting to wonder if her older sister's tales were just comforting lies, especially because there's nothing fantastic about her own life -- permanently disabled and in constant pain from childhood polio. In 1909, after a two-year absence, Od reappears with a suitcase supposedly full of weapons and a promise to rescue Tru." (Publisher's note)

"Winters has woven an intricate and innovative pattern of structure, genre, and history that cannot fail to capture readers' imaginations." Kirkus

★ The **steep** and thorny way. By Cat Winters. Amulet Books 2016 352 p.

Grades: 8 9 10 11 12

1. Ghosts -- Fiction 2. Murder -- Fiction 3. Prejudices -- Fiction 4. Racially mixed people -- Fiction 5. Oregon -- History -- 20th century -- Fiction 6. Historical fiction

9781419719158, $17.95

LC 2015022705

This novel, by Cat Winters, is a re-setting of William Shakespeare's Hamlet in 1920s Oregon. "Hanalee [Denney's] . . . father, Hank Denney, died a year ago, hit by a drunk-driving teenager. Now her father's killer is out of jail and back in town, and he claims that Hanalee's father wasn't killed by the accident at all but, instead, was poisoned by the doctor who looked after him-who happens to be Hanalee's new stepfather." (Publisher's Note)

"A fast-paced read with multiple twists, the novel delivers a history lesson wrapped inside a murder mystery and ghost story. Winters deftly captures the many injustices faced by marginalized people in the years following World War I as well as a glimmer of hope for the better America to come. A riveting story of survival, determination, love, and friendship." Kirkus

Wise, Tama

Street dreams. Bold Strokes Books 2012 264 p. $13.95

Grades: 9 10 11 12

1. Hip-hop culture -- Fiction 2. Gay men -- Fiction 3. Street life -- Fiction 4. Graffiti -- Fiction

ISBN 1602826501; 9781602826502

LC 2011279902

In this novel by Tama Wise "Tyson Rua has more than his fair share of problems growing up in South Auckland. . . . Now Tyson's fallen in love at first sight. Only thing is, it's another guy. Living life on the sidelines of the local hip-hop scene, Tyson finds that to succeed in becoming a local graffiti artist or in getting the man of his dreams, he's going to have to get a whole lot more involved. And that means more problems." (Publisher's note)

Wiseman, Eva

Puppet; a novel. Tundra Books 2009 243p $17.95

Grades: 7 8 9 10 11 12

1. Prejudices -- Fiction 2. Jews -- Hungary -- Fiction

ISBN 978-0-88776-828-6; 0-88776-828-8

"Times are hard in Julie Vamosi's Hungarian village in the late nineteenth-century, and the townspeople . . . blame the Jews. After Julie's best friend, Esther, . . . disappears, the rumor spreads that the Jews cut her throat and drained her blood to drink with their Passover matzos. . . . Based on the records of a trial in 1883, this searing novel dramatizes virulent anti-Semitism from the viewpoint of a Christian child. . . . The climax is electrifying." Booklist

Withers, Pam

Andreo's race. Pam Withers. Tundra Books of Northern New York 2015 224 p.

Grades: 9 10 11 12

1. Contests 2. Adopted children -- Fiction 3. Human trafficking -- Fiction

1770497668; 9781770497665, $12.99; 9781770497672

LC 2014934267

In Pam Wither's novel "just as sixteen-year-old Andreo, skilled in death-defying ironman events in wilderness regions, is about to compete in rugged Bolivia, he and his friend Raul (another Bolivian adoptee) begin to suspect that their adoptive parents have unwittingly acquired them illegally. Plotting to use the upcoming race to pursue the truth, they veer on an epic journey to locate Andreo's birth parents, only to find themselves hazardously entangled with a gang of baby traffickers." (Publisher's note)

"The simple, straightforward language, surprise twist, and nonstop action will appeal to reluctant readers looking for a thrilling novel." SLJ

First descent. Tundra Books 2011 265p $17.95

Grades: 7 8 9 10

1. Colombia -- Fiction 2. Kayaks and kayaking -- Fiction

ISBN 978-1-77049-257-8; 1-77049-257-7

"Seventeen-year-old champion slalom kayaker Rex Scruggs is determined to kayak Colombia's Furioso River, when he meets a young woman, an Andean indigena, who both aids Rex in his quest and puts him in the crosshairs of Colombia's battling guerrillas and paramilitaries. . . . Withers flings the reader from one perilous adventure to another." Booklist

Wittlinger, Ellen

Hard love. Simon & Schuster Bks. for Young Readers 1999 224p hardcover o.p. pa $8.99

Grades: 7 8 9 10

1. Lesbians -- Fiction 2. Authorship -- Fiction

ISBN 0-689-82134-4; 0-689-84154-X pa

LC 98-6668

Michael L. Printz Award honor book, 2000

"John, cynical yet vulnerable, thinks he's immune to emotion until he meets bright, brittle Marisol, the author of

his favorite zine. He falls in love, but Marisol, a lesbian, just wants to be friends. A love story of a different sort—funny, poignant, and thoughtful." Booklist

Followed by: Love & lies: Marisol's story (2008)

Love & lies; Marisol's story. Simon & Schuster Books for Young Readers 2008 245p $16.99

Grades: 7 8 9 10

1. Lesbians -- Fiction 2. Authorship -- Fiction 3. Massachusetts -- Fiction

ISBN 978-1-4169-1623-9; 1-4169-1623-7

LC 2007-18330

When Marisol, a self-confident eighteen-year-old lesbian, moves to Cambridge, Massachusetts to work and try to write a novel, she falls under the spell of her beautiful but deceitful writing teacher, while also befriending a shy, vulnerable girl from Indiana.

"The emotional morass of Marisol's life . . . is complex and realistic; it will draw in both fans of the earlier novel . . . and realistic-fiction readers seeking a love story with depth." Bull Cent Child Books

★ **Parrotfish**. Simon & Schuster Books for Young Readers 2007 294p $16.99

Grades: 7 8 9 10

1. School stories 2. Family life -- Fiction 3. Transgender people -- Fiction

ISBN 978-1-4169-1622-2; 1-4169-1622-9

LC 2006-9689

Grady, a transgender high school student, yearns for acceptance by his classmates and family as he struggles to adjust to his new identity as a male.

"The author demonstrates well the complexity faced by transgendered people and makes the teen's frustration with having to fit into a category fully apparent." Publ Wkly

★ **Sandpiper**. Simon & Schuster Books for Young Readers 2005 227p hardcover o.p. pa $6.99

Grades: 9 10 11 12

1. Dating (Social customs) -- Fiction

ISBN 0-689-86802-2; 1-4169-3651-3 pa

LC 2004-7576

When The Walker, a mysterious boy who walks constantly, intervenes in an argument between Sandpiper and a boy she used to see, their lives become entwined in ways that change them both.

"While heavy on message and mature in subject matter, the novel is notable for the bold look it takes at relationships and at the myth that oral sex is not really sex." SLJ

Wizner, Jake

Spanking Shakespeare. Random House Children's Books 2007 287p $15.99; lib bdg $18.99

Grades: 8 9 10

1. School stories 2. Authorship -- Fiction

ISBN 978-0-375-84085-2; 978-0-375-94085-9 lib bdg

LC 2006-27035

Shakespeare Shapiro navigates a senior year fraught with feelings of insecurity while writing the memoir of his embarrassing life, worrying about his younger brother being cooler than he is, and having no prospects of ever getting a girlfriend.

"Raw, sexual, cynical, and honest, this book belongs on library shelves and gift lists." Voice Youth Advocates

Wolf, Allan

New found land; Lewis and Clark's voyage of discovery: a novel. Candlewick Press 2004 500p map $18.99

Grades: 7 8 9 10

    1. Lewis and Clark Expedition (1804-1806) -- Fiction

ISBN 0-7636-2113-7

                                   LC 2003-65254

The letters and thoughts of Thomas Jefferson, members of the Corps of Discovery, their guide Sacagawea, and Captain Lewis's Newfoundland dog, all tell of the historic exploratory expedition to seek a water route to the Pacific Ocean.

"This is an extraordinary, engrossing book that would appeal most to serious readers, but it should definitely be added to any collection." SLJ

Includes glossary and bibliographical references

★ The **watch** that ends the night; voices from the Titanic. Candlewick Press 2011 466p $21.99

Grades: 7 8 9 10

    1. Novels in verse 2. Shipwrecks -- Fiction 3. Titanic (Steamship) -- Fiction

ISBN 978-0-7636-3703-3

                                   LC 2010040150

Recreates the 1912 sinking of the Titanic as observed by millionaire John Jacob Astor, a beautiful young Lebanese refugee finding first love, "Unsinkable" Molly Brown, Captain Smith, and others including the iceberg itself.

"A lyrical, monumental work of fact and imagination that reads like an oral history revved up by the drama of the event." Kirkus

Who killed Christopher Goodman?: based on a true crime. Allan Wolf. Candlewick Press 2017 288 p.

Grades: 8 9 10 11 12

    1. Murder -- Investigation -- Fiction; 2. Violence -- Fiction; 3. Teenagers -- Fiction

ISBN 0763656135; 9780763656133, $16.99

This book, by Allan Wolf, "examines the circumstances of one boy's inexplicable murder and the fateful summer leading up to it. Everybody likes Chris Goodman.... He wears those funny bell-bottoms and he really likes the word ennui and he shakes your hand when he meets you, but he's also the kind of guy who's always up for a good time.... Everybody likes Chris Goodman, which makes it especially shocking when he's murdered." (Publisher's note)

Wolf, Jennifer Shaw

Breaking beautiful; Jennifer Shaw Wolf. Walker 2012 356 p. (hardcover) $16.99

Grades: 9 10 11 12

    1. Siblings -- Fiction 2. Date rape -- Fiction 3. Traffic accidents -- Fiction 4. Twins -- Fiction 5. Memory -- Fiction 6. Dating violence -- Fiction 7. Mystery and detective stories 8. Brothers and sisters -- Fiction 9. Dating (Social customs) -- Fiction

ISBN 0802723527; 9780802723529

                                   LC 2011010944

This novel, by Jennifer Shaw Wolf, follows "Allie[, who] lost everything the night her boyfriend, Trip, died in a horrible car accident—including her memory of the event. As their small town mourns his death, Allie is afraid to remember because doing so means delving into what she's kept hidden for so long: the horrible reality of their abusive relationship. . . . Can she reach deep enough to remember that night so she can finally break free?" (Publisher's note)

Wolff, Virginia Euwer

★ **Make** lemonade. Holt & Co. 1993 200p $17.95; pa $7.95

Grades: 8 9 10 11 12

    1. Novels in verse 2. Poverty -- Fiction 3. Babysitters -- Fiction 4. Teenage mothers -- Fiction

ISBN 978-0-8050-2228-5; 0-8050-2228-7; 978-0-8050-8070-4 pa; 0-8050-8070-8 pa

                                   LC 92-41182

"Fourteen-year-old LaVaughn accepts the job of babysitting Jolly's two small children but quickly realizes that the young woman, a seventeen-year-old single mother, needs as much help and nurturing as her two neglected children. The four become something akin to a temporary family, and through their relationship each makes progress toward a better life. Sixty-six brief chapters, with words arranged on the page like poetry, perfectly echo the patterns of teenage speech." Horn Book Guide

Other titles in this trilogy are:

This full house (2009)

True believer (2001)

Wolitzer, Meg

★ **Belzhar;** a novel; Meg Wolitzer. Dutton Books for Young Readers. 2014 272p $17.99

Grades: 9 10 11 12

    1. Boarding schools -- Fiction 2. Dating (Social customs) -- Fiction 3. Emotional problems -- Fiction 4. Friendship -- Fiction 5. Schools -- Fiction

ISBN: 0525423052; 9780525423058

                                   LC 2014010747

"When Jam suffers a terrible trauma and feels isolated by grief, her parents send her to the Wooden Barn, a boarding school for "highly intelligent, emotionally fragile" teens. Once there she is enrolled in a class with only five specially selected students where they exclusively read Sylvia Plath... While the conclusion is a touch heavy-handed, older teen readers, especially rabid Plath fans, will relish Wolitzer's deeply respectful treatment of Jam's realistic emotional struggle." Booklist

Wood, Fiona

Cloudwish. By Fiona Wood. Little, Brown & Co. 2016 320 p.

Grades: 7 8 9 10

    1. Dating (Social life and customs) -- Fiction 2. Magic -- Fiction 3. Vietnamese -- Australia -- Fiction 4. Wishes -- Fiction 5. Australia -- Fiction

ISBN 9780316242134, $54; 9780316242127, $17.99

                                   LC 2015036989

First published in 2015 by Pan Macmillan Australia PTY, Ltd.

In this novel by Fiona Wood, "Vân Uoc tries to stick to her reality—keeping a low profile as a scholarship student at her prestigious Melbourne private school, managing her mother's PTSD from a traumatic emigration from Vietnam, and admiring Billy from afar. Until she makes a wish that inexplicably (possibly magically) comes true. Billy actually notices her. . . . . [But] Vân Uoc can't help but wonder why Billy has suddenly fallen for her." (Publisher's note)

" It's an inspiring story with a sympathetic heroine, who will especially appeal to those who feel pressured to follow paths they don't want to travel." Pub Wkly

Wooding, Chris
The **haunting** of Alaizabel Cray. Orchard Bks. 2004 292p $16.95; pa $7.99
Grades: 7 8 9 10
1. Horror fiction 2. Supernatural -- Fiction 3. London (England) -- Fiction
ISBN 0-439-54656-7; 0-439-59851-6 pa
LC 2003-69108
First published 2001 in the United Kingdom
In a world similar to Victorian London, Thaniel, a seventeen-year-old hunter of deadly, demonic creatures called the wych-kin, takes in a lost, possessed girl, and becomes embroiled in a plot to unleash evil on the world
"Eerie and exhilarating. . . . [The author] fuses together his best storytelling skills . . . to create a fabulously horrific and ultimately timeless underworld." SLJ

Havoc; illustrated by Dan Chernett. Scholastic Press 2010 396p il $16.99
Grades: 6 7 8 9
1. Magic -- Fiction 2. Good and evil -- Fiction 3. Comic books, strips, etc. -- Fiction
ISBN 978-0-545-16045-2; 0-545-16045-6
"As Seth makes his way back into Malice with the talismanic Shard and joins the effort to mount an attack on the dread Deadhouse, a new ally, Alicia, nervously tracks the House's sinister master Tall Jake to the decrepit English psychiatric hospital where Grendel—the mad, disturbed, misshapen graphic artist (and maybe god?) who has created both the comic and the world it depicts—is imprisoned. . . . This features expertly meshed multiple plotlines, colorful supporting characters . . . frequent eerie skitterings and sudden feelings of dread plus nonstop action that breaks, occasionally, from prose into graphic-novel–style panels festooned with noisy sound effects." Kirkus

★ **Malice**; illustrated by Dan Chernett. Scholastic Press 2009 377p il $14.99; pa $8.99
Grades: 6 7 8 9 10
1. Horror fiction 2. Comic books, strips, etc. -- Fiction
ISBN 978-0-545-16043-8; 0-545-16043-X; 978-0-545-16044-5 pa; 0-545-16044-8 pa
Everyone's heard the rumors. Call on Tall Jake and he'll take you to Malice, a world that exists inside a horrifying comic book. A place most kids never leave. Seth and Kady think it's all a silly myth. But then their friend disappears.
"This nail-biter will keep readers glued to the story until the very last page is turned. . . . Seth and Kady are strong and exciting characters." SLJ

Poison. Orchard Bks. 2005 273p $16.99; pa $7.99
Grades: 7 8 9 10
1. Fantasy fiction 2. Fairies -- Fiction 3. Storytelling -- Fiction
ISBN 0-439-75570-0; 0-439-75571-9 pa
LC 2005-02174
First published 2003 in the United Kingdom
When Poison leaves her home in the marshes of Gull to retrieve the infant sister who was snatched by the fairies, she and a group of unusual friends survive encounters with the inhabitants of various Realms, and Poison herself confronts a surprising destiny.
"Poison's story should please crowds of horror fans who like their books fast-paced, darkly atmospheric, and melodramatic." SLJ

Silver; Chris Wooding. Scholastic Press 2014 320 p. (hc) $17.99
Grades: 7 8 9 10 11 12
1. Horror fiction 2. School stories 3. Survival -- Fiction 4. Boarding schools -- Fiction 5. Communicable diseases -- Fiction
ISBN 0545603927; 9780545603928
LC 2013014037
In this young adult science fiction horror novel, by Chris Wooding, "without warning, a horrifying infection will spread across the school grounds [of Mortingham Boarding Academy], and a group of students with little in common will find themselves barricaded in a classroom, fighting for their lives. Some will live. Some will die. And then it will get even worse." (Publisher's note)
"When strange insects assault a remote boarding school in England, the kids try to save the day in this tense page-turner...Skillfully managed subplots keep the pages flying. It looks like the end of the world is nigh.... It's just all kinds of white-knuckle fun." (Kirkus)

Velocity. Chris Wooding. Scholastic Press 2017 325 p.
Grades: 7 8 9 10
1. Automobile mechanics -- Australia -- Fiction; 2. Automobile racing -- Fiction; 3. Dystopian fiction; 4. Female friendship -- Fiction; 5. Friendship -- Fiction; 6. Science fiction; 7. Women automobile racing drivers -- Australia -- Fiction; 8. Australia -- Fiction
9780545944946, $18.99; 9781338042788; 0545944945
LC 2016030469
In this book, by Chris Wooding, "Cassica and Shiara are best friends. They couldn't be more different, but their differences work to their advantage -- especially when they're drag racing. Cassica is fearless and determined, making her the perfect driver for daring, photo-finish victories. Shiara is intelligent and creative, able to build cars out of scrap and formulate daring strategies from the passenger's seat." (Publisher's note)
"An action-packed, wild ride with unexpected twists and turns and characters readers care about -- call it a dystopia with heart." Kirkus
"First published in the United Kingdom in 2015 by Scholastic Children's Books" -- Copyright page.

Woods, Brenda

Emako Blue. G. P. Putnam's Sons 2004 124p $15.99

Grades: 7 8 9 10

    1. African Americans -- Fiction

    ISBN 0-399-24006-3

                           LC 2003-16647

Monterey, Savannah, Jamal, and Eddie have never had much to do with each other until Emako Blue shows up at chorus practice, but just as the lives of the five Los Angeles high school students become intertwined, tragedy tears them apart.

"This short, succinct, and poignant story of friendship, family, and overwhelming sadness will leave some readers in tears." SLJ

Woods, Elizabeth Emma

Choker; [by] Elizabeth Woods. Simon & Schuster Books for Young Readers 2011 233p $16.99

Grades: 9 10 11 12

    1. School stories 2. Friendship -- Fiction 3. Mental illness -- Fiction

    ISBN 978-1-4424-1233-0

                           LC 2010-34672

Teenaged Cara, solitary and bullied in high school, is delighted to reconnect with her childhood best friend Zoe whose support and friendship help Cara gain self-confidence, even as her classmates start dying.

"Terrific pacing and mounting suspense lead to a resolution that may not surprise savvy readers but is nonetheless chilling." Booklist

Woodson, Jacqueline

★ **After** Tupac and D Foster. G.P. Putnam's Sons 2008 153p $15.99

Grades: 7 8 9 10

    1. Poets 2. Actors 3. Rap musicians 4. Friendship -- Fiction 5. African Americans -- Fiction

    ISBN 978-0-399-24654-8

                           LC 2007-23725

A Newbery honor book, 2009

In the New York City borough of Queens in 1996, three girls bond over their shared love of Tupac Shakur's music, as together they try to make sense of the unpredictable world in which they live.

"The subtlety and depth with which the author conveys the girls' relationships lend this novel exceptional vividness and staying power." Publ Wkly

Behind you. Putnam 2004 118p $15.99; pa $7.99

Grades: 7 8 9 10

    1. Death -- Fiction 2. New York (N.Y.) -- Fiction 3. African Americans -- Fiction

    ISBN 978-0-399-23988-5; 0-399-23988-X; 978-0-14-241554-2 pa; 0-14-241554-5 pa

    Sequel to: If you come softly

After fifteen-year-old Jeremiah is mistakenly shot by police, the people who love him struggle to cope with their loss as they recall his life and death, unaware that 'Miah is watching over them.

"Woodson writes with impressive poetry about race, love, death, and what grief feels like—the things that 'snap the heart' and her characters' open strength and wary optimism will resonate with many teens." Booklist

★ **Beneath** a meth moon; Jacqueline Woodson. Nancy Paulsen Books 2012 181p

Grades: 9 10 11 12

    1. Teenagers -- Drug use -- Fiction 2. Hurricane Katrina, 2005 -- Fiction 3. Iowa -- Fiction 4. Grief -- Fiction 5. Runaways -- Fiction 6. Drug abuse -- Fiction 7. Methamphetamine -- Fiction 8. Pass Christian (Miss.) -- Fiction

    ISBN 9780399252501

                           LC 2011046799

In this novel, "Laurel, her father, and her little brother are reeling from the deaths of her mother and grandmother, who refused to leave their home in Pass Christian, Mississippi, during Hurricane Katrina. As they try to start life over in a new town, things look better for Laurel: she meets a sympathetic new friend named Kaylee, becomes a cheerleader, and starts dating T-Boom. Their first night together, though, T-Boom introduces her to meth, and she becomes instantly addicted. Her addiction progresses quickly, and when Kaylee confronts her and her father finds her stash, she runs away and lives on the streets, begging for money and trying desperately to stay high." (Bulletin of the Center for Children's Books)

★ **From** the notebooks of Melanin Sun. G.P. Putnam's Sons 2010 126p $17.99; pa $7.99

Grades: 7 8 9 10

    1. Lesbians -- Fiction 2. African Americans -- Fiction 3. Mother-son relationship -- Fiction

    ISBN 978-0-399-25280-8; 0-399-25280-0; 978-0-14-241641-9 pa; 0-14-241641-X pa

                           LC 2009011314

A reissue of the title first published 1995 by Blue Sky Press

A Coretta Scott King honor book, 1996

Almost-fourteen-year-old Melanin Sun's comfortable, quiet life is shattered when his mother reveals she has fallen in love with a woman

"Offering no easy answers, Woodson teaches the reader that love can lead to acceptance of all manner of differences." Publ Wkly

If you come softly. Putnam 1998 181p $15.99; pa $5.99

Grades: 7 8 9 10

    1. Race relations -- Fiction 2. New York (N.Y.) -- Fiction 3. African Americans -- Fiction

    ISBN 0-399-23112-9; 0-698-11862-6 pa

                           LC 97-32212

ALA YALSA Margaret A. Edwards Award (2006)

After meeting at their private school in New York, fifteen-year-old Jeremiah, who is black and whose parents are separated, and Ellie, who is white and whose mother has twice abandoned her, fall in love and then try to cope with people's reactions

"The gentle and melancholy tone of this book makes it ideal for thoughtful readers and fans of romance." Voice Youth Advocates

Another title about Jeremiah is:

Behind you (2004)

Lena; by Jacqueline Woodson. 1st G.P. Putnam's Sons ed.; G. P. Putnam's Sons 2006 135p $17.99

Grades: 6 7 8 9

1. Sisters -- Fiction 2. Runaway teenagers -- Fiction

ISBN 0-399-24469-7

LC 2005032666

A reissue of the title first published 1999 by Delacorte Press

ALA YALSA Margaret A. Edwards Award (2006)

Thirteen-year-old Lena and her younger sister Dion mourn the death of their mother as they hitchhike from Ohio to Kentucky while running away from their abusive father.

"Soulful, wise and sometimes wrenching, this taut story never loses its grip on the reader." Publ Wkly

Miracle's boys. Putnam 2000 133p $15.99; pa $5.99

Grades: 9 10 11 12

1. Orphans -- Fiction 2. Brothers -- Fiction 3. New York (N.Y.) -- Fiction 4. African Americans -- Fiction

ISBN 0-399-23113-7; 0-698-11916-9 pa

LC 99-40050

ALA YALSA Margaret A. Edwards Award (2006)

Twelve-year-old Lafayette's close relationship with his older brother Charlie changes after Charlie is released from a detention home and blames Lafayette for the death of their mother

"The fast-paced narrative is physically immediate, and the dialogue is alive with anger and heartbreak." Booklist

Woolston, Blythe

★ **Black** helicopters; Blythe Woolston. Candlewick Press 2013 176 p. $15.99

Grades: 9 10 11 12

1. Dystopias 2. Adventure fiction 3. Survivalism -- Fiction

ISBN 0763661465; 9780763661465

LC 2012942619

This young adult suspense novel, by Blythe Woolston, follows "a teenage girl. A survivalist childhood. And now a bomb strapped to her chest. . . . With Da unexpectedly gone and no home to return to, [the] teenage . . . Valkyrie . . . and her big brother must bring their message to the outside world--a not-so-smart place where little boys wear their names on their backpacks and young men don't pat down strangers before offering a lift." (Publisher's note)

Catch & release; Blythe Woolston. Carolrhoda Lab 2012 210 p.

Grades: 9 10 11 12

1. Fishing -- Fiction 2. Friendship -- Fiction 3. Automobile travel -- Fiction 4. Communicable diseases -- Fiction 5. People with disabilities -- Fiction 6. Trout -- Fiction 7. West (U.S.) -- Fiction 8. Disfigured

persons -- Fiction

ISBN 0761377557; 9780761377559

LC 2011009630

In this book, "[e]ighteen-year-old Polly recounts her road trip with Odd, a fellow survivor of the disease that killed five others from their small town, in D'Elegance, his Gramma's old baby-blue Cadillac. Fishing is ostensibly the purpose of their outing, and it symbolically charts the way the two teens process their disabilities. . . . Polly once had a boyfriend and a sense of a normal future. . . . Odd Estes lost a foot as well as some football buddies, and although the two barely knew each other before, they both now struggle to accommodate their good fortune in surviving and their misfortune of disability. . . . Odd and Polly move from isolation to a mutual connection that helps them deal with their pain." (Kirkus)

★ The **Freak** Observer. Carolrhoda Lab 2010 202p $16.95

Grades: 8 9 10 11 12

1. Post-traumatic stress disorder -- Fiction

ISBN 978-0-7613-6212-8; 0-7613-6212-6

LC 2010-989

Suffering from a crippling case of post-traumatic stress disorder, sixteen-year-old Loa Lindgren tries to use her problem solving skills, sharpened in physics and computer programming, to cure herself.

"Woolston's talent for dialogue and her unique approach to scenes make what sounds standard about this story feel fresh and vital. . . . A strong . . . [novel] about learning to see yourself apart from the reflection you cast off others." Booklist

★ **Martians**. Blythe Woolston. Candlewick Press 2015 224 p.

Grades: 9 10 11 12

1. Science fiction 2. Consumption (Economics) -- Fiction

9780763677565, $16.99; 0763677566

LC 2015931430

In this novel, by Blythe Woolston, set "in a near-future world of exurban decay studded with big box stores, daily routine revolves around shopping-for those who can. For Zoë, the mission is simpler: live. . . . With a handful of other disaffected, forgotten kids, Zoë must find her place in a world that has consumed itself beyond redemption." (Publisher's note)

"Imagination shines through the bleak but poetic prose, love and kindness prove hearty, and once again, life proves that roses not only do, but always will, grow in concrete. Dystopian aficionados, budding social pundits, and readers who enjoy quirky characters, settings, and challenges will find a lot to love here." VOYA

Wrede, Patricia C., 1953-

Across the Great Barrier; Patricia C. Wrede. Scholastic Press 2011 339p (Frontier magic) $16.99

Grades: 7 8 9 10 11 12

1. Fantasy 2. Magic -- Fiction 3. Twins -- Fiction 4. Brothers and sisters -- Fiction 5. Frontier and pioneer

life -- Fiction
ISBN 978-0-545-03343-5; 0-545-03343-8;
9780545033435

LC 2011032260

Eff is an unlucky thirteenth child. Her twin brother, Lan, is a powerful seventh son of a seventh son. And yet, Eff is the one who saved the day for the settlements west of the Great Barrier. Her unique ways of doing magic and seeing the world, and her fascination with the magical creatures and land in the Great Plains push Eff to work toward joining an expedition heading west. But things are changing on the frontier.

"Splendid worldbuilding and deliciously complex characterization continue to be the hallmarks of this standout fantasy." Kirkus

The **Far** West; Patricia C. Wrede. Scholastic Press 2012 378 p. $17.99
Grades: 7 8 9 10 11 12

1. Steampunk fiction; 2. Fantasy fiction; 3. Fantasy; 4. Magic -- Fiction; 5. Twins -- Fiction; 6. Friendship -- Fiction
ISBN 0545033446; 9780545033442

LC 2012288790

This young adult speampunk novel, by Patricia C. Wrede, concludes the "Frontier Magic" trilogy. "Eff is an unlucky thirteenth child . . . but also the seventh daughter in her family. Her twin brother, Lan, is a powerful double seventh son. Her life at the edge of the Great Barrier Spell is different from anyone else's that she knows. . . . With Lan, William, Professor Torgeson, Wash, and Professor Ochiba, Eff finds that nothing on the wild frontier is as they expected." (Publisher's note)

Sorcery and Cecelia, or, The enchanted chocolate pot; being the correspondence of two young ladies of quality regarding various magical scandals in London and the country. [by] Patricia C. Wrede and Caroline Stevermer. Harcourt 2003 316p $17; pa $6.95
Grades: 7 8 9 10

1. Cousins -- Fiction 2. Supernatural -- Fiction
ISBN 0-15-204615-1; 0-15-205300-X pa

LC 2002-38706

In 1817 in England, two young cousins, Cecilia living in the country and Kate in London, write letters to keep each other informed of their exploits, which take a sinister turn when they find themselves confronted by evil wizards

"This is a fun story that quickly draws in the reader." Voice Youth Advocates

Other titles about Kate and Cecilia are:
The grand tour (2004)
The mislaid magician (2006)

The **thirteenth** child. Scholastic Press 2009 344p (Frontier magic) $16.99
Grades: 7 8 9 10 11 12

1. School stories 2. Fantasy fiction 3. Magic -- Fiction 4. Twins -- Fiction 5. Frontier and pioneer life -- Fiction
ISBN 978-0-545-03342-8; 0-545-03342-X

LC 2008-34048

Eighteen-year-old Eff must finally get over believing she is bad luck and accept that her special training in Aphrikan

magic, and being the twin of the seventh son of a seventh son, give her extraordinary power to combat magical creatures that threaten settlements on the western frontier.

Wrede "creates a rich world where steam dragons seem as normal as bears, and a sympathetic character in Eff." Publ Wkly

Followed by Across the Great Barrier (2011)

Wright, Bil

Putting makeup on the fat boy. Simon & Schuster Books for Young Readers 2011 219p $16.99
Grades: 7 8 9 10 11 12

1. School stories 2. Cosmetics -- Fiction 3. Gay teenagers -- Fiction 4. Hispanic Americans -- Fiction 5. Single parent family -- Fiction
ISBN 978-1-4169-3996-2; 1-4169-3996-2

LC 2010032450

"Carlos, 16 and fabulous, just knows he's going to be famous. Cocky but playful—'I had just the slightest touch of color in my cheeks. I'd given myself a manicure. I looked beyond excellent!'—Carlos strides purposefully toward his goal: Makeup artist to the stars. Zipping around Manhattan, he obtains employment with a hip, prestigious cosmetics company in Macy's and nabs a position working for the star of a Saturday Night Live equivalent." Kirkus

"Obviously, there's a whole lot going on in Wright's novel, but it's handled deftly and, for the most part, believably. Best of all, Carlos is not completely defined by his homosexuality." Booklist

When the black girl sings; [by] Bil Wright. Simon & Schuster Books for Young Readers 2007 266p $16.99; pa $5.99
Grades: 6 7 8 9 10

1. Divorce -- Fiction 2. Adoption -- Fiction 3. African Americans -- Fiction
ISBN 978-1-4169-3995-5; 1-4169-3995-4; 978-1-4169-4003-6 pa; 1-4169-4003-0 pa

LC 2006030837

Adopted by white parents and sent to an exclusive Connecticut girls' school where she is the only black student, fourteen-year-old Lahni Schuler feels like an outcast, particularly when her parents separate, but after attending a local church where she hears gospel music for the first time, she finds her voice.

"Readers will enjoy the distinctive characters, lively dialogue, and palette of adolescent and racial insecurities in this contemporary, upbeat story." SLJ

Wright, Denis

Violence 101; a novel. G. P. Putnam's Sons 2010 213p $16.99
Grades: 8 9 10

1. Genius -- Fiction 2. Violence -- Fiction 3. New Zealand -- Fiction 4. Reformatories -- Fiction 5. Race relations -- Fiction
ISBN 978-0-399-25493-2; 0-399-25493-5

LC 2010-02851

First published 2007 in New Zealand

In a New Zealand reformatory, Hamish Graham, an extremely intelligent fourteen-year-old who believes in the compulsory study of violence, learns that it is not always the answer.

"Wright's novel is clever and biting, a tragedy of society's failure to deal with kids like Hamish and a satire of society's winking condemnations of violence. Hamish's actions can be revolting, despite his justifications, but he still draws empathy as a product of the environment at large. Hardly a comfortable book to read, but a gripping one." Publ Wkly

Wulffson, Don L.

Soldier X. Viking 2001 226p $15.99; pa $6.99

Grades: 7 8 9 10

1. World War, 1939-1945 -- Fiction 2. World War, 1939-1945 -- Campaigns -- Soviet Union
ISBN 0-670-88863-X; 0-14-250073-9 pa

LC 99-49418

In 1943 sixteen-year-old Erik experiences the horrors of war when he is drafted into the German army and sent to fight on the Russian front

"Erik's first-person narrative records battlefield sequences with an unflinching—and occasionally numbing—brutality, in a story notable for its unusual perspective." Horn Book Guide

Wunder, Wendy

★ The **museum** of intangible things. Wendy Wunder. Razorbill 2014 295p $17.99

Grades: 8 9 10 11 12

1. Automobile travel -- Fiction 2. Best friends -- Fiction 3. Female friendship -- Fiction 4. Manic-depressive illness -- Fiction 5. Runaways -- Fiction
ISBN 1595145141; 9781595145147

LC 2013030169

"As Hannah and best friend Zoe (diagnosed bipolar) embark on a cross-country road trip, Zoe gives Hannah "intangible lessons" (e.g., Hannah learns insouciance when they overnight in an IKEA). When Zoe's irrationality gets scary, Hannah learns betrayal and, later, forgiveness. With each lesson, Hannah becomes more confident, building her own distinct identity. Meanwhile, Zoe is a complex character--intelligent, loyal, and funny." Horn Book

★ The **probability** of miracles. Razorbill 2011 360p $17.99

Grades: 8 9 10 11 12

1. Death -- Fiction 2. Maine -- Fiction 3. Cancer -- Fiction 4. Miracles -- Fiction
ISBN 978-1-59514-368-6; 1-59514-368-8

"Faced with death, one teen discovers life in this bittersweet debut. . . . Cynical and loner Campbell Cooper (an Italian-Samoan-American) gave up on magic after her parents divorced, her father died and she developed neuroblastoma. . . . Having exhausted Western medicine, her single mother suggests spending the summer after Cam's graduation in Promise, Maine, a hidden town . . . known to have mysterious healing powers. . . . Exploring both sides of Cam's heritage, the story unfolds through narration as beautiful as the sun's daily 'everlasting gobstopper descent behind the lighthouse.' Irreverent humor, quirky small-town charm and surprises along the way help readers brace themselves for the tearjerker ending." Kirkus

Wung-Sung, Jesper

The **last** execution. Jesper Wung-Sung; translation by Lindy Falk van Rooyen. Atheneum Books for Young Readers 2016 144 p.

Grades: 10 11 12

1. Executions and executioners -- Fiction 2. Denmark -- Fiction
9781481429658, $17.99; 9781481429665

LC 2015033461

This book, by Jesper Wung-Sung, is "based on the . . . true story of the last execution in Denmark's history. . . . Niels Nielson, a young peasant, was sentenced to death by beheading on the dubious charges of arson and murder. Does he have the right to live despite what he is accused of? That is the question the townsfolk ask as the countdown begins." (Publisher's note)

"This bleak Danish import imagines the last day of a real-life execution victim in 1853 Svendborg, Denmark. The observations of various townspeople—interspersed with the fifteen-year-old boy's own memories of poverty, rejection, loss, and finally rage—reveal the world that led the boy to his crime and his fate. Rich with symbolism, historical criticism, and contemporary resonance, this is an unflinching examination of capitol punishment." Horn Book

Original text was published in 2010.

Wyatt, Melissa

Funny how things change. Farrar, Straus & Giroux 2009 196p $16.95

Grades: 9 10 11 12

1. Artists -- Fiction 2. Mountains -- Fiction 3. Country life -- Fiction 4. West Virginia -- Fiction
ISBN 978-0-374-30233-7; 0-374-30233-2

LC 2008-16190

Remy, a talented, seventeen-year-old auto mechanic, questions his decision to join his girlfriend when she starts college in Pennsylvania after a visiting artist helps him to realize what his family's home in a dying West Virginia mountain town means to him.

"Laconic but full of heart, smart, thoughtful and proudly working-class, Remy makes a fresh and immensely appealing hero." Kirkus

Wynne-Jones, Tim

★ **Blink** & Caution. Candlewick Press 2011 342p $16.99

Grades: 9 10 11 12

1. Crime -- Fiction 2. Guilt -- Fiction 3. Canada -- Fiction 4. Runaway teenagers -- Fiction
ISBN 978-0-7636-3983-9; 0-7636-3983-4

LC 2010-13563

Two teenagers who are living on the streets and barely getting by become involved in a complicated criminal plot, and make an unexpected connection with each other

"The short, punchy sentences Wynne-Jones fires like buckshot; the joy, fear, and doubt that punctuate the teens' every action. This is gritty, sure, but more than that, it's smart, and earns every drop of its hopeful finish." Booklist

★ The **emperor** of any place. Tim Wynne-Jones. Candlewick Press 2015 336 p.

Grades: 9 10 11 12

1. World War, 1939-1945 -- Fiction 2. Grandparent-grandchild relationship -- Fiction 3. Father-son relationship -- Fiction
9780763669737, $17.99

LC 2014953457

In this book, by Tim Wynne-Jones, "when Evan's father dies suddenly, Evan finds a hand-bound yellow book on his desk—a book his dad had been reading when he passed away. The book is the diary of a Japanese soldier stranded on a small Pacific island in WWII. Why was his father reading it? What is in this account that Evan's grandfather, whom Evan has never met before, fears so much that he will do anything to prevent its being seen? And what could this possibly mean for Evan?" (Publisher's note)

"Without spelling out the metaphoric significance of the story within the story, Wynne-Jones provides enough hints for readers to make connections and examine the lines between war and peace, as well as hate and love." Pub Wkly

The **uninvited**. Candlewick Press 2009 351p $16.99

Grades: 10 11 12

1. Canada -- Fiction 2. Vacations -- Fiction 3. Father-daughter relationship -- Fiction
ISBN 978-0-7636-3984-6; 0-7636-3984-2

LC 2009-7520

After a disturbing freshman year at New York University, Mimi is happy to get away to her father's remote Canadian cottage only to discover a stranger living there who has never heard of her or her father and who is convinced that Mimi is responsible for leaving sinister tokens around the property.

"This suspenseful and deftly crafted family drama will appeal to older teens who are exploring their options beyond high school." Voice Youth Advocates

Yancey, Richard

★ The **5th** Wave; Rick Yancey. G.P. Putnam's Sons, an imprint of Penguin Group (USA) Inc. 2013 480 p. (hardcover) $18.99

Grades: 9 10 11 12

1. Science fiction 2. Extraterrestrial beings -- Fiction 3. War -- Fiction 4. Survival -- Fiction
ISBN 0399162410; 9780399162411

LC 2012047622

In this post-apocalyptic novel, by Rick Yancey, "on a lonely stretch of highway, Cassie runs from Them. The beings who only look human, who roam the countryside killing anyone they see. Who have scattered Earth's last survivors. To stay alone is to stay alive, Cassie believes, until she meets Evan Walker. Beguiling and mysterious, Evan Walker may be Cassie's only hope for rescuing her brother--or even saving herself." (Publisher's note)

"Yancey makes a dramatic 180 from the intellectual horror of his Monstrumologist books to open a gripping SF trilogy about an Earth decimated by an alien invasion. The author fully embraces the genre, while resisting its more sensational tendencies... It's a book that targets a broad commercial audience, and Yancey's aim is every bit as good as Cassie's." Pub Wkly

The **final** descent; Rick Yancey. Simon & Schuster Books for Young Readers 2013 320 p. (Monstrumologist) (hardback) $18.99

Grades: 9 10 11 12

1. Monsters -- Fiction 2. Apprentices -- Fiction 3. Horror stories 4. Orphans -- Fiction 5. Supernatural -- Fiction
ISBN 144245153X; 9781442451537

LC 2013015811

In this final installment of Rick Yancey's Monstrumologist series, "Will Henry, now 16, often drunk and colder than ever, helps Monstrumologist Pellinore Warthrop track down the T. cerrejonensis, a giant, snakelike critter that poisons its human prey then swallows them whole. At the same time, the novel also fast-forwards decades later to 1911, when Will returns to care for an elderly Warthrop and then reverts back to when he was first taken in by his employer." (Kirkus Reviews)

The **infinite** sea. Rick Yancey. Putnam Publishing Group 2014 300 p. (5th wave)

Grades: 9 10 11 12

1. Extraterrestrial beings -- Fiction 2. Science fiction 3. Survival -- Fiction 4. War -- Fiction 5. Apocalyptic fiction
0399162429; 9780399162428, $18.99

LC 2014022058

In this science fiction novel, by Rick Yancey, book 2 in the "5th Wave" series, "surviving the first four waves was nearly impossible. Now Cassie Sullivan finds herself in a new world, a world in which the fundamental trust that binds us together is gone. As the 5th Wave rolls across the landscape, Cassie, Ben, and Ringer are forced to confront the Others' ultimate goal: the extermination of the human race." (Publisher's note)

"Yancey's prose remains unimpeachable-every paragraph is laden with setting, theme, and emotion-and he uses it toward a series of horrifying set pieces, including a surgery scene that will have your pages sopping with sweat." Booklist

★ The **monstrumologist**; [by] William James Henry; edited by Rick Yancey. Simon & Schuster Books for Young Readers 2009 454p il $17.99; pa $9.99

Grades: 9 10 11 12

1. Orphans -- Fiction 2. Monsters -- Fiction 3. Apprentices -- Fiction 4. Supernatural -- Fiction
ISBN 978-1-4169-8448-1; 1-4169-8448-8; 978-1-4169-8449-8 pa; 1-4169-8449-6 pa

LC 2009-4562

ALA YALSA Printz Award Honor Book (2010)

In 1888, twelve-year-old Will Henry chronicles his apprenticeship with Dr. Warthrop, a scientist who hunts and studies real-life monsters, as they discover and attempt to destroy a pod of Anthropophagi.

"As the action moves from the dissecting table to the cemetery to an asylum to underground catacombs, Yancey keeps the shocks frequent and shrouded in a splattery miasma of blood, bone, pus, and maggots. . . . Yancey's prose is stentorian and wordy, but it weaves a world that possesses a Lovecraftian logic and hints at its own deeply satisfying mythos. . . . 'Snap to!' is Warthrop's continued demand of Will, but readers will need no such needling." Booklist

Other titles in this series include:

The curse of the wendigo (2010)

The Isle of Blood (2011)

The final descent (2013)

Yee, F. C.

★ The **epic** crush of Genie Lo. A novel by F.C. Yee. Amulet Books 2017 310 p.

Grades: 7 8 9 10

1. Oakland (Calif.); 2. California -- Fiction; 3. Supernatural -- Fiction; 4. High school students -- Fiction

9781683351221, $15.54; 9781419725487, $18.99

LC 2017018271

In this book, by F.C. Yee, "the struggle to get into a top-tier college consumes sixteen-year-old Genie's every waking thought. But when she discovers she's a celestial spirit who's powerful enough to bash through the gates of heaven with her fists, her perfectionist existence is shattered. Enter Quentin, a transfer student from China whose tone-deaf assertiveness beguiles Genie to the brink of madness." (Publisher's note)

"Hard-driving, hyperachieving Chinese-American sophomore Genie Lo may have to put her take-no-prisoners rush to the Ivy Leagues aside so she can save the world, or at least the local region of California currently under attack by Chinese demons.... Loads of action, a touch of comedy, a bit of well-controlled lust, and even some serious discussion of Eastern philosophy should leave readers eager for a return performance." Bulletin of the Center for Children's Books

Yee, Lisa

The **kidney** hypothetical, or, how to ruin your life in seven days. Lisa Yee. Arthur A. Levine Books 2015 272 p.

Grades: 9 10 11 12

1. Brothers -- Fiction 2. Families -- California -- Marina del Rey -- Fiction 3. Family life -- Fiction 4. Friendship -- Fiction 5. High schools -- California -- Marina del Rey -- Fiction 6. High schools -- Fiction 7. Marina del Rey (Calif.) -- Fiction 8. Schools -- Fiction 9. High school students -- Fiction 10. Dating (Social customs) -- Fiction

0545230942; 0545230950; 9780545230940, $17.99; 9780545230957

LC 2014005332

In this novel by Lisa Yee "Higgs Boson Bing has seven days left before his perfect high school career is completed. Then it's on to Harvard to fulfill the fantasy portrait of success that he and his parents have cultivated for the past four years. But something's not right. And when Higgs's girlfriend presents him with a seemingly innocent hypothetical question about whether or not he'd give her a kidney . . . the exposed fault lines reach straight down to the foundations of his life." (Publisher's note)

"With whip-smart writing, a fast-paced plot, plenty of humor, and just enough mystery to keep readers on edge, this is an emotional journey about breaking free of family, friends, and duty to discover what makes you happy." Booklist

Yee, Paul

Learning to fly; [by] Paul Yee. Orca Book Pub. 2008 108p (Orca soundings) $16.95

Grades: 7 8 9 10

1. Chinese -- Fiction 2. Drug abuse -- Fiction 3. Friendship -- Fiction 4. Immigrants -- Fiction 5. Prejudices -- Fiction 6. Native Americans -- Fiction

ISBN 978-1-55143-955-6; 1-55143-955-7

"Jason Chen, 17, wants to leave his small town in Canada and return to China. . . . His white high-school teachers do not know how smart he is, and his classmates jeer at him. Driven to join the crowd of potheads, he bonds especially with his Native American classmate, Charles ('Chief'). Narrated in Jason's wry, first-person, present-tense narrative, Yee's slim novel packs in a lot. . . . The clipped dialogue perfectly echoes the contemporary scene, the harsh prejudice felt by the new immigrant and the Native American, and their gripping friendship story." Booklist

Yep, Laurence, 1948-

★ **Dragonwings**; Golden Mountain chronicles: 1903. Harper & Row 1975 248p lib bdg $16.89; pa $6.99

Grades: 6 7 8 9

1. Chinese Americans -- Fiction

ISBN 0-06-026738-0 lib bdg; 0-06-440085-9 pa

A Newbery Medal honor book, 1976

"In 1903 Moon Shadow, eight years old, leaves China for the 'Land of the Golden Mountains,' San Francisco, to be with his father, Windrider, a father he has never seen. There, beset by the trials experienced by most foreigners in America, Moonrider shares his father's dream—to fly. This dream enables Windrider to endure the mockery of the other Chinese, the poverty he suffers in this hostile place—the land of the white demons—and his loneliness for his wife and his own country." Shapiro. Fic for Youth. 3d edition

Yolen, Jane

Curse of the Thirteenth Fey; the True Tale of Sleeping Beauty. Jane Yolen. Philomel Books 2012 290 p. $16.99

Grades: 6 7 8 9 10

1. Curses -- Fiction 2. Fairy tales 3. Elves -- Fiction 4. Magic -- Fiction 5. Fairies -- Fiction 6. Prophecies -- Fiction 7. Family life -- Fiction

ISBN 0399256644; 9780399256646

LC 2011038847

In author Jane Yolen's book, "Gorse is the thirteenth . . . in a family of fairies tied to the evil king's land and made to do his bidding. . . . When accident-prone Gorse falls ill just as the family is bid to bless the new princess . . . [she] races to the castle with the last piece of magic the family has left. . . . But that is when accident, mayhem, and magic combine to drive Gorse's story into the unthinkable, threatening the baby, the kingdom, and all." (Publisher's note)

Dragon's blood. Harcourt 2004 303p (Pit dragon chronicles) pa $6.95

Grades: 6 7 8 9

1. Fantasy fiction 2. Dragons -- Fiction

ISBN 0-15-205126-0

LC 2003-56661

A reissue of the title first published 1982 by Delacorte Press

Jakkin, a bond boy who works as a Keeper in a dragon nursery on the planet Austar IV, secretly trains a fighting pit dragon of his own in hopes of winning his freedom

"An original and engrossing fantasy." Horn Book

Other titles in this series are:

Heart's blood (2004)

Sending of dragons (2004)

Dragon's heart (2009)

★ The **Rogues**; [by] Jane Yolen & Robert J. Harris. Philomel Books 2007 277p $18.99

Grades: 7 8 9 10

    1. Adventure fiction

    ISBN 978-0-399-23898-7

LC 2006-26434

After his family is evicted from their Scottish farm, fifteen-year-old Roddy forms an unlikely friendship with a notorious rogue who helps him outwit a tyrant landlord in order to find a family treasure and make his way to America.

"The suspense mounts and the plot races along flawlessly in this excellent historical adventure." Booklist

Troll Bridge; a rock 'n' roll fairy tale. [by] Jane Yolen and Adam Stemple. 1st ed.; Starscape 2006 240p $16.95; pa $5.99

Grades: 7 8 9 10

    1. Fairy tales 2. Musicians -- Fiction

    ISBN 0-7653-1426-6; 0-7653-5284-2 pa

LC 2005034517

Sixteen-year-old harpist prodigy Moira is transported to a strange and mystical wilderness, where she finds herself in the middle of a deadly struggle between a magical fox and a monstrous troll.

"The story ends with a grand twist that is totally satisfying. The writing is filled with humor and straightforward prose, and the song lyrics are so well written that one can almost hear the music that accompanies them." SLJ

Yoo, Paula

Good enough. HarperTeen 2008 322p $16.99; lib bdg $17.89

Grades: 7 8 9 10

    1. Violinists -- Fiction 2. Korean Americans -- Fiction

    ISBN 978-0-06-079085-1; 978-0-06-079086-8 lib bdg

LC 2007-02985

A Korean American teenager tries to please her parents by getting into an Ivy League college, but a new guy in school and her love of the violin tempt her in new directions.

"The frequent lists, . . . SAT questions, and even spam recipes are, like Patti's convincing narration, filled with laugh-out-loud lines, but it's the deeper questions about growing up with immigrant parents, confronting racism, and how best to find success and happiness that will stay with readers." Booklist

Yoon, Nicola

★ **Everything**, everything. Nicola Yoon. Delacorte Press 2015 320 p.

    1. Allergy -- Fiction 2. Friendship -- Fiction 3. Love

-- Fiction 4. Racially mixed people -- Fiction 5. Romance fiction

9780553496642, $18.99

LC 2015002950

This young adult novel, by Nicola Yoon, tells "the story of Maddy, a girl who's literally allergic to the outside world, and Olly, the boy who moves in next door . . . and becomes the greatest risk she's ever taken. This . . . novel unfolds via vignettes, diary entries, illustrations, and more." (Publisher's note)

★ The **Sun** Is Also a Star. By Nicola Yoon. Random House Childrens Books 2016 384 p.

Grades: 8 9 10 11 12

    1. Korean Americans -- Fiction 2. Teenagers -- Fiction 3. Jamaican Americans -- Fiction 4. Immigrants -- Fiction

0553496689; 0553496697; 9780553496680; 9780553496697, $21.99

National Book Award Finalist: Young People's Literature (2016); Coretta Scott King/John Steptoe New Talent Author Award (2017); Printz Honor Book (2017)

In this book, by Nicola Yoon, "it is Natasha's last day in New York City, where she has lived for 10 years. Her family, living as undocumented immigrants in a small Brooklyn apartment, are being deported to Jamaica after her father's arrest for drunk driving. Natasha is scouring the city for a chance to stay in the United States legally. She wants the normal teen existence of her peers." (Publisher's note)

"With appeal to cynics and romantics alike, this profound exploration of life and love tempers harsh realities with the beauty of hope in a way that is both deeply moving and satisfying." Kirkus

Young, Moira

Blood red road. Margaret K. McElderry Books 2011 512p (Dustlands trilogy) $17.99

Grades: 6 7 8 9 10

    1. Science fiction 2. Twins -- Fiction 3. Orphans -- Fiction 4. Siblings -- Fiction 5. Kidnapping -- Fiction

    ISBN 978-1-4424-2998-7; 1-4424-2998-4

LC 2011-03423

"When 18-year-old Saba's father is killed and her twin brother, Lugh, is kidnapped, she sets out to rescue him, along with their younger sister, Emmi, and Saba's intelligent raven, Nero. Their travels across the desert wasteland bring them to a violent city in which Saba is forced to fight for her life in an arena. When she escapes with the help of a group of women warriors, she and her new allies (including a handsome and infuriating male warrior named Jack) try to prevent Lugh from being sacrificed. Readers will . . . be riveted by the book's fast-paced mix of action and romance. It's a natural for Hunger Games fans." Publ Wkly

Yovanoff, Brenna

Fiendish. Brenna Yovanoff. Razorbill 2014 352 p.

Grades: 9 10 11 12

    1. Love -- Fiction 2. Magic -- Fiction 3. Supernatural -- Fiction

1595146385; 9781595146380, $17.99

LC 2013047610

In this book, by Brenna Yovanoff, "when Clementine was a child, dangerous and inexplicable things started happening in New South Bend. The townsfolk blamed the fiendish people out in the Willows and burned their homes to the ground. But magic kept Clementine alive, walled up in the cellar for ten years, until a boy named Fisher sets her free. Back in the world, Clementine sets out to discover what happened all those years ago. But the truth gets muddled in her dangerous attraction to Fisher." (Publisher's note)

"When Clementine, in a magical coma for years, is awakened, eerie things (grotesquely mutated animals, animated plants, uncanny weather) begin to happen. Clementine must sift through the mysteries of her childhood to figure out what's causing the wild magic. Yovanoff's worldbuilding is sophisticated and precise. Powerful, haunting prose brings to life a world overflowing with wild magic, seething prejudice, and base fear." Horn Book

★ **Places** no one knows. Brenna Yovanoff. Delacorte Press 2016 384 p.
Grades: 9 10 11 12
    1. Dreams -- Fiction 2. High schools -- Fiction 3. Schools -- Fiction 4. Self-perception -- Fiction 5. Sleep -- Fiction 6. School stories
9780553522631, $17.99; 9780553522648
                  LC 2015015299

In this novel, by Brenna Yovanoff, "Waverly Camdenmar spends her nights . . . [with] the tiny, nagging suspicion that there's more to life than student council and GPAs. Marshall Holt is a loser. He drinks on school nights and gets stoned in the park. . . . But then one night Waverly falls asleep and dreams herself into Marshall's bedroom. . . . In Waverly's dreams, the rules have changed. But in her days, she'll have to decide if it's worth losing everything for a boy who barely exists." (Publisher's note)

"There are two Waverly Camdenmars. One is the Waverly everyone sees: smart, driven, untouchable. The other is the Waverly who runs at night until her feet bleed, who spends hours meticulously analyzing her fellow students so she knows how to behave, and who, one night, dreams herself into the bedroom of Marshall Holt, a thoughtful slackerstoner with a troubled home life who shouldn't even be on her radar. As her nighttime wanderings continue and their connection grows, Waverly must decide if he is something she wants in her waking life as well. . . . This is a tightly woven, luminously written novel that captures the uncertain nature of high school and the difficult path of self-discovery." Booklist

★ The **replacement**. Razorbill 2010 343p $17.99
Grades: 9 10 11 12
    1. Fantasy fiction 2. Death -- Fiction 3. Siblings -- Fiction 4. Supernatural -- Fiction 5. Missing children -- Fiction
ISBN 978-1-59514-337-2; 1-59514-337-8
                  LC 2010-36066
Sixteen-year-old Mackie Doyle knows that he replaced a human child when he was just an infant, and when a friend's sister disappears he goes against his family's and town's deliberate denial of the problem to confront the beings that dwell under the town, tampering with human lives.

"Yovanoff's spare but haunting prose creates an atmosphere shrouded in gloom and secrecy so that readers, like Mackie, must attempt to make sense of a situation ruled by chaos and fear. The ethical complications of the town's deal with the creatures of Mayhem are clearly presented but never overwrought, while Mackie's problematic relationship to the townspeople as both an outsider and a savior is poignantly explored." Bull Cent Child Books

Zadoff, Allen

★ **Boy** Nobody; a novel by Allen Zadoff. 1st ed. Little, Brown, and Co. 2013 352 p. (hardcover) $18
Grades: 9 10 11 12
    1. Assassins -- Fiction 2. Undercover operations -- Fiction 3. Teenagers -- Conduct of life -- Fiction 4. Schools -- Fiction 5. High schools -- Fiction 6. Conduct of life -- Fiction 7. Interpersonal relations -- Fiction
ISBN 0316199680; 9780316199681
                  LC 2012029484
In this book by Allen Zadoff, the "unnamed 16-year-old protagonist lost his identity when he was kidnapped and his parents murdered. Forced into a grueling training program, the teen now gets sent on undercover missions, befriending the children of powerful targets, getting invited to their houses, and killing their parents. He never questions his orders or actions until he's given five days to infiltrate a ritzy private school and kill the mayor of New York City." (Publishers Weekly)

I am the mission: a novel. By Allen Zadoff. Little, Brown and Co. 2014 432 p. (Unknown Assassin)
Grades: 9 10 11 12
    1. Assassins -- Fiction; 2. Brainwashing -- Fiction; 3. Adventure fiction
0316199699; 9780316199698, $18; 9780316255042
                  LC 2013024561
In this young adult adventure novel by Allen Zadoff, part of The Unknown Assassin series, "Boy Nobody, haunted by the outcome of his last assignment, is given a new mission. . . . His objective: take out Eugene Moore, the owner of a military training and indoctrination camp for teenagers. . . . It sounds simple, but a previous operative couldn't do it. He lost the mission and is presumed dead. Boy Nobody is confident he can finish the job. Quickly." (Publisher's note)

"Zadoff has crafted another highly suspenseful, compulsively readable futuristic thriller with an agreeably intricate plot and a sympathetic-though often cold-blooded-protagonist." Booklist

Zail, Suzy

Playing for the commandant; Suzy Zail . Candlewick Press. 2014 245p $16.99
Grades: 7 8 9 10 11 12
    1. Concentration camps -- Fiction 2. Historical fiction 3. Birkenau (Concentration camp) -- Fiction 4. Pianists -- Fiction 5. Holocaust, 1933-1945 —Fiction
ISBN: 0763664030; 9780763664039
                  LC 2013955694
"Hanna, 15, is a talented pianist living in Hungary in 1944, until the SS storms the ghetto and takes her and her family to Birkenau. The camp is a horror, but Hanna and her sister manage to survive. When word gets out that Hanna

is a gifted musician, she is selected to play piano daily in the commandant's drawing room...Zail's story is as gut-wrenching as any Holocaust tale, particularly when, upon their liberation by Russian troops, Hanna discovers that her own dehumanizing experiences in the labor camp were nothing compared to the barbarity that occurred in the extermination camps. The haunting, matter-of-fact tone of Hanna's story will likely resonate with teens learning about the Holocaust." Booklist

Zappia, Francesca

★ **Eliza** and her monsters. Francesca Zappia. Greenwillow Books, an Imprint of HarperCollins Publishers 2017 Iv, 385 p. Illustration
Grades: 9 10 11 12

> 1. Depression (Psychology) -- Fiction; 2. Teenage girls -- Fiction; 3. Internet -- Fiction
> 9780062290137, $17.99; 9780062290151

> LC 2017934160

In this book, by Francesca Zappia, "Eliza Mirk is shy, weird, smart, and friendless. Online, Eliza is LadyConstellation, the anonymous creator of a popular webcomic... with millions of followers...Then Wallace Warland transfers to her school, and Eliza begins to wonder if a life offline might be worthwhile. But when Eliza's secret is accidentally shared . . ., everything she's built -- her story, her relationship with Wallace, and even her sanity -- begins to fall apart." (Publisher's note)

"A wrenching depiction of depression and anxiety, respectful to fandom, online-only friendships, and the benefits and dangers of internet fame." Kirkus

Zarr, Sara

★ **Gem** & Dixie. Sara Zarr. Harpercollins Childrens Books 2017 288 p.
Grades: 8 9 10 11 12

> 1. Dysfunctional families -- Fiction; 2. Runaway teenagers -- Fiction; 3. Sisters -- Fiction
> 9780062434623, $16.99; 0062434594; 9780062434593, $17.99

In this book, by Sara Zarr, "Gem has never known what it is to have security. She's never known an adult she can truly rely on. But the one constant in her life has been Dixie. Gem grew up taking care of her sister when no one else could.... Even as Gem and Dixie have grown apart, they've always had each other. When their dad returns home for the first time in years and tries to insert himself back into their lives, Gem finds herself with an unexpected opportunity." (Publisher's note)

"A thoughtful work that will resonate with Zarr's many fans and those who appreciate contemplative, character-driven novels." SLJ

★ **How** to save a life; Sara Zarr. Little, Brown 2011 341 p. $17.99
Grades: 6 7 8 9 10 11 12

> 1. Adoption -- Fiction 2. Bereavement -- Fiction 3. Mother-daughter relationship -- Fiction 4. Colorado -- Fiction 5. Pregnancy -- Fiction 6. Family life -- Fiction
> ISBN 9780316036061

> LC 2010045832

Told from their own viewpoints, seventeen-year-old Jill, in grief over the loss of her father, and Mandy, nearly nineteen, are thrown together when Jill's mother agrees to adopt Mandy's unborn child but nothing turns out as they had anticipated.

"Filled with so many frustrations, so many dilemmas needing reasonable solutions, and so much hope and faith in the midst of sadness, Zarr's novel is a rich tapestry of love and survival that will resonate with even the most cynical readers." Booklist

★ The **Lucy** variations; by Sara Zarr. 1st ed. Little, Brown and Co. 2013 320 p. (hardcover) $17.99
Grades: 7 8 9 10 11 12

> 1. Pianists -- Fiction 2. Brothers and sisters -- Fiction 3. Ability -- Fiction 4. San Francisco (Calif.) -- Fiction 5. Family life -- California -- Fiction 6. Self-actualization (Psychology) -- Fiction
> ISBN 031620501X; 9780316205016

> LC 2012029852

In this novel, by Sara Zarr, "Lucy Beck-Moreau once had a promising future as a concert pianist. . . . Now, at sixteen, it's over. A death, and a betrayal, led her to walk away. That leaves her talented ten-year-old brother, Gus, to shoulder the full weight of the Beck-Moreau family expectations. Then Gus gets a new piano teacher who is young, kind, and interested in helping Lucy rekindle her love of piano--on her own terms." (Publisher's note)

"The third-person narration focuses entirely on Lucy but allows readers enough distance to help them understand her behavior in ways Lucy cannot. Occasional flashbacks fill out the back story. The combination of sympathetic main character and unusual social and cultural world makes this satisfying coming-of-age story stand out." Kirkus

★ **Once** was lost. Little, Brown 2009 217p $16.99
Grades: 7 8 9 10

> 1. Clergy -- Fiction 2. Alcoholism -- Fiction 3. Kidnapping -- Fiction 4. Christian life -- Fiction
> ISBN 978-0-316-03604-7; 0-316-03604-8

> LC 2009-25187

As the tragedy of a missing girl unfolds in her small town, fifteen-year-old Samara, who feels emotionally abandoned by her parents, begins to question her faith.

"This multilayered exploration of the intersection of the spiritual life and imperfect people features suspense and packs an emotional wallop." SLJ

Roomies; Sara Zarr and Tara Altebrando. Little, Brown and Company 2014 288 p. $18
Grades: 9 10 11 12

> 1. Roommates -- Fiction 2. Teenage girls -- Fiction 3. Email -- Fiction 4. Friendship -- Fiction 5. Dating (Social customs) -- Fiction 6. Family life -- California -- Fiction 7. Family life -- New Jersey -- Fiction
> ISBN 0316217492; 9780316217491

> LC 2012048431

"Jersey girl Elizabeth (EB) and San Franciscan Lauren, soon to be college roommates, correspond throughout the summer; chapters with alternating perspectives unwrap each girl's backstory, personality, and coming-to-terms with changes looming on the horizon. The premise will have mass appeal with teens who fantasize about their post-high-school futures, and the authors succeed in presenting two distinct and relatable narrative voices." (Horn Book)

★ **Story** of a girl; a novel. Little, Brown 2006 192p $16.99

Grades: 10 11 12

1. California -- Fiction 2. Family life -- Fiction

ISBN 978-0-316-01453-3; 0-316-01453-2

LC 2005-28467

In the three years since her father caught her in the back seat of a car with an older boy, sixteen-year-old Deanna's life at home and school has been a nightmare, but while dreaming of escaping with her brother and his family, she discovers the power of forgiveness.

"This highly recommended novel will find a niche with older, more mature readers because of frank references to sex and some x-rated language." Voice Youth Advocates

★ **Sweethearts**. Little, Brown and Co. 2008 217p $16.99

Grades: 8 9 10 11 12

1. Love stories 2. School stories 3. Utah -- Fiction 4. Weight loss -- Fiction

ISBN 978-0-316-01455-7; 0-316-01455-9

LC 2007-41099

After losing her soul mate, Cameron, when they were nine, Jennifer, now seventeen, transformed herself from the unpopular fat girl into the beautiful and popular Jenna, but Cameron's unexpected return dredges up memories that cause both social and emotional turmoil.

"Zarr's writing is remarkable. . . . She conveys great delicacy of feeling and shades of meaning, and the realistic, moving ending will inspire excellent discussion." Booklist

Zeises, Lara M.

The **sweet** life of Stella Madison; [by] Lara Zeises. Delacorte Press 2009 230p $16.99; lib bdg $19.99

Grades: 9 10 11 12

1. Food -- Fiction 2. Journalism -- Fiction 3. Family life -- Fiction 4. Dating (Social customs) -- Fiction

ISBN 978-0-385-73146-1; 0-385-73146-9; 978-0-385-90178-9 lib bdg; 0-385-90178-X lib bdg

LC 2008-32024

Seventeen-year-old Stella struggles with the separation of her renowned chef parents, writing a food column for the local paper even though she is a junk food addict, and having a boyfriend but being attracted to another.

The author "has created a refreshing protagonist sure to captivate readers, who will enjoy following along as she learns about romance through food, and vice versa." SLJ

Zentner, Jeff

★ **Goodbye** days. Jeff Zentner. Crown Books for Young Readers 2017 404 p.

Grades: 8 9 10 11 12

1. Best friends -- Fiction; 2. Distracted driving -- Fiction; 3. Friendship -- Fiction; 4. Grief -- Fiction; 5. Guilt -- Fiction; 6. Text messaging (Cell phone systems) and

traffic accidents -- Fiction; 7. Traffic accidents -- Fiction

9780553524086; 9780553524062, $17.99; 9780553524079

LC 2016008248

This novel, by Jeff Zentner, "asks what you would do if you could spend one last day with someone you lost. Where are you guys? Text me back. That's the last message Carver Briggs will ever send his three best friends, Mars, Eli, and Blake. He never thought that it would lead to their death. Now Carver can't stop blaming himself for the accident and even worse, a powerful judge is pressuring the district attorney to open up a criminal investigation." (Publisher's note)

"A fine cautionary tale and journey toward wisdom, poignant and realistic." Kirkus

★ The **serpent** king. Jeff Zentner. Crown Books for Young Readers 2016 384 p.

Grades: 9 10 11 12

1. Country life -- Fiction 2. Friendship -- Fiction 3. Self-actualization (Psychology) -- Fiction 4. Teenagers -- Fiction 5. Bildungsromans

9780553524024, $17.99; 9780553524031

LC 2014044883

William C. Morris Award (2017)

In this novel, by Jeff Zentner, "Dill has had to wrestle with vipers his whole life-at home, as the only son of a Pentecostal minister who urges him to handle poisonous rattlesnakes, and at school, where he faces down bullies who target him. . . . He and his fellow outcast friends must try to make it through their senior year of high school without letting the small-town culture destroy their creative spirits and sense of self." (Publisher's note)

"Characters, incidents, dialogue, the poverty of the rural South, enduring friendship, a desperate clinging to strange faiths, fear of the unknown, and an awareness of the courage it takes to survive, let alone thrive, are among this fine novel's strengths. Zentner writes with understanding and grace—a new voice to savor." Kirkus

Zettel, Sarah

Bad luck girl; Sarah Zettel. Random House Inc. 2014 357p $17.99

Grades: 7 8 9 10

1. Fairies -- Fiction 2. Magic -- Fiction 3. Racially mixed people -- Fiction 4. Chicago (Ill.) -- Fiction

ISBN: 0375869409; 9780375869402; 9780375969409

LC 2013013855

In this concluding volume to the author's American fairy trilogy, "half-fairy, half-human Callie . . . has reunited with her family, thus starting a war between the two fairy kingdoms. Fleeing Los Angeles for Chicago, Callie realizes that to end the war she must stand and fight. Zettel brings the street life, locales, and culture of jazz-age Chicago into the imagery of her fantasy, packing the story with incident and adventure." Horn Book

Dust girl; Sarah Zettel. Random House 2012 292 p. (trade : alk. paper) $17.99

Grades: 6 7 8 9

1. Fairies -- Fiction 2. Voyages and travels -- Fiction 3. Father-daughter relationship -- Fiction 4. Magic --

Fiction
ISBN 9780375869389; 9780375873812;
9780375969386; 9780375983184

LC 2011043310

In this book, "a mixed-race girl in Dust Bowl Kansas discovers her long-lost father isn't just a black man: He's a fairy. . . . [A] strange man . . . tells Callie secrets of her never-met father. Soon Callie's walking the dusty roads with Jack, a ragged white kid. . . . Callie and Jack dodge fairy politics and dangers, from grasshopper people to enchanted food to magic movie theaters--but the conventional dangers are no less threatening." (Kirkus Reviews)

Golden girl; by Sarah Zettel. 1st ed. Random House Inc. 2013 308 p. (The American fairy trilogy) (hardcover) $17.99; (library) $20.99
Grades: 7 8 9 10

    1. Fantasy fiction 2. Voyages and travels 3. Magic -- Fiction 4. Fairies -- Fiction 5. Racially mixed people -- Fiction 6. Hollywood (Los Angeles, Calif.) -- History -- 20th century -- Fiction
ISBN 0375869395; 9780375869396; 9780375969393

LC 2013006238

In this book, it's 1935, and Callie LeRoux has journeyed to Hollywood from Slow Run, Kan., in search of her white human mother and black fairy father. A fairy kidnap attempt is foiled by none other than the famous Renaissance man Paul Robeson, a human who seems impervious to fairy magic. . . . Callie just wants to find her parents and get the heck out of Dodge, but with a prophecy hanging over her head, it won't be easy." (Kirkus Reviews)

Palace of Spies; being a true, accurate, and complete account of the scandalous and wholly remarkable adventures of Margaret Preston Fitzroy... by Sarah Zettel. Harcourt, Houghton Mifflin Harcourt 2013 368 p. (Palace of spies) $16.99
Grades: 8 9 10

    1. Spies -- Fiction 2. London (England) -- Fiction 3. Great Britain -- History -- 1714-1837 -- Fiction 4. Love -- Fiction 5. Orphans -- Fiction 6. Courts and courtiers -- Fiction 7. London (England) -- History -- 18th century -- Fiction
ISBN 0544074114; 9780544074118

LC 2012046366

"In eighteenth-century London, destitute orphan Peggy Fitzroy agrees to impersonate the recently deceased spy Lady Francesca as maid of honor to Princess Caroline. With a war of succession, jilted love, and religious turmoil in the mix, Peggy must navigate intrigue and shady liaisons to uncover the truth behind her predecessor's death. The feisty narrator and lush period details will garner fans for this new series." (Horn Book)

Zevin, Gabrielle

    All these things I've done. Farrar Straus Giroux 2011 354p $16.99
Grades: 8 9 10 11 12

    1. Science fiction 2. Celebrities -- Fiction 3. Family life -- Fiction 4. New York (N.Y.) -- Fiction 5. Organized

crime -- Fiction
ISBN 978-0-374-30210-8

LC 2010035873

In a future where chocolate and caffeine are contraband, teenage cellphone use is illegal, and water and paper are carefully rationed, sixteen-year-old Anya Balanchine finds herself thrust unwillingly into the spotlight as heir apparent to an important New York City crime family.

"Offering the excitement of a crime drama and the allure of forbidden romance, this introduction to a reluctant Godfather-in-the-making will pique the interest of dystopia-hungry readers." Publ Wkly

Because it is my blood; Gabrielle Zevin. Farrar Straus Giroux 2012 350 p. $17.99
Grades: 7 8 9 10

    1. Crime -- Fiction 2. Criminals -- Fiction 3. High school students -- Fiction 4. Science fiction 5. Mexico -- Fiction 6. Violence -- Fiction 7. Chocolate -- Fiction 8. Celebrities -- Fiction 9. New York (N.Y.) -- Fiction 10. Organized crime -- Fiction 11. Oaxaca de Juárez (Mexico) -- Fiction 12. Family life -- New York (State) -- New York -- Fiction
ISBN 0374380740; 9780374380748

LC 2011036991

In Gabrielle Zeven's book, "Anya Balanchine is determined to follow the straight and narrow . . . since her release from Liberty Children's Facility . . . Unfortunately, her criminal record is making it hard for her to do that. No high school wants her with a gun possession charge . . . But when old friends return demanding that certain debts be paid, Anya is thrown right back into the criminal world that she had been determined to escape." (Macmillan)

Elsewhere. Farrar, Straus & Giroux 2005 275p $16; pa $6.95
Grades: 7 8 9 10

    1. Death -- Fiction 2. Future life -- Fiction
ISBN 0-374-32091-8; 0-312-36746-5 pa

LC 2004-56279

After fifteen-year-old Liz Hall is hit by a taxi and killed, she finds herself in a place that is both like and unlike Earth, where she must adjust to her new status and figure out how to "live."

"Zevin's third-person narrative calmly, but surely guides readers through the bumpy landscape of strongly delineated characters dealing with the most difficult issue that faces all of us. A quiet book that provides much to think about and discuss." SLJ

Memoirs of a teenage amnesiac. Farrar, Straus and Giroux 2007 271p $17; pa $8.99
Grades: 7 8 9 10

    1. School stories 2. Amnesia -- Fiction 3. Friendship -- Fiction
ISBN 978-0-374-34946-2; 0-374-34946-0; 978-0-312-56128-4 pa; 0-312-56128-8 pa

LC 2006-35287

After a nasty fall, Naomi realizes that she has no memory of the last four years and finds herself reassessing every aspect of her life.

This is a "sensitive, joyful novel. . . . Pulled by the the heart-bruising love story, readers will pause to contemplate irresistible questions." Booklist

Zhang, Amy

Falling into place. By Amy Zhang. Greenwillow Books 2014 304 p.

Grades: 9 10 11 12

 1. Conduct of life -- Fiction 2. Emotional problems -- Fiction 3. High schools -- Fiction 4. Interpersonal relations -- Fiction 5. Schools -- Fiction 6. Suicide -- Fiction 7. Teenagers -- Suicide
0062295047; 9780062295040, $17.99

           LC 2014018247

In this young adult novel by Amy Zhang, "one cold fall day, high school junior Liz Emerson steers her car into a tree. . . . [This] nonlinear novel pieces together the short and devastating life of Meridian High's most popular junior girl. Mass, acceleration, momentum, force—Liz didn't understand it in physics, and even as her Mercedes hurtles toward the tree, she doesn't understand it now." (Publisher's note)

"Although the subject matter is heavy and there are a few easily brushed-off awkward moments, the breezy yet powerful and exceptionally perceptive writing style, multifaceted characters, surprisingly hopeful ending, and pertinent contemporary themes frame an engrossing, thought-provoking story that will be snapped up by readers." SLJ

This Is Where the World Ends. By Amy Zhang. Harpercollins Childrens Books 2016 304 p. Illustration

Grades: 9 10 11 12

 1. Secrets -- Fiction 2. Friendship -- Fiction 3. Missing persons -- Fiction
0062383043; 9780062383044, $17.99

This book, by Amy Zhang, is "about best friends on a collision course with the real world. . . . Janie and Micah, Micah and Janie. That's how it's been ever since elementary school, when Janie Vivien moved next door. Janie says Micah is everything she is not. . . . It's the perfect friendship-as long as no one finds out about it. But then Janie goes missing and everything Micah thought he knew about his best friend is colored with doubt." (Publisher's note)

"Edgy, taut, and compelling, this is a story of unrequited love, betrayal, and apocalyptic changes using lyrical language wrought with symbolism. . . . . The breadth of topics covered, figurative language employed, page-turning suspense, and spot-on delivery render this novel a must-have for high school libraries." SLJ

Zhang, Kat, 1991-

Once we were; the second book in the Hybrid chronicles. Kat Zhang. HarperTeen 2014 340 p. $17.99

Grades: 8 9 10 11 12

 1. Science fiction 2. Sisters -- Fiction 3. Identity (Psychology) -- Fiction 4. Resistance to government -- Fiction 5. Identity -- Fiction 6. Government, Resistance to -- Fiction
ISBN 0062114905; 9780062114907; 9780062114914

           LC 2013032811

In this sequel to "What's Left of Me," by Kat Zhang, "Eva and Addie struggle to share their body as they clash over romance and join the fight for hybrid freedom. . . . Addie and Eva escaped imprisonment at a horrific psychiatric hospital. Now they should be safe, living among an underground hybrid movement. But safety is starting to feel constricting. Faced with the possibility of being in hiding forever, the girls are eager to help bring about change—now." (Publisher's note)

"Because sisters Addie and Eva grew up hiding their hybrid nature, they're now learning—along with readers -- some of the nuances of what it means for two souls to share one body...Zhang has a unique challenge: she must give each character two distinct personalities, which she skillfully manages. While this book lacks some of the freshness of What's Left of Me (HarperCollins, 2012), simply by virtue of being a sequel, the lovely, atmospheric storytelling is still very much present. Zhang has envisioned a complex, unique world and deftly brings it to life." (School Library Journal)

What's left of me. Harper 2012 343 p. $17.99

Grades: 8 9 10 11 12

 1. Twins 2. Dystopian fiction 3. Science fiction
ISBN 0062114875; 9780062114877

           LC 2012289047

This novel, by Kat Zhang, is the first book of the young adult science fiction "Hybrid Chronicles." "Eva and Addie started out the same way as everyone else--two souls woven together in one body, taking turns controlling their movements. . . . Finally Addie was pronounced healthy and Eva was declared gone. Except, she wasn't. . . . For the past three years, Eva has clung to the remnants of her life, . . . for a chance to smile, to twirl, to speak, Eva will do anything." (Publisher's note)

Zindel, Paul

★ The **Pigman**; a novel. Harper & Row 1968 182p hardcover o.p. pa $6.99

Grades: 7 8 9 10

 ISBN 0-06-026828-X; 0-06-0757353-3 pa
 ALA YALSA Margaret A. Edwards Award (2002)

"John Conlan and Lorraine Jensen, high school sophomores, are both troubled young people who have problems at home. They become friendly with an elderly widower, Mr. Pignati, who welcomes them into his home and shares with them his simple pleasures, including his collection of ceramic pigs, of which he is proud. When the Pigman, as the young people call him, goes to the hospital after a heart attack, they take advantage of his house for a party that becomes destructive. The consequences are tragic and propel the two young friends into more responsible behavior." Shapiro. Fic for Youth. 3d edition

 Another title about the Pigman is:
 The Pigman's legacy (1980)

Zink, Michelle

Guardian of the Gate. Little, Brown 2010 340p $17.99

Grades: 7 8 9 10

 1. Magic -- Fiction 2. Twins -- Fiction 3. Sisters -- Fiction 4. Supernatural -- Fiction 5. Good and evil

-- Fiction

ISBN 978-0-316-03447-0; 0-316-03447-9

Sequel to: Prophecy of the sisters (2009)

In 1891 London, sixteen-year-old orphan Lia Milthorpe continues her quest to end an ancient prophecy requiring her to search for missing pages and human "keys" and develop her powers for an inevitable final confrontation with her twin sister Alice.

"An intense and captivating story that gives a whole new meaning to sibling rivalry." Voice Youth Advocates

Prophecy of the sisters. Little, Brown 2009 343p $17.99

Grades: 7 8 9 10

1. Twins -- Fiction 2. Sisters -- Fiction 3. Supernatural -- Fiction 4. Good and evil -- Fiction

ISBN 978-0-316-02742-7; 0-316-02742-1

LC 2008-45290

In late nineteenth-century New York state, wealthy sixteen-year-old twin sisters Lia and Alice Milthorpe find that they are on opposite sides of an ancient prophecy that has destroyed their parents and seeks to do even more harm.

"This arresting story takes readers to other planes of existence." Booklist

Followed by: Guardian of the gate (2010)

Zinn, Bridget

Poison; by Bridget Zinn. 1st ed. Disney/Hyperion Books 2013 276 p. (hardcover) $16.99

Grades: 7 8 9 10 11 12

1. Occult fiction 2. Fantasy fiction 3. Fantasy 4. Magic -- Fiction 5. Heroes -- Fiction 6. Princesses -- Fiction 7. Impersonation -- Fiction 8. Fugitives from justice -- Fiction

ISBN 1423139933; 9781423139935

LC 2012008693

In this novel, sixteen-year-old "Kyra is on the run. She may be one of the Kingdom of Mohr's most highly skilled potions masters, but she has also just tried—and failed—to poison Princess Ariana. And Kyra is determined to finish her mission even if it means killing her best friend. . . . In order to save her kingdom from a nefarious plot, Kyra will have to come to terms with all the gifts she possesses." (School Library Journal)

Zoboi, Ibi

★ **American** street. Ibi Zoboi. Harpercollins Childrens Books 2017 336 p.

Grades: 9 10 11 12

1. Haitians -- United States -- Fiction; 2. Immigrants -- Fiction; 3. Mother-daughter relationship -- Fiction

0062473042; 9780062473042, $17.99

LC 2017006125

National Book Award Finalist: Young People's Literature (2017)

In this novel, by Ibi Zoboi, "on the corner of American Street and Joy Road, Fabiola Toussaint thought she would finally find une belle vie -- a good life. But after they leave Port-au-Prince, Haiti, Fabiola's mother is detained by U.S. immigration, leaving Fabiola to navigate her loud American cousins, Chantal, Donna, and Princess; the grittiness of De-

troit's west side; a new school; and a surprising romance, all on her own." (Publisher's note)

"Mixing gritty street life with the tenderness of first love, Haitian Vodou, and family bonds, the book is at once chilling, evocative, and reaffirming." Pub Wkly

Zorn, Claire

Protected. Claire Zorn. Sourcebooks Fire 2017 276 p.

Grades: 9 10 11 12

1. Bullying -- Fiction; 2. Counseling -- Fiction; 3. Death -- Fiction; 4. Friendship -- Fiction; 5. Grief -- Fiction; 6. Self-realization -- Fiction; 7. Australia -- Fiction; 8. Bullies -- Fiction

9781492652137, $17.99; 9781492652144

LC 2016050932

In this novel, by Claire Zorn, "Hannah has survived high school by putting up walls. At first, they were meant to protect her from the relentless bullying that no one would defend her from, not even her popular older sister, Katie. Then Katie died, and, in a cruel twist of fate, Hannah's daily torment abruptly stopped. Now the walls try to shut it all out.... Then...friendship comes knocking in the form of new student Josh Chamberlain." (Publisher's note)

"Though the book tackles important issues, it reaches far beyond these flash points into a fully developed exploration of the aftermath of tragedy through strong characterization and genuine emotional appeal." Kirkus

Originally published: Australia: University of Queensland Press, 2014.

Zusak, Markus, 1975-

★ The **book** thief. Knopf 2006 552p il $16.95; lib bdg $18.99

Grades: 8 9 10 11 12

1. Death -- Fiction 2. Jews -- Germany -- Fiction 3. Books and reading -- Fiction 4. Holocaust, 1933-1945 -- Fiction 5. World War, 1939-1945 -- Fiction

ISBN 0-375-83100-2; 0-375-93100-7 lib bdg

LC 2005-08942

Michael L. Printz Award honor book, 2007

Trying to make sense of the horrors of World War II, Death relates the story of Liesel—a young German girl whose book-stealing and storytelling talents help sustain her family and the Jewish man they are hiding, as well as their neighbors.

"This hefty volume is an achievement—a challenging book in both length and subject, and best suited to sophisticated older readers." Publ Wkly

Bridge of Clay. Markus Zusak. Alfred A. Knopf 2018 544 p.

Grades: 10 11 12

1. Abandoned children -- Fiction; 2. Bridges -- Design and construction -- Fiction; 3. Brothers -- Fiction; 4. Family life -- Fiction; 5. Secrets -- Fiction; 6. Family secrets -- Fiction

1984830155; 9780375594595; 9781984830159, $26; 9781984830166

LC 2018013864

This book, by Markus Zusak, presents the "story of five brothers who bring each other up in a world run by their own rules. As the Dunbar boys love and fight and learn to reckon with the adult world, they discover the moving secret behind their father's disappearance. At the center of the Dunbar family is Clay, a boy who will build a bridge -- for his family, for his past, for greatness, for his sins, for a miracle." (Publisher's note)

★ **I** am the messenger. Knopf 2005 357p hardcover o.p. pa $8.95

Grades: 9 10 11 12

1. Mystery fiction

ISBN 0-375-83099-5; 0-375-83667-5 pa

LC 2003-27388

Michael L. Printz Award honor book, 2006

After capturing a bank robber, nineteen-year-old cab driver Ed Kennedy begins receiving mysterious messages that direct him to addresses where people need help, and he begins getting over his lifelong feeling of worthlessness

"Zusak's characters, styling, and conversations are believably unpretentious, well conceived, and appropriately raw. Together, these key elements fuse into an enigmatically dark, almost film-noir atmosphere where unknowingly lost Ed Kennedy stumbles onto a mystery—or series of mysteries—that could very well make or break his life." SLJ

AUTHOR, TITLE, AND SUBJECT INDEX

This index to the books in the collection includes author, title, and subject entries; added entries for publishers' series, illustrators, joint authors, and editors of works entered under title; and name and subject cross-references; all arranged in one alphabet.

Acevedo, Elizabeth, ca. 1988-

The poet X: a novel

Aceves, Fred

The closest I've come

      a star-swept sea. Peterfreund, D.

      a war-tossed sea. Elliot, L.

      the Great Barrier. Wrede, P. C.

      the universe. Revis, B.

ACTION AND ADVENTURE FICTION

Silvera, A. They both die at the end

ACTORS AND ACTRESSES -- FICTION

Shukert, R. Love me

ACTORS -- FICTION

Johnson, M. Scarlett fever

Lockhart, E. Dramarama

Mantchev, L. Eyes like stars

Sones, S. One of those hideous books where the mother dies

Woodson, J. After Tupac and D Foster

ACTRESSES -- FICTION

Berry, N. The Notorious Pagan Jones

Rennison, L. The taming of the tights

Shukert, R. Love me

Adams, Richard

Watership Down

Adaptation. Lo, M.

ADDICTION -- FICTION

Bastedo, J. Cut Off

Adeyemi, Tomi

Children of blood and bone

ADIRONDACK MOUNTAINS (N.Y.) -- FICTION

Kephart, B. Wild blues

ADJUSTMENT (PSYCHOLOGY)

Jensen, C. Skyscraping

Adlington, L. J.

The diary of Pelly D

ADOLESCENCE -- FICTION

Acevedo, E. The poet X: a novel

Alsaid, A. Let's Get Lost

Calame, D. Swim the fly

Gansworth, E. Give me some truth: a novel with paintings

Grossman, N. A world away

ADOLESCENTS

See Teenagers

ADOPTED CHILDREN -- FICTION

Benway, R. Far from the tree

Gibney, S. See no color

Grey, M. The girl at midnight

Withers, P. Andreo's race

ADOPTEES -- FICTION

Kearney, M. The girl in the mirror

ADOPTION -- FICTION

Burg, A. E. All the broken pieces

Dowswell, P. The Auslander

Gibney, S. See no color

Johnson, A. Heaven

Kearney, M. The girl in the mirror

Kephart, B. Small damages

Sáenz, B. A. The inexplicable logic of my life

Smith, A. 1959-. The Alex Crow

Wein, E. Black dove, white raven

ADULTERY -- FICTION

Mankell, H. Shadow of the leopard

Sugiura, M. It's not like it's a secret

ADVENTURE AND ADVENTURERS -- FICTION

Cameron, S. Rook

Crossan, S. Breathe

Funke, C. Fearless

Golden, C. The sea wolves

Kephart, B. Wild blues

Lake, N. Hostage Three

Lee, S. Under a painted sky

Lippert-M., K. Tabula rasa

Lloyd-Jones, E. Illusive

Lowitz, L. Jet Black and the ninja wind.

McDonald, I. Empress of the sun

McQuerry, M. D. The Peculiars

Nix, G. A confusion of princes

Schreiber, J. Perry's killer playlist

Smith, A. G. The Devil's engine

Tintera, A. Reboot

Tripp, B. The accidental highwayman: being the tale of Kit Bristol, his horse Midnight, a mysterious princess, and sundry magical persons besides

Tubb, K. O. The 13th sign

Turner, M. W. Thick as thieves

Wegelius, J. The murderer's ape

Wein, E. Black dove, white raven

ADVENTURE FICTION

Ahdieh, R. Flame in the mist

Bacigalupi, P. The doubt factory

Bastedo, J. Cut Off

Block, F. L. The island of excess love

Bobet, L. Above

Carson, R. The crown of embers

Coben, H. Seconds away

Colfer, E. Airman

Doctorow, C. Homeland

Falkner, B. The project

Friesner, E. M. Nobody's princess

Funke, C. Reckless

Gavin, R. 3 of a kind

Gilman, D. The devil's breath

Golden, C. The sea wolves

Golden, C. The wild

Grant, K. M. How the hangman lost his heart

Hamilton, A. Traitor to the throne

Henderson, J. The Triumph of Death

Horowitz, A. Stormbreaker

Johnston, E. K. Prairie fire

Johnston, E. K. The story of Owen

Johnston, E. K. A thousand nights

Kephart, B. Wild blues

Kittredge, C. The nightmare garden

Landers, M. Starfall

Lippert-M., K. Tabula rasa
Lupica, M. Hero
MacHale, D. J. The merchant of death
MacHale, D. J. The pilgrims of Rayne
MacHale, D. J. SYLO
Marillier, J. Shadowfell
Mary-Todd, J. Shot down
McCaughrean, G. The death-defying Pepper Roux
McCaughrean, G. The glorious adventures of the Sunshine
  Queen
McGinnis, M. The female of the species
McKernan, V. Shackleton's stowaway
Mieville, C. Railsea
Miller, M. Shadow run
Moran, K. Bloodline
Mourlevat, J. Winter's end
Mowll, J. Operation Red Jericho
Mowll, J. Operation Storm City
Mowll, J. Operation typhoon shore
Mussi, S. The door of no return
Nix, G. A confusion of princes
O'Brien, J. Day of the assassins
Park, L. S. Click
Pike, A. Glitter
Pratchett, T. Dodger
Sangster, C. Last star burning
Schreiber, J. Au revoir, crazy European chick
Schreiber, J. Perry's killer playlist
Smith, A. G. The Devil's engine
Somper, J. Demons of the ocean
Stroud, J. Heroes of the valley
Summers, C. This is not a test
Tayleur, K. Killer Pizza: the slice
Tripp, B. The accidental highwayman: being the tale of Kit
  Bristol, his horse Midnight, a mysterious princess, and sundry
  magical persons besides
Tucholke, A. G. Between the spark and the burn
Turner, M. W. The thief
Van Diepen, A. Takedown
Woolston, B. Black helicopters
Yolen, J. The Rogues
Zadoff, A. I am the mission

ADVENTURE STORIES
See also Adventure fiction
Cameron, S. Rook
Schrefer, E. Threatened
Smith, A. G. The Devil's engine
Stohl, M. Black Widow

ADVENTURE TELEVISION PROGRAMS
See also Television programs

ADVENTURE TRAVEL
See also Travel; Voyages and travels

ADVICE COLUMNISTS -- FICTION
Weston, C. Speed of life

ADVICE COLUMNS -- FICTION
Bjorkman, L. Miss Fortune Cookie
Weston, C. Speed of life

AESTHETICS -- FICTION
Headley, J. C. North of beautiful

AFFECTION
See Friendship; Love

AFGHANISTAN -- FICTION
Doller, T. Something like normal
Staples, S. F. Under the Persimmon tree

AFGHAN WAR, 2001- -- FICTION
Doller, T. Something like normal

AFRICA -- FICTION
Kinch, M. The blending time
Kinch, M. The fires of New SUN
Kinch, M. The rebels of New SUN
Stratton, A. Chanda's secrets
Stratton, A. Chanda's wars

AFRICAN AMERICAN GIRLS -- FICTION
Moon, S. Sparrow

AFRICAN AMERICANS -- BIOGRAPHY
Shabazz, I. X

AFRICAN AMERICANS -- FICTION
Alexander, K. The crossover
Alexander, K. He said, she said
Alexander, K. Swing
Anderson, M. T. The astonishing life of Octavian Nothing,
  traitor to the nation
Blythe, C. Revenge of a not-so-pretty girl
Bolden, T. Crossing Ebenezer Creek
Booth, C. Bronxwood
Booth, C. Tyrell
Brockenbrough, M. The game of Love and Death
Brooks, B. The moves make the man; a novel
Buckhanon, K. Upstate
Coles, J. Tyler Johnson was here
Davis, T. S. A la carte
Davis, T. S. Mare's war
Dudley, D. L. Caleb's wars
Feinstein, J. Foul trouble
Flake, S. G. Bang!.
Flake, S. G. Pinned
Frank, E. R. Dime
Gibney, S. Dream country
Gibney, S. See no color
Giles, L. Fake ID
Grant, C. Teenie
Grimes, N. Bronx masquerade
Grimes, N. A girl named Mister
Grimes, N. Jazmin's notebook
Houston, J. New boy
Ireland, J. Dread nation
Johnson, A. Heaven
Johnson, A. Sweet, hereafter
Johnson, A. Toning the sweep
Lee, S. Under a painted sky
Lester, J. Day of tears
Lester, J. Guardian
Lester, J. Time's memory
Lipsyte, R. The contender

Lyons, M. E. Letters from a slave boy
Lyons, M. E. Letters from a slave girl
Maldonado, T. Secret Saturdays
Mattison, B. T. Unsigned hype; a novel
McDonald, J. Chill wind
McDonald, J. Harlem Hustle
McKissack, F. Shooting star
Moon, S. Sparrow
Moses, S. P. Joseph
Moses, S. P. The legend of Buddy Bush
Myers, W. D. All the right stuff
Myers, W. D. Amiri & Odette; a love story
Myers, W. D. The Cruisers
Myers, W. D. Darius & Twig
Nelson, Vaunda Micheaux. No crystal stair
Oakes, S. The sacred lies of Minnow Bly
Paulsen, G. Nightjohn
Perez, A. Out of darkness
Reynolds, J. Boy in the black suit
Simone, Ni-Ni. Upgrade U
Smith, S. L. Flygirl
Smith, S. The other side of dark
Stone, N. Dear Martin
Tamani, L. Calling my name
Taylor, M. D. The land
Taylor, M. D. Roll of thunder, hear my cry
Thomas, A. The hate u give
Van Diepen, A. Takedown
Volponi, P. Black and white
Walker, B. F. Black boy/white school
Walter, J. My name is not Friday
Waltman, K. Slump
Watson, R. Piecing me together
Weatherford, C. B. Becoming Billie Holiday
Williams-Garcia, R. Like sisters on the homefront
Williams, L. A. When Kambia Elaine flew in from
   Neptune
Winston, S. The Kayla chronicles.
Woods, B. Emako Blue
Woodson, J. After Tupac and D Foster
Woodson, J. Behind you
Woodson, J. From the notebooks of Melanin Sun
Woodson, J. If you come softly
Woodson, J. Miracle's boys

AFRICAN AMERICANS -- HARLEM (NEW YORK, N.Y.) -- FICTION
Myers, W. D. All the right stuff

AFRICAN AMERICANS -- FICTION
Bolden, T. Crossing Ebenezer Creek
Tamani, L. Calling my name

AFRICAN AMERICANS -- HISTORY
Patrick, D. L. A matter of souls.

AFRICAN AMERICANS -- SOUTHERN STATES -- FICTION
Patrick, D. L. A matter of souls.

AFRICAN AMERICAN TEENAGE GIRLS -- FICTION
Frank, E. R. Dime

Moon, S. Sparrow

AFRICAN AMERICAN TEENAGE GIRLS -- WASHINGTON (STATE) -- SEATTLE -- FICTION
Brockenbrough, M. The game of Love and Death

AFRICAN AMERICAN TEENAGERS -- FICTION
Jackson, T. D. Allegedly: a novel

AFRICAN AMERICAN WOMEN
See also Women

AFRICAN AMERICAN YOUTH -- FICTION
Blythe, C. Revenge of a not-so-pretty girl
Volponi, P. The Final Four

AFRICANS -- FICTION
Park, L. S. A long walk to water

AFRICANS -- UNITED STATES -- FICTION
Cooney, C. B. Diamonds in the shadow

AFRO-AMERICAN WOMEN
See African American women

After Eli. Rupp, R.
After. Prose, F.
After ever after. Sonnenblick, J.
After the first death. Cormier, R.
After the rain. Mazer, N. F.
After Tupac and D Foster. Woodson, J.

AFTERLIFE
See Future life

Aftermath. Armstrong, Kelley
Afterworlds. Westerfeld, S.

Agard, John
The young inferno

AGORAPHOBIA -- FICTION
Whaley, J. C. Highly illogical behavior

Ahdieh, Renée
Flame in the mist
The rose and the dagger
Smoke in the sun
The wrath and the dawn

Ahmed, Samira
Love, hate & other filters

AIDS (DISEASE) -- FICTION
Meaker, M. Night kites
Minchin, A. The beat goes on
Sheinmel, C. Positively
Stratton, A. Chanda's secrets

AIR PILOTS -- FICTION
Smith, S. L. Flygirl
Wein, E. Black dove, white raven
Wein, E. Code name Verity
Wein, E. Rose under fire

AIRCRAFT ACCIDENTS -- FICTION
Scott, E. Miracle

Airhead. Cabot, M.
Airman. Colfer, E.

AIRPLANES -- FICTION
Colfer, E. Airman
Horvath, P. The Corps of the Bare-Boned Plane

AIRSHIPS -- FICTION
McDonald, I. Empress of the sun

Almond, David

Half a creature from the sea
Kit's wilderness

A song for Ella Grey
The tightrope walkers
The true tale of the monster Billy Dean
      perfect. Katcher, B.
      for the ride. Dessen, S.

ALOPECIA AREATA -- FICTION

Friend, N. How we roll

Alsaid, Adi

Let's Get Lost
Never Always Sometimes
North of happy

Alsenas, Linas

Beyond clueless

Altebrando, Tara

The Leaving
      Rush, J.

ALTERNATIVE HISTORIES

Caine, R. Ink and bone
Cameron, S. The dark unwinding
Grant, M. Front Lines
Hesse, K. Safekeeping
Rutkoski, M. The shadow society

Alvarez, Julia

Before we were free
      a catch. Richmond, P.
      a witch. MacCullough, C.

ALZHEIMER'S DISEASE -- FICTION

Miller, S. A lite too bright

Amateau, Gigi

A certain strain of peculiar
    amateurs. Shepard, Sara

Amato, Mary

Get happy
    amazing Maurice and his educated rodents. Pratchett, T.

AMAZONS -- FICTION

Hoffman, A. The foretelling

AMBASSADORS -- FICTION

Carter, A. Embassy row #1: all fall down

AMBITION -- FICTION

Rivers, K. Love
      Anne is dead and gone. Rosenfield, K.

American ace. Nelson, M.

American Girls: A Novel. Umminger, A.

American road trip. Flores-Scott, P.

AMERICANS -- ETHIOPIA -- FICTION

Wein, E. Black dove, white raven

AMERICANS -- FRANCE -- FICTION

Perkins, S. Isla and the happily ever after: a novel

AMERICAN SHORT STORIES

Giles, L. Fresh ink
Patrick, D. L. A matter of souls.

AMERICAN SIGN LANGUAGE

Ferris, J. Of sound mind

AMERICANS -- IRAN -- FICTION

Khorram, A. Darius the Great is not okay

AMERICANS -- LIBERIA -- FICTION

Gibney, S. Dream country

AMERICANS -- MEXICO -- FICTION

Talley, R. Our own private universe

American street. Zoboi, I.

AMHERST (MASS.) -- FICTION

Hubbard, J. R. And we stay

AMHERST (MASS.) -- HISTORY -- 19TH CENTURY FICTION

MacColl, M. Nobody's secret

AMIN, IDI

Nanji, S. Child of dandelions

Amiri & Odette; a love story. Myers, W. D. 1937-2014

AMISH -- FICTION

Bickle, L. The hallowed ones
Bickle, L. The outside
Grossman, N. A world away

AMNESIA -- FICTION

Cameron, S. The Forgetting
Cameron, S. The knowing
Cook, E. With malice
Lockhart, E. We were liars
Lowry, L. Son
McQuein, J. L. Arclight

AMPUTEES -- FICTION

Bingham, K. Shark girl
Friend, N. How we roll
Mankell, H. Shadow of the leopard
Oakes, S. The sacred lies of Minnow Bly
Rorby, G. The outside of a horse; a novel
Van Draanen, W. The running dream
Venkatraman, P. A time to dance
Voigt, C. Izzy, willy-nilly
Waldorf, H. Tripping

AMTRAK -- FICTION

Arnold, A. Love & other train wrecks

The **Amulet** of Samarkand. Stroud, J.

AMUSEMENT PARKS -- FICTION

Shusterman, N. Full tilt; a novel

Amy Chelsea Stacie Dee. Thompson, M. G.

AMYOTROPHIC LATERAL SCLEROSIS -- FICTION

Benwell, S. The last leaves falling

Amy & Roger's epic detour. Matson, M.

The **anatomy** of wings. Foxlee, K.

ANCIENT SCROLLS -- FICTION

Kagawa, J. Shadow of the Fox

Ancient, strange, and lovely. Fletcher, S.

And I darken. White, K.

And in the morning. Wilson, J.

Anderson, Jodi Lynn

Midnight at the Electric
Speak
Twisted
Wintergirls

Anderson, Laurie Halse
The impossible knife of memory
Anderson, M. T.
The astonishing life of Octavian Nothing, traitor to the nation

Landscape with invisible hand
Anderson, Natalie C.
City of Saints & Thieves
Andreo's race. Withers, P.
Andreu, Maria E.
The secret side of empty
Andrews, Jesse
The Haters
Me & Earl & the dying girl
Munmun
    Then the Sky Exploded. Poulsen, D.
    then things fall apart. Tibensky, A.
    the ocean was our sky. Ness, P.
    we stay. Hubbard, J. R.
Angelfire. Moulton, C. A.
ANGELS -- FICTION
Brockenbrough, M. Devine intervention
Cameron, S. Out of the blue
Hand, C. Unearthly
Moulton, C. A. Angelfire
Shirvington, J. Embrace
Taylor, L. Daughter of smoke and bone
Taylor, L. Days of blood & starlight
Taylor, L. Dreams of gods & monsters
ANGELS -- TEEN FICTION
Cameron, S. Out of the blue
ANGER -- FICTION
Oshiro, M. Anger is a gift.
    is a gift. Oshiro, M.
    young man. Lynch, C.
    thongs and full-frontal snogging. Rennison, L.
ANIMAL ABUSE
See Animal welfare
ANIMAL BEHAVIOR -- FICTION
Tan, S. Tales from the inner city
ANIMAL RESCUE -- FICTION
Schrefer, E. Threatened
ANIMALS -- ANATOMY
See also Anatomy
ANIMAL SANCTUARIES -- FICTION, E.
Endangered. Schrefer, E.
ANIMALS -- COLOR
See also Color
ANIMALS -- DISEASES
See also Diseases
ANIMALS -- FICTION
Flinn, A. Cloaked
Napoli, D. J. Storm
ANIMALS -- FOLKLORE
See also Folklore
ANIMALS -- HABITS AND BEHAVIOR -- FICTION
Tan, S. Tales from the inner city

ANIMALS, MYTHICAL -- FICTION
Ritter, W. The dire king.
ANIMISM
See also Religion
Anna and the French kiss. Perkins, S.
Anna and the Swallow Man. Savit, G.
Annexed. Dogar, S.
ANOREXIA NERVOSA -- FICTION
Anderson, J. L. Wintergirls
George, M. Looks
Kaslik, I. Skinny
Price, N. Zoe letting go
Vrettos, A. M. Skin
Another Faust. Nayeri, D.
Another kind of cowboy. Juby, S.
Another Pan. Nayeri, D.
Anstey, Cindy
Carols and chaos
Love, lies and spies
ANTARCTICA -- FICTION
McCaughrean, G. The white darkness
White, A. Surviving Antarctica
Anthem for Jackson Dawes. Bryce, C.
Anthony, Jessica
Chopsticks
ANTHROPOLOGY -- FICTION
Pearson, J. The rites & wrongs of Janice Wills
ANTI-APARTHEID MOVEMENT
See also Civil rights; South Africa -- Race relations
ANTI-APARTHEID MOVEMENTS -- SOUTH AFRICA -- FICTION
Raina, A. When morning comes
Antieau, Kim
Broken moon
ANTIETAM (MD.), BATTLE OF
See also United States -- History -- 1861-1865, Civil War -- Campaigns
The **anti-prom.** McDonald, A.
ANTISEMITISM -- FICTION
Sanders, S. Rachel's secret
ANTI-UTOPIAS
See Dystopias
ANTI-WAR STORIES
See War stories
Antsy does time. Shusterman, N.
ANXIETY DISORDERS -- FICTION
Green, J. Turtles all the way down
Kinsella, S. Finding Audrey
Mac, C. 10 things I can see from here
ANXIETY -- FICTION
Kinsella, S. Finding Audrey
Mac, C. 10 things I can see from here
Oshiro, M. Anger is a gift.
Anya's war. Alban, A.
ANYWAR, RICKY RICHARD
Hutton, K. Soldier boy
APARTHEID

Abdel-Fattah, R. The lines we cross

AUSTRALIA -- FICTION
Abdel-Fattah, R. The lines we cross
Buzo, L. Love and other perishable items
Crowley, C. Words in deep blue
Foxlee, K. The anatomy of wings
Foxlee, K. The midnight dress
Groth, D. Munro vs. the coyote
Hartnett, S. Butterfly
Hartnett, S. Thursday's child
Herrick, S. By the river
Herrick, S. The wolf
Howell, S. Girl defective
James, R. Beautiful malice
Jinks, C. Evil genius
Jinks, C. Genius squad
Jinks, C. The genius wars
Larbalestier, J. Magic lessons
Marsden, J. Incurable
Marsden, J. The other side of dawn
Marsden, J. Tomorrow, when the war began.
Marsden, J. While I live
Moriarty, J. Feeling sorry for Celia
Moriarty, J. The ghosts of Ashbury High
Silvey, C. Jasper Jones
Wakefield, V. Friday never leaving
Wilkinson, L. Pink
Williams, G. Beatle meets Destiny
Wood, F. Cloudwish
Wooding, C. Velocity
Zorn, C. Protected

AUSTRALIA -- POLITICS AND GOVERNMENT -- 21ST CENTURY -- JUVENILE LITERATURE
Abdel-Fattah, R. The lines we cross

AUTHORS -- FICTION
Bjorkman, L. My invented life
Chambers, A. Dying to know you
Engle, M. Firefly letters
Golden, C. The wild
Klein, L. M. Ophelia
Marsden, J. Hamlet: a novel
Sales, L. Tonight the streets are ours
Scieszka, J. Who done it? an investigation of murder most foul.
Sheth, K. Keeping corner
Silbert, L. The intelligencer
Tibensky, A. And then things fall apart
Westerfeld, S. Afterworlds

AUTHORSHIP -- FICTION
Cooney, C. B. Janie face to face
Grimes, N. Jazmin's notebook
Hemphill, S. Hideous love
Johnson, M. Suite Scarlett
Lauren, C. Autoboyography
Lubar, D. Sleeping freshmen never lie
Myers, W. D. Darius & Twig
Nance, A. Daemon Hall
Nance, A. Return to Daemon Hall: evil roots

Redgate, R. Final draft
Scieszka, J. Who done it? an investigation of murder most foul.
Selfors, S. Mad love
Wittlinger, E. Hard love
Wittlinger, E. Love & lies
Wizner, J. Spanking Shakespeare.

AUTISM -- FICTION
Coker, R. Chasing Jupiter
Kehoe, S. W. The sound of letting go

Autoboyography. Lauren, C.

AUTOMOBILE MECHANICS -- AUSTRALIA -- FICTION
Wooding, C. Velocity

AUTOMOBILE RACING -- FICTION
Weaver, W. Saturday night dirt
Wooding, C. Velocity

AUTOMOBILE TRAVEL -- FICTION
Alsaid, A. Let's Get Lost
Borris, A. Crash into me
Bray, L. Going bovine
Brown, J. Perfect escape
Flores-Scott, P. American road trip
Leno, K. The lost & found
Lockhart, E. How to be bad
Matson, M. Amy & Roger's epic detour
Rabb, M. Kissing in America
Resau, L. Red glass
Sanchez, A. Rainbow road
Vawter, V. Copyboy
Woolston, B. Catch & release
Wunder, W. The museum of intangible things

Avasthi, Swati
Chasing Shadows
Split

AVENGERS (FICTIONAL CHARACTERS)
Stohl, M. Black Widow

Avery, Lara
The memory book

Aveyard, Victoria
King's cage
Red queen

Avi, 1937-
City of orphans
Crispin
Nothing but the truth
Traitor's gate

Axelrod, Kate
The law of loving others: a novel

Ayarbe, Heidi
Compulsion

Ayres, Katherine
North by night

B
BABYSITTERS -- FICTION
Prose, F. the turning

De la Peña, M. Ball don't lie
Deuker, C. Swagger
Feinstein, J. Foul trouble
Feinstein, J. Last shot
Lupica, M. Miracle on 49th Street
Lupica, M. Summer ball
Mackel, K. Boost
Murdock, C. G. Front and center
Soto, G. Taking sides
Volponi, P. Black and white
Waltman, K. Slump

BASKETBALL PLAYERS -- FICTION
Simone, Ni-Ni. Upgrade U

Bass, Karen
Summer of fire

Bass, Ron
On thin ice

Bassoff, Leah
Lost girl found

Bastedo, Jamie
Cut Off
   batboy Lupica, M.

BATH (ENGLAND) -- FICTION
Pitcher, A. Ketchup clouds

BATMAN (FICTIONAL CHARACTER) -- FICTION
Lu, M. Batman: Nightwalker
      Nightwalker. Lu, M.
   dress. Efaw, A.

Bauer, Joan
Hope was here

Bauman, Beth Ann
Rosie & Skate

Bayard, Louis
Lucky strikes
   my enemy. McDonald, I.

BEACHES -- FICTION
Bancks, T. Mac Slater hunts the cool
Han, J. The summer I turned pretty
Nelson, B. The y came from below

Beam, Cris

Beanball. Fehler, G.

Beard, Philip
Dear Zoe

BEARS -- FICTION
Pattou, E. East
      bones: a Jackaby novel. Ritter, W.
      Flinn, A.
      Napoli, D. J.,
   beast of Noor. Carey, J. L.
      Spangler, B.
         goes on. Minchin, A.
      meets Destiny. Williams, G.
   the band. Calame, D.

Beaudoin, Sean
Wise Young Fool

Beaufrand, Mary Jane
The rise and fall of the Gallivanters
Useless Bay

The **beautiful** and the cursed. Morgan, P.
Beautiful broken girls. Savage, K.
Beautiful malice. James, R.
Beautiful Music for Ugly Children. Cronn-Mills, K.
Beauty; a retelling of the story of Beauty & the beast. McKinley, R.

BEAUTY CONTESTS -- FICTION
Bray, L. Beauty queens
Murphy, J. Dumplin'

BEAUTY, PERSONAL -- FICTION
Clayton, D. The Belles
Friend, N. My life in black and white
Rainfield, C. Stained
Rudnick, P., 1957- Gorgeous

Beauty queens. Bray, L.
Because I am furniture. Chaltas, T.

Bechard, Margaret
Hanging on to Max

Beck. Peet, Mal
Beck. Rosoff, M.
Becoming Billie Holiday. Weatherford, C. B.

Bedford, Martyn
Flip

BEES -- FICTION
McKinley, R. Chalice

Beetle Boy. Willey, M.
Before we were free. Alvarez, J.

BEHAVIOR
See Human behavior

Behind you. Woodson, J.
Beige. Castellucci, C.
Being Audrey Hepburn: a novel. Kriegman, M.

BELACQUA, LYRA (FICTITIOUS CHARACTER) -- FICTION
Pullman, P. La Belle Sauvage

BELFAST (NORTHERN IRELAND) -- FICTION
Wilkinson, S. Taking Flight

Bell, Hilari
Fall of a kingdom
Forging the sword
The last knight

Bell, Joanne
Juggling fire

Belladonna. Finn, M.
The **Belles.** Clayton, D.

Belleza, Rhoda
Empress of a thousand skies

Belzhar. Wolitzer, M.
Beneath. Woodson, J.

Bennett, Holly
Shapeshifter

Bennett, Jenn
Alex, approximately
Starry eyes

Benway, Robin
Far from the tree
Benwell, Sarah
The last leaves falling
BEREAVEMENT -- FICTION
Beard, P. Dear Zoe
Bryant, J. Pieces of Georgia
Cooney, C. B. If the witness lied
Danticat, E. Untwine
Davies, J. Lost
Davis, R. F. Chasing AllieCat
Foxlee, K. The anatomy of wings
Frank, E. R. Wrecked
Franklin, E. The half life of planets
Friend, N. Perfect
Hale, M. The goodbye season
Herlong, M. The great wide sea
Horvath, P. The Corps of the Bare-Boned Plane
Hutchinson, S. D. The five stages of Andrew Brawley
Jaden, D. Losing Faith
James, R. Beautiful malice
Johnson, J. J. The theory of everything
Kittle, K. Reasons to be happy
Knowles, J. See you at Harry's
Matson, M. Amy & Roger's epic detour
Moskowitz, H. Gone, gone, gone.
Nelson, J. The sky is everywhere
Nolan, H. Crazy
Ockler, S. Fixing Delilah
O'Connell, M. The sharp time
Peterson, L. J. Beyond repair
Pieces Lynch, C.
Plum, A. Die for me
Proimos, J. 12 things to do before you crash and burn
Rabb, M. Kissing in America
Rupp, R. After Eli
Schroeder, L. Chasing Brooklyn
Sheinmel, C. Positively
Sones, S. One of those hideous books where the mother dies
Summers, C. Fall for anything
Thompson, H. Orchards
Verday, J. The Hollow
Watkins, S. What comes after
Williams, C. L. Waiting
Berk, Ari
Death watch
Berlin Boxing Club. Sharenow, R.
BERLIN (GERMANY) -- FICTION
Dowswell, P. The Auslander
Kephart, B. Going over
Sharenow, R. The Berlin Boxing Club
BERLIN WALL (1961-1989) -- FICTION
Berry, N. The Notorious Pagan Jones
Kephart, B. Going over
Bernard, Romily
Find me
Berry, Julie

All the truth that's in me
The passion of Dolssa
Berry, Nina
The Notorious Pagan Jones
The **best** bad luck I ever had. Levine, K.
BEST FRIENDS -- FICTION
Alexander, K. Swing
Armstrong, K. Aftermath
Barnard, S. Fragile like us
Bliss, B. We'll fly away
Carter, A. Not if I save you first
Cook, E. With malice
Deracine, A. Driving by starlight
Derting, K. The last echo
Emond, S. Bright lights, dark nights
Flake, S. G. Pinned
Haas, A. Dangerous girls
Howard, J. J. That time I joined the circus
Howland, L. Nantucket blue
Hutchinson, S. D. At the edge of the universe
Johnson, J. J. The theory of everything
Johnston, E. K. Exit, pursued by a bear
Karim, S. That thing we call a heart
Kenneally, M. Coming up for air
Keplinger, K. Run
Keyser, A. J. Pointe
King, A. S. Glory O'Brien's history of the future: a novel
Lockhart, E. Genuine fraud
Lo, M. A line in the dark
Matson, M. Since you've been gone
McCahan, E. Love and other foreign words
McGarry, K. Only a breath apart
Moracho, C. A good idea
Myers, W. D. Darius & Twig
Oliver, L. Requiem
Priest, C. I Am Princess X.
Rivers, K. Love
Salomon, P. A. All those broken angels
Scelsa, K. Fans of the impossible life
Sharpe, T. Far from you
Skuse, C. J. Rockoholic
Stone, T. I. Little do we know
Strohmeyer, S. Smart girls get what they want
Watson, R. This side of home
Williams, S. Twinmaker
Wunder, W. The museum of intangible things
Zentner, J. Goodbye days
BETRAYAL -- FICTION
Bardugo, L. The language of thorns
Devlin, C. Tell me something real
Thomas, K. Little monsters
The **betrayal** of Maggie Blair. Laird, E.
Betting Game. O'Connor, H.
Betts, A. J.
Zac and Mia
Between the devil and the deep blue sea. Tucholke, A. G.
Between the spark and the burn. Tucholke, A. G.

here and forever. Scott, E.

shades of gray. Sepetys, R.

sisters. Badoe, A.

Two Skies. O'Sullivan, J.

two worlds. Kirkpatrick, K.

us Baxters. Hegedus, B.

Between. Warman, J.

BEVERLY HILLS (CALIF.) -- FICTION

Block, F. L. Teen spirit

that girl. Toten, T.

Bewitching season. Doyle, M.

clueless. Alsenas, L.

repair. Peterson, L. J.

the chocolate war. Cormier, R.

Bick, Ilsa J.

The Sin eater's confession

Bickle, Laura

The hallowed ones

The outside

BICYCLE RACING -- FICTION

Renn, D. Latitude zero

BICYCLES AND BICYCLING -- FICTION

Renn, D. Latitude zero

BICYCLES -- FICTION

Renn, D. Latitude zero

crunch. Hautman, P.

Dose of Lucky. Jocelyn, M.

fat disaster. Fehlbaum, B.

field Lupica, M.

Lie. Mayhew, J.

Mouth & Ugly Girl. Oates, J. C.

Bigelow, Lisa Jenn

Starting from here

BIGOTRY

See Prejudices; Toleration

BILDUNGSROMANS

Acevedo, E. The poet X: a novel

Almond, D. The tightrope walkers

Alsaid, A. Let's Get Lost

Alsaid, A. North of happy

Axelrod, K. The law of loving others: a novel

Combs, S. Breakfast served anytime

Coyle, K. Vivian Apple at the end of the world

Coyle, K. Vivian Apple needs a miracle

Danforth, E. M. The miseducation of Cameron Post

Dessen, S. The moon and more

Diederich, P. Playing for the Devil's Fire

Foley, J. A. Neighborhood girls

Gansworth, E. Give me some truth: a novel with paintings

Grossman, N. A world away

Jägerfeld, J. Me on the Floor, Bleeding

Johnson, L. Muchacho

King, E. R. The hundredth queen

Kreslehner, G. I Don't Live Here Anymore

Kriegman, M. Being Audrey Hepburn: a novel

Lynch, J. N. My beautiful hippie

Marsh, K. Jepp, who defied the stars

McCahan, E. The lake effect

Moriarty, J. Feeling sorry for Celia

Mukherjee, S. Gemini

Murphy, J. Ramona Blue

Myers, W. D. All the right stuff

Ness, P. Release

Peet, M. Beck

Powell, W. C. Expiration day

Rocco, J. Swim that rock

Rosoff, M. Beck

Rupp, R. After Eli

Sáenz, B. A. Aristotle and Dante discover the secrets of the universe

Skilton, S. Bruised

Stiefvater, M. The raven king

Sugiura, M. It's not like it's a secret

Sweeney, D. The minnow

Tamani, L. Calling my name

Warman, J. The world beneath: one South African boy's struggle to be free

Weston, R. P. Blues for Zoey

Zentner, J. The serpent king

Bilen, Tracy

What she left behind

Billie Standish was here. Crocker, N.

Billingsley, Franny

Chime

Bingham, Kelly

Formerly shark girl

Shark girl

BIOETHICS -- FICTION

Werlin, N. Double helix

BIOGRAPHICAL FICTION

Atkins, J. Stone mirrors

BIOMEDICAL ENGINEERING

Grant, M. Eve & Adam

BIOTERRORISM -- FICTION

Bickle, L. The hallowed ones

The **bird** and the blade. Bannen, M.

BIRDS -- FICTION

Whaley, J. C. Where things come back

BIRKENAU (CONCENTRATION CAMP) -- FICTION

Zail, S. Playing for the commandant

BIRTH DEFECTS -- FICTION

Rosen, R. Every crooked pot

Shreve, S. The lovely shoes

Birthmarked. O'Brien, C. M.

BIRTHMARKS -- FICTION

Rainfield, C. Stained

BISEXUAL HIGH SCHOOL STUDENTS -- FICTION

Talley, R. Our own private universe

BISEXUALITY -- FICTION

Blake, A. H. Girl made of stars

Brennan, S. R. In other lands

Colbert, B. Little & Lion

Lauren, C. Autoboyography

Tregay, S. Love & leftovers; a novel in verse

for blood. Graudin, R.
Bloodhound. Pierce, T.
blood keeper. Gratton, T.
Bloodline. Moran, K.
Bloodline rising. Moran, K.
red horse. Grant, K. M.
red road. Young, M.
Rose Rebellion. Eves, R.
Bloor, Edward

Tangerine
bloods. De la Cruz, M.
flame. Grant, K. M.
noon. Westerfeld, S.
BLUE RIDGE MOUNTAINS -- FICTION
Hensley, J. N. Rites of passage
sword. McKinley, R.
thread. Feldman, R. T.
Schmatz, P.
Bluescreen. Wells, D.
for Zoey. Weston, R. P.
Blume, Judy
Forever
Tiger eyes
Blumenthal, Deborah
Mafia girl
Blundell, Judy
What I saw and how I lied
Blythe, Carolita
Revenge of a not-so-pretty girl
patrol. Thomas, E.
BOARDING SCHOOLS -- FICTION
Carriger, G. Curtsies & conspiracies
Carriger, G. Etiquette & espionage
Hubbard, J. R. And we stay
Johnson, M. The madness underneath
Johnson, M. The shadow cabinet
Kindl, P. A school for brides
Miranda, M. Hysteria
Perkins, S. Isla and the happily ever after: a novel
Philpot, C. Even in paradise
Richmond, P. Always a catch
Rowell, R. Carry on: a novel
Wolitzer, M. Belzhar
Wooding, C. Silver
Bobet, Leah

An inheritance of ashes
Bock, Caroline

Bodeen, S. A.
The Compound
The raft
body finder. Derting, K.
BODYGUARDS -- FICTION
Kincaid, S. J. The diabolic
Salisbury, M. The Sin Eater's daughter

BODY IMAGE -- FICTION
Miller, S. J. The art of starving
Rainfield, C. Stained
Body slammed. Villareal, R.
Bolden, Tonya
Crossing Ebenezer Creek
Boll, Rosemarie
The second trial
BOMBINGS -- FICTION
Abawi, A. A land of permanent goodbyes
Bond, Gwenda
Fallout
Bones of Faerie. Simner, J. L.
BONOBO -- FICTION
Schrefer, E. Endangered
Booked. Alexander, K.
The **book** jumper. Gläser, M.
Book of a thousand days. Hale, S.
The **book** of blood and shadow. Wasserman, R.
The **Book** of Broken Hearts. Ockler, S.
The **book** of Mordred. Vande Velde, V.
The **book** of Pearl. De Fombelle, T.
BOOKS AND READING -- FICTION
Alexander, K. Booked
Chee, T. The speaker
Gläser, M. The book jumper
Iturbe, A. The librarian of Auschwitz
Mantchev, L. Eyes like stars
Petrucha, S. The Rule of Won
Rupp, R. After Eli
Schoenherr, I. The Speaker
Tubb, K. O. The 13th sign
Zusak, M. The book thief
BOOKSELLERS AND BOOKSELLING -- FICTION
Nelson, V. M. No crystal stair
BOOKS -- FICTION
Caletti, D. Essential maps for the lost
BOOKSTORES -- FICTION
Crowley, C. Words in deep blue
BOOKSTORES -- NEW YORK (STATE) -- NEW YORK
Nelson, V. M. No crystal stair
The **book** thief. Zusak, M.
Boone, Martina
Compulsion
Boost. Mackel, K.
Booth, Coe
Bronxwood
Tyrell
Booth, Molly
Saving Hamlet
Born confused. Desai Hidier, T.
Borris, Albert
Crash into me
BORZOI -- FICTION
O'Brien, A. Lara's gift
BOSTON (MASS.) -- FICTION
Kluger, S. My most excellent year

BRITISH -- UNITED STATES -- FICTION

Elliot, L. Across a war-tossed sea

BRITTANY (FRANCE) -- HISTORY -- 1341-1532 -- FICTION

LaFevers, R. Grave mercy

LaFevers, R. Mortal heart

Brockenbrough, Martha

Devine intervention

The game of Love and Death

      memory. Combres, E.

      moon. Antieau, K.

BRONTË FAMILY ABOUT

Dunkle, C. The house of dead maids

BRONX (NEW YORK, N.Y.) -- FICTION

Booth, C. Bronxwood

Booth, C. Tyrell

Grimes, N. Bronx masquerade

Quintero, S. Efrain's secret

Rice-Gonzalez, C. Chulito

Silvera, A. More happy than not

      masquerade. Grimes, N.

Bronxwood. Booth, C.

Brooklyn, burning. Brezenoff, S.

BROOKLYN (NEW YORK, N.Y.) -- FICTION

Blythe, C. Revenge of a not-so-pretty girl

Brezenoff, S. Brooklyn, burning

Frank, E. R. Life is funny

Grant, C. Teenie

McDonald, J. Off -color

Moon, S. Sparrow

Older, D. J. Shadowhouse fall

Reynolds, J. Boy in the black suit

Reynolds, J. When I was the greatest

Wang, C. The takedown

Brooks, Bruce

The moves make the man; a novel

Brooks, Kevin

The bunker diary

BROTHELS -- FICTION

Scott, V. Violet Grenade

BROTHERS AND SISTERS -- FICTION

Adeyemi, T. Children of blood and bone

Ahdieh, R. Smoke in the sun

Andrews, J. Munmun

Arcos, C. The re will come a time

Bayard, L. Lucky strikes

Beaufrand, M. J. Useless Bay

Blake, A. H. Girl made of stars

Bolden, T. Crossing Ebenezer Creek

Brewer, Z. The cemetery boys

Brown, J. Perfect escape

Coker, R. Chasing Jupiter

Colbert, B. Little & Lion

Cousins, D. Waiting for Gonzo

Daley, J. R. Jesus Jackson

Davis, T. S. Happy families

Dennard, S. Something strange and deadly

Goelman, A. The path of names

Groth, D. Munro vs. the coyote

Hopkinson, N. The Chaos

Kagawa, J. Talon

Katcher, B. The improbable theory of Ana and Zak

Keyser, A. J. The way back from broken

Kizer, A. A matter of days

Leno, K. The lost & found

London, A. Black wings beating

McCarthy, A. Just fly away

McLaughlin, L. The Free

Morgan, P. The beautiful and the cursed

Porter, S. When I Cast Your Shadow

Price, L. Starters

Reynolds, J. When I was the greatest

Roth, V. Carve the mark

Scott, M. The enchantress

Sedgwick, M. She is not invisible

Shusterman, N. Dry

Sonnenblick, J. Falling over sideways

Stork, F. X. Disappeared

Tahir, S. An ember in the ashes: a novel

Tahir, S. A Torch Against the Night

Vanhee, J. Engines of the broken world

Walrath, D. Like water on stone

Webber, K. The heartbeats of Wing Jones

Wein, E. Black dove, white raven

Wiggins, B. Cured

Williams, C. L. Waiting

Wolf, J. S. Breaking beautiful

Wrede, P. C. Across the Great Barrier

BROTHERS AND SISTERS -- MEXICO -- CIUDAD JUÁREZ -- FICTION

Stork, F. X. Disappeared

BROTHERS -- DEATH -- FICTION

Alsaid, A. North of happy

Armstrong, K. Aftermath

Chan, G. The disappearance

Daley, J. R. Jesus Jackson

Porter, S. When I Cast Your Shadow

BROTHERS -- FICTION

Alexander, K. The crossover

Armstrong, K. Aftermath

Avasthi, S. Split

Black, H. Black heart

Black, H. Red glove

Black, H. The white cat

Bloor, E. Tangerine

Brennan, S. R. The demon's lexicon

Casella, J. Thin space

Coles, J. Tyler Johnson was here

Crossan, S. Moonrise

Doller, T. Something like normal

Elliot, L. Across a war-tossed sea

Fisher, C. Darkwater

Flores-Scott, P. American road trip

Funke, C. Fearless

Maciel, A. Tease
McNeil, G. I'm not your manic pixie dream girl
Miller, S. J. The art of starving
Russell, C. Songs about a girl
Scelsa, K. Fans of the impossible life
Scott, V. Violet Grenade
Summers, C. All the rage
Zorn, C. Protected
Bunce, Elizabeth C.
  A curse dark as gold
  Liar's moon
  Star crossed
Bunheads. Flack, S.
  bunker diary. Brooks, K.
Bunker, Lisa
  Felix Yz
Bunting, Eve
  The pirate captain's daughter
Burd, Nick
  The vast fields of ordinary
Burg, Ann E.
  All the broken pieces
Burgess, Melvin

  beneath the baobab tree. Nwaubani, A. T.
  MacCready, R. M.
  onions. Soto, G.
BURIED TREASURE -- FICTION
  Lowitz, L. Jet Black and the ninja wind.
  Mussi, S. The door of no return
  my heart. Naidoo, B.
  burning sky. Thomas, S.
BURNS AND SCALDS -- FICTION
  Katcher, B. Playing with matches
Burns, Laura J.

Butcher, Kristin

  Lange, E. J.
  y. Hartnett, S.
Buzo, Laura
  Love and other perishable items
  kill. Fantaskey, B.
  the river. Herrick, S.

C

CABALA -- FICTION
  Goelman, A. The path of names
Cabot, Meg
  Airhead
  All-American girl
  The princess diaries
Caine, Rachel
  Ash and quill. Rachel Caine
  Ink and bone

Prince of Shadows
Calame, Don
  Beat the band
  Swim the fly
Caleb's wars. Dudley, D. L.
Caletti, Deb
  Essential maps for the lost
  The fortunes of Indigo Skye
  A heart in a body in the world
  The last forever
  The secret life of Prince Charming
  The six rules of maybe
  Stay
CALIFORNIA -- FICTION
  Bennett, J. Alex, approximately
  Bennett, J. Starry eyes
  Castan, M. Fighting for Dontae
  Colbert, B. Little & Lion
  Gardner, F. The second life of Ava Rivers
  Gilbert, K. L. Picture us in the light
  Hurwin, D. Freaks and revelations
  Jimenez, F. Reaching out
  Lester, J. S. Black, white, other
  Nelson, J. I'll give you the sun
  Shusterman, N. Dry
  Stevenson, S. J. The Latte Rebellion
  Sugiura, M. It's not like it's a secret
  Yee, F. C. The epic crush of Genie Lo
CALIFORNIA -- GOLD DISCOVERIES
  Carson, R. Walk on Earth a Stranger
CALIFORNIA, SOUTHERN -- FICTION
  Arcos, C. Out of reach
Call me Maria. Ortiz Cofer, J.
The **call.** O'Guilin, P.
Callahan, Erin
  The art of escaping
Calling my name. Tamani, L.
Calvin. Leavitt, M.
CAMBODIAN AMERICANS -- FICTION
  Schmidt, G. D. Trouble
CAMBRIDGE (ENGLAND) -- FICTION
  Moriarty, J. A corner of white
  Moriarty, J. The cracks in the kingdom
  Moriarty, J. A tangle of gold
Camel rider. Mason, P.
Cameron, Peter
  Someday this pain will be useful to you
Cameron, Sharon
  The dark unwinding
  The Forgetting
  The knowing
  Rook
Cameron, Sophie
  Out of the blue
Caminar. Brown, S.
Camp So-and-So. McCoy, M.
CAMPING -- FICTION

the mark. Roth, V.
Casanova, Mary

Casella, Jody
Thin space
Cashore, Kristin
Bitterblue

Graceling
Jane, unlimited
Castan, Mike
Fighting for Dontae
Castellucci, Cecil

Boy proof
First day on Earth
The queen of cool
Castle, Jennifer
You look different in real life
CASTLES -- FICTION
Kindl, P. Keeping the castle
Castor, H. M.

Catching fire. Collins, S.
      & release. Woolston, B.
      rider. Lyne, J. H.
CATHOLIC SCHOOLS -- FICTION
Alsenas, L. Beyond clueless
Blythe, C. Revenge of a not-so-pretty girl
Henry, K. Heretics Anonymous
Catmull, Katherine
The radiant road: a novel
CATS -- FICTION
Bow, E. Plain Kate
Deedy, C. A. The Cheshire Cheese cat
Murdock, C. G. Wisdom's kiss
Pratchett, T. The amazing Maurice and his educated rodents
Rossetti, R. The girl with borrowed wings
CATWOMAN (FICTIONAL CHARACTER)
Maas, S. J. Catwoman: soulstealer
Catwoman: soulstealer. Maas, S. J.
Cavallaro, Brittany
The Last of August
CELEBRITIES -- FICTION
Castle, J. You look different in real life
Griffin, A. The unfinished life of Addison Stone
Zevin, G. All these things I've done
CELEBRITY CHEFS -- FICTION
Alsaid, A. North of happy
CEMETERIES -- FICTION
Brewer, Z. The cemetery boys
      cemetery boys. Brewer, Z.
CENSORSHIP -- FICTION
Selzer, A. How to get suspended and influence people
      center of everything. Moriarty, L.
CENTRAL AMERICA -- FICTION
Hubbard, K. Wanderlove

CENTRAL PARK (NEW YORK, N.Y.) -- FICTION
Forman, G. I have lost my way
CEREBRAL PALSY -- FICTION
Johnson, H. M. Accidents of nature
Kamata, S. Gadget Girl
Trueman, T. Life happens next; a novel
CEREBROVASCULAR DISEASE -- FICTION
Sonnenblick, J. Falling over sideways
A **certain** slant of light. Whitcomb, L.
A **certain** strain of peculiar. Amateau, G.
Chalice. McKinley, R.
Challenger. Shusterman, N.
Chaltas, Thalia
Because I am furniture
Chambers, Aidan
Dying to know you
Postcards from no man's land
Chan, Crystal
All that I can fix
The **chance** you won't return. Cardi, A.
Chanda's secrets. Stratton, A.
Chanda's wars. Stratton, A.
Changers book one. Cooper, T.
Chan, Gillian
The disappearance
The **Chaos.** Hopkinson, N.
The **Chaos.** Ward, R.
Chapman, Fern Schumer
Is it night or day?
Chapman, Lara
Flawless
Character, driven. Lubar, D.
CHARACTERS AND CHARACTERISTICS IN
       LITERATURE -- FICTION
Gläser, M. The book jumper
Rowell, R. Fangirl
CHARACTERS IN LITERATURE -- FICTION
Gläser, M. The book jumper
Howard, A. G. Unhinged
Leavitt, M. Calvin
CHARISMA (PERSONALITY TRAIT) -- FICTION
Parker, A. C. Astray
Chasing AllieCat. Davis, R. F.
Chasing boys. Tayleur, K.
Chasing Brooklyn. Schroeder, L.
Chasing Jupiter. Coker, R.
Chasing Shadows. Avasthi, S.
Cheat. Butcher, K.
CHEATING (EDUCATION) -- FICTION
Brown, J. Perfect escape
Butcher, K. Cheat
CHEERLEADING -- FICTION
Barnes, J. L. The Squad
Johnston, E. K. Exit, pursued by a bear
Valentine, A. How (not) to find a boyfriend
Chee, Traci
The speaker

Chen, Justina
Return to me
CHEROKEE INDIANS -- FICTION
Gensler, S. The revenant
CHEROKEE NATIONAL FEMALE SEMINARY --
FICTION
Gensler, S. The revenant
Cheshire Cheese cat. Deedy, C. A.
CHESS -- FICTION
Wallace, R. Perpetual check
Cheva, Cherry
DupliKate
Chibbaro, Julie

CHICAGO (IL.) -- FICTION
Ahmed, S. Love, hate & other filters
Cisneros, S. The house on Mango Street
Elkeles, S. How to ruin my teenage life
Fletcher, C. Ten cents a dance
Foley, J. A. Neighborhood girls
Hamilton, K. When the stars threw down their spears
Martinez, J. Virtuosity
Sanchez, E. L. I Am Not Your Perfect Mexican Daughter
Zettel, S. Bad luck girl
CHILD ABUSE -- FICTION
Avasthi, S. Split
Chaltas, T. Because I am furniture
Crocker, N. Billie Standish was here
Crutcher, C. Staying fat for Sarah Byrnes
Dessen, S. Lock and key
Felin, M. S. Touching snow
Giles, A. Now is everything
Hernandez, D. Suckerpunch
Klass, D. You don't know me
MacCullough, C. Stealing Henry
Roe, R. A list of cages
Schmidt, G. D. Orbiting Jupiter
Shusterman, N. Bruiser
Summers, C. This is not a test
Watkins, S. What comes after
Werlin, N. The rules of survival
CHILD AUTHORS -- FICTION
Willey, M. Beetle Boy
of dandelions. Nanji, S.
CHILDREN
Crowe, C. Mississippi trial, 1955
Dogar, S. Annexed
children and the wolves. Rapp, A.
CHILDREN AND WAR -- FICTION
Almond, D. The true tale of the monster Billy Dean
CHILDREN OF ALCOHOLICS -- FICTION
Castellucci, C. First day on Earth
MacCready, R. M. Buried
Palmer, R. The Corner of Bitter and Sweet
Children of blood and bone. Adeyemi, T.
CHILDREN OF DIVORCED PARENTS -- FICTION
Arnold, A. Love & other train wrecks

Kreslehner, G. I Don't Live Here Anymore
Mesrobian, C. Just a girl
CHILDREN OF DRUG ADDICTS -- FICTION
Alexander, K. Solo
Blair, J. Leap of Faith
Murdoch, E. If you find me
CHILDREN OF GAY PARENTS -- FICTION
Friend, N. The other F-word
Gardner, W. You're Welcome
Kenneally, M. Stealing Parker
Polisner, G. In sight of stars
Sáenz, B. A. The inexplicable logic of my life
Tregay, S. Love & leftovers; a novel in verse
CHILDREN OF IMMIGRANTS -- FICTION
Girard, M.-E. Girl Mans Up
CHILDREN OF MURDER VICTIMS -- FICTION
Ellis, K. Breaker
CHILDREN OF PARENTS WITH DISABILITIES --
FICTION
Sonnenblick, J. Falling over sideways
CHILDREN OF POLICE -- FICTION
Foley, J. A. Neighborhood girls
CHILDREN OF POLITICIANS -- FICTION
De la Cruz, M. Someone to love
CHILDREN OF PRISONERS -- FICTION
Bao, K. Dove arising
Foley, J. A. Neighborhood girls
CHILDREN'S SECRETS -- FICTION
Pitcher, A. Ketchup clouds
CHILDREN'S STORIES
Lu, M. Warcross
CHILDREN -- TRAVEL
Hubbard, K. Wanderlove
CHILDREN WITH DISABILITIES -- ABUSE OF --
FICTION
Edwards, J. Earth star
CHILDREN WITH DISABILITIES -- FICTION
Castan, M. Fighting for Dontae
CHILDREN WITH MENTAL DISABILITIES -- FICTION
Hamilton, K. Tyger tyger
CHILD SEXUAL ABUSE -- FICTION
Atkins, C. The file on Angelyn Stark
Chaltas, T. Because I am furniture
Deuker, C. Swagger
Doyle, B. Boy O'Boy
Lyga, B. Boy toy
Mazer, N. F. The missing girl
Rainfield, C. Scars
Sanchez, A. Bait
Scott, E. Living dead girl
Williams, C. L. Glimpse
Childs, Tera Lynn
Oh. My. Gods
Sweet venom
Chill wind. McDonald, J.
Chima, Cinda Williams
The Crimson Crown

The Demon King

The warrior heir

Billingsley, F.

CHIMERA (GREEK MYTHOLOGY) -- FICTION

Taylor, L. Days of blood & starlight

Taylor, L. Dreams of gods & monsters

CHIMPANZEES -- FICTION

Dickinson, P. Eva

Schrefer, E. Threatened

CHINA -- FICTION

Fine, S. Of Metal and Wishes

Liu, J. Girls on the line

Mowll, J. Operation Storm City

Mowll, J. Operation typhoon shore

Napoli, D. J. Bound

CHINA -- HISTORY -- YÜAN DYNASTY

McCaughrean, G. The kite rider; a novel

CHINATOWN (SAN FRANCISCO, CALIF.) -- FICTION

Bjorkman, L. Miss Fortune Cookie

CHINESE AMERICANS -- FICTION

Bjorkman, L. Miss Fortune Cookie

Gilbert, K. L. Picture us in the light

Lee, S. Outrun the moon

Lee, S. Under a painted sky

Lo, M. A line in the dark

Namioka, L. Mismatch

Shinn, S. Gateway

Yep, L. Dragonwings

CHINESE -- FICTION

Yee, P. Learning to fly

CHOCOLATE -- FICTION

Selfors, S. The sweetest spell

chocolate war. Cormier, R.

CHOCTAW INDIANS -- FICTION

Tingle, T. House of purple cedar

CHOCTAW INDIANS -- OKLAHOMA -- FICTION

Tingle, T. House of purple cedar

CHOICE -- FICTION

Kirby, J. Golden

Stirling, T. When my heart was wicked

Villareal, R. Body slammed

CHOICE (PSYCHOLOGY) -- FICTION

Heppermann, C. Ask Me How I Got Here

West, K. Pivot point

West, K. Split second

Choi, Sook Nyul

Year of impossible goodbyes

Woods, E. E.

Chokshi, Roshani

The star-touched queen

Chopsticks. **Anthony, J.**

chosen one. Williams, C. L.

CHRISTIAN FUNDAMENTALISM -- FICTION

Coyle, K. Vivian Apple at the end of the world

Coyle, K. Vivian Apple needs a miracle

Danforth, E. M. The miseducation of Cameron Post

Nader, E. Escape from Eden

CHRISTIAN HERESIES -- FICTION

Berry, J. The passion of Dolssa

CHRISTIAN LIFE -- FICTION

Bickle, L. The hallowed ones

Brande, R. Evolution, me, & other freaks of nature

Cranse, P. All the major constellations

Despain, B. The dark Divine

Dickerson, M. The merchant's daughter

Fixmer, E. Down from the mountain

Grimes, N. A girl named Mister

Jaden, D. Losing Faith

Mattison, B. T. Unsigned hype; a novel

McVoy, T. E. Pure

White, R. A month of Sundays

CHRISTMAS -- FICTION

Anstey, C. Carols and chaos

Asher, J. What light

Christy. Marshall, C.

The **chronicles** of Vladimir Tod. Brewer, Z.

Chulito. Rice-Gonzalez, C.

Chupeco, Rin

The Girl from the Well

CHURCH GROUP WORK -- FICTION

Talley, R. Our own private universe

The **circuit.** Jimenez, F.

CIRCUS -- FICTION

Howard, J. J. That time I joined the circus

Lam, L. Pantomime

Cisneros, Sandra

The house on Mango Street

CITY AND TOWN LIFE -- FICTION

French, G. Grit

Knowles, J. Read between the lines

Oliver, L. Panic

Tan, S. Tales from the inner city

CITY AND TOWN LIFE -- KANSAS -- FICTION

Wasserman, R. The waking dark

City boy. Michael, J.

The **City** in the Lake. Neumeier, R.

City of ashes. Clare, C.

City of a Thousand Dolls. Forster, M.

City of orphans. Avi, 1937-

City of Saints & Thieves. Anderson, N. C.

CIUDAD JUÁREZ (MEXICO) -- FICTION

Stork, F. X. Disappeared

CIVIL RIGHTS -- FICTION

Doctorow, C. Homeland

Doctorow, C. Little brother

CLAIRVOYANCE -- FICTION

Chen, J. Return to me

King, A. S. Glory O'Brien's history of the future: a novel

Nadol, J. The mark

Nadol, J. The vision

Stiefvater, M. The Raven Boys

CLANS -- FICTION

Eshbaugh, J. Obsidian and stars

Clare, Cassandra

COLONIZATION -- FICTION

Blair, K. Tangled planet

COLOR -- FICTION

Moriarty, J. A corner of white

Moriarty, J. The cracks in the kingdom

Moriarty, J. A tangle of gold

COLORADO -- FICTION

Peters, J. A. She loves you, she loves you not--

Stiefvater, M. All the crooked saints.

COMA -- FICTION

Cranse, P. All the major constellations

Magoon, K. 37 things I love (in no particular order)

Mass, W. Heaven looks a lot like the mall; a novel

Scott, E. Between here and forever

COMA -- PATIENTS -- FICTION

Webber, K. The heartbeats of Wing Jones

COMBAT -- FICTION

Silver, E. Rush

Combres, Elisabeth

Broken memory

Combs, Sarah

Breakfast served anytime

COMIC BOOKS, STRIPS, ETC. -- FICTION

Priest, C. I Am Princess X.

Wooding, C. Havoc

COMING OF AGE -- FICTION

Axelrod, K. The law of loving others: a novel

Bickle, L. The hallowed ones

Bickle, L. The outside

Coyle, K. Vivian Apple at the end of the world

Coyle, K. Vivian Apple needs a miracle

Cummings, P. The journey back

Diederich, P. Playing for the Devil's Fire

Flores-Scott, P. American road trip

Hahn, M. D. Mister Death's blue-eyed girls

Howell, S. Girl defective

Kamata, S. Gadget Girl

Kriegman, M. Being Audrey Hepburn: a novel

Lynch, J. N. My beautiful hippie

Macvie, M. The ocean in my ears

Myers, W. D. All the right stuff

Powell, W. C. Expiration day

Sáenz, B. A. Aristotle and Dante discover the secrets of the universe

Simner, J. L. Faerie after

Sweeney, D. The minnow

Tashjian, J. The gospel according to Larry

Wakefield, V. Friday never leaving

Weston, R. P. Blues for Zoey

COMING OUT (SEXUAL ORIENTATION) -- FICTION

Alsenas, L. Beyond clueless

Barakiva, M. One man guy

Daniels, A. Dreadnought

Goslee, S. J. Whatever

Jones, A. G. Fire song

Lennon, T. When love comes to town

Rice-Gonzalez, C. Chulito

Silvera, A. More happy than not

Coming up for air. Kenneally, M.

COMMUNAL LIVING -- FICTION

Finneyfrock, K. Starbird Murphy and the world outside

Heathfield, L. Seed

Reed, A. Over you

COMMUNICABLE DISEASES -- FICTION

Bickle, L. The hallowed ones

Wells, D. Partials

Wooding, C. Silver

Woolston, B. Catch & release

COMMUNICATION -- FICTION

Trueman, T. Life happens next; a novel

COMMUNISM -- FICTION

Mackall, D. D. Eva underground

COMMUNIST COUNTRIES -- FICTION

Marsden, C. My Own Revolution

COMMUNITY COLLEGE STUDENTS -- FICTION

Oelke, L. Nice try, Jane Sinner

COMMUNITY LIFE -- FICTION

Berry, J. All the truth that's in me

Martinez, C. G. Pig Park

Rosenfield, K. Amelia Anne is dead and gone

Templeman, M. The glass casket

COMMUNITY SERVICE (PUNISHMENT) -- FICTION

Lu, M. Batman: Nightwalker

COMPETITION (PSYCHOLOGY) -- FICTION

Aldredge, B. Sasquatch, love, and other imaginary things

Juby, S. The fashion committee

Williams, K. Pizza, love, and other stuff that made me famous

COMPOSERS -- FICTION

Bowman, A. D. Summer bird blue

Collins, P. L. Hidden voices

Dunlap, S. E. The musician's daughter.

Weil, C. I'm glad I did

The **Compound.** Bodeen, S. A.

Compulsion. Ayarbe, H.

Compulsion. Boone, M.

COMPULSIVE BEHAVIOR -- FICTION

Omololu, C. J. Dirty little secrets

COMPULSIVE EATING -- FICTION

Fehlbaum, B. Big fat disaster

Griffin, N. Just wreck it all

COMPUTER CRIMES -- FICTION

Lu, M. Wildcard

COMPUTER GAMES -- FICTION

Cheva, C. DupliKate

Pratchett, T. Only you can save mankind

COMPUTER HACKERS -- FICTION

Bernard, R. Find me

Doctorow, C. Homeland

Gagnon, M. Don't let go

Gagnon, M. Don't Look Now

Gagnon, M. Don't turn around

Lu, M. Warcross

Lu, M. Wildcard

COMPUTER PROGRAMS -- FICTION

COOKING -- FICTION
Alsaid, A. North of happy
Davis, T. S. A la carte
Kephart, B. Small damages
Lewis, S. The secret ingredient
Williams, K. Pizza, love, and other stuff that made me famous

Cooney, Caroline B., 1947-
Code orange
Diamonds in the shadow
The face on the milk carton
If the witness lied
Janie face to face
The voice on the radio
Whatever happened to Janie?
What Janie found.

Cooper, Susan
Over sea, under stone

Cooper, T.
Changers book one

COPPER MINES AND MINING -- FICTION
Wallace, S. N. Muckers

Copyboy. Trunfio, A.

Copyboy. Vawter, V.

COPYRIGHT -- FICTION
Doctorow, C. Pirate cinema
Katsoulis, G. S. All rights reserved

Córdova, Zoraida
Labyrinth lost

Cormier, Robert
After the first death
Beyond the chocolate war
The chocolate war
I am the cheese
Corner of Bitter and Sweet. Palmer, R.
corner of white. Moriarty, J.

Cornwell, Betsy
Mechanica

Venturess

CORPORATIONS -- CORRUPT PRACTICES -- FICTION
Bacigalupi, P. The doubt factory
Corps of the Bare-Boned Plane. Horvath, P.

Corthron, Kara Lee
The truth of right now

Cosimano, Elle
Holding Smoke

COSTUME -- FICTION
Perkins, S. Lola and the boy next door

Coulthurst, Audrey
Of Fire and Stars

COUNSELING -- FICTION
Zorn, C. Protected

COUNTERCULTURE -- FICTION
Doctorow, C. Homeland

COUNTERFEITS AND COUNTERFEITING -- FICTION
Anstey, C. Carols and chaos
Pierce, T. Bloodhound

COUNTRY LIFE -- FICTION
Levine, K. The best bad luck I ever had
Magnin, J. Carrying Mason
Michael, J. City boy
Napoli, D. J. Alligator bayou
White, R. A month of Sundays
Wyatt, M. Funny how things change
Zentner, J. The serpent king

COUNTRY MUSIC -- FICTION
Supplee, S. Somebody everybody listens to
Whitaker, A. Wildflower

COURAGE -- FICTION
Bartoletti, S. C. The boy who dared
Deuker, C. Payback time
Roth, V. Allegiant
Roth, V. Divergent
Roth, V. Insurgent
Wilkinson, S. Taking Flight
A **court** of thorns and roses. Maas, S. J.

COURTS AND COURTIERS -- FICTION
Ahdieh, R. Smoke in the sun
Aveyard, V. King's cage
Black, H. The cruel prince
Hand, C. My Lady Jane
Hartman, R. Seraphina
Hartman, R. Shadow scale
Hartman, R. Tess of the road
Kincaid, S. J. The diabolic
Kincaid, S. J. The empress
LaFevers, R. Grave mercy
Longshore, K. Brazen
Maas, S. J. Throne of glass
Marsh, K. Jepp, who defied the stars
Murdock, C. G. Princess Ben
Pike, A. Glitter
Thomas, R. Long may she reign
Zettel, S. Palace of Spies

COURTSHIP -- FICTION
Kindl, P. A school for brides
Kindl, P. Keeping the castle
Robert, Na'ima B. She wore red trainers: A Muslim Love Story

Cousins, Dave
Waiting for Gonzo

COUSINS -- FICTION
French, G. Grit
Horvath, P. The Corps of the Bare-Boned Plane
Lecesne, J. Absolute brightness
Levitin, S. Strange relations
Meyerhoff, J. Queen of secrets
Mills, E. First & then
Minchin, A. The beat goes on
Perera, A. Guantanamo boy
Stiefvater, M. All the crooked saints
Thomas, E. Boarder patrol
Thompson, M. G. Amy Chelsea Stacie Dee
Wagner, L. R. Hold tight, don't let go
Wrede, P. C. Sorcery and Cecelia

Staying fat for Sarah Byrnes

Whale talk
of the giraffe. Oron, J.

CRYONICS
Whaley, J. C. Noggin

CRYSTAL CITY INTERNMENT CAMP (CRYSTAL CITY, TEX.) -- FICTION
Hesse, M. The war outside

CUBA -- FICTION
Engle, M. Firefly letters

CUBAN AMERICANS -- FICTION
Dole, M. L. Down to the bone

CULTS -- FICTION
Brewer, Z. The cemetery boys
Fahy, T. R. The unspoken
Finneyfrock, K. Starbird Murphy and the world outside
Fixmer, E. Down from the mountain
Hautman, P. Eden West
Heathfield, L. Seed
Jaden, D. Losing Faith
Nader, E. Escape from Eden
Oakes, S. The sacred lies of Minnow Bly
Parker, A. C. Astray
Parker, A. C. Gated
Smith-Ready, J. This side of salvation
Williams, C. L. The chosen one

CULTURE CONFLICT -- FICTION
Kerbel, D. Mackenzie, lost and found
Ostlere, C. Karma
Powell, K. The Merit Birds

Cummings, Priscilla
Blindsided
The journey back
Red kayak
Wiggins, B.
dark as gold. Bunce, E. C.
of the Thirteenth Fey. Yolen, J.

CURSES -- FICTION
Yolen, J. Curse of the Thirteenth Fey
Columbus. Tal, E.
& conspiracies. Carriger, G.
McCormick, P.
Off. Bastedo, J.

CUTTING (SELF-MUTILATION) -- FICTION
Oates, J. C. Two or three things I forgot to tell you
Rainfield, C. Scars
secret. Marillier, J.

CYBERBULLYING -- FICTION
Davis, L. I swear
Laidlaw, S. J. Fifteen lanes
Littman, S. Backlash
Wang, C. The takedown

CYBERTERRORISM -- PREVENTION -- FICTION
Klavan, A. MindWar: a novel

CYCLING -- FICTION
Bradbury, J. Shift

Cypess, Leah
Death sworn
Mistwood
Nightspell

CYRANO DE BERGERAC, 1619-1655 ABOUT
McCaughrean, G. Cyrano

CYSTIC FIBROSIS -- FICTION
Moskowitz, H. Teeth

CZECHOSLOVAKIA -- FICTION
Marsden, C. My Own Revolution

CZECH REPUBLIC -- FICTION
Taylor, L. Days of blood & starlight

D

Daemon Hall. Nance, A.
Dairy Queen. Murdock, C. G.
Daley, James Ryan
Jesus Jackson
Damico, Gina
Croak
Hellhole
Rogue
Scorch
Wax
Damned. Holder, N.
DANCE -- FICTION
Dixon, H. Entwined
Venkatraman, P. A time to dance
Dance of thieves. Pearson, M. E.
DANCERS -- FICTION
Fletcher, C. Ten cents a dance
Kephart, B. House of Dance
Lieberman, L. Off pointe
Winston, S. The Kayla chronicles.
Danforth, Emily M.
The miseducation of Cameron Post
Dangerous angels. Block, F. L.
Dangerous girls. Haas, A.
Daniels, April
Dreadnought
Danticat, Edwidge
Untwine
Dao, Julie C.
Forest of a thousand lanterns
Dare You to. McGarry, K.
DARFUR (SUDAN) -- FICTION
Whitman, S. The milk of birds
Darius the Great is not okay. Khorram, A.
Darius & Twig. Myers, W. D. 1937-2014
DARK AGES
See Middle Ages
The **dark** city. Fisher, C.
The **dark** Divine. Despain, B.
The **darkest** corners. Thomas, K.
Dark song. Giles, G.
Dark sons. Grimes, N.

dark unwinding. Cameron, S.

Darkwater. Fisher, C.

Darrows, Eva

Dead little mean girl

    & Lily's book of dares. Cohn, R.

DATE RAPE -- FICTION

Johnston, E. K. Exit, pursued by a bear

Padian, M. Wrecked

Wolf, J. S. Breaking beautiful

DATING (SOCIAL CUSTOMS) -- FICTION

Ahmed, S. Love, hate & other filters

Albertalli, B. What if it's us

Arnold, E. K. What girls are made of

Barnholdt, L. Through to you

Barzak, C. The gone away place

Bauman, B. A. Rosie & Skate

Bennett, J. Alex, approximately

Bennett, J. Starry eyes

Bigelow, L. J. Starting from here

Block, F. L. Teen spirit

Brewer, Z. The cemetery boys

Burd, N. The vast fields of ordinary

Caletti, D. Stay

Cann, K. Consumed

Carter, A. Perfect scoundrels

Cohn, R. Naomi and Ely's no kiss list

Colbert, B. Little & Lion

Demetrios, H. Bad romance

Dessen, S. Along for the ride

Dessen, S. Once and for all

Dessen, S. The moon and more

Doktorski, J. S. Famous last words

Doktorski, J. S. The summer after you and me

Elkeles, S. Perfect chemistry

Ellsworth, L. Unforgettable

Emond, S. Bright lights, dark nights

Fantaskey, B. Buzz kill.

Fitzpatrick, H. What I thought was true

Flack, S. Bunheads

Friend, N. How we roll

Friend, N. My life in black and white

Goo, M. I believe in a thing called love

Goo, M. The way you make me feel

Goslee, S. J. Whatever

Grant, C. Teenie

Han, J. To all the boys I've loved before

Handler, D. Why we broke up

Hartinger, B. Three truths and a lie

Hautman, P. The big crunch

Hautman, P. What boys really want

Howland, L. Nantucket blue

Johnson, M. Scarlett fever

Karim, S. Skunk girl

Katcher, B. Almost perfect

Katcher, B. Playing with matches

Kerr, M. E. If I love you, am I trapped forever?

King, A. S. Reality Boy

Kisner, A. Dear Rachel Maddow

Lauren, C. Autoboyography

Levithan, D. Hold me closer: the Tiny Cooper story

Lindstrom, E. Not if I see you first

Littlefield, S. Infected

Lo, M. A line in the dark

Lockhart, E. Real live boyfriends

Lockhart, E. The boy book

Lockhart, E. The boyfriend list

Lockhart, E. The treasure map of boys

Luper, E. Seth Baumgartner's love manifesto

Mackler, C. Guyaholic; a story of finding, flirting, forgetting . .

    . and the boy who changes everything

Macvie, M. The ocean in my ears

Madigan, L. K. Flash burnout; a novel

Matson, M. Since you've been gone

McCahan, E. The lake effect

McNeil, G. I'm not your manic pixie dream girl

McVoy, T. E. Pure

Menon, S. When Dimple met Rishi

Mills, E. First & then

Murphy, J. Dumplin'

Murphy, J. Puddin

Namioka, L. Mismatch

Naylor, P. R. Incredibly Alice

Ormsbee, K. Tash hearts Tolstoy

Patrick, C. Forgotten

Patrick, C. The Originals

Paulsen, G. Crush; the theory, practice, and destructive

    properties of love

Reinhardt, D. Tell us something true

Rennison, L. Are these my basoomas I see before me? final

    confessions of Georgia Nicolson

Rennison, L. Stop in the name of pants!

Rennison, L. The taming of the tights

Rosenfield, K. Amelia Anne is dead and gone

Rowell, R. Carry on: a novel

Rowell, R. Eleanor & Park

Saeed, A. Written in the stars

Scheidt, E. L. Uses for boys

Silvera, A. More happy than not

Simone, Ni-Ni. Upgrade U

Sones, S. What my girlfriend doesn't know

Sones, S. What my mother doesn't know

Spangler, B. Beast

Stone, T. I. Little do we know

Strasser, T. Price of duty

Talley, R. What We Left Behind

Tharp, T. The spectacular now

Tibensky, A. And then things fall apart

Trigiani, A. Viola in reel life

Trigiani, A. Viola in the spotlight

Valentine, A. How (not) to find a boyfriend

Vivian, S. Not that kind of girl

Voorhees, C. The brothers Torres

Walton, J. Words on bathroom walls

Warman, J. Where the truth lies

Watson, R. This side of home
Wettersten, L. My faire lady
Whitaker, A. Wildflower
Willey, M. Beetle Boy
Williams, G. Beatle meets Destiny
Wittlinger, E. Sandpiper
Wolf, J. S. Breaking beautiful
Wolitzer, M. Belzhar
Wood, F. Cloudwish
Yee, L. The kidney hypothetical
Zeises, L. M. The sweet life of Stella Madison

DATING (SOCIAL CUSTOMS) -- RELIGIOUS ASPECTS -- FICTION
Robert, Na'ima B. She wore red trainers: A Muslim Love Story

DATING VIOLENCE -- FICTION
Connor, L. The things you kiss goodbye
Rosenfield, K. Amelia Anne is dead and gone
Wolf, J. S. Breaking beautiful

Daughter of smoke and bone. Taylor, L.
Daughter of the pirate king. Levenseller, T.
Davies, Jacqueline

Davies, Jocelyn
The odds of lightning
Davies, Stephen
Outlaw
Davis, Lane
I swear
Davis, Rebecca Fjelland
Chasing AllieCat
Davis, Tanita S.
Happy families
A la carte
Mare's war
Dawn, Sasha
Splinter
of tears. Lester, J.
of the assassins. O'Brien, J.
of blood & starlight. Taylor, L.
Dayton, Arwen Elys
Stronger, faster, and more beautiful
De Gramont, Nina
Every little thing in the world
De la Cruz, Melissa
Blue bloods
Someone to love
De la Peña, Matt
Ball don't lie
The living
de Vigan, Delphine
No and me
Locke went to prom. Katcher, B.
Dead connection. Price, C.
DEAD -- FICTION
Barzak, C. The gone away place
Block, F. L. Teen spirit
Bow, E. Sorrow's knot

Brockenbrough, M. Devine intervention
Casella, J. Thin space
Chupeco, R. The Girl from the Well
Cox, S. The Dead Girls Detective Agency
Cypess, L. Nightspell
Dennard, S. Something strange and deadly
Derting, K. The body finder
Derting, K. The last echo
Huntley, A. The everafter
McBride, L. Hold me closer, necromancer
Noel, A. Radiance
Plum, A. Die for me
Ruiz Zafon, C. The Prince of Mist
Shepard, S. The lying game
Suma, N. R. Imaginary girls
Tintera, A. Reboot
Warman, J. Between
Westerfeld, S. Afterworlds
The **Dead** Girls Detective Agency. Cox, S.
The **dead** girls of Hysteria Hall. **Alender, K.**
The **dead** I know. Gardner, S.
Dead is a battlefield. Perez, M.
Deadline. Crutcher, C.
Dead little mean girl. Darrows, E.
Deadly. Chibbaro, J.
The **deadly** sister. Schrefer, E.
DEAF CULTURE -- FICTION
Gardner, W. You're Welcome
DEAF -- FICTION
Ferris, J. Of sound mind
Na, A. Wait for me
Dear Martin. Stone, N.
Dear Rachel Maddow. Kisner, A.
Dear Zoe. Beard, P.
DEATH
Burgess, M. The hit
Caletti, D. The last forever
Daley, J. R. Jesus Jackson
The **death**-defying Pepper Roux. McCaughrean, G.
Death, Dickinson, and the demented life of Frenchie Garcia.
Torres Sanchez, J.
DEATH -- FICTION
Alsaid, A. North of happy
Anderson, J. L. Wintergirls
Arcos, C. The re will come a time
Avasthi, S. Chasing Shadows
Beard, P. Dear Zoe
Block, F. L. Pretty dead
Blume, J. Tiger eyes
Bowman, A. D. Summer bird blue
Brockenbrough, M. The game of Love and Death
Burgess, M. The hit
Caletti, D. The last forever
Coles, J. Tyler Johnson was here
Crane, E. M. Skin deep
Crutcher, C. Deadline
Cummings, P. Red kayak

Little's still not dead. Rubin, L.

DEPORTATION -- FICTION

McCall, G. G. All the stars denied

DEPRESSED PERSONS -- FICTION

Barnard, S. Fragile like us

DEPRESSION (PSYCHOLOGY) -- FICTION

Caletti, D. Essential maps for the lost

Hutchinson, S. D. We are the ants

Khorram, A. Darius the Great is not okay

Ockler, S. Fixing Delilah

Vizzini, N. It's kind of a funny story

Zappia, F. Eliza and her monsters

DEPRESSION, MENTAL -- FICTION

Khorram, A. Darius the Great is not okay

DEPRESSIONS -- 1929 -- FICTION

Bayard, L. Lucky strikes

McCall, G. G. All the stars denied

Peet, M. Beck

Rosoff, M. Beck

DEPRESSIONS -- 1929 -- UNITED STATES -- FICTION

Barnaby, H. Wonder show

Deracine, Anat

Driving by starlight

Derting, Kimberly

The body finder

Desires of the dead

The last echo

The pledge

Desai Hidier, Tanuja

Born confused

DESERTS -- FICTION

Hamilton, A. Hero at the fall.

Kinch, M. The fires of New SUN

Kinch, M. The rebels of New SUN

Mason, P. Camel rider

Rossetti, R. The girl with borrowed wings

of the dead. Derting, K.

Despain, Bree

The dark Divine

DESPOTISM -- FICTION

Mourlevat, J. Winter's end

Dessen, Sarah

Along for the ride

Just listen

Lock and key

The moon and more

Once and for all

DeStefano, Lauren

Perfect ruin

all cars. Nelson, B.

DETECTIVE AND MYSTERY STORIES

Carter, A. Perfect scoundrels

Landman, T. Hell and high water

Mason, S. Running girl

McClintock, N. About that night

Thomas, K. The darkest corners

DETECTIVES -- FICTION

Latham, J. Scarlett undercover

DETROIT (MICH.) -- FICTION

Whelan, G. See what I see

Deuker, Carl

Gym candy

High heat

Painting the black

Payback time

Runner

Swagger

DEVELOPMENTAL PSYCHOLOGY

See also Psychology

The **devil** and Winnie Flynn. Ostow, M.

DEVIL -- FICTION

Clare, C. City of ashes

Damico, G. Hellhole

Gill, D. M. Soul enchilada

Napoli, D. J. The wager

Nayeri, D. Another Faust

The **devil's** breath. Gilman, D.

The **Devil's** engine. Smith, A. G.

The **devil** you know. Doller, T.

Devine, Eric

Press play

Devine intervention. Brockenbrough, M.

Devlin, Calla

Tell me something real

DeWoskin, Rachel

Blind

Dhar, Payal

Eat the sky, drink the ocean

DIABETES -- FICTION

Hautman, P. Sweetblood

The **diabolic.** Kincaid, S. J.

Diamond boy. Williams, M.

DIAMOND MINES AND MINING -- FICTION

Williams, M. Diamond boy

Diamonds in the shadow. Cooney, C. B.

DIARIES -- FICTION

Arcos, C. The re will come a time

Ayres, K. North by night

Brooks, K. The bunker diary

Chibbaro, J. Deadly

Kirby, J. Golden

Miller, S. A lite too bright

Nielsen, S. The reluctant journal of Henry K. Larsen

Oelke, L. Nice try, Jane Sinner

Patterson, J. Homeroom diaries

Powell, W. C. Expiration day

Price, N. Zoe letting go

Quintero, I. Gabi, a girl in pieces

Rennison, L. Are these my basoomas I see before me? final confessions of Georgia Nicolson

Rennison, L. Stop in the name of pants!

Schlitz, L. A. The hired girl.

Herrick, S. The wolf
King, A. S. Still life with tornado
DOMESTICS -- FICTION
Chibbaro, J. Deadly
DOMINICAN AMERICANS -- FICTION
Acevedo, E. The poet X: a novel
Myers, W. D. Darius & Twig
Williams, I. Water in May
DOMINICAN REPUBLIC -- HISTORY -- 1930-1961
Alvarez, J. Before we were free
DONATION OF ORGANS, TISSUES, ETC. -- FICTION
Pieces Lynch, C.
DONNER PARTY -- FICTION
Brown, S. To stay alive
   let go. Gagnon, M.
   Look Now. Gagnon, M.
   turn around. Gagnon, M.
door in the moon. Fisher, C.
Doormat; a novel. McWilliams, K.
door of no return, Mussi, S.
   crossing. Tal, E.
   helix. Werlin, N.
   Valentine, J.
doubt factory. Bacigalupi, P.
   arising. Bao, K.
Downes, Patrick
Ten miles one way
   from the mountain. Fixmer, E.
Downsiders. Shusterman, N.
DOWN SYNDROME -- FICTION
Hyde, C. R. The year of my miraculous reappearance
Trueman, T. Life happens next; a novel
   to the bone. Dole, M. L.
Dowswell, Paul
The Auslander
Doyle, Brian
Boy O'Boy
Pure Spring
Doyle, Marissa
Bewitching season
Doyle, Roddy
A greyhound of a girl
DRACULA, COUNT (FICTIONAL CHARACTER) -- FICTION
Maniscalco, K. Hunting Prince Dracula
DRAG CULTURE -- FICTION
St. James, J. Freak show
Dragongirl. McCaffrey, T. J.
Dragonhaven. McKinley, R.
Dragon's blood. Yolen, J.
DRAGONS -- FICTION
Barron, T. A. Merlin's dragon
Carey, J. L. Dragon's Keep
Carey, J. L. Dragonswood
Carey, J. L. In the time of dragon moon
Fforde, J. The last Dragonslayer
Fletcher, S. Ancient, strange, and lovely

Fletcher, S. Dragon's milk
Hahn, R. A creature of moonlight
Hartman, R. Seraphina
Hartman, R. Shadow scale
Hartman, R. Tess of the road
Johnston, E. K. Prairie fire
Johnston, E. K. The story of Owen
Kagawa, J. Shadow of the Fox
Kagawa, J. Talon
McCaffrey, T. J. Dragongirl
McKinley, R. Dragonhaven
Paolini, C. Eragon
Vaughn, C. Voices of dragons
Yolen, J. Dragon's blood
Dragon's Keep. Carey, J. L.
Dragon's milk. Fletcher, S.
Dragonswood. Carey, J. L.
Dragonwings. Yep, L.
Dramarama. Lockhart, E.
DRAMATISTS
Bjorkman, L. My invented life
Klein, L. M. Ophelia
Marsden, J. Hamlet: a novel
Silbert, L. The intelligencer
Draw the line. Linn, L.
Dread nation. Ireland, J.
Dreadnought. Daniels, A.
Dream country. Gibney, S.
DREAMS -- FICTION
Arbuthnott, G. The Keepers' tattoo
Bray, L. Lair of dreams: a Diviners novel
Dimaline, C. The marrow thieves
Gardner, S. The dead I know
King, A. S. Everybody sees the ants
O'Brien, Caragh M. The vault of dreamers
Schroeder, L. Chasing Brooklyn
Stiefvater, M. Blue lily, lily blue
Stiefvater, M. The dream thieves
Warman, J. Where the truth lies
Yovanoff, B. Places no one knows
Dreams of gods & monsters. Taylor, L.
Dreams of the dead. Randall, T.
Dream Things True. Marquardt, M. F.
DRESSMAKING -- FICTION
Jones, K. Murder, magic, and what we wore
Driving by starlight. Deracine, A.
DROPOUTS -- FICTION
O'Connell, M. The sharp time
Oelke, L. Nice try, Jane Sinner
Drop. Papademetriou, L.
DROUGHTS -- FICTION
Shusterman, N. Dry
The **drowned** cities. Bacigalupi, P.
DRUG ABUSE -- FICTION
Arcos, C. Out of reach
Burgess, M. Smack
Hernandez, D. Suckerpunch

Zhang, K. What's left of me
DYSTOPIAS -- FICTION
  Katsoulis, G. S. All rights reserved
  Wooding, C. Velocity
  Woolston, B. Black helicopters

E

Earthbound. Pike, A.
Earthgirl. Cowan, J.
  earth, my butt, and other big, round things. Mackler, C.
EARTHQUAKES -- FICTION
  Block, F. L. Love in the time of global warming
  Lake, N. In darkness
  Lee, S. Outrun the moon
  Wagner, L. R. Hold tight, don't let go
    star. Edwards, J.
EAST HARLEM (NEW YORK, N.Y.)
  Manzano, S. The revolution of Evelyn Serrano
EAST INDIAN AMERICANS -- FICTION
  Ahmed, S. Love, hate & other filters
  Born confused. Desai Hidier, T.
  Menon, S. When Dimple met Rishi
  Patel, S. Rani Patel in full effect
  Perkins, M. You bring the distant near
  Westerfeld, S. Afterworlds
EAST INDIANS -- FICTION
  Nanji, S. Child of dandelions
    Pattou, E.
    the sky, drink the ocean. Dhar, P.
    the sky, drink the ocean. Roy, A.
EATING DISORDERS -- FICTION
  Fehlbaum, B. Big fat disaster
  Griffin, N. Just wreck it all
  Lange, E. J. Butter
  Miller, S. J. The art of starving
  Price, N. Zoe letting go
EATING HABITS
  Lange, E. J. Butter
ECCENTRICS AND ECCENTRICITIES -- FICTION
  Cameron, S. The dark unwinding
  Foxlee, K. The midnight dress
  King, A. S. Glory O'Brien's history of the future: a novel
ECOLOGY -- FICTION
  Nelson, B. Destroy all cars
ECUADOR -- FICTION
  Farinango, M. V. The Queen of Water
  Renn, D. Latitude zero
  Resau, L. The indigo notebook
    West. Hautman, P.
  edge. Smith, R.
EDINBURGH (SCOTLAND) -- TEEN FICTION
  Cameron, S. Out of the blue
Edwards, Janet
  Earth star
Edwardson, Debby Dahl
  Blessing's bead

My name is not easy
Efaw, Amy
  Battle dress
Efrain's secret. Quintero, S.
Egan, Catherine
  Julia vanishes
Ehrenhaft, Daniel
  Friend is not a verb
ELDERLY MEN -- FICTION
  Chambers, A. Dying to know you
Eleanor & Park. Rowell, R.
An **elephant** in the garden. Morpurgo, M.
Elephant run. Smith, R.
ELEPHANTS -- FICTION
  Morpurgo, M. An elephant in the garden
  Smith, R. Elephant run
ELEPORTATION -- FICTION
  Williams, S. Twinmaker
The **eleventh** plague. Hirsch, J.
Eliza and her monsters. Zappia, F.
Elkeles, Simone
  How to ruin my teenage life
  Perfect chemistry
Ellen, Laura
  Blind spot
Elliot, Laura
  Across a war-tossed sea
Elliott, David
  Bull
Elliott, Laura
  Hamilton and Peggy!: a revolutionary friendship
Ellis, Kat
  Breaker
Ellsworth, Loretta
  Unforgettable
Elston, Ashley
  The rules for disappearing
ELVES -- FICTION
  Yolen, J. Curse of the Thirteenth Fey
Elwood, Tessa
  Split the sun
E-MAIL -- FICTION
  Kisner, A. Dear Rachel Maddow
Emako Blue. Woods, B.
Embassy row #1: all fall down. Carter, A.
An **ember** in the ashes: a novel. Tahir, S.
Embrace. Shirvington, J.
EMIGRATION AND IMMIGRATION -- FICTION
  Abdel-Fattah, R. The lines we cross
  Abdel-Fattah, R. The lines we cross
  Andreu, M. E. The secret side of empty
  Marquardt, Marie F. The radius of us
Emilie & the hollow world. Wells, M.
Emond, Stephen
  Bright lights, dark nights
  Winter town
EMOTION RECOGNITION -- FICTION

McCreight, K. The scattering

EMOTIONAL INTELLIGENCE -- FICTION

McCreight, K. The scattering

EMOTIONAL PROBLEMS -- FICTION

Carter, C. Me, him, them, and it

Gardner, S. The dead I know

Johnston, E. K. Exit, pursued by a bear

King, A. S. Reality Boy

Luedeke, L. Smashed

Niven, J. All the bright places

Price, N. Zoe letting go

Rainfield, C. Scars

Schmidt, G. D. Orbiting Jupiter

Webber, K. The heartbeats of Wing Jones

Willey, M. Beetle Boy

Wolitzer, M. Belzhar

EMOTIONAL PROBLEMS OF CHILDREN -- FICTION

Kaplan, A. E. Grendel's guide to love and war

EMOTIONAL PROBLEMS OF TEENAGERS -- FICTION

Nielsen, S. Optimists die first

Webber, K. The heartbeats of Wing Jones

EMOTIONS -- FICTION

Hardinge, F. A face like glass

McCreight, K. The scattering

Niven, J. All the bright places

Roat, S. H. How to Disappear

Sutton, K. Some quiet place

   emperor of any place. Wynne-Jones, T.

EMPERORS -- FICTION

Kincaid, S. J. The empress

EMPLOYMENT AGENCIES -- FICTION

Fforde, J. The last Dragonslayer

EMPRESSES -- FICTION

Dao, J. C. Forest of a thousand lanterns

Kincaid, S. J. The empress

   empress. Kincaid, S. J.

Empress of a thousand skies. Belleza, R.

Empress of the sun. McDonald, I.

Empress of the world. Ryan, S.

   empty kingdom. Wein, E.

Enchantment Lake: a Northwoods mystery. Preus, M.

   enchantment of ravens. Rogerson, M.

Enchantress from the stars. Engdahl, S. L.

   enchantress. Scott, M.

Endangered. Schrefer, E.

   game. Card, O. S.

   Price, L.

   games. **Martin, T. M.**

END OF THE WORLD -- FICTION

Coyle, K. Vivian Apple at the end of the world

Coyle, K. Vivian Apple needs a miracle

Hutchinson, S. D. The apocalypse of Elena Mendoza

Smith-Ready, J. This side of salvation

   enemy has a face. Miklowitz, G. D.

Engdahl, Sylvia Louise

Enchantress from the stars

   of the broken world. Vanhee, J.

ENGLAND -- FICTION

Almond, D. A song for Ella Grey

Almond, D. Half a creature from the sea

Almond, D. The tightrope walkers

Buckley-Archer, L. The many lives of John Stone

Conaghan, B. When Mr. Dog bites

Cousins, D. Waiting for Gonzo

Doctorow, C. Pirate cinema

Fisher, C. Darkwater

Johnson, M. The madness underneath

Johnson, M. The shadow cabinet

Mason, S. Running girl

Mayhew, J. The Big Lie

Moriarty, J. A corner of white

Moriarty, J. A tangle of gold

Moriarty, J. The cracks in the kingdom

Morpurgo, M. Listen to the Moon

Pitcher, A. Ketchup clouds

Pitcher, A. My sister lives on the mantelpiece

Pitcher, A. Silence is goldfish: a novel

Powell, L. The Master of Misrule

Powell, W. C. Expiration day

Pullman, P. La Belle Sauvage

Reeve, P. Scrivener's moon

Rennison, L. The taming of the tights

Terry, T. Fractured

Valentine, J. Double

Ward, R. Infinity

ENGLAND -- SOCIAL LIFE AND CUSTOMS -- 19TH CENTURY -- FICTION

Kindl, P. A school for brides

Kindl, P. Keeping the castle

Engle, Margarita

Firefly letters

Enthusiasm. Shulman, P.

Entwined. Dixon, H.

ENVIRONMENTAL DEGRADATION -- FICTION

Crossan, S. Breathe

ENVIRONMENTAL MOVEMENT -- FICTION

Cowan, J. Earthgirl

Henry, A. Torched

ENVIRONMENTAL PROTECTION -- FICTION

Gilman, D. The devil's breath

McDonald, A. Boys, bears, and a serious pair of hiking boots

The **epic** crush of Genie Lo. Yee, F. C.

EPIDEMICS -- FICTION

Condie, A. Reached

Griffin, E. Z. Light years

Howe, K. Conversion

Kagawa, J. The Eternity Cure

Kizer, A. A matter of days

London, A. Guardian

Lucier, M. A death-struck year

Sangster, C. Last star burning

Treggiari, J. Ashes, ashes

Wiggins, B. Stung

EPIDEMIOLOGY -- FICTION

Chibbaro, J. Deadly

EPILEPSY -- FICTION

Oakes, S. The arsonist

Philbrick, W. R. The last book in the universe

Thomas, L. Nowhere near you

EPISTOLARY FICTION

Moriarty, J. A corner of white

Moriarty, J. Feeling sorry for Celia

Pitcher, A. Ketchup clouds

Paolini, C.

EROS (GREEK DEITY) -- FICTION

Selfors, S. Mad love

Erskine, Kathryn

Quaking

from Eden. Nader, E.

ESCAPES -- FICTION

Gagnon, M. Strangelets

Nader, E. Escape from Eden

Riggs, R. Hollow city

Smith, A. G. Lockdown

Turtschaninoff, M. Naondel

Turtschaninoff, M. Naondel

ESCAPES -- FICTION

Turtschaninoff, M. Naondel

Turtschaninoff, M. Naondel

ESCAPES (AMUSEMENTS) -- FICTION

Callahan, E. The art of escaping

Escaping from Houdini. Maniscalco, K.

Escaping the tiger. Manivong, L.

Eshbaugh, Julie

Obsidian and stars

ESKIMOS -- FICTION, K. Between two worlds, Kirkpatrick

Hoban, R. Soonchild

ESPIONAGE -- FICTION

Carriger, G. Curtsies & conspiracies

Carriger, G. Etiquette & espionage

Wein, E. Code name Verity

ESSAYISTS

Sheth, K. Keeping corner

Essential maps for the lost. Caletti, D.

Estrella's quinceanera. Alegria, M.

ETCHING

See also Art; Pictures

Eternity Cure. Kagawa, J.

ETHIOPIA -- HISTORY -- 1889-1974 -- FICTION

Wein, E. Black dove, white raven

ETHNIC RELATIONS -- FICTION

Abdel-Fattah, R. The lines we cross

Abdel-Fattah, R. The lines we cross

Etiquette & espionage. Carriger, G.

ETIQUETTE -- FICTION

Carriger, G. Curtsies & conspiracies

Carriger, G. Etiquette & espionage

EUROPE -- FICTION

Johnson, M. 13 little blue envelopes

Lee, M. The gentleman's guide to vice and virtue

Schreiber, J. Perry's killer playlist

EUROPE -- HISTORY -- 1918-1945 -- FICTION

De Fombelle, T. The book of Pearl

Ruiz Zafon, C. The Prince of Mist

EUROPE -- HISTORY -- 16TH CENTURY -- FICTION

Marsh, K. Jepp, who defied the stars

EUROPE -- HISTORY -- 18TH CENTURY -- FICTION

Lee, M. The gentleman's guide to vice and virtue

EURYDICE (GREEK MYTHOLOGICAL CHARACTER) -- FICTION

Almond, D. A song for Ella Grey

Eva. Dickinson, P.

Eva underground. Mackall, D. D.

Eve & Adam. Grant, M.

Even in paradise. Philpot, C.

Even the darkest stars. Fawcett, H.

Even the darkest stars. Rens, K.

The **everafter.** Huntley, A.

Everbound. Ashton, B.

Everless. Holland, S.

Everlost. Shusterman, N.

Everneath. Ashton, B.

Everybody sees the ants. King, A. S.

Every crooked pot. Rosen, R.

Every day. Levithan, D.

Every little thing in the world. De Gramont, N.

Everything that makes you. McStay, M.

Everything. Yoon, N.

Eves, Rosalyn

Blood Rose Rebellion

Evil genius. Jinks, C.

EVOLUTION -- FICTION

Brande, R. Evolution, me, & other freaks of nature

Card, O. S. Ruins

Evolution, me, & other freaks of nature. Brande, R.

EXECUTIONS AND EXECUTIONERS -- FICTION

LaFevers, R. Grave mercy

Salisbury, M. The Sin Eater's daughter

Wung-Sung, J. last execution

Exile. Osterlund, A.

EXILES -- FICTION

Carleson, J. C. The tyrant's daughter

Exit, pursued by a bear. Johnston, E. K.

Exit strategy. Potter, R.

EXPERIMENTS -- FICTION

Gagnon, M. Don't let go

Gagnon, M. Don't Look Now

Gagnon, M. Don't turn around

Expiration day. Powell, W. C.

EXPLORERS

McKernan, V. Shackleton's stowaway

EXPLOSIONS -- FICTION

Perez, A. Out of darkness

Exposed. Marcus, K.

EXTRASENSORY PERCEPTION -- FICTION

Brant, W. Zenn diagram

Derting, K. The body finder

Derting, K. Desires of the dead

Gee, M. Salt
St. Crow, L. Strange angels
Ward, R. The Chaos
Ward, R. Num8ers
    Westerfeld, S.

EXTRATERRESTRIAL BEINGS -- FICTION
Anderson, M. T. Landscape with invisible hand
Bunker, L. Felix Yz
Castellucci, C. First day on Earth
Grant, M. Monster
Lo, M. Adaptation
Lo, M. Inheritance
Silver, E. Rush
Wallenfels, S. POD
Yancey, R. infinite sea
Yancey, R. The 5th Wave
    of the crow. Peacock, S.
    like stars. Mantchev, L.
    of the emperor. Salisbury, G.

EYRE, JANE (FICTITIOUS CHARACTER)
Hand, C. My plain Jane

F
    like glass. Hardinge, F.
    on the milk carton. Cooney, C. B.

FACTORIES -- FICTION
Bryant, M. E. Glow
Bunce, E. C. A curse dark as gold
Davies, J. Lost
Liu, J. Girls on the line
    after. Simner, J. L.
    winter. Simner, J. L

Fahy, Thomas Richard
The unspoken

FAIRIES -- FICTION
Black, H. The cruel prince
Block, F. L. The waters & the wild
Carey, J. L. Dragonswood
Carey, J. L. In the time of dragon moon
Catmull, K. The radiant road: a novel
Fisher, C. The door in the moon
Healey, K. Guardian of the dead
Larbalestier, J. How to ditch your fairy
Lo, M. Ash
Lo, M. Huntress
Maas, S. J. A court of thorns and roses
Marr, M. Wicked lovely
O'Guilin, P. The call
Pike, A. Wings
Pratchett, T. The shepherd's crown
Rogerson, M. An enchantment of ravens
Simner, J. L. Bones of Faerie
Simner, J. L. Faerie after
Simner, J. L. Faerie winter
Stiefvater, M. Ballad; a gathering of faerie
Taylor, L. Blackbringer

Taylor, L. Silksinger
Thompson, K. The new policeman
Tripp, B. The accidental highwayman: being the tale of Kit Bristol, his horse Midnight, a mysterious princess, and sundry magical persons besides
Yolen, J. Curse of the Thirteenth Fey
Zettel, S. Bad luck girl
Zettel, S. Dust girl
Zettel, S. Golden girl

FAIRS
Dennard, S. Something strange and deadly

FAIRY TALES -- FICTION
Ahdieh, R. The wrath and the dawn
Albert, M. The Hazel Wood
Cornwell, B. Mechanica
Cornwell, B. Venturess
De Fombelle, T. The book of Pearl
Flinn, A. Cloaked
George, J. D. Princess of glass
George, J. D. Princess of the midnight ball
George, J. D. Sun and moon, ice and snow
Hale, S. The Goose girl
Johnston, E. K. A thousand nights
Lo, M. Ash
Lo, M. Huntress
McKinley, R. Beauty; a retelling of the story of Beauty & the beast
Murdock, C. G. Princess Ben
Murdock, C. G. Wisdom's kiss
Myers, W. D. Amiri & Odette; a love story
Napoli, D. J. Beast
Napoli, D. J. The magic circle
Napoli, D. J. The wager
Pattou, E. East
Templeman, M. The glass casket
Yolen, J. Curse of the Thirteenth Fey
Yolen, J. Troll Bridge

FAITH -- FICTION
Berry, J. The passion of Dolssa
Coker, R. Chasing Jupiter
Daley, J. R. Jesus Jackson
Gilbert, K. L. Conviction
Hautman, P. Eden West
Henry, K. Heretics Anonymous

Faith, hope, and Ivy June. Naylor, P. R.
Fake ID. Giles, L.

FALCONRY -- FICTION
London, A. Black wings beating

FALCONS -- FICTION
Whitman, E. Wildwing

Falkner, Brian
Brain Jack
The project

Fallen Grace. Hooper, M.
Fall for anything. Summers, C.
Falling over sideways. Sonnenblick, J.
Fall of a kingdom. Bell, H.

Bond, G.

Falls, Kat

Inhuman

FALSE ACCUSATION -- FICTION

Grace, A. In too deep

FAME -- FICTION

Johnston, E. K. Prairie fire

Johnston, E. K. The story of Owen

King, A. S. Reality Boy

Noel, A. Unrivaled

Ormsbee, K. Tash hearts Tolstoy

Rudnick, P., 1957- Gorgeous

Russell, C. Songs about a girl

Shukert, R. Love me

Skuse, C. J. Rockoholic

Tashjian, J. The gospel according to Larry

Whitaker, A. Wildflower

FAMILIARS (SPIRITS) -- FICTION

Pullman, P. La Belle Sauvage

FAMILIES -- ARIZONA -- FICTION

Flood, N. B. Soldier sister, fly home

FAMILIES -- AUSTRALIA -- FICTION

Abdel-Fattah, R. The lines we cross

FAMILIES -- CALIFORNIA -- MARINA DEL REY -- FICTION

Yee, L. The kidney hypothetical

FAMILIES -- FICTION

Amato, M. Get happy

Block, F. L. Love in the time of global warming

Brashares, A. The whole thing together

Caine, R. Prince of Shadows

Casanova, M. Frozen

Corthron, K. L. The truth of right now

Córdova, Z. Labyrinth lost

Fowley-Doyle, M. The accident season

Frank, E. R. Dime

Hardinge, F. A skinful of shadows

Hemphill, S. Sisters of glass

Karim, S. That thing we call a heart

Katsoulis, G. S. All rights reserved

Kephart, B. One thing stolen

Laskin, P. L. Ronit & Jamil

Littman, S. Backlash

Lockhart, E. We were liars

McCarthy, A. Just fly away

McLaughlin, L. The Free

McLemore, A. -M. Wild beauty

Mesrobian, C. Just a girl

Miller, M. Shadow run

Miller, S. J. The art of starving

Pitcher, A. Ketchup clouds

Porter, S. When I Cast Your Shadow

Rosenfield, K. Inland

Roth, V. Allegiant

Roth, V. Insurgent

Stiefvater, M. All the crooked saints

Sáenz, B. A. Aristotle and Dante discover the secrets of the

universe

Sáenz, B. A. The inexplicable logic of my life

Tamani, L. Calling my name

FAMILIES -- FLORIDA -- FICTION

Mills, E. First & then

FAMILIES -- MASSACHUSETTS -- CONCORD -- FICTION

MacColl, M. The revelation of Louisa May

FAMILIES -- NEW JERSEY -- FICTION

Blume, J. Forever

FAMILIES OF DRUG ADDICTS -- FICTION

Arcos, C. Out of reach

FAMILIES -- PENNSYLVANIA -- FICTION

Alender, K. The dead girls of Hysteria Hall

FAMILIES -- TEXAS -- FICTION

Tamani, L. Calling my name

FAMILY -- FICTION

Amato, M. Get happy

Davis, T. S. Happy families

Demetrios, H. Something real

King, A. S. Everybody sees the ants

Rupp, R. After Eli

FAMILY LIFE

Keplinger, K. A midsummer's nightmare

Lockhart, E. We were liars

Van Draanen, W. Flipped

FAMILY LIFE -- ALASKA -- FICTION

Macvie, M. The ocean in my ears

FAMILY LIFE -- ARIZONA -- FICTION

Flood, N. B. Soldier sister, fly home

FAMILY LIFE -- AUSTRALIA -- FICTION

Abdel-Fattah, R. The lines we cross

Howell, S. Girl defective

FAMILY LIFE -- CALIFORNIA -- FICTION

Colbert, B. Little & Lion

Gilbert, K. L. Picture us in the light

Lynch, J. N. My beautiful hippie

FAMILY LIFE -- CALIFORNIA -- LOS ANGELES -- FICTION

Arcos, C. The re will come a time

FAMILY LIFE -- CANADA -- FICTION

Hopkinson, N. The Chaos

Johnston, E. K. Prairie fire

Johnston, E. K. The story of Owen

Martin, C. K. K. Yesterday

FAMILY LIFE -- CONNECTICUT -- FICTION

Matson, M. Since you've been gone

FAMILY LIFE -- ENGLAND -- FICTION

Burgess, M. The hit

Conaghan, B. When Mr. Dog bites

Cousins, D. Waiting for Gonzo

Pitcher, A. Ketchup clouds

Terry, T. Slated

FAMILY LIFE -- FICTION

Abdel-Fattah, R. The lines we cross

Aldredge, B. Sasquatch, love, and other imaginary things

Alender, K. The dead girls of Hysteria Hall

Schmidt, G. D. Trouble
Scott, E. Miracle
Sharenow, R. The Berlin Boxing Club
Silvey, C. Jasper Jones
Sitomer, A. L. The secret story of Sonia Rodriguez
Sloan, H. G. I'll be there
Smith-Ready, J. This side of salvation
Sonnenblick, J. After ever after
Sonnenblick, J. Falling over sideways
Sorosiak, C. Wild blue wonder
Spinelli, J. Smiles to go
Standiford, N. Confessions of the Sullivan sisters
Standiford, N. How to say goodbye in Robot
Stevenson, S. J. The Latte Rebellion
Strasser, T. Price of duty
Surface tension; a novel in four summers. Runyon, B.
Tal, E. Cursing Columbus
Thompson, H. Orchards
Tregay, S. Love & leftovers; a novel in verse
Trigiani, A. Viola in the spotlight
Venkatraman, P. Climbing the stairs
Vlahos, L. The Scar Boys
Warman, J. Between
Warman, J. Where the truth lies
West, K. Split second
Whaley, J. C. Where things come back
Whitaker, A. Wildflower
White, R. A month of Sundays
Williams, C. L. The chosen one
Williams, C. L. Miles from ordinary; a novel
Williams-Garcia, R. Like sisters on the homefront
Williams, G. Beatle meets Destiny
Williams, S. D. Palace beautiful
Wilson, D. L. Firehorse
Wittlinger, E. Parrotfish
Yee, L. The kidney hypothetical
Yolen, J. Curse of the Thirteenth Fey
Zeises, L. M. The sweet life of Stella Madison
Zusak, M. Bridge of Clay

FAMILY LIFE -- FLORIDA -- FICTION
Mills, E. First & then
FAMILY LIFE -- FLORIDA -- MIAMI -- FICTION
Danticat, E. Untwine
FAMILY LIFE -- GEORGIA -- FICTION
Coker, R. Chasing Jupiter
FAMILY LIFE-- GERMANY--FICTION
Kephart, B. Going over
FAMILY LIFE -- HAWAII -- FICTION
Patel, S. Rani Patel in full effect
FAMILY LIFE -- ILLINOIS -- CHICAGO -- FICTION
Ahmed, S. Love, hate & other filters
Martinez, C. G. Pig Park
FAMILY LIFE -- ILLINOIS -- FICTION
Stone, T. I. Time between us
FAMILY LIFE -- JAPAN -- FICTION
Lowitz, L. Jet Black and the ninja wind.
FAMILY LIFE -- KANSAS -- FICTION

Schantz, S. E. Fig
FAMILY LIFE -- LIBERIA -- FICTION
Gibney, S. Dream country
FAMILY LIFE -- MASSACHUSETTS -- CONCORD -- FICTION
MacColl, M. The revelation of Louisa May
FAMILY LIFE -- MASSACHUSETTS -- FICTION
Friend, N. How we roll
Thompson, H. The language inside
FAMILY LIFE -- MINNESOTA -- FICTION
Gibney, S. Dream country
FAMILY LIFE -- MISSOURI -- KANSAS CITY -- FICTION
Whaley, J. C. Noggin
FAMILY LIFE -- NEW JERSEY -- FICTION
Bryant, M. E. Glow
Doktorski, J. S. The summer after you and me
FAMILY LIFE -- NEW YORK (STATE) -- BROOKLYN -- FICTION
Reynolds, J. Boy in the black suit
Reynolds, J. When I was the greatest
FAMILY LIFE -- NEW YORK (STATE) -- FICTION
Johnson, J. J. The theory of everything
FAMILY LIFE -- NEW YORK (STATE) -- NEW YORK -- FICTION
Perkins, M. You bring the distant near
FAMILY LIFE -- NORTH CAROLINA
Moses, S. P. The legend of Buddy Bush
FAMILY LIFE -- OHIO -- FICTION
Barzak, C. The gone away place
FAMILY LIFE -- OREGON -- FICTION
Reed, A. The Nowhere Girls.
FAMILY LIFE -- PENNSYLVANIA -- FICTION
Andrews, J. Me & Earl & the dying girl
FAMILY LIFE -- PENNSYLVANIA -- HERSHEY -- FICTION
Finneyfrock, K. The sweet revenge of Celia Door
FAMILY LIFE -- RHODE ISLAND -- FICTION
Callahan, E. The art of escaping
FAMILY LIFE -- RUSSIA -- FICTION
O'Brien, A. Lara's gift
FAMILY LIFE -- SYRIA -- FICTION
Abawi, A. A land of permanent goodbyes
Abawi, A. A land of permanent goodbyes
FAMILY LIFE -- TENNESSEE -- FICTION
Vawter, V. Copyboy
FAMILY LIFE -- TEXAS -- FICTION
Fehlbaum, B. Big fat disaster
McCall, G. G. All the stars denied
Temblador, A. Secrets of the Casa Rosada
FAMILY LIFE -- UTAH -- FICTION
Lauren, C. Autoboyography
FAMILY LIFE -- VIRGINIA -- FICTION
Lyne, J. H. Catch rider
FAMILY LIFE -- WASHINGTON (STATE) -- SEATTLE -- FICTION
Trueman, T. Life happens next; a novel
FAMILY PROBLEMS -- FICTION

Anderson, L. H. The impossible knife of memory
Arnold, E. K. What girls are made of
Beaufrand, M. J. The rise and fall of the Gallivanters
Bennett, J. Starry eyes
Bliss, B. We'll fly away
Blythe, C. Revenge of a not-so-pretty girl
Bowman, A. D. Starfish
Carter, C. Me, him, them, and it
Castan, M. Fighting for Dontae
Chan, C. All that I can fix
Chen, J. Return to me
Crossan, S. Moonrise
Crossan, S. One
Doller, T. Something like normal
Fehlbaum, B. Big fat disaster
Ferris, J. Of sound mind
Gardner, F. The second life of Ava Rivers
Henry, K. Heretics Anonymous
Juby, S. The Truth Commission
Kehoe, S. W. The sound of letting go
Keplinger, K. A midsummer's nightmare
King, A. S. Ask the passengers
King, A. S. Reality Boy
Kirby, J. Golden
Kriegman, M. Being Audrey Hepburn: a novel
Lyga, B. Bang
McCahan, E. The lake effect
McGarry, K. Only a breath apart
McLaughlin, L. The Free
Pitcher, A. My sister lives on the mantelpiece
Quintero, I. Gabi, a girl in pieces
Reed, A. Over you
Sales, L. Tonight the streets are ours
Scelsa, K. Fans of the impossible life
Stone, T. I. Little do we know
Summers, C. This is not a test
Sutton, K. Some quiet place
Vlahos, L. Life in a fishbowl
Willey, M. Beetle Boy
Williams, C. L. Waiting
Williams, I. Water in May

FAMILY SECRETS -- FICTION
Alexander, K. Solo
Beaufrand, M. J. Useless Bay
Benway, R. Far from the tree
Carey, E. Heap House
Devlin, C. Tell me something real
Fowley-Doyle, M. The accident season
Giles, A. Now is everything
Haddix, M. P. Full ride
Hardinge, F. A skinful of shadows
Jensen, C. Skyscraping
King, A. S. Still life with tornado
Littlefield, S. Infected
Long, H. Sophie someone
Lowitz, L. Jet Black and the ninja wind.
Martinez, J. Kiss kill vanish

McCarthy, A. Just fly away
Murdoch, E. If you find me
Nelson, M. American ace
Stiefvater, M. Blue lily, lily blue
Zusak, M. Bridge of Clay

FAMILY VIOLENCE -- FICTION
Bilen, T. What she left behind
King, A. S. Still life with tornado
Famous last words. Doktorski, J. S.

FANATICISM -- FICTION
Fixmer, E. Down from the mountain

FAN FICTION
Rowell, R. Fangirl
Fangirl. Rowell, R.
Fans of the impossible life. Scelsa, K.
Fantaskey, Beth
Buzz kill
Jessica's guide to dating on the dark side

FANTASY -- FICTION
Ahdieh, R. The rose and the dagger
Almond, D. Skellig
Arbuthnott, G. The Keepers' tattoo
Ashton, B. Everneath
Bardugo, L. Crooked kingdom
Bardugo, L. Ruin and rising
Bardugo, L. Shadow and bone
Bardugo, L. Siege and storm
Bardugo, L. Six of crows
Barrett, T. The Stepsister's Tale
Barron, T. A. Merlin's dragon
Barron, T. A. The lost years of Merlin
Bashardoust, M. Girls made of snow and glass
Bell, H. Fall of a kingdom
Bell, H. Forging the sword
Bell, H. The last knight
Bennett, H. Shapeshifter
Berk, A. Death watch
Black, H. The cruel prince
Bobet, L. Above
Bobet, L. An inheritance of ashes
Bow, E. Plain Kate
Bow, E. The Scorpion Rules
Brennan, S. R. In other lands
Bunce, E. C. Liar's moon
Bunce, E. C. Star crossed
Caine, R. Ash and quill
Cameron, S. The dark unwinding
Carey, J. L. Dragonswood
Carey, J. L. Dragon's Keep
Carey, J. L. In the time of dragon moon
Carey, J. L. The beast of Noor
Carson, R. The bitter kingdom
Carson, R. The crown of embers
Carson, R. The girl of fire and thorns
Casella, J. Thin space
Cashore, K. Bitterblue
Cashore, K. Graceling

Chee, T. The speaker
Chima, C. W. The Crimson Crown
Chima, C. W. The Demon King
Chima, C. W. The warrior heir
Chokshi, R. The star-touched queen
Clement-Davies, D. The sight
Cluess, J. A shadow bright and burning
Coakley, L. Witchlanders
Condie, A. Crossed
Condie, A. Matched
Cooper, S. Over sea, under stone
Cooper, T. Changers book one
Croggon, A. The Naming
Cypess, L. Death sworn
Cypess, L. Mistwood
Damico, G. Scorch
Daniels, A. Dreadnought
Dennard, S. Truthwitch
Derting, K. The pledge
Dickinson, P. The ropemaker
Dimaline, C. The marrow thieves
Duey, K. Sacred scars
Egan, C. Julia vanishes
Fawcett, H. Even the darkest stars
Fire. Cashore, K.
Fisher, C. The dark city
Fisher, C. The door in the moon
Fletcher, S. Ancient, strange, and lovely
Fletcher, S. Dragon's milk
Flinn, A. Beastly
Forster, M. City of a Thousand Dolls
Frost, G. Shadowbridge
Funke, C. Fearless
Funke, C. Reckless
Gaiman, N. The Sleeper and the Spindle
Gaughen, A. C. Reign the earth
Gee, M. Salt
George, J. D. Sun and moon, ice and snow
Goto, H. Half World
Graudin, R. Blood for blood
Grey, M. The girl at midnight
Hahn, R. A creature of moonlight
Hale, S. Book of a thousand days
Hamilton, A. Hero at the fall.
Hamilton, A. Traitor to the throne
Hamilton, K. Tyger tyger
Hardinge, F. A face like glass
Hardinge, F. A skinful of shadows
Harland, R. Worldshaker
Harris, J. Runemarks
Hartley, A. J. Steeplejack
Hartman, R. Seraphina
Hartman, R. Shadow scale
Heilig, H. For a muse of fire
Heilig, H. The Girl from Everywhere
Hocking, A. Wake
Hodge, R. Crimson bound

Hodge, R. Cruel Beauty
Holland, S. Everless
Hubbard, A. Ripple
Humphreys, C. The hunt of the unicorn
Jacobs, J. H. The twelve-fingered boy
Jeschonek, R. T. My favorite band does not exist
Kagawa, J. Shadow of the Fox
Kagawa, J. Talon
Kagawa, J. The forever song
King, E. R. The hundredth queen
Kittredge, C. The Iron Thorn
Kittredge, C. The nightmare garden
Lam, L. Pantomime
Lanagan, M. The brides of Rollrock Island
Lasky, K. Lone wolf
Legrand, C. Furyborn
Legrand, C. Sawkill girls
London, A. Black wings beating
Maas, S. J. A court of thorns and roses
Maas, S. J. Throne of glass
MacHale, D. J. The merchant of death
MacHale, D. J. The pilgrims of Rayne
Marillier, J. Raven flight
Marillier, J. Shadowfell
Marr, M. Wicked lovely
McCaffrey, T. J. Dragongirl
McKinley, R. Chalice
McKinley, R. Dragonhaven
McKinley, R. Pegasus
McKinley, R. The blue sword
McKinley, R. The hero and the crown
McLemore, A. -M. When the moon was ours
McNeal, T. Far far away
McQuein, J. L. Arclight
McQuerry, M. D. The Peculiars
Mieville, C. Un Lun Dun
Moriarty, J. A corner of white
Moriarty, J. The cracks in the kingdom
Moskowitz, H. Teeth
Mourlevat, J. Winter's end
Nayeri, D. Another Pan
Neumeier, R. The City in the Lake
Neumeier, R. The keeper of the mist
Nicholson, W. Seeker
Nix, G. Clariel: the lost Abhorsen
Paolini, C. Eragon
Pierce, T. Alanna: the first adventure
Pierce, T. Bloodhound
Pierce, T. First test
Pierson, D. C. Crap kingdom
Pike, A. Wings
Porter, S. When I Cast Your Shadow
Pratchett, T. The amazing Maurice and his educated rodents
Pratchett, T. The shepherd's crown
Pratchett, T. The Wee Free Men
Pullman, P. The golden compass
Redwine, C. J. The wish granter: a Ravenspire novel

Kaslik, I. Skinny

King, A. S. Glory O'Brien's history of the future: a novel

Lake, N. Hostage Three

Les Becquets, D. Season of ice

Lupica, M. Miracle on 49th Street

Mackall, D. D. Eva underground

Marshall, K. I am still alive

McCarthy, A. Just fly away

McQuerry, M. D. The Peculiars

North, P. Starglass

Oates, J. C. Freaky green eyes

O'Brien, A. Lara's gift

Robert, Na'ima B. From Somalia with love

Rorby, G. The outside of a horse; a novel

Rosen, R. Every crooked pot

Rossetti, R. The girl with borrowed wings

Shepherd, M. Her Dark Curiosity

Sones, S. One of those hideous books where the mother dies

Stuber, B. Crossing the tracks

Summers, C. Fall for anything

Treichel, E. A series of small maneuvers

Valentine, J. Fire color one

Waller, S. B. The Forbidden Orchid

Whelan, G. See what I see

Wynne-Jones, T. uninvited

Zettel, S. Dust girl

FATHER-SON RELATIONSHIP -- FICTION

Alexander, K. Solo

Alsaid, A. North of happy

Berk, A. Death watch

Bruchac, J. Wolf mark

Crutcher, C. Ironman

Deuker, C. Gym candy

Gavin, R. 3 of a kind

Gilbert, K. L. Conviction

Going, K. L. King of the screwups

Gratz, A. Samurai shortstop

Grimes, N. Dark sons

Hartnett, S. Golden Boys

Herlong, M. The great wide sea

Hernandez, D. Suckerpunch

Jimenez, F. Reaching out

Kerr, M. E. If I love you, am I trapped forever?

Luper, E. Bug boy

Luper, E. Seth Baumgartner's love manifesto

Lupica, M. The big field

Lupica, M. Hero

Lyga, B. I hunt killers

Lynch, C. Hothouse

Mankell, H. A bridge to the stars

McDonald, I. Be my enemy

McGhee, A. What I leave behind

Morpurgo, M. Listen to the Moon

Nolan, H. Crazy

Proimos, J. 12 things to do before you crash and burn

Sloan, H. G. I'll be there

Smith, R. Peak

Stewart, M. Riverkeep

Thomas, R. Rats saw God

Villareal, R. Body slammed

Volponi, P. Hurricane song

Wallace, R. Perpetual check

Willey, M. Beetle Boy

Wynne-Jones, T. The emperor of any place

FATHERS -- DEATH -- FICTION

Polisner, G. In sight of stars

FATHERS -- FICTION

Barnaby, H. Wonder show

Barratt, M. The wild man

Bilen, T. What she left behind

Bodeen, S. A. The Compound

Caletti, D. The secret life of Prince Charming

Davis, T. S. Happy families

Deuker, C. High heat

Fleischman, P. Seek

Maetani, V. E. Ink & ashes

Matson, M. Amy & Roger's epic detour

Nelson, M. American ace

Pitcher, A. Silence is goldfish: a novel

Resau, L. The indigo notebook

Resau, L. The jade notebook

Sedgwick, M. She is not invisible

Tayleur, K. Chasing boys

Valentine, J. Me, the missing, and the dead

FATHERS AND DAUGHTERS -- FICTION

Amato, M. Get happy

Bacigalupi, P. The doubt factory

Bennett, J. Alex, approximately

Bigelow, L. J. Starting from here

Cabot, M. The princess diaries

Carter, A. Not if I save you first

Doller, T. The devil you know

Jensen, C. Skyscraping

Keplinger, K. A midsummer's nightmare

Lake, N. Hostage Three

Mac, C. 10 things I can see from here

McCarthy, A. Just fly away

Rush, J. Altered

Sonnenblick, J. Falling over sideways

Sugiura, M. It's not like it's a secret

Thomas, R. Long may she reign

Treichel, E. A series of small maneuvers

Valentine, J. Fire color one

FATHERS AND SONS -- FICTION

Alexander, K. The crossover

Alexander, K. Solo

Crowe, C. Mississippi trial, 1955

Emond, S. Bright lights, dark nights

Gavin, R. 3 of a kind

Gilbert, K. L. Conviction

Konigsberg, B. Honestly Ben

Lubar, D. Character, driven

Lyga, B. I hunt killers

McGhee, A. What I leave behind

& then. Mills, E.

Fisher, Catherine
The dark city
Darkwater
The door in the moon
FISHERS -- FICTION
Parker, S. M. The rattled bones
FISHING -- FICTION
Rocco, J. Swim that rock
Between Two Skies. O'Sullivan, J.
Woolston, B. Catch & release
Fitzpatrick, Becca
Black ice
Fitzpatrick, Huntley
My life next door
What I thought was true
    stages of Andrew Brawley. Hutchinson, S. D.
    Delilah. Ockler, S.
Fixmer, Elizabeth
Down from the mountain
Flack, Sophie
Bunheads
Flake, Sharon G.

    a Sky Chasers novel. Ryan, A. K.
    in the mist. Ahdieh, R.
FLAMEL, NICOLAS, D. 1418 -- FICTION
Scott, M. The enchantress
    burnout; a novel. Madigan, L. K.
Flawless. Chapman, L.
Fleischman, Paul

Fletcher, Christine
Ten cents a dance
Fletcher, Susan
Ancient, strange, and lovely
Dragon's milk
FLIGHT -- FICTION
Reeve, P. A Web of Air
Flinn, Alex
Beastly
Breathing underwater
Cloaked
A kiss in time
    Bedford, M.
      Van Draanen, W.
Flood, Nancy Bo
Soldier sister, fly home
FLOODS -- FICTION
Napoli, D. J. Storm
Richards, J. Three rivers rising
FLORENCE (ITALY) -- FICTION
Kephart, B. One thing stolen
Flores-Scott, Patrick
American road trip
FLORIDA -- FICTION

Blundell, J. What I saw and how I lied
Doller, T. The devil you know
Howard, J. J. That time I joined the circus
McCarthy, S. C. True fires
Mills, E. First & then
St. James, J. Freak show
FLOWERS -- FICTION
Hahn, R. A creature of moonlight
Flygirl. Smith, S. L.
FLYING -- FICTION
Rossetti, R. The girl with borrowed wings
Foley, Jessie Ann
Neighborhood girls
FOLKLORE
Oh, E. A thousand beginnings and endings: 15 retellings of
    Asian myths and legends
FOLKLORE -- RUSSIA
Bardugo, L. Shadow and bone
FOOD -- FICTION
Zeises, L. M. The sweet life of Stella Madison
FOOTBALL -- FICTION
Cohen, J. C. Leverage
Deuker, C. Gym candy
Deuker, C. Payback time
Herbach, G. Stupid fast
Lipsyte, R. Raiders night
Lynch, C. Hit count
Lynch, C. Inexcusable
McKissack, F. Shooting star
Murdock, C. G. Dairy Queen
Murdock, C. G. The off season
Richmond, P. Always a catch
Tharp, T. Knights of the hill country
Wallace, S. N. Muckers
FOOTBALL PLAYERS -- FICTION
Mills, E. First & then
For a muse of fire. Heilig, H.
The **Forbidden** Orchid. Waller, S. B.
FORCED MARRIAGE -- FICTION
Saeed, A. Written in the stars
FOREIGN STUDY -- FICTION
Perkins, S. Anna and the French kiss
Perkins, S. Isla and the happily ever after: a novel
Forest of a thousand lanterns. Dao, J. C.
The **Forest** of Hands and Teeth. Ryan, C.
FORESTS AND FORESTRY -- FICTION
Hahn, R. A creature of moonlight
The **foretelling.** Hoffman, A.
Forever, again. Laurie, V.
Forever. Blume, J.
Forever in blue. Brashares, A.
The **forever** song. Kagawa, J.
The **Forgetting.** Cameron, S.
Forging the sword. Bell, H.
FORGIVENESS -- FICTION
Carter, A. Not if I save you first
Forgotten. Patrick, C.

keeps. Friend, N.

Forman, Gayle
  I have lost my way

Formerly shark girl. Bingham, K.

Forster, Miriam
  City of a Thousand Dolls
  the win. Doctorow, C.

FORTUNE -- FICTION
  Stokes, P. Girl against the universe
  fortunes of Indigo Skye. Caletti, D.
  Mosley, W.

FOSTER CHILDREN -- FICTION
  Bernard, R. Find me

FOSTER HOME CARE -- FICTION
  Bernard, R. Find me
  Booth, C. Bronxwood
  De la Peña, M. Ball don't lie
  Gagnon, M. Don't let go
  Gagnon, M. Don't Look Now
  Gagnon, M. Don't turn around
  Patterson, J. Homeroom diaries
  Rutkoski, M. The shadow society
  Scelsa, K. Fans of the impossible life
  Schmidt, G. D. Orbiting Jupiter
  trouble. Feinstein, J.

FOUNDLINGS -- FICTION
  Murdoch, E. If you find me

FOUR ELEMENTS (PHILOSOPHY) -- FICTION
  Gaughen, A. C. Reign the earth
  -Four-Two. Hughes, D.

Fowley-Doyle, Moïra
  The accident season

Foxlee, Karen
  The anatomy of wings
  The midnight dress

FRACTURED FAIRY TALES
  Cornwell, B. Mechanica
  Gaiman, N. The Sleeper and the Spindle

Fractured. Terry, T.
  like us. Barnard, S.

Fragments. Wells, D.

FRANCE -- FICTION
  Berry, J. The passion of Dolssa
  Cameron, S. Rook
  Kamata, S. Gadget Girl
  Perkins, S. Anna and the French kiss
  Perkins, S. Isla and the happily ever after: a novel
  Resau, L. The ruby notebook

FRANCE -- HISTORY -- CHARLES VIII, 1483- 1498 -- FICTION
  LaFevers, R. Grave mercy
  LaFevers, R. Mortal heart

FRANCE -- HISTORY -- 0-1328 -- FICTION
  Grant, K. M. Blue flame

FRANCE -- HISTORY -- 1940-1945, GERMAN OCCUPATION -- FICTION
  Macdonald, M. Odette's secrets

Wein, E. Code name Verity

FRANCE -- HISTORY -- LOUIS IX, 1226-1270 -- FICTION
  Berry, J. The passion of Dolssa

FRANCE -- HISTORY -- THIRD REPUBLIC -- 1870-1940 -- FICTION
  Morgan, P. The beautiful and the cursed

FRANK, ANNE, 1929-1945 ABOUT
  Dogar, S. Annexed

Frank, E. R.
  Dime
  Life is funny
  Wrecked

Franklin, Emily
  The half life of planets

Frank, Lucy
  Two girls staring at the ceiling

The **Freak** Observer. Woolston, B.

Freak show. St. James, J.

Freakboy. Clark, K. E.

Freaks and revelations. Hurwin, D.

Freaks like us. Vaught, S.

Freaky green eyes. Oates, J. C.

FREEDMEN -- FICTION
  Bolden, T. Crossing Ebenezer Creek

FREEDOM -- FICTION
  Anderson, M. T. The astonishing life of Octavian Nothing, traitor to the nation

The **freedom** maze. Sherman, D.

FREEDOM OF EXPRESSION -- FICTION
  Katsoulis, G. S. Access restricted

FREEDOM OF SPEECH -- FICTION
  Myers, W. D. The Cruisers

The **Free.** McLaughlin, L.

French, Gillian
  Grit

Fresh ink. Giles, L.

Friday never leaving. Wakefield, V.

Friend is not a verb. Ehrenhaft, D.

Friend, Natasha
  Bounce
  How we roll
  For keeps
  My life in black and white
  The other F-word
  Perfect
  Threads and flames

FRIENDSHIP -- FICTION
  Aceves, F. The closest I've come
  Albertalli, B. Leah on the offbeat
  Albertalli, B. Simon vs. the Homo Sapiens agenda
  Alexander, K. Booked
  Alexander, K. Swing
  Almond, D. A song for Ella Grey
  Alsaid, A. Let's Get Lost
  Alsaid, A. Never Always Sometimes
  Alsenas, L. Beyond clueless
  Amato, M. Get happy

Anderson, J. L. Midnight at the Electric
Anderson, J. L. Wintergirls
Andrews, J. Me & Earl & the dying girl
Andrews, J. The Haters
Avery, L. The memory book
Barnard, S. Fragile like us
Barnes, J. Tales of the Madman Underground
Barzak, C. The gone away place
Beam, C. I am J
Beaufrand, M. J. The rise and fall of the Gallivanters
Bennett, J. Starry eyes
Benwell, S. The last leaves falling
Berry, J. The passion of Dolssa
Betts, A. J. Zac and Mia
Bjorkman, L. Miss Fortune Cookie
Bliss, B. We'll fly away
Block, F. L. Dangerous angels
Block, F. L. The island of excess love
Block, F. L. Weetzie Bat
Born confused. Desai Hidier, T.
Bradbury, J. Shift
Brashares, A. Forever in blue
Brashares, A. Girls in pants
Brashares, A. The second summer of the sisterhood
Brashares, A. The sisterhood of the traveling pants
Brennan, S. R. In other lands
Brooks, B. The moves make the man; a novel
Brothers, M. Weird Girl and What's His Name
Bryce, C. Anthem for Jackson Dawes
Buzo, L. Love and other perishable items
Caletti, D. The last forever
Callahan, E. The art of escaping
Cameron, S. The Forgetting
Cameron, S. The knowing
Carter, A. Not if I save you first
Chambers, A. Dying to know you
Chan, G. The disappearance
Chapman, L. Flawless
Cole, B. The goats
Connelly, N. O. Into the hurricane
Cook, E. With malice
Corthron, K. L. The truth of right now
Crane, E. M. Skin deep
Cranse, P. All the major constellations
Crocker, N. Billie Standish was here
Crossan, S. Breathe
Crutcher, C. Staying fat for Sarah Byrnes
Cummings, P. Red kayak
Davies, J. The odds of lightning
De Gramont, N. Every little thing in the world
Dennard, S. Truthwitch
Deracine, A. Driving by starlight
Derting, K. Desires of the dead
Derting, K. The last echo
Dessen, S. Just listen
Dinnison, K. You and me and him
Dubosarsky, U. The golden day

Duiker, K. S. The hidden star
Dunagan, T. M. The salvation of Miss Lucretia
Elliott, L. Hamilton and Peggy!: a revolutionary friendship
Elston, A. The rules for disappearing
Emond, S. Bright lights, dark nights
Farrey, B. With or without you
Ferris, J. Of sound mind
Flake, S. G. Pinned
Foley, J. A. Neighborhood girls
Foxlee, K. The midnight dress
Frank, L. Two girls staring at the ceiling
Friend, N. My life in black and white
Frost, H. Hidden
George, M. Looks
Giles, G. Girls like us
Girard, M.-E. Girl Mans Up
Going, K. L. Fat kid rules the world
Goslee, S. J. Whatever
Graff, L. Lost in the sun
Green, J. Turtles all the way down
Haas, A. Dangerous girls
Halpern, J. Into the wild nerd yonder
Han, J. The summer I turned pretty
Hardinge, F. A skinful of shadows
Hartinger, B. Project Sweet Life
Hartinger, B. Three truths and a lie
Hautman, P. Invisible
Hautman, P. What boys really want
Hegedus, B. Between us Baxters
Hemmings, K. H. Juniors
Herbach, G. Nothing special
Hesse, M. The war outside
Hitchcock, B.-S. The smell of other people's houses
Howard, J. J. That time I joined the circus
Howe, K. Conversion
Howell, S. Girl defective
Howland, L. Nantucket blue
Hubbard, J. R. Try not to breathe
Huntley, A. The everafter
Jackson, T. D. Monday's not coming
James, R. Beautiful malice
Johnson, J. J. The theory of everything
Johnston, E. K. Exit, pursued by a bear
Johnston, E. K. Prairie fire
Juby, S. Another kind of cowboy
Juby, S. The fashion committee
Kaplan, A. E. Grendel's guide to love and war
Kaplan, A. We regret to inform you
Karim, S. That thing we call a heart
Kenneally, M. Coming up for air
Kephart, B. The heart is not a size
Keplinger, K. Run
Keyser, A. J. Pointe
Khorram, A. Darius the Great is not okay
Kinch, M. The fires of New SUN
Kinch, M. The rebels of New SUN
King, A. S. Glory O'Brien's history of the future: a novel

Yee, L. The kidney hypothetical
Yee, P. Learning to fly
Yoon, N. Everything
Zentner, J. Goodbye days
Zentner, J. The serpent king
Zorn, C. Protected

FRIENDSHIP IN ADOLESCENCE -- FICTION
McCreight, K. The scattering

Friesner, Esther M.
Nobody's princess
    Somalia with love. Robert, Na'ima B.
    the notebooks of Melanin Sun. Woodson, J.
    and center. Murdock, C. G.

FRONTIER AND PIONEER LIFE -- FICTION
Nelson, J. On the volcano
Paulsen, G. Woods runner
Wrede, P. C. Across the Great Barrier
Wrede, P. C. The thirteenth child
    Lines. Grant, M.

Frost, Gregory
Shadowbridge

Frost, Helen
The braid
Crossing stones
Hidden
Keesha's house

Frost, Mark
Alliance
    Casanova, M.

FUGITIVE SLAVES -- FICTION
Ayres, K. North by night
MacColl, M. The revelation of Louisa May

FUGITIVE SLAVES -- UNITED STATES -- HISTORY -- 19TH CENTURY -- FICTION
MacColl, M. The revelation of Louisa May

FUGITIVES FROM JUSTICE
Cummings, P. The journey back

FUGITIVES FROM JUSTICE -- FICTION
Belleza, R. Empress of a thousand skies
Blair, J. Leap of Faith
Cummings, P. The journey back
Keplinger, K. Run
Miranda, M. Soulprint
Sangster, C. Last star burning
Shusterman, N. Thunderhead
Shusterman, N. UnSouled
Shusterman, N. UnWholly
Simmons, K. Three
Tahir, S. A Torch Against the Night
Zinn, B. Poison

Fukuda, Andrew
The Prey
    ride. Haddix, M. P.
    tilt; a novel. Shusterman, N.

FUND-RAISING -- FICTION
Weston, R. P. Blues for Zoey

FUNDAMENTALISM -- FICTION

Coyle, K. Vivian Apple at the end of the world
Coyle, K. Vivian Apple needs a miracle

FUNERAL HOMES -- FICTION
Gardner, S. The dead I know
Reynolds, J. Boy in the black suit

FUNERAL RITES AND CEREMONIES -- FICTION
Hooper, M. Fallen Grace
Reynolds, J. Boy in the black suit

Funke, Cornelia, 1958-
Fearless
Reckless

Funny how things change. Wyatt, M.

Furyborn. Legrand, C.

FUTURE LIFE -- FICTION
Ashton, B. Everbound
Brockenbrough, M. Devine intervention
Cox, S. The Dead Girls Detective Agency
Damico, G. Croak
Damico, G. Rogue
Damico, G. Scorch
Noel, A. Radiance
Schmatz, P. Lizard radio
Shusterman, N. Everlost
Warman, J. Between
Wells, D. Bluescreen
Whitcomb, L. A certain slant of light
The **future** of us. Asher, J.

G

Gabi, a girl in pieces. Quintero, I.

GABON -- FICTION
Schrefer, E. Threatened

Gadget Girl. Kamata, S.

Gagnon, Michelle
Don't let go
Don't Look Now
Don't turn around
Strangelets

Gaiman, Neil
Interworld
The Sleeper and the Spindle

Galante, Cecilia
The sweetness of salt

GAMBLING -- FICTION
Abrahams, P. Reality check
Hautman, P. All-in
Luper, E. Bug boy
Papademetriou, L. Drop
The **game** of Love and Death. Brockenbrough, M.
The **game** of triumphs. Powell, L.

GAMES -- FICTION
Grant, M. Messenger of Fear
Oliver, L. Panic
Powell, L. The game of triumphs
Powell, L. The Master of Misrule
Gandhi, Mahatma, 1869-1948 About

Sheth, K. Keeping corner

GANGS -- FICTION
Anderson, N. C. City of Saints & Thieves
Avi. City of orphans
Bruton, C. I Predict a Riot
Castan, M. Fighting for Dontae
Elkeles, S. Perfect chemistry
Graudin, R. The walled city
Lake, N. In darkness
Marquardt, Marie F. The radius of us
Maxwell, L. The last magician
Perez, A. H. The knife and the butterfly
Voorhees, C. The brothers Torres

Gansworth, Eric
Give me some truth: a novel with paintings

GARDENS -- FICTION
McLemore, A. -M. Wild beauty

Gardner, Faith
The second life of Ava Rivers

Gardner, Scot
The dead I know

Gardner, Whitney
You're Welcome

GARGOYLES -- FICTION
Morgan, P. The beautiful and the cursed

Garner, Em
Contaminated
Mercy mode
    Parker, A. C.
Gateway. Shinn, S.
Gathering blue. Lowry, L.
Gaughen, A. C.
Reign the earth
Gavin, Rohan
3 of a kind

GAWAIN (LEGENDARY CHARACTER) -- FICTION
Morris, G. The squire's tale

GAY FATHERS -- FICTION
Jensen, C. Skyscraping

GAY MEN -- FICTION
Federle, T. The great American whatever
Hutchinson, S. D. At the edge of the universe
Hutchinson, S. D. We are the ants
Lee, M. The gentleman's guide to vice and virtue
Silvera, A. They both die at the end
Wise, T. Street dreams

GAY TEENAGERS -- FICTION
Albertalli, B. Simon vs. the Homo Sapiens agenda
Barakiva, M. One man guy
Burd, N. The vast fields of ordinary
Cohn, R. Naomi and Ely's no kiss list
Dinnison, K. You and me and him
Farrey, B. With or without you
Harrison, R. Looking for group
Hurwin, D. Freaks and revelations
Hutchinson, S. D. At the edge of the universe
Hutchinson, S. D. The five stages of Andrew Brawley

Jones, A. G. Fire song
Juby, S. Another kind of cowboy
Knowles, J. See you at Harry's
Konigsberg, B. Honestly Ben
Lennon, T. When love comes to town
Levithan, D. Boy meets boy
Levithan, D. Hold me closer: the Tiny Cooper story
Levithan, D. Two boys kissing
Linn, L. Draw the line
Miller, S. J. The art of starving
Moskowitz, H. Gone, gone, gone.
Ness, P. Release
Pearce, J. As you wish
Rice-Gonzalez, C. Chulito
Sanchez, A. Getting it
Sanchez, A. Rainbow boys
Sanchez, A. Rainbow High
Sanchez, A. Rainbow road
Silvera, A. History is all you left me
Silvera, A. More happy than not
Silvera, A. They both die at the end
Sloan, B. A tale of two summers
St. James, J. Freak show
Sáenz, B. A. Aristotle and Dante discover the secrets of the universe
Whaley, J. C. Highly illogical behavior
Wilson, M. What they always tell us

GAY YOUTH -- FICTION
Rice-Gonzalez, C. Chulito

GAYS -- FICTION
Albertalli, B. Simon vs. the Homo Sapiens agenda
Albertalli, B. What if it's us
Alsenas, L. Beyond clueless
Barakiva, M. One man guy
Danforth, E. M. The miseducation of Cameron Post
Dinnison, K. You and me and him
Federle, T. The great American whatever
Finneyfrock, K. The sweet revenge of Celia Door
Goslee, S. J. Whatever
Hutchinson, S. D. The five stages of Andrew Brawley
Lennon, T. When love comes to town
Leslea, N. October mourning
Levithan, D. Hold me closer: the Tiny Cooper story
Levithan, D. Two boys kissing
Linn, L. Draw the line
London, A. Guardian
London, A. Proxy
Mitchell, S. All out: the no-longer-secret stories of queer teens throughout the ages
Nelson, J. I'll give you the sun
Ness, P. Release
Quintero, I. Gabi, a girl in pieces
Scelsa, K. Fans of the impossible life
Silvera, A. History is all you left me
Silvera, A. More happy than not
Whaley, J. C. Highly illogical behavior

GAZA -- FICTION

Glimpse. Williams, C. L.
    Pike, A.
    glorious adventures of the Sunshine Queen. McCaughrean, G.
    O'Brien's history of the future: a novel. King, A. S.
    Bryant, M. E.
    Ryan, A. K.
    goats. Cole, B.

GOBLINS -- FICTION
  Hamilton, K. Tyger tyger
  Hamilton, K. When the stars threw down their spears
  McQuerry, M. D. The Peculiars

GODDESSES -- FICTION
  Salisbury, M. The Sin Eater's daughter

GODDESSES, GREEK -- FICTION
  Hahn, R. The shadow behind the stars
    Hautman, P.

GODS -- FICTION
  LaFevers, R. Grave mercy
  LaFevers, R. Mortal heart

GODS AND GODDESSES--FICTION
  Hahn, R. The shadow behind the stars
  Halam, A. Snakehead

Goelman, Ari
  The path of names
    bovine. Bray, L.
    going. Nye, N. S.

Going, K. L.
  Fat kid rules the world
  King of the screwups
    over. Kephart, B.
    Boys. Hartnett, S.

Golden, Christopher
  The sea wolves
  The wild
    golden compass. Pullman, P.
    golden day. Dubosarsky, U.
    girl. Zettel, S.
    Kirby, J.

GOLD MINES AND MINING -- FICTION
  Golden, C. The wild

GOLF -- FICTION
  Fichera, L. Hooked
  Luper, E. Seth Baumgartner's love manifesto
    gone away place. Barzak, C.
    gone, gone. Moskowitz, H.
    Grant, M.

Gonzalez, Julie
  Imaginary enemy

Goo, Maurene
  I believe in a thing called love
  The way you make me feel

GOOD AND EVIL
  Chupeco, R. The Girl from the Well

GOOD AND EVIL -- FICTION
  Cann, K. Consumed
  Cann, K. Possessed.

  Catmull, K. The radiant road: a novel
  Cooper, S. Over sea, under stone
  Frost, M. Alliance
  Grant, M. Gone
  Grant, M. Messenger of Fear
  Jinks, C. Evil genius
  Jinks, C. Genius squad
  Jinks, C. The genius wars
  Kagawa, J. Shadow of the Fox
  Lecesne, J. Absolute brightness
  MacCullough, C. Always a witch
  MacCullough, C. Once a witch
  Meyer, M. Renegades
  O'Guilin, P. The call
  Sedgwick, M. White crow
  Taylor, L. Dreams of gods & monsters
  Taylor, L. Silksinger
  Tucholke, A. G. Between the spark and the burn
  White, K. And I darken
  White, K. Now I rise
  Wooding, C. Havoc
  Zink, M. Guardian of the Gate
  Zink, M. Prophecy of the sisters

Goodbye days. Zentner, J.
The **goodbye** season. Hale, M.
Good enough. Yoo, P.
A **good** idea. Moracho, C.
A **good** idea. Moracho, Cristina
A **good** long way. Saldana, R.
The **Goose** girl. Hale, S.
Gorgeous. Rudnick, P., 1957-

GORILLAS -- FICTION
  Wegelius, J. The murderer's ape

Goslee, S. J.
  Whatever
The **gospel** according to Larry. Tashjian, J.

GOSSIP -- FICTION
  Harrington, H. Speechless
  King, A. S. Ask the passengers
Goth girl rising, Lyga, B.

GOTHIC ROMANCES
  Tucholke, A. G. Between the spark and the burn

Goto, Hiromi
  Half World

GOVERNESSES -- FICTION
  Hand, C. My plain Jane

GOVERNMENT, RESISTANCE TO -- FICTION
  Adeyemi, T. Children of blood and bone
  Aveyard, V. King's cage
  Bao, K. Dove arising
  Condie, A. Reached
  Garner, E. Mercy mode
  Oliver, L. Requiem
  Peterfreund, D. Across a star-swept sea
  Raina, A. When morning comes
  Simmons, K. Article 5

Grace, Amanda

In too deep

Graceling. Cashore, K.

GRADING AND MARKING (EDUCATION)

Strohmeyer, S. Smart girls get what they want

GRAFFITI -- FICTION

Gardner, W. You're Welcome

Wise, T. Street dreams

Graff, Lisa

Lost in the sun

GRANDFATHERS -- FICTION

Crowe, C. Mississippi trial, 1955

Gill, D. M. Soul enchilada

Kephart, B. House of Dance

Kerr, M. E. Gentlehands

King, A. S. Everybody sees the ants

Mazer, N. F. After the rain

Miller, S. A lite too bright

Morpurgo, M. Half a man

GRANDMOTHERS -- FICTION

Amateau, G. A certain strain of peculiar

Block, F. L. Teen spirit

Davis, T. S. Mare's war

Johnson, A. Toning the sweep

Katcher, B. Deacon Locke went to prom

Lester, J. S. Black, white, other

Manzano, S. The revolution of Evelyn Serrano

Standiford, N. Confessions of the Sullivan sisters

Temblador, A. Secrets of the Casa Rosada

GRANDPARENT AND CHILD -- FICTION

Katcher, B. Deacon Locke went to prom

Morpurgo, M. Half a man

GRANDPARENT-GRANDCHILD RELATIONSHIP --
FICTION

Block, F. L. Teen spirit

Wynne-Jones, T. The emperor of any place

GRANDPARENTS -- FICTION

Khorram, A. Darius the Great is not okay

Meyerhoff, J. Queen of secrets

GRAND TOURS (EDUCATION) -- FICTION

Lee, M. The gentleman's guide to vice and virtue

Grant, Christopher

Grant, K. M.

Blood red horse

Blue flame

How the hangman lost his heart.

Grant, Michael, 1954-

Eve & Adam

Front Lines

Messenger of Fear

Monster

Silver stars

Gratton, Tessa

The blood keeper

Gratz, Alan

Samurai shortstop

Graudin, Ryan

Blood for blood

Invictus

The walled city

Wolf by wolf

Grave mercy. LaFevers. R.

Gray, Claudia

Defy the stars

Defy the worlds

The **great** American whatever. Federle, T.

A **great** and terrible beauty. Bray, L.

GREAT-AUNTS -- FICTION

Preus, M. Enchantment Lake: a Northwoods mystery

GREAT BRITAIN -- FICTION

Almond, D. Kit's wilderness

Bedford, M. Flip

Bray, L. A great and terrible beauty

Bray, L. Rebel angels

Bray, L. The sweet far thing

Burgess, M. Smack

Cann, K. Consumed

Cann, K. Possessed.

Dunkle, C. B. The house of dead maids

Lloyd, S. The carbon diaries 2015

Malley, G. The Declaration

Minchin, A. The beat goes on

Morpurgo, M. Private Peaceful

Mussi, S. The door of no return

Rennison, L. Angus, thongs and full-frontal snogging

Rennison, L. Are these my basoomas I see before me? final
    confessions of Georgia Nicolson

Rennison, L. Stop in the name of pants!

Robert, Na'ima B. Boy vs. girl.

Sedgwick, M. White crow

Tripp, B. The accidental highwayman: being the tale of Kit
    Bristol, his horse Midnight, a mysterious princess, and sundry
    magical persons besides

GREAT BRITAIN -- HISTORY -- 1485-1603

Silbert, L. The intelligencer

GREAT BRITAIN -- HISTORY -- CIVIL WAR, 1642-1649
    -- FICTION

Hardinge, F. A skinful of shadows

GREAT BRITAIN -- HISTORY -- EDWARD VII, 1901-1910
    -- FICTION

Fisher, C. Darkwater

Waller, S. B. A mad

GREAT BRITAIN -- HISTORY -- 0-1066 -- FICTION

Moran, K. Bloodline

Moran, K. Bloodline rising

Reeve, P. Here lies Arthur

Vande Velde, V. The book of Mordred

GREAT BRITAIN -- HISTORY -- 1714- 1837 -- FICTION

Kindl, P. A school for brides

Zettel, S. Palace of Spies

GREAT BRITAIN -- HISTORY -- 1789-1820 -- FICTION

Anstey, C. Love, lies and spies

Kindl, P. A school for brides: a story of maidens, mystery, and matrimony

Kindl, P. Keeping the castle

GREAT BRITAIN -- HISTORY -- 1837-1901 -- FICTION

Pratchett, T. Dodger

GREAT BRITAIN -- HISTORY -- 1936- 1945 -- FICTION

Wein, E. Code name Verity

GREAT BRITAIN -- HISTORY -- GEORGE III, 1760- 1820 -- FICTION

Anstey, C. Carols and chaos

Tripp, B. The accidental highwayman: being the tale of Kit Bristol, his horse Midnight, a mysterious princess, and sundry magical persons besides

GREAT BRITAIN -- HISTORY -- GEORGE VI, 1936-1952 -- FICTION

Carriger, G. Curtsies & conspiracies

Carriger, G. Etiquette & espionage

GREAT BRITAIN -- HISTORY -- HENRY VII, 1485-1509 -- FICTION

Castor, H. M. VIII

GREAT BRITAIN -- HISTORY -- HENRY VIII, 1509-1547 -- FICTION

Castor, H. M. VIII

Longshore, K. Brazen

GREAT BRITAIN -- HISTORY -- 1800-1837 -- FICTION

Jones, K. Murder, magic, and what we wore

GREAT BRITAIN -- HISTORY -- 1066-1154, NORMAN PERIOD -- FICTION

Carey, J. L. Dragon's Keep

GREAT BRITAIN -- HISTORY -- 1066- 1154, NORMAN PERIOD -- FICTION

Whitman, E. Wildwing

GREAT BRITAIN -- HISTORY -- 1154-1399, PLANTAGENETS -- FICTION

Coventry, S. The queen's daughter

GREAT BRITAIN -- HISTORY -- 19TH CENTURY -- FICTION

Hooper, M. Fallen Grace

Peacock, S. Eye of the crow

GREAT BRITAIN -- HISTORY -- 1485-1603, TUDORS -- FICTION

Castor, H. M. VIII

GREAT BRITAIN -- HISTORY -- VICTORIA, 1837-1901 -- FICTION

Bailey, K. Legacy of the clockwork key

Cameron, S. The dark unwinding

Carey, E. Heap House

Cluess, J. A poison dark and drowning

Hooper, M. Velvet

Kirby, M. J. A taste for monsters

Maniscalco, K. Escaping from Houdini

Maniscalco, K. Stalking Jack the Ripper

GREAT DEPRESSION, 1929-1939 -- FICTION

Ingold, J. Hitch

Laskas, G. M. The miner's daughter

Peterson, L. J. Silver rain

Falls. Watkins, S.

great god Pan. Napoli, D. J.

The **great** wide sea. Herlong, M.

GREEK AMERICANS -- FICTION

Connor, L. The things you kiss goodbye

GREEK MYTHOLOGY -- FICTION

Hahn, R. The shadow behind the stars

Taylor, L. Dreams of gods & monsters

GREENHOUSE EFFECT -- FICTION

Bass, R. On thin ice

Green, John

Turtles all the way down

Grendel's guide to love and war. Kaplan, A. E.

A **greyhound** of a girl. Doyle, R.

GREY, JANE, -- LADY, -- 1537-1554 -- FICTION

Hand, C. My Lady Jane

Grey, Melissa

The girl at midnight

GRIEF -- FICTION

Alsaid, A. Let's Get Lost

Arcos, C. The re will come a time

Bowman, A. D. Summer bird blue

Caletti, D. A heart in a body in the world

Caletti, D. Essential maps for the lost

Caletti, D. The last forever

Cameron, S. Out of the blue

Cashore, K. Jane, unlimited

Coles, J. Tyler Johnson was here

Danticat, E. Untwine

Darrows, E. Dead little mean girl

Federle, T. The great American whatever

Hahn, M. D. Mister Death's blue-eyed girls

Howland, L. Nantucket blue

Hutchinson, S. D. The five stages of Andrew Brawley

Johnson, J. J. The theory of everything

Kearney, M. The girl in the mirror

Keyser, A. J. The way back from broken

Kirby, J. Things we know by heart

LaCour, N. We Are Okay

Macvie, M. The ocean in my ears

Magoon, K. 37 things I love (in no particular order)

Mayhew, J. Red ink

McGhee, A. What I leave behind

Moon, S. Sparrow

Moskowitz, H. Gone, gone, gone.

Nelson, J. I'll give you the sun

Nielsen, S. The reluctant journal of Henry K. Larsen

O'Connell, M. The sharp time

Pieces Lynch, C.

Pitcher, A. Ketchup clouds

Pitcher, A. My sister lives on the mantelpiece

Pixley, M. Ready to fall

Rabb, M. Kissing in America

Reynolds, J. Boy in the black suit

Sanchez, E. L. I Am Not Your Perfect Mexican Daughter

Silvera, A. History is all you left me

Silvera, A. More happy than not

Smith-Ready, J. This side of salvation

Sorosiak, C. Wild blue wonder

Spears, K. Breakaway: a novel
Sweeney, D. The minnow
Torres Sanchez, J. Death, Dickinson, and the demented life of
  Frenchie Garcia
Treichel, E. A series of small maneuvers
Turrisi, K. Just a normal Tuesday
Wallace, S. N. Muckers
Weston, C. Speed of life
Williams, C. L. Waiting
Woodson, J. Beneath
Zentner, J. Goodbye days
Zorn, C. Protected

GRIEF -- TEEN FICTION
Cameron, S. Out of the blue

Griffin, Adele
All you never wanted
The Julian game
The unfinished life of Addison Stone
Where I want to be

Griffin, Claire J.
Nowhere to run

Griffin, Emily Ziff
Light years

Griffin, N.
Just wreck it all

GRIM REAPER (SYMBOLIC CHARACTER) -- FICTION
Damico, G. Rogue

Grimes, Nikki
Bronx masquerade
Dark sons
A girl named Mister
Jazmin's notebook

GRIMM, JACOB, 1785-1863 ABOUT
McNeal, T. Far far away
    French, G.

Grossman, Nancy
A world away

Groth, Darren
Munro vs. the coyote

GROUP HOMES -- FICTION
Chan, G. The disappearance

**GUANTANAMO BAY NAVAL BASE (CUBA) --
    DETENTION CAMP -- FICTION**
Perera, A. Guantanamo boy
Guantanamo boy. Perera, A.
Guardian. Lester, J.
Guardian. London, A.
Guardian angel house. Clark, K.

GUARDIAN ANGELS -- FICTION
Brockenbrough, M. Devine intervention
Guardian of the dead. Healey, K.
Guardian of the Gate. Zink, M.

GUATEMALA -- FICTION
Brown, S. Caminar
Resau, L. Red glass

GUIDES (PERSONS)
O'Dell, S. Streams to the river, river to the sea

GUILT -- FICTION
Billingsley, F. Chime
Chaltas, T. Because I am furniture
Graff, L. Lost in the sun
Griffin, N. Just wreck it all
Knowles, J. Living with Jackie Chan
Lyga, B. Bang
Marcus, K. Exposed
Matson, M. Amy & Roger's epic detour
Miranda, M. Soulprint
Northrop, M. Gentlemen
Pitcher, A. Ketchup clouds
Scott, E. Love you hate you miss you
Thompson, M. G. Amy Chelsea Stacie Dee
Wynne-Jones, T. Blink & Caution
Zentner, J. Goodbye days
Guitar boy. Auch, M. J.

GUITARS -- FICTION
Auch, M. J. Guitar boy
Guy in real life. Brezenoff, S.
Guyaholic; a story of finding, flirting, forgetting . . . and the boy
            who changes everything. Mackler, C.
Gym candy. Deuker, C.

GYMNASTICS -- FICTION
Cohen, J. C. Leverage

GYPSIES -- FICTION
Dunlap, S. E. The musician's daughter.
Sedgwick, M. My swordhand is singing

H

Haas, Abigail
Dangerous girls
Habibi. Nye, N. S.

HACKERS -- FICTION
Kaplan, A. We regret to inform you
Lu, M. Wildcard

HACKTIVISM -- FICTION
Doctorow, C. Homeland

Haddix, Margaret Peterson
Full ride
Just Ella
Uprising

Hahn, Mary Downing, 1937-
Mister Death's blue-eyed girls

Hahn, Rebecca
A creature of moonlight
The shadow behind the stars

Haines, Kathryn Miller
The girl is murder
The girl is trouble

HAITI -- FICTION
Lake, N. In darkness
Wagner, L. R. Hold tight, don't let go

**HAITI -- HISTORY -- REVOLUTION, 1791-1804 --
    FICTION**
Lake, N. In darkness

lies Arthur. Reeve, P.
    Anonymous. Henry, K.

Herlong, Madaline
The great wide sea

Hernandez, David
Suckerpunch
    Lupica, M.
    hero and the crown. McKinley, R.
    at the fall. Hamilton, A.

HEROES -- FICTION
Meyer, M. Renegades
Strasser, T. Price of duty
Zinn, B. Poison

HEROES AND HEROINES -- FICTION
Lyga, B. Hero-type
Pierson, D. C. Crap kingdom
    of the valley. Stroud, J.
    -type. Lyga, B.

Herrick, Steven
By the river
The wolf

HERSHEY (PA.) -- FICTION
Finneyfrock, K. The sweet revenge of Celia Door

Hesse, Karen
Safekeeping

Hesse, Monica
Girl in the blue coat
The war outside
    Hall. Hawkins, R.
    Frost, H.

HIDDEN CHILDREN (HOLOCAUST)
Macdonald, M. Odette's secrets
    hidden star. Duiker, K. S.
    voices. Collins, P. L.
    love. Hemphill, S.
    heat. Deuker, C.
    illogical behavior. Whaley, J. C.

HIGH SCHOOL DROPOUTS -- FICTION
Oelke, L. Nice try, Jane Sinner

HIGH SCHOOL GIRLS -- FICTION
Jägerfeld, J. Me on the Floor, Bleeding
Roat, S. H. How to Disappear

HIGH SCHOOLS -- CALIFORNIA -- MARINA DEL REY
    -- FICTION
Yee, L. The kidney hypothetical

HIGH SCHOOLS -- FICTION
Aceves, F. The closest I've come
Ahmed, S. Love, hate & other filters
Albertalli, B. Simon vs. the Homo Sapiens agenda
Alexander, K. He said, she said
Alsenas, L. Beyond clueless
Andrews, J. Me & Earl & the dying girl
Backes, M. M. The princesses of Iowa
Bigelow, L. J. Starting from here
Bliss, B. We'll fly away
Bond, G. Fallout
Callahan, E. The art of escaping

Carleson, J. C. The tyrant's daughter
Casella, J. Thin space
Clark, K. E. Freakboy
Coben, H. Seconds away
Cousins, D. Waiting for Gonzo
Cronn-Mills, K. Beautiful Music for Ugly Children
Crossan, S. One
Crutcher, C. Period 8
Demetrios, H. Bad romance
Derting, K. The last echo
DeWoskin, R. Blind
Dinnison, K. You and me and him
Ellen, L. Blind spot
Elston, A. The rules for disappearing
Emond, S. Bright lights, dark nights
Fantaskey, B. Buzz kill.
Fehlbaum, B. Big fat disaster
Finneyfrock, K. Starbird Murphy and the world outside
Finneyfrock, K. The sweet revenge of Celia Door
Flake, S. G. Pinned
George, M. The difference between you and me
Goo, M. I believe in a thing called love
Goslee, S. J. Whatever
Grace, A. In too deep
Griffin, N. Just wreck it all
Haddix, M. P. Full ride
Harrington, H. Speechless
Hemmings, K. H. Juniors
Howe, K. Conversion
Hubbard, J. R. And we stay
Jensen, C. Skyscraping
Johnston, E. K. Exit, pursued by a bear
Johnston, E. K. Prairie fire
Johnston, E. K. The story of Owen
Juby, S. The Truth Commission
Kaplan, A. We regret to inform you
Kehoe, S. W. The sound of letting go
Kenneally, M. Coming up for air
Keplinger, K. That's not what happened
Kiely, B. Tradition
King, A. S. Ask the passengers
Knowles, J. Read between the lines
Lauren, C. Autoboyography
Leavitt, M. Calvin
Lindstrom, E. Not if I see you first
Linn, L. Draw the line
Luedeke, L. Smashed
Maciel, A. Tease
Macvie, M. The ocean in my ears
Magoon, K. 37 things I love (in no particular order)
Mathieu, J. Moxie: a novel
Mesrobian, C. Just a girl
Mills, E. First & then
Ness, P. The rest of us just live here
Oseman, A. Solitaire
O'Brien, Caragh M. The vault of dreamers
O'Connell, M. The sharp time

Sedgwick, M. White crow
Shusterman, N. Full tilt; a novel
Stewart, M. The sacrifice box
Tayleur, K. Killer Pizza
Tayleur, K. Killer Pizza: the slice
Tucholke, A. G. Between the devil and the deep blue sea
Wasserman, R. The waking dark
Wooding, C. The haunting of Alaizabel Cray
Wooding, C. Silver

HORROR STORIES
Alender, K. The dead girls of Hysteria Hall
Brewer, Z. The cemetery boys
Chupeco, R. The Girl from the Well
Delaney, J. A new darkness
Dennard, S. Something strange and deadly
Garner, E. Contaminated
Garner, E. Mercy mode
Henderson, J. The Triumph of Death
Moulton, C. A. Angelfire
Summers, C. This is not a test
Yancey, R. final descent

HORROR TALES
Alender, K. The dead girls of Hysteria Hall
Ireland, J. Dread nation
Kagawa, J. The forever song
Kiernan, C. Into the grey
Roux, M. House of furies

HORSEMANSHIP -- FICTION
Juby, S. Another kind of cowboy
Kenneally, M. Racing Savannah
Lyne, J. H. Catch rider
Whitney, K. A. The perfect distance
Wilkinson, S. Taking Flight

HORSE RACING -- FICTION
Luper, E. Bug boy

HORSES -- FICTION
Finn, M. Belladonna
Flood, N. B. Soldier sister, fly home
Grant, K. M. Blood red horse
Juby, S. Another kind of cowboy
Kenneally, M. Racing Savannah
Lyne, J. H. Catch rider
Rorby, G. The outside of a horse; a novel
Stiefvater, M. The scorpio races
Wilson, D. L. Firehorse

HORSE SHOWS -- FICTION
Lyne, J. H. Catch rider

Horvath, Polly
The Corps of the Bare-Boned Plane

HOSPICES (TERMINAL CARE) -- FICTION
Seamon, H. Somebody up there hates you

HOSPITALS -- FICTION
Bryce, C. Anthem for Jackson Dawes
Frank, L. Two girls staring at the ceiling
Hutchinson, S. D. The five stages of Andrew Brawley
Lippert-M., K. Tabula rasa

HOSTAGES -- FICTION

Bow, E. The Scorpion Rules
Fitzpatrick, B. Black ice
Lake, N. Hostage Three
Van Diepen, A. Takedown

Hostage Three. Lake, N.

HOTELS AND MOTELS -- FICTION
Johnson, M. Scarlett fever
Johnson, M. Suite Scarlett
Roux, M. House of furies

Hothouse. Lynch, C.

HOUDINI, HARRY, 1874-1926 -- FICTION
Maniscalco, K. Escaping from Houdini

The **hound** of Rowan, Neff, Henry H.

Hourglass. McEntire, M.

HOUSEHOLD EMPLOYEES -- FICTION
Anstey, C. Carols and chaos
Budhos, M. T. Tell us we're home
Cann, K. Consumed
Dunkle, C. B. The house of dead maids
Hale, M. The goodbye season
Murdock, C. G. Wisdom's kiss
Roux, M. House of furies
Schlitz, L. A. The hired girl.
Stuber, B. Crossing the tracks

House of Dance. Kephart, B.

The **house** of dead maids. Dunkle, C. B.

House of furies. Roux, M.

House of purple cedar. Tingle, T.

The **house** on Mango Street. Cisneros, S.

HOUSES -- FICTION
Carey, E. Heap House

HOUSTON (TEX.) -- FICTION
Williams, L. A. When Kambia Elaine flew in from Neptune

Houston, Julian
New boy

How the hangman lost his heart. Grant, K. M.

How to be bad. Lockhart, E.

How to build a house. Reinhardt, D.

How to Disappear. Roat, S. H.

How to ditch your fairy. Larbalestier, J.

How (not) to find a boyfriend. Valentine, A.

How to get suspended and influence people. Selzer, A.

How to ruin my teenage life. Elkeles, S.

How to steal a car. Hautman, P.

How we roll. Friend, N.

Howard, A. G.
Unhinged

Howard, J. J.
That time I joined the circus

HOWARD, MARY, LADY, 1519- 1557 -- FICTION
Longshore, K. Brazen

Howe, Katherine
Conversion

Howell, Simmone
Girl defective

How to say goodbye in Robot. Standiford, N.

Howland, Leila

Nantucket blue

Hrdlitschka, Shelley
Allegra
Sister wife

Hubbard, Amanda

Hubbard, Jennifer R.
Paper covers rock
Try not to breathe
And we stay

Hubbard, Kirsten
Wanderlove

HÜBENER, HELMUTH, 1925-1942 ABOUT
Bartoletti, S. C. The boy who dared

Hughes, Dean
Four-Four-Two
Search and destroy

HUMAN-ALIEN ENCOUNTERS -- FICTION
Lo, M. Inheritance
McDonald, I. Empress of the sun

HUMAN-ANIMAL RELATIONSHIPS -- FICTION
Ness, P. And the ocean was our sky
Stiefvater, M. Sinner
Tan, S. Tales from the inner city
Wegelius, J. The murderer's ape

HUMAN BEINGS -- FICTION
Dayton, A. E. Stronger, faster, and more beautiful

HUMAN BEINGS -- GENETIC ENGINEERING -- MORAL AND ETHICAL ASPECTS -- FICTION
Kincaid, S. J. The empress

HUMAN CLONING -- FICTION
Patrick, C. The Originals

HUMAN TRAFFICKING -- FICTION
Sedgwick, M. Saint death
Withers, P. Andreo's race

HUMOROUS FICTION
Andrews, J. The Haters
Calame, D. Beat the band
Damico, G. Wax
Goslee, S. J. Whatever
Paulsen, G. Crush; the theory, practice, and destructive properties of love
Pierson, D. C. Crap kingdom
Rubin, L. Denton Little's still not dead
Scieszka, J. Who done it? an investigation of murder most foul.

HUMOROUS STORIES
Andrews, J. Me & Earl & the dying girl
Damico, G. Hellhole
Damico, G. Rogue
Damico, G. Scorch
Damico, G. Wax
Goslee, S. J. Whatever
Paulsen, G. Crush; the theory, practice, and destructive properties of love
Pratchett, T. Dodger
Rennison, L. The taming of the tights
Scieszka, J. Who done it? an investigation of murder most foul.

Humphreys, Chris
The hunt of the unicorn

The **hundredth** queen. King, E. R.

The **Hunger** Games. Collins, S.

Hunt for the bamboo rat. Salisbury, G.

HUNTING -- FICTION
Mary-Todd, J. Shot down

Hunting Prince Dracula. Maniscalco, K.

Huntley, Amy
The everafter

The **hunt** of the unicorn. Humphreys, C.

Huntress. Lo, M.

Hurley, Tonya
Ghostgirl

HURRICANE KATRINA
Between Two Skies. O'Sullivan, J.

HURRICANE KATRINA, 2005 -- FICTION
Volponi, P. Hurricane song
Woodson, J. Beneath

Hurricane song. Volponi, P.

HURRICANES -- FICTION
Connelly, N. O. Into the hurricane
Kephart, B. This is the story of you

Hurwin, Davida
Freaks and revelations

Hurwitz, Gregg
The rains

Hush. Napoli, D. J.

Hutchinson, Shaun David
The apocalypse of Elena Mendoza
At the edge of the universe
The five stages of Andrew Brawley
We are the ants

Hutton, Keely
Soldier boy

HUTU (AFRICAN PEOPLE) -- FICTION
Combres, E. Broken memory

Hyde, Catherine Ryan
Jumpstart the world
The year of my miraculous reappearance

HYPOCHONDRIA -- FICTION
Raf, M. The symptoms of my insanity

Hysteria. Miranda, M.

I

I am J. Beam, C.
I Am Not Your Perfect Mexican Daughter. Sanchez, E. L.
I Am Princess X. Priest, C.
I am still alive. Marshall, K.
I am the cheese. Cormier, R.
I am the messenger. Zusak, M.
I am the mission. Zadoff, A.
I believe in a thing called love. Goo, M.
I crawl through it.. King, A. S.
I Don't Live Here Anymore. Kreslehner, G.
I have lost my way. Forman, G.

hunt killers Lyga, B.

know it's over. Martin, C. K. K.

know what you did last summer. Duncan, L.

swear. Davis, L.

be there. Sloan, H. G.

not your manic pixie dream girl. McNeil, G.

Ibbitson, John

The Landing

IDENTITY -- FICTION

Ali, S. K. Saints and misfits: a novel

Altebrando, T. The Leaving.

Bennett, J. Alex, approximately

Blumenthal, D. Mafia girl

Bow, E. Sorrow's knot

Bowman, A. D. Starfish

Buckley-Archer, L. The many lives of John Stone

Casanova, M. Frozen

Castle, J. You look different in real life

Catmull, K. The radiant road: a novel

Cooney, C. B. Janie face to face

Dawn, S. Splinter

Gardner, F. The second life of Ava Rivers

Gibney, S. See no color

Gibney, S. See no color

Hahn, R. A creature of moonlight

Hartman, R. Seraphina

Hopkins, E. The you I've never known

Hopkinson, N. The Chaos

Jägerfeld, J. Me on the Floor, Bleeding

King, A. S. Ask the passengers

Konigsberg, B. Honestly Ben

Lowry, L. Son

Macdonald, M. Odette's secrets

Manzano, S. The revolution of Evelyn Serrano

McQuein, J. L. Arclight

McQuerry, M. D. The Peculiars

Nelson, M. American ace

Ortiz Cofer, J. Call me Maria

Pitcher, A. Silence is goldfish: a novel

Reeve, P. Scrivener's moon

Roth, V. Insurgent

Rush, J. Altered

Rutkoski, M. The shadow society

Sáenz, B. A. The inexplicable logic of my life

Shusterman, N. UnSouled

Shusterman, N. UnWholly

Tashjian, J. The gospel according to Larry

Terry, T. Fractured

Terry, T. Slated

Valentine, J. Double

Walker, B. F. Black boy/white school

Wells, D. Fragments

Whaley, J. C. Noggin

IDENTITY (PHILOSOPHICAL CONCEPT) -- FICTION

Karim, S. That thing we call a heart

Roth, V. Allegiant

IDENTITY (PSYCHOLOGY) -FICTION

Albertalli, B. Leah on the offbeat

Beam, C. I am J

Clark, K. E. Freakboy

Cooper, T. Changers book one

Friend, N. The other F-word

Giles, L. Fresh ink

Kearney, M. The girl in the mirror

Kincaid, S. J. The empress

Konigsberg, B. Honestly Ben

Mitchell, S. All out: the no-longer-secret stories of queer teens throughout the ages

Oakes, S. The arsonist

Pitcher, A. Silence is goldfish: a novel

Roth, V. Divergent

Starmer, A. Spontaneous

Terry, T. Fractured

Vivian, S. The list

Wells, D. Fragments

Wilkinson, L. Pink

IDENTITY -- FICTION HIGH SCHOOLS -- FICTION

Martin, C. K. K. Yesterday

IDENTITY (PHILOSOPHICAL CONCEPT) -- FICTION

Oakes, S. The arsonist

IDENTITY (PSYCHOLOGY) -- FICTION

Friend, N. The other F-word

Hardinge, F. A skinful of shadows

Konigsberg, B. Honestly Ben

Mitchell, S. All out: the no-longer-secret stories of queer teens throughout the ages

If he had been with me. Nowlin, L.

If I could fly. Ortiz Cofer, J.

If I love you, am I trapped forever?. Kerr, M. E.

If I Was Your Girl. Russo, M.

If the witness lied. Cooney, C. B.

If you come softly. Woodson, J.

If you find me. Murdoch, E.

Ignite the stars. Milan, M.

ILLEGAL ALIENS -- FICTION

Marquardt, Marie F. The radius of us

Restrepo, B. Illegal

Illegal. Restrepo, B.

ILLEGITIMATE CHILDREN OF ROYALTY -- FICTION

Redwine, C. J. The wish granter: a Ravenspire novel

I'll give you the sun. Nelson, J.

ILLINOIS -- FICTION

Keplinger, K. A midsummer's nightmare

Nadol, J. The vision

Rapp, A. Under the wolf, under the dog

Rutkoski, M. The shadow society

Stone, T. I. Time between us

Illuminae. Kaufman, A.

Illuminae. Kristoff, J.

Illusive. Lloyd-Jones, E.

IMAGINARY CREATURES -- FICTION

Hamilton, K. When the stars threw down their spears

Ritter, W. Beastly bones: a Jackaby novel

Imaginary enemy. Gonzalez, J.

INFLUENZA -- FICTION
Edwardson, D. D. Blessing's bead
Lucier, M. A death-struck year
Williams, S. D. Palace beautiful
Ingold, Jeanette

Inheritance. Lo, M.
INHERITANCE AND SUCCESSION -- FICTION
Albert, M. The Hazel Wood
Cameron, S. The dark unwinding
Carter, A. Perfect scoundrels
Hardinge, F. A skinful of shadows
Nix, G. A confusion of princes
Standiford, N. Confessions of the Sullivan sisters
   inheritance of ashes. Bobet, L.
Inhuman. Falls, K.
   and bone. Caine, R.
   & ashes. Maetani, V. E.
   Sun, A.
      Rosenfield, K.
INQUISITION -- FICTION
Berry, J. The passion of Dolssa
INSURGENCY -- FICTION
Crossan, S. Breathe
Dowswell, P. The Auslander
Marillier, J. Raven flight
Marillier, J. Shadowfell
North, P. Starglass
Tahir, S. A reaper at the gates
Wein, E. Code name Verity
Insurgent. Roth, V.
   intelligencer. Silbert, L.
INTELLIGENCE SERVICE -- FICTION
Cormier, R. I am the cheese
Intensely Alice. Naylor, P. R.
INTERGENERATIONAL RELATIONS -- FICTION
Price, L. Starters
INTERNET -- FICTION
Doctorow, C. Pirate cinema
Zappia, F. Eliza and her monsters
INTERNET AND TEENAGERS
Bastedo, J. Cut Off
INTERNET GAMES -- FICTION
Doctorow, C. For the win
Lu, M. Warcross
Lu, M. Wildcard
INTERNET INDUSTRY -- FICTION
Wells, D. Bluescreen
INTERNET TELEVISION -- FICTION
Oelke, L. Nice try, Jane Sinner
Ormsbee, K. Tash hearts Tolstoy
INTERNET TELEVISION -- PRODUCTION AND DIRECTION -- FICTION
Ormsbee, K. Tash hearts Tolstoy
INTERNSHIP PROGRAMS -- FICTION
Cornwell, B. Tides
Doktorski, J. S. Famous last words

INTERPERSONAL ATTRACTION -- FICTION
Abdel-Fattah, R. The lines we cross
Abdel-Fattah, R. The lines we cross
INTERPERSONAL COMMUNICATION -- FICTION
McCahan, E. Love and other foreign words
INTERPERSONAL RELATIONS -- FICTION
Acevedo, E. The poet X: a novel
Alsaid, A. Let's Get Lost
Alsaid, A. North of happy
Alsenas, L. Beyond clueless
Arnold, A. Love & other train wrecks
Bjorkman, L. Miss Fortune Cookie
Brashares, A. The whole thing together
Brooks, K. The bunker diary
Casella, J. Thin space
Chambers, A. Dying to know you
Chibbaro, J. Deadly
Conaghan, B. When Mr. Dog bites
Connelly, N. O. Into the hurricane
Damico, G. Hellhole
DeWoskin, R. Blind
Dirkes, C. Sucktown
Ellis, K. Breaker
Forman, G. I have lost my way
Geiger, J. C. Wildman
Harrington, H. Speechless
Harrison, R. Looking for group
Haston, M. The end of our story
Hautman, P. What boys really want
Haydu, C. A. OCD love story
Hemmings, K. H. Juniors
Hopkinson, N. The Chaos
Howland, L. Nantucket blue
Hubbard, J. R. And we stay
Hubbard, J. R. Try not to breathe
Hutchinson, S. D. At the edge of the universe
Johnson, J. J. The theory of everything
Kephart, B. Small damages
Levithan, D. Every day
Lewis, S. The secret ingredient
Magoon, K. 37 things I love (in no particular order)
Martin, C. K. K. Yesterday
McCahan, E. Love and other foreign words
McStay, M. Everything that makes you
Meyer, M. Renegades
Mills, W. All we have left
Moriarty, J. A corner of white
Moriarty, J. A tangle of gold
Murphy, J. Ramona Blue
Ness, P. Release
O'Connell, M. The sharp time
Paulsen, G. Crush; the theory, practice, and destructive properties of love
Perez, M. Dead is a battlefield
Pieces Lynch, C.
Reinhardt, D. Tell us something true
Rupp, R. After Eli

Cashore, K. Jane, unlimited
Fitzpatrick, H. What I thought was true
Horvath, P. The Corps of the Bare-Boned Plane
Kephart, B. This is the story of you
Lanagan, M. The brides of Rollrock Island
Moskowitz, H. Teeth
Parker, S. M. The rattled bones
Pratchett, T. Nation
Sedgwick, M. Midwinterblood
Venkatraman, P. Island's end

ISLANDS -- SOUTH CAROLINA -- FICTION
Boone, M. Compulsion
of blood and stone. Lucier, M.

ISLES OF SHOALS
Cornwell, B. Tides

ISRAEL-ARAB CONFLICTS -- FICTION
Laird, E. A little piece of ground

ISRAELIS -- FICTION
Elkeles, S. How to ruin my teenage life
Laskin, P. L. Ronit & Jamil

ISRAEL -- FICTION
Laskin, P. L. Ronit & Jamil

ISTANBUL (TURKEY) -- FICTION
White, K. Now I rise

**ISTANBUL (TURKEY) -- HISTORY -- 15TH CENTURY
-- FICTION**
White, K. Now I rise

ITALIAN AMERICANS -- FICTION
Napoli, D. J. Alligator bayou

ITALO- ETHIOPIAN WAR, 1935-1936 -- FICTION
Wein, E. Black dove, white raven

ITALY -- FICTION
Cook, E. With malice
Kephart, B. One thing stolen

ITALY -- HISTORY -- 1559-1789 -- FICTION
Caine, R. Prince of Shadows

ITALY -- HISTORY -- 15TH CENTURY -- FICTION
Strauss, V. Passion blue
's kind of a funny story. Vizzini, N.
not like it's a secret. Sugiura, M.

Iturbe, Antonio
The librarian of Auschwitz
willy-nilly. Voigt, C.

J

Jackson, Tiffany D.
Allegedly: a novel
Monday's not coming

JACK, THE RIPPER -- FICTION
Kirby, M. J. A taste for monsters
Maniscalco, K. Stalking Jack the Ripper

**JACK THE RIPPER MURDERS, LONDON, ENGLAND,
1888 -- FICTION**
Kirby, M. J. A taste for monsters

Jacobs, John Hornor
The Shibboleth

The twelve-fingered boy
The **jade** notebook. Resau, L.

Jaden, Denise
Losing Faith

Jae-Jones, S.
Wintersong

Jaffe, Michele
Bad kitty
Rosebush

Jägerfeld, Jenny
Me on the Floor, Bleeding

JAMAICAN AMERICANS -- FICTION
Yoon, N. The Sun Is Also a Star

James, Rebecca
Beautiful malice

Jane, unlimited. Cashore, K.

Janie face to face. Cooney, C. B.

Jansen, Hanna
Over a thousand hills I walk with you

JAPAN -- FICTION
Benwell, S. The last leaves falling
Lowitz, L. Jet Black and the ninja wind.
Randall, T. Dreams of the dead
Randall, T. Spirits of the Noh
Sun, A. Ink
Thompson, H. The language inside
Thompson, H. Orchards

**JAPAN -- HISTORY -- TOKUGAWA PERIOD, 1600-1868
-- FICTION**
Ahdieh, R. Smoke in the sun

JAPANESE -- UNITED STATES -- FICTION
Preus, M. Heart of a samurai

**JAPANESE AMERICANS -- EVACUATION AND
RELOCATION, 1942-1945 -- FICTION**
Hughes, D. Four-Four-Two
The war outside. Hesse, Monica

JAPANESE AMERICANS -- FICTION
Maetani, V. E. Ink & ashes
Namioka, L. Mismatch
Salisbury, G. Eyes of the emperor
Salisbury, G. Hunt for the bamboo rat
Sugiura, M. It's not like it's a secret

Jaramillo, Ann
La linea

Jasper Jones. Silvey, C.

Jazmin's notebook. Grimes, N.

JAZZ -- FICTION
Kehoe, S. W. The sound of letting go

JAZZ MUSIC -- FICTION
Volponi, P. Hurricane song
Weatherford, C. B. Becoming Billie Holiday

JAZZ MUSICIANS -- FICTION
Townley, R. Sky; a novel in three sets and an encore

JEALOUSY -- FICTION
Hautman, P. What boys really want

Jensen, Cordelia
Skyscraping

who defied the stars. Marsh, K,

JERUSALEM -- FICTION
Kerbel, D. Mackenzie, lost and found
Stroud, J. The Ring of Solomon

Jeschonek, Robert T.
My favorite band does not exist
  guide to dating on the dark side. Fantaskey, B.
  Jackson. Daley, J. R.
 Black and the ninja wind. Lowitz, L.

JEWISH-ARAB RELATIONS -- FICTION
Nye, N. S. Habibi

JEWISH GHETTOS
Sax, A. The war within these walls

JEWISH REFUGEES -- FICTION
Alban, A. Anya's war
Chapman, F. S. Is it night or day?

JEWISH WOMEN -- FICTION
Feldman, R. T. Blue thread

JEWS -- CHINA -- FICTION
Alban, A. Anya's war

JEWS -- ETHIOPIA -- FICTION
Oron, J. Cry of the giraffe

JEWS -- FICTION
Elkeles, S. How to ruin my teenage life
Friend, N. Threads and flames
Graudin, R. Blood for blood
Levitin, S. Strange relations
Lieberman, L. Lauren Yanofsky hates the holocaust
Mazer, H. The last mission
North, P. Starglass
Stamper, V. What the night sings
Tal, E. Cursing Columbus
Tal, E. Double crossing
Thor, A. Deep sea

JEWS -- FRANCE --FICTION
Macdonald, M. Odette's secrets

JEWS -- GERMANY -- FICTION
Chapman, F. S. Is it night or day?
Iturbe, A. The librarian of Auschwitz
Sharenow, R. The Berlin Boxing Club
Zusak, M. The book thief

JEWS -- GERMANY -- HISTORY -- 1933-1945 -- FICTION
Iturbe, A. The librarian of Auschwitz

JEWS -- HUNGARY -- FICTION
Clark, K. Guardian angel house
Wiseman, E. Puppet

JEWS -- NETHERLANDS -- FICTION
Hesse, M. Girl in the blue coat

JEWS -- PERSECUTIONS -- FICTION
Oron, J. Cry of the giraffe

JEWS -- POLAND -- FICTION
Sax, A. The war within these walls

JEWS -- SWEDEN -- FICTION
Thor, A. Deep sea

JEWS -- UNITED STATES -- FICTION
Aldredge, B. Sasquatch, love, and other imaginary things
Andrews, J. Me & Earl & the dying girl

Chapman, F. S. Is it night or day?
Crowder, M. Audacity
Goelman, A. The path of names
Meyerhoff, J. Queen of secrets
Miklowitz, G. D. The enemy has a face
Pixley, M. Ready to fall
Reinhardt, D. The things a brother knows

Jimenez, Francisco
Breaking through
The circuit
Reaching out

Jinks, Catherine
Evil genius
Genius squad
The genius wars
Living hell

JOAN, OF ENGLAND, 1165-1199 ABOUT
Coventry, S. The queen's daughter

Jocelyn, Marthe
A Big Dose of Lucky

Joe Rat. Barratt, M.

Johnson, Angela
Heaven
Sweet, hereafter
Toning the sweep

Johnson, Harriet McBryde
Accidents of nature

Johnson, J. J.
The theory of everything

Johnson, Lindsay Lee
Worlds apart

Johnson, LouAnne
Muchacho

Johnson, Maureen
13 little blue envelopes
The madness underneath
The name of the star
Scarlett fever
The shadow cabinet
Suite Scarlett
Truly devious: a mystery

Johnson, Varian
Saving Maddie

Johnston, E. K.
Exit, pursued by a bear
Prairie fire
The story of Owen
That inevitable Victorian thing
A thousand nights

Jones, Adam Garnet
Fire song

Jones, Kelly
Murder, magic, and what we wore

Joseph. Moses, S. P.

JOURNALISM -- FICTION
Bauer, J. Peeled
Doktorski, J. S. Famous last words

Winston, S. The Kayla chronicles.
Zeises, L. M. The sweet life of Stella Madison

JOURNALISTS

Sheth, K. Keeping corner

JOURNALISTS -- FICTION

Deuker, C. Payback time
Feinstein, J. Last shot
Renn, D. Latitude zero
journey back. Cummings, P.

Juby, Susan

Another kind of cowboy
The fashion committee
Getting the girl
The Truth Commission

JUDAISM -- RELATIONS -- CHRISTIANITY -- FICTION

Sanders, S. Rachel's secret
fire. Bell, J.
Julian game. Griffin, A.
vanishes. Egan, C.
Williams-Garcia, R.
Jumping off swings. Knowles, J.
Jumpstart the world. Hyde, C. R.
Hemmings, K. H.
a girl. Mesrobian, C.
a normal Tuesday. Turrisi, K.
Ella. Haddix, M. P.
fly away. McCarthy, A.
for you to know. Harness, C.
listen. Dessen, S.
wreck it all. Griffin, N.

JUSTICE -- FICTION

Damico, G. Croak
Grant, M. Messenger of Fear

JUVENILE DELINQUENCY

Beaudoin, S. Wise Young Fool

JUVENILE DELINQUENCY -- ENGLAND -- FICTION

Mason, S. Running girl

JUVENILE DELINQUENCY -- FICTION

Berry, N. The Notorious Pagan Jones
Griffin, C. J. Nowhere to run
Hinton, S. E. The outsiders
Mason, S. Running girl
McLaughlin, L. The Free
Perez, A. H. The knife and the butterfly
Rapp, A. The children and the wolves
Suma, N. R. The walls around us: a novel
Thompson, K. Creature of the night
Watkins, S. Juvie

JUVENILE DETENTION HOMES -- FICTION

Beaudoin, S. Wise Young Fool
Cosimano, E. Holding Smoke
Cummings, P. The journey back
Jacobs, J. H. The twelve-fingered boy
Oakes, S. The sacred lies of Minnow Bly
Perez, A. H. The knife and the butterfly
Suma, N. R. The walls around us: a novel

JUVENILE PROSTITUTION -- FICTION

Frank, E. R. Dime
Leavitt, M. My book of life by Angel
Scott, V. Violet Grenade
Scott, V. Violet Grenade
Juvie. Watkins, S.

K

Kagawa, Julie

The Eternity Cure
The forever song
The immortal rules
Shadow of the Fox
Talon

Kamata, Suzanne

Gadget Girl

KANSAS -- FICTION

Moriarty, L. The center of everything
Nadol, J. The mark
Wasserman, R. The waking dark

KANSAS -- HISTORY -- 20TH CENTURY -- FICTION

Schantz, S. E. Fig

Kaplan, A. E.

Grendel's guide to love and war

Kaplan, Ariel

We regret to inform you

Karim, Sheba

Skunk girl
That thing we call a heart

Karma. Ostlere, C.

Kaslik, Ibolya

Skinny

Katcher, Brian

Almost perfect
Deacon Locke went to prom
The improbable theory of Ana and Zak
Playing with matches

Katsoulis, Gregory Scott

Access restricted
All rights reserved

Kaufman, Amie

Gemina
Illuminae
Obsidio

KAYAKS AND KAYAKING -- FICTION

Withers, P. First descent
The **Kayla** chronicles. Winston, S.

Kearney, Meg

The girl in the mirror
The **keeper** of the mist. Neumeier, R.
The **Keepers'** tattoo. Arbuthnott, G.
Keeping corner. Sheth, K.
Keeping the castle. Kindl, P.
Keesha's house. Frost, H.

Kehoe, Stasia Ward

The sound of letting go

KELLER, HELEN, 1880-1968 ABOUT

Miller, S. Miss Spitfire

Kelly, Tara
Harmonic feedback

Kenneally, Miranda
Coming up for air
Racing Savannah
Stealing Parker

KENTUCKY -FICTION
Combs, S. Breakfast served anytime
Mary-Todd, J. Shot down

KENYA -- FICTION
Naidoo, B. Burn my heart

Kephart, Beth
Going over
The heart is not a size
House of Dance
One thing stolen
Small damages
This is the story of you
Undercover

Kephart, Beth
Wild blues

Keplinger, Kody
A midsummer's nightmare

That's not what happened

Kerbel, Deborah
Mackenzie, lost and found

Kerr, M. E.
Gentlehands
If I love you, am I trapped forever?
        clouds. Pitcher, A.

Keyser, Amber J.

The way back from broken

KGB -- FICTION
Smith, L. Sekret

Khorram, Adib
Darius the Great is not okay

Khoury, Jessica

KIDNAPPING -- FICTION
Altebrando, T. The Leaving.
Antieau, K. Broken moon
Berry, J. All the truth that's in me
Blair, J. Leap of Faith
Bloor, E. Taken
Brooks, K. The bunker diary
Carey, J. L. In the time of dragon moon
Carter, A. Not if I save you first
Chee, T. The speaker
Chee, T. The speaker
Cooney, C. B. The face on the milk carton
Cooney, C. B. Janie face to face
Cooney, C. B. Whatever happened to Janie?
Cooney, C. B. What Janie found
Crutcher, C. Period 8

Davies, S. Outlaw
DeStefano, L. Wither
Duncan, L. Killing Mr. Griffin
Giles, G. What happened to Cass McBride?.
Hamilton, A. Hero at the fall.
Hamilton, A. Traitor to the throne
Hautman, P. Snatched
Hopkins, E. The you I've never known
Lo, M. Inheritance
Mahoney, K. The iron witch
Mazer, N. F. The missing girl
McClintock, N. Taken
McDonald, I. Be my enemy
Nwaubani, A. T. Buried beneath the baobab tree
Paulsen, G. Woods runner
Rainfield, C. Stained
Rapp, A. The children and the wolves
Sandler, K. Rebellion
Schoenherr, I. The Speaker
Scott, E. Living dead girl
Skuse, C. J. Rockoholic
Stork, F. X. Disappeared
Stratton, A. Chanda's wars
Thompson, M. G. Amy Chelsea Stacie Dee
Young, M. Blood red road

KIDNAPPING -- MEXICO -- CIUDAD JUÁREZ --
        FICTION
Stork, F. X. Disappeared
The **kidney** hypothetical. Yee, L.

Kiely, Brendan
Tradition

Kiernan, Celine
Into the grey
The **killer** in me. Harrison, M.
Killer Pizza. Tayleur, K.
Killer Pizza: the slice. Tayleur, K.
Killing Mr. Griffin. Duncan, L.

Kincaid, S. J.
The diabolic
The empress

Kinch, Michael
The blending time
The fires of New SUN
The rebels of New SUN

Kindl, Patrice
Keeping the castle
A school for brides

King, A. S.
Ask the passengers
Everybody sees the ants
Glory O'Brien's history of the future: a novel
I crawl through it.
Please ignore Vera Dietz
Reality Boy
Still life with tornado
The **Kingdom** of little wounds. Cokal, S.

King, Emily R.

The hundredth queen

KING, MARTIN LUTHER, JR., 1929-1968 -- FICTION

Stone, N. Dear Martin

    of Ithaka. Barrett, T.

    of the screwups. Going, K. L.

KINGS AND RULERS -- FICTION

Ahdieh, R. The wrath and the dawn

Aveyard, V. Red queen

Bannen, M. The bird and the blade

Bunce, E. C. Star crossed

Carleson, J. C. The tyrant's daughter

Carson, R. The girl of fire and thorns

Cypess, L. Mistwood

Cypess, L. Nightspell

Dixon, H. Entwined

Hand, C. My Lady Jane

Hodge, R. Crimson bound

Johnston, E. K. A thousand nights

Kincaid, S. J. The empress

Lucier, M. Isle of blood and stone

Marr, M. Wicked lovely

Moriarty, J. A tangle of gold

Neumeier, R. The keeper of the mist

    cage. Aveyard, V.

KINGS -- FICTION

Hartman, R. Seraphina

Reeve, P. Here lies Arthur

Stroud, J. The Ring of Solomon

Vande Velde, V. The book of Mordred

Wein, E. The lion hunter

KINGS, QUEENS, RULERS, ETC. -- FICTION

Carey, J. L. In the time of dragon moon

Carson, R. The bitter kingdom

Carson, R. The crown of embers

Castor, H. M. VIII

Chima, C. W. The Crimson Crown

Johnston, E. K. A thousand nights

Longshore, K. Brazen

Moriarty, J. A tangle of gold

Neumeier, R. The keeper of the mist

Salisbury, M. The Sin Eater's daughter

Turner, M. W. Thick as thieves

Kinsella, Sophie

Finding Audrey

Kirby, Jessi

Golden

Things we know by heart

Kirby, Matthew J.

A taste for monsters

Kirkpatrick, Katherine

Between two worlds

Kisner, Adrienne

Dear Rachel Maddow

    in America. Rabb, M.

    in time. Flinn, A.

    kill vanish. Martinez, J.

    rider; a novel. McCaughrean, G.

KITES -- FICTION

McCaughrean, G. The kite rider; a novel

Kit's wilderness. Almond, D.

Kittle, Katrina

Reasons to be happy

Kittredge, Caitlin

The Iron Thorn

The nightmare garden

Kizer, Amber

A matter of days

Klages, Ellen

Out of left field

Klass, David

Firestorm

You don't know me

Klass, Sheila Solomon

Soldier's secret

Klause, Annette Curtis

Blood and chocolate

The silver kiss

Klavan, Andrew

MindWar: a novel

Klein, Lisa M.

Ophelia

KLEPTOMANIA -- FICTION

Kephart, B. One thing stolen

Kluger, Steve

My most excellent year

The **knife** and the butterfly. Perez, A. H.

KNIGHTS AND KNIGHTHOOD -- FICTION

Bell, H. The last knight

Grant, K. M. Blue flame

Morris, G. The squire's tale

Pierce, T. Alanna: the first adventure

Pierce, T. First test

Vande Velde, V. The book of Mordred

Knights of the hill country. Tharp, T.

KNOTS AND SPLICES -- FICTION

Bow, E. Sorrow's knot

The **knowing.** Cameron, S.

Knowles, Jo

See you at Harry's

Jumping off swings

Living with Jackie Chan

Read between the lines

Konigsberg, Bill

Honestly Ben

KOREA -- FICTION

Choi, S. N. Year of impossible goodbyes

KOREAN AMERICANS -- FICTION

Goo, M. I believe in a thing called love

Na, A. Wait for me

Yoon, N. The Sun Is Also a Star

Yoo, P. Good enough

KRAUS, DITA, 1929-

Iturbe, A. The librarian of Auschwitz

Kreslehner, Gabi

I Don't Live Here Anymore

Kriegman, Mitchell

Being Audrey Hepburn: a novel

Kuehn, Stephanie

When I am through with you

KUWAITI AMERICANS -- FICTION

Oakes, S. The arsonist

L

Belle Sauvage. Pullman, P.

linea. Jaramillo, A.

LABOR MOVEMENT -- FICTION

Crowder, M. Audacity

Labyrinth lost. Córdova, Z.

LABYRINTHS -- FICTION

Goelman, A. The path of names

carte. Davis, T. S.

LaCour, Nina

We Are Okay

LaFevers, Robin

Grave mercy

Mortal heart

Laidlaw, S. J.

Fifteen lanes

Laird, Elizabeth

The betrayal of Maggie Blair

A little piece of ground

of dreams: a Diviners novel. Bray, L.

effect. McCahan, E.

Lake, Nick

In darkness

Hostage Three

Satellite

LAKES -- FICTION

Les Becquets, D. Season of ice

Preus, M. Enchantment Lake: a Northwoods mystery

Lam, Laura

Pantomime

Lanagan, Margo

The brides of Rollrock Island

of permanent goodbyes. Abawi, A.

land. Taylor, M. D.

Landers, Melissa

Starfall

Landing. Ibbitson, J.

Landman, Tanya

Hell and high water

Landscape with invisible hand. Anderson, M. T.

Lane, Andrew

Rebel fire

Lange, Erin Jade

LANGUAGE AND LANGUAGES -- FICTION

Derting, K. The pledge

language inside. Thompson, H.

language of thorns. Bardugo, L.

LAOS -- FICTION

Powell, K. The Merit Birds

LARAMIE (WYO.) -- FICTION

Leslea, N. October mourning

Lara's gift. O'Brien, A.

Larbalestier, Justine

How to ditch your fairy

Liar

Magic lessons

LAS VEGAS (NEV.) -- FICTION

Gavin, R. 3 of a kind

Hautman, P. All-in

Jaffe, M. Bad kitty

Laskas, Gretchen Moran

The miner's daughter

Laskin, Pamela L.

Ronit & Jamil

Lasky, Kathryn

Ashes

Lone wolf

The **last** book in the universe. Philbrick, W. R.

Last chance for Paris. McNicoll, S.

The **last** Dragonslayer. Fforde, J.

The **last** echo. Derting, K.

The **last** execution. Wung-Sung, J.

The **last** forever. Caletti, D.

The **last** knight. Bell, H.

The **last** leaves falling. Benwell, S.

The **last** magician. Maxwell, L.

The **last** mission. Mazer, H.

Last night I sang to the monster; a novel. Sáenz, B. A.

The **Last** of August. Cavallaro, B.

Last shot. Feinstein, J.

Last star burning. Sangster, C.

The **latent** powers of Dylan Fontaine Lurie, A.

Latham, Jennifer

Scarlett undercover

LATIN AMERICANS -- NEW YORK (STATE) -- NEW YORK -- FICTION

Rice-Gonzalez, C. Chulito

LATINOS (U.S.) -- FICTION

Córdova, Z. Labyrinth lost

Latitude zero. Renn, D.

The **Latte** Rebellion. Stevenson, S. J.

Lauren, Christina

Autoboyography

Lauren Yanofsky hates the holocaust. Lieberman, L.

Laurie, Victoria

Forever, again

The **law** of loving others: a novel. Axelrod, K.

Leah on the offbeat. Albertalli, B.

Leap of Faith. Blair, J.

LEARNING DISABILITIES -- FICTION

Flake, S. G. Pinned

Learning to fly. Yee, P.

The **Leaving.** Altebrando, T.

Leavitt, Lindsey

Sean Griswold's head

Leavitt, Martine

My book of life by Angel

Lecesne, James
Absolute brightness

Lee, Mackenzi
The gentleman's guide to vice and virtue

Lee, Stacey
Outrun the moon
Under a painted sky
    of the clockwork key. Bailey, K.
  legend of Buddy Bush. Moses, S. P.

Legrand, Claire
Furyborn
Sawkill girls

LEMLICH, CLARA, 1886-1982 -- FICTION
Crowder, M. Audacity
    Woodson, J.

Lennon, Tom
When love comes to town

Leno, Katrina
The lost & found

Leonard, Julia Platt
Cold case

LEOPARD -- FICTION
Smith, R. The edge

Les Becquets, Diane
Season of ice

LESBIAN TEENAGERS -- FICTION
Albertalli, B. The upside of unrequited
Girard, M.-E. Girl Mans Up
Mac, C. 10 things I can see from here
Sugiura, M. It's not like it's a secret
Talley, R. Pulp
Talley, R. What We Left Behind

LESBIANISM -- FICTION
Talley, R. Pulp

LESBIANS -- FICTION
Bigelow, L. J. Starting from here
Danforth, E. M. The miseducation of Cameron Post
Dole, M. L. Down to the bone
George, M. The difference between you and me
Hopkins, E. The you I've never known
King, A. S. Ask the passengers
Lo, M. Adaptation
Lo, M. Huntress
Lo, M. A line in the dark
Love & lies. Wittlinger, E.
Mac, C. 10 things I can see from here
Mitchell, S. All out: the no-longer-secret stories of queer teens
  throughout the ages
Murphy, J. Ramona Blue
Peters, J. A. She loves you, she loves you not--
Rainfield, C. Scars
Ryan, S. Empress of the world
Sugiura, M. It's not like it's a secret

Talley, R. Our own private universe
Talley, R. Pulp
Westerfeld, S. Afterworlds
Wittlinger, E. Hard love
Woodson, J. From the notebooks of Melanin Sun

Leslea, Newman
October mourning

Lester, Joan Steinau
Black, white, other

Lester, Julius
Day of tears
Guardian
Time's memory

Let's Get Lost. Alsaid, A.

LETTERS -- FICTION
Alexander, K. Swing
Beard, P. Dear Zoe
Bliss, B. We'll fly away
Bryant, M. E. Glow
Buckhanon, K. Upstate
Handler, D. Why we broke up
Lyons, M. E. Letters from a slave boy
Lyons, M. E. Letters from a slave girl
Menon, S. When Dimple met Rishi
Pitcher, A. Ketchup clouds
Price, N. Zoe letting go
Stone, N. Dear Martin
Thomas, L. Nowhere near you
Whitman, S. The milk of birds

Letters from a slave boy. Lyons, M. E.
Letters from a slave girl. Lyons, M. E.

LEUKEMIA -- FICTION
Andrews, J. Me & Earl & the dying girl
Devlin, C. Tell me something real
Sonnenblick, J. Drums

Levenseller, Tricia
Daughter of the pirate king

Leverage. Cohen, J. C.

Levine, Ellen, 1939-2012
In trouble

Levine, Kristin
The best bad luck I ever had

Levithan, David
Boy meets boy
Every day
Hold me closer: the Tiny Cooper story
Love is the higher law
Two boys kissing

Levitin, Sonia
Strange relations

LEWIS AND CLARK EXPEDITION (1804-1806) --
        FICTION
Wolf, A. New found land

LEWIS, EDMONIA
Atkins, J. Stone mirrors

Lewis, Stewart
The secret ingredient

AUTHOR, TITLE AND SUBJECT INDEX
THIRD EDITION

me. Shukert, R.

& other train wrecks. Arnold, A.

Rivers, K.

LOVE STORIES

Almond, D. The tightrope walkers

Ashton, B. Everbound

Ashton, B. Everneath

Bardugo, L. Ruin and rising

Black, H. Black heart

Blume, J. Forever

Carey, J. L. Dragonswood

Chapman, L. Flawless

Cohn, R. Dash & Lily's book of dares

Cole, K. Poison princess

Cooney, C. B. Janie face to face

Cornwell, B. Tides

Cypess, L. Death sworn

Derting, K. The last echo

DeStefano, L. Sever

Doller, T. Something like normal

Emond, S. Winter town

Fichera, L. Hooked

Fine, S. Of Metal and Wishes

Fink, M. The summer I got a life

Fitzpatrick, H. My life next door

Fitzpatrick, H. What I thought was true

Gratton, T. The blood keeper

Hale, S. Book of a thousand days

Hamilton, K. When the stars threw down their spears

Haydu, C. A. OCD love story

Hemphill, S. Sisters of glass

Hodge, R. Cruel Beauty

Hubbard, A. Ripple

Kagawa, J. The immortal rules

Kephart, B. Going over

Kindl, P. Keeping the castle

King, A. S. Ask the passengers

Kirby, J. Golden

LaFevers, R. Grave mercy

Lam, L. Pantomime

Levithan, D. Every day

Lo, M. Ash

Lo, M. Huntress

Lo, M. Inheritance

Madison, B. September Girls

Mafi, T. Shatter me

Martin, C. K. K. I know it's over

McGarry, K. Dare You to

Morgan, P. The beautiful and the cursed

Moskowitz, H. Gone, gone, gone.

Myers, W. D. Amiri & Odette; a love story

Nelson, J. I'll give you the sun

Nowlin, L. If he had been with me

Ockler, S. The Book of Broken Hearts

Parker, A. C. Gated

Plum, A. Die for me

Pratchett, T. Dodger

Rennison, L. The taming of the tights

Roth, V. Allegiant

Rowell, R. Eleanor & Park

Scheidt, E. L. Uses for boys

Selfors, S. Mad love

Selfors, S. The sweetest spell

Simone, Ni-Ni. Upgrade U

Spears, K. Sway

Stiefvater, M. Forever

Stiefvater, M. The scorpio races

Stone, T. I. Time between us

Sun, A. Ink

Taylor, L. Daughter of smoke and bone

Tregay, S. Love & leftovers; a novel in verse

Trueman, T. Life happens next; a novel

Walton, L. The Strange and beautiful sorrows of Ava Lavender

West, K. Pivot point

West, K. Split second

Williams, G. Beatle meets Destiny

Zarr, S. Sweethearts

Love you hate you miss you. Scott, E.

Lowitz, Leza

Jet Black and the ninja wind

Lowry, Lois

Gathering blue

The giver

Son

LOYALTY -- FICTION

Milan, M. Ignite the stars

Roth, V. Allegiant

Lubar, David

Character, driven

Sleeping freshmen never lie

Lucier, Makiia

A death-struck year

Isle of blood and stone

LUCK -- FICTION

Smith, J. E. Windfall

Stokes, P. Girl against the universe

Lucky strikes. Bayard, L.

Lucky. Vail, R.

Luedeke, Lisa

Smashed

Lu, Marie

Batman: Nightwalker

Warcross

Wildcard

Lundin, Britta

Ship it

Luper, Eric

Bug boy

Seth Baumgartner's love manifesto

Lupica, Mike

The batboy

The big field

Hero

Miracle on 49th Street

Callahan, E. The art of escaping

Carson, R. The bitter kingdom

Carson, R. The crown of embers

Carson, R. The girl of fire and thorns

Carson, R. Walk on Earth a Stranger

Catmull, K. The radiant road: a novel

Chima, C. W. The warrior heir

Clayton, D. The Belles

Cluess, J. A poison dark and drowning

Cluess, J. A shadow bright and burning

Cornwell, B. Mechanica

Cornwell, B. Venturess

Coulthurst, A. Of Fire and Stars

Cypess, L. Death sworn

Cypess, L. Mistwood

Córdova, Z. Labyrinth lost

Dennard, S. Something strange and deadly

Dickinson, P. The ropemaker

Dixon, H. Entwined

Doyle, M. Bewitching season

Duey, K. Sacred scars

Duiker, K. S. The hidden star

Egan, C. Julia vanishes

Fawcett, H. Even the darkest stars

Fforde, J. The last Dragonslayer

Flinn, A. Cloaked

Foxlee, K. The midnight dress

Funke, C. Fearless

Funke, C. Reckless

Gaughen, A. C. Reign the earth

Goelman, A. The path of names

Gratton, T. The blood keeper

Hahn, R. A creature of moonlight

Hamilton, K. Tyger tyger

Hamilton, K. When the stars threw down their spears

Harris, J. Runemarks

Hartman, R. Shadow scale

Healey, K. Guardian of the dead

Heilig, H. For a muse of fire

Hodge, R. Crimson bound

Hodge, R. Cruel Beauty

Johnston, E. K. A thousand nights

Jones, K. Murder, magic, and what we wore

Kittredge, C. The nightmare garden

Lam, L. Pantomime

Lanagan, M. The brides of Rollrock Island

Larbalestier, J. How to ditch your fairy

Larbalestier, J. Magic lessons

Legrand, C. Furyborn

Mahoney, K. The iron witch

Mantchev, L. Eyes like stars

Marillier, J. Cybele's secret

Marillier, J. Raven flight

Marillier, J. Shadowfell

Marillier, J. Wildwood dancing

Maxwell, L. The last magician

McBride, L. Hold me closer, necromancer

McKinley, R. Pegasus

McLemore, A. -M. When the moon was ours

McLemore, A. -M. Wild beauty

Moriarty, J. A corner of white

Moriarty, J. A tangle of gold

Moriarty, J. The cracks in the kingdom

Morris, G. The squire's tale

Mosley, W. 47

Murdock, C. G. Princess Ben

Neff, H. H. The hound of Rowan

Neumeier, R. The City in the Lake

Neumeier, R. The keeper of the mist

Nix, G. Clariel: the lost Abhorsen

Nix, G. Frogkisser

Okorafor, N. Akata warrior

Older, D. J. Shadowhouse fall

Reeve, P. Here lies Arthur

Rens, K. Even the darkest stars

Ritter, W. The dire king.

Rowell, R. Carry on: a novel

Rudnick, P., 1957- Gorgeous

Ruiz Zafon, C. The Prince of Mist

Sanderson, B. The Rithmatist

Scott, M. The alchemyst

Scott, M. The enchantress

Selfors, S. The sweetest spell

Simner, J. L. Bones of Faerie

Simner, J. L. Faerie after

Simner, J. L. Faerie winter

Stiefvater, M. All the crooked saints.

Stiefvater, M. Ballad; a gathering of faerie

Stiefvater, M. Blue lily, lily blue

Stiefvater, M. The dream thieves

Stiefvater, M. The raven boys

Stiefvater, M. The raven king

Stirling, T. When my heart was wicked

Strauss, V. Passion blue

Stroud, J. The Ring of Solomon

Taylor, L. Blackbringer

Thomas, S. The burning sky

Tiernan, C. Immortal beloved

Tripp, B. The accidental highwayman: being the tale of Kit Bristol, his horse Midnight, a mysterious princess, and sundry magical persons besides

Werlin, N. Impossible

Wood, F. Cloudwish

Wooding, C. Havoc

Wrede, P. C. Across the Great Barrier

Wrede, P. C. The Far West

Wrede, P. C. The thirteenth child

Yolen, J. Curse of the Thirteenth Fey

Yovanoff, B. Fiendish

Zettel, S. Bad luck girl

Zettel, S. Dust girl

Zettel, S. Golden girl

Zink, M. Guardian of the Gate

Zinn, B. Poison

lessons. Larbalestier, J.

MAGIC MIRRORS

Fisher, C. The door in the moon

MAGIC REALISM (LITERATURE)

Davies, J. The odds of lightning

MAGIC TRICKS -- FICTION

Callahan, E. The art of escaping

Goelman, A. The path of names

Maniscalco, K. Escaping from Houdini

MAGICIANS -- FICTION

Chima, C. W. The Crimson Crown

Maxwell, L. The last magician

Magnin, Joyce

Carrying Mason

Magoon, Kekla

37 things I love (in no particular order)

Mahoney, Karen

The iron witch

MAINE -- FICTION

French, G. Grit

Les Becquets, D. Season of ice

Oliver, L. Requiem

Parker, S. M. The rattled bones

Walker, B. F. Black boy/white school

Wunder, W. The probability of miracles

MAJOR LEAGUE BASEBALL (ORGANIZATION) --
FICTION

White, E. E. A season of daring greatly

lemonade. Wolff, V. E.

Maldonado, Torrey

Secret Saturdays

Malley, Gemma

The Declaration

MANCHESTER (ENGLAND) -- FICTION

Burgess, M. The hit

Pitcher, A. Silence is goldfish: a novel

mango-shaped space; a novel. Mass, W.

MANHATTAN PROJECT (U.S.) -- FICTION

Poulsen, David A. And Then the Sky Exploded

MANIC-DEPRESSIVE ILLNESS -- FICTION

Colbert, B. Little & Lion

Downes, P. Ten miles one way

Heilig, H. For a muse of fire

Selfors, S. Mad love

Wunder, W. The museum of intangible things

Maniscalco, Kerri

Escaping from Houdini

Hunting Prince Dracula

Stalking Jack the Ripper

MANITOBA -- FICTION

Buffie, M. Winter shadows

Manivong, Laura

Escaping the tiger

Mankell, Henning

A bridge to the stars

Shadow of the leopard

MANNERS AND CUSTOMS -- FICTION

Katsoulis, G. S. All rights reserved

Mantchev, Lisa

Eyes like stars

MAN-WOMAN RELATIONSHIP -- FICTION

Alexander, K. He said, she said

Brockenbrough, M. The game of Love and Death

Coulthurst, A. Of Fire and Stars

Handler, D. Why we broke up

Laskin, P. L. Ronit & Jamil

McGarry, K. Dare You to

Rossi, V. Under the never sky

The **many** lives of John Stone. Buckley-Archer, L.

Manzano, Sonia

The revolution of Evelyn Serrano

MAORIS -- FICTION

Healey, K. Guardian of the dead

MAPS -- FICTION

Lucier, M. Isle of blood and stone

Marcus, Kimberly

Exposed

Maresi. Turtschaninoff, M.

Mare's war. Davis, T. S.

MARIJUANA -- FICTION

Dirkes, C. Sucktown

Marillier, Juliet

Cybele's secret

Raven flight

Shadowfell

Wildwood dancing

MARINA DEL REY (CALIF.) -- FICTION

Yee, L. The kidney hypothetical

MARINE POLLUTION -- FICTION

Nelson, B. The y came from below

Mariz, Rae

The Unidentified

The **mark.** Nadol, J.

MARLOWE, CHRISTOPHER, 1564-1593 ABOUT

Silbert, L. The intelligencer

Marquardt, Marie F.

Dream Things True

The radius of us

Marr, Melissa

Wicked lovely

MARRIAGE -- FICTION

DeStefano, L. Wither

Kindl, P. Keeping the castle

Kindl, P. A school for brides: a story of maidens, mystery, and
matrimony

Oliver, L. Requiem

Robert, Na'ima B. She wore red trainers: A Muslim Love Story

The **marrow** thieves. Dimaline, C.

Marsden, Carolyn, 1950-

My Own Revolution

Sahwira; an African friendship

MARS (PLANET) -- FICTION

Gill, D. M. Black hole sun

Rivers, K. Love

Marsden, John, 1950-
Hamlet: a novel
Incurable
The other side of dawn
Tomorrow, when the war began
While I live

Marsh, Katherine
Jepp, who defied the stars
The night tourist

Marshall, Catherine
Christy

Marshall, Kate
I am still alive

MARTIAL ARTS -- FICTION
Skilton, S. Bruised
Uehashi, N. Moribito; Guardian of the Spirit

Martians. Woolston, B.

Martin, C. K. Kelly
I know it's over
The lighter side of life and death
Yesterday

Martinez, Claudia Guadalupe
Pig Park

Martinez, Jessica
Kiss kill vanish
Virtuosity

Martinez, Victor
Parrot in the oven; a novel

Martin, T. Michael
The end games

MARY, BLESSED VIRGIN, SAINT ABOUT
Grimes, N. A girl named Mister

MARYLAND -- FICTION
Cummings, P. Blindsided
Cummings, P. The journey back
Lyga, B. Hero-type
Naylor, P. R. Intensely Alice

Mary-Todd, Jonathan
Shot down
McClintock, N.

MASKS (FACIAL) -- FICTION
Hardinge, F. A face like glass

Mason, Prue
Camel rider

Mason, Simon
Running girl

Mass, Wendy
Heaven looks a lot like the mall; a novel
A mango-shaped space; a novel

MASSACHUSETTS -- FICTION
Friend, N. For keeps
Friend, N. How we roll
Howe, K. Conversion
Konigsberg, B. Honestly Ben
Lo, M. A line in the dark
Love & lies. Wittlinger, E.
Thompson, H. The language inside

Tiernan, C. Immortal beloved

MASSACRE SURVIVORS -- FICTION
Caletti, D. A heart in a body in the world
Keplinger, K. That's not what happened

MASS MURDER INVESTIGATION -- FICTION
Armstrong, K. Aftermath

The **Master** of Misrule. Powell, L.

Matched. Condie, A.

Mathieu, Jennifer
Moxie: a novel

Matson, Morgan
Amy & Roger's epic detour
Since you've been gone

A **matter** of days. Kizer, A.

A **matter** of souls. Patrick, D. L.

MATTHEW, THE APOSTLE, SAINT ABOUT
Gormley, B. Poisoned honey

Mattison, Booker T.
Unsigned hype; a novel

MATURATION (PSYCHOLOGY) -- FICTION
Buzo, L. Love and other perishable items

Maximum Ride: the angel experiment. Patterson, J.

Maxwell, Lisa
The last magician

Mayhew, Julie
The Big Lie
Red ink

Mazer, Harry
A boy at war
The last mission
Snow bound

Mazer, Norma Fox
After the rain
The missing girl

Mazunte (mexico) -- Fiction
Resau, L. The jade notebook

McBay, Bruce
Waiting for Sarah

McBride, Lish
Hold me closer, necromancer

McCaffrey, Todd J.
Dragongirl

McCahan, Erin
The lake effect
Love and other foreign words

McCall, Guadalupe Garcia
All the stars denied
Shame the Stars

McCarthy, Andrew
Just fly away

McCarthy, Susan Carol
True fires

McCaughrean, Geraldine
The death-defying Pepper Roux
The glorious adventures of the Sunshine Queen
The kite rider; a novel
The white darkness

Lippert-M., K. Tabula rasa
Martin, C. K. K. Yesterday
Miranda, M. Hysteria
Patrick, C. Forgotten
Polisner, G. The memory of things
Rainfield, C. Scars
Richards, N. D. Six months later
Rush, J. Altered
Silvera, A. More happy than not
Terry, T. Fractured
Terry, T. Slated
Warman, J. Where the truth lies
West, K. Split second
Wolf, J. S. Breaking beautiful
memory of things. Polisner, G.

MEMPHIS (TENN.) -- HISTORY -- 20TH CENTURY -- FICTION
Vawter, V. Copyboy

Menon, Sandhya
When Dimple met Rishi

MENTAL ILLNESS -- FICTION
Anthony, J. Chopsticks
Arnold, D. Mosquitoland
Axelrod, K. The law of loving others: a novel
Barratt, M. Joe Rat
Colbert, B. Little & Lion
Downes, P. Ten miles one way
Griffin, A. Where I want to be
Halpern, J. Get well soon
Halpern, J. Have a nice day
Haston, M. The end of our story
Hautman, P. Invisible
Heilig, H. For a muse of fire
Howard, A. G. Unhinged
Leavitt, M. Calvin
Nolan, H. Crazy
Scelsa, K. Fans of the impossible life
Schantz, S. E. Fig
Sloan, H. G. I'll be there
Steiger, A. J. When my heart joins the thousand
Toten, T. Beware that girl
Vaught, S. Freaks like us
Walton, J. Words on bathroom walls
Williams, C. L. Miles from ordinary; a novel
Woods, E. E. Choker

MENTAL ILLNESS -- TREATMENT -- FICTION
Walton, J. Words on bathroom walls

MENTALLY ILL -- FICTION
Cardi, A. The chance you won't return
McGinnis, M. A madness so discreet

MENTALLY ILL -- INSTITUTIONAL CARE -- FICTION
Hubbard, J. R. Try not to breathe

MENTORING -- FICTION
Myers, W. D. All the right stuff
Watson, R. Piecing me together

MERCENARY SOLDIERS -- FICTION
Taylor, L. Silksinger

The **merchant** of death. MacHale, D. J.
The **merchant's** daughter. Dickerson, M.
Mercy mode. Garner, E.
The **Merit** Birds. Powell, K.

MERLIN (LEGENDARY CHARACTER) -- FICTION
Barron, T. A. The lost years of Merlin
Merlin's dragon. Barron, T. A.

MERMAIDS AND MERMEN -- FICTION
Braxton-Smith, A. Merrow
Madison, B. September Girls
Moskowitz, H. Teeth

MERMEN -- FICTION
Moskowitz, H. Teeth

MERRICK, JOSEPH CAREY, 1862-1890 -- FICTION
Kirby, M. J. A taste for monsters
Merrow. Braxton-Smith, A.

Mesrobian, Carrie
Just a girl
Messenger of Fear. Grant, M.

METAMORPHOSIS -- FICTION
Stiefvater, M. Sinner

METAPHYSICS -- FICTION
Kittredge, C. The nightmare garden

METEORS -- FICTION
Wallach, T. We all looked up

METHAMPHETAMINE -- FICTION
Arcos, C. Out of reach
Woodson, J. Beneath

MEXICAN-AMERICAN BORDER REGION -- FICTION
Sedgwick, M. Saint death

MEXICAN AMERICAN FAMILIES -- FICTION
Sanchez, E. L. I Am Not Your Perfect Mexican Daughter

MEXICAN AMERICANS -- FICTION
Alegria, M. Estrella's quinceanera
Canales, V. The tequila worm
Castan, M. Fighting for Dontae
Cisneros, S. The house on Mango Street
De la Peña, M. The living
Flores-Scott, P. American road trip
Jimenez, F. Breaking through
Jimenez, F. The circuit
Jimenez, F. Reaching out
Johnson, L. Muchacho
Martinez, V. Parrot in the oven; a novel
McCall, G. G. All the stars denied
Perez, A. Out of darkness
Perez, A. What can(t) wait
Quintero, I. Gabi, a girl in pieces
Sáenz, B. A. Aristotle and Dante discover the secrets of the universe
Sáenz, B. A. He forgot to say good-bye
Sáenz, B. A. The inexplicable logic of my life
Sáenz, B. A. Sammy and Juliana in Hollywood
Saldana, R. A good long way
Sanchez, A. Bait
Sanchez, A. Getting it
Sanchez, A. So hard to say

AUTHOR, TITLE AND SUBJECT INDEX
THIRD EDITION

Sanchez, E. L. I Am Not Your Perfect Mexican Daughter
Sitomer, A. L. The secret story of Sonia Rodriguez
Soto, G. Buried onions
Temblador, A. Secrets of the Casa Rosada
Villareal, R. Body slammed
Wallace, S. N. Muckers
Whitney, K. A. The perfect distance

MEXICAN AMERICAN TEENAGERS -- FICTION
Stiefvater, M. All the crooked saints.

MEXICANS -- FICTION
Jaramillo, A. La linea
Restrepo, B. Illegal

MEXICANS -- UNITED STATES -- FICTION
Alsaid, A. North of happy

MEXICO CITY (MEXICO) -- FICTION
Diederich, P. Playing for the Devil's Fire

MEXICO -- FICTION
Diederich, P. Playing for the Devil's Fire
Resau, L. The jade notebook
Resau, L. Red glass
Sedgwick, M. Saint death
Sedgwick, M. Saint death
Stork, F. X. Disappeared

Meyerhoff, Jenny
Queen of secrets

Meyer, Marissa
Renegades

MEYERS ODETTE ABOUT
Macdonald, M. Odette's secrets

MIAMI (FLA.) -- FICTION
Danticat, E. Untwine

MICE -- FICTION
Deedy, C. A. The Cheshire Cheese cat

Michaelis, Antonia
Tiger moon

Michael, Jan
City boy

MICHAUX, LEWIS H., 1885-1976 ABOUT
Nelson, V. M. No crystal stair

MICHIGAN -- FICTION
Potter, R. Exit strategy

MICHIGAN, LAKE -- FICTION
McCahan, E. The lake effect

MIDDLE AGES -- FICTION
Avi. Crispin
Coventry, S. The queen's daughter
Dickerson, M. The merchant's daughter Grant, K. M. Blood
  red horse
Grant, K. M. Blue flame
Moran, K. Bloodline
Moran, K. Bloodline rising
Napoli, D. J. Hush
Stroud, J. Heroes of the valley

MIDDLE EAST -- FICTION
Carleson, J. C. The tyrant's daughter

**MIDDLE EAST -- POLITICS AND GOVERNMENT --
  FICTION**

Carleson, J. C. The tyrant's daughter

MIDDLE SCHOOLS -- FICTION
Castan, M. Fighting for Dontae
Gilman, C. Professor Gargoyle
Myers, W. D. The Cruisers
Vail, R. Unfriended

Midnight at the Electric. Anderson, J. L.
Midnight charter. Whitley, D.
The **midnight** dress. Foxlee, K.
A **midsummer's** nightmare. Keplinger, K.
Midwinterblood. Sedgwick, M.

MIDWIVES -- FICTION
O'Brien, C. M. Birthmarked

Mieville, China
Railsea
Un Lun Dun

MIGRANT LABOR -- FICTION
Jimenez, F. Breaking through
Jimenez, F. The circuit

Mikaelsen, Ben
Ghost of Spirit Bear

Miklowitz, Gloria D.
The enemy has a face

Milan, Maura
Ignite the stars

Miles from ordinary; a novel. Williams, C. L.
Miles Morales: Spider-Man. Reynolds, J.

MILITARY BASES -- FICTION
Duble, K. B. Phantoms in the snow

MILITARY EDUCATION -- FICTION
Efaw, A. Battle dress

**MILITARY EDUCATION -- NEW YORK (STATE) -- WEST
  POINT**
Efaw, A. Battle dress

MILITARY PERSONNEL -- UNITED STATES -- FICTION
Doller, T. Something like normal

MILITARY TRAINING -- FICTION
Hensley, J. N. Rites of passage

MILITIA MOVEMENTS -- FICTION
Bao, K. Dove arising
The **milk** of birds. Whitman, S.

Miller, Michael
Shadow run

Miller, Sam J
The art of starving

Miller, Samuel
A lite too bright
A **million** suns. Revis, B.

Mills, Emma
First & then

Mills, Wendy
All we have left

Minchin, Adele
The beat goes on
Mindblind. Roy, J. R.
MindWar: a novel. Klavan, A.
The **miner's** daughter. Laskas, G. M.

MINERS -- FICTION

Gill, D. M. Black hole sun

MINES AND MINERAL RESOURCES -- FICTION

Williams, M. Diamond boy

MINNEAPOLIS (MINN.) -- FICTION

Gibney, S. Dream country

MINNESOTA -- FICTION

Brezenoff, S. Guy in real life

Delsol, W. Stork

Preus, M. Enchantment Lake: a Northwoods mystery

Weaver, W. Saturday night dirt

MINNESOTA -- HISTORY -- 20TH CENTURY -- FICTION

Casanova, M. Frozen

MINNESOTA -- FICTION

Mesrobian, C. Just a girl

minnow. Sweeney, D.

MINOTAUR (GREEK MYTHOLOGY)

Elliott, D. Bull

MINOTAUR (GREEK MYTHOLOGY) -- FICTION

Elliott, D. Bull

on 49th Street Lupica, M.

Miracle's boys. Woodson, J.

Scott, E.

MIRACLES -- FICTION

Hutchinson, S. D. The apocalypse of Elena Mendoza

Stiefvater, M. All the crooked saints.

Wunder, W. The probability of miracles

Miranda, Megan

Hysteria

Soulprint

MIRRORS

Fisher, C. The door in the moon

miseducation of Cameron Post. Danforth, E. M.

Mismatch. Namioka, L.

Fortune Cookie. Bjorkman, L.

Peregrine's home for peculiar children. Riggs, R.

MISSING CHILDREN -- FICTION

Altebrando, T. The Leaving.

Anthony, J. Chopsticks

Beaufrand, M. J. The rise and fall of the Gallivanters

Beaufrand, M. J. Useless Bay

Crutcher, C. Period 8

Gardner, F. The second life of Ava Rivers

Hartnett, S. What the birds see

Hesse, M. Girl in the blue coat

Kephart, B. Wild blues

Lucier, M. Isle of blood and stone

Oliver, L. Vanishing girls

Priest, C. I Am Princess X.

Salomon, P. A. All those broken angels

Tharp, T. Mojo

Thomas, K. Little monsters

Tromly, S. Trouble is a friend of mine

Valentine, J. Double

Vaught, S. Freaks like us

Yovanoff, B. The replacement

missing girl. Mazer, N. F.

MISSING PERSONS -- FICTION

Abrahams, P. Reality check

Bell, J. Juggling fire

Bilen, T. What she left behind

Bradbury, J. Shift

Cantor, J. The September sisters

Coben, H. Shelter

Coyle, K. Vivian Apple needs a miracle

Crutcher, C. Period 8

Dawn, S. Splinter

Diederich, P. Playing for the Devil's Fire

Doyle, M. Bewitching season

Dubosarsky, U. The golden day

Flinn, A. Cloaked

French, G. Grit

Gavin, R. 3 of a kind

Green, J. Turtles all the way down

Haines, K. M. The girl is murder

Hautman, P. The obsidian blade

Hutchinson, S. D. At the edge of the universe

Hutchinson, S. D. The apocalypse of Elena Mendoza

Jackson, T. D. Monday's not coming

King, A. S. Everybody sees the ants

Les Becquets, D. Season of ice

Liu, J. Girls on the line

Lucier, M. Isle of blood and stone

McClintock, N. About that night

McNeal, T. Far far away

Miklowitz, G. D. The enemy has a face

Moriarty, J. A corner of white

Moriarty, J. A tangle of gold

Moriarty, J. The cracks in the kingdom

Northrop, M. Gentlemen

Peterson, L. J. Silver rain

Resau, L. The jade notebook

Roecker, L. The lies that bind

Sedgwick, M. She is not invisible

Smith-Ready, J. This side of salvation

Summers, C. All the rage

Valentine, J. Me, the missing, and the dead

Vaught, S. Freaks like us

Wells, M. Emilie & the hollow world

Whaley, J. C. Where things come back

Winters, C. Odd & true

MISSISSIPPI -- FICTION

Taylor, M. D. Roll of thunder, hear my cry

MISSISSIPPI -- RACE RELATIONS

Crowe, C. Mississippi trial, 1955

Mississippi trial, 1955. Crowe, C.

MISSOURI -- FICTION

Katcher, B. Almost perfect

Katcher, B. Playing with matches

Mister Death's blue-eyed girls. Hahn, M. D.

Mistwood. Cypess, L.

Mitchell, Saundra

All out: the no-longer-secret stories of queer teens throughout the ages

Mockingbirds. Whitney, D.
Mockingjay. Collins, S.
MOHAWK INDIANS -- FICTION
Carvell, M. Sweetgrass basket
Carvell, M. Who will tell my brother?
    Tharp, T.
MOLOKAI (HAWAII) -- FICTION
Patel, S. Rani Patel in full effect
Molope, Kagiso Lesego
This book betrays my brother
Monday's not coming. Jackson, T. D.
MONEYMAKING PROJECTS -- FICTION
Coker, R. Chasing Jupiter
Monster. Grant, M.
MONSTERS -- FICTION
Bardugo, L. Shadow and bone
Bardugo, L. Siege and storm
Bobet, L. An inheritance of ashes
Childs, T. L. Sweet venom
Delaney, J. A new darkness
Gilman, C. Professor Gargoyle
Golden, C. The sea wolves
Moulton, C. A. Angelfire
Randall, T. Spirits of the Noh
Ritter, W. Beastly bones: a Jackaby novel
Rowell, R. Carry on: a novel
Schwab, V. Our Dark Duet
Scott, M. The enchantress
Smith, A. G. The Devil's engine
Tayleur, K. Killer Pizza
Tayleur, K. Killer Pizza: the slice
Winters, C. Odd & true
Yancey, R. The monstrumologist
Yancey, R. final descent
    monstrumologist. Yancey, R.
MONTANA -- FICTION
Danforth, E. M. The miseducation of Cameron Post
Ingold, J. Hitch
Price, C. The interrogation of Gabriel James
    of Sundays. White, R.
    moon and more. Dessen, S.
MOON -- FICTION
Bao, K. Dove arising
Harstad, J. 172 hours on the moon
Moonrise. Crossan, S.
Moon, Sarah
Sparrow
Moracho, Cristina
A good idea
Moran, Katy
Bloodline
Bloodline rising
MORDRED (LEGENDARY CHARACTER) -- FICTION
Vande Velde, V. The book of Mordred
    happy than not. Silvera, A.
    than this. Ness, P.
Morgan, Page

The beautiful and the cursed
Moriarty, Jaclyn
A corner of white
The cracks in the kingdom
Feeling sorry for Celia
The ghosts of Ashbury High
A tangle of gold
Moriarty, Laura
The center of everything
Moribito; Guardian of the Spirit. Uehashi, N.
Moribito II; Guardian of the Darkness. Uehashi, N.
MORMONS -- FICTION
Lauren, C. Autoboyography
Morpurgo, Michael
An elephant in the garden
Half a man
Listen to the Moon
Private Peaceful
Morris, Gerald
The squire's tale
Mortal heart. LaFevers. R.
Morton-Shaw, Christine
The riddles of Epsilon
Moses, Shelia P.
Joseph
The legend of Buddy Bush
Moskowitz, Hannah
Gone, gone, gone
Teeth
Mosley, Walter
47
Mosquitoland. Arnold, D.
MOTHER AND CHILD -- FICTION
Lowry, L. Son
MOTHER-CHILD RELATIONSHIP -- FICTION
Lowry, L. Son
MOTHER-DAUGHTER RELATIONSHIP -- FICTION
Arnold, D. Mosquitoland
Arnold, E. K. Infandous
Axelrod, K. The law of loving others: a novel
Bassoff, L. Lost girl found
Bowman, A. D. Starfish
Braxton-Smith, A. Merrow
Budhos, M. T. Tell us we're home
Cardi, A. The chance you won't return
Carey, J. L. Dragon's Keep
Carter, A. Embassy row #1: all fall down
Casanova, M. Frozen
Dawn, S. Splinter
Fixmer, E. Down from the mountain
Friend, N. For keeps
Goto, H. Half World
Grant, M. Eve & Adam
Hale, M. The goodbye season
Howard, A. G. Unhinged
Hyde, C. R. Jumpstart the world
Kamata, S. Gadget Girl

Kephart, B. House of Dance
MacCready, R. M. Buried
MacCullough, C. Stealing Henry
Martinez, J. Virtuosity
Mayhew, J. Red ink
McDonald, J. Off-color
Moriarty, L. The center of everything
Mulder, M. Out of the box
Na, A. Wait for me
Oakes, S. The arsonist
Oates, J. C. Freaky green eyes
Omololu, C. J. Dirty little secrets
Palmer, R. The Corner of Bitter and Sweet
Reed, A. Over you
Resau, L. The indigo notebook
Resau, L. The jade notebook
Resau, L. The ruby notebook
Sanchez, E. L. I Am Not Your Perfect Mexican Daughter
Schantz, S. E. Fig
Selfors, S. Mad love
Shreve, S. The lovely shoes
Simmons, K. Article 5
Simner, J. L. Faerie winter
Stirling, T. When my heart was wicked
White, E. E. The President's daughter
Williams, C. L. Glimpse
Williams, C. L. Miles from ordinary; a novel
Zoboi, I. American street

MOTHERS AND DAUGHTERS -- FICTION
Albert, M. The Hazel Wood
Arnold, D. Mosquitoland
Arnold, E. K. Infandous
Axelrod, K. The law of loving others: a novel
Bashardoust, M. Girls made of snow and glass
Blythe, C. Revenge of a not-so-pretty girl
Bowman, A. D. Starfish
Bowman, A. D. Summer bird blue
Dawn, S. Splinter
Devlin, C. Tell me something real
Elwood, T. Split the sun
Fixmer, E. Down from the mountain
Haddix, M. P. Full ride
Howard, J. J. That time I joined the circus
Kirby, J. Golden
Mathieu, J. Moxie: a novel
Moon, S. Sparrow
Oakes, S. The arsonist
Sanchez, E. L. I Am Not Your Perfect Mexican Daughter
Schantz, S. E. Fig
Sepetys, R. Out of the Easy
Sonnenblick, J. Falling over sideways
Stirling, T. When my heart was wicked
Valentine, J. Fire color one

MOTHERS AND SONS -- FICTION
Benwell, S. The last leaves falling
Damico, G. Hellhole

MOTHERS -- DEATH -- FICTION

Redwine, C. J. The wish granter: a Ravenspire novel

MOTHERS -- DEATH -- TEEN FICTION
Cameron, S. Out of the blue

MOTHERS -- FICTION
Cameron, S. Out of the blue
Garner, E. Contaminated
Lewis, S. The secret ingredient
Lowry, L. Son
Peters, J. A. She loves you, she loves you not--
Raf, M. The symptoms of my insanity
Shaw, S. Safe

MOTHER-SON RELATIONSHIP -- FICTION
Barnes, J. Tales of the Madman Underground
Benwell, S. The last leaves falling
Lupica, M. The batboy
Lynch, C. Angry young man
Moses, S. P. Joseph
Powell, K. The Merit Birds
Woodson, J. From the notebooks of Melanin Sun

MOTION PICTURE INDUSTRY -- FICTION
Umminger, A. American Girls: A Novel

MOTION PICTURE PRODUCERS AND DIRECTORS -- FICTION
Bruton, C. I Predict a Riot

MOTION PICTURES -- FICTION
Castellucci, C. Boy proof
Selzer, A. How to get suspended and influence people

MOTION PICTURES -- PRODUCTION AND DIRECTION -- FICTION
Doctorow, C. Pirate cinema

MOTORCYCLE RACING -- FICTION
Graudin, R. Wolf by wolf

Moulton, Courtney Allison
Angelfire

MOUNTAIN BIKING -- FICTION
Davis, R. F. Chasing AllieCat

MOUNTAINEERING -- FICTION
Fawcett, H. Even the darkest stars
Rens, K. Even the darkest stars
Smith, R. The edge
Smith, R. Peak

MOUNTAINEERING -- HINDU KUSH MOUNTAINS (AFGHANISTAN AND PAKISTAN) -- FICTION
Smith, R. The edge

MOUNTAINS -- FICTION
Wyatt, M. Funny how things change

Mourlevat, Jean-Claude
Winter's end

The **moves** make the man; a novel. Brooks, B.

MOVING -- FICTION
Bennett, J. Alex, approximately
Chen, J. Return to me
Coben, H. Shelter
Cousins, D. Waiting for Gonzo
Fehlbaum, B. Big fat disaster
Friend, N. Bounce
Hand, C. Unearthly

Wisdom's kiss

Murphy, Julie

Dumplin'

Ramona Blue.
  museum of intangible things. Wunder, W.

MUSIC -- FICTION

Hartman, R. Seraphina

Thompson, K. The new policeman

MUSICALS -- FICTION

Alsenas, L. Beyond clueless

Levithan, D. Hold me closer: the Tiny Cooper story
  musician's daughter. Dunlap, S. E.

MUSICIANS -- FICTION

Amato, M. Get happy

Andrews, J. The Haters

Anthony, J. Chopsticks

Auch, M. J. Guitar boy

Beaudoin, S. Wise Young Fool

Brezenoff, S. Brooklyn, burning

Castellucci, C. Beige

Collins, P. L. Hidden voices

Dunlap, S. E. The musician's daughter.

Going, K. L. Fat kid rules the world

Martinez, J. Virtuosity

McClintock, N. Out of tune

Nelson, B. Rock star, superstar

Nelson, J. The sky is everywhere

Skuse, C. J. Rockoholic

Smith-Ready, J. Shade

Smith-Ready, J. Shift

Sonnenblick, J. Notes from the midnight driver

Stamper, V. What the night sings

Stiefvater, M. Ballad; a gathering of faerie

Weston, R. P. Blues for Zoey

Whitaker, A. Wildflower

Yolen, J. Troll Bridge

MUSLIM FAMILIES -- AUSTRALIA -- FICTION

Abdel-Fattah, R. The lines we cross

MUSLIMS -- AUSTRALIA -- FICTION

Abdel-Fattah, R. The lines we cross

MUSLIMS -- FICTION

Abawi, A. A land of permanent goodbyes

Abawi, A. A land of permanent goodbyes

Ahmed, S. Love, hate & other filters

Ali, S. K. Saints and misfits: a novel

Budhos, M. T. Watched.

Karim, S. Skunk girl

Karim, S. That thing we call a heart

Mafi, T. A very large expanse of sea

Mills, W. All we have left

Perera, A. Guantanamo boy

Robert, Na'ima B. Boy vs. girl.

Robert, Na'ima B. From Somalia with love

Robert, Na'ima B. She wore red trainers: A Muslim Love Story

MUSLIMS -- UNITED STATES -- FICTION

Ali, S. K. Saints and misfits: a novel

Mussi, Sarah

The door of no return

MUTATION (BIOLOGY) -- FICTION

Reeve, P. Scrivener's moon

MUTISM -- FICTION

Chan, G. The disappearance

My beautiful hippie Lynch, J. N.

My big mouth. Hannan, P.

My book of life by Angel. Leavitt, M.

My brother, my sister, and I. Watkins, Y. K.

My faire lady. Wettersten, L.

My favorite band does not exist. Jeschonek, R. T.

My invented life. Bjorkman, L.

My Lady Jane. Hand, C.

My life in black and white. Friend, N.

My life next door. Fitzpatrick, H.

My most excellent year. Kluger, S.

My name is not easy. Edwardson, D. D.

My name is not Friday. Walter, J.

My Own Revolution. Marsden, C.

My plain Jane. Hand, C.

My sister lives on the mantelpiece. Pitcher, A.

My swordhand is singing. Sedgwick, M.

Myers, Walter Dean

All the right stuff

Carmen; an urban adaptation of the opera

The Cruisers

Darius & Twig

Myers, W. D. Amiri & Odette; a love story

MYSTERY AND DETECTIVE STORIES

Altebrando, T. The Leaving.

Beaufrand, M. J. Useless Bay

Bernard, R. Find me

Bray, L. The diviners

Bray, L. Lair of dreams: a Diviners novel

Cook, E. With malice

Cox, S. The Dead Girls Detective Agency

Crutcher, C. Period 8

Damico, G. Wax

Dawn, S. Splinter

Ellen, L. Blind spot

Fantaskey, B. Buzz kill.

Foxlee, K. The midnight dress

Gavin, R. 3 of a kind

Giles, L. Fake ID

Griffin, A. The unfinished life of Addison Stone

Haas, A. Dangerous girls

Harrison, M. The killer in me

Hartinger, B. Three truths and a lie

Hesse, M. Girl in the blue coat

Howell, S. Girl defective

Kindl, P. A school for brides

Latham, J. Scarlett undercover

Laurie, V. Forever, again

Maetani, V. E. Ink & ashes

Maniscalco, K. Escaping from Houdini

Maniscalco, K. Stalking Jack the Ripper

Mason, S. Running girl
Moracho, C. A good idea
Moracho, C. A good idea
Ostow, M. The devil and Winnie Flynn
Preus, M. Enchantment Lake: a Northwoods mystery
Rebel fire. Lane, A.
Renn, D. Latitude zero
Ritter, W. Beastly bones: a Jackaby novel
Rosenfield, K. Amelia Anne is dead and gone
Salomon, P. A. All those broken angels
Savage, K. Beautiful broken girls
Sedgwick, M. She is not invisible
Sharpe, T. Far from you
Shepard, Sara The amateurs
Tharp, T. Mojo
Thomas, K. The darkest corners
Tromly, S. Trouble is a friend of mine
Vaught, S. Freaks like us
Wein, E. The pearl thief
Wolf, J. S. Breaking beautiful

MYSTERY AND DETECTIVE STORIES MYSTERY FICTION -- FICTION

Wegelius, J. The murderer's ape

MYSTERY FICTION

Altebrando, T. The Leaving.
Anthony, J. Chopsticks
Avi. City of orphans
Beaufrand, M. J. Useless Bay
Blundell, J. What I saw and how I lied
Bradbury, J. Wrapped
Bray, L. A great and terrible beauty
Bray, L. The diviners
Bray, L. Lair of dreams: a Diviners novel
Bray, L. Rebel angels
Bray, L. The sweet far thing
Bunce, E. C. Liar's moon
Coben, H. Seconds away
Coben, H. Shelter
Cox, S. The Dead Girls Detective Agency
Daley, J. R. Jesus Jackson
Damico, G. Croak
Damico, G. Wax
Dawn, S. Splinter
Derting, K. The body finder
Dubosarsky, U. The golden day
Duncan, L. I know what you did last summer
Duncan, L. Locked in time
Dunlap, S. E. The musician's daughter.
Ellen, L. Blind spot
Ellis, K. Breaker
Feinstein, J. Last shot
Forster, M. City of a Thousand Dolls
Gagnon, M. Strangelets
Gavin, R. 3 of a kind
Goelman, A. The path of names
Hahn, M. D. Mister Death's blue-eyed girls
Haines, K. M. The girl is murder

Haines, K. M. The girl is trouble
Harrison, M. The killer in me
Hartinger, B. Three truths and a lie
Hartley, A. J. Steeplejack
Harvey, A. Haunting Violet
Hautman, P. Snatched
Healey, K. The shattering
Jaffe, M. Bad kitty
Jaffe, M. Rosebush
Johnson, M. The madness underneath
Johnson, M. Truly devious: a mystery
Juby, S. Getting the girl
Kirby, J. Golden
Laurie, V. Forever, again
Leonard, J. P. Cold case
Lo, M. Adaptation
Lu, M. Batman: Nightwalker
Lyga, B. I hunt killers
MacColl, M. Nobody's secret
Maetani, V. E. Ink & ashes
Maniscalco, K. Escaping from Houdini
Maniscalco, K. Stalking Jack the Ripper
Martin, C. K. K. Yesterday
Mason, S. Running girl
McClintock, N. Masked
McClintock, N. Out of tune
McGinnis, M. A madness so discreet
Moracho, C. A good idea
Mulligan, A. Trash
Osterlund, A. Aurelia
Ostow, M. The devil and Winnie Flynn
Peacock, S. Eye of the crow
Preus, M. Enchantment Lake: a Northwoods mystery
Rebel fire. Lane, A.
Renn, D. Latitude zero
Roecker, L. The Liar Society
Rosenfield, K. Amelia Anne is dead and gone
Salomon, P. A. All those broken angels
Savage, K. Beautiful broken girls
Schrefer, E. The deadly sister
Scieszka, J. Who done it? an investigation of murder most foul.
Sedgwick, M. She is not invisible
Sepetys, R. Out of the Easy
Shepard, Sara The amateurs
Shepard, S. The lying game
Silbert, L. The intelligencer
Silvey, C. Jasper Jones
Simukka, S. As Red As Blood
Summers, C. Fall for anything
Tharp, T. Mojo
Thomas, E. Boarder patrol
Thomas, K. The darkest corners
Tromly, S. Trouble is a friend of mine
Tucholke, A. G. Between the devil and the deep blue sea
Valentine, J. Double
Wasserman, R. The book of blood and shadow
Wein, E. The pearl thief

Wells, R. E. Feedback
Zusak, M. I am the messenger
MYTHOLOGY, ASIAN -- FICTION
Oh, E. A thousand beginnings and endings: 15 retellings of
Asian myths and legends
MYTHOLOGY, CELTIC -- FICTION
O'Guilin, P. The call
MYTHOLOGY, GREEK -- FICTION
Almond, D. A song for Ella Grey
Elliott, D. Bull
Hahn, R. The shadow behind the stars
Taylor, L. Days of blood & starlight

N

Wait for me
Nader, Elisa
Escape from Eden
Nadol, Jen
The mark
The vision
Naidoo, Beverley
Burn my heart
Nakahama, Manjiro, 1827-1898 About
Preus, M. Heart of a samurai
name of the star. Johnson, M.
NAMIBIA -- FICTION
Gilman, D. The devil's breath
Naming. Croggon, A.
Namioka, Lensey
Mismatch
Nance, Andrew
Daemon Hall
Return to Daemon Hall: evil roots
Nanji, Shenaaz
Child of dandelions
Nantucket blue. Howland, L.
NANTUCKET ISLAND (MASS.) -- FICTION
Howland, L. Nantucket blue
and Ely's no kiss list. Cohn, R.
Naondel. Turtschaninoff, M.
Napoli, Donna Jo
Alligator bayou

The great god Pan

The magic circle
The smile

The wager
NASHVILLE (TENN.) -- FICTION
Supplee, S. Somebody everybody listens to
Whitaker, A. Wildflower
NATCHITOCHES (LA.) -- FICTION
Elston, A. The rules for disappearing

NATIONAL SECURITY -- UNITED STATES
Littlefield, S. Infected
NATIONAL SOCIALISM -- FICTION
Bartoletti, S. C. The boy who dared
Dowswell, P. The Auslander
Falkner, B. The project
Graudin, R. Blood for blood
Lasky, K. Ashes
Mayhew, J. The Big Lie
Sharenow, R. The Berlin Boxing Club
Nation. Pratchett, T.
NATIVE AMERICANS -- FICTION
Bruchac, J. Wolf mark
Edwardson, D. D. My name is not easy
Gansworth, E. Give me some truth: a novel with paintings
O'Dell, S. Island of the Blue Dolphins
O'Dell, S. Streams to the river, river to the sea
Paulsen, G. Woods runner
Quigley, D. Apple in the middle
Yee, P. Learning to fly
NATURAL DISASTERS -- FICTION
De la Peña, M. The living
NAVAJO INDIANS -- FICTION
Bruchac, J. Code talker
Flood, N. B. Soldier sister, fly home
O'Dell, S. Sing down the moon
Nayeri, Daniel
Another Faust
Another Pan
Nayeri, Dina
Nayeri, D. Another Faust
Nayeri, D. Another Pan
Naylor, Phyllis Reynolds
Alice in April
Alice in rapture, sort of
Faith, hope, and Ivy June
Incredibly Alice
Intensely Alice
Reluctantly Alice
NAZIS -- FICTION
Graudin, R. Blood for blood
Wein, E. Code name Verity
NEAR-DEATH EXPERIENCES -- FICTION
Gagnon, M. Strangelets
Vlahos, L. The Scar Boys
NEBRASKA -- FICTION
Reed, A. Over you
Neff, Henry H.
The hound of Rowan
NEIGHBORHOOD -- FICTION
Hartnett, S. Golden Boys
Martinez, C. G. Pig Park
Reynolds, J. When I was the greatest
Watson, R. This side of home
Neighborhood girls. Foley, J. A.
NEIGHBORS -- FICTION
Littman, S. Backlash

Nelson, Blake
Destroy all cars
Recovery Road
Rock star, superstar
The y came from below
Nelson, James
On the volcano
Nelson, Jandy
I'll give you the sun
The sky is everywhere
Nelson, Marilyn
American ace
Nemesis. Reichs, B.
Ness, Patrick
And the ocean was our sky
More than this
Release
The rest of us just live here
NETHERLANDS -- FICTION
Chambers, A. Postcards from no man's land
Dogar, S. Annexed
**NETHERLANDS -- HISTORY -- 1940-1945, GERMAN
OCCUPATION -- FICTION**
Hesse, M. Girl in the blue coat
Neumeier, Rachel
The City in the Lake
The keeper of the mist
The white road of the moon.
NEUROFIBROMATOSIS -- FICTION
Kirby, M. J. A taste for monsters
Always Sometimes. Alsaid, A.
blood. McPhee, P.
boy. Houston, J.
darkness. Delaney, J.
NEW ENGLAND -- FICTION
Ritter, W. The dire king.
**NEW ENGLAND -- HISTORY -- 19TH CENTURY --
FICTION**
Ritter, W. Beastly bones: a Jackaby novel
**NEW ENGLAND -- SOCIAL LIFE AND CUSTOMS -- 19TH
CENTURY -- FICTION**
Ritter, W. The dire king.
found land. Wolf, A.
NEW HAMPSHIRE -- FICTION
Tregay, S. Love & leftovers; a novel in verse
NEW JERSEY -- FICTION
Bauman, B. A. Rosie & Skate
Budhos, M. T. Tell us we're home
Doktorski, J. S. The summer after you and me
Kephart, B. This is the story of you
Kriegman, M. Being Audrey Hepburn: a novel
Lecesne, J. Absolute brightness
Plum-Ucci, C. Fire will fall
Plum-Ucci, C. Streams of Babel
NEW JERSEY -- HISTORY -- 20TH CENTURY -- FICTION
Bryant, M. E. Glow
NEW LONDON (TEX.) -- HISTORY -- 20TH CENTURY

-- FICTION
Perez, A. Out of darkness
NEW MEXICO -- FICTION
Johnson, L. Muchacho
Sáenz, B. A. Sammy and Juliana in Hollywood
NEW ORLEANS (LA.) -- FICTION
Sepetys, R. Out of the Easy
Smith, S. L. Orleans
Tiernan, C. Balefire
Tubb, K. O. The 13th sign
Volponi, P. Hurricane song
**NEW ORLEANS (LA.) -- HISTORY -- 20TH CENTURY --
FICTION**
Sepetys, R. Out of the Easy
The **new** policeman. Thompson, K.
NEWSPAPER EMPLOYEES -- FICTION
Vawter, V. Copyboy
NEWSPAPERS -- FICTION
Dirkes, C. Sucktown
Doktorski, J. S. Famous last words
Kerr, M. E. If I love you, am I trapped forever?
Myers, W. D. The Cruisers
NEW YORK (N.Y.) -- FICTION
Albertalli, B. What if it's us
Brashares, A. The here and now
Budhos, M. T. Ask me no questions
Budhos, M. T. Watched.
Cabot, M. Airhead
Cameron, P. Someday this pain will be useful to you
Clare, C. City of ashes
Cohn, R. Dash & Lily's book of dares
Cohn, R. Naomi and Ely's no kiss list
Cohn, R. Nick & Norah's infinite playlist
Cooney, C. B. Code orange
Cooney, C. B. Janie face to face
Cox, S. The Dead Girls Detective Agency
Davies, J. Lost
De la Cruz, M. Blue bloods
Ehrenhaft, D. Friend is not a verb
Falkner, B. Brain Jack
Felin, M. S. Touching snow
Flack, S. Bunheads
Forman, G. I have lost my way
Friend, N. Threads and flames
Griffin, A. The unfinished life of Addison Stone
Haines, K. M. The girl is murder
Howard, J. J. That time I joined the circus
Johnson, M. Scarlett fever
Johnson, M. Suite Scarlett
Larbalestier, J. Magic lessons
Levithan, D. Love is the higher law
Lurie, A. The latent powers of Dylan Fontaine
MacCullough, C. Once a witch
Mackler, C. The earth, my butt, and other big, round things
McDonald, J. Chill wind
Myers, W. D. Darius & Twig
Nayeri, D. Another Faust

Perkins, M. You bring the distant near
Polisner, G. In sight of stars
Sales, L. Tonight the streets are ours
Schreiber, J. Au revoir, crazy European chick
Shusterman, N. Downsiders
Silvera, A. More happy than not
Silvera, A. They both die at the end
Smith, A. G. The Devil's engine
Tal, E. Cursing Columbus
Treggiari, J. Ashes, ashes
Vizzini, N. It's kind of a funny story
Westerfeld, S. Afterworlds
Weston, C. Speed of life
Woodson, J. Behind you
Woodson, J. If you come softly
Woodson, J. Miracle's boys

NEW YORK (STATE) -- FICTION
Arnold, A. Love & other train wrecks
Bauer, J. Peeled
Castle, J. You look different in real life
Johnson, J. J. The theory of everything
Karim, S. Skunk girl
Levine, E. In trouble
Luper, E. Bug boy
Mazer, N. F. The missing girl
Suma, N. R. Imaginary girls
Surface tension; a novel in four summers. Runyon, B.
Vlahos, L. The Scar Boys

NEW YORK (N.Y.) -- HISTORY -- 1898-1951 -- FICTION
Bray, L. The diviners
Bray, L. Lair of dreams: a Diviners novel
Chibbaro, J. Deadly
Crowder, M. Audacity

NEW YORK (N.Y.) -- HISTORY -- 20TH CENTURY -- FICTION
Jensen, C. Skyscraping
Manzano, S. The revolution of Evelyn Serrano
Townley, R. Sky; a novel in three sets and an encore

NEW YORK (STATE) -- HISTORY -- 20TH CENTURY -- FICTION
Gansworth, E. Give me some truth: a novel with paintings

NEW YORK (N.Y.) -- HISTORY -- 20TH CENTURY -- YOUNG ADULT FICTION
Maxwell, L. The last magician

NEW ZEALAND -- FICTION
Healey, K. Guardian of the dead
Healey, K. The shattering
Wright, D. Violence 101

NEZ PERCE INDIANS -- FICTION
O'Dell, S. Thunder rolling in the mountains
    try, Jane Sinner. Oelke, L.
Nicholson, William

    & Norah's infinite playlist. Cohn, R.
Nielsen, Susin
Optimists die first.
The reluctant journal of Henry K. Larsen

NIGERIA -- FICTION
Okorafor, N. Akata warrior
Nightjohn. Paulsen, G.
Night kites. Meaker, M.
The **nightmare** garden. Kittredge, C.
NIGHTMARES -- FICTION
Chee, T. The speaker
Chee, T. The speaker
Schoenherr, I. The Speaker
Nightspell. Cypess, L.
The **night** tourist. Marsh, K.
NINETEEN SIXTIES -- FICTION
Sorosiak, C. Wild blue wonder
Weil, C. I'm glad I did
NINJA -- FICTION
Lowitz, L. Jet Black and the ninja wind.
Niven, Jennifer
All the bright places
Holding up the universe
Nix, Garth
Clariel: the lost Abhorsen
A confusion of princes
Nix, Garth
Frogkisser
Nix Minus One. MacLean, J.
NOAH'S ARK -- FICTION
Napoli, D. J. Storm
No and me. de Vigan, D.
NOBILITY -- FICTION
Clayton, D. The Belles
Johnston, E. K. That inevitable Victorian thing
Nobody's princess. Friesner, E. M.
Nobody's secret. MacColl, M.
No crystal stair. Nelson, V. M.
Noel, Alyson
Radiance
Unrivaled
Noggin. Whaley, J. C.
Nolan, Han
Crazy
NORSE MYTHOLOGY -- FICTION
Harris, J. Runemarks
North by night. Ayres, K.
NORTH CAROLINA -- FICTION
Hubbard, J. R. Paper covers rock
Pearson, J. The rites & wrongs of Janice Wills
Watkins, S. What comes after
North of beautiful. Headley, J. C.
North of happy. Alsaid, A.
North, Phoebe
Starglass
Northrop, Michael
Gentlemen
Trapped
Notes from my captivity. Parks, K.
Notes from the midnight driver. Sonnenblick, J.
Noteworthy. Redgate, R.

but the truth. Avi, 1937-
  special. Herbach, G.
   Teller, J.
if I save you first. Carter, A.
if I see you first. Lindstrom, E.
Notorious Pagan Jones. Berry, N.
that kind of girl. Vivian, S.
the girls you're looking for. Safi, A. M.

NOVELISTS
Engle, M. Firefly letters
Golden, C. The wild
Tibensky, A. And then things fall apart

NOVELS IN VERSE
Agard, J. The young inferno
Alexander, K. The crossover
Alexander, K. Swing
Atkins, J. Stone mirrors
Bingham, K. Shark girl
Burg, A. E. All the broken pieces
Chaltas, T. Because I am furniture
Clark, K. E. Freakboy
Crossan, S. Moonrise
Crossan, S. One
Crowder, M. Audacity
Elliott, D. Bull
Engle, M. Firefly letters
Fehler, G. Beanball
Frank, L. Two girls staring at the ceiling
Frost, H. The braid
Frost, H. Crossing stones
Frost, H. Hidden
Grimes, N. Dark sons
Grimes, N. A girl named Mister
Hemphill, S. Hideous love
Hemphill, S. Sisters of glass
Hemphill, S. Wicked girls
Heppermann, C. Ask Me How I Got Here
Herrick, S. The wolf
Jensen, C. Skyscraping
Kearney, M. The girl in the mirror
Kehoe, S. W. The sound of letting go
Leavitt, M. My book of life by Angel
Leslea, N. October mourning
Macdonald, M. Odette's secrets
MacLean, J. Nix Minus One
Marcus, K. Exposed
Myers, W. D. Amiri & Odette; a love story
Nelson, M. American ace
Ostlere, C. Karma
Reynolds, J. Long way down
Richards, J. Three rivers rising
Schroeder, L. Chasing Brooklyn
Schroeder, L. Far from you
Sones, S. What my mother doesn't know
Thompson, H. The language inside
Thompson, H. Orchards
Tregay, S. Love & leftovers; a novel in verse

Venkatraman, P. A time to dance
Walrath, D. Like water on stone
Weatherford, C. B. Becoming Billie Holiday
Williams, C. L. Glimpse
Wolf, A.The watch that ends the night
Wolff, V. E. Make lemonade

NOVELS IN VERSE -- FICTION
Brown, S. To stay alive
The **Nowhere** Girls. Reed, A.
Nowhere near you. Thomas, L.
Nowhere to run. Griffin, C. J.
Now I rise. White, K.
Now is everything. Giles, A.
Now is the time for running. Williams, M.

Nowlin, Laura
If he had been with me
Num8ers. Ward, R.

NUNS -- FICTION
Clark, K. Guardian angel house
LaFevers, R. Mortal heart
Strauss, V. Passion blue

NURSES -- FICTION
Dunlap, S. E. In the shadow of the lamp
Lucier, M. A death-struck year

Nuzum, K. A.
A small white scar

Nwaubani, Adaobi Tricia
Buried beneath the baobab tree

Nye, Naomi Shihab
Going going
Habibi

O

Oakes, Stephanie
The arsonist.
The sacred lies of Minnow Bly

OAKLAND (CALIF.)
Yee, F. C. The epic crush of Genie Lo

Oates, Joyce Carol
Big Mouth & Ugly Girl
Freaky green eyes
Two or three things I forgot to tell you

OBEDIENCE -- FICTION
Bacigalupi, P. Tool of war

OBESITY -- FICTION
Crutcher, C. Staying fat for Sarah Byrnes
Deuker, C. Payback time
George, M. Looks
Going, K. L. Fat kid rules the world
Lange, E. J. Butter
Mackler, C. The earth, my butt, and other big, round things
Niven, J. Holding up the universe
Rex, A. Fat vampire; a never coming of age story.

O'Brien, Annemarie
Lara's gift
O'Brien, Caragh M.

Birthmarked

The vault of dreamers

O'Brien, Johnny

Day of the assassins

O'Brien, Robert C.

Z for Zachariah

OBSESSIVE-COMPULSIVE DISORDER -- FICTION

Ayarbe, H. Compulsion

Brown, J. Perfect escape

De la Peña, M. Ball don't lie

Green, J. Turtles all the way down

Haydu, C. A. OCD love story

MacCready, R. M. Buried

Silvera, A. History is all you left me

Obsidian and stars. Eshbaugh, J.

    obsidian blade. Hautman, P.

        Kaufman, A.

OCCULT FICTION

Ashton, B. Everbound

Ashton, B. Everneath

Bickle, L. The outside

Black, H. The coldest girl in Coldtown

Carey, J. L. Dragonswood

Casella, J. Thin space

Cole, K. Poison princess

Fukuda, A. The Prey

Henderson, J. The Triumph of Death

Hoban, R. Soonchild

Hocking, A. Wake

Johnson, M. The madness underneath

Levithan, D. Every day

Marillier, J. Raven flight

Martin, C. K. K. Yesterday

McNeal, T. Far far away

Pike, A. Earthbound

Simner, J. L. Faerie after

Stiefvater, M. The dream thieves

Sutton, K. Some quiet place

Taylor, L. Daughter of smoke and bone

Taylor, L. Days of blood & starlight

Tubb, K. O. The 13th sign

West, K. Pivot point

Winters, C. In the shadow of blackbirds.

Zinn, B. Poison

OCCULTISM -- FICTION

Bray, L. The diviners

Older, D. J. Shadowhouse fall

Stiefvater, M. Blue lily, lily blue

Stiefvater, M. The Raven Boys

    love story. Haydu, C. A.

OCEAN -- FICTION

Rosenfield, K. Inland

    ocean in my ears. Macvie, M.

OCEAN TRAVEL -- FICTION

Maniscalco, K. Escaping from Houdini

Ockler, Sarah

The Book of Broken Hearts

Fixing Delilah

O'Connell, Mary

The sharp time

O'Connor, Heather

Betting Game

O'Connor, Sheila

Sparrow Road

October mourning. Leslea, N.

The **odds** of lightning. Davies, J.

Odd & true. Winters, C.

O'Dell, Scott

Island of the Blue Dolphins

Sing down the moon

Streams to the river, river to the sea

Thunder rolling in the mountains

Odette's secrets. Macdonald, M.

ODYSSEUS (GREEK MYTHOLOGY) -- FICTION

Barrett, T. King of Ithaka

Oelke, Lianne

Nice try, Jane Sinner

Off -color. McDonald, J.

OFFENSES AGAINST THE PERSON -- FICTION

Landman, T. Hell and high water

Of Fire and Stars. Coulthurst, A.

Off pointe. Lieberman, L.

The **off** season. Murdock, C. G.

Of Metal and Wishes. Fine, S.

Of sound mind. Ferris, J.

O'Guilin, Peadar

The call

Oh, Ellen

A thousand beginnings and endings: 15 retellings of Asian myths and legends

OHIO -- FICTION

Anderson, J. L. Twisted

Barnes, J. Tales of the Madman Underground

Barzak, C. The gone away place

Haddix, M. P. Full ride

OHIO -- HISTORY -- 19TH CENTURY -- FICTION

McGinnis, M. A madness so discreet

Oh. My. Gods. Childs, T. L.

OJIBWA INDIANS -- FICTION

Jones, A. G. Fire song

OKLAHOMA -- FICTION

Gensler, S. The revenant

Tharp, T. Knights of the hill country

Tharp, T. The spectacular now

Tingle, T. House of purple cedar

OKLAHOMA -- HISTORY -- LAND RUSH, 1893 --
        FICTION

Tingle, T. House of purple cedar

Okorafor, Nnedi

Akata warrior

OLD AGE -- FICTION

Blythe, C. Revenge of a not-so-pretty girl

McCahan, E. The lake effect

Sonnenblick, J. Notes from the midnight driver

O'Connell, M. The sharp time
Peet, M. Beck
Petrucha, S. Teen
Price, L. Starters
Reeve, P. A Web of Air
Reeve, P. Fever Crumb
Resau, L. Red glass
Rosoff, M. Beck
Ryan, C. The Forest of Hands and Teeth
St. Crow, L. Strange angels
Schoenherr, I. The Speaker
Smith, J. E. Windfall
Smith, S. The other side of dark
Stiefvater, M. The scorpio races
Stratton, A. Chanda's wars
Unsworth, T. The one safe place: a novel
Van Draanen, W. Runaway
Walrath, D. Like water on stone
Walter, J. My name is not Friday
Ward, R. The Chaos
Woodson, J. Miracle's boys
Yancey, R. The monstrumologist
Yancey, R. final descent
Young, M. Blood red road
Zettel, S. Palace of Spies

ORPHANS -- GABON -- FICTION
Schrefer, E. Threatened
ORPHEUS (GREEK MYTHOLOGICAL CHARACTER) -- FICTION
Almond, D. A song for Ella Grey
Ortiz Cofer, Judith
Call me Maria
If I could fly
Oseman, Alice
Solitaire
Oshiro, Mark
Anger is a gift
OSTEOGENESIS IMPERFECTA -- PATIENTS -- FICTION
Steiger, A. J. When my heart joins the thousand
Osterlund, Anne
Aurelia

Ostlere, Cathy

Ostow, Micol
The devil and Winnie Flynn
O'Sullivan, Joanne
Between Two Skies
other F-word. Friend, N.
other side of dark. Smith, S.
other side of dawn. Marsden, J.
Dark Duet. Schwab, V.
own private universe. Talley, R.
Davies, S.
of darkness. Perez, A.
of left field. Klages, E.
of reach. Arcos, C.

Out of the blue. Cameron, S.
Out of the box. Mulder, M.
Out of the Easy. Sepetys, R.
Out of tune. McClintock, N.
Outrun the moon. Lee, S.
The **outside.** Bickle, L.
The **outside** of a horse; a novel. Rorby, G.
The **outsiders.** Hinton, S. E.
Over a thousand hills I walk with you. Jansen, H.
Over sea, under stone. Cooper, S.
OVERWEIGHT PERSONS -- FICTION
Fehlbaum, B. Big fat disaster
Griffin, N. Just wreck it all
Murphy, J. Dumplin'
OVERWEIGHT TEENAGERS -- FICTION
Fehlbaum, B. Big fat disaster
Murphy, J. Puddin
Over you. Reed, A.

P

PACIFISM -- FICTION
Duble, K. B. Phantoms in the snow
PACIFISTS -- FICTION
Sheth, K. Keeping corner
Padian, Maria
Wrecked
PAINTERS -- FICTION
Bryant, M. E. Glow
Finn, M. Belladonna
Rogerson, M. An enchantment of ravens
PAINTING, MODERN -- FICTION
Bryant, M. E. Glow
Painting the black. Deuker, C.
PAKISTAN -- FICTION
Antieau, K. Broken moon
Saeed, A. Written in the stars
Staples, S. F. Shabanu; daughter of the wind
Staples, S. F. Under the Persimmon tree
PAKISTANI AMERICAN TEENAGE GIRLS
Saeed, A. Written in the stars
PAKISTANI AMERICANS -- FICTION
Karim, S. Skunk girl
Saeed, A. Written in the stars
PAKISTANIS -- GREAT BRITAIN -- FICTION
Robert, Na'ima B. Boy vs. girl.
Palace beautiful. Williams, S. D.
Palace of Spies. Zettel, S.
PALESTINIAN ARABS -- FICTION
Clinton, C. A stone in my hand
Laskin, P. L. Ronit & Jamil
Miklowitz, G. D. The enemy has a face
Palmer, Robin
The Corner of Bitter and Sweet
Geek charming
PAN (GREEK DEITY) -- FICTION
Napoli, D. J. The great god Pan

Brewer, Z. The cemetery boys
Friend, N. My life in black and white

Peet, Mal

PEGASUS (GREEK MYTHOLOGY) -- FICTION
McKinley, R. Pegasus
   McKinley, R.

PENNSYLVANIA -- FICTION
Alender, K. The dead girls of Hysteria Hall
Leavitt, L. Sean Griswold's head
Richards, J. Three rivers rising
Thomas, K. The darkest corners

PEN PALS -- FICTION
Albertalli, B. Simon vs. the Homo Sapiens agenda
Whitman, S. The milk of birds

PEOPLE WITH DISABILITIES -- FICTION
Bunker, L. Felix Yz
Castan, M. Fighting for Dontae
Clements, A. Things not seen
DeWoskin, R. Blind
Ellen, L. Blind spot
Ferris, J. Of sound mind
Fink, M. The summer I got a life
Flake, S. G. Pinned
Friend, N. How we roll
Giles, G. Girls like us
Johnson, H. M. Accidents of nature
Kamata, S. Gadget Girl
Kephart, B. Wild blues
Keplinger, K. Run
Lindstrom, E. Not if I see you first
Oakes, S. The arsonist
Oakes, S. The sacred lies of Minnow Bly
O'Guilin, P. The call
Sedgwick, M. She is not invisible
Selfors, S. The sweetest spell
Thomas, L. Nowhere near you
Trueman, T. Life happens next; a novel
Van Draanen, W. The running dream
Venkatraman, P. A time to dance
Winters, C. Odd & true
Woolston, B. Catch & release

PEOPLE WITH MENTAL DISABILITES -- FICTION
Castan, M. Fighting for Dontae
Hamilton, K. When the stars threw down their spears
Hooper, M. Fallen Grace
Magnin, J. Carrying Mason
Nuzum, K. A. A small white scar
Williams, M. Now is the time for running

PEOPLE WITH PHYSICAL DISABILITIES -- FICTION
Lowry, L. Gathering blue
McBay, B. Waiting for Sarah
Selfors, S. The sweetest spell

Perera, Anna
Guantanamo boy

Perez, Ashley Hope
The knife and the butterfly

Out of darkness
What can(t) wait

Perez, Marlene
Dead is a battlefield

Perfect chemistry. Elkeles, S.

The **perfect** distance. Whitney, K. A.

Perfect escape. **Brown, J.**

Perfect. Friend, N.

PERFECTION -- FICTION
Dayton, A. E. Stronger, faster, and more beautiful

Perfect ruin. DeStefano, L.

Perfect scoundrels. Carter, A.

PERFORMING ARTS -- FICTION
McLemore, A. -M. The weight of feathers
Rennison, L. The taming of the tights

PERFORMING ARTS HIGH SCHOOLS -- FICTION
Hrdlitschka, S. Allegra

PERFUMES -- FICTION
Perez, M. Dead is a battlefield

Period 8. Crutcher, C.

Perkins, Mitali
You bring the distant near.

Perkins, Stephanie
Anna and the French kiss
Isla and the happily ever after: a novel
Lola and the boy next door

Perpetual check. Wallace, R.

Perry's killer playlist. Schreiber, J.

PERSEUS (GREEK MYTHOLOGY)
Halam, A. Snakehead

PERSIAN MYTHOLOGY -- FICTION
Bell, H. Fall of a kingdom

Persistence of memory. Atwater-Rhodes, A.

PERSONAL APPEARANCE -- FICTION
Chapman, L. Flawless
Clayton, D. The Belles
Griffin, A. All you never wanted
Kittle, K. Reasons to be happy
Vivian, S. The list

PERSONALITY -- FICTION
Roth, V. Insurgent

Peterfreund, Diana
Across a star-swept sea

PETER PAN (FICTIONAL CHARACTER)
Nayeri, D. Another Pan

Peters, Julie Anne
She loves you, she loves you not--

Peterson, Lois J.
Beyond repair
Silver rain
Triskellion 2: The burning

Petrucha, Stefan
The Rule of Won
Split
Teen

Phantoms in the snow. Duble, K. B.

PHILADELPHIA (PA.) -- HISTORY -- 19TH CENTURY

AUTHOR, TITLE AND SUBJECT INDEX
THIRD EDITION

-- FICTION

Dennard, S. Something strange and deadly

Philbrick, W. R.

The last book in the universe

PHILIPPINES -- HISTORY -- JAPANESE OCCUPATION, 1942-1945 -- FICTION

Salisbury, G. Hunt for the bamboo rat

Philpot, Chelsey

Even in paradise

PHOSPHORUS -- PHYSIOLOGICAL EFFECT -- FICTION

Kirby, M. J. A taste for monsters

PHOTOGRAPHERS -- FICTION

Madigan, L. K. Flash burnout; a novel

PHOTOGRAPHY -- FICTION

Bick, I. J. The Sin eater's confession

King, A. S. Glory O'Brien's history of the future: a novel

Marcus, K. Exposed

Russell, C. Songs about a girl

PHOTOJOURNALISM -- FICTION

Park, L. S. Click

PHYSICIANS -- FICTION

McGinnis, M. A madness so discreet

PIANISTS -- FICTION

Lynch, J. N. My beautiful hippie

Richmond, P. Always a catch

Zail, S. Playing for the commandant

PIANO MUSIC -- FICTION

Anthony, J. Chopsticks

us in the light. Gilbert, K. L.

Lynch, C.

of Georgia. Bryant, J.

me together. Watson, R.

Pierce, Tamora

Alanna: the first adventure

Bloodhound

First test

Pierson, D. C.

Crap kingdom

PIGEONS -- FICTION

Ortiz Cofer, J. If I could fly

Pigman. Zindel, P.

Park. Martinez, C. G.

Pike, Aprilynne

Earthbound

pilgrims of Rayne. MacHale, D. J.

Pink, Randi

Into white

Wilkinson, L.

Flake, S. G.

pirate captain's daughter. Bunting, E.

cinema. Doctorow, C.

PIRATE RADIO BROADCASTING -- FICTION

Stiefvater, M. All the crooked saints.

PIRATES -- FICTION

Bunting, E. The pirate captain's daughter

Golden, C. The sea wolves

Lake, N. Hostage Three

Levenseller, T. Daughter of the pirate king

Somper, J. Demons of the ocean

Vaughn, C. Steel

Pitcher, Annabel

Ketchup clouds

My sister lives on the mantelpiece

Silence is goldfish: a novel

PITTSBURGH (PA.) -- FICTION

Andrews, J. Me & Earl & the dying girl

Pivot point. West, K.

Pixley, Marcella

Ready to fall.

Pizza, love, and other stuff that made me famous. Williams, K.

Places no one knows. Yovanoff, B.

PLAGIARISM -- FICTION

Hautman, P. What boys really want

Kaufman, A. Illuminae

Kristoff, J. Illuminae

PLAGUE -- FICTION

Gray, C. Defy the worlds

Plain Kate. Bow, E.

Planesrunner. McDonald, I.

PLANTATION LIFE -- FICTION

Sherman, D. The freedom maze

PLANTS -- FICTION

Pike, A. Wings

Plath, Sylvia About

Tibensky, A. And then things fall apart

Played. Fichera, L.

Playing for the commandant. Zail, S.

Playing for the Devil's Fire. Diederich, P.

Playing with matches. Katcher, B.

Please ignore Vera Dietz. King, A. S.

The **pledge.** Derting, K.

Plum, Amy

Die for me

Plum-Ucci, Carol

Fire will fall

Streams of Babel

POACHING -- FICTION

Fletcher, S. Ancient, strange, and lovely

POD. Wallenfels, S.

The **poet** X: a novel. Acevedo, E.

POETRY -- COLLECTIONS

Leslea, N. October mourning

POETRY -- FICTION

Finneyfrock, K. The sweet revenge of Celia Door

Hubbard, J. R. And we stay

Kephart, B. Undercover

POETRY SLAMS -- FICTION

Acevedo, E. The poet X: a novel

POETS -- FICTION

Acevedo, E. The poet X: a novel

Bjorkman, L. My invented life

Klein, L. M. Ophelia

MacColl, M. Nobody's secret

Marsden, J. Hamlet: a novel

Schmidt, G. D. The Wednesday wars

Tibensky, A. And then things fall apart

Woodson, J. After Tupac and D Foster

    Keyser, A. J.

poison dark and drowning. Cluess, J.

    princess. Cole, K.

    Zinn, B.

POISONING -- FICTION
Thomas, R. Long may she reign

POISONS AND POISONING -- FICTION
Thomas, R. Long may she reign

POISONS -- FICTION
Salisbury, M. The Sin Eater's daughter

POKER -- FICTION
Hautman, P. All-in

Volponi, P. The hand you're dealt

POLAND -- FICTION
Mackall, D. D. Eva underground

Savit, G. Anna and the Swallow Man

POLAND -- HISTORY -- OCCUPATION, 1939-1945 -- FICTION
Savit, G. Anna and the Swallow Man

Sax, A. The war within these walls

POLAR BEAR -- FICTION
Bass, R. On thin ice

POLICE BRUTALITY -- FICTION
Reynolds, J. All American Boys

Stone, N. Dear Martin

POLICE CORRUPTION -- ILLINOIS -- CHICAGO -- FICTION
Foley, J. A. Neighborhood girls

POLICE -- FICTION
Pierce, T. Bloodhound

POLICE SHOOTINGS -- FICTION
Coles, J. Tyler Johnson was here

Thomas, A. The hate u give

POLIOMYELITIS -- FICTION
Winters, C. Odd & true

POLISH AMERICANS -- FICTION
Friend, N. Threads and flames

Polisner, Gae

    The memory of things

    In sight of stars.

POLITICAL ACTIVISTS -- FICTION
Nye, N. S. Going going

POLITICAL CORRUPTION -- FICTION
Mulligan, A. Trash

POLITICAL LEADERS -- FICTION
Sheth, K. Keeping corner

POLITICIANS -- FICTION
Hartley, A. J. Firebrand

POLITICS -- FICTION
Lupica, M. Hero

White, E. E. The President's daughter

POLITICS, PRACTICAL -- FICTION

Doctorow, C. Homeland

Fitzpatrick, H. My life next door

POLLUTION -- FICTION
Petrucha, S. Teen

POLYGAMY -- FICTION
Fixmer, E. Down from the mountain

Hrdlitschka, S. Sister wife

Williams, C. L. The chosen one

POOR -- FICTION
Badoe, A. Between sisters

Barrett, T. The Stepsister's Tale

Booth, C. Tyrell

Lyne, J. H. Catch rider

Shabazz, I. X

POPULAR MUSIC -- FICTION
Russell, C. Songs about a girl

Weil, C. I'm glad I did

POPULARITY -- FICTION
Backes, M. M. The princesses of Iowa

Calame, D. Beat the band

Griffin, A. All you never wanted

Halpern, J. Into the wild nerd yonder

Hurley, T. Ghostgirl

Juby, S. Getting the girl

Kittle, K. Reasons to be happy

Palmer, R. Geek charming

Pearce, J. As you wish

Roat, S. H. How to Disappear

Sales, L. This song will save your life

Vail, R. Unfriended

Valentine, A. How (not) to find a boyfriend

Wang, C. The takedown

PORT-AU-PRINCE (HAITI) -- FICTION
Wagner, L. R. Hold tight, don't let go

Porter, Sarah

    When I Cast Your Shadow

PORTLAND (OR.) -- FICTION
Lucier, M. A death-struck year

Watson, R. This side of home

PORTLAND (OR.) -- HISTORY -- 20TH CENTURY -- FICTION
Lucier, M. A death-struck year

Positively. Sheinmel, C.

Possessed. Cann, K.

Postcards from no man's land. Chambers, A.

POST-TRAUMATIC STRESS DISORDER -- FICTION
Anderson, L. H. The impossible knife of memory

Caletti, D. A heart in a body in the world

Doller, T. Something like normal

Flores-Scott, P. American road trip

Hodkin, M. The unbecoming of Mara Dyer

Leno, K. The lost & found

Scott, E. Miracle

Strasser, T. Price of duty

Tharp, T. Badd

Watkins, S. Great Falls

White, E. E. Long may she reign

Woolston, B. The Freak Observer

Potter, Ryan

Exit strategy

Poulsen, David

And Then the Sky Exploded

POVERTY -- FICTION

Avi. Traitor's gate

Bayard, L. Lucky strikes

Fletcher, C. Ten cents a dance

Hartnett, S. Thursday's child

Hooper, M. Fallen Grace

Kephart, B. The heart is not a size

Mulligan, A. Trash

Shulman, M. Scrawl

Wolff, V. E. Make lemonade

Powell, Kelley

The Merit Birds

Powell, Laura

The game of triumphs

The Master of Misrule

Powell, William Campbell

Expiration day

PRACTICAL JOKES -- FICTION

Cousins, D. Waiting for Gonzo

Oseman, A. Solitaire

Pattou, E. Ghosting

PRAGUE (CZECH REPUBLIC) -- FICTION

Taylor, L. Days of blood & starlight

Wasserman, R. The book of blood and shadow
  fire. Johnston, E. K.

Pratchett, Terry

The amazing Maurice and his educated rodents

Dodger

Only you can save mankind

The shepherd's crown

The Wee Free Men

PREGNANCY -- FICTION

Caletti, D. The six rules of maybe

Carter, C. Me, him, them, and it

Cousins, D. Waiting for Gonzo

De Gramont, N. Every little thing in the world

Grimes, N. A girl named Mister

Hoban, R. Soonchild

Kephart, B. Small damages

Knowles, J. Jumping off swings

Levine, E. In trouble

Liu, J. Girls on the line

Martin, C. K. K. I know it's over

McWilliams, K. Doormat; a novel

Quintero, I. Gabi, a girl in pieces

Werlin, N. Impossible

Williams, I. Water in May

PREHISTORIC PEOPLES -- FICTION

Eshbaugh, J. Obsidian and stars

PREJUDICES -- FICTION

Aceves, F. The closest I've come

Adeyemi, T. Children of blood and bone

Bock, C. LIE

Buffie, M. Winter shadows

Fine, S. Of Metal and Wishes

Houston, J. New boy

Hughes, D. Four-Four-Two

Hurwin, D. Freaks and revelations

King, A. S. Ask the passengers

Levine, K. The best bad luck I ever had

Mafi, T. A very large expanse of sea

Namioka, L. Mismatch

Napoli, D. J. Alligator bayou

Nwaubani, A. T. Buried beneath the baobab tree

Perera, A. Guantanamo boy

St. James, J. Freak show

Schmidt, G. D. Trouble

Selfors, S. The sweetest spell

Venkatraman, P. Climbing the stairs

Walsh, A. A. Long Way from Home

Wein, E. The pearl thief

Winters, C. The steep and thorny way

Wiseman, E. Puppet

Yee, P. Learning to fly

PREPARATORY SCHOOLS -- FICTION

Kiely, B. Tradition

Konigsberg, B. Honestly Ben

Oates, J. C. Two or three things I forgot to tell you

Walker, B. F. Black boy/white school

PREPARATORY SCHOOLS -- MASSACHUSETTS --
FICTION

Konigsberg, B. Honestly Ben

The **President's** daughter. White, E. E.

PRESIDENTS -- FICTION

Cabot, M. All-American girl

Nanji, S. Child of dandelions

White, E. E. Long may she reign

Press play. Devine, E.

Pretty dead. Block, F. L.

Preus, Margi

Enchantment Lake: a Northwoods mystery

Heart of a samurai

The **Prey.** Fukuda, A.

The **Prey.** Isbell, T.

Price, Charlie

Dead connection

The interrogation of Gabriel James

Price, Lissa

Enders

Starters

Price, Nora

Zoe letting go

Price of duty. Brown, D.

Price of duty. Strasser, T.

Priest, Cherie

I Am Princess X

The **Prince** of Mist. Ruiz Zafon, C.

Prince of Shadows. Caine, R.

PRINCES -- FICTION

Bardugo, L. Ruin and rising
Black, H. The cruel prince
Klein, L. M. Ophelia
Maas, S. J. Throne of glass
Marsden, J. Hamlet: a novel
Miller, M. Shadow run
Nix, G. A confusion of princes
O'Brien, J. Day of the assassins
Rogerson, M. An enchantment of ravens
Rudnick, P., 1957- Gorgeous
Salisbury, M. The Sin Eater's daughter
Wein, E. The empty kingdom
Wein, E. The lion hunter
    Ben. Murdock, C. G.
  princess diaries. Cabot, M.
    of glass. George, J. D.
  princesses of Iowa. Backes, M. M.
    of the midnight ball. George, J. D.

PRINCESSES -- FICTION
Aveyard, V. King's cage
Aveyard, V. Red queen
Belleza, R. Empress of a thousand skies
Bow, E. The Scorpion Rules
Cabot, M. The princess diaries
Carey, J. L. Dragon's Keep
Chima, C. W. The Demon King
Cokal, S. The Kingdom of little wounds
Coulthurst, A. Of Fire and Stars
Coventry, S. The queen's daughter
Dixon, H. Entwined
Flinn, A. Cloaked
Flinn, A. A kiss in time
George, J. D. Princess of glass
Haddix, M. P. Just Ella
Hahn, R. A creature of moonlight
Hale, S. The Goose girl
Johnston, E. K. That inevitable Victorian thing
Landers, M. Starfall
Levenseller, T. Daughter of the pirate king
McKinley, R. Pegasus
Michaelis, A. Tiger moon
Moriarty, J. A corner of white
Moriarty, J. The cracks in the kingdom
Murdock, C. G. Princess Ben
Murdock, C. G. Wisdom's kiss
Napoli, D. J. Hush
Nix, G. Frogkisser
Osterlund, A. Aurelia
Osterlund, A. Exile
Redwine, C. J. The wish granter: a Ravenspire novel
Tripp, B. The accidental highwayman: being the tale of Kit
  Bristol, his horse Midnight, a mysterious princess, and sundry
  magical persons besides
White, K. And I darken
White, K. Now I rise
Zinn, B. Poison

PRINCESSES -- ROMANIA -- TRANSYLVANIA --

FICTION
White, K. And I darken

PRISONERS' FAMILIES -- FICTION
Crossan, S. Moonrise

PRISONERS -- FICTION
Bliss, B. We'll fly away
Buckhanon, K. Upstate
Colfer, E. Airman
Maas, S. J. Throne of glass
Miranda, M. Soulprint
Perera, A. Guantanamo boy
Smith, A. G. Lockdown

PRISONERS OF WAR -- FICTION
Dudley, D. L. Caleb's wars
Mazer, H. The last mission
Salisbury, G. Hunt for the bamboo rat
Smith, R. Elephant run
Wein, E. Code name Verity
Wein, E. Rose under fire

PRIVATE INVESTIGATORS -- FICTION
Latham, J. Scarlett undercover
Ritter, W. Beastly bones: a Jackaby novel
Ritter, W. The dire king.

Private Peaceful. Morpurgo, M.

PRIVATE SCHOOLS -- FICTION
Fisher, C. Darkwater
Johnson, M. Truly devious: a mystery
Lee, S. Outrun the moon
Philpot, C. Even in paradise
Redgate, R. Noteworthy
Rowell, R. Carry on: a novel
Walker, B. F. Black boy/white school
Wells, R. E. Feedback

The **probability** of miracles. Wunder, W.

PROCUREMENT OF ORGANS, TISSUES, ETC
Dimaline, C. The marrow thieves

PRODUCERS AND DIRECTORS -- FICTION
Menon, S. When Dimple met Rishi

Professor Gargoyle. Gilman, C.

Proimos, James
  12 things to do before you crash and burn

The **project.** Falkner, B.

Project Sweet Life. Hartinger, B.

Promise the night. MacColl, M.

PROMS -- FICTION
Katcher, B. Deacon Locke went to prom

PROPHECIES -- FICTION
Carson, R. The bitter kingdom
Carson, R. The crown of embers
Carson, R. The girl of fire and thorns
Cole, K. Poison princess
Hahn, R. The shadow behind the stars
Legrand, C. Furyborn
Yolen, J. Curse of the Thirteenth Fey

Prophecy of the sisters. Zink, M.

Prose, Francine
  After

The turning

PROSOPAGNOSIA -- FICTION

Niven, J. Holding up the universe

PROSTITUTION -- FICTION

Frank, E. R. Dime

Leavitt, M. My book of life by Angel

Scott, V. Violet Grenade

Sepetys, R. Out of the Easy

Protected. Zorn, C.

PROTEST MOVEMENTS -- FICTION

Alexander, K. He said, she said

Doctorow, C. Pirate cinema

George, M. The difference between you and me

PROTEST MOVEMENTS -- NEW YORK (STATE) -- NEW YORK

Manzano, S. The revolution of Evelyn Serrano

PROVENCE (FRANCE) -- HISTORY -- 13TH CENTURY -- FICTION

Berry, J. The passion of Dolssa

London, A.

PRUSSIA -- FICTION

Sepetys, R. Salt to the sea

PSYCHIATRIC HOSPITAL PATIENTS -- FICTION

Polisner, G. In sight of stars

PSYCHIATRIC HOSPITALS -- FICTION

Alender, K. The dead girls of Hysteria Hall

Halpern, J. Get well soon

Jacobs, J. H. The Shibboleth

Johnson, L. L. Worlds apart.

McCormick, P. Cut

Vizzini, N. It's kind of a funny story

PSYCHIC ABILITY -- FICTION

Brant, W. Zenn diagram

Bray, L. The diviners

Bray, L. Lair of dreams: a Diviners novel

Derting, K. The last echo

McCreight, K. The scattering

Miller, S. J. The art of starving

Neumeier, R. The white road of the moon

Ostow, M. The devil and Winnie Flynn

Smith, L. Sekret

Ward, R. Infinity

West, K. Split second

PSYCHIC TRAUMA -- FICTION

Johnston, E. K. Exit, pursued by a bear

Rosenfield, K. Inland

PSYCHICS -- FICTION

Bray, L. Lair of dreams: a Diviners novel

West, K. Split second

PSYCHOLOGICAL ABUSE -- FICTION

Demetrios, H. Bad romance

PSYCHOLOGICAL FICTION

Hartinger, B. Three truths and a lie

Hutchinson, S. D. We are the ants

King, A. S. I crawl through it

Lockhart, E. Genuine fraud

Rapp, A. The children and the wolves

Rosenfield, K. Inland

Thompson, M. G. Amy Chelsea Stacie Dee

PSYCHOPATHS -- FICTION

Doller, T. The devil you know

Hopkins, E. The you I've never known

Lyga, B. I hunt killers

Rainfield, C. Stained

Toten, T. Beware that girl

PSYCHOTHERAPY -- FICTION

Giles, G. Right behind you

Haydu, C. A. OCD love story

Lyga, B. Goth girl rising

Moon, S. Sparrow

Sáenz, B. A. Last night I sang to the monster; a novel

PSYCHOTHERAPY PATIENTS -- FICTION

Polisner, G. In sight of stars

PUBERTY -- FICTION

Raf, M. The symptoms of my insanity

PUBLIC WELFARE -- FICTION

McDonald, J. Chill wind

Puddin. Murphy, J.

PUERTO RICAN FAMILIES -- FICTION

Older, D. J. Shadowhouse fall

PUERTO RICANS -- FICTION

Manzano, S. The revolution of Evelyn Serrano

Ortiz Cofer, J. Call me Maria

Ortiz Cofer, J. If I could fly

PUERTO RICANS -- FICTION

Older, D. J. Shadowhouse fall

PUERTO RICANS -- NEW YORK (STATE) -- NEW YORK -- FICTION

Older, D. J. Shadowhouse fall

PUERTO RICAN YOUTH -- NEW YORK (STATE) -- NEW YORK -- FICTION

Older, D. J. Shadowhouse fall

Pullman, Philip

The golden compass

La Belle Sauvage

Pulp. Talley, R.

PUNK ROCK MUSIC -- FICTION

Beaufrand, M. J. The rise and fall of the Gallivanters

Castellucci, C. Beige

Punkzilla. Rapp, A.

Puppet. Wiseman, E.

Pure. McVoy, T. E.

Pure Spring. Doyle, B.

PURITANS -- FICTION

Speare, E. G. The witch of Blackbird Pond

Q

Quaking. Erskine, K.

QUARANTINE -- FICTION

Falls, K. Inhuman

The **queen** of cool. Castellucci, C.

Queen of secrets. Meyerhoff, J.

Queen of Water. Farinango, M. V.

queen's daughter. Coventry, S.

QUEENS -- FICTION

Carson, R. The bitter kingdom

Cashore, K. Bitterblue

Chima, C. W. The Crimson Crown

Chokshi, R. The star-touched queen

Cokal, S. The Kingdom of little wounds

Coventry, S. The queen's daughter

Rinaldi, A. The redheaded princess

Salisbury, M. The Sin Eater's daughter

Thomas, R. Long may she reign

QUEENS -- FICTION

Bashardoust, M. Girls made of snow and glass

Thomas, R. Long may she reign

QUESTS (EXPEDITIONS) -- FICTION

King, E. R. The hundredth queen

Legrand, C. Furyborn

Quigley, Dawn

Apple in the middle

QUINCEAÑERA (SOCIAL CUSTOM) -- FICTION

Alegria, M. Estrella's quinceanera

Quintero, I.

Gabi, a girl in pieces

Quintero, Sofia

Efrain's secret

QUINTUPLETS -- FICTION

Beaufrand, M. J. Useless Bay

R

RABBITS -- FICTION

Adams, R. Watership Down

Rabb, Margo

Kissing in America

RACE RELATIONS -- FICTION

Brockenbrough, M. The game of Love and Death

De la Peña, M. Ball don't lie

Dudley, D. L. Caleb's wars

Dunagan, T. M. The salvation of Miss Lucretia

Emond, S. Bright lights, dark nights

Hegedus, B. Between us Baxters

Kirkpatrick, K. Between two worlds

Lester, J. Guardian

Lester, J. S. Black, white, other

Levine, K. The best bad luck I ever had

Lizzie Bright and the Buckminster boy. Schmidt, G. D.

Marsden, C. Sahwira; an African friendship

McCall, G. G. All the stars denied

McCarthy, S. C. True fires

Moses, S. P. The legend of Buddy Bush

Myers, W. D. The Cruisers

Naidoo, B. Burn my heart

Patrick, D. L. A matter of souls.

Perez, A. Out of darkness

Raina, A. When morning comes

Reynolds, J. All American Boys

Sherman, D. The freedom maze

Smith, S. The other side of dark

Stone, N. Dear Martin

Taylor, M. D. The land

Volponi, P. Black and white

Walker, B. F. Black boy/white school

Wallace, S. N. Muckers

Wein, E. Black dove, white raven

Woodson, J. If you come softly

Wright, D. Violence 101

Rachel's secret. Sanders, S.

RACIALLY MIXED PEOPLE -- FICTION

Bowman, A. D. Starfish

Buffie, M. Winter shadows

Cann, K. Consumed

Carey, J. L. In the time of dragon moon

Chan, C. All that I can fix

Crutcher, C. Whale talk

Gill, D. M. Soul enchilada

Griffin, E. Z. Light years

Hopkinson, N. The Chaos

Jocelyn, M. A Big Dose of Lucky

Keyser, A. J. The way back from broken

Landman, T. Hell and high water

Lester, J. S. Black, white, other

Maldonado, T. Secret Saturdays

McDonald, J. Off -color

Nelson, M. American ace

Redgate, R. Final draft

Schrefer, E. Endangered

Stevenson, S. J. The Latte Rebellion

Taylor, M. D. The land

Thompson, H. Orchards

Voorhees, C. The brothers Torres

Wang, C. The takedown

Webber, K. The heartbeats of Wing Jones

Weston, R. P. Blues for Zoey

Winters, C.The steep and thorny way

Yoon, N. Everything

Zettel, S. Bad luck girl

Zettel, S. Golden girl

RACIAL PROFILING IN LAW ENFORCEMENT

Stone, N. Dear Martin

RACING -- FICTION

Stiefvater, M. The scorpio races

Racing Savannah. Kenneally, M.

RACISM -- FICTION

Coles, J. Tyler Johnson was here

Crowe, C. Mississippi trial, 1955

Gibney, S. Dream country

Parker, S. M. The rattled bones

Reynolds, J. All American Boys

Shabazz, I. X

Stone, N. Dear Martin

Taylor, M. D. Roll of thunder, hear my cry

Radiance. Noel, A.

The **radiant** road: a novel. Catmull, K.

RADIATION -- FICTION
Bryant, M. E. Glow
RADIATION -- PHYSIOLOGICAL EFFECT
Bryant, M. E. Glow
RADIO -- FICTION
Fleischman, P. Seek
RADIO PROGRAMS -- FICTION
Cooney, C. B. The voice on the radio
radius of us. Marquardt, Marie F.
Raf, Mindy
The symptoms of my insanity
Bodeen, S. A.
night. Lipsyte, R.
RAILROADS -- FICTION
Mieville, C. Railsea
RAILROAD TRAVEL -- FICTION
Arnold, A. Love & other train wrecks
Miller, S. A lite too bright
Mieville, C.
Rainbow boys. Sanchez, A.
Rainbow High. Sanchez, A.
Rainbow road. Sanchez, A.
Rainfield, Cheryl

Stained
RAIN FORESTS -- FICTION
Khoury, J. Origin
rains. Hurwitz, G.
RAMADAN -- FICTION
Robert, Na'ima B. Boy vs. girl.
RAMA (HINDU DEITY) -- FICTION
Sattar, A. Ramayana: an illustrated retelling
Zohra, S. Ramayana: an illustrated retelling
Ramayana: an illustrated retelling. Sattar, A.
Ramayana: an illustrated retelling. Zohra, S.
Blue. Murphy, J.
RANCH LIFE -- FICTION
Amateau, G. A certain strain of peculiar
Mabry, S. All the wind in the world
RANCH LIFE -- SOUTHWESTERN STATES -- FICTION
Mabry, S. All the wind in the world
RANCH LIFE -- SPAIN -- FICTION
Kephart, B. Small damages
Randall, Thomas
Dreams of the dead
Spirits of the Noh
Patel in full effect. Patel, S.
RAP MUSIC -- FICTION
Alexander, K. The crossover
Mattison, B. T. Unsigned hype; a novel
McDonald, J. Harlem Hustle
RAP MUSICIANS
Woodson, J. After Tupac and D Foster
RAPE -- FICTION
Anderson, J. L. Speak
Blake, A. H. Girl made of stars
Crocker, N. Billie Standish was here

French, G. Grit
Grace, A. In too deep
Hartzler, A. What we saw
Johnston, E. K. Exit, pursued by a bear
Kiely, B. Tradition
Levine, E. In trouble
Lipsyte, R. Raiders night
Lynch, C. Inexcusable
Marcus, K. Exposed
McGhee, A. What I leave behind
Molope, K. L. This book betrays my brother
O'Neill, L. Asking for it
Reed, A. The Nowhere Girls.
Shaw, S. Safe
Summers, C. All the rage
Whitney, D. The Mockingbirds
RAPE -- INVESTIGATION -- FICTION
Padian, M. Wrecked
RAPE VICTIMS -- FICTION
Johnston, E. K. Exit, pursued by a bear
Rapp, Adam
The children and the wolves
Punkzilla
Under the wolf, under the dog
RATS -- FICTION
Pratchett, T. The amazing Maurice and his educated rodents
Rats saw God. Thomas, R.
The **rattled** bones. Parker, S. M.
Raven flight. Marillier, J.
RAVENSBRUCK (CONCENTRATION CAMP) -- FICTION
Wein, E. Rose under fire
Raven's gate. Horowitz, A.
Reached. Condie, A.
Reaching out. Jimenez, F.
Read between the lines. Knowles, J.
READING -- FICTION
Castan, M. Fighting for Dontae
Paulsen, G. Nightjohn
Ready to fall. Pixley, M.
Reality Boy. King, A. S.
Reality check. Abrahams, P.
REALITY -- FICTION
King, A. S. I crawl through it
REALITY TELEVISION PROGRAMS -- FICTION
Aldredge, B. Sasquatch, love, and other imaginary things
Demetrios, H. Something real
King, A. S. Reality Boy
O'Brien, Caragh M. The vault of dreamers
Oelke, L. Nice try, Jane Sinner
Vlahos, L. Life in a fishbowl
Williams, K. Pizza, love, and other stuff that made me famous
Real live boyfriends. Lockhart, E.
A **reaper** at the gates. Tahir, S.
Reasons to be happy. Kittle, K.
Rebel angels. Bray, L.
Rebel fire. Lane, A.
Rebellion. Sandler, K.

rebels of New SUN. Kinch, M.
   Tintera, A.
Reckless. Funke, C.
RECLUSES -- FICTION
   Callahan, E. The art of escaping
RECONCILIATION -- FICTION
   Alexander, K. Solo
RECORD STORES -- FICTION
   Howell, S. Girl defective
Recovery Road. Nelson, B.
RECYCLING -- FICTION
   Bacigalupi, P. Ship Breaker
Redgate, Riley
   Final draft
   Noteworthy
     glass. Resau, L.
     glove. Black, H.
     redheaded princess. Rinaldi, A.
     ink. Mayhew, J.
     kayak. Cummings, P.
     moon at Sharpsburg. Wells, R.
     queen. Aveyard, V.
Redwine, C. J.
   The wish granter: a Ravenspire novel
Reed, Amy
   Over you
   The Nowhere Girls.
Reeve, Philip
   Fever Crumb
   Here lies Arthur
   Scrivener's moon
   A Web of Air
REFORMATORIES -- FICTION
   Wright, D. Violence 101
REFUGEE CAMPS -- FICTION
   Wagner, L. R. Hold tight, don't let go
REFUGEES -- AUSTRALIA -- FICTION
   Abdel-Fattah, R. The lines we cross
REFUGEES -- FICTION
   Abawi, A. A land of permanent goodbyes
   Abdel-Fattah, R. The lines we cross
   Anderson, N. C. City of Saints & Thieves
   Bacigalupi, P. The drowned cities
   Bassoff, L. Lost girl found
   Coates, J. L. A hare in the elephant's trunk
   Cooney, C. B. Diamonds in the shadow
   Gibney, S. Dream country
   Hartley, A. J. Firebrand
   Manivong, L. Escaping the tiger
   Park, L. S. A long walk to water
   Sepetys, R. Salt to the sea
   Stamper, V. What the night sings
   Thor, A. Deep sea
   Wagner, L. R. Hold tight, don't let go
   Whitman, S. The milk of birds
   Williams, M. Now is the time for running
REFUSE AND REFUSE DISPOSAL -- FICTION

   Mulligan, A. Trash
REGENCY NOVELS -- FICTION
   Kindl, P. Keeping the castle
REHABILITATION -- FICTION
   Price, N. Zoe letting go
Reichs, Brendan
   Nemesis
Reign the earth. Gaughen, A. C.
REINCARNATION -- FICTION
   Laurie, V. Forever, again
   Miranda, M. Soulprint
   Moulton, C. A. Angelfire
   Sedgwick, M. Midwinterblood
Reinhardt, Dana
   How to build a house
   Tell us something true
   The things a brother knows
   We are the goldens
Release, Ness, P.
RELIEF WORKERS -- FICTION
   Park, L. S. A long walk to water
RELIGION -- FICTION
   Bunce, E. C. Star crossed
   Coyle, K. Vivian Apple at the end of the world
   Coyle, K. Vivian Apple needs a miracle
   Daley, J. R. Jesus Jackson
   Hautman, P. Godless
   Hautman, P. The obsidian blade
   Johnson, V. Saving Maddie
   Levitin, S. Strange relations
RELIGIOUS LEADERS -- FICTION
   Parker, A. C. Astray
   Parker, A. C. Gated
RELIGIOUS LIFE -- FICTION
   Parker, A. C. Astray
The **reluctant** journal of Henry K. Larsen. Nielsen, S.
Reluctantly Alice. Naylor, P. R.
REMARRIAGE -- FICTION
   Friend, N. Bounce
   Graff, L. Lost in the sun
   Keplinger, K. A midsummer's nightmare
   Martin, C. K. K. The lighter side of life and death
RENAISSANCE -- FICTION
   Marsh, K. Jepp, who defied the stars
   Napoli, D. J. The smile
RENAISSANCE FAIRS -- FICTION
   Wettersten, L. My faire lady
Renegades. Meyer, M.
Renn, Diana
   Latitude zero
Rennison, Louise
   Angus, thongs and full-frontal snogging
   Are these my basoomas I see before me? final confessions of
     Georgia Nicolson
   Stop in the name of pants!
   The taming of the tights
Rens, Kristin

behind you. Giles, G.

Rinaldi, Ann

The redheaded princess

   Ring of Solomon. Stroud, J.

      Hubbard, A.

      and fall of the Gallivanters. Beaufrand, M. J.

RISK-TAKING (PSYCHOLOGY) -- FICTION

Oliver, L. Panic

   of passage. Hensley, J.

      & wrongs of Janice Wills. Pearson, J.

   Rithmatist. Sanderson, B.

Ritter, William

Beastly bones: a Jackaby novel

The dire king

Riverkeep. Stewart, M.

RIVERS -- FICTION

Stewart, M. Riverkeep

Rivers, Karen

Roat, Sharon Huss

How to Disappear

ROBBERS AND OUTLAWS -- FICTION

Egan, C. Julia vanishes

Lloyd-Jones, E. Illusive

Tripp, B. The accidental highwayman: being the tale of Kit
Bristol, his horse Midnight, a mysterious princess, and sundry
magical persons besides

Robert, Na'ima B.

Boy vs. girl

She wore red trainers: A Muslim Love Story

From Somalia with love

ROBOTS -- FICTION

Carriger, G. Curtsies & conspiracies

Carriger, G. Etiquette & espionage

Gray, C. Defy the stars

Gray, C. Defy the worlds

Powell, W. C. Expiration day

Wells, D. Fragments

Wells, D. Partials

Wells, D. Ruins

Wells, R. E. Feedback

Rocco, John

Swim that rock

ROCK MUSIC -- FICTION

Ehrenhaft, D. Friend is not a verb

Franklin, E. The half life of planets

Hannan, P. My big mouth

Kelly, T. Harmonic feedback

Nelson, B. Rock star, superstar

Skuse, C. J. Rockoholic

Weil, C. I'm glad I did

ROCK MUSICIANS -- FICTION

Cohn, R. Nick & Norah's infinite playlist

Skuse, C. J. Rockoholic

   star, superstar. Nelson, B.

Rockoholic. Skuse, C. J.

Roecker, Laura

The Liar Society

The lies that bind

Roe, Robin

A list of cages

Rogerson, Margaret

An enchantment of ravens

Rogue. Damico, G.

The **Rogues.** Yolen, J.

ROLE MODELS -- FICTION

White, E. E. A season of daring greatly

ROLE PLAYING -- FICTION

Brezenoff, S. Guy in real life

Powell, L. The Master of Misrule

Roll of thunder, hear my cry. Taylor, M. D.

ROMANCE FICTION

Ahdieh, R. The rose and the dagger

Albertalli, B. The upside of unrequited

Almond, D. A song for Ella Grey

Alsaid, A. Never Always Sometimes

Anstey, C. Carols and chaos

Anstey, C. Love, lies and spies

Axelrod, K. The law of loving others: a novel

Barrett, T. The Stepsister's Tale

Brockenbrough, M. The game of Love and Death

Cameron, S. Rook

Connor, L. The things you kiss goodbye

Corthron, K. L. The truth of right now

Crowley, C. Words in deep blue

Demetrios, H. Bad romance

Dessen, S. Once and for all

Fichera, L. Played

Fine, S. Of Metal and Wishes

Goo, M. The way you make me feel

Kephart, B. One thing stolen

Laskin, P. L. Ronit & Jamil

Laurie, V. Forever, again

Longshore, K. Brazen

Mafi, T. Shatter me

Mafi, T. A very large expanse of sea

McCahan, E. The lake effect

McCahan, E. Love and other foreign words

McLemore, A. -M. The weight of feathers

McNeil, G. I'm not your manic pixie dream girl

Mills, W. All we have left

Nielsen, S. Optimists die first

Niven, J. Holding up the universe

Pearson, M. E. Dance of thieves

Perkins, S. Isla and the happily ever after: a novel

Rabb, M. Kissing in America

Russo, M. If I Was Your Girl

Rutkoski, M. The winner's crime

Salisbury, M. The Sin Eater's daughter

Sedgwick, M. Midwinterblood

Silvera, A. They both die at the end

Smith, J. E. Windfall

Steiger, A. J. When my heart joins the thousand

Stiefvater, M. Sinner

Zarr, S. Gem & Dixie

Runemarks. Harris, J.

    Keplinger, K.

      Deuker, C.

    running dream. Van Draanen, W.

RUNNING -- FICTION

  Caletti, D. A heart in a body in the world

  Childs, T. L. Oh. My. Gods.

  Myers, W. D. Darius & Twig

  Van Draanen, W. The running dream

  Webber, K. The heartbeats of Wing Jones

Running girl. Mason, S.

Running loose. Crutcher, C.

Runyon, Brent

  Surface tension; a novel in four summers

Rupp, Rebecca

  After Eli

RURAL SCHOOLS -- FICTION

  Keplinger, K. That's not what happened

  , J. Altered

Rush, Jennifer

  Altered

    Silver, E.

Russell, Chris

  Songs about a girl

RUSSIA -- FICTION

  Bardugo, L. Siege and storm

RUSSIA -- HISTORY -- 1904-1914 -- FICTION

  O'Brien, A. Lara's gift

RUSSIAN AMERICANS -- FICTION

  Crowder, M. Audacity

  Tal, E. Cursing Columbus

Russo, Meredith

  If I Was Your Girl

Rutkoski, Marie

  The shadow society

  The winner's crime

  The winner's curse

RWANDA -- FICTION

  Combres, E. Broken memory

  Jansen, H. Over a thousand hills I walk with you

Ryan, Amy Kathleen

  Flame; a Sky Chasers novel

Ryan, Carrie

  The Forest of Hands and Teeth

Ryan, Sara

  Empress of the world

S

Sachar, Louis

  The cardturner; a novel about a king, a queen, and a joker

    sacred lies of Minnow Bly. Oakes, S.

      scars. Duey, K.

    sacrifice box. Stewart, M.

SACRIFICE -- FICTION

Bardugo, L. The language of thorns

The **sacrifice** of Sunshine Girl. McKenzie, P.

Saeed, Aisha

  Written in the stars

Sáenz, Benjamin Alire

  Aristotle and Dante discover the secrets of the universe

  He forgot to say good-bye

  The inexplicable logic of my life

  Last night I sang to the monster; a novel

  Sammy and Juliana in Hollywood

Safekeeping. Hesse, K.

Safe. Shaw, S.

Safi, Aminah Mae

  Not the girls you're looking for.

Sahwira; an African friendship. Marsden, C.

SAILING -- FICTION

  Herlong, M. The great wide sea

Saint death. Sedgwick, M.

SAINT KILDA (VIC.) -- FICTION

  Howell, S. Girl defective

SAINTS

  Grimes, N. A girl named Mister

Saints and misfits: a novel. Ali, S. K.

St. Crow, Lili

  Strange angels

St. James, James

  Freak show

Saldana, Rene

  A good long way

SALEM (MASS.) -- FICTION

  Hemphill, S. Wicked girls

  Howe, K. Conversion

Sales, Leila

  This song will save your life

  Tonight the streets are ours

Salisbury, Graham

  Eyes of the emperor

  Hunt for the bamboo rat

Salisbury, Melinda

  The Sin Eater's daughter

Salomon, Peter Adam

  All those broken angels

Salt. Gee, M.

Salt to the sea. Sepetys, R.

SALVADORAN AMERICANS -- FICTION

  Kephart, B. Wild blues

  Perez, A. H. The knife and the butterfly

The **salvation** of Miss Lucretia. Dunagan, T. M.

Sammy and Juliana in Hollywood. Sáenz, B. A.

SAMPSON, DEBORAH, 1760-1827 ABOUT

  Klass, S. S. Soldier's secret

SAMURAI -- FICTION

  Ahdieh, R. Flame in the mist

  Ahdieh, R. Smoke in the sun

Samurai shortstop. Gratz, A.

SAN ANTONIO (TEX.) -- FICTION

  Villareal, R. Body slammed

Bancks, T. Mac Slater hunts the cool
Barnes, J. L. The Squad
Barnes, J. Tales of the Madman Underground
Bauer, J. Peeled
Bigelow, L. J. Starting from here
Bjorkman, L. Miss Fortune Cookie
Bjorkman, L. My invented life
Block, F. L. The waters & the wild
Bond, G. Fallout
Brande, R. Evolution, me, & other freaks of nature
Brewer, Z. The chronicles of Vladimir Tod
Budhos, M. T. Ask me no questions
Butcher, K. Cheat
Calame, D. Beat the band
Carriger, G. Etiquette & espionage
Carvell, M. Sweetgrass basket
Carvell, M. Who will tell my brother?
Castellucci, C. The queen of cool
Castle, J. You look different in real life
Chaltas, T. Because I am furniture
Chapman, L. Flawless
Cheva, C. DupliKate
Childs, T. L. Oh. My. Gods.
Coben, H. Shelter
Cohen, J. C. Leverage
Cohn, R. Shrimp
Conaghan, B. When Mr. Dog bites
Cooney, C. B. Code orange
Cormier, R. Beyond the chocolate war
Cormier, R. The chocolate war
Crutcher, C. Deadline
Crutcher, C. Ironman
Crutcher, C. Period 8
Crutcher, C. Running loose
Crutcher, C. Whale talk
Cummings, P. Blindsided
Delsol, W. Stork
Derting, K. Desires of the dead
Despain, B. The dark Divine
Dessen, S. Just listen
Deuker, C. Gym candy
Deuker, C. High heat
Deuker, C. Painting the black
Deuker, C. Payback time
Devine, E. Press play
Dinnison, K. You and me and him
Duey, K. Sacred scars
Duncan, L. Killing Mr. Griffin
Edwardson, D. D. My name is not easy
Elkeles, S. Perfect chemistry
Ellsworth, L. Unforgettable
Erskine, K. Quaking
Fehler, G. Beanball
Finneyfrock, K. The sweet revenge of Celia Door
Friend, N. For keeps
Gensler, S. The revenant
George, M. Looks

Giles, G. Shattering Glass
Gilman, C. Professor Gargoyle
Grant, C. Teenie
Gratz, A. Samurai shortstop
Griffin, A. The Julian game
Griffin, C. J. Nowhere to run
Grimes, N. Bronx masquerade
Halpern, J. Into the wild nerd yonder
Hand, C. Unearthly
Hannan, P. My big mouth
Hartinger, B. Geography Club
Hautman, P. The big crunch
Hautman, P. Blank confession
Hawkins, R. Hex Hall
Healey, K. Guardian of the dead
Hemmings, K. H. Juniors
Henderson, J. Vampire rising
Hensley, J. N. Rites of passage
Hodkin, M. The unbecoming of Mara Dyer
Houston, J. New boy
Hrdlitschka, S. Allegra
Hubbard, J. R. Paper covers rock
Hurley, T. Ghostgirl
Hyde, C. R. Jumpstart the world
Jaden, D. Losing Faith
Jinks, C. Evil genius
Johnson, L. Muchacho
Johnson, M. The name of the star
Johnson, M. Scarlett fever
Juby, S. Getting the girl
Karim, S. Skunk girl
Katcher, B. Almost perfect
Katcher, B. Playing with matches
Kenneally, M. Stealing Parker
Kephart, B. Undercover
Kerr, M. E. If I love you, am I trapped forever?
Kindl, P. A school for brides
Kittle, K. Reasons to be happy
Klass, D. You don't know me
Knowles, J. Read between the lines
Leavitt, L. Sean Griswold's head
Levithan, D. Two boys kissing
Lindstrom, E. Not if I see you first
Lockhart, E. The boy book
Lockhart, E. The boyfriend list
Lockhart, E. The disreputable history of Frankie Landau-Banks
Lockhart, E. Dramarama
Lockhart, E. Real live boyfriends
Lockhart, E. The treasure map of boys
Lubar, D. Sleeping freshmen never lie
Lyga, B. The astonishing adventures of Fanboy & Goth Girl
Lyga, B. Boy toy
Lyga, B. Goth girl rising
Lyga, B. Hero-type
Lynch, C. Inexcusable
Mackey, W. K. Throwing like a girl
Mackler, C. The earth, my butt, and other big, round things

Acevedo, E. The poet X: a novel
Aceves, F. The closest I've come
Ahmed, S. Love, hate & other filters
Albertalli, B. Simon vs. the Homo Sapiens agenda
Alexander, K. He said, she said
Alsenas, L. Beyond clueless
Andrews, J. Me & Earl & the dying girl
Armstrong, K. Aftermath
Backes, M. M. The princesses of Iowa
Bliss, B. We'll fly away
Blythe, C. Revenge of a not-so-pretty girl
Bond, G. Fallout
Brennan, S. R. In other lands
Bunker, L. Felix Yz
Caletti, D. A heart in a body in the world
Callahan, E. The art of escaping
Carleson, J. C. The tyrant's daughter
Carriger, G. Curtsies & conspiracies
Carriger, G. Etiquette & espionage
Casella, J. Thin space
Castan, M. Fighting for Dontae
Clark, K. E. Freakboy
Coben, H. Seconds away
Conaghan, B. When Mr. Dog bites
Cousins, D. Waiting for Gonzo
Cronn-Mills, K. Beautiful Music for Ugly Children
Crossan, S. One
Crutcher, C. Period 8
Demetrios, H. Bad romance
Derting, K. The last echo
DeWoskin, R. Blind
Dinnison, K. You and me and him
Emond, S. Bright lights, dark nights
Fehlbaum, B. Big fat disaster
Finneyfrock, K. Starbird Murphy and the world outside
Finneyfrock, K. The sweet revenge of Celia Door
Fisher, C. Darkwater
Foxlee, K. The midnight dress
George, M. The difference between you and me
Goo, M. I believe in a thing called love
Goslee, S. J. Whatever
Grace, A. In too deep
Griffin, N. Just wreck it all
Haddix, M. P. Full ride
Harrington, H. Speechless
Hemmings, K. H. Juniors
Henry, K. Heretics Anonymous
Hensley, J. N. Rites of passage
Hubbard, J. R. And we stay
Jensen, C. Skyscraping
Johnson, M. The madness underneath
Johnson, M. The shadow cabinet
Johnston, E. K. Exit, pursued by a bear
Juby, S. The Truth Commission
Kaplan, A. We regret to inform you
Katcher, B. The improbable theory of Ana and Zak
Kenneally, M. Coming up for air

Keplinger, K. That's not what happened
Keplinger, K. That's not what happened
Kicly, B. Tradition
Kindl, P. A school for brides
King, A. S. Ask the passengers
Konigsberg, B. Honestly Ben
Lauren, C. Autoboyography
Leavitt, M. Calvin
Lindstrom, E. Not if I see you first
Linn, L. Draw the line
Macvie, M. The ocean in my ears
Magoon, K. 37 things I love (in no particular order)
Martin, C. K. K. Yesterday
Mathieu, J. Moxie: a novel
Mesrobian, C. Just a girl
Mills, E. First & then
Myers, W. D. The Cruisers
Oseman, A. Solitaire
O'Brien, Caragh M. The vault of dreamers
Perez, A. Out of darkness
Perkins, S. Isla and the happily ever after: a novel
Philpot, C. Even in paradise
Pixley, M. Ready to fall
Reed, A. The Nowhere Girls.
Richmond, P. Always a catch
Rowell, R. Carry on: a novel
Rowell, R. Eleanor & Park
Ryan, S. Empress of the world
Sales, L. Tonight the streets are ours
Schantz, S. E. Fig
SCHOOL SHOOTINGS -- FICTION
Smith, A. G. The Devil's engine
Smith-Ready, J. This side of salvation
Sonnenblick, J. Falling over sideways
Thor, A. Deep sea
Tromly, S. Trouble is a friend of mine
Vail, R. Unfriended
Walker, B. F. Black boy/white school
Wallace, S. N. Muckers
Wallach, T. We all looked up
Waltman, K. Slump
Wang, C. The takedown
Watson, R. Piecing me together
West, K. Pivot point
West, K. Split second
Wolitzer, M. Belzhar
Yee, L. The kidney hypothetical
Yovanoff, B. Places no one knows
Zadoff, A. Boy Nobody
Schrefer, Eliot
The deadly sister
Endangered
Threatened
Schreiber, Joe
Au revoir, crazy European chick
Perry's killer playlist
Schroeder, Lisa

O'Brien, Caragh M. The vault of dreamers
O'Brien, C. M. Birthmarked
O'Brien, J. Day of the assassins
O'Brien, J. Z for Zachariah
Oliver, L. Requiem
Patterson, J. Maximum Ride: the angel experiment
Peterfreund, D. Across a star-swept sea
Philbrick, W. R. The last book in the universe
Pike, A. Earthbound
Pike, A. Glitter
Powell, W. C. Expiration day
Price, L. Enders
Price, L. Starters
Reeve, P. A Web of Air
Reeve, P. Fever Crumb
Reeve, P. Scrivener's moon
Reichs, B. Nemesis
Revis, B. Across the universe
Revis, B. A million suns
Revis, B. Shades of Earth
Rossi, V. Under the never sky
Roth, V. Allegiant
Roth, V. Carve the mark
Roth, V. Divergent
Roth, V. The fates divide
Roth, V. Insurgent
Rush, J. Altered
Rutkoski, M. The shadow society
Ryan, A. K. Flame; a Sky Chasers novel
Ryan, A. K. Glow
Sandler, K. Rebellion
Sandler, K. Tankborn
Sedgwick, M. The ghosts of heaven.
Shusterman, N. Scythe
Shusterman, N. Thunderhead
Shusterman, N. UnSouled
Shusterman, N. UnWholly
Shusterman, N. Unwind
Silver, E. Rush
Simmons, K. Article 5
Simmons, K. Three
Skurzynski, G. The Virtual War
Sleator, W. The duplicate
Smith, A. 1959-. The Alex Crow
Smith, A. G. The Devil's engine
Smith, A. G. Lockdown
Smith, S. L. Orleans
Smythe, J. P. Way down dark
Terrill, C. All our yesterdays
Terry, T. Fractured
Terry, T. Slated
Thomas, L. Nowhere near you
Tintera, A. Reboot
Treggiari, J. Ashes, ashes
Unsworth, T. The one safe place: a novel
Vanhee, J. Engines of the broken world
Wallenfels, S. POD

Ward, R. The Chaos
Ward, R. Num8ers
Wasserman, R. The waking dark
Wells, D. Fragments
Wells, D. Partials
Wells, D. Ruins
Wells, R. E. Feedback
Wells, R. E. Variant
Wendig, C. Under the Empyrean Sky
Werlin, N. Double helix
Westerfeld, S. Blue noon
Westerfeld, S. Extras
Whaley, J. C. Noggin
White, A. Surviving Antarctica
Whitley, D. Midnight charter
Wiggins, B. Cured
Wiggins, B. Stung
Williams, S. Twinmaker
Wooding, C. Velocity
Woolston, B. Martians
Yancey, R. infinite sea
Yancey, R. The 5th Wave
Young, M. Blood red road
Zevin, G. All these things I've done
Zhang, K. What's left of me

SCIENCE FICTION -- CONGRESSES -- FICTION
Katcher, B. The improbable theory of Ana and Zak

Scieszka, Jon, 1954
Who done it? an investigation of murder most foul

Scorch. Damico, G.

Scored. McLaughlin, L.

The **Scorpion** Rules. Bow, E.

The **Scorpio** Races. Stiefvater, M.

SCOTLAND -- FICTION
Frost, H. The braid

SCOTLAND -- HISTORY -- 17TH CENTURY -- FICTION
Laird, E. The betrayal of Maggie Blair

SCOTLAND -- HISTORY -- 20TH CENTURY -- FICTION
Wein, E. The pearl thief

Scott, Elizabeth
Between here and forever
Living dead girl
Love you hate you miss you
Miracle

SCOTTISH TRAVELLERS (NOMADIC PEOPLE) --
FICTION
Wein, E. The pearl thief

Scott, Michael
The alchemyst
The enchantress

Scott, Victoria
Violet Grenade

Scrawl. Shulman, Mark

SCREENWRITERS -- FICTION
Federle, T. The great American whatever

Scrivener's moon. Reeve, P.

SCULPTORS -- FICTION

Arnold, E. K. Infandous

Atkins, J. Stone mirrors

    Shusterman, N.

SEAFARING LIFE -- FICTION

Bunting, E. The pirate captain's daughter

Seamon, Hollis

Somebody up there hates you

SEA MONSTERS -- FICTION

Stewart, M. Riverkeep

    Griswold's head. Leavitt, L.

    and destroy. Hughes, D.

SEASIDE RESORTS -- FICTION

Hocking, A. Wake

    of daring greatly. White, E. E.

    of ice. Les Becquets, D.

SEA STORIES

Golden, C. The sea wolves

Heilig, H. The Girl from Everywhere

SEATTLE (WASH.) -- FICTION

Katcher, B. The improbable theory of Ana and Zak

Lockhart, E. Real live boyfriends

Lockhart, E. The treasure map of boys

McBride, L. Hold me closer, necromancer

Trueman, T. Life happens next; a novel

SEATTLE (WASH.) -- HISTORY -- 20TH CENTURY -- FICTION

Brockenbrough, M. The game of Love and Death

    wolves. Golden, C.

  second life of Ava Rivers. Gardner, F.

    away. Coben, H.

  second summer of the sisterhood. Brashares, A.

  second trial. Boll, R.

SECRECY -- FICTION

Alender, K. The dead girls of Hysteria Hall

Bannen, M. The bird and the blade

Callahan, E. The art of escaping

Cameron, S. The knowing

French, G. Grit

Keplinger, K. Run

Keplinger, K. That's not what happened

Lo, M. Adaptation

Lowry, L. Son

Lucier, M. Isle of blood and stone

Mabry, S. All the wind in the world

McCarthy, A. Just fly away

McLaughlin, L. The Free

Oates, J. C. Two or three things I forgot to tell you

Patrick, C. Revived

Sanchez, E. L. I Am Not Your Perfect Mexican Daughter

Scott, V. Violet Grenade

Toten, T. Beware that girl

Walton, J. Words on bathroom walls

SECRETARIES -- FICTION

Turner, M. W. Thick as thieves

  secret ingredient. Lewis, S.

  secret life of Prince Charming. Caletti, D.

    Saturdays. Maldonado, T.

The **secret** side of empty. Andreu, M. E.

SECRETS -- FICTION

Albertalli, B. Simon vs. the Homo Sapiens agenda

Alender, K. The dead girls of Hysteria Hall

Arnold, E. K. Infandous

Bobet, L. An inheritance of ashes

Caletti, D. Essential maps for the lost

Callahan, E. The art of escaping

Cameron, S. Rook

Cypess, L. Death sworn

French, G. Grit

Haddix, M. P. Full ride

Harrington, H. Speechless

Hartinger, B. Three truths and a lie

Hartman, R. Seraphina

Jensen, C. Skyscraping

Keplinger, K. Run

Keplinger, K. That's not what happened

Latham, J. Scarlett undercover

Lowitz, L. Jet Black and the ninja wind.

Lucier, M. Isle of blood and stone

Mason, S. Running girl

McLaughlin, L. The Free

Oates, J. C. Two or three things I forgot to tell you

Pitcher, A. Ketchup clouds

Resau, L. The jade notebook

Richards, N. D. Six months later

Rosenfield, K. Inland

Rutkoski, M. The winner's crime

Scott, V. Violet Grenade

Stiefvater, M. The dream thieves

Stone, T. I. Little do we know

Temblador, A. Secrets of the Casa Rosada

Thomas, K. The darkest corners

Thompson, M. G. Amy Chelsea Stacie Dee

Toten, T. Beware that girl

Weil, C. I'm glad I did

Zusak, M. Bridge of Clay

SECRET SOCIETIES -- FICTION

Bailey, K. Legacy of the clockwork key

Frost, M. Alliance

Gier, K. Ruby red

Hensley, J. N. Rites of passage

Okorafor, N. Akata warrior

Roecker, L. The Liar Society

Roecker, L. The lies that bind

Stohl, M. Black Widow

Tharp, T. Mojo

Whitney, D. The Mockingbirds

Secrets of the Casa Rosada. Temblador, A.

The **secret** story of Sonia Rodriguez. Sitomer, A. L.

Sedgwick, Marcus

The ghosts of heaven

Midwinterblood

My swordhand is singing

Revolver

Saint death

She is not invisible

White crow

  no color. Gibney, S.

  what I see. Whelan, G.

  you at Harry's. Knowles, J.

    Heathfield, L.

    Fleischman, P.

    Nicholson, W.

SEGREGATION -- FICTION

Dudley, D. L. Caleb's wars

SEGREGATION IN EDUCATION -- FICTION

McCarthy, S. C. True fires

  Smith, L.

SELECTIVE MUTISM -- FICTION

Berry, J. All the truth that's in me

Casanova, M. Frozen

Chan, G. The disappearance

Pitcher, A. Silence is goldfish: a novel

Wallach, T. Thanks for the trouble

SELF-ACCEPTANCE -- FICTION

Friend, N. How we roll

Friend, N. My life in black and white

Gibney, S. See no color

Miller, S. J. The art of starving

Ness, P. Release

Winfrey, K. Things Jolie needs to do before she bites it

SELF-ACTUALIZATION -- FICTION

Kriegman, M. Being Audrey Hepburn: a novel

SELF-ACTUALIZATION (PSYCHOLOGY) -- FICTION

Chen, J. Return to me

Forman, G. I have lost my way

Geiger, J. C. Wildman

Hartman, R. Seraphina

King, A. S. Reality Boy

Magoon, K. 37 things I love (in no particular order)

Zentner, J. The serpent king

SELF-ACTUALIZATION (PSYCHOLOGY) IN ADOLESCENCE -- FICTION

Lee, M. The gentleman's guide to vice and virtue

SELF-CONFIDENCE -- FICTION

McStay, M. Everything that makes you

SELF-CONSCIOUSNESS

Friend, N. My life in black and white

Griffin, A. All you never wanted

Schantz, S. E. Fig

SELF-ESTEEM -- FICTION

Acevedo, E. The poet X: a novel

Murphy, J. Dumplin'

Oates, J. C. Two or three things I forgot to tell you

Patel, S. Rani Patel in full effect

Vawter, V. Copyboy

Vivian, S. The list

SELF-ESTEEM IN ADOLESCENCE -- FICTION

Murphy, J. Puddin

SELF-HELP GROUPS -- FICTION

Henry, K. Heretics Anonymous

Reinhardt, D. Tell us something true

Spangler, B. Beast

SELF-MUTILATION -- FICTION

Anderson, J. L. Wintergirls

Griffin, N. Just wreck it all

McCormick, P. Cut

Rainfield, C. Scars

Selfors, Suzanne

Mad love

The sweetest spell

SELF-PERCEPTION -- FICTION

Bowman, A. D. Starfish

Chambers, A. Dying to know you

De la Cruz, M. Someone to love

Doktorski, J. S. Famous last words

Friend, N. My life in black and white

Galante, C. The sweetness of salt

Halpern, J. Have a nice day

McDonald, A. Boys, bears, and a serious pair of hiking boots

Shulman, M. Scrawl

Skilton, S. Bruised

Van Draanen, W. Flipped

Vivian, S. The list

Yovanoff, B. Places no one knows

SELF-PERCEPTION IN WOMEN -- FICTION

White, E. E. A season of daring greatly

SELF-REALIZATION -- FICTION

Bigelow, L. J. Starting from here

Braxton-Smith, A. Merrow

Geiger, J. C. Wildman

Grossman, N. A world away

Lewis, S. The secret ingredient

Matson, M. Since you've been gone

Richmond, P. Always a catch

Sales, L. Tonight the streets are ours

Strauss, V. Passion blue

Talley, R. What We Left Behind

Tharp, T. Mojo

Umminger, A. American Girls: A Novel

Wallach, T. We all looked up

Zorn, C. Protected

SELKIES -- FICTION

Cornwell, B. Tides

Lanagan, M. The brides of Rollrock Island

Selzer, Adam

How to get suspended and influence people

SENILE DEMENTIA -- FICTION

Gardner, S. The dead I know

SEPARATION (PSYCHOLOGY) -- FICTION

Lowry, L. Son

Wagner, L. R. Hold tight, don't let go

Sepetys, Ruta

Out of the Easy

Salt to the sea

Between shades of gray

September Girls. Madison, B.

The **September** sisters. Cantor, J.

SEPTEMBER 11 TERRORIST ATTACKS, 2001 -- FICTION

SHAKESPEARE, WILLIAM, 1564-1616 -- FICTION
Booth, M. Saving Hamlet
SHAKESPEARE, WILLIAM, 1564-1616 HAMLET --
FICTION
Booth, M. Saving Hamlet
SHAMANS -- FICTION
Hoban, R. Soonchild
the Stars. McCall, G. G.
Shan, Darren
The thin executioner
Shapeshifter. Bennett, H.
SHAPESHIFTING -- FICTION
Kagawa, J. Talon
Rossetti, R. The girl with borrowed wings
Sharenow, Rob
The Berlin Boxing Club
SHARK ATTACKS -- FICTION
Bingham, K. Formerly shark girl
girl. Bingham, K.
Sharpe, Tess
Far from you
sharp time. O'Connell, M.
Shattering Glass. Giles, G.
shattering. Healey, K.
me. Mafi, T.
Shaw, Susan

Tunnel vision
Sheinmel, Courtney
Positively
is not invisible. Sedgwick, M.
Shelley, Percy Bysshe 1792-1822 About
Hemphill, S. Hideous love
loves you, she loves you not-- Peters, J. A.
Coben, H.
Shepard, Matthew, d. 1998 About
Leslea, N. October mourning
Shepard, Sara
The amateurs
The lying game
Shepherd, Megan
Her Dark Curiosity
shepherd's crown. Pratchett, T.
Sherman, Delia
The freedom maze
SHERMAN'S MARCH TO THE SEA -- FICTION
Bolden, T. Crossing Ebenezer Creek
Sheth, Kashmira
Keeping corner
wore red trainers: A Muslim Love Story. Robert, Na'ima B.
Shibboleth. Jacobs, J. H.
Bradbury, J.
Smith-Ready, J.
Shinn, Sharon
Gateway
Breaker. Bacigalupi, P.
SHIPBUILDING -- FICTION

Almond, D. The tightrope walkers
Ship it. Lundin, B.
SHIPS -- FICTION
Mowll, J. Operation typhoon shore
Ness, P. And the ocean was our sky
SHIPWRECKS -- FICTION
Ruiz Zafon, C. The Prince of Mist
Wolf, A.The watch that ends the night
Shirvington, Jessica
Embrace
Shiver. Stiefvater, M.
SHOEMAKERS -- FICTION
Shreve, S. The lovely shoes
SHOES -- FICTION
Flinn, A. Cloaked
SHONA (AFRICAN PEOPLE) -- FICTION
Williams, M. Diamond boy
SHOOTERS OF FIREARMS -- FICTION
Hamilton, A. Hero at the fall.
Shooting star. McKissack, F.
SHOPPING CENTERS AND MALLS -- FICTION
Mass, W. Heaven looks a lot like the mall; a novel
SHORT STORIES
Dhar, P. Eat the sky, drink the ocean
Giles, L. Fresh ink
Oh, E. A thousand beginnings and endings: 15 retellings of
Asian myths and legends
Patrick, D. L. A matter of souls.
Roy, A. Eat the sky, drink the ocean
Tan, S. Tales from the inner city
SHORT STORIES, AMERICAN
Giles, L. Fresh ink
SHORT STORIES -- COLLECTIONS
Almond, D. Half a creature from the sea
Bardugo, L. The language of thorns
SHORT STORY WRITERS
Golden, C. The wild
Shot down. Mary-Todd, J.
Showalter, Gena
Intertwined
Shreve, Susan
The lovely shoes
Shrimp. Cohn, R.
Shukert, Rachel
Love me
Shulman, Mark
Scrawl
Shulman, Polly
Enthusiasm
Shusterman, Neal
Antsy does time
Bruiser
Challenger
Downsiders
Dry
Everlost
Full tilt; a novel

The Schwa was here

Thunderhead
UnDivided
UnSouled
UnWholly
Unwind
SIBERIA (RUSSIA) -- FICTION
Parks, K. Notes from my captivity
SIBLING RIVALRY -- FICTION
Griffin, A. All you never wanted
SIBLINGS -- FICTION
Ahdieh, R. Smoke in the sun
Andrews, J. Munmun
Antieau, K. Broken moon
Arcos, C. Out of reach
Bayard, L. Lucky strikes
Bolden, T. Crossing Ebenezer Creek
Brown, J. Perfect escape
Cooney, C. B. If the witness lied
Davies, S. Outlaw
Ehrenhaft, D. Friend is not a verb
Flores-Scott, P. American road trip
Halpern, J. Into the wild nerd yonder
Harvey, A. Hearts at stake
Hopkinson, N. The Chaos
Hyde, C. R. The year of my miraculous reappearance
Jaramillo, A. La linea
Knowles, J. See you at Harry's
MacCullough, C. Stealing Henry
McEntire, M. Hourglass
McNicoll, S. Last chance for Paris
Molope, K. L. This book betrays my brother
Mowll, J. Operation Red Jericho
Mowll, J. Operation Storm City
Mowll, J. Operation typhoon shore
Parkinson, S. Long story short
Peterson, W. Triskellion 2: The burning
Robert, Na'ima B. Boy vs. girl.
Ruiz Zafon, C. The Prince of Mist
Scott, M. The alchemyst
Sedgwick, M. Revolver
Shusterman, N. Bruiser
Shusterman, N. Dry
Spinelli, J. Smiles to go
Tharp, T. Badd
Voigt, C. Homecoming
Vrettos, A. M. Skin
Werlin, N. The rules of survival
Williams, C. L. Waiting
Williams, G. Beatle meets Destiny
Wolf, J. S. Breaking beautiful
Young, M. Blood red road
Yovanoff, B. The replacement
SICILY (ITALY) -- FICTION
Coventry, S. The queen's daughter
SICK -- FICTION

Beaufrand, M. J. The rise and fall of the Gallivanters
Burns, L. J. Crave
Chibbaro, J. Deadly
Damico, G. Hellhole
Whelan, G. See what I see
White, R. A month of Sundays
This **side** of salvation. **Smith-Ready, J.**
Sidekicks. Ferraiolo, J. D.
SIDESHOWS -- FICTION
Barnaby, H. Wonder show
Siege and storm. Bardugo, L.
The **sight.** Clement-Davies, D.
Silbert, Leslie
The intelligencer
SILENCE -- FICTION
Katsoulis, G. S. Access restricted
Silence is goldfish: a novel. Pitcher, A.
Silksinger. Taylor, L.
Silvera, Adam
History is all you left me
More happy than not
They both die at the end
Silver, Eve
Rush
The **silver** kiss. Klause, A. C.
Silver rain. Peterson, L. J.
Silver stars. Grant, M.
Silver. Wooding, C.
Silvey, Craig
Jasper Jones
Simmons, Kristen
Article 5
Three
Simner, Janni Lee
Bones of Faerie
Faerie after
Faerie winter
Simon vs. the Homo Sapiens agenda. Albertalli, B.
Simone, Ni-Ni
Upgrade U
Simukka, Salla
As Red As Blood
Since you've been gone. Matson, M.
The **Sin** eater's confession. Bick, I. J.
The **Sin** Eater's daughter. Salisbury, M.
SIN -- FICTION
Fisher, C. Darkwater
Sing down the moon. O'Dell, S.
SINGERS -- FICTION
Forman, G. I have lost my way
Ortiz Cofer, J. If I could fly
Supplee, S. Somebody everybody listens to
Weatherford, C. B. Becoming Billie Holiday
SINGLE-PARENT FAMILIES -- FICTION
Aceves, F. The closest I've come
Arnold, E. K. Infandous
Benwell, S. The last leaves falling

Block, F. L. Teen spirit
Caletti, D. The fortunes of Indigo Skye
Coles, J. Tyler Johnson was here
Damico, G. Hellhole
Doller, T. The devil you know
Emond, S. Bright lights, dark nights
Foxlee, K. The midnight dress
Herrick, S. By the river
Howard, J. J. That time I joined the circus
Kamata, S. Gadget Girl
Katcher, B. Almost perfect
Klages, E. Out of left field
Kriegman, M. Being Audrey Hepburn: a novel
Lyga, B. Bang
Lynch, C. Angry young man
Lyne, J. H. Catch rider
Maldonado, T. Secret Saturdays
McDonald, J. Off -color
McGhee, A. What I leave behind
Moriarty, L. The center of everything
Ockler, S. Fixing Delilah
Patrick, C. The Originals
Rapp, A. The children and the wolves
Resau, L. The indigo notebook
Resau, L. The jade notebook
Resau, L. The ruby notebook
Rosenfield, K. Inland
Russell, C. Songs about a girl
Silvera, A. More happy than not
Valentine, J. Me, the missing, and the dead
    Stiefvater, M.

SINO-JAPANESE CONFLICT, 1937-1945 -- FICTION
Alban, A. Anya's war

SIRENS (MYTHOLOGY) -- FICTION
Hocking, A. Wake
Hubbard, A. Ripple
    sisterhood of the traveling pants. Brashares, A.

SISTERS
Friend, N. My life in black and white

SISTERS -- DEATH -- FICTION
Nielsen, S. Optimists die first
Sanchez, E. L. I Am Not Your Perfect Mexican Daughter

SISTERS -- FICTION
Alender, K. Bad girls don't die
Alender, K. The dead girls of Hysteria Hall
Anderson, N. C. City of Saints & Thieves
Bass, K. Summer of fire
Bauman, B. A. Rosie & Skate
Beard, P. Dear Zoe
Billingsley, F. Chime
Bjorkman, L. My invented life
Black, H. The cruel prince
Bobet, L. An inheritance of ashes
Bowman, A. D. Summer bird blue
Bryant, M. E. Glow
Bunce, E. C. A curse dark as gold
Caletti, D. The six rules of maybe

Cantor, J. The September sisters
Carvell, M. Sweetgrass basket
Childs, T. L. Sweet venom
Crossan, S. One
Cypess, L. Nightspell
Danticat, E. Untwine
Davies, J. Lost
Davis, T. S. Mare's war
Devlin, C. Tell me something real
Doyle, M. Bewitching season
Elliott, L. Hamilton and Peggy!: a revolutionary friendship
Flood, N. B. Soldier sister, fly home
Foxlee, K. The anatomy of wings
Frost, H. The braid
Galante, C. The sweetness of salt
Gardner, F. The second life of Ava Rivers
Graudin, R. The walled city
Griffin, A. Where I want to be
Han, J. To all the boys I've loved before
Hocking, A. Wake
Holder, N. Crusade
Hooper, M. Fallen Grace
Jaden, D. Losing Faith
Jae-Jones, S. Wintersong
Juby, S. The Truth Commission
Kaslik, I. Skinny
Littman, S. Backlash
MacCullough, C. Once a witch
Marillier, J. Cybele's secret
Marillier, J. Wildwood dancing
Mazer, N. F. The missing girl
McCahan, Love and other foreign words
McLemore, A. -M. Blanca & Roja
McNally, J. The looking glass
Morgan, P. The beautiful and the cursed
Mukherjee, S. Gemini
Murdoch, E. If you find me
Na, A. Wait for me
Nelson, J. The sky is everywhere
Nix, G. Frogkisser
Oliver, L. Vanishing girls
Patrick, C. The Originals
Pearce, J. Sisters red
Plum, A. Die for me
Reinhardt, D. We are the Goldens
Sanchez, E. L. I Am Not Your Perfect Mexican Daughter
Savage, K. Beautiful broken girls
Schrefer, E. The deadly sister
Scott, E. Between here and forever
Shepard, S. The lying game
Standiford, N. Confessions of the Sullivan sisters
Suma, N. R. Imaginary girls
Tahir, S. A reaper at the gates
Thomas, K. The darkest corners
Thor, A. Deep sea
Tiernan, C. Balefire
Watkins, S. Juvie

Watson, R. This side of home
Whitney, D. The Mockingbirds
Williams, C. L. Glimpse
Winters, C. Odd & true
Woodson, J. Lena
Zarr, S. Gem & Dixie
Zink, M. Guardian of the Gate
Zink, M. Prophecy of the sisters
 of glass. Hemphill, S.
 red. Pearce, J.
 wife. Hrdlitschka, S.

SITA (HINDU DEITY) -- FICTION
Sattar, A. Ramayana: an illustrated retelling
Zohra, S. Ramayana: an illustrated retelling

Sitomer, Alan Lawrence
The secret story of Sonia Rodriguez
 months later. Richards, N. D.
 of crows. Bardugo, L.
  rules of maybe. Caletti, D.

SIZE -- FICTION
Andrews, J. Munmun

SKATEBOARDING -- FICTION
Hornby, N. Slam
 Almond, D.

SKIING -- FICTION
Thomas, E. Boarder patrol

Skilton, Sarah
Bruised
 . Vrettos, A. M.
 deep. Crane, E. M.
skinful of shadows. Hardinge, F.
 Kaslik, I.
 girl. Karim, S.

Skurzynski, Gloria
The Virtual War

Skuse, C. J.
Rockoholic
 a novel in three sets and an encore. Townley, R.
 is everywhere. Nelson, J.

Skyscraping. Jensen, C.
 Hornby, N.
 Terry, T.

SLAVERY -- FICTION
Anderson, M. T. The astonishing life of Octavian Nothing,
 traitor to the nation
Ayres, K. North by night
Bannen, M. The bird and the blade
Bolden, T. Crossing Ebenezer Creek
Engle, M. Firefly letters
Gibney, S. Dream country
Lester, J. Day of tears
Lester, J. S. Black, white, other
Lester, J. Time's memory
Lyons, M. E. Letters from a slave boy
MacColl, M. The revelation of Louisa May
Mosley, W. 47
Napoli, D. J. Hush

Paulsen, G. Nightjohn
Rutkoski, M. The winner's curse.
Shan, D. The thin executioner
Sherman, D. The freedom maze
Turner, M. W. Thick as thieves
Walter, J. My name is not Friday

SLAVERY -- UNITED STATES -- FICTION
Anderson, M. T. The astonishing life of Octavian Nothing,
 traitor to the nation
Walter, J. My name is not Friday

SLAVES -- FICTION
Lyons, M. E. Letters from a slave girl
Moran, K. Bloodline rising
Tahir, S. An ember in the ashes: a novel

SLAVIC MYTHOLOGY
Bardugo, L. Shadow and bone

Sleator, William
The duplicate

SLEEP -- FICTION
Bray, L. Lair of dreams: a Diviners novel
Gaiman, N. The Sleeper and the Spindle
Yovanoff, B. Places no one knows
The **Sleeper** and the Spindle. Gaiman, N.
Sleeping freshmen never lie. Lubar, D.

SLEEPWALKING -- FICTION
Gardner, S. The dead I know

Sloan, Brian
A tale of two summers

Sloan, Holly Goldberg
I'll be there

Slump. Waltman, K.

Smack. Burgess, M.

SMALL BUSINESS -- FICTION
Nye, N. S. Going going
Small damages. Kephart, B.
A **small** white scar. Nuzum, K. A.

SMALLPOX -- FICTION
Cooney, C. B. Code orange
Smart girls get what they want. Strohmeyer, S.
Smashed Luedeke, L.
The **smell** of other people's houses. Hitchcock, B.-S.
The **smile.** Napoli, D. J.
Smiles to go. Spinelli, J.

Smith, Alexander Gordon
The Devil's engine
Lockdown

Smith, Andrew, 1959-
The Alex Crow

Smith, Jennifer E.
Windfall

Smith, Lindsay
Sekret

Smith, Roland
The edge
Elephant run
Peak

Smith, Sarah

The other side of dark
Smith, Sherri L.

Orleans
Smith-Ready, Jeri

This side of salvation
     in the sun. Ahdieh, R.
SMUGGLING -- FICTION
  Deuker, C. Runner
  Sedgwick, M. Saint death
Smythe, J. P.
  Way down dark
Snakehead. Halam, A.
Snatched. Hautman, P.
    bound. Mazer, H.
SNOW -- FICTION
  Schroeder, L. Far from you
SNOW LEOPARD -- FICTION
  Smith, R. The edge
SNOWBOARDING -- FICTION
  Thomas, E. Boarder patrol
    far from the bamboo grove. Watkins, Y. K.
    you want to be a wizard. Duane, D.
SOCCER -- FICTION
  Alexander, K. Booked
  Ayarbe, H. Compulsion
  Bloor, E. Tangerine
  O'Connor, H. M. Betting game
  Williams, M. Now is the time for running
SOCIAL ACTION -- FICTION
  Caletti, D. A heart in a body in the world
  McDonald, A. Boys, bears, and a serious pair of hiking boots
  Nelson, B. Destroy all cars
SOCIAL CHANGE -- FICTION
  Levithan, D. Two boys kissing
SOCIAL CLASSES -- FICTION
  Abrahams, P. Reality check
  Aldredge, B. Sasquatch, love, and other imaginary things
  Andrews, J. Munmun
  Aveyard, V. King's cage
  Barratt, M. The wild man
  Bloor, E. Taken
  Budhos, M. T. Tell us we're home
  Bunce, E. C. Liar's moon
  Bunce, E. C. Star crossed
  Croggon, A. Black spring
  Derting, K. The pledge
  Elkeles, S. Perfect chemistry
  Farinango, M. V. The Queen of Water
  Fitzpatrick, H. What I thought was true
  Haines, K. M. The girl is murder
  Harland, R. Worldshaker
  Harvey, A. Haunting Violet
  Hinton, S. E. The outsiders
  Holland, S. Everless

Kerr, M. E. Gentlehands
Kindl, P. Keeping the castle
Lo, M. A line in the dark
London, A. Guardian
London, A. Proxy
Lyne, J. H. Catch rider
Peterfreund, D. Across a star-swept sea
Richards, J. Three rivers rising
Roth, V. Allegiant
Roth, V. Divergent
Roth, V. Insurgent
Whitman, E. Wildwing
SOCIAL CONFLICT -- FICTION
  Myers, W. D. All the right stuff
SOCIAL ISOLATION -- FICTION
  Johnston, E. K. Exit, pursued by a bear
SOCIAL MEDIA -- FICTION
  Katcher, B. Deacon Locke went to prom
  Roat, S. H. How to Disappear
  Vail, R. Unfriended
  Wang, C. The takedown
SOCIAL PROBLEMS -- FICTION
  Davies, S. Outlaw
SOCIETY OF FRIENDS -- FICTION
  Erskine, K. Quaking
SOFTBALL -- FICTION
  Mackey, W. K. Throwing like a girl
So hard to say. Sanchez, A.
Soldier boy. Hutton, K.
Soldier sister, fly home. Flood, N. B.
Soldier X. Wulffson, D. L
SOLDIERS -- FICTION
  Bacigalupi, P. The drowned cities
  Bacigalupi, P. Tool of war
  Brennan, S. R. In other lands
  Duble, K. B. Phantoms in the snow
  Frost, H. Crossing stones
  Gray, C. Defy the stars
  Gray, C. Defy the worlds
  Hughes, D. Four-Four-Two
  Hutton, K. Soldier boy
  Klass, S. S. Soldier's secret
  Mafi, T. Shatter me
  Murdock, C. G. Wisdom's kiss
  Paulsen, G. Woods runner
  Reinhardt, D. The things a brother knows
  Simmons, K. Article 5
  Strasser, T. Price of duty
  Tintera, A. Reboot
Soldier's secret. Klass, S. S.
Solitaire. Oseman, A.
Solo. Alexander, K.
Solomon, King of Israel About
  Stroud, J. The ring of Solomon
Some girls are. Summers, C.
Some quiet place. Sutton, K.
Somebody everybody listens to. Supplee, S.

Somebody up there hates you. Seamon, H.

Someday this pain will be useful to you. Cameron, P.

Someone to love. De la Cruz, M.

Something like normal. Doller, T.

Something real. Demetrios, H.

Something strange and deadly. Dennard, S.

Somper, Justin

Demons of the ocean

Lowry, L.

Sones, Sonya

One of those hideous books where the mother dies

What my girlfriend doesn't know

What my mother doesn't know

for Ella Grey. **Almond, D.**

about a girl. Russell, C.

SONGWRITERS AND SONGWRITING

Weil, C. I'm glad I did

Sonnenblick, Jordan

After ever after

Falling over sideways

Notes from the midnight driver

Zen and the art of faking it

war. Hobbs, V.

Soonchild. Hoban, R.

someone. Long, H.

and Cecelia. Wrede, P. C.

Sorosiak, Carlie

Wild blue wonder

Sorrow's knot. Bow, E.

Soto, Gary

Buried onions

Taking sides

enchilada. Gill, D. M.

SOUL -- FICTION

Brockenbrough, M. Devine intervention

Damico, G. Croak

Fisher, C. Darkwater

Miranda, M. Soulprint

Soulprint. Miranda, M.

SOULS -- FICTION

Moulton, C. A. Angelfire

sound of letting go. Kehoe, S. W.

SOUP KITCHENS -- FICTION

Myers, W. D. All the right stuff

SOUTH AFRICA -- FICTION

Raina, A. When morning comes

Van de Ruit, J. Spud

SOUTH AFRICA -- RACE RELATIONS -- FICTION

Raina, A. When morning comes

Warman, J. The world beneath: one South African boy's struggle to be free

SOUTH CAROLINA -- FICTION

Boone, M. Compulsion

Johnson, V. Saving Maddie

SOUTHERN STATES -- FICTION

Dunagan, T. M. The salvation of Miss Lucretia

Lester, J. Guardian

Patrick, D. L. A matter of souls.

SOUTHERN STATES -- HISTORY -- FICTION

Patrick, D. L. A matter of souls.

SOUTHWESTERN STATES -- FICTION

Mabry, S. All the wind in the world

SOVIET UNION -- FICTION

Sepetys, R. Between shades of gray

SOVIET UNION -- HISTORY -- 1953-1985 -- FICTION

Smith, L. Sekret

SPACE AND TIME -- FICTION

Gaiman, N. Interworld

Hautman, P. The obsidian blade

Larbalestier, J. Magic lessons

McEntire, M. Hourglass

Petrucha, S. Split

Powell, L. The game of triumphs

Powell, L. The Master of Misrule

Sedgwick, M. The ghosts of heaven.

Shinn, S. Gateway

Stone, T. I. Time between us

Thompson, K. The new policeman

Williams, S. Twinmaker

SPACE COLONIES -- FICTION

Bao, K. Dove arising

Card, O. S. Pathfinder

Card, O. S. Ruins

Revis, B. Shades of Earth

SPACE FLIGHT -- FICTION

Revis, B. A million suns

SPACE FLIGHT TO THE MOON -- FICTION

Harstad, J. 172 hours on the moon

SPACE SHIPS -- FICTION

Landers, M. Starfall

Smythe, J. P. Way down dark

SPACE STATIONS -- FICTION

Kaufman, A. Gemina

Kristoff, J. Gemina

Lake, N. Satellite

SPACE TRAVELERS -- FICTION

Blair, K. Tangled planet

SPACE VEHICLES -- FICTION

Revis, B. Across the universe

Smythe, J. P. Way down dark

SPAIN -- FICTION

Kephart, B. Small damages

SPAIN -- HISTORY -- 20TH CENTURY -- FICTION

Spangler, Brie

Beast

SPANISH AMERICANS -- FICTION

Weston, C. Speed of life

Spanking Shakespeare. Wizner, J.

Sparrow. Moon, S.

Sparrow Road. O'Connor, S.

Speak. Anderson, J. L.

The **speaker.** Chee, T.

The **Speaker.** Schoenherr, I.

Speare, Elizabeth George
The witch of Blackbird Pond
Spears, Kat
Breakaway: a novel

SPECIAL EDUCATION -- FICTION
King, A. S. Reality Boy
Trueman, T. Life happens next; a novel
spectacular now. Tharp, T.
Speechless. Harrington, H.
of life. Weston, C.
SPIDER-MAN (FICTIONAL CHARACTER)
Reynolds, J. Miles Morales: Spider-Man.
SPIES -- FICTION
Anstey, C. Love, lies and spies
Avi. Traitor's gate
Barnes, J. L. The Squad
Bradbury, J. Wrapped
Bruchac, J. Wolf mark
Hartley, A. J. Firebrand
Horowitz, A. Stormbreaker
Leonard, J. P. Cold case
Littlefield, S. Infected
Lu, M. Wildcard
Paulsen, G. Woods runner
Peterfreund, D. Across a star-swept sea
Plum-Ucci, C. Fire will fall
Plum-Ucci, C. Streams of Babel
Pullman, P. La Belle Sauvage
Salisbury, G. Hunt for the bamboo rat
Smith, L. Sekret
Zettel, S. Palace of Spies
Spinelli, Jerry
Smiles to go
Stargirl
SPIRIT POSSESSION -- FICTION
Hardinge, F. A skinful of shadows
SPIRITS -- FICTION
Block, F. L. Teen spirit
Boone, M. Compulsion
Porter, S. When I Cast Your Shadow
of the Noh. Randall, T.
SPIRITUALISM -- FICTION
Harvey, A. Haunting Violet
In the shadow of blackbirds. Winters, C.
SPIRITUALISTS -- FICTION
Hooper, M. Velvet
Dawn, S.
Avasthi, S.
second. West, K.
the sun. Elwood, T.
Spontaneous. Starmer, A.
SPORTS BETTING
O'Connor, H. M. Betting game
SPORTS INJURIES -- FICTION
Lynch, C. Hit count
SPORTS TOURNAMENTS -- FICTION

Volponi, P. The Final Four
Spud. Van de Ruit, J.
SPY STORIES
Baldwin, K. A School for Unusual Girls
Carriger, G. Etiquette & espionage
Peterfreund, D. Across a star-swept sea
Salisbury, G. Hunt for the bamboo rat
The **Squad.** Barnes, J. L.
The **squire's** tale. Morris, G.
Stained. Rainfield, C.
Stalking Jack the Ripper. Maniscalco, K.
Stamper, Vesper
What the night sings
Standiford, Natalie
Confessions of the Sullivan sisters
How to say goodbye in Robot
Staples, Suzanne Fisher
Under the Persimmon tree
Shabanu; daughter of the wind
Star crossed. Bunce, E. C.
Starbird Murphy and the world outside. Finneyfrock, K.
Starfall. Landers, M.
Starfish. Bowman, A. D.
Stargirl. Spinelli, J.
Starglass. North, P.
Starmer, Aaron
Spontaneous
Starry eyes. Bennett, J.
Starters. Price, L.
Starting from here. Bigelow, L. J.
The **star-touched** queen. Chokshi, R.
STARVATION -- FICTION
Miller, S. J. The art of starving
Stay. Caletti, D.
Staying fat for Sarah Byrnes. Crutcher, C.
Stealing Henry. MacCullough, C.
Stealing Parker. Kenneally, M.
STEAMPUNK FICTION
Carriger, G. Curtsies & conspiracies
Hartley, A. J. Steeplejack
Kittredge, C. The nightmare garden
Mieville, C. Railsea
Reeve, P. Scrivener's moon
Wrede, P. C. The Far West
Steel. Vaughn, C.
STEEL-WORKS
Fine, S. Of Metal and Wishes
The **steep** and thorny way. Winters, C.
Steeplejack. Hartley, A. J.
Steiger, A. J.
When my heart joins the thousand
STEPFAMILIES -- FICTION
Arnold, D. Mosquitoland
Barrett, T. The Stepsister's Tale
Childs, T. L. Oh. My. Gods.
Dessen, S. Along for the ride
Friend, N. Bounce

Crossing the tracks
  Wiggins, B.
  fast. Herbach, G.
Sturtevant, Katherine
  A true and faithful narrative
STUTTERING -- FICTION
  Vawter, V. Copyboy
SUBWAYS -- FICTION
  Shusterman, N. Downsiders
Suckerpunch. Hernandez, D.
Sucktown. Dirkes, C.
SUDAN -- FICTION
  Whitman, S. The milk of birds
SUDAN -- HISTORY -- CIVIL WAR, 1983-2005 -- FICTION
  Bassoff, L. Lost girl found
  Coates, J. L. A hare in the elephant's trunk
  Park, L. S. A long walk to water
SUDAN -- HISTORY -- DARFUR CONFLICT, 2003- -- FICTION
  Whitman, S. The milk of birds
Sugiura, Misa
  It's not like it's a secret
SUICIDAL BEHAVIOR -- FICTION
  Littman, S. Backlash
SUICIDE -- FICTION
  Arcos, C. The re will come a time
  Asher, J. Thirteen reasons why
  Borris, A. Crash into me
  Connelly, N. O. Into the hurricane
  Davis, L. I swear
  Foxlee, K. The anatomy of wings
  Giles, A. Now is everything
  Giles, G. What happened to Cass McBride?.
  Healey, K. The shattering
  Hubbard, J. R. And we stay
  Hubbard, J. R. Try not to breathe
  Jones, A. G. Fire song
  King, A. S. Glory O'Brien's history of the future: a novel
  Lange, E. J. Butter
  Littman, S. Backlash
  Maciel, A. Tease
  McGhee, A. What I leave behind
  Moon, S. Sparrow
  Niven, J. All the bright places
  Polisner, G. In sight of stars
  Rapp, A. Under the wolf, under the dog
  Sales, L. This song will save your life
  Summers, C. Fall for anything
  Thompson, H. Orchards
  Torres Sanchez, J. Death, Dickinson, and the demented life of Frenchie Garcia
  Turrisi, K. Just a normal Tuesday
  Williams, C. L. Glimpse
  Williams, K. Absent
    Scarlett. Johnson, M.
SULTANS -- FICTION
  Hamilton, A. Hero at the fall.

Suma, Nova Ren
  Imaginary girls
  The walls around us: a novel
The **summer** after you and me. Doktorski, J. S.
Summer ball Lupica, M.
Summer bird blue. Bowman, A. D.
SUMMER EMPLOYMENT -- FICTION
  Buckley-Archer, L. The many lives of John Stone
  Dessen, S. Once and for all
  Hartinger, B. Project Sweet Life
  McCahan, E. The lake effect
  Wettersten, L. My faire lady
SUMMER -- FICTION
  Doktorski, J. S. The summer after you and me
  French, G. Grit
  Han, J. The summer I turned pretty
  Howland, L. Nantucket blue
  Karim, S. That thing we call a heart
  Lockhart, E. We were liars
  Madison, B. September Girls
  McCoy, M. Camp So-and-So.
  Naylor, P. R. Intensely Alice
  Potter, R. Exit strategy
The **summer** I got a life. Fink, M.
The **summer** I turned pretty. Han, J.
Summer of fire. Bass, K.
SUMMER RESORTS -- FICTION
  Doktorski, J. S. The summer after you and me
  Rosenfield, K. Amelia Anne is dead and gone
Summers, Courtney
  All the rage
  Fall for anything
  Some girls are
  This is not a test
Sun, Amanda
  Ink
Sun and moon, ice and snow. George, J. D.
The **Sun** Is Also a Star. Yoon, N.
Sunrise. Mullin, M.
SUPERHEROES -- FICTION
  Bond, G. Fallout
  Daniels, A. Dreadnought
  Ferraiolo, J. D. Sidekicks
  Frost, M. Alliance
  Lloyd-Jones, E. Illusive
  Lupica, M. Hero
  Meyer, M. Renegades
  Reynolds, J. Miles Morales: Spider-Man.
  Stohl, M. Black Widow
SUPERMAN (FICTITIOUS CHARACTER) -- FICTION
  Bond, G. Fallout
SUPERNATURAL BEINGS -- FICTION
  Stewart, M. The sacrifice box
SUPERNATURAL -- FICTION
  Almond, D. Clay
  Armentrout, J. L. White Hot Kiss
  Asher, J. The future of us

AUTHOR, TITLE AND SUBJECT INDEX
THIRD EDITION

SUPERVILLAINS -- FICTION

Meyer, M. Renegades

Supplee, Suzanne

Somebody everybody listens to

  tension; a novel in four summers. Runyon, B.

Surrender. Hartnett, S.

SURVIVAL AFTER AIRPLANE ACCIDENTS, SHIPWRECKS, ETC. -- FICTION

Bodeen, S. A. The Compound

Bodeen, S. A. The raft

Bray, L. Beauty queens

De la Peña, M. The living

Herlong, M. The great wide sea

Mary-Todd, J. Shot down

McKernan, V. Shackleton's stowaway

Napoli, D. J. Storm

Pratchett, T. Nation

SURVIVAL -- FICTION

Anderson, M. T. Landscape with invisible hand

Bacigalupi, P. The drowned cities

Bacigalupi, P. Tool of war

Bennett, J. Starry eyes

Block, F. L. Love in the time of global warming

Block, F. L. The island of excess love

Carter, A. Not if I save you first

Collins, S. Catching fire

Collins, S. Mockingjay

Collins, S. The Hunger Games

Connelly, N. O. Into the hurricane

Crossan, S. Breathe

De la Peña, M. The living

DeStefano, L. Sever

Falls, K. Inhuman

Fitzpatrick, B. Black ice

Gagnon, M. Strangelets

Garner, E. Mercy mode

Grant, M. Monster

Graudin, R. The walled city

Harrison, M. The killer in me

Isbell, T. The Prey

Kephart, B. This is the story of you

Keyser, A. J. The way back from broken

Kinch, M. The fires of New SUN

Kinch, M. The rebels of New SUN

King, E. R. The hundredth queen

Kizer, A. A matter of days

Kuehn, S. When I am through with you

Lake, N. Hostage Three

Lake, N. In darkness

Littlefield, S. Infected

Martin, T. M. The end games

Mary-Todd, J. Shot down

O'Guilin, P. The call

Parker, A. C. Astray

Parker, A. C. Gated

Reichs, B. Nemesis

Roth, V. Carve the mark

Roth, V. The fates divide

Salisbury, G. Hunt for the bamboo rat

Sangster, C. Last star burning

Savit, G. Anna and the Swallow Man

Scott, E. Miracle

Shusterman, N. Dry

Shusterman, N. UnSouled

Shusterman, N. UnWholly

Smith, R. The edge

Smythe, J. P. Way down dark

Stamper, V. What the night sings

Summers, C. This is not a test

Unsworth, T. The one safe place: a novel

Wells, D. Fragments

Wells, D. Partials

Wells, R. E. Feedback

Wiggins, B. Cured

Wiggins, B. Stung

Williams, M. Diamond boy

Wooding, C. Silver

Yancey, R. infinite sea

Yancey, R. The 5th Wave

SURVIVALISM -- FICTION

Woolston, B. Black helicopters

SURVIVAL SKILLS -- FICTION

Bodeen, S. A. The raft

Fukuda, A. The Prey

Harrison, M. The killer in me

Kephart, B. This is the story of you

Marshall, K. I am still alive

Mary-Todd, J. Shot down

O'Guilin, P. The call

Parker, A. C. Astray

Rainfield, C. Stained

Savit, G. Anna and the Swallow Man

Shusterman, N. UnWholly

Smythe, J. P. Way down dark

Wells, D. Fragments

Williams, M. Diamond boy

Surviving Antarctica. White, A.

SUSPENSE FICTION

Cameron, S. Rook

Ellis, K. Breaker

McCoy, M. Camp So-and-So.

Simukka, S. As Red As Blood

Wasserman, R. The book of blood and shadow

Sutton, Kelsey

Some quiet place

Swagger. Deuker, C.

SWANS -- FICTION

McLemore, A. -M. Blanca & Roja

Sway, Spears, K.

SWEDEN -- HISTORY -- GUSTAV V, 1907-1950 -- FICTION

Thor, A. Deep sea

Sweeney, Diana

The minnow

The **sweet** far thing. Bray, L.

The **sweet** life of Stella Madison. Zeises, L. M.

sweet revenge of Celia Door. Finneyfrock, K.
    venom. Childs, T. L.
    hereafter. Johnson, A.
Sweetblood. Hautman, P.
    sweetest spell. Selfors, S.
Sweetgrass basket. Carvell, M.
Sweethearts. Zarr, S.
    sweetness of salt. Galante, C.
SWIMMING -- FICTION
  Calame, D. Swim the fly
  Crutcher, C. Staying fat for Sarah Byrnes
  Crutcher, C. Stotan!
  Crutcher, C. Whale talk
  Kenneally, M. Coming up for air
    that rock. Rocco, J.
    the fly. Calame, D.
SWINDLERS AND SWINDLING -- FICTION
  Black, H. Red glove
  Black, H. The white cat
  Carter, A. Perfect scoundrels
  Hooper, M. Fallen Grace
  Luper, E. Bug boy
  Preus, M. Enchantment Lake: a Northwoods mystery
    Alexander, K.
      MacHale, D. J.
    symptoms of my insanity. Raf, M.
SYNESTHESIA -- FICTION
  Ellsworth, L. Unforgettable
  Griffin, E. Z. Light years
  Mass, W. A mango-shaped space; a novel
SYRIA -- FICTION
  Abawi, A. A land of permanent goodbyes

T

    rasa. Lippert-M., K.
TAE KWON DO -- FICTION
  Skilton, S. Bruised
Tahir, Sabaa
  An ember in the ashes: a novel
  A reaper at the gates
  A Torch Against the Night
Takedown. Van Diepen, A.
    takedown. Wang, C.
      Bloor, E.
      McClintock, N.
      Flight. Wilkinson, S.
      sides. Soto, G.

  Cursing Columbus
  Double crossing
    of two summers. Sloan, B.
TALES -- ASIA -- FICTION
  Oh, E. A thousand beginnings and endings: 15 retellings of
  Asian myths and legends
    from the inner city. Tan, S.
    of the Madman Underground. Barnes, J.

TALISMANS -- FICTION
  Strauss, V. Passion blue
Talley, Robin
  Our own private universe
  Pulp
  What We Left Behind
Talon. Kagawa, J.
Tamani, Liara
  Calling my name
The **taming** of the tights. Rennison, L.
TAMPA (FLA.) -- FICTION
  Aceves, F. The closest I've come
Tan, Shaun
  Tales from the inner city
Tangerine. Bloor, E.
A **tangle** of gold. Moriarty, J.
Tangled planet. Blair, K.
Tankborn. Sandler, K.
TAROT -- FICTION
  Cole, K. Poison princess
  Powell, L. The game of triumphs
  Powell, L. The Master of Misrule
Tash hearts Tolstoy. Ormsbee, Kathryn
Tash, Sarvenaz
  The geek's guide to unrequited love
Tashjian, Janet
  The gospel according to Larry
A **taste** for monsters. Kirby, M. J.
TATTOOING -- FICTION
  Arbuthnott, G. The Keepers' tattoo
Tayleur, Karen
  Chasing boys
  Killer Pizza
  Killer Pizza: the slice
Taylor, Laini
  Blackbringer
  Daughter of smoke and bone
  Days of blood & starlight
  Dreams of gods & monsters
  Silksinger
  Strange the Dreamer
Taylor, Mildred D.
  The land
  Roll of thunder, hear my cry
TEACHERS -- FICTION
  Gensler, S. The revenant
  Gilman, C. Professor Gargoyle
  Marshall, C. Christy
  Northrop, M. Gentlemen
  Schmatz, P. Bluefish
  Volponi, P. The hand you're dealt
TEACHER-STUDENT RELATIONSHIP -- FICTION
  Atkins, C. The file on Angelyn Stark
  French, G. Grit
  Hrdlitschka, S. Allegra
  O'Connell, M. The sharp time
  Reinhardt, D. We are the Goldens

Toten, T. Beware that girl
  Maciel, A.

TECHNOLOGY -- FICTION
McDonald, I. Be my enemy
Reeve, P. Scrivener's moon

TEENAGE BOYS -- FICTION
Daley, J. R. Jesus Jackson
Levithan, D. Boy meets boy
Groth, D. Munro vs. the coyote

TEENAGE BOYS -- WASHINGTON (STATE) -- SEATTLE -- FICTION
Brockenbrough, M. The game of Love and Death

TEENAGE FATHERS
Knowles, J. Living with Jackie Chan

TEENAGE FATHERS -- FICTION
Bechard, M. Hanging on to Max
Hornby, N. Slam
Schmidt, G. D. Orbiting Jupiter

TEENAGE GIRLS -- CRIMES AGAINST -- ENGLAND -- FICTION
Mason, S. Running girl

TEENAGE GIRLS -- FICTION
Acevedo, E. The poet X: a novel
Anderson, J. L. Midnight at the Electric
Andreu, M. E. The secret side of empty
Avasthi, S. Chasing Shadows
Aveyard, V. Red queen
Barnard, S. Fragile like us
Between Two Skies. O'Sullivan, J.
Clayton, D. The Belles
Connor, L. The things you kiss goodbye
Darrows, E. Dead little mean girl
De la Cruz, M. Someone to love
Deracine, A. Driving by starlight
Fine, S. Of Metal and Wishes
Foley, J. A. Neighborhood girls
Frank, L. Two girls staring at the ceiling
Giles, A. Now is everything
Green, J. Turtles all the way down
Heathfield, L. Seed
Howell, S. Girl defective
Jocelyn, M. A Big Dose of Lucky
Johnston, E. K. Exit, pursued by a bear
Katsoulis, G. S. All rights reserved
Kriegman, M. Being Audrey Hepburn: a novel
Laidlaw, S. J. Fifteen lanes
Lindstrom, E. Not if I see you first
McKenzie, P. The sacrifice of Sunshine Girl
Molope, K. L. This book betrays my brother
Moriarty, J. Feeling sorry for Celia
Murphy, J. Puddin
Oelke, L. Nice try, Jane Sinner
Patterson, J. Homeroom diaries
Quigley, D. Apple in the middle
Rabb, M. Kissing in America
Raf, M. The symptoms of my insanity
Redwine, C. J. The wish granter: a Ravenspire novel

Roux, M. House of furies
Safi, A. M. Not the girls you're looking for
Sugiura, M. It's not like it's a secret
Wettersten, L. My faire lady
Zappia, F. Eliza and her monsters

TEENAGE MOTHERS -- FICTION
McDonald, J. Chill wind
Sweeney, D. The minnow
Werlin, N. Impossible
Williams-Garcia, R. Like sisters on the homefront
Wolff, V. E. Make lemonade

TEENAGE PREGNANCY -- FICTION
Carter, C. Me, him, them, and it
Heppermann, C. Ask Me How I Got Here
Jackson, T. D. Allegedly: a novel
Kephart, B. Small damages
Sweeney, D. The minnow

TEENAGERS -- ALCOHOL USE -- FICTION
Luedeke, L. Smashed

TEENAGERS -- CONDUCT OF LIFE -- FICTION
Blythe, C. Revenge of a not-so-pretty girl
Grace, A. In too deep
Haas, A. Dangerous girls
Herbach, G. Nothing special
Lyga, B. I hunt killers
Scheidt, E. L. Uses for boys
Wakefield, V. Friday never leaving
Zadoff, A. Boy Nobody

TEENAGERS -- DRUG USE -- FICTION
Burgess, M. The hit
Woodson, J. Beneath

TEENAGERS -- FICTION
Almond, D. The tightrope walkers
Alsaid, A. Let's Get Lost
Armstrong, K. Aftermath
Asher, J. What light
Beaudoin, S. Wise Young Fool
Blake, A. H. Girl made of stars
Brewer, Z. The cemetery boys
Carleson, J. C. The tyrant's daughter
De Fombelle, T. The book of Pearl
De la Cruz, M. Someone to love
DeWoskin, R. Blind
Ellen, L. Blind spot
Emond, S. Winter town
Eshbaugh, J. Obsidian and stars
Finneyfrock, K. The sweet revenge of Celia Door
Fisher, C. Darkwater
Fitzpatrick, H. My life next door
Gagnon, M. Don't turn around
Gansworth, E. Give me some truth: a novel with paintings
Hitchcock, B.-S. The smell of other people's houses
Jacobs, J. H. The twelve-fingered boy
Johnson, L. Muchacho
Katcher, B. The improbable theory of Ana and Zak
King, A. S. Everybody sees the ants
King, A. S. I crawl through it

of the road. Hartman, R.

TEXAS -- FICTION

Canales, V. The tequila worm

Fehlbaum, B. Big fat disaster

Hale, M. The goodbye season

Mathieu, J. Moxie: a novel

McCall, G. G. Shame the Stars

Murphy, J. Dumplin'

Murphy, J. Puddin

Restrepo, B. Illegal

Saldana, R. A good long way

Scott, V. Violet Grenade

Tamani, L. Calling my name

TEXAS -- HISTORY -- 20TH CENTURY -- FICTION

Temblador, A. Secrets of the Casa Rosada

TEXT MESSAGING (CELL PHONE SYSTEMS) AND TRAFFIC ACCIDENTS -- FICTION

Zentner, J. Goodbye days

for the trouble. Wallach, T.

Tharp, Tim

Knights of the hill country

The spectacular now

inevitable Victorian thing. Johnston, E. K.

thing we call a heart. Karim, S.

time I joined the circus. Howard, J. J.

not what happened. Keplinger, K.

THEATER -- FICTION

Alsenas, L. Beyond clueless

Bjorkman, L. My invented life

Booth, M. Saving Hamlet

Heilig, H. For a muse of fire

Mantchev, L. Eyes like stars

Martin, C. K. K. The lighter side of life and death

McCaughrean, G. The glorious adventures of the Sunshine Queen

McWilliams, K. Doormat; a novel

Naylor, P. R. Incredibly Alice

Pixley, M. Ready to fall

Rennison, L. Are these my basoomas I see before me? final confessions of Georgia Nicolson

Sloan, B. A tale of two summers

Trigiani, A. Viola in the spotlight

Wilkinson, L. Pink

THEFT -- FICTION

Bardugo, L. Six of crows

Carter, A. Perfect scoundrels

Hautman, P. How to steal a car

Kephart, B. One thing stolen

theory of everything. Johnson, J. J.

will come a time. Arcos, C.

THESEUS (GREEK MYTHOLOGY)

Elliott, D. Bull

THESEUS, KING OF ATHENS -- FICTION

Elliott, D. Bull

They both die at the end. Silvera, A.

They came from below. Nelson, B.

Thick as thieves. Turner, M. W.

The **thief.** Turner, M. W.

THIEVES -- FICTION

Bardugo, L. Crooked kingdom

Bunce, E. C. Liar's moon

Bunce, E. C. Star crossed

Carter, A. Heist Society

Graudin, R. Invictus

Hartley, A. J. Firebrand

Michaelis, A. Tiger moon

Pearson, M. E. Dance of thieves

Turner, M. W. The thief

The **thin** executioner. Shan, D.

The **things** a brother knows. Reinhardt, D.

Things Jolie needs to do before she bites it. Winfrey, K.

Things not seen. Clements, A.

Things that are. Clements, A.

12 things to do before you crash and burn. Proimos, J.

Things we know by heart. Kirby, J.

The **things** you kiss goodbye. Connor, L.

Thin space. Casella, J.

Thirteen reasons why. Asher, J.

The **thirteenth** child. Wrede, P. C.

This book betrays my brother. Molope, K. L.

This dark endeavor. Oppel, K.

This is not a test. Summers, C.

This is the story of you. Kephart, B.

This song will save your life. Sales, L.

This side of home. Watson, R.

Thomas, Angie

The hate u give

Thomas, Erin

Boarder patrol

Thomas, Kara

The darkest corners

Little monsters

Thomas, Leah

Nowhere near you

Thomas, Rhiannon

Long may she reign

Thomas, Rob

Rats saw God

Thomas, Sherry

The burning sky

Thompson, Holly

The language inside

Orchards

Thompson, Kate

Creature of the night

The new policeman

Thompson, Mary G.

Amy Chelsea Stacie Dee

Thor, Annika

Deep sea

A **thousand** beginnings and endings: 15 retellings of Asian

Silbert, L. The intelligencer
vision. Shaw, S.
TURKEY -- FICTION
Marillier, J. Cybele's secret
TURKEY -- HISTORY -- MEHMED II, 1451-1481 --
FICTION
White, K. Now I rise
TURKEY -- HISTORY -- OTTOMAN EMPIRE, 1288-1918
-- FICTION
Walrath, D. Like water on stone
Turner, Megan Whalen
Thick as thieves
The thief
turning. Prose, F.
Turrisi, Kim
Just a normal Tuesday
all the way down. Green, J.
Turtschaninoff, Maria

Naondel
TUSCARORA INDIANS -- FICTION
Gansworth, E. Give me some truth: a novel with paintings
TUSCARORA NATION RESERVATION (N.Y.) -- FICTION
Gansworth, E. Give me some truth: a novel with paintings
TUTORS AND TUTORING -- FICTION
Brant, W. Zenn diagram
TUTSI (AFRICAN PEOPLE) -- FICTION
Combres, E. Broken memory
twelve-fingered boy. Jacobs, J. H.
Twinmaker. Williams, S.
TWINS -- FICTION
Albertalli, B. The upside of unrequited
Alexander, K. The crossover
Arcos, C. There will come a time
Billingsley, F. Chime
Blake, A. H. Girl made of stars
Bodeen, S. A. The Compound
Brewer, Z. The cemetery boys
Casella, J. Thin space
Coles, J. Tyler Johnson was here
Crossan, S. One
Danticat, E. Untwine
Davis, T. S. Happy families
Doktorski, J. S. The summer after you and me
Doyle, M. Bewitching season
Duncan, L. Stranger with my face
Fisher, C. Darkwater
Gardner, F. The second life of Ava Rivers
Isbell, T. The Prey
Kiernan, C. Into the grey
London, A. Black wings beating
McNicoll, S. Last chance for Paris
Menon, S. When Dimple met Rishi
Nelson, J. I'll give you the sun
Nuzum, K. A. A small white scar
Oppel, K. This dark endeavor
Peterson, W. Triskellion 2: The burning

Porter, S. When I Cast Your Shadow
Redwine, C. J. The wish granter: a Ravenspire novel
Robert, Na'ima B. Boy vs. girl.
Scott, M. The alchemyst
Scott, M. The enchantress
Shepard, S. The lying game
Shusterman, N. Bruiser
Somper, J. Demons of the ocean
Tiernan, C. Balefire
Watson, R. This side of home
Wiggins, B. Cured
Williams, G. Beatle meets Destiny
Wolf, J. S. Breaking beautiful
Wrede, P. C. Across the Great Barrier
Wrede, P. C. The Far West
Wrede, P. C. The thirteenth child
Young, M. Blood red road
Zhang, K. What's left of me
Zink, M. Guardian of the Gate
Zink, M. Prophecy of the sisters
Twisted. Anderson, J. L.
Two boys kissing. Levithan, D.
Two girls staring at the ceiling. Frank, L.
Two or three things I forgot to tell you. Oates, J. C.
Tyger tyger. Hamilton, K. R.
Tyler Johnson was here. Coles, J.
TYPHOID FEVER -- FICTION
Chibbaro, J. Deadly
Typhoid Mary, d. 1938 About
Chibbaro, J. Deadly
The **tyrant's** daughter. Carleson, J. C.
Tyrell. Booth, C.

U

Uehashi, Nahoko
Moribito; Guardian of the Spirit
Moribito II; Guardian of the Darkness
UGANDA -- FICTION
Hutton, K. Soldier boy
Nanji, S. Child of dandelions
UGANDA -- HISTORY -- 1979- -- FICTION
Hutton, K. Soldier boy
Umminger, Alison
American Girls: A Novel
Umubyeyi, Jeanne d'Arc, 1986- About
Jansen, H. Over a thousand hills I walk with you
Un Lun Dun. Mieville, C.
UNAUTHORIZED IMMIGRANTS -- FICTION
Gilbert, K. L. Picture us in the light
Marquardt, M. F. Dream Things True
The **unbecoming** of Mara Dyer. Hodkin, M.
UNCLES -- FICTION
Arbuthnott, G. The Keepers' tattoo
Bray, L. The diviners
Bunce, E. C. A curse dark as gold
Cameron, S. The dark unwinding

Coben, H. Seconds away
Coben, H. Shelter
Duble, K. B. Phantoms in the snow
Going, K. L. King of the screwups
Hautman, P. The obsidian blade
Horvath, P. The Corps of the Bare-Boned Plane
Ibbitson, J. The Landing
Knowles, J. Living with Jackie Chan
Laird, E. The betrayal of Maggie Blair
Lyne, J. H. Catch rider
Mowll, J. Operation Red Jericho
Mowll, J. Operation typhoon shore
Napoli, D. J. Alligator bayou
Proimos, J. 12 things to do before you crash and burn
Sachar, L. The cardturner; a novel about a king, a queen, and a

a painted sky. Lee, S.
Undercover. Kephart, B.
UNDERCOVER OPERATIONS -- FICTION
Budhos, M. T. Watched.
Klavan, A. MindWar: a novel
Tahir, S. An ember in the ashes: a novel
Zadoff, A. Boy Nobody
UNDERGROUND AREAS -- FICTION
Hardinge, F. A face like glass
UNDERGROUND MOVEMENTS -- FICTION
North, P. Starglass
UNDERGROUND RAILROAD -- FICTION
Ayres, K. North by night
MacColl, M. The revelation of Louisa May
**UNDERGROUND RAILROAD -- MASSACHUSETTS --
FICTION**
MacColl, M. The revelation of Louisa May
UNDERTAKERS AND UNDERTAKING -- FICTION
Gardner, S. The dead I know
Nadol, J. The vision
Reynolds, J. Boy in the black suit
the Empyrean Sky. Wendig, C.
the never sky. Rossi, V.
the wolf, under the dog. Rapp, A.
the Persimmon tree. Staples, S. F.
UnDivided. Shusterman, N.
Unearthly. Hand, C.
unfinished life of Addison Stone. Griffin, A.
Unforgettable. Ellsworth, L.
Unfriended. Vail, R.
Unhinged. Howard, A. G.
UNICORNS -- FICTION
Humphreys, C. The hunt of the unicorn
Unidentified. Mariz, R.
uninvited. Wynne-Jones, T.
**UNITED STATES. ARMY AIR FORCES. BOMBARDMENT
GROUP**
Nelson, M. American ace
**UNITED STATES. ARMY. REGIMENTAL COMBAT
TEAM, 442ND -- FICTION**
Hughes, D. Four-Four-Two

**UNITED STATES -- DEPT. OF HOMELAND SECURITY
-- FICTION**
Doctorow, C. Homeland
Doctorow, C. Little brother
**UNITED STATES -- FEDERAL BUREAU OF
INVESTIGATION -- FICTION**
Derting, K. Desires of the dead
**UNITED STATES -- HISTORY -- CIVIL WAR, 1861-1865
-- FICTION**
Bolden, T. Crossing Ebenezer Creek
Walter, J. My name is not Friday
Wells, R. Red moon at Sharpsburg
**UNITED STATES -- HISTORY -- 1775-1783, REVOLUTION
-- FICTION**
Anderson, M. T. The astonishing life of Octavian Nothing,
traitor to the nation
Klass, S. S. Soldier's secret
**UNITED STATES -- HISTORY -- REVOLUTION, 1775-1783
--NAVAL OPERATIONS, BRITISH -- FICTION**
Anderson, M. T. The astonishing life of Octavian Nothing,
traitor to the nation
**UNITED STATES -- IMMIGRATION AND EMIGRATION
-- FICTION**
Andreu, M. E. The secret side of empty
UNITED STATES. MARINE CORPS -- FICTION
Doller, T. Something like normal
**UNITED STATES. NATIONAL AERONAUTICS AND
SPACE ADMINISTRATION -- FICTION**
Harstad, J. 172 hours on the moon
UNIVERSITIES AND COLLEGES -- FICTION
Cooney, C. B. Janie face to face
Padian, M. Wrecked
Unrivaled. Noel, A.
Unsigned hype; a novel. Mattison, B. T.
UnSouled. Shusterman, N.
The **unspoken.** Fahy, T. R.
Unsworth, Tania
The one safe place: a novel
Untwine. Danticat, E.
UnWholly. Shusterman, N.
Unwind. Shusterman, N.
Upgrade U. Simone, Ni-Ni
Uprising. Haddix, M. P.
The **upside** of unrequited. Albertalli, B.
Upstate. Buckhanon, K.
URBAN ANIMALS -- FICTION
Tan, S. Tales from the inner city
URBAN RENEWAL -- FICTION
Watson, R. This side of home
Useless Bay. Beaufrand, M. J.
Uses for boys. Scheidt, E. L.
UTAH -- FICTION
Lauren, C. Autoboyography
Zarr, S. Sweethearts
UTOPIAN FICTION
Parker, A. C. Astray
UTOPIAS -- FICTION

DeStefano, L. Perfect ruin
Parker, A. C. Astray
Parker, A. C. Gated

V

VACATION HOMES -- FICTION
Brashares, A. The whole thing together
VACATIONS -- FICTION
Han, J. The summer I turned pretty
Surface tension; a novel in four summers. Runyon, B.
Wynne-Jones, T. uninvited
VACCINES -- FICTION
Lloyd-Jones, E. Illusive
Vail, Rachel

Unfriended
Valentine, Allyson
How (not) to find a boyfriend
Valentine, Jenny
Double
Fire color one
Me, the missing, and the dead
   rising. Henderson, J.
VAMPIRES -- FICTION
Atwater-Rhodes, A. Persistence of memory
Bickle, L. The outside
Black, H. The coldest girl in Coldtown
Block, F. L. Pretty dead
Brewer, Z. The chronicles of Vladimir Tod
Burns, L. J. Crave
De la Cruz, M. Blue bloods
Fantaskey, B. Jessica's guide to dating on the dark side
Harvey, A. Hearts at stake
Henderson, J. The Triumph of Death
Henderson, J. Vampire rising
Holder, N. Crusade
Holder, N. Damned
Kagawa, J. The Eternity Cure
Kagawa, J. The forever song
Kagawa, J. The immortal rules
Klause, A. C. The silver kiss
Maniscalco, K. Hunting Prince Dracula
Rex, A. Fat vampire; a never coming of age story.
Sedgwick, M. My swordhand is singing
Showalter, G. Intertwined
Somper, J. Demons of the ocean
St. Crow, L. Strange angels
VANCOUVER (B.C.) -- FICTION
Leavitt, M. My book of life by Angel
Van de Ruit, John

Vande Velde, Vivian
The book of Mordred
Van Diepen, Allison
Takedown
Van Draanen, Wendelin

Flipped
Runaway
The running dream
Vanhee, Jason
Engines of the broken world
Vanishing girls. Oliver, L.
Variant. Wells, R. E.
The **vast** fields of ordinary. Burd, N.
Vaughn, Carrie
Steel
Voices of dragons
Vaught, Susan
Freaks like us
The **vault** of dreamers. O'Brien, C.
Vawter, Vince
Copyboy
Vegan virgin Valentine. Mackler, C.
Velocity. Wooding, C.
Velvet. Hooper, M.
VENDETTA -- FICTION
Boone, M. Compulsion
Caine, R. Prince of Shadows
McLemore, A. -M. The weight of feathers
Van Diepen, A. Takedown
VENICE (ITALY) -- FICTION
Collins, P. L. Hidden voices
Hemphill, S. Sisters of glass
VENICE (LOS ANGELES, CALIF.) -- FICTION
Arnold, E. K. Infandous
Venkatraman, Padma
Climbing the stairs
Island's end
A time to dance
Venturess. Cornwell, B.
Verday, Jessica
The Hollow
VERMONT -- FICTION
Galante, C. The sweetness of salt
Ockler, S. Fixing Delilah
VERONA (ITALY) -- HISTORY -- 16TH CENTURY --
   FICTION
Caine, R. Prince of Shadows
VERSAILLES (FRANCE) -- 18TH CENTURY -- FICTION
Pike, A. Glitter
A **very** large expanse of sea. Mafi, T.
VETERANS -- FICTION
Anderson, L. H. The impossible knife of memory
Doller, T. Something like normal
Morpurgo, M. Half a man
Rorby, G. The outside of a horse; a novel
Watkins, S. Great Falls
VETERINARY MEDICINE -- FICTION
Wilson, D. L. Firehorse
VICTIMS OF BULLYING -- FICTION
Miller, S. J. The art of starving
VICTIMS OF CRIMES -- FICTION
Kephart, B. Wild blues

Marquardt, Marie F. The radius of us

VIDEO GAMERS -- FICTION
Bond, G. Fallout
Klavan, A. MindWar: a novel

VIDEO GAMES -- FICTION
Bond, G. Fallout
Brezenoff, S. Guy in real life
Klavan, A. MindWar: a novel

VIDEO RECORDING -- FICTION
Bancks, T. Mac Slater hunts the cool
Trigiani, A. Viola in reel life

VIETNAMESE AMERICANS -- FICTION
Burg, A. E. All the broken pieces

VIETNAMESE -- AUSTRALIA -- FICTION
Wood, F. Cloudwish

VIETNAM WAR, 1961-1975 -- FICTION
Burg, A. E. All the broken pieces
Hobbs, V. Sonny's war
Hughes, D. Search and destroy
King, A. S. Everybody sees the ants

VIETNAM WAR, 1961-1975-- FICTION
Lynch, J. N. My beautiful hippie
Castor, H. M.

VILLAGES -- FICTION
Edwardson, D. D. Blessing's bead
Hinwood, C. The returning
Sedgwick, M. White crow
Templeman, M. The glass casket

Villareal, Ray
Body slammed

VINTAGE CLOTHING -- FICTION
O'Connell, M. The sharp time
in reel life. Trigiani, A.
in the spotlight. Trigiani, A.

VIOLENCE -- FICTION
Bock, C. LIE
Cohen, J. C. Leverage
Davis, R. F. Chasing AllieCat
Flake, S. G. Bang!.
Giles, G. Shattering Glass
Kinch, M. The blending time
Kinch, M. The fires of New SUN
Kinch, M. The rebels of New SUN
Lake, N. In darkness
Nelson, J. On the volcano
Ostlere, C. Karma
Pattou, E. Ghosting
Quintero, S. Efrain's secret
Sáenz, B. A. Sammy and Juliana in Hollywood
Silver, E. Rush
Smythe, J. P. Way down dark
Soto, G. Buried onions
Wolf, A. Who killed Christopher Goodman?
Wright, D. Violence 101
101. Wright, D.
Grenade. Scott, V.
Grenade. Scott, V.

VIOLINISTS
Collins, P. L. Hidden voices

VIOLINISTS -- FICTION
Ibbitson, J. The Landing
Martinez, J. Virtuosity
Yoo, P. Good enough

VIRGIL. AENEID -- FICTION
Block, F. L. The island of excess love

VIRGIN BIRTH -- FICTION
Hutchinson, S. D. The apocalypse of Elena Mendoza

VIRGINIA -- FICTION
Elliot, L. Across a war-tossed sea
Kaplan, A. E. Grendel's guide to love and war
Lyne, J. H. Catch rider

VIRGINIA -- HISTORY -- REVOLUTION, 1775- 1783 -- FICTION
Anderson, M. T. The astonishing life of Octavian Nothing, traitor to the nation

VIRGINIA -- HISTORY -- 20TH CENTURY -- FICTION
Bayard, L. Lucky strikes

VIRTUAL REALITY -- FICTION
Bond, G. Fallout
Cheva, C. DupliKate
Klavan, A. MindWar: a novel
Skurzynski, G. The Virtual War
The **Virtual** War. Skurzynski, G.

Virtuosity. Martinez, J.

VIRUS DISEASES -- FICTION
Falls, K. Inhuman
Grant, M. Monster
Kizer, A. A matter of days
Smith, S. L. Orleans

VIRUSES -- FICTION
Smith, S. L. Orleans

The **vision.** Nadol, J.

VISIONS -- FICTION
Block, F. L. The island of excess love
O'Brien, A. Lara's gift

Vivaldi, Antonio, 1678-1741 About
Collins, P. L. Hidden voices

Vivian Apple at the end of the world. Coyle, K.

Vivian Apple needs a miracle. Coyle, K.

Vivian, Siobhan
The list
Not that kind of girl

Vizzini, Ned
It's kind of a funny story

Vlahos, Len
Life in a fishbowl
The Scar Boys

VODOU
Dunagan, T. M. The salvation of Miss Lucretia

VOICE -- FICTION
Casanova, M. Frozen

The **voice** on the radio. Cooney, C. B.

Voices of dragons. Vaughn, C.

Voigt, Cynthia

Homecoming

Izzy, willy-nilly

VOLCANOES -- FICTION

Mullin, M. Ashfall

Mullin, M. Sunrise

Nelson, J. On the volcano

Volponi, Paul

Black and white

The Final Four

The hand you're dealt

Hurricane song

VOLUNTEER WORK -- FICTION

Kephart, B. The heart is not a size

Reinhardt, D. How to build a house

Voorhees, Coert

The brothers Torres

VOYAGES AND TRAVELS

Cummings, P. The journey back

Kizer, A. A matter of days

Zettel, S. Golden girl

VOYAGES AND TRAVELS -- FICTION

Arnold, D. Mosquitoland

Block, F. L. Love in the time of global warming

Brothers, M. Perfect escape

Cummings, P. The journey back

Hesse, K. Safekeeping

Johnson, M. 13 little blue envelopes

Kittredge, C. The nightmare garden

Lo, M. Huntress

Lucier, M. Isle of blood and stone

Marillier, J. Raven flight

Marillier, J. Shadowfell

Marsh, K. Jepp, who defied the stars

McQuerry, M. D. The Peculiars

Osterlund, A. Exile

Rossetti, R. The girl with borrowed wings

Shan, D. The thin executioner

Waldorf, H. Tripping

Wiggins, B. Cured

Zettel, S. Dust girl

Vrettos, Adrienne Maria

W

wager. Napoli, D. J.

Wagner, Laura Rose

Hold tight, don't let go

WAITERS AND WAITRESSES -- FICTION

Caletti, D. The fortunes of Indigo Skye

Finneyfrock, K. Starbird Murphy and the world outside

for me. Na, A.

Williams, C. L.

for Gonzo. Cousins, D.

for Sarah. McBay, B.

Wakefield, Vikki

Friday never leaving

Wake. Hocking, A.

Waldorf, Heather

Tripping

WALES -- FICTION

Skuse, C. J. Rockoholic

Walker, Brian F.

Black boy/white school

Walk on Earth a Stranger. Carson, R.

Wallace, Rich

Perpetual check

Wrestling Sturbridge

Wallace, Sandra Neil

Muckers

Wallach, Tommy

Thanks for the trouble

We all looked up

The **walled** city. Graudin, R.

Wallenfels, Stephen

POD

Waller, Sharon Biggs

The Forbidden Orchid

A mad

The **walls** around us: a novel. Suma, N. R.

Walrath, Dana

Like water on stone

Walsh, Alice

A Long Way from Home

Walter, Jon

My name is not Friday

Waltman, Kevin

Slump

Walton, Julia

Words on bathroom walls

Walton, Leslye

The Strange and beautiful sorrows of Ava Lavender

Wanderlove. Hubbard, K.

Wang, Corrie

The takedown

WAR CORRESPONDENTS -- FICTION

Sorosiak, C. Wild blue wonder

Warcross. Lu, M.

Ward, Rachel

The Chaos

Infinity

Num8ers

WAR -- FICTION

Bacigalupi, P. The drowned cities

Berry, J. All the truth that's in me

Bobet, L. An inheritance of ashes

Strasser, T. Price of duty

Yancey, R. infinite sea

Yancey, R. The 5th Wave

The **war** outside. Hesse, M.

The **war** within these walls. Sax, A.

Warman, Janice

The world beneath: one South African boy's struggle to be free

Warman, Jessica

Between

Where the truth lies

    warrior heir. Chima, C. W.

WAR STORIES

Bobet, L. An inheritance of ashes

Brown, S. Caminar

Coakley, L. Witchlanders

Frost, H. Crossing stones

Grey, M. The girl at midnight

Hartman, R. Shadow scale

Hinwood, C. The returning

Marsden, J. Incurable

Marsden, J. The other side of dawn

Marsden, J. Tomorrow, when the war began.

Marsden, J. While I live

Mason, P. Camel rider

McDonald, I. Empress of the sun

Moran, K. Bloodline

Pratchett, T. Only you can save mankind

Ryan, A. K. Flame; a Sky Chasers novel

Stratton, A. Chanda's wars

WARSAW (POLAND) -- HISTORY -- WARSAW GHETTO
        UPRISING, 1943 -- FICTION

Sax, A. The war within these walls

WASHINGTON (D.C.) -- FICTION

White, E. E. The President's daughter

WASHINGTON (STATE) -- FICTION

Caletti, D. The fortunes of Indigo Skye

Caletti, D. Stay

Derting, K. Desires of the dead

Derting, K. The last echo

Deuker, C. Gym candy

Finneyfrock, K. Starbird Murphy and the world outside

Kelly, T. Harmonic feedback

Lockhart, E. The boyfriend list

Wasserman, Robin

The book of blood and shadow

The waking dark

    watch that ends the night. Wolf, A.

Watched. Budhos, M. T.

WATER -- FICTION

Park, L. S. A long walk to water

    in May. Williams, I.

Watership Down. Adams, R.

    waters & the wild. Block, F. L.

Watkins, Steve

Great Falls

What comes after

Watkins, Yoko Kawashima

My brother, my sister, and I

So far from the bamboo grove

Watson, Renée

Piecing me together

This side of home

    Damico, G.

WAX FIGURES -- FICTION

Damico, G. Wax

The **way** back from broken. Keyser, A. J.

Way down dark. Smythe, J. P.

The **way** you make me feel. Goo, M.

We all looked up. Wallach, T.

We Are Okay. LaCour, N.

We are the ants. Hutchinson, S. D.

We are the Goldens. Reinhardt, D.

We regret to inform you. Kaplan, A.

We were liars. Lockhart, E.

WEALTH -- FICTION

Caletti, D. The fortunes of Indigo Skye

Carter, A. Perfect scoundrels

Hemmings, K. H. Juniors

Kiely, B. Tradition

Lockhart, E. We were liars

Smith, J. E. Windfall

Vail, R. Lucky

Valentine, J. Fire color one

WEATHER -- FICTION

Brown, S. To stay alive

Weatherford, Carole Boston

Becoming Billie Holiday

Weaver, Will

Saturday night dirt

A **Web** of Air. Reeve, P.

Webber, Katherine

The heartbeats of Wing Jones

WEBCOMICS -- FICTION

Priest, C. I Am Princess X.

WEBLOGS -- FICTION

Bancks, T. Mac Slater hunts the cool

Cowan, J. Earthgirl

WEB SITES -- FICTION

Bancks, T. Mac Slater vs. the city

Tashjian, J. The gospel according to Larry

WEDDINGS -- FICTION

Ahdieh, R. Smoke in the sun

Dessen, S. Once and for all

Holland, S. Everless

Rutkoski, M. The winner's crime

The **Wednesday** wars. Schmidt, G. D.

The **Wee** Free Men. Pratchett, T.

Weetzie Bat. Block, F. L.

Wegelius, Jakob

The murderer's ape

The **weight** of feathers. McLemore, A. -M.

Weil, Cynthia

I'm glad I did

Wein, Elizabeth

Black dove, white raven

Code name Verity

The empty kingdom

The lion hunter

The pearl thief

Rose under fire

Weird Girl and What's His Name. Brothers, M.

Now I rise
>**white** road of the moon. Neumeier, R.

White, Ruth
A month of Sundays

Whitley, David
Midnight charter

Whitman, Emily
Wildwing

Whitman, Sylvia
The milk of birds

Whitney, Daisy
The Mockingbirds

Whitney, Kim Ablon
The perfect distance
>done it? an investigation of murder most foul. Scieszka, J.
>killed Christopher Goodman?. Wolf, A.

>**whole** thing together. Brashares, A.
>will tell my brother?. Carvell, M.
>we broke up. Handler, D.
>>girls. Hemphill, S.
>lovely. Marr, M.

WIDOWS -- FICTION
Sheth, K. Keeping corner

WIFE ABUSE -- FICTION
Boll, R. The second trial

Wiggins, Bethany

>**wild.** Golden, C.
>beauty. McLemore, A. -M.
>blues. Kephart, B.
>blue wonder. Sorosiak, C.

Wildcard. Lu, M.

WILDERNESS AREAS -- FICTION
De Gramont, N. Every little thing in the world
McDonald, A. Boys, bears, and a serious pair of hiking boots
Nelson, J. On the volcano

WILDERNESS SURVIVAL -- FICTION
Bell, J. Juggling fire
Bodeen, S. A. The raft
Brown, S. To stay alive
Carter, A. Not if I save you first
Fitzpatrick, B. Black ice
Golden, C. The wild
Keyser, A. J. The way back from broken
Kuehn, S. When I am through with you
Mason, P. Camel rider
Mazer, H. Snow bound
McCaughrean, G. The white darkness
McClintock, N. Taken
Mullin, M. Ashfall
Mullin, M. Sunrise
O'Dell, S. Island of the Blue Dolphins
Parks, K. Notes from my captivity
Rorby, G. Lost in the river of grass
Smith, R. The edge
Waldorf, H. Tripping

Wildflower. Whitaker, A.

WILDLIFE CONSERVATION -- FICTION
Schrefer, E. Endangered

WILDLIFE RESCUE -- FICTION
Schrefer, E. Endangered
Schrefer, E. Threatened

The **wild** man. Barratt, M.

Wildman. Geiger, J. C.

Wildwing. Whitman, E.

Wildwood dancing. Marillier, J.

Wilkinson, Lili
Pink

Wilkinson, Sheena
Taking Flight

Willey, Margaret
Beetle Boy

Williams, Carol Lynch
The chosen one
Glimpse
Miles from ordinary; a novel
Waiting

Williams, Gabrielle
Beatle meets Destiny

Williams-Garcia, Rita
Jumped
Like sisters on the homefront

Williams, Ismee
Water in May

Williams, Kathryn
Pizza, love, and other stuff that made me famous

Williams, Katie
Absent

Williams, Lori Aurelia
When Kambia Elaine flew in from Neptune

Williams, Michael
Diamond boy
Now is the time for running

Williams, Sarah DeFord
Palace beautiful

Williams, Sean
Twinmaker

Wilson, Diane L.
Firehorse

Wilson, John
And in the morning

Wilson, Martin
What they always tell us

Windfall. Smith, J. E.

Winfrey, Kerry
Things Jolie needs to do before she bites it

Wings. Pike, A.

The **winner's** crime. Rutkoski, M.
The **winner's** curse. Rutkoski, M.

Winston, Sherri
The Kayla chronicles

Wintergirls. Anderson, J. L.

Winters, Cat

Odd & true

In the shadow of blackbirds

The steep and thorny way

Winter's end. Mourlevat,, J.

shadows. Buffie, M.

Wintersong. Jae-Jones, S.

WINTER STORMS -- FICTION

Arnold, A. Love & other train wrecks

town. Emond, S.

WISCONSIN -- FICTION

Bauer, J. Hope was here

Bick, I. J. The Sin eater's confession

Farrey, B. With or without you

Fink, M. The summer I got a life

Sutton, K. Some quiet place

Wisdom's kiss. Murdock, C. G.

Wise, Tama

Street dreams

Young Fool. Beaudoin, S.

Wiseman, Eva.

wish granter: a Ravenspire novel. Redwine, C. J.

WISHES -- FICTION

Fine, S. Of Metal and Wishes

Pearce, J. As you wish

Wood, F. Cloudwish

witch of Blackbird Pond. Speare, E. G.

WITCHCRAFT -- FICTION

Atwater-Rhodes, A. Persistence of memory

Bow, E. Plain Kate

Brignull, I. The Hawkweed Prophecy

Chima, C. W. The Demon King

Coakley, L. Witchlanders

Croggon, A. Black spring

Córdova, Z. Labyrinth lost

Dao, J. C. Forest of a thousand lanterns

Delaney, J. A new darkness

Dennard, S. Truthwitch

Egan, C. Julia vanishes

Flinn, A. A kiss in time

Hawkins, R. Hex Hall

Hemphill, S. Wicked girls

Henderson, J. The Triumph of Death

Horowitz, A. Raven's gate

Howe, K. Conversion

Laird, E. The betrayal of Maggie Blair

Lanagan, M. The brides of Rollrock Island

MacCullough, C. Always a witch

MacCullough, C. Once a witch

Napoli, D. J. The magic circle

Pratchett, T. The shepherd's crown

Pratchett, T. The Wee Free Men

Rowling, J. K., 1965- Harry Potter and the Sorcerer's Stone.

Speare, E. G. The witch of Blackbird Pond

Stroud, J. The Ring of Solomon

Templeman, M. The glass casket

Tiernan, C. Balefire

Witchlanders. Coakley, L.

With malice. Cook, E.

With or without you. Farrey, B.

Wither. DeStefano, L.

Withers, Pam

Andreo's race

First descent

Without warning. Hamley, D.

WITNESSES -- FICTION

Elston, A. The rules for disappearing

Giles, L. Fake ID

Hartzler, A. What we saw

Johnson, M. The name of the star

Shaw, S. Tunnel vision

WITNESS PROTECTION PROGRAMS -- FICTION

Elston, A. The rules for disappearing

Giles, L. Fake ID

Wittlinger, Ellen

Hard love

Love & lies

Parrotfish

Sandpiper

WIZARDS -- FICTION

Chima, C. W. The Crimson Crown

Duane, D. So you want to be a wizard

Nix, G. Frogkisser

Wizner, Jake

Spanking Shakespeare

Wizner, J. Spanking Shakespeare.

Wolf, Allan

New found land

The watch that ends the night

Who killed Christopher Goodman?

Wolf by wolf. Graudin, R.

The **wolf.** Herrick, S.

Wolf, Jennifer Shaw

Breaking beautiful

Wolf mark. Bruchac, J.

Wolff, Virginia Euwer

Make lemonade

Wolitzer, Meg

Belzhar

WOLVES -- FICTION

Clement-Davies, D. The sight

Golden, C. The wild

Lasky, K. Lone wolf

McNicoll, S. Last chance for Paris

Stiefvater, M. Sinner

WOMEN AIR PILOTS -- FICTION

MacColl, M. Promise the night

Smith, S. L. Flygirl

Wein, E. Code name Verity

WOMEN ARTISTS -- FICTION

Strauss, V. Passion blue

WOMEN ATHLETES -- FICTION

White, E. E. A season of daring greatly

WOMEN AUTOMOBILE RACING DRIVERS --

Lee, M. The gentleman's guide to vice and virtue
young inferno, Agard, J.

Young, Moira
  Blood red road

YOUNG WOMEN -- FICTION
  Atkins, C. The file on Angelyn Stark
  King, E. R. The hundredth queen
  Rosenfield, K. Amelia Anne is dead and gone
  Schlitz, L. A. The hired girl.
      Welcome. Gardner, W.

YOUTHS' WRITINGS
  Bao, K. Dove arising
  Moulton, C. A. Angelfire
  Silvera, A. More happy than not
  Thomas, K. The darkest corners

YOUTH WITH AUTISM SPECTRUM DISORDERS -- FICTION
  Steiger, A. J. When my heart joins the thousand

YOUTUBE (ELECTRONIC RESOURCE) -- FICTION
  Lyga, B. Bang

Yovanoff, Brenna
  Fiendish
  Places no one knows
  The replacement

YUKON RIVER VALLEY (YUKON AND ALASKA) -- FICTION
  Golden, C. The wild

Z

  and Mia. Betts, A. J.

Zadoff, Allen
  Boy Nobody
  I am the mission

Zail, Suzy
  Playing for the commandant

Zappia, Francesca
  Eliza and her monsters

Zarr, Sara
  Gem & Dixie
  Sweethearts

Zeises, Lara M.
  The sweet life of Stella Madison
     and the art of faking it. Sonnenblick, J.

ZEN BUDDHISM -- FICTION
  Sonnenblick, J. Zen and the art of faking it
     diagram. Brant, W.

Zentner, Jeff
  Goodbye days
  The serpent king
     Westerfeld, S.

Zettel, Sarah
  Bad luck girl
  Dust girl

  Golden girl
  Palace of Spies

Zevin, Gabrielle
  All these things I've done

Z for Zachariah. O'Brien, R. C.

Zhang, Kat
  What's left of me

ZIMBABWE -- FICTION
  Williams, M. Diamond boy
  Williams, M. Now is the time for running

Zindel, Paul
  The Pigman

Zindel, P. The Pigman

ZINES -- FICTION
  Mathieu, J. Moxie: a novel

Zink, Michelle
  Guardian of the Gate
  Prophecy of the sisters

Zinn, Bridget
  Poison

Zipped. McNeal, L.

Zipped. McNeal, T.

Zoboi, Ibi
  American street

ZODIAC -- FICTION
  Tubb, K. O. The 13th sign

Zoe letting go. Price, N.

Zohra, Sonali
  Ramayana: an illustrated retelling

ZOMBIES -- FICTION
  Dennard, S. Something strange and deadly
  Hurwitz, G. The rains
  Ireland, J. Dread nation
  Maberry, J. Rot & ruin
  Martin, T. M. The end games
  Ness, P. The rest of us just live here
  Perez, M. Dead is a battlefield
  Ritter, W. The dire king.
  Ryan, C. The Forest of Hands and Teeth
  Summers, C. This is not a test

ZOONOSES -- FICTION
  Keyser, A. J. Pointe

ZOOS -- FICTION
  Castellucci, C. The queen of cool
  Hamilton, K. When the stars threw down their spears

ZOOS -- FICTION, 1914-1918 -- FICTION
  Morpurgo, M. An elephant in the garden

Zorn, Claire
  Protected

Zusak, Markus, 1975-
  The book thief
  Bridge of Clay
  I am the messenger

PRINTZ AWARD WINNERS

The American Library Association's (ALA) Young Adult Library Services Association (YALSA) established this award in 2000 to recognize literary excellence in young adult literature. Each year, one title is granted the Printz Award, and up to four honor books are recognized. Please note the following list contains only award winners within the scope of YOUNG ADULT FICTION CORE COLLECTION and does not include nonfiction and/or graphic novel winners of this award.

Author	Title	Year Granted
Myers, Walter Dean	*Monster*	2000
Almond, David	*Kit's Wilderness*	2001
Na, An	*A Step From Heaven*	2002
Chambers, Aidan	*Postcards from No Man's Land*	2003
Johnson, Angela	*The First Part Last*	2004
Rosoff, Meg	*How I Live Now*	2005
Green, John	*Looking for Alaska*	2006
Yang, Gene	*American Born Chinese*	2007
McCaughrean, Geraldine	*The White Darkness*	2008
Marchetta, Melina	*Jellicoe Road*	2009
Bray, Libba	*Going Bovine*	2010
Bacigalupi, Paolo	*Ship Breaker*	2011
Whaley, John Corey	*Where Things Come Back*	2012
Lake, Nick	*In Darkness*	2013
Sedgwick, Marcus	*Midwinterblood*	2014
Nelson, Jandy	*I'll Give You the Sun*	2015
Ruby, Laura	*Bone Gap*	2016
Lewis, John	*March*	2017
LaCour, Nina	*We Are Okay*	2018
Acevedo, Elizabeth	*The Poet X*	2019

MORRIS AWARD WINNERS

The William C. Morris YA Debut Award is awarded to the debut work of a young adult author. It recognizes the work's overall excellence and the appeal of the work to a wide range of teen readers. Please note the following list contains only award winners within the scope of YOUNG ADULT FICTION CORE COLLECTION and does not include nonfiction and/or graphic novel winners of this award.

Author	Title	Year Granted
Bunce, Elizabeth C.	*A Curse Dark As Gold*	2009
Madigan, L. K.	*Flash Burnout*	2010
Woolston, Blythe	*The Freak Observer*	2011
Whaley, John Corey	*Where Things Come Back*	2012
Hartman, Rachel	*Seraphina*	2013
Kuehn, Stephanie	*Charm & Strange*	2014
Quintero, Isabel	*Gabi. A Girl in Pieces*	2015
Albertalli, Becky	*Simon vs. the Homo Sapiens Agenda*	2016
Zentner, Jeff	*The Serpent King*	2017
Tomas, Angie	*The Hate U Give*	2018
Khorram, Adib	*Darius the Great is Not Okay*	2019